# *Civil Procedure*

## **How to use** your Connected Casebook

**Step 1:** Go to **www.CasebookConnect.com** and redeem your access code to get started.

**Access Code:**

**Step 2:** Go to your **BOOKSHELF** and select your Connected Casebook to start reading, highlighting, and taking notes in the margins of your e-book.

**Step 3:** Select the **STUDY** tab in your toolbar to access a variety of practice materials designed to help you master the course material. These materials may include explanations, videos, multiple-choice questions, flashcards, short answer, essays, and issue spotting.

**Step 4:** Select the **OUTLINE** tab in your toolbar to access chapter outlines that automatically incorporate your highlights and annotations from the e-book. Use the My Notes area for copying, pasting, and editing your book notes or creating new notes.

**Step 5:** If your professor has enrolled your class, you can select the **CLASS INSIGHTS** tab and compare your own study center results against the average of your classmates.

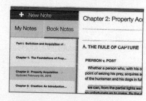

### Is this a used casebook? Access code already scratched off?

You can purchase the Digital Version and still access all of the powerful tools listed above.
Please visit CasebookConnect.com and select Catalog to learn more.

PLEASE NOTE: Each access code can only be used once. This access code will expire one year after the discontinuation of the corresponding print title and must be redeemed before then. CCH reserves the right to discontinue this program at any time for any business reason. For further details, please see the Casebook Connect End User Agreement.

PIN: 9111149521 BabcCivP6

03463

ASPEN CASEBOOK SERIES

# *Civil Procedure*

## Cases and Problems

*Sixth Edition*

*Barbara Allen Babcock*
**Judge John Crown Professor of Law, Emerita**
**Stanford Law School**

*Toni M. Massaro*
**Regents' Professor, Milton O. Riepe Chair in**
**Constitutional Law, and Dean Emerita**
**University of Arizona College of Law**

*Norman W. Spaulding*
**Nelson Bowman Sweitzer and Marie B. Sweitzer**
**Professor of Law**
**Stanford Law School**

 Wolters Kluwer

Published by Wolters Kluwer in New York.

Wolters Kluwer Legal & Regulatory U.S. serves customers worldwide with CCH, Aspen Publishers, and Kluwer Law International products. (www.WKLegaledu.com)

To contact Customer Service, e-mail customer.service@wolterskluwer.com, call 1-800-234-1660, fax 1-800-901-9075, or mail correspondence to:

Wolters Kluwer
Attn: Order Department
PO Box 990
Frederick, MD 21705

Printed in the United States of America.

5 6 7 8 9 0

ISBN 978-1-4548-7645-8

**Library of Congress Cataloging-in-Publication Data**

Names: Babcock, Barbara Allen, author. | Massaro, Toni Marie, 1955- author. | Spaulding, Norman W., author.
Title: Civil procedure: cases and problems / Barbara Allen Babcock, Judge John Crown Professor of Law, Emerita, Stanford Law School; Toni M. Massaro, Regents' Professor, Milton O. Riepe Chair in Constitutional Law, and Dean Emerita, University of Arizona College of Law; Norman W. Spaulding, Nelson Bowman Sweitzer and Marie B. Sweitzer Professor of Law, Stanford Law School.
Description: Sixth edition. | New York : Wolters Kluwer, 2017. | Includes index.
Identifiers: LCCN 2017000455 | ISBN 9781454876458
Subjects: LCSH: Civil procedure—United States. | LCGFT: Casebooks.
Classification: LCC KF8839 .B33 2017 | DDC 347.73/5—dc23
LC record available at https://lccn.loc.gov/2017000455

## About Wolters Kluwer Legal & Regulatory U.S.

Wolters Kluwer Legal & Regulatory U.S. delivers expert content and solutions in the areas of law, corporate compliance, health compliance, reimbursement, and legal education. Its practical solutions help customers successfully navigate the demands of a changing environment to drive their daily activities, enhance decision quality and inspire confident outcomes.

Serving customers worldwide, its legal and regulatory portfolio includes products under the Aspen Publishers, CCH Incorporated, Kluwer Law International, ftwilliam.com and MediRegs names. They are regarded as exceptional and trusted resources for general legal and practice-specific knowledge, compliance and risk management, dynamic workflow solutions, and expert commentary.

*To Tom, Jerry, and Ticien,*
*Our better halves.*

# Summary of Contents

# Contents

## 2 *Constructing a Civil Lawsuit* — 295

# 3 *Discovery of the Adversary's Case*                                499

# 6  *More Complex Litigation*                                      *911*

# *Preface*

The famous legal realist Karl Llewellyn once observed that law can be really known only "through the spectacles of procedure." This casebook is designed to help you learn this new way of seeing. Sometimes, as in the first case, the effect of procedure on substantive rights is glaringly obvious—a creditor attempts to use a procedure called "garnishment" to seize the wages of Ms. Sniadach *before* the creditor has proved in court that the debt is owed. In other instances the connection between procedural and substantive law is more subtle. But Llewellyn was right. You will soon begin to see this connection everywhere. That is in no small part because the rule of law itself is dependent on due process of law—no theory of rights or justice can be established or sustained without fair, transparent, participatory, and affordable rules for the resolution of disputes.

From the very first edition of this casebook we have selected cases that reveal the power of procedure in the lives of ordinary Americans, especially those for whom access to law has not come easily. Struggles for civil rights and civil liberties—for the full legal recognition of women, minorities and other disenfranchised groups in American society—are always also procedural in nature. It is no accident that the connection between substance and procedure is most vivid in these cases.

This casebook also sets critiques of the modern adversary system alongside praise songs for the noble service profession you are training to enter. On the one hand, the cost and delay of litigation have been a constant source of popular frustration with the adversary system and with the legal profession. Many important reform movements have tapped into that popular frustration or sought to check it. On the other hand, at critical moments in the history of our nation, courageous lawyers have stepped forward to defend due process of law and other democratic values. As you begin the study of procedure, consider what assumptions about professionalism are embedded in the rules governing litigation. And we invite you to ask what choices you would have made as counsel for the parties in the cases you will read.

As the Sixth Edition goes to press, the nation is recovering from the most profound economic crisis since the Great Depression, reeling from a bruising presidential election in which the value of equal justice under law has itself been challenged, and struggling to respond to social justice movements that have revealed profound disparities in the way civil and criminal justice is administered. Now more than ever we believe in starting the course with the enduring values that define procedural law: the belief in the power of rules to constrain government decision makers and fellow citizens; the commitment to equal access to law; the desire for efficiency and rationality in dispute resolution; the peculiarly American zest for adversarial exchange; and the belief in meaningful participation in decisions affecting one's substantive legal rights.

With this grounding in procedural first principles, we turn to doctrines defining the power of courts over the parties and subject matter of a dispute ("jurisdiction"). Subsequent chapters provide a survey of each stage of the modern litigation process: the rules governing the initial filings that notify the court and litigation opponents of the nature of the controversy ("pleading"); the rules governing the exchange of information relevant to the dispute ("discovery"); techniques for disposing of a case before trial (settlement and "summary judgment"); the balance of power between a judge and jury during trial; the management of complex litigation; and finally, doctrines that define the finality of a judgment ("repose" or "preclusion").

Over the last decade, the Supreme Court has been particularly active in the area of procedure. It has modified the architecture of pre-trial litigation in a series of important decisions regarding jurisdiction, pleading, the certification of class actions, and summary judgment. The Court has narrowed the number of fora in which a dispute may be litigated and intervened in new and surprising ways to enhance the power of judges to dispose of cases early in litigation. It also has strictly limited the rights of consumers and employees to avoid contract provisions requiring that they forgo litigation and submit their disputes to private resolution through arbitration. Although the full effects remain uncertain, these developments have sharpened an already precipitous decline in the number of cases that go to trial. And yet both bench and bar seem, as much as ever, to rely on jury trial for the model and measure of due process of law. We have structured the new cases and materials to highlight this seeming contradiction.

The Advisory Committee for Civil Rules has also been active, particularly in the area of discovery, and we have taken up new amendments in detail in the new edition. We have expanded materials on the increasingly difficult and important issues surrounding the preservation, storage, and disclosure of digital data. Discovery now dominates modern law practice, and the development of digital data, metadata, and new means of storage and recovery, among other technological advances, has complicated nearly all the traditional burdens and opportunities of discovery practice. We have also retained coverage of cases and readings on Rule 11 sanctions and sanctions in discovery practice, in order to prompt reflection on ethical standards of practice and what it means to be committed to an adversary system. Finally, we have continued to expand the treatment of emerging doctrines governing transnational litigation. Throughout the text we have sought to place greater emphasis on empirical studies of the practical consequences of procedural change, as well as the relationship between procedural rules and both ethical and social understandings of the lawyering role.

For the new edition, invaluable assistance with research was provided by a cadre of dedicated students at Stanford Law School: Brittany L. Benjamin, Joe DeMott, Samuel A. Martin, Tierney O'Rourke, Max Schoening, Rachel Rose Suhr, and Michelle Wu. We are deeply indebted to them for their hard work, keen editorial insights, and enthusiasm in every phase of production. Ms. O'Rourke and Ms. Wu were instrumental from the very earliest planning and research phases of the new edition. Ginny Smith provided invaluable, prompt, and highly professional administrative support. We are grateful as well to the fine editors at Wolters-Kluwer for assistance with the new edition and to Troy Froebe and his team for outstanding assistance with production.

Finally, we would like to give special thanks to our fellow procedure teachers who have been so generous over the years with comments, ideas, and suggestions to improve the casebook. The book is better for it and the joys of teaching the subject have been amplified by our lively engagement with those who share our passion for procedure. When we launched the "due process" approach to teaching civil procedure many years ago, we had no expectation that it would become the dominant approach to the introductory course. That it remains so relevant today is a credit to the wisdom of our intellectual mentor Paul Carrington. And for being so much more than a mentor, Toni and Norman wish to thank Barbara. She is an inspiration to us, as she has been to generations of students who, in *every* encounter with her, have found warm comfort, wise counsel, boundless good cheer, and insight into the joys of the practice of law.

> *Barbara A. Babcock*
> *Toni M. Massaro*
> *Norman W. Spaulding*

December 2016

# *Acknowledgments*

We wish to thank those who have given permission for the use of excerpts from the following articles and books:

ABA Model Rules of Professional Conduct, 2012 Edition. Copyright © 2013 by the American Bar Association. Reprinted with permission. Copies of ABA Model Rules of Professional Conduct, 2008. Editions are available from Service Center, American Bar Association, 321 North Clark Street, Chicago, IL 60654, 1-800-285-2221. This information or any portion thereof may not be copied or disseminated in any form or by any means or stored in an electronic database or retrieval system without the express written consent of the American Bar Association.

Babcock, Barbara A., A Place in the Palladium: Women's Rights and Jury Service, 61 U. Cin. L. Rev. 1139 (1993). Copyright © 1993 by the University of Cincinnati. Reprinted by permission of the author and the Cincinnati Law Review from the Cincinnati Law Review, Vol. 61.

Canby, Hon. William C., Tribal Court, Federal Court, State Court: A Jurisdiction Primer, Arizona Attorney (July 1993). Copyright © 1993 State Bar of Arizona. Reprinted by permission of the author and Arizona Attorney.

Friedenthal, Jack H., Mary Kay Kane, and Arthur R. Miller, Civil Procedure (3rd ed. 1999) Copyright © 1999 by West Publishing Corporation. Reprinted with permission of the authors and West Publishing Corporation from Civil Procedure 3rd ed., pp. 629-631.

Higginbotham, A. Leon, The Case of Missing Black Judges, N.Y. Times, July 29, 1992, Op-Ed. Copyright © 1992 by the New York Times Company. Reprinted by permission.

Kagan, Robert, Adversarial Legalism: The American Way of Law, pp.6-16 (2001).

Landers, Jonathan M., Of Legalized Blackmail and Legalized Theft: Consumer Class Actions and the Substance Procedure Dilemma, 47 S. Cal. L. Rev. 842 (1974). Reprinted by permission of the author and the Southern California Law Review from the Southern California Law Review, Vol. 47, pp. 845-847.

Levy, Jerome S. and Robert C. Prather, Sr., Texas Practice Guide, ADR Strategies, 3:10. Copyright © 1998 by Thomson West. Reprinted with permission of Thomson West.

Margolick, David, The Long Road Back for a Disgraced Patrician, N.Y. Times, Jan. 19, 1990, as reprinted in the S.F. Chronicle, Jan. 28, 1990.

Nelson, William E., Americanization of the Common Law: The Impact of Legal Change on Massachusetts Society, 1760-1830, 69-78, 86-87 (1975).

Perdue, Wendy, Sin, Scandal, and Substantive Due Process: Personal Jurisdiction and Pennoyer Reconsidered, 62 Wash. L. Rev. 479 (1987). Reprinted by permission of the author and the Washington Law Review, from the Washington Law Review, Vol. 62, pp. 480-490.

Purcell, Edward Jr., Geography as Litigation Weapon: Forum Selection Clauses and the Rehnquist Court. Originally published in 40 UCLA L. Rev. 423, 446-449 (1992). Copyright © 1992 by The Regents of the University of California. All Rights Reserved. Reprinted by permission of the author, UCLA Law Review, and Fred B. Rothman & Company.

Purcell, Edward Jr., Litigation and Inequality: Federal Diversity Jurisdiction in Industrial America, 1870-1958 (1992). Copyright © 1992 by Oxford University Press, Inc. Reprinted by permission of the author and Oxford University Press, Inc.

Restatement Second of Judgments §§ 17-29, 86-87 (ALI 1982). Copyright © 1982 by the American Law Institute. Reprinted with permission.

Rhode, Deborah L., Professional Responsibility: Teaching Ethics by the Pervasive Method (1994). Copyright © 1994 by Deborah L. Rhode. Published by Little, Brown and Company. Reprinted by permission of the author and Little, Brown and Company.

Spaulding, Norman W., The Enclosure of Justice: Courthouse Architecture, Due Process, and the Dead Metaphor of Trial, 24 Yale J.L. & Hum. 311 (2012). Reprinted with permission.

Tyler, Tom, Why People Obey the Law (1990). Published by Yale University Press. Copyright © 1990 by Yale University. Reprinted with permission by the author and Yale University Press.

Welles, Edmund O., They Also Serve, San Jose Mercury News, Dec. 28, 1986, at 4. Copyright © 1986 by the San Jose Mercury News. Reprinted with permission from the San Jose Mercury News.

Winters, Glenn R., Selection of Judges — An Historical Introduction, 44 Tex. L. Rev. 1081 (1966). Copyright © 1966 by the Texas Law Review Association. Reprinted by permission.

Zampano, Robert, "From the Bench" Settlement Strategies for Trial Judges, Litigation Magazine, Volume 22, No. 1, Fall 1995, pp. 3-6.

Zweifach, Lawrence J., Deposition Strategy in the Framework of an Overall Discovery Plan (PLI 1992). Copyright © by the Practicing Law Institute. Reprinted by permission of the Practicing Law Institute.

# *Special Notice on Citations*

Some citations have been omitted from case excerpts without notation, including parallel citations, string citations, and footnotes. Other omissions are indicated with ellipses or bracketed text. We have preserved the original footnote numbers for those notes that have been retained; editors' footnotes are designated with an asterisk and the notation "Eds." when they occur within an excerpt.

# Civil Procedure

# 1   *Due Process of Law*

## A.   NOTICE AND THE OPPORTUNITY TO BE HEARD

### Problem Case: The Due Process Game

In your second week of law school, you find a letter from the President of the University in your mailbox. On official letterhead, it reads:

> You have been accused of a serious Honor Code violation. Please discontinue class attendance immediately and make arrangements to leave campus.

What further information would you want from the University? What procedures would you expect? What kind of hearing would you seek? Would you want someone else to speak for you? What sort of decision maker would you desire? What rights would you assume? Are your assumptions about rights dependent on whether you are innocent or guilty of the violation? On the severity of the penalty?

Most Americans, especially law students, will construct a fairly elaborate model for deciding whether there was an Honor Code violation and what penalty should apply. A sense of the process due, of how facts should be found, and what results should follow is part of the larger, as well as the legal, culture of our society.

Due process, both as aspiration and as method, is at the heart of our study of procedure. Rules, statutes, formal and informal decision making must all meet a due process standard. The U.S. Supreme Court has spoken on the subject in many settings. Sometimes, the process due is only what the legislature says must be done before the government takes property or liberty.

Even then, however, the government must notify the persons affected and afford them some chance to "tell the other side." How much notice, what kind of hearing—these are the due process questions. Here is a recent Supreme Court case on due process, followed by interpretive and explanatory notes. This first section introduces the core of our study and our method in this book. Each unit starts with a problem case, followed by cases and materials for solving it. In reading these, think about the problem case; how does the doctrine fit with your intuitions about due process?

## 1.   The Process Due: Of Context and Subtext

Our first case begins with Christine Sniadach. She allegedly owed a bill for some eyeglasses. Her optometrist hired a collection agency, whose lawyer filed suit demanding the money. The court then issued a preliminary order directing Ms. Sniadach's employer to hold in escrow a part of her weekly wage of $63.18, so that there would be a pool of money from which to pay a judgment against her. The procedure that allowed the collection agency to seize part of Ms. Sniadach's wages directly from her employer right at the beginning of the suit is called a garnishment action.

Ms. Sniadach never had a chance to contest the order before it was sent to her employer. Represented by the legal arm of the National Association for the Advancement of Colored People (NAACP), Ms. Sniadach took her case to the Supreme Court, arguing that wage garnishment, as it was practiced in Wisconsin and many other states, denied the debtor due process of law.

The case is short and concerns what may seem to be a fairly minor aspect of debtor-creditor litigation procedure, but it is widely credited as sparking a revolution in procedural due process. As you read the case, think about the factors that make Sniadach's situation an appealing one for a test case. And think about why garnishment poses a due process problem at all.

### *Sniadach v. Family Finance Corp.*
395 U.S. 337 (1969)

Mr. Justice Douglas delivered the opinion of the Court.

Respondents instituted a garnishment action against petitioner as defendant and Miller Harris Instrument Co., her employer, as garnishee. The complaint alleged a claim of $420 on a promissory note. The garnishee filed its answer stating it had wages of $63.18 under its control earned by petitioner and unpaid, and that it would pay one-half to petitioner as a subsistence allowance[1] and hold the other half subject to the order of the court.

Petitioner moved that the garnishment proceedings be dismissed for failure to satisfy the due process requirements of the Fourteenth Amendment. The Wisconsin Supreme Court sustained the lower state court in approving the procedure. The case is here on a petition for a writ of certiorari.

---

1. Wis. Stat. § 267.18(2)(a) provides:

> When wages or salary are the subject of garnishment action, the garnishee shall pay over to the principal defendant on the date when such wages or salary would normally be payable a subsistence allowance, out of the wages or salary then owing in the sum of $25 in the case of an individual without dependents or $40 in the case of an individual with dependents; but in no event in excess of 50 per cent of the wages or salary owing. Said subsistence allowance shall be applied to the first wages or salary earned in the period subject to said garnishment action.

The Wisconsin statute gives a plaintiff 10 days in which to serve the summons and complaint on the defendant after service on the garnishee. In this case petitioner was served the same day as the garnishee. She nonetheless claims that the Wisconsin garnishment procedure violates that due process required by the Fourteenth Amendment, in that notice and an opportunity to be heard are not given before the *in rem* seizure of the wages. What happens in Wisconsin is that the clerk of the court issues the summons at the request of the creditor's lawyer; and it is the latter who by serving the garnishee sets in motion the machinery whereby the wages are frozen. They may, it is true, be unfrozen if the trial of the main suit is ever had and the wage earner wins on the merits. But in the interim the wage earner is deprived of his enjoyment of earned wages without any opportunity to be heard and to tender any defense he may have, whether it be fraud or otherwise.

Such summary procedure may well meet the requirements of due process in extraordinary situations. Cf. Fahey v. Mallonee, 332 U.S. 245, 253-254 [(1947)]; Ewing v. Mytinger & Casselberry, Inc., 339 U.S. 594, 598-600 [(1950)]; Ownbey v. Morgan, 256 U.S. 94, 110-112 [(1921)]; Coffin Bros. & Co. v. Bennett, 277 U.S. 29, 31 [(1928)]. But in the present case no situation requiring special protection to a state or creditor interest is presented by the facts; nor is the Wisconsin statute narrowly drawn to meet any such unusual condition. Petitioner was a resident of this Wisconsin community and *in personam* jurisdiction was readily obtainable.

The question is not whether the Wisconsin law is a wise law or unwise law. Our concern is not what philosophy Wisconsin should or should not embrace. We do not sit as a super-legislative body. In this case the sole question is whether there has been a taking of property without that procedural due process that is required by the Fourteenth Amendment. We have dealt over and over again with the question of what constitutes 'the right to be heard' (Schroeder v. New York, 371 U.S. 208, 212 [(1962)]) within the meaning of procedural due process. See Mullane v. Central Hanover Bank & Trust Co., 339 U.S. 306, 314 [(1950)]. In the latter case we said that the right to be heard "has little reality or worth unless one is informed that the matter is pending and can choose for himself whether to appear or default, acquiesce or contest." 339 U.S., at 314. In the context of this case the question is whether the interim freezing of the wages without a chance to be heard violates procedural due process.

A procedural rule that may satisfy due process for attachments in general, see McKay v. McInnes, 279 U.S. 820 [(1929)], does not necessarily satisfy procedural due process in every case. The fact that a procedure would pass muster under a feudal regime does not mean it gives necessary protection to all property in its modern forms. We deal here with wages—a specialized type of property presenting distinct problems in our economic system. We turn then to the nature of that property and problems of procedural due process.

A prejudgment garnishment of the Wisconsin type is a taking which may impose tremendous hardship on wage earners with families to support.

Until a recent Act of Congress,[4] Section 304 of which forbids discharge of employees on the ground that their wages have been garnished, garnishment often meant the loss of a job. Over and beyond that was the great drain on family income. As stated by Congressman Reuss:[5]

> The idea of wage garnishment in advance of judgment, of trustee process, of wage attachment, or whatever it is called is a most inhuman doctrine. It compels the wage earner, trying to keep his family together, to be driven below the poverty level.

Recent investigations of the problem have disclosed the grave injustices made possible by prejudgment garnishment whereby the sole opportunity to be heard comes after the taking. Congressman Sullivan, Chairman of the House Subcommittee on Consumer Affairs who held extensive hearings on this and related problems stated:

> What we know from our study of this problem is that in a vast number of cases the debt is a fraudulent one, saddled on a poor ignorant person who is trapped in an easy credit nightmare, in which he is charged double for something he could not pay for even if the proper price was called for, and then hounded into giving up his pound of flesh, and being fired besides. 114 Cong. Rec. 1832.

The leverage of the creditor on the wage earner is enormous. The creditor tenders not only the original debt but the "collection fees" incurred by his attorneys in the garnishment proceedings:

> The debtor whose wages are tied up by a writ of garnishment, and who is usually in need of money, is in no position to resist demands for collection fees. If the debt is small, the debtor will be under considerable pressure to pay the debt and collection charges in order to get his wages back. If the debt is large, he will often sign a new contract of 'payment schedule' which incorporates these additional charges.[6]

Apart from those collateral consequences, it appears that in Wisconsin the statutory exemption granted the wage earner[7] is "generally insufficient to support the debtor for any one week."[8]

---

4. [The Consumer Credit Protection Act of 1968,] 82 Stat. 146, Act of May 29, 1968.

5. 114 Cong. Rec. 1832.

6. Comment, Wage Garnishment in Washington—An Empirical Study, 43 Wash. L. Rev. 743, 753 (1968). And see Comment, Wage Garnishment as a Collection Device, 1967 Wis. L. Rev. 759.

7. See n. 1, supra.

8. Comment, Wage Garnishment as a Collection Device, 1967 Wis. L. Rev. 759, 767.

The result is that a prejudgment garnishment of the Wisconsin type may as a practical matter drive a wage earning family to the wall.[9] Where the taking of one's property is so obvious, it needs no extended argument to conclude that absent notice and a prior hearing this prejudgment garnishment procedure violates the fundamental principles of due process.

*Reversed.*

MR. JUSTICE HARLAN, concurring.

Particularly in light of my Brother Black's dissent, I think it not amiss for me to make explicit the precise basis on which I join the Court's opinion. The "property" of which petitioner has been deprived is the use of the garnished portion of her wages during the interim period between the garnishment and the culmination of the main suit. Since this deprivation cannot be characterized as *de minimis*, she must be accorded the usual requisites of procedural due process: notice and a prior hearing. . . .

From my standpoint, I do not consider that the requirements of "notice" and "hearing" are satisfied by the fact that the petitioner was advised of the garnishment simultaneously with the garnishee, or by the fact that she will not permanently lose the garnished property until after a plenary adverse adjudication of the underlying claim against her, or by the fact that relief from the garnishment may have been available in the interim under less than clear circumstances. . . . Apart from special situations, some of which are referred to in this Court's opinion, I think that due process is afforded only by the kinds of "notice" and "hearing" which are aimed at establishing the validity, or at least the probable validity, of the underlying claim against the alleged debtor before he can be deprived of his property or its unrestricted use. I think this is the thrust of the past cases in this Court. See, e.g., Mullane v. Central Hanover Bank & Trust Co., 339 U.S. 306, 313 (1950). . . .

MR. JUSTICE BLACK, dissenting.

The Court here holds unconstitutional a Wisconsin statute permitting garnishment before a judgment has been obtained against the principal debtor. The law, however, requires that notice be given to the principal debtor and authorizes him to present all of his legal defenses at the regular hearing and trial of the case. The Wisconsin law is said to violate the "fundamental principles of due process." Of course the Due Process Clause of the Fourteenth Amendment contains no words that indicate that this Court has power to

---

9. "For a poor man—and whoever heard of the wage of the affluent being attached?—to lose part of his salary often means his family will go without the essentials. No man sits by while his family goes hungry or without heat. He either files for consumer bankruptcy and tries to begin again, or just quits his job and goes on relief. Where is the equity, the common sense, in such a process?" Congressman Gonzales, 114 Cong. Rec. 1833. For the impact of garnishment on personal bankruptcies see H.R. Rep. No. 1040, 90th Cong., 1st Sess., 20-21.

play so fast and loose with state laws. The arguments the Court makes to reach what I consider to be its unconstitutional conclusion, however, show why it strikes down this state law. It is because it considers a garnishment law of this kind to be bad state policy, a judgment I think the state legislature, not this Court, has power to make. The Court shows it believes the garnishment policy to be a "most inhuman doctrine"; that it "compels the wage earner, trying to keep his family together, to be driven below the poverty level". . . .

The foregoing emotional rhetoric might be very appropriate for Congressmen to make against some phases of garnishment laws. Indeed, the quoted statements were made by Congressmen during a debate over a proposed federal garnishment law. The arguments would also be appropriate for Wisconsin's legislators to make against that State's garnishment laws. But made in a Court opinion, holding Wisconsin's law unconstitutional, they amount to what I believe to be a plain, judicial usurpation of state legislative power to decide what the State's laws shall be. . . . The Court thus steps back into the due process philosophy which brought on President Roosevelt's Court fight. Arguments can be made for outlawing loan sharks and installment sales companies but such decisions, I think, should be made by state and federal legislators, and not by this Court. . . .

Every argument implicit in . . . my Brother Harlan's views has been, in my judgment, satisfactorily answered in the opinion of the Supreme Court of Wisconsin in this case—an outstanding opinion on constitutional law. That opinion shows that petitioner was not required to wait until the "culmination of the main suit," that is, the suit between the creditor and the petitioner. In fact the case now before us was not a final determination of the merits of that controversy but was, in accordance with well-established state court procedure, the result of a motion made by the petitioner to dismiss the garnishment proceedings. With reference to my Brother Harlan's statement that petitioner's deprivation could not be characterized as *de minimis*, it is pertinent to note that the garnishment was served on her and her employer on the same day, November 21, 1966; that she, without waiting for a trial on the merits filed a motion to dismiss the garnishment on December 23, 1966, which motion was denied by the Circuit Court on April 18, 1967; and that it is that judgment which is before us today. The amount of her wages held up by the garnishment was $31.59. The amount of interest on the wages withheld even if computed at 10% annually would have been about $3. Whether that would be classified as *de minimis* I do not know and in fact it is not material to know for the decision of this case. . . .

The indebtedness of petitioner was evidenced by a promissory note, but petitioner's affidavit in support of the motion to dismiss, according to the Wisconsin Supreme Court contained no allegation that she is not indebted thereon to the plaintiff. Of course if it had alleged that, or if it had shown in some other way that this was not a good-faith lawsuit against her, the

Wisconsin opinion shows that this could have disposed of the whole case on the summary motion.

Another ground of unconstitutionality, according to the state court, was that the Act permitted a defendant to post a bond and secure the release of garnished property and that this provision denied equal protection of the law "to persons of low income." With reference to this ground, the Wisconsin court said:

> Appellant has made no showing that she is a person of low income and unable to post a bond. 37 Wis. 2d, at 167.

Another ground of unconstitutionality urged was that since many employers discharged garnished employees for being unreliable, the law threatened the gainful employment of many wage earners. This contention the Supreme Court of Wisconsin satisfactorily answered by saying that petitioner had "made no showing that her own employer reacted in this manner."

. . .

The state court . . . pointed out that the garnishment proceedings did not involve "any final determination of the title to a defendant's property, but merely preserve(d) the status quo thereof pending determination of the principal action." 37 Wis. 2d, at 169. The court then relied on McInnes v. McKay, 127 Me. 110 [(Me. 1928)]. That suit related to a Maine attachment law which, of course, is governed by the same rule as garnishment law. See "garnishment," Bouvier's Law Dictionary; see also Pennoyer v. Neff, 95 U.S. 714 (1877). The Maine law was subjected to practically the same challenges that Brother Harlan and the Court raise against this Wisconsin law. About that law the Supreme Court of Maine said:

> But, although an attachment may, within the broad meaning of the preceding definition, deprive one of property, yet conditional and temporary as it is, and part of the legal remedy and procedure by which the property of a debtor may be taken in satisfaction of the debt, if judgment be recovered, we do not think it is the deprivation of property contemplated by the Constitution. And if it be, it is not a deprivation without 'due process of law' for it is a part of a process, which during its proceeding gives notice and opportunity for hearing and judgment of some judicial or other authorized tribunal. The requirements of 'due process of law' and 'law of the land' are satisfied. 127 Me. 110.

This Court did not even consider the challenge to the Maine law worthy of a Court opinion but affirmed it in a *per curiam* opinion, 279 U.S. 820, on the authority of two prior decisions of this Court.

The Supreme Court of Wisconsin, in upholding the constitutionality of its law also cited the following statement of our Court made in Rothschild v. Knight, 184 U.S. 334, 341 [(1902)]:

> To what actions the remedy of attachment may be given is for the legislature of a State to determine and its courts to decide. . . .

The Supreme Court of Wisconsin properly pointed out:

> The ability to place a lien upon a man's property, such as to temporarily deprive him of its beneficial use, without any judicial determination of probable cause dates back not only to medieval England but also to Roman times. 37 Wis. 2d, at 171.

The State Supreme Court then went on to point out a statement made by Mr. Justice Holmes in Jackman v. Rosenbaum Co., 260 U.S. 22, 31 [(1922)]:

> The Fourteenth Amendment, itself a historical product, did not destroy history for the States and substitute mechanical compartments of law all exactly alike. If a thing has been practiced for two hundred years by common consent, it will need a strong case for the Fourteenth Amendment to affect it, as is well illustrated by Ownbey v. Morgan, 256 U.S. 94, 104 [(1921)].

The *Ownbey* case, which was one of the two cited by this Court in its *per curiam* affirmance of McInnes v. McKay, supra, sustained the constitutionality of a Delaware attachment law.

In the first sentence of the argument in her brief, petitioner urges that this Wisconsin law 'is contrary to public policy'; the Court apparently finds that a sufficient basis for holding it unconstitutional. This holding savors too much of the "Natural Law," "Due Process," "Shock-the-conscience" test of what is constitutional for me to agree to the decision. See my dissent in Adamson v. California, 332 U.S. 46, 68 [(1947)].

## Note: Due Process as Notice and a Chance to Be Heard

The first step in due process analysis is to determine whether life, liberty, or property is at stake. In *Sniadach*, it is property—Ms. Sniadach's right to the full use of the wages she had earned. Other classic due process cases have held that various government benefits are a form of property and that the government must give beneficiaries notice and a chance to be heard before these benefits are revoked. In one of the most famous cases, for example, the Court held that due process required notice and a right to be heard prior to the termination of welfare benefits under the federal Aid to Families with Dependent Children program and a parallel state law. Goldberg v. Kelly, 397 U.S. 254 (1970). As in *Sniadach*, the Court emphasized in *Goldberg* that "termination of aid pending resolution of a controversy over eligibility may deprive an eligible recipient of the very means by which to live while he waits. His need to concentrate upon finding the means for daily subsistence, in turn, adversely affects his ability to seek redress from the welfare bureaucracy." 397 U.S. at 264. In our problem case, does the student have a property interest in attending college, or is it more of a liberty, or associational interest? Though the short opinion in *Sniadach* spoke only to the peculiar hardships of wage garnishment, it dramatically affected other state procedures regulating the relationship between debtors and creditors. You can anticipate some of the possibilities in Justice Black's concern that the case would affect Maine's procedure for prejudgment "attachment" of property. *Sniadach* had even broader implications because, in *any* civil suit for money damages, not just breach of contract claims central to debtor-creditor disputes, the defendant is a potential debtor. If she loses, she will owe the plaintiff damages. That means every plaintiff has an incentive to use prejudgment seizures of the defendant's assets to safeguard means of satisfying the judgment if she prevails. *Sniadach* opened all forms of prejudgment seizure of property to attack if the associated procedures were deficient.

After *Sniadach* was decided both the legal community and creditors anxiously awaited the next case. The long legal journey of Margarita Fuentes to the Supreme Court started with her visit to a Legal Services Office in Miami, Florida. See C. Michael Abbott and Donald C. Peters, Fuentes v. Shevin: A Narrative of Federal Test Litigation in the Legal Services Program, 57 Iowa L. Rev. 955 (1972). Fuentes had purchased a stove and a stereo and fallen behind on her payments. One day the sheriff came to her house waving a writ of replevin, unplugged both items, and carted them away. Again the Court wrote broadly and based its decision squarely on the lack of notice before seizure of the property. Fuentes v. Shevin, 407 U.S. 67 (1972) (holding that prejudgment replevin without notice and opportunity to be heard violates due process).

Though the Florida statute was called "replevin," it was like the provisions of virtually all states that allowed pretrial repossession of property in which both creditor and debtor had some interest. In Louisiana the procedure allowing prejudgment attachment of property was entitled "sequestration." Just two years after *Fuentes,* that statute was upheld. Mitchell v. W.T. Grant Co., 416 U.S. 600 (1974). Lawrence Mitchell allegedly owed $574.17 on a stove, stereo, refrigerator, and washing machine when they were seized from him.

In an unusually bitter dissent, Justice Stewart, writing for three members of the Court, said that *Mitchell* was "constitutionally indistinguishable from *Fuentes.*" 416 U.S. at 634 (Stewart, J., dissenting). But the majority found that the statute was saved by provisions for the exercise of real judicial discretion in issuing prejudgment orders, the posting of a bond, and a quick postseizure hearing.

Essentially *Mitchell* held that it was possible for creditors' remedies to pass constitutional muster. But the final case in the series, North Georgia Finishing, Inc. v. Di-Chem, Inc., 419 U.S. 601 (1975), holding Georgia's prejudgment attachment statute unconstitutional, made plain that due process scrutiny was still alive:

> Here, a bank account, surely a form of property, was impounded and, absent a bond, put totally beyond use during the pendency of the litigation on the

> alleged debt, all by a writ of garnishment issued by a court clerk without notice or opportunity for an early hearing and without participation by a judicial officer.

Id. at 606.

For almost 20 years, the Supreme Court did not speak again on the subject of prejudgment remedies. The action moved instead to the state legislatures, which scrambled to revise their procedures in order to reach the proper balance between the property interests of both creditors and debtors, plaintiffs, and defendants, as well as commercial actors.

One state's typical efforts to update its prejudgment remedies were in the background of the 1991 Supreme Court opinion in Connecticut v. Doehr, 501 U.S. 1 (1991). In that case, a personal quarrel led to the placing of a lien on Doehr's house in connection with a tort action for assault and battery. Relying on the *Sniadach* line, the Court held that, as applied in this case, the Connecticut statute violated due process.

Though it revived procedural due process in a rather dramatic way, *Doehr* was different because it involved real property. All the prior cases had dealt with some form of personalty and the physical seizure of the property itself, which triggered due process concerns. What other types of attachments might fall within *Doehr*'s scope? See, for instance, Shaumyan v. O'Neill, 987 F.2d 122 (2d Cir. 1993), upholding the application of the same Connecticut statute involved in *Doehr* in a case where homeowners were dissatisfied with painting and repairs on their house and refused to pay. The contractors sued in state court and obtained an attachment of the home without either a prior hearing or the posting of a bond.

Think about the interaction of legislatures and courts that this set of cases illustrates. Does it seem like a good way for the legal system to operate, or do you agree with the judge who dissented from the Second Circuit's earlier holding that the *Doehr* statute was unconstitutional? He wrote:

> The Due Process Clause is not a code of civil procedure. . . . An *ex parte* prejudgment attachment of real estate does not deprive the owner of any possessory rights in his property. At most, it impairs the market value of the property during the brief interval between the *ex parte* attachment and "expeditious" adversary hearing required by state law. . . .

Pinsky v. Duncan, 898 F.2d 852 (2d Cir. 1990) (Newman, J., dissenting).

Note how much the personnel of the Court has changed since Sniadach was decided. Almost three decades later, Justice Scalia wrote for a unanimous court in Gilbert v. Homar, 520 U.S. 924 (1997), that a university's failure to provide notice and a hearing before suspending a university police officer without pay did not violate the officer's right to due process. The officer had been arrested and formally charged with a felony drug charge, which was dropped a few days later.

## Note: Private Actors and Due Process

In the problem case, we do not specify whether the university is public or private. Only the government is required by the Constitution to render due process in its dealings, so the second part of the due process calculus is determining whether there is state action.

As you will learn in other courses, the line between private and official conduct is sometimes blurred such that it is difficult to decide whether state action is present. In one sense, even the thoroughly "private" decision to ask an obnoxious party guest to leave one's house could be characterized as having "official" force to the extent that state property laws determine who owns certain property, subject to interests of others. Yet the Court clearly would not treat the homeowner's eviction of the guest as an action that triggers due process constraints. Less clear is whether the self-help actions of private creditors should be subject to due process simply because state laws regulate some aspects of these contractual relationships. See Flagg Bros., Inc. v. Brooks, 436 U.S. 149 (1978) (holding there was no state action in the sale of a debtor's goods by a warehouse that had the goods in its possession and under state law had a lien for unpaid storage charges).

In general, you may assume that when the challenged actions are those of the "state" itself—such as the admission decisions of a public (but not private) employer—then they satisfy state action and thereby may implicate constitutional rights. This does not mean that private actions are *legal* simply because they are beyond constitutional reach. On the contrary, actions that would be unconstitutional in the public sector likewise may be unlawful in private spheres based on statutory, contract, tort, or other law.

## Note: The Mathews Test

Once we know that a deprivation of life, liberty, or property occurs as a result of state action, the due process analysis shifts to a balancing test. Can you see what interests the Court weighed in *Sniadach*? Does it matter whether the creditor is right that Ms. Sniadach owes the money for the glasses? Against what ideals of fair procedure is the Court judging the Wisconsin garnishment statute?

The modern balancing test for determining when notice and a hearing must precede the deprivation of life, liberty, or property, and for deciding how complete the hearing must be, is set out in Mathews v. Eldridge, 424 U.S. 319 (1976). In that case, the Court considered whether an evidentiary hearing must precede the termination of Social Security disability benefits. The Court set out the balancing test as follows:

> . . . In *Fuentes v. Shevin*, 407 U.S., at 96-97, the Court said only that, in a replevin suit between two private parties, the initial determination required something more than an *ex parte* proceeding before a court clerk. Similarly, *Bell v.*

*Burson,* 402 U.S., at 540, held, in the context of the revocation of a state-granted driver's license, that due process required only that the pre-revocation hearing involve a probable cause determination as to the fault of the licensee, noting that the hearing "need not take the form of a full adjudication of the question of liability." *See also North Georgia Finishing, Inc. v. Di-Chem, Inc.,* 419 U.S. 601, 607 (1975). More recently, in *Arnett v. Kennedy, supra,* we sustained the validity of procedures by which a federal employee could be dismissed for cause. They included notice of the action sought, a copy of the charge, reasonable time for filing a written response, and an opportunity for an oral appearance. Following dismissal, an evidentiary hearing was provided. 416 U.S. at 142-146.

These decisions underscore the truism that "[d]ue process,' unlike some legal rules, is not a technical conception with a fixed content unrelated to time, place and circumstances." Cafeteria Workers v. McElroy, 367 U.S. 886, 895 (1961). "[D]ue process is flexible, and calls for such procedural protections as the particular situation demands." Morrissey v. Brewer, 408 U.S. 471, 481 (1972). Accordingly, resolution of the issue whether the administrative procedures provided here are constitutionally sufficient requires analysis of the governmental and private interests that are affected. *More precisely, our prior decisions indicate that identification of the specific dictates of due process generally requires consideration of three distinct factors: first, the private interest that will be affected by the official action; second, the risk of an erroneous deprivation of such interest through the procedures used, and the probable value, if any, of additional or substitute procedural safeguards; and, finally, the Government's interest, including the function involved and the fiscal and administrative burdens that the additional or substitute procedural requirement would entail.*

424 U.S. at 333-335 (emphasis added). Applying these factors, the Court held that no evidentiary hearing was necessary before the government terminated Social Security disability payments because there is an "elaborate" agency review process in which the beneficiary is given notice of the proposed termination, has an opportunity to review the relevant medical reports and other evidence in the case file, and is allowed to submit additional evidence and respond in writing before the termination decision is made. Id. at 338-340.

Unlike in *Goldberg,* the Court emphasized, "[e]ligibility for disability benefits . . . is not based on financial need," so the "disabled worker's need is likely to be less than that of a welfare recipient" and "[i]n addition to the possibility of access to private resources, other forms of government assistance will become available where the termination of disability benefits places a worker or his family below the subsistence level." Id. at 340-342. The risk of error in existing procedures was relatively low in the Court's view because a medical assessment is a more "easily documented decision than the typical determination of welfare entitlement. In the latter case, a wide variety of information may be deemed relevant, and issues of witness credibility and veracity are often crucial to the decisionmaking process." Id. at 343-344. The government's interest in "conserving scarce fiscal and administrative resources" was significant (every dollar that goes to an undeserving beneficiary diminishes the resources for those who truly need it), and the Court emphasized the "wise admonishment of Mr. Justice Frankfurter that differences in the origin and function of administrative agencies 'preclude wholesale transplantation of the rules of procedure, trial and review which have evolved from the history and experience of courts. The judicial model of an evidentiary hearing is neither a required, nor even the most effective method of decisionmaking in all circumstances.' FCC v. Pottsville Broadcasting Co., 309 U.S. 134, 143 (1940). . . . The essence of due process is the requirement that 'a person in jeopardy of serious loss [be given] notice of the case against him and opportunity to meet it.' Joint Anti-Fascist Comm. v. McGrath, 341 U.S. at 171-72 (Frankfurter, J., concurring)." Id. at 348-349.

The *Mathews* balancing test is the culmination of a profound evolution in thought about what constitutes due process of law. Chapter 39 of the Magna Carta provides that:

> No free man shall be seized or imprisoned or stripped of his rights or possessions, or outlawed or exiled, or deprived of his standing in any other way, nor will we proceed with force against him, or send others to do so, except by the lawful judgment of his equals or by the law of the land.

Chapter 40 provides that "[t]o no one will we sell, to no one deny or delay right or justice." Toni M. Massaro and E. Thomas Sullivan, quote both chapters in pages 7-8, The Arc of Due Process in American Constitutional Law 7-8 (2013). Massaro and Sullivan emphasize that in early English constitutional thought, "[i]t was not until a 1354 reissue of the charter that the phrase 'due process of law' was included, but by the end of the fourteenth century the due process check against arbitrary government forces was firmly established within the charter." Id. Even then, "development of a truly robust rule of law structure with due process protections did not take place . . . because of the influence of divine right" and deference to parliament—English courts assumed that the process parliament authorized was the process that was "due." Id.

In America, Massaro and Sullivan continue, the earliest treatments of due process by courts

> held that the law of the land was simply a guarantee that citizens would be subject to whatever laws had been passed by the legislature, and that they would not be subject to foreign or arbitrary power. This interpretation of due process 'stated an uncontroversial principle that was expected to be trivial.' This may explain why the Due Process Clause of the Fifth Amendment was included with little, if any, debate. It also may explain why the Due Process Clause was not addressed by the United States Supreme Court for sixty-five years after its inclusion, even though the Court was actively interpreting other provisions.

Id. at 81-82. Notice that, on this view of procedural due process (that whatever process the legislature sets out is "due") Ms. Sniadach would have no recourse against the Wisconsin garnishment statute. "This limited interpretation eventually fell from common use . . . even though it occasionally found support from certain members of the Court . . . ." Id. at 82. The first major shift in the nineteenth century was the development of a historical test that examined the challenged procedure against "those settled usages and modes of proceeding existing in the common and statue law of England . . . which were shown not to have been unsuited to their civil and political condition." Id. at 83. Could Ms. Sniadach have prevailed on this "settled usages" test?

What kinds of settled usages, other than those embedded in statutes, might a court look to? See Norman W. Spaulding, The Enclosure of Justice: Courthouse Architecture, Due Process, and the Dead Metaphor of Trial, 24 Yale J.L. & Hum. 311 (2012) ("Due process . . . has a readily identifiable spatial structure with deep historical and cultural resonance. It is the trial courtroom. And notwithstanding perennial accusations that due process of law is a guarantee of '. . . indefinite content,' courts and legal commentators have systematically relied upon the courtroom trial as an organizing metaphor. . . . [M]odern courts are constantly imagining the adversarial space of the trial courtroom as they decide what procedures should govern pre-trial . . . alternative forms of dispute resolution, and the operation of the modern administrative state.").

The modern *Mathews* balancing test, Massaro and Sullivan emphasize, developed gradually over the course of the twentieth century without ever completely displacing the "settled usages" approach. The Arc of Due Process in American Constitutional Law at 87. They point in particular to the significance of Justice Frankfurter's distillation of the virtues of a more flexible approach in his concurring opinion in a case relied on by the majority in *Mathews*, by Justice Harlan in his attempt to answer Justice Black's dissent in *Sniadach*, and in many other cases:

> "[D]ue process," unlike some legal rules, is not a technical conception with a fixed content unrelated to time, place and circumstances. Expressing as it does in its ultimate analysis respect enforced by law for that feeling of just treatment which has been evolved through centuries of Anglo-American constitutional history and civilization, "due process" cannot be imprisoned within the treacherous limits of any formula. Representing a profound attitude of fairness between man and man, and more particularly between the individual and government, "due process" is compounded of history, reason, the past course of decisions, and stout confidence in the strength of the democratic faith which we profess. Due process is not a mechanical instrument. It is not a yardstick. It is a process. It is a delicate process of adjustment inescapably involving the exercise of judgment by those whom the Constitution entrusted with the unfolding of the process.

Id. at 86-87 (quoting Joint Anti-Fascist Comm., 341 U.S. at 162-163 (Frankfurter, J., concurring)).

As Massaro and Sullivan conclude, "[d]espite the changes in the standard for determining what process is due for an individual in a certain context over time, the purpose of these procedures has remained the same: to assure that the government makes fair and accurate adjudicatory decisions." Id. at 88.

## Note: Due Process and Postjudgment Remedies

*Sniadach* was decided in 1969, five years after President Johnson declared an "unconditional war" on poverty in his State of the Union address. The series of legislative initiatives that followed to "relieve the symptoms of poverty . . . and, above all, to prevent it," have been condemned as "a catastrophe" by critics and praised as expressing our deep commitment as a society to the "dignity and potential of every human being" by others. See https://www.washingtonpost.com/news/wonk/wp/2014/01/08/everything-you-need-to-know-about-the-war-on-poverty/. One of the reasons the NAACP became involved in cases like Ms. Sniadach's is that civil rights leaders saw the potential of the president's initiative to unify social movements — a policy that could advance civil rights by addressing broader legal and social conditions that perpetuate economic disparities. Part of the most vigorous exchanges among the Justices in *Sniadach* concerns whether the majority was using the Due Process Clause of the Fourteenth Amendment in the service of the war on poverty.

In the wake of the Great Recession attention has returned to widespread economic disparities and racial injustice in debtor-creditor relations. The excerpt that follows is part of a civil complaint — the pleading filed to initiate a lawsuit — drafted by the Civil Advocacy Clinics at the Saint Louis University School of Law and other public interest lawyers. This particular complaint involves debt collection practices by a city bordering Ferguson, Missouri. After issuing traffic citations and fines for other minor violations of the municipal code, the City of Jennings holds indigent defendants who cannot not afford bail in custody until they agree to plead guilty. The guilty plea is then used as the basis for a civil judgment requiring payment of the fines, fees, costs, and late payment penalties. In order to collect, the city issues arrest warrants for non-payment and missed payments, and it holds arrestees in indefinite detention in its municipal jails to induce them to pay. Because the city budget depends in part on the revenue from its fines and penalties, it has a strong incentive to use aggressive collection practices. Information about these practices came to light after the Department of Justice published its report on widespread racial discrimination in the administration of criminal justice in and around Ferguson.

The *Sniadach-Fuentes* line of cases addressed due process defects in *prejudgment* remedies that favored creditors. As you read the excerpts of the complaint below, consider how those cases, and the *Mathews* balancing test, might apply to *postjudgment* collection practices.

*Jenkins v. The City of Jennings*
4:15-cv-00252
Filed February 8, 2015
United States District Court for the Eastern District of Missouri

## CLASS ACTION COMPLAINT

### INTRODUCTION

1. The Plaintiffs in this case are each impoverished people who were jailed by the City of Jennings because they were unable to pay a debt owed to the City from traffic tickets or other minor offenses. In each case, the City imprisoned a human being solely because the person could not afford to make a monetary payment. Although the Plaintiffs pleaded that they were unable to pay due to their poverty, each was kept in jail indefinitely and none was afforded a lawyer or the inquiry into their ability to pay that the United States Constitution requires. . . .

2. Once locked in the Jennings jail, impoverished people owing debts to the City endure grotesque treatment. They are kept in overcrowded cells; they are denied toothbrushes, toothpaste, and soap; they are subjected to the stench of excrement and refuse in their congested cells; they are surrounded by walls smeared with mucus, blood, and feces; they are kept in the same clothes for days and weeks without access to laundry or clean undergarments; they step on top of other inmates, whose bodies cover nearly the entire uncleaned cell floor, in order to access a single shared toilet that the City does not clean; they huddle in cold temperatures with a single thin blanket even as they beg guards for warm blankets; they develop untreated illnesses and infections in open wounds that spread to other inmates; they sleep next to a shower space overgrown with mold and slimy debris; they endure days and weeks without being allowed to use the shower; women are not given adequate hygiene products for menstruation, and the lack of trash removal has on occasion forced women to leave bloody napkins in full view on the cell floor where inmates sleep; they are routinely denied vital medical care and prescription medication, even when their families beg to be allowed to bring medication to the jail; they are provided food so insufficient and lacking in nutrition that inmates are forced to compete to perform demeaning janitorial labor for extra food rations and exercise; and they must listen to the screams of other inmates being beaten or tased or in shrieking pain from unattended medical issues as they sit in their cells without access to books, legal materials, television, or natural light. Perhaps worst of all, they do not know when they will be allowed to leave.

3. In each of the past two years, inmates have committed suicide in the Jennings jail after being confined there solely because they did not have enough money to buy their freedom. Others have attempted to take their own lives under similar conditions.

4. These physical abuses and deprivations are accompanied by other pervasive humiliations. Jennings jail guards routinely taunt impoverished

people when they are unable to pay for their release, telling them that they will be released whenever jail staff "feels" like letting them go. As described in detail below, jail staff routinely laugh at the inmates and humiliate them with discriminatory and degrading epithets about their poverty and their physical appearance.

5. City officials and employees—through their conduct, decisions, training and lack of training, rules, policies, and practices—have built a municipal scheme designed to brutalize, to punish, and to profit. The architecture of this illegal scheme has been in place for many years.[1]

6. In 2014, the City of Jennings issued an average of more than 2.1 arrest warrants per household and almost 1.4 arrest warrants for every adult, mostly in cases involving unpaid debt for tickets. . . .

7. The City's modern debtors' prison scheme has been increasingly profitable to the City of Jennings, earning millions of dollars over the past several years. It has also devastated the City's poor, trapping them for years in a cycle of increased fees, debts, extortion, and cruel jailings. The families of indigent people borrow money to buy their loved ones out of jail at rates arbitrarily set by jail officials, only for them later to owe more money to the City of Jennings from increased fees and surcharges. Thousands of people like the Plaintiffs take money from their disability checks or sacrifice money that is desperately needed by their families for food, diapers, clothing, rent, and utilities to pay ever increasing court fines, fees, costs, and surcharges. They are told by City officials that, if they do not pay, they will be thrown in jail. The cycle repeats itself, month after month, for years.

8. The treatment of Samantha Jenkins, Edward Brown, Keilee Fant, Byeon Wells, Meldon Moffit, Allison Nelson, Herbert Nelson Jr., and Tonya DeBerry reveals systemic illegality perpetrated by the City of Jennings against some of its poorest people. . . .

9. By and through their attorneys and on behalf of a class of similarly situated impoverished people, the Plaintiffs seek in this civil action the vindication of their fundamental rights, compensation for the violations that they suffered, injunctive relief assuring that their rights will not be violated again, and a declaration that the City's conduct is unlawful. In the year 2015, these practices have no place in our society. . . .

171. Tonya DeBerry is a 52-year-old woman. Over the past 13 years, she has been jailed repeatedly by the City of Jennings because of unpaid court fines and costs. Over that time period, she has paid thousands of dollars to Jennings for fines, costs, surcharges, and added fees. . . .

---

1. See, e.g., T.E. Lauer, Prolegomenon to Municipal Court Reform in Missouri, 31 Mo. L. Rev. 69, 93 (1966) ("Our municipal jails are, in almost every case, nothing but calabooses suited at best for temporary detention. The worst of them are comparable with medieval dungeons of the average class; they are the shame of our cities."); id. at 88 ("[I]t seems that many citizens of the state are being confined needlessly in our city jails. . . ."); id. at 85 ("[I]t is disgraceful that we do not appoint counsel in our municipal courts to represent indigent persons accused of ordinance violations."); id. at 90 ("It is clear that many municipalities have at times conceived of their municipal courts in terms of their revenue-raising ability. . . .").

173. On one occasion in 2012, Ms. DeBerry arrived late to the Jennings court while proceedings were going on. She had arrived to make her monthly $100 payment. She was told that the doors to the public proceedings were locked because the court was too crowded, and officers refused to let her enter to make her payment. The court officer told her to call the Jennings clerk the next day. Ms. DeBerry called the next day, and the City clerk told her that the City would not accept payment because she was a day late. The City told her that there was now a warrant out for her arrest because she had not paid the previous evening. She was told that she now had to pay a "bond" of $400. When Ms. DeBerry asked what that meant, the City clerk explained that she would be arrested if she did not pay $400 and that her debts had increased because, pursuant to City policy, a warrant fee had been added to her costs. In order to remove the warrant and avoid arrest, she had to pay $400. Ms. DeBerry could not afford to pay $400 to remove the warrant.

174. In September 2012, Ms. DeBerry was again arrested and held in the Jennings jail because of her non-payment. Jail staff threatened her with indefinite incarceration unless she paid approximately $700. It took her family two days to borrow and raise the $700 necessary to pay for her release.

175. In January 2014, Ms. DeBerry was again arrested because of her non-payment. When she was brought to the jail, she was told that she would not be released unless she paid $2,400 because that was the amount of her total debt to the City from old fines and costs. She was then told that she would be released for $1,400. She stated that she was poor and that she could not afford to pay anywhere near that amount. After two nights in jail, the City reduced her release amount to $100, and her family came to the jail and bought her release.

176. For years, Ms. DeBerry has been afraid to leave her own home for fear that she would be arrested on warrants for non-payment and held for days or weeks until someone could borrow enough money to free her. Ms. DeBerry is disabled and depends on federal disability support and food stamps to survive. . . .

178. As with the other Plaintiffs, the threat of being jailed for non-payment by Jennings has been a constant fact of everyday life for Ms. DeBerry and her family for years. It affects every decision to leave their home every day, including going to the grocery store or going to church. . . .

181. Ms. DeBerry has paid many thousands of dollars to Jennings for ballooning costs, fines, surcharges, and fees.

182. During her time in the Jennings jail, Ms. DeBerry was forced to endure grotesque conditions similar to those endured by the other Plaintiffs described in this Complaint. . . .

184. As with all of the other Plaintiffs, the City of Jennings never made any meaningful inquiry into Ms. DeBerry's indigence prior to jailing her or keeping her in jail for non-payment. Nor did the City consider any alternatives to incarceration or provide her with an attorney. . . .

187. It is the policy and practice of the City of Jennings to use its municipal court and its jail as significant sources of revenue generation for the

City. The money to be brought into the City through the municipal court is budgeted by the City in advance.[15] As a result, the entire municipal government apparatus, including municipal court officials and City jailors, has a significant incentive to operate the court and the jail in a way that maximizes revenues, not justice.

188. Decisions regarding the operation of the court and the jail—including but not limited to the assessment of fines, fees, costs,[16] and surcharges; the availability and conditions of payment plans; the setting of amounts required for release from jail; the issuance and withdrawal of arrest warrants; and the non-appointment of an attorney—are significantly influenced by and based on maximizing revenues collected rather than on legitimate penological considerations. . . .

190. Over the past five years, the City of Jennings, according to its public records, has earned more than $3.5 million dollars from its municipal court fines, fees, costs, and surcharges.[17] The population of the City of Jennings, including children, is 14,700.

### i.  Arbitrary and Indefinite Detention of the Indigent

191. As each of the Plaintiffs' cases illustrates, the City of Jennings has adopted a policy and practice of arresting people when they owe unpaid debt from judgments on old traffic tickets and other minor offenses. When those arrestees are booked at the Jennings jail, they are told by jail staff that they can be released immediately, but only if they pay cash to the City of Jennings. If they cannot pay the City, they are told that they will be held in jail indefinitely. . . .

194. It is and has been the policy and practice of the City of Jennings to gradually and incrementally reduce the amount of money required to buy a person's freedom. . . .

195. Inmates find out about these incremental reductions by asking jail staff every morning what their new release amount is. Some days they are told that the release amount has remained the same, and other days they are told that it has been reduced. Inmates are then usually given an opportunity to use the telephone to call family or friends who might be able to come up with enough money to pay for their release. The incremental reductions do not happen as the result of any formal adversarial process in which the inmate participates. . . .

15. The City uses the money collected through these procedures to help fund the City jail, to pay Municipal Court judicial salaries, to pay City Attorney's Office salaries, and to fund other portions of the City budget.

16. Missouri Law requires costs to be waived for the indigent, see Mo. Code § 479.260, but the City ignores that law.

17. The City also uses its jail to earn significant additional revenue by renting its jail space to other neighboring municipalities and knowingly keeps in its jail people who cannot afford to make payments to the other municipalities.

197. These policies and practices have created a culture of fear among the City's poorest residents, who are afraid even to appear at the payment window or in City court to explain their indigence because they know they will be jailed by the City without any meaningful process. The same fear motivates many very poor City residents to sacrifice expenditures on food, clothing, utilities, sanitary home repairs, and other basic necessities of life in order to scrape together money to pay traffic debt to the City. . . .

200. When providing information to inmates, the City refers in practice to the amount of cash required for a person's release at any given moment as the person's "bond," even though the money is applied toward old unpaid debts and is set, re-set, reduced, bargained, and eventually waived without any formal process or consideration of any of the lawful considerations related to Missouri's statutory bail system. Nor is the amount set in relation to any particular pending charge for which legal proceedings are imminent. Indeed, inmates often do not even have future court dates set and are held indefinitely without being brought to court. If a person subsequently misses any future "payment" date, the City, without any meaningful legal adversarial process, confiscates any previous amounts paid by the person to secure their release from jail and resets the person's debts. The City also adds a "warrant" fee for the person's missed payment date without any legal process.[18] In this way, many impoverished people end up paying thousands of dollars over a period of many years to the City based on a small number of relatively inexpensive initial tickets. . . .

### ii. Debt-Collection Proceedings in the Jennings Municipal Court

203. It is and has been the policy and practice of the City of Jennings to conduct a "confined docket" every Tuesday evening. At that docket, some (but not all) inmates who have been unable to secure enough money for their release from custody are brought before the City clerks, City prosecutor, and City judge. As a matter of policy and practice, inmates are not provided counsel by the City even though the City is represented by an experienced prosecutor at such proceedings.

204. During the "confined docket," inmates are told by City officials that they will remain in jail unless they can make monetary payments based on the total amount of debt that they owe.[21] Inmates are told that they will

---

18. For example, the person is not arraigned on any new charge for failure to appear prior to the "warrant" fee being added, and the person is not given a meaningful opportunity to present a defense to the elements of such a potential charge or appointed an attorney to defend her on any new charge. The money is simply added to the person's debts.

21. Because the City holds court only one time per week, those arrested on new offenses or warrants who cannot afford the amount of money set by the City often languish in jail for nearly a week before seeing a judicial officer. Inmates arrested on new charges (as opposed to previously unpaid debts) are told that they will not be released from custody prior to trial unless and until they make generically determined monetary payments. Arrestees who are not indigent and who can afford the scheduled monetary payment are released immediately after booking.

remain in jail unless they pay even though it is the policy and practice of the City of Jennings not to provide them with an attorney and not to conduct any meaningful inquiry into their ability to pay or alternatives to incarceration as required by the United States Constitution.[22]

205. Inmates are not advised of their relevant rights under federal or Missouri law, including applicable constitutional rights and state-law defenses and procedures. . . .

207. It is the policy and practice of the City to lock the court and building doors while conducting its "confined docket," thereby illegally barring the public from observing arraignments, plea hearings, compliance hearings, debt-collecting proceedings, and all other public proceedings in open and closed cases in which a person is incarcerated.[23]

208. In general, it is and has been the policy and practice of the City of Jennings to conduct a "payment docket" on Tuesday evenings at the Jennings municipal complex. It is the policy and practice of the City to hold this "payment docket" after the "confined docket." The stated purpose of this docket is to collect payments from debtors who are too poor to pay off their entire debt to the City from old judgments.

209. As with confined inmates, a person can end this debt-collection process at any time by paying what she owes to the City in full. If a person is too poor to end this process, her closed "case" can go on for years and years in perpetuity after the entry of a civil judgment assessing financial penalties, with the City imposing additional fees and surcharges for late payments and threatening incarceration for missed payments.

210. On Tuesday nights, a line of several hundred people usually forms outside the building waiting to be let into the municipal complex for the "payment docket." The crowd consists almost entirely of low-income people of color.

211. Jennings municipal policy dictates that any person owing traffic or other debt to the City need not appear in court if the person can afford to make a payment of $100 or more to the city clerk during the previous month.

212. All people who are too poor to pay at least $100 toward their debts are told by City officials that they are required to appear in the courtroom at the "payment docket."

---

22. Because no inquiry is made into ability to pay, no inquiry is likewise made into the reasons for non-payment or alternatives to incarceration.

23. The building doors are often opened, as a matter of practice, before the end of the confined docket so that the courtroom can be filled with those waiting for the "payment docket," which immediately follows the confined docket on Tuesday evenings. Thus, as a matter of practice, those waiting for the "payment docket" are often able to hear the City prosecutor and City judge threatening those who cannot afford their debts with longer jail terms and sending those unable to pay back to the City jail. When the public is permitted into the courtroom during the "payment docket," the proceedings are conducted as a matter of policy and practice as private bench conferences, with the defendant standing at the bench with the judge. The courtroom audience is unable to hear the content of the proceedings, other than the words of the judge, who speaks into a microphone. No transcripts or audio recordings of proceedings are available.

213. The courtroom is usually filled with hundreds of people, often making the wait hours for those unable to make significant payments.

214. At the "payment docket," courtroom police staff instructs audience members that those paying more money will be called first. The courtroom police staff calls a list of descending dollar amounts between $100 and $25 and instructs those paying each amount to line up when the number is called. The officer informs the audience by shouting to the entire room that anyone who cannot pay at least $25 will be considered a "no pay."

215. After the officer instructs audience members that if they cannot afford at least $25, they are not permitted to pay and will be classified as a "no pay," some audience members typically leave the building.

216. The officer instructs the audience that repeated appearances without payment will result in the person being jailed.

217. Those not making a payment or unable to come up with at least $25 are also told by the City clerk who collects payments that they "must" start paying. Officers also inform audience members that they will check "no pay" people for warrants in other municipalities. . . .

219. The City prosecutor and City judge do not conduct indigence or ability-to-pay hearings. . . .

220. The City prosecutor and City judge conduct no meaningful individualized process prior to ordering people to make generic monthly payments. Payment plans are set without any adversarial process and without any individualized inquiry into the circumstances of a debtor. Those jailed for unpaid debts (i.e. for not making their ordered payments) are not appointed an attorney, even though the City is represented by an experienced prosecutor.

221. In addition to the difficulty of mounting constitutional and statutory arguments and defenses in the face of an experienced prosecutor, navigating the origin of the numerous fees and surcharges imposed by Jennings and determining whether they are even validly assessed by the City in any particular case is a complicated inquiry. This inquiry involves the application of state law and procedure; local law and practice; multiple court files, accounting documents, and receipts over a period of years; and constitutional law to a person's lengthy case history. . . .

224. The City employs a materially different set of procedures for those people who [can afford to] retain private counsel. It is and has been the policy and practice of the City of Jennings to remove existing arrest warrants and schedule new court dates for those debtors who retain a private lawyer. Unrepresented people are told that there is no way to clear their warrants unless they pay the City.

### Note: Jennings, Ferguson, and Procedural Due Process

The Complaint goes on to state a number of causes of action. Many concern substantive constitutional rights under the Fourth Amendment (regarding the improper use of warrants by the city) and the Eighth Amendment's prohibition on excessive fines and unconstitutional prison conditions. But for our purposes the most fundamental and pervasive constitutional violation is that the city's debt collection practices contradict the core principles of procedural due process. Taking what you have learned from *Sniadach* and *Mathews*, what specific practices on the part of the city concern you the most?

As you might expect in light of the shocking allegations in the complaint, and the backdrop of the earlier Department of Justice report on Ferguson, see U.S. Department of Justice, Civil Rights Division, Investigation of the Ferguson Police Department (March 4, 2015), the federal district court entered a permanent injunction against the city in 2016 and the city entered into negotiations for a multi-million dollar settlement to compensate the plaintiffs. See Joint Motion for Preliminary Approval of Class Action Settlement, Civ. Action No.: 4:15-CV-00252-CEJ (E.D. Mo. July 8, 2016); Campbell Robertson, Missouri City to Pay $4.7 Million to Settle Suit Over Jailing Practices, N.Y. Times, July 15, 2016.

If you were a resident of Jennings, how would the city's practices have affected your view of the city government? The local courts? Law enforcement? Fifty years after *Sniadach*, what explains the city's use of debt collection procedures so out of line with basic standards of procedural fairness? Are you surprised to learn that the court and the city's lawyers were complicit in its practices?

In the materials that follow we will study close cases and rich debates about the cost, efficiency, and ethical integrity of the adversary system. You will see that there is much to debate. *Jenkins* is a welcome reminder at the start of those studies that there are profound reasons why the guarantee of due process appears twice in the Constitution. Optimal dispute resolution procedures are and ought to be open to debate, but there is no debating the relationship between basic human dignity and the constitutional minimum of notice and a meaningful right to be heard.

## Note: Critiques of Due Process Balancing

As we will see shortly in cases concerning the right to counsel, the balancing mandated by *Mathews* often comes out in favor of the government and of restricted rather than elaborate process. *Mathews* itself is an example of that. The Court concluded that due process does not demand an evidentiary hearing. A more recent example is Hamdi v. Rumsfeld, 542 U.S. 507 (2004). After the attacks of September 11, 2001 by the al Qaeda terrorist network, the United States invaded Afghanistan. An American citizen, Yaser Esam Hamdi, was captured on the field of battle by the Northern Alliance and turned over to the U.S. military. He was detained and interrogated in Afghanistan before being transferred to the Naval Base in Guantanamo Bay, Cuba, in January 2002. When his U.S. citizenship was confirmed a few months later he was transferred to a naval brig in Charleston, South Carolina. Hamdi's father challenged his son's detention by filing an action in federal court asserting that his son had been in Afghanistan to do relief work, that he had been in the country less than two months before being captured, and that he was not properly classified as an "enemy combatant." The government responded by filing a declaration by an intelligence officer asserting that Hamdi was "affiliated" with the Taliban.

The central question was what procedures the government had to follow in determining whether Hamdi was indeed an enemy combatant. Justice O'Connor, writing for a plurality, applied the *Mathews* balancing test and concluded that while the government had to provide an evidentiary hearing to protect Hamdi's liberty interest in establishing that he was not subject to indefinite detention as an enemy combatant, hearsay should be allowed, the government should enjoy a presumption in favor of its evidence, and the adjudicator need not be a judicial officer. These procedural modifications, Justice O'Connor concluded, were necessary to protect the government's national security interests in a time of war.

A few months after the case was decided, the government released Hamdi from the naval brig under negotiated terms. By that time, Hamdi had been detained without charges for almost three years. To secure his release, Hamdi agreed to give up his U.S. citizenship, to be deported to Saudi Arabia, and to abide by travel restrictions prohibiting him from returning to the United States or going to Israel, the West Bank, the Gaza Strip, Syria, Afghanistan, or Pakistan. He also was required to waive any right to sue the United States for the harm caused by his detention.

Justices Scalia and Stevens, an unlikely duo, dissented on the ground that a U.S. citizen either must be charged and tried or released. Far from providing a reliable measure of due process, they complained, *Mathews* balancing invites the Court "to prescribe what procedural protections *it* thinks appropriate" and adopt a "Mr. Fix-it Mentality" well beyond the competence and authority of the judicial branch. Id. at 575-576 (Scalia, J., dissenting). Justice Thomas's separate dissent in *Hamdi* attacked the balancing test as well. He argued that due process balancing has no place in matters of national security. And even if it were applicable, he added, the plurality got the balance wrong by giving excessive weight to Hamdi's interests and insufficient weight to the government's. His dissent parallels arguments Justice Rehnquist once raised regarding the subjectivity of the *Mathews* factors:

> In *Goldberg* we required a full-fledged trial-type hearing, and in *Mathews* we declined to require any pretermination process other than those required by the statute. *At times this balancing process looks as if it were undertaken with a thumb on the scale, depending on the result the Court desired.* . . . The lack of any principled standards in this area means that these procedural due process cases will recur time and time again. Every different set of facts will present a new issue on what process was due and when.

Cleveland Bd. of Educ. v. Loudermill, 470 U.S. 532, 562, n.* (1985) (Rehnquist, J., dissenting) (emphasis added). You can see that although Justice Black provided the lone dissent in *Sniadach*, his concerns about expanding procedural due process protections based on the sentiments of individual Justices have resonated with the modern Court.

There are equally strong criticisms of the *Mathews* balancing test from the left. Professor Jerry Mashaw's critique has been particularly influential, as his qualms about the case resonate with so many people. Jerry Mashaw, The Supreme Court's Due Process Calculus for Administrative Adjudication: Three Factors in Search of a Theory of Value, 44 U. Chi. L. Rev. 28 (1976). His primary concern is that the Court's account of the values of due process was incomplete. Due process is not only about the risk of error, but also about individual dignity, equality, and tradition. Yet nothing in *Mathews* refers to these important aspects of "fair procedure." Moreover, although the due process calculus set forth in *Mathews* appears scientific, it actually is highly subjective and manipulable. How is the judge to measure the risk of error referred to in the test? As Mashaw says, "the calculus asks unanswerable questions. For example, what is the social value, and the social cost, of continuing disability payments until after an oral hearing for persons initially determined to be ineligible?" Id. at 48. Finally, Mashaw argues that the Bill of Rights is "meant to insure individual liberty in the face of contrary collective action." Id. at 49. This suggests that the *Mathews* calculus is focusing on constitutionally irrelevant factors by emphasizing state interest rather than individual liberty. Thus, whether or not the result in *Mathews* was defensible, according to Mashaw the due process test it deploys was not well conceived.

Yet this critique may ignore the positive features of *Mathews*, especially its realistic appraisal of the significance of procedural costs to procedural rights, and of how any basic constitutional test must be flexible enough to apply to a vast range of due process scenarios. Particularly in the context of administrative law, which *Mathews* addressed, procedural costs must be taken seriously, given the number of hearings involved. Moreover, one must consider that administrative procedures are intended to be an alternative to civil litigation. If due process is construed to require a full-blown adversary hearing in every instance, then most alternative forms of dispute resolution would violate due process.

## 2.   Notice: The Constitutional Dimension

### Problem Case: The Elusive Defendant

You are a lawyer consulted by Paulette Peinture, who has a grievance against Gisele Fourchette, international art dealer and all-around world citizen. Peinture was employed to redecorate Fourchette's fabulous condominium for $1 million dollars. Some weeks into the work, Fourchette suddenly shouted, "I loathe this faux belle époque junk," and shoved the decorator, causing her to fall and dislocate her shoulder. Fourchette then picked up a vase on loan from a gallery and smashed it against the newly papered wall. In ordering Peinture out of the apartment forever, Fourchette said she didn't intend to pay for the work previously done. Peinture's assistant witnessed these events.

Fourchette has the lifestyle of a very rich woman, but preliminary investigation shows few liquid assets. On the other hand, she owns three late-model luxury cars and the condominium and undoubtedly has some money in a local checking account. Although a resident of the state, she retains her Swiss citizenship, and has five other residences all over the world. The incident itself suggests a certain instability and Fourchette's frequent travels might make her difficult to bring to court.

Nevertheless, you decide to file suit in federal district court in your state claiming damages for breach of contract and tortious assault. You tell your associate to do everything possible to make sure Fourchette has adequate notice, starting (but not concluding) with meeting the requirements of Fed. R. Civ. P. 4.

Your associate first scanned Rule 4 and mailed a copy of the summons to Fourchette at the condominium address. He then faxed a copy of the summons to her condominium, as well as to three art galleries in town where Fourchette is known to have business dealings. He also sent her an e-mail greeting card with the message, "You are being sued" and the law firm's return number on it.

Not satisfied that he had done everything possible, your associate hired a company called "You Sue, We Deliver" to effect in-hand service. The company took the papers to the condominium address, where they were met at the door by Roxanne DeSilva, Fourchette's elderly housekeeper, one of five assistants at the place. DeSilva would later testify that she took some papers from "a kid, a teenager who couldn't be more than 16 years old."

When he learned that Fourchette was in town as a defendant in an unrelated criminal trial, your associate mailed a copy of the summons and complaint to Fourchette's lawyer in that case. Even more ingeniously, he employed an actor to pose as a birthday messenger to deliver the papers to Fourchette on the courthouse steps as she emerged from the criminal trial. Singing "A Summons and Complaint Just for You" to a familiar tune, the actor gave, and Fourchette took, a birthday cake, under which the papers rested.

Fourchette has now moved to dismiss the complaint on the basis that she did not receive proper notice and was therefore denied due process of law. Federal courts have interpreted Rule 4(e)(2)(B) to permit service of process against a person who has multiple homes if the "dwelling or usual place of abode" selected by the plaintiff has "sufficient indicia of permanence." See National Development Co. v. Triad Holding Corp. & Adnan Khashoggi, 930 F.2d 253 (2d Cir. 1991) (service upheld against citizen of Saudi Arabia at multi-million dollar New York City apartment owned for fifteen years, elaborately remodeled, and listed as a residence on bail application in connection with a separate criminal matter; defendant claimed he "resided" in a ten-acre, six-villa compound in Riyadh, and that the New York apartment was just one of twelve locations around the world where he passed time, but was staying in New York when his housekeeper was served). How will you respond to the motion that she has been denied due process in this action?

## Greene v. Lindsey
456 U.S. 444 (1982)

JUSTICE BRENNAN delivered the opinion of the Court.

Appellees Linnie Lindsey, Barbara Hodgens, and Pamela Ray are tenants in a Louisville, Ky., housing project. Appellants are the Sheriff of Jefferson County, Ky., and certain unnamed Deputy Sheriffs charged with responsibility for serving process in forcible entry and detainer actions. In 1975, the Housing Authority of Louisville initiated detainer actions against each of appellees, seeking repossession of their apartments. Service of process was made pursuant to Ky. Rev. Stat. § 454.030 (1975), which states:

> If the officer directed to serve notice on the defendant in forcible entry or detainer proceedings cannot find the defendant on the premises mentioned in the writ, he may explain and leave a copy of the notice with any member of the defendant's family thereon over sixteen (16) years of age, and if no such person is found he may serve the notice by posting a copy thereof in a conspicuous place on the premises. The notice shall state the time and place of meeting of the court.

In each instance, notice took the form of posting a copy of the writ of forcible entry and detainer on the door of the tenant's apartment.[1] Appellees claim never to have seen these posted summonses; they state that they did not learn of the eviction proceedings until they were served with writs of possession, executed after default judgments had been entered against them, and after their opportunity for appeal had lapsed.

Thus without recourse in the state courts, appellees filed this suit as a class action in the United States District Court for the Western District of

---

1. "Posting" refers to the practice of placing the writ on the property by use of a thumbtack, adhesive tape, or other means. App. 74, 77 (deposition of process servers). Appellants describe the usual method of effecting service pursuant to § 454.030 in the following terms:

> The officer of the court who is charged with serving notice in a forcible entry and detainer action, usually a Jefferson County Deputy Sheriff, takes the following steps in notifying a tenant. First the officer goes to the apartment in an effort to effectuate personal in-hand service. Second, if the named tenant is absent or will not appear at the door, personal in-hand service is made on any member of the tenant's family over sixteen years of age. Finally, if no one answers the door, a copy of the notice is posted on the premises, usually the door.

Brief for Appellants 3.

Kentucky, seeking declaratory and injunctive relief under 42 U.S.C. § 1983.*
They claimed that the notice procedure employed as a predicate to these
eviction proceedings did not satisfy the minimum standards of constitutionally adequate notice described in Mullane v. Central Hanover Bank &
Trust Co., 339 U.S. 306 (1950), and that the Commonwealth of Kentucky
had thus failed to afford them the due process of law guaranteed by the
Fourteenth Amendment. Named as defendants were the Housing Authority
of Louisville, several public officials charged with responsibility over particular Louisville public housing projects, Joseph Greene, the Jefferson
County Sheriff, and certain known and unknown Deputy Sheriffs.

On cross-motions for summary judgment, the District Court granted
judgment for appellants. In an unreported opinion, the court noted that
some 70 years earlier, in Weber v. Grand Lodge of Kentucky, F. & A.M.,
169 F. 522 (1909), the Court of Appeals for the Sixth Circuit had held that
constructive notice by posting on the door of a building, pursuant to the
predecessor statute to § 454.030, provided an adequate constitutional basis
upon which to commence an eviction action, on the ground that it was
reasonable for the State to presume that a notice posted on the door of the
building in dispute would give the tenant actual notice in time to contest
the action. Although the District Court recognized that "conditions have
changed since the decision in *Weber* . . . and . . . that there is undisputed
testimony in this case that notices posted on the apartment doors of tenants are often removed by other tenants," App. 41-42, the court nevertheless
concluded that the procedures employed did not deny due process in light
of the fact "that posting only comes into play after the officer directed to
serve notice cannot find the defendant on the premises," id. at 42.

The Court of Appeals for the Sixth Circuit reversed the grant of summary judgment in favor of appellants and remanded the case for further
proceedings. . . .[2] We noted probable jurisdiction, 454 U.S. 938 (1981), and
now affirm.

"The fundamental requisite of due process of law is the opportunity to
be heard." Gannis v. Ordean, 234 U.S. 385, 394 (1914). And the "right to be
heard has little reality or worth unless one is informed that the matter is

---

* [Section 1983 provides in full: "Every person who, under color of any statute, ordinance, regulation, custom, or usage, of any State or Territory, subjects, or causes to be subjected, any citizen of the United States or other person within the jurisdiction thereof to
the deprivation of any rights, privileges, or immunities secured by the Constitution and
laws, shall be liable to the party injured in an action at law, suit in equity, or other proper
proceeding for redress." — Eds.]

2. The Court of Appeals concluded that "[r]equiring Kentucky to provide notice by mail
when personal service proves infeasible will not be overly burdensome. The cost will be
minimal, and the state's conceded interest in providing a summary procedure for settlement of landlord-tenant disputes will not be seriously circumscribed." 649 F.2d, at 428. The
court then noted with approval the provisions of the New York counterpart of § 454.030,
which provides that when notice is served by posting, a copy of the petition must be
sent by registered or certified mail within a day of the posting. Ibid., citing Velazquez v.
Thompson, 451 F.2d 202, 205 (2d Cir. 1971).

pending and can choose for himself whether to appear or default, acquiesce or contest," *Mullane*, supra, at 314. Personal service guarantees actual notice of the pendency of a legal action; it thus presents the ideal circumstance under which to commence legal proceedings against a person, and has traditionally been deemed necessary in actions styled *in personam*. McDonald v. Mabee, 243 U.S. 90, 92 (1917). Nevertheless, certain less rigorous notice procedures have enjoyed substantial acceptance throughout our legal history; in light of this history and the practical obstacles to providing personal service in every instance, we have allowed judicial proceedings to be prosecuted in some situations on the basis of procedures that do not carry with them the same certainty of actual notice that inheres in personal service. But we have also clearly recognized that the Due Process Clause does prescribe a constitutional minimum: "An elementary and fundamental requirement of due process in any proceeding which is to be accorded finality is *notice reasonably calculated, under all the circumstances, to apprise interested parties of the pendency of the action* and afford them an opportunity to present their objections." *Mullane*, 339 U.S. at 314 (emphasis added). It is against this standard that we evaluate the procedures employed in this case. . . .

It is, of course, reasonable to assume that a property owner will maintain superintendence of his property, and to presume that actions physically disturbing his holding will come to his attention. See *Mullane*, supra, at 316. The frequent restatement of this rule impresses upon the property owner the fact that a failure to maintain watch over his property may have significant legal consequences for him, providing a spur to his attentiveness, and a consequent reinforcement to the empirical foundation of the principle. Upon this understanding, a State may in turn conclude that in most cases, the secure posting of a notice on the property of a person is likely to offer that property owner sufficient warning of the pendency of proceedings possibly affecting his interests.

The empirical basis of the presumption that notice posted upon property is adequate to alert the owner or occupant of property of the pendency of legal proceedings would appear to make the presumption particularly well founded where notice is posted at a residence. With respect to claims affecting the continued possession of that residence, the application of this presumption seems particularly apt: If the tenant has a continuing interest in maintaining possession of the property for his use and occupancy, he might reasonably be expected to frequent the premises; if he no longer occupies the premises, then the injury that might result from his not having received actual notice as a consequence of the posted notice is reduced. Short of providing personal service, then, posting notice on the door of a person's home would, in many or perhaps most instances, constitute not only a constitutionally acceptable means of service, but indeed a singularly appropriate and effective way of ensuring that a person who cannot conveniently be served personally is actually apprised of proceedings against him.

But whatever the efficacy of posting in many cases, it is clear that, in the circumstances of this case, merely posting notice on an apartment door does not satisfy minimum standards of due process. In a significant number of instances, reliance on posting pursuant to the provisions of § 454.030 results in a failure to provide actual notice to the tenant concerned. Indeed, appellees claim to have suffered precisely such a failure of actual notice. As the process servers were well aware, notices posted on apartment doors in the area where these tenants lived were "not infrequently" removed by children or other tenants before they could have their intended effect. Under these conditions, notice by posting on the apartment door cannot be considered a "reliable means of acquainting interested parties of the fact that their rights are before the courts." *Mullane,* 339 U.S. at 315.

Of course, the reasonableness of the notice provided must be tested with reference to the existence of "feasible and customary" alternatives and supplements to the form of notice chosen. Ibid. In this connection, we reject appellants' characterization of the procedure contemplated by § 454.030 as one in which "'posting' is used as a method of service only as a last resort." To be sure, the statute requires the officer serving notice to make a visit to the tenant's home and to attempt to serve the writ personally on the tenant or some member of his family. But if no one is at home at the time of that visit, as is apparently true in a "good percentage" of cases, posting follows forthwith. Neither the statute, nor the practice of the process servers, makes provision for even a second attempt at personal service, perhaps at some time of day when the tenant is more likely to be at home. The failure to effect personal service on the first visit hardly suggests that the tenant has abandoned his interest in the apartment such that mere *pro forma* notice might be held constitutionally adequate. Cf. *Mullane,* 339 U.S., at 317-318.

As noted by the Court of Appeals, and as we noted in *Mullane,* the mails provide an "efficient and inexpensive means of communication," id., at 319, upon which prudent men will ordinarily rely in the conduct of important affairs, id., at 319-320. Notice by mail in the circumstances of this case would surely go a long way toward providing the constitutionally required assurance that the State has not allowed its power to be invoked against a person who has had no opportunity to present a defense despite a continuing interest in the resolution of the controversy. Particularly where the subject matter of the action also happens to be the mailing address of the defendant, and where personal service is ineffectual, notice by mail may reasonably be relied upon to provide interested persons with actual notice of judicial proceedings. We need not go so far as to insist that in order to "dispense with personal service the substitute that is most likely to reach the defendant is the least that ought to be required," McDonald v. Mabee, 243 U.S., 90, 92 (1917), in order to recognize that where an inexpensive and efficient mechanism such as mail service is available to enhance the reliability of an otherwise unreliable notice procedure, the State's continued exclusive reliance on an ineffective means of service is not notice "reasonably calculated to reach those who could easily be informed by other means at hand." *Mullane,* supra, at 319.

We conclude that in failing to afford appellees adequate notice of the proceedings against them before issuing final orders of eviction, the State has deprived them of property without the due process of law required by the Fourteenth Amendment. The judgment of the Court of Appeals is therefore *Affirmed*.

Justice O'Connor, with whom The Chief Justice and Justice Rehnquist join, dissenting.

Today, the Court holds that the Constitution prefers the use of the Postal Service to posted notice. The Court reaches this conclusion despite the total absence of any evidence in the record regarding the speed and reliability of the mails. The sole ground for the Court's result is the scant and conflicting testimony of a handful of process servers in Kentucky. On this flimsy basis, the Court confidently overturns the work of the Kentucky Legislature and, by implication, that of at least 10 other States. I must respectfully dissent. . . .

Kentucky's forcible entry and detainer action is a summary proceeding for quickly determining whether or not a landlord has the right to immediate possession of leased premises and, if so, for enabling the landlord speedily to obtain the property from the person in wrongful possession. Ky. Rev. Stat. §§ 383.200, 383.210 (1972). As this Court has recognized, such circumstances call for special procedures:

> There are unique factual and legal characteristics of the landlord-tenant relationship that justify special statutory treatment inapplicable to other litigants. The tenant is, by definition, in possession of the property of the landlord; unless a judicially supervised mechanism is provided for what would otherwise be swift repossession by the landlord himself, the tenant would be able to deny the landlord the rights of income incident to ownership by refusing to pay rent and by preventing sale or rental to someone else. Many expenses of the landlord continue to accrue whether a tenant pays his rent or not. Speedy adjudication is desirable to prevent subjecting the landlord to undeserved economic loss and the tenant to unmerited harassment and dispossession when his lease or rental agreement gives him the right to peaceful and undisturbed possession of the property. Lindsey v. Normet, 405 U.S. 56, 72-73 (1972).

The means chosen for making service of process, therefore, must be prompt and certain, for otherwise the principal purpose of a forcible entry and detainer action could be thwarted before the judicial proceedings even began.

The Kentucky statute meets this need. . . .

The Court, however, holds that notice via the mails is so far superior to posted notice that the difference is of constitutional dimension. How the Court reaches this judgment remains a mystery, especially since the Court is unable, on the present record, to evaluate the risks that notice mailed to public housing projects might fail due to loss, misdelivery, lengthy delay, or theft. Furthermore, the advantages of the mails over posting, if any, are far from obvious. It is no secret, after all, that unattended mailboxes are subject to plunder by thieves. Moreover, unlike the use of the mails, posting notice at least gives assurance that the notice has gotten as far as the tenant's door.

## *Notes and Questions*

1. Note that the Court in *Greene* did not hold that posting is always unconstitutional; rather, the circumstances were such that posting was an unreliable method of service in light of the available alternatives. What is the basis for this conclusion?

2. Service by posting has a long historical pedigree that may make the result in *Greene* surprising. After all, if due process is informed by one's reasonable expectations about the process due, including the notice due, then the long history of permitting notice by posting suggests that the practice is constitutional. Moreover, as you saw in Justice Harlan's concurring opinion in *Sniadach*, and as you will see in connection with personal jurisdiction later in the chapter, some members of the current Court believe that traditional practices are extremely important measures of due process. How do you imagine these Justices would have ruled in *Greene*? Revisit this question after you have read Burnham v. Superior Court, 495 U.S. 604 (1990), infra.

## *Note: Mullane v. Central Hanover Bank and Tr. Co.*

The practice of serving individuals by publication was rendered constitutionally suspect in Mullane v. Central Hanover Bank & Tr. Co., 339 U.S. 306 (1950), one of the cases relied on by the majority in *Sniadach*. *Mullane* involved a common trust fund administered by the Central Hanover Bank. The New York banking statute permitted smaller trust estates to be pooled into a larger fund, enabling small investors to afford professional money managers. State law required the trustee of the fund to petition the New York Surrogate Court to settle or audit its activities as trustee. Pursuant to statute, the trustee gave notice of the petition by publishing it in a local newspaper. And months earlier, when each participating trust fund first invested in the common fund, known beneficiaries of the pooled trust had been mailed notice of the procedure for settling the pooled trust.

The court appointed Mullane as representative of all persons with an interest in the income of the common fund and appointed Vaughan as representative of all persons with an interest in the principal of the fund. Mullane challenged the proceeding on the grounds, inter alia, that process had not been served personally on nonresident beneficiaries of the trust and that service by publication violated due process. The Court held that the statutory notice by publication was adequate only for those beneficiaries whose whereabouts were unknown or whose rights were conjectural when the action began. Known beneficiaries, whose whereabouts were reasonably ascertainable, were entitled to notice by mail. The Court in *Mullane* also set forth the general standard for constitutionally sufficient notice that appears in *Greene*.

The Supreme Court has continued to invoke the standard of *Mullane*—notice "reasonably calculated" to apprise interested parties—in a wide range of notice settings. In Dusenbery v. United States, 534 U.S. 161

(2002), the Court held, in a 5-4 decision, that notice by certified mail is sufficient to put a prisoner on notice of the administrative forfeiture of cash seized at the time of his arrest. The prisoner claimed he did not receive the certified letter, and that the Bureau of Prisons could have assured actual delivery of the letter to him while he was incarcerated. The majority disagreed, observing that actual notice is not required by *Mullane* and that the methods used were reasonably certain to inform the prisoner.

## Note: Jones v. Flowers

Certified mail was good enough for service on prisoners in *Dusenbery*, but the Court rejected service by certified mail on a taxpayer in Jones v. Flowers, 547 U.S. 220 (2006). Gary Jones bought a house on North Bryan Street in Little Rock, Arkansas, in 1967. He lived there with his wife until they separated in 1993 and Jones moved into an apartment. He continued to pay the mortgage on the house to a mortgage company that deducted and paid the property taxes each month. Once the house was paid off, however, Jones neglected to pay the property taxes and the property was certified as delinquent. In 2000, the State Lands Commissioner mailed a notice of delinquency to Jones at the North Bryan address via certified mail. No one was home, and no one came to the post office in the next 15 days to retrieve the letter, so it was returned to the Commissioner "unclaimed."

In 2002, a few weeks before the property was to be sold at public auction, the Commissioner published a notice of public sale in the *Arkansas Democrat Gazette*. Jones did not come forward. Although no bids were received at the auction, Linda Flowers made an offer a few months later, and the Commissioner again sent a certified letter to Jones at the North Bryan address stating that the land would be sold to Flowers if he did not pay his back taxes. The letter was returned unclaimed and the property, estimated to be worth $80,000, was sold to Flowers for $21,042.15. Flowers then brought proceedings to evict Jones's daughter from the property.

Jones did not learn of the tax sale until his daughter brought him the notice of unlawful detainer Flowers had served on her. Jones responded by filing an action in state court claiming that the Commissioner's attempts at notice were constitutionally deficient under *Mullane* and thus a taking of private property without due process of law. The state trial and appellate courts agreed with the Commissioner that two certified letters are all state law requires and, citing *Dusenbery*, all the process Jones was due under the Constitution.

Writing for the majority, Chief Justice Roberts observed that while due process "does not require that a property owner receive actual notice before the government may take his property," id. at 226, when the government learns that its chosen method of notice has failed, *Mullane* requires that the government take additional steps. Following *Greene*, the Court observed that the Commissioner could have resent the letter by regular mail or posted notice at the house. Id. at 229. As the Court admonished:

We do not think that a person who actually desired to inform a real property owner of an impending tax sale of a house he owns would do nothing when a certified letter sent to the owner is returned unclaimed. If the Commissioner prepared a stack of letters to mail to delinquent taxpayers, handed them to the postman, and then watched as the departing postman accidentally dropped the letters down a storm drain, one would certainly expect the Commissioner's office to prepare a new stack of letters and send them again. No one "desirous of actually informing" the owners would simply shrug his shoulders as the letters disappeared and say "I tried." Failure to follow up would be unreasonable, despite the fact that the letters were reasonably calculated to reach their intended recipients when delivered to the postman. . . .

In prior cases, we have required the government to consider unique information about an intended recipient regardless of whether a statutory scheme is reasonably calculated to provide notice in the ordinary case. In Robinson v. Hanrahan, we held that notice of forfeiture proceedings sent to a vehicle owner's home address was inadequate when the State knew that the property owner was in prison. 409 U.S. at 40. In Covey v. Town of Somers, 351 U.S. 141 (1956), we held that notice of foreclosure by mailing, posting, and publication was inadequate when town officials knew that the property owner was incompetent and without a guardian's protection. Id. at 146-147.

The Commissioner points out that in these cases, the State was aware of such information *before* it calculated how best to provide notice. But it is difficult to explain why due process would have settled for something less if the government had learned after notice was sent, but before the taking occurred, that the property owner was in prison or was incompetent. Under *Robinson* and *Covey*, the government's knowledge that notice pursuant to the normal procedure was ineffective triggered an obligation on the government's part to take additional steps to effect notice. That knowledge was one of the "practicalities and peculiarities of the case," *Mullane*, supra, at 314-315, that the Court took into account in determining whether constitutional requirements were met. It should similarly be taken into account in assessing the adequacy of notice in this case. . . .

It is certainly true, as the Commissioner and Solicitor General contend, that the failure of notice in a specific case does not establish the inadequacy of the attempted notice; in that sense, the constitutionality of a particular procedure for notice is assessed *ex ante*, rather than *post hoc*. But if a feature of the State's chosen procedure is that it promptly provides additional information to the government about the effectiveness of notice, it does not contravene the *ex ante* principle to consider what the government does with that information in assessing the adequacy of the chosen procedure. After all, the State knew *ex ante* that it would promptly learn whether its effort to effect notice through certified mail had succeeded. It would not be inconsistent with the approach the Court has taken in notice cases to ask, with respect to a procedure under which telephone calls were placed to owners, what the State did when no one answered. Asking what the State does when a notice letter is returned unclaimed is not substantively different.

Id. at 1716-1717. The Court rejected the Commissioner's argument that notice was reasonably calculated to reach Jones because he was under a legal obligation to keep his address up to date with the tax assessor. It noted, however, that the Commissioner was under no obligation to check to see if Jones's address had changed after he took reasonable additional steps such as resending and posting notice.

Three Justices dissented, arguing that notice by certified mail to an owner's record address should be all that due process requires and insisting that the sufficiency of a state's method of notice must be assessed *ex ante*, at the time notice in any case is sent, not *ex post*, when considerations that go to whether a particular defendant actually received notice inevitably creep in.

Why would resending or posting have improved notice to Jones if he no longer lived at the property? Perhaps, despite its disclaimer, the majority is in effect requiring actual notice. The Court also may have inadvertently resuscitated posting as an alternative or supplemental way of giving notice. Maybe when the notice pertains to an inhabited dwelling, posting is actually better than certified mail, though the Court's larger point is surely that those giving notice must attend to context in choosing a method of service and implementing it.

## 3.   Notice: Constitutional Requirements Ritualized: Rule 4

Rule 4 sets out specifically how to give notice. While a lawyer may want to do more than required, she must not do less. Has the associate in the problem case succeeded in giving notice? In meeting the requirements of the Rule?

In its original version, Rule 4 assumed that in-hand delivery of a summons, often by a federal marshal, would be the usual form of service. Major changes in 1983 and 1993 moved mail delivery, with waiver of further service, to the heart of the process. As one commentator rather wistfully noted: "The awesome impact of the sheriff arriving in armor and on horseback . . . and the authority of the sovereign sealed in the hot, red wax of earlier times has been replaced by a bland manila envelope carrying a postage stamp that may celebrate notions of love or poetry." Kent Sinclair, Service of Process: Rethinking the Theory and Procedure of Serving Process Under Federal Rule 4(c), 73 Va. L. Rev. 1183, 1188-1189 (1987).

It took many years, and repeated expressions of preference for mail by the Supreme Court, like those in *Greene*, before Rule 4 was changed significantly. Now, however, waiver of service by mail is standard. See Fed. R. Civ. P. 4(d). The next reforms appear to be coming more quickly. Rule 5(b)(2)(E), effective December 2001, now allows electronic service on parties who give their written consent. Such service is complete upon transmission. See also Rule 6(d) (providing an additional three days to respond to a paper served via electronic means).

In the first federal appellate case to address the point, the U.S. Court of Appeals for the Ninth Circuit held that a foreign defendant could be served via e-mail. Rio Properties, Inc. v. Rio Int'l Interlink, 284 F.3d 1007

(9th Cir. 2002). The court noted that Rule 4(f)(3) permits courts to direct service "by other means not prohibited by international agreement," and concluded that e-mail service fell within this rule and satisfied due process. The defendant in question had a Web site and had structured its business such that it could only be contacted via e-mail. See also In re Int'l Telemedia Assocs., Inc., 245 B.R. 713 (Bankr. N.D. Ga. 2000) (holding that e-mail service was authorized under Rule 4(f)(3) where it was the only means of communication between plaintiff and defendant).

The Ninth Circuit is not the only court to permit e-mail service. Snyder v. Alternate Energy, Inc., 857 N.Y.S.2d 442 (Civ. Ct. 2008), allowed e-mail service under New York state law provisions permitting the court to direct the manner of service upon individuals and corporations alike when the other methods outlined in the state rules proved "impracticable." Plaintiffs had unsuccessfully attempted to locate the defendants' physical whereabouts and contact them via telephone, but were in frequent contact with defendants over e-mail and instant messenger software. Noting the "pervasive role the internet plays in today's world," id. at 443, and citing *Rio* and *Telemedia*, id. at 447-448, the court crafted an order requiring that plaintiffs e-mail service on two consecutive dates with "prominent subject line[s] indicating that what was being sent were legal papers in an attachment that was to be opened immediately." Id. at 449. "To better insure the effectiveness of the notice to defendants," the court also required plaintiffs to send paper copies of the e-mailed documents to the defendants' last known physical addresses, and contact them at their last known phone numbers. Id. The court concluded its opinion by stating that the "broad constitutional principle" underlying judicially devised alternative service "unshackles the . . . courts from anachronistic methods of service and permits them entry into the technological renaissance." Id. at 449 (quoting *Rio*, 284 F.3d at 1017). Compare Hollow v. Hollow, 747 N.Y.S.2d 704 (S. Ct. Oswego Cty. 2002) (e-mail service is proper on a defendant in divorce proceedings who was living in a secure compound in Saudi Arabia, where armed guards had been instructed to turn away process servers), with Liberty Media Holdings, LLC v. Sheng Gan, 2012 WL 122862 (D. Colo. Jan. 17, 2012) (denying motion for e-mail service due to uncertainty about which e-mail address defendant uses and whether defendant "has held these addresses out to the public as a preferred means of contact"), and Kowalski v. Anova Food, LLC, 2012 WL 3308884 (D. Haw. Aug. 10, 2012) (denying motion for e-mail service where plaintiff presented no evidence of evasion by defendant, no evidence defendant's physical location was concealed, and no evidence of attempts to serve defendant in Malta). Kevin W. Lewis discusses the developing case law in E-Service: Ensuring the Integrity of International Email Service of Process, 13 Roger Williams U. L. Rev. 285 (2008).

Is serving process through a social networking site such as Facebook more or less controversial than using e-mail? An Australian court has authorized service via Facebook for notice of a default judgment. See Nick Abrahams, Australian Court Serves Documents via Facebook, Sydney Morning Herald,

Dec. 12, 2008. Melodie M. Dan suggests that service by social networking sites may be superior to e-mail service in her article, Social Networking Sites: A Reasonably Calculated Method to Effect Service of Process, 1 Case W. Res. J.L. Tech. & Internet 183 (2010). And a U.S. federal court has authorized service under Rule 4(f) via Twitter against a Kuwaiti bank and others for damages arising from their financial relationship with ISIS and ISIS sponsored attacks in Iraq and Syria. See Venkat Balasurbramani, Federal Court Authorizes Service of Process Via Twitter, October 1, 2016, http://blog.ericgoldman.org/archives/2016/10/federal-court-authorizes-service-of-process-via-twitter.htm.

Experiments with electronic filing of pleadings and motions with the court may further encourage electronic service of process. Many state courts and federal district courts have set up systems for online filing. The Advisory Committee on Rules of Civil Procedure has amended Rule 5(d)(3) to authorize all federal district courts by local rule to require papers to be filed, signed, or verified electronically, as long as the rules provide "reasonable exceptions." And under Rule 5(b)(3), the same papers can be served on parties using the court's electronic case management system. So once initial service of the summons and complaint occurs under Rule 4, most other papers in the case (motions, pleadings, notices, etc., see Rule 5(a)) can be filed and served electronically. Electronic case management systems are now pervasive in the federal courts and many courts use the same system to distribute orders to the parties.

Despite modern innovations, personal service has continued to play a major role, and will likely do so even under the waiver of service revision, which still contemplates hand delivery as the major fallback if service by mail should fail.

In most places these days, personal service is seldom done by the sheriff or marshal. Rather, professionals hired by the litigant seek out both easy-to-find and reclusive defendants. One commentator says that this "curious band of white collar soldiers of fortune" often supplies the "grease that gets the ponderous wheels of justice turning." Here is his description of the business of one such office:

> Batzi's (the 26-year-old owner) business ebbs and flows with the season. This time of year he hears a lot from one client, Western Appliance. People whose budgets were blown on Christmas are falling behind on the freezer payments. He works on a lot of child support cases in August and September. "A lot of ex-wives are taking their husbands back to court to get more money for the kid's clothes for school." July and August are the petty crime months when kids are out of school with too much time on their hands. "People are getting divorced all the time—except December. . . . They try to stick it through till the first of the year for tax reasons." In the fall Batzi serves a lot of roofers—the rainy season has begun, exposing shoddy work done the season before.
>
> To serve papers, a process server can do anything short of impersonating an officer of the law. He can lie about his identity or intent. Batzi always

carries a change of clothes in the back of his car for disguise. He delights in making "gag" phone calls to people he is tracking down, verifying their presence by informing them that they have just won a lifetime subscription to *Field and Stream.* . . .

Edward O. Welles, They Also Serve, San Jose Mercury West, Dec. 28, 1986, at 4.

A lawyer's magazine details the consumer's point of view:

"Early in my practice," says Marc Alan Fong, a partner with Fong & Fong of Oakland, "I had some bad experiences with gutter service. I was looking for the cheapest way to serve, and cheapest isn't always the best."

Indeed, "gutter service"—the unauthorized drop-off or posting of papers—is the bane of the process-serving industry. Incompetent process servers can easily ruin a case by slipping papers through a mail slot, leaving them with an unauthorized substitute or even falsifying proof of service and tossing the actual documents. For an attorney, this unethical practice leads to loss of time, costly re-servicing and default judgments. The process server may also face a suit by the person mis-served.

Problems range from the mundane to the melodramatic. First, there's the task of locating the person to be served. Since process servers are generally regarded as door-to-door salesmen specializing in bad news, it's not surprising that all but the most pedestrian jobs require some degree of ingenuity. Seasoned veterans talk romantically about all-night stakeouts, scaling third-story ledges and devising elaborate ruses to trick a recalcitrant subject into identifying himself.

And there is always the prospect of violence. Some irate recipients of process, particularly in bitter domestic cases, take too literally the classical notion of killing the messenger.

"I've been threatened, chased, and had guns pointed under my nose," says Judith A. Cochran, owner of A and T Legal Process Service in Oakland. "One guy led a German shepherd right up against my jugular." Another time, Cochran served the owners of a circus while elephants trained in a yard next to the house. When Cochran handed over the papers, the housemaid energetically beckoned to the elephants in an indecipherable foreign tongue. "The elephants trumpeted and came running towards me," says Cochran. "I don't know to this day whether they were coming after me, or if they were just frightened by the maid."

Fred Setterberg, Service with a Smile: Selecting the Right Process Server, 5 Cal. Law. 55 (July 1985).

Whatever choices the lawyer makes about the method of service, delay is dangerous. For one thing, statutes of limitation in some jurisdictions run until service of process is complete. Filing the complaint in court is not enough to stop the statute of limitations from running. Second, Rule 4(m) gives plaintiffs 90 days to effect service before the court "must dismiss the action without prejudice . . . or order that service be made within a specified time." And as the following case shows, the technicalities of Rule 4 must be observed precisely in effecting service.

## *Mid-Continent Wood Products v. Harris*
936 F.2d 297 (7th Cir. 1991)

COFFEY, CIRCUIT JUDGE.

Lawrence A. Harris appeals the district court's order denying his Rule 60(b)(4) motion to vacate and dismiss a default judgment on the grounds of improper service of process. We reverse.

## I. Facts and Disposition Below

Harris Plywood, Inc. ("Harris Plywood") purchased lumber from the plaintiff, Mid-Continent Wood Products, Inc. ("Mid-Continent") on three separate occasions between May and August of 1980. When Harris Plywood failed to make any payments on the three shipments, the parties entered into negotiations in October 1980 and Harris agreed that the amount due would bear interest at the rate of fourteen percent per annum and that payments would commence within a few weeks. After Harris Plywood failed to make any payments, Mid-Continent filed suit in April 1981 for breach of contract. The parties entered into negotiations for a second time and after these discussions proved fruitless, Mid-Continent filed a motion for a default judgment. On October 28, 1981, the district court granted Mid-Continent's motion for a default judgment in Mid-Continent Wood Products, Inc. v. Harris Plywood, Inc., in the amount of $28,544.75. Instead of executing on the default judgment, Mid-Continent accepted a promissory note for the judgment amount from the defendant Lawrence Harris, President of Harris Plywood, in December of 1981. When Harris failed to pay the amount due, Mid-Continent filed this action to collect on Harris' promissory note.

Mid-Continent makes clear that (to state it mildly) it had a rather difficult time locating Harris and serving him with the complaint and summons. Initially, Mid-Continent attempted to serve Harris personally through a U.S. Marshal in December 1982. One month later on January 5, 1983, the marshal again attempted service by certified mail at Harris' place of employment, Superb Realty Corporation. Harris denied receipt of this mailing.

Mid-Continent states it next attempted service in May 1983 through a private process server at what was thought to be Harris' residence at 13 Secor Drive, Port Washington, New York. On two separate occasions the server attempted personal service but found no one at the address. On the third attempt, the server left the complaint and summons attached to the door of the residence, and followed this up by mailing another copy addressed to Harris at the same address.

At the request of the district court, Mid-Continent's attorney sent a letter on June 3, 1983, to the residence at 13 Secor Drive in order to notify Harris of an upcoming status hearing. A copy of this letter was also sent to Harris' counsel of record in the previous lawsuit, Samuel Panzer. Neither the letter to Harris nor the copy sent to Harris' attorney included copies of the complaint and summons. Harris' attorney contacted Mid-Continent on June 9, 1983, and proposed a settlement in which Harris would pay the entire amount due on the note in monthly installments. Mid-Continent's attorney rejected the offer and stated that if the full amount was not received, Mid-Continent would seek a judgment order against Harris. Nevertheless, Harris' attorney confirmed in writing Harris' intention of forwarding a check and promissory notes in partial satisfaction of the amount due under Harris' guaranty. As promised by Harris' attorney, a mailing arrived from Superb Realty, Harris' place of business, containing a check for $1,000.00 signed on behalf of Superb Realty and three notes for $1,000.00 each, also signed by agents acting on behalf of Superb Realty. On June 16, 1983, Mid-Continent's attorney again informed Harris' attorney that no settlement for less than the full amount would suffice and that if full payment was not received before the next status hearing on June 28, 1983, Mid-Continent would seek a default judgment against Harris. When no further payments were made, Mid-Continent obtained a default judgment against Harris on July 20, 1983, in the amount of $24,549.92.

After securing the judgment, Mid-Continent alleges that it attempted but was unable to locate Harris' assets for some time for purposes of executing on the judgment. Six years later, in June of 1989, Mid-Continent located certain assets of Harris' in Massachusetts and attempted to execute upon the 1983 judgment. However, on August 31, 1989, Harris filed a motion for relief in the district court pursuant to Rule 60(b)(4) of the Federal Rules of Civil Procedure[3] claiming that because service on him did not properly comply with Rule 4 of the Federal Rules of Civil Procedure, the district court lacked personal jurisdiction over him at the time of the entry of judgment in 1983 and further that he never received a copy of the complaint and summons in this action. In support of his motion, Harris offered exhibits and affidavits stating that he never resided at 13 Secor Drive, Port Washington, New York, but stated that he lived at 15 Secor Drive, Port Washington, New York in 1983. He further stated that no one at 13 Secor Drive ever brought any documents pertaining to the case to his house at 15 Secor Drive. The district court issued an opinion denying Harris' motion to vacate and dismiss the default judgment on the grounds of improper service of process on November 1, 1989. While the district court acknowledged in its opinion that service upon Harris did not strictly comply with Rule 4, it nonetheless determined that strict compliance was unnecessary because of: 1) Harris' "actual knowledge of the lawsuit" based on Harris' former attorney's negotiations with Mid-Continent; 2) Mid-Continent's diligent efforts "to obtain technically proper service upon Harris"; and 3) Harris' evasive conduct in responding to the attempts at service of process.

---

3. Rule 60(b)(4) provides relief from a final judgment when the judgment is void.

## II.  Issue for Review

The issue before us is whether a district court may formulate its own test to determine whether to assert personal jurisdiction over a defendant in the absence of service of complaint and summons in accordance with Rule 4 of the Federal Rules of Civil Procedure.

## III.  Discussion

. . . The district court found that Mid-Continent's attempted service of process on Harris did not comply with Rule 4. The district court then proceeded to devise a three-part test and fashioned an exception to the usual requirements of strict compliance with Rule 4:

> When the cases are examined, three requirements present themselves as requisite to finding an exception to strict compliance. First, it is imperative to upholding faulty service that the defendant actually know of a lawsuit. . . . Second, the server must show that he duly tried to serve the defendant properly; in other words, show that more than a minimum effort was made and that the service actually made on the defendant came reasonably close to satisfying the requirements. This is often stated in terms of the plaintiff having "substantially complied" with Rule 4's mandate. . . . Third, the equities of the situation must warrant an exception from the usual strict compliance requirement. Specifically, the focus here is on the conduct of the defendant in responding to the situation.

The district court determined that these three factors "point clearly toward an exception from strict compliance in this case."

Rule 4(d)(1)* provides that the complaint and summons shall, with respect to an individual defendant who is not an infant or incompetent, be made:

> by delivering a copy of the summons and of the complaint to the individual personally or by leaving copies thereof at the individual's dwelling house or usual place of abode with some person of suitable age and discretion then residing therein or by delivering a copy of the summons and of the complaint to an agent authorized by appointment or by law to receive service of process.

The Supreme Court recently addressed the issue of judicially created rules authorizing the service of process:

> We would consider it unwise for a court to make its own rule authorizing service of summons. It seems likely that Congress has been acting on the

---

* [The provision of the Rule referred to in the case as Rule 4(d)(1) now appears as Rule 4(e)(2). — EDS.]

assumption that federal courts cannot add to the scope of service of summons Congress has authorized. . . . The strength of this long-standing assumption, and the network of statutory enactments and judicial decisions tied to it, argue strongly against devising common law service of process provisions at this late date for at least two reasons. First, since Congress concededly has the power to limit service of process, circumspection is called for in going beyond what Congress has authorized. Second, as statutes and rules have always provided the measures for service, courts are inappropriate forums for deciding whether to extend them. Omni Capital International v. Rudolf Wolff & Company, Ltd., 484 U.S. 97 (1987).

This court has previously stated that a liberal construction of the rules of service of process "cannot be utilized as a substitute for the plain legal requirement as to the manner in which service of process may be had." United States v. Mollenhauer Laboratories, Inc., 267 F.2d 260, 262 (7th Cir. 1959).

. . . [T]he factors considered by the district court have questionable validity, and as a result, the district court's three-part test must fail. The first factor the district court considered in determining the jurisdictional question concerning Harris was its finding that Harris had "actual knowledge of the lawsuit" based on Harris' former attorney's negotiations with Mid-Continent. The district court quotes Armco, Inc. v. Penrod-Stauffer Building Systems, Inc. for the proposition that "[w]hen there is actual notice, every technical violation of the rule or failure of strict compliance may not invalidate the service of process." 733 F.2d 1087, 1089 (4th Cir. 1984). However, the appellate court in *Armco* found the service of process to be invalid despite the defendant's knowledge of the suit and thus, the trial court was without jurisdiction and the default judgment was void. Id. at 1089.

This court has long recognized that valid service of process is necessary in order to assert personal jurisdiction over a defendant. Rabiolo v. Weinstein, 357 F.2d 167 (7th Cir. 1966). Moreover, it is well recognized that a "defendant's actual notice of the litigation . . . is insufficient to satisfy Rule 4's requirements."

In a case similar to ours, the District Court for the Northern District of Indiana held that a defendant's knowledge of a lawsuit will not serve to "cure the deficiencies in service." Bennett v. Circus U.S.A., 108 F.R.D. 142, 148 (1985). In *Bennett*, the plaintiff was unable to locate the defendant and attempted service of the complaint and summons by sending them certified mail to the law firm which had represented the defendant in a previous matter.

. . . [T]he *Bennett* court initially held that service of the summons and complaint upon the defendant's attorney was insufficient because the attorney had not been specifically appointed as an agent to accept service of process. Next, the court rejected the plaintiff's argument that the court had personal jurisdiction over the defendant because the defendant knew of the lawsuit prior to the entry of the default judgment. . . .

We agree with the *Bennett* court and hold that actual knowledge of the existence of a lawsuit is insufficient to confer personal jurisdiction over a defendant in the absence of valid service of process. Even though Harris may have had knowledge of the lawsuit as a result of Harris' former attorney's negotiations with Mid-Continent, "actual notice alone is insufficient to give the court the jurisdiction necessary to allow it to enter a judgment against a defendant." Id. Thus, the district court's reliance on actual notice in determining that it had personal jurisdiction over Harris is erroneous.

The second part of the district court's three-part test focused on whether "the service actually made on the defendant came reasonably close to satisfying the requirements [of Rule 4]." The district court characterized this factor as whether the plaintiff "substantially complied" with Rule 4's mandate. The district court determined that Mid-Continent "tried diligently to obtain technically proper service upon Harris." The court further noted that these attempts "were sufficient to result in settlement discussions between the parties."

This court is reluctant to find jurisdiction based upon whether Mid-Continent "tried diligently" to serve Harris. Indeed, the extent to which the plaintiff "tried" to serve process should not be a factor as to whether a federal court has personal jurisdiction over a defendant. Rather, the requirements of Rule 4 are satisfied only when the plaintiff is successful in serving the complaint and summons on the defendant.

The district court cites United Food & Commercial Workers Union v. Alpha Beta Company, 736 F.2d 1371 (9th Cir. 1984), for its erroneous conclusion that a plaintiff need only come "reasonably close" to satisfying the requirements of Rule 4. However, *United Food* is applicable only to those cases in which the "substantial compliance" is used to prevent a technical error in the form of the documents under Rule 4 from defeating an otherwise proper and successful delivery of process. . . . Thus, to the extent that the "substantial compliance" doctrine has any validity, it is applicable to only those cases such as *United Food*, where it was involved to prevent a purely technical error in the form of the documents under Rule 4 from invalidating an otherwise proper and successful delivery of process.

Even if we agreed with the district court's interpretation of the "substantial compliance" doctrine (which we do not), the facts lead us to believe that ours is a case of "substantial *non*-compliance." The extent of Mid-Continent's efforts to obtain service on Harris consisted of the following: 1) one certified mailing of the complaint and summons to a business address of Harris (which Harris denies receiving), and neither the envelope containing the complaint and summons nor the return receipt evidencing delivery were ever returned; 2) three attempts at personal service by a private process server over a four-day period at an incorrect address; and 3) a noncertified mailing to the same incorrect address.

The district court also cites the settlement discussions between the parties' attorneys as proof that the above-cited attempts at service were sufficient. However, nowhere in Rule 4 is there an exception for settlement discussions in the absence of the usual requirements of proper service of process, nor does the district court cite any case law in support of this proposition. . . .

The third and final factor of the district court's three-part test is whether the "equities" of the case warrant an exception from the usual strict compliance requirement: "Specifically, the focus here is on the conduct of the defendant in responding to the situation." The court cites evasion of process by the defendant as "the most typical example" of this kind of conduct. . . .

The cases cited by the district court involve clear-cut examples of evasion: both involve defendants who specifically refused to acknowledge service and are thus distinguishable. The facts in the case before us fall short of establishing clear and convincing evidence of evasion on the part of the defendant. Unlike the defendants in *Nikwei* and *Benage,* there is no evidence that Harris either refused to accept his mail or actually received mail service but refused to acknowledge it. The district court infers evasion on the part of Harris because of the repeated, *though faulty,* attempts at service of process by Mid-Continent. As we stated supra, valid service of process is a must in order to assert personal jurisdiction over a defendant. Furthermore, the district court found that Harris had acted inequitably by allowing his attorney to engage in settlement discussions with Mid-Continent's attorney and then challenging the service of process six years after the judgment was entered: "Defendant in this case simply sat on his potential defense until the plaintiff finally found some of his assets and only then attempted to assert it." While we certainly do not condone Harris' or his attorney's conduct, we are of the opinion that the record falls short of supporting a finding of evasion or inequitable conduct by Harris.

## IV. Conclusion

The three-part test devised by the district court to uphold the default judgment entered against Harris fails to support an exception to the service of process requirements of Rule 4. Therefore, the district court's order denying Harris' Rule 60(b)(4) motion to vacate and dismiss the default judgment on the grounds of improper service of process is *reversed.*

## *Notes and Questions*

1. Some might consider *Mid-Continent* the worst kind of insistence on legal technicality, while others might view it as the best example of the rule of law. What are the arguments for these two positions? What would happen if judges did *not* insist on the technicalities of Rule 4?

2. If, as in *Mid-Continent,* a default judgment has already been entered, the defendant will have to move to vacate the judgment under Rule 60(b)(4). The defendant will bear the burden of proving she is entitled to relief even though the plaintiff normally has the burden of establishing the court's power to hear the case and its power to bind the defendant to any judgment. In *Mid-Continent,* the court held that it did not matter that Harris

had actual notice of the litigation against him: Rule 4 had to be followed to obtain personal jurisdiction over him.

But actual notice is not totally irrelevant when a default judgment is challenged. It can affect the burden of proof on a motion to vacate. The Second, Seventh, and Ninth Circuits have held that a defendant who had actual notice of the litigation carries a "substantial burden" of proving that service was improper, particularly when the plaintiff presents a return of service signed by the process server. SEC v. Internet Sols. for Bus. Inc., 509 F.3d 1161, 1163 (9th Cir. 2007) (following Burda Media, Inc. v. Viertel, 417 F.3d 292, 299 (2d Cir. 2005)); O'Brien v. R.J. O'Brien & Assocs. Inc., 998 F.2d 1394, 1398 (7th Cir. 1993); Bally Exp. Corp. v. Balicar, Ltd., 804 F.2d 398, 400-401 (7th Cir. 1986). In *Internet Solutions*, the SEC presented a signed return of service by a process server with a "long and reputable" history and a sworn declaration from the process server claiming that the defendant verified his identity before accepting the summons and complaint for securities fraud. 509 F.3d at 1166. After moving to vacate the $100,000 default judgment, the defendant conceded he knew about the lawsuit but claimed he was at a meeting in another town the day the process server supposedly effected service. Id. Neither the district court nor the Ninth Circuit was convinced:

> Each time Shaw's story was challenged he came up with new and often contradictory evidence to support his version of the facts. In the face of the process server's sworn affidavits, and given the district court's credibility findings in favor of the process server and against Shaw, we find that Shaw did not meet his burden to prove by strong and convincing evidence that he was not served with process.

Id. at 1167 (characterizing e-mail correspondence suggesting defendant might have been out of town as "rank hearsay").

3. Courts are not always as inflexible regarding strict compliance with the Rule 4 mandates as the court was in *Mid-Continent*. Consider the following passage from Ortiz v. County of Westchester, 1994 WL 419815 11147 (S.D.N.Y. 1994):

> On March 11, 1994, Plaintiff sent to defendant Jackson, by first class mail, a copy of the Summons and Complaint, Plaintiff's First Discovery Demand, a postage prepaid envelope, and two copies of a form entitled "Notice of Acknowledgement of Receipt of Summons and Complaint" (the "Acknowledgment"). The Acknowledgement asserted that service was being effected pursuant to Fed. R. Civ. P. 4(c)(2)(C)(ii). Although Jackson signed the Acknowledgement and returned it without objection to Plaintiff's counsel, who filed it with the Court, Jackson now asserts that service upon him was ineffective. He contends that at the time Plaintiff attempted to effect such service, the method used was invalid, having been superseded by amendments to the Federal Rules of Civil Procedure which took effect December 1, 1993. On this basis, Defendants seek dismissal of the claims against Jackson pursuant to Rule 12(b)(5). . . .

Because the new waiver procedure comports substantially with the former mail service provision, the return of the Acknowledgment by Jackson to Plaintiff's counsel, together with the subsequent filing of the same with the Court, constitutes a waiver of service of process under Rule 4(d). The new Rule 4(d), like the Former Rule 4(c)(2)(C)(ii), aims to eliminate unnecessary costs of service; it effects little change other than the name of the provision, reflecting that "it is more accurate to describe the communication sent to the defendant [formerly the Acknowledgement] as a request for a waiver of formal service. . . ." Fed. R. Civ. P. 4, 28 U.S.C.A., Advisory Committee Notes to 1993 Amendments at 115 (Supp. 1994). Thus, the former service by mail provision and the current waiver of service provision are functional equivalents and Plaintiff's attempt to effect service of process pursuant to the old rule is valid, having been met with Jackson's compliance in returning the Acknowledgment.

In *Mid-Continent*, the Seventh Circuit heaps scorn on the district court's substantial compliance theory and its attention to the defendant's evasiveness. *United Food*, the Ninth Circuit case cited by the district court, is distinguished as dealing exclusively with technical error in the form of the documents served, not falling short in the method of service authorized by Rule 4. As it happens, the Ninth Circuit's approach to substantial compliance is now consistent with the district court's analysis. In Travelers Cas. & Sur. Co. v. Brenneke, 551 F.3d 1132 (9th Cir. 2009), the Ninth Circuit upheld service of process upon an evasive defendant where the process server saw the defendant in the window, "held the summons and complaint out towards the window, and announced in a loud voice 'You are served,'" and observed the defendant watch the server place the documents on the doorstep. 551 F.3d at 1134. The defendant was known to the server from effecting service in other lawsuits and the server had made four prior attempts at personal service in the instant case at the defendant's home. No one came to the door even when there were multiple cars in the driveway. On the night of the fifth attempt "an adult male answering to the name of [the defendant] responded" to the intercom "but never opened the door." That's when the "window" service occurred. The Ninth Circuit reasoned:

> Sufficient service may be found where there is a good faith effort to comply with the requirements of Rule 4(e)(2) which has resulted in placement of the summons and complaint within the defendant's immediate proximity and further compliance with Rule 4(e)(2) is only prevented by the defendant's knowing and intentional actions to evade service.

Id. at 1136.

Note the differences among proper service of process in the sense of (a) whether proper *methods* for service are deployed, versus (b) whether the contents of the process are sufficient, versus (c) (explored later) whether the court to which the defendant is haled has power over that defendant or the defendant's property. If anything is improper, the defendant in federal court may move to dismiss the action on the grounds of "improper service."

Some state procedure codes require that the defendant distinguish among these types of process defects.

## Note: Serving and Being Served

Rule 4(e)(2)(B) requires that persons served be of "suitable age and discretion." What does it say about the person doing the serving? See 4(c). In Benny v. Pipes, 799 F.2d 489 (9th Cir. 1986), *cert. denied*, 484 U.S. 870 (1987), a suit by prisoners against their guards, a fellow prisoner served process on the defendant guards. The guards threw the summons in the trash and then suffered a default judgment. The Ninth Circuit held that "Rule 4 means precisely what it says: save for those few special situations expressly enumerated in the Rule, *any* person over 18, who is not a party to the suit, may serve the summons and complaint." Id. at 494.

If, as in the problem case, there is a contest over the underlying facts of service, where should the court look first to determine them? See Rule 4(*l*). It is, however, to avoid such disputes that the mail and waiver provisions in 4(d) were added. What incentives to waive are built into the Rule?

The Rule also provides for service in special situations—such as upon minors, incompetents, the non-monolithic U.S. government—and upon corporations. See Rule 4(g), (i), and (h).

How about seizure of the defendant's assets in the jurisdiction as a way to give notice, as well as to assure that a judgment will be paid? Would you consider it in the problem case? Remember the line of cases starting with *Sniadach* in the first part of this chapter. See Rule 4(n).

## Note: Serving Process Abroad

Globalization and the rise of multinational corporations have made suits in federal court against foreign individuals and corporations quite common, but these defendants often do not have a presence in the United States making them amenable to service under Rule 4(e). Rule 4(f) sets out procedures for serving individuals in foreign countries; Rule 4(j) covers service upon foreign governments; Rule 4(k)(2) provides for personal jurisdiction over defendants who may not have sufficient contacts with any one state, a common problem with foreign defendants; and Rule 4(h)(2) directs that service on foreign corporations shall be effected in the same manner as service on foreign individuals.

Rule 4(f)(1) refers to an important treaty governing international service of process called the Hague Convention on the Service Abroad of Judicial and Extrajudicial Documents in Civil or Commercial Matters. Ratified in 1965 to standardize and simplify service of process in international civil suits, the Hague Convention requires each member country to establish a "Central Authority" to receive documents from other member countries. Each Central Authority may set certain rules for the form of documents it receives (e.g., that the documents be translated into the language of the receiving country), and as long as the documents comply with those requirements, the Convention requires the Central Authority to effect service of process.

Because the United States is a signatory, any attempt to hale a foreign defendant into federal court by service abroad must begin with a method of service recognized by the Convention, or, as Rule 4(f)(1) states, another international agreement. Relying on the Central Authority in the defendant's country is standard, but the Convention explicitly provides that it does not "interfere" with other methods, including "the freedom to send judicial documents, by postal channels, directly to persons abroad," as long as "the State of destination does not object." Hague Convention, Article 10(a); see also Brockmeyer v. May, 383 F.3d 798 (9th Cir. 2004) (noting split among Circuit Courts over whether the reference to "send[ing] judicial documents" in Article 10(a) includes service of process by mail; joining the Second Circuit in holding that "send" includes "serve"). Tempting as it may be to just drop a summons and complaint in the mail, any alternative method chosen also must be valid under Rule 4, see *Brockmeyer,* 383 F.3d at 804 ("[I]n order for the postal channel to be utilized, it is necessary that it be authorized by the law of the forum state."), and U.S. courts demand strict compliance. Id. at 804-806 (invalidating service on a British defendant by regular mail because Rule 4(f)(2)(C)(ii) demands "mail requiring a signed receipt . . . dispatched by the clerk of the court"*; narrowly construing Rule 4(f)(2)(A) as limited to personal service).

This may seem quite technical, and it is true that plaintiffs still trip up on the minutiae, but it is an improvement over the pre-Convention system.

What about international organizations? Can they be served wherever their headquarters are located? Typically, international organizations enter into a "Headquarters Agreement" with the sovereign states in which they have their headquarters. These agreements commonly prohibit service of process upon the headquarters without the express consent of the organization's leadership. This can make it very difficult to effect service on an international organization.

In Prewitt Enters. Inc. v. Org. of Petroleum Exporting Countries, 353 F.3d 916 (11th Cir. 2003), the plaintiff, a gas station owner in Birmingham, Alabama, filed a complaint in federal district court alleging OPEC had engaged in a price-fixing conspiracy with non-member states to limit the production and export of oil. Plaintiff attempted service on OPEC by having the clerk of the court send a copy of the complaint by registered, return-service mail to OPEC's headquarters in Vienna, Austria. Although OPEC received and signed for the complaint, it failed to appear and the district court entered a default judgment. When OPEC received a copy of the order from the triumphant plaintiff, it immediately filed a motion to set aside

---

* [The restyled Rule 4(f)(2)(C)(ii) states "using any form of mail that the clerk addresses and sends to the individual and that requires a signed receipt." —Eds.]

the default judgment and for dismissal on grounds of insufficient service of process. The Eleventh Circuit affirmed the dismissal, agreeing with the district court that 1) service upon an international organization is governed by Rule 4(h), which provides that service on a corporation or association (including foreign corporations and associations) "shall be effected . . . *in any manner prescribed for individuals by subdivision (f)* except personal delivery"[†]; and 2) that OPEC could not legally be served by any means listed in Rule 4(f) without its consent because of its Headquarters Agreement with the Austrian government. Id. at 921-928.

## 4.   Improper Conduct to Effect Service

*Wyman v. Newhouse*
93 F.2d 313 (2d Cir. 1937)

MANTON, CIRCUIT JUDGE.

This appeal is from a judgment entered dismissing the complaint on motion before trial. The action is on a judgment entered by default in a Florida state court, a jury having assessed the damages. The recovery there was for money loaned, money advanced for appellee, and for seduction under promise of marriage.

Appellee's answer pleads facts supporting his claim that he was fraudulently enticed into the Florida jurisdiction, appellant's state of residence, for the sole purpose of service of process. . . .

The affidavits submitted by the appellee deemed to be true for the purpose of testing the alleged error dismissing the complaint established that he was a resident of New York and never lived in Florida. On October 25, 1935, while appellee was in Salt Lake City, Utah, he received a telegram from the appellant, which read: "Account illness home planning leaving. Please come on way back. Must see you." Upon appellee's return to New York he received a letter from appellant stating that her mother was dying in Ireland; that she was leaving the United States for good to go to her mother; that she could not go without seeing the appellee once more; and that she wanted to discuss her affairs with him before she left. Shortly after the receipt of this letter, they spoke to each other on the telephone, whereupon the appellant repeated, in a hysterical and distressed voice, the substance of her letter. Appellee promised to go to Florida in a week or ten days and agreed to notify her when he would arrive. This he did, but before leaving New York by plane he received a letter couched in endearing terms and expressing love and affection for him, as well as her delight at his coming. Before leaving New York, appellee telegraphed appellant, suggesting arrangements for their accommodations together while in Miami, Fla.

[†] [The restyled text of this rule reads: "must be served . . . in any manner prescribed by Rule 4(f) for serving an individual, except personal delivery under (f)(2)(C)(i)." — EDS.]

She telegraphed him at a hotel in Washington, D.C., where he was to stop en route, advising him that the arrangements requested had been made. Appellee arrived at 6 o'clock in the morning at the Miami Airport and saw the appellant standing with her sister some 75 feet distant. He was met by a deputy sheriff who, upon identifying appellee, served him with process in a suit for $500,000. A photographer was present who attempted to take his picture. Thereupon a stranger introduced himself and offered to take appellee to his home, stating that he knew a lawyer who was acquainted with the appellant's attorney. . . . Appellee did not retain the Florida attorney to represent him. He returned to New York by plane that evening and consulted his New York counsel, who advised him to ignore the summons served in Florida. He did so, and judgment was entered by default. . . .

These facts and reasonable deductions therefrom convincingly establish that the appellee was induced to enter the jurisdiction of the state of Florida by a fraud perpetrated upon him by the appellant in falsely representing her mother's illness, her intention to leave the United States, and her love and affection for him, when her sole purpose and apparent thought was to induce him to come within the Florida jurisdiction so as to serve him in an action for damages. Appellant does not deny making these representations. All her statements of great and undying love were disproved entirely by her appearance at the airport and participation in the happenings there. She never went to Ireland to see her mother, if indeed the latter was sick at all.

In asking for judgment based on these Florida proceedings, appellant relies upon article 4, section 1, of the United States Constitution, providing that "Full Faith and Credit shall be given in each State to the public Acts, Records, and Judicial Proceedings of every other State." Congress has provided that judicial proceedings duly authenticated, "shall have such faith and credit given to them in every court within the United States as they have by law or usage in the courts of the State from which they are taken." 28 U.S.C.A. § 687. The first inquiry is what faith and credit would be given to this judgment within the state of Florida. On these facts, the service of process was fraudulent, and under the circumstances we think would have been vacated there. . . .

This judgment is attacked for fraud perpetrated upon the appellee which goes to the jurisdiction of the Florida court over his person. A judgment procured fraudulently, as here, lacks jurisdiction and is null and void. The appellee was not required to proceed against the judgment in Florida. His equitable defense in answer to a suit on the judgment is sufficient. A judgment recovered in a sister state, through the fraud of the party procuring the appearance of another, is not binding on the latter when an attempt is made to enforce such judgment in another state.

### Note: Impropriety and Immunity from Service of Process

*Wyman* is the classic case drawing the line against trickery and undignified behavior when such tactics induce a defendant to enter the jurisdiction.

Along the same lines is Tickle v. Barton, 95 S.E.2d 427 (W. Va. 1956), which found that service was fraudulently effected when the plaintiff lured the defendant to town by calls about a football banquet honoring his son. The dissent pointed out that the banquet was actually held and that the defendant knew a suit was pending against him in the country to which he traveled.

Generally, however, courts are sympathetic to the efforts to serve elusive defendants. Typical is another old favorite, Sawyer v. LaFlamme, 185 A.2d 466 (Vt. 1962), where the defendant was not only served, but physically held to answer the complaint after being invited and entreated to come to Vermont to settle the case. In holding that this was not fraudulent behavior, the court relied on the fact that the plaintiff's lawyer made no promises about what would happen if the defendant appeared. Can you distinguish *Tickle* from *Sawyer*? How would you distinguish either case from the tactics described at the beginning of this section that process servers use to identify the defendant and effectuate personal service?

There is a common law immunity-from-process rule of long standing to protect *witnesses* who come from outside the jurisdiction to testify in cases unrelated to the one in which some plaintiff seeks to serve them. Because the purpose is to encourage people to appear and testify, many courts have refused to apply this common law standard to litigants themselves (who have other incentives for appearing) or to witnesses who appear voluntarily rather than under subpoena. Lamb v. Schmitt, 285 U.S. 222 (1932), is the only Supreme Court case on the subject. There an attorney who had come into a state to set aside a fraudulent conveyance was served in an action to recover funds paid as fees in the main suit. The trial court denied the attorney immunity because the two proceedings were integrally related so that service of process in the second suit would not impede but rather would facilitate the administration of justice in the principal case. The Supreme Court made it clear that the immunity is for the benefit of the trial court's processes and is not "a right of the person against whom service is sought." The Court also indicated that whether to allow such immunity is a matter of considerable trial court discretion.

## B. WHAT KIND OF HEARING DOES DUE PROCESS REQUIRE?

### Problem Case: The Well-Meaning Legislator

You are the legislative assistant for State Senator Veliz, who has asked for your advice about a proposed piece of legislation, summarized below. Specifically, the Senator (who is a lawyer and well-versed in the applicable law) wants to know if the legislation comports with the procedural due process requirements of the Fourteenth Amendment.

Prepare a memorandum that discusses the *procedural due process* implications of each section of the bill. Be specific in identifying any due process problems and the reasons you think they exist. Also discuss any changes or additions that you think would help to protect the bill from a successful procedural due process challenge.

Conclude your memorandum with some observations on whether the bill is a good idea from a procedural standpoint, e.g., is it fair and does it properly take into account the various interests that enter the due process calculation?

*Proposed Legislation:*

Preamble: WHEREAS, the state of California seeks to assure the prompt, inexpensive, and nonadversarial resolution of all domestic disputes and disputes that involve juveniles, and WHEREAS adversarial process imposes undue expense and delay, exacerbates domestic disharmony, and ill serves the interests of all affected parties, the state adopts the following procedures for permanent and temporary termination of foster parent placements.

Section A. When the Department of Child Protective Services (CPS) has any reason to believe that a child placed by the state in a foster care home is in peril of physical, mental, or emotional abuse, CPS may intervene immediately and remove the child from the custody of the foster parent(s).

Section B. Within 24 hours of removing the child from the custody of the foster parent(s), CPS shall mail notice to the home address of the foster parent(s), stating that the child is in the protective custody of the state, pending a hearing to determine whether the allegations of peril are well founded.

Section C. A hearing shall be commenced within 5 days of delivery of the notice described in (B). Written notice of the time, date, and place of the hearing must be delivered to the home address of the foster parent(s) at least 24 hours before the scheduled hearing.

Section D. The hearing shall be held before an impartial arbitrator, appointed by the state. At the hearing, the arbitrator shall conduct all questioning of relevant parties. No party shall be represented by counsel at this hearing.

Section E. If the arbitrator finds the evidence of peril is well founded, he or she shall enter an order removing any and all other foster children from the foster care home and barring any future placements of foster children in the home of the censured foster parent(s).

Section F. Appeal of the arbitrator's decision may be had by the foster parent(s) or CPS by filing a complaint in the California Superior (trial) court. No attorney shall be provided at state expense for the foster parents on such appeals.

Look back to the due process game problem case at the beginning of this chapter. Did you want a lawyer, or at least an advocate other than yourself, to present your case? Think about the *Jenkins* case too. How might counsel have made a difference in protecting low-income residents from the City of Jennings's debt collection practices?

Having a lawyer is the "top of the line" of due process and is also the chief cost of a meaningful hearing. Think about when a lawyer's skills are needed to make the system fair. The introduction of a lawyer into the case, at least in the United States, brings with it the adversary approach. Most lawyers would not feel competent or adequate unless they zealously represented their clients, and under the state malpractice laws and bar rules that govern lawyers, professional sanctions and malpractice liability could be imposed on an advocate who fails to zealously represent her clients. Codes of ethics enforced by state bar associations and many of the rules we will study in the pages that follow take cognizance of the interests of third parties, but fidelity to the client's (lawful) interests is paramount. It is not too soon in your legal education to start asking whether and why such professional responsibility should trump personal morality or natural human response to a situation. Should we endorse a role that, as one philosopher put it, promotes "institutionalized immunity from the requirements of conscience" in the legal profession? David Luban, Lawyers and Justice: An Ethical Study at xxi (1988). Compare Norman W. Spaulding, The Rule of Law in Action: A Defense of Adversary System Values, 93 Cornell L. Rev. 1377 (2008).

This is a difficult question that not only admits of many answers, but raises other, deeper questions. Is law separate from morality? Will the truth emerge from a clash of zealous advocates who put their clients' interests before societal interests? Can a lawyer give good legal advice without talking about the moral, economic, and political consequences of her client's legal position and/or the likely impact on third parties? Can a lawyer identify and make the best legal arguments for a client if she confuses her own moral, economic, and political views with what the law requires or permits? If lawyers are *not* held to be immune from the requirements of conscience, will unpopular, controversial, or morally suspect clients be represented in the legal system? Who will agree to take their cases?

A lawyer for each side totally devoted to that side's cause is the hallmark of the adversary system. The following excerpts discuss this and other essential attributes of the system. As you read, think about what it means to make a lawyer's representation a requisite of the constitutional guarantee of due process.

*Robert Kagan, Adversarial Legalism:*
*The American Way of Law*
Pages 6-16 (2001)

**American Legal Exceptionalism**

Everywhere in the modern world legal control of social, political, and economic life is intensifying (Galanter, 1992; Dewees et al., 1991). Law grows from the relentless pressures of technological change, geographic mobility, global economic competition, and environmental pollution—all of which generate social and economic disruption, new risks to health and security, new forms of injustice, and new cultural challenges to traditional norms. Some citizens, riding the waves of change, demand new rights of inclusion, political access, and economic opportunity. Others, threatened by the change, demand legal protection from harm and loss of control. Democratic governments pass laws and issue judicial rulings responsive to both sets of demands (Schuck, 2000; Kagan, 1995).

In some spheres of activity, such as land use regulation and worker protection, Western European polities typically have more restrictive laws than does the United States. Compared to the United States, Japan has a more detailed and extensive set of legally mandated product standards and premarket testing requirements (Edelman, 1988: 292, Vogel, 1990). . . . An increasing number of nations, as well as the European Union, now have active constitutional courts, supporting Torbjorn Vallinder's (1995: 13) claim of a worldwide trend toward the "judicialization of politics," defined as "(1) the expansion of the province of courts or the judges at the expense of politicians and/or the administrators . . . or . . . (2) the spread of judicial decision making methods outside the judicial province proper."

The United States, however, has a unique legal "style." That is the message of an accumulating body of careful cross-national studies. . . . For one social problem after another, the studies show, the American system for making and implementing public policy and resolving disputes is distinctive. "It generally entails (1) more complex bodies of legal rules; (2) more formal, adversarial procedures for resolving political and scientific disputes; (3) more costly forms of legal contestation; (4) stronger, more punitive legal sanctions; (5) more frequent judicial review of and intervention into administrative decisions and processes; (6) more political controversy about legal rules and institutions; (7) more politically fragmented, less closely coordinated decision making systems; and (8) more legal uncertainty and instability."

Comparative studies are hardly necessary, moreover, to show that in no other democracy is litigation so often employed by contestants in political struggles over the delineation of electoral district boundaries, the management of forests, the breakup of business monopolies, the appropriate funding level for inner-city versus suburban public schools, or the effort to discourage cigarette smoking. In no other countries are the money damages assessed in environmental and tort suits nearly so high, or have major manufacturers been driven into bankruptcy by liability claims. . . . The United States has by far the world's largest cadre of special "cause lawyers" seeking to influence public policy and institutional practices by means of innovative litigation. In no other country are lawyers so entrepreneurial in seeking out new kinds of business, so eager to challenge authority, or so quick to propose new liability-expanding legal theories. . . .

## What Is Adversarial Legalism?

All these legal propensities are manifestations of what I call "adversarial legalism"—a method of policymaking and dispute resolution with two salient characteristics. The first is *formal legal contestation*—competing interests and disputants readily invoke legal rights, duties and procedural requirements, backed by recourse to formal law enforcement, strong legal penalties, litigation, and/or judicial review. The second is *litigant activism*—a style of legal contestation in which the assertion of claims, the search for controlling legal arguments, and the gathering and submission of evidence are dominated not by judges or government officials but by disputing parties or interests, acting primarily through lawyers. Organizationally, adversarial legalism typically is associated with and is embedded in decision-making institutions in which *authority is fragmented* and in which *hierarchical control is relatively weak.*

These defining features of adversarial legalism have two characteristic consequences. The first is costliness—litigant-controlled, adversarial decision making tends to be particularly complex, protracted and costly. The second is legal uncertainty—when potent adversarial advocacy is combined with fragmented, relatively nonhierarchical decision-making authority, legal norms are particularly malleable and complex, and legal decisions are particularly variable and unpredictable. It is the combination of costliness and legal uncertainty that makes adversarial legalism especially fearsome and controversial.

Table 2 contrasts adversarial legalism with other modes of policy implementation and dispute resolution. The horizontal dimension refers to legal formality—the extent to which contending parties or interests, as well as government officials, invoke and insist on conformity to written legal procedures and preexisting legal rights and duties. . . .

The vertical dimension of Table 2 concerns the extent to which the implementation or decision-making process is hierarchical—dominated by an official decisionmaker, applying authoritative norms or standards—as opposed to participatory—that is, influenced by disputing parties and their lawyers, their normative arguments, and the evidence they deem relevant. Taking each of these dimensions to their extreme form produces four "ideal types."

**TABLE 2**
**Modes of Policy Implementation and Dispute Resolution**

| *Organization of decision-making authority* | *Decision-making style* | | |
|---|---|---|---|
| | INFORMAL | $\longleftrightarrow$ | FORMAL |
| HIERARCHICAL | Expert or political judgment | | Bureaucratic legalism |
| $\updownarrow$ | | | |
| PARTICIPATORY | Negotiation/mediation | | Adversarial legalism |

### Negotiation/Mediation

A process in the lower left quadrant of Table 2 is adversarial in the sense that it is dominated by the contending parties, not by an authoritative

governmental decision maker. But it is informal or nonlegalistic, since neither procedures nor normative standards are dictated by formal law. One
example would be dispute resolution by negotiation, with or without lawyers. . . . The quadrant would also include mediation, whereby an "official"
third party attempts to induce contending parties to agree on a policy or
settlement but refrains from imposing a settlement based on law or official
policy.

### Expert/Political Judgment

The more an official decision maker or institution (as opposed to the contending interests) controls the process and the standards for decision, and
the more authoritative and final the institution's decisions are, the more
"hierarchical" the process. As suggested by the upper left quadrant in
Table 2, hierarchical processes can be legally informal. For example . . . [in]
Japan disputes over fault in motor vehicle accidents typically are resolved
by special traffic police who rush to the scene, question the parties, "ham-
mer out a consensual story as to what happened," and file a detailed report
on their findings (Tanase, 1990: 651-674).

### Bureaucratic Legalism

A policy-implementing or decision-making process characterized by a high
degree of hierarchical authority and legal formality (the upper right quadrant of Table 2) resembles the ideal-typical bureaucratic process as analyzed
by Max Weber. Governance by means of bureaucratic legalism emphasizes
uniform implementation of centrally devised rules, vertical accountability,
and official responsibility for fact-finding. The more hierarchical the system, the more restricted the role for legal representation and influence by
affected citizens or contending interests. In contemporary democracies the
pure case of bureaucratic legalism usually is softened in some respects, but
it is an ideal systematically pursued, for example, by tax collection agencies. Also tending toward this ideal are German and French courts, where
bureaucratically recruited and embedded judges—not the parties' lawyers
and not lay juries—dominate both the evidence-gathering and the decision-making processes (Langbein, 1994). . . .

### Adversarial Legalism

The lower right quadrant of Table 2 includes policy-implementing and
decision processes that are procedurally formalistic but in which hierarchy
is weak and party influence on the process is strong. American methods
for compensating victims of highway and medical accidents, for example,
prominently include a decentralized and adversarial tort law system driven
by claimants and their lawyers, as contrasted with Western European
compensation systems, which operate primarily though social insurance or benefit-payment bureaucracies. In American civil and criminal

adjudication, the introduction of evidence and invocation of legal rules are dominated not by the judge (as in Europe) but by the contending parties' lawyers. . . . From a comparative perspective, American judges are more political, their decisions less uniform (Levin, 1972: 193-221; Rowland and Carp, 1983: 109-134). . . . Lay jurors, whose decisions are not explained and largely shielded from hierarchical review, still play an important role in the American system, which reduces legal certainty and magnifies the influence of skillful advocacy.

Similarly, compared to European democracies, regulatory decision making in the United States entails many more legal formalities—complex legal rules concerning public notice and comment, restrictions on ex parte and other informal contacts with decisionmakers, legalistically specified evidentiary and scientific standards, mandatory official "findings" and responses to interest group arguments. . . . But hierarchical authority is correspondingly weak. . . . Agency decisions are frequently challenged in court by dissatisfied parties and reversed by judges, who dictate further changes in administrative policymaking routines. Lawyers, scientists, and economists hired by contending industry and advocacy groups play a large role in presenting evidence and arguments. Overall, the clash of adversarial argument has a larger influence on decisions than in other countries' regulatory systems, where policy decisions are characterized by a combination of political and expert judgment and consultation with affected interests (Badaracco, 1985; Brickman et al., 1985).

No modern democratic legal system is characterized entirely by any of the quadrants in Table 2. National legal styles are not monolithic. . . . British libel law is more threatening to the press than American libel law, which has been restricted by judicial interpretations of the First Amendment (Weaver and Bennett, 1993). The German Constitutional Court, interpreting a more recent and more detailed constitution than the U.S. Constitution, has been more activist than the U.S. Supreme Court in some important policy areas, thereby stimulating a good deal of constitutional litigation (Currie, 1990; Landfried, 1995: 113). Adversarial legalism can and does occur in more "cooperation"-oriented nations, such as the Netherlands and Japan (Niemeijer, 1989: 121-152; Upham, 1987). . . .

Conversely, Americans often refrain from and disparage adversarial legalism. Contrary to one popular belief, ordinary people often do not demand tougher laws, prosecutions, and lawsuits for every kind of offense. Research indicates that accident victims, disappointed purchasers, and regulatory inspectors who encounter violations generally do *not* resort to law suits as their first recourse (Hensler et al., 1991; Miller and Sarat, 1981; Bardach and Kagan, 1982). They are often willing to submit to bureaucratic or expert judgment or negotiate solutions to their legal claims. Politicians and legal elites often devise less adversarial, less costly alternatives to adversarial litigation—juvenile courts, family courts, small claims courts, workers' compensation tribunals, commercial arbitration, mandatory mediation, negotiated rulemaking and compliance plans, and so on.

American judges and legislatures periodically issue rulings and enact statutes that are designed to *discourage* lawsuits and appeals; the 1980s and 1990s saw a wave of such efforts to dampen adversarial legalism. . . .

Yet viewed in comparative perspective, the United States is distinctive in both dimensions. It is especially inclined to encourage the use of adversarial litigation to implement public policies and resolve disputes. And . . . adversarial legalism as a matter of day-to-day practice is far more common in the United States than in other democracies. . . .

The dual aspect of adversarial legalism—as decision-making structure or method and as day-to-day practice—is crucial to understanding its social consequences. It means that adversarial legalism's importance cannot be measured by litigation or adjudication rates alone, any more than the significance of nuclear weapons rests in the frequency of nuclear war. For example, even if only a small minority of aggrieved persons or organizations actually file lawsuits that result in jury trials, the mere threat of costly and potentially punitive adversarial litigation can deter malpractice by hospitals, business organizations and government bodies. . . .

## The Roots of Adversarial Legalism

. . . Students of comparative politics have long observed that in relation to other economically advanced democracies, the United States "has a strong society but a weak state" (Krasner, 1978: 61). Among the rich democracies, American government is the most easily penetrated by organized interest groups and extracts less tax revenue as a proportion of gross national product (Steinmo, 1993; Wilensky, 1975). In a comparative analysis of political cultures, Seymour Martin Lipset (1996: 21) writes that due to its long-standing emphasis on individualism and mistrust of government, "America began and continues as the most antistatist, legalistic, and rights-oriented nation." American government, accordingly, is designed to fragment and limit power. Both the federal and the state constitutions subject governmental power to crosscutting institutional checks and judicially enforceable individual rights. . . .

A structurally fragmented state is especially open to popular and interest group demands. And in contemporary societies—far richer, better informed, and with higher expectations than any in human history—citizens demand a great deal of their government. . . . But getting . . . things from an institutionally fragmented, tax-averse, "antistatist" political system, as in the United States, presents a problem.

American adversarial legalism, therefore, can be viewed as arising from a fundamental tension between two powerful elements: first, a political culture (or set of popular political attitudes) that expects and demands comprehensive governmental protections from serious harm, injustice, and environmental dangers—and hence a powerful, activist government—and, second, a set of governmental structures that reflect mistrust of concentrated power and hence that limit and fragment political and governmental authority.

Adversarial legalism helps resolve the tension. In a "weak," structurally fragmented state, lawsuits and courts provide "nonpolitical," nonstatist mechanisms through which individuals can demand high standards of justice from government. Lawsuits and courts empower interest groups to prod the government to implement ambitious public policies. It is only a slight oversimplification to say that in the United States, lawyers, legal rights, judges, and lawsuits are the functional equivalent of the large central bureaucracies that dominate governance in high-tax, activist welfare states. . . .

But this kind of "responsive law" . . . is a "high-risk strategy" of governance. With its high costs and penalties, and with its responsiveness to private claims, adversarial litigation enables ideologues or opportunists to use the law as a tool for exploitation. In its eagerness to put aside legal formalism in order to seek good outcomes, responsive law generates high levels of legal unpredictability, at least when it is implemented through adversarial legalism. . . .

## Notes and Questions

1. What are the defining attributes of adversarial legalism? Stephan Landsman offers the following definition: "The central precept of the adversary process is that out of the sharp clash of proofs presented by adversaries in a highly structured forensic setting is most likely to come the information upon which a neutral and passive decision maker can base the resolution of a litigated dispute acceptable to both the parties and society." Stephan Landsman, Readings on Adversarial Justice: The American Approach to Adjudication 2 (1988).

2. Professor Kagan concludes with the observation that the adversary system is costly and an inefficient way to meet modern demands for justice. How relevant is efficiency to justice? There is, of course, the time-worn expression that justice delayed is justice denied. Is this the kind of inefficiency he is describing? We are all also familiar with the expression "rubber-stamping." Are hasty, superficial procedures for decision making any less pernicious than inefficient ones? Efficiency, you will see, looms large in all efforts to define due process in the American legal system.

3. Professor Kagan argues that adversarial legalism is used and abused by a wide range of institutions, interest groups, and individuals. Which social groups would fare the worst if access to courts for social change was restricted and people had to bring their grievances to the politically accountable, majoritarian branches of government? Which social groups would fare the best?

## Note: The Common Understanding of Due Process

One goal of public adjudication is to resolve disputes in a manner acceptable to the parties and to society. This suggests that laypeople's procedural expectations should be a primary factor in determining what process is due in a given setting.

Professor Tom Tyler has tried, in different sociological contexts, to measure the expectations of laypeople. His conclusions below are based on telephone interviews with 1,575 citizens of Chicago, Illinois, identified through a random selection process. The respondents were interviewed about their views of the police and courts in Chicago and about their level of behavioral compliance with the law. Does his study suggest that the adversarial model is an inadequate account of procedural justice? That nonadversarial procedures might be acceptable to the parties and society for at least some disputes?

### Tom R. Tyler, Why People Obey the Law
Pages 137-138, 143, 147-148 (1990)

Citizens are not using any simple, unidimensional approach to assessing procedural justice. Instead, they pay attention to seven distinct aspects of procedure: the authorities' motivation, honesty, bias, and ethicality; their opportunities for representation; the quality of the decisions; and the opportunity for correcting errors. Each of these seven aspects of procedure has a significant independent influence on judgments about procedural justice. Both aspects of procedure related to decision making and those unrelated to it are important to judgments of procedural justice. The elements of procedural justice most directly linked to decision making are judgments about the neutrality of the decision-making procedure. People believe that decisions should be made by neutral, unbiased decision makers, and they expect the decision makers to be honest and to make their decisions based on objective information about the issues.

People also feel that procedures are fairer when they believe they have had some control in the decision-making procedure. Such control includes having the opportunity to present one's arguments, being listened to, and having one's view considered. As previously noted, this influence includes elements of control over the decisions made, but also includes interpersonal issues not directly linked to decision making. Procedural fairness is further linked to interpersonal aspects of the decision-making procedure. People place great weight on being treated politely and having respect shown both for their rights and for themselves as people. In addition, assessments of procedural fairness are strongly linked to judgments about whether the authorities being dealt with are trying to be fair. These interpersonal factors were not of minor importance. Inferences about the effort to be fair were the most important criterion of procedural fairness; concerns about politeness and rights (jointly labeled ethicality) were the second-most important.

Clearly, there are important noninstrumental elements to the meaning of procedural justice. . . .

. . . [T]he meaning of procedural justice changes in response to the nature of the experience that citizens have with legal authorities. Apparently, individuals do not have a single schema of a fair procedure that they apply on all occasions, but instead are concerned with different issues in different circumstances. As a result, it is likely that there are no universally fair procedures for allocation and the resolution of disputes. . . .

If citizens are allowed to convey to authorities their suggestions for solving problems, they feel that their experience is procedurally fairer, and this judgment in turn leads their experience to have positive effects on their views about legal authorities. Such process control effects are larger than the effects of control over the decisions made by the third party. In addition, process control effects increase in magnitude as the outcomes involved become more important. When people feel that they had an opportunity to present their evidence but that they had no influence over the decisions made by the authorities, they may have several possible reactions. First, they may feel a lack of influence and decision control, and these feelings may lead to a loss of support for the authorities that made decisions without heeding their views. This reaction reflects an instrumental perspective. It is a reaction based on the lack of correspondence between the person's advocated outcomes and the outcomes actually obtained. Alternatively, people may react favorably to the opportunity to present their views, even if their views had no effect on the decision made. This has been called the value-expressive effect (Tyler, Rasinski, and Spodick 1985) because the value of process control is not linked to its impact on outcomes.

That process control without decision control generally enhances judgments of fairness and support for the authorities is a result consistent with the value-expressive perspective on process control. People do not seem sensitive only to whether their opportunity to speak influences decisions made by a third party. The implication for legal authorities is that they can gain public support by setting up decision-making structures that allow opportunities for process control. Irrespective of whether their long-term accountability is based on the quality of the outcomes they produce, authorities can clearly obtain short-term support from their constituents by providing opportunities for process control. For authorities motivated to follow policies that are sound in the long term, this discretionary authority gives them the flexibility to do so (see Tyler, Rasinski, and Griffin 1986).

Unfortunately, value-expressive effects also provide opportunities to authorities less interested in helping people: opportunities to mislead and beguile the public by providing chances to speak not linked to any short or long-term influence over decisions (Tyler and McGraw 1986). If the focus on having opportunities to speak draws people's attention away from the tangible benefits they might receive from the authorities, it makes "false consciousness" possible. People may be satisfied in situations that should be viewed as unfair if judged on objective grounds. . . .

A recent analysis of the content of the speeches of revolutionary leaders found that the speeches focused heavily on distributive justice as opposed to procedural justice (Martin, Scully, and Levitt 1986). Perhaps revolutionary leaders recognize that successfully undermining the legitimacy of existing authorities involves directing people's attention toward distributive injustices. . . .

## *Notes and Questions*

1. To what extent should the "common understanding" of due process inform the constitutional standard? Does it matter if these common understandings change over time, or should the Constitution be interpreted solely against the backdrop of the framers' common understandings? If the framers' intentions should govern, do studies like Tyler's suggest that inquiries into these intentions may be quite complicated—even impossible?

2. Look at the significance of participants' control over process and their satisfaction with the outcomes. What are the implications of this finding for the due process game in the problem case and the *Jenkins* case at the beginning of the chapter? For administrators and others who want to deflect complaints about their decisions?

3. Tyler suggests that process preferences are socialized, not intellectualized. Does this mean our taste for due process is wholly learned, not innate? Can it be unlearned? If so, are there educational implications of this study, as well as legal ones? When do you think you learned your process preferences? From whom?

4. Having read Tyler's account, what do you make of Kagan's claim that adversarial legalism results more from structural than cultural factors?

5. The extent to which procedural expectations become culturally ingrained has a significant, practical effect on projects like the American Law Institute's (ALI) effort to draft Transnational Rules of Civil Procedure that would "harmonize" differences among the procedural laws of national legal systems. Such a project immediately encounters skepticism about the possibility, if not the desirability, of "global" procedural rules. One profound obstacle is the difference between the common-law systems—e.g., in the United States—and civil law systems—e.g., in France. In civil law systems, most law derives from legislatively created codes, whereas in common law systems, judges have authority to craft new rules in response to new circumstances. The adversary system, as we know it, and the ideas of due process explored in this chapter, developed in common law systems. There are understandable objections to any transnational procedure that takes as its baseline characteristic U.S. procedure.

In light of both concerns, ALI reporters Geoffrey C. Hazard, Jr., and Michele Taruffo conclude as follows:

> [A] system of procedure acceptable generally throughout the world could not include jury trial and would require much more limited discovery than is

typical in the United States. This in turn leads us to conclude that the scope of the proposed Transnational Civil Rules should exclude personal-injury and wrongful-death actions, because barring jury trial in such cases would be unacceptable in the United States. Hence, the scope is now conceived in terms of "business disputes."

Preface, The American Law Institute, Transnational Rules of Civil Procedure, Preliminary Draft No. 2, March 17, 2000. Despite these limitations, the reporters remain optimistic. The Proposed Final Draft, issued in March 2004 and joined by the International Institute for the Unification of Private Law, emphasizes that "the cost and distress resulting from legal conflict can be mitigated by reducing differences in legal systems, whereby the same or similar 'rules of the game' apply no matter where the participants may find themselves." The Principles were published in 2006.

There is a basic tension here between the need to harmonize and standardize procedural rules in the age of e-commerce and global trade, and the cultural and other adverse consequences of imposing any "dominant" cultural model of procedure on "nondominant," dissenting systems. Yet isn't procedural standardizing inescapable, whether through intergovernmental agreements or through private contractual arrangements between commercial actors?

Assume that you are a participant in the ongoing debates about transnational procedure. What would you insist upon, as procedural minima? Would you be willing to sacrifice trial by jury in civil cases? Party-conducted discovery of the opposing party's evidence? The right to counsel?

The work of the American Law Institute on Transnational Rules of Civil Procedure is significant, but international arbitration, rather than litigation, is the dominant method of resolving many private international law disputes. One of the core advantages of arbitration over litigation is precisely that the parties enjoy flexibility in setting the procedures that will govern the process. The International Chamber of Commerce, which runs the International Court of Arbitration, emphasizes that "arbitration procedure is driven by 'party autonomy,' that is, choices made by the parties themselves about how they want the dispute to be dealt with." http://www.icc-wbo.org/products-and-services/arbitration-and-adr/arbitration/. This is a world apart from constitutionally mandated procedures.

### *Lassiter v. Department of Social Services*
452 U.S. 18 (1981)

JUSTICE STEWART delivered the opinion of the Court.

In the late Spring of 1975, after hearing evidence that the petitioner, Abby Gail Lassiter, had not provided her infant son William with proper medical care, the District Court of Durham County, N.C., adjudicated him a neglected child and transferred him to the custody of the Durham County Department of Social Services, the respondent here. A year later, Ms.

Lassiter was charged with first-degree murder, was convicted of second-degree murder, and began a sentence of 25 to 40 years of imprisonment. In 1978 the Department petitioned the court to terminate Ms. Lassiter's parental rights because, the Department alleged, she "has not had any contact with the child since December of 1975" and

> has willfully left the child in foster care for more than two consecutive years without showing that substantial progress has been made in correcting the conditions which led to the removal of the child, or without showing a positive response to the diligent efforts of the Department of Social Services to strengthen her relationship to the child, or to make and follow through with constructive planning for the future of the child.

Ms. Lassiter was served with the petition and with notice that a hearing on it would be held. Although her mother had retained counsel for her in connection with an effort to invalidate the murder conviction, Ms. Lassiter never mentioned the forthcoming hearing to him (or, for that matter, to any other person except, she said, to "someone" in the prison). At the behest of the Department of Social Services' attorney, she was brought from prison to the hearing, which was held August 31, 1978. The hearing opened, apparently at the judge's insistence, with a discussion of whether Ms. Lassiter should have more time in which to find legal assistance. Since the court concluded that she "has had ample opportunity to seek and obtain counsel prior to the hearing of this matter, and [that] her failure to do so is without just cause," the court did not postpone the proceedings. Ms. Lassiter did not aver that she was indigent, and the court did not appoint counsel for her.

A social worker from the respondent Department was the first witness. She testified that in 1975 the Department "received a complaint from Duke Pediatrics that William had not been followed in the pediatric clinic for medical problems and that they were having difficulty in locating Ms. Lassiter. . . ." She said that in May of 1975 a social worker had taken William to the hospital, where doctors asked that he stay "because of breathing difficulties [and] malnutrition and [because] there was a great deal of scarring that indicated that he had a severe infection that had gone untreated." The witness further testified that except for one "prearranged" visit and a chance meeting on the street, Ms. Lassiter had not seen William after he had come into the State's custody, and that neither Ms. Lassiter nor her mother had "made any contact with the Department of Social Services regarding that child." When asked whether William should be placed in his grandmother's custody, the social worker said he should not, since the grandmother "has indicated to me on a number of occasions that she was not able to take responsibility for the child" and since "I have checked with people in the community and from Ms. Lassiter's church who also feel that this additional responsibility would be more than she can handle." The social worker added that William has not seen his grandmother since the chance meeting in July of '76 and that was the only time.

After the direct examination of the social worker, the judge said:

> I notice we made extensive findings in June of '75 that you were served with papers and called the social services and told them you weren't coming; and the serious lack of medical treatment. And, as I have said in my findings of the 16th day of June '75, the Court finds that the grandmother, Ms. Lucille Lassiter, mother of Abby Gail Lassiter, filed a complaint on the 8th day of May, 1975, alleging that the daughter often left the children, Candina, Felicia and William L. with her for days without providing money or food while she was gone.

Ms. Lassiter conducted a cross-examination of the social worker, who firmly reiterated her earlier testimony. The judge explained several times, with varying degrees of clarity, that Ms. Lassiter should only ask questions at this stage; many of her questions were disallowed because they were not really questions, but arguments.

Ms. Lassiter herself then testified, under the judge's questioning, that she had properly cared for William. Under cross-examination, she said that she had seen William more than five or six times after he had been taken from her custody and that, if William could not be with her, she wanted him to be with her mother since "He knows us. Children know they family. . . . They know they people, they know they family and that child knows us anywhere. . . . I got four more other children. Three girls and a boy and they know they little brother when they see him."

Ms. Lassiter's mother was then called as a witness. She denied, under the questioning of the judge, that she had filed the complaint against Ms. Lassiter, and on cross-examination she denied both having failed to visit William when he was in the State's custody and having said that she could not care for him.

The court found that Ms. Lassiter "has not contacted the Department of Social Services about her child since December 1975, has not expressed any concern for his care and welfare, and has made no efforts to plan for his future." Because Ms. Lassiter thus had "willfully failed to maintain concern or responsibility for the welfare of the minor," and because it was "in the best interests of the minor," the court terminated Ms. Lassiter's status as William's parent.

On appeal, Ms. Lassiter argued only that, because she was indigent, the Due Process Clause of the Fourteenth Amendment entitled her to the assistance of counsel, and that the trial court had therefore erred in not requiring the State to provide counsel for her. The North Carolina Court of Appeals decided that "[w]hile this State action does invade a protected area of individual privacy, the invasion is not so serious or unreasonable as to compel us to hold that appointment of counsel for indigent parents is constitutionally mandated." In the Matter of William L. Lassiter, 43 N.C. App. 525, 527, 259 S.E.2d 336, 337. The Supreme Court of North Carolina summarily denied Ms. Lassiter's application for discretionary review, 299 N.C. 120, 262 S.E.2d 6, and we granted certiorari to consider the petitioner's claim under the Due Process Clause of the Fourteenth Amendment, [449] U.S. [819] 1980. . . .

The pre-eminent generalization that emerges from this Court's precedents on an indigent's right to appointed counsel is that such a right has been recognized to exist only where the litigant may lose his physical liberty if he loses the litigation. Thus, when the Court overruled the principle of Betts v. Brady, 316 U.S. 455 [(1942)], that counsel in criminal trials need be appointed only where the circumstances in a given case demand it, the Court did so in the case of a man sentenced to prison for five years. Gideon v. Wainwright, 372 U.S. 335 [(1963)].

And thus Argersinger v. Hamlin, 407 U.S. 25 [(1967)], established that counsel must be provided before any indigent may be sentenced to prison, even where the crime is petty and the prison term brief.

That it is the defendant's interest in personal freedom, and not simply the special Sixth and Fourteenth Amendments right to counsel in criminal cases, which triggers the right to appointed counsel is demonstrated by the Court's announcement in In re Gault, 387 U.S. 1 [(1965)], that "the Due Process Clause of the Fourteenth Amendment requires that in respect of proceedings to determine delinquency *which may result in commitment to an institution in which the juvenile's freedom is curtailed,*" the juvenile has a right to appointed counsel even [though] those proceedings may be styled "civil" and not "criminal." Id., at 41 . . . (emphasis added). Similarly, four of the five Justices who reached the merits in Vitek v. Jones, 445 U.S. 480 [(1980)], concluded that an indigent prisoner is entitled to appointed counsel before being involuntarily transferred for treatment to a state mental hospital. The fifth Justice differed from the other four only in declining to exclude the "possibility that the required assistance may be rendered by a competent layman in some cases." Id., at 497 [(1980)] (separate opinion of Powell, J.).

Significantly, as a litigant's interest in personal liberty diminishes, so does his right to appointed counsel. In Gagnon v. Scarpelli, 411 U.S. 778 [(1973)], . . . the Court gauged the due process rights of a previously sentenced probationer at a probation-revocation hearing. In Morrissey v. Brewer, 408 U.S. 471, 480 [(1972)], which involved an analogous hearing to revoke parole, the Court had said: "Revocation deprives an individual, not of the absolute liberty to which every citizen is entitled, but only of the conditional liberty properly dependent on observance of special parole restrictions." Relying on that discussion, the Court in *Scarpelli* declined to hold that indigent probationers have, per se, a right to counsel at revocation hearings, and instead left the decision whether counsel should be appointed to be made on a case-by-case basis. . . .

The case of Mathews v. Eldridge, 424 U.S. 319, 335 [(1976)], propounds three elements to be evaluated in deciding what due process requires, viz., the private interests at stake, the government's interest, and the risk that the procedures used will lead to erroneous decisions. We must balance these elements against each other, and then set their net weight in the scales against the presumption that there is a right to appointed counsel only where the indigent, if he is unsuccessful, may lose his personal freedom.

This Court's decisions have by now made plain beyond the need for multiple citation that a parent's desire for and right to "the companionship, care, custody and management of his or her children" is an important interest that "undeniably warrants deference and, absent a powerful countervailing interest, protection." Stanley v. Illinois, 405 U.S. 645, 651 [(1972)]. Here the State has sought not simply to infringe upon that interest, but to end it. If the State prevails, it will have worked a unique kind of deprivation. Cf. May v. Anderson, 345 U.S. 528, 533 [(1953)]; Armstrong v. Manzo, 380 U.S. 545 [(1965)]. A parent's interest in the accuracy and justice of the decision to terminate his or her parental status is, therefore, a commanding one.

Since the State has an urgent interest in the welfare of the child, it shares the parent's interest in an accurate and just decision. For this reason, the State may share the indigent parent's interest in the availability of appointed counsel. If, as our adversary system presupposes, accurate and just results are most likely to be obtained through the equal contest of opposed interests, the State's interest in the child's welfare may perhaps best be served by a hearing in which both the parent and the State acting for the child are represented by counsel, without whom the contest of interests may become unwholesomely unequal. North Carolina itself acknowledges as much by providing that where a parent files a written answer to a termination petition, the State must supply a lawyer to represent the child. N.C. Gen. Stat. § 7A-289.29 (Supp. 1979).

The State's interests, however, clearly diverge from the parent's insofar as the State wishes the termination decision to be made as economically as possible and thus wants to avoid both the expense of appointed counsel and the cost of the lengthened proceedings his presence may cause. But though the State's pecuniary interest is legitimate, it is hardly significant enough to overcome private interests as important as those here, particularly in light of the concession in the respondent's brief that the "potential costs of appointed counsel in termination proceedings . . . is [sic] admittedly *de minimis* compared to the costs in all criminal actions."

Finally, consideration must be given to the risk that a parent will be erroneously deprived of his or her child because the parent is not represented by counsel. North Carolina law now seeks to assure accurate decisions by establishing the following procedures: A petition to terminate parental rights may be filed only by a parent seeking the termination of the other parent's rights, by a county department of social services or licensed child-placing agency with custody of the child, or by a person with whom the child has lived continuously for the two years preceding the petition. N.C.G.S. § 7A-289.24. A petition must describe facts sufficient to warrant a finding that one of the grounds for termination exists, N.C.G.S. § 7A-289.25(6), and the parent must be notified of the petition and given 30 days in which to file a written answer to it, N.C.G.S. § 7A-289.27. If that answer denies a material allegation, the court must, as has been noted, appoint a lawyer as the child's guardian *ad litem* and must conduct a special hearing to resolve the issues raised by the petition and the answer. N.C.G.S. § 7A-289.29. If the parent files no answer, "the court shall issue an order terminating all parental and custodial rights . . . ; provided the court shall order a hearing on the petition and may examine the petitioner or others on the facts alleged in the petition." N.C.G.S. § 7A-289.28. Findings of fact are made by a court sitting without a jury and must "be based on clear," cogent, and "convincing evidence." N.C.G.S. § 7A-289.30. Any party may appeal who gives notice of appeal within 10 days after the hearing. N.C.G.S. § 7A-289.34.

The respondent argues that the subject of a termination hearing—the parent's relationship with her child—far from being abstruse, technical, or unfamiliar, is one as to which the parent must be uniquely well informed and to which the parent must have given prolonged thought. The respondent also contends that a termination hearing is not likely to produce difficult points of evidentiary law, or even of substantive law, since the evidentiary problems peculiar to criminal trials are not present and since the standards for termination are not complicated. In fact, the respondent reports, the North Carolina Departments of Social Services are themselves sometimes represented at termination hearings by social workers instead of by lawyers.

Yet the ultimate issues with which a termination hearing deals are not always simple, however commonplace they may be. Expert medical and psychiatric testimony, which few parents are equipped to understand and fewer still to confute, is sometimes presented. The parents are likely to be people with little education, who have had uncommon difficulty in dealing with life, and who are, at the hearing, thrust into a distressing and disorienting situation. That these factors may combine to overwhelm an uncounselled parent is evident from the findings some courts have made.

. . . Thus, courts have generally held that the State must appoint counsel for indigent parents at termination proceedings. State ex rel. Heller v. Miller, 61 Ohio St. 2d 6, 399 N.E.2d 66 (1980); Dept. of Public Welfare v. J. K.B., 393 N.E.2d 406 (Mass. 1979); Matter of Chad S., 580 P.2d 983 (Okla. Sup. Ct. 1978); In re Myricks, 85 Wash. 2d 252, 533 P.2d 841 (1975); Crist v. Division of Youth and Family Services, 128 N.J. Super. 402, 320 A.2d 203 (N.J. Super. Ct. 1974); Danforth v. Maine Dept. of Health and Welfare, 303 A.2d 794 (Me. Sup. Ct. 1973); In re Freisz, 190 Neb. 347, 208 N.W.2d 259 (1973). The respondent is able to point to no presently authoritative case, except for the North Carolina judgment now before us, holding that an indigent parent has no due process right to appointed counsel in termination proceedings. . . .

If, in a given case, the parent's interests were at their strongest, the State's interests were at their weakest, and the risks of error were at their peak, it could not be said that the *Eldridge* factors did not overcome the presumption against the right to appointed counsel, and that due process did not therefore require the appointment of counsel. But since the *Eldridge* factors will not always be so distributed, and since "due process is not so rigid as to require that the significant interests in informality, flexibility and economy must always be sacrificed," Gagnon v. Scarpelli, supra, 411 U.S. at 788, neither can we say that the Constitution requires the appointment of counsel in every parental termination proceeding. We therefore adopt the standard found appropriate in *Gagnon v. Scarpelli,* and leave the decision whether due process calls for the appointment of counsel for indigent parents in termination proceedings to be answered in the first instance by the trial court, subject, of course, to appellate review. . . .

Here, as in *Scarpelli*, "[i]t is neither possible nor prudent to attempt to formulate a precise and detailed set of guidelines to be followed in determining when the providing of counsel is necessary to meet the applicable due process requirements," since here, as in that case, "[t]he facts and circumstances . . . are susceptible of almost infinite variation. . . ." Supra, 411 U.S. at 788. . . . Nevertheless, because child-custody litigation must be concluded as rapidly as is consistent with fairness,[7] we decide today whether the trial judge denied Ms. Lassiter due process of law when he did not appoint counsel for her.

The respondent represents that the petition to terminate Ms. Lassiter's parental rights contained no allegations of neglect or abuse upon which criminal charges could be based, and hence Ms. Lassiter could not well have argued that she required counsel for that reason. The Department of Social Services was represented at the hearing by counsel, but no expert witnesses testified and the case presented no especially troublesome points of law, either procedural or substantive. While hearsay evidence was no doubt admitted, and while Ms. Lassiter no doubt left incomplete her defense that the Department had not adequately assisted her in rekindling her interest in her son, the weight of the evidence that she had few sparks of such interest was sufficiently great that the presence of counsel for Ms. Lassiter could not have made a determinative difference. True, a lawyer might have done more with the argument that William should live with Ms. Lassiter's mother—but that argument was quite explicitly made by both Lassiters, and the evidence that the elder Ms. Lassiter had said she could not handle another child, that the social worker's investigation had led to a similar conclusion, and that the grandmother had displayed scant interest in the child once he had been removed from her daughter's custody was, though controverted, sufficiently substantial that the absence of counsel's guidance on this point did not render the proceedings fundamentally unfair. Finally, a court deciding whether due process requires the appointment of counsel need not ignore a parent's plain demonstration that she is not interested in attending a hearing. Here, the trial court had previously found that Ms. Lassiter had expressly declined to appear at the 1975 child custody hearing, Ms. Lassiter had not even bothered to speak to her retained lawyer after being notified of the termination hearing, and the court specifically found that Ms. Lassiter's failure to make an effort to contest the termination proceeding was without cause. In view of all these circumstances, we hold that the trial court did not err in failing to appoint counsel for Ms. Lassiter. . . .

7. According to the respondent's brief, William Lassiter is now living "in a preadoptive home with foster parents committed for formal adoption to become his legal parents." He cannot be legally adopted, nor can his status otherwise be finally clarified, until this litigation ends.

In its Fourteenth Amendment, our Constitution imposes on the States the standards necessary to ensure that judicial proceedings are fundamentally fair. A wise public policy, however, may require that higher standards be adopted than those minimally tolerable under the Constitution. Informed opinion has clearly come to hold that an indigent parent is entitled to the assistance of appointed counsel not only in parental termination proceedings, but in dependency and neglect proceedings as well. Most significantly, 33 States and the District of Columbia provide statutorily for the appointment of counsel in termination cases. The Court's opinion today in no way implies that the standards increasingly urged by informed public opinion and now widely followed by the States are other than enlightened and wise.

For the reasons stated in this opinion, the judgment is affirmed. *It is so ordered.* . . .

Justice Blackmun, with whom Justice Brennan and Justice Marshall join, dissenting.

The Court today denies an indigent mother the representation of counsel in a judicial proceeding initiated by the State of North Carolina to terminate her parental rights with respect to her youngest child. The Court most appropriately recognizes that the mother's interest is a "commanding one," . . . and it finds no countervailing state interest of even remotely comparable significance. . . . Nonetheless, the Court avoids what seems to me the obvious conclusion that due process requires the presence of counsel for a parent threatened with judicial termination of parental rights, and instead, revives an ad hoc approach thoroughly discredited nearly 20 years ago in Gideon v. Wainwright, 372 U.S. 335 (1963). Because I believe that the unique importance of a parent's interest in the care and custody of his or her child cannot constitutionally be extinguished through formal judicial proceedings without the benefit of counsel, I dissent. . . .

The method chosen by North Carolina to extinguish parental rights resembles in many respects a criminal prosecution. Unlike the probation revocation procedure reviewed in Gagnon v. Scarpelli, on which the Court so heavily relies, the termination procedure is distinctly formal and adversarial. The State initiates the proceedings by filing a petition in district court, N.C. Gen. Stat. §§ 7A-289.23 and 7A-289.25 (Supp. 1979), and serving a summons on the parent, § 7A-289.27(1). A state judge presides over the adjudicatory hearing that follows, and the hearing is conducted pursuant to the formal rules of evidence and procedure. N.C. Gen. Stat. § 1A-1, Rule 1 (Supp. 1979). In general, hearsay is inadmissible and records must be authenticated. See, e.g., § 1A-1, Rules 1, 43, 44, 46.

In addition, the proceeding has an obvious accusatory and punitive focus. In moving to terminate a parent's rights, the State has concluded that it no longer will try to preserve the family unit, but instead will marshal an array of public resources to establish that the parent-child separation must be made permanent. The State has legal representation through the county attorney. This lawyer has access to public records concerning the family and to professional social workers who are empowered to investigate the family situation and to testify against the parent. The State's legal representative may also call upon experts in family relations, psychology, and medicine to bolster the State's case. And, of course, the State's counsel himself is an expert in the legal standards and techniques employed at the termination proceeding, including the methods of cross-examination.

In each of these respects, the procedure devised by the State vastly differs from the informal and rehabilitative probation revocation decision in *Scarpelli*. . . . Indeed, the State here has prescribed virtually all the attributes of a formal trial as befits the severity of the loss at stake in the termination decision—every attribute, that is, except counsel for the defendant parent. The provision of counsel for the parent would not alter the character of the proceeding, which is already adversarial, formal, and quintessentially legal. It, however, would diminish the prospect of an erroneous termination, a prospect that is inherently substantial, given the gross disparity in power and resources between the State and the uncounselled indigent parent.

The prospect of error is enhanced in light of the legal standard against which the defendant parent is judged. As demonstrated here, that standard commonly adds another dimension to the complexity of the termination proceeding. Rather than focusing on the facts of isolated acts or omissions, the State's charges typically address the nature and quality of complicated ongoing relationships among parent, child, other relatives, and even unrelated parties. . . .

The legal issues posed by the State's petition are neither simple nor easily defined. The standard is imprecise and open to the subjective values of the judge. A parent seeking to prevail against the State must be prepared to adduce evidence about his or her personal abilities and lack of fault, as well as proof of progress and foresight as a parent that the State would deem adequate and improved over the situation underlying a previous adverse judgment of child neglect. The parent cannot possibly succeed without being able to identify material issues, develop defenses, gather and present sufficient supporting nonhearsay evidence, and conduct cross-examination of adverse witnesses.

The Court, of course, acknowledges that these tasks "may combine to overwhelm an uncounselled parent." I submit that that is a profound understatement. Faced with a formal accusatory adjudication, with an adversary—the State—that commands great investigative and prosecutorial resources, with standards that involve ill-defined notions of fault and adequate parenting, and with the inevitable tendency of a court to apply subjective values or to defer to the State's "expertise," the defendant parent plainly is outstripped if he or she is without the assistance of "'the guiding hand of counsel.'" In re Gault, 387 U.S. [1, 36 (1967)], quoting Powell v. Alabama, 287 U.S. 45, 69 (1932). When the parent is indigent, lacking in education, and easily intimidated by figures of authority, the imbalance may well become insuperable. . . .

The problem of inadequate representation is painfully apparent in the present case. . . .

At the termination hearing, the State's sole witness was the county worker who had met petitioner on the one occasion at the prison. This worker had been assigned to William's case in August 1977, yet much of her testimony concerned events prior to that date; she represented these events as contained in the agency record. . . . Petitioner failed to uncover this weakness in the worker's testimony. That is hardly surprising, for there is no indication that an agency record was introduced into evidence or was present in court, or that petitioner or the grandmother ever had an opportunity to review any such record. The social worker also testified about her conversations with members of the community. In this hearsay testimony, the witness reported the opinion of others that the grandmother could not handle the additional responsibility of caring for the fifth child. . . . There is no indication that these community members were unavailable to testify, and the country attorney did not justify the admission of the hearsay. Petitioner made no objection to its admission. . . .

. . . An experienced attorney might have translated petitioner's reaction and emotion into several substantive legal arguments. The State charged petitioner with failing to arrange a "constructive plan" for her child's future or to demonstrate a "positive response" to the Department's intervention. A defense would have been that petitioner had arranged for the child to be cared for properly by his grandmother, and evidence might have been adduced to demonstrate the adequacy of the grandmother's care of the other children. The Department's own "diligence" in promoting the family's integrity was never put in issue during the hearing, yet it is surely significant in light of petitioner's incarceration and lack of access to her child. Finally, the asserted willfulness of petitioner's lack of concern could obviously have been attacked since she was physically unable to regain custody or perhaps even to receive meaningful visits during 21 of the 24 months preceding the action.

Petitioner plainly has not led the life of the exemplary citizen or model parent. It may well be that if she were accorded competent legal representation, the ultimate result in this particular case would be the same. But the issue before the Court is not petitioner's character; it is whether she was given a meaningful opportunity to be heard when the State moved to terminate absolutely her parental rights. In light of the unpursued avenues of defense, and of the experience petitioner underwent at the hearing, I find virtually incredible the Court's conclusion today that her termination proceeding was fundamentally fair. To reach that conclusion, the Court simply ignores the defendant's obvious inability to speak effectively for herself, a factor the Court has found to be highly significant in past cases. . . .

I respectfully dissent.

[Dissenting opinion of Justice Stevens omitted.]

## Note: Adding Lawyers: A Functional Approach

You may be wondering how Ms. Lassiter got her case all the way to the U.S. Supreme Court without a lawyer. At the close of the termination proceeding, the trial judge informed her of the right to appeal, and gave her the name and address of the North Central Legal Assistance Program, a free legal aid office for indigents. She contacted them immediately after the hearing. The record is silent about why the judge did not inform her of the availability of free counsel before the hearing.

In their brief to the Supreme Court, Lassiter's attorneys emphasized three ways in which a lawyer could have helped her present her case: by effectively cross-examining the social worker, who was the only witness against her; by contesting the accuracy and hearsay nature of the secondhand and carelessly maintained records of the social service agency; and by helping her and her mother tell their side of the story on direct examination. As it was, Ms. Lassiter delivered most of her direct testimony in response to impatient and sometimes hostile questions by the court.

The National Center on Women and Family Law, Inc., framed the ways in which counsel could significantly decrease the risk of an erroneous decision: 1) by presenting defenses that the parent would be unlikely to come up with on her own; 2) by ensuring that the state's burden of proof is met and supported by reliable evidence; and 3) by protecting the client against bias and impropriety. Excerpts from the *Lassiter* briefs and transcripts offer concrete examples of these points. See Elizabeth G. Thornburg, The Story of *Lassiter:* The Importance of Counsel in an Adversary Setting, in Kevin M. Clermont, Civil Procedure Stories 489 (2004).

The adversary courtroom setting of *Lassiter* makes the absence of a lawyer very striking. Think about a lawyer's due process role in other kinds of hearings and proceedings. A related case study is Lucie White, Subordination, Rhetorical Survival Skills, and Sunday Shoes: Notes on the Hearing of Mrs. G., 38 Buff. L. Rev. 1 (1990). She tells the story of a poor woman engaged in an administrative hearing at a welfare office, and asks whether there might be a humanist model of due process that would allow more meaningful participation by the clients in the decisions that affect their lives.

Finally, for a view that the occasional introduction of counsel at hearings meant to be informal is not an unmixed blessing, see Richard Lempert and Karl Monsma, Lawyers and Informal Justice: The Case of a Public Housing Eviction Board, 51 Law & Contemp. Probs. 135 (1988).

In M.L.B. v. S.L.J., 519 U.S. 102 (1996), the Court faced another case terminating a mother's parental interests in her children. Under Mississippi procedures, the mother had a judicial hearing and was represented by counsel. An appeal was allowed from this procedure, but only upon payment of the costs of preparing a record. In this case, that would be over $2,000.

M.L.B. argued in the Supreme Court that conditioning her right to appeal on payment of this sum when she was indigent denied her due process of law. Citing *Lassiter* for the proposition that "the interest of parents in their relationship with their children is sufficiently fundamental to come within the finite class of liberty interests protected by the Fourteenth Amendment," 519 U.S. at 119 (quoting Santosky v. Kramer, 455 U.S. 745, 774 (1982) (Rehnquist, J., dissenting)), the Court held that a transcript must be provided to M.L.B. Read together, the two cases would seem to assure a transcript but not a lawyer to use it effectively. How can you reconcile these cases? Is this a case in which the identity of the judge might make a difference in the outcome?

### Note: Lawyers and Due Process

In the problem case of *The Well-Meaning Legislator,* would you design a process with lawyers in it? At what point are lawyers necessary to fundamental fairness? One way to think about this is to consider the place of the adversary tradition, which assures each side an appropriate chance to present its case. In our civil procedure, the adversary tradition is linked to a much grander principle, the rule of law — that is, the impersonal application of generally accepted principles to disputes. Both are embraced in the deathless words of due process forbidding the government to deprive any person of "life, liberty, or property, without due process of law."

Due process links the adversary tradition to the rule of law in several ways. For example, the accurate application of law depends on knowing what the underlying facts of the particular case are. The expression of and competition between the adversaries' ideas is thought by many observers to be the best (or at least the most culturally compatible) means for learning the facts. Moreover, the effort to apply independent legal principles lends an appearance of impartiality to the adversary tournament, which can enhance the satisfaction of the contestants.

Yet despite their linkage, the rule of law and the adversary tradition are sometimes rivals. The latter seeks to gratify the individual by glorifying her procedural rights while the former focuses on the whole society or its leadership by seeking to enforce society's substantive commands.

This rivalry has economic and ethical dimensions. In economic terms, the decisional process is a scarce resource. A limited amount of time and treasure can be invested in the resolution of any dispute. Thus, the value of any substantive right must be discounted by the cost of enforcement: If the cost to the individual is too high, the "right" is a deception and the game is unfair and ungratifying. But if the cost to the public is exorbitant, the right is contrary to the general interest. Consequently, if we are to be effective in the enforcement of substantive law, we cannot be too fastidious about costly adversary procedures; and if we are to provide fair opportunity for adversary competition, we cannot be excessively demanding about the absolute accuracy and consistent application of substantive principles.

The ethical aspect of the uneasy relationship between the adversary tradition and the rule of law lies in the ambivalence we have about the role of professional advocates. If fidelity to client were unqualified, the advocate would be bound to subvert the process by purposefully twisting the law. On the other hand, if a lawyer's fidelity to the law were absolute, the adversary relationship would be undermined by self-defeating advocacy. This particular tension is beyond complete reconciliation, and it is complicated by the fact that legal rules are often ambiguous. Even if the lawyer's duty to the law is absolute, it is not at all obvious what obligations would follow from such absolute fidelity. Alternatively, if the lawyer's duty to the client is absolute, legal indeterminacy can make it difficult to identify the boundaries of a client's entitlements, and thus difficult to say how far it is fair to push for that client. Add to this the fact that we are a culturally and morally pluralistic society and you will begin to grasp the depth of the tensions that define the role of professional advocates. See Norman W. Spaulding, Reinterpreting Professional Identity, 74 U. Colo. L. Rev. 1 (2003).

The advocate's skills apply to both the adversary tradition and the rule of law ideal. As the client's representative, the lawyer should maintain a professional detachment in order to present the case at the level of abstraction needed to apply the law, and, of course, to say "no" to the client when the law so requires. Also, the advocate's learning and verbal skill may influence the selection of the legal principle to be applied by judge and jury. The blend of the adversary tradition and the rule of law that makes due process is thus further intertwined with the development and availability of professional skills, attitudes, and learning.

## 1. Access to Lawyers: The Price of Advice

If the outcome of *Lassiter* (no lawyer at state expense unless the judge so orders) disturbs you, what do you propose as a solution? Legislative action? An appeal to private attorneys to handle such cases pro bono? Mandatory referral to a legal aid attorney?

Rather than have the loser pay the fees of the prevailing party, the so-called American Rule is that each party in a lawsuit bears its own attorneys' fees. As the Supreme Court has put it: "[S]ince litigation is at best uncertain one should not be penalized for merely defending or prosecuting a lawsuit, and . . . the poor might be unjustly discouraged from instituting actions to vindicate their rights. . . . Also, the time, expense, and difficulties of proof inherent in litigating the question of what constitutes reasonable attorney's fees would pose substantial burdens for judicial administration." Fleischmann Distilling Co. v. Maier Brewing Co., 386 U.S. 714, 718 (1967).

But the American Rule is riddled with statutory exceptions on both the federal and state level. For example, under the Civil Rights Attorney's Fees Act of 1976, 42 U.S.C. § 1988, courts are given discretion to award "a reasonable attorney's fee" to the prevailing party to induce competent counsel to bring civil rights cases seeking equitable relief or small monetary awards. Service and commercial contracts of all kinds increasingly include a clause providing that in the case of litigation the loser will pay attorneys' fees. Moreover, there have been recent proposals for civil justice reform that include a "loser pays" rule in *all* cases. The proponents argue that this reform is necessary to prevent plaintiffs from filing insubstantial suits in the hope that defendants will settle to avoid the expense of defending the action. Opponents, which include the ABA section on litigation, argue that the rule would deter many meritorious lawsuits and impose a regressive tax on the right to litigate.

Regardless of how the fees are paid, they must be "reasonable," insofar as the legal profession treats the charging of unreasonable fees as a matter of ethics. The Bar of every state has adopted a code that includes some provision similar to that of the ABA Model Rules of Professional Conduct:

### Rule 1.5(a) Fees

(a)  A lawyer shall not make an agreement for, charge, or collect and unreasonable fee or an unreasonable amount for expenses. The factors to be considered in determining the reasonableness of a fee include the following:

(1) the time and labor required, the novelty and difficulty of the questions involved, and the skill requisite to perform the legal service properly;

(2) the likelihood, if apparent to the client, that the acceptance of the particular employment will preclude other employment by the lawyer;

(3) the fee customarily charged in the locality for similar legal services;

(4) the amount involved and the results obtained;

(5) the time limitations imposed by the client or by the circumstances;

(6) the nature and length of the professional relationship with the client;

(7) the experience, reputation, and ability of the lawyer or lawyers performing the services; and

(8) whether the fee is fixed or contingent.

## a.  The Contingent Fee

While defendants usually pay their attorneys by the hour or a set fee for their services, contingent fee contracts are common for plaintiffs in the collection of commercial debts, personal injury claims, treble damage antitrust suits, minority shareholder litigation, condemnation proceedings, and will contests. Ninety-six percent of individual personal injury plaintiffs pay their lawyers on a contingent fee basis. Samuel R. Gross and Kent D. Syverud, Don't Try: Civil Jury Verdicts in a System Geared to Settlement, 44 UCLA L. Rev. 1, 15 (1996). Prospective clients usually welcome the contingent fee not only because it relieves them of the immediate burden of litigation costs, but also because they perceive that lawyers having a stake in their claims will be more aggressive.

Other observers have complained of this aggression, attributing to it certain unethical side effects such as the improper coaching of witnesses. On the other hand, the lawyer on contingent fee is sometimes accused of selling out his client by premature settlement of large claims. And even where there is no early settlement, critics have assailed contingent fee agreements according to which lawyers sometimes take over 40 percent of the plaintiff's damage award. Recent scholarship has highlighted abuses in the collection of contingency fees by so-called settlement mills—personal injury law firms organized to aggressively advertise, sign high percentages of plaintiff clients, delegate many tasks in the representation to non-lawyers, and settle cases rather than go to trial. In one such firm, Nora Engstrom found that cases were ordinarily settled after just "two-to-three hours of attorney time." Nora Freeman Engstrom, Run-of-the-Mill Justice, 22 Geo. J. Legal Ethics 1485, 1526 (2009).

Although the professional codes of most states and the ABA Model Rules generally approve contingent fee arrangements in all but domestic relations and criminal cases, there is widespread unease with the practice. See Lester Brickman, Lawyer Barons: What Their Contingency Fees Really Cost America (2011).

### b.   Other Methods for Providing Legal Services

#### i.   *Government-Provided Legal Services*

Even if the American Rule means you don't have to pay the other side's fees if you lose, you still have to "pay to play"—whether by contingency fee or some other arrangement, you must typically pay a lawyer to represent you. As part of the War on Poverty in the 1960s, the federal government established civil legal services offices for those unable to pay. The Legal Services Corporation Act once was funded at over $100 million a year to provide legal help to the indigent through a network of legal aid agencies spread over the country.

The early years of Legal Aid were turbulent because, for instance, poverty lawyers and their clients sued state institutions in "test" cases and, in the minds of some, stirred up litigation and cost to the taxpayers without regard to the overall needs of the community. Consider the *Fuentes* case described earlier in this chapter. Without legal aid lawyers, Ms. Fuentes would never have fought the repossession of her stove and stereo all the way to the U.S. Supreme Court. Similarly, Ms. Lassiter appealed the termination of her parental rights with the help of lawyers paid by the federal government.

As the Legal Aid program matured, its first conservative critics, concerned about subsidizing law reform and class warfare, have in some instances been replaced by those who charge that the original ideals of the program have not been realized, or even that they have been betrayed. For critical analyses of the Legal Aid program and community lawyering, see Gary Bellow, Turning Solutions into Problems: The Legal Aid Experience, 34 NLADA Briefcase 106 (1977); Gerald P. Lopez, Rebellious Lawyering: One Chicano's Vision of Progressive Law Practice (1992); Ann Southworth, Taking the Lawyer

Out of Progressive Lawyering, 46 Stan. L. Rev. 213 (1993); see also D. James Greiner and Cassandra Wolos Pattanayak, Randomized Evaluation in Legal Assistance: What Difference Does Representation (Offer and Actual Use) Make?, 121 Yale L.J. 2118 (2012); Leon Neyfakh, Free Legal Advice—But Does it Work?, Boston Globe, Dec. 23, 2012. The problems with the legal aid system pointed out by Gary Bellow are several. First, most cases dealt with in legal services offices are treated perfunctorily, unless the client's case presents an interesting or unique legal problem. Second, clients have very little control over their cases; lawyers present the options they see and effectively make the decisions. Third, many lawyers too narrowly define the client's concerns, focusing only on the "legal" problem presented. Finally, many cases result in settlements that may not be desirable for the client. Lopez presents an alternative vision of community lawyering, advocating more collaboration between clients and attorneys, and focusing on political mobilization rather than litigation. Southworth, in her critique of Lopez's model, makes additional suggestions to help lawyers facilitate clients' assertion of control and best use their lawyering skills to make a difference.

By the turn of the century, federally funded legal services had been greatly weakened over the years by legislation that cut the budgets of the programs and that restricted sharply the kinds of cases to which federally funded legal services could be applied. Congress cut the budget of the Legal Services Corporation by about one third in 1996 and passed restrictions that prohibited legal aid lawyers from participating in certain kinds of law reform. Some of these restrictions have been struck down because they interfere with the attorney-client relationship and First Amendment rights. See Legal Servs. Corp. v. Velasquez, 531 U.S. 533 (2001) (striking down statutory provisions that prohibited legal aid lawyers representing welfare beneficiaries from raising challenges to welfare rules that led to the denial of benefits for their clients). Writing for the majority in *Velasquez*, Justice Kennedy emphasized that

> [r]estricting LSC attorneys in advising their clients and in presenting arguments and analyses to the courts distorts the legal system by altering the attorneys' traditional role . . . . [According to the statute,] upon determining [that] a question of statutory validity is present in any anticipated or pending case or controversy, the LSC-funded attorney must cease the representation at once. . . . The Constitution does not permit the Government to confine litigants and their attorneys in this manner. We must be vigilant when Congress imposes rules and conditions which in effect insulate its own laws from legitimate judicial challenge.

531 U.S. at 534, 544, 548. Other restrictions, however, such as the ban on representing undocumented aliens, prison inmates, and accused drug dealers, and the ban on filing class action lawsuits, remain.

Overall, as David Luban describes, the effect is that legal aid and other public interest legal organizations do not even begin to meet the legal needs of the poor:

Law is a $100 billion per year industry. Of that $100 billion, however, less than $1 billion is dedicated to delivering legal services to low-income Americans. Put in terms of people rather than dollars, there is about one lawyer for every 240 nonpoor Americans, but only one lawyer for every 9,000 Americans whose low income would qualify them for legal aid. Forty-five million Americans qualify for civil legal aid, and they are served by a mere 4,000 legal-aid lawyers plus an estimated 1,000 to 2,000 additional poor people's lawyers. Although the myth persists that the very rich and the very poor have no trouble getting lawyers (because the rich have money and the poor qualify for legal aid), and that only the middle class is squeezed, these numbers reveal the true scarcity of lawyers and services available to low-income people. In very real effect, low-income Americans are denied access to justice. The reason is simple: one lawyer per 9,000 clients.

David Luban, Taking Out the Adversary: The Assault on Progressive Public-Interest Lawyers, 91 Cal. L. Rev. 209, 211-213 (2003); see also Erwin Chemerinsky, Closing the Courthouse Doors to Civil Rights Litigants, 5 U. Pa. J. Const. L. 537 (2003). On the history of efforts to ensure legal services for the poor, see Alan W. Houseman and Linda E. Perle, Securing Equal Justice for All: A Brief History of Civil Legal Assistance in the United States (2003); Ruth Bader Ginsburg, Access to Justice: The Social Responsibility of Lawyers, In Pursuit of the Public Good: Access to Justice in the United States, 7 Wash. U. J.L. & Pol'y 1 (2001).

### ii.   *Group Legal Services*

The American Bar Association Model Rules of Professional Conduct encourage limited use of group legal service plans, which are plans that, like group health care plans, enable consumers to purchase legal services at substantial savings by participating in a group program that covers certain legal services.

### iii.   *The Prepayment Movement*

In many European systems, the costs of some kinds of litigation are distributed among large numbers of users and potential users of the legal system through various schemes of insurance, often private but sometimes public.

This approach to the access problem first made an appearance in the United States during the 1930s, when automobile clubs began to provide insurance against legal costs associated with the purchase and use of automobiles. Such insurance plans were often successfully resisted by the organized bar, which enforced rules against advertising, rules against the presence of intermediaries between lawyers and clients, and rules against unauthorized practice of law by intermediary associations or corporations.

Such resistance was overcome in NAACP v. Button, 371 U.S. 415 (1963), which held that Virginia could not prohibit the NAACP from paying the legal costs of its members in school desegregation litigation; the Virginia law prohibiting third-party payment of costs was said in this instance to violate the First Amendment rights of the group members.

### iv.   *Private Agreements*

Just as parties can waive or modify other rights by contract, they also can contract to pay attorneys' fees that they would otherwise not have to pay. In Burger King v. Rudzewicz, 471 U.S. 462 (1985), which we will study in the next section, a franchise agreement provided that "[i]n any litigation to enforce the terms of this Agreement, the prevailing party shall be paid by the other party all costs, including attorney's fees, incurred as a result of the legal action." This sort of arrangement is common in contracts between commercial actors.

Historically, lawyers were prohibited from receiving litigation funds from third parties willing to help finance litigation costs in exchange for a percentage of any recovery. The policy behind common law doctrines forbidding "champerty," "maintenance" and "barratry" was that allowing outside funding might stir up litigation. Recently, however, the ancient objections have been largely overcome and litigation funding is a lucrative business. See Assoc. of the Bar of the City of New York, Committee on Professional Ethics, Formal Opinion 2011-2012: Third Party Litigation Financing (discussing the development of third-party litigation funding in the 1990s; estimating the aggregate amount of litigation financing at over $1 billion; and concluding that it is not per se unethical to enter into a "non-recourse litigation financing arrangement with a third party lender" where the borrower who loses is not personally liable to the lender); see also Jonathan T. Molot, The Feasibility of Litigation Markets, 89 Ind. L.J. 171 (2014).

### v.   *Pro Bono Legal Services*

Lawyers are encouraged to provide legal services on a pro bono basis to clients who cannot afford their services and who may not qualify for legal aid. Should this obligation be a mandatory one? Would making it mandatory violate the lawyer's constitutional rights?

In fact, the American Bar Association's requirements for pro bono are nonmandatory—that is, they take the form of rules *not* subject to disciplinary action. The ethical guideline, embodied in Model Rule of Professional Conduct 6.1, is reprinted below:

Every lawyer has a professional responsibility to provide legal services to those unable to pay. A lawyer should aspire to render at least (50) hours of

pro bono publico services per year. In fulfilling this responsibility, the lawyer should:

(a)   provide a substantial majority of the (50) hours of legal services
without fee or expectation of fee to:
(1) persons of limited means; or
(2) charitable, religious, civic, community, governmental and
educational organizations in matters which are designed primarily to address the needs of persons of limited means; and

(b)   provide any additional services through:
(1) delivery of legal services at no fee or substantially reduced
fee to individuals, groups or organizations seeking to secure or
protect civil rights, civil liberties or public rights, or charitable,
religious, civic, community, governmental and educational organizations in matters in furtherance of their organizational purposes, where the payment of standard legal fees would significantly deplete the organization's economic resources or would be
otherwise inappropriate;
(2) delivery of legal services at a substantially reduced fee to
persons of limited means; or
(3) participation in activities for improving the law, the legal
system or the legal profession.

In addition, a lawyer should voluntarily contribute financial support to organizations that provide legal services to persons of limited means.

In addition to providing pro bono service on a volunteer basis, lawyers are
expected to accept appointments by courts to represent indigent litigants or
defendants. ABA Model Rule 6.2 provides that a "lawyer shall not seek to
avoid appointment by a tribunal to represent a person except for good cause,
such as: (a) representing the client is likely to result in violation of the Rules
of Professional Conduct or other law; (b) representing the client is likely to
result in an unreasonable financial burden on the lawyer; or (c) the client or
the cause is so repugnant to the lawyer as to be likely to impair the client-
lawyer relationship or the lawyer's ability to represent the client." See also
United States v. Dillon, 346 F.2d 633, 635 (9th Cir. 1965) (holding that lawyers
implicitly consent to court-compelled representation by appointment in part
because it is an established tradition of lawyers as officers of the court).

Rules governing the appointment of lawyers by courts for service appear
in other places as well. The statute providing for in forma pauperis proceedings, 28 U.S.C. § 1915, places a similar obligation on lawyers, though
the case law illustrates the nonenforceable nature of these rules. See, e.g.,
Mallard v. U.S. Dist. Court, 490 U.S. 296 (1989).

In reality, although there are instances of dedication and altruism, state
bars and courts have consistently rejected proposals to create mandatory
pro bono programs, and, as Deborah Rhode reports, "few lawyers come
close to satisfying the American Bar Association's" 50-hour aspiration.
"Recent estimates," she adds, "suggest that most attorneys do not perform
significant pro bono work, and that only between ten and twenty percent of

those who do are assisting low-income clients." Deborah L. Rhode, Cultures of Commitment: Pro Bono for Lawyers and Law Students, in Ethics in Practice: Lawyers' Roles, Responsibilities and Regulation 264 (2000); see also Norman W. Spaulding, The Prophet and the Bureaucrat: Positional Conflicts of Interest in Service Pro Bono Publico, 50 Stan. L. Rev. 1395 (1998). Whether other states will follow New York's innovation remains to be seen.

### vi.  *Lay Competition*

One of the classic arguments for pro bono service is that lawyers enjoy a monopoly on the provision of legal advice. It is a crime in many states to engage in the unauthorized practice of law, and bar associations have aggressively protected their turf by lobbying for strict enforcement of unauthorized practice rules against non-lawyers. In exchange for the monopoly rights, so the argument goes, lawyers should ensure that the needs of those who cannot afford a lawyer are met. But in the gap between the bar's pro bono aspirations and the mass of unmet legal needs among the poor, low-income, and middle classes, there is now a burgeoning market for inexpensive information about the law and legal process produced by non-lawyers. This includes publishers of so-called legal form books and, increasingly, software programs that guide users through the creation of legal instruments such as wills, contracts, real estate leases, and trusts. Lay purveyors have responded to prosecutions for unauthorized practice by arguing that the First Amendment protects their business—that they have a right to produce, and citizens have a right to purchase, information about how to protect one's legal interests. See Unauthorized Practice of Law Comm. v. Parsons Tech., Inc., 1999 WL 47235 (N.D. Tex. 1999) (software that helps users choose the correct legal form and customizes the forms selected by users constitutes unauthorized practice of law), *vacated by* Unauthorized Practice of Law Comm. v. Parsons Tech., Inc., 179 F.3d 956 (5th Cir. 1999) (vacating lower court decision after Texas legislature amended state rules on unauthorized practice to permit software that helps users with basic legal forms).

More recently, online companies like LegalZoom have been sued by state bar associations for unauthorized practice and false advertising. See Janson v. LegalZoom.com, Inc., 802 F. Supp. 2d 1053 (W.D. Mo. 2011) (holding that LegalZoom violates Missouri's unauthorized practice of law statutes); Catherine J. Lanctot, Does LegalZoom Have First Amendment Rights?: Some Thoughts About Freedom of Speech and the Unauthorized Practice of Law, 20 Temp. Pol. & Civ. Rts. L. Rev. 255 (2011); Ronald W. Staudt, All the Wild Possibilities: Technology That Attacks Barriers to Access to Justice, 42 Loy. L.A. L. Rev. 1117 (2009).

### c.  Access to Justice as a Fundamental Right

Rather obviously, civil cases can address rights that are as significant as many involved in criminal proceedings. *Lassiter,* which involved child custody, is an excellent example. Thus you can appreciate why some commentators have urged the U.S. Supreme Court to find a constitutional right to counsel. Indeed, Professor Frank Michelman has argued that litigating, like voting, is "preservative of all rights" and thus may deserve comparable constitutional protection. Frank I. Michelman, The Supreme Court and Litigation Access Fees: The Right to Protect One's Rights—Part 1, 1973 Duke L.J. 1153 (1974).

Professor Deborah Rhode summarizes other commentators' resistance to such arguments as follows:

> As a threshold matter, how could such rights to counsel be limited? If money were no object, what would deter parties from pursuing trivial claims and inflicting unwarranted costs, not only on the state but also on innocent opponents? . . .
>
> A more fundamental concern involves the magnitude of assistance necessary to assure truly effective representation in civil matters. While efforts to measure legal needs present substantial methodological problems, existing studies suggest the scope of the problem. In a national sample of households at or below 125 percent of the government poverty line, 43 percent of those surveyed reported civil legal problems in the last year; for about 80 percent of those problems, no legal assistance was available. Major areas of unmet need involved claims concerning medical treatment (14.6 percent), public benefits (13.4 percent), utilities (12 percent), family issues (12 percent), discrimination (11 percent), consumer disputes (10 percent) and housing (9 percent). Moreover, these studies have obvious limitations. They measure only subjective perception, and if parties lack awareness of potential claims, these would not be reported. Nor do such surveys generally measure group needs or collective problems, such as environmental risks or inequitable educational financing.

Deborah L. Rhode, Professional Responsibility: Ethics by the Pervasive Method 542-543 (1994).

Absent a right to counsel at state expense, litigants who cannot afford legal counsel must rely on the other methods for paying lawyers—for example, the contingency fee, legal aid, and pro bono—described above.

In the next two cases, the Supreme Court deals with the question of whether lawyers are necessary to due process in two very different settings. As you read, think how the Court views the work of lawyers and their contributions to efficiency.

### *Walters v. National Association of Radiation Survivors*
473 U.S. 305 (1985)

JUSTICE REHNQUIST delivered the opinion of the Court. . . .

## I

Congress has by statute established an administrative system for granting service-connected death or disability benefits to veterans. See 38 U.S.C.

§§ 301 et seq. The amount of the benefit award is not based upon need, but upon service connection—that is, whether the disability is causally related to an injury sustained in the service—and the degree of incapacity caused by the disability. A detailed system has been established by statute and Veterans' Administration (VA) regulation for determining a veteran's entitlement, with final authority resting with an administrative body known as the Board of Veterans' Appeals (BVA). Judicial review of VA decisions is precluded by statute. The controversy in this case centers on the opportunity for a benefit applicant or recipient to obtain legal counsel to aid in the presentation of his claim to the VA. Section 3404(c) of Title 38 provides:

> The Administrator shall determine and pay fees to agents or attorneys recognized under this section in allowed claims for monetary benefits under laws administered by the Veterans' Administration. Such fees—...
>    (2) shall not exceed $10 with respect to any one claim. . . .

Section 3405 provides criminal penalties for any person who charges fees in excess of the limitation of § 3404.

Appellees here are two veterans' organizations, three individual veterans, and a veteran's widow. . . .

Appellees contended in the District Court that the fee limitation provision of § 3404 denied them any realistic opportunity to obtain legal representation in presenting their claims to the VA and hence violated their rights under the Due Process Clause of the Fifth Amendment and under the First Amendment. The District Court agreed with the appellees on both of these grounds, and entered a nationwide "preliminary injunction" barring appellants from enforcing the fee limitation. 589 F. Supp. 1302 (1984). To understand fully the posture in which the case reaches us it is necessary to discuss the administrative scheme in some detail.

Congress began providing veterans pensions in early 1789, and after every conflict in which the Nation has been involved Congress has, in the words of Abraham Lincoln, "provided for him who has borne the battle, and his widow and his orphan." The VA was created by Congress in 1930, and since that time has been responsible for administering the congressional program for veterans' benefits. In 1978, the year covered by the report of the Legal Services Corporation to Congress that was introduced into evidence in the District Court, approximately 800,000 claims for service-connected disability or death and pensions were decided by the 58 regional offices of the VA. Slightly more than half of these were claims for service-connected disability or death, and the remainder were pension claims. Of the 800,000 total claims in 1978, more than 400,000 were allowed, and some 379,000 were denied. Sixty-six thousand of these denials were contested at the regional level; about a quarter of these contests were dropped, 15% prevailed on reconsideration at the local level, and the remaining 36,000 were appealed to the BVA. At that level some 4,500, or 12%, prevailed, and another 13% won a remand for further proceedings. Although these figures are from 1978, the statistics in evidence indicate that the figures remain fairly constant from year to year.

As might be expected in a system which processes such a large number of claims each year, the process prescribed by Congress for obtaining disability benefits does not contemplate the adversary mode of dispute resolution utilized by courts in this country. It is commenced by the submission of a claim form to the local veterans agency, which form is provided by the VA either upon request or upon receipt of notice of the death of a veteran. Upon application a claim generally is first reviewed by a three-person "rating board" of the VA regional office—consisting of a medical specialist, a legal specialist, and an "occupational specialist." A claimant is "entitled to a hearing at any time on any issue involved in a claim. . . ." 38 C.F.R. § 3.103(c) (1984). Proceedings in front of the rating board "are *ex parte* in nature," § 3.103(a); no Government official appears in opposition. The principal issues are the extent of the claimant's disability and whether it is service connected. The board is required by regulation "to assist a claimant in developing the facts pertinent to his claim," § 3.103(a), and to consider any evidence offered by the claimant. In deciding the claim the board generally will request the applicant's Armed Service and medical records, and will order a medical examination by a VA hospital. Moreover, the board is directed by regulation to resolve all reasonable doubts in favor of the claimant.

After reviewing the evidence the board renders a decision either denying the claim or assigning a disability "rating" pursuant to detailed regulations developed for assessing various disabilities. Money benefits are calculated based on the rating. The claimant is notified of the board's decision and its reasons, and the claimant may then initiate an appeal by filing a "notice of disagreement" with the local agency. If the local agency adheres to its original decision it must then provide the claimant with a "statement of the case"—a written description of the facts and applicable law upon which the board based its determination—so that the claimant may adequately present his appeal to the BVA. Hearings in front of the BVA are subject to the same rules as local agency hearings—they are *ex parte*, there is no formal questioning or cross-examination, and no formal rules of evidence apply. The BVA's decision is not subject to judicial review.

The process is designed to function throughout with a high degree of informality and solicitude for the claimant. There is no statute of limitations, and a denial of benefits has no formal res judicata effect; a claimant may resubmit as long as he presents new facts not previously forwarded. Although there are time limits for submitting a notice of disagreement and although a claimant may prejudice his opportunity to challenge factual or legal decisions by failing to challenge them in that notice, the time limit is quite liberal—up to one year—and the VA boards are instructed to read any submission in the light most favorable to the claimant.

Perhaps more importantly for present purposes, however, various veterans' organizations across the country make available trained service agents, free of charge, to assist claimants in developing and presenting their claims. These service representatives are contemplated by the VA statute, and they are recognized as an important part of the administrative scheme. . . .

In support of their claim that the present statutory and administrative scheme violates the Constitution, appellees submitted affidavits and declarations of 16 rejected claimants or recipients and 24 practicing attorneys, depositions of several VA employees, and various exhibits. The District Court held a hearing and then issued a 52-page opinion and order granting the requested "preliminary injunction." . . .

. . . In holding that the process described above was "fundamentally unfair," the court relied on the analysis developed by this Court in Mathews v. Eldridge, supra, in which we stated the factors that must be weighed in determining what process is due an individual subject to a deprivation. . . .

In applying this test the District Court relied heavily on appellees' evidence; it noted that the veterans' interest in receiving benefits was significant in that many recipients are disabled, and totally or primarily dependent on benefits for their support. 589 F. Supp. at 1315. With respect to the likelihood of error under the present system, and the value of the additional safeguard of legal representation, it first noted that some of the appellees had been represented by service agents and had been dissatisfied with their representation, and had sought and failed to obtain legal counsel due solely to the fee limitation. The court found that absent expert legal counsel claimants ran a significant risk of forfeiting their rights, because of the highly complex issues involved in some cases. VA processes, the court reasoned, allow claimants to waive points of disagreement on appeal, or to waive appeal altogether by failing to file the notice of disagreement; in addition, claimants simply are not equipped to engage in the factual or legal development necessary in some cases, or to spot errors made by the administrative boards. . . .

. . . In defining the process necessary to ensure "fundamental fairness" we have recognized that the Clause does not require that "the procedures used to guard against an erroneous deprivation . . . be so comprehensive as to preclude any possibility of error," Mackey v. Montrym, 443 U.S. 1, 13 (1979), and in addition we have emphasized that the marginal gains from affording an additional procedural safeguard often may be outweighed by the societal cost of providing such a safeguard. . . .

The Government interest, which has been articulated in congressional debates since the fee limitation was first enacted in 1862 during the Civil War, has been this: that the system for administering benefits should be managed in a sufficiently informal way that there should be no need for the employment of an attorney to obtain benefits to which a claimant was entitled, so that the claimant would receive the entirety of the award without having to divide it with a lawyer. . . .

There can be little doubt that invalidation of the fee limitation would seriously frustrate the oft-repeated congressional purpose for enacting it. Attorneys would be freely employable by claimants to veterans' benefits, and the claimant would as a result end up paying part of the award, or its equivalent, to an attorney. But this would not be the only consequence of striking down the fee limitation that would be deleterious to the congressional plan.

A necessary concomitant of Congress' desire that a veteran not need a representative to assist him in making his claim was that the system should be as informal and nonadversarial as possible. This is not to say that complicated factual inquiries may be rendered simple by the expedient of informality, but surely Congress desired that the proceedings be as informal and nonadversarial as possible. The regular introduction of lawyers into the proceedings would be quite unlikely to further this goal. . . .

Knowledgeable and thoughtful observers have made the same point in other language:

> To be sure, counsel can often perform useful functions even in welfare cases or other instances of mass justice; they may bring out facts ignored by or unknown to the authorities, or help to work out satisfactory compromises. But this is only one side of the coin. Under our adversary system the role of counsel is not to make sure the truth is ascertained but to advance his client's cause by any ethical means. Within the limits of professional propriety, causing delay and sowing confusion not only are his right but may be his duty. The appearance of counsel for the citizen is likely to lead the government to provide one — or at least to cause the government's representative to act like one. The result may be to turn what might have been a short conference leading to an amicable result into a protracted controversy. . . .
>
> These problems concerning counsel and confrontation inevitably bring up the question whether we would not do better to abandon the adversary system in certain areas of mass justice. . . . While such an experiment would be a sharp break with our tradition of adversary process, that tradition, which has come under serious general challenge from a thoughtful and distinguished judge, was not formulated for a situation in which many thousands of hearings must be provided each month.

Friendly, Some Kind of Hearing, 123 U. Pa. L. Rev. 1267, 1287-1290 (1975).

Thus, even apart from the frustration of Congress' principal goal of wanting the veteran to get the entirety of the award, the destruction of the fee limitation would bid fair to complicate a proceeding which Congress wished to keep as simple as possible. It is scarcely open to doubt that if claimants were permitted to retain compensated attorneys the day might come when it could be said that an attorney might indeed be necessary to present a claim properly in a system rendered more adversary and more complex by the very presence of lawyer representation. It is only a small step beyond that to the situation in which the claimant who has a factually simple and obviously deserving claim may nonetheless feel impelled to retain an attorney simply because so many other claimants retain attorneys. And this additional complexity will undoubtedly engender greater administrative costs, with the end result being that less Government money reaches its intended beneficiaries. . . .

. . . Simple factual questions are capable of resolution in a nonadversarial context, and it is less than crystal clear why *lawyers* must be available to identify possible errors in *medical* judgment. . . .

Justice Stevens, with whom Justice Brennan and Justice Marshall join, dissenting.

The Court does not appreciate the value of individual liberty. It may well be true that in the vast majority of cases a veteran does not need to employ a lawyer, and that the system of processing veterans benefit claims, by and large, functions fairly and effectively without the participation of retained counsel. Everyone agrees, however, that there are at least some complicated cases in which the services of a lawyer would be useful to the veteran and, indeed, would simplify the work of the agency by helping to organize the relevant facts and to identify the controlling issues. What is the reason for denying the veteran the right to counsel of his choice in such cases? The Court gives us two answers: First, the paternalistic interest in protecting the veteran from the consequences of his own improvidence; and second, the bureaucratic interest in minimizing the cost of administering the benefit program. I agree that both interests are legitimate, but neither provides an adequate justification for the restraint on liberty imposed by the $10-fee limitation. . . .

## II

The Court's opinion blends its discussion of the paternalistic interest in protecting veterans from unscrupulous lawyers and the bureaucratic interest in minimizing the cost of administration in a way that implies that each interest reinforces the other. Actually the two interests are quite different and merit separate analysis.

In my opinion, the bureaucratic interest in minimizing the cost of administration is nothing but a red herring. Congress has not prohibited lawyers from participating in the processing of claims for benefits and there is no reason why it should. The complexity of the agency procedures can be regulated by limiting the number of hearings, the time for argument, the length of written submissions, and in other ways, but there is no reason to believe that the *agency's* cost of administration will be increased because a claimant is represented by counsel instead of appearing *pro se.* The informality that the Court emphasizes is desirable because it no doubt enables many veterans, or their lay representatives, to handle their claims without the assistance of counsel. But there is no reason to assume that lawyers would add confusion rather than clarity to the proceedings. As a profession, lawyers are skilled communicators dedicated to the service of their clients. Only if it is assumed that the average lawyer is incompetent or unscrupulous can one rationally conclude that the efficiency of the agency's work would be undermined by allowing counsel to participate whenever a veteran is willing to pay for his services. I categorically reject any such assumption.

The fact that a lawyer's services are unnecessary in most cases, and might even be counterproductive in a few, does not justify a total prohibition on their participation in all pension claim proceedings. . . .

The paternalistic interest in protecting the veteran from his own improvidence would unquestionably justify a rule that simply prevented lawyers from overcharging their clients. Most appropriately, such a rule might require agency approval, or perhaps judicial review, of counsel fees. It might also establish a reasonable ceiling, subject to exceptions for especially complicated cases. In fact, I assume that the $10-fee limitation was justified by this interest when it was first enacted in 1864. But time has brought changes in the value of the dollar, in the character of the legal profession, in agency procedures, and in the ability of the veteran to proceed without the assistance of counsel. . . .

. . . [T]he statute is unconstitutional for a reason that is more fundamental than its apparent irrationality. What is at stake is the right of an individual to consult an attorney of his choice in connection with a controversy with the Government. In my opinion that right is firmly protected by the Due Process Clause of the Fifth Amendment and by the First Amendment.

The Court recognizes that the Veterans' Administration's procedures must provide claimants with due process of law, but then concludes that the constitutional requirement is satisfied because the appellees have not proved that the "probability of error under the present system" is unacceptable. In short, if 80 or 90 percent of the cases are correctly decided, why worry about those individuals whose claims have been erroneously rejected and who might have prevailed if they had been represented by counsel?

The fundamental error in the Court's analysis is its assumption that the individual's right to employ counsel of his choice in a contest with his sovereign is a kind of second-class interest that can be assigned a material value and balanced on a utilitarian scale of costs and benefits. It is true that the veteran's right to benefits is a property right and that in fashioning the procedures for administering the benefit program, the Government may appropriately weigh the value of additional procedural safeguards against their pecuniary costs. It may, for example, properly decide not to provide free counsel to claimants. But we are not considering a procedural right that would involve any cost to the Government. We are concerned with the individual's right to spend his own money to obtain the advice and assistance of independent counsel in advancing his claim against the Government.

In all criminal proceedings, that right is expressly protected by the Sixth Amendment. As I have indicated, in civil disputes with the Government I believe that right is also protected by the Due Process Clause of the Fifth Amendment and by the First Amendment. If the Government, in the guise of a paternalistic interest in protecting the citizen from his own improvidence, can deny him access to independent counsel of his choice, it can change the character of our free society. Even though a dispute with the sovereign may only involve property rights, or as in this case a statutory entitlement, the citizen's right of access to the independent, private bar is itself an aspect of liberty that is of critical importance in our democracy. Just as I disagree with the present Court's crabbed view of the concept of "liberty," so do I reject its apparent unawareness of the function of the independent lawyer as a guardian of our freedom.

In my view, regardless of the nature of the dispute between the sovereign and the citizen—whether it be a criminal trial, a proceeding to terminate parental rights, a claim for social security benefits, a dispute over welfare benefits, or a pension claim asserted by the widow of a soldier who was killed on the battlefield—the citizen's right to consult an independent lawyer and to retain that lawyer to speak on his or her behalf is an aspect of liberty that is priceless. It should not be bargained away on the notion that a totalitarian appraisal of the mass of claims processed by the Veterans' Administration does not identify an especially high probability of error. Unfortunately, the reason for the Court's mistake today is all too obvious. It does not appreciate the value of individual liberty.

### *Note: The Second Act—Legislation*

After ten years of debate, in which the *Walters* case was an important spur, Congress passed the Veterans Judicial Review Act of 1988, 102 Stat. 4105 (38 U.S.C. § 4063) (popularly known as the JRA). In sum, the JRA established a Court of Veterans' Appeals (CVA) that was empowered to review the previously final decisions of the Board of Veterans' Appeals, and also made the decisions of the CVA subject to review by the U.S. Court of Appeals for the Federal Circuit.

In removing the $10 cap on the cost of representation, Congress responded to hearings replete with stories of injured veterans denied their rights because they could not negotiate the intricacies of hearings without representation and because there was no appeal from unjust adverse decisions. S. Rep. No. 418, 100th Cong., 2d Sess. (1988).

For a full discussion of the intricacies of the law, see Barton F. Stichman, The Veterans' Judicial Review Act of 1988: Congress Introduces Courts and Attorneys to Veterans' Benefit Proceedings, 23 Clearinghouse Rev. 515 (1989). He summarizes the attorneys' fees provisions as follows:

> For services rendered in cases appealed to the CVA, the appellant and his or her representative are free to negotiate any fee agreement they desire . . . [though] the advocate must file a copy of the fee agreement with the CVA which may order a reduction if it finds that the fee agreed upon is "excessive or unreasonable." The CVA need not take affirmative action to approve a fee agreement. CVA review of the reasonableness of particular fee agreements can be initiated by motion of the CVA itself or by one of the parties, including apparently, the VA. A decision by the CVA on the reasonableness of a fee is final and cannot be appealed to any other court.

## *Note: Further* **Walters** *Proceedings in the Lower Courts*

The Supreme Court found that the fee-cap statute was not unconstitutional on its face, leaving open the question of whether it might be unconstitutionally applied. On remand, Federal District Judge Marilyn Hall Patel ruled the fee cap unconstitutional when applied to a particular type of plaintiff, notably those who claimed exposure to ionizing radiation and were *not* covered by the Veteran's Review Act of 1988. Nat'l Ass'n of Radiation Survivors v. Derwinski, 782 F. Supp. 1392, 1394, 1407-1408 (N.D. Cal. 1991).

The final act of the due process drama occurred in the Ninth Circuit when it reversed Judge Patel in a long opinion that considered her specific findings and compared them to the observations of the Supreme Court in *Walters*. Nat'l Ass'n of Radiation Survivors v. Derwinski, 994 F.2d 583 (9th Cir. 1992), *cert. denied sub nom.* Nat'l Ass'n of Radiation Survivors v. Brown, 510 U.S. 1023 (1993). Typical of the court's skepticism about the value attorneys would add to the process is the following passage:

> The Supreme Court in *Walters* stated that it is less than crystal clear why *lawyers* must be available to identify possible errors in *medical* judgment. *Walters*, 473 U.S. at 330. The district court found that [ionizing radiation] claims present many tasks for which attorneys particularly are well suited. Attorneys could secure government documents with relevant information, help claimants avoid procedural errors, enhance the effective use of medical and scientific experts, conduct detailed factual development, and prepare briefs. *Derwinski*, 782 F. Supp. at 1406. The government concedes that attorneys could assist with a number of tasks but asserts that this does not indicate that lawyers are necessary to ensure procedural fairness in the adjudication of IR claims. See *Walters*, 473 U.S. at 331.
>
> In support of its finding, the district court stated that "evidence demonstrates that IR claimants who employ attorneys have had significantly higher success rates than those relying on service representatives." *Derwinski*, 782 F. Supp. at 1407. The evidence referenced in that quote showed that in IR claims handled by lawyers the claims were granted in 5 out of 31 cases (16%) while in IR claims not handled by lawyers the claims were granted in 35 out of 5,456 cases (.6%).

## *Turner v. Rogers*
564 U.S. 431 (2011)

JUSTICE BREYER delivered the opinion of the Court.

South Carolina's Family Court enforces its child support orders by threatening with incarceration for civil contempt those who are (1) subject to a child support order, (2) able to comply with that order, but (3) fail to do so. We must decide whether the Fourteenth Amendment's Due Process Clause requires the State to provide counsel (at a civil contempt hearing) to an indigent person potentially faced with such incarceration.

We conclude that whereas here the custodial parent (entitled to receive the support) is unrepresented by counsel, the State need not provide counsel to the noncustodial parent (required to provide the support). But we attach an important caveat, namely, that the State must nonetheless have in place alternative procedures that assure a fundamentally fair determination of the critical incarceration-related question, whether the supporting parent is able to comply with the support order.

## I

### A

South Carolina family courts enforce their child support orders in part through civil contempt proceedings. Each month the family court clerk reviews outstanding child support orders, identifies those in which the supporting parent has fallen more than five days behind, and sends that parent an order to "show cause" why he should not be held in contempt. S.C. Rule Family Ct. 24 (2011). The "show cause" order and attached affidavit refer to the relevant child support order, identify the amount of the arrearage, and set a date for a court hearing. At the hearing that parent may demonstrate that he is not in contempt, say, by showing that he is not able to make the required payments. See Moseley v. Mosier, 279 S.C. 348, 351 (1983) ("When the parent is unable to make the required payments, he is not in contempt"). If he fails to make the required showing, the court may hold him in civil contempt. And it may require that he be imprisoned unless and until he purges himself of contempt by making the required child support payments (but not for more than one year regardless). See S.C. Code Ann. § 63-3-620 (Supp. 2010) (imprisonment for up to one year of "adult who willfully violates" a court order); Price v. Turner, 387 S.C. 142, 145 (2010) (civil contempt order must permit purging of contempt through compliance).

### B

In June 2003 a South Carolina family court entered an order, which (as amended) required petitioner, Michael Turner, to pay $51.73 per week to respondent, Rebecca Rogers, to help support their child. (Rogers' father, Larry Price, currently has custody of the child and is also a respondent before this Court.) Over the next three years, Turner repeatedly failed to pay the amount due and was held in contempt on five occasions. The first four times he was sentenced to 90 days' imprisonment, but he ultimately paid the amount due (twice without being jailed, twice after spending two or three days in custody). The fifth time he did not pay but completed a 6-month sentence.

After his release in 2006 Turner remained in arrears. On March 27, 2006, the clerk issued a new "show cause" order. And after an initial postponement due to Turner's failure to appear, Turner's civil contempt hearing took place on January 3, 2008. Turner and Rogers were present, each without representation by counsel.

The hearing was brief. The court clerk said that Turner was $5,728.76 behind in his payments. The judge asked Turner if there was "anything you want to say." Turner replied,

> "Well, when I first got out, I got back on dope. I done meth, smoked pot and everything else, and I paid a little bit here and there. And, when I finally did get to working, I broke my back, back in September. I filed for disability and SSI. And, I didn't get straightened out off the dope until I broke my back and laid up for two months. And, now I'm off the dope and everything. I just hope that you give me a chance. I don't know what else to say. I mean, I know I done wrong, and I should have been paying and helping her, and I'm sorry. I mean, dope had a hold to me."

The judge then said, "[o]kay," and asked Rogers if she had anything to say. After a brief discussion of federal benefits, the judge stated,

> "If there's nothing else, this will be the Order of the Court. I find the Defendant in willful contempt. I'm [going to] sentence him to twelve months in the Oconee County Detention Center. He may purge himself of the contempt and avoid the sentence by having a zero balance on or before his release. I've also placed a lien on any SSI or other benefits."

The judge added that Turner would not receive good-time or work credits, but "[i]f you've got a job, I'll make you eligible for work release." When Turner asked why he could not receive good-time or work credits, the judge said, "[b]ecause that's my ruling."

The court made no express finding concerning Turner's ability to pay his arrearage (though Turner's wife had voluntarily submitted a copy of Turner's application for disability benefits). Nor did the judge ask any follow up questions or otherwise address the ability-to-pay issue. After the hearing, the judge filled out a prewritten form titled "Order for Contempt of Court," which included the statement:

> "Defendant (was) (was not) gainfully employed and/or (had) (did not have) the ability to make these support payments when due."

But the judge left this statement as is without indicating whether Turner was able to make support payments.

## C

While serving his 12-month sentence, Turner, with the help of *pro bono* counsel, appealed. He claimed that the Federal Constitution entitled him to counsel at his contempt hearing. The South Carolina Supreme Court decided Turner's appeal after he had completed his sentence. And it rejected his "right to counsel" claim. The court pointed out that civil contempt differs significantly from criminal contempt. The former does not require all the "constitutional safeguards" applicable in criminal proceedings. 387 S.C., at 145. And the right to government-paid counsel, the Supreme Court held, was one of the "safeguards" not required. Id.

Turner sought certiorari. In light of differences among state courts (and some federal courts) on the applicability of a "right to counsel" in civil contempt proceedings enforcing child support orders, we granted the writ.

## II

[The Court held that the case was not moot even though Turner completed his 12-month sentence in 2009. The Court reasoned that his dispute with the state was "capable of repetition" yet "evading review" because of the short sentences to which Turner was exposed:]

Turner has frequently failed to make his child support payments. He has been the subject of several civil contempt proceedings. He has been imprisoned on several of those occasions. Within months of his release from the imprisonment here at issue he was again the subject of civil contempt proceedings. And he was again imprisoned, this time for six months. As of December 9, 2010, Turner was $13,814.72 in arrears, and another contempt hearing was scheduled for May 4, 2011.

[If no exception to ordinary mootness rules were made, his appeals of these short sentences would never reach the Supreme Court prior to his release.]

## III

### A

We must decide whether the Due Process Clause grants an indigent defendant, such as Turner, a right to state-appointed counsel at a civil contempt proceeding, which may lead to his incarceration. This Court's precedents provide no definitive answer to that question. This Court has long held that the Sixth Amendment grants an indigent defendant the right to state-appointed counsel in a criminal case. Gideon v. Wainwright, 372 U.S. 335 (1963). And we have held that this same rule applies to criminal contempt proceedings (other than summary proceedings). United States v. Dixon, 509 U.S. 688, 696 (1993).

But the Sixth Amendment does not govern civil cases. Civil contempt differs from criminal contempt in that it seeks only to "coerc[e] the defendant to do" what a court had previously ordered him to do. Gompers v. Bucks Stove & Range Co., 221 U.S. 418, 442 (1911). A court may not impose punishment "in a civil contempt proceeding when it is clearly established that the alleged contemnor is unable to comply with the terms of the order." Hicks

v. Feiock, 485 U.S. 624, 638, n.9 (1988). And once a civil contemnor complies with the underlying order, he is purged of the contempt and is free. Id., at 633 (he "carr[ies] the keys of [his] prison in [his] own pockets").

Consequently, the Court has made clear (in a case not involving the right to counsel) that, where civil contempt is at issue, the Fourteenth Amendment's Due Process Clause allows a State to provide fewer procedural protections than in a criminal case. Id., at 637-41 (State may place the burden of proving inability to pay on the defendant).

This Court has decided only a handful of cases that more directly concern a right to counsel in civil matters. And the application of those decisions to the present case is not clear. On the one hand, the Court has held that the Fourteenth Amendment requires the State to pay for representation by counsel in a civil "juvenile delinquency" proceeding (which could lead to incarceration). In re Gault, 387 U.S. 1, 35-42 (1967). Moreover, in Vitek v. Jones, 445 U.S. 480, 496-497 (1980), a plurality of four Members of this Court would have held that the Fourteenth Amendment requires representation by counsel in a proceeding to transfer a prison inmate to a state hospital for the mentally ill. Further, in Lassiter v. Department of Social Servs. of Durham Cty., 452 U.S. 18 (1981), a case that focused upon civil proceedings leading to loss of parental rights, the Court wrote that the

> "pre-eminent generalization that emerges from this Court's precedents on an indigent's right to appointed counsel is that such a right has been recognized to exist only where the litigant may lose his physical liberty if he loses the litigation." Id., at 25.

And the Court then drew from these precedents "the presumption that an indigent litigant has a right to appointed counsel only when, if he loses, he may be deprived of his physical liberty." Id., at 26-27.

On the other hand, the Court has held that a criminal offender facing revocation of probation and imprisonment does not ordinarily have a right to counsel at a probation revocation hearing. Gagnon v. Scarpelli, 411 U.S. 778 (1973); see also Middendorf v. Henry, 425 U.S. 25 (1976) (no due process right to counsel in summary court-martial proceedings). And, at the same time, *Gault*, *Vitek*, and *Lassiter* are readily distinguishable. The civil juvenile delinquency proceeding at issue in *Gault* was "little different" from, and "comparable in seriousness" to, a criminal prosecution. 387 U.S., at 28, 36. In *Vitek*, the controlling opinion found no right to counsel. 445 U.S., at 499-500 (Powell, J., concurring in part) (assistance of mental health professionals sufficient). And the Court's statements in *Lassiter* constitute part of its rationale for denying a right to counsel in that case. We believe those statements are best read as pointing out that the Court previously had found a right to counsel "only" in cases involving incarceration, not that a right to counsel exists in all such cases (a position that would have been difficult to reconcile with *Gagnon*).

## B

Civil contempt proceedings in child support cases constitute one part of a highly complex system designed to assure a noncustodial parent's regular payment of funds typically necessary for the support of his children. Often the family receives welfare support from a state-administered federal program, and the State then seeks reimbursement from the noncustodial parent. Other times the custodial parent (often the mother, but sometimes the father, a grandparent, or another person with custody) does not receive government benefits and is entitled to receive the support payments herself.

The Federal Government has created an elaborate procedural mechanism designed to help both the government and custodial parents to secure the payments to which they are entitled. See generally Blessing v. Freestone, 520 U.S. 329, 333 (1997) (describing the "interlocking set of cooperative federal-state welfare programs" as they relate to child support enforcement); 45 CFR pt. 303 (2010) (prescribing standards for state child support agencies). These systems often rely upon wage withholding, expedited procedures for modifying and enforcing child support orders, and automated data processing. But sometimes States will use contempt orders to ensure that the custodial parent receives support payments or the government receives reimbursement. Although some experts have criticized this last-mentioned procedure, and the Federal Government believes that "the routine use of contempt for non-payment of child support is likely to be an ineffective strategy," the Government also tells us that "coercive enforcement remedies, such as contempt, have a role to play." Brief for United States as Amicus Curiae. South Carolina, which relies heavily on contempt proceedings, agrees that they are an important tool.

We here consider an indigent's right to paid counsel at such a contempt proceeding. It is a civil proceeding. And we consequently determine the "specific dictates of due process" by examining the "distinct factors" that this Court has previously found useful in deciding what specific safeguards the Constitution's Due Process Clause requires in order to make a civil proceeding fundamentally fair. Mathews v. Eldridge, 424 U.S. 319, 335 (1976) (considering fairness of an administrative proceeding). As relevant here those factors include (1) the nature of "the private interest that will be affected," (2) the comparative "risk" of an "erroneous deprivation" of that interest with and without "additional or substitute procedural safeguards," and (3) the nature and magnitude of any countervailing interest in not providing "additional or substitute procedural requirement[s]." Id.

The "private interest that will be affected" argues strongly for the right to counsel that Turner advocates. That interest consists of an indigent defendant's loss of personal liberty through imprisonment. The interest in securing that freedom, the freedom "from bodily restraint," lies "at the core of the liberty protected by the Due Process Clause." Foucha v. Louisiana, 504 U.S. 71, 80 (1992). And we have made clear that its threatened loss through legal proceedings demands "due process protection." Addington v. Texas, 441 U.S. 418, 425 (1979).

Given the importance of the interest at stake, it is obviously important to assure accurate decision making in respect to the key "ability to pay" question. Moreover, the fact that ability to comply marks a dividing line between civil and criminal contempt, *Hicks*, 485 U.S., at 635, n.7, reinforces the need for accuracy. That is because an incorrect decision (wrongly classifying the contempt proceeding as civil) can increase the risk of wrongful incarceration by depriving the defendant of the procedural protections (including counsel) that the Constitution would demand in a criminal proceeding. See, e.g., *Dixon*, 509 U.S., at 696 (proof beyond a reasonable doubt, protection from double jeopardy); Codispoti v. Pennsylvania, 418 U.S. 506, 512-513, 517 (1974) (jury trial where the result is more than six months' imprisonment). And since 70% of child support arrears nationwide are owed by parents with either no reported income or income of $10,000 per year or less, the issue of ability to pay may arise fairly often.

On the other hand, the Due Process Clause does not always require the provision of counsel in civil proceedings where incarceration is threatened. See *Gagnon*, 411 U.S. 778. And in determining whether the Clause requires a right to counsel here, we must take account of opposing interests, as well as consider the probable value of "additional or substitute procedural safeguards." *Mathews*, supra, at 335.

Doing so, we find three related considerations that, when taken together, argue strongly against the Due Process Clause requiring the State to provide indigents with counsel in every proceeding of the kind before us.

First, the critical question likely at issue in these cases concerns, as we have said, the defendant's ability to pay. That question is often closely related to the question of the defendant's indigence. But when the right procedures are in place, indigence can be a question that in many—but not all—cases is sufficiently straightforward to warrant determination prior to providing a defendant with counsel, even in a criminal case. Federal law, for example, requires a criminal defendant to provide information showing that he is indigent, and therefore entitled to state-funded counsel, before he can receive that assistance. See 18 U.S.C. § 3006A(b).

Second, sometimes, as here, the person opposing the defendant at the hearing is not the government represented by counsel but the custodial parent unrepresented by counsel. See Dept. of Health and Human Services, Office of Child Support Enforcement, Understanding Child Support Debt: A Guide to Exploring Child Support Debt in Your State 5, 6 (2004) (51% of nationwide arrears, and 58% in South Carolina, are not owed to the government). The custodial parent, perhaps a woman with custody of one or more children, may be relatively poor, unemployed, and unable to afford counsel. Yet she may have encouraged the court to enforce its order through contempt. Cf. Tr. Contempt Proceedings (Sept. 14, 2005) (Rogers asks court, in light of pattern of nonpayment, to confine Turner). She may be able to provide the court with significant information. Cf. id. (Rogers describes where Turner lived and worked). And the proceeding is ultimately for her benefit.

A requirement that the State provide counsel to the noncustodial parent in these cases could create an asymmetry of representation that would "alter significantly the nature of the proceeding." *Gagnon*, supra, at 787. Doing so could mean a degree of formality or delay that would unduly slow payment to those immediately in need. And, perhaps more important for present purposes, doing so could make the proceedings less fair overall, increasing the risk of a decision that would erroneously deprive a family of the support it is entitled to receive. The needs of such families play an important role in our analysis.

Third, as the Solicitor General points out, there is available a set of "substitute procedural safeguards," *Mathews*, 424 U.S., at 335, which, if employed together, can significantly reduce the risk of an erroneous deprivation of liberty. They can do so, moreover, without incurring some of the drawbacks inherent in recognizing an automatic right to counsel. Those safeguards include (1) notice to the defendant that his "ability to pay" is a critical issue in the contempt proceeding; (2) the use of a form (or the equivalent) to elicit relevant financial information; (3) an opportunity at the hearing for the defendant to respond to statements and questions about his financial status (e.g., those triggered by his responses on the form); and (4) an express finding by the court that the defendant has the ability to pay. See Brief for United States as Amicus Curiae 23-25. In presenting these alternatives, the Government draws upon considerable experience in helping to manage statutorily mandated federal-state efforts to enforce child support orders. It does not claim that they are the only possible alternatives, and this Court's cases suggest, for example, that sometimes assistance other than purely legal assistance (here, say, that of a neutral social worker) can prove constitutionally sufficient. Cf. *Vitek*, 445 U.S., at 499-500 (Powell, J., concurring in part) (provision of mental health professional). But the Government does claim that these alternatives can assure the "fundamental fairness" of the proceeding even where the State does not pay for counsel for an indigent defendant.

While recognizing the strength of Turner's arguments, we ultimately believe that the three considerations we have just discussed must carry the day. In our view, a categorical right to counsel in proceedings of the kind before us would carry with it disadvantages (in the form of unfairness and delay) that, in terms of ultimate fairness, would deprive it of significant superiority over the alternatives that we have mentioned. We consequently hold that the Due Process Clause does not automatically require the provision of counsel at civil contempt proceedings to an indigent individual who is subject to a child support order, even if that individual faces incarceration (for up to a year). In particular, that Clause does not require the provision of counsel where the opposing parent or other custodian (to whom support funds are owed) is not represented by counsel and the State provides alternative procedural safeguards equivalent to those we have mentioned (adequate notice of the importance of ability to pay, fair opportunity to present, and to dispute, relevant information, and court findings).

We do not address civil contempt proceedings where the underlying child support payment is owed to the State, for example, for reimbursement of welfare funds paid to the parent with custody. Those proceedings more closely resemble debt-collection proceedings. The government is likely to have counsel or some other competent representative. And this kind of proceeding is not before us. Neither do we address what due process requires in an unusually complex case where a defendant "can fairly be represented only by a trained advocate." *Gagnon*, 411 U.S., at 788; see also Reply Brief for Petitioner 18-20 (not claiming that Turner's case is especially complex).

## IV

The record indicates that Turner received neither counsel nor the benefit of alternative procedures like those we have described. He did not receive clear notice that his ability to pay would constitute the critical question in his civil contempt proceeding. No one provided him with a form (or the equivalent) designed to elicit information about his financial circumstances. The court did not find that Turner was able to pay his arrearage, but instead left the relevant "finding" section of the contempt order blank. The court nonetheless found Turner in contempt and ordered him incarcerated. Under these circumstances Turner's incarceration violated the Due Process Clause.

We vacate the judgment of the South Carolina Supreme Court and remand the case for further proceedings not inconsistent with this opinion.

*It is so ordered.*

JUSTICE THOMAS, with whom JUSTICE SCALIA joins, and with whom THE CHIEF JUSTICE and JUSTICE ALITO join as to Parts I-B and II, dissenting.

. . .

## I

The only question raised in this case is whether the Due Process Clause of the Fourteenth Amendment creates a right to appointed counsel for all indigent defendants facing incarceration in civil contempt proceedings. It does not.

## A

Under an original understanding of the Constitution, there is no basis for concluding that the guarantee of due process secures a right to appointed counsel in civil contempt proceedings. It certainly does not do so to the extent that the Due Process Clause requires "'that our Government must proceed according to the "law of the land"—that is, according to written constitutional and statutory provisions.'" Hamdi v. Rumsfeld, 542 U.S. 507, 589 (2004) (Thomas, J., dissenting) (quoting In re Winship, 397 U.S. 358, 382 (1970) (Black, J., dissenting)). No one contends that South Carolina law entitles Turner to appointed counsel. Nor does any federal statute or constitutional provision so provide. . . .

Appointed counsel is also not required in civil contempt proceedings under a somewhat broader reading of the Due Process Clause, which takes it to approve "'[a] process of law . . . [that] can show the sanction of settled usage.'" Weiss v. United States, 510 U.S. 163, 197 (1994) (Scalia, J., concurring in part and concurring in judgment) (quoting Hurtado v. California, 110 U.S. 516, 528 (1884)). Despite a long history of courts exercising contempt authority, Turner has not identified any evidence that courts appointed counsel in those proceedings. See Mine Workers v. Bagwell, 512 U.S. 821, 831 (1994) (describing courts' traditional assumption of "inherent contempt authority"); see also 4 W. Blackstone, Commentaries on the Laws of England 280-285 (1769) (describing the "summary proceedings" used to adjudicate contempt). . . .

## B

Even under the Court's modern interpretation of the Constitution, the Due Process Clause does not provide a right to appointed counsel for all indigent defendants facing incarceration in civil contempt proceedings. . . .

[I]f the Due Process Clause created a right to appointed counsel in all proceedings with the potential for detention, then the Sixth Amendment right to appointed counsel would be unnecessary. Under Turner's theory, every instance in which the Sixth Amendment guarantees a right to appointed counsel is covered also by the Due Process Clause. The Sixth Amendment, however, is the only constitutional provision that even mentions the assistance of counsel; the Due Process Clause says nothing about counsel. Ordinarily, we do not read a general provision to render a specific one superfluous. Cf. Morales v. Trans World Airlines, Inc., 504 U.S. 374, 384 (1992) ("[I]t is a commonplace of statutory construction that the specific governs the general"). The fact that one constitutional provision expressly provides a right to appointed counsel in specific circumstances indicates that the Constitution does not also *sub silentio* provide that right far more broadly in another, more general, provision. . . .

After countless factors weighed, mores evaluated, and practices surveyed, the Court has not determined that due process principles of fundamental fairness categorically require counsel in any context outside criminal proceedings. See, e.g., Lassiter v. Department of Social Servs. of Durham Cty., 452 U.S. 18, 31-32 (1981); Wolff v. McDonnell, 418 U.S. 539, 569-570 (1974); see also Walters v. National Assn. of Radiation Survivors, 473 U.S. 305, 307-308, 320-326 (1985); Goss v. Lopez, 419 U.S. 565, 583 (1975). . . .

## III

. . . [T]here is yet another reason not to undertake the Mathews v. Eldridge balancing test here. That test weighs an individual's interest against that of the Government. It does not account for the interests of the child and custodial parent, who is usually the child's mother. But their interests are the very reason for the child support obligation and the civil contempt proceedings that enforce it.

When fathers fail in their duty to pay child support, children suffer. See Cancian, Meyer, & Han, Child Support: Responsible Fatherhood and the Quid Pro Quo, 635 Annals Am. Acad. Pol. & Soc. Sci. 140, 153 (2011) (finding that child support plays an important role in reducing child poverty in single-parent homes); cf. Sorensen & Zibman, Getting to Know Poor Fathers Who Do Not Pay Child Support, 75 Soc. Serv. Rev. 420, 423 (2001) (finding that children whose fathers reside apart from them are 54 percent more likely to live in poverty than their fathers). Nonpayment or inadequate payment can press children and mothers into poverty. M. Garrison, The Goals and Limits of Child Support Policy, in Child Support: The Next Frontier 16 (J. Oldham & M. Melli eds. 2000); see also Dept. of Commerce, Census Bureau, T. Grall, Custodial Mothers and Fathers and Their Child Support: 2007, pp. 4-5 (2009) (hereinafter Custodial Mothers and Fathers) (reporting that 27 percent of custodial mothers lived in poverty in 2007).

The interests of children and mothers who depend on child support are notoriously difficult to protect. See, e.g., Hicks v. Feiock, 485 U.S. 624, 644 (1988) (O'Connor, J., dissenting) ("The failure of enforcement efforts in this area has become a national scandal"). Less than half of all custodial parents receive the full amount of child support ordered; 24 percent of those owed support receive nothing at all. Custodial Mothers and Fathers 7; see also Dept. of Health and Human Services, Office of Child Support Enforcement, FY 2008 Annual Report to Congress, App. III, Table 71 (showing national child support arrears of $105.5 billion in 2008). In South Carolina alone, more than 139,000 noncustodial parents defaulted on their child support obligations during 2008, and at year end parents owed $1.17 billion in total arrears. Id.

That some fathers subject to a child support agreement report little or no income "does not mean they do not have the ability to pay any child support." Dept. of Health and Human Services, H. Sorensen, L. Sousa, & S. Schaner, Assessing Child Support Arrears in Nine Large States and the Nation 22 (2007) (prepared by The Urban Institute) (hereinafter Assessing Arrears). Rather, many "deadbeat dads" "opt to work in the underground economy" to "shield their earnings from child support enforcement efforts." Mich. Sup. Ct., Task Force Report: The Underground Economy 10 (2010) (hereinafter Underground Economy). To avoid attempts to garnish their wages or otherwise enforce the support obligation, "deadbeats" quit their jobs, jump from job to job, become self-employed, work under the table, or engage in illegal activity.[6] See Waller & Plotnick, Effective Child Support Policy for Low-Income Families: Evidence from Street Level Research, 20 J. Pol'y Analysis & Mgmt. 89, 104 (2001); Assessing Arrears 22-23.

---

6. In this case, Turner switched between eight different jobs in three years, which made wage withholding difficult. Most recently, Turner sold drugs in 2009 and 2010 but paid not a penny in child support during those years.

Because of the difficulties in collecting payment through traditional enforcement mechanisms, many States also use civil contempt proceedings to coerce "deadbeats" into paying what they owe. The States that use civil contempt with the threat of detention find it a "highly effective" tool for collecting child support when nothing else works. Compendium of Responses Collected by the U.S. Dept. of Health and Human Services Office of Child Support Enforcement (Dec. 28, 2010). For example, Virginia, which uses civil contempt as "a last resort," reports that in 2010 "deadbeats" paid approximately $13 million "either before a court hearing to avoid a contempt finding or after a court hearing to purge the contempt finding." Id. Other States confirm that the mere threat of imprisonment is often quite effective because most contemners "will pay . . . rather than go to jail." Id.; see also Underground Economy C-2 ("Many judges . . . report that the prospect of [detention] often causes obligors to discover previously undisclosed resources that they can use to make child support payments").

This case illustrates the point. After the family court imposed Turner's weekly support obligation in June 2003, he made no payments until the court held him in contempt three months later, whereupon he paid over $1,000 to avoid confinement. Three more times, Turner refused to pay until the family court held him in contempt—then paid in short order.

. . . Whether "deadbeat dads" should be threatened with incarceration is a policy judgment for state and federal lawmakers, as is the entire question of government involvement in the area of child support. See Elrod & Dale, Paradigm Shifts and Pendulum Swings in Child Custody, 42 Fam. L.Q. 381, 382 (2008) (observing the "federalization of many areas of family law"). This and other repercussions of the shift away from the nuclear family are ultimately the business of the policymaking branches. See, e.g., D. Popenoe, Family in Decline in America, reprinted in War Over the Family 3, 4 (2005) (discussing "four major social trends" that emerged in the 1960's "to signal a widespread 'flight'" from the "nuclear family"); Krause, Child Support Reassessed, 24 Fam. L.Q. 1, 16 (1990) ("Easy-come, easy-go marriage and casual cohabitation and procreation are on a collision course with the economic and social needs of children"); M. Boumil & J. Friedman, Deadbeat Dads 23-24 (1996) ("Many [children of deadbeat dads] are born out of wedlock. . . . Others have lost a parent to divorce at such a young age that they have little conscious memory of it").

* * *

I would affirm the judgment of the South Carolina Supreme Court because the Due Process Clause does not provide a right to appointed counsel in civil contempt hearings that may lead to incarceration. As that is the only issue properly before the Court, I respectfully dissent.

### Notes and Questions

1. *Turner* is consistent with *Lassiter* in a number of respects. The *Turner* Court holds, as in *Lassiter*, that there is no right to counsel unless the

circumstances make the presence of counsel imperative. And, as in *Lassiter*, it looks for additional procedural safeguards in making the determination whether to require counsel categorically. Recall that in *Lassiter*, the Court takes pains to observe that North Carolina's procedures for terminating parental rights are elaborate, and therefore reduce the risk of error. In *Turner*, the Court concludes that additional safeguards are constitutionally required. On the other hand, unlike in *Lassiter*, civil contempt proceedings threaten the core interest in physical liberty (avoiding unjustified confinement by the state). The cases prior to *Lassiter*, and *Lassiter* itself, suggest that where physical liberty is at issue, counsel must be provided. See Brooke D. Coleman, Prison Is Prison, 88 Notre Dame L. Rev. 1399 (2013) (arguing that because deprivation of physical liberty is a consequence of criminal prosecution and civil contempt proceedings, counsel is constitutionally required in both settings). What factors do you think influenced the *Turner* majority to deviate from this view of the right to counsel?

2. Most of the procedural guarantees in the Bill of Rights address criminal investigation and trial. If Justice Thomas is right that one cannot read broader rights into the Due Process Clause than the Constitution expressly recognizes in other more specific provisions, what limits does he think the Due Process Clause imposes in civil proceedings?

3. The Court in *Turner* appears to have refined and extended the contextual analysis it developed in *Walters*. The majority in both cases seems concerned with the respects in which introducing counsel would alter the nature of the proceedings. What assumptions about how counsel behave and how veterans' benefits and child support contempt determinations ordinarily proceed underlie the Court's conclusion that lawyers would change things for the worse? See D. James Greiner and Cassandra Wolos Pattanayak, Randomized Evaluation in Legal Assistance: What Difference Does Representation (Offer and Actual Use) Make?, 121 Yale L.J. 2118 (2012) (reporting results of empirical evaluation of clinical program providing counsel at Harvard Legal Aid and finding no statistically significant difference in outcomes where legal representation was provided by the legal aid bureau) ("Despite the best and continuing efforts of the civil *Gideon* and access to justice movements, and the need for greater funding for legal services provision, it may be time to face the fact that there will never be enough funding to provide a full attorney-client relationship with a competent lawyer to all low-income persons interacting with, or contemplating interaction with, the legal system. This is probably true even in areas of so-called 'basic human needs.' If these assertions turn out to approximate the truth, then triaging of legal services is unavoidable. We must learn to triage well."). A provocative response to the Greiner and Pattanayak article was published by nationally recognized clinical law professors and advocates of access to legal services for the poor. See Jeffrey Selbin, Jeanne Charn, Anthony Alfieri, and Stephen Wizner, Service Delivery, Resource Allocation, and Access to Justice: Geiner and Pattanayak and the Research Imperative, 122 Yale L.J. Online 45 (2012).

## *Note: Tennessee v. Lane*

So far, we have talked about access to the courts in terms of access to counsel, notice, and the right to be heard. But the right of "access" can be impaired in even more basic ways. Consider the case of George Lane. He is a paraplegic and uses a wheelchair. In August 1998, he was compelled to appear in county court in Tennessee to face two misdemeanor criminal charges. When he arrived at the courthouse, he learned that all the courtrooms were located on the second floor and that the building had no elevator, so he left his wheelchair and dragged himself up two flights of stairs to get to the courtroom. When he arrived for his second appearance in October, he refused to drag himself up again, sending word to the court that he would not crawl to the courtroom and that he did not want to put his safety at risk by being carried up by police officers. The court ordered Lane arrested and held in contempt for "failure to appear." In subsequent proceedings, to avoid another contempt citation, Lane remained at the bottom of the stairs while his attorney shuttled between him and the courtroom.

Lane then filed a separate civil action against the state of Tennessee, contending that the state violated Title II of the Americans with Disabilities Act (ADA), which requires that public entities ensure access to disabled persons. The State moved to dismiss the case on the ground that it is immune from suits brought by private individuals to enforce federal law. See U.S. Const. amend. XI. However, the Supreme Court upheld the district court's denial of the motion to dismiss, emphasizing that the right of access to the courts under the Due Process Clause is a fundamental right and that Congress has the power under Section 5 of the Fourteenth Amendment to legislate to ensure that disabled persons are not deprived of this fundamental right. Tennessee v. Lane, 541 U.S. 509 (2004). See also id. at 523 (discussing defendant's Sixth Amendment right of confrontation "to be present at all stages of the trial where his absence might frustrate the fairness of the proceedings" (quoting Faretta v. California, 422 U.S. 806, 816 (1975))). The Court cited a report before Congress in 1990 when it voted on the ADA showing that "76% of public services and programs housed in state-owned buildings were inaccessible to and unusable by persons with disabilities." Id. at 527. The Court concluded that the ADA's duty to accommodate disabled persons in gaining access to public facilities "is perfectly consistent with the well-established due process principle that, within the limits of practicability, a State must afford to all individuals a meaningful opportunity to be heard in its courts." Id. at 532 (internal quotation marks and citations omitted). "[O]rdinary considerations of cost and convenience alone cannot justify a State's failure to provide individuals with a meaningful right of access to the courts." Id. at 533 (internal quotation marks and citations omitted).

## C.   DUE PROCESS AND JURISDICTION: THE LIMITS OF STATE POWER OVER PERSONS AND PROPERTY

### Problem Case: An Unhappy Wanderer

Luckett, a Californian returning from a visit in Arizona, left the interstate highway to visit a rest stop, the Last Chance Curio Shop. Last Chance is advertised on billboards along the highway. It specializes in the sale of Navajo wares and Navajo replicas made in Hong Kong. Luckett passed up the curios, made use of the plumbing facility, and purchased a soft drink from the vending machine.

Shortly after she left Last Chance and just inside the California border, the bottle exploded, causing her car to leave the road. She was injured and her new car was totally wrecked.

Luckett would like to sue Last Chance and/or the Arizona bottler in a California court. In contemplation of such an action, her counsel has conducted an investigation that reveals that:

1. Last Chance gets its Hong Kong curios from a Long Beach, California, importer. Title probably passes to Last Chance in Hong Kong.
2. The Arizona bottler is actually a franchise of a large nationwide soft drink company that is headquartered in Los Angeles. The beverages sold in Last Chance's vending machine are made and bottled in Arizona, and the Arizona bottler has never visited the franchisor's California offices. Yet the franchise contract provides that California law governs it, and that financial transactions and other paperwork must be forwarded to the Los Angeles headquarters.

Can California constitutionally exercise jurisdiction over this claim against the Arizona bottler? Against Last Chance? If a shipment of Last Chance's goods can be found in Long Beach? If Luckett can serve process on the bottler's headquarters in Los Angeles?

## 1.   Introduction: State Boundaries and Jurisdiction

The concept that courts must have jurisdiction—the authority to speak—is rooted in the State's power over the people and property within its boundaries. Until well into the sixteenth century, the physical expression of this power occurred when plaintiffs used the writ of *capias ad respondendum*, which directed the sheriff to arrest defendants and bring them before the court. Today service of process substitutes for bodily seizure—but behind that innocent-looking piece of paper titled "Summons" stands the full coercive power of the State.

The State is also sovereign over all tangible property located within its borders. When there is a dispute over title, a writ of attachment symbolically seizes the property and gives the court *in rem* jurisdiction to adjudicate the conflicting claims of ownership. In theory, the court has jurisdiction over only the property, or *res*, and not over the people claiming ownership of it. In practice, of course, seizure of the property effectively forces the claimants to come in and defend their interests or suffer a default judgment extinguishing their claims.

Attachment was also the traditional basis for *quasi in rem* jurisdiction, which allowed seizure of a defendant's property even when the property was not related to the claim before the court. Once the court had control of the defendant's property, it could adjudicate the unrelated claim against him—an action for breach of contract, for example—and then, if the defendant lost, order a judicial sale of the property to satisfy the judgment. As with regular *in rem* jurisdiction, a court exercising *quasi in rem* jurisdiction had power over only the property. If the seized property was worth less than the plaintiff's damages on the contract claim, for example, the court had no power to enter an *in personam* judgment against the defendant for the difference.

All three classes of jurisdiction—*capias ad respondendum, in rem,* and *quasi in rem*—are based on ancient notions of territoriality, that is, the State's (and therefore the court's) power over property and persons within its borders. The first case to turn territorial conceptions of jurisdiction into constitutional requirements, and to define these requirements as due process limits on state power, was Pennoyer v. Neff, 95 U.S. 714 (1877), which was technically overruled in 1977, exactly 100 years after it was decided. Shaffer v. Heitner, 433 U.S. 186 (1977). Yet the case remains important because its central holding is still vital—that due process of law is the measure of personal jurisdiction.

We present the *Pennoyer* case through a legal historian's account rather than that of an appellate judge. Think about the differences between the disciplines of law and history in the way facts are stated and used.

## 2.   Pennoyer v. Neff: The Human Drama

*Wendy Perdue, Sin, Scandal, and Substantive Due Process:*
*Personal Jurisdiction and* Pennoyer *Reconsidered*
62 Wash. L. Rev. 479, 481-489 (1987)

Our story begins with a young man, Marcus Neff, heading across the country by covered wagon train, presumably to seek his fortune. Neff left Iowa in early 1848 at the age of 24, joining a wagon train of five companies of wagons. At that time, the question of Oregon statehood was being considered in Congress, and there was much speculation that large tracts of the vast, undeveloped land of Oregon would be made available to homesteaders. The speculation proved to be correct and Marcus Neff was one of the earliest settlers to claim land under the Oregon Donation Act.

To qualify for land under the Donation Act, one had to be a citizen living in Oregon and had to submit a request for land by December 1, 1850. Interestingly, Neff's land request was originally dated December 15, 1850, which would have made it too late, but "December" was crossed out and "September" written in above. This is the first instance of many to suggest that events surrounding Pennoyer v. Neff may have been tainted by fraud and deception.

Not surprisingly, registration of a Donation Act claim required a certain amount of paperwork. In addition to the initial claim, the homesteader was required after four years to submit the affidavits of two disinterested persons affirming that the homesteader had cultivated the land for his own use. Neff secured two affidavits, which were submitted prematurely in 1853 and resubmitted in 1856. The 1856 submission should have entitled Neff to receive a patent to the land, but the government was notoriously slow in processing claims, and ten years passed before Neff received his land patent.

Early in 1862 Neff made the unfortunate decision to consult a local Portland attorney, J. H. Mitchell. Although the nature of the legal services is unclear, Neff may have consulted Mitchell in an attempt to expedite the paperwork concerning his land patent. Neff was illiterate, and at the time he consulted Mitchell the government had still not issued his patent. Mitchell, moreover, specialized in land matters. In mid-1862, several months after Neff first consulted Mitchell, another affidavit was filed on Neff's behalf. Several months thereafter Neff received a document from the government certifying that he had met the criteria for issuance of a patent.

Whatever Neff's reasons for seeking Mitchell's legal services, he certainly could have done better in his choice of lawyers. "J. H. Mitchell" was actually the Oregon alias of one John Hipple. Hipple had been a teacher in Pennsylvania who, after being forced to marry the 15-year-old student whom he had seduced, left teaching and took up law. He practiced with a partner for several years, but apparently concluded that it was time to move on to greener pastures. Thus, in 1860 Hipple headed west taking with him four thousand dollars of client money and his then current paramour, a local school teacher. They made their way to California where Hipple abandoned the teacher, ostensibly because she was sick and her medical expenses had become too burdensome, and moved on to Portland, Oregon. There, using the name John H. Mitchell, he quickly established himself as a successful lawyer, specializing in land litigation and railroad right-of-way cases. He also remarried without bothering to divorce his first wife. As one historian has observed, Mitchell's success as a lawyer cannot be attributed to either intellectual or oratorical skills; rather, his strengths included exceptional political instincts, a generous disposition, and a friendly handshake. What he lacked in ethics and ability, he made up for with persistence and desire for success. In his subsequent political career, he became known as a man whose "political ethics justified any means that would win the battle."[33]

Mitchell's ethical standards as a lawyer were no higher than his ethics as a politician. As the *Oregonian* observed: "His political methods are indeed pitched on a sufficiently low scale, but not below his methods as a lawyer." Given Mitchell's reputation, one might at least question whether Neff in fact owed the money Mitchell claimed was due. Neff paid Mitchell $6.50, but Mitchell claimed he was owed an additional $209. Although Mitchell's services were rendered between early 1862 and mid-1863, Mitchell waited several years to take legal action against Neff, perhaps purposely waiting until Neff left the state.

On November 3, 1865, Mitchell filed suit against Neff in Oregon state court, seeking $253.14 plus costs. Mitchell secured jurisdiction under Oregon statute section 55, which provided that if the defendant, after due diligence, cannot be found within the state, he may be served by publication. Mitchell supplied an affidavit in which he asserted that Neff was living somewhere in California and could not be found. Mitchell provided no details as to what he had done to locate Neff, and given Mitchell's lack of scruples, one might wonder whether Neff's whereabouts were indeed unknown to Mitchell and whether Mitchell made any attempt to locate Neff. Notice of the lawsuit was published for six weeks in the *Pacific Christian Advocate,* a weekly newspaper published under the authority of the Methodist Episcopal Church and devoted primarily to religious news and inspirational articles.

In initiating the litigation, Mitchell made what ultimately proved to be a critical mistake. Mitchell's affidavit asserted that Neff owned property, but he did not attach the property at that time. Mitchell most likely neglected this step because Oregon law did not appear to require attachment as a prerequisite for reliance on section 55.

A default judgment in the amount of $294.98 was entered against Neff on February 19, 1866. Although Mitchell had an immediate right to execute on the judgment, he waited until early July 1866 to seek a writ of execution, possibly waiting for the arrival of Neff's land patent. The title, which was sent from Washington, D.C. on March 22, 1866, would have taken several months to arrive in Oregon, and thus probably arrived in Oregon shortly before Mitchell sought the writ of execution. Interestingly, although Mitchell had alleged that Neff could not be found, the Oregon land office apparently had no difficulty delivering the patent to Neff.

Under Oregon law, to secure execution one had to obtain a writ of execution and post and publish notice for four weeks. All of the steps were apparently taken. On August 7, 1866, the property was sold at a sheriff's

---

33. [J. Gaston, The Centennial History of Oregon 1811-1912, at 665 (1912).] Mitchell had an extremely successful political career. He was first elected to the State Senate in 1862, became president of the State Senate in 1864, was seven times a candidate for the United States Senate, and was elected in four of those contests.

auction for $341.60. Notably, the buyer was not Sylvester Pennoyer, as the Supreme Court opinion and commentators have implied. The property was purchased by none other than J. H. Mitchell, who three days later assigned the property to Sylvester Pennoyer. Pennoyer had much in common with Mitchell. He, like Mitchell, was a Portland lawyer, involved in politics, and active in real estate speculation. There is no evidence available on whether Pennoyer had actual knowledge of, or connection to, the original action, though it is certainly possible. Moreover, since he took title through Mitchell, it is not clear that he should have been treated as a true innocent third-party purchaser.

It appears that for the next eight years Pennoyer peacefully minded his own business, doing those things one would expect of any property owner—he paid the taxes, cut some timber, and sold a small portion of the land. The peace was broken in 1874 when Neff reappeared on the scene. . . .

The case of Neff v. Pennoyer was filed in federal court on September 10, 1874, and the ensuing battle confirms that vindictive and protracted litigation is not a recent phenomenon. Neff apparently had prospered in California. He had settled in San Joaquin with a wife and family, as well as servants, property, and livestock. He was prepared, however, to leave his home in California and move himself, his wife, and his daughter to Oregon for a year to pursue his various legal actions.

## 3.   Pennoyer v. Neff: The Legal Story

Even putting personalities aside, right and justice were clearly with Marcus Neff and nineteenth-century law supplied adequate doctrine for his protection. The lower court decided in his favor by interpreting Oregon's jurisdictional statutes; it found that Mitchell's affidavit describing his efforts to notify Neff failed to meet statutory requirements. Therefore, the default judgment in Mitchell v. Neff was void because it was entered by a court without jurisdiction.

On Pennoyer's appeal to the U.S. Supreme Court, Justice Field brushed aside the lower court's statutory argument but found another jurisdictional defect instead. Mitchell had failed to attach the property *before filing suit.* Establishing a course that held for 100 years, the Court declared: "The authority of every tribunal is necessarily restricted by the territorial limits of the State in which it is established." Pennoyer v. Neff, 95 U.S. at 720. The Court continued:

> [T]he property here in controversy sold under the judgment rendered was not attached, nor in any way brought under the jurisdiction of the court. Its first connection with the case was caused by a levy of the execution. It was not, therefore, disposed of pursuant to any adjudication, but only in enforcement of a personal judgment, having no relation to the property, rendered against a non-resident without service of process upon him in the action, or his appearance therein.

Id. Then, having decided the case, the Court went on to discuss *in personam* jurisdiction more generally:

> [E]very State possesses exclusive jurisdiction and sovereignty over persons and property within its territory. . . . [N]o State can exercise direct jurisdiction and authority over persons or property without its territory. . . . The several States are of equal dignity and authority, and the independence of one implies the exclusion of power from all others. . . . [T]he laws of one State have no operation outside of its territory, except so far as is allowed by comity; . . . no tribunal established by it can extend its process beyond that territory so as to subject either persons or property to its decisions. "Any exertion of authority of this sort beyond this limit," says Story, "is a mere nullity, and incapable of binding such persons or property in any other tribunals." Story, Confl. Laws, sect. 539.

*If the property is in the state and it the suit concerns the property, the state has jurisdiction*

Id. at 722-723.

In short, each state's complete power within its own boundaries completely excluded any exercise of extraterritorial jurisdiction by another state. Thus, the limits of judicial power under *Pennoyer* were defined by the dotted lines on a map of the United States. In this rigidly geographical scheme, the distinction between a writ of attachment obtained before judgment to perfect jurisdiction over property and a writ of execution obtained after the fact to enforce an *in personam* judgment assumed constitutional significance.

But Justice Field did not stop with his observations on territoriality and personal jurisdiction. He went on to strike down the state's original action—the entry of "jurisdictionless" judgment—on the ground that it deprived Neff of his property without due process of law.

Justice Field was not speaking in the due process terms that we have dealt with earlier in this chapter—notice and the opportunity to be heard; these, in an unarticulated sense, had been the bases of the lower court opinion. Rather, he established due process as a regulatory canon for the relations among the sovereign states:

> Since the adoption of the Fourteenth Amendment to the Federal Constitution, the validity of such judgments [those rendered against nonresidents] may be directly questioned, and their enforcement in the State resisted, on the ground that proceedings in a court of justice to determine the personal rights and obligations of parties over whom that court has no jurisdiction do not constitute due process of law. . . . [A] tribunal [must be] competent by its constitution—that is, by the law of its creation—to pass upon the subject-matter of the suit; and, if that involves merely a determination of the personal liability of the defendant, he must be brought within its jurisdiction by service of process within the State, or his voluntary appearance.

95 U.S. at 733.

In the background of *Pennoyer* was not only the Fourteenth Amendment (adopted less than a decade before the opinion) but also Article IV of the

Constitution itself, which requires that "Full Faith and Credit shall be given in each State to the judicial proceedings of every other state." This means that a *valid* judgment of another state or federal court must be enforced according to its terms, without relitigating the underlying claims or defenses. But a judgment entered without obtaining personal jurisdiction over the defendant is invalid and void.

What *Pennoyer* did in the paragraph quoted above was to "identif[y] the test under the Full Faith and Credit clause with the test under the Due Process Clause, making a judgment which would not be enforceable beyond the borders of the state unenforceable within its boundaries. . . ." Philip Kurland, The Supreme Court, the Due Process Clause and the *In Personam* Jurisdiction of State Courts From *Pennoyer* to *Denckla*: A Review, 25 U. Chi. L. Rev. 569 (1958). In short, *Pennoyer* declared that a judgment entered without jurisdiction was unenforceable even by the state that rendered it and even on property within the state's borders. The legal effects of the great old case have reverberated through the twentieth century. Here is the end of the human drama as related by Professor Perdue:

> The opening salvo between Neff and Pennoyer was fired when Neff sued to evict Pennoyer, but the war did not end there. After Pennoyer lost the eviction suit, and costs were awarded against him, he battled bitterly over the amount of those costs. Neff was again the winner, and adding insult to injury, he proceeded to sue Pennoyer again — this time to recover money damages sustained as a result of Pennoyer cutting down timber on the property. Pennoyer counter-claimed to collect property taxes that he had paid from 1866 to 1875. The counterclaim was dismissed and Pennoyer's defense of the damage action proved to be the closest that he got to a victory: the jury found for Neff but awarded only nominal damages.
>
> When the dust had settled, Pennoyer, whom the Supreme Court assumed was a bona fide purchaser for value, was left holding the bag. Pennoyer had purchased the land for "valuable consideration" and paid taxes on it for a number of years, yet he found himself evicted, with nothing to show for his money and subject to suit for trespass for entering the land he thought he owned. There is no evidence that Pennoyer did or could ever recover the loss from anyone.
>
> Following the litigation, Neff disappeared into obscurity; not so Pennoyer and Mitchell. Pennoyer went on to be Governor of Oregon, but he remained bitter about his defeat in Pennoyer v. Neff. Ten years after the Supreme Court decision, in his inaugural address as governor, Pennoyer decried that decision as a usurpation of state power. He remained a vociferous critic of the Supreme Court, urging at one point that the entire Court should be impeached, explaining: "We have during this time been living under a government not based upon the Federal Constitution, but under one created by the plausible sophistries of John Marshall. . . . Our constitutional government has been supplanted by a judicial oligarchy."

Perdue, supra, 62 Wash. L. Rev. at 487-488.

By the early twentieth century, the notion that a state's judicial power stopped abruptly at its territorial boundary was being strained by the increasingly interstate character of American society. The modern business corporation and the automobile were two developments that exacerbated the *Pennoyer* restraints; each could inflict damage in a state without necessarily leaving the sort of jurisdictional footprints that *Pennoyer* required. The states responded by enacting statutes based on a theory of "consent" to jurisdiction, which *Pennoyer* had approved.

A Massachusetts statute, for example, declared that by using the state's highways, an out-of-state motorist was deemed to have appointed the state registrar as agent for service of process in actions arising out of accidents on the highways. Jurisdiction under the statute was sustained in Hess v. Pawloski, 274 U.S. 352 (1927). And most states had statutes requiring foreign corporations to appoint a local agent for service of process as a condition of conducting business within the state. If the corporation failed to do so, it was deemed to have appointed a state official, such as the secretary of state, by virtue of undertaking to transact business in the state. The extent and nature of business activities necessary to support this implication of consent to jurisdiction was the subject of considerable litigation. Smolik v. Phila. & Reading Co., 222 F. 148 (S.D.N.Y. 1915), *aff'd sub nom.* Penn. Fire Ins. Co. v. Gold Issue Mining Co., 243 U.S. 93 (1917).

The doctrine of implied consent to jurisdiction was a classic example of a "legal fiction" that served to bridge a period of transition in the development of the law. In International Shoe Co. v. Washington, 326 U.S. 310 (1945), the Supreme Court cast those fictions aside, and made explicit the underlying basis of these decisions: due process does not necessarily *require* the States to adhere to the unbending territorial limits on jurisdiction set forth in *Pennoyer.* Burnham v. Superior Court, 495 U.S. 604 (1990).

## 4. Minimum Contacts and Substantial Justice

### Problem Case: Contact Without Commerce

On December 1, 2012, 15 residents of the state of Nevada brought suit in Nevada federal district court against FibreLite, a California company with its principal place of business near Lake Tahoe in Truckee, California. The plaintiffs claim that FibreLite caused a variety of respiratory diseases and complications through emissions of air pollution from its manufacturing facility in Truckee. They claim that prevailing winds regularly carry emissions from the FibreLite plant into Nevada where they live. The plaintiffs further claim that the emissions are illegal under state and federal law and they seek damages for their personal injuries. Their damages vary: The average claim is $2 million and the lowest is $500,000. All plaintiffs currently live outside of Reno in a valley on the eastern slope of the Sierras.

FibreLite admits in its answer that it releases certain air pollutants, including sulfur dioxide and nitrogen oxides, as a part of its process for manufacturing lightweight materials for thermal insulated clothing as well as ski and snowboard components. It has a permit from the EPA, but for the last decade it has regularly exceeded the permit allowances. In its answer to the complaint, FibreLite admits knowledge that the alleged pollutants from its plant cross the border into Nevada.

FibreLite sells no products in Nevada. It has no offices there and none of its employees live there. All of its products are sold in California, all of its print and TV marketing is in California, and its Web page simply has contact information, profiles of corporate officers, and descriptions of its products as well as the consumer goods into which they are incorporated.

Do you think it would be consistent with due process of law for a Nevada federal court to exercise personal jurisdiction over FibreLite?

## *International Shoe Co. v. Washington*
326 U.S. 310 (1945)

CHIEF JUSTICE STONE delivered the opinion of the Court.

The questions for decision are (1) whether, within the limitations of the due process clause of the Fourteenth Amendment, appellant, a Delaware corporation, has by its activities in the State of Washington rendered itself amenable to proceedings in the courts of that state to recover unpaid contributions to the state unemployment compensation fund exacted by the state statutes, and (2) whether the state can exact those contributions consistently with the due process clause of the Fourteenth Amendment. . . .

In this case notice of assessment for the years in question was personally served upon a sales solicitor employed by appellant in the State of Washington, and a copy of the notice was mailed by registered mail to appellant at its address in St. Louis, Missouri. Appellant appeared specially before the office of unemployment and moved to set aside the order and notice of assessment on the ground that the service upon appellant's salesman was not proper service upon appellant; that appellant was not a corporation of the State of Washington and was not doing business within the state; that it had no agent within the state upon whom service could be made; and that appellant is not an employer and does not furnish employment within the meaning of the statute. . . .

The facts, as found by the appeal tribunal and accepted by the state Superior Court and Supreme Court, are not in dispute. Appellant is a Delaware corporation, having its principal place of business in St. Louis, Missouri, and is engaged in the manufacture and sale of shoes and other footwear. It maintains places of business in several states, other than Washington, at which its manufacturing is carried on and from which its merchandise is distributed interstate through several sales units or branches located outside the State of Washington.

Appellant has no office in Washington and makes no contracts either for sale or purchase of merchandise there. It maintains no stock of merchandise in that state and makes there no deliveries of goods in intrastate commerce. During the years from 1937 to 1940, now in question, appellant employed eleven to thirteen salesmen under direct supervision and control of sales managers located in St. Louis. These salesmen resided in Washington; their principal activities were confined to that state; and they were compensated by commissions based upon the amount of their sales. The commissions for each year totaled more than $31,000. Appellant supplies its salesmen with a line of samples, each consisting of one shoe of a pair, which they display to prospective purchasers. On occasion they rent permanent sample rooms, for exhibiting samples, in business buildings, or rent rooms in hotels or business buildings temporarily for that purpose. The cost of such rentals is reimbursed by appellant.

The authority of the salesmen is limited to exhibiting their samples and soliciting orders from prospective buyers, at prices and on terms fixed by appellant. The salesmen transmit the orders to appellant's office in St. Louis for acceptance or rejection, and when accepted the merchandise for filling the orders is shipped f.o.b. from points outside Washington to the purchasers within the state. All the merchandise shipped into Washington is invoiced at the place of shipment from which collections are made. No salesman has authority to enter into contracts or make collections.

The Supreme Court of Washington was of opinion that the regular and systematic solicitation of orders in the state by appellant's salesmen, resulting in a continuous flow of appellant's product into the state, was sufficient to constitute doing business in the state so as to make appellant amenable to suit in its courts. But it was also of opinion that there were sufficient additional activities shown to bring the case within the rule frequently stated, that solicitation within a state by the agents of a foreign corporation plus some additional activities there are sufficient to render the corporation amenable to suit brought in the courts of the state to enforce an obligation arising out of its activities there. International Harvester Co. v. Kentucky, 234 U.S. 579, 587 [(1914)]. The court found such additional activities in the salesmen's display of samples sometimes in permanent display rooms, and the salesmen's residence within the state, continued over a period of years, all resulting in a substantial volume of merchandise regularly shipped by appellant to purchasers within the state. . . .

Historically the jurisdiction of courts to render judgment *in personam* is grounded on their *de facto* power over the defendant's person. Hence his presence within the territorial jurisdiction of court was prerequisite to its rendition of a judgment personally binding him. Pennoyer v. Neff, 95 U.S. 714, 733 [(1877)]. But now that the *capias ad respondendum* has given way to personal service of summons or other form of notice, due process requires only that in order to subject a defendant to a judgment *in personam,* if he be not present within the territory of the forum, *he have certain minimum contacts with it* such that the maintenance of the suit does not offend "traditional notions of fair play and substantial justice." Milliken v. Meyer, 311 U.S. 457, 463 [(1940)]. . . .

Since the corporate personality is a fiction, although a fiction intended to be acted upon as though it were a fact, Klein v. Board of Supervisors, 282 U.S. 19, 24 [(1930)], it is clear that unlike an individual its "presence" without, as well as within, the state of its origin can be manifested only by activities carried on in its behalf by those who are authorized to act for it. To say that the corporation is so far "present" there as to satisfy due process requirements, for purposes of taxation or the maintenance of suits against it in the courts of the state, is to beg the question to be decided. For the terms "present" or "presence" are used merely to symbolize those activities of the corporation's agent within the state which courts will deem to be sufficient to satisfy the demands of due process. L. Hand, J., in Hutchinson v. Chase & Gilbert, 45 F.2d 139, 141 [(2d Cir. 1930)]. Those demands may be met by such contacts of the corporation with the state of the forum as make it reasonable, in the context of our federal system of government, to require the corporation to defend the particular suit which is brought there. An "estimate of the inconveniences" which would result to the corporation from a trial away from its "home" or principal place of business is relevant in this connection. Hutchinson v. Chase & Gilbert, supra, 141.

"Presence" in the state in this sense has never been doubted when the activities of the corporation there have not only been continuous and systematic, but also give rise to the liabilities sued on, even though no consent to be sued or authorization to an agent to accept service of process has been given. . . . Conversely it has been generally recognized that the casual presence of the corporate agent or even his conduct of single or isolated items of activities in a state in the corporation's behalf are not enough to subject it to suit on causes of action unconnected with the activities there. To require the corporation in such circumstances to defend the suit away from its home or other jurisdiction where it carries on more substantial activities has been thought to lay too great and unreasonable a burden on the corporation to comport with due process.

While it has been held in cases on which appellant relies that continuous activity of some sorts within a state is not enough to support the demand that the corporation be amenable to suits unrelated to that activity, there have been instances in which the continuous corporate operations within a state were thought so substantial and of such a nature as to justify suit against it on causes of action arising from dealings entirely distinct from those activities.

Finally, although the commission of some single or occasional acts of the corporate agent in a state sufficient to impose an obligation or liability on the corporation has not been thought to confer upon the state authority to enforce it, other such acts, because of their nature and quality and the circumstances of their commission, may be deemed sufficient to render the corporation liable to suit. Cf. . . . Hess v. Pawloski, 274 U.S. 352 (1927).

True, some of the decisions holding the corporation amenable to suit have been supported by resort to the legal fiction that it has given its consent to service and suit, consent being implied from its presence in the state through the acts of its authorized agents. But more realistically it may be said that those authorized acts were of such a nature as to justify the fiction. . . .

It is evident that the criteria by which we mark the boundary line between those activities which justify the subjection of a corporation to suit, and those which do not, cannot be simply mechanical or quantitative. The test is not merely, as has sometimes been suggested, whether the activity, which the corporation has seen fit to procure through its agents in another state, is a little more or a little less. International Harvester Co. v. Kentucky, supra, 587. Whether due process is satisfied must depend rather upon the quality and nature of the activity in relation to the fair and orderly administration of the laws which it was the purpose of the due process clause to insure. That clause does not contemplate that a state may make binding a judgment *in personam* against an individual or corporate defendant with which the state has no contacts, ties, or relations. Cf. Pennoyer v. Neff, supra; Minnesota Commercial Assn. v. Benn, 261 U.S. 140 [(1923)].

But to the extent that a corporation exercises the privilege of conducting activities within a state, it enjoys the benefits and protection of the laws of that state. The exercise of that privilege may give rise to obligations, and, so far as those obligations arise out of or are connected with the activities within the state, a procedure which requires the corporation to respond to a suit brought to enforce them can, in most instances, hardly be said to be undue. . . .

Applying these standards, the activities carried on in behalf of appellant in the State of Washington were neither irregular nor casual. They were systematic and continuous throughout the years in question. They resulted in a large volume of interstate business, in the course of which appellant received the benefits and protection of the laws of the state, including the right to resort to the courts for the enforcement of its rights. The obligation which is here sued upon arose out of those very activities. It is evident that these operations establish sufficient contacts or ties with the state of the forum to make it reasonable and just, according to our traditional conception of fair play and substantial justice, to permit the state to enforce the obligations which appellant has incurred there. Hence we cannot say that the maintenance of the present suit in the State of Washington involves an unreasonable or undue procedure. . . .

We are likewise unable to conclude that the service of the process within the state upon an agent . . . was not sufficient notice of the suit. . . .

Nor can we say that the mailing of the notice of suit to appellant by registered mail at its home office was not reasonably calculated to apprise appellant of the suit. . . .

Justice Black, concurring.

[I]t is unthinkable that the vague due process clause was ever intended to prohibit a State from regulating or taxing a business carried on within its boundaries simply because this is done by agents of a corporation organized and having its headquarters elsewhere. To read this into the due process clause would in fact result in depriving a State's citizens of due process by taking from the State the power to protect them in their business dealings within its boundaries with representatives of a foreign corporation. Nothing could be more irrational or more designed to defeat the function of our federative system of government. Certainly a State, at the very least, has power to tax and sue those dealing with its citizens within its boundaries, as we have held before. . . . It is true that this Court did use the terms "fair play" and "substantial justice" in explaining the philosophy underlying the holding that it could not be "due process of law" to render a personal judgment against a defendant without notice to and an opportunity to be heard by him. . . .

[This] did not mean thereby that all legislative enactments which this Court might deem to be contrary to natural justice ought to be held invalid under the due process clause. None of the cases purport to support or could support a holding that a State can tax and sue corporations only if its action comports with this Court's notions of "natural justice." I should have thought the Tenth Amendment settled that.

I believe that the Federal Constitution leaves to each State, without any "ifs" or "buts," a power to tax and to open the doors of its courts for its citizens to sue corporations whose agents do business in those States. Believing that the Constitution gave the States that power, I think it a judicial deprivation to condition its exercise upon this Court's notion of "fair play," however appealing that term may be. Nor can I stretch the meaning of due process so far as to authorize this Court to deprive a State of the right to afford judicial protection to its citizens on the ground that it would be more "convenient" for the corporation to be sued somewhere else.

### Note: The World After International Shoe

As the second great constitutional case on personal jurisdiction, *International Shoe* reaffirmed the due process basis of *Pennoyer* but cut the analysis loose from the mooring of territoriality and set it upon the uncharted sea of "minimum contacts" and "fair play and substantial justice." The Court does emphasize the corporation's continuous contacts with the state, which would indicate that it was "present" in Washington, but also stresses that the state's claim arises from the very activities that provide the basis for jurisdiction. Much ink in opinions and commentary has flowed over cases that fall in between: where the corporation's activities are "continuous and systematic" but do *not* give rise to the liabilities sued upon; or where there are only "isolated items of activity in a state," but these activities are closely connected with the plaintiff's cause of action.

In McGee v. International Life Ins. Co., 355 U.S. 220 (1957), a resident of California purchased an insurance policy from an Arizona company that was later acquired by International Life Insurance Co. The policy holder received premium notices in California and made remittances. Upon his death, his mother, the beneficiary, sought double indemnity; she brought suit in California, serving the state insurance commissioner and notifying the defendant by registered mail, in accordance with California insurance laws. The insurer defaulted. The beneficiary sought to enforce the resulting judgment by means of an action in Texas. The Supreme Court held that Texas courts were obliged to recognize the validity of the California judgment even though International Life had no office or agent in California and did not solicit any business there apart from the policy with McGee. "It is sufficient for purposes of due process that the suit was based on a contract which had substantial connection with that State. . . . California has a manifest interest in providing effective means of redress for its residents when their insurers refuse to pay claims." Id. at 223.

Another famous case was Gray v. Am. Radiator & Standard Sanitary Corp., 22 Ill. 2d 432 (1961), in which the Illinois court found that it had jurisdiction over an Ohio manufacturer of valves. The defendant had sold his valves to a Pennsylvania manufacturer of water heaters who in turn had sold a heater to an Illinois resident who was ultimately injured by an explosion, allegedly resulting from a defective valve. The court upheld jurisdiction even though "[t]he record fails to disclose whether defendant has done any other business in Illinois, either directly or indirectly." 22 Ill. 2d at 438. See also Buckeye Boiler Co. v. Superior Court of L.A. Cty., 71 Cal. 2d 893 (1969).

The possibilities suggested by *McGee* and *Gray* invited a wave of so-called long-arm statutes, in which states undertook to define the circumstances under which they would attempt to exercise jurisdiction over nonresident defendants. Some states took an expansive approach. See, e.g., Cal. Civ. Proc. Code § 410.10: "A court of this state may exercise jurisdiction on any basis not inconsistent with the Constitution of this state or of the United States." Other states, however, chose not to open the doors of their courts to the full extent permitted by the Constitution. An early model was Ill. Rev. Stat. 1959, ch. 100, para. 17:

(1) Any person, whether or not a citizen or resident of this State, who in person or through an agent does any of the acts hereinafter enumerated, thereby submits such person, and, if an individual, his personal representative, to the jurisdiction of the courts of this State as to any cause of action arising from the doing of any of such acts:
   (a) The transaction of any business within this State;
   (b) The commission of a tortious act within this State;
   (c) The ownership, use, or possession of any real estate situated in this State;
   (d) Contracting to insure any person, property or risk located within this State at the time of contracting. . . .

For 35 years, states expanded their reach over nonresidents, particularly corporate defendants. In only two cases—once believed to be limited to their factual contexts—did the Court deny a state court's effort to exercise jurisdiction. In the first case, Hanson v. Denckla, 357 U.S. 235 (1958), the Court held that a Florida court did not have jurisdiction over a Delaware trust company that had entered into a trust agreement with Dora Donner. Donner was a resident of Pennsylvania when the trust was formed. She later moved to Florida, where she eventually died. Although the trust company continued to perform tasks in connection with the trust after she moved to

Florida, the Court concluded that the trustee's ties to Florida were too slight for minimum contacts:

> The unilateral activity of those who claim some relationship with a non-resident defendant cannot satisfy the requirement of contact with the forum State. The application of that rule will vary with the quality and nature of the defendant's activity, but it is essential in each case that there be some act by which the defendant purposefully avails itself of the privilege of conducting activities within the forum State, thus invoking the benefits and protections of its laws.

Id. at 253.

In the second case denying jurisdiction, Kulko v. Superior Court, 436 U.S. 84 (1978), the Court held unconstitutional California's exercise of jurisdiction over a New York father who was sued for divorce, full child custody, and increased child support payments by his former wife, a California resident. California courts had held that by consenting to his daughter's move to California to live with her mother, he had "purposefully availed" himself of the benefits and protections of California. Id. at 89.

The Supreme Court reversed, reasoning that "[a] father who agrees, in the interests of family harmony and his children's preferences, to allow them to spend more time in California than was required under a separation agreement" does not meet the "purposeful avail[ment]" standard. Id. at 94. Additionally, the Kulkos' separation was completed in New York, and "basic considerations of fairness point decisively in favor of [that state as the] proper forum for adjudication of this case. . . . It is appellant who has remained in the State of the marital domicile." Id. at 97. Finally, the Court reiterated that "appellant did no more than acquiesce in the stated preference of one of his children to live with her mother in California. This single act is surely not one that a reasonable parent would expect to result in the substantial financial burden and strain of litigating a child-support suit in a forum 3,000 miles away."

## Note: Litigating Personal Jurisdiction

Consider the following comments of Professor Winton Woods:

> We need constantly to remind ourselves that personal jurisdiction decisions are usually made in the dimly-lit factual arena of the initial choice of forum. Moreover, they are made by trial lawyers with no admitted expertise in constitutional adjudication, but who claim great skill at common law argumentation concerning fairness and equity. At this preliminary litigation juncture, simplicity and clarity of doctrine are principles with stature equal to that of coherency.

Winton D. Woods, Carnival Cruise Lines v. Shute: An Amicus Inquiry into the Future of "Purposeful Availment," 36 Wayne L. Rev. 1393, 1396 (1990).

Is it easy to determine where a corporation has "minimum contacts" or where it has "purposefully directed" its commercial activities? Would a simple, bright-line test be preferable to the context-sensitive due process analysis we now have?

The complexities of the law of personal jurisdiction prompt many lawyers simply to avoid confronting them whenever possible. The simplest way to do this, of course, is to file the action in a forum that clearly has power over the defendant, and in most cases there is such a forum. Whatever the attractions of a questionable forum, the expenses of waging a jurisdiction battle and the likely prolonging of the litigation often lead lawyers to decline a case or to refer the client instead to a lawyer in the forum where jurisdiction is most likely to be established.

Yet when questions of personal jurisdiction do arise, they are fundamental to fairness and to the ability of our procedural system to deal with the nationalization and globalization of commerce.

How exactly does the defendant's lawyer raise the question of personal jurisdiction? There are two principal methods of attack: collateral and direct. By far the more important of these is the direct attack, outlined briefly here and presented more fully in its tactical dimensions in Chapter 2.

The risky indirect, or collateral, attack on personal jurisdiction is raised by doing nothing in response to the service of the summons and complaint. A default judgment will probably be entered; when the plaintiff seeks to execute on the judgment, the defendant can argue that it is void because it was entered by a court without personal jurisdiction. A void judgment is not enforceable as a matter of due process and of full faith and credit. In addition to personal jurisdiction, the requisites of a valid and enforceable judgment are subject matter jurisdiction and notice to the defendant.

Collateral attack is not for the faint-hearted or risk-averse, however, because the defendant who loses his jurisdictional argument cannot then argue the merits of his defense. These he has defaulted away. The only objections that can be raised on collateral attack are those that go to the power of the court entering the default judgment.

The much more common method of objecting is to raise the issue in the court where the plaintiff asserts jurisdiction. Note that an objection to personal jurisdiction is waived if it is not made in the first response to the complaint filed in the action, whether that is an answer or a motion prior to answering. See Fed. R. Civ. P. 12.

In the direct attack procedure, the defendant who loses on personal jurisdiction may then go on to defend on the merits. If there is an appeal, she may argue that the lower court erred in its ruling on personal jurisdiction. To put it another way, a defendant does not submit to the jurisdiction of the court by moving on to defend the merits. Typically, in state and appellate courts, those who contest jurisdiction directly must wait for a final judgment in the trial court before appealing its assertion of jurisdiction.

Finally, although procedure on contesting personal jurisdiction varies in its details from state to state, the overall approach is close to that of the federal system, outlined above. A few states still provide for "special" and a few for "limited" appearances to contest jurisdiction. The theory behind these practices is that a court must have jurisdiction to decide whether it has jurisdiction, or that by coming in and contesting jurisdiction, a defendant submits to the court's power. In such states, a special appearance must be made for the purpose of objecting to jurisdiction. Similarly, in some places a defendant in a *quasi in rem* action makes a "limited appearance" to defend his cause without exposing himself to an *in personam* judgment that would be enforceable against all of his assets, wherever they may be located.

### Note: General and Specific Jurisdiction

The Court in *International Shoe* acknowledged cases in which "the continuous corporate operations within a state were thought *so substantial* and of such a nature as to justify suit against it on causes of action arising from dealings entirely distinct from those activities." 326 U.S. at 318 (emphasis added). The Court later restated this principle in Helicopteros Nacionales de Colom., S.A. v. Hall, 466 U.S. 408 (1984), as follows: "Even when the cause of action does not arise out of or relate to the foreign corporation's activities in the forum State, due process is not offended by a State's subjecting the corporation to its *in personam* jurisdiction when there are sufficient contacts between the State and the foreign corporation." Id. at 414.

Where the defendant's activities in the forum are not "continuous" and "substantial" enough to satisfy this test, then the Court's minimum contacts analysis is the standard. In these cases it matters whether the dispute "arises out of" or is "related to" the defendant's forum ties. Courts refer to the first type of "dispute-blind" jurisdiction as *general jurisdiction*. The latter "dispute-specific" type of jurisdiction is called *specific jurisdiction*.

Be aware that the term "general jurisdiction" has multiple meanings. It not only refers to the personal jurisdiction concept described in this section, but also can refer to subject matter jurisdiction of some courts. Likewise, the term "limited jurisdiction" may surface in both contexts. It may avoid confusion later to be aware now that the terms have different meanings in different contexts.

The rest of the Supreme Court cases in this chapter were decided since 1978. As you read them, be especially alert to the distinction between statutory and constitutional limits on jurisdiction. You will note that the statutory question is always considered first, since the constitutional issue does not arise unless the state purports to exercise jurisdiction. Note also the different styles of argument and the various roles that statutory arguments play in shaping the constitutional issues. We treat first the development of disagreement in the Supreme Court about the proper boundaries of minimum contacts analysis for specific jurisdiction. Cases on general jurisdiction follow.

## 5.   Minimum Contacts and Foreseeability

### Problem Case: Contacts in the Stream of Commerce

Revisit the facts of the problem case Contacts Without Commerce just before *International Shoe.* Assume now that FibreLite blames any emissions beyond federal limits at the Truckee plant on defects in a smokestack filter manufactured by FreshAir, a Korean company with its principal place of business in Seoul, South Korea. FibreLite acquires these filters as part of a smokestack assembly system from PurePuff, a Texas partnership with its principal place of business in Arkansas. PurePuff assembles and installs complete smokestack filtration systems from component parts. FibreLite's filtration system was assembled in Texas by PurePuff and installed at the Truckee facility by PurePuff staff in 2010. PurePuff has maintained and updated the filters every year since then.

Plaintiffs move to amend their complaint to add FreshAir and PurePuff and properly serve them with the amended complaint. FreshAir makes no sales in Nevada, has no offices or employees there, and has no advertising in the state. Its U.S. sales are exclusively to PurePuff. Sales to PurePuff constitute just 5 percent of FreshAir's global revenue. Still, every power plant and many other businesses in Nevada use PurePuff filtration systems with FreshAir filters set to meet state and federal emissions standards. Nevada sales constitute 55 percent of PurePuff's revenue and it employs ten salespeople to cover the state. The sales staff occupies an office in Las Vegas owned by PurePuff and is supervised by a partner living there. The company also owns a field office in Reno for trips to northern Nevada clients as well as a lavish condominium just off the strip in Las Vegas for corporate retreats.

FreshAir's CEO submits an affidavit in support of the company's motion to dismiss under 12(b)(2) stating:

> I am fully aware that PurePuff sells filtration systems primarily in the western U.S., but because PurePuff provides maintenance and service, FreshAir has no relationship with end users and does not track the flow of its products beyond the point of sale to PurePuff.
>
> We do not tailor our filters for any specific U.S. market. Instead, the filters meet specifications provided by PurePuff for all states in which that company sells smokestack filtration systems.

How should the court rule on FreshAir's motion to dismiss? What result if PurePuff moves to dismiss for lack of personal jurisdiction as well?

### *World-Wide Volkswagen Corp. v. Woodson*
585 P.2d 351 (Okla. 1978)

BARNES, J.

This case concerns an original action brought on behalf of World-Wide Volkswagen Corporation and Seaway Volkswagen, Inc., in which the petitioners ask this Court to assume original jurisdiction and issue a writ of prohibition, prohibiting the respondent trial judge, the Honorable Charles S. Woodson, from exercising personal jurisdiction over the petitioners, through service under the Uniform Interstate and International Procedure Act, as adopted in Oklahoma at 12 O.S. 1971, §§ 1701.01 et seq., commonly referred to as the Oklahoma Long-Arm Statute.

The test for applying Long-Arm jurisdiction in Oklahoma is to determine whether the exercise of jurisdiction is authorized by statute, and, if so, whether such exercise of jurisdiction is consistent with the constitutional requirements of due process.

After examining Oklahoma's Long-Arm Statute and the facts present in this case, we conclude that jurisdiction over the nonresident petitioners is authorized by statute.

The facts before us in this case are as follows: In September of 1977, an Audi automobile, driven by Kay Eloise Robinson, was struck in the rear by an automobile being driven by a party not involved in the case before us. Mrs. Robinson and her two children, Eva May and George Samuel, were seriously injured in that collision when the gasoline tank of their Audi automobile ruptured, causing a fire in the passenger compartment of that car. As a result of that collision, manufacturers products liability actions were brought on behalf of Mrs. Robinson, her husband and her children against (1) the manufacturer of the automobile, Volkswagenwerk Aktiengesellschaft; (2) against the U.S. importer of the automobile, Volkswagen of America, Inc.; (3) against the distributor of the automobile, World-Wide Volkswagen Corporation; and (4) against the retail dealer who sold the Robinsons the car, Seaway Volkswagen, Inc.

It is World-Wide Volkswagen, distributor of Audis in Connecticut, New York and New Jersey, and Seaway Volkswagen, Inc., the dealer who sold the car, that petition this Court seeking a writ of prohibition. . . .

In the case before us, the respondents contend that the courts of Oklahoma have jurisdiction over the petitioners because they caused a tortious injury in this State, giving rise to jurisdiction under the provisions of 12 O.S. 1971, § 1701.03(a)(3) or (4).

Title 12 O.S. 1971, § 1701.03, provides in part:

> (a) A court may exercise personal jurisdiction over a person, who acts directly or by an agent, as to a cause of action or claim for relief arising from the person's: . . .
>> (3) causing tortious injury in this state *by an act or omission in this state;*
>> (4) causing tortious injury in this state *by an act or omission outside* this state *if he regularly does or solicits business or engages in any other persistent course of conduct, or derives substantial revenue from goods used or consumed or services rendered, in this state.* . . . (Emphasis added)

While it is true that the alleged acts or omissions of the petitioners allegedly caused tortious injury in this State, none of the acts or omissions alleged took place in this State. The defects in the product allegedly existed at the time the product left the hands of the petitioners, and at that time the automobile was not, and had not been, in the State of Oklahoma. We therefore conclude that no acts or omissions on the part of the petitioners took place within the State. In attempting to convince us that acts or omissions of the petitioners did take place within the State, the respondents rely on Gray v. American Radiator & Standard Sanitary Corp., 22 Ill. 2d 432, 176 N.E.2d 761 (1961).

We do not find the analysis used in Gray v. American Radiator, supra, persuasive. In that case, the Illinois Supreme Court was interpreting a provision of the Illinois Revised Statutes which provided that a nonresident, who either in person or through an agent *commits a tortious act within Illinois,* submits to the jurisdiction of Illinois, and may be served by means of the State Long-Arm Statute. In determining whether the manufacturer of a defective safety valve, which was allegedly defective at the time of manufacture in Ohio, committed a "tortious act" in the State of Illinois, the Court held that a tort had been committed within the jurisdiction because the injury which resulted from the defect occurred in Illinois. In so ruling, the Court held that the place of a wrong is where the last event necessary to render the actor liable takes place, and that the last act to render the manufacturer liable was the sustaining of an injury in Illinois by the plaintiff.

Our statute is *unlike* the Illinois statute. The Illinois statute merely requires that a tortious act be committed within Illinois. The Illinois court ruling makes a party subject to Illinois jurisdiction if his acts ultimately result in tortious injury within Illinois. Our statute requires more than the occurrence of tortious injury within the State before a party is subject to personal jurisdiction. . . .

. . . Accordingly, we hold that the acts or omissions of the petitioners, which are alleged in the petition, were not acts or omissions in this State, and therefore no power to exercise personal jurisdiction over the petitioners existed by virtue of the provisions of 12 O.S. 1971, § 1701.03(a)(3).

We next consider whether the power to exercise personal jurisdiction over the petitioners existed by virtue of 12 O.S. 1971, § 1701.03(a)(4). . . .

In the case before us, the product being sold and distributed by the petitioners is by its very design and purpose so mobile that petitioners can foresee its possible use in Oklahoma. This is especially true of the distributor, who has the exclusive right to distribute such automobile in New York, New Jersey and Connecticut. The evidence presented below demonstrated that goods sold and distributed by the petitioners were used in the State of Oklahoma, and under the facts we believe it reasonable to infer, given the retail value of the automobile, that the petitioners derive substantial income from automobiles which from time to time are used in the State of Oklahoma. This being the case, we hold that under the facts presented, the trial court was justified in concluding that the petitioners derive substantial revenue from goods used or consumed in this State. . . .

[The court then concluded that this assertion of jurisdiction did not violate due process. — EDS.]

## Notes and Questions

1. The Oklahoma Supreme Court opinion first examines the Oklahoma long-arm statute before turning to the constitutional analysis. This is the order in which the jurisdiction issue commonly is addressed, as courts prefer to avoid constitutional issues when possible. If the state long-arm statute does not permit the assertion of jurisdiction, then the court need not reach the difficult constitutional question of whether the assertion would violate due process under the Fourteenth Amendment. What are the efficiencies of this approach? What other policy issues support it?

2. As you might imagine, states have strong incentives in this area to draft long-arm measures that go to the limits of due process. Why? Is there any reason a state might not extend its reach to the maximum extent possible?

3. Despite the incentives to draft long-arm measures that go to the limits of due process, not all states have amended their rules to take advantage of this power. In practice you may encounter three types of long-arm rules, two of which look identical on the books. The first is the type that California, to take one example, has adopted. This "one-step" measure simply asserts, as shown supra, that the state courts have jurisdiction "to the limits of due process," thereby collapsing the state law test into the constitutional one. Be aware, however, that state courts still may interpret such a measure to require a higher, or different, level of contacts than the federal due process case law requires.

Other states list the conditions under which a court will have jurisdiction. Yet some state courts have interpreted this language to go to the limits of due process, making the statute operationally identical to the one-step measures described above. These might be described as "quasi two-step" measures, insofar as they appear to require two separate analyses—state law and constitutional—but case law reveals that the analysis is the same. Why would state courts interpret language in this manner? Have they usurped legislative power in doing so?

Still other states, dwindling in numbers, have a true two-step process and do not interpret their long-arm statutes to be coterminous with the Fourteenth Amendment. Distinguishing between this type of true two-step statute and the quasi two-step statute is impossible without research into the case law interpreting the scope of long-arm jurisdiction.

What kind of long-arm statute did Oklahoma have when its Supreme Court decided *World-Wide Volkswagen*?

We now turn to the U.S. Supreme Court's review of the Oklahoma decision. Note that the Court does not reconsider whether the Oklahoma court properly interpreted its long-arm statute, only whether that interpretation violated due process. Why? Whose word is final on the issue of a state statute's meaning?

## *World-Wide Volkswagen Corp. v. Woodson*
444 U.S. 286 (1980)

JUSTICE WHITE delivered the opinion of the Court.

The issue before us is whether, consistently with the Due Process Clause of the Fourteenth Amendment, an Oklahoma court may exercise *in personam* jurisdiction over a nonresident automobile retailer and its wholesale distributor in a products-liability action, when the defendants' only connection with Oklahoma is the fact that an automobile sold in New York to New York residents became involved in an accident in Oklahoma. . . .

The facts presented to the District Court showed that World-Wide is incorporated and has its business office in New York. It distributes vehicles, parts, and accessories, under contract with Volkswagen, to retail dealers in New York, New Jersey, and Connecticut. Seaway, one of these retail dealers, is incorporated and has its place of business in New York. Insofar as the record reveals, Seaway and World-Wide are fully independent corporations whose relations with each other and with Volkswagen and Audi are contractual only. Respondents adduced no evidence that either World-Wide or Seaway does any business in Oklahoma, ships or sells any products to or in that State, has an agent to receive process there, or purchases advertisements in any media calculated to reach Oklahoma. In fact, as respondents' counsel conceded at oral argument, Tr. of Oral Arg. 32, there was no showing that any automobile sold by World-Wide or Seaway has ever entered Oklahoma with the single exception of the vehicle involved in the present case. . . .

As has long been settled, and as we reaffirm today, a state court may exercise personal jurisdiction over a nonresident defendant only so long as there exist "minimum contacts" between the defendant and the forum State. International Shoe Co. v. Washington, supra, at 316. The concept of minimum contacts, in turn, can be seen to perform two related, but distinguishable, functions. It protects the defendant against the burdens of litigating in a distant or inconvenient forum. And it acts to ensure that the States, through their courts, do not reach out beyond the limits imposed on them by their status as coequal sovereigns in a federal system.

The protection against inconvenient litigation is typically described in terms of "reasonableness" or "fairness." We have said that the defendant's contacts with the forum State must be such that maintenance of the suit "does not offend 'traditional notions of fair play and substantial justice.'" International Shoe Co. v. Washington, supra, at 316, quoting Milliken v. Meyer, 311 U.S. 457, 463 (1940). The relationship between the defendant and the forum must be such that it is "reasonable . . . to require the corporation to defend the particular suit which is brought there." 326 U.S., at 317. Implicit in this emphasis on reasonableness is the understanding that the burden on the defendant, while always a primary concern, will in an appropriate case be considered in light of other relevant factors, including the forum State's interest in adjudicating the dispute, see McGee v. International Life Ins. Co., 355 U.S. 220, 223 (1957); the plaintiff's interest in obtaining convenient and effective relief, see Kulko v. California Superior Court, [436 U.S. 84, 92 (1978),] at least when that interest is not adequately protected by the plaintiff's power to choose the forum, cf. Shaffer v. Heitner, 433 U.S. 186, 211, n.37 (1977); the interstate judicial system's interest in obtaining the most efficient resolution of controversies; and the shared interest of the several States in furthering fundamental substantive social policies, see Kulko v. California Superior Court, supra, at 93, 98.

The limits imposed on state jurisdiction by the Due Process Clause, in its role as guarantor against inconvenient litigation, have been substantially relaxed over the years. As we noted in McGee v. International Life Ins. Co., supra, at 222-223, this trend is largely attributable to a fundamental transformation in the American economy:

> Today many commercial transactions touch two or more States and may involve parties separated by the full continent. With this increasing nationalization of commerce has come a great increase in the amount of business conducted by mail across state lines. At the same time modern transportation and communication have made it much less burdensome for a party sued to defend himself in a State where he engages in economic activity.

The historical developments noted in *McGee*, of course, have only accelerated in the generation since that case was decided.

Nevertheless, we have never accepted the proposition that state lines are irrelevant for jurisdictional purposes, nor could we, and remain faithful to the principles of interstate federalism embodied in the Constitution. The economic interdependence of the States was foreseen and desired by the Framers. In the Commerce Clause, they provided that the Nation was to be a common market, a "free trade unit" in which the States are debarred from acting as separable economic entities. H. P. Hood & Sons, Inc. v. Du Mond, 336 U.S. 525, 538 (1949). But the Framers also intended that the States retain many essential attributes of sovereignty, including, in particular, the sovereign power to try causes in their courts. The sovereignty of each State, in turn, implied a limitation on the sovereignty of all of its sister States — a limitation express or implicit in both the original scheme of the Constitution and the Fourteenth Amendment. Even if the defendant would suffer minimal or no inconvenience from being forced to litigate before the tribunals of another State; even if the forum State has a strong interest in applying its law to the controversy; even if the forum State is the most convenient location for litigation, the Due Process Clause, acting as an instrument of interstate federalism, may sometimes act to divest the State of its power to render a valid judgment. Hanson v. Denckla, supra, at 251, 254.

Applying these principles to the case at hand, we find in the record before us a total absence of those affiliating circumstances that are a necessary predicate to any exercise of state-court jurisdiction. Petitioners carry on no activity whatsoever in Oklahoma. They close no sales and perform no services there. They avail themselves of none of the privileges and benefits of Oklahoma law. They solicit no business there either through salespersons or through advertising reasonably calculated to reach the State. Nor does the record show that they regularly sell cars at wholesale or retail to Oklahoma customers or residents or that they indirectly, through others, serve or seek to serve the Oklahoma market. In short, respondents seek to base jurisdiction on one, isolated occurrence and whatever inferences can be drawn therefrom: the fortuitous circumstance that a single Audi automobile, sold in New York to New York residents, happened to suffer an accident while passing through Oklahoma.

It is argued, however, that because an automobile is mobile by its very design and purpose it was "foreseeable" that the Robinsons' Audi would cause injury in Oklahoma. Yet "foreseeability" alone has never been a sufficient benchmark for personal jurisdiction under the Due Process Clause. . . . In Kulko v. California Superior Court, 436 U.S. 84 (1978), it was surely "foreseeable" that a divorced wife would move to California from New York, the domicile of the marriage, and that a minor daughter would live with the mother. Yet we held that California could not exercise jurisdiction in a child-support action over the former husband who had remained in New York.

If foreseeability were the criterion, a local California tire retailer could be forced to defend in Pennsylvania when a blowout occurs there, see Erlanger Mills, Inc. v. Cohoes Fibre Mills, Inc. 239 F.2d 502, 507 (4th Cir. 1956); a Wisconsin seller of a defective automobile jack could be haled before a distant court for damage caused in New Jersey, Reilly v. Phil Tolkan Pontiac, Inc., 372 F. Supp. 1205 (D.N.J. 1974), or a Florida soft drink concessionaire could be summoned to Alaska to account for injuries happening there, see Uppgren v. Executive Aviation Services, Inc., 304 F. Supp. 165, 170-171 (D. Minn. 1969). Every seller of chattels would in effect appoint the chattel his agent for service of process. His amenability to suit would travel with the chattel. . . .[11]

This is not to say, of course, that foreseeability is wholly irrelevant. But the foreseeability that is critical to due process analysis is not the mere likelihood that a product will find its way into the forum State. Rather, it is that the defendant's conduct and connection with the forum State are such that he should reasonably anticipate being haled into court there. See Kulko v. California Superior Court, supra at 97-98; Shaffer v. Heitner, 433 U.S. at 216; and see id. at 217-219 (Stevens, J., concurring in judgment). The Due Process

---

11. Respondents' counsel, at oral argument . . . sought to limit the reach of the foreseeability standard by suggesting that there is something unique about automobiles. It is true that automobiles are uniquely mobile . . . , that they did play a crucial role in the expansion of personal jurisdiction through the fiction of implied consent, e.g., Hess v. Pawloski, 274 U.S. 352, 47 S. Ct. 632 (1927), and that some of the cases have treated the automobile as a "dangerous instrumentality." But today, under the regime of *International Shoe*, we see no difference for jurisdictional purposes between an automobile and any other chattel. The "dangerous instrumentality" concept apparently was never used to support personal jurisdiction; and to the extent it has relevance today it bears not on jurisdiction but on the possible desirability of imposing substantive principles of tort law such as strict liability.

Clause, by ensuring the "orderly administration of the laws," International Shoe Co. v. Washington, 326 U.S. at 319, gives a degree of predictability to the legal system that allows potential defendants to structure their primary conduct with some minimum assurance as to where that conduct will and will not render them liable to suit.

When a corporation "purposefully avails itself of the privilege of conducting activities within the forum State," Hanson v. Denckla, 357 U.S. [235,] 253 [1958], it has clear notice that it is subject to suit there, and can act to alleviate the risk of burdensome litigation by procuring insurance, passing the expected costs on to customers, or, if the risks are too great, severing its connection with the State. Hence if the sale of a product of a manufacturer or distributor such as Audi or Volkswagen is not simply an isolated occurrence, but arises from the efforts of the manufacturer or distributor to serve, directly or indirectly, the market for its product in other States, it is not unreasonable to subject it to suit in one of those States if its allegedly defective merchandise has there been the source of injury to its owner or to others. The forum State does not exceed its powers under the Due Process Clause if it asserts personal jurisdiction over a corporation that delivers its products into the stream of commerce with the expectation that they will be purchased by consumers in the forum State. Cf. Gray v. American Radiator & Standard Sanitary Corp., 22 Ill. 2d 432, 176 N.E.2d 761 (1961).

But there is no such or similar basis for Oklahoma jurisdiction over World-Wide or Seaway in this case. Seaway's sales are made in Massena, [New York]. World-Wide's market, although substantially larger, is limited to dealers in New York, New Jersey, and Connecticut. There is no evidence of record that any automobiles distributed by World-Wide are sold to retail customers outside this tristate area. It is foreseeable that the purchasers of automobiles sold by World-Wide and Seaway may take them to Oklahoma. But the mere "unilateral activity of those who claim some relationship with a nonresident defendant cannot satisfy the requirement of contact with the forum State." Hanson v. Denckla, supra, at 253.

In a variant on the previous argument, it is contended that jurisdiction can be supported by the fact that petitioners earn substantial revenue from goods used in Oklahoma. The Oklahoma Supreme Court so found, 585 P.2d at 354-355, drawing the inference that because one automobile sold by petitioners had been used in Oklahoma, others might have been used there also. While this inference seems less than compelling on the facts of the instant case, we need not question the court's factual findings in order to reject its reasoning.

This argument seems to make the point that the purchase of automobiles in New York, from which the petitioners earn substantial revenue, would not occur *but for* the fact that the automobiles are capable of use in distant States like Oklahoma. Respondents observe that the very purpose of an automobile is to travel, and that travel of automobiles sold by petitioners is facilitated by an extensive chain of Volkswagen service centers throughout the country, including some in Oklahoma. However, financial benefits accruing to the defendant from a collateral relation to the forum State will not support jurisdiction if they do not stem from a constitutionally cognizable contact with that State. See Kulko v. California Superior Court, 436 U.S. at 94-95. In our view, whatever marginal revenues petitioners may receive by virtue of the fact that their products are capable of use in Oklahoma is far too attenuated a contact to justify that State's exercise of *in personam* jurisdiction over them.

Because we find that petitioners have no "contacts, ties, or relations" with the State of Oklahoma, International Shoe Co. v. Washington, supra, at 319, the judgment of the Supreme Court of Oklahoma is

*Reversed.*

JUSTICE BRENNAN, dissenting. . . .

. . . [T]he interest of the forum State and its connection to the litigation is strong. The automobile accident underlying the litigation occurred in Oklahoma. The plaintiffs were hospitalized in Oklahoma when they brought suit. Essential witnesses and evidence were in Oklahoma. See Shaffer v. Heitner, 433 U.S. at 208. The State has a legitimate interest in enforcing its laws designed to keep its highway system safe, and the trial can proceed at least as efficiently in Oklahoma as anywhere else.

The petitioners are not unconnected with the forum. Although both sell automobiles within limited sales territories, each sold the automobile which in fact was driven to Oklahoma where it was involved in an accident. It may be true, as the Court suggests, that each sincerely intended to limit its commercial impact to the limited territory, and that each intended to accept the benefits and protection of the laws only of those States within the territory. But obviously these were unrealistic hopes that cannot be treated as an automatic constitutional shield.

An automobile simply is not a stationary item or one designed to be used in one place. An automobile is *intended* to be moved around. Someone in the business of selling large numbers of automobiles can hardly plead ignorance of their mobility or pretend that the automobiles stay put after they are sold. It is not merely that a dealer in automobiles foresees that they will move. The dealer actually intends that the purchasers will use the automobiles to travel to distant States where the dealer does not directly "do business." The sale of an automobile does *purposefully* inject the vehicle into the stream of interstate commerce so that it can travel to distant States. See *Kulko*, 436 U.S. at 94; Hanson v. Denckla, 357 U.S. 235, 253 (1958). . . .

The Court accepts that a State may exercise jurisdiction over a distributor which "serves" that State "indirectly" by "deliver[ing] its products into the stream of commerce with the expectation that they will be purchased by consumers in the forum State." It is difficult to see why the Constitution should distinguish between a case involving goods which reach a distant State through a chain of distribution and a case involving goods which reach the same State because a consumer, using them as the dealer knew the customer would, took them there. In each case the seller purposefully injects the goods into the stream of commerce and those goods predictably are used in the forum State.

Furthermore, an automobile seller derives substantial benefits from States other than its own. A large part of the value of automobiles is the extensive, nationwide network of highways. Significant portions of that network have been constructed by and are maintained by the individual States, including Oklahoma. The States, through their highway programs, contribute in a very direct and important way to the value of petitioners' businesses. Additionally, a network of other related dealerships with their service departments operates throughout the country under the protection of the laws of the various States, including Oklahoma, and enhances the value of petitioners' businesses by facilitating their customers' traveling. . . .

JUSTICE MARSHALL, with whom JUSTICE BLACKMUN joins, dissenting. . . .

This is a difficult case, and reasonable minds may differ as to whether respondents have alleged a sufficient "relationship among the defendant[s], the forum, and the litigation," Shaffer v. Heitner, 433 U.S. 186, 204 (1977), to satisfy the requirements of *International Shoe*. I am concerned, however, that the majority has reached its result by taking an unnecessarily narrow view of petitioners' forum-related conduct. . . . [T]he basis for the assertion of jurisdiction is not the happenstance that an individual over whom petitioners had no control made a unilateral decision to take a chattel with him to a distant State. Rather, jurisdiction is premised on the deliberate and purposeful actions of the defendants themselves in choosing to become part of a nationwide, indeed a global, network for marketing and servicing automobiles.

Petitioners are sellers of a product whose utility derives from its mobility. . . . Petitioners know that their customers buy cars not only to make short trips, but also to travel long distances. In fact, the nationwide service network with which they are affiliated was designed to facilitate and encourage such travel. Seaway would be unlikely to sell many cars if authorized service were available only in Massena, N.Y. Moreover, local dealers normally derive a substantial portion of their revenues from their service operations and thereby obtain a further economic benefit from the opportunity to service cars which were sold in other States. It is apparent that petitioners have not attempted to minimize the chance that their activities will have effects in other States; on the contrary, they have chosen to do business in a way that increases that chance, because it is to their economic advantage to do so. . . .

JUSTICE BLACKMUN, dissenting. . . .

For me, a critical factor in the disposition of the litigation is the nature of the instrumentality under consideration. It has been said that we are a nation on wheels. What we are concerned with here is the automobile and its peripatetic character. . . . To expect that any new automobile will remain in the vicinity of its retail sale—like the 1914 electric car driven by the proverbial "little old lady"—is to blink at reality. The automobile is intended for distance as well as for transportation within a limited area.

It therefore seems to me not unreasonable—and certainly not unconstitutional and beyond the reach of the principles laid down in International Shoe Co. v. Washington, 326 U.S. 310 (1945), and its progeny—to uphold Oklahoma jurisdiction over this New York distributor and this New York dealer when the accident happened in Oklahoma. . . .

## *Notes and Questions*

1. Would it have mattered if the Robinsons had told the retailer that they were headed for Oklahoma? If they had been from a neighboring state and been injured there, rather than a distant one?

2. What do you think of Justice Brennan's "hey, hop on a plane" approach? Isn't the burden of distant litigation easily overstated, given modern procedure and technology? What, exactly, is the burden of distant litigation?

3. If the test for minimum contacts had to do with one's reasonable expectations, then why couldn't the expectations simply be changed by an announcement that all states heretofore will have nationwide service of process? Or that all manufacturers, distributors, and sellers of mobile products can anticipate being sued wherever they cause injury within the United States? If strict liability is justifiable, why isn't "strict amenability"?

4. Justice White states that the sovereignty of each state implies a limitation on the sovereignty of others, and suggests that this interstate sovereignty factor is relevant to the personal jurisdiction puzzle. Yet the defendant has always been able to consent to jurisdiction, even by a state with which he has no minimum contacts. How can an individual waive a state's sovereignty interests?

In Insurance Corp. of Ireland v. Compagnie des Bauxites de Guinee, 456 U.S. 694, 702 n.10 (1982), Justice White revisited this aspect of *World-Wide Volkswagen*, and offered this explanation:

> It is true that we have stated that the requirement of personal jurisdiction, as applied to the state courts, reflects an element of federalism and the character of state sovereignty vis-à-vis other States. . . . The restriction on state sovereign power described in *World-Wide Volkswagen Corp.*, however, must be seen as ultimately a function of the individual liberty interest preserved by the Due Process Clause. That Clause is the only source of the personal jurisdiction requirement and the clause itself makes no mention of federalism concerns. Furthermore, if the federalism concept operated as an independent restriction on the sovereign power of the court, it would not be possible to waive the personal jurisdiction requirement: Individual actions cannot change the powers of sovereignty, although the individual can subject himself to powers from which he may otherwise be protected.

So what, then, is the proper role of the sovereignty factor in the personal jurisdiction calculus?

5. Look at the Court's reference to Gray v. American Radiator. How are the two cases different? How does the Court's apparent approval of *Gray* modify the *World-Wide Volkswagen* test for jurisdiction in product liability cases?

## Note: The Robinson Saga

Think of yourself as the lawyer for the Robinsons. Why might you prefer to litigate in Oklahoma rather than New York or Arizona? In many cases involving personal jurisdiction, the most interesting question is why the plaintiff chose the questionable forum since there is almost always some relatively uncontestable place where he could sue instead.

Often the answer turns on the other advantages that the plaintiff's lawyer hoped (or the defendant's lawyer feared) would come from filing in a particular forum. From some of the statements and pleadings in the subsequent litigation in the Robinson case, outlined below, it appears that the decision to fight for jurisdiction over the retailer and distributor was based on the mistaken assumption that their presence would destroy potential diversity in the case, and thus prevent its removal to federal court. (In fact, diversity might not have been destroyed because the Robinsons arguably were no longer citizens of New York, though whether they had effectively established a new domicile was contested.) You will learn about such intricacies of subject matter jurisdiction later in this chapter.

The reason the Robinsons' original trial attorney preferred state over federal courts was that he believed his style would be better appreciated by the more local jury drawn from the state court pool. The county where the Robinsons' gas tank caught fire was, moreover, noted for the size of plaintiffs' verdicts that the local juries returned.

After the Supreme Court opinion releasing the retailer and distributor from the case, the Robinsons' fortunes took further sad and protracted turns. The remaining defendants (the importer and the manufacturer) removed the case to federal court based on diversity of citizenship. A jury found for the defendants, and the Robinsons appealed. In Robinson v. Audi NSU Auto Union Aktiengesellschaft, 739 F.2d 1481 (10th Cir. 1984), the court reversed as to the importer, holding that the trial judge improperly excluded evidence that the importer had prior knowledge that the fuel tank design was dangerous.

Back in the trial court, the judge granted summary judgment for the defendant importer on the basis of an Oklahoma Supreme Court decision, handed down after the Robinsons' appeal, holding that an importer cannot be held responsible for a defect attributable solely to the manufacturing process. This time the Robinsons lost on appeal. Robinson v. Volkswagen of America, 803 F.2d 572 (10th Cir. 1986). With new counsel, the Robinsons turned to malpractice claims against their original lawyers, as well as fraud claims against some of the defendants and their lawyers. Some of these were lost. See, e.g., Robinson v. Volkswagenwerk, 940 F.2d 1369 (10th

Cir. 1991), *cert. denied sub nom.* Herzfeld & Rubin v. Robinson, 502 U.S. 1091 (1992). See Charles W. Adams, World-Wide Volkswagen v. Woodson—The Rest of the Story, 72 Neb. L. Rev. 1122 (1993).

Looking back over the course of the litigation, we can now see that the Robinsons' physical injuries started with an exploding gas tank, and their legal wounds with the questionable and expensive tactical decision to join the retailer and regional distributor and to fight to keep them in the case, even though there were other "deep-pocket" defendants subject to personal jurisdiction in Oklahoma.

## *Note: Why Does the Forum Matter?*

In the following excerpt, Edward Purcell describes how geography can become a litigation weapon that is especially powerful when deployed against individual parties of modest means:

> The deterrent effects of geography are numerous and weighty. The threshold task of merely retaining counsel in a distant location, which may seem routine to attorneys and judges, is profoundly daunting to ordinary people. The very decision to retain an attorney is so troublesome, in fact, that most claimants are content to accept a settlement without one. The result of that commonplace decision, as numerous studies have repeatedly shown, is that such claimants almost invariably obtain much less from their adversaries than they otherwise would. . . .
>
> If a claimant does eventually retain an attorney, he may likely begin by securing counsel who resides near his home and outside of the contractual forum state. In such a case, his hopes are immediately subject to two related risks that geography creates. First, the claimant's leverage in negotiating a settlement is minimized because he has not yet established his willingness or capacity to bring suit in the contractual forum, or even to hire an attorney in the forum state. Second, his local attorney has a strong incentive to arrange an out-of-court settlement—especially if she is acting, as she most probably is, under a contingent fee agreement—in order to maximize her return and prevent the great bulk of the fee from eventually going to an attorney in the contractual forum state. Those facts by themselves increase the likelihood that the claimant will wind up with a relatively low and unfavorable out-of-court settlement.
>
> If the claimant does secure representation in the distant contractual forum, he begins to shoulder other and more palpable burdens. He may, for example, wind up with two attorneys, one local and one in the contractual forum, an arrangement that can complicate the representation and drive up his costs. Further, his need to rely on a distant attorney compounds his anxieties and uncertainties. The distant attorney is an unknown quantity. The claimant has fewer reasons to trust her, and the possibility that some subtle conflict of interest may emerge between the client and his distant attorney increases. The claimant can scarcely monitor the distant attorney's performance closely, and any attempt to do so would drive up his costs yet again. For her part, the attorney in the contractual forum is not particularly

concerned with her reputation in the relatively remote town where her client lives, and she most likely does not represent or hope to represent other individuals or organizations from her client's distant home town.

Once litigation begins, the process quickly piles on additional burdens. One is the obvious need to travel and communicate over long distances, which makes the suit more costly as well as more inconvenient in terms of both litigation planning and client-attorney consultation. Another is the compounded costs and risks created by the attorney's need to communicate with the client's witnesses and to prepare them for depositions and trial testimony. The party may either have to pay additional travel costs for in-person meetings or risk the creation of potentially discoverable documents that could spur additional and costly motion practice and, if disclosed, weaken the party's position in negotiations and at trial. A third burden is the likely additional delays involved in prosecuting the case, as distance and inconvenience combine to complicate various pretrial events and to remove from the attorney the spur of a human client who can or does present himself in person at his attorney's office. A fourth burden is the added cost of participating in a distant trial, including the costs and risks involved in securing the attendance of witnesses at such a location. All of these burdens will be especially heavy if the plaintiff's claim arises from events in his home state and many or all of his witnesses reside there.

Yet another burden is the fact that, whatever else happens, psychologically the claimant feels more cut off, more vulnerable, and even more anxious than he otherwise would. That burden is magnified by the fact that the attorneys representing his corporate adversary feel relatively comfortable and secure litigating in their home court. Those attorneys are, moreover, fully aware of the extra-legal burdens the plaintiff is facing. Consciously or unconsciously, they will tend to drive a harder bargain, hold off settling for a longer period in the hope of obtaining increasingly more favorable terms, and drag their feet while forcing the out-of-state litigant continually to press for action at each stage of the litigation.

Edward A. Purcell, Jr., Geography as a Litigation Weapon: Consumers, Forum-Selection Clauses, and the Rehnquist Court, 40 UCLA L. Rev. 423, 446-449 (1992).

## *Note: Choice of Law*

Simply because a court has jurisdiction over the defendant does not necessarily mean it has the power to apply its substantive laws to the controversy. It may, however, apply its own procedural rules—though the distinction between procedural and substantive rules is sometimes hazy.

If the applicable substantive law is federal, then the court—federal or state—will apply that federal law to the matter. Where an action is based on state law but has multistate features—such as in *World-Wide Volkswagen*—the forum may be obliged to apply the substantive law of another jurisdiction rather than its own. The choice of law decision depends on two sets of constraints.

First, each state has its own statutory rules regarding which law to apply, called "conflicts" laws. Second, the U.S. Supreme Court has held that due process and full faith and credit limitations prevent a state from applying its own laws to a controversy unless it has "a significant contact or significant aggregation of contacts, creating state interests, such that choice of its law is neither arbitrary nor fundamentally unfair." Allstate Ins. Co. v. Hague, 449 U.S. 302, 312-313 (1981) (plurality opinion). See also Phillips Petroleum Co. v. Shutts, 472 U.S. 797 (1985). In defining fundamental fairness for choice of law purposes, the Court has relied on factors that track closely the factors relevant to "minimum contacts." While in theory the inquiries are distinct, they tend to converge such that a court with personal jurisdiction typically will also have constitutional power to apply its state law to the controversy.

Full treatment of the range of choice of law problems in state courts is beyond the scope of this text. For discussion of the substantive law applied to a controversy brought in a federal court on the basis of diversity jurisdiction, see Chapter 6.

## 6.  Directing a "Product" Toward a Forum State: Minimum Contacts and Fair Play in a Post-Modern Age

### Problem Case: A Troubled Young Man

Dr. Anna Froid is a psychiatrist who lives and works in San Francisco. One of her patients is a deeply troubled 19-year-old man named Alvin Baites. She has been treating Alvin with medication and psychotherapy since October 1987. During the course of his treatment, Alvin has expressed repeatedly his hatred of his family, including his widower father, who lives in Sedona, Arizona, and his two sisters, Ellen Baites Plath of Washington state and Sally Baites of Jefferson City, Missouri.

The holidays are always a time of particular unhappiness and frustration for Alvin. During two prior Christmas seasons, Alvin became violent and irrational after drinking heavily at employee Christmas parties. Though he did not harm anyone, Alvin was institutionalized for several months in 1988, after the second episode. Dr. Froid knows all of this, since Alvin was under her care at that time.

During the fall of 1990, Alvin seemed to be making some progress. New medication was helping, and his level of anger toward others decreased modestly as therapy continued. Shortly before the Christmas holidays, however, Alvin seemed to suffer a setback. Dr. Froid linked this regression to the impending holidays and Alvin's plans to spend Christmas with his father and sisters in Arizona. Dr. Froid increased the dosage of his medication, but she did not renew her usual warning about mixing alcohol with the medication, since it was typed on the vial.

Alvin flew home to Arizona for the holidays. The visit reintroduced old family tensions, which triggered a violent argument between Alvin and his family. Unhinged by a combination of medication, alcohol, and stress,

Alvin lost control and struck and injured his father and sisters. Alvin has again been hospitalized, this time in Arizona. At his request, Dr. Froid flew to Arizona to see him there. She consulted with his doctors and talked to Alvin for 50 minutes. Dr. Froid left Arizona in the evening of the day she arrived there.

Her only other contact with Arizona is a one-quarter interest in a rental property in Scottsdale, Arizona. She has never visited the property or indeed been in Arizona except for her visit to Alvin.

Mr. Baites (Alvin's father) has filed a lawsuit against Dr. Froid in Arizona, alleging that she had a duty to warn foreseeable plaintiffs such as him of Alvin's violent tendencies.

Assume, *arguendo*, that the Arizona long-arm rules provide, in relevant part:

**Section 1.03**

(a) A court may exercise personal jurisdiction over a person, who acts directly or by an agent as to a claim arising from the person's . . .

(3) causing tortious injury by an act or omission in this state; or

(4) causing tortious injury in this state by an act or omission outside this state if he or she regularly does or solicits business, or engages in any other persistent course of conduct, or derives substantial revenue from goods used or consumed or services rendered, in this state; or meets the conditions of (5) of this section.

(5) having an interest in, using, or possessing real property in this state. . . .

Can Arizona constitutionally exercise jurisdiction over Mr. Baites's claim against Dr. Froid? If process was served on her when she visited Alvin in the hospital?

## Note: Keeton v. Hustler Magazine, Inc.

In *Keeton v. Hustler Magazine, Inc.*, 465 U.S. 770 (1984), Kathy Keeton, a New York resident, sued *Hustler* magazine, an Ohio corporation head-quartered in California, for libel in U.S. District Court in New Hampshire. Keeton had originally filed suit in Ohio, but the court held she was time barred there. She then initiated the same action in New Hampshire, where the statute of limitations for libel claims is longer than in most states. The only connection between the forum state and *Hustler* magazine was the monthly sale of 10,000 to 15,000 copies of the magazine there.

Both the district court and the court of appeals dismissed Keeton's complaint, holding that her lack of contacts rendered the State's interest "too attenuated" for an assertion of personal jurisdiction. The court of appeals also pointed out that it would be "unfair" to the magazine to allow jurisdiction under New Hampshire's exceptionally long statute of limitations, especially since the "single publication rule" relied on in libel cases would mean that the New Hampshire court would have to award a prevailing Keeton damages equivalent to the total harm she had suffered, rather than just that sustained in New Hampshire.

The Supreme Court reversed, holding that *Hustler*'s "regular circulation of magazines in the forum State is sufficient to support an assertion of jurisdiction in a libel action based on the contents of the magazine" since "regular monthly sales of thousands of magazines cannot by any stretch of the imagination be characterized as random, isolated, or fortuitous." The Court reasoned that, despite the fact that Keeton was unknown in New Hampshire, the state still had an interest in "employ[ing] its libel laws to discourage the deception of its citizens." The Court also pointed to New Hampshire's "substantial interest" in abiding by the "single publication rule," which preserves judicial resources nationwide by prohibiting multiple libel actions against the same defendant in different states.

Finally, the Court brushed aside concerns about the unfairness of subjecting *Hustler* to the state's unusual approach to libel suits, finding that "[t]he chance duration of statutes of limitations in nonforum jurisdictions has nothing to do with the contacts among respondent, New Hampshire, and this multistate libel action."

In a companion case, Calder v. Jones, 465 U.S. 783 (1984), the Court again addressed the issue of personal jurisdiction in a libel context. In this case, Shirley Jones, the entertainer, sued the editor of the *National Enquirer* and a writer in California for libel related to a defamatory piece about Jones in the magazine. Jones lives in California, the editor and staff writer in Florida. The Court held that the editor and writer reasonably should have anticipated that litigation might be initiated in the home state of a libel plaintiff. Though a plaintiff's domicile is not always a proper forum, where the plaintiff resides can be relevant to a minimum contacts analysis in some cases. The Court noted that this was an intentional tort that involved a particular target, Shirley Jones, and that the writer and editor would have realized at the time of writing and publishing the piece that the injury would be felt primarily where the plaintiff lives. In such a case, the plaintiff's domicile was a proper forum. Moreover, the Court pointed out, more issues of the *National Enquirer* are sold in California — the hub of the entertainment industry — than in any other state.

More recently the Supreme Court has emphasized that a defendant's mere awareness that her conduct will have concrete effects on the plaintiff in a particular forum, absent other more direct contact with the forum, is not a sufficient basis for personal jurisdiction. In Walden v. Fiore, Gina Fiore and Keith Gipson filed a civil rights suit in Nevada federal court against a DEA agent who seized $97,000 in cash from them when they changed flights in Atlanta, Georgia, after a trip to Puerto Rico. When the DEA agent questioned them at the Atlanta airport, Fiore explained that she and Gipson were professional gamblers and that the cash was their gambling "bank" and winnings from the trip. The DEA agent nevertheless seized the cash, stating that it would be returned later if they could prove the money had a legitimate source. The agent filled out a probable cause affidavit to support a forfeiture proceeding against Fiore and Gipson even though their attorney had submitted proper documentation to establish the legitimacy of the funds. The funds were returned nine months later when federal prosecutors decided not to file a forfeiture complaint.

The district court granted Officer Walden's motion to dismiss for want of personal jurisdiction on the ground that "even if [Walden] caused harm to respondents in Nevada while knowing they lived in Nevada, that fact alone did not confer jurisdiction." Walden v. Fiore, 134 S.Ct. 1115, 1120 (2014). The Ninth Circuit reversed on the ground that Officer Walden "'expressly aimed' his submission of the allegedly false affidavit at Nevada by submitting the affidavit with knowledge that it would affect persons with a 'significant connection' to Nevada." Id. In a unanimous decision, the Supreme Court reversed. Taking pains to distinguish *Calder*, the Court emphasized that the plaintiff "cannot be the only link between the defendant and the forum. Rather, it is the defendant's conduct that must form the necessary connection with the forum State. . . . These same principles apply when intentional torts are involved. In that context, it is likewise insufficient to rely on a defendant's 'random, fortuitous, or attenuated contacts' or on the 'unilateral activity' of a plaintiff." Id. at 1122-1123. Jurisdiction was upheld in *Calder*, the Court acknowledged, but the focus there was on

> the various contacts the defendants had created with California (and not just with the plaintiff) by writing the allegedly libelous story. We found those forum contacts to be ample . . . . The crux of *Calder* was that the reputation-based "effects" of the alleged libel connected the defendants to California, not just to the plaintiff. . . . However scandalous a newspaper article might be, it can lead to a loss of reputation only if communicated to (and read and understood by) third persons. . . . Indeed, because publication to third persons is a necessary element of libel . . . the defendants' intentional tort activity actually occurred *in* California.

Id. at 1123-1124. Officer Walden, by contrast, "never traveled to, conducted activities within, contacted anyone in, or sent anything or anyone to Nevada. . . . [His] actions in Georgia did not create sufficient contacts with Nevada simply because he allegedly directed his conduct at plaintiffs whom he knew had Nevada connections." Id. at 1124-1125. Plaintiffs may have suffered harm in Nevada by being unable to use their seized money there, but "[r]egardless of where a plaintiff lives or works, an injury is jurisdictionally relevant only insofar as it shows that the defendant has formed a contact with the forum State. The proper question is not where the plaintiff experienced a particular injury or effect but whether the defendant's conduct connects him to the forum in a meaningful way." Id. at 1125.

Even outside the context of intentional torts the Court has struggled with the issue of when extraterritorial conduct has a sufficient, direct impact on the forum to justify jurisdiction there. In the following case the Court addresses the matter in an international context, but is unable to agree on how courts ought to approach this issue. Which opinion do you find most persuasive?

## *Asahi Metal Indus. Co. v. Superior Court*
480 U.S. 102 (1987)

[JUSTICE O'CONNOR delivered the opinion of a Court that was severely fractured on all but the statement of facts and a few paragraphs of standard due process analysis. We print excerpts from these parts first. — EDS.]

### I

On September 23, 1978, on Interstate Highway 80 in Solano County, California, Gary Zurcher lost control of his Honda motorcycle and collided with a tractor. Zurcher was severely injured, and his passenger and wife, Ruth Ann Moreno, was killed. In September 1979, Zurcher filed a product liability action in the Superior Court of the State of California in and for the County of Solano. Zurcher alleged that the 1978 accident was caused by a sudden loss of air and an explosion in the rear tire of the motorcycle, and alleged that the motorcycle tire, tube, and sealant were defective. Zurcher's complaint named, *inter alia*, Cheng Shin Rubber Industrial Co., Ltd. (Cheng Shin), the Taiwanese manufacturer of the tube. Cheng Shin in turn filed a cross-complaint seeking indemnification from its codefendants and from petitioner, Asahi Metal Industry Co., Ltd. (Asahi), the manufacturer of the tube's valve assembly. Zurcher's claims against Cheng Shin and the other defendants were eventually settled and dismissed, leaving only Cheng Shin's indemnity action against Asahi.

California's long-arm statute authorizes the exercise of jurisdiction "on any basis not inconsistent with the Constitution of this state or of the United States." Cal. Civ. Proc. Code Ann. § 410.10 (West 1973). Asahi moved to quash Cheng Shin's service of summons, arguing the State could not exert jurisdiction over it consistent with the Due Process Clause of the Fourteenth Amendment.

In relation to the motion, the following information was submitted by Asahi and Cheng Shin. Asahi is a Japanese corporation. It manufactures tire valve assemblies in Japan and sells the assemblies to Cheng Shin, and to several other tire manufacturers, for use as components in finished tire tubes. Asahi's sales to Cheng Shin took place in Taiwan. The shipments from Asahi to Cheng Shin were sent from Japan to Taiwan. Cheng Shin bought and incorporated into its tire tubes 150,000 Asahi valve assemblies in 1978; 500,000 in 1979; 500,000 in 1980; 100,000 in 1981; and 100,000 in 1982. Sales to Cheng Shin accounted for 1.24 percent of Asahi's income in 1981 and 0.44 percent in 1982. Cheng Shin alleged that approximately 20 percent of its sales in the United States are in California. Cheng Shin purchases valve assemblies from other suppliers as well, and sells finished tubes throughout the world.

In 1983 an attorney for Cheng Shin conducted an informal examination of the valve stems of the tire tubes sold in one cycle store in Solano County. The attorney declared that of the approximately 115 tire tubes in the store, 97 were purportedly manufactured in Japan or Taiwan, and of those 97, 21 valve stems were marked with the circled letter "A," apparently Asahi's trademark. Of the 21 Asahi valve stems, 12 were incorporated into Cheng Shin tire tubes. The store contained 41 other Cheng Shin tubes that incorporated the valve assemblies of other manufacturers. An affidavit of a manager of Cheng Shin whose duties included the purchasing of component parts stated: "'In discussions with Asahi regarding the purchase of valve stem assemblies the fact that my Company sells tubes throughout the world and specifically the United States has been discussed. I am informed and believe that Asahi was fully aware that valve stem assemblies sold to my Company and to others would end up throughout the United States and in California.'" An affidavit of the president of Asahi, on the other hand, declared that Asahi "'has never contemplated that its limited sales of tire valves to Cheng Shin in Taiwan would subject it to lawsuits in California.'" The record does not include any contract between Cheng Shin and Asahi.

Primarily on the basis of the above information, the Superior Court denied the motion to quash summons, stating: "Asahi obviously does business on an international scale. It is not unreasonable that they defend claims of defect in their product on an international scale." Order Denying Motion to Quash Summons.

The Court of Appeal of the State of California issued a peremptory writ of mandate commanding the Superior Court to quash service of summons. The court concluded that "it would be unreasonable to require Asahi to respond in California solely on the basis of ultimately realized foreseeability that the product into which its component was embodied would be sold all over the world including California."

The Supreme Court of the State of California reversed and discharged the writ issued by the Court of Appeal. The court observed: "Asahi has no offices, property or agents in California. It solicits no business in California and has made no direct sales [in California]." 39 Cal. 3d 35, 705 P.2d 543 (1985). Moreover, "Asahi did not design or control the system of distribution that carried its valve assemblies into California." Id. at 48, 702 P.2d at 549. Nevertheless, the court found the exercise of jurisdiction over Asahi to be consistent with the Due Process Clause. It concluded that Asahi knew that some of the valve assemblies sold to Cheng Shin would be incorporated into tire tubes sold in California, and that Asahi benefited indirectly from the sale in California of products incorporating its components. The court considered Asahi's intentional act of placing its components into the stream of commerce — that is, by delivering the components to Cheng Shin in Taiwan — coupled with Asahi's awareness that some of the components would eventually find their way into California, sufficient to form the basis for state court jurisdiction under the Due Process Clause.

We granted certiorari and now reverse.

[All but Justice Scalia agreed with the following part of the opinion (labeled in the Opinion as Part II(B)). — EDS.]

The strictures of the Due Process Clause forbid a state court to exercise personal jurisdiction over Asahi under circumstances that would offend "'traditional notions of fair play and substantial justice.'"

We have previously explained that the determination of the reasonableness of the exercise of jurisdiction in each case will depend on an evaluation of several factors. A court must consider the burden on the defendant, the interests of the forum State, and the plaintiff's interest in obtaining relief. It must also weigh in its determination "the interstate judicial system's interest in obtaining the most efficient resolution of controversies; and the shared interest of the several States in furthering fundamental substantive social policies." Cf. *World-Wide Volkswagen*, 444 U.S. at 292 (citations omitted).

A consideration of these factors in the present case clearly reveals the unreasonableness of the assertion of jurisdiction over Asahi, even apart from the question of the placement of goods in the stream of commerce.

Certainly the burden on the defendant in this case is severe. Asahi has been commanded by the Supreme Court of California not only to traverse the distance between Asahi's headquarters in Japan and the Superior Court of California in and for the County of Solano, but also to submit its dispute with Cheng Shin to a foreign nation's judicial system. The unique burdens placed upon one who must defend oneself in a foreign legal system should have significant weight in assessing the reasonableness of stretching the long arm of personal jurisdiction over national borders.

When minimum contacts have been established, often the interests of the plaintiff and the forum in the exercise of jurisdiction will justify even the serious burdens placed on the alien defendant. In the present case, however, the interests of the plaintiff and the forum in California's assertion of jurisdiction over Asahi are slight. All that remains is a claim for indemnification asserted by Cheng Shin, a Taiwanese corporation, against Asahi. The transaction on which the indemnification claim is based took place in Taiwan; Asahi's components were shipped from Japan to Taiwan. Cheng Shin has not demonstrated that it is more convenient for it to litigate its indemnification claim against Asahi in California rather than in Taiwan or Japan.

Because the plaintiff is not a California resident, California's legitimate interests in the dispute have considerably diminished. The Supreme Court of California argued that the State had an interest in "protecting its consumers by ensuring that foreign manufacturers comply with the state's safety standards." The State Supreme Court's definition of California's interest, however, was overly broad. The dispute between Cheng Shin and Asahi is primarily about indemnification rather than safety standards. Moreover, it is not at all clear at this point that California law should govern the question whether a Japanese corporation should indemnify a Taiwanese corporation on the basis of a sale made in Taiwan and a shipment of goods from Japan to Taiwan. The possibility of being haled into a California court as a result of an accident involving Asahi's components undoubtedly creates an additional deterrent to the manufacture of unsafe components; however, similar pressures will be placed on Asahi by the purchasers of its components as long as those who use Asahi components in their final products, and sell those products in California, are subject to the application of California tort law.

*World-Wide Volkswagen* also admonished courts to take into consideration the interests of the "several States," in addition to the forum State, in the efficient judicial resolution of the dispute and the advancement of substantive policies. In the present case, this advice calls for a court to consider the procedural and substantive policies of other *nations* whose interests are affected by the assertion of jurisdiction by the California court. The procedural and substantive interests of other nations in a state court's assertion of jurisdiction over an alien defendant will differ from case to case. In every case, however, those interests, as well as the Federal Government's interest in its foreign relations policies, will be best served by a careful inquiry into the reasonableness of the assertion of jurisdiction in the particular case, and an unwillingness to find the serious burdens on an alien defendant outweighed by minimal interests on the part of the plaintiff or the forum State. "Great care and reserve should be exercised when extending our notions of personal jurisdiction into the international field." United States v. First National City Bank, 379 U.S. 378, 404 (1965) (Harlan, J., dissenting). See Born, Reflections on Judicial Jurisdiction in International Cases, 17 Ga. J. Int'l & Comp. L. 1 (1987).

Considering the international context, the heavy burden on the alien defendant, and the slight interests of the plaintiff and the forum State, the exercise of personal jurisdiction by a California court over Asahi in this instance would be unreasonable and unfair.

[JUSTICE O'CONNOR, joined by JUSTICES REHNQUIST, POWELL, and SCALIA, put forth the following theory.—EDS.]

The Due Process Clause of the Fourteenth Amendment limits the power of a state court to exert personal jurisdiction over a nonresident defendant. . . . Most recently we have reaffirmed . . . that minimum contacts must have a basis in "some act by which the defendant purposefully avails itself of the privilege of conducting activities within the forum State, thus invoking the benefits and protections of its laws." Burger King [Corp. v. Rudzewicz, 471 U.S. 462, 475 (1985)]. "Jurisdiction is proper . . . where the contacts proximately result from actions by the defendant *himself* that create a 'substantial connection' with the forum State." Ibid., quoting McGee v. International Life Insurance Co.[, 355 U.S. 220, 223 (1957)].

Applying the principle that minimum contacts must be based on an act of the defendant, the Court in World-Wide Volkswagen Corp. v. Woodson, 444 U.S. 286 (1980), rejected the assertion that a *consumer's* unilateral act of bringing the defendant's product into the forum State was a sufficient constitutional basis for personal jurisdiction over the defendant. It had been argued in *World-Wide Volkswagen* that because an automobile retailer and its wholesale distributor sold a product mobile by design and purpose, they could foresee being haled into court in the distant States into which their customers might drive. The Court rejected this concept of foreseeability as an insufficient basis for jurisdiction under the Due Process Clause. Id. at 295-296. The Court disclaimed, however, the idea that "foreseeability is wholly irrelevant" to personal jurisdiction, concluding that "[t]he forum State does not exceed its powers under the Due Process Clause if it asserts personal jurisdiction over a corporation that delivers its products into the stream of commerce with the expectation that they will be purchased by consumers in the forum State." . . .

In *World-Wide Volkswagen* itself, the state court sought to base jurisdiction not on any act of the defendant, but on the foreseeable unilateral actions of the consumer. Since *World-Wide Volkswagen,* lower courts have been confronted with cases in which the defendant acted by placing a product in the stream of commerce, and the stream eventually swept defendant's product into the forum State, but the defendant did nothing else to purposefully avail itself of the market in the forum State. Some courts have understood the Due Process Clause, as interpreted in *World-Wide Volkswagen,* to allow an exercise of personal jurisdiction to be based on no more than the defendant's act of placing the product in the stream of commerce. Other courts have understood the Due Process Clause and the above-quoted language in *World-Wide Volkswagen* to require the action of the defendant to be more purposefully directed at the forum State than the mere act of placing a product in the stream of commerce.

The reasoning of the Supreme Court of California in the present case illustrates the former interpretation of *World-Wide Volkswagen.* The Supreme Court of California held that, because the stream of commerce eventually brought some valves Asahi sold Cheng Shin into California, Asahi's awareness that its valves would be sold in California was sufficient to permit California to exercise jurisdiction over Asahi consistent with the requirements of the Due Process Clause. The Supreme Court of California's position was consistent with those courts that have held that mere foreseeability or awareness was a constitutionally sufficient basis for personal jurisdiction if the defendant's product made its way into the forum State while still in the stream of commerce.

Other courts, however, have understood the Due Process Clause to require something more than that the defendant was aware of its product's entry into the forum State through the stream of commerce in order for the State to exert jurisdiction over the defendant. In the present case, for example, the State Court of Appeal did not read the Due Process Clause, as interpreted by *World-Wide Volkswagen,* to allow "mere foreseeability that the product will enter the forum state [to] be enough by itself to establish jurisdiction over the distributor and retailer." . . .

We now find this latter position to be consonant with the requirements of due process. The "substantial connection" between the defendant and the forum State necessary for a finding of minimum contacts must come about by *an action of the defendant purposefully directed toward the forum State.*

The placement of a product into the stream of commerce, without more, is not an act of the defendant purposefully directed toward the forum State. Additional conduct of the defendant may indicate an intent or purpose to serve the market in the forum State, for example, designing the product for the market in the forum State, advertising in the forum State, establishing channels for providing regular advice to customers in the forum State, or marketing the product through a distributor who has agreed to serve as the sales agent in the forum State. But a defendant's awareness that the stream of commerce may or will sweep the product into the forum State does not convert the mere act of placing the product into the stream into an act purposefully directed toward the forum State.

Assuming, *arguendo*, that respondents have established Asahi's awareness that some of the valves sold to Cheng Shin would be incorporated into tire tubes sold in California, respondents have not demonstrated any action by Asahi to purposefully avail itself of the California market.

[JUSTICES BRENNAN, WHITE, MARSHALL, and BLACKMUN wrote separately to disagree with the "stream of commerce theory" propounded by the four plurality Justices. — EDS.]

. . . This is one of those rare cases in which "minimum requirements inherent in the concept of 'fair play and substantial justice' . . . defeat the reasonableness of jurisdiction even [though] the defendant has purposefully engaged in forum activities." [*Burger King*, 471 U.S. at 477-478.] . . .

. . . The stream of commerce refers not to unpredictable currents or eddies, but to the regular and anticipated flow of products from manufacture to distribution to retail sale. As long as a participant in this process is aware that the final product is being marketed in the forum State, the possibility of a lawsuit there cannot come as a surprise. Nor will the litigation present a burden for which there is no corresponding benefit. A defendant who has placed goods in the stream of commerce benefits economically from the retail sale of the final product in the forum State, and indirectly benefits from the State's laws that regulate and facilitate commercial activity. These benefits accrue regardless of whether that participant directly conducts business in the forum State, or engages in additional conduct directed toward that State. Accordingly, most courts and commentators have found that jurisdiction premised on the placement of a product into the stream of commerce is consistent with the Due Process Clause, and have not required a showing of additional conduct.

[Finally, JUSTICE STEVENS, joined by JUSTICES WHITE and BLACKMUN, wrote the following. — EDS.]

. . . [E]ven assuming [the validity of the stream-of-commerce-*plus* theory of the plurality, the opinion] misapplies it to the facts of this case. The plurality seems to assume that an unwavering line can be drawn between "mere awareness" that a component will find its way into the forum State and "purposeful availment" of the forum's market. Over the course of its dealings with Cheng Shin, Asahi has arguably engaged in a higher quantum of conduct than "[t]he placement of a product into the stream of commerce, without more. . . ." Whether or not this conduct rises to the level of purposeful availment requires a constitutional determination that is affected by the volume, the value, and the hazardous character of the components.

### Note: Foreign Corporations, Private and State-Owned

We know from *Asahi* that privately held foreign corporations may be subject to suit in American courts if the due process requirements set out in *International Shoe* are met. The Court is in disarray over how those requirements should apply to the case, but no one questions the amenability of a foreign corporation to suit in circumstances where it would be fundamentally fair.

Foreign governments, by contrast, are not "persons" protected by the Due Process Clause. So as long as the court has *subject matter* jurisdiction and the requirements of the Foreign Sovereign Immunities Act have been met, suits may be filed against them in American courts without worrying about personal jurisdiction. See Continental Transfert Technique, Ltd. v. Fed. Gov't of Nigeria, 697 F. Supp. 2d 46, 56 (D.D.C. 2010).

Much less obvious is how to treat state-owned corporations. In GSS Group Ltd. v. National Port Authority, 774 F. Supp. 2d 134 (D.D.C. 2011), a Liberian state-owned corporation moved to dismiss a suit brought to enforce a $44 million arbitration award. Noting that the port authority could sue and be sued "in its own name" in Liberia, is responsible for its own finances, receives no state subsidies, and exists primarily for "commercial" purposes, the court concluded that ordinary due process limits on the exercise of personal jurisdiction should apply: "Because the NPA does not possess the characteristics of a sovereign nation . . . it functions more like a private corporation than a foreign government for the purposes of a Fifth Amendment analysis. It therefore may not be haled into an American court without having a sufficient quantum of minimum contacts with the United States." Id. at 141. The court then dismissed the suit because the plaintiff made no showing that NPA had sufficient minimum contacts with the United States.

### Note: Criticism of Asahi

Commentators have been very critical of *Asahi*. The mixed messages of the split Court and the addition of factors that are not analytically distinct from minimum contacts are common grounds of the almost universal condemnation.

Another objection is that the plurality creates confusion in an effort to prevent jurisdictional surprise. Why should it be necessary, as Justice O'Connor suggests, that a component part manufacturer *do* something directed toward the forum? Why isn't actual or constructive awareness that the products reach the forum state enough?

A significant post-*Asahi* issue is whether the case modifies the stream of commerce analysis set forth in *World-Wide Volkswagen*. If a product exits the chain of distribution in the forum and causes injury there, are all parties "up the chain" amenable to process there? Or is some additional forum-directed conduct required, as Justice O'Connor suggests? For more than two decades, lawyers, lower courts, and law students (!) have lamented the confusion *Asahi* created. So when the Court granted certiorari in the following case in 2010, all were hopeful that the Court (or at least five Justices) would be prepared to speak with one voice. As you will read below, these hopes were unfulfilled.

## *J. McIntyre Machinery, Ltd. v. Nicastro*
564 U.S. 873 (2011)

JUSTICE KENNEDY announced the judgment and delivered the opinion of the Court, in which THE CHIEF JUSTICE, JUSTICE SCALIA, and JUSTICE THOMAS join.

. . . The rules and standards for determining when a State does or does not have jurisdiction over an absent party have been unclear because of decades-old questions left open in Asahi Metal Industry Co. v. Superior Court of Cal., Solano Cty., 480 U.S. 102 (1987).

Here, the Supreme Court of New Jersey, relying in part on *Asahi*, held that New Jersey's courts can exercise jurisdiction over a foreign manufacturer of a product so long as the manufacturer "knows or reasonably should know that its products are distributed through a nationwide distribution system that might lead to those products being sold in any of the fifty states." Nicastro v. McIntyre Machinery America, Ltd., 987 A.2d 575, 591, 592 (N.J. 2010). Applying that test, the court concluded that a British manufacturer of scrap metal machines was subject to jurisdiction in New Jersey, even though at no time had it advertised in, sent goods to, or in any relevant sense targeted the State.

That decision cannot be sustained. Although the New Jersey Supreme Court issued an extensive opinion with careful attention to this Court's cases and to its own precedent, the "stream of commerce" metaphor carried the decision far afield. Due process protects the defendant's right not to be coerced except by lawful judicial power. As a general rule, the exercise of judicial power is not lawful unless the defendant "purposefully avails itself of the privilege of conducting activities within the forum State, thus invoking the benefits and protections of its laws." Hanson v. Denckla, 357 U.S. 235, 253 (1958). There may be exceptions, say, for instance, in cases involving an intentional tort. But the general rule is applicable in this products-liability case, and the so-called "stream-of-commerce" doctrine cannot displace it.

**I**

This case arises from a products-liability suit filed in New Jersey state court. Robert Nicastro seriously injured his hand while using a metal-shearing machine manufactured by J. McIntyre Machinery, Ltd. (J. McIntyre). The accident occurred in New Jersey, but the machine was manufactured in England, where J. McIntyre is incorporated and operates. The question here is whether the New Jersey courts have jurisdiction over J. McIntyre, notwithstanding the fact that the company at no time either marketed goods in the State or shipped them there. Nicastro was a plaintiff in the New Jersey trial court and is the respondent here; J. McIntyre was a defendant and is now the petitioner.

At oral argument in this Court, Nicastro's counsel stressed three primary facts in defense of New Jersey's assertion of jurisdiction over J. McIntyre.

First, an independent company agreed to sell J. McIntyre's machines in the United States. J. McIntyre itself did not sell its machines to buyers in this country beyond the U.S. distributor, and there is no allegation that the distributor was under J. McIntyre's control.

Second, J. McIntyre officials attended annual conventions for the scrap recycling industry to advertise J. McIntyre's machines alongside the distributor. The conventions took place in various States, but never in New Jersey.

Third, no more than four machines (the record suggests only one), including the machine that caused the injuries that are the basis for this suit, ended up in New Jersey.

In addition to these facts emphasized by respondent, the New Jersey Supreme Court noted that J. McIntyre held both United States and European patents on its recycling technology. 987 A.2d, at 579. It also noted that the U.S. distributor "structured [its] advertising and sales efforts in accordance with" J. McIntyre's "direction and guidance whenever possible," and that "at least some of the machines were sold on consignment to" the distributor. 987 A.2d, at 579.

. . . Jurisdiction was proper, in [the state] court's view, because the injury occurred in New Jersey; because petitioner knew or reasonably should have known "that its products are distributed through a nationwide distribution system that might lead to those products being sold in any of the fifty states"; and because petitioner failed to "take some reasonable step to prevent the distribution of its products in this State." 987 A.2d, at 592.

Both the New Jersey Supreme Court's holding and its account of what it called "[t]he stream-of-commerce doctrine of jurisdiction," 987 A.2d, at 594, were incorrect, however. This Court's *Asahi* decision may be responsible in part for that court's error regarding the stream of commerce, and this case presents an opportunity to provide greater clarity.

## II

. . . As a general rule, neither statute nor judicial decree may bind strangers to the State. Cf. Burnham v. Superior Court of Cal., County of Marin, 495 U.S. 604, 608-609 (1990) (opinion of Scalia, J.) (invoking "the phrase *coram non judice,* 'before a person not a judge' — meaning, in effect, that the proceeding in question was not a *judicial* proceeding because lawful judicial authority was not present, and could therefore not yield a *judgment*.").

A court may subject a defendant to judgment only when the defendant has sufficient contacts with the sovereign "such that the maintenance of the suit does not offend traditional notions of fair play and substantial justice." International Shoe Co. v. Washington, 326 U.S. 310, 316 (1945). Free form notions of fundamental fairness divorced from traditional practice cannot transform a judgment rendered in the absence of authority into law. As a general rule, the sovereign's exercise of power requires some act by which the defendant "purposefully avails itself of the privilege of conducting activities within the forum State, thus invoking the benefits and protections of its laws," *Hanson*, 357 U.S., at 253, though in some cases, as with an intentional tort, the defendant might well fall within the State's authority by reason of his attempt to obstruct its laws. In products-liability cases like this one, it is the defendant's purposeful availment that makes jurisdiction consistent with "traditional notions of fair play and substantial justice."

A person may submit to a State's authority in a number of ways. There is, of course, explicit consent. *E.g.*, Insurance Corp. of Ireland v. Compagnie des Bauxites de Guinee, 456 U.S. 694, 703 (1982). Presence within a State at the time suit commences through service of process is another example. See *Burnham*. Citizenship or domicile—or, by analogy, incorporation or principal place of business for corporations—also indicates general submission to a State's powers. Goodyear Dunlop Tires Operations, S.A. v. Brown. Each of these examples reveals circumstances, or a course of conduct, from which it is proper to infer an intention to benefit from and thus an intention to submit to the laws of the forum State. These examples support exercise of the general jurisdiction of the State's courts and allow the State to resolve both matters that originate within the State and those based on activities and events elsewhere. Helicopteros Nacionales de Colombia, S.A. v. Hall, 466 U.S. 408, and n.9 (1984). By contrast, those who live or operate primarily outside a State have a due process right not to be subjected to judgment in its courts as a general matter.

There is also a more limited form of submission to a State's authority for disputes that "arise out of or are connected with the activities within the state." *International Shoe Co.*, supra, at 319. Where a defendant "purposefully avails itself of the privilege of conducting activities within the forum State, thus invoking the benefits and protections of its laws," *Hanson*, supra, at 253, it submits to the judicial power of an otherwise foreign sovereign to the extent that power is exercised in connection with the defendant's activities touching on the State. . . .

The imprecision arising from *Asahi*, for the most part, results from its statement of the relation between jurisdiction and the "stream of commerce." The stream of commerce, like other metaphors, has its deficiencies as well as its utility. It refers to the movement of goods from manufacturers through distributors to consumers, yet beyond that descriptive purpose its meaning is far from exact. This Court has stated that a defendant's placing goods into the stream of commerce "with the expectation that they will be purchased by consumers within the forum State" may indicate purposeful availment. World-Wide Volkswagen Corp. v. Woodson, 444 U.S. 286, 298 (1980) (finding that expectation lacking). But that statement does not amend the general rule of personal jurisdiction. It merely observes that a defendant may in an appropriate case be subject to jurisdiction without entering the forum—itself an unexceptional proposition—as where manufacturers or distributors "seek to serve" a given State's market. Id., at 295. The principal inquiry in cases of this sort is whether the defendant's activities manifest an intention to submit to the power of a sovereign. In other words, the defendant must "purposefully avai[l] itself of the privilege of conducting activities within the forum State, thus invoking the benefits and protections of its laws." *Hanson,* supra at 253; *Insurance Corp.,* supra, at 704-705 ("[A]ctions of the defendant may amount to a legal submission to the jurisdiction of the court"). Sometimes a defendant does so by sending its goods rather than its agents. The defendant's transmission of goods permits the exercise of jurisdiction only where the defendant can be said to have targeted the forum; as a general rule, it is not enough that the defendant might have predicted that its goods will reach the forum State.

In *Asahi,* an opinion by Justice Brennan for four Justices outlined a different approach. It discarded the central concept of sovereign authority in favor of considerations of fairness and foreseeability. As that concurrence contended, "jurisdiction premised on the placement of a product into the stream of commerce [without more] is consistent with the Due Process Clause," for "[a]s long as a participant in this process is aware that the final product is being marketed in the forum State, the possibility of a lawsuit there cannot come as a surprise." 480 U.S., at 117. It was the premise of the concurring opinion that the defendant's ability to anticipate suit renders the assertion of jurisdiction fair. In this way, the opinion made foreseeability the touchstone of jurisdiction.

The standard set forth in Justice Brennan's concurrence was rejected in an opinion written by Justice O'Connor; but the relevant part of that opinion, too, commanded the assent of only four Justices, not a majority of the Court. . . .

Since *Asahi* was decided, the courts have sought to reconcile the competing opinions. But Justice Brennan's concurrence, advocating a rule based on general notions of fairness and foreseeability, is inconsistent with the premises of lawful judicial power. This Court's precedents make clear that it is the defendant's actions, not his expectations, that empower a State's courts to subject him to judgment. . . .

Two principles are implicit in the foregoing. First, personal jurisdiction requires a forum-by-forum, or sovereign-by-sovereign, analysis. The question is whether a defendant has followed a course of conduct directed at the society or economy existing within the jurisdiction of a given sovereign, so that the sovereign has the power to subject the defendant to judgment concerning that conduct. Personal jurisdiction, of course, restricts "judicial power not as a matter of sovereignty, but as a matter of individual liberty," for due process protects the individual's right to be subject only to lawful power. *Insurance Corp.*, 456 U.S., at 702. But whether a judicial judgment is lawful depends on whether the sovereign has authority to render it.

The second principle is a corollary of the first. Because the United States is a distinct sovereign, a defendant may in principle be subject to the jurisdiction of the courts of the United States but not of any particular State. This is consistent with the premises and unique genius of our Constitution. Ours is "a legal system unprecedented in form and design, establishing two orders of government, each with its own direct relationship, its own privity, its own set of mutual rights and obligations to the people who sustain it and are governed by it." U.S. Term Limits, Inc. v. Thornton, 514 U.S. 779, 838 (1995) (Kennedy, J., concurring). For jurisdiction, a litigant may have the requisite relationship with the United States Government but not with the government of any individual State. That would be an exceptional case, however. If the defendant is a domestic domiciliary, the courts of its home State are available and can exercise general jurisdiction. And if another State were to assert jurisdiction in an inappropriate case, it would upset the federal balance, which posits that each State has a sovereignty that is not subject to unlawful intrusion by other States. Furthermore, foreign corporations will often target or concentrate on particular States, subjecting them to specific jurisdiction in those forums.

It must be remembered, however, that although this case and *Asahi* both involve foreign manufacturers, the undesirable consequences of Justice Brennan's approach are no less significant for domestic producers. The owner of a small Florida farm might sell crops to a large nearby distributor, for example, who might then distribute them to grocers across the country. If foreseeability were the controlling criterion, the farmer could be sued in Alaska or any number of other States' courts without ever leaving town. And the issue of foreseeability may itself be contested so that significant expenses are incurred just on the preliminary issue of jurisdiction. Jurisdictional rules should avoid these costs whenever possible. . . .

## III

. . . Here the question concerns the authority of a New Jersey state court to exercise jurisdiction, so it is petitioner's purposeful contacts with New Jersey, not with the United States, that alone are relevant.

Respondent has not established that J. McIntyre engaged in conduct purposefully directed at New Jersey. . . . The British manufacturer had no office in New Jersey; it neither paid taxes nor owned property there; and it neither advertised in, nor sent any employees to, the State. Indeed, after discovery the trial court found that the "defendant does not have a single contact with New Jersey short of the machine in question ending up in this state." These facts may reveal an intent to serve the U.S. market, but they do not show that J. McIntyre purposefully availed itself of the New Jersey market.

* * *

Due process protects petitioner's right to be subject only to lawful authority. At no time did petitioner engage in any activities in New Jersey that reveal an intent to invoke or benefit from the protection of its laws. New Jersey is without power to adjudge the rights and liabilities of J. McIntyre, and its exercise of jurisdiction would violate due process. The contrary judgment of the New Jersey Supreme Court is

*Reversed.*

JUSTICE BREYER, with whom JUSTICE ALITO joins, concurring in the judgment.

The Supreme Court of New Jersey adopted a broad understanding of the scope of personal jurisdiction based on its view that "[t]he increasingly fast-paced globalization of the world economy has removed national borders as barriers to trade." Nicastro v. McIntyre Machinery America, Ltd., 987 A.2d 575, 577 (2010). I do not doubt that there have been many recent changes in commerce and communication, many of which are not anticipated by our precedents. But this case does not present any of those issues. So I think it unwise to announce a rule of broad applicability without full consideration of the modern-day consequences. . . .

## I

. . . None of our precedents finds that a single isolated sale, even if accompanied by the kind of sales effort indicated here, is sufficient. Rather, this Court's previous holdings suggest the contrary. The Court has held that a single sale to a customer who takes an accident-causing product to a different State (where the accident takes place) is not a sufficient basis for asserting jurisdiction. See World-Wide Volkswagen Corp. v. Woodson, 444 U.S. 286 (1980). And the Court, in separate opinions, has strongly suggested that a single sale of a product in a State does not constitute an adequate basis for asserting jurisdiction over an out-of-state defendant, even if that defendant places his goods in the stream of commerce, fully aware (and hoping) that such a sale will take place. See Asahi Metal Industry Co. v. Superior Court of Cal., Solano Cty., 480 U.S. 102, 111, 112 (1987).

Here, the relevant facts found by the New Jersey Supreme Court show no "regular . . . flow" or "regular course" of sales in New Jersey; and there is no "something more," such as special state-related design, advertising, advice, marketing, or anything else. . . .

Accordingly, on the record present here, resolving this case requires no more than adhering to our precedents.

## II

### A

The plurality seems to state strict rules that limit jurisdiction where a defendant does not "inten[d] to submit to the power of a sovereign" and cannot "be said to have targeted the forum." But what do those standards mean when a company targets the world by selling products from its Web site? And does it matter if, instead of shipping the products directly, a company consigns the products through an intermediary (say, Amazon. com) who then receives and fulfills the orders? And what if the company markets its products through popup advertisements that it knows will be viewed in a forum? Those issues have serious commercial consequences but are totally absent in this case.

### B

But though I do not agree with the plurality's seemingly strict no-jurisdiction rule, I am not persuaded by the absolute approach adopted by the New Jersey Supreme Court and urged by respondent and his amici. Under that view, a producer is subject to jurisdiction for a products liability action so long as it "knows or reasonably should know that its products are distributed through a nationwide distribution system that might lead to those products being sold in any of the fifty states." 987 A.2d, at 592. In the context of this case, I cannot agree.

. . . I cannot reconcile so automatic a rule with the constitutional demand for "minimum contacts" and "purposefu[l] avail[ment]," each of which rest upon a particular notion of defendant-focused fairness. Id., at 291, 297. A rule like the New Jersey Supreme Court's would permit every State to assert jurisdiction in a products-liability suit against any domestic manufacturer who sells its products (made anywhere in the United States) to a national distributor, no matter how large or small the manufacturer, no matter how distant the forum, and no matter how few the number of items that end up in the particular forum at issue. What might appear fair in the case of a large manufacturer which specifically seeks, or expects, an equal-sized distributor to sell its product in a distant State might seem unfair in the case of a small manufacturer (say, an Appalachian potter) who sells his product (cups and saucers) exclusively to a large distributor, who resells a single item (a coffee mug) to a buyer from a distant State (Hawaii). I know too little about the range of these or in-between possibilities to abandon in favor of the more absolute rule what has previously been this Court's less absolute approach.

. . .

It may be that a larger firm can readily "alleviate the risk of burdensome litigation by procuring insurance, passing the expected costs on to customers, or, if the risks are too great, severing its connection with the State." *World-Wide Volkswagen*, supra, at 297. But manufacturers come in many shapes and sizes. It may be fundamentally unfair to require a small Egyptian shirt maker, a Brazilian manufacturing cooperative, or a Kenyan coffee farmer, selling its products through international distributors, to respond to products-liability tort suits in virtually every State in the United States, even those in respect to which the foreign firm has no connection at all but the sale of a single (allegedly defective) good. And a rule like the

New Jersey Supreme Court suggests would require every product manufacturer, large or small, selling to American distributors to understand not only the tort law of every State, but also the wide variance in the way courts within different States apply that law. See, e.g., Dept. of Justice, Bureau of Justice Statistics Bulletin, Tort Trials and Verdicts in Large Counties, 2001, p. 11 (reporting percentage of plaintiff winners in tort trials among 46 populous counties, ranging from 17.9% (Worcester, Mass.) to 69.1% (Milwaukee, Wis.)).

## C

. . . Accordingly, though I agree with the plurality as to the outcome of this case, I concur only in the judgment of that opinion and not its reasoning.

JUSTICE GINSBURG, with whom JUSTICE SOTOMAYOR and JUSTICE KAGAN join, dissenting.

A foreign industrialist seeks to develop a market in the United States for machines it manufactures. It hopes to derive substantial revenue from sales it makes to United States purchasers. Where in the United States buyers reside does not matter to this manufacturer. Its goal is simply to sell as much as it can, wherever it can. It excludes no region or State from the market it wishes to reach. But, all things considered, it prefers to avoid products liability litigation in the United States. To that end, it engages a U.S. distributor to ship its machines stateside. Has it succeeded in escaping personal jurisdiction in a State where one of its products is sold and causes injury or even death to a local user?

Under this Court's pathmarking precedent in International Shoe Co. v. Washington, 326 U.S. 310 (1945), and subsequent decisions, one would expect the answer to be unequivocally, "No." But instead, six Justices of this Court, in divergent opinions, tell us that the manufacturer has avoided the jurisdiction of our state courts, except perhaps in States where its products are sold in sizeable quantities. Inconceivable as it may have seemed yesterday, the splintered majority today "turn[s] the clock back to the days before modern long-arm statutes when a manufacturer, to avoid being haled into court where a user is injured, need only Pilate-like wash its hands of a product by having independent distributors market it." Weintraub, A Map Out of the Personal Jurisdiction Labyrinth, 28 U.C. Davis L. Rev. 531, 555 (1995).

## I

On October 11, 2001, a three-ton metal shearing machine severed four fingers on Robert Nicastro's right hand. Alleging that the machine was a dangerous product defectively made, Nicastro sought compensation from the machine's manufacturer, J. McIntyre Machinery Ltd. (McIntyre UK). Established in 1872 as a United Kingdom corporation, and headquartered in Nottingham, England, McIntyre UK "designs, develops and manufactures a complete range of equipment for metal recycling." The company's product line, as advertised on McIntyre UK's Web site, includes "metal shears, balers, cable and can recycling equipment, furnaces, casting equipment and . . . the world's best aluminium dross processing and cooling system." McIntyre UK holds both United States and European patents on its technology.

The machine that injured Nicastro, a "McIntyre Model 640 Shear," sold in the United States for $24,900 in 1995, and features a "massive cutting capacity." According to McIntyre UK's product brochure, the machine is "use[d] throughout the [w]orld." McIntyre UK represented in the brochure that, by "incorporat[ing] off-the-shelf hydraulic parts from suppliers with international sales outlets," the 640 Shear's design guarantees serviceability "wherever [its customers] may be based." The instruction manual advises "owner[s] and operators of a 640 Shear [to] make themselves aware of [applicable health and safety regulations]," including "the American National Standards Institute Regulations (USA) for the use of Scrap Metal Processing Equipment."

Nicastro operated the 640 Shear in the course of his employment at Curcio Scrap Metal (CSM) in Saddle Brook, New Jersey. "New Jersey has long been a hotbed of scrap-metal businesses. . . ." See Drake, The Scrap-Heap Rollup Hits New Jersey, Business News New Jersey, June 1, 1998, p. 1. In 2008, New Jersey recycling facilities processed 2,013,730 tons of scrap iron, steel, aluminum, and other metals—more than any other State—outpacing Kentucky, its nearest competitor, by nearly 30 percent. Von Haaren, Themelis, & Goldstein, The State of Garbage in America, BioCycle, Oct. 2010, p. 19.

CSM's owner, Frank Curcio, "first heard of [McIntyre UK's] machine while attending an Institute of Scrap Metal Industries [(ISRI)] convention in Las Vegas in 1994 or 1995, where [McIntyre UK] was an exhibitor." [Quoting complaint]. ISRI "presents the world's largest scrap recycling industry trade show each year." Id. The event attracts "owners [and] managers of scrap processing companies" and others "interested in seeing—and purchasing—new equipment." Id. According to ISRI, more than 3,000 potential buyers of scrap processing and recycling equipment attend its annual conventions, "primarily because th[e] exposition provides them with the most comprehensive industry-related shopping experience concentrated in a single, convenient location." Id. Exhibitors who are ISRI members pay $3,000 for 10' x 10' booth space. Id.

McIntyre UK representatives attended every ISRI convention from 1990 through 2005. Id. These annual expositions were held in diverse venues across the United States; in addition to Las Vegas, conventions were held 1990-2005 in New Orleans, Orlando, San Antonio, and San Francisco. Id. McIntyre UK's president, Michael Pownall, regularly attended ISRI conventions. Id. He attended ISRI's Las Vegas convention the year CSM's owner first learned of, and saw, the 640 Shear. Id. McIntyre UK exhibited its products at ISRI trade shows, the company acknowledged, hoping to reach "anyone interested in the machine from anywhere in the United States." Id.

Although McIntyre UK's U.S. sales figures are not in the record, it appears that for several years in the 1990's, earnings from sales of McIntyre UK products in the United States "ha[d] been good" in comparison to "the rest of the world." (Letter from Sally Johnson, McIntyre UK's Managing Director, to Gary and Mary Gaither, officers of McIntyre UK's exclusive distributor in the United States (Jan. 13, 1999)). In response to interrogatories, McIntyre UK stated that its commissioning engineer had installed the company's equipment in several States—Illinois, Iowa, Kentucky, Virginia, and Washington.

From at least 1995 until 2001, McIntyre UK retained an Ohio-based company, McIntyre Machinery America, Ltd. (McIntyre America), "as its exclusive distributor for the entire United States." *Nicastro*, 945 A.2d 92, 104. Though similarly named, the two companies were separate and independent entities with "no commonality of ownership or management." 945 A.2d, at 95. In invoices and other written communications, McIntyre America described itself as McIntyre UK's national distributor, "America's Link" to "Quality Metal Processing Equipment" from England.

In a November 23, 1999 letter to McIntyre America, McIntyre UK's president spoke plainly about the manufacturer's objective in authorizing the exclusive distributorship: "All we wish to do is sell our products in the [United] States—and get paid!" [Quoting Complaint.] Notably, McIntyre America was concerned about U.S. litigation involving McIntyre UK products, in which the distributor had been named as a defendant. McIntyre UK counseled McIntyre America to respond personally to the litigation, but reassured its distributor that "the product was built and designed by McIntyre Machinery in the UK and the buck stops here—if there's something wrong with the machine." Id. Answering jurisdictional interrogatories, McIntyre UK stated that it had been named as a defendant in lawsuits in Illinois, Kentucky, Massachusetts, and West Virginia. And in correspondence with McIntyre America, McIntyre UK noted that the manufacturer had products liability insurance coverage.

Over the years, McIntyre America distributed several McIntyre UK products to U.S. customers, including, in addition to the 640 Shear, McIntyre UK's "Niagara" and "Tardis" systems, wire strippers, and can machines. In promoting McIntyre UK's products at conventions and demonstration sites and in trade journal advertisements, McIntyre America looked to McIntyre UK for direction and guidance. To achieve McIntyre UK's objective, i.e., "to sell [its] machines to customers throughout the United States," *Nicastro*, 945 A.2d, at 97, "the two companies [were acting] closely in concert with each other," id., McIntyre UK never instructed its distributor to avoid certain States or regions of the country; rather, as just noted, the manufacturer engaged McIntyre America to attract customers "from anywhere in the United States."

In sum, McIntyre UK's regular attendance and exhibitions at ISRI conventions was surely a purposeful step to reach customers for its products "anywhere in the United States." At least as purposeful was McIntyre UK's engagement of McIntyre America as the conduit for sales of McIntyre UK's machines to buyers "throughout the United States." Given McIntyre UK's endeavors to reach and profit from the United States market as a whole, Nicastro's suit, I would hold, has been brought in a forum entirely appropriate for the adjudication of his claim. He alleges that McIntyre UK's shear machine was defectively designed or manufactured and, as a result, caused injury to him at his workplace. The machine arrived in Nicastro's New Jersey workplace not randomly or fortuitously, but as a result of the U.S. connections and distribution system that McIntyre UK deliberately arranged. On what sensible view of the allocation of adjudicatory authority could the place of Nicastro's injury within the United States be deemed off limits for his products liability claim against a foreign manufacturer who targeted the United States (including all the States that constitute the Nation) as the territory it sought to develop?

## II

A few points on which there should be no genuine debate bear statement at the outset. First, all agree, McIntyre UK surely is not subject to general (all-purpose) jurisdiction in New Jersey courts, for that foreign-country corporation is hardly "at home" in New Jersey. See Goodyear Dunlop Tires Operations, S.A. v. Brown. . . .

Second, no issue of the fair and reasonable allocation of adjudicatory authority among States of the United States is present in this case. New Jersey's exercise of personal jurisdiction over a foreign manufacturer whose dangerous product caused a workplace injury in New Jersey does not tread on the domain, or diminish the sovereignty, of any sister State. Indeed, among States of the United States, the State in which the injury occurred would seem most suitable for litigation of a products liability tort claim. See World-Wide Volkswagen Corp. v. Woodson, 444 U.S. 286, 297 (1980) (if a manufacturer or distributor endeavors to develop a market for a product in several States, it is reasonable "to subject it to suit in one of those States if its allegedly defective [product] has there been the source of injury"); 28 U.S.C. § 1391(a)-(b) (in federal-court suits, whether resting on diversity or federal-question jurisdiction, venue is proper in the judicial district "in which a substantial part of the events or omissions giving rise to the claim occurred").

Third, the constitutional limits on a state court's adjudicatory authority derive from considerations of due process, not state sovereignty. As the Court clarified in Insurance Corp. of Ireland v. Compagnie des Bauxites de Guinee, 456 U.S. 694 (1982):

> The restriction on state sovereign power described in *World-Wide Volkswagen Corp.* . . . must be seen as ultimately a function of the individual liberty interest preserved by the Due Process Clause. That Clause is the only source of the personal jurisdiction requirement and the Clause itself makes no mention of federalism concerns. Furthermore, if the federalism concept operated

> as an independent restriction on the sovereign power of the court, it would not be possible to waive the personal jurisdiction requirement: Individual actions cannot change the powers of sovereignty, although the individual can subject himself to powers from which he may otherwise be protected.

Id., at 703, n.10. See also Shaffer v. Heitner, 433 U.S. 186, and n.20 (1977) (recognizing that "the mutually exclusive sovereignty of the States [is not] the central concern of the inquiry into personal jurisdiction").

Finally, in *International Shoe* itself, and decisions thereafter, the Court has made plain that legal fictions, notably "presence" and "implied consent," should be discarded, for they conceal the actual bases on which jurisdiction rests. See 326 U.S., at 316, 318; Hutchinson v. Chase & Gilbert, 45 F.2d 139, 141 (2d Cir. 1930) (L. Hand, J.) ("nothing is gained by [resort to words that] concea[l] what we do"). "[T]he relationship among the defendant, the forum, and the litigation" determines whether due process permits the exercise of personal jurisdiction over a defendant, *Shaffer,* 433 U.S., at 204, and "fictions of implied consent" or "corporate presence" do not advance the proper inquiry, id., at 202.

Whatever the state of academic debate over the role of consent in modern jurisdictional doctrines, the plurality's notion that consent is the animating concept draws no support from controlling decisions of this Court. Quite the contrary, the Court has explained, a forum can exercise jurisdiction when its contacts with the controversy are sufficient; invocation of a fictitious consent, the Court has repeatedly said, is unnecessary and unhelpful. See, e.g., Burger King Corp. v. Rudzewicz, 471 U.S. 462, 472 (1985) (Due Process Clause permits "forum . . . to assert specific jurisdiction over an out-of-state defendant who has not consented to suit there"); McGee v. International Life Ins. Co., 355 U.S. 220, 222 (1957) ("[T]his Court [has] abandoned 'consent,' 'doing business,' and 'presence' as the standard for measuring the extent of state judicial power over [out-of-state] corporations.").

## III

This case is illustrative of marketing arrangements for sales in the United States common in today's commercial world. A foreign-country manufacturer engages a U.S. company to promote and distribute the manufacturer's products, not in any particular State, but anywhere and everywhere in the United States the distributor can attract purchasers. The product proves defective and injures a user in the State where the user lives or works. Often, as here, the manufacturer will have liability insurance covering personal injuries caused by its products. See Cupp, Redesigning Successor Liability, 1999 U. Ill. L. Rev. 845, 870-871 (noting the ready availability of products liability insurance for manufacturers and citing a study showing, "between 1986 and 1996, [such] insurance cost manufacturers, on average, only sixteen cents for each $100 of product sales").

. . . The modern approach to jurisdiction over corporations and other legal entities, ushered in by *International Shoe*, gave prime place to reason and fairness. Is it not fair and reasonable, given the mode of trading of which this case is an example, to require the international seller to defend at the place its products cause injury? Do not litigational convenience and choice-of-law considerations point in that direction? . . . Is not the burden on McIntyre UK to defend in New Jersey fair, i.e., a reasonable cost of transacting business internationally, in comparison to the burden on Nicastro to go to Nottingham, England to gain recompense for an injury he sustained using McIntyre's product at his workplace in Saddle Brook, New Jersey?

McIntyre UK dealt with the United States as a single market. Like most foreign manufacturers, it was concerned not with the prospect of suit in State X as opposed to State Y, but rather with its subjection to suit anywhere in the United States. . . . As a McIntyre UK officer wrote in an e-mail to McIntyre America: "American law—who needs it?!" (e-mail dated April 26, 1999 from Sally Johnson to Mary Gaither). . . .

In sum, McIntyre UK, by engaging McIntyre America to promote and sell its machines in the United States, "purposefully availed itself " of the United States market nationwide, not a market in a single State or a discrete collection of States. McIntyre UK thereby availed itself of the market of all States in which its products were sold by its exclusive distributor. "Th[e] 'purposeful availment' requirement," this Court has explained, simply "ensures that a defendant will not be haled into a jurisdiction solely as a result of 'random,' 'fortuitous,' or 'attenuated' contacts." *Burger King*, 471 U.S., at 475. Adjudicatory authority is appropriately exercised where "actions by the defendant *himself*" give rise to the affiliation with the forum. Id. How could McIntyre UK not have intended, by its actions targeting a national market, to sell products in the fourth largest destination for imports among all States of the United States and the largest scrap metal market?

Courts, both state and federal, confronting facts similar to those here, have rightly rejected the conclusion that a manufacturer selling its products across the USA may evade jurisdiction in any and all States, including the State where its defective product is distributed and causes injury. . . . See, e.g., Tobin v. Astra Pharmaceutical Prods., Inc., 993 F.2d 528, 544 (6th Cir. 1993); A. Uberti & C. v. Leonardo, 892 P.2d 1354, 1362 (1995).

## IV

### A

While this Court has not considered in any prior case the now-prevalent pattern presented here—a foreign-country manufacturer enlisting a U.S. distributor to develop a market in the United States for the manufacturer's products—none of the Court's decisions tug against the judgment made by the New Jersey Supreme Court. McIntyre contends otherwise, citing *World-Wide Volkswagen*, and *Asahi*.

. . . Notably, the foreign manufacturer of the Audi in *World-Wide Volkswagen* did not object to the jurisdiction of the Oklahoma courts and the U.S. importer abandoned its initially stated objection. 444 U.S., at 288, and n.3. And most relevant here, the Court's opinion indicates that an objection to jurisdiction by the manufacturer or national distributor would have been unavailing. . . .

. . . Asahi, unlike McIntyre UK, did not itself seek out customers in the United States, it engaged no distributor to promote its wares here, it appeared at no tradeshows in the United States, and, of course, it had no Web site advertising its products to the world. Moreover, Asahi was a component-part manufacturer with "little control over the final destination of its products once they were delivered into the stream of commerce." *A. Uberti*, 892 P.2d, at 1361. It was important to the Court in *Asahi* that "those who use Asahi components in their final products, and sell those products in California, [would be] subject to the application of California tort law." 480 U.S., at 115 (majority opinion). To hold that *Asahi* controls this case would, to put it bluntly, be dead wrong.

## B

The Court's judgment also puts United States plaintiffs at a disadvantage in comparison to similarly situated complainants elsewhere in the world. Of particular note, within the European Union, in which the United Kingdom is a participant, the jurisdiction New Jersey would have exercised is not at all exceptional. The European Regulation on Jurisdiction and the Recognition and Enforcement of Judgments provides for the exercise of specific jurisdiction "in matters relating to tort . . . in the courts for the place where the harmful event occurred." Council Reg. 44/2001, Art. 5, 2001 O.J. (L. 12) 4. The European Court of Justice has interpreted this prescription to authorize jurisdiction either where the harmful act occurred or at the place of injury. See Handelskwekerij G.J. Bier B.V. v. Mines de Potasse d'Alsace S.A., 1976 E. C. R. 1735, 1748-1749. . . .

\* \* \*

. . . While I dissent from the Court's judgment, I take heart that the plurality opinion does not speak for the Court, for that opinion would take a giant step away from the "notions of fair play and substantial justice" underlying *International Shoe*. 326 U.S., at 316.

## Notes and Questions

1. After more than 20 years and several new additions to the Court, not much has changed. As in *Asahi*, four Justices adhere to the requirement of purposeful availment. Brennan's stream of commerce analysis has lost a vote, but three Justices remain committed. And a most unlikely pair appear to think it was a mistake for the Court to have taken up the case at all.

2. In what may turn out to be a significant sentence, Justice Breyer signaled that he believes purposeful availment is a constitutionally required component of personal jurisdiction. But he also suggests that he thinks the plurality's approach is too strict, allowing companies with a global reach to avoid personal jurisdiction in fora where they should be held to suit.

Other aspects of the concurring opinion indicate that Justice Breyer may not have taken the opportunity to consider the details of the Court's earlier cases closely. He states that none of the Court's prior decisions uphold jurisdiction on the basis of a "single, isolated sale." He cites *World-Wide Volkswagen* to support this proposition, but that case turned heavily on the unilateral activity of the Robinsons—bringing the car to Oklahoma and then seeking to force the New York distributor and dealer to answer there. He does not cite *McGee*, which involved a single insurance policy issued in California by a Texas insurer. Nor does he cite Gray v. American Radiator and Sanitary Corp., in which the Illinois Supreme Court concluded Illinois courts could exercise jurisdiction over an Ohio valve manufacturer who made a defective valve that was incorporated into a water heater in Pennsylvania and subsequently sold in Illinois, where it exploded and injured the plaintiff. The case was cited by numerous state courts in the heyday of broad minimum contacts analysis. It was also cited prominently and favorably in the majority opinion of the Supreme Court in *World-Wide Volkswagen*. Justice White wrote:

> The forum State does not exceed its powers under the Due Process Clause if it asserts personal jurisdiction over a corporation that delivers its products into the stream of commerce with the expectation that they will be purchased by consumers in the forum State. Cf. Gray v. American Radiator & Standard Sanitary Corp., 22 Ill. 2d 432, 176 N.E.2d 761 (1961).

444 U.S. at 297-298.

Justice Breyer also rejects the approach taken by the New Jersey Supreme Court in part on the ground that it would subject producers to suit in any forum in which their products cause injury. He worries in particular about a small business being held to suit in a far-flung forum of an injured consumer's choosing. But, unlike McIntyre, a small business would have a strong argument that holding it to suit in a distant forum is unreasonable. Recall that there were eight votes in *Asahi* to deny personal jurisdiction on the ground that, whatever one thought of the company's contacts with California, holding it to suit there would be fundamentally unfair. Presumably, the claim of a small company would be stronger even if its contact with the forum was more direct than the indemnification dispute at issue in *Asahi*.

3. Is there another state that can exercise personal jurisdiction over McIntyre, or will plaintiffs have to hire a lawyer and sue in the United Kingdom? Consider McIntyre's relationship with its U.S. distributor. McIntyre has many contacts with the state in which its U.S. distributor has its principal place of business. McIntyre and its U.S. distributor are in relatively constant contact via e-mail, phone, and fax, and, as importantly,

they are presumably in a long-term contractual relationship. What about Nevada, where the company attends conventions to promote its machines?

4. The plurality goes out of its way to make foreseeability analysis seem unworkable by emphasizing what a company does — its intentional activity. But isn't foreseeability just a way of summarizing or inferring what a company knows based on what it does? If New Jersey recycling facilities process more scrap metal than any other state in the nation, and McIntyre machines end up in the state, it's reasonable to infer that McIntyre intends its machines to be sold there, or, if you like, it's foreseeable that its distributor will make sales there. Indeed, its U.S. distributor would likely be fired and replaced if it failed to make sales in New Jersey. And this is a much more predictable form of foreseeability than what troubled the Court in *World-Wide Volkswagen* (where the mobility of a car made the choices of a consumer much more relevant to the possible fora where suit could be brought than the choices and actions of the manufacturer).

5. Take a look again at the nature of the contacts in *International Shoe*, especially all the things the company did to avoid having a corporate presence in the state of Washington. Do you think that if the plurality in *Nicastro* were on the Court in 1945 it would have upheld the exercise of personal jurisdiction in that case? If your answer is yes, what contacts do you think are most salient?

6. *Nicastro* 2.0. The J. McIntyre Machinery company dissolved in 2013, but it split off its metal shearing manufacturing business into another entity called JMC, a foreign corporation with its principal place of business in, you guessed it, Nottingham, England. For at least a decade prior to acquiring McIntyre, JMC had a distribution agreement for all its U.S. sales with Strip Technology, a Texas corporation located in Fort Worth. JMC transferred title on all its metal shearing and other products by contract to Strip Technology. The two companies arranged for Strip Technology to receive payment for its services in England and JMC had no control or ownership interest in the distributor. One of JMC's metal shearing machines was sold by Strip Technology to a metal recycling facility in, you guessed it, New Jersey, where Anthony Benitez sustained severe injuries in 2011 while operating the machine. He sued JMC in federal court in New Jersey and JMC moved to dismiss for lack of personal jurisdiction, claiming it is a UK corporation with no assets, offices, employees, or business in the state of New Jersey. Benitez v. JMC Recycling Sys., Ltd., 97 F. Supp. 3d 576 (D.N.J. 2015). A company director filed a declaration adding that the company attends no trade shows in New Jersey and that no employees have traveled there to conduct business.

The court granted the motion to dismiss, reasoning that "[a]s in *Nicastro*, the facts here reveal only JMC's intent to serve the U.S. market . . . . Strip Technology, whose distribution relationship with JMC has apparently concluded, was not a subsidiary of JMC and the two entities shared no commonality of ownership or management. Further, Plaintiff does not allege that JMC directed Strip Technology to serve the New Jersey market in particular." Id. at 583. Under these circumstances, the court concluded, there was no evidence of purposeful availment. Although jurisdictional discovery is allowed under Third Circuit precedent unless the plaintiff's claim is "clearly frivolous," the court concluded it was not proper here because the plaintiff was unable to suggest "with reasonable particularity the possible existence of contacts" between JMC and New Jersey. Id. at 584.

For an example of a court taking account of the nature of the defendant's distribution channels and upholding personal jurisdiction, see Hart v. Bed Bath & Beyond, Inc., 48 F. Supp. 3d 837, 843 (D. Md. 2014) (specific personal jurisdiction over defendant Losorea Packaging grounded in part on company's reliance "on a clearly defined network of distributors for the ultimate sale of the [citronella eco-]fuel gel" alleged to have burned plaintiffs; even though Losorea Packaging did not personally make sales in Maryland, it bottled and packaged the fuel gel knowing that Bed Bath & Beyond (BBB) would sell the fuel gel in its stores, and BBB in fact sold 1,992 bottles of fuel gel in Maryland) ("The present case is not one in which a lone item or just a few items happened to wind up in this state. Instead, this case folds into the scenario portrayed by Justice Breyer, where a defendant, 'instead of shipping the products directly . . . consigns the product through an intermediary . . . who then receives and fulfills the orders.' . . . '[T]he distribution channel formed by [defendant] was intentionally established.'") (quoting *Nicastro* and circuit precedent); see also Gerk v. CL Med. SARL, 2016 WL 1259363 (C.D. Ill. 2016) (upholding specific personal jurisdiction against transnational defendant who sent multiple devices to Illinois hospitals, exhibited its products at Illinois conferences, and advertised in the state; although defendant had a U.S. distributor targeting the entire country, the defendant and distributor had a close relationship, including common ownership and management).

## 7.   Contacts and Contracts

The identity of the parties is a constant, though usually subtextual, issue in personal jurisdiction cases. As you look back on the cases, most of them deal with bringing a distant defendant to the plaintiff's home court. Add to the mix that the defendant is a multistate corporation and the plaintiff an injured individual, and you have a potent recipe for extending jurisdiction.

So far, we have dealt with fairness determinations after the fact; now we turn to the possibility of deciding in advance the location of some future lawsuit. Here, principles of contract law, as well as of waiver, enter the jurisdictional calculus. The identity of the parties remains important here as well, coming into play in the decisions about whether a contract was fair or fairly agreed to, or whether execution of its terms violates due process of law.

### *Burger King Corp. v. Rudzewicz*
471 U.S. 462 (1985)

JUSTICE BRENNAN delivered the opinion of the Court.

The State of Florida's long-arm statute extends jurisdiction to "[a]ny person, whether or not a citizen or resident of this state," who, *inter alia,* "[b]reach[es] a contract in this state by failing to perform acts required by the contract to be performed in this state," so long as the cause of action arises from the alleged contractual breach. Fla. Stat. § 48.193(1)(g) (Supp. 1984). The United States District Court for the Southern District of Florida, sitting in diversity, relied on this provision in exercising personal jurisdiction over a Michigan resident who allegedly had breached a franchise agreement with a Florida corporation by failing to make required payments in Florida. The question presented is whether this exercise of long-arm jurisdiction offended "traditional conception[s] of fair play and substantial justice" embodied in the Due Process Clause of the Fourteenth Amendment. International Shoe Co. v. Washington, 326 U.S. 310, 320 (1945).

# I

## A

Burger King Corporation is a Florida corporation whose principal offices are in Miami. It is one of the world's largest restaurant organizations, with over 3,000 outlets in the 50 States, the Commonwealth of Puerto Rico, and 8 foreign nations. Burger King conducts approximately 80% of its business through a franchise operation that the company styles the "Burger King System"—"a comprehensive restaurant format and operating system for the sale of uniform and quality food products." Burger King licenses its franchisees to use its trademarks and service marks for a period of 20 years and leases standardized restaurant facilities to them for the same term. In addition, franchisees acquire a variety of proprietary information concerning the "standards, specifications, procedures and methods for operating a Burger King Restaurant." They also receive market research and advertising assistance, ongoing training in restaurant management,[2] and accounting, cost-control, and inventory-control guidance. By permitting franchisees to tap into Burger King's established national reputation and to benefit from proven procedures for dispensing standardized fare, this system enables them to go into the restaurant business with significantly lowered barriers to entry.

In exchange for these benefits, franchisees pay Burger King an initial $40,000 franchise fee and commit themselves to payment of monthly royalties, advertising and sales promotion fees, and rent computed in part from monthly gross sales. Franchisees also agree to submit to the national organization's exacting regulation of virtually every conceivable aspect of their operations. Burger King imposes these standards and undertakes its rigid regulation out of conviction that "[u]niformity of service, appearance, and

---

2. Mandatory training seminars are conducted at Burger King University in Miami and at Whopper College Regional Training Centers around the country.

quality of product is essential to the preservation of the Burger King image and the benefits accruing therefrom to both Franchisee and Franchisor."

Burger King oversees its franchise system through a two-tiered administrative structure. The governing contracts provide that the franchise relationship is established in Miami and governed by Florida law, and call for payment of all required fees and forwarding of all relevant notices to the Miami headquarters. The Miami headquarters sets policy and works directly with its franchisees in attempting to resolve major problems. Day-to-day monitoring of franchisees, however, is conducted through a network of 10 district offices which in turn report to the Miami headquarters.

The instant litigation grows out of Burger King's termination of one of its franchisees, and is aptly described by the franchisee as "a divorce proceeding among commercial partners." The appellee John Rudzewicz, a Michigan citizen and resident, is the senior partner in a Detroit accounting firm. In 1978, he was approached by Brian MacShara, the son of a business acquaintance, who suggested that they jointly apply to Burger King for a franchise in the Detroit area. MacShara proposed to serve as the manager of the restaurant if Rudzewicz would put up the investment capital; in exchange, the two would evenly share the profits. Believing that MacShara's idea offered attractive investment and tax-deferral opportunities, Rudzewicz agreed to the venture.

Rudzewicz and MacShara jointly applied for a franchise to Burger King's Birmingham, Michigan, district office in the autumn of 1978. The application was forwarded to Burger King's Miami headquarters, which entered into a preliminary agreement with them in February 1979. During the ensuing four months it was agreed that Rudzewicz and MacShara would assume operation of an existing facility in Drayton Plains, Michigan. MacShara attended the prescribed management courses in Miami during this period, see no. 2, supra, and the franchisees purchased $165,000 worth of restaurant equipment from Burger King's Davmor Industries division in Miami. Even before the final agreements were signed, however, the parties began to disagree. . . . During these disputes Rudzewicz and MacShara negotiated both with the Birmingham district office and with the Miami headquarters.[7] With some misgivings, Rudzewicz and MacShara finally obtained limited concessions from the Miami headquarters,[8] signed the final agreements, and commenced operations in June 1979. By signing the final agreements, Rudzewicz obligated himself personally to payments exceeding $1 million over the 20-year franchise relationship.

7. Although Rudzewicz and MacShara dealt with the Birmingham district office on a regular basis, they communicated directly with the Miami headquarters in forming the contracts; moreover, they learned that the district office had "very little" decision-making authority and accordingly turned directly to headquarters in seeking to resolve their disputes.

8. They were able to secure a $10,439 reduction in rent for the third year.

The Drayton Plains facility apparently enjoyed steady business during the summer of 1979, but patronage declined after a recession began later that year. Rudzewicz and MacShara soon fell far behind in their monthly payments to Miami. Headquarters sent notices of default, and an extended period of negotiations began among the franchisees, the Birmingham district office, and the Miami headquarters. After several Burger King officials in Miami had engaged in prolonged but ultimately unsuccessful negotiations with the franchisees by mail and by telephone,[9] headquarters terminated the franchise and ordered Rudzewicz and MacShara to vacate the premises. They refused and continued to occupy and operate the facility as a Burger King restaurant.

## B

Burger King commenced the instant action in the United States District Court for the Southern District of Florida in May 1981. . . . Burger King alleged that Rudzewicz and MacShara had breached their franchise obligations "within [the jurisdiction of] this district court" by failing to make the required payments "at plaintiff's place of business in Miami, Dade Country, Florida," and also charged that they were tortiously infringing its trademarks and service marks through their continued, unauthorized operation as a Burger King restaurant. Burger King sought damages, injunctive relief, and costs and attorney's fees. Rudzewicz and MacShara entered special appearances and argued, *inter alia,* that because they were Michigan residents and because Burger King's claim did not "arise" within the Southern District of Florida, the District Court lacked personal jurisdiction over them. The District Court denied their motions after a hearing, holding that, pursuant to Florida's long-arm statute, "a non-resident Burger King franchisee is subject to the personal jurisdiction of this Court in actions arising out of its franchise agreements." . . .

After a 3-day bench trial, the court again concluded that it had "jurisdiction over the subject matter and the parties to this cause." Finding that Rudzewicz and MacShara had breached their franchise agreements with Burger King and had infringed Burger King's trademarks and service marks, the court entered judgment against them, jointly and severally, for $228,875 in contract damages. The court also ordered them "to immediately close Burger King Restaurant Number 775 from continued operation or to immediately give the keys and possession of said restaurant to Burger King Corporation," found that they had failed to prove any of the required

---

9. Miami's policy was to "deal directly" with franchisees when they began to encounter financial difficulties, and to involve district office personnel only when necessary. In the instant case, for example, the Miami office handled all credit problems, ordered cost-cutting measures, negotiated for a partial refinancing of the franchisees' debts, communicated directly with the franchisees in attempting to resolve the dispute, and was responsible for all termination matters.

elements of their counterclaim, and awarded costs and attorney's fees to Burger King.

Rudzewicz appealed to the Court of Appeals for the Eleventh Circuit.[11] A divided panel of that Circuit reversed the judgment, concluding that the District Court could not properly exercise personal jurisdiction over Rudzewicz pursuant to Fla. Stat. § 48.193(1)(g) (Supp. 1984) because "the circumstances of the Drayton Plains franchise and the negotiations which led to it left Rudzewicz bereft of reasonable notice and financially unprepared for the prospect of franchise litigation in Florida." Burger King Corp. v. MacShara, 724 F.2d 1505, 1513 (1984). Accordingly, the panel majority concluded that "[j]urisdiction under these circumstances would offend the fundamental fairness which is the touchstone of due process." Ibid. . . .

## II

### A

The Due Process Clause protects an individual's liberty interest in not being subject to the binding judgments of a forum with which he has established no meaningful "contacts, ties, or relations." International Shoe Co. v. Washington, 326 U.S., at 319.[13] . . .

Where a forum seeks to assert specific jurisdiction over an out-of-state defendant who has not consented to suit there this "fair warning" requirement is satisfied if the defendant has "purposefully directed" his activities at residents of the forum, Keeton v. Hustler Magazine, Inc., 465 U.S. 770, 774 (1984). . . . And with respect to interstate contractual obligations, we have emphasized that parties who "reach out beyond one state and create continuing relationships and obligations with citizens of another state" are subject to regulation and sanctions in the other State for the consequences of their activities. . . .

Jurisdiction in these circumstances may not be avoided merely because the defendant did not *physically* enter the forum State. Although territorial presence frequently will enhance a potential defendant's affiliation with a State and reinforce the reasonable foreseeability of suit there, it is an inescapable fact of modern commercial life that a substantial amount of business is transacted solely by mail and wire communications across state lines, thus obviating the need for physical presence within a State in which

11. MacShara did not appeal his judgment. See Burger King Corp. v. MacShara, 724 F.2d 1505, 1506, n.1 (11th Cir. 1984). In addition, Rudzewicz entered into a compromise with Burger King and waived his right to appeal the District Court's finding of trademark infringement and its entry of injunctive relief. . . .

13. Although this protection operates to restrict state power, it "must be seen as ultimately a function of the individual liberty interest preserved by the Due Process Clause" rather than as a function "of federalism concerns." Insurance Corp. of Ireland v. Compagnie des Bauxites de Guinee, 456 U.S. 694, 702-703, n.10 (1982).

business is conducted. So long as a commercial actor's efforts are "purposefully directed" toward residents of another State, we have consistently rejected the notion that an absence of physical contacts can defeat personal jurisdiction there. Keeton v. Hustler Magazine, Inc., supra. . . .

## B

. . . [W]e believe there is substantial record evidence supporting the District Court's conclusion that the assertion of personal jurisdiction over Rudzewicz in Florida for the alleged breach of his franchise agreement did not offend due process. . . .

In this case, no physical ties to Florida can be attributed to Rudzewicz other than MacShara's brief training course in Miami. Rudzewicz did not maintain offices in Florida and, for all that appears from the record, has never even visited there. Yet this franchise dispute grew directly out of "a contact which had a *substantial* connection with that State." McGee v. International Life Insurance Co., 355 U.S. at 223 (emphasis added). Eschewing the option of operating an independent local enterprise, Rudzewicz deliberately "reach[ed] out beyond" Michigan and negotiated with a Florida corporation for the purchase of a long-term franchise and the manifold benefits that would derive from affiliation with a nationwide organization. Upon approval, he entered into a carefully structured 20-year relationship that envisioned continuing and wide-reaching contacts with Burger King in Florida. . . .

The Court of Appeals concluded, however, that in light of the supervision emanating from Burger King's district office in Birmingham, Rudzewicz reasonably believed that "the Michigan office was for all intents and purposes the embodiment of Burger King" and that he therefore had no "reason to anticipate a Burger King suit outside of Michigan." 724 F.2d at 511.

This reasoning overlooks substantial record evidence indicating that Rudzewicz most certainly knew that he was affiliating himself with an enterprise based primarily in Florida. The contract documents themselves emphasize that Burger King's operations are conducted and supervised from the Miami headquarters, that all relevant notices and payments must be sent there, and that the agreements were made in and enforced from Miami. Moreover, the parties' actual course of dealing repeatedly confirmed that decisionmaking authority was vested in the Miami headquarters and that the district office served largely as an intermediate link between the headquarters and the franchisees. When problems arose over building design, site-development fees, rent computation, and the defaulted payments, Rudzewicz and MacShara learned that the Michigan office was powerless to resolve their disputes and could only channel their communications to Miami. Throughout these disputes, the Miami headquarters and the Michigan franchisees carried on a continuous course of direct communications by mail and by telephone, and it was the Miami headquarters that made the key negotiating decisions out of which the instant litigation arose.

Moreover, we believe the Court of Appeals gave insufficient weight to provisions in the various franchise documents providing that all disputes would be governed by Florida law. The franchise agreement, for example, stated:

> This Agreement shall become valid when executed and accepted by BKC at Miami, Florida; it shall be deemed made and entered into in the State of Florida and shall be governed and construed under and in accordance with the laws of the State of Florida. The choice of law designation does not require that all suits concerning this Agreement be filed in Florida.

The Court of Appeals reasoned that choice-of-law provisions are irrelevant to the question of personal jurisdiction. . . . Nothing in our cases . . . suggests that a choice-of-law *provision* should be ignored in considering whether a defendant has "purposefully invoked the benefits and protections of a State's laws" for jurisdictional purposes. Although such a provision standing alone would be insufficient to confer jurisdiction, we believe that, when combined with the 20-year interdependent relationship Rudzewicz established with Burger King's Miami headquarters, it reinforced his deliberate affiliation with the forum State and the reasonable foreseeability of possible litigation there. As Judge Johnson argued in his dissent below, Rudzewicz "purposefully availed himself of the benefits and protections of Florida's laws" by entering into contracts expressly providing that those laws would govern franchise disputes.[24]

Nor has Rudzewicz pointed to other factors that can be said persuasively to outweigh the considerations discussed above and to establish the *unconstitutionality* of Florida's assertion of jurisdiction. We cannot conclude that Florida had no "legitimate interest in holding [Rudzewicz] answerable on a claim related to" the contacts he had established in that State.[25] Moreover, although Rudzewicz has argued at some length that Michigan's Franchise Investment Law, Mich. Comp. Laws §§ 445.1501 et seq. (1979), governs many aspects of this franchise relationship, he has not demonstrated how Michigan's acknowledged interest might possibly render jurisdiction in Florida *unconstitutional*. Finally, the Court of Appeals' assertion that the

---

24. . . . The lease also provided for binding arbitration in Miami of certain condemnation disputes, and Rudzewicz conceded the validity of this provision at oral argument. Although it does not govern the instant dispute, this provision also should have made it apparent to the franchisees that they were dealing directly with the Miami headquarters and that the Birmingham district office was *not* "for all intents and purposes the embodiment of Burger King."

25. Complaining that "when Burger King is the plaintiff, you won't 'have it your way' because it sues all franchisees in Miami," Rudzewicz contends that Florida's interest in providing a convenient forum is negligible given the company's size and ability to conduct litigation anywhere in the country. We disagree. Absent compelling considerations, a defendant who has purposefully derived commercial benefit from his affiliations in a forum may not defeat jurisdiction there simply because of his adversary's greater net wealth.

Florida litigation "severely impaired [Rudzewicz's] ability to call Michigan witnesses who might be essential to his defense and counterclaim," 724 F.2d at 1511-1512, and n.10, is wholly without support in the record. And even to the extent that it is inconvenient for a party who has minimum contacts with a forum to litigate there, such considerations most frequently can be accommodated through a change of venue. Although the Court has suggested that inconvenience may at some point become so substantial as to achieve *constitutional* magnitude, this is not such a case.

The Court of Appeals also concluded, however, that the parties' dealings involved "a characteristic disparity of bargaining power" and "elements of surprise," and that Rudzewicz "lacked fair notice" of the potential for litigation in Florida because the contractual provisions suggesting to the contrary were merely "boilerplate declarations in a lengthy printed contract." United States v. United States Gypsum Co., 333 U.S. 364, 395 (1948). Rudzewicz presented many of these arguments to the District Court, contending that Burger King was guilty of misrepresentation, fraud, and duress; that it gave insufficient notice in its dealings with him; and that the contract was one of adhesion. After a 3-day bench trial, the District Court found that Burger King had made no misrepresentations, that Rudzewicz and MacShara "were and are experienced and sophisticated businessmen," and that "at no time" did they "ac[t] under economic duress or disadvantage imposed by" Burger King. . . . Federal Rule of Civil Procedure 52(a) requires that "[f]indings of fact shall not be set aside unless clearly erroneous,"* and neither Rudzewicz nor the Court of Appeals has pointed to record evidence that would support a "definite and firm conviction" that the District Court's findings are mistaken. To the contrary, Rudzewicz was represented by counsel throughout these complex transactions and, as Judge Johnson observed in dissent below, was himself an experienced accountant "who for five months conducted negotiations with Burger King over the terms of the franchise and lease agreements, and who obligated himself personally to contracts requiring over time payments that exceeded $1 million." 724 F.2d at 1514. Rudzewicz was able to secure a modest reduction in rent and other concessions from Miami headquarters[;] moreover, to the extent that Burger King's terms were inflexible, Rudzewicz presumably decided that the advantages of affiliating with a national organization provided sufficient commercial benefits to offset the detriments.

## III

Notwithstanding these considerations, the Court of Appeals apparently believed that it was necessary to reject jurisdiction in this case as a prophylactic measure, reasoning that an affirmance of the District Court's

---

* [The restyled Rule 52(a) provides that, "Findings of fact, whether based on oral or other evidence, must not be set aside unless clearly erroneous, and the reviewing court must give due regard to the trial court's opportunity to judge the witnesses' credibility." Eds.]

judgment would result in the exercise of jurisdiction over "out-of-state consumers to collect payments due on modest personal purchases" and would "sow the seeds of default judgments against franchisees owing smaller debts." Kulko v. Superior Court, 436 U.S. 84, 92 (1978). We share the Court of Appeals' broader concerns and therefore reject any talismanic jurisdictional formulas; "the facts of each case must [always] be weighed" in determining whether personal jurisdiction would comport with "fair play and substantial justice." . . .

. . . The judgment of the Court of Appeals is accordingly reversed, and the case is remanded for further proceedings consistent with this opinion.

*It is so ordered.*

JUSTICE POWELL took no part in the consideration or decision of this case.
JUSTICE STEVENS, with whom JUSTICE WHITE joins, dissenting.

In my opinion there is a significant element of unfairness in requiring a franchisee to defend a case of this kind in the forum chosen by the franchisor. It is undisputed that appellee maintained no place of business in Florida, that he had no employees in that State, and that he was not licensed to do business there. Appellee did not prepare his French fries, shakes, and hamburgers in Michigan, and then deliver them into the stream of commerce "with the expectation that they [would] be purchased by consumers in" Florida. To the contrary, appellee did business only in Michigan, his business, property, and payroll taxes were payable in that State, and he sold all of his products there.

Throughout the business relationship, appellee's principal contacts with appellant were with its Michigan office. Notwithstanding its disclaimer, the Court seems ultimately to rely on nothing more than standard boilerplate language contained in various documents to establish that appellee "'purposefully availed himself of the benefits and protections of Florida's laws.'" Such superficial analysis creates a potential for unfairness not only in negotiations between franchisors and their franchisees but, more significantly, in the resolution of the disputes that inevitably arise from time to time in such relationships. . . .

Accordingly, I respectfully dissent.

## Notes and Questions

1. *Burger King* followed after the signal in *World-Wide Volkswagen* to retract the long arm, yet it is fairly unrestrained in its explication of Florida's interest. Although suit was filed in a federal district court, the governing law is the Florida long-arm statute. This occurs by operation of Fed. R. Civ. P. 4.

Read Rule 4 and think about whether the federal courts are entitled to extend their reach beyond that of the state in which they sit. Could there be nationwide service of process by federal courts, without regard to the jurisdictional boundaries of individual states? Note that one congressional act, the interpleader statute, provides that a federal court subpoena may reach any state. 28 U.S.C. § 2361.

Given that federal courts in some cases thus have broader service reach than any state court, should parties' reasonable expectations of being haled into a foreign court extend to this broadest range whenever the matter could be filed in federal court?

2. *Burger King* offers some guidance for future cases in which a plaintiff seeks to sue a nonresident defendant in a contract dispute. The Court identifies several factors to consider. These factors fall into two groups: those that are contained within the contract itself and those that are external to the contract. As to the first group, what contract terms would improve the chances that a party to the contract would be amenable to process in a particular jurisdiction? Post–*Burger King,* what changes do you imagine occurred in contract negotiations among sophisticated commercial actors?

3. Is there reason to believe that a nonresident seller is more vulnerable to jurisdiction in the state where the buyer lives than a nonresident buyer is in the state where the seller lives? Think about the problem case of Durand v. Intact Hearing, below, and the effect of *Burger King* on actions brought by a seller of goods against a stay-at-home individual consumer.

In Quill v. North Dakota, 504 U.S. 298 (1992), the U.S. Supreme Court held that a nonresident mail order firm was amenable to process in a suit to collect a sales-type tax from the firm. Although the firm had no office, plant, or salespeople there, it mailed catalogues and items worth millions of dollars in annual sales to North Dakota customers. What if one of the consumers failed to pay her bill? Would she be amenable to process in the state where the mail order firm is located? Is an L.L. Bean customer at risk of suit in Freeport, Maine?

4. Whether you think *Burger King* was correctly decided depends partly on whether you see Rudzewicz and MacShara as competent commercial actors or two little guys from Detroit. In this regard, consider the remark of a civil procedure student at Stanford in Fall 1993:

> I found the two perspectives of the Burger King restaurant in Michigan interesting. The corporation itself viewed the restaurant as part of a large chain with specific quality control measures, price standards, and a uniform nationwide reputation to preserve. The dissent viewed the restaurant as "a local concern serving, at best, a neighborhood or a community." I relate to the latter since I live in an urban area where you can walk from one Burger King to another. Although you can get the same food at another Burger King, the one in your neighborhood is *your* Burger King.

## 8.  Persons or Property Within the State

### Problem Case: Just Passing Through

You are an associate with a law firm in San Jose, California. As part of your firm's pro bono obligation, you take on the defense of a case against a local 70-year-old widow, Dinah Durand. Durand was recently served with a summons while sitting in the Phoenix, Arizona, airport en route to her brother's funeral in Richmond, Virginia. The plaintiff is Intact Hearing, Inc., based in Phoenix.

The complaint correctly alleges that Dinah Durand ordered from Intact an in-ear hearing aid, but paid only one installment: the one that accompanied her order. The cost of the hearing aid was $1,200, payable in 12 monthly installments.

You learn that Durand ordered the hearing aid by mail after seeing it advertised on television as a "revolutionary new break-through." But when it arrived, she was extremely disappointed to find that, in her words, "it was a piece of plastic junk that made things louder but not clearer." Along with the aid, she received a piece of paper labeled Acceptance of Order and 11 payment envelopes. The Acceptance form had a schedule of payments due and in large letters at the top stated "Arizona Courts Have Jurisdiction over Any Disputes Under This Agreement." All payments, like the first, were to be mailed to the company in Phoenix, Arizona.

Durand sent the hearing aid back in one of the envelopes provided for the monthly payments and simply threw away all further correspondence from the company. After nine months of this, a company representative telephoned her and warned that if she did not pay the balance due within seven days, she would be sued. Durand told the representative that she had sent the aid back and that he wouldn't be able to sue her in any event because she was leaving the next morning at 6:05 A.M. for Richmond, Virginia, and wouldn't be back for more than seven days. The company representative happened to know that there was a 6:05 flight from San Jose, California, to Richmond that had a plane change in Phoenix. With a quick call to a travel agent, he confirmed that this was the only 6:05 flight to Richmond originating from an airport in or near San Jose.

The company representative passed this information on to the company lawyers and told them as well that "she claims to have returned the aid, but that's what they all say." Since it was already afternoon, the lawyers decided not to institute a search of the company's mail room or to talk to the mail room personnel, but instead quickly filled in Durand's name and the relevant dates on their form complaint, filed it in the Arizona district court (the state trial court), and hired a process server to deliver the complaint and summons to Dinah Durand during her stop-over in Phoenix. She says she was humiliated when a beefy red-faced man thrust the papers at her and said loudly: "Here's a complaint against you, lady. I guess you can hear that."

Assume that the Arizona long-arm provision reads as stated on p. 136 above in the problem case of the "Troubled Young Man."

What would be your advice to Ms. Durand? Do you have legitimate objections to the exercise of personal jurisdiction by Arizona? Would you raise them by motion or by taking a default judgment in Arizona? What policy considerations and other considerations would enter your decision about how and whether to object to personal jurisdiction? How would you raise them?

If you were an appellate judge deciding whether jurisdiction was properly exercised, how would you vote, and why?

*International Shoe* and all its case and statute progeny explicitly and implicitly rejected the principle that presence of the defendant or his property was *essential* for jurisdiction. Unanswered for many years, and still not definitively decided, was whether the presence of either is *sufficient* for the constitutional exercise of jurisdiction.

Recall that under *Pennoyer*, both types of presence-based jurisdiction were constitutional. Presence of a person in the forum—sometimes called "transient" or "gotcha" jurisdiction—would suffice for any lawsuit against the defendant, even if the defendant had no other ties to the state and the lawsuit arose out of activities elsewhere. Moreover, the jurisdiction over the defendant would be general, which in this context means that the defendant's liability would extend to the full value of her (nonexempt) assets.

Presence of a person's property (not self) in the forum was also sufficient for jurisdiction under *Pennoyer*. But the defendant's liability in a case based on attachment of property—called "attachment jurisdiction"—typically was limited to the value of the property attached. Thus the defendant's financial exposure was more limited than if she were physically present and served during the forum visit (though in some states the moment the defendant appeared to defend against that attachment she was deemed to "consent" to *in personam* and thus general jurisdiction over her).

The following chart outlines the four ways in which a court might attempt to obtain jurisdiction over a nonresident:

| *In personam (person-based)* | *Quasi in rem, in rem (property-based)* |
|---|---|
| 1. Nonresident served outside the forum | 3. Attachment of property unrelated to lawsuit |
| 2. Nonresident served within the forum | 4. Attachment of property related to lawsuit |

We have already addressed in depth the post-*Pennoyer* response to the first category, that is, lawsuits in which a nonresident is served outside the forum. The statutory and case law developments from *International Shoe* onward established that jurisdiction over the nonresident will be constitutional if the defendant has minimum contacts with the forum and it is reasonable for the court to assert jurisdiction.

At the same time, most legal actors assumed that minimum contacts provided an alternative to traditional territorial jurisdiction—that *in rem* and *quasi in rem* jurisdiction were essentially unaffected by modern notions of fair play and substantial justice. The great expansions of state court jurisdiction took place on a track that paralleled traditional territorial authority over property.

But in a pattern similar to the pressure put on territoriality by the development of the automobile and the corporation, new forms of highly mobile property whose situs was uncertain finally brought the due process analysis of *International Shoe* to bear on the *quasi in rem* hybrid jurisdiction. Shaffer v. Heitner, 433 U.S. 186 (1977), overruled *Pennoyer* in so many words and held that *"all assertions of state-court jurisdiction must be evaluated according to the standards set forth in* International Shoe *and its progeny. . . ."* Id. at 212 (emphasis added). A Delaware statute permitted its state courts to take jurisdiction of a case where the plaintiff sequestered any property of the defendant located within the state. The plaintiff in *Shaffer* filed a shareholder derivative suit against Greyhound bus line and officers and directors of the company, asserting jurisdiction by sequestering and preventing the transfer of 82,000 common stock and options of the corporation. That was made possible not because the stock was "in" Delaware, but rather because Delaware corporations law treated the stock of any Delaware corporation as formally in the state. The Supreme Court rejected this theory of jurisdiction, finding no minimum contacts because the defendants had never set foot in Delaware and no elements of the cause of action took place in Delaware. The mere statutory "presence" of the stock in the state was insufficient.

For the first time, minimum contacts provided the basis for *limiting*, rather than expanding, traditional bases of jurisdiction. After *Shaffer* was decided, Delaware enacted a new law that afforded its courts jurisdiction over officers and directors of Delaware corporations in cases related to their corporate activities. 10 Del. Code § 3114. Is that statute constitutional? That is, are these contacts always sufficient for the assertion of specific jurisdiction by a Delaware court? See Armstrong v. Pomerance, 423 A.2d 174 (Del. 1980) (holding the statute is constitutional).

The Court's logic in *Shaffer* suggested that a nonresident who is served within the forum *cannot* be amenable to process there *unless* she has "minimum contacts" with the state. Read on, and see how *Shaffer* forms the historical backdrop for the surprising decision of Burnham v. Superior Court. *Burnham* dealt with category two—*in personam* jurisdiction based on physical presence in the forum. *Shaffer* dealt with category three and, by implication, category four—jurisdiction based on the presence of property related to the lawsuit.

### Burnham v. Superior Court
495 U.S. 604 (1990)

JUSTICE SCALIA announced the judgment of the Court and delivered an opinion in which CHIEF JUSTICE REHNQUIST and JUSTICE KENNEDY join, and in which JUSTICE WHITE joins with respect to Parts I, II-A, II-B, and II-C.

The question presented is whether the Due Process Clause of the Fourteenth Amendment denies California courts jurisdiction over a nonresident, who was personally served with process while temporarily in that State, in a suit unrelated to his activities in the State.

## I

Petitioner Dennis Burnham married Francie Burnham in 1976, in West Virginia. In 1977, the couple moved to New Jersey, where their two children were born. In July 1987, the Burnhams decided to separate. They agreed that Mrs. Burnham, who intended to move to California, would take custody of the children. Shortly before Mrs. Burnham departed for California that same month, she and petitioner agreed that she would file for divorce on grounds of "irreconcilable differences."

In October 1987, petitioner filed for divorce in New Jersey state court on grounds of "desertion." Petitioner did not, however, obtain an issuance of summons against his wife and did not attempt to serve her with process. Mrs. Burnham, after unsuccessfully demanding that petitioner adhere to their prior agreement to submit to an "irreconcilable differences" divorce, brought suit for divorce in California state court in early January 1988.

In late January, petitioner visited southern California on business, after which he went north to visit his children in the San Francisco Bay area, where his wife resided. He took the older child to San Francisco for the weekend. Upon returning the child to Mrs. Burnham's home on January 24, 1988, petitioner was served with a California court summons and a copy of Mrs. Burnham's divorce petition. He then returned to New Jersey.

Later that year, petitioner made a special appearance in the California Superior Court, moving to quash the service of process on the ground that the court lacked personal jurisdiction over him because his only contacts with California were a few short visits to the State for the purposes of conducting business and visiting his children. The Superior Court denied the motion, and the California Court of Appeal denied mandamus relief, rejecting petitioner's contention that the Due Process Clause prohibited California courts from asserting jurisdiction over him because he lacked "minimum contacts" with the State. The court held it to be "a valid jurisdictional predicate for *in personam* jurisdiction" that the "defendant [was] present in the forum state and personally served with process."

## II

### A

The proposition that the judgment of a court lacking jurisdiction is void traces back to the English Year Books. . . . Traditionally that proposition was embodied in the phrase *coram non judice*, "before a person not a judge"—meaning, in effect, that the proceeding in question was not a *judicial* proceeding because lawful judicial authority was not present, and could therefore not yield a *judgment.* American courts invalidated, or denied recognition to, judgments that violated this common-law principle long before the Fourteenth Amendment was adopted. In Pennoyer v. Neff, 95 U.S. 714, 732 (1878), we announced that the judgment of a court lacking personal jurisdiction violated the Due Process Clause of the Fourteenth Amendment as well.

To determine whether the assertion of personal jurisdiction is consistent with due process, we have long relied on the principles traditionally followed by American courts in marking out the territorial limits of each State's authority. That criterion was first announced in Pennoyer v. Neff, in which we stated that due process "mean[s] a course of legal proceedings according to those rules and principles which have been established in our systems of jurisprudence for the protection and enforcement of private rights," id. at 733, including the "well-established principles of public law respecting the jurisdiction of an independent State over persons and property," id. at 722. In what has become the classic expression of the criterion, we said in International Shoe Co. v. Washington, 326 U.S. 310 (1945), that a state court's assertion of personal jurisdiction satisfies the Due Process Clause if it does not violate "'traditional notions of fair play and substantial justice.'" Id. at 316 (quoting Milliken v. Meyer, 311 U.S. 457, 463 (1940)).

Since *International Shoe*, we have only been called upon to decide whether these "traditional notions" permit States to exercise jurisdiction over absent defendants in a manner that deviates from the rules of jurisdiction applied in the 19th century. We have held such deviations permissible, but only with respect to suits arising out of the absent defendant's contacts with the State. The question we must decide today is whether due process requires a similar connection between the litigation and the defendant's contacts with the State in cases where the defendant is physically present in the State at the time process is served upon him.

## B

Among the most firmly established principles of personal jurisdiction in American tradition is that the courts of a State have jurisdiction over nonresidents who are physically present in the State. The view developed early that each State had the power to hale before its courts any individual who could be found within its borders, and that once having acquired jurisdiction over such a person by properly serving him with process, the State could retain jurisdiction to enter judgment against him, no matter how fleeting his visit. . . .

. . . Particularly striking is the fact that, as far as we have been able to determine, *not one* American case from the period (or, for that matter, not one American case until 1978) held, or even suggested, that in-state personal service on an individual was insufficient to confer personal jurisdiction. . . .

This American jurisdictional practice is, moreover, not merely old; it is continuing. It remains the practice of, not only a substantial number of the States, but as far as we are aware *all* the States and the Federal Government—if one disregards (as one must for this purpose) the few opinions since 1978 that have erroneously said, on grounds similar to those that petitioner presses here, that this Court's due process decisions render the practice unconstitutional. We do not know of a single state or federal statute, or a single judicial decision resting upon state law, that has abandoned in-state service as a basis of jurisdiction. Many recent cases reaffirm it.

## C

Despite this formidable body of precedent, petitioner contends, in reliance on our decisions applying the *International Shoe* standard, that in the absence of "continuous and systematic" contacts with the forum, a nonresident defendant can be subjected to judgment only as to matters that arise out of or relate to his contacts with the forum. This argument rests on a thorough misunderstanding of our cases. . . . [The Court goes on to discuss the development of due process analysis in state court jurisdiction cases from *Pennoyer* forward. EDS.]

. . . Our opinion in *International Shoe* made explicit . . . [that] due process does not necessarily *require* the States to adhere to the unbending territorial limits on jurisdiction set forth in *Pennoyer*. The validity of assertion of jurisdiction over a nonconsenting defendant who is not present in the forum depends upon whether "the quality and nature of [his] activity" in relation to the forum renders such jurisdiction consistent with "'traditional notions of fair play and substantial justice.'" . . .

. . . As *International Shoe* suggests, the defendant's litigation-related "minimum contacts" may take the place of physical presence as the basis for jurisdiction. . . .

Nothing in *International Shoe* or the cases that have followed it, however, offers support for the very different proposition petitioner seeks to establish today: that a defendant's presence in the forum is not only unnecessary to validate novel, nontraditional assertions of jurisdiction, but is itself no longer sufficient to establish jurisdiction. That proposition is unfaithful to both elementary logic and the foundations of our due process jurisprudence. The distinction between what is needed to support novel procedures and what is needed to sustain traditional ones is fundamental, as we observed over a century ago:

> [A] process of law, which is not otherwise forbidden, must be taken to be due process of law, if it can show the sanction of settled usage both in England and in this country; but it by no means follows that nothing else can be due process of law. . . . [That which], in substance, has been immemorially the actual law of the land . . . therefor[e] is due process of law. But to hold that such a characteristic is essential to due process of law, would be to deny every quality of the law but its age, and to render it incapable of progress or improvement. It would be to stamp upon our jurisprudence the unchangeableness attributed to the laws of the Medes and Persians. Hurtado v. California, 110 U.S. 516, 528-529 (1884).

The short of the matter is that jurisdiction based on physical presence alone constitutes due process because it is one of the continuing traditions of our legal system that define the due process standard of "traditional notions of fair play and substantial justice." That standard was developed by *analogy* to "physical presence," and it would be perverse to say it could now be turned against that touchstone of jurisdiction.

### D

Petitioner's strongest argument, though we ultimately reject it, relies upon our decision in Shaffer v. Heitner, 433 U.S. 186 (1977). . . .

It goes too far to say, as petitioner contends, that *Shaffer* compels the conclusion that a State lacks jurisdiction over an individual unless the litigation arises out of his activities in the State. *Shaffer,* like *International Shoe,* involved jurisdiction over an *absent defendant,* and it stands for nothing more than the proposition that when the "minimum contact" that is a substitute for physical presence consists of property ownership it must, like other minimum contacts, be related to the litigation. . . . *Shaffer* was saying, in other words, not that all bases for the assertion of *in personam* jurisdiction (including, presumably, in-state service) must be treated alike and subjected to the "minimum contacts" analysis of *International Shoe;* but rather that *quasi in rem* jurisdiction, that fictional "ancient form," and *in personam* jurisdiction, are really one and the same and must be treated alike—leading to the conclusion that *quasi in rem* jurisdiction, i.e., that form of *in personam* jurisdiction based upon a "property ownership" contact and by definition unaccompanied by personal, in-state service, must satisfy the litigation-relatedness requirement of *International Shoe.* The logic of *Shaffer'*s holding—which places all suits against absent nonresidents on the same constitutional footing, regardless of whether a separate Latin label is attached to one particular basis of contact—does not compel the conclusion that physically present defendants must be treated identically to absent ones. . . .

It is fair to say, however, that while our holding today does not contradict *Shaffer,* our basic approach to the due process question is different. We have conducted no independent inquiry into the desirability or fairness of the prevailing in-state service rule, leaving that judgment to the legislatures that are free to amend it; for our purposes, its validation is its pedigree, as the phrase *"traditional notions* of fair play and substantial justice" makes clear. *Shaffer* did conduct such an independent inquiry, asserting that "'traditional notions of fair play and substantial justice' can be as readily offended by the perpetuation of ancient forms that are no longer justified as by the adoption of new procedures that are inconsistent with the basic values of our constitutional heritage." 433 U.S., at 212. Perhaps that assertion can be sustained when the "perpetuation of ancient forms" is engaged in by only a very small minority of the States.[4] Where, however, as in the

---

4. *Shaffer* may have involved a unique state procedure in one respect: Justice Stevens noted that Delaware was the only State that treated the place of incorporation as the situs of corporate stock when both owner and custodian were elsewhere. See 433 U.S. at 218 (opinion concurring in judgment).

present case, a jurisdictional principle is both firmly approved by tradition and still favored, it is impossible to imagine what standard we could appeal to for the judgment that it is "no longer justified." . . .

## III

A few words in response to Justice Brennan's opinion concurring in the judgment: It insists that we apply "contemporary notions of due process" to determine the constitutionality of California's assertion of jurisdiction. But our analysis today comports with that prescription, at least if we give it the only sense allowed by our precedents. The "contemporary notions of due process" applicable to personal jurisdiction are the enduring "*traditional* notions of fair play and substantial justice" established as the test by *International Shoe*. By its very language, that test is satisfied if a state court adheres to jurisdictional rules that are generally applied and have always been applied in the United States.

But the concurrence's proposed standard of "contemporary notions of due process" requires more: It measures state-court jurisdiction not only against traditional doctrines in this country, including current state-court practice, but also against each Justice's subjective assessment of what is fair and just. Authority for that seductive standard is not to be found in any of our personal jurisdiction cases. It is, indeed, an outright break with the test of "traditional notions of fair play and substantial justice," which would have to be reformulated "*our* notions of fair play and substantial justice."

The subjectivity, and hence inadequacy, of this approach becomes apparent when the concurrence tries to explain *why* the assertion of jurisdiction in the present case meets its standard of continuing-American-tradition-*plus*-innate-fairness. Justice Brennan lists the "benefits" Mr. Burnham derived from the State of California—the fact that, during the few days he was there, "[h]is health and safety [were] guaranteed by the State's police, fire, and emergency medical services; he [was] free to travel on the State's roads and waterways; he likely enjoy[ed] the fruits of the State's economy." Three days' worth of these benefits strike us as powerfully inadequate to establish, as an abstract matter, that it is "fair" for California to decree the ownership of all Mr. Burnham's worldly goods acquired during the 10 years of his marriage, and the custody over his children. We daresay a contractual exchange swapping those benefits for that power would not survive the "unconscionability" provision of the Uniform Commercial Code. Even less persuasive are the other "fairness" factors alluded to by Justice Brennan. It would create "an asymmetry," we are told, if Burnham were *permitted* (as he is) to appear in California courts as a plaintiff, but were not *compelled* to appear in California courts as defendant; and travel being as easy as it is nowadays, and modern procedural devices being so convenient, it is no great hardship to appear in California courts. The problem with these assertions is that they justify the exercise of jurisdiction over *everyone, whether or not* he ever comes to California. The only "fairness" elements setting

Mr. Burnham apart from the rest of the world are the three days' "benefits" referred to above—and even those, do not set him apart from many other people who have enjoyed three days in the Golden State (savoring the fruits of its economy, the availability of its roads and police services) but who were fortunate enough not to be served with process while they were there and thus are not (simply by reason of that savoring) subject to the general jurisdiction of California's courts. See, e.g., Helicopteros Nacionales de Colombia v. Hall, 466 U.S. [408,] 414-416 [(1986)]. In other words, even if one agreed with Justice Brennan's conception of an equitable bargain, the "benefits" we have been discussing would explain why it is "fair" to assert general jurisdiction over Burnham-returned-to-New-Jersey-after-service only at the expense of proving that it is also "fair" to assert general jurisdiction over Burnham-returned-to-New-Jersey-*without*-service—which we *know* does not conform with "contemporary notions of due process." . . .

. . . Nothing we say today prevents individual States from limiting or entirely abandoning the in-state-service basis of jurisdiction. And nothing prevents an overwhelming majority of them from doing so, with the consequence that the "traditional notions of fairness" that this Court applies may change. But the States have overwhelmingly declined to adopt such limitation or abandonment, evidently not considering it to be progress.[5] The question is whether, armed with no authority other than individual Justices' perceptions of fairness that conflict with both past and current practice, this Court can compel the States to make such a change on the ground that "due process" requires it. We hold that it cannot. . . .

Because the Due Process Clause does not prohibit the California courts from exercising jurisdiction over petitioner based on the fact of in-state service of process, the judgment is

*Affirmed.*

JUSTICE WHITE, concurring in part and concurring in the judgment.

I join Parts I, II-A, II-B, and II-C of Justice Scalia's opinion and concur in the judgment of affirmance. The rule allowing jurisdiction to be obtained over a nonresident by personal service in the forum State, without more, has been and is so widely accepted throughout this country that I could not possibly strike it down, either on its face or as applied in this case, on

---

5. I find quite unacceptable as a basis for this Court's decisions Justice Brennan's view that "the *raison d'être* of various constitutional doctrines designed to protect out-of-staters, such as the Art. IV Privileges and Immunities Clause and the Commerce Clause," entitles this Court to brand as "unfair," and hence unconstitutional, the refusal of all 50 States "to limit or abandon bases of jurisdiction that have become obsolete." "Due process" (which is the constitutional text at issue here) does not mean that process which shifting majorities of this Court feel to be "due"; but that process which American society—self-interested American society, which expresses its judgments in the laws of self-interested States—has traditionally considered "due." The notion that the Constitution, through some penumbra emanating from the Privileges and Immunities Clause and the Commerce Clause, establishes this Court as a Platonic check upon the society's greedy adherence to its traditions can only be described as imperious.

the ground that it denies due process of law guaranteed by the Fourteenth Amendment. Although the Court has the authority under the Amendment to examine even traditionally accepted procedures and declare them invalid, e.g., Shaffer v. Heitner, 433 U.S. 186 (1977), there has been no showing here or elsewhere that as a general proposition the rule is so arbitrary and lacking in common sense in so many instances that it should be held violative of due process in every case. Furthermore, until such a showing is made, which would be difficult indeed, claims in individual cases that the rule would operate unfairly as applied to the particular nonresident involved need not be entertained. At least this would be the case where presence in the forum State is intentional, which would almost always be the fact. Otherwise, there would be endless, fact-specific litigation in the trial and appellate courts, including this one. Here, personal service in California, without more, is enough, and I agree that the judgment should be affirmed.

JUSTICE BRENNAN, with whom JUSTICE MARSHALL, JUSTICE BLACKMUN, and JUSTICE O'CONNOR join, concurring in the judgment.

I agree with Justice Scalia that the Due Process Clause of the Fourteenth Amendment generally permits a state court to exercise jurisdiction over a defendant if he is served with process while voluntarily present in the forum State.[1] I do not perceive the need, however, to decide that a jurisdictional rule that "'has been immemorially the actual law of the land,'" quoting Hurtado v. California, 110 U.S. 516, 528 (1884), automatically comports with due process simply by virtue of its "pedigree." Although I agree that history is an important factor in establishing whether a jurisdictional rule satisfies due process requirements, I cannot agree that it is the *only* factor such that all traditional rules of jurisdiction are, *ipso facto*, forever constitutional. Unlike Justice Scalia, I would undertake an "independent inquiry into the . . . fairness of the prevailing in-state service rule." I therefore concur only in the judgment.

## I

I believe that the approach adopted by Justice Scalia's opinion today—reliance solely on historical pedigree—is foreclosed by our decisions in International Shoe Co. v. Washington, 326 U.S. 310 (1945), and Shaffer v. Heitner, 433 U.S. 186 (1977). . . . The critical insight of *Shaffer* is that all rules of jurisdiction, even ancient ones, must satisfy contemporary notions of due process. . . . We recognized that "'[t]raditional notions of fair play and substantial justice' can be as readily offended by the perpetuation of

---

1. I use the term "transient jurisdiction" to refer to jurisdiction premised solely on the fact that a person is served with process while physically present in the forum State.

ancient forms that are no longer justified as by the adoption of new procedures that are inconsistent with the basic values of our constitutional heritage." Id. at 212 (citations omitted). I agree with this approach and continue to believe that "the minimum-contacts analysis developed in *International Shoe* . . . represents a far more sensible construct for the exercise of state-court jurisdiction than the patchwork of legal and factual fictions that has been generated from the decision in Pennoyer v. Neff." Id. at 219 (citation omitted) (Brennan, J., concurring in part and dissenting in part). . . .

## II

Tradition, though alone not dispositive, is of course *relevant* to the question whether the rule of transient jurisdiction is consistent with due process.[7] Tradition is salient not in the sense that practices of the past are automatically reasonable today; indeed, under such a standard, the legitimacy of transient jurisdiction would be called into question because the rule's historical "pedigree" is a matter of intense debate. . . . I find the historical background relevant because, however murky the jurisprudential origins of transient jurisdiction, the fact that American courts have announced the rule for perhaps a century (first in dicta, more recently in holdings) provides a defendant voluntarily present in a particular State *today* "clear notice that [he] is subject to suit" in the forum. World-Wide Volkswagen Corp. v. Woodson, 444 U.S. at 297. . . .

By visiting the forum State, a transient defendant actually "avail[s]" himself, Burger King [v. Rudzewicz, 471 U.S. 462, 476 (1985)], of significant benefits provided by the State. His health and safety are guaranteed by the State's police, fire, and emergency medical services; he is free to travel on the State's roads and waterways; he likely enjoys the fruits of the State's economy as well. . . .

The potential burdens on a transient defendant are slight. "'[M]odern transportation and communications have made it much less burdensome for a party sued to defend himself'" in a State outside his place of residence. *Burger King*, supra, at 474, quoting McGee v. International Life Ins. Co., 355 U.S. 220, 223 (1957). That the defendant has already journeyed at least once

---

7. I do not propose that the "contemporary notions of due process" to be applied are no more than "each Justice's subjective assessment of what is fair and just." Rather, the inquiry is guided by our decisions beginning with International Shoe Co. v. Washington, 326 U.S. 310 (1945), and the specific factors that we have developed to ascertain whether a jurisdictional rule comports with "traditional notions of fair play and substantial justice." See, e.g., Asahi Metal Industry Co. v. Superior Court of California, Solano County, 480 U.S. 102, 113 (1987) (noting "several factors," including "the burden on the defendant, the interests of the forum State, and the plaintiff's interest in obtaining relief"). This analysis may not be "mechanical or quantitative," *International Shoe*, 326 U.S. at 319, but neither is it "freestanding," or dependent on personal whim. Our experience with this approach demonstrates that it is well within our competence to employ.

before to the forum—as evidenced by the fact that he was served with process there—is an indication that suit in the forum likely would not be prohibitively inconvenient. Finally, any burdens that do arise can be ameliorated by a variety of procedural devices.[13] For these reasons, as a rule the exercise of personal jurisdiction over a defendant based on his voluntary presence in the forum will satisfy the requirements of due process.

In this case, it is undisputed that petitioner was served with process while voluntarily and knowingly in the State of California. I therefore concur in the judgment.

JUSTICE STEVENS, concurring in the judgment.

As I explained in my separate writing, I did not join the Court's opinion in Shaffer v. Heitner, 433 U.S. 186 (1977), because I was concerned by its unnecessarily broad reach. Id. at 217-219 (opinion concurring in judgment). The same concern prevents me from joining either Justice Scalia's or Justice Brennan's opinion in this case. For me, it is sufficient to note that the historical evidence and consensus identified by Justice Scalia, the consideration of fairness identified by Justice Brennan, and the common sense displayed by Justice White, all combine to demonstrate that this is, indeed, a very easy case. Accordingly, I agree that the judgment should be affirmed.

## Notes and Questions

1. Is reasonableness irrelevant, post-*Burnham*, whenever a defendant is served in the forum? This case is like *Asahi* in showing a fractured Court and in leaving the reader with no clear sense of direction. Do you agree with Professor Mary Twitchell that "the case leaves us with the unpalatable result of a clear rule with two mutually destructive explanations of how the rule fits into our jurisprudence"? *Burnham* and Constitutionally Permissible Levels of Harm, 22 Rutgers L.J. 659, 667 (1991).

What is the impact of a plurality opinion? Is there any reason to give Justice Scalia's four-vote rationale more weight than Justice Brennan's four-vote rationale? Why does Justice Scalia's opinion appear first? What is the unanimous part of the opinion? Do you sympathize with Justice Stevens's "a pox on both your houses" approach?

---

13. For example, in the federal system, a transient defendant can avoid protracted litigation of a spurious suit through a motion to dismiss for failure to state a claim or through a motion for summary judgment. Fed. Rules Civ. Proc. 12(b)(6) and 56. He can use relatively inexpensive methods of discovery, such as oral deposition by telephone (Rule 30(b)(7)), deposition upon written questions (Rule 31), interrogatories (Rule 33), and requests for admission (Rule 36), while enjoying protection from harassment (Rule 26(c)), and possibly obtaining costs and attorney's fees for some of the work involved (Rules 37(a)(4), (b)-(d)). Moreover, a change of venue may be possible. 28 U.S.C. § 1404. In state court, many of the same procedural protections are available, as is the doctrine of *forum non conveniens*, under which the suit may be dismissed. See generally Abrams, Power, Convenience, and the Elimination of Personal Jurisdiction in the Federal Courts, 58 Ind. L. J. 1, 23-25 (1982).

2. Look again at Justice White's concurrence. Is he placing a burden on the defendant to show that jurisdiction is arbitrary in a particular case, or in so many cases that it is unreasonable in every case? Is the latter showing one that a defendant can ever make? Is it the correct inquiry under due process, which—one might argue—is an individual-centered right that assures due process to *each* defendant rather than to *most* of them over time?

3. None of the opinions in *Burnham* pays much heed to the Court's 1978 decision in *Kulko*. Why not? Although *Burnham* did not overrule *Kulko*, and is superficially easy to distinguish because Ezra Kulko was not served in California, isn't the Court's reasoning in *Kulko* hard to reconcile with either the result or the plurality opinions in *Burnham*?

4. Among the most interesting of the issues raised by *Burnham* is the struggle between Justice Scalia and Justice Brennan over the role of tradition in constitutional interpretation. What is the best case one can make in favor of the static approach proposed by Justice Scalia, which emphasizes tradition-bound interpretation? What is the best case for the dynamic approach to interpretation that Justice Brennan believes is appropriate? Is it "imperious"? Is the excerpt from Tom Tyler on page 60, regarding the common understanding of fair process, relevant to this discussion?

Obviously, quite a bit more is at stake in this debate over original intent, tradition, and Platonic checks than simply the vitality of transient jurisdiction. *Burnham* is but one illustration of a fundamental question that recurs in constitutional law: What are the proper limits of judicial review in this area? Yet *Burnham* is an excellent vehicle for launching that debate in the context of procedure, given its straightforward facts and potentially harsh results.

We encourage you to approach this important issue from the standpoint of one seeking to develop the arguments on both sides as fully as possible, rather than as one committed *ab initio* to a particular result. Remember that the composition of the judiciary can and does change over time. So, too, does society. If you embrace the dynamic approach to interpretation, does it matter to you who is doing the interpreting? Should it? Likewise, if you endorse the static approach, have you thought about how you would determine what "our traditions" are? As of what date would you pinpoint the applicable tradition? Does your experience with jurisdiction issues thus far assure you that legislators "know what they are doing" when they draft a jurisdiction statute? Or are the interpretation and refining of jurisdiction issues best left to the judiciary? Should judges be "imperious"?

*Burnham* inspired a flurry of scholarly activity, mostly critical. For a sampling of concerns about the decision by commentators with a procedural bent, see The Future of Personal Jurisdiction: A Symposium on Burnham v. Superior Court, 22 Rutgers L.J. 559 (1991). For other commentary on *Burnham*, see Earl M. Maltz, Personal Jurisdiction and Constitutional Theory—A Comment on Burnham v. Superior Court, 22 Rutgers L.J. 689 (1991); Linda J. Silberman, Reflections on Burnham v. Superior Court: Toward Presumptive Rules of Jurisdiction and Implications for Choice of Law, 22 Rutgers L.J. 569 (1991); Russell J. Weintraub, An Objective Basis for Rejecting Transient Jurisdiction, 22 Rutgers L.J. 611 (1991); see also Richard B. Cappalli, Locke as the Key: A Unifying and Coherent Theory of *In Personam* Jurisdiction, 43 Case W. Res. L. Rev. 97 (1992); Robert Taylor-Manning, An Easy Case Makes Bad Law — Burnham v. Superior Court of California, 66 Wash. L. Rev. 623 (1991).

*Burnham* deals with general jurisdiction when the defendant is personally served while physically present in the forum state. A defendant is also subject to general jurisdiction in her "home" state. For an individual defendant, that is the state where she is domiciled. For a corporate defendant, the state of incorporation is thought to satisfy the substantial "continuous and systematic" test for general jurisdiction. For decades, uncertainty has lingered in the lower courts about whether a corporation may have a sufficiently large commercial footprint to have more than one "home" state. The Court took up this issue in the following case.

### *Goodyear Dunlop Tires Operations, S.A. v. Brown*
564 U.S. 915 (2011)

JUSTICE GINSBURG delivered the opinion of the Court.

. . . Are foreign subsidiaries of a United States parent corporation amenable to suit in state court on claims unrelated to any activity of the subsidiaries in the forum State? . . .


I

On April 18, 2004, a bus destined for Charles de Gaulle Airport overturned on a road outside Paris, France. Passengers on the bus were young soccer players from North Carolina beginning their journey home. Two 13-year-olds, Julian Brown and Matthew Helms, sustained fatal injuries. The boys' parents, respondents in this Court, filed a suit for wrongful-death damages in the Superior Court of Onslow County, North Carolina, in their capacity as administrators of the boys' estates. Attributing the accident to a tire that failed when its plies separated, the parents alleged negligence in the "design, construction, testing, and inspection" of the tire. 681 S.E.2d, at 384.

Goodyear Luxembourg Tires, SA (Goodyear Luxembourg), Goodyear Lastikleri T.A.S. (Goodyear Turkey), and Goodyear Dunlop Tires France, SA (Goodyear France), petitioners here, were named as defendants. Incorporated in Luxembourg, Turkey, and France, respectively, petitioners are indirect subsidiaries of Goodyear USA, an Ohio corporation also named as a defendant in the suit. Petitioners manufacture tires primarily for sale in European and Asian markets. Their tires differ in size and construction from tires ordinarily sold in the United States. They are designed to carry significantly heavier loads, and to serve under road conditions and speed limits in the manufacturers' primary markets.

In contrast to the parent company, Goodyear USA, which does not contest the North Carolina courts' personal jurisdiction over it, petitioners are not registered to do business in North Carolina. They have no place of business, employees, or bank accounts in North Carolina. They do not design, manufacture, or advertise their products in North Carolina. And they do not solicit business in North Carolina or themselves sell or ship tires to North Carolina customers. Even so, a small percentage of petitioners' tires (tens of thousands out of tens of millions manufactured between 2004 and 2007) were distributed within North Carolina by other Goodyear USA affiliates. These tires were typically custom ordered to equip specialized vehicles such as cement mixers, waste haulers, and boat and horse trailers. Petitioners state, and respondents do not here deny, that the type of tire involved in the accident, a Goodyear Regional RHS tire manufactured by Goodyear Turkey, was never distributed in North Carolina.

Petitioners moved to dismiss the claims against them for want of personal jurisdiction. The trial court denied the motion, and the North Carolina Court of Appeals affirmed. Acknowledging that the claims neither "related to, nor . . . ar[o]se from, [petitioners'] contacts with North Carolina," the Court of Appeals confined its analysis to "general rather than specific jurisdiction," which the court recognized required a "higher threshold" showing: A defendant must have "continuous and systematic contacts" with the forum. 681 S.E.2d, at 388. That threshold was crossed, the court determined, when petitioners placed their tires "in the stream of interstate commerce without any limitation on the extent to which those tires could be sold in North Carolina." 681 S.E.2d, at 394.

Nothing in the record, the court observed, indicated that petitioners "took any affirmative action to cause tires which they had manufactured to be shipped into North Carolina." 681 S.E.2d, at 392. The court found, however, that tires made by petitioners reached North Carolina as a consequence of a "highly-organized distribution process" involving other Goodyear USA subsidiaries. 681 S.E.2d, at 394. Petitioners, the court noted, made "no attempt to keep these tires from reaching the North Carolina market." 681 S.E.2d, at 393. Indeed, the very tire involved in the accident, the court observed, conformed to tire standards established by the U.S. Department of Transportation and bore markings required for sale in the United States. Id. As further support, the court invoked North Carolina's "interest in providing a forum in which its citizens are able to seek redress for [their] injuries," and noted the hardship North Carolina plaintiffs would experience "[were they] required to litigate their claims in France," a country to which they have no ties. 681 S.E.2d, at 394. The North Carolina Supreme Court denied discretionary review. Brown v. Meter, 695 S.E.2d 756 (N.C. 2010).

We granted certiorari . . . .

## II

### A

. . . The canonical opinion in this area remains *International Shoe*, 326 U.S. 310, in which we held that a State may authorize its courts to exercise personal jurisdiction over an out-of-state defendant if the defendant has "certain minimum contacts with [the State] such that the maintenance of the suit does not offend 'traditional notions of fair play and substantial justice.'" Id., at 316 (quoting *Meyer*, 311 U.S., at 463).

Endeavoring to give specific content to the "fair play and substantial justice" concept, the Court in *International Shoe* classified cases involving out-of-state corporate defendants. First, as in *International Shoe* itself, jurisdiction unquestionably could be asserted where the corporation's in-state activity is "continuous and systematic" and that activity gave rise to the episode-in-suit. 326 U.S., at 317. Further, the Court observed, the commission of certain "single or occasional acts" in a State may be sufficient to render a corporation answerable in that State with respect to those acts, though not with respect to matters unrelated to the forum connections. Id., at 318. The heading courts today use to encompass these two *International Shoe* categories is "specific jurisdiction." Adjudicatory authority is "specific" when the suit "aris[es] out of or relate[s] to the defendant's contacts with the forum." *Helicopteros*, 466 U.S., at 414, n.8.

*International Shoe* distinguished from cases that fit within the "specific jurisdiction" categories, "instances in which the continuous corporate operations within a state [are] so substantial and of such a nature as to justify suit against it on causes of action arising from dealings entirely distinct from those activities." 326 U.S., at 318. Adjudicatory authority so grounded is today called "general jurisdiction." *Helicopteros*, 466 U.S., at 414, n.9. For an individual, the paradigm forum for the exercise of general jurisdiction is the individual's domicile; for a corporation, it is an equivalent place, one in which the corporation is fairly regarded as at home. . . .

In only two decisions postdating *International Shoe*, discussed infra, has this Court considered whether an out-of-state corporate defendant's in-state contacts were sufficiently "continuous and systematic" to justify the exercise of general jurisdiction over claims unrelated to those contacts: Perkins v. Benguet Consol. Mining Co., 342 U.S. 437 (1952); and *Helicopteros*, 466 U.S. 408 . . . .

## B

To justify the exercise of general jurisdiction over petitioners, the North Carolina courts relied on the petitioners' placement of their tires in the "stream of commerce." The stream-of-commerce metaphor has been invoked frequently in lower court decisions permitting "jurisdiction in products liability cases in which the product has traveled through an extensive chain of distribution before reaching the ultimate consumer." 18 W. Fletcher, Cyclopedia of the Law of Corporations § 8640.40, p. 133 (rev. ed. 2007). Typically, in such cases, a nonresident defendant, acting outside the forum, places in the stream of commerce a product that ultimately causes harm inside the forum.

Many States have enacted long-arm statutes authorizing courts to exercise specific jurisdiction over manufacturers when the events in suit, or some of them, occurred within the forum state. For example, the "Local Injury; Foreign Act" subsection of North Carolina's long-arm statute authorizes North Carolina courts to exercise personal jurisdiction in "any action claiming injury to person or property within this State arising out of [the defendant's] act or omission outside this State," if, "in addition[,] at or about the time of the injury," "[p]roducts . . . manufactured by the defendant were used or consumed, within this State in the ordinary course of trade." N.C. Gen. Stat. Ann. § 1-75.4(4)(b) (2009). As the North Carolina Court of Appeals recognized, this provision of the State's long-arm statute "does not apply to this case," for both the act alleged to have caused injury (the fabrication of the allegedly defective tire) and its impact (the accident) occurred outside the forum.

The North Carolina court's stream-of-commerce analysis elided the essential difference between case-specific and all-purpose (general) jurisdiction. Flow of a manufacturer's products into the forum, we have explained, may bolster an affiliation germane to specific jurisdiction. . . . But ties serving to bolster the exercise of specific jurisdiction do not warrant a determination that, based on those ties, the forum has general jurisdiction over a defendant.

A corporation's "continuous activity of some sorts within a state," *International Shoe* instructed, "is not enough to support the demand that the corporation be amenable to suits unrelated to that activity." 326 U.S., at 318. Our 1952 decision in Perkins v. Benguet Consol. Mining Co., remains "[t]he textbook case of general jurisdiction appropriately exercised over a foreign corporation that has not consented to suit in the forum." Donahue v. Far Eastern Air Transport Corp., 652 F.2d 1032, 1037 (D.C. Cir. 1981).

Sued in Ohio, the defendant in Perkins was a Philippine mining corporation that had ceased activities in the Philippines during World War II. To the extent that the company was conducting any business during and immediately after the Japanese occupation of the Philippines, it was doing so in Ohio: the corporation's president maintained his office there, kept the company files in that office, and supervised from the Ohio office "the necessarily limited wartime activities of the company." *Perkins*, 342 U.S., at 447-448. Although the claim-in-suit did not arise in Ohio, this Court ruled that it would not violate due process for Ohio to adjudicate the controversy. Ibid.; see Keeton v. Hustler Magazine, Inc., 465 U.S. 770, 779-780, n.11 (1984) (Ohio's exercise of general jurisdiction was permissible in Perkins because "Ohio was the corporation's principal, if temporary, place of business").

We next addressed the exercise of general jurisdiction over an out-of-state corporation over three decades later, in *Helicopteros*. In that case, survivors of United States citizens who died in a helicopter crash in Peru instituted wrongful-death actions in a Texas state court against the owner and operator of the helicopter, a Colombian corporation. The Colombian corporation had no place of business in Texas and was not licensed to do business there. "Basically, [the company's] contacts with Texas consisted of sending its chief executive officer to Houston for a contract-negotiation session; accepting into its New York bank account checks drawn on a Houston bank; purchasing helicopters, equipment, and training services from [a Texas enterprise] for substantial sums; and sending personnel to [Texas] for training." 466 U.S., at 416. These links to Texas, we determined, did not "constitute the kind of continuous and systematic general business contacts . . . found to exist in *Perkins*," and were insufficient to support the exercise of jurisdiction over a claim that neither "ar[o]se out of . . . no[r] related to" the defendant's activities in Texas. Id., at 415-416.

*Helicopteros* concluded that "mere purchases [made in the forum State], even if occurring at regular intervals, are not enough to warrant a State's assertion of [general] jurisdiction over a nonresident corporation in a cause of action not related to those purchase transactions." Id., at 418. We see no reason to differentiate from the ties to Texas held insufficient in *Helicopteros*, the sales of petitioners' tires sporadically made in North Carolina through intermediaries. Under the sprawling view of general jurisdiction urged by respondents and embraced by the North Carolina Court of Appeals, any substantial manufacturer or seller of goods would be amenable to suit, on any claim for relief, wherever its products are distributed. But cf. *World-Wide Volkswagen*, 444 U.S., at 296 (every seller of chattels does not, by virtue of the sale, "appoint the chattel his agent for service of process").

Measured against *Helicopteros* and *Perkins*, North Carolina is not a forum in which it would be permissible to subject petitioners to general jurisdiction. Unlike the defendant in *Perkins*, whose sole wartime business activity was conducted in Ohio, petitioners are in no sense at home in North Carolina. Their attenuated connections to the State fall far short of the [sic] "the continuous and systematic general business contacts" necessary to empower North Carolina to entertain suit against them on claims unrelated to anything that connects them to the State. *Helicopteros*, 466 U.S., at 416 . . . .

\* \* \*

For the reasons stated, the judgment of the North Carolina Court of Appeals is
*Reversed.*

## Notes and Questions

1. Take a look back at Section II.B. of the Court's decision. It seems clear that the incidental flow of goods into a particular state will no longer be sufficient for general jurisdiction. But is the flow of goods into the forum state now irrelevant to general jurisdiction? How else should we interpret Justice Ginsburg's statement that "ties serving to bolster the exercise of specific jurisdiction do not warrant a determination that, based on those ties, the forum has general jurisdiction over a defendant"? Or her statement that "continuous activity of some sorts within a state" is not enough to support general jurisdiction? She seems to be saying general jurisdiction turns on activity beyond mere sales volume. What if a majority or supermajority of sales occur in a state in which the defendant has no corporate presence?

2. The Court notes that the parent company, Goodyear USA, did not contest personal jurisdiction in North Carolina. Why do you think that is so? Assuming a money judgment against Goodyear USA would be adequate to compensate plaintiffs, why do you think they wanted to have the foreign subsidiaries in the case? The appeal of personal jurisdiction up to the Supreme Court suggests they felt strongly about the issue.

3. *Goodyear* is primarily concerned with the test for general jurisdiction, but the case also turns on the relationship between a parent corporation and its subsidiary. The Court revisited the parent-subsidiary relationship in another recent case. As in *Goodyear*, the Court stressed that the number of jurisdictions in which a defendant may be considered at "home" is relatively small.

## Daimler AG v. Bauman
134 S. Ct. 746 (2014)

JUSTICE GINSBURG delivered the opinion of the Court.

This case concerns the authority of a court in the United States to entertain a claim brought by foreign plaintiffs against a foreign defendant based on events occurring entirely outside the United States. The litigation commenced in 2004, when twenty-two Argentinian residents filed a complaint in the United States District Court for the Northern District of California against DaimlerChrysler Aktiengesellschaft (Daimler), a German public stock company, headquartered in Stuttgart, that manufactures Mercedes-Benz vehicles in Germany. The complaint alleged that during Argentina's 1976–1983 "Dirty War," Daimler's Argentinian subsidiary, Mercedes-Benz Argentina (MB Argentina) collaborated with state security forces to kidnap, detain, torture, and kill certain MB Argentina workers, among them, plaintiffs or persons closely related to plaintiffs. Damages for the alleged human-rights violations were sought from Daimler under the laws of the United States, California, and Argentina. Jurisdiction over the lawsuit was predicated on the California contacts of Mercedes-Benz USA, LLC (MBUSA), a subsidiary of Daimler incorporated in Delaware with its principal place of business in New Jersey. MBUSA distributes Daimler-manufactured vehicles to independent dealerships throughout the United States, including California.

The question presented is whether the Due Process Clause of the Fourteenth Amendment precludes the District Court from exercising jurisdiction over Daimler in this case, given the absence of any California connection to the atrocities, perpetrators, or victims described in the complaint. Plaintiffs invoked the court's general or all-purpose jurisdiction. California, they urge, is a place where Daimler may be sued on any and all claims against it, wherever in the world the claims may arise. For example, as plaintiffs' counsel affirmed, under the proffered jurisdictional theory, if a Daimler-manufactured vehicle overturned in Poland, injuring a Polish driver and passenger, the injured parties could maintain a design defect suit in California. Exercises of personal jurisdiction so exorbitant, we hold, are barred by due process constraints on the assertion of adjudicatory authority.

# I

. . . [P]laintiffs asserted claims under the Alien Tort Statute, 28 U.S.C. § 1350, as well as claims for wrongful death and intentional infliction of emotional distress under the laws of California and Argentina. The incidents recounted in the complaint center on MB Argentina's plant in Gonzalez Catan, Argentina; no part of MB Argentina's alleged collaboration with Argentinian authorities took place in California or anywhere else in the United States. . . .

Daimler moved to dismiss the action for want of personal jurisdiction. Opposing the motion, plaintiffs submitted declarations and exhibits purporting to demonstrate the presence of Daimler itself in California. Alternatively, plaintiffs maintained that jurisdiction over Daimler could be founded on the California contacts of MBUSA, a distinct corporate entity that, according to plaintiffs, should be treated as Daimler's agent for jurisdictional purposes.

MBUSA, an indirect subsidiary of Daimler, is a Delaware limited liability corporation. MBUSA serves as Daimler's exclusive importer and distributor in the United States, purchasing Mercedes-Benz automobiles from Daimler in Germany, then importing those vehicles, and ultimately distributing them to independent dealerships located throughout the Nation. Although MBUSA's principal place of business is in New Jersey, MBUSA has multiple California-based facilities, including a regional office in Costa Mesa, a Vehicle Preparation Center in Carson, and a Classic Center in Irvine. According to the record developed below, MBUSA is the largest supplier of luxury vehicles to the California market. In particular, over 10% of all sales of new vehicles in the United States take place in California, and MBUSA's California sales account for 2.4% of Daimler's worldwide sales.

The relationship between Daimler and MBUSA is delineated in a General Distributor Agreement, which sets forth requirements for MBUSA's distribution of Mercedes-Benz vehicles in the United States. That agreement established MBUSA as an "independent contracto[r]" that "buy[s] and sell[s] [vehicles] . . . as an independent business for [its] own account." App. 179a. The agreement "does not make [MBUSA] . . . a general or special agent, partner, joint venturer or employee of DAIMLERCHRYSLER or any DaimlerChrysler Group Company"; MBUSA "ha[s] no authority to make binding obligations for or act on behalf of DAIMLERCHRYSLER or any DaimlerChrysler Group Company." Id.

After allowing jurisdictional discovery on plaintiffs' agency allegations, the District Court granted Daimler's motion to dismiss. Daimler's own affiliations with California, the court first determined, were insufficient to support the exercise of all-purpose jurisdiction over the corporation. Next, the court declined to attribute MBUSA's California contacts to Daimler on an agency theory, concluding that plaintiffs failed to demonstrate that MBUSA acted as Daimler's agent.

The Ninth Circuit [reversed] . . . . We granted certiorari to decide whether, consistent with the Due Process Clause of the Fourteenth Amendment, Daimler is amenable to suit in California courts for claims involving only foreign plaintiffs and conduct occurring entirely abroad.

## II

. . . California's long-arm statute allows the exercise of personal jurisdiction to the full extent permissible under the U.S. Constitution. We therefore inquire whether the Ninth Circuit's holding comports with the limits imposed by federal due process.

## III

. . . Since *International Shoe*, "specific jurisdiction has become the centerpiece of modern jurisdiction theory, while general jurisdiction [has played] a reduced role." *Goodyear*, 131 S. Ct., at 2854 (quoting Twitchell, The Myth of General Jurisdiction, 101 Harv. L. Rev. 610, 628 (1988)). . . .

Our post-*International Shoe* opinions on general jurisdiction, by comparison, are few. "[The Court's] 1952 decision in Perkins v. Benguet Consol. Mining Co. remains the textbook case of general jurisdiction appropriately exercised over a foreign corporation that has not consented to suit in the forum." *Goodyear*, 131 S.Ct., at 2856. . . .

The next case on point, *Helicopteros*, . . . held that the [Colombian] company's Texas connections did not resemble the "continuous and systematic general business contacts . . . found to exist in *Perkins*." [466 U.S. at 416.] "[M]ere purchases, even if occurring at regular intervals," we clarified, "are not enough to warrant a State's assertion of *in personam* jurisdiction over a nonresident corporation in a cause of action not related to those purchase transactions." Id., at 418.

Most recently, in *Goodyear*, we answered the question: "Are foreign subsidiaries of a United States parent corporation amenable to suit in state court on claims unrelated to any activity of the subsidiaries in the forum State?" 131 S. Ct., at 2850. . . . Although the placement of a product into the stream of commerce "may bolster an affiliation germane to *specific* jurisdiction," we explained, such contacts [on the part of a foreign subsidiary] "do not warrant a determination that, based on those ties, the forum has *general* jurisdiction over a defendant." Id., at 2857. As *International Shoe* itself teaches, a corporation's "continuous activity of some sorts within a state is not enough to support the demand that the corporation be amenable to suits unrelated to that activity." 326 U.S., at 318. Because Goodyear's foreign subsidiaries were "in no sense at home in North Carolina," we held, those subsidiaries could not be required to submit to the general jurisdiction of that State's courts. 131 S. Ct., at 2857.

As is evident from *Perkins, Helicopteros,* and *Goodyear,* general and specific jurisdiction have followed markedly different trajectories post-*International Shoe.* Specific jurisdiction has been cut loose from *Pennoyer's* sway, but we have declined to stretch general jurisdiction beyond limits traditionally recognized. . . .

## IV

With this background, we turn directly to the question whether Daimler's affiliations with California are sufficient to subject it to the general (all-purpose) personal jurisdiction of that State's courts. In the proceedings below, the parties agreed on, or failed to contest, certain points we now take as given. . . . While plaintiffs ultimately persuaded the Ninth Circuit to impute MBUSA's California contacts to Daimler on an agency theory, at no point have they maintained that MBUSA is an alter ego of Daimler.

Daimler, on the other hand, failed to object below to plaintiffs' assertion that the California courts could exercise all-purpose jurisdiction over MBUSA. We will assume then, for purposes of this decision only, that MBUSA qualifies as at home in California.

### A

In sustaining the exercise of general jurisdiction over Daimler, the Ninth Circuit relied on an agency theory, determining that MBUSA acted as Daimler's agent for jurisdictional purposes and then attributing MBUSA's California contacts to Daimler. The Ninth Circuit's agency analysis derived from Circuit precedent considering principally whether the subsidiary "performs services that are sufficiently important to the foreign corporation that if it did not have a representative to perform them, the corporation's own officials would undertake to perform substantially similar services." 644 F.3d, at 920 (quoting Doe v. Unocal Corp., 248 F.3d 915, 928 (9th Cir. 2001).

This Court has not yet addressed whether a foreign corporation may be subjected to a court's general jurisdiction based on the contacts of its in-state subsidiary. Daimler argues, and several Courts of Appeals have held, that a subsidiary's jurisdictional contacts can be imputed to its parent only when the former is so dominated by the latter as to be its alter ego. The Ninth Circuit adopted a less rigorous test based on what it described as an "agency" relationship. Agencies, we note, come in many sizes and shapes: "One may be an agent for some business purposes and not others so that the fact that one may be an agent for one purpose does not make him or her an agent for every purpose." 2A C. J. S., Agency § 43, p. 367

(2013) (footnote omitted).[13] A subsidiary, for example, might be its parent's agent for claims arising in the place where the subsidiary operates, yet not its agent regarding claims arising elsewhere. The Court of Appeals did not advert to that prospect. But we need not pass judgment on invocation of an agency theory in the context of general jurisdiction, for in no event can the appeals court's analysis be sustained.

The Ninth Circuit's agency finding rested primarily on its observation that MBUSA's services were "important" to Daimler, as gauged by Daimler's hypothetical readiness to perform those services itself if MBUSA did not exist. Formulated this way, the inquiry into importance stacks the deck, for it will always yield a pro-jurisdiction answer: "Anything a corporation does through an independent contractor, subsidiary, or distributor is presumably something that the corporation would do 'by other means' if the independent contractor, subsidiary, or distributor did not exist." 676 F.3d, at 777 (O'Scannlain, J., dissenting from denial of rehearing en banc). The Ninth Circuit's agency theory thus appears to subject foreign corporations to general jurisdiction whenever they have an in-state subsidiary or affiliate, an outcome that would sweep beyond even the "sprawling view of general jurisdiction" we rejected in *Goodyear*. 131 S. Ct., at 2856.

## B

Even if we were to assume that MBUSA is at home in California, and further to assume MBUSA's contacts are imputable to Daimler, there would still be no basis to subject Daimler to general jurisdiction in California, for Daimler's slim contacts with the State hardly render it at home there.

*Goodyear* made clear that only a limited set of affiliations with a forum will render a defendant amenable to all-purpose jurisdiction there. "For an individual, the paradigm forum for the exercise of general jurisdiction is the individual's domicile; for a corporation, it is an equivalent place, one in which the corporation is fairly regarded as at home." 131 S. Ct., at 2853-54. With respect to a corporation, the place of incorporation and principal place of business are "paradig[m] . . . bases for general jurisdiction." Id., at 735. Those affiliations have the virtue of being unique—that is, each ordinarily indicates only one place—as well as easily ascertainable. Cf. Hertz Corp.

---

13. Agency relationships, we have recognized, may be relevant to the existence of *specific* jurisdiction. "[T]he corporate personality," *International Shoe* observed, "is a fiction, although a fiction intended to be acted upon as though it were a fact." Id., at 316. See generally 1 W. Fletcher, Cyclopedia of the Law of Corporations § 30, p. 30 (Supp. 2012–2013) ("A corporation is a distinct legal entity that can act only through its agents."). As such, a corporation can purposefully avail itself of a forum by directing its agents or distributors to take action there. See, *e.g., Asahi*, 480 U.S., at 112 (opinion of O'Connor, J.) (defendant's act of "marketing [a] product through a distributor who has agreed to serve as the sales agent in the forum State" may amount to purposeful availment); *International Shoe*, 326 U.S., at 318 ("the commission of some single or occasional acts of the corporate agent in a state" may sometimes "be deemed sufficient to render the corporation liable to suit" on related claims). . . . It does not inevitably follow, however, that similar reasoning applies to *general* jurisdiction. . . .

v. Friend, 559 U.S. 77, 94 (2010) ("Simple jurisdictional rules . . . promote greater predictability."). These bases afford plaintiffs recourse to at least one clear and certain forum in which a corporate defendant may be sued on any and all claims.

*Goodyear* did not hold that a corporation may be subject to general jurisdiction *only* in a forum where it is incorporated or has its principal place of business; it simply typed those places paradigm all-purpose forums. Plaintiffs would have us look beyond the exemplar bases *Goodyear* identified, and approve the exercise of general jurisdiction in every State in which a corporation "engages in a substantial, continuous, and systematic course of business." That formulation, we hold, is unacceptably grasping.

. . . [T]he words "continuous and systematic" were used in *International Shoe* to describe instances in which the exercise of *specific* jurisdiction would be appropriate. See 326 U.S., at 317 (jurisdiction can be asserted where a corporation's in-state activities are not only "continuous and systematic, but also give rise to the liabilities sued on"). Turning to all-purpose jurisdiction, in contrast, *International Shoe* speaks of "instances in which the continuous corporate operations within a state [are] so substantial and of such a nature as to justify suit . . . *on causes of action arising from dealings entirely distinct from those activities.*" Id., at 318 (emphasis added). See also Twitchell, Why We Keep Doing Business With Doing-Business Jurisdiction, 2001 U. Chi. Legal Forum 171, 184 (*International Shoe* "is clearly not saying that dispute-blind jurisdiction exists whenever 'continuous and systematic' contacts are found."). Accordingly, the inquiry under *Goodyear* is not whether a foreign corporation's in-forum contacts can be said to be in some sense "continuous and systematic," it is whether that corporation's "affiliations with the State are so 'continuous and systematic' as to render [it] essentially at home in the forum State." 131 S. Ct., at 2851.[19]

Here, neither Daimler nor MBUSA is incorporated in California, nor does either entity have its principal place of business there. If Daimler's California activities sufficed to allow adjudication of this Argentina-rooted case in California, the same global reach would presumably be available in every other State in which MBUSA's sales are sizable. Such exorbitant exercises of all-purpose jurisdiction would scarcely permit out-of-state defendants "to structure their primary conduct with some minimum assurance as to where that conduct will and will not render them liable to suit." *Burger King Corp.*, 471 U.S., at 472.

It was therefore error for the Ninth Circuit to conclude that Daimler, even with MBUSA's contacts attributed to it, was at home in California, and

---

19. We do not foreclose the possibility that in an exceptional case, see, *e.g., Perkins,* a corporation's operations in a forum other than its formal place of incorporation or principal place of business may be so substantial and of such a nature as to render the corporation at home in that State. But this case presents no occasion to explore that question, because Daimler's activities in California plainly do not approach that level. It is one thing to hold a corporation answerable for operations in the forum State, quite another to expose it to suit on claims having no connection whatever to the forum State.

hence subject to suit there on claims by foreign plaintiffs having nothing to do with anything that occurred or had its principal impact in California.[20]

## C

Finally, the transnational context of this dispute bears attention. The Court of Appeals emphasized, as supportive of the exercise of general jurisdiction, plaintiffs' assertion of claims under the Alien Tort Statute and the Torture Victim Protection Act of 1991. See 644 F.3d, at 927 ("American federal courts, be they in California or any other state, have a strong interest in adjudicating and redressing international human rights abuses."). Recent decisions of this Court, however, have rendered plaintiffs' ATS and TVPA claims infirm. See Kiobel v. Royal Dutch Petroleum Co., 133 S. Ct. 1659, 1669 (2013) (presumption *against* extraterritorial application controls claims under the ATS); Mohamad v. Palestinian Authority, 132 S. Ct. 1702, 1705 (2012) (only natural persons are subject to liability under the TVPA).

The Ninth Circuit, moreover, paid little heed to the risks to international comity its expansive view of general jurisdiction posed. Other nations do not share the uninhibited approach to personal jurisdiction advanced by the Court of Appeals in this case. In the European Union, for example, a corporation may generally be sued in the nation in which it is "domiciled," a term defined to refer only to the location of the corporation's "statutory seat," "central administration," or "principal place of business." European Parliament and Council Reg. 1215/2012, Arts. 4(1) and 63(1), 2012 O.J. (L. 351) 7, 18. See also id., Art. 7(5), 2012 O.J. 7 (as to "a dispute *arising out of the operations of a branch, agency or other establishment*," a corporation may be sued "in the courts for the place where the branch, agency or other establishment is situated" (emphasis added)). The Solicitor General informs us, in this regard, that "foreign governments' objections to some domestic courts' expansive views of general jurisdiction have in the past impeded

---

20. To clarify in light of Justice Sotomayor's opinion concurring in the judgment, the general jurisdiction inquiry does not "focu[s] solely on the magnitude of the defendant's in-state contacts." General jurisdiction instead calls for an appraisal of a corporation's activities in their entirety, nationwide and worldwide. A corporation that operates in many places can scarcely be deemed at home in all of them. Otherwise, "at home" would be synonymous with "doing business" tests framed before specific jurisdiction evolved in the United States. Nothing in *International Shoe* and its progeny suggests that "a particular quantum of local activity" should give a State authority over a "far larger quantum of . . . activity" having no connection to any in-state activity. Feder, *supra*, at 694.

Justice Sotomayor would reach the same result, but for a different reason. Rather than concluding that Daimler is not at home in California, Justice Sotomayor would hold that the exercise of general jurisdiction over Daimler would be unreasonable "in the unique circumstances of this case." In other words, she favors a resolution fit for this day and case only. True, a multipronged reasonableness check was articulated in *Asahi*, 480 U.S., at 113-14, but not as a free-floating test. Instead, the check was to be essayed when *specific* jurisdiction is at issue. See also *Burger King*, 471 U.S. 476-78. First, a court is to determine whether the connection between the forum and the episode-in-suit could justify the exercise of specific jurisdiction. Then, in a second step, the court is to consider several additional factors to assess the reasonableness of entertaining the case. When a corporation is genuinely at home in the forum State, however, any second-step inquiry would be superfluous. . . .

negotiations of international agreements on the reciprocal recognition and enforcement of judgments." U.S. Brief 2 (citing Juenger, The American Law of General Jurisdiction, 2001 U. Chi. Legal Forum 141, 161-62).

* * *

For the reasons stated, the judgment of the United States Court of Appeals for the Ninth Circuit is

*Reversed.*

JUSTICE SOTOMAYOR, concurring in the judgment.

I agree with the Court's conclusion that the Due Process Clause prohibits the exercise of personal jurisdiction over Daimler in light of the unique circumstances of this case. I concur only in the judgment, however, because I cannot agree with the path the Court takes to arrive at that result.

. . . The problem, the Court says, is not that Daimler's contacts with California are too few, but that its contacts with other forums are too many. In other words, the Court does not dispute that the presence of multiple offices, the direct distribution of thousands of products accounting for billions of dollars in sales, and continuous interaction with customers throughout a State would be enough to support the exercise of general jurisdiction over some businesses. Daimler is just not one of those businesses, the Court concludes, because its California contacts must be viewed in the context of its extensive "nationwide and worldwide" operations. In recent years, Americans have grown accustomed to the concept of multinational corporations that are supposedly "too big to fail"; today the Court deems Daimler "too big for general jurisdiction."

. . . [T]he Court's focus on Daimler's operations outside of California ignores the lodestar of our personal jurisdiction jurisprudence: A State may subject a defendant to the burden of suit if the defendant has sufficiently taken advantage of the State's laws and protections through its contacts in the State; whether the defendant has contacts elsewhere is immaterial. . . .

# I

. . . Whether the reasonableness prong should apply in the general jurisdiction context is . . . a question we have never decided,[1] and it is one on which I can appreciate the arguments on both sides. But . . . I would decide this case under the reasonableness prong without foreclosing future consideration of whether that prong should be limited to the specific jurisdiction context.

---

1. The Courts of Appeals have uniformly held that the reasonableness prong does in fact apply in the general jurisdiction context. See Metropolitan Life Ins. Co. v. Robertson-Ceco Corp., 84 F.3d 560, 573 (2d Cir. 1996) ("[E]very circuit that has considered the question has held, implicitly or explicitly, that the reasonableness inquiry is applicable to all questions of personal jurisdiction, general or specific").

We identified the factors that bear on reasonableness in Asahi Metal Industry Co. v. Superior Court of Cal., Solano Cty., 480 U.S. 102 (1987) . . . .

The same considerations resolve this case. It involves Argentine plaintiffs suing a German defendant for conduct that took place in Argentina. Like the plaintiffs in *Asahi*, respondents have failed to show that it would be more convenient to litigate in California than in Germany, a sovereign with a far greater interest in resolving the dispute. *Asahi* thus makes clear that it would be unreasonable for a court in California to subject Daimler to its jurisdiction.

## II

. . . [Turning to the nature of defendant's contacts with California] Daimler conceded at the start of this litigation that MBUSA is subject to general jurisdiction based on its California contacts. We therefore do not know the full extent of those contacts, though what little we do know suggests that Daimler was wise to concede what it did. MBUSA imports more than 200,000 vehicles into the United States and distributes many of them to independent dealerships in California, where they are sold. MBUSA's California sales account for 2.4% of Daimler's worldwide sales, which were $192 billion in 2004. And 2.4% of $192 billion is $4.6 billion, a considerable sum by any measure. MBUSA also has multiple offices and facilities in California, including a regional headquarters.

But the record does not answer a number of other important questions. Are any of Daimler's key files maintained in MBUSA's California offices? How many employees work in those offices? Do those employees make important strategic decisions or oversee in any manner Daimler's activities? These questions could well affect whether Daimler is subject to general jurisdiction. After all, this Court upheld the exercise of general jurisdiction in *Perkins*—which the majority refers to as a "textbook case" of general jurisdiction—on the basis that the foreign defendant maintained an office in Ohio, kept corporate files there, and oversaw the company's activities from the State. California-based MBUSA employees may well have done similar things on Daimler's behalf. But because the Court decides the issue without a developed record, we will never know.

## III

While the majority's decisional process is problematic enough, I fear that process leads it to an even more troubling result.

## A

Until today, our precedents had established a straightforward test for general jurisdiction: Does the defendant have "continuous corporate operations within a state" that are "so substantial and of such a nature as to justify suit against it on causes of action arising from dealings entirely distinct from those activities"? International Shoe Co. v. Washington, 326 U.S. 310, 318 (1945). In every case where we have applied this test, we have focused solely on the magnitude of the defendant's in-state contacts, not the relative magnitude of those contacts in comparison to the defendant's contacts with other States. . . .

This approach follows from the touchstone principle of due process in this field, the concept of reciprocal fairness. When a corporation chooses to invoke the benefits and protections of a State in which it operates, the State acquires the authority to subject the company to suit in its courts. . . . The majority's focus on the extent of a corporate defendant's out-of-forum contacts is untethered from this rationale. After all, the degree to which a company intentionally benefits from a forum State depends on its interactions with that State, not its interactions elsewhere. . . .

Had the majority applied our settled approach, it would have had little trouble concluding that Daimler's California contacts rise to the requisite level, given the majority's assumption that MBUSA's contacts may be attributed to Daimler and given Daimler's concession that those contacts render MBUSA "at home" in California. . . . We used the phrase "at home" to signify that in order for an out-of-state defendant to be subject to general jurisdiction, its continuous and substantial contacts with a forum State must be akin to those of a local enterprise that actually is "at home" in the State.[8]

8. The majority views the phrase "at home" as serving a different purpose—that of requiring a comparison between a defendant's in-state and out-of-state contacts. *Ante*, n. 20. That cannot be the correct understanding though, because among other things it would cast grave doubt on *Perkins*—a case that *Goodyear* pointed to as an exemplar of general jurisdiction, 131 S. Ct., at 2855-56. For if *Perkins* had applied the majority's newly minted proportionality test, it would have come out the other way.

The majority apparently thinks that the Philippine corporate defendant in *Perkins* did not have meaningful operations in places other than Ohio. But one cannot get past the second sentence of *Perkins* before realizing that is wrong. That sentence reads: "The corporation has been carrying on in Ohio a continuous and systematic, but limited, part of its general business." 342 U.S., at 438. Indeed, the facts of the case set forth by the Ohio Court of Appeals show just how "limited" the company's Ohio contacts—which included a single officer keeping files and managing affairs from his Ohio home office—were in comparison with its "general business" operations elsewhere. By the time the suit was commenced, the company had resumed its considerable mining operations in the Philippines, "'rebuilding its properties'" there and purchasing "'machinery, supplies and equipment.'" 88 Ohio App., at 123-24. Moreover, the company employed key managers in other forums, including a purchasing agent in San Francisco and a chief of staff in the Philippines. Id., at 124. The San Francisco purchasing agent negotiated the purchase of the company's machinery and supplies "'on the direction of the Company's Chief of Staff in Manila,'" Id., a fact that squarely refutes the majority's assertion that "[a]ll of Benguet's activities were directed by the company's president from within Ohio," *ante*, at 756, n. 8. And the vast majority of the company's board of directors meetings took place outside Ohio, in locations such as Washington, New York, and San Francisco. 88 Ohio App., at 125.

In light of these facts, it is all but impossible to reconcile the result in *Perkins* with the proportionality test the majority announces today. . . .

Under this standard, Daimler's concession that MBUSA is subject to general jurisdiction in California (a concession the Court accepts) should be dispositive. For if MBUSA's California contacts are so substantial and the resulting benefits to MBUSA so significant as to make MBUSA "at home" in California, the same must be true of Daimler when MBUSA's contacts and benefits are viewed as its own. Indeed, until a footnote in its brief before this Court, even Daimler did not dispute this conclusion for eight years of the litigation.

**B**

. . . Just as it was fair to say in the 1940's that an out-of-state company could enjoy the benefits of a forum State enough to make it "essentially at home" in the State, it is fair to say today that a multinational conglomerate can enjoy such extensive benefits in multiple forum States that it is "essentially at home" in each one.

In any event, to the extent the majority is concerned with the modern-day consequences of *International Shoe*'s conception of personal jurisdiction, there remain other judicial doctrines available to mitigate any resulting unfairness to large corporate defendants. Here, for instance, the reasonableness prong may afford petitioner relief. In other cases, a defendant can assert the doctrine of *forum non conveniens* if a given State is a highly inconvenient place to litigate a dispute. See Gulf Oil Corp. v. Gilbert, 330 U.S. 501, 508-09 (1947). In still other cases, the federal change of venue statute can provide protection. See 28 U.S.C. § 1404(a) (permitting transfers to other districts "[f]or the convenience of parties and witnesses" and "in the interests of justice"). And to the degree that the majority worries these doctrines are not enough to protect the economic interests of multinational businesses (or that our longstanding approach to general jurisdiction poses "risks to international comity"), the task of weighing those policy concerns belongs ultimately to legislators, who may amend state and federal long-arm statutes in accordance with the democratic process. Unfortunately, the majority short circuits that process by enshrining today's narrow rule of general jurisdiction as a matter of constitutional law.

**C**

. . . [T]he majority's approach creates the incongruous result that an individual defendant whose only contact with a forum State is a one-time visit will be subject to general jurisdiction if served with process during that visit, Burnham v. Superior Court of Cal., County of Marin, 495 U.S. 604 (1990), but a large corporation that owns property, employs workers, and does billions of dollars' worth of business in the State will not be, simply because the corporation has similar contacts elsewhere (though the visiting individual surely does as well).

. . . [T]he ultimate effect of the majority's approach will be to shift the risk of loss from multinational corporations to the individuals harmed by their actions. Under the majority's rule, for example, a parent whose child is maimed due to the negligence of a foreign hotel owned by a multinational conglomerate will be unable to hold the hotel to account in a single U.S. court, even if the hotel company has a massive presence in multiple States. See, e.g., Meier v. Sun Int'l Hotels, Ltd., 288 F.3d 1264 (11th Cir. 2002). Similarly, a U.S. business that enters into a contract in a foreign country to sell its products to a multinational company there may be unable to seek relief in any U.S. court if the multinational company breaches the contract, even if that company has considerable operations in numerous U.S. forums. See, e.g., Walpex Trading Co. v. Yacimientos Petroliferos Fiscales Bolivianos, 712 F. Supp. 383 (S.D.N.Y. 1989). Indeed, the majority's approach would preclude the plaintiffs in these examples from seeking recourse anywhere in the United States even if no other judicial system was available to provide relief. I cannot agree with the majority's conclusion that the Due Process Clause requires these results. . . .

––––––––––––––––

## Notes and Questions

1. Reread footnote 19 of the majority opinion. The Court takes care to note that it has not eliminated the possibility that a defendant may be subject to general personal jurisdiction in a forum other than its state of incorporation or its principal place of business. What kinds of facts do you think would prompt the Court to recognize general jurisdiction based on the amount of business or manufacturing conducted in that state? How significant is it that Daimler is a foreign multinational corporation?

2. This is an intriguing case for considering the relationship between substantive and procedural law. Unlike in *Goodyear*, there is no domestic U.S. entity that will remain in the case as a defendant—here, plaintiffs' entire case fails once personal jurisdiction fails against Daimler AG. But that is partly an effect of the structure of the substantive laws involved—statutes designed to permit foreigners to sue in U.S. courts for injuries that occurred overseas. Once those statutes were narrowly construed by the Supreme Court (see the Court's reference to *Kiobel* at the end of the majority opinion), the due process objections to hailing a foreign multinational corporation to a U.S. forum become more salient, don't they?

3. Should reasonableness be an element of general personal jurisdiction analysis? Justice Sotomayor points out that the circuit courts of appeals had assumed the answer was yes, but the majority flatly rejects this. Some of the majority's hostility to importing reasonableness analysis surely has to do with the conviction that it is always "reasonable" for dispute-blind litigation to occur against a defendant in her "home" state. But some of the majority's hostility to importing reasonableness analysis must also derive from concern about variation in outcomes if lower courts are granted discretion to decide what constitutes a reasonable assertion of general jurisdiction.

4. Even if you believe the Court should have upheld jurisdiction in this case, doesn't it strike you as strange that the plaintiffs should be able to sue in a California federal court for injuries arising from decades-old conduct in Argentina by the Argentinian subsidiary of a German corporation and on the basis of present contacts of the company's U.S. subsidiary with California? Alternatively, if you think the Court got the jurisdictional analysis right, how do you respond to Justice Sotomayor's concern that the Court is retreating to outdated ideas about due process in response to twenty-first century complexities of globalization and the increasingly pervasive economic influence of vast multinational corporations?

5. Notice that one powerful effect of a narrow test for general jurisdiction — a test that restricts general jurisdiction to forums in which the defendant can truly be said to be "at home" — is that the defendant will enjoy all the advantages of being "at home" in dispute-blind litigation. Both judge and jury will hale from a state in which the defendant's presence is truly substantial. See Shovah v. Roman Catholic Diocese of Albany, 745 F.3d 30 (2d Cir. 2014) (reversing district court's refusal to grant motion to dismiss; concluding there is no general jurisdiction in Vermont federal court against a former New York priest and his Diocese for sexual abuse of a minor). The Diocese in *Shovah* was a New York corporation covering fourteen New York counties. It did not own real property, maintain an office, or have financial accounts in Vermont, but over a ten-year period 6 of the Diocese's more than 100 parishes were located near the Vermont border. Those parishes served Vermont residents, employed Vermont residents, did business with Vermont vendors, circulated the Diocese newspaper in Vermont, accepted Vermont students into Diocese schools, received philanthropic gifts from Vermont residents, and occasionally commissioned priests to celebrate Sunday mass in Vermont churches. Id. at 34.

As in *Daimler,* the Second Circuit dismissed these contacts as insufficient for general jurisdiction by comparing them to the much more extensive presence of the Diocese in New York. For example, while the Diocese employed 21 Vermont vendors, it employed 698 New York vendors; it received just 0.080 percent of its more than $67 million in philanthropic gifts from Vermont; and only 12 Vermont students enrolled in its schools. Id. The court also emphasized that each parish is a "separate religious corporation." Id. "Daimler's contacts with the forum were far more substantial than the Diocese's with Vermont. . . . [E]ven had the district court imputed the six border parishes' Vermont contacts to the Diocese, its jurisdictional determination would not stand." Id. at 40. See also Brown v. Lockheed Martin Corp., 814 F.3d 619 (2d Cir. 2016).

Other lower courts have been reluctant to find general personal jurisdiction on the basis of mere business activity within the forum state. See, e.g., Freedman v. Suntrust Banks, Inc., 139 F. Supp. 3d 271 (D.D.C. 2015) (Florida loan applicant denied general jurisdiction in D.C. federal court in suit against Georgia bank and its wholly owned Virginia subsidiary for violations of the Fair Housing Act and Equal Credit Opportunity Act; neither company was incorporated, had its principal place of business, or had "substantial, continuous, and extensive business contacts" in D.C.); Siswanto v. Airbus, 153 F. Supp. 3d 1024 (N.D. Ill. 2015) (no general personal jurisdiction in suit brought by estates of passengers who died in air crash; contacts by Airbus subsidiaries cannot be imputed to Airbus because parent did not exercise "an unusually high degree of control" over the subsidiaries); Carmouche v. Tamborlee Mgmt., Inc., 789 F.3d 1201 (11th Cir. 2015) (Panamanian company not subject to general personal jurisdiction in Florida despite holding a Florida bank account, a post office box sometimes listed on contracts as its principal place of business, insurance contracts with Florida insurers, filing financial statements with the Florida government, maintaining membership in a trade organization based in the state, and selecting the Southern District of Florida as the forum for litigation in contracts with a cruise company); Kipp v. Ski Enterprise Corp. of Wis., 783 F.3d 695 (7th Cir. 2015) (annual attendance at a trade show, passive website, solicitation of business in Illinois, and significant percentage of customers hailing from Illinois insufficient to hold Wisconsin ski resort operator to suit in Illinois); Sonera Holding B.V. v. Cukurova Holding A.S., 750 F.3d 221 (2d Cir. 2014) (Turkish conglomerate not subject to general jurisdiction in New York based on business activities in the forum including sales on stock exchange, contracts to provide digital television content, an office, and negotiations with New York equity funds); Senne v. Kan. City Royals Baseball Corp., 105 F. Supp. 3d 981 (N.D. Cal. 2015) (out-of-state Major League Baseball teams not subject to personal jurisdiction in California in Fair Labor Standards Act class action filed by current and former players on the basis of regular travel to the state to play games, regular scouting in the state, having employees based in California, and membership in an organization that has teams in the state); Farber v. Tennant Truck Lines, Inc., 84 F. Supp. 3d 421 (E.D. Pa. 2015) (no general personal jurisdiction in Pennsylvania where defendant had made over 4,600 deliveries and pick-ups in the state between 2010 and 2014, earned about 3.4 percent of its total revenue in the state from 2010 to 2013, owned vehicles traveling around 500,000 miles in the state from 2010 to 2014, purchased around 80,000 gallons of gas in the state from 2010 to 2014, paid over $500,000 to the state from 2010 to 2014, employed three individuals in the state at the time of the accident, and filed and paid nominal corporate taxes to the state from 2010 to 2013).

## 9.   Persons and Property in Cyberspace

### Problem Case: The Ubiquitous Defendant

You are a law clerk for a federal district court judge in Washington, D.C., who is considering a motion to dismiss for lack of personal jurisdiction. She has asked you to draft an opinion for her in the case of Marcus Neff, a U.S. congressman from Oregon, who is suing Sylvester Sleeze for the tort of defamation.

Sleeze is the editor of *The Naked Truth*, an electronic gossip magazine focusing on the doings of politicians and people in the entertainment industry. Anyone in the world may access his magazine through his Web site, www.thenakedtruth.com, after registering a free user name and obtaining a free password. The site relies on word-of-mouth to gain readers and does not pay to advertise itself.

A few months ago, the lead story, printed under the headline "Vicious Rumor," was to the effect that Marcus Neff, "the scion of a long line of Oregonians," was guilty of repeated acts of domestic violence against his wife, over a period of many years. The Neff story appeared on the Web site 24 hours a day for three days, during which the Web site received 30,000 hits (visitors to the Web site), significantly more than the usual 3,000-hit total for each new posting. There is no way to tell how many of these hits were from the District of Columbia, or how many visitors to the Web site read the Neff story.

If untrue, the publication is clearly an actionable tort under D.C. law. Less clear is whether this court has personal jurisdiction over Sleeze, who is a resident of Los Angeles, where he puts out the magazine from his home computer.

During the time period involved in this suit, Sleeze was trying to develop a regular list of subscribers to whom he e-mailed each new edition of *The Naked Truth*. At the time of the Neff story, there were a few thousand subscribers. But since the e-mail address gives no geographical information, Sleeze did not know precisely how many of these were in D.C. At oral argument, however, counsel for Sleeze said that, in a preliminary effort to locate subscribers geographically, they had traced several hundred to Los Angeles, but only a few dozen to D.C.

*The Naked Truth* Web site has hyperlinks that allow visitors to the Web site to connect with other publications, some of which are based in D.C. At the Web site, and in the e-mailed editions of the report, Sleeze seeks financial contributions to the magazine, but he has received very few so far, and only one or two from D.C.

Visitors to the Web site may leave comments and gossip of their own on the Web site. Again, since e-mail identities are not generally geographical, it is impossible to say how much of the interaction on the Web site comes from D.C.

Sleeze has been to D.C. only once over the last five years, for the christening of his niece. His sister paid his way, and while he was in town he appeared on C-SPAN (a nationwide cable TV service) to talk about putting out an electronic magazine. He did not pay for the airtime, nor was he paid for appearing. Sleeze has not advertised his magazine in any media located in D.C.

The D.C. long-arm statute provides for personal jurisdiction over anyone who:

(1) causes tortious injury in the District of Columbia by an act or omission in the District of Columbia, or

(2) causes tortious injury by an act or omission outside the District of Columbia if he reasonably expects the act to have consequences in the District of Columbia *and* derives substantial revenue from interstate or international commerce.

## Introduction: Personal Jurisdiction and Cyberspace

Almost overnight (especially quick in legal time), the World Wide Web has become a force in the global economy, as well as a part of the daily lives of millions. The Web's new and unstructured interactions stir up all sorts of litigation. People sue over the use and ownership of intellectual property such as domain names. Torts are committed, contracts made and broken in cyberspace. Where is the center of gravity of such lawsuits, and where is the location of the wrongs sued upon? Where can the plaintiff make the defendant appear?

The challenge is fairness to the defendant who is, in one sense, everywhere and, at the same time, potentially nowhere. Should a person who causes harm, as in our problem case, be held to suit wherever the Internet reaches? Technological change has often shaped concepts of due process. Think about how the early Internet cases compare with the impact of the automobile and the corporate form of doing business on jurisdiction.

Appellate courts are beginning to decide important cases dealing with the Internet and jurisdiction; still, much of the law is in the form of trial court opinions. Virtually all of these apply traditional jurisdictional analysis, looking first to the scope of the local long-arm statute, then to due process fairness in the usual sense. Though courts and commentators often mention the Web's potential to revolutionize state court jurisdiction, the cases so far are only beginning to face these implications.

### *Zippo Mfg. Co. v. Zippo Dot Com*
952 F. Supp. 1119 (W.D. Pa. 1997)

McLaughlin, District Judge.

This is an Internet domain name[1] dispute. At this stage of the controversy, we must decide the constitutionally permissible reach of Pennsylvania's Long Arm Statute, 42 Pa. C.S.A. § 5322, through cyberspace. Plaintiff Zippo Manufacturing Corporation ("Manufacturing") has filed a five count complaint against Zippo Dot Com, Inc. ("Dot Com") alleging trademark dilution, infringement, and false designation under the Federal Trademark Act, 15 U.S.C. §§ 1051-1127. In addition, the Complaint alleges causes of action based on state law trademark dilution under 54 Pa. C.S.A. § 1124, and seeks equitable accounting and imposition of a constructive trust. Dot Com has moved to dismiss for lack of personal jurisdiction. . . . For the reasons set forth below, Defendant's motion is denied.

---

1. Domain names serve as a primary identifier of an Internet user. Panavision Intern., L. P. v. Toeppen, 938 F. Supp. 616 (C.D. Cal. 1996). Businesses using the Internet commonly use their business names as part of the domain name (e.g., IBM.com). Id. The designation ".com" identifies the user as a commercial entity. Id.

## I.  Background

The facts relevant to this motion are as follows. Manufacturing is a Pennsylvania corporation with its principal place of business in Bradford, Pennsylvania. Manufacturing makes, among other things, well known "Zippo" tobacco lighters. Dot Com is a California corporation with its principal place of business in Sunnyvale, California. Dot Com operates an Internet Web site and an Internet news service and has obtained the exclusive right to use the domain names "zippo.com", "zippo.net" and "zipponews.com" on the Internet.[3]

Dot Com's Web site contains information about the company, advertisements, and an application for its Internet news service. The news service itself consists of three levels of membership — "public/free," "Original," and "Super." Each successive level offers access to a greater number of Internet newsgroups. A customer who wants to subscribe to either the "Original" or "Super" level of service, fills out an online application that asks for a variety of information including the person's name and address. Payment is made by credit card over the Internet or the telephone. The application is then processed and the subscriber is assigned a password which permits the subscriber to view and/or download Internet newsgroup messages that are stored on the Defendant's server in California.

Dot Com's contacts with Pennsylvania have occurred almost exclusively over the Internet. Dot Com's offices, employees and Internet servers are located in California. Dot Com maintains no offices, employees or agents in Pennsylvania. Dot Com's advertising for its service to Pennsylvania residents involves posting information about its service on its Web page, which is accessible to Pennsylvania residents via the Internet. Defendant has approximately 140,000 paying subscribers worldwide. Approximately two percent (3,000) of those subscribers are Pennsylvania residents. These subscribers have contracted to receive Dot Com's service by visiting its Web site and filling out the application. Additionally, Dot Com has entered into agreements with seven Internet access providers in Pennsylvania to permit their subscribers to access Dot Com's news service. Two of these providers are located in the Western District of Pennsylvania.

The basis of the trademark claims is Dot Com's use of the word "Zippo" in the domain names it holds, in numerous locations in its Web site and in the heading of Internet newsgroup messages that have been posted by Dot Com subscribers. When an Internet user views or downloads a newsgroup message posted by a Dot Com subscriber, the word "Zippo" appears in the "Message-ID" and "Organization" sections of the heading. The news message itself, containing text and/or pictures, follows. Manufacturing points

---

3. Dot Com has registered these domain names with Network Solutions, Inc. which has contracted with the National Science Foundation to provide registration services for Internet domain names. Once a domain name is registered to one user, it may not be used by another.

out that some of the messages contain adult oriented, sexually explicit subject matter. . . .

## III. Discussion

### A. *Personal Jurisdiction*

#### 1. The Traditional Framework

Our authority to exercise personal jurisdiction in this case is conferred by state law. Fed. R. Civ. P. 4(e); Mellon Bank (East) FSFS, N.A. v. Farino, 960 F.2d 1217, 1221 (3d Cir. 1992). The extent to which we may exercise that authority is governed by the Due Process Clause of the Fourteenth Amendment to the Federal Constitution. Kulko v. Superior Court of California, 436 U.S. 84, 91 (1978).

Pennsylvania's long arm jurisdiction statute is codified at 42 Pa. C.S.A. § 5322(a). The portion of the statute authorizing us to exercise jurisdiction here permits the exercise of jurisdiction over non-resident defendants upon "(2) Contracting to supply services or things in this Commonwealth." 42 Pa. C.S.A. § 5322(a). It is undisputed that Dot Com contracted to supply Internet news services to approximately 3,000 Pennsylvania residents and also entered into agreements with seven Internet access providers in Pennsylvania. Moreover, even if Dot Com's conduct did not satisfy a specific provision of the statute, we would nevertheless be authorized to exercise jurisdiction to the "fullest extent allowed under the Constitution of the United States." 42 Pa. C.S.A. § 5322(b).

The constitutional limitations on the exercise of personal jurisdiction differ depending upon whether a court seeks to exercise general or specific jurisdiction over a non-resident defendant. *Mellon*, 960 F.2d at 1221. General jurisdiction permits a court to exercise personal jurisdiction over a nonresident defendant for non-forum related activities when the defendant has engaged in "systematic and continuous" activities in the forum state. Helicopteros Nacionales de Colombia, S.A. v. Hall, 466 U.S. 408, 414-416 (1984). In the absence of general jurisdiction, specific jurisdiction permits a court to exercise personal jurisdiction over a non-resident defendant for forum-related activities where the "relationship between the defendant and the forum falls within the 'minimum contacts' framework" of International Shoe Co. v. Washington, 326 U.S. 310 (1945), and its progeny. *Mellon*, 960 F.2d at 1221. Manufacturing does not contend that we should exercise general personal jurisdiction over Dot Com. Manufacturing concedes that if personal jurisdiction exists in this case, it must be specific.

A three-pronged test has emerged for determining whether the exercise of specific personal jurisdiction over a non-resident defendant is appropriate: (1) the defendant must have sufficient "minimum contacts" with the forum state, (2) the claim asserted against the defendant must arise out of those contacts, and (3) the exercise of jurisdiction must be reasonable. Id.

## 2. The Internet and Jurisdiction

In Hanson v. Denckla, the Supreme Court noted that "[a]s technological progress has increased the flow of commerce between States, the need for jurisdiction has undergone a similar increase." Hanson v. Denckla, 357 U.S. 235, 250-251 (1958). Twenty seven years later, the Court observed that jurisdiction could not be avoided "merely because the defendant did not *physically* enter the forum state." *Burger King*, 471 U.S. at 476. The Court observed that:

> [I]t is an inescapable fact of modern commercial life that a substantial amount of commercial business is transacted solely by mail and wire communications across state lines, thus obviating the need for physical presence within a State in which business is conducted.

Id.

Enter the Internet, a global "'super-network' of over 15,000 computer networks used by over 30 million individuals, corporations, organizations, and educational institutions worldwide." Panavision Intern., L.P. v. Toeppen, 938 F. Supp. 616 (C.D. Cal. 1996). "In recent years, businesses have begun to use the Internet to provide information and products to consumers and other businesses." Id. The Internet makes it possible to conduct business throughout the world entirely from a desktop. With this global revolution looming on the horizon, the development of the law concerning the permissible scope of personal jurisdiction based on Internet use is in its infant stages. The cases are scant. Nevertheless, our review of the available cases and materials[5] reveals that the likelihood that personal jurisdiction can be constitutionally exercised is directly proportionate to the nature and quality of commercial activity that an entity conducts over the Internet. This sliding scale is consistent with well developed personal jurisdiction principles. At one end of the spectrum are situations where a defendant clearly does business over the Internet. If the defendant enters into contracts with residents of a foreign jurisdiction that involve the knowing and repeated transmission of computer files over the Internet, personal jurisdiction is proper. *E.g.*, CompuServe, Inc. v. Patterson, 89 F.3d 1257 (6th Cir. 1996). At the opposite end are situations where a defendant has simply posted information on an Internet Web site which is accessible to users in foreign jurisdictions. A passive Web site that does little more than make information available to those who are interested in it is not grounds for the exercise of personal jurisdiction. *E.g.*, Bensusan Restaurant Corp., v. King, 937 F. Supp. 295 (S.D.N.Y. 1996). The middle ground is occupied by interactive Web sites where a user can exchange information with the host computer. In these

---

5. See generally, Robert A. Bourque and Kerry L. Konrad, Avoiding Jurisdiction Based on Internet Web Site, New York Law Journal (Dec. 10, 1996); David Bender, Emerging Personal Jurisdiction Issues on the Internet, 453 PLI/Pat 7 (1996); Comment, Richard S. Zembek, Jurisdiction and the Internet: Fundamental Fairness in the Networked World of Cyberspace, 6 Alb. L.J. Sci. & Tech. 339 (1996).

cases, the exercise of jurisdiction is determined by examining the level of interactivity and commercial nature of the exchange of information that occurs on the Web site. *E.g.,* Maritz, Inc. v. Cybergold, Inc., 947 F. Supp. 1328 (E.D. Mo. 1996).

Traditionally, when an entity intentionally reaches beyond its boundaries to conduct business with foreign residents, the exercise of specific jurisdiction is proper. *Burger King,* 471 U.S. at 475. Different results should not be reached simply because business is conducted over the Internet. In CompuServe, Inc. v. Patterson, 89 F.3d 1257 (6th Cir. 1996), the Sixth Circuit addressed the significance of doing business over the Internet. In that case, Patterson, a Texas resident, entered into a contract to distribute shareware[6] through CompuServe's Internet server located in Ohio. *CompuServe,* 89 F.3d at 1260. From Texas, Patterson electronically uploaded thirty-two master software files to CompuServe's server in Ohio via the Internet. Id. at 1261. One of Patterson's software products was designed to help people navigate the Internet. Id. When CompuServe later began to market a product that Patterson believed to be similar to his own, he threatened to sue. Id. CompuServe brought an action in the Southern District of Ohio, seeking a declaratory judgment. Id. The District Court granted Patterson's motion to dismiss for lack of personal jurisdiction and CompuServe appealed. Id. The Sixth Circuit reversed, reasoning that Patterson had purposefully directed his business activities toward Ohio by knowingly entering into a contract with an Ohio resident and then "deliberately and repeatedly" transmitted files to Ohio. Id. at 1264-1266.

In Maritz, Inc. v. Cybergold, Inc., 947 F. Supp. 1328 (E.D. Mo. 1996), the defendant had put up a Web site as a promotion for its upcoming Internet service. The service consisted of assigning users an electronic mailbox and then forwarding advertisements for products and services that matched the users' interests to those electronic mailboxes. *Maritz,* 947 F. Supp. at 1330. The defendant planned to charge advertisers and provide users with incentives to view the advertisements. Id. Although the service was not yet operational, users were encouraged to add their address to a mailing list to receive updates about the service. Id. The court rejected the defendant's contention that it operated a "passive Web site." Id. at 1333-34. The court reasoned that the defendant's conduct amounted to "active solicitations" and "promotional activities" designed to "develop a mailing list of Internet users" and that the defendant "indiscriminately responded to every user" who accessed the site. Id. at 1333-34.

Inset Systems, Inc. v. Instruction Set, 937 F. Supp. 161 (D. Conn. 1996), represents the outer limits of the exercise of personal jurisdiction based on the Internet. In *Inset Systems,* a Connecticut corporation sued a Massachusetts corporation in the District of Connecticut for trademark infringement

---

6. "Shareware" is software which a user is permitted to download and use for a trial period, after which the user is asked to pay a fee to the author for continued use. *CompuServe,* 89 F.3d at 1260.

based on the use of an Internet domain name. *Inset Systems*, 937 F. Supp. at 162. The defendant's contacts with Connecticut consisted of posting a Web site that was accessible to approximately 10,000 Connecticut residents and maintaining a toll free number. Id. at 165. The court exercised personal jurisdiction, reasoning that advertising on the Internet constituted the purposeful doing of business in Connecticut because "unlike television and radio advertising, the advertisement is available continuously to any Internet user." Id. at 165.

Bensusan Restaurant Corp. v. King, 937 F. Supp. 295 (S.D.N.Y. 1996), reached a different conclusion based on a similar Web site. In *Bensusan,* the operator of a New York jazz club sued the operator of a Missouri jazz club for trademark infringement. *Bensusan*, 937 F. Supp. at 297. The Internet Web site at issue contained general information about the defendant's club, a calendar of events and ticket information. Id. However, the site was not interactive. Id. If a user wanted to go to the club, she would have to call or visit a ticket outlet and then pick up tickets at the club on the night of the show. Id. The court refused to exercise jurisdiction based on the Web site alone, reasoning that it did not rise to the level of purposeful availment of that jurisdiction's laws. The court distinguished the case from *CompuServe,* supra, where the user had "'reached out' from Texas to Ohio and 'originated and maintained' contacts with Ohio." Id. at 301.

Pres-Kap, Inc. v. System One, Direct Access, Inc., 636 So. 2d 1351 (Fla. App. 1994), *review denied,* 645 So. 2d 455 (Fla. 1994), is not inconsistent with the above cases. In *Pres-Kap,* a majority of a three-judge intermediate state appeals court refused to exercise jurisdiction over a consumer of an online airline ticketing service. *Pres-Kap* involved a suit on a contract dispute in a Florida court by a Delaware corporation against its New York customer. *Pres-Kap*, 636 So. 2d at 1351-1352. The defendant had leased computer equipment which it used to access an airline ticketing computer located in Florida. Id. The contract was solicited, negotiated, executed and serviced in New York. Id. at 1352. The defendant's only contact with Florida consisted of logging onto the computer located in Florida and mailing payments for the leased equipment to Florida. Id. at 1353. *Pres-Kap* is distinguishable from the above cases and the case at bar because it addressed the exercise of jurisdiction over a consumer of online services as opposed to a seller. When a consumer logs onto a server in a foreign jurisdiction he is engaging in a fundamentally different type of contact than an entity that is using the Internet to sell or market products or services to residents of foreign jurisdictions. The *Pres-Kap* court specifically expressed concern over the implications of subjecting users of "online" services with contracts with out-of-state networks to suit in foreign jurisdictions. Id. at 1353.

### 3. Application to This Case

First, we note that this is not an Internet advertising case in the line of *Inset Systems* and *Bensusan,* supra. Dot Com has not just posted information on a Web site that is accessible to Pennsylvania residents who are connected to the Internet. This is not even an interactivity case in the line of *Maritz,* supra. Dot Com has done more than create an interactive Web site through which it exchanges information with Pennsylvania residents in hopes of using that information for commercial gain later. We are not being asked to determine whether Dot Com's Web site alone constitutes the purposeful availment of doing business in Pennsylvania. This is a "doing business over the Internet" case in the line of *CompuServe,* supra. We are being asked to determine whether Dot Com's conducting of electronic commerce with Pennsylvania residents constitutes the purposeful availment of doing business in Pennsylvania. We conclude that it does. Dot Com has contracted with approximately 3,000 individuals and seven Internet access providers in Pennsylvania. The intended object of these transactions has been the downloading of the electronic messages that form the basis of this suit in Pennsylvania.

We find Dot Com's efforts to characterize its conduct as falling short of purposeful availment of doing business in Pennsylvania wholly unpersuasive. At oral argument, Defendant repeatedly characterized its actions as merely "operating a Web site" or "advertising." Dot Com also cites to a number of cases from this Circuit which, it claims, stand for the proposition that merely advertising in a forum, without more, is not a sufficient minimal contact.[7] This argument is misplaced. Dot Com has done more than advertise on the Internet in Pennsylvania. Defendant has sold passwords to approximately 3,000 subscribers in Pennsylvania and entered into seven contracts with Internet access providers to furnish its services to their customers in Pennsylvania.

Dot Com also contends that its contacts with Pennsylvania residents are "fortuitous" within the meaning of *World-Wide Volkswagen,* 444 U.S. 286 (1980). Defendant argues that it has not "actively" solicited business in Pennsylvania and that any business it conducts with Pennsylvania residents has resulted from contacts that were initiated by Pennsylvanians who visited the Defendant's Web site. The fact that Dot Com's services have been consumed in Pennsylvania is not "fortuitous" within the meaning of *World-Wide Volkswagen.* In *World-Wide Volkswagen,* a couple that had purchased a vehicle in New York, while they were New York residents, were injured while driving that vehicle through Oklahoma and brought suit in an Oklahoma state court. *World-Wide Volkswagen,* 444 U.S. at 288. The [defendant] did not sell its vehicles in Oklahoma and had not made an effort to establish business relationships in Oklahoma. Id. at 295. The Supreme Court characterized the [defendant's] ties with Oklahoma as fortuitous because they resulted entirely out the fact that the plaintiffs had driven their car into that state. Id.

---

7. Defendant has cited to: Gehling v. St. George's School of Medicine, Ltd., 773 F.2d 539 (3d Cir. 1985); Fields v. Ramada Inn Inc., 816 F. Supp. 1033 (E.D. Pa. 1993); and Garofalo v. Praiss, 1990 WL 97800 (E.D. Pa. 1990). We note that these cases all involve the issue of whether advertising can rise to the level of "systematic and continuous" contacts for the purpose of general jurisdiction.

Here, Dot Com argues that its contacts with Pennsylvania residents are fortuitous because Pennsylvanians happened to find its Web site or heard about its news service elsewhere and decided to subscribe. This argument misconstrues the concept of fortuitous contacts embodied in *World-Wide Volkswagen*. Dot Com's contacts with Pennsylvania would be fortuitous within the meaning of *World-Wide Volkswagen* if it had no Pennsylvania subscribers and an Ohio subscriber forwarded a copy of a file he obtained from Dot Com to a friend in Pennsylvania or an Ohio subscriber brought his computer along on a trip to Pennsylvania and used it to access Dot Com's service. That is not the situation here. Dot Com repeatedly and consciously chose to process Pennsylvania residents' applications and to assign them passwords. Dot Com knew that the result of these contracts would be the transmission of electronic messages into Pennsylvania. The transmission of these files was entirely within its control. Dot Com cannot maintain that these contracts are "fortuitous" or "coincidental" within the meaning of *World-Wide Volkswagen*. When a defendant makes a conscious choice to conduct business with the residents of a forum state, "it has clear notice that it is subject to suit there." *World-Wide Volkswagen*, 444 U.S. at 297. Dot Com was under no obligation to sell its services to Pennsylvania residents. It freely chose to do so, presumably in order to profit from those transactions. If a corporation determines that the risk of being subject to personal jurisdiction in a particular forum is too great, it can choose to sever its connection to the state. Id. If Dot Com had not wanted to be amenable to jurisdiction in Pennsylvania, the solution would have been simple—it could have chosen not to sell its services to Pennsylvania residents.

Next, Dot Com argues that its forum-related activities are not numerous or significant enough to create a "substantial connection" with Pennsylvania. Defendant points to the fact that only two percent of its subscribers are Pennsylvania residents. However, the Supreme Court has made clear that even a single contact can be sufficient. *McGee*, 355 U.S. at 223. The test has always focused on the "nature and quality" of the contacts with the forum and not the quantity of those contacts. *International Shoe*, 326 U.S. at 320. The Sixth Circuit also rejected a similar argument in *CompuServe* when it wrote that the contacts were "deliberate and repeated even if they yielded little revenue." *CompuServe*, 89 F.3d at 1265.

We also conclude that the cause of action arises out of Dot Com's forum-related conduct in this case. The Third Circuit has stated that "a cause of action for trademark infringement occurs where the passing off occurs." Cottman Transmission Systems Inc. v. Martino, 36 F.3d 291, 294 (citing Tefal, S.A. v. Products Int'l Co., 529 F.2d 495, 496 n.1 (3d Cir. 1976)); Indianapolis Colts v. Metro. Baltimore Football, 34 F.3d 410 (7th Cir. 1994). . . .

In *Indianapolis Colts,* also case cited by the Third Circuit in *Cottman,* an Indiana National Football League franchise sued a Maryland Canadian Football League franchise in the Southern District of Indiana, alleging trademark infringement. *Indianapolis Colts*, 34 F.3d at 411. On appeal, the Seventh Circuit held that personal jurisdiction was appropriate in Indiana because trademark infringement is a tort-like injury and a substantial amount of the injury from the alleged infringement was likely to occur in Indiana. Id. at 412.

In the instant case, both a significant amount of the alleged infringement and dilution, and resulting injury have occurred in Pennsylvania. The object of Dot Com's contracts with Pennsylvania residents is the transmission of the messages that Plaintiff claims dilute and infringe upon its trademark. When these messages are transmitted into Pennsylvania and viewed by Pennsylvania residents on their computers, there can be no question that the alleged infringement and dilution occur in Pennsylvania. Moreover, since Manufacturing is a Pennsylvania corporation, a substantial amount of the injury from the alleged wrongdoing is likely to occur in Pennsylvania. Thus, we conclude that the cause of action arises out of Dot Com's forum-related activities under the authority of both *Tefal* and *Indianapolis Colts,* supra.

Finally, Dot Com argues that the exercise of jurisdiction would be unreasonable in this case. We disagree. There can be no question that Pennsylvania has a strong interest in adjudicating disputes involving the alleged infringement of trademarks owned by resident corporations. We must also give due regard to the Plaintiff's choice to seek relief in Pennsylvania. *Kulko,* 436 U.S. at 92. These concerns outweigh the burden created by forcing the Defendant to defend the suit in Pennsylvania, especially when Dot Com consciously chose to conduct business in Pennsylvania, pursuing profits from the actions that are now in question. The Due Process Clause is not a "territorial shield to interstate obligations that have been voluntarily assumed." *Burger King,* 471 U.S. at 474. . . .

## IV.  Conclusion

We conclude that this Court may appropriately exercise personal jurisdiction over the Defendant. . . .

## *Note: Traditional Concepts*

The legal contracts between "Dot Com" and its Pennsylvania customers are really driving the outcome, aren't they? Does the existence of the Web add to the analysis or is this just *Burger King* in cyberspace? Compare the jurisdictional facts in *Zippo* with those in the problem case. Are they equally compelling cases for exercising jurisdiction? What do you make of the "reasonableness" analysis in the penultimate paragraph of the opinion? Are Internet vendors open to suit anywhere they have clients? Almost anywhere?

If you were a lawyer representing a Web entrepreneur, like Sleeze in our problem case, how would you advise him to avoid potential worldwide personal jurisdiction? One device for websites selling products is the "click-wrap agreement" that includes a choice of venue clause, which a consumer must agree to before being allowed to buy anything. Stomp Inc. v. NeatO, LLC, 61 F. Supp. 2d 1074 (C.D. Cal. 1999).

*Zippo*'s "sliding scale test" is now the rule in a number of circuits. See, e.g., Shrader v. Biddinger, 633 F.3d 1235, 1242 (10th Cir. 2011) (describing *Zippo* test as an "heuristic adjunct to, rather than a substitute for, traditional jurisdictional analysis"); Johnson v. Arden, 614 F.3d 785, 796 (8th Cir. 2010); Best Van Lines, Inc. v. Walker, 490 F.3d 239 (2d Cir. 2007) (using the *Zippo* test to frame the inquiry into whether the defendant transacted any business in the jurisdiction); Carefirst of Md., Inc. v. Carefirst Pregnancy Ctrs., Inc., 334 F.3d 390 (4th Cir. 2003); Toys "R" Us, Inc. v. Step Two, S.A., 318 F.3d 446, 452 (3d Cir. 2003) (calling *Zippo* the "seminal authority regarding personal jurisdiction based upon the operation of an Internet web site"); Neogen Corp. v. Neo Gen Screening, Inc., 282 F.3d 883 (6th Cir. 2002), *followed in* One Media IP Ltd. V.S.A.A.R. SrL, 122 F. Supp. 3d 705 (M.D. Tenn. 2015) (no personal jurisdiction where defendant's Web site did not directly contract with consumers in Tennessee or offer allegedly infringing music recordings for sale); Mink v. AAAA Dev. LLC, 190 F.3d 333, 336 (5th Cir. 1999); Cybersell, Inc. v. Cybersell, Inc., 130 F.3d 414 (9th Cir. 1997).

However, a number of lower courts have signaled their willingness to disregard the *Zippo* framework. See, e.g., Illinois v. Hemi Group LLC, 622 F.3d 754, 758-759 (7th Cir. 2010) ("We wish to point out that we have done the entire minimum contacts analysis without resorting to the sliding scale approach first developed in *Zippo*. . . . This was not a mistake . . . . [W]e think the traditional due process inquiry . . . is not so difficult to apply to cases involving Internet contacts. . . ."); Caiazzo v. Am. Royal Arts Corp., 73 So. 3d 245, 254 (Fla. Dist. Ct. App. 2011) ("No Florida court has actually adopted the *Zippo* factors and we are not inclined to do so either."); Kauffman Racing Equip., L.L.C v. Roberts, 930 N.E.2d 784 (2010) ("When the Internet activity in question is non-commercial in nature, the *Zippo* analysis offers little to supplement the traditional framework. . . .") (internal quotations omitted); Shamsuddin v. Vitamin Research Prods., 346 F. Supp. 2d 804, 811 (D. Md. 2004) (holding that "website interactivity may have some bearing on the jurisdictional analysis, but it does not control the outcome"); Howard v. Mo. Bone & Joint Ctr., Inc., 869 N.E.2d 207, 212 (Ill. App. 5th 2007) (calling the *Zippo* sliding-scale approach "arbitrary" and concluding that "the web page's level of interactivity is irrelevant"). See also Sayeedi v. Walser, 835 N.Y.S.2d 840, 845-846 (Civ. Ct. 2007) (expressing skepticism about the relevance of *Zippo*'s interactivity analysis where buyers and sellers who connect through an auction site such as eBay "cannot be said themselves to control eBay's degree of commercial interactivity any more than a buyer and seller at Sotheby's can be said to be responsible for the premises or to control the auctioneer").

Several articles, however, have argued that the *Zippo* test should be abandoned. See, e.g., Eric C. Hawkins, General Jurisdiction and Internet Contacts: What Role, If Any, Should the *Zippo* Sliding Scale Test Play in the Analysis?, 74 Fordham L. Rev. 2371 (2006); Bunmi Awoyemi, *Zippo* Is Dying, Should It Be Dead?: The Exercise of Personal Jurisdiction by U.S. Federal Courts over

Non-Domiciliary Defendants in Trademark Infringement Lawsuits Arising Out of Cyberspace, 9 Marq. Intell. Prop. L. Rev. 37 (2005).

Two courts have gone further than *Zippo*, holding that Internet companies with interactive, commercially successful Web sites may be subject to *general* jurisdiction in any state where sales and use of the Web site are substantial. See Gator.com Corp. v. L.L. Bean, Inc., 341 F.3d 1072, 1079-1080 (9th Cir. 2003), *rehearing en banc granted by* 366 F.3d 789 (2004) (finding general jurisdiction arising from L.L. Bean's "highly interactive, as opposed to 'passive,' website," its extensive Internet catalogue sales in California, and its targeted electronic advertising in the state), *dismissed as moot by* 398 F.3d 1125 (9th Cir. 2005) (en banc); Gorman v. Ameritrade Holding Corp., 293 F.3d 506, 512-513 (D.C. Cir. 2002) (finding general jurisdiction where D.C. customers of defendant online brokerage firm used the Web site to open accounts, transmit funds to those accounts electronically, use the accounts to buy and sell securities, and enter into bidding contracts with the defendant). But particularly since *Goodyear*, courts have rejected looking to the degree of interactivity to determine general personal jurisdiction. See CollegeSource, Inc. v. AcademyOne, Inc., 653 F.3d 1066, 1075-1076 (9th Cir. 2011) ("Interactive websites where a user can exchange information with the host computer are now extremely common. If the maintenance of an interactive website were sufficient to support general jurisdiction in every forum in which users interacted with the website, the eventual demise of all restrictions on the personal jurisdiction of state courts would be the inevitable result.") (internal quotations and citations omitted).

### Note: Substance and Procedure

The nature of the Internet comes up first in connection with personal jurisdiction. In many cases, the issue is also central to the merits. What kinds of facts would Plaintiff Neff want to show about *The Naked Truth* Web site at the trial? Questions about who owns what in cyberspace are often contested in huge, bet-the-store jury trials, replete with many experts and multi-media presentations.

One of the most interesting trials of the twentieth century was the government's case against Microsoft for antitrust violations and unfair competition. Though it was tried by a judge, the intense media and market interest gave it the flavor and community connection of a jury trial. The existential features of the Web and who controls access to it were at issue in the case, and much of the evidence was in electronic form, including crucial e-mails. See, e.g., U.S. v. Microsoft: How a Case Gained Momentum, N.Y. Times, June 9, 2000, at A1; Laureen Seeger and Beth Rogers, Computer Compliance Issues: U.S. v. Microsoft & E-mail, 1121 PLI/Corp. 11 (1999). The case also required the trial judge to master the intricacies of contemporary computer markets and technology, fomenting discussions of the judiciary's institutional competence to deal with emerging technological issues. For further discussion of issues surrounding the *Microsoft* trial, see Steve Bickerstaff,

Shackles on the Giant: How the Federal Government Created Microsoft, Personal Computers, and the Internet, 78 Tex. L. Rev. 1 (1999); Symposium, United States v. Microsoft, 31 Conn. L. Rev. 1245 (1999).

## *Note: Enforceability*

One concern for a judge ruling on personal jurisdiction is whether he or she will be able to enter enforceable judgments. Distant defendants with only Web contacts in the forum state may be able simply to ignore court orders. Consider, for instance, the case of the toymaker, Mattel Inc., the manufacturer of the Barbie doll. It owns Cyber Patrol, a popular Internet filtering program intended to help parents block children's access to harmful sites, and also used by libraries and schools.

Two computer enthusiasts, one in Canada and one in Sweden, each independently designed programs to defeat Cyber Patrol, and posted them for free on the Internet. Mattel sued, claiming violation of the Cyber Patrol copyright. Mattel filed its case in Massachusetts, and the two original defendants caved in immediately, stipulating to the entry of a far-ranging injunction against not only the named defendants but "all persons in active concert or participation" with them. All these "un-named parties" were enjoined from "publishing the software source code and binaries known as 'Cphack.exe' or any derivative thereof."

The injunction would presumably cover the hundred or so other people in the United States and elsewhere who had set up mirror sites of the original two, from which Cphack.exe could be downloaded and used. None of these people received notice or had the opportunity to be heard. Few have ever been in Massachusetts. Are they bound by the injunction? Should they be bound? What is the remedy if they continue to display their Web sites? See Microsystems Software, Inc. v. Scandinavia Online AB, 98 F. Supp. 2d 74 (D. Mass. 2000). See also Chapter 5, section B, infra.

## *Note: Purposeful Availment and Dot-Com Litigation Overseas*

How can a Web-based company protect itself against judgments obtained by foreign users in foreign courts? Popular search engines are especially susceptible to foreign litigation because they are used by people all around the world and they must constantly balance the goal of providing open access to wide-ranging Internet content against the risk that content accessed through their search engines will offend users and/or the law where users are logging on. To give but one example, Yahoo! runs chat rooms and an auction Web site. Nazi rhetoric has surfaced in some of its chat rooms and Nazi paraphernalia has appeared for sale on its auction Web site. In 2004, two French organizations filed suit in French court against Yahoo! alleging violations of the French Criminal Code, which prohibits exhibition of Nazi propaganda for sale and the purchase or possession of such material by French citizens, and other French hate speech laws. The Web site www. fr.yahoo.com, run by the company's subsidiary in France, edits the Web site to exclude all Nazi material, but French users can easily access the unedited American Web site. The French court granted an injunction requiring Yahoo!, among other things, "to destroy all Nazi-related messages, images, and text stored on its server, particularly any Nazi relics, objects, insignia, emblems, and flags on its auction site, and to remove any excerpts from *Mein Kampf* and *Protocole des Sages de Sion*, books promoting Nazism." Yahoo! Inc. v. La Ligue Contre le Racisme et L'Antisemitisme, 379 F.3d 1120, 1122 (9th Cir. 2004). The injunction authorized sanctions of about $13,300 U.S. *per day* for failure to comply.

Rather than comply with or appeal the decision in France, Yahoo! filed a complaint in the Northern District of California seeking a declaration that the French court's orders were unenforceable in the United States because they abridge the First Amendment. The French organizations responded by moving to dismiss the complaint for want of personal jurisdiction. The district court denied the motion, holding that it could exercise specific jurisdiction because the French organizations had (1) sent a cease and desist letter to Yahoo!'s corporate headquarters in Santa Clara, California, demanding that Yahoo! remove the offending Nazi material, (2) used the United States Marshals Service to effect service on Yahoo! in California, and (3) asked the French court for an injunction ordering Yahoo! to make changes to its Web sites. Id. at 1124. The court decided that these actions met the purposeful availment requirement, because, like the libelous newspaper article in Calder v. Jones, see *supra* p. 138, they were "'expressly aim[ed]'" at Yahoo! in California. Id. at 1124 (quoting *Calder*).

The Ninth Circuit reversed on appeal, noting that *Calder*'s "express aiming" test requires that the conduct aimed at the forum state must be "wrongful," like the intentionally tortious article the journalist and editor in *Calder* were sued for publishing. The French organization's actions, by contrast, were simply efforts to enforce French law — efforts, the court stressed, that a French court had already deemed legitimate. Id. at 1125-1126. A lengthy dissenting opinion argued that wrongful conduct is only one form of express aiming that can meet the purposeful availment requirement. Id. at 1132 ("[A]lthough an intentional tortious act clearly satisfies the *Calder* 'effects test,' . . . so too can other conduct 'targeted' or 'expressly aimed' at residents of the forum state") (Brunetti, J., dissenting opinion).

In 2006, after rehearing the case en banc, the Ninth Circuit reversed the panel decision, finding the exercise of personal jurisdiction proper. The court pointed out that if conduct had to be wrongful in order to create personal jurisdiction, a court would lose its jurisdiction, and hence its ability to decide a case, the moment it ruled the questionable conduct to be permissible. *Yahoo!*, 433 F.3d 1199, 1208 (2006). In evaluating the French organization's contacts with the forum state, the court agreed with earlier decisions that the cease and desist letter alone was not enough to establish minimum contacts. See Inamed Corp. v. Kuzmak, 249 F.3d 1356 (Fed. Cir. 2001); Bancroft & Masters, Inc. v. Augusta Nat'l Inc., 223 F.3d 1082 (9th Cir.

2000); Cascade Corp. v. Hiab-Foco AB, 619 F.2d 36 (9th Cir. 1980). But taken together with the interim orders from the French court, the Ninth Circuit found sufficient contacts for personal jurisdiction.

Additionally, whether or not the French court had infringed Yahoo!'s First Amendment rights, the court noted that enforcement of the fines was highly unlikely because "American courts do not enforce monetary fines or penalties awarded by foreign courts." *Yahoo!*, 433 F.3d at 1211. A plurality of the court further held that the First Amendment question was not ripe, and remanded the case to the district court to be dismissed without prejudice. The lawsuit appears to have had an impact on online companies despite the dismissal. Recently, Twitter voluntarily agreed to remove anti-Semitic tweets after being threatened with litigation by a French organization. That decision came a day after the company blocked the account of a neo-Nazi group that is banned in Germany. Eleanor Beardsley, French Tweet Sweep Shows Twitter's Local Struggles, National Public Radio, Oct. 20, 2012.

## 10.   Waiving Due Process Objections by Agreement: Autonomy or Adhesion?

### Problem Case: A Hidden Forum Selection Clause?

In January 2012, the County of Travis, Texas, decided to replace its manual voting machines with electronic voting machines. On January 31, 2012, the County entered a contract with Failsafe Voting Machines to purchase 1,000 Electronic Voting Units ("EVUs"), manufactured by AccuVote, Inc. Failsafe provided software, marketing, distribution, and maintenance for the AccuVote EVUs. Failsafe's contract with the County contained a warranty clause promising that the EVUs would perform without any problem recording a vote, any inaccuracy tallying votes, or any mechanical or software defects causing voting delays. Failsafe further warranted that its machines would meet any and all standards for electronic voting machines provided by federal law. Under the contract, the County paid the complete purchase price of $5 million up front.

The EVUs were used in a handful of polling places for the Spring 2012 primaries and the June 2012 special elections. Based on their solid performance, the County decided to use them county-wide for a multi-page ballot in the November 2012 general elections. This time, the machines malfunctioned badly. When voters scrolled the ballot on screen to reach additional pages, the EVUs shut down. The power failures caused long lines at polling places, delays of up to five hours, and, in some instances, voters left the lines in frustration without voting. Matters grew worse after the polls closed when the software designed to count the votes miscalculated the results and sent the incorrect data to the press. It took two days of recounting to certify and announce the correct results of the election, making it the most costly and error-ridden in the County's history.

In March 2013, the County decided to return to its manual voting machines. Immediately after sending the defective EVUs back to Failsafe on March 15, 2013, the County filed and properly served a complaint against Failsafe seeking $5 million for breach of contract, breach of warranty, and fraud, in the U.S. District Court for the Western District of Texas.

Failsafe is a Japanese corporation. The County is Failsafe's only Texas client and represents 50 percent of its total global revenue. The company's CEO, CFO, and COO, as well as its entire U.S. sales and software force, worked in Austin, Texas. Each EVU Failsafe delivers to its customers comes wrapped in protective packaging. On the surface of the part of the packaging that covers the EVU screen, the company always inserts a two-inch square card with the following text printed in 7-point font:

> — READ BEFORE OPENING —
> Purchaser agrees that any claim regarding the performance of this machine brought, at any time, against Failsafe Voting Machines shall be brought ONLY in the courts of Japan. Use of this machine constitutes acceptance of the foregoing.

The County disregarded these cards on the packaging when it filed suit in Texas federal court because it cannot afford to litigate its case against Failsafe in Japan and its lawyers advised that the provision may not be enforceable since volunteer election officers responsible for opening and booting up the EVUs claimed not to have noticed them.

Failsafe has moved to dismiss the complaint under Rule 12(b)(2). Is the Texas federal court obliged to enforce the forum selection provision? If not, does the court have personal jurisdiction over Failsafe?

As we saw in *Burger King*, parties can by private agreement affect what law will be applied to a controversy. Whether and when courts will respect these choice of law clauses depends on several practical and policy considerations, including the extent to which the agreement was freely negotiated.

What principle justifies giving effect to a forum selection clause? How knowing and voluntary must the execution of the clause (versus the entire contract) be to warrant giving that clause effect? Read on to see what the U.S. Supreme Court has said on the matter.

In Shute v. Carnival Cruise Lines, 783 P.2d 78 (Wash. 1989), Eulala Shute, a Washington resident, fell while touring the galley of the cruise ship *Tropicale* while it was off the coast of Mexico. She had purchased her ticket in Washington through a travel agent who forwarded the payment to Carnival's headquarters in Miami. The cruise sailed from Los Angeles to Puerto Vallarta, Mexico.

Factors cutting for the exercise of jurisdiction were Carnival's advertisements in local newspapers, its provision of brochures to travel agents within the state, and its periodic seminars for travel agents in order to update them on Carnival's offerings. Carnival also pays a 10 percent commission on proceeds from tickets sold for Carnival cruises. On the other hand, Carnival is a Panamanian corporation with its principal place of business in Miami. It is not registered to do business in Washington, owns no property, and maintains no office or bank account there. None of its ships call at Washington ports.

The suit was filed in federal district court, which held that it had no jurisdiction. Initially, the Ninth Circuit reversed and found that there was jurisdiction. The court then withdrew its opinion and certified to the Supreme Court of Washington the question whether the long-arm statute applied to Carnival Cruise Lines. In deciding that its statute would bring Carnival Cruise Lines to Washington to defend, the state Supreme Court held that its statute requires that three factors must coincide:

(1) The nonresident defendant or foreign corporation must purposefully do some act or consummate some transaction in the forum state;

(2) the cause of action must arise from, or be connected with, such act or transaction; and

(3) the assumption of jurisdiction by the forum state must not offend traditional notions of fair play and substantial justice, consideration being given to the quality, nature, and extent of the activity in the forum state, the relative convenience of the parties, the benefits and protection of the laws of the forum state afforded the respective parties, and the basic equities of the situation.

783 P.2d at 80. The Washington court concluded:

We adopt the "but for" test of Shute v. Carnival Cruise Lines, 863 F.2d 1437 (9th Cir. 1988), *withdrawn*, 872 F.2d 930 (1989), and hold that there is sufficient connection between the Shutes' claim and Carnival's Washington contacts to support long-arm jurisdiction under RCW 4.28.185. "But for" Carnival's "transaction of any business within this state," Mrs. Eulala Shute would not have been injured on respondent's cruise ship. Therefore her claim "arises from" Carnival's Washington contacts within the meaning of Washington's long-arm statute.

Id. at 82.

Thus, as it was litigated through the courts below, *Carnival Cruise* was shaping up to be the next major case on personal jurisdiction, dealing with the sending of advertising messages and other intangibles through the commercial stream. The question on which the U.S. Supreme Court granted certiorari was: "Can a state long-arm statute constitutionally reach a defendant whose activities in the forum state are insubstantial and bear only a tenuous relationship to the cause of action?" But this question was not to be decided.

### *Carnival Cruise Lines v. Shute*
499 U.S. 585 (1991)

JUSTICE BLACKMUN delivered the opinion of the Court.

In this admiralty case we primarily consider whether the United States Court of Appeals for the Ninth Circuit correctly refused to enforce a forum-selection clause contained in tickets issued by petitioner Carnival Cruise Lines, Inc., to respondents Eulala and Russel Shute.

**I**

The Shutes, through an Arlington, Wash., travel agent, purchased passage for a 7-day cruise on petitioner's ship, the *Tropicale*. Respondents paid the fare to the agent who forwarded the payment to petitioner's headquarters in Miami, Fla. Petitioner then prepared the tickets and sent them to respondents in the State of Washington. The face of each ticket, at its left-hand lower corner, contained this admonition:

SUBJECT TO CONDITIONS OF
CONTRACT ON LAST PAGES
**IMPORTANT!** PLEASE READ CONTRACT
ON LAST PAGES 1, 2, 3

The following appeared on "contract page 1" of each ticket:

**Terms and Conditions of Passage Contract Ticket**

3. (a) The acceptance of this ticket by the person or persons named hereon as passengers shall be deemed to be an acceptance and agreement by each of them of all of the terms and conditions of this Passage Contract Ticket.
8. It is agreed by and between the passenger and the Carrier that all disputes and matters whatsoever arising under, in connection with or incident to this Contract shall be litigated, if at all, in and before a Court located in the State of Florida, U.S.A., to the exclusion of the Courts of any other state or country.

The last quoted paragraph is the forum-selection clause at issue. . . .

Turning to the forum-selection clause, the Court of Appeals acknowledged that a court concerned with the enforceability of such a clause must begin its analysis with The Bremen v. Zapata Off-Shore Co., 407 U.S. 1 (1972), where this Court held that forum-selection clauses, although not "historically . . . favored," are "prima facie valid." Id., at 9-10. See [Shute v. Carnival Cruise Lines,] 897 F.2d at 388 [9th Cir. 1990]. The appellate court concluded that the forum clause should not be enforced because it "was not freely bargained for." Id. at 389. As an "independent justification" for refusing to enforce the clause, the Court of Appeals noted that there was evidence in the record to indicate that "the Shutes are physically and financially incapable of pursuing this litigation in Florida" and that the enforcement of the clause would operate to deprive them of their day in court and thereby contravene this Court's holding in *The Bremen*. 897 F.2d at 389.

We granted certiorari to address the question whether the Court of Appeals was correct in holding that the District Court should hear respondents' tort claim against petitioner. 498 U.S. at 807-808 (1990). Because we find the forum-selection clause to be dispositive of this question, we need not consider petitioner's constitutional argument as to personal jurisdiction.

We begin by noting the boundaries of our inquiry. First, this is a case in admiralty, and federal law governs the enforceability of the forum-selection clause we scrutinize. Second, we do not address the question whether respondents had sufficient notice of the forum clause before entering the contract for passage. Respondents essentially have conceded that they had notice of the forum-selection provision. Additionally, the Court of Appeals evaluated the enforceability of the forum clause under the assumption, although "doubtful," that respondents could be deemed to have had knowledge of the clause.

Within this context, respondents urge that the forum clause should not be enforced because, contrary to this Court's teachings in *The Bremen*, the clause was not the product of negotiation, and enforcement effectively would deprive respondents of their day in court. . . .

Both petitioner and respondents argue vigorously that the Court's opinion in *The Bremen* governs this case, and each side purports to find ample support for its position in that opinion's broad-ranging language. This seeming paradox derives in large part from key factual differences between this case and *The Bremen*, differences that preclude an automatic and simple application of *The Bremen*'s general principles to the facts here.

In *The Bremen*, this Court addressed the enforceability of a forum-selection clause in a contract between two business corporations. An American corporation, Zapata, made a contract with Unterweser, a German corporation, for the towage of Zapata's ocean-going drilling rig from Louisiana to a point in the Adriatic Sea off the coast of Italy. The agreement provided that any dispute arising under the contract was to be resolved in the London Court of Justice. After a storm in the Gulf of Mexico seriously damaged the rig, Zapata ordered Unterweser's ship to tow the rig to Tampa, Fla., the nearest point of refuge. Thereafter, Zapata sued Unterweser in admiralty in federal court at Tampa. Citing the forum clause, Unterweser moved to dismiss. The District Court denied Unterweser's motion, and the Court of Appeals for the Fifth Circuit, sitting en banc on rehearing, and by a sharply divided vote, affirmed. 446 F.2d 907 (1971).

This Court vacated and remanded, stating that, in general, "a freely negotiated private international agreement, unaffected by fraud, undue influence, or overweening bargaining power, such as that involved here, should be given full effect." 407 U.S. at 12-13 (footnote omitted). The Court further generalized that "in the light of present-day commercial realities and expanding international trade we conclude that the forum clause should control absent a strong showing that it should be set aside." Id. at 15. The Court did not define precisely the circumstances that would make it unreasonable for a court to enforce a forum clause. Instead, the Court discussed a number of factors that made it reasonable to enforce the clause at issue in *The Bremen* and that, presumably, would be pertinent in any determination whether to enforce a similar clause.

In this respect, the Court noted that there was "strong evidence that the forum clause was a vital part of the agreement, and [that] it would be unrealistic to think that the parties did not conduct their negotiations, including fixing the monetary terms, with the consequences of the forum clause figuring prominently in their calculations." Id. at 14 (footnote omitted).

Further, the Court observed that it was not "dealing with an agreement between two Americans to resolve their essentially local disputes in a remote alien forum," and that in such a case, "the serious inconvenience of the contractual forum to one or both of the parties might carry greater weight in determining the reasonableness of the forum clause." Id. at 17. The Court stated that even where the forum clause establishes a remote forum for resolution of conflicts, "the party claiming [unfairness] should bear a heavy burden of proof." Ibid.

In applying *The Bremen*, the Court of Appeals in the present litigation took note of the foregoing "reasonableness" factors and rather automatically decided that the forum-selection clause was unenforceable because, unlike the parties in *The Bremen*, respondents are not business persons and did not negotiate the terms of the clause with petitioner. Alternatively, the Court of Appeals ruled that the clause should not be enforced because enforcement effectively would deprive respondents of an opportunity to litigate their claim against petitioner. *The Bremen* concerned a "far from routine transaction between companies of two different nations contemplating the tow of an extremely costly piece of equipment from Louisiana across the Gulf of Mexico and the Atlantic Ocean, through the Mediterranean Sea to its final destination in the Adriatic Sea." Id. at 13. These facts suggest that, even apart from the evidence of negotiation regarding the forum clause, it was entirely reasonable for the Court in *The Bremen* to have expected Unterweser and Zapata to have negotiated with care in selecting a forum for the resolution of disputes arising from their special towing contract.

In contrast, respondents' passage contract was purely routine and doubtless nearly identical to every commercial passage contract issued by petitioner and most other cruise lines. In this context, it would be entirely unreasonable for us to assume that respondents—or any other cruise passenger—would negotiate with petitioner the terms of a forum-selection clause in an ordinary commercial cruise ticket. Common sense dictates that a ticket of this kind will be a form contract the terms of which are not subject to negotiation, and that an individual purchasing the ticket will not have bargaining parity with the cruise line. But by ignoring the crucial differences in the business contexts in which the respective contracts were executed, the Court of Appeals' analysis seems to us to have distorted somewhat this Court's holding in *The Bremen*.

In evaluating the reasonableness of the forum clause at issue in this case, we must refine the analysis of *The Bremen* to account for the realities of form passage contracts. As an initial matter, we do not adopt the Court of Appeals' determination that a nonnegotiated forum-selection clause in a form ticket contract is never enforceable simply because it is not the subject of bargaining. Including a reasonable forum clause in a form contract of this kind well may be permissible for several reasons: First, a cruise line has a special interest in limiting the fora in which it potentially could be subject to suit. Because a cruise ship typically carries passengers from many locales, it is not unlikely that a mishap on a cruise could subject the cruise line to litigation in several different fora. Additionally, a clause establishing *ex ante* the forum for dispute resolution has the salutary effect of dispelling any confusion about where suits arising from the contract must be brought and defended, sparing litigants the time and expense of pretrial motions to determine the correct forum and conserving judicial resources that otherwise would be devoted to deciding those motions. Finally, it stands to reason that passengers who purchase tickets containing a forum clause like that at issue in this case benefit in the form of reduced fares reflecting the savings that the cruise line enjoys by limiting the fora in which it may be sued.

We also do not accept the Court of Appeals' "independent justification" for its conclusion that *The Bremen* dictates that the clause should not be enforced because "[t]here is evidence in the record to indicate that the Shutes are physically and financially incapable of pursuing this litigation in Florida." 897 F.2d at 389. We do not defer to the Court of Appeals' findings of fact. In dismissing the case for lack of personal jurisdiction over petitioner, the District Court made no finding regarding the physical and financial impediments to the Shutes' pursuing their case in Florida. The Court of Appeals' conclusory reference to the record provides no basis for this Court to validate the finding of inconvenience. . . . In the present case, Florida is not a "remote alien forum," nor—given the fact that Mrs. Shute's accident occurred off the coast of Mexico—is this dispute an essentially local one inherently more suited to resolution in the State of Washington than in Florida. In light of these distinctions, and because respondents do not claim lack of notice of the forum clause, we conclude that they have not satisfied the "heavy burden of proof" required to set aside the clause on grounds of inconvenience.

It bears emphasis that forum-selection clauses contained in form passage contracts are subject to judicial scrutiny for fundamental fairness. In this case, there is no indication that petitioner set Florida as the forum in which disputes were to be resolved as a means of discouraging cruise passengers from pursuing legitimate claims. Any suggestion of such a bad-faith motive is belied by two facts: Petitioner has its principal place of business in Florida, and many of its cruises depart from and return to Florida ports. Similarly, there is no evidence that petitioner obtained respondents' accession to the forum clause by fraud or overreaching. Finally, respondents have conceded that they were given notice of the forum provision and, therefore, presumably retained the option of rejecting the contract with impunity. In the case before us, therefore, we conclude that the Court of Appeals erred in refusing to enforce the forum-selection clause. . . .

The judgment of the Court of Appeals is reversed.

*It is so ordered.*

JUSTICE STEVENS, with whom JUSTICE MARSHALL joins, dissenting.

The Court prefaces its legal analysis with a factual statement that implies that a purchaser of a Carnival Cruise Lines passenger ticket is fully and fairly notified about the existence of the choice of forum clause in the fine print on the back of the ticket. Even if this implication were accurate, I would disagree with the Court's analysis. But, given the Court's preface, I begin my dissent by noting that only the most meticulous passenger is likely to become aware of the forum-selection provision. I have therefore appended to this opinion a facsimile of the relevant text, using the type size that actually appears in the ticket itself. A careful reader will find the forum-selection clause in the 8th of the 25 numbered paragraphs.

Of course, many passengers, like the respondents in this case, will not have an opportunity to read paragraph 8 until they have actually purchased their tickets. By this point, the passengers will already have accepted the condition set forth in paragraph 16(a), which provides that "[t]he Carrier shall not be liable to make any refund to passengers in respect of . . . tickets wholly or partly not used by a passenger." Not knowing whether or not that provision is legally enforceable, I assume that the average passenger would accept the risk of having to file suit in Florida in the event of an injury, rather than canceling—without a refund—a planned vacation at the last minute. The fact that the cruise line can reduce its litigation costs, and therefore its liability insurance premiums, by forcing this choice on its passengers does not, in my opinion, suffice to render the provision reasonable. . . .

Forum-selection clauses in passenger tickets involve the intersection of two strands of traditional contract law that qualify the general rule that courts will enforce the terms of a contract as written. Pursuant to the first strand, courts traditionally have reviewed with heightened scrutiny the terms of contracts of adhesion, form contracts offered on a take-or-leave basis by a party with stronger bargaining power to a party with weaker power. Some commentators have questioned whether contracts of adhesion can justifiably be enforced at all under traditional contract theory because the adhering party generally enters into them without manifesting knowing and voluntary consent to all their terms.

The common law, recognizing that standardized form contracts account for a significant portion of all commercial agreements, has taken a less extreme position and instead subjects terms in contracts of adhesion to scrutiny for reasonableness. Judge J. Skelly Wright set out the state of the law succinctly in Williams v. Walker-Thomas Furniture Co., 350 F.2d 445, 449-450 (1965) (footnotes omitted):

> Ordinarily, one who signs an agreement without full knowledge of its terms might be held to assume the risk that he has entered a one-sided bargain. But when a party of little bargaining power, and hence little real choice, signs a commercially unreasonable contract with little or no knowledge of its terms, it is hardly likely that his consent, or even an objective manifestation of his consent, was ever given to all of the terms. In such a case the usual rule that the terms of the agreement are not to be questioned should be abandoned and the court should consider whether the terms of the contract are so unfair that enforcement should be withheld.

The second doctrinal principle implicated by forum-selection clauses is the traditional rule that "contractual provisions, which seek to limit the place or court in which an action may . . . be brought, are invalid as contrary to public policy." See Dougherty, Validity of Contractual Provision Limiting Place or Court in Which Action May Be Brought, 31 A.L.R. 4th 404, 409 § 3 (1984). Although adherence to this general rule has declined in recent years, particularly following our decision in The Bremen v. Zapata Off-Shore Co., 407 U.S. 1 (1972), the prevailing rule is still that forum-selection clauses are not enforceable if they were not freely bargained for, create additional expense for one party, or deny one party a remedy. A forum-selection clause in a standardized passenger ticket would clearly have been unenforceable under the common law before our decision in *The Bremen,* and, in my opinion, remains unenforceable under the prevailing rule today. . . .

I respectfully dissent.

## Notes and Questions

1. The Court in *Carnival Cruise* suggests that forum selection clauses should be enforced only if they are fundamentally fair. Yet it upheld a small-type forum clause against the Shutes. Is the concept of fundamental fairness related to due process?

2. The Supreme Court's decision in *Carnival Cruise* has been the subject of criticism from many angles. A sampling of the criticism is listed here. For the contracts perspective, see Patrick J. Borchers, Forum Selection Agreements in the Federal Courts after *Carnival Cruise*: A Proposal for Congressional Reform, 67 Wash. L. Rev. 55 (1992); for an economic perspective, see Lee Goldman, My Way and the Highway: The Law and Economics of Choice of Forum Clauses in Consumer Form Contracts, 86 Nw. U. L. Rev. 700 (1992). For the personal jurisdiction perspective, see John McKinley Kirby, Consumer's Right to Sue at Home Jeopardized Through Forum Selection Clause in Carnival Cruise Lines v. Shute, 70 N.C. L. Rev. 888 (1992); Edward A. Purcell, Jr., Geography as a Litigation Weapon: Consumers, Forum-Selection Clauses, and the Rehnquist Court, 40 UCLA L. Rev. 423 (1992); David H. Taylor, The Forum Selection Clause: A Tale of Two Concepts, 66 Temp. L. Rev. 785 (1993); Linda S. Mullenix, Forum-Shoppers Should Discover a Wider Market, Nat'l L.J., Aug. 19, 1991, at S12.

For an especially thorough examination of the consequences of forum selection clauses, see Walter W. Heiser, Forum Selection Clauses in State Court: Limitations on Enforcement After *Stewart* and *Carnival Cruise*, 45 Fla. L. Rev. 361 (1993). And for an important historical study of forum selection clause enforcement, see David Marcus, The Perils of Contract Procedure: A Revised History of Forum Selection Clauses in the Federal Courts, 82 Tul. L. Rev. 973 (2008).

3. Notwithstanding the criticism, lower courts generally have followed the Court's lead. But see Walker v. Carnival Cruise Lines, 107 F. Supp. 2d 1135 (N.D. Cal. 2000) (refusing to enforce a forum selection clause in a suit alleging that Carnival Cruise violated the Americans with Disabilities Act by failing to provide accessible accommodations on a cruise ship; the court

reasoned that, in combination, "plaintiffs' physical disabilities and economic constraints are so severe that . . . they would preclude plaintiffs from
having their day in court" if they had to travel to bring suit against Carnival
Cruise); id. at 1143 ("This Court is persuaded that enforcing defendants'
forum selection clause, under the circumstances presented here, would
contravene the strong national policy of eradicating disability discrimination and promoting full and equal access to the legal system for civil rights
plaintiffs."). See also O'Brien v. Okemo Mountain, Inc., 17 F. Supp. 2d 98
(D. Conn. 1998) (inadequate notice on lift ticket rendered forum selection
clause unenforceable). For its part, Carnival Cruise Lines continues to rely
upon judicial enforcement of forum selection clauses limiting litigation to
South Florida courts near its headquarters in Miami. See Curt Anderson,
Cruise Lawsuits Are In, But Carnival Cruise Has Advantage, Assoc. Press,
Feb. 21, 2013.

Some courts have even extended the enforceability of forum selection
clauses to third parties. In Medtronic, Inc. v. Endologix, Inc., 530 F. Supp.
2d 1054 (D. Minn. 2008), a district court held that Medtronic (a heart valve
manufacturer with a long-standing corporate presence in Minnesota)
could bind not only two former employees who had signed employment
contracts that included forum selection clauses requiring litigation in
Minnesota state court, but also their new employer. The court reasoned that
"[a]lthough Endologix did not sign those agreements, a third party may be
bound by a forum-selection clause where it is 'closely related to the dispute
such that it becomes foreseeable that it will be bound.'" Id. at 1056 (quoting
and following Marano Enters. of Kan. v. Z-Teca Rests., L.P., 254 F.3d 753,
757 (8th Cir. 2001)). The court concluded that Endologix could "reasonably
foresee being bound by the forum-selection clause" because the litigation
arose from Endologix's decision to hire the two former Medtronic employees, it knew of the agreements the employees had signed with Medtronic,
and it shared a common interest with the employees in defending against
the Medtronic suit. Id. at 1057. Even if Endologix could not be bound as a
third party, the court continued, the forum selection clauses precluded the
employees from giving their consent to Endologix's attempt to remove the
case from Minnesota state court. Id.

4. All of us, in our online activity, have agreed to forum selection clauses
we have not read because they are tucked into "clickwrap agreements."
Typically, if a court finds the clickwrap agreement enforceable, it will
also enforce the forum clause contained in that agreement. See Fteja v.
Facebook, Inc., 841 F. Supp. 2d 829 (S.D.N.Y. 2012); Segal v. Amazon.com,
Inc., 763 F. Supp. 2d 1367 (S.D. Fla. 2011); TradeComet.com LLC v. Google,
Inc., 693 F. Supp. 2d 370 (S.D.N.Y. 2010). See also Corporate Counsel's Guide
to Licensing § 16:6 (2012) (gathering cases).

There are two exceptions. First, where the forum designated in the contract has lax consumer protection laws, courts in states with more robust
consumer protection laws have found the forum selection clause void as a
matter of public policy. See Dix v. ICT Group, Inc., 106 P.3d 841, 845 (Wash
Ct. App. 2005), *aff'd*, 161 P.3d 1016 (Wash. 2007) (holding that Washington's

Consumer Protection Act made AOL's forum selection clause unenforceable); Am. Online, Inc. v. Superior Court, 108 Cal. Rptr. 2d 699 (Cal. Ct. App. 2001) (holding that the enforcement of AOL's forum selection clause was the functional equivalent of a contractual waiver of the consumer protections under the California Consumer's Legal Remedies Act, and therefore barred); Am. Online, Inc. v. Pasieka, 870 So. 2d 170 (Fla. Dist. Ct. App. 2004) (holding that the Florida Deceptive and Unfair Trade Practices Act and Florida Free Gift Advertising Law barred enforcement of AOL's forum selection clause). But see Am. Online, Inc. v. Booker, 781 So. 2d 423 (Fla. Dist. Ct. App. 2001) (upholding AOL's forum selection clause); Koch v. Am. Online, Inc., 139 F. Supp. 2d 690 (D. Md. 2000) (upholding AOL's forum selection clause).

Second, sometimes the consumer isn't given the option of reviewing the contract. Instead, "the license terms provide that using a Web site constitutes agreement to a contract whether the user knows it or not." Mark A. Lemley, Terms of Use, 91 Minn. L. Rev. 459, 460 (2006). Forum selection clauses in these so-called browse wrap agreements have occasionally been struck down. See Jerez v. JD Closeouts, LLC, 943 N.Y.S.2d 392, 398 (Dist. Ct. 2012) (holding forum selection clause invalid where it was "buried" and "submerged" on a Web page that could only be found by clicking on an inconspicuous link on the company's "About Us" page); Hoffman v. Supplements Togo Mgmt., LLC, 18 A.3d 210, 212 (App. Div. 2011) (holding that a forum selection clause was unenforceable where "defendants' website was evidently structured in an unfair manner so that the clause would not appear on a purchaser's computer screen unless he or she scrolled down to display the 'submerged' clause before adding the product to his or her electronic 'shopping cart.'"). But see Molnar v. 1-800-Flowers.com, Inc., CV 08-0542 CAS JCx, 2008 WL 4772125 (C.D. Cal. Sept. 29, 2008).

5. What language must a party use to require litigation in the *state* courts of a forum and prevent a federal court from deciding the case? The circuit courts are divided. In the Fifth Circuit, if a forum selection clause refers generically to a specific county, either the state or federal courts sitting in that county may decide the case. See Alliance Health Group, LLC v. Bridging Health Options, LLC, 553 F.3d 397 (5th Cir. 2008). But see Excell, Inc. v. Sterling Boiler & Mech., Inc., 106 F.3d 318 (10th Cir. 1997) (clause providing "venue shall lie in the County of El Paso" required litigation in state court even though a federal court was located in that county). See also Simonoff v. Expedia, Inc., 643 F.3d 1202 (9th Cir. 2011) (disagreeing with *Excell*).

6. What is the proper motion to file to invoke a forum selection clause? A Rule 12(b)(3) motion to dismiss? A motion to dismiss under 28 U.S.C. § 1406(a) for improper venue? Where the forum selection clause specifies a *federal* forum, the Supreme Court has supplied a clear answer. The proper motion is for a change of venue under 28 U.S.C. § 1404(a). See Atlantic Marine Constr. Co. v. U.S. Dist. Ct. Western Dist. Tex., 134 S. Ct. 568 (2013). Unlike with an ordinary motion for change of venue, however, "plaintiff's choice of forum merits no weight" and the parties "waive the right to challenge the preselected forum as inconvenient or less convenient for themselves or their witnesses." Id. at 581-82. That leaves the district court

to "consider arguments about public-interest factors only." Id. at 582. But because "those factors will rarely defeat a transfer motion, the practical result is that forum-selection clauses should control except in unusual cases." Id. Finally, although a § 1404(a) transfer ordinarily carries with it the choice-of-law rules of the original venue, that rule does not apply when the § 1404(a) transfer enforces a forum selection clause. Id.

In the same case, the Court indicated that where a forum selection clause points to a *state* or *foreign* forum rather than a federal forum, the proper motion to file is a motion dismiss for *forum non conveniens* — the traditional procedural tool upon which § 1404(a) was modeled. Indeed, "because both § 1404(a) and the *forum non conveniens* doctrine from which it derives entail the same balancing-of-interests standard, courts should evaluate a forum-selection clause pointing to a nonfederal forum in the same way they evaluate a forum-selection clause pointing to a federal forum." Id. at 580. Section 1404(a) and *forum non conveniens* doctrine are covered in detail in Chapter 6. For present purposes, you need only recognize that there are specific procedural tools for enforcing a forum selection clause.

7. In *Carnival Cruise,* the Court treated the issues of personal jurisdiction and forum selection clauses as analytically distinct. Yet by effectively upholding Florida jurisdiction over the case, the Court may have missed the boat. Perhaps the *plaintiffs* have a due process right, akin to that of non-resident defendants, not to be forced to litigate in a foreign forum.

Due process for defendants requires that a court have personal jurisdiction over them before entering judgment. Thus, a forum selection clause operates against a defendant as a waiver of personal jurisdiction in the specified forum, limiting venue to that forum. Against a plaintiff, a forum selection clause forces an individual to bring suit in a specified place. Isn't there a parallel due process concern? See John McKinley Kirby, Consumer's Right to Sue at Home Jeopardized Through Forum Selection Clause in Carnival Cruise Line v. Shute, 70 N.C. L. Rev. 888 (1992).

Just as the Shutes were deemed to have entered into a valid contract designating the forum in which litigation would occur, a party may enter a private agreement waiving its constitutional right to *notice* by providing that service of process shall be made in a specific manner or upon a specific person. See Nat'l Equip. Rental, Ltd. v. Szukhent, 375 U.S. 311 (1964) ("[I]t is settled . . . that parties to a contract may agree in advance to submit to the jurisdiction of a given court, to permit notice to be served by the opposing party, or even to waive notice altogether."; in an action to recover unpaid rent on farm equipment, service upheld where contract designated relative of an officer of the leasing company as an agent for service against lessees, residents of Michigan).

Under what circumstances should people be allowed to give up (or waive) their constitutional right to due process? This question arises with respect to all aspects of due process — notice, the right to a hearing, and, as you just saw above, personal jurisdiction. Waiver of due process rights can come in many forms; a somewhat crude example of such a waiver — waiving notice and the opportunity to be heard — is that of a Texas bank which responded to *Fuentes*, page 9 *supra*, by requiring loan applicants to sign this form:

IN THE EVENT I/WE DEFAULT IN ANY OF THE OBLIGATIONS IMPOSED BY THIS CONTRACT, I/WE HEREBY WAIVE NOTICE AND HEARING AND AGREE THAT THE COLLATERAL MAY BE REPOSSESSED.

If you were the bank's lawyer, what advice would you give them about whether they can seize the savings account of a defaulting debtor who has signed this form? What considerations would enter into your advice?

A form of this type, known as a "cognovit note," was upheld by the Court against a due process claim in D.H. Overmyer Co. v. Frick Co., 405 U.S. 174 (1972). The Court described a cognovit note as an "ancient legal device by which the debtor consents in advance to the holder's obtaining a judgment without notice or hearing, and possibly even with the appearance, on the debtor's behalf, of an attorney designated by the holder." Id. at 176. But the Court noted specifically that its holding applied in

> the commercial world . . . and is not controlling precedent for other facts of other cases. For example, where the contract is one of adhesion, where there is great disparity in bargaining power, and where the debtor receives nothing for the cognovit provision, other legal consequences may ensue.

Id. at 188.

## Note: Applying the Case Law

Review your understanding of the Court's personal jurisdiction case law by analyzing the following questions:

1. Should placement of advertisements in internationally circulated magazines constitute a sufficient tie to a U.S. forum, where the plaintiff in a defamation suit resides in the forum and experienced injuries there, but the defendant, a French advertising agency, had no other ties to the forum and the allegedly defamatory publication was written in French and was aimed at French consumers? See Noonan v. Winston Co., 135 F.3d 85 (1st Cir. 1998) (finding contacts with the forum insufficient to establish jurisdiction).

2. In a breach of contract case, are only the parties' dealings with respect to the disputed contracts relevant, or are all of defendant's contacts with the state relevant, however dissimilar in terms of time, geography, or substance? See R.A.R., Inc. v. Turner Diesel, Ltd., 107 F.3d 1272 (7th Cir. 1997) (concluding that prior sales transactions between a foreign corporation and an Illinois corporation were not sufficiently related to a later contract to establish minimum contacts for purposes of jurisdiction).

3. What if a Hong Kong hotel that solicited a Massachusetts firm's business is sued in Massachusetts in a wrongful death action arising from the death of a firm employee in the hotel swimming pool? See Nowak v. Tak How Invs., Ltd., 94 F.3d 708 (1st Cir. 1996), *cert. denied,* 520 U.S. 1155 (1997) (finding personal jurisdiction because the hotel's solicitation of business in Massachusetts brought plaintiffs to the hotel and was therefore related to the drowning that gave rise to the suit).

4. Should California courts have jurisdiction over Washington-based fast food franchisees named as defendants in a cross-complaint filed by a California meat processor? The meat processor was a defendant in an action brought by franchisees whose customers were exposed to E-coli bacteria. The E-coli bacteria were traced to the hamburgers processed at a California plant. The cross-plaintiff claimed that the Washington franchisee failed to cook the hamburgers properly, and sought both damages and indemnification for any liability in the main action. The Washington franchisee had contractual arrangements with the California-based franchiser, including a forum selection clause and choice of law provision pointing toward California and California law, respectively. Were the tort claims listed in the cross-complaint sufficiently related to the franchisee's California contacts to satisfy due process? See Vons Cos. v. Seabest Foods, Inc., 926 P.2d 1085 (Cal. 1997) (finding purposeful availment by cross-defendants because of ongoing franchise relationship with California franchiser).

5. Is a Bennington, Vermont doctor who regularly treats patients from New York amenable to process in New York, in a malpractice suit filed by a New York resident who was seen by the doctor in Vermont? See Ingraham v. Carroll, 687 N.E.2d 1293 (N.Y. 1997) (holding that although the doctor could anticipate that his actions might cause injury in New York, he did not derive substantial revenue from interstate or international commerce; a physician's services are "inherently personal, and local, in nature").

6. If nine out of 69,000 accounts at a Louisiana bank are owned by six customers in Kentucky, should a Kentucky district court have personal jurisdiction over the Louisiana bank? The Kentucky residents signed up for online banking through the company's Web site and accessed their bank accounts by obtaining a password at the Web site. The plaintiff, a Kentucky banking and financial services company, sued the Louisiana bank for trademark infringement. In Cmty. Tr. Bancorp, Inc. v. Cmty. Tr. Fin. Corp., 692 F.3d 469 (6th Cir. 2012), the Sixth Circuit avoided addressing the district court's conclusion that providing passwords and granting online access to Kentucky customers knowing they would use them continuously and systematically to access their accounts is purposeful availment. Instead, it reversed the finding of personal jurisdiction on the ground that plaintiff's trademark action is unrelated to the online banking contacts of a handful of Kentucky customers. "It is not enough that there be some connection between the in-state activity and the cause of action—that connection must be *substantial*." Id. at 472-473.

# D.   DUE PROCESS AND THE DUAL COURT SYSTEM: A FIRST LOOK AT SUBJECT MATTER JURISDICTION AND VENUE

## Problem Case: The Due Process Game (Part Two)

Assume that a public university expels an undergraduate without a hearing of any kind. The student decides to sue the University on two grounds: violation of due process under the Fourteenth Amendment and breach of an implied contract based on the terms of the Student Handbook, which sets forth a list of grounds for expulsion. The student's position is that she violated none of the stated grounds for expulsion, and that the school cannot expel her for reasons not listed in the Handbook. Moreover, she contends, she was entitled to notice and a hearing regarding the University's basis for the expulsion and a chance to respond to the accusations.

Could the student file this action in a federal district court? In a state court? In either? Does the University have any control over the choice of forum?

## 1.   A Dual Court System

The federal and state courts have distinct and overlapping jurisdiction, such that some actions may be brought in either system whereas others may be brought in only one of them. In general, state courts are courts of "general jurisdiction" and federal courts are courts of "limited jurisdiction." This means that state courts have broader subject matter jurisdiction than do federal courts. On rare occasions, however, an action may fall within the exclusive jurisdiction of the federal courts, and would thus be heard only by a federal judge.

To understand the division of judicial power and labor between the federal and state courts, one must review the U.S. Constitution. The Constitution says that the federal government, including the federal judiciary, has only as much power as the Constitution allows. That is, under the Tenth Amendment, all powers not expressly given to the federal government are reserved to the states and to the people.

### a.   Legislative Authority—Federal Versus State

In general, Congress has power over matters of national concern, which include matters involving interstate commerce, money, naturalization, post offices, roads, and a host of other concerns that require national legislation and control. Article I of the Constitution sets forth these areas of federal concern, and adds that the power to control these issues includes the power to make all laws that are "necessary and proper" for executing that authority. The most significant basis for congressional action is the Commerce

Clause, which has been interpreted to justify broad-reaching federal legislation over a wide range of private activities. For example, the U.S. Congress has passed laws that prevent any business that employs a modest number of employees from discriminating against its employees on the basis of race, gender, ethnicity, or religion. This intervention of federal legislative authority into private, local businesses has been held to be constitutional because the business may affect interstate commerce, which Congress has the right to regulate.

Simply because Congress has the power to legislate in an area, however, does not mean that it must do so. Nor does it mean that states are powerless to draft legislation that addresses the same matter. When a state law and a federal law conflict, however, the federal law trumps the state law, under the Supremacy Clause (Article VI). Moreover, federal law may preempt state law in areas where there is congressional intention to do so or where there is a particularly compelling reason not to allow both federal and state standards to control that subject.

### b.   Federal Judicial Authority

Just as Congress possesses limited legislative authority, the federal courts have limited judicial authority. Again, the explanation lies in the constitutional allocation of power.

First, read Article III of the Constitution. In Section 1, Congress is given the power to establish the "inferior" federal courts. Thus the only court that Congress cannot abolish, or that does not exist subject to congressional discretion, is the U.S. Supreme Court.

Now read Section 2 of Article III. This sets forth the major areas of subject matter jurisdiction for the federal courts. It cites the types of cases that can be litigated in federal (as opposed to state) courts. The two most significant areas include cases that arise between "citizens of different states" (diversity jurisdiction) and cases "arising under this Constitution, the laws of the United States, and Treaties made" (federal question jurisdiction).

The Court, pursuant to its authority under Marbury v. Madison, 5 U.S. (1 Cranch) 137 (1803), to determine the meaning and scope of the Constitution, has interpreted Article III fairly liberally. For example, the Court has interpreted the phrase "between citizens of different states" to mean merely that at least one of the plaintiffs is from a different state than at least one defendant or adverse party. Complete diversity of all plaintiffs from all defendants is not *constitutionally* required.

The Court has been even more generous in construing the phrase "arising under." It is enough, according to the Court, if federal law is an "ingredient" of the dispute; it need not be central or the gravamen of the matter. Thus, for example, the Court said that the Constitution is satisfied when a federal court hears a case that involves a federally chartered bank, even if the case turns entirely on state law. The federal charter gives the bank its legal existence and thus its capacity to sue or be sued. This federal law is an original ingredient that, though a slender reed, is enough to satisfy Article III. Osborn v. Bank of United States, 22 U.S. (9 Wheat.) 738, 819-823 (1824).

Finally, the Court has interpreted Article III to permit federal courts to hear state law claims, even when they arise between citizens of the same state, provided that the state law claims grow out of the same "common nucleus of operative facts" as a claim that meets Article III requirements. That is, if there is a solid federal subject matter jurisdiction "trunk," then the court can hear state claim "branches" from that trunk. The test is one of factual connectedness. The current name applied to this "branch" jurisdiction is *supplemental* jurisdiction. Older terms for this type of jurisdiction are *pendent* and *ancillary*, or *incidental*, jurisdiction.

The foregoing passages, however, describe only the constitutional possibilities of federal court jurisdiction—the limits to which Congress *could* go in giving the courts subject matter jurisdiction. The power that federal courts actually have been given by Congress is, according to the Supreme Court, much narrower. The statutory power of the federal courts has been construed to be much narrower than the constitutional potential power described above. The key statutes are 28 U.S.C. §§ 1331, 1332, 1367, and 1441. We will concentrate here on the basic statutes, leaving discussion of supplemental jurisdiction to Chapter 6.

## 2. Federal Diversity Jurisdiction

### Problem Case: Down with Diversity! Viva Diversity!

Assume that you are a member of Congress. The Congress is poised to vote on a bill that would—once and for all—abolish federal court diversity jurisdiction. After reviewing the history of diversity jurisdiction and the legal literature debating its current usefulness, you rise and speak out on the matter. What position will you take? What arguments will you raise in support of your position?

### a. Determining Diversity of Citizenship

The federal diversity jurisdiction statute, 28 U.S.C. § 1332, permits federal courts to exercise jurisdiction in actions between "citizens of different States" where the amount in controversy exceeds $75,000. The federal courts' diversity jurisdiction is not exclusive. The litigant may choose either state or federal court to hear the claim. If the plaintiff does choose state court, however, the defendant may be entitled to remove the action to federal court, provided that the defendant is not a resident of the state in which the original action was filed and all other requirements of removal are met. 28 U.S.C. §§ 1446-1447.

The basic requirements of the modern diversity statute may be summarized as follows:

- All plaintiffs must be diverse from all defendants, absent a clear statutory or decisional exception. That is, *complete diversity* is required by the statute, though this is not constitutionally compelled. See Strawbridge v. Curtiss, 7 U.S. (3 Cranch) 267 (1806).
- Diversity of citizenship for an individual is determined by examining where she resides and has the intention of remaining indefinitely.
- A corporation is a citizen, for purposes of diversity, both where it is incorporated and where it has its principal place of business. The principal place of business is the corporation's "nerve center," which often (but not always) means the central office where corporate decision makers are located.
- For other types of businesses, such as partnerships, unincorporated associations, or business trusts, different rules apply—partnerships, for instance, are citizens, for purposes of diversity, of every state in which a partner resides. To determine these rules one must consult decisional law.
- In assessing citizenship, the court generally looks to the status of the parties at the time the action is filed. Thus if the parties are diverse at the start of the lawsuit, the court does not lose jurisdiction simply because the parties later become nondiverse. One exception to this occurs when a case is removed from state court to federal court. Diversity generally must exist both when the action is filed in state court and when the petition for removal to federal court is filed.
- Another important exception to the time-of-filing rule is that defects in diversity jurisdiction usually can be cured by dismissing the nondiverse party when the defect in jurisdiction is discovered.
- The amount in controversy may sometimes be satisfied by aggregating claims within the lawsuit. The summary on page 262, infra, reviews how courts have tended to interpret the amount-in-controversy requirement when multiple parties or claims are involved; a complete treatment, and coverage of 28 U.S.C. § 1367, are reserved for Chapter 6.
- If the plaintiff requests an injunction, rather than money damages, the amount-in-controversy requirement may still be satisfied, provided the value of the controversy exceeds $75,000. Courts have taken several approaches to calculating this value, including 1) assessing the value of the injunction to the plaintiff, 2) assessing the cost of complying with the injunction for the defendant, and 3) analyzing both value to plaintiff and cost to defendant and allowing jurisdiction if either one exceeds $75,000.

## Problems

Test your understanding of the basic rules by answering the following hypotheticals. Are the diversity jurisdiction requirements satisfied?

1. *A*, a citizen of Nebraska, sues *B*, a citizen of Delaware, and *C*, a citizen of Nebraska, for $100,000 (each) in federal court.

2. *A*, a citizen of Nebraska, sues *B*, a corporation that is incorporated in Maryland and has its principal place of business in Nebraska, for $100,000 in federal court.
3. *A*, a corporation that is incorporated in Delaware and has its principal place of business in Alaska, sues *B*, a corporation that is incorporated in Delaware and has its principal place of business in California, for $100,000 in federal court.
4. *A*, a citizen of Maine, and *B*, a citizen of Maine, sue *C*, a citizen of Arizona, for $100,000 (each) in federal court.

The following cases and materials demonstrate how courts have interpreted statutory diversity jurisdiction requirements.


## Mas v. Perry
489 F.2d 1396 (5th Cir. 1974)

AINSWORTH, CIRCUIT JUDGE.

[Plaintiffs were a married couple who met while graduate students at Louisiana State University. They were married at Mrs. Mas's home in Jackson, Mississippi, after which they returned to LSU for two more years. They then moved to Park Ridge, Illinois. They sued their Louisiana landlord in federal district court in Louisiana for damages resulting from his undetected use of two-way mirrors to watch them in their bedroom during three of the first four months of their marriage before their move out of state. The husband was a French national; the wife was originally from Mississippi. The landlord challenged the federal court filing on the ground that the wife was not diverse from him. At the time of trial, the couple's intention was to return to Baton Rouge while Mr. Mas completed his Ph.D. They were undecided as to where they would go thereafter. The trial court held that the wife retained her Mississippi citizenship. — EDS.]

It has long been the general rule that complete diversity of parties is required in order that diversity jurisdiction obtain; that is, no party on one side may be a citizen of the same State as any party on the other side. Strawbridge v. Curtiss, [7 U.S. (3 Cranch) 267 (1806)]. This determination of one's State citizenship for diversity purposes is controlled by federal law, not by the law of any State. As is the case in other areas of federal jurisdiction, the diverse citizenship among adverse parties must be present at the time the complaint is filed. Jurisdiction is unaffected by subsequent changes in the citizenship of the parties. The burden of pleading the diverse citizenship is upon the party invoking federal jurisdiction and if the diversity jurisdiction is properly challenged, that party also bears the burden of proof.

To be a citizen of a State within the meaning of section 1332, a natural person must be both a citizen of the United States and a domiciliary of that State. For diversity purposes, citizenship means domicile; mere residence in the State is not sufficient.

A person's domicile is the place of "his true, fixed, and permanent home and principal establishment, and to which he has the intention of returning whenever he is absent therefrom. . . ." [Stine v. Moore, 213 F.2d 446, 448 (5th Cir. 1954).] A change of domicile may be effected only by a combination of two elements: (a) taking up residence in a different domicile with (b) the intention to remain there.

It is clear that at the time of her marriage, Mrs. Mas was a domiciliary of the State of Mississippi. While it is generally the case that the domicile of the wife—and, consequently, her State citizenship for purposes of diversity jurisdiction—is deemed to be that of her husband, we find no precedent for extending this concept to the situation here, in which the husband is a citizen of a foreign state but resides in the United States. Indeed, such a fiction would work absurd results on the facts before us. If Mr. Mas were considered a domiciliary of France—as he would be since he had lived in Louisiana as a student-teaching assistant prior to filing this suit—then Mrs. Mas would also be deemed a domiciliary, and thus, fictionally at least, a citizen of France. She would not be a citizen of any State and could not sue in a federal court on that basis; nor could she invoke the alienage jurisdiction to bring her claim in federal court, since she is not an alien. On the other hand, if Mrs. Mas's domicile were Louisiana, she would become a Louisiana citizen for diversity purposes and could not bring suit with her husband against appellant, also a Louisiana citizen, on the basis of diversity jurisdiction. These are curious results under a rule arising from the theoretical identity of person and interest of the married couple.

An American woman is not deemed to have lost her United States citizenship solely by reason of her marriage to an alien. 8 U.S.C. § 1489. Similarly, we conclude that for diversity purposes a woman does not have her domicile or State citizenship changed solely by reason of her marriage to an alien.

Mrs. Mas's Mississippi domicile was disturbed neither by her year in Louisiana prior to her marriage nor as a result of the time she and her husband spent at LSU after their marriage, since for both periods she was a graduate assistant at LSU.

Though she testified that after her marriage she had no intention of returning to her parents' home in Mississippi, Mrs. Mas did not effect a change of domicile since she and Mr. Mas were in Louisiana only as students and lacked the requisite intention to remain there. Until she acquires a new domicile, she remains a domiciliary, and thus a citizen, of Mississippi. . . .

[The court's discussion of the jurisdictional amount is omitted. Eds.]

Thus the power of the federal district court to entertain the claims of appellees in this case stands on two separate legs of diversity jurisdiction: a claim by an alien against a State citizen; and an action between citizens of different States. We also note, however, the propriety of having the federal district court entertain a spouse's action against a defendant, where the district court already has jurisdiction over a claim, arising from the same transaction, by the other spouse against the same defendant. In the case before us, such a result is particularly desirable. The claims of Mr. and Mrs. Mas arise from the same operative facts, and there was almost complete interdependence between their claims with respect to the proof required and the issues raised at trial. Thus, since the district court has jurisdiction of Mr. Mas's action, sound judicial administration militates strongly in favor of federal jurisdiction of Mrs. Mas's claim.

*Affirmed.*


## Note: The Domicile of Married Women

Under the common law, a wife automatically assumed her husband's domicile upon marriage, based primarily upon the assumption that the husband was the breadwinner and could therefore determine where the family would live. Over time, exceptions were created if, for instance, the wife was providing the main financial support for the family. See Herma Hill Kay, Sex-Based Discrimination 177-183 (2d ed. 1981). The court in *Mas* created another exception—that of a female U.S. citizen marrying a foreign national. Since *Mas*, the common-law rule has been successfully challenged under the Equal Protection Clause as well as under Louisiana's equal rights amendment. Samuel v. Univ. of Pittsburgh, 375 F. Supp. 1119 (W.D. Pa. 1974), *decision to decertify class vacated*, 538 F.2d 991 (3d Cir. 1976); Craig v. Craig, 365 So. 2d 1298 (La. 1978). Today, although many spouses are of the same domicile, most courts are quick to accept evidence to the contrary and consider each individual's domicile separately.


## Tanzymore v. Bethlehem Steel Corp.
457 F.2d 1320 (3d Cir. 1972)

GIBBONS, CIRCUIT JUDGE.

Appellant Tanzymore filed a complaint in the District Court for the Eastern District of Pennsylvania seeking damages from Bethlehem Steel Corporation for personal injuries. The complaint alleges that Mr. Tanzymore is "a domiciliary of 7418 Lenwood Street, Apartment 3, City of Cleveland, State of Ohio," and that Bethlehem is a Delaware corporation with its principal place of business in the Eastern District of Pennsylvania. Bethlehem filed an answer, and took Mr. Tanzymore's deposition. When the deposition was filed Bethlehem moved to dismiss the action on the ground that the district court lacked jurisdiction because the controversy is not wholly between citizens of different states. No affidavits were filed by Mr. Tanzymore in opposition to the motion. The court considered the briefs filed by the parties, heard argument on the motion, and without holding an evidentiary hearing, on the basis of Mr. Tanzymore's deposition concluded that there was no diversity of citizenship between the parties and dismissed the complaint. In its opinion, 325 F. Supp. 891, the court stated:

> Both the deposition[s] taken of the plaintiff, and his work record [as disclosed therein], indicate[s] that he is at best a resident of Pennsylvania, and may, in fact, be a citizen of no state. . . . This Court is unable to find that plaintiff is a citizen of the state of Ohio.

This appeal followed.[1] On appeal Mr. Tanzymore concedes, as he must, that determination of the underlying jurisdictional facts may be made by the court. Wetmore v. Rymer, 169 U.S. 115 (1898). Nor does he dispute that where a jurisdictional fact is traversed the burden of showing that the federal court has jurisdiction rests upon the plaintiff. Gibbs v. Buck, 307 U.S. 66, 72 (1939). He contends only that in a case in which the pleadings and depositions show a dispute as to the jurisdictional facts that dispute may not be resolved by the court without an evidentiary hearing. Mr. Tanzymore's deposition does contain the naked assertion that he intended at all times to remain an Ohio domiciliary, but virtually nothing else in the deposition is consistent with the conclusive assertion.[2] Nevertheless, he contends, it was

---

1. We are advised that a timely suit has been filed in a Pennsylvania court.
2. In his deposition Tanzymore testified as follows:

**Examination by Mr. Holland [Bethlehem's Attorney]**

Q. Assuming that it was in May or along about May of 1966 or '65 that you first went to work for Young & Posen, I would like you to tell me where you went to work for them.
A. Philadelphia, Pennsylvania, at the Gulf Oil Company.
Q. All right. Now, before you went to work for Young & Posen at the Gulf Oil plant in Philadelphia, where did you work?
A. I worked for Lachat Construction Company in Baltimore, Maryland—Lachat Steel Construction Company, Baltimore, Maryland. . . .
Q. What is your permanent home address now?
A. 307 East Fourth Street, Bethlehem, Pennsylvania.
Q. And what is 307 East Fourth Street: Is it an apartment or a house or a—
A. This is a lady got a house, and she rent me a room and helps me about, because I can't—I am unable to help myself.
Q. And your accommodations there, then, are a room?
A. Right.
Q. Do you take your meals with this landlady?
A. Up until she unable to cook for me. Now I have to eat in lunchrooms.
Q. How long have you lived at 307 East Fourth Street?
A. Umm, six months. . . .
A. 543 North New Street.
Q. That's in Bethlehem?
Q. Were you living at the American Hotel—
A. When I got hurt, correct.
Q. —when you were working at the Bethlehem Steel?
Q. Were all of these jobs that you did at Bethlehem Steel right after each other, or did you have assignments somewhere else in between?
A. We had assignment elsewhere. I went down into West Virginia, and then I had an assignment of staying at home until the other job got ready to be done.
A. Oh, I lived in Cleveland, Ohio, off and on, ever since '65. Off and on. . . .

improper to resolve the disputed domicile issue against him without giving him the opportunity to testify in an evidentiary hearing.

Appellant's argument confuses the court's role in deciding a motion for summary judgment under Fed. R. Civ. P. 56 with its role in making a

---

Q.   [Y]ou are not registered to vote?

A.   No. . . .

A.   Well, hell, my license expired in—it must be, for my automobile, what the hell—'63.

Q.   And at the time this accident occurred, you didn't own one?

A:   Correct.

Q.   Would I be correct in assuming that you haven't owned one since 1963?

A.   Correct.

Q.   Now, Mr. Tanzymore, at the place where you presently live on 307 East Fourth Street, do you own furnishings in that house?

A.   Yeah. I bought my bed, tables, chairs. I have to sleep in a hospital bed, due to my discs in my back resting on the nerves of my spine.

Q.   Do you get mail at that address?

A.   Yes, I do.

Q.   The postmen [sic] delivers the mail to 307—

A.   No, he deliver to the front house. I live in the back house.

Q.   Well, what was that address?

A.   543—

Q.   —North New. Did you own any of the furnishings at that residence?

A.   No, I didn't own any. I had the same furniture I have now. I was buying the same stuff that I am buying now.

Q.   And did you get your mail at that address also?

A.   I did so.

Q.   Do you have any furnishings—beds, chairs, sofas, television set, or anything like that—

A.   I got a television set, I got a hospital bed. I got a stand, I got a table and five chairs, I got three sheets, I got one blanket, I got two pillows, I got a water glass that I put water aside of the bed on. I got a flower and a pot, about yea long and yea high (demonstrating). I have three suits of clothes, I got a dozen pocket handkerchiefs, a dozen pair of underwears, I got six pair of socks, and I have three neckties. . . .

Q.   Do you own any things like these—clothing or furniture—that you keep anywhere else? . . .

A.   No, I don't. Not now I don't.

Q.   When was the last time that you did?

A.   1967.

Q.   Mr. Tanzymore, do you own any real estate?

A.   No, I don't.

Q.   Any land?

A.   No.

Q.   Lots?

Q.   You don't maintain any bank accounts in any other cities?

A.   No.

Q.   You don't have a safe deposit box in any bank anywhere?

A.   No, I don't.

Q.   Do you maintain any memberships in any clubs any places other than Bethlehem?

A.   No. I don't.

**Examination by Mr. Baratta [Mr. Tanzymore's attorney]**

Q.   Now, the address that you gave us in Cleveland, was that a house?

A.   Yes. Apartment house.

jurisdictional determination pursuant to 28 U.S.C. § 1359[3] and Fed. R. Civ. P. 12(h)(3).[4] Since 1875, when the predecessor to 28 U.S.C. § 1359 was first enacted, when a question of federal jurisdiction is raised either by a party as here, or by the court on its own motion, the court may inquire, by affidavits or otherwise, into the facts as they exist. Wetmore v. Rymer, 169 U.S. [115,] 120-121 [(1898)]. McNutt v. General Motors Acceptance Corp., 298 U.S. 178, 184-190 (1936); KVOS, Inc. v. Associated Press, 299 U.S. 269, 278 (1936); Gibbs v. Buck, 307 U.S. [66,] 71, 72 [(1939)]; Land v. Dollar, 330 U.S. 731, 735 (1947). In Wetmore v. Rymer, the Court wrote:

> But the questions might arise in such a shape that the court might consider and determine them without the intervention of a jury. And it would appear to have been the intention of congress to leave the mode of raising and trying such issues to the discretion of the trial judge.

---

Q. Did you own that house?
A. No. Rent. I rented a room there, with another lady and her—you know, her family.
Q. Did you own any furniture that was in that particular apartment?
A. No. All that was furnished. That house was a furnished house.
Q. A furnished apartment?
A. Yes.
Q. Did you have a lease?
A. No. Just rent weekly—monthly.
A. My operator license. They expired in 1963.
Q. All right. What state issued that license?
A. Seattle, Washington.
Q. At the time of your accident did you have any bank accounts in Cleveland, Ohio?
A. No. At the time of my accident, no.
Q. At the time of your accident or immediately before the accident, and immediately after the accident did you receive any mail at the Cleveland address that you gave us?
A. No. No.
A. I haven't been back to Cleveland, Ohio, since I left.

**Examination by Mr. Holland**

Q. But you have since made Bethlehem your home?
A. I made Bethlehem my home on the—under my doctor, I made Pennsylvania my home, under my doctors throughout Pennsylvania. When I say "throughout Pennsylvania" I mean I may be under this doctor if I felt like I wasn't going to get well, like I did before. I'd go somewhere where I can. Due to that, due to all the business of my accident—the same as this meeting here, I can't be in Cleveland and attend your meeting here. All of this stuff comes under the heading of my accident, that I have to stay here until somebody do something about me, other than God himself.

3. § 1359. Parties Collusively Joined or Made: "A district court shall not have jurisdiction of a civil action in which any party, by assignment or otherwise, has been improperly or collusively made or joined to invoke the jurisdiction of such court."

4. Waiver or Preservation of Certain Defenses: "(3) Whenever it appears by suggestion of the parties or otherwise that the court lacks jurisdiction of the subject matter, the court shall dismiss the action."

169 U.S. at 121. More recently in Gibbs v. Buck, the Court wrote:

> As there is no statutory direction for procedure upon an issue of jurisdiction, the mode of its determination is left to the trial court.

307 U.S. at 71-72.

Shortly after our decision in McSparran v. Weist, 402 F.2d 867 (3d Cir. 1968), *cert. denied sub nom.* Fritzinger v. Weist, 395 U.S. 903 (1969), in which we directed that the district courts make inquiry into diversity manufactured by the appointment of out of state guardians, we had occasion to suggest a standard for the exercise of discretion in the method of determining the jurisdictional issue. In Groh v. Brooks, 421 F.2d 589, 594 (3d Cir. 1970), Judge Stahl wrote:

> If a plaintiff whose assertion of federal jurisdiction is challenged by a motion to dismiss fails to bring forth any factual material to support his claim to jurisdiction, then dismissal may properly be granted against him. However, it should clearly appear from the record that plaintiff has had an opportunity to present facts, either by way of affidavit or in an evidentiary hearing, in support of his position that diversity was not manufactured. (footnotes omitted)

Here the attorney for Tanzymore had an opportunity to cross examine him at the deposition. He did so. There was an opportunity, unavailed of, to file affidavits in opposition to the motion to dismiss. The district court, having discretion as to the procedure to be followed in making its jurisdictional determination, exercised that discretion reasonably in deciding the motion on the basis of the deposition. Had parts of the deposition tended to support Mr. Tanzymore's conclusory statement of domicile and had he then requested an evidentiary hearing to resolve the conflict a different procedure might have been appropriate.

Compare Seideman v. Hamilton, 275 F.2d 224 (3d Cir. 1960), in which we approved the procedure of the court's hearing evidence on the issue of diversity and Shahmoon Industries Inc. v. Imperato, 338 F.2d 449 (3d Cir. 1964), in which this court *sua sponte* returned the case to the district court to enlarge the record on a diversity issue by taking additional evidence. While these cases teach that an evidentiary hearing may be appropriate they do not hold that such a hearing is always required so long as the court has afforded the plaintiff notice and a fair opportunity to be heard. We will not set aside its reasonable exercise of discretion as to the mode of determination of the jurisdictional facts. A different rule applies, of course, where a summary disposition reaches the merits of the claim rather than the jurisdiction of the court. Compare Fed. R. Civ. P. 56(c), 65(a).

Mr. Tanzymore also contends that the district court decision is a holding which accepts the doctrine of cases such as Pannill v. Roanoke Times Co., 252 F. 910 (W.D. Va. 1918), which hold that a person may be "stateless" and that such a stateless person cannot create diversity of citizenship for purposes of 28 U.S.C. § 1332. See also Clapp v. Stearns & Co., 229 F. Supp. 305

(S.D.N.Y. 1964); Factor v. Pennington Press, Inc., 238 F. Supp. 630 (N.D. Ill. 1964). He urges that we reject this doctrine.

The district court did speculate that Mr. Tanzymore may be a stateless person, but this is not its holding. The plaintiff had the burden of alleging a basis for federal jurisdiction. Fed. R. Civ. P. 8(a)(1). When the jurisdictional allegations were traversed he had the burden of supporting those allegations. McNutt v. General Motors Acceptance Corp., 298 U.S. at 182-189; KVOS v. Associated Press, 299 U.S. at 276-277; Nelson v. Keefer, 451 F.2d 289 (3d Cir. 1971). The holding was only that Mr. Tanzymore failed to meet the burden of establishing that he was, as he alleged, a citizen of Ohio.[5] Since he had the burden of establishing the basis of federal jurisdiction which he alleged, and failed to carry that burden, we need inquire no further for it was his obligation, not that of the court, to establish his citizenship.

The judgment of the district court dismissing the complaint for want of jurisdiction will be affirmed.

## Note: The Citizenship of Corporations

*Mas* and *Tanzymore* concern the citizenship of individuals for purposes of determining diversity jurisdiction. In a global economy, there are inherent difficulties in determining the citizenship of corporations — difficulties not wholly unlike those we have seen in personal jurisdiction analysis. Over the years, the circuit courts developed divergent tests for determining corporate citizenship. All corporations are obviously citizens of the state in which they are incorporated, but what if a company has its corporate offices in another state, and core manufacturing facilities and staff in yet another? What if a company derives substantial revenue from a state? In 2010, the Supreme Court finally stepped in, clarifying that a corporation is a citizen of the state in which it is incorporated and of the state in which it has its "nerve center."

## *Hertz Corp. v. Friend*
559 U.S. 77 (2010)

JUSTICE BREYER delivered the opinion of the Court.

The federal diversity jurisdiction statute provides that "a corporation shall be deemed to be a citizen of any State by which it has been incorporated

---

5. The complaint actually alleges only that Mr. Tanzymore is a "domiciliary" of Ohio:

A naked averment that one is a "domiciliary" or a "resident" of a state is insufficient. The statute requires that the averment be that one is a "citizen" of a state. "The whole record, however, may be looked to, for the purpose of curing a defective averment of citizenship, . . . and if the requisite citizenship is anywhere expressly averred in the record, or facts are therein stated which in legal intendment constitute such allegation, that is sufficient."

Sun Printing & Pub. Assn. v. Edwards, 194 U.S. 377, 382 (1904).

*and of the State where it has its principal place of business."* 28 U.S.C. § 1332(c)(1) (emphasis added). We seek here to resolve different interpretations that the Circuits have given this phrase. In doing so, we place primary weight upon the need for judicial administration of a jurisdictional statute to remain as simple as possible. And we conclude that the phrase "principal place of business" refers to the place where the corporation's high level officers direct, control, and coordinate the corporation's activities. Lower federal courts have often metaphorically called that place the corporation's "nerve center." We believe that the "nerve center" will typically be found at a corporation's headquarters.

## I

In September 2007, respondents Melinda Friend and John Nhieu, two California citizens, sued petitioner, the Hertz Corporation, in a California state court. They sought damages for what they claimed were violations of California's wage and hour laws. And they requested relief on behalf of a potential class composed of California citizens who had allegedly suffered similar harms.

Hertz filed a notice seeking removal to a federal court. 28 U.S.C. § 1332(d)(2). Hertz claimed that the plaintiffs and the defendant were citizens of different States. §§ 1332(a)(1), (c)(1). Hence, the federal court possessed diversity-of-citizenship jurisdiction. Friend and Nhieu, however, claimed that the Hertz Corporation was a California citizen, like themselves, and that, hence, diversity jurisdiction was lacking.

To support its position, Hertz submitted a declaration by an employee relations manager that sought to show that Hertz's "principal place of business" was in New Jersey, not in California. The declaration stated, among other things, that Hertz operated facilities in 44 States; and that California—which had about 12% of the Nation's population—accounted for 273 of Hertz's 1,606 car rental locations; about 2,300 of its 11,230 full-time employees; about $811 million of its $4.371 billion in annual revenue; and about 3.8 million of its approximately 21 million annual transactions, i.e., rentals. The declaration also stated that the "leadership of Hertz and its domestic subsidiaries" is located at Hertz's "corporate headquarters" in Park Ridge, New Jersey; that its "core executive and administrative functions . . . are carried out" there and "to a lesser extent" in Oklahoma City, Oklahoma; and that its "major administrative operations . . . are found" at those two locations.

The District Court of the Northern District of California accepted Hertz's statement of the facts as undisputed. But it concluded that, given those facts, Hertz was a citizen of California. In reaching this conclusion, the court applied Ninth Circuit precedent, which instructs courts to identify a corporation's "principal place of business" by first determining the amount of a corporation's business activity State by State. If the amount of activity is "significantly larger" or "substantially predominates" in one State, then that State is the corporation's "principal place of business." If there is no such State, then the "principal place of business" is the corporation's "'nerve center,'" i.e., the place where "'the majority of its executive and administrative functions are performed.'"

Applying this test, the District Court found that the "plurality of each of the relevant business activities" was in California, and that "the differential between the amount of those activities" in California and the amount in "the next closest state" was "significant." Hence, Hertz's "principal place of business" was California, and diversity jurisdiction was thus lacking. The District Court consequently remanded the case to the state courts.

. . . The Ninth Circuit affirmed in a brief memorandum opinion. Hertz filed a petition for certiorari. And, in light of differences among the Circuits in the application of the test for corporate citizenship, we granted the writ.

## III

We begin our "principal place of business" discussion with a brief review of relevant history. The Constitution provides that the "judicial Power shall extend" to "Controversies . . . between Citizens of different States." Art. III, § 2. This language, however, does not automatically confer diversity jurisdiction upon the federal courts. Rather, it authorizes Congress to do so and, in doing so, to determine the scope of the federal courts' jurisdiction within constitutional limits.

Congress first authorized federal courts to exercise diversity jurisdiction in 1789 when, in the First Judiciary Act, Congress granted federal courts authority to hear suits "between a citizen of the State where the suit is brought, and a citizen of another State." § 11, 1 Stat. 78. The statute said nothing about corporations. In 1809, Chief Justice Marshall, writing for a unanimous Court, described a corporation as an "invisible, intangible, and artificial being" which was "certainly not a citizen." Bank of United States v. Deveaux, 5 Cranch 61, 86 (1809). But the Court held that a corporation could invoke the federal courts' diversity jurisdiction based on a pleading that the corporation's shareholders were all citizens of a different State from the defendants, as "the term citizen ought to be understood as it is used in the constitution, and as it is used in other laws. That is, to describe the real persons who come into court, in this case, under their corporate name." Id., at 91-92.

In Louisville, C. & C. R. Co. v. Letson, 2 How. 497 (1844), the Court modified this initial approach. It held that a corporation was to be deemed an artificial person of the State by which it had been created, and its citizenship for jurisdictional purposes determined accordingly. Id., at 558-559. Ten years later, the Court in Marshall v. Baltimore & Ohio R. Co., 16 How. 314 (1854), held that the reason a corporation was a citizen of its State of incorporation was that, for the limited purpose of determining corporate citizenship, courts could conclusively (and artificially) presume that a corporation's *shareholders* were citizens of the State of incorporation. Id., at 327-328.

And it reaffirmed *Letson.* 16 How., at 325-26. Whatever the rationale, the practical upshot was that, for diversity purposes, the federal courts considered a corporation to be a citizen of the State of its incorporation.

In 1928 this Court made clear that the "state of incorporation" rule was virtually absolute. It held that a corporation closely identified with State A could proceed in a federal court located in that State as long as the corporation had filed its incorporation papers in State B, perhaps a State where the corporation did no business at all. See Black and White Taxicab & Transfer Co. v. Brown and Yellow Taxicab & Transfer Co., 276 U.S. 518 [(1928)] (refusing to question corporation's reincorporation motives and finding diversity jurisdiction). Subsequently, many in Congress and those who testified before it pointed out that this interpretation was at odds with diversity jurisdiction's basic rationale, namely, opening the federal courts' doors to those who might otherwise suffer from local prejudice against out-of-state parties. See, e.g., S. Rep. No. 530, 72d Cong., 1st Sess., 2, 4-7 (1932). Through its choice of the State of incorporation, a corporation could manipulate federal-court jurisdiction, for example, opening the federal courts' doors in a State where it conducted nearly all its business by filing incorporation papers elsewhere. . . . Although various legislative proposals to curtail the corporate use of diversity jurisdiction were made, none of these proposals were enacted into law.

At the same time as federal dockets increased in size, many judges began to believe those dockets contained too many diversity cases. A committee of the Judicial Conference of the United States [returned to] the matter [in the 1950s]. . . .

Among its observations, the committee found a general need "to prevent frauds and abuses" with respect to jurisdiction. Id., at 14. The committee recommended against eliminating diversity cases altogether. Id., at 28. Instead it recommended, along with other proposals, a statutory amendment that would make a corporation a citizen both of the State of its incorporation and any State from which it received more than half of its gross income. Id., at 14-15 (requiring corporation to show that "less than fifty per cent of its gross income was derived from business transacted within the state where the Federal court is held"). If, for example, a citizen of California sued (under state law in state court) a corporation that received half or more of its gross income from California, that corporation would not be able to remove the case to federal court, even if Delaware was its State of incorporation.

During the spring and summer of 1951 committee members circulated their report and attended circuit conferences at which federal judges discussed the report's recommendations. Reflecting those criticisms, the committee filed a new report in September, in which it revised its corporate citizenship recommendation. It now proposed that "'a corporation shall be deemed a citizen of the state of its original creation . . . [and] shall also be deemed a citizen of a state where it has its principal place of business.'" Judicial Conference of the United States, Report of the Committee on Jurisdiction and Venue 4 (Sept. 24, 1951) (hereinafter Sept. Committee

Rept.)—the source of the present-day statutory language. The committee wrote that this new language would provide a "simpler and more practical formula" than the "gross income" test. Sept. Committee Rept. 2. It added that the language "ha[d] a precedent in the jurisdictional provisions of the Bankruptcy Act." Id., at 2-3.

In mid-1957 the committee presented its reports to the House of Representatives Committee on the Judiciary. Judge Albert Maris, representing Judge John Parker (who had chaired the Judicial Conference Committee), discussed various proposals that the Judicial Conference had made to restrict the scope of diversity jurisdiction. In respect to the "principal place of business" proposal, he said that the relevant language "ha[d] been defined in the Bankruptcy Act." House Hearings 37. He added:

> . . . I think the courts have generally taken the view that where a corporation's interests are rather widespread, the principal place of business is an actual rather than a theoretical or legal one. It is the actual place where its business operations are coordinated, directed, and carried out, which would ordinarily be the place where its officers carry on its day-to-day business, where its accounts are kept, where its payments are made, and not necessarily a State in which it may have a plant, if it is a big corporation, or something of that sort. . . .

The House Committee reprinted the Judicial Conference Committee Reports along with other reports and relevant testimony and circulated it to the general public "for the purpose of inviting further suggestions and comments." Subsequently, in 1958, Congress both codified the courts' traditional place of incorporation test and also enacted into law a slightly modified version of the Conference Committee's proposed "principal place of business" language.

## IV

The phrase "principal place of business" has proved more difficult to apply than its originators likely expected. Decisions under the Bankruptcy Act did not provide the firm guidance for which Judge Maris had hoped because courts interpreting bankruptcy law did not agree about how to determine a corporation's "principal place of business." Compare Burdick v. Dillon, 144 F. 737, 738 (1st Cir. 1906) (holding that a corporation's "principal office, rather than a factory, mill, or mine . . . constitutes the 'principal place of business'"), with Continental Coal Corp. v. Roszelle Bros., 242 F. 243, 247 (6th Cir. 1917) (identifying the "principal place of business" as the location of mining activities, rather than the "principal office"); see also Friedenthal, New Limitations on Federal Jurisdiction, 11 Stan. L. Rev. 213, 223 (1959) ("The cases under the Bankruptcy Act provide no rigid legal formula for the determination of the principal place of business").

After Congress' amendment, courts were similarly uncertain as to where to look to determine a corporation's "principal place of business" for diversity purposes. If a corporation's headquarters and executive offices were in the same State in which it did most of its business, the test seemed straightforward. The "principal place of business" was located in that State.

But suppose those corporate headquarters, including executive offices, are in one State, while the corporation's plants or other centers of business activity are located in other States? In 1959 a distinguished federal district judge, Edward Weinfeld, relied on the Second Circuit's interpretation of the Bankruptcy Act to answer this question in part:

> Where a corporation is engaged in far-flung and varied activities which are carried on in different states, its principal place of business is the nerve center from which it radiates out to its constituent parts and from which its officers direct, control and coordinate all activities without regard to locale, in the furtherance of the corporate objective. The test applied by our Court of Appeals, is that place where the corporation has an "office from which its business was directed and controlled"—the place where "all of its business was under the supreme direction and control of its officers."

*Scot Typewriter Co.,* 170 F. Supp., at 865.

Numerous Circuits have since followed this rule, applying the "nerve center" test for corporations with "far-flung" business activities.

*Scot*'s analysis, however, did not go far enough. For it did not answer what courts should do when the operations of the corporation are not "far-flung" but rather limited to only a few States. When faced with this question, various courts have focused more heavily on where a corporation's actual business activities are located.

Perhaps because corporations come in many different forms, involve many different kinds of business activities, and locate offices and plants for different reasons in different ways in different regions, a general "business activities" approach has proved unusually difficult to apply. Courts must decide which factors are more important than others: for example, plant location, sales or servicing centers; transactions, payrolls, or revenue generation.

The number of factors grew as courts explicitly combined aspects of the "nerve center" and "business activity" tests to look to a corporation's "total activities," sometimes to try to determine what treatises have described as the corporation's "center of gravity." . . . Not surprisingly, different circuits (and sometimes different courts within a single circuit) have applied these highly general multifactor tests in different ways.

This complexity may reflect an unmediated judicial effort to apply the statutory phrase "principal place of business" in light of the general purpose of diversity jurisdiction, i.e., an effort to find the State where a corporation is least likely to suffer out-of-state prejudice when it is sued in a local court, Pease v. Peck, 18 How. 595, 599 (1856). But, if so, that task seems doomed to failure. After all, the relevant purposive concern—prejudice against an out-of-state party—will often depend upon factors that courts cannot easily measure, for example, a corporation's image, its history, and its advertising, while the factors that courts can more easily measure, for example, its office or plant location, its sales, its employment, or the nature of the goods or services it supplies, will sometimes bear no more than a distant relation to the likelihood of prejudice. At the same time, this approach is at war with administrative simplicity. And it has failed to achieve a nationally uniform interpretation of federal law, an unfortunate consequence in a federal legal system.

## V

### A

. . . We conclude that "principal place of business" is best read as referring to the place where a corporation's officers direct, control, and coordinate the corporation's activities. It is the place that Courts of Appeals have called the corporation's "nerve center." And in practice it should normally be the place where the corporation maintains its headquarters—provided that the headquarters is the actual center of direction, control, and coordination, i.e., the "nerve center," and not simply an office where the corporation holds its board meetings (for example, attended by directors and officers who have traveled there for the occasion).

Three sets of considerations, taken together, convince us that this approach, while imperfect, is superior to other possibilities. First, the statute's language supports the approach. The statute's text deems a corporation a citizen of the "State where it has its principal place of business." 28 U.S.C. § 1332(c)(1). The word "place" is in the singular, not the plural. The word "principal" requires us to pick out the "main, prominent" or "leading" place. 12 Oxford English Dictionary 495 (2d ed. 1989) (def. (A)(I)(2)). . . .

A corporation's "nerve center," usually its main headquarters, is a single place. The public often (though not always) considers it the corporation's main place of business. And it is a place within a State. By contrast, the application of a more general business activities test has led some courts, as in the present case, to look, not at a particular place within a State, but incorrectly at the State itself, measuring the total amount of business activities that the corporation conducts there and determining whether they are "significantly larger" than in the next-ranking State.

This approach invites greater litigation and can lead to strange results, as the Ninth Circuit has since recognized. Namely, if a "corporation may be deemed a citizen of California on th[e] basis" of "activities [that] roughly reflect California's larger population . . . nearly every national retailer—no matter how far flung its operations—will be deemed a citizen of California for diversity purposes." Davis v. HSBC Bank Nev., N.A., 557 F.3d 1026, 1029-1030 (2009). But why award or decline diversity jurisdiction on the basis of a State's population, whether measured directly, indirectly (say proportionately), or with modifications?

Second, administrative simplicity is a major virtue in a jurisdictional statute. Complex jurisdictional tests complicate a case, eating up time and money as the parties litigate, not the merits of their claims, but which court is the right court to decide those claims. . . . Judicial resources too are at stake. Courts have an independent obligation to determine whether subject-matter jurisdiction exists, even when no party challenges it. So courts benefit from straightforward rules under which they can readily assure themselves of their power to hear a case.

Simple jurisdictional rules also promote greater predictability. Predictability is valuable to corporations making business and investment decisions. Predictability also benefits plaintiffs deciding whether to file suit in a state or federal court.

A "nerve center" approach, which ordinarily equates that "center" with a corporation's headquarters, is simple to apply *comparatively speaking*. The metaphor of a corporate "brain," while not precise, suggests a single location. By contrast, a corporation's general business activities more often lack a single principal place where they take place. That is to say, the corporation may have several plants, many sales locations, and employees located in many different places. If so, it will not be as easy to determine which of these different business locales is the "principal" or most important "place."

Third, the statute's legislative history, for those who accept it, offers a simplicity-related interpretive benchmark. The Judicial Conference provided an initial version of its proposal that suggested a numerical test. A corporation would be deemed a citizen of the State that accounted for more than half of its gross income. The Conference changed its mind in light of criticism that such a test would prove too complex and impractical to apply. That history suggests that the words "principal place of business" should be interpreted to be no more complex than the initial "half of gross income" test. A "nerve center" test offers such a possibility. A general business activities test does not.

## B

We recognize that there may be no perfect test that satisfies all administrative and purposive criteria. We recognize as well that, under the "nerve center" test we adopt today, there will be hard cases. For example, in this era of telecommuting, some corporations may divide their command and coordinating functions among officers who work at several different locations, perhaps communicating over the Internet. That said, our test nonetheless points courts in a single direction, towards the center of overall direction, control, and coordination. . . .

We also recognize that the use of a "nerve center" test may in some cases produce results that seem to cut against the basic rationale for 28 U.S.C. § 1332. For example, if the bulk of a company's business activities visible to the public take place in New Jersey, while its top officers direct those activities just across the river in New York, the "principal place of business" is New York. One could argue that members of the public in New Jersey would be *less* likely to be prejudiced against the corporation than persons in New York—yet the corporation will still be entitled to remove a New Jersey state case to federal court. And note too that the same corporation would be unable to remove a New York state case to federal court, despite the New York public's presumed prejudice against the corporation.

We understand that such seeming anomalies will arise. However, in view of the necessity of having a clearer rule, we must accept them. . . .

The burden of persuasion for establishing diversity jurisdiction, of course, remains on the party asserting it. When challenged on allegations of jurisdictional facts, the parties must support their allegations by competent proof. And when faced with such a challenge, we reject suggestions such as, for example, the one made by petitioner that the mere filing of a form like the Securities and Exchange Commission's Form 10-K listing a corporation's "principal executive offices" would, without more, be sufficient proof to establish a corporation's "nerve center." Such possibilities would readily permit jurisdictional manipulation, thereby subverting a major reason for the insertion of the "principal place of business" language in the diversity statute. Indeed, if the record reveals attempts at manipulation—for example, that the alleged "nerve center" is nothing more than a mail drop box, a bare office with a computer, or the location of an annual executive retreat—the courts should instead take as the "nerve center" the place of actual direction, control, and coordination, in the absence of such manipulation.

## VI

Petitioner's unchallenged declaration suggests that Hertz's center of direction, control, and coordination, its "nerve center," and its corporate headquarters are one and the same, and they are located in New Jersey, not in California. Because respondents should have a fair opportunity to litigate their case in light of our holding, however, we vacate the Ninth Circuit's judgment and remand the case for further proceedings consistent with this opinion.

*It is so ordered.*

### Notes and Questions

1. Since *Hertz Corp.* was decided the lower courts have begun to grapple with the proper application of the "nerve center" test for determining a corporation's principal place of business. In Cent. W. Va. Energy Co. v. Mountain State Carbon, LLC, 636 F.3d 101 (4th Cir. 2011), two coal companies, one a West Virginia citizen and the other a Virginia citizen, sued Mountain State Carbon, LLC, along with its member and parent companies. Plaintiffs alleged that Mountain State wrongfully refused to accept coal deliveries, thereby breaching a supply agreement. The suit was brought in federal court in West Virginia on the basis of diversity jurisdiction.

Mountain State and Severstal Wheeling, a Mountain State member company, moved to dismiss the complaint on the ground that diversity was not complete. They argued that Severstal Wheeling's principal place of business was in West Virginia, the same state as one of the plaintiffs. The district court granted the motion and dismissed the complaint for want of subject matter jurisdiction. In finding that West Virginia was Severstal Wheeling's principal place of business, the court concentrated on the fact that the locus of Severstal's day-to-day operations was Wheeling, West Virginia. It also noted Severstal's "visibility in and involvement with the Wheeling community."

The Fourth Circuit reversed, observing that although Severstal's day-to-day operations, including purchasing, product sales, managing environmental compliance, and carrying out human resources functions, were conducted in West Virginia, none of these factors had any relevance to application of the *Hertz Corp.* "nerve center" test. Instead, the court pointed out that Severstal Wheeling's officers directed, controlled, and coordinated its activities from Dearborn, Michigan. Seven of its eight officers—including the CEO, COO, CFO, general counsel, and secretary—had their offices in Michigan. Only one officer maintained an office in West Virginia. None of Severstal's directors were located in West Virginia, while two were based in Michigan. Moreover, in its corporate filings with the states of West Virginia, Ohio, and Michigan, Severstal listed its Dearborn address as its principal place of business.

The Fourth Circuit emphasized that neither "daily" nor "management" is used in the Supreme Court's holding in *Hertz Corp.*, and the omissions were consistent with the Court's decision to eschew a "place of operations" test, under which the location of a corporation's day-to-day activities is a relevant factor in determining its principal place of business. The proper inquiry for determining a corporation's principal place of business under *Hertz Corp.* is simply "where [its] . . . high level officers direct, control, and coordinate the corporation's activities." But see Agostini v. Piper Aircraft Corp., 2012 WL 646025 (E.D. Pa. Feb. 29, 2012) (distinguishing *Mountain State Carbon*; the mere capacity of officers to exercise corporate control at a location within a state does not make that location the principal place of business).

2. Note that the party invoking diversity jurisdiction has the burden of proving it. Consider the steps you might take to establish this on behalf of an individual client. What questions would you need to ask the client? What other evidence would you seek? Where would you obtain that evidence? In what form would you present it to the court?

Challenges to diversity jurisdiction are made via a motion to dismiss under Rule 12(b)(1). Occasionally the pleadings disclose a fatal defect—where the truth of the allegations is not contested, no outside evidence is necessary because the defect appears on the face of the complaint. Some courts call this a "facial attack." Where the allegations of the pleadings are disputed, as in *Tanzymore*, "the party opposing the motion must furnish affidavits or other evidence necessary to satisfy its burden of establishing subject matter jurisdiction." Safe Air for Everyone v. Meyer, 373 F.3d 1035, 1039 (9th Cir. 2004).

Even though the party invoking diversity jurisdiction has the burden of proving it, opponents who would prefer to be in state court have ample incentive to investigate the issue for themselves. Failure to do so can be costly. See Belleville Catering Co. v. Champaign Mkt. Place, L.L.C., 350 F.3d 691 (7th Cir. 2003).

In *Belleville Catering,* the case went all the way to trial, ending in a $220,000 verdict for defendants on a counterclaim against plaintiffs. On appeal, the court raised *sua sponte* the question whether all the members of Champaign Market Place were indeed diverse (the parties had incorrectly assumed that limited liability companies are treated like corporations for diversity of citizenship analysis). Several members of Champaign Market Place, as it happened, were nondiverse, prompting the Seventh Circuit to dismiss the case for lack of subject matter jurisdiction and to order counsel "to perform, without additional fees, any further services that are necessary to bring this suit to a conclusion in state court, or via settlement. That way the clients will pay just once for the litigation." Id. at 694. The court admonished: "The costs of a doomed foray into federal court should fall on the lawyers who failed to do their homework, not on the hapless clients. . . . Lawyers for defendants, as well as plaintiffs, must investigate rather than assume jurisdiction. . . ." Id. at 693-694.

*Belleville Catering* is a case in which neither party caught a defect in diversity jurisdiction that was present from the very start of the case. What do you think should happen if the citizenship status of a nondiverse party changes during litigation? Under the standard "time-of-filing" rule, post-filing changes in citizenship are not relevant, so the result should be the same—dismissal for lack of subject matter jurisdiction. But this has not stopped parties and sympathetic lower courts from trying to forge exceptions to avoid the harsh consequences of the time-of-filing rule. In Grupo Dataflux v. Atlas Glob. Group, L.P., 541 U.S. 567 (2004), the Supreme Court rejected the Fifth Circuit's attempt to create an exception to the time-of-filing rule where the composition of a partnership changes. When the complaint for state law breach of contract was filed, Atlas, a Texas partnership, had two partners who were Mexican citizens. Grupo Dataflux was a Mexican corporation, so there were aliens on both sides, see 28 U.S.C. § 1332(a)(2), but the case went all the way through a jury trial resulting in a $750,000 award for Atlas before Grupo Dataflux caught the jurisdictional defect and filed a motion to dismiss. The Fifth Circuit reversed the lower court's dismissal because the Mexican partners left Atlas a month before the trial began (thus altering its citizenship) and because Grupo Dataflux failed to raise the defect until after court time and resources had been expended on a jury trial. In a sharply divided decision, the Supreme Court reversed, holding that the traditional time-of-filing rule should apply even though the citizenship of Atlas changed, and even though the case had proceeded to a jury verdict before Grupo Dataflux raised the defect. As the majority opinion emphasized,

[t]o our knowledge, the Court has never approved a deviation from the rule articulated by Chief Justice Marshall in 1829 that "[w]here there is *no* change of party, a jurisdiction depending on the condition of the party is governed by that condition, as it was at the commencement of the suit."

541 U.S. at 574. Does this holding embrace a venerable but inefficient rule? Why not punish Grupo Dataflux for its lack of diligence in raising the jurisdictional defect? What interests does the time-of-filing rule serve? Atlas and the dissenting opinion raised these questions and received the following response in the majority opinion:

The time-of-filing rule is what it is precisely because the facts determining jurisdiction are subject to change, and because constant litigation in response to that change would be wasteful. . . . Atlas and Dataflux have thus far litigated this case for more than 6½ years, including 3½ years over a conceded jurisdictional defect. Compared with the *one month* it took the Magistrate Judge to apply the time-of-filing rule . . . when the jurisdictional problem was brought to her attention, this waste counsels strongly against any course that would impair the certainty of our jurisdictional rules and thereby encourage similar jurisdictional litigation.

Id. at 580-82. Are you persuaded?

3. Recall the controversy in *World-Wide Volkswagen* regarding whether the Robinsons were diverse from all of the defendants in the action. Their lawyer sought to prevent removal of the action from state court to federal court by adding defendants who were not diverse from the Robinsons and those who were. This is permissible, provided that the parties are not nominal parties, in which case their citizenship may be disregarded for diversity purposes. See, e.g., Rose v. Giamatti, 721 F. Supp. 906 (S.D. Ohio 1989) (holding that the Cincinnati Reds and Major League Baseball were nominal parties in the action by Pete Rose against A. Bartlett Giamatti, then Commissioner of Baseball).

Likewise, the court will disregard the citizenship of fictitious parties, also known as Doe allegations. See 28 U.S.C. § 1441(a) (providing that, for purposes of removal, "the citizenship of defendants sued under fictitious names shall be disregarded").

4. What about citizens of foreign countries who are joined to a suit between citizens of different states? 28 U.S.C. § 1332(a)(3) provides for federal jurisdiction in suits between "citizens of different States and in which citizens or subjects of a foreign state are additional parties." In this context, courts have held that "the presence of foreigners on both sides of a diversity case does not destroy diversity" so long as there are properly diverse U.S. citizens on both sides of the case. Tango Music, LLC v. DeadQuick Music, Inc., 348 F.3d 244, 245 (7th Cir. 2003). The plain language of the statute suggests the same result should follow even if foreigners from the same country are on both sides of the litigation. Id. at 245-246. How would you distinguish *Grupo Dataflux*?

5. The circuits are split, however, on how to treat trusts. The Supreme Court has held that in a suit by individual trustees authorized to manage trust assets and sue on behalf of the trust, the citizenship of the trustees and not the beneficiaries of the trust is assessed for diversity purposes. Navarro Savings Assoc. v. Lee, 446 U.S. 458, 465-466 (1980). The Court did not address how to assess citizenship when the trust itself is a party to a suit. Some circuit courts have extended *Navarro* and held that the citizenship of the trust is always that of the trustee or trustees. See Hicklin Eng'g, L.C. v. Bartell, 439 F.3d 346, 348 (7th Cir. 2006); Johnson v. Columbia Props. Anchorage, LP, 437 F.3d 894, 899 (9th Cir. 2006). The Eleventh Circuit has held that the beneficiaries of a trust are the only relevant group for diversity purposes. See Riley v. Merrill Lynch, 292 F.3d 1334, 1338 (11th Cir. 2002). After canvassing the prior law, the Third Circuit recently held that the proper approach is to look to the citizenship of *both* the trustees and beneficiaries. Emerald Inv'rs Tr. v. Gaunt Parsippany Partners, 492 F.3d 192, 203-205 (3d Cir. 2007). The court placed special emphasis on the Supreme Court's holding in Carden v. Arkoma Assocs., 494 U.S. 185 (1990), that the citizenship of all members of an artificial entity must be assessed for diversity purposes. *Emerald Inv'rs,* 492 F.3d at 200. It also stressed that a broad citizenship rule serves federalism principles by keeping state law cases out of federal court unless diversity is truly complete. Id. at 204. The court remanded for a full evidentiary hearing to determine the citizenship of all beneficiaries and trustees of the plaintiff trust as well as the citizenship of all partners of defendant limited partnership.

What about the relationship between parent and subsidiary corporations? Specifically, what should a court do when a nondiverse parent company assigns its legal claims to a diverse subsidiary? What should a court do when a nondiverse subsidiary assigns legal claims to a diverse parent? These are complex issues involving corporations doctrine, but a few basic principles are clear. First, some courts apply a presumption of collusion—that is, a presumption that diversity jurisdiction has been improperly manufactured under 28 U.S.C. § 1359—when a nondiverse parent company assigns its claims to a diverse subsidiary "engaged in no business other than the prosecution of that claim." Prudential Oil Corp. v. Phillips Petroleum Co., 546 F.2d 469, 476 (2d Cir. 1976) (extended beyond parent-subsidiary relationships in Airlines Reporting Corp. v. S & N Travel, Inc., 58 F.3d 857 (2d Cir. 1995)). The reason is fairly straightforward: A subsidiary whose only business is to create diversity jurisdiction for bringing legal claims on behalf of a parent company is nothing short of a forum selection scam. If it were legal to do this, companies could simply create subsidiaries anytime they wanted to avoid the normal limits on diversity jurisdiction.

Different concerns are implicated when a nondiverse *subsidiary* assigns claims to a diverse *parent.* Here, the parent already may be on the hook for liabilities of the subsidiary or otherwise involved in the events leading to litigation. Still, the circuits are split. The Ninth Circuit has applied a presumption of collusion. See Nike, Inc. v. Comercial Iberica de Exclusivas Deportivas, S.A., 20 F.3d 987, 991-992 (9th Cir. 1994). The Eleventh Circuit, by contrast, applies no presumption. See Ambrosia Coal & Constr. Co. v. Pages Morales, 482 F.3d 1309, 1314-1315 (11th Cir. 2007) (following Seventh Circuit decision, Herzog Contracting Corp. v. McGowen Corp., 976 F.2d 1062, 1067 (7th Cir. 1992) (holding that "no inference of collusive invocation of jurisdiction can be drawn from the simple fact that assignor and assignee are under common ownership")). The Eleventh Circuit emphasized that a number of factors are relevant to determining whether an assignment of claims is collusive: whether the assignor has retained an interest in the assigned claim, whether consideration was exchanged, and whether the assignee has any previous connection to the matter. *Ambrosia Coal*, 482 F.2d at 1315. In the case before it, the court determined that the subsidiary had not collusively assigned its claim to its parent because there was evidence that the parent had funded the real estate purchase at issue and had actively participated in the suit. Id. at 1316.

6. In *Mas*, the court held that Mrs. Mas remained a Mississippi domiciliary even though she had no intention of returning there because she had not acquired a new domicile; she was living in Louisiana as a student but "lacked the requisite intention to remain there." This is the so-called presumption of continuing domicile. See Padilla-Mangual v. Pavia Hosp., 516 F.3d 29, 31-32 (1st Cir. 2008). The presumption is overcome by evidence of presence or residence in another state and evidence of intent to remain there. Although things like registering to vote; paying taxes; owning or leasing real or personal property; working; and holding bank accounts, licenses, and church or club memberships are all traditional indicia of intent to remain, notice that most of these activities would be most applicable to a person of means. The First Circuit has emphasized that none of these "typical indicia of domicile are required in order to change one's domicile"; they are only examples. Id. at 33.

In *Padilla*, the district court of Puerto Rico dismissed plaintiff's suit for damages from allegedly negligent medical treatment for lack of diversity, concluding that he had not altered his presumed domicile of Puerto Rico by moving to Florida. The court

> focused on Padilla's apparent failure to cultivate the sort of ties traditionally viewed as manifesting an expression of domicile: "Padilla does not work nor has he indicated that he is looking for work in Florida. He does not go to school. He does not own or rent any real property in Florida. He does not belong to any clubs, nor does he attend a church. He does not have any bank accounts. He has not registered or exercised the right to vote. Other than his driver's license and a stated desire to stay there, Padilla doesn't seem to have established any real presence in Florida."

Id. The district court also rejected Padilla's claim that his physical condition prevented him from working or going to school.

The First Circuit reversed, pointing to record evidence including: two declarations, one by Padilla, and another by his mother, that he is a resident of Florida with no intention to return to Puerto Rico and plans to stay in

Florida; copies of payments and charges from four places in Florida where Padilla claimed he had lived; and a copy of a Florida driver's license. Id. at 32. The court noted that "[a]ny number of explanations are possible" for the absence of traditional indicia of domicile—among them "physical or mental incapacity, religious objections, to name a few." Id. at 34.

> The point is that where a party has declared his intent to change and remain in his new domicile, and the opposing written submissions do not demonstrate the falsity of the declaration with reasonable certainty, the absence of typical indicia of domicile is not determinative. More is required of the district court before it concludes that a plaintiff has not met his burden and overcome the presumption. We agree with our sister circuits that in these circumstances an evidentiary hearing is appropriate.

Id. The court remanded for such a hearing.

7. There is an indication at the end of *Tanzymore* that the district court thought Mr. Tanzymore might be "stateless." That would mean he is not a citizen of a state entitled to invoke the diversity jurisdiction of any federal court. See Newman-Green, Inc. v. Alfonzo-Larrain, 490 U.S. 826, 828 (1989). The Third Circuit did not take up the question, deciding instead that Mr. Tanzymore simply failed to meet his burden of establishing that he was in fact a citizen of Ohio. Other courts have, however, dismissed a case for want of complete diversity when it appears one of the parties is indeed "stateless." See Thompson v. Deloitte & Touche LLP, 503 F. Supp. 2d 1118, 1123-1125 (S.D. Iowa 2007) (granting motion to dismiss for want of diversity jurisdiction on ground that U.S. limited liability partnership with one stateless partner, a U.S. citizen living in Asia with no domicile in the United States, who was not registered to vote in the United States, with no U.S. residence for state income tax purposes, and who planned to continue living and working in Asia "indefinitely," renders entire firm stateless); Nat'l City Bank v. Aronson, 474 F. Supp. 2d 925 (S.D. Ohio 2007) (remanding case and awarding attorneys' fees to plaintiff for defendants' improper removal upon finding that a defendant beneficiary of trust living and planning to remain in New Zealand was stateless despite owning a residence in Colorado, holding a Colorado bank account to pay U.S. bills, possessing a Colorado driver's license, owning two cars registered in the state, retaining two state academic certifications, actively serving on a board for a religious organization in the state, and residing in the home for nearly six months in 2005).

8. There are two exceptions to the diversity statute: probate and domestic relations claims. Such claims cannot be brought in federal court, regardless of the diversity of the parties. The root of these exceptions lies in the historical division of labor among courts. While probate and domestic relations claims once were heard by the ecclesiastical courts, only actions "of a civil nature in law or equity" were covered by the diversity statute. The historical treatment has persisted because of a modern sense that states have greater expertise in these matters of "local" concern, though this characterization is certainly debatable.

Teasing out matters that fall within the states' exclusive probate jurisdiction from overlapping matters that do not can be difficult. Although it is clear that the federal courts will not probate a will or assume control of property that is in the custody of a state court, this does not mean they cannot hear actions against administrators, executors, and other claimants that are related to such property.

Similarly subtle distinctions can arise in connection with the domestic relations exception. In Ankenbrandt v. Richards, 504 U.S. 689 (1992), the Court held that despite the exception the federal court could hear an action in which plaintiff sued her ex-husband for abuse of the children while they were visiting their father. Federal courts may not issue divorce, child custody, or alimony decrees, but they can hear tort actions that arise within domestic relations. Anna Nicole Smith's widely reported, and ultimately successful, efforts to establish her right to the multi-million dollar estate of her deceased husband offer a case in point. Smith, whose real name was Vickie Lynn Marshall, married Texas millionaire J. Howard Marshall in 1994 after a three-year courtship. J. Howard died a year later without having provided for Vickie in his will. Although he had apparently promised to provide for her security via a "catch-all" trust, his will at the time of his death left his estate to one of his sons, E. Pierce Marshall.

In 1997, while J. Howard's estate was in probate proceedings in Texas state court, Vickie filed for bankruptcy in the U.S. Bankruptcy Court for the Central District of California. Federal bankruptcy courts have exclusive jurisdiction over bankruptcy petitions.

Hostilities between Vickie and Pierce broke out almost immediately, with Vickie making public charges that Pierce had engaged in forgery, fraud, and overreaching to win control of his father's estate. Pierce responded by jumping into the bankruptcy proceedings. He filed a "proof of claim" with the bankruptcy court, seeking a declaration that his separate cause of action against Vickie for defamation was not a dischargeable debt. Since Pierce had submitted himself to the jurisdiction of the bankruptcy court by filing his objections, Vickie then filed a counterclaim against Pierce asserting that he had tortiously interfered with the estate gift J. Howard intended to give her.

The bankruptcy court entered judgment for Vickie on her counterclaim, finding that J. Howard had in fact directed his lawyers to prepare a trust for Vickie consisting of half the appreciation of his assets from the date of their marriage, but that Pierce had conspired to suppress or destroy the trust instrument and to strip his father of his assets by backdating, altering, and otherwise falsifying documents, arranging for surveillance of his father and Vickie, and presenting documents to his father under false pretenses. The court awarded Vickie $449 million, less any recovery she made in the Texas probate proceeding, and, on "overwhelming evidence" of Pierce's maliciousness and fraud, $25 million in punitive damages. At the same time, in the Texas proceeding, Pierce succeeded in convincing the probate court that his father's existing will was valid, making Pierce the heir to the entire estate.

The case reached the Supreme Court on Pierce's claim that the federal bankruptcy court judgment was void for want of subject matter jurisdiction due to the probate exception. Marshall v. Marshall, 547 U.S. 293 (2006). Resolving a division in the circuit courts over what sorts of actions by a bankruptcy court "interfere with the probate proceedings," Id. at 311 (quoting Markham v. Allen, 326 U.S. 490, 494 (1946)), the Court held that a bankruptcy court impermissibly "interferes" with probate proceedings only when it "'disturb[s] or affect[s] the possession of property in the custody of a state court.'" Id. (quoting *Markham*, 326 U.S. at 494). As the Court reasoned:

> [T]he probate exception reserves to state probate courts the probate or annulment of a will and the administration of a decedent's estate; it also precludes federal courts from endeavoring to dispose of property that is in the custody of a state probate court. But it does not bar federal courts from adjudicating matters outside those confines and otherwise within federal jurisdiction.

Id. at 311-312. Vickie's tort claim seeking an *in personam* judgment against Pierce was therefore within the jurisdiction of the bankruptcy court. She did not "seek to reach a *res* in the custody of a state court," her claim did not "involve the administration of an estate, the probate of a will, or any other purely probate matter," and it raised common tort issues as to which state probate courts possess "no special proficiency . . . in handling." Id. at 312. The Court also rejected the Texas Probate Court's attempt to claim exclusive jurisdiction: "'[A] State cannot create a transitory cause of action and at the same time destroy the right to sue on that transitory cause of action in any court having jurisdiction.'" Id. at 314 (quoting Tenn. Coal, Iron & R.R. Co. v. George, 233 U.S. 354, 360 (1914)).

## b. Historical Backdrop and Current Controversies

The history of diversity jurisdiction is long and conflict-ridden. Unlike federal question jurisdiction, which was not granted fully to the federal courts until after the Civil War, diversity jurisdiction was granted in the first Judiciary Act of 1789. The founders felt strongly that federal courts must be given power to hear conflicts between citizens of different states, lest nonresidents be subject to biased judgments by plaintiffs' home courts.

Whether the diversity option actually was essential to protecting nonresident parties from state court bias, however, was and is contested. In a detailed study of federal diversity jurisdiction from 1870 to 1958, Edward Purcell concludes that the diversity option often worked to the strategic advantage of astute corporate defendants of the late 1800s and early 1900s in ways that had little or nothing to do with local bias. Edward A. Purcell, Jr., Litigation and Inequality: Federal Diversity Jurisdiction in Industrial America, 1870-1958 (1992). Corporate lawyers would petition for removal to federal courts, which often sat in cities far from the plaintiffs' homes. Id. at 45-50. The distance factor, coupled with the more pro-business law then available in federal courts, id. at 59-60, made federal court a highly attractive option for corporations. To block the removal, plaintiffs either would discount their claims at the pleading stage and allege less than the jurisdictional amount that then applied to diversity cases ($500), or settle. As Purcell reports, the corporations had significant leverage in these settlement negotiations because of the diversity option. Id. at 63. Those most affected by the combination of procedural and substantive advantages afforded corporations by federal diversity were plaintiffs whose injuries were the most serious. For these plaintiffs to avoid removal, they had to discount their claims far more steeply than parties with less serious injuries. Id. at 100. None of these machinations was inspired by the "fear of state court bias" so often invoked as the primary reason for federal court diversity jurisdiction.

The 95th Congress, in 1978, came close to abolishing diversity jurisdiction — the bill passed the House but died in the Senate. See Thomas D. Rowe, Jr., Abolishing Diversity Jurisdiction: The Silver Lining, 66 A.B.A. J. 177 (1980); see also Thomas D. Rowe, Jr., Abolishing Diversity Jurisdiction: Positive Side Effects and Potential for Further Reforms, 92 Harv. L. Rev. 963 (1979). Commenting on the bill, Professor Rowe argued that abolishing the random benefits and manipulable aspects of diversity jurisdiction might not be such a bad thing, after all. He says that abolishing diversity jurisdiction would: result in a "sheer reduction in the incidence of difficult jurisdictional and procedural issues," particularly complete diversity; facilitate judicial reform of federal pendent and ancillary jurisdiction and procedures for removal of actions from state court to federal court; and pave the way for further reforms in federal practice. Id. at 178. To arguments that not all state courts are equipped to handle foreign service of process, multistate discovery, and interstate enforcement of judgments, Rowe responded that the abolition of diversity jurisdiction might give them just the incentive they need to develop their capacities. Id. at 180.

Other legal scholars disagree. For example, Professors Moore and Weckstein have suggested that "[t]he large number of diversity cases brought to the federal courts and their apparently satisfactory disposition is itself evidence of the value of diversity jurisdiction." James William Moore & Donald T. Weckstein, Diversity Jurisdiction: Past, Present, and Future, 43 Tex. L. Rev. 1, 19 n.116 (1964). They even argue that diversity jurisdiction be expanded at the federal level, to help build federal common law and expound national rules of conflict of laws. Id. at 20.

Daniel J. Meador has taken a third approach, suggesting that rather than abolishing diversity jurisdiction altogether or restricting it with periodic adjustments to the amount in controversy, a more effective controlling device would be to eliminate diversity cases based on subject matter, particularly personal injury. Daniel J. Meador, A New Approach to Limiting Diversity Jurisdiction, 46 A.B.A. J. 383 (1960).

Although bills to abolish diversity jurisdiction have been perennially introduced, none has succeeded thus far. Thus, diversity cases continue to be an important part of the federal court dockets. Diversity cases accounted for 51,992, or 20 percent, of total federal civil cases in 1974, and 49,793, or 19 percent, of total federal civil cases filed in 1988. Compare this with the early days, when the 368 cases heard by the federal courts between 1790 and 1815 constituted over 57 percent of the total cases heard. The 1996 amendment to 28 U.S.C. § 1332, which raised the amount in controversy to $75,000, did not lower the number of filings. In 2008, 88,457 diversity cases were filed, 34 percent of all federal civil cases. However, the number fell dramatically in 2015, down 38 percent to 40,697, just under 25 percent of all federal civil filings.

### c.  Joinder and the Amount in Controversy

In addition to establishing complete diversity of citizenship, the party invoking federal diversity jurisdiction must demonstrate that the amount in controversy is greater than $75,000.

The jurisdictional amount stated in 28 U.S.C. § 1332 can be difficult to calculate. Questions immediately arise that cannot be resolved on the face of the statute, such as whether two plaintiffs can aggregate their claims against one defendant to meet the jurisdictional amount. Most of these questions have been answered by case law that construes the statute. Some of them also require an understanding of 28 U.S.C. § 1367, which addresses supplemental jurisdiction. In each example below, we assume the action is based *solely* on diversity. We summarize the case law under 28 U.S.C. § 1332 and the basic rules that it establishes. We leave a more thorough examination of § 1367 and supplemental jurisdiction to Chapter 6.

1. Two or more claims of *one* plaintiff against a defendant *can* be aggregated to reach the amount-in-controversy requirement, even if the claims are factually unrelated.

   P v. D

   | P claim(1) $45,000 | + | P claim(2) $31,000 | = | Amount in controversy $76,000 *meets requirement* |
   |---|---|---|---|---|

2. The claims of *more than one* plaintiff, each of which fails to meet the amount-in-controversy requirement standing alone, *cannot* be aggregated to reach the jurisdictional amount if the plaintiffs' claims are *separate and distinct* (that is, not asserting one right). But if at least one plaintiff's claims, standing alone, meets the amount-in-controversy requirement, the related claims of additional plaintiffs joined under Rule 20 may be joined even if those claims are below the amount-in-controversy requirement.[*]

---

[*] For more on the subtleties of this rule for complex litigation, see the section on supplemental jurisdiction in Chapter 6.

3. There is no aggregation of a plaintiff's claims against multiple defendants. Thus where P's claim against D(1) does not meet the amount-in-controversy requirement, it does not matter that P's claim against D(2), when added to P's claim against D(1), would meet that amount.

4. A defendant's compulsory counterclaim** against the plaintiff falls within the supplemental jurisdiction of the court and thus *can* be heard even if it does not meet the amount-in-controversy requirement.

5. If, on the other hand, D's counterclaim falls below the amount in controversy and is unrelated to plaintiff's claim, then it is *not* within the court's supplemental jurisdiction and must be dismissed.

6. As in situation 1 above, separate counterclaims of a single defendant against a single plaintiff *can* be aggregated to reach the amount-in-controversy requirement. This is true regardless of whether the counterclaims are compulsory or permissive.

### Note: Litigating Subject Matter Jurisdiction

Review the mechanics of litigating personal jurisdiction, discussed in section C of this chapter. Now read Fed. R. Civ. P. 12(b)(1). Assume that a claim filed in a federal district court is arguably, but not certainly, outside the court's subject matter jurisdiction, and that dismissal for lack of personal jurisdiction over the defendant is clearly warranted. May the court address only the dispositive personal jurisdiction issue and thereby avoid the thorny subject matter jurisdiction dispute? Or must the subject matter jurisdiction be faced first, given that it is foundational? In Ruhrgas AG v. Marathon Oil Co., 526 U.S. 574 (1999), the Court held that:

> [In] cases removed from state court to federal court, as in cases originating in federal court, there is no unyielding jurisdictional hierarchy. Customarily, a federal court first resolves doubts about its jurisdiction over the subject matter, but there are circumstances in which a district court appropriately accords priority to a personal jurisdiction inquiry.

Id. at 578. The Court concluded that the case before it was one in which treatment of personal jurisdiction issues first was appropriate, because the challenge to personal jurisdiction involved no complex state law questions and was easier to resolve than the "difficult and novel" subject matter jurisdiction issue. Id. at 579.

---

** A "compulsory" counterclaim is one that arises out of the transaction or occurrence that is the subject matter of the opposing party's claims. See Fed. R. Civ. P. 13(a).

## 3.   Federal Question Jurisdiction: Statutory Requirements

### Problem Case: Making a Federal Case

Can this case properly be brought in federal court?

|  |  |  |
|---|---|---|
| Heidi Gesund | ) | |
| | ) | |
| v. | ) | COMPLAINT |
| | ) | |
| The Vita-Men, | ) | |
| Inc. | ) | |

### JURISDICTION

1. Jurisdiction is based on 28 U.S.C. § 1331; this is a case arising under the laws of the United States.

### PARTIES

2. Plaintiff Heidi Gesund is a citizen of Albuquerque, New Mexico. She is a professional bodybuilder who has over the past decade won state, national, and world titles in the women's division of the sport.

3. Defendant, trading under the name The Vita-Men, is a company incorporated under the laws of New Mexico and doing business in that state with its principal place of business in Albuquerque.

### CAUSE OF ACTION

4. Defendants have advertised on radio, television, and in the print media that their product, Mineral Magic, contains an all-natural vitamin formula guaranteed to enhance muscle tone.

5. On or about June 25, 2015, Plaintiff Heidi Gesund purchased 100 doses of Mineral Magic, and between that date and July 10, 2015, she consumed a total of 40 doses of the product in preparation for a national bodybuilding competition to be held in Albuquerque on July 12, 2015.

6. On the eve of the competition, Plaintiff awoke with a disturbing medical condition characterized by severe swelling of the muscular tissue and the appearance of unsightly, thick black hairs, which now cover her entire body; plaintiff is a natural blonde.

7. On information and belief, Mineral Magic contains synthetic testosterone, as well as other animal and human hormones, that have not been adequately tested or approved by the federal Food and Drug Administration.

8. On information and belief, Mineral Magic is sold and distributed in violation of FDA rules and regulations, and is unsafe for human consumption.

WHEREFORE, plaintiff demands judgment against The Vita-Men in the sum of one million dollars and costs.

––––––––––––––––

The Court has interpreted federal question statutory jurisdiction to mean that the federal courts may hear a case under 28 U.S.C. § 1331 provided that federal law has a *substantial* and *direct* bearing on the case. (Recall that the constitutional possibilities may be much broader; the federal law need only be an "ingredient" of the dispute.) In the easiest examples, this statutory test is met because the claim is based directly on an alleged violation of a federal statute. Thus, for example, § 1331 is clearly satisfied if a plaintiff alleges that the defendant violated Title VII of the Civil Rights Act of 1964, a federal statute that protects workers against discrimination. The court inevitably must construe the federal law in order to resolve the dispute, and Title VII explicitly creates a cause of action. The plaintiff therefore has a right to litigate this matter in federal court, if she wishes.

Note, however, that she instead may choose to litigate in state court, because the state courts have *concurrent* power over all federal claims unless they fall within the *exclusive* judicial authority of the federal courts. That is, simply because a federal statute is involved does not mean that she *must* litigate in federal court, but that she *can* do so, if she wishes. When Congress wants to prevent state courts from adjudicating federal law, it explicitly provides for exclusive federal jurisdiction.

A more difficult question arises when an action not based directly on a federal statute requires the court to construe a federal law in order to dispose of the case. For example, parties might agree under a contract that *A* will deliver to *B* goods that meet certain federal standards. If *B* sues *A* for breach of contract, alleging that the goods fail to meet these federal standards, then a case based on the state law of contract necessarily will entail federal law as well. The courts have said, in essence, that whether the presence of federal law in the case is enough to "federalize" it under § 1331 is a matter of degree, rather like proximate cause.

In this section, we want to enable you to recognize the nature of federal claims in our dual court system, while at the same time assuring you that complete understanding must await a course in federal jurisdiction. We begin with an exercise in identifying federal claims. We then turn to one of the earliest cases limiting federal court jurisdiction, Louisville & Nashville R.R. Co. v. Mottley, 211 U.S. 149 (1908). Finally, we discuss Merrell Dow Pharm. v. Thompson, 478 U.S. 804 (1986), and Grable & Sons Metal Prods., Inc. v. Darue Eng'g & Mfg., 545 U.S. 308 (2005), the two most significant modern cases dealing with limits on federal question jurisdiction.

The following case excerpt summarizes the current test for determining whether a case "arises under" federal law and thus poses a federal question justifying the jurisdiction of the federal courts. Which of the cases that follow the excerpt seem to satisfy the test?

## *Franchise Tax Board v. Construction Laborers Vacation Trust*
463 U.S. 1 (1983)

Justice Brennan delivered the opinion of the Court.

Since the first version of § 1331 was enacted, Act of Mar. 3, 1875, ch. 137, § 1, 18 Stat. 470, the statutory phrase "arising under the Constitution, laws, or treaties of the United States" has resisted all attempts to frame a single, precise definition for determining which cases fall within, and which cases fall outside, the original jurisdiction of the district courts. . . .

The most familiar definition of the statutory "arising under" limitation is Justice Holmes' statement, "A suit arises under the law that creates the cause of action." American Well Works Co. v. Layne & Bowler Co., 241 U.S. 257, 260 (1916). However, it is well settled that Justice Holmes' test is more useful for describing the vast majority of cases that come within the district courts' original jurisdiction than it is for describing which cases are beyond district court jurisdiction. We have often held that a case "arose under" federal law where the vindication of a right under state law necessarily turned on some construction of federal law, see, e.g., Smith v. Kansas City Title & Trust Co., 255 U.S. 180 (1921); Hopkins v. Walker, 244 U.S. 486 (1917), and even the most ardent proponent of the Holmes test has admitted that it has been rejected as an exclusionary principle, see Flournoy v. Wiener, 321 U.S. 253, 270-72 (1944) (Frankfurter, J., dissenting). See also T. B. Harms Co. v. Eliscu, 339 F.2d 823, 827 (2d Cir. 1964) (Friendly, J.). Leading commentators have suggested that for purposes of § 1331 an action "arises under" federal law "if in order for the plaintiff to secure the relief sought he will be obliged to establish both the correctness and the applicability to his case of a proposition of federal law." P. Bator, P. Mishkin, D. Shapiro & H. Wechsler, Hart and Wechsler's The Federal Courts and the Federal System 889 (2d ed. 1973); cf. T. B. Harms Co., supra, at 827 ("a case may 'arise under' a law of the United States if the complaint discloses a need for determining the meaning or application of such a law"). . . .

. . . "[A] right or immunity created by the Constitution or laws of the United States must be an element, and an essential one, of the plaintiff's cause of action." Gully v. First National Bank in Meridian, 299 U.S. 109, 112 (1936). . . . Even though state law creates appellant's causes of action, its case might still "arise under" the laws of the United States if a well-pleaded complaint established that its right to relief under state law requires resolution of a substantial question of federal law in dispute between the parties. . . .

. . . Under our interpretations, Congress has given the lower federal courts jurisdiction to hear, originally or by removal from a state court, only those cases in which a well-pleaded complaint establishes either that federal law creates the cause of action or that the plaintiff's right to relief necessarily depends on resolution of a substantial question of federal law. . . .

### a.   Some Easy Cases

Below are short summaries of claims filed in federal court under the federal question statute. Can you see why they might satisfy the statute?

*Bender v. City of St. Ann*, 816 F. Supp. 1372 (E.D. Mo. 1993). Deli owner brought § 1983 action alleging constitutional violations stemming from enforcement of ordinance restricting the number of commercial signs his establishment could display.

*Hudson v. Nat'l Acad. of Scis., Inst. of Med.*, 816 F. Supp. 774 (D.D.C. 1993). Title VII race discrimination case was filed by former employee of non-profit corporation alleging discrimination in failure to promote, retaliation in nonselection for promotion, harassment, demotion based on race, and discriminatory termination.

*Ware v. Howard Univ.*, 816 F. Supp. 737 (D.D.C. 1993). University employee brought action against university alleging violations of Age Discrimination in Employment Act (ADEA).

*Adler v. Berg Harmon Assocs.*, 816 F. Supp. 919 (S.D.N.Y. 1993). Investors in limited partnership interests in real estate tax shelters brought suit against joint venture which syndicated and promoted sale of interests, its parent corporations, and corporate officer. Investors asserted violations of the Securities Exchange Act of 1934, the Racketeer Influenced and Corrupt Organizations Act (RICO), common-law fraud, negligence, and breach of fiduciary duty.

### b.   The Well-Pleaded Complaint Requirement

The above cases should reinforce for you the first requirement of federal question jurisdiction: that federal courts may hear a case if federal law has a substantial and direct bearing on the case. A second requirement is that the federal question must appear on the face of the "well-pleaded" complaint. Simply put, the plaintiff's claim—not the defendant's response—must include the federal question. Below is the famous case that established this limitation on federal court power. To understand *Mottley*, you need to appreciate that "well-pleaded" does not mean *actually* pleaded in the complaint filed with the court. Rather, "well-pleaded" here means the least the plaintiff needed to include in the complaint to state fully her complaint against the defendant, without anticipating defendant's likely response to that claim. Read on to find out what happened to the Mottley crew.

### *Louisville & Nashville R.R. Co. v. Mottley*
211 U.S. 149 (1908)

Statement by JUSTICE MOODY.

The appellees (husband and wife), being residents and citizens of Kentucky, brought this suit in equity in the circuit court of the United

States for the western district of Kentucky against the appellant, a railroad company and a citizen of the same state. The object of the suit was to compel the specific performance of the following contract:

> Louisville, Ky., Oct. 2d, 1871. The Louisville & Nashville Railroad Company, in consideration that E. L. Mottley and wife, Annie E. Mottley, have this day released company from all damages or claims for damages for injuries received by them on the 7th of September, 1871, in consequence of a collision of trains on the railroad of said company at Randolph's Station, Jefferson County, Kentucky, hereby agrees to issue free passes on said railroad and branches now existing or to exist, to said E. L. & Annie E. Mottley for the remainder of the present year, and thereafter to renew said passes annually during the lives of said Mottley and wife or either of them.

The bill alleged that in September, 1871, plaintiffs, while passengers upon the defendant railroad, were injured by the defendant's negligence, and released their respective claims for damages in consideration of the agreement for transportation during their lives, expressed in the contract. It is alleged that the contract was performed by the defendant up to January 1, 1907, when the defendant declined to renew the passes. The bill then alleges that the refusal to comply with the contract was based solely upon that part of the act of Congress of June 29, 1906 (34 Stat. at L. 584, chap. 3591), which forbids the giving of free passes or free transportation. The bill further alleges: First, that the act of Congress referred to does not prohibit the giving of passes under the circumstances of this case; and, second, that, if the law is to be construed as prohibiting such passes, it is in conflict with the 5th Amendment of the Constitution, because it deprives the plaintiffs of their property without due process of law. The defendant demurred to the bill. The judge of the circuit court overruled the demurrer, entered a decree for the relief prayed for, and the defendant appealed directly to this court. . . .

JUSTICE MOODY, after making the foregoing statement, delivered the opinion of the court:

Two questions of law were raised by the demurrer to the bill, were brought here by appeal, and have been argued before us. They are, first, whether that part of the act of Congress of June 29, 1906 (34 Stat. at L. 584, chap. 3591), which forbids the giving of free passes or the collection of any different compensation for transportation of passengers than that specified in the tariff filed, makes it unlawful to perform a contract for transportation of persons who, in good faith, before the passage of the act, had accepted such contract in satisfaction of a valid cause of action against the railroad; and, second, whether the statute, if it should be construed to render such a contract unlawful, is in violation of the 5th Amendment of the Constitution of the United States. We do not deem it necessary, however, to consider either of these questions, because, in our opinion, the court below was without jurisdiction of the cause. Neither party has questioned that jurisdiction, but it is the duty of this court to see to it that the jurisdiction of the circuit court, which is defined and limited by statute, is not exceeded. This duty we have frequently performed of our own motion.

There was no diversity of citizenship, and it is not and cannot be suggested that there was any ground of jurisdiction, except that the case was a "suit . . . arising under the Constitution or laws of the United States." 25 Stat. at L. 434, chap. 866. It is the settled interpretation of these words, as used in this statute, conferring jurisdiction, that a suit arises under the Constitution and laws of the United States only when the plaintiff's statement of his own cause of action shows that it is based upon those laws or that Constitution. It is not enough that the plaintiff alleges some anticipated defense to his cause of action, and asserts that the defense is invalidated by some provision of the Constitution of the United States. Although such allegations show that very likely, in the course of the litigation, a question under the Constitution would arise, they do not show that the suit, that is, the plaintiff's original cause of action, arises under the Constitution. . . .

It is ordered that the judgment be reversed and the case remitted to the circuit court with instructions to dismiss the suit for want of jurisdiction.

### Note: The Aftermath of Mottley

Assume that you are the lawyer for the Mottleys and must turn to redrafting the complaint. Try your hand at rewriting the complaint so that it does not anticipate the defendant's response.

Your efforts are likely to reflect real life in which the lawyer for the Mottleys could not draft a federal question complaint, and so turned to state court. Naturally, the railroad responded by raising the authority of the federal statute for its actions. Again the case made its way to the U.S. Supreme Court, which construed the statute to uphold the railroad's action in rescinding the passes. Louisville & Nashville R.R. Co. v. Mottley, 219 U.S. 467 (1911). Thus, two long and expensive journeys led to a dead end for the Mottleys.

The Court reaffirmed the well-pleaded complaint rule in Rivet v. Regions Bank of Louisiana, 522 U.S. 470 (1998). See further discussion of *Rivet* in Chapters 6 and 7. See also Holmes Group, Inc. v. Vornado Air Circulation Syst., Inc., 535 U.S. 826 (2002) (holding that a federal patent infringement claim asserted as a counterclaim did not create federal subject matter jurisdiction because the well-pleaded complaint, not the counterclaim, determines whether a civil action "arises under" federal patent law).

At first glance, the Declaratory Judgment Act, 28 U.S.C. § 2201, which allows potential defendants like the railroad to become plaintiffs instead and test whether they are excused from renewing passes like those granted the Mottleys, would seem an avenue for a more fair and speedy resolution of questions like that about the statute in *Mottley*. In Skelly Oil Co. v. Phillips Petroleum Co., 339 U.S. 667 (1950), however, the Supreme Court held that the Declaratory Judgment Act did not alter the jurisdiction of the federal courts, so that if plaintiffs like the Mottleys could not plead "well" in the federal courts, neither could defendants like the railroad who did not want to wait to be sued before determining the constitutionality and viability of their potential defenses.

For discussion of federal question jurisdiction in the Declaratory Judgment and Labor Management Relations Act § 301(a) context, which discusses (and distinguishes) *Skelly Oil Co.,* see Textron Lycoming Reciprocating Engine Div. Arvo Corp. v. United Auto. Aerospace and Agric. Implement Workers of Am., Int'l Union and Its Local 787, 523 U.S. 653 (1998). The Court noted that "[n]o decision of this Court has squarely confronted and explicitly upheld federal-question jurisdiction on the basis of the anticipatory claim against which the declaratory-judgment plaintiff presents a non-federal defense." 523 U.S. at 659, 660. Although it acknowledged that the Declaratory Judgment Act might be read to allow such anticipation, past cases have not presented that issue, and have had language to suggest "that the declaratory-judgment plaintiff must himself have a federal claim." Id. at 660. See also Household Bank v. JFS Group, 320 F.3d 1249, 1251 (11th Cir. 2003) (joining seven other circuits in holding that "federal-question jurisdiction exists in a declaratory judgment action if the plaintiff has alleged facts in a well-pleaded complaint which demonstrate that the defendant could file a coercive action arising under federal law").

### c.   Hard Cases: What Kinds of "Mixed" Claims Arise Under Federal Law?

### Problem Case: More Than a Hidden Forum Selection Clause . . .

Revisit the facts of the litigation involving failed voting machines just before *Carnival Cruise.* Recall that Failsafe's contract with the County contained a warranty clause promising that the EVUs would perform without any problem recording a vote, any inaccuracy tallying votes, or any mechanical or software defects causing voting delays. Failsafe further warranted that its machines would meet any and all standards for electronic voting machines provided by *federal* law. Assume now that the only relevant federal law provides:

> All electronic voting machines sold for use in local, state, and federal elections shall perform at least as well as the manual voting machines they replace. The Department of Justice shall have exclusive authority to bring suit for statutory damages of $1000 per occurrence for failure to meet this standard as well as any appropriate equitable relief. "Occurrence" means any instance of substandard performance by an electronic voting machine. Performance resulting in no delays or errors in the final vote tally shall be a complete defense to a claim for statutory damages.

The County is a citizen of Texas for diversity purposes. Failsafe is a Japanese corporation. The County is Failsafe's only Texas client and represents 50 percent of its total global revenue. The company's CEO, CFO, COO, as well as its entire U.S. sales and software force, worked in Austin, Texas. However, it relocated all of these employees to Nevada on April 1, 2013, two weeks after the complaint was filed. The company hoped to save labor costs and minimize taxes by moving to Nevada. Lawyers for the County filed the complaint in federal court in Texas knowing that Failsafe planned to move its principal place of business to Nevada in the spring.

The causes of action stated in the complaint are for fraud, breach of contract, and breach of warranty. Failsafe has moved to dismiss the complaint under Rule 12(b)(1). Does the court have either arising under or diversity jurisdiction?

In Merrell Dow Pharmaceutical v. Thompson, 478 U.S. 804 (1986), the U.S. Supreme Court addressed the question whether a federal statute *must* provide an express or implied private right of action when a plaintiff seeks to rely on that statute as the basis for federal jurisdiction over *state* law claims. A private right of action is created when a statute gives to private persons, not merely public authorities, the power to enforce the rights created by the statute through litigation. This happens in one of two ways. Either the statute expressly provides for this private right of action, or a court may conclude that such a right is implied by the statute, despite the absence of explicit congressional language granting such a right. Either way, if a private right of action exists, private citizens ordinarily can bring suit in state or federal court. See Mims v. Arrow Financial Services, LLC, 132 S. Ct. 740, 748-749 (2012) ("When federal law creates a private right of action and furnishes the substantive rules of decision, the claim arises under federal law, and district courts possess federal-question jurisdiction under § 1331.").

However, not all statutes that impose particular legal obligations can be enforced by private citizens, even though the statutes likely were drafted to protect those citizens. Many areas of federal law are enforced exclusively by federal agencies. If, for example, Congress were to pass a law regulating the disposal of chemical waste by certain industries, the law may be enforceable only by the government rather than by private individuals harmed by a company's failure to comply with those disposal regulations. Private individuals might be able to sue in state court, say for personal injuries arising from the pollution, but not for violation of the federal statute.

More difficult is the question whether such a state law personal injury claim could be filed in *federal* court, assuming there is no diversity jurisdiction. If the state tort law standard of liability is affected by a claim that federal regulatory standards have been violated, then federal issues are a necessary part of the plaintiff's prima facie case. That makes it a classic "mixed" case in which state law provides the cause of action, but federal law affects liability and will have to be adjudicated for the plaintiff to prevail. Even so, there is still the question whether the federal issue is "substantial" under the well-pleaded complaint rule.

If Congress has *not* created an express or implied private right of action in federal court for these cases, granting § 1331 jurisdiction could sweep into federal court many cases in which state law provides the cause of action and is the core of the case. So one could conclude that federalism requires restricting the definition of "substantial" federal issues in mixed cases to instances in which Congress has allowed private rights of action. On the other hand, relegating mixed cases of this kind exclusively to the state courts by denying § 1331 jurisdiction would mean that some aspects of the enforcement of a federal regulatory scheme would not receive nationally uniform application. What makes a federal issue "substantial," on this view, is not whether Congress has gone out of its way to say so, but rather, whether the regulatory scheme Congress established is one that calls for the expertise, independence, and uniformity federal courts can provide. One approach gives more weight to federalism in setting the boundaries of arising under jurisdiction, the other gives more weight to the Supremacy Clause.

In *Merrell Dow*, the Court endorsed the first approach. It appeared to hold that without an express or implied federal right of action, there is no § 1331 jurisdiction. The parties conceded that Congress had not either expressly or impliedly created a federal cause of action against pharmaceutical companies for the misbranding of drugs under the Federal Food, Drug, and Cosmetic Act. The Court reasoned:

> We . . . conclude that the congressional determination that there should be no federal remedy for the violation of this federal statute is tantamount to a congressional conclusion that the presence of a claimed violation of the statute as an element of a state cause of action is insufficiently "substantial" to confer federal-question jurisdiction. . . . Petitioner's concern about the uniformity of interpretation, moreover, is considerably mitigated by the fact that, even if there is no original district court jurisdiction for these kinds of action, this Court retains power to review the decision of a federal issue in a state cause of action. . . .

478 U.S. at 814-816.

Lower courts were sharply divided about the implications of *Merrell Dow*. Some read the decision as holding that federal question jurisdiction is strictly limited to cases in which the plaintiff has a private right of action in federal court. The language quoted above supports this reading. However, other courts tried to square the case with long-standing Supreme Court precedents, not overruled in *Merrell Dow*, recognizing federal question jurisdiction in mixed cases where there was no private right of action. In these earlier cases, the Court took a contextual approach to determining whether the federal issue was substantial enough to warrant adjudication in federal court.

The following case resolved some of the confusion surrounding *Merrell Dow*. *Grable* began as a suit to "quiet title" to land in Michigan seized and resold by the IRS to pay for back taxes. Like the tort law claims in *Merrell Dow*, a suit to resolve a dispute regarding title to land is typically a matter of state common law property doctrine. Plaintiff, the original owner, brought suit in state court against the company that bought the land at an IRS sale. As the case describes in Section II below, there is a specific statutory vehicle for accomplishing this called "removal." See 28 U.S.C. § 1441. Removal jurisdiction is discussed in some detail in Chapter 6. For now, you need only know that for a defendant to remove a case to federal court, the case must meet the same test for federal question jurisdiction under § 1331 we have been examining here. As you read, pay close attention to how the Court treats *Merrell Dow*.

### *Grable & Sons Metal Products, Inc. v. Darue Engineering & Mfg.*
545 U.S. 308 (2005)

JUSTICE SOUTER delivered the opinion of the Court.

The question is whether want of a federal cause of action to try claims of title to land obtained at a federal tax sale precludes removal to federal court of a state action with nondiverse parties raising a disputed issue of federal title law. We answer no, and hold that the national interest in providing a federal forum for federal tax litigation is sufficiently substantial to support the exercise of federal question jurisdiction over the disputed issue on removal, which would not distort any division of labor between the state and federal courts, provided or assumed by Congress.

### I

In 1994, the Internal Revenue Service seized Michigan real property belonging to petitioner Grable & Sons Metal Products, Inc., to satisfy Grable's federal tax delinquency. Title 26 U.S.C. § 6335 required the IRS to give notice of the seizure, and there is no dispute that Grable received actual notice by certified mail before the IRS sold the property to respondent Darue Engineering & Manufacturing. Although Grable also received notice of the sale itself, it did not exercise its statutory right to redeem the property within 180 days of the sale, § 6337(b)(1), and after that period had passed, the Government gave Darue a quitclaim deed. § 6339.

Five years later, Grable brought a quiet title action in state court, claiming that Darue's record title was invalid because the IRS had failed to notify Grable of its seizure of the property in the exact manner required by § 6335(a), which provides that written notice must be "given by the Secretary to the owner of the property [or] left at his usual place of abode or business." Grable said that the statute required personal service, not service by certified mail.

Darue removed the case to Federal District Court as presenting a federal question, because the claim of title depended on the interpretation of the notice statute in the federal tax law. The District Court declined to remand the case at Grable's behest after finding that the "claim does pose a significant question of federal law," Tr. 17 (Apr. 2, 2001), and ruling that Grable's lack of a federal right of action to enforce its claim against Darue did not bar the exercise of federal jurisdiction. . . .

The Court of Appeals for the Sixth Circuit affirmed. 377 F.3d 592 (2004). On the jurisdictional question, the panel thought it sufficed that the title claim raised an issue of federal law that had to be resolved, and implicated a substantial federal interest (in construing federal tax law). The court went on to affirm the District Court's judgment on the merits. We granted certiorari on the jurisdictional question alone, to resolve a split within the Courts of Appeals on whether Merrell Dow Pharmaceuticals Inc. v. Thompson, 478 U.S. 804 (1986), always requires a federal cause of action as a condition for exercising federal-question jurisdiction.[2] We now affirm.

## II

Darue was entitled to remove the quiet title action if Grable could have brought it in federal district court originally, 28 U.S.C. § 1441(a), as a civil action "arising under the Constitution, laws, or treaties of the United States," § 1331. This provision for federal-question jurisdiction is invoked by and large by plaintiffs pleading a cause of action created by federal law (e.g., claims under 42 U.S.C. § 1983). There is, however, another longstanding, if less frequently encountered, variety of federal "arising under" jurisdiction, this Court having recognized for nearly 100 years that in certain cases federal question jurisdiction will lie over state-law claims that implicate significant federal issues. E.g., Hopkins v. Walker, 244 U.S. 486, 490-491 (1917). The doctrine captures the commonsense notion that a federal court ought to be able to hear claims recognized under state law that nonetheless turn on substantial questions of federal law, and thus justify resort to the experience, solicitude, and hope of uniformity that a federal forum offers on federal issues, see ALI, Study of the Division of Jurisdiction Between State and Federal Courts 164-166 (1968).

The classic example is Smith v. Kansas City Title & Trust Co., 255 U.S. 180 (1921), a suit by a shareholder claiming that the defendant corporation could not lawfully buy certain bonds of the National Government because their issuance was unconstitutional. Although Missouri law provided the cause of action, the Court recognized federal-question jurisdiction because the principal issue in the case was the federal constitutionality of the bond issue. *Smith* thus held, in a somewhat generous statement of the scope of the doctrine, that a state-law claim could give rise to federal-question jurisdiction so long as it "appears from the [complaint] that the right to relief depends upon the construction or application of [federal law]." Id. at 199.

---

2. Compare Seinfeld v. Austen, 39 F.3d 761, 764 (7th Cir. 1994) (finding that federal-question jurisdiction over a state-law claim requires a parallel federal private right of action), with Ormet Corp. v. Ohio Power Co., 98 F.3d 799, 806 (4th Cir. 1996) (finding that a federal private action is not required).

The *Smith* statement has been subject to some trimming to fit earlier and later cases recognizing the vitality of the basic doctrine, but shying away from the expansive view that mere need to apply federal law in a state-law claim will suffice to open the "arising under" door. As early as 1912, this Court had confined federal-question jurisdiction over state-law claims to those that "really and substantially involv[e] a dispute or controversy respecting the validity, construction or effect of [federal] law." Shulthis v. McDougal, 225 U.S. 561, 569 (1912). This limitation was the ancestor of Justice Cardozo's later explanation that a request to exercise federal-question jurisdiction over a state action calls for a "common-sense accommodation of judgment to [the] kaleidoscopic situations" that present a federal issue, in "a selective process which picks the substantial causes out of the web and lays the other ones aside." Gully v. First Nat. Bank in Meridian, 299 U.S. 109, 117-118 (1936). It has in fact become a constant refrain in such cases that federal jurisdiction demands not only a contested federal issue, but a substantial one, indicating a serious federal interest in claiming the advantages thought to be inherent in a federal forum. E.g., Chicago v. International College of Surgeons, 522 U.S. 156, 164 (1997); *Merrell Dow,* supra, at 814, and n.12; Franchise Tax Bd. of Cal. v. Construction Laborers Vacation Trust for Southern Cal., 463 U.S. 1, 28 (1983).

But even when the state action discloses a contested and substantial federal question, the exercise of federal jurisdiction is subject to a possible veto. For the federal issue will ultimately qualify for a federal forum only if federal jurisdiction is consistent with congressional judgment about the sound division of labor between state and federal courts governing the application of § 1331. Thus, *Franchise Tax Bd.* explained that the appropriateness of a federal forum to hear an embedded issue could be evaluated only after considering the "welter of issues regarding the interrelation of federal and state authority and the proper management of the federal judicial system." Id. at 8. Because arising-under jurisdiction to hear a state-law claim always raises the possibility of upsetting the state-federal line drawn (or at least assumed) by Congress, the presence of a disputed federal issue and the ostensible importance of a federal forum are never necessarily dispositive; there must always be an assessment of any disruptive portent in exercising federal jurisdiction. See also *Merrell Dow,* supra, at 810.

These considerations have kept us from stating a "single, precise, all-embracing" test for jurisdiction over federal issues embedded in state-law claims between nondiverse parties. Christianson v. Colt Industries Operating Corp., 486 U.S. 800, 821 (1988) (Stevens, J., concurring). We have not kept them out simply because they appeared in state raiment, as Justice Holmes would have done, see *Smith,* supra, at 214 (dissenting opinion), but neither have we treated "federal issue" as a password opening federal courts to any state action embracing a point of federal law. Instead, the question is, does a state-law claim necessarily raise a stated federal issue, actually disputed and substantial, which a federal forum may entertain without disturbing any congressionally approved balance of federal and state judicial responsibilities.

## III

### A

This case warrants federal jurisdiction. Grable's state complaint must specify "the facts establishing the superiority of [its] claim," Mich. Ct. Rule 3.411(B)(2)(c) (West 2005), and Grable has premised its superior title claim on a failure by the IRS to give it adequate notice, as defined by federal law. Whether Grable was given notice within the meaning of the federal statute is thus an essential element of its quiet title claim, and the meaning of the federal statute is actually in dispute; it appears to be the only legal or factual issue contested in the case. The meaning of the federal tax provision is an important issue of federal law that sensibly belongs in a federal court. The Government has a strong interest in the "prompt and certain collection of delinquent taxes," United States v. Rodgers, 461 U.S. 677, 709 (1983), and the ability of the IRS to satisfy its claims from the property of delinquents requires clear terms of notice to allow buyers like Darue to satisfy themselves that the Service has touched the bases necessary for good title. The Government thus has a direct interest in the availability of a federal forum to vindicate its own administrative action, and buyers (as well as tax delinquents) may find it valuable to come before judges used to federal tax matters. Finally, because it will be the rare state title case that raises a contested matter of federal law, federal jurisdiction to resolve genuine disagreement over federal tax title provisions will portend only a microscopic effect on the federal-state division of labor. See n.3, infra.

This conclusion puts us in venerable company, quiet title actions having been the subject of some of the earliest exercises of federal-question jurisdiction over state-law claims. . . .[3]

### B

Merrell Dow Pharmaceuticals Inc. v. Thompson, 478 U.S. 804 (1986), on which Grable rests its position, is not to the contrary. *Merrell Dow* considered a state tort claim resting in part on the allegation that the defendant drug company had violated a federal misbranding prohibition, and was thus presumptively negligent under Ohio law. Id. at 806. The Court assumed that federal law would have to be applied to resolve the claim, but after

---

3. The quiet title cases also show the limiting effect of the requirement that the federal issue in a state-law claim must actually be in dispute to justify federal-question jurisdiction. In Shulthis v. McDougal, 225 U.S. 561 (1912), this Court found that there was no federal question jurisdiction to hear a plaintiff's quiet title claim in part because the federal statutes on which title depended were not subject to "any controversy respecting their validity, construction, or effect." Id. at 570. As the Court put it, the requirement of an actual dispute about federal law was "especially" important in "suit[s] involving rights to land acquired under a law of the United States," because otherwise "every suit to establish title to land in the central and western states would so arise [under federal law], as all titles in those States are traceable back to those laws." Id. at 569-570.

closely examining the strength of the federal interest at stake and the implications of opening the federal forum, held federal jurisdiction unavailable. Congress had not provided a private federal cause of action for violation of the federal branding requirement, and the Court found "it would . . . flout, or at least undermine, congressional intent to conclude that federal courts might nevertheless exercise federal-question jurisdiction and provide remedies for violations of that federal statute solely because the violation . . . is said to be a . . . 'proximate cause' under state law." Id. at 812.

Because federal law provides for no quiet title action that could be brought against Darue, Grable argues that there can be no federal jurisdiction here, stressing some broad language in *Merrell Dow* (including the passage just quoted) that on its face supports Grable's position, see Note, Mr. *Smith* Goes to Federal Court: Federal Question Jurisdiction over State Law Claims Post-*Merrell Dow*, 115 Harv. L. Rev. 2272, 2280-2282 (2002) (discussing split in Circuit Courts over private right of action requirement after *Merrell Dow*). But an opinion is to be read as a whole, and *Merrell Dow* cannot be read whole as overturning decades of precedent, as it would have done by effectively adopting the Holmes dissent in *Smith*, see supra, at 5, and converting a federal cause of action from a sufficient condition for federal-question jurisdiction into a necessary one.

In the first place, *Merrell Dow* disclaimed the adoption of any bright-line rule, as when the Court reiterated that "in exploring the outer reaches of § 1331, determinations about federal jurisdiction require sensitive judgments about congressional intent, judicial power, and the federal system." 478 U.S. at 810. The opinion included a lengthy footnote explaining that questions of jurisdiction over state-law claims require "careful judgments," id. at 814, about the "nature of the federal interest at stake," id., at 814, n.12 (emphasis deleted). And as a final indication that it did not mean to make a federal right of action mandatory, it expressly approved the exercise of jurisdiction sustained in *Smith*, despite the want of any federal cause of action available to *Smith*'s shareholder plaintiff. 478 U.S. at 814, n.12. *Merrell Dow* then, did not toss out, but specifically retained the contextual enquiry that had been *Smith*'s hallmark for over 60 years. At the end of *Merrell Dow*, Justice Holmes was still dissenting.

Accordingly, *Merrell Dow* should be read in its entirety as treating the absence of a federal private right of action as evidence relevant to, but not dispositive of, the "sensitive judgments about congressional intent" that § 1331 requires. The absence of any federal cause of action affected *Merrell Dow*'s result two ways. The Court saw the fact as worth some consideration in the assessment of substantiality. But its primary importance emerged when the Court treated the combination of no federal cause of action and no preemption of state remedies for misbranding as an important clue to Congress's conception of the scope of jurisdiction to be exercised under § 1331. The Court saw the missing cause of action not as a missing federal door key, always required, but as a missing welcome mat, required in the circumstances, when exercising federal jurisdiction over a state misbranding action would have attracted a horde of original filings and removal cases raising other state claims with embedded federal issues. For if the federal labeling standard without a federal cause of action could get a state claim into federal court, so could any other federal standard without a federal cause of action. And that would have meant a tremendous number of cases.

One only needed to consider the treatment of federal violations generally in garden variety state tort law. "The violation of federal statutes and regulations is commonly given negligence per se effect in state tort proceedings." Restatement (Third) of Torts (proposed final draft) § 14, Comment *a*. See also W. Keeton, D. Dobbs, R. Keeton, & D. Owen, Prosser and Keeton on Torts, § 36, p. 221, n.9 (5th ed. 1984) ("[T]he breach of a federal statute may support a negligence per se claim as a matter of state law" (collecting authority)). A general rule of exercising federal jurisdiction over state claims resting on federal mislabeling and other statutory violations would thus have heralded a potentially enormous shift of traditionally state cases into federal courts. Expressing concern over the "increased volume of federal litigation," and noting the importance of adhering to "legislative intent," *Merrell Dow* thought it improbable that the Congress, having made no provision for a federal cause of action, would have meant to welcome any state-law tort case implicating federal law "solely because the violation of the federal statute is said to [create] a rebuttable presumption [of negligence] . . . under state law." 478 U.S. at 811-812 (internal quotation marks omitted). In this situation, no welcome mat meant keep out. *Merrell Dow*'s analysis thus fits within the framework of examining the importance of having a federal forum for the issue, and the consistency of such a forum with Congress's intended division of labor between state and federal courts.

As already indicated, however, a comparable analysis yields a different jurisdictional conclusion in this case. Although Congress also indicated ambivalence in this case by providing no private right of action to Grable, it is the rare state quiet title action that involves contested issues of federal law, see n.3, supra. Consequently, jurisdiction over actions like Grable's would not materially affect, or threaten to affect, the normal currents of litigation. Given the absence of threatening structural consequences and the clear interest the Government, its buyers, and its delinquents have in the availability of a federal forum, there is no good reason to shirk from federal jurisdiction over the dispositive and contested federal issue at the heart of the state-law title claim.

## IV

The judgment of the Court of Appeals, upholding federal jurisdiction over Grable's quiet title action, is affirmed.

*It is so ordered.*

[The concurring opinion of Justice Thomas is omitted.]

## Note: Reconciling Grable and Merrell Dow

1. *Grable* holds that while the presence of a private cause of action is sufficient to establish federal question jurisdiction, it is not necessary. Instead, the Court endorses the long-standing "contextual enquiry" focusing on whether allowing cases into federal court will upset "the sound division of labor between state and federal courts," or, more precisely, the "congressionally approved balance of federal and state judicial responsibilities." Allowing jurisdiction in *Grable* presented no threat to the federal/state balance, at least in part, the Court reasoned, because state title cases involving disputed issues of federal law are rare (unlike state tort cases involving violations of federal standards like *Merrell Dow*, which are quite common and would therefore overwhelm the federal courts). Does that mean there is a presumption against federal question jurisdiction whenever a federal issue involved in state law claims arises frequently? Shouldn't cases that frequently present important, contested issues of federal law be heard in federal court?

For recent scholarship on *Grable*, see Elizabeth Y. McCuskey, Clarity and Clarification: Grable Federal Questions in the Eyes of Their Beholders, 91 Neb. L. Rev. 387 (2012); Andrew Brandt, *Grable* on the Ground: Mitigating Unchecked Jurisdictional Discretion, 44 U.C. Davis L. Rev. 1153 (2011); F. Andrew Hessick III, The Common Law of Federal Question Jurisdiction, 60 Ala. L. Rev. 895 (2009); Gil Seinfeld, The Federal Courts as a Franchise: Rethinking the Justifications for Federal Question Jurisdiction, 97 Cal. L. Rev. 95 (2009); Ann Woolhandler and Michael G. Collins, Federal Courts, Practice & Procedure: Federal Question Jurisdiction and Justice Holmes, 84 Notre Dame L. Rev. 2151 (2009); Frederic M. Bloom, Jurisdiction's Noble Lie, 61 Stan. L. Rev. 971 (2009).

2. Because *Grable* doesn't overrule *Merrell Dow*, it is still important to ask whether an express or implied private cause of action is provided in the federal law invoked as part of a state law claim. When the federal statute expressly creates a cause of action, this is easy work—the statute says private individuals can sue to enforce the rights it protects. But how do we know when Congress has created a private right of action by implication?

In Alexander v. Sandoval, 532 U.S. 275 (2001), the Supreme Court established a very high threshold for finding an implied right of action. Plaintiffs filed a class action lawsuit seeking to enjoin enforcement of an English-only requirement for the Alabama state driver's license examination. They alleged that the requirement had the effect of discriminating against plaintiffs on the basis of national origin in violation of Title VI of the Civil Rights Act of 1964. The Supreme Court held that no private right of action could be brought for plaintiffs' disparate impact claim. Writing for the majority, Justice Scalia insisted that statutory text is dispositive. The fact that Congress has legislated a private right to be free from discrimination is irrelevant unless Congress also legislates a private remedy. He added that when a statute focuses on an agency's regulatory authority "rather than the individuals protected [it] create[s] no implication of an intent to confer rights on a particular class of persons." The relevant provision of Title VI was purely regulatory in this respect. Finally, he added that where a statute provides for one method of enforcement expressly, courts must conclude that "Congress intended to preclude others." Here, the relevant provision of Title VI empowers federal agencies to terminate the funding of entities that violate the statute's anti-discrimination mandate.

*Sandoval* does not overrule earlier cases in which the Court had implied private rights of action. Nevertheless, it is difficult to imagine the circumstances in which the Court would recognize any new implied rights of action. See, e.g., Stoneridge Inv. Partners v. Scientific-Atlanta, 552 U.S. 148 (2008) (concluding that the implied right of action previously found in the Securities Exchange Act does not extend to customers or suppliers of the investment company); Gonzaga Univ. v. Doe, 536 U.S. 273 (2002) (holding that federal law that requires schools and colleges to protect the privacy of student educational records does not establish a private right of action for improper disclosures). If Congress were clear enough to meet Scalia's strict test, wouldn't the proper conclusion be that Congress had *expressly* provided a private right of action?

3. Since *Grable*, the Court has continued to take a dim view of assertions of federal question jurisdiction where Congress has not explicitly "set out the welcome mat." In Empire Healthchoice Assurance, Inc. v. McVeigh, 547 U.S. 677 (2006), a 5-4 majority of the Court rejected federal question jurisdiction over an action to recover health care payments made to an injured federal employee after the employee prevailed in a tort action against the individuals responsible for his injuries. Although the plaintiff was a private insurer and the cause of action for reimbursement a standard state law claim, the company provided health benefits to federal employees under a federally regulated contract, the action for reimbursement against the federal employee was authorized by that contract, and the contract required that any reimbursements obtained be returned to the Federal Employees Health Benefits Fund, against which private insurance carriers draw to pay for benefits of enrolled federal employees.

While conceding that "distinctly federal interests are involved," id. at 696, the majority placed great weight on the fact that "Congress has not expressly created a federal right of action enabling insurance carriers like Empire to sue health-care beneficiaries in federal court to enforce reimbursement rights. . . ." Id. at 693. Indeed, the Court drew a further inference against federal question jurisdiction for reimbursement actions from the fact that the statute creating the program expressly recognized a right for beneficiaries to sue in federal court if carriers denied benefits. "Had Congress found it necessary or proper to extend federal jurisdiction further, in particular, to encompass contract-derived reimbursement claims between carriers and insured workers, it would have been easy enough for Congress to say so." Id. at 696. Even the statute's broad federal preemption provision (which states that the contract provisions the government negotiates with private carriers "shall supersede and preempt any State or local law" on questions relating to "the nature or extent of coverage or benefits," id. at 685) was insufficient to convince the Court that Congress intended reimbursement claims to be adjudicated in federal court. Id. at 698. The Court found the case "poles apart from *Grable*," because plaintiff's reimbursement claim was fact-bound, would not aid the resolution of future cases, and "was triggered, not by the action of any federal department, agency, or service, but by the settlement of a personal-injury action launched in state court. . . ." Id. at 700.

Justice Breyer, in dissent, emphasized the incongruity of denying federal question jurisdiction where

> the statute is federal, the program it creates is federal, the program's beneficiaries are federal employees working throughout the country, the Federal Government pays all relevant costs, and the Federal Government receives all relevant payments. The private carrier's only role in this scheme is to administer the health benefits plan for the federal agency in exchange for a fixed service charge.

Id. at 704.

But the majority flatly rejected the view that a case arises under federal law simply because the dispute concerns the application of terms in a federal contract. "[U]niform federal law need not be applied to all questions in federal government litigation, even in cases involving government contracts. The prudent course, we have recognized, is often to adopt the ready-made body of state law as the federal rule of decision until Congress strikes a different accommodation." Id. at 691-692. Absent evidence of a "significant conflict . . . between an identifiable federal policy or interest and the operation of state law . . . there is no cause to displace state law, much less to lodge this case in federal court." Id. at 693.

As in *Merrell Dow*, the central inquiry for the majority is whether Congress has expressly created a federal right of action. Why should it make a difference, in distinguishing *Grable*, that this case involves adjudication of facts, whereas *Grable* presented a fairly pure question of law? Does the majority give adequate weight to the interest in uniformity in the law that governs the health benefits of federal employees?

In 2013, the Supreme Court again applied *Grable* to require dismissal of a state law cause of action with a necessary federal issue. Gunn v. Minton, 133 S. Ct. 1059 (2013). Minton, a software programmer, lost a federal patent infringement lawsuit over a computer program and network he designed to facilitate securities trading. The court determined that Minton's patent was invalid because he marketed the patent more than a year before applying for a federal patent — the so-called "on sale" bar to patentability.

Minton blamed the law firm that represented him for the loss and sued the firm for malpractice in Texas state court. The state trial court granted summary judgment to the law firm, concluding that even if the firm had raised a possible exception to the "on-sale" bar in a timely fashion, Minton still would have lost the infringement suit. On appeal, Minton argued, for the first time, that the Texas state courts (which he had chosen) did not have subject matter jurisdiction because the malpractice lawsuit involved questions of federal patent law and federal courts have exclusive jurisdiction over "any civil action arising under any Act of Congress relating to patents." 28 U.S.C. § 1338(a). He moved to have the trial court decision vacated and the suit dismissed so that he could start over in federal court.

The Texas appellate court refused to dismiss the case and the Texas Supreme Court reversed. In a unanimous decision, the U.S. Supreme Court applied the *Grable* framework for assessing mixed cases and reinstated the appellate court's decision that there is no federal question jurisdiction.

First, with respect to necessity, the Court emphasized that in Milton's malpractice case a federal patent question is raised on the face of the plaintiff's well-pleaded complaint, and it is "actually disputed." *Minton*, 133 S. Ct. at 1065. It must therefore be resolved for plaintiff to prevail:

> Under Texas law, a plaintiff alleging legal malpractice must establish four elements: (1) that the defendant attorney owed the plaintiff a duty; (2) that the attorney breached that duty; (3) that the breach was the proximate cause of the plaintiff's injury; and (4) that damages occurred. See Alexander v. Turtur & Associates, Inc., 146 S.W.3d 113, 117 (Tex. 2004). In cases like this one, in which the attorney's alleged error came in failing to make a particular argument, the causation element requires a "case within a case" analysis of whether, had the argument been made, the outcome of the earlier litigation would have been different. To prevail on his legal malpractice claim, therefore, Minton must show that he would have prevailed in his federal patent infringement case if only petitioners had timely made an [argument for an exception to the "on-sale" bar]. That will necessarily require application of patent law to the facts of Minton's case.

Id.

With respect to substantiality, the Court emphasized that the question is not whether the federal issue matters a lot to the parties in the case, but whether it is the kind of issue that implicates the distinctive purposes of federal court jurisdiction:

> As our past cases show, however, it is not enough that the federal issue be significant to the particular parties in the immediate suit; that will *always* be true when the state claim "necessarily raise[s]" a disputed federal issue, as *Grable* separately requires. The substantiality inquiry under *Grable* looks instead to the importance of the issue to the federal system as a whole.
>
> In *Grable* itself, for example, [we] emphasized the Government's "strong interest" in being able to recover delinquent taxes through seizure and sale of property, which in turn "require[d] clear terms of notice to allow buyers . . . to satisfy themselves that the Service has touched the bases necessary for good title." 545 U.S. at 315. . . .
>
> A second illustration of the sort of substantiality we require comes from Smith v. Kansas City Title & Trust Co., 255 U.S. 180 (1921), which *Grable* described as "[t]he classic example" of a state claim arising under federal

law. 545 U.S. at 312. . . . [T]he relevant point was not the importance of the question to the parties alone but rather the importance more generally of a determination that the Government "securities were issued under an unconstitutional law, and hence of no validity." Ibid.

Here, the federal issue carries no such significance. Because of the backward-looking nature of a legal malpractice claim, the question is posed in a merely hypothetical sense: *If* Minton's lawyers had raised a timely [exception to the "on-sale" bar], would the result in the patent infringement proceeding have been different? No matter how the state courts resolve that hypothetical "case within a case," it will not change the real-world result of the prior federal patent litigation. Minton's patent will remain invalid.

Nor will allowing state courts to resolve these cases undermine "the development of a uniform body of [patent] law." Bonito Boats, Inc. v. Thunder Craft Boats, Inc., 489 U.S. 141, 162 (1989). Congress ensured such uniformity by vesting exclusive jurisdiction over actual patent cases in the federal district courts and exclusive appellate jurisdiction in the Federal Circuit. See 28 U.S.C. §§ 1338(a), 1295(a)(1). In resolving the non-hypothetical patent questions those cases present, the federal courts are of course not bound by state court case-within-a-case patent rulings. See Tafflin v. Levitt, 493 U.S. 455, 465 (1990). In any event, the state court case-within-a-case inquiry asks what would have happened in the prior federal proceeding if a particular argument had been made. In answering that question, state courts can be expected to hew closely to the pertinent federal precedents. It is those precedents, after all, that would have applied had the argument been made.

As for more novel questions of patent law that may arise for the first time in a state court "case within a case," they will at some point be decided by a federal court in the context of an actual patent case, with review in the Federal Circuit. If the question arises frequently, it will soon be resolved within the federal system, laying to rest any contrary state court precedent; if it does not arise frequently, it is unlikely to implicate substantial federal interests. The present case is "poles apart from *Grable*," in which a state court's resolution of the federal question "would be controlling in numerous other cases." *Empire Healthchoice Assurance, Inc.*, 547 U.S., at 700.

Minton also suggests that state courts' answers to hypothetical patent questions can sometimes have real-world effect on other patents through issue preclusion. Minton, for example, has filed what is known as a "continuation patent" application related to his original patent. See 35 U.S.C. § 120. He argues that, in evaluating this separate application, the patent examiner could be bound by the Texas trial court's interpretation of the scope of Minton's original patent. . . . Minton has not identified any case finding such preclusive effect based on a state court decision. But even assuming that a state court's case-within-a-case adjudication may be preclusive under some circumstances, the result would be limited to the parties and patents that had been before the state court. Such "fact-bound and situation-specific" effects are not sufficient to establish federal arising under jurisdiction. *Empire Healthchoice Assurance, Inc.*, 547 U.S. at 701.

Nor can we accept the suggestion that the federal courts' greater familiarity with patent law means that legal malpractice cases like this one belong in federal court. It is true that a similar interest was among those we considered in *Grable*, 545 U.S., at 314. But the possibility that a state court will incorrectly resolve a state claim is not, by itself, enough to trigger the federal courts' exclusive patent jurisdiction, even if the potential error finds its root in a misunderstanding of patent law . . . .

It follows from the foregoing that *Grable*'s fourth requirement is also not met. That requirement is concerned with the appropriate "balance of federal and state judicial responsibilities." Ibid. We have already explained the absence of a substantial federal issue within the meaning of *Grable.* The States, on the other hand, have "a special responsibility for maintaining standards among members of the licensed professions." Ohralik v. Ohio State Bar Assn., 436 U.S. 447, 460 (1978). Their "interest . . . in regulating lawyers is especially great since lawyers are essential to the primary governmental function of administering justice, and have historically been officers of the courts." Goldfarb v. Virginia State Bar, 421 U.S. 773, 792 (1975). We have no reason to suppose that Congress—in establishing exclusive federal jurisdiction over patent cases—meant to bar from state courts state legal malpractice claims simply because they require resolution of a hypothetical patent issue.

Id. at 1066-1068. The Court rejected another claim of exclusive federal jurisdiction in Merrill Lynch v. Manning, 136 S. Ct. 1562 (2016) (construing exclusive federal jurisdiction provisions in Securities Exchange Act of 1934 governing short sale of stock as applying only when the plaintiff's claim "arises under" federal law; remanding to state court where plaintiff's complaint stated only state law causes of action and merely made reference to federal short sale regulations).

4. *Grable* and *Minton* reaffirm that federal question jurisdiction exists for cases arising under state law only if "necessar[y] . . . actually disputed and substantial" federal issues are presented in the complaint. From *Mottley,* we know that anticipated defenses do not create federal question jurisdiction. What if a plaintiff pleads a substantial federal issue *to overcome an anticipated defense*? In California Shock Trauma Air Rescue v. State Compensation Insurance Fund, 636 F.3d 538 (9th Cir. 2011), the plaintiff sued to recover unpaid fees for ambulance services provided to workers injured on the job. Only state law causes of action were pled in the complaint. But anticipating that defendants would contend they paid fees consistent with state workers' compensation law, plaintiff alleged that state workers' compensation law would be preempted by the Federal Aviation Act. The Ninth Circuit ordered the case dismissed, reasoning that plaintiff's federal preemption argument was not an essential element of its state law claims.

## 4. Tribal Courts

Often overlooked in studies of jurisdiction is that within the geographical boundaries of the United States is Native American territory, within which tribes have judicial authority along with, in certain circumstances, the states and the federal government. Below, we present a Supreme Court case dealing with the issue of tribal jurisdiction in civil cases. We then turn to an analysis by Judge William C. Canby Jr., outlining the main features of civil tribal court authority. As you read these materials, consider the radically different historical trajectory of tribal jurisdiction relative to our study of civil jurisdiction in state and federal court. Notice, however, that concepts of sovereignty, territoriality, the status of the litigants, and the relationship between the dispute and the forum, though considerably more complex in this context, are still present. For a fuller account of federal Indian law, see David H. Getches, Charles F. Wilkinson and Robert A. Williams Jr., Federal Indian Law: Cases and Materials (5th ed. 2004). For a discussion of the interrelationship of tribal, federal, and state courts, see Judith Resnick, Dependent Sovereigns: Indian Tribes, States and the Federal Courts, 56 U. Chi. L. Rev. 671 (1989).

## *Williams v. Lee*
358 U.S. 217 (1959)

Mr. JUSTICE BLACK delivered the opinion of the Court.

Respondent, who is not an Indian, operates a general store in Arizona on the Navajo Indian Reservation under a license required by federal statute. He brought this action in the Superior Court of Arizona against petitioners, a Navajo Indian and his wife who live on the Reservation, to collect for goods sold them there on credit. Over petitioners' motion to dismiss on the ground that jurisdiction lay in the tribal court rather than in the state court, judgment was entered in favor of respondent. The Supreme Court of Arizona affirmed, holding that since no Act of Congress expressly forbids their doing so Arizona courts are free to exercise jurisdiction over civil suits by non-Indians against Indians though the action arises on an Indian reservation. 83 Ariz. 241. Because this was a doubtful determination of the important question of state power over Indian affairs, we granted certiorari.

Originally the Indian tribes were separate nations within what is now the United States. Through conquest and treaties they were induced to give up complete independence and the right to go to war in exchange for federal protection, aid, and grants of land. When the lands granted lay within States these governments sometimes sought to impose their laws and courts on the Indians. Around 1830 the Georgia Legislature extended its laws to the Cherokee Reservation despite federal treaties with the Indians which set aside this land for them. The Georgia statutes forbade the Cherokees from enacting laws or holding courts and prohibited outsiders from being on the Reservation except with permission of the State Governor. The constitutionality of these laws was tested in Worcester v. State of Georgia, 6 Pet. 515, when the State sought to punish a white man, licensed by the Federal Government to practice as a missionary among the Cherokees, for his refusal to leave the Reservation. Rendering one of his most courageous and eloquent opinions, Chief Justice Marshall held that Georgia's assertion of power was invalid.

The Cherokee nation . . . is a distinct community, occupying its own territory . . . in which the laws of Georgia can have no force, and which the citizens of Georgia have no right to enter, but with the assent of the Cherokees themselves, or in conformity with treaties, and with the acts of Congress. The whole intercourse between the United States and this nation, is, by our constitution and laws, vested in the government of the United States. 6 Pet. at page 561.

Despite bitter criticism and the defiance of Georgia which refused to obey this Court's mandate in *Worcester* the broad principles of that decision came to be accepted as law. Over the years this Court has modified these principles in cases where essential tribal relations were not involved and where the rights of Indians would not be jeopardized, but the basic policy of *Worcester* has remained. Thus, suits by Indians against outsiders in state courts have been sanctioned. And state courts have been allowed to try non-Indians who committed crimes against each other on a reservation. But if the crime was by or against an Indian, tribal jurisdiction or that expressly conferred on other courts by Congress has remained exclusive.[5] Essentially, absent governing Acts of Congress, the question has always been whether the state action infringed on the right of reservation Indians to make their own laws and be ruled by them.

Congress has also acted consistently upon the assumption that the States have no power to regulate the affairs of Indians on a reservation. To assure adequate government of the Indian tribes it enacted comprehensive statutes in 1834 regulating trade with Indians and organizing a Department of Indian Affairs. 4 Stat. 729, 735. Not satisfied solely with centralized government of Indians, it encouraged tribal governments and courts to become stronger and more highly organized. See, e.g., the Wheeler-Howard Act, §§ 16, 17, 48 Stat. 987, 988, 25 U.S.C. §§ 476, 477, 25 U.S.C.A. §§ 476, 477. Congress has followed a policy calculated eventually to make all Indians full-fledged participants in American society. This policy contemplates criminal and civil jurisdiction over Indians by any State ready to assume the burdens that go with it as soon as the educational and economic status of the Indians permits the change without disadvantage to them. See H.R. Rep. No. 848, 83d Cong., 1st Sess. 3, 6, 7 (1953). Significantly, when Congress has wished the States to exercise this power it has expressly granted them the jurisdiction which Worcester v. State of Georgia had denied.

No departure from the policies which have been applied to other Indians is apparent in the relationship between the United States and the Navajos. On June 1, 1868, a treaty was signed between General William T. Sherman,

---

5. For example, Congress has granted to the federal courts exclusive jurisdiction upon Indian reservations over 11 major crimes. And non-Indians committing crimes against Indians are now generally tried in federal courts. See 18 U.S.C. §§ 437-439, 1151-1163, 18 U.S.C.A. §§ 437-439, 1151-1163.

for the United States, and numerous chiefs and headmen of the "Navajo nation or tribe of Indians."[7] At the time this document was signed the Navajos were an exiled people, forced by the United States to live crowded together on a small piece of land on the Pecos River in eastern New Mexico, some 300 miles east of the area they had occupied before the coming of the white man. In return for their promises to keep peace, this treaty "set apart" for "their permanent home" a portion of what had been their native country, and provided that no one, except United States Government personnel, was to enter the reserved area. Implicit in these treaty terms, as it was in the treaties with the Cherokees involved in Worcester v. State of Georgia, was the understanding that the internal affairs of the Indians remained exclusively within the jurisdiction of whatever tribal government existed. Since then, Congress and the Bureau of Indian Affairs have assisted in strengthening the Navajo tribal government and its courts. See the Navajo-Hopi Rehabilitation Act of 1950, § 6, 64 Stat. 46, 25 U.S.C. § 636, 25 U.S.C.A. § 636; 25 CFR §§ 11.1 through 11.87NH. The Tribe itself has in recent years greatly improved its legal system through increased expenditures and better-trained personnel. Today the Navajo Courts of Indian Offenses exercise broad criminal and civil jurisdiction which covers suits by outsiders against Indian defendants. No Federal Act has given state courts jurisdiction over such controversies. In a general statute Congress did express its willingness to have any State assume jurisdiction over reservation Indians if the State Legislature or the people vote affirmatively to accept such responsibility. To date, Arizona has not accepted jurisdiction, possibly because the people of the State anticipate that the burdens accompanying such power might be considerable.

There can be no doubt that to allow the exercise of state jurisdiction here would undermine the authority of the tribal courts over Reservation affairs and hence would infringe on the right of the Indians to govern themselves. It is immaterial that respondent is not an Indian. He was on the Reservation and the transaction with an Indian took place there. The cases in this Court have consistently guarded the authority of Indian governments over their reservations. Congress recognized this authority in the Navajos in the Treaty of 1868, and has done so ever since. If this power is to be taken away from them, it is for Congress to do it.

*Reversed.*

---

7. 15 Stat. 667. In 16 Stat. 566 (1871), Congress declared that no Indian tribe or nation within the United States should thereafter be recognized as an independent power with whom the United States could execute a treaty but provided that this should not impair the obligations of any treaty previously ratified. Thus the 1868 treaty with the Navajos survived this Act.

### *William C. Canby Jr., American Indian Law*
Pages 124-128, 131-133, 138-141, 199-208 (2004)

## Chapter VII

### A.  Introduction

The most complex problems in the field of Indian Law arise in jurisdictional disputes among the federal government, the tribes and the states.

To resolve those problems it is essential to know the basic limits of jurisdiction of each of the three contending powers. . . .

### B.  Indian Country

After many years of change and development, the concept of Indian country was given its present definition by Congress in 1948. 18 U.S.C. § 1151 provides:

> [T]he term "Indian country," as used in this chapter, means (a) all land within the limits of any Indian reservation under the jurisdiction of the United States government, notwithstanding the issuance of any patent, and including rights-of-way running through the reservation, (b) all dependent Indian communities within the borders of the United States whether within the original or subsequently acquired territory thereof, and whether within or without the limits of a state, and (c) all Indian allotments, the Indian titles to which have not been extinguished, including rights-of-way running through the same.

Although this definition is for purposes of the criminal code, it is also used for civil jurisdiction. . . .

Subsection (a) includes all of the territory within an Indian reservation. It is most important to note that even land owned by non-Indians in fee simple . . . is still "Indian country" if it is within the exterior boundaries of an Indian reservation. There exist within many reservations large tracts of land long since settled by non-Indians, and even entire towns incorporated by non-Indians under state law, but all of those tracts and towns are Indian country for purposes of jurisdiction. . . .

Although the mere opening up of a reservation for non-Indian settlement does not remove the newly settled lands from Indian country, a congressional decision to abandon the reservation status of those lands does. In cases where Congress has opened reservations to heavy settlement, there is often a difficult question of fact whether the intent was to permit non-Indians to live and own land on a reservation or whether it was to extinguish a portion of the reservation (to "diminish" the reservation) and open it for settlement as public, non-Indian land. . . .

In Solem v. Bartlett, 465 U.S. 463 (1984), the Court . . . stated that . . . "[e]xplicit reference to cession or other language evidencing the present and total surrender of all tribal interests" was strongly indicative of intent to diminish, and created an almost insurmountable presumption when combined with a commitment to compensate the tribe for the opened land. 465 U.S. at 470-71. Even without language of cession, a diminishment could be found from other factors, although it would not lightly be implied. The other factors were the manner in which the transaction was arranged or considered at the time; subsequent treatment of the area by the concerned governments; and later demographic consequences of the opening. . . .

Subsection (b) of 18 U.S.C. § 1151 . . . is a codification of the Supreme Court's holding in United States v. Sandoval, 231 U.S. 28 (1913). That case involved the New Mexico Pueblos, which held their land in fee simple under Spanish grants and which were not formally designated as reservations. The Court held that the Pueblo lands were Indian country nevertheless, since the Pueblos were wards dependent upon the federal government's guardianship. . . .

Subsection (c) of § 1151 is self-explanatory; it includes within Indian country any allotment that is either still in trust . . . or is owned in fee by an Indian with a restriction on alienation in favor of the United States. . . . Such allotments are Indian country whether or not they are located within a reservation.

## C.  Historical Background of Jurisdiction in Indian Country

In colonial days, the Indian territory was entirely the province of the tribes, and they had jurisdiction in fact and theory over all persons and subjects present there. Shortly after the Revolution, federal jurisdiction was extended to non-Indians committing crimes against Indians in Indian territory, as part of the overall federal policy of providing a buffer between the non-Indian and Indian populations. Federal jurisdiction was further extended in 1817 to cover crimes by both Indians and non-Indians in Indian country with the notable exception of crimes by Indians against Indians; the latter were left entirely to be dealt with by tribal law or custom. . . .

One of the basic premises underlying the constitutional allocation of Indian affairs to the federal government was that the states could not be relied upon to deal fairly with the Indians. Severe limitations upon the exercise of state power in Indian territory therefore seemed implicit in the nation's early Indian policy, but the extent of these limitations was not dealt with authoritatively until John Marshall's decision in the second of the famous Cherokee cases, Worcester v. Georgia, 31 U.S. 515 (1832). At the heart of the case lay Georgia's attempt to exercise total jurisdiction within Cherokee territory—to divide that territory among several Georgia counties, to apply Georgia law to all persons within the area, and to prohibit the Cherokees from exercising any governmental powers of their own. Chief Justice Marshall's opinion for the Court totally rejected Georgia's attempt, and characterized Cherokee territory as one "in which the laws of Georgia can have no force. . . ." 31 U.S. at 561. . . .

For fifty years, Marshall's view that state law and power could not intrude into Indian country held sway. Then a major change occurred in

United States v. McBratney, 104 U.S. 621 (1881). In that case a non-Indian had been convicted in federal circuit court of murdering another non-Indian on the Ute reservation in Colorado. The Supreme Court, in a highly doubtful construction of the applicable federal statutes, first held that the federal court could exercise criminal jurisdiction only over places within the exclusive jurisdiction of the federal government. If the state had any jurisdiction over this crime, then the federal court necessarily had none. The state of Colorado must have jurisdiction, the Court ruled, because Congress had admitted it to the union "upon an equal footing with the original States" and no exception was made for jurisdiction over the Ute reservation. The laws of Colorado therefore extend throughout the state, including the Ute reservation, insofar as they relate to crimes by non-Indians against non-Indians. The federal conviction was reversed, and the lower court was directed to deliver the defendant to state authorities. . . .

In both theoretical and practical terms . . . the decision[] had an enormous and complicating impact on the law of jurisdiction in Indian country, for they made it impossible ever after to deal with questions of state jurisdiction on a purely geographical basis. Marshall's rule in *Worcester* that state laws can have no force in Indian country had several virtues, but perhaps the greatest was simplicity. When tribal and state powers were viewed in purely territorial terms, it was necessary only to discover the location of a transaction or occurrence in order to determine which of two competing systems of law and courts had control over it. *McBratney* [and its progeny], on the other hand, require not only a determination of location, but also an inquiry into the nature of the subject matter and the identity of the parties involved in the case. They open the door to judicial balancing of state and tribal interests whenever arguable questions of jurisdiction arise. . . .

## F.  *Present Division of Civil Jurisdiction in Indian Country*

### 2.1   Tribal Civil Jurisdiction

#### a.   General Civil Litigation

The civil jurisdiction of tribal courts, unlike their criminal jurisdiction, is subject to no statutory limit on the relief courts may grant. . . .

With regard to subject matter, tribal courts have exclusive jurisdiction over a suit by any person against an Indian for a claim arising in Indian country. Williams v. Lee, 358 U.S. 217 (1959). Necessarily, then, the tribe has exclusive jurisdiction over disputes between tribal members arising on the reservation. It also has exclusive jurisdiction over wholly internal tribal subject matter, such as membership disputes. The exclusive jurisdiction recognized by Williams v. Lee had always been assumed to extend to suits against Indians from recognized tribes other than the one upon whose reservation the claim arose, but the Supreme Court in recent years has rendered this assumption unsafe. . . . In Washington v. Confederated Tribes of the Colville Indian Reservation, 447 U.S. 134 (1980), the Court permitted a state to impose a sales tax on Indians making purchases on a reservation other than their own. The Court stated that, "[f]or most practical purposes those Indians stand on the same footing as non-Indians resident on the reservation." 447 U.S. at 161. Then, in Strate v. A-1 Contractors, 520 U.S. 438 (1997), the Court held that a tribal court had no jurisdiction over a dispute between "nonmembers" arising out of a vehicle accident on a state right-of-way within the reservation. In *Strate*, the nonmembers were non-Indians, but the Court talked only of nonmembers and tribal members in drawing a line of adjudicatory jurisdiction. . . .

In addition to their exclusive jurisdiction over reservation-based claims against tribal members, tribal courts also probably have the power to adjudicate claims against tribal members domiciled or present within their territory even though those claims arose outside of Indian country. Many tribes, however, have chosen not to exercise such jurisdiction.

Much recent litigation has been concerned with the power of tribal courts to entertain claims against non-Indian (or nonmember) defendants that arise in Indian country. For years the tribes made no attempt to exercise that power by compulsion; some tribal codes still provide for such jurisdiction only when the non-Indian defendant stipulates to it. Recently, however, numbers of tribes have revised their codes to permit their tribal courts generally to exercise jurisdiction over non-Indians for reservation-based claims. A non-Indian defendant contested such jurisdiction in National Farmers Union Ins. Cos. v. Crow Tribe, 471 U.S. 845 (1985). The Supreme Court did not resolve the question, but deferred to the tribal court so that it could determine its jurisdiction in the first instance. . . .

[The Crow Tribe decision, along with language in Iowa Mutual Ins. Co. v. LaPlante, 480 U.S. 9 (1987),] encouraged many tribes, and numbers of lower courts, to assume that tribal courts could exercise general civil jurisdiction over all reservation-based litigation, particularly if one of the parties was the tribe or a tribal member. The seeds of a narrower view had already been planted, however, in Montana v. United States, 450 U.S. 544 (1981). *Montana* held that an Indian tribe had no authority to regulate hunting and fishing by non-Indians on non-Indian-owned fee land within the reservation. The Court stated that the tribe's domestic dependent sovereignty extended only to self-government and the control of internal relations. Hunting and fishing by non-Indians on non-Indian fee lands was neither. *Montana* at one point went considerably farther, however, and announced a general proposition that "the inherent sovereign powers of an Indian tribe do not extend to the activities of nonmembers of the tribe." The only exceptions were (1) that a tribe could regulate "activities of nonmembers who enter consensual relationships with the tribe or its members," as through commercial dealings, and (2) that a tribe could exercise "civil authority over the conduct of non-Indians on fee lands within its reservation when that conduct threatens or has some direct effect on the political integrity, the economic security, or the health or welfare of the tribe." *Montana*, 450 U.S. at 565-66.

The Supreme Court carried *Montana* a step farther in 1997, when it held that a tribal court had no jurisdiction over litigation between nonmembers arising out of a vehicle accident on a state highway within a reservation. Strate v. A-1 Contractors, 520 U.S. 438 (1997). The Court narrowed the statement in *LaPlante* that civil jurisdiction over non-Indian activities within a reservation "presumptively lies in the tribal courts"; that statement, according to *Strate*, meant nothing more than that the tribal court presumptively had jurisdiction over those non-Indian activities that the tribe could regulate under *Montana*. . . . The Court also stated that the second *Montana* exception should be read narrowly, in light of *Montana*'s description of tribal authority as the power to punish tribal offenders, to determine membership, and to regulate the domestic relations and inheritance for members.

## 5.  Venue

Selecting the proper forum for a dispute also involves the rules of venue. Unlike personal jurisdiction or subject matter jurisdiction restrictions on the plaintiff's choice of forum, venue restrictions are purely statutory and not constitutionally mandated. The rules of venue attempt to allocate court business in a reasonable and efficient manner, mindful of the interests of the litigants and the judicial system.

The primary sources of venue requirements in the federal courts are 28 U.S.C. §§ 1391 and 1392. There also are specialty venue statutes for particular types of actions, such as shareholder's derivative suits. See, e.g., 28 U.S.C. § 1401. Note that § 1391 was amended in 1990 and again in 2011. The Federal Courts Jurisdiction and Venue Clarification Act of 2011, Public Law No. 112-63, took effect January 6, 2012.

At this point we deal with venue in its simplest form: choosing a court within a state's boundaries. More complicated issues, and more aggressive gaming, occur with the possibility of venue transfers among federal courts in a multistate system. We deal with these statutes—28 U.S.C. §§ 1404 and 1406—in Chapter 6.

## Applying the Basic Federal Venue Statutes

Read 28 U.S.C. §§ 1391 and 1392 and Fed. R. Civ. P. 12(b)(3) and (h)(1) carefully, and then attempt to answer the following questions:

1. Who can object to improper venue? Can the court raise this issue *sua sponte,* or is this solely a defendant-centered concern?

2. How does a party raise an objection to improper venue? See Fed. R. Civ. P. 12(b)(3) and (h)(1). What happens if the defendant fails to make the

objection in the answer or pre-answer motion? What happens if the defendant makes a timely motion and it is granted? Return to this last question after you have studied the venue transfer statutes, 28 U.S.C. §§ 1404 and 1406.

3. Note that where a person or a corporation "resides" for purposes of the venue statute may differ from "domicile" for purposes of determining diversity jurisdiction. For an individual, residence and domicile typically are the same. But for a corporation, they are not.

A defendant corporation "resides" in any judicial district in which it is subject to personal jurisdiction. If the state has more than one district, then each district is treated like a separate state for determining this.

A plaintiff or defendant corporation is "domiciled" in the state(s) where it is incorporated *and* where it has its principal place of business ("dual citizenship").

4. Where would venue be proper in the following cases? If you would need additional information to determine this, what would it be?

a. *P*, a resident of California, sues *D*(1), a resident of the northern district of Illinois, and *D*(2), a resident of the southern district of Illinois, in federal court. The sole basis for federal court jurisdiction is diversity. The action concerns a car accident that occurred in southern Illinois.

b. *P*, a resident of California, sues *D*(1), who lives in Arkansas, and *D*(2), who lives in Tennessee, in federal court. The action is based on federal question jurisdiction and concerns a contract that was entered into and executed in California.

c. *P* is a corporation that is incorporated in Delaware and does business throughout the northeast. *D* is a corporation that is incorporated in Maine and that has its principal place of business in Maine. It does business solely in Maine, Vermont, and New Hampshire. *P* sues *D* in federal court, based solely on diversity, regarding the sale by *D* to *P* of a defective machine. The machine was shipped from Maine to *P*'s plant in Vermont.

## Review Problem: Choosing Systems in Retrospect

Now that you have mastered the territorial restrictions on forum selection (personal jurisdiction and venue) as well as the power restrictions imposed by the subject matter jurisdiction rules, you should test your skills by answering the following questions based on the hypothetical of the "Troubled Young Man."

> A patient of a San Francisco-based psychiatrist injures his father, an Arizona resident, in Arizona. The father wishes to sue the California psychiatrist on the theory that she had a duty to warn the Arizonan of her patient's foreseeable violent acts toward his father. All therapy took place in California. The psychiatrist knew that her patient was going to visit his father in Arizona and increased his medication to ease the inevitable stress of family encounters.

1. Would a state court have subject matter jurisdiction?

2. Would a federal district court have subject matter jurisdiction, assuming there is an adequate amount in controversy?

3. Where would personal jurisdiction over Dr. Froid be found?

4. Assuming that a federal court would have jurisdiction to hear the dispute, where within the federal system would venue be proper?

5. What law would govern Dr. Froid's liability — federal or state?

# 2  *Constructing a Civil Lawsuit*

## Problem Case: The Due Process Game (Part Three)

Recall the due process game, which we encountered in Chapter 1. Assume that the student was expelled without the requisite notice and opportunity to be heard, and now wishes to file an action in federal court complaining that the expulsion was unlawful. Which of the following do you think should be included in the complaint?

1) All facts concerning the expulsion. (What should be included in "all facts"?)
2) The specific law that is violated by the expulsion.
3) The basis for federal court power to hear the matter.
4) The specific relief requested, e.g., money damages or injunctive relief.

What are the costs of demanding that a plaintiff include this information? Of allowing the plaintiff to plead less information? How much research should the plaintiff's lawyer do to verify what she learns from her client? Can the lawyer plead facts she doesn't yet know to be true but hopes to prove during trial?

Do you think that the plaintiff should also be allowed to include information about another, unrelated matter that involves one or all of the same defendants? What if, for example, the administrator had hit the student's car in the school parking lot? Could this tort action be included in the due process lawsuit against the same administrator?

Assume that the student alleges only the due process violation. Assume also that the defendant believes that the facts are not as the student alleges, that the student has no legal right to recover even if the facts as alleged are true, and that since the time for complaining about the matter has passed, the lawsuit is too late. Should the defendant be able to make all three objections, or must he choose one and stick to it?

What if, after the complaint and defendant's response have been filed, additional facts come to light that change the facts alleged in the complaint? Should the plaintiff be allowed to amend the complaint? Required to do so?

---

In the following sections, we will consider all of these questions from a historical and a contemporary perspective. As the materials will explain, attitudes about pleadings and the amount of work pleadings should do to narrow and resolve the claims have changed dramatically over time. At one point, pleadings, which dominated pretrial practice, were expected to produce one and only one issue for trial. In 1938, however, the law of federal pleading rejected this view of the paper conversation and liberalized the rules. Plaintiffs were allowed merely to state the basic facts of the dispute in order to put the defendant on notice of the nature of the case. Gone were the days of artful pleaders and the triumph of arcane pleading form over litigation substance.

The changes produced their own forms of abuse, however, including a perceived rise in insubstantial claims that cost defendants time and money, as defendants no longer could rely on the burdens of pleading to weed out the frivolous pleaders. Proceduralists remain divided about the proper role of pleading in establishing the contours of a lawsuit. Indeed, the divisions may be sharper than ever, and Congress and the courts have altered the balance struck in 1938. Plaintiffs, of course, prefer less strict rules in order to move the case forward without the burden of elaborate and expensive investigation prior to filing. Defendants prefer rules that require plaintiffs to uncover facts that support their claims before the defendant must answer these claims. No rule, as we shall see, is costless or uncontroversial among the lawyers who best know the litigation implications of pleading obligations.

We begin with the history of pleading, which remains relevant to modern-day pleading in three ways: first, some modern terminology and practices reflect the older locutions; second, the right to trial by jury in civil cases depends in part on whether the right in question would have been heard on the "law" or "equity" side of the old courts of England; and third, knowing the history of modern pleading gives the modern lawyer a richer sense of the problems the new rules hoped to cure. This history also may be an important corrective to some contemporary reformers' claims about the benefits of tailoring pleading rules to particular substantive rights and increasing the burden on the plaintiff to establish her case before she may compel the defendant to reveal possibly inculpating facts.

## A.   A BRIEF HISTORY OF CIVIL PROCEDURE

In modern usage, pleadings are the documents that initially frame a lawsuit: the plaintiff's complaint, the defendant's answer, and possibly the plaintiff's reply to new matters raised in the answer. There has long been considerable controversy about the function of pleadings—whether they serve merely to notify the court and the parties that a legal dispute is beginning, to screen frivolous cases out of the system, or to define and limit the issues for trial. Some background on the ancestry of today's pretrial procedure aids the understanding of the cycles of reform and reaction that characterize the practice of pleading.

## 1.  Common Law Procedure

### a.  The Pleading Process

The first pleadings were oral exchanges in court between the parties. The exchanges quickly came to adhere to established patterns; thus, in debt, the plaintiff would orally swear: "In the name of the living God, as I money demand, so have I lack of that which [defendant's name] promised me when I mine to him sold." To this the defendant would make an appropriate, equally formulaic response.

The first lawyers entered the picture as assistants to the parties in their oral pleas to the court. Early in the Norman period, it became the custom to make a record of oral altercations by entering them on the plea roll, which was maintained by a clerk. In 1256, Bracton's Note Book was published. This study of the plea rolls increased attention to the written words. Plucknett explains the natural result of this new focus:

> [C]ounsel no longer directed their attention solely to the oral words; on the contrary, it is plain that their great concern was to get some things on the record, and to keep other things off. Pleading was therefore the art of saying things in court in such a way as to produce a particular result on the roll. . . .
>
> . . . It demanded great learning and still greater skill from the serjeants [lawyers] for they were in effect settling the pleadings in the heat of battle, and in the presence of the adversary. On the other hand, there was the substantial advantage that the court joined in the discussion, which thus sometimes became a round-table conference of judges and counsel who joined in trying to find a way of pleading a cause which would bring out the real points. . . .
>
> Then [in the fifteenth century] a change took place: instead of leaving it to the clerks to enroll a case in accordance with their own ideas of the way it was pleaded, the legal profession provided the clerks with drafts of the entries they desired to have. . . . By this means the lawyers secured absolute control of what was written on the rolls. . . .

Theodore Plucknett, A Concise History of the Common Law 405-407 (5th ed. 1956).

Over the centuries two basic rules that were originally sensible and straightforward were elaborated until common law pleading became arcane and accessible only to the most skilled. The first rule was that the plea must abide the writ. The writs were a kind of order, or form of action, that the King's courts issued to begin a suit. Even if a plaintiff alleged a good case under, for instance, the writ of trespass, his suit would be thrown out of court if he pleaded some aspect of moral fault; this could be included only in a pleading under the writ of trespass on the case. The rigidity of the writ system meant that legal fictions arose as parties sought to bring the facts of their cases within established writs. At the same time that such fictions abounded, new forms of action were devised to meet society's increasing complexity.

The second rule was that the pleading exchange must proceed until a single issue emerged. Roy McDonald, Alternative Pleading, 48 Mich. L. Rev. 311, 314-317 (1950), explains:

> As is well known, the unique object of classical common law pleading was to reduce litigation to a single issue of law or fact. The dominant precept which had been developed to effectuate this objective was that the "facts" be alleged with certainty. Three subordinate rules—that pleadings not be duplicitous, or repugnant, or in the alternative—tended to the "chief object . . . that the parties be brought to issue, and that the issue be material, single and certain in its quality." Apologists had supported the requirement with argument as to economy and expedience: the decision of one material issue would dispose of the controversy, so it was unnecessary to consider more. This, of course, was true, provided one did not inquire too closely into the justice of the decision. . . .
>
> . . . The classical common law rule was that so long as new matter responsive to the immediately preceding pleading of the opponent could be introduced without departure, the exchange continued, each pleading limited to its single issue, until the parties ultimately clashed head-on at a single point.
>
> Such rules were by their very nature incompatible with alternative pleadings. Accordingly, alternatives were prohibited upon the theory that the party must take a stand and notify his opponent with precision as to his contention. Neither party could assert in a single count or defense two theories, either of which independently would sustain his claim or defense, and each of which would require a separate response. . . .

By the early eighteenth century, several methods emerged to avoid the hazards of single-issue pleading. Most notable among these were the "common counts," which were pattern pleadings used for simple contract actions, known as assumpsit. For instance, under the "indebitatus" count, the plaintiff could simply state that at the defendant's request he had furnished him with goods and services at an agreed price, that the plaintiff had demanded the price, and defendant had not paid. Similarly, in the "in quantum valebant" count the plaintiff alleged that he had delivered goods for which no price was agreed upon; the "in quantum meruit" count was used for services performed where no price was agreed.

But ease in pleading was the exception, and by the nineteenth century, legal technicalities had earned their still-surviving bad name. In an ironic twist, the first reform efforts made matters worse by insisting on even greater precision in pleadings. The Hilary Rules of 1834 had the effect of increasing the number of dispositions based on shortcomings in the pleadings, rather than permanently settling pleading rules promptly with a minimal number of cases being decided on the basis of pleading technicalities, as proponents of the reform claimed would happen.

### b.  The Writ System

No overview of the history of pleading would be complete without a glance at the type of actions covered by the common law writs and their relationship to modern substantive law. The principal writs were those of debt, covenant, account, assumpsit (special and general), trespass, trespass on the case, ejectment, trover, detinue, and replevin.

Each writ had its own procedure, as we have seen, and each covered its own distinct form of legal wrong. The distinctions between some of them — such as trespass and trespass on the case — were rather fine, however, making writ selection a sometimes complex decision that would doom the pleading if made incorrectly. These precursors to your modern common law subjects — contracts, property, and torts — included actions to recover property, breach of contracts (express and implied in law or fact), assault and battery, theft of personal property, trespass onto real property, negligence, injuries to reputation, nuisances, actions to try title to land, actions to recover damages for conversion of or injury to personal property, and actions to recover property wrongfully taken or detained.

In the mighty writ of trespass and its offshoot — trespass on the case — lie the history of much of modern tort and property law. The writ of assumpsit gave rise to much of modern contract law. Students may want to examine their casebooks in all of these courses to see whether they contain early English cases involving trespass, case, or assumpsit. The historical distinction between trespass and trespass on the case, to take one important example, is the root of the modern distinction between intentional torts and negligence.

Perhaps the most interesting, even amusing, bit of writ history is that of ejectment. It underwent a series of modifications that transformed ejectment from a literal matter of physical ejectment of a hostile person on the owner's land, to a staged performance (with live "actors" — so-called John Does and Richard Roes engaged to act out for the landowner the steps necessary to bring the matter of trying his title to the land before the court), to fictitious allegations of entry onto the land, lease, and ouster without an actual entry or ouster.

As the following excerpt from Professor William E. Nelson's study of procedural reform in post-Revolutionary Massachusetts describes, the writ system made for an exceedingly complex pleading regime. And the complexities generated resentment, especially among farmers and other working class people who believed that the legal system should be accessible to the common citizen. Many decisions turned on technicalities rather than the merits, leaving litigants without redress for wrongs while enhancing not only the power and purse of lawyers but the undemocratic authority of judge-made law inherited from England:

> Although the [state] Constitution of 1780 had enjoined that "every subject . . . ought to obtain right and justice freely," the costs of litigation were such that

many agrarian debtors felt that right and justice were unobtainable. To them "judicial proceeding[s]" appeared so "intricate" that their usual outcome was only "to throw an honest man out of three quarters of his property" if he put his case to law. Agrarian leaders were determined "to vindicate the rights of the poor against the aggressions of power and violence."

The reform movement was in part directed against the legal profession. . . . Their remedy was to abolish lawyers and have every litigant plead his own cause. Some concessions were made to this antiprofessionalism during the 1780s: litigants were granted permission by statute to plead their own cause, they were forbidden to employ more than two attorneys simultaneously in any one case, and they were permitted to employ as attorneys persons not admitted to the bar. But then the bar regrouped and fought vigorously and successfully to resist any further concessions and to erode those already granted. . . .

[Another] way the reformers sought to make justice freely and equally accessible was by simplifying the rules of procedure. They contended that "the state of pleading in this Commonwealth [had become such] that an honest man . . . [could] not obtain" right and justice "without being obliged to employ a lawyer, at a great expense. . . ." "Artful men in England," they explained, "ha[d] so entangled the mode of managing a cause with the nice distinction of special pleas (and . . . [the courts in Massachusetts had] unfortunately adopted the pernicious practice) that in short justice . . . [could] scarcely be obtained unless it [was] dearly purchased." . . .

The reformers sought to abandon technical and outmoded pleading forms and to have judgments rendered "according to the merits of the case. . . ." "[P]leas," it was urged, should "be simple, and the clerk [should be] authorized to write them in short form for each of the parties." There was no "occasion or need . . . of all the parade of written pleas, replications, rejoinders, etc., etc. in common trials at law," since all that a court needed to know was "the fact, the law, and the equity of the case"; then the issue of causes would not "depend upon adroitness of advocates . . . [but] upon their intrinsic justice." . . .

Although the system of common law pleading was not the principal cause of the high cost of litigation, it was a factor. . . .

Under the common law system a plaintiff was required to name the form of action under which he was bringing his suit. If he did "not name . . . his plea," "give any name to this his Action," or "declare . . . in an action of Debt or Trespass on the Case, or in any other Action or Plea known in the Register or in the Law," his writ would be abated. Writs were also abated when a plaintiff brought the wrong cause of action—trespass, for example, instead of a case for obstructing the flow of water to a milldam; case instead of debt on a bond; debt instead of trespass for a statutory penalty for cutting the plaintiff's trees; debt and detinet, a variety of debt, instead of detinet only on an administrator's bond.

Each form of action, moreover, had its own form of general denial, so called because it imported an absolute and complete denial by a defendant of each and every allegation in a plaintiff's declaration. . . . If the defendant pleaded the wrong general issue . . . then judgment would be given on demurrer for the plaintiff.

If a defendant did not wish to plead the general issue, he could plead specially. . . . Special pleas could be of a great variety, depending upon the circumstances of a defendant's case. . . .

The response to a special plea by a defendant was a replication by the plaintiff, traversing or confessing and avoiding the special plea. That could be followed by a rejoinder by the defendant, followed in turn by a surrejoinder, a rebutter, and a surrebutter. A number of technical rules made special pleading a supremely refined and difficult art. First, a plea was required to be single—that is, it could contain only one factual allegation; moreover, a party could set forth only one plea, unless he obtained the court's permission to plead double. Second, a party's plea had to answer his opponent's allegations in every material point. A plea also had to be direct, positive, and nonargumentative, certain as to time, place, and persons, capable of trial and properly averred in the common form—"and this he is ready to verify." A final rule was that the defendant could not put in a special plea that amounted merely to a denial of all or part of the plaintiff's charge but had to advance some new fact not mentioned in the declaration. . . .

After the plaintiff had selected the correct writ, he was required to have it served on the defendant . . . [and the] plaintiff also had to be certain that all the parties who ought to be joined in the litigation were joined and that the parties who ought not to be joined were not. Rules on this subject were quite technical. Joint obligors and joint promissors, for example, both had to be joined in a suit on their promise. . . . Joint bailors, on the other hand, did not have to sue their bailee together, and agents were not required to be joined in suits against their principals. . . .

The most technical of all the pleading rules was one requiring parties to litigation to be precisely identified. Pursuant to this requirement, civil and criminal actions were dismissed when there was no person by the exact name and description given the named defendant. Civil and criminal actions were similarly dismissed for failing to state the full name of a party to the writ or for misspelling or otherwise misstating a party's name—either his Christian name or his surname. There was an even greater need for certainty in naming parties in suits involving corporate litigants, and here too writs were abated for misnomers.

In addition to making a plaintiff give all parties their proper names, the law required him to state correctly without any misspelling the town and county in which all parties resided. . . . [T]he plaintiff also had to state correctly the addition, that is the occupation or social rank, of both plaintiff and defendant. Failure to do so was ground for abatement of a writ. . . .

More suits were abated or dismissed for improper additions than on any other ground, and much elaborate learning proliferated on the subject of additions: one finds the bench and bar of the Superior Court debating, for instance, whether the description of a blacksmith should include a nailer, and whether a militia captain was a gentleman by way of commission, reputation, or courtesy. . . .

Even before Shay's Rebellion, in which high litigation costs, high taxes, and lack of currency were the chief complaints, the courts and the legal profession had begun to take hesitant steps toward reform. . . . Reform occurred piecemeal, as individual lawyers, either lacking precise knowledge of common law pleading rules or seeking some strategic advantage in litigation at hand, entered pleas that were not in proper form. . . . The courts, sensing the validity of reformers' complaints about the undue expense of technical pleading rules and seeing that reduced adherence to form threatened no tangible interest of the law or of the legal profession, often decided to permit counsel either to ignore or to amend the informality. As various decisions of this sort cumulated over time, the ancient system of common law pleading was destroyed, and new rules of pleading emerged in its place. . . .

By the early nineteenth century, then, the emerging concern in pleading was with substance, not with form. This concern was of great significance, for it compelled the bench and the bar to think about law in substantive categories, such as "tort" and "contract," rather than in the old procedural categories of trespass, assumpsit, and the like.

William E. Nelson, Americanization of the Common Law: The Impact of Legal Change on Massachusetts Society, 1760-1830, at 69-78 (1975).

Nelson emphasizes that the transition away from the writ system was not without "consequences that were unforeseen and that required compensatory modification of other rules of law." Id. at 86. These problems are worth enumerating here, as you will see that they resurface in our study of the modern pleading rules that emerged from the nineteenth-century rejection of the writ system.

> One advantage of common law pleading is that in addition to giving parties notice of the essence of each others' claims it narrows the issues that can arise upon trial by requiring the parties to select before trial, at least in part, the legal theory they plan to pursue. Particularly if the parties have engaged in special pleading, the issues on which litigation will turn are precisely identified before trial begins. With the abolition of common law pleading, issues were no longer formulated and defined before trial but during the very course of trial, as the parties offered evidence and made legal contentions on the basis of that evidence. . . . [P]reparation for trial [thus] became more difficult and hazardous; as one defendant argued, the complaint to which he had to respond was "so general, that it . . . [was] impossible [that] any man . . . [could] prepare to defend himself in the same. . . ." Whereas litigants at common law had often had to prepare evidence only on a small number of precisely defined issues, a litigant under the new pleading system had to prepare to meet many potential issues, only some of which would arise. Moreover, he faced the danger that issues he had never anticipated might be brought up and that he might "be surprised by a piece of evidence which at another time he could have explained or answered."

Id. at 86-87.

Can you imagine any procedural tools that would address these problems? Is it more efficient to force parties to plead to and try a single issue, or to have more liberal pleading and grant new trials if a litigant is unfairly surprised by unanticipated or undiscovered evidence? Nelson reports that, after the reforms in Massachusetts,

> [n]ewly discovered evidence became . . . the most common cause for granting new trials. As a general matter, new trials were granted whenever a party had not had adequate opportunity to present his claim. . . . Although common law pleading was antiquated, unduly technical, and expensive, and

hence in need of reform, it nonetheless provided a working system for the trial of cases.

Id. at 87.

Again, recall that each had its own procedure, which included its own method of proof. In the next section we take up the matter of methods of proof, with special emphasis on the evolution of the trial by jury and the decline of wager of law, trial by battle, and—most students' personal favorite—trial by ordeal.

### c.   Methods of Proof

Before the emergence of the jury as a method of proof, the common law system employed wager of law, trial by battle, and the ordeal as mechanisms for determining the victor in litigation. The jury system eventually replaced these older methods, for reasons that should become obvious as you learn more about each.

Wager of law, abolished in 1833, referred to a litigant's use of oaths to "make his law." For example, in a debt action the defendant would solemnly swear that he owed the plaintiff nothing. He then would bring in *compurgators*, or "oath helpers," who would swear that the defendant's oath was clean. The defendant might say the following: "By the Lord, I am guiltless both in deed and counsel of the charge of which N. accuses me." To which the compurgators would swear, "By the Lord, the oath is clear and unperjured which M. has sworn."

The purpose of these oaths was not to convince the court, or to submit the defendant to cross-examination; it was to bring upon the swearers the wrath of God if they lied. Yet the wrath of God was not all these oath helpers had to fear. By swearing for the defendant, they put their worth as well as their souls on the line, for the price of swearing falsely was to lose one's *wergeld* (the value, set in monetary terms, of each person, which varied with one's status—each person quite literally had his "price"), as well as community respect and confidence. People who lived in small agrarian communities depended heavily on their neighbors and needed a good reputation.

How many compurgators one needed depended on the defendant's rank. A person of low rank or bad character might be required to produce three times the usual number of compurgators, or be required to undergo the ordeal. In many respects, the wager of law was less about truth than about community support for the defendant.

Trial by battle, abolished in 1819, is self-explanatory; less obvious was the provision for hiring a champion, thus transforming the battle into one of economic, rather than physical strength. (Some would say that this method of proof resembles most closely modern methods of proof, though parties now hire the best legal rather than physical competitors.)

And, of course, there was the ordeal, abolished in 1215 by the Lateran Council, but still used well into the fifteenth century. The ordeal is traced by some historians to a certain Bishop Poppo, who preached to the Jutlanders

(Danes) with no success. Frustrated by his failures, Bishop Poppo asked the Jutlanders whether they might believe his message was divine if he could touch a hot iron and suffer no harm. Receiving an affirmative response, Bishop Poppo allegedly heated an iron glove until red hot, put his hand inside, and withdrew it uninjured. The Danes apparently were impressed.

The theory behind the ordeal, perhaps based on Numbers 5:12-13, was that God would spare the innocent. One ordeal required the party to carry a one-pound red-hot iron a distance of nine feet. The party's hands would then be bound for three days. If his hands healed, he was innocent; if not, he was deemed guilty. Similarly, a party might be ordered to put his hand in a boiling cauldron and pull out a stone. A third ordeal was to bind a party with rope and throw him into the river. If he sank, he was innocent, because the water would reject the guilty. (Being proved innocent seems small comfort, though, if it meant being tied up at the bottom of the river.) Such methods were bound to produce some bad results, as the community witnessed some innocent (in the modern sense) people deemed guilty in the eyes of God. The Church effectively ended the practice in 1215 by withdrawing its support.

The most enduringly important common law method of proof was the trial by jury, though its early form bore little resemblance to its modern counterpart. The early jury was a group of neighbors who were sworn to tell the truth about something they had observed, usually in an effort to preserve the King's rights. They were summoned by a royal officer to give impartial testimony about their knowledge. As such, the early jurors were more like modern-day witnesses than jurors. Moreover, the right to trial by jury was a matter of royal prerogative, not a common right. Benefit of that right was one that the King could give or sell to people in his grace. This gave rise to the expression "One could not wage law against the King." This meant that when the King was the plaintiff, one had to submit to trial by jury, which then included certain incentives for jurors to find for the crown. The right to a trial of one's peers is traced to the Magna Carta, but the notion then was that the Barons at Runnymede should be entitled to trial by *their* "peers" — noblemen, not lower echelon citizens.

Over time, of course, the right to trial by jury became available to all citizens who filed writs that carried with them this method of proof. Moreover, jurors no longer were selected on the basis of their knowledge of a controversy; on the contrary, actual knowledge would disqualify a person from serving as a juror in the case.

Today, under the Seventh Amendment, the right to trial by jury in civil cases hinges primarily on whether the right in question was one that would have fallen on the common law (versus equity) side of Anglo-American jurisdiction. This means that modern actions sounding in tort and contract, as well as many in property, could involve jury trials should one of the parties request it in a timely manner. You will learn more about how this analysis goes in Chapter 5's section on the right to jury trial.

As the discussion below on equity jurisdiction will explain, another guide to whether one is entitled to a trial by jury is the relief requested. If it is money damages, this often—though not always—means that the action is one at law and jury triable.

### d. Equity

Adding to the confusion of the common law system was the existence of a separate court system, Chancery, which administered a body of "equitable" doctrine applying to allegations of fraud, mistake, and breach of fiduciary duty. The Court of Chancery differed from the common law courts in important ways. First, Chancery developed the concept of formal pretrial proceedings through which parties could learn facts beyond the pleadings—"discovery" in modern parlance. But this ameliorative alternative to the burden of pleading was soon itself weighted with Byzantine complexity and protracted delays, made infamous by Dickens in *Bleak House*. Second, the Chancery trial had no jury; the judge decided questions of fact. Finally, Chancery had remedies unavailable at common law, where the only favorable plaintiff's outcome was an award of monetary damages. The Chancellor typically issued affirmative orders requiring that the rightful situation be effected—orders that were the ancestors of the modern injunction.

Resort to Chancery was proper only when an action at law was inadequate, either because the court of law was unfair or unwilling to do justice, or because the available common law writs and their remedies were inadequate. The system was not meant to act contrary to the principles of the law courts, but as an essential supplement to them.

Unlike actions at law, which were considered actions against property (*in rem*), equity acted against the person (*in personam*). The order of the Chancellor was a personal order against the affected party, and was enforceable by contempt power and imprisonment, if necessary. A judgment at law would operate against the party's property, such that the court (through the sheriff) would enforce the judgment by attaching the property in an execution on the judgment, selling it, and satisfying the plaintiff's judgment through the proceeds of the sale. Any balance, minus costs, was returned to the defendant.

Chancery was a highly discretionary and flexible system, prompting the remark by Selden that equitable relief depended on the "size of the Chancellor's foot." The reason for this discretion, again, makes sense in light of the origins of equity. In its earliest forms, equity was not a formal system of judicial relief, but the Chancellor's response to an individual's appeal. There was no need to employ the common law methods of proof, such as a jury or wager of law since the Chancellor's action was an administrative and political response to a dispute.

By the fifteenth century, however, the Chancellor was clearly acting as a judge, and was recognized as such. In ruling on the petitions, the Chancellor invoked moral grounds that continue to influence one's right to secure an equitable remedy. For example, "clean hands" were necessary before one could receive equitable relief. Likewise, delay ("laches") might defeat one's right to recover, even if no formal statute of limitations barred recovery. Conduct that misled an opponent or otherwise caused him to rely on a state of affairs might "estop" one from disrupting his expectations.

The remedies available in equity included injunctions, specific performance, restitution, constructive trusts, equitable liens, and remedies for fiduciary misconduct, among others. Recall that in Chapter 1, we dealt with the flexible equitable doctrines in considering whether injunctions, wage garnishment, and attachment of property without an *ex ante* adversary hearing may violate due process.

The subjects commonly heard in equity rather than in law included matters involving the enforcement of uses or trusts, those involving mortgage foreclosures, family matters, and equitable conversion. The need for a system like equity to relieve the unforgiving nature of law, and the interplay between the two, is well illustrated by a mortgage foreclosure example. The mortgage itself is a contract between the mortgagor and mortgagee that typically provides that failure to make timely payments constitutes a material breach. Legal title, as readers with mortgages will know, is held by the lender, and does not pass to the borrower unless he makes timely payments, as prescribed by the mortgage agreement. The term *legal* title is important here, and refers to title acknowledged on the law side of the common law courts.

The harshness of mortgage law, enforced by the law side of common law courts, was that a borrower who paid a significant number of payments, but who later defaulted on the mortgage, was deemed to have breached the contract and thereby lost the value of any payments he already made. Moreover, he had no chance to redeem the mortgage.

Over time, equity recognized the severity of this result and came to respect the borrower's right to recovery of the money already paid — called *equity* today, and now you know why.

In the early seventeenth century, equity courts acted to soften further the hard edges of the law of mortgage by providing a right of redemption to the borrower even in the absence of fraud or mistake in the making of the mortgage. It tempered the redemption opportunity, though, by giving the lender the right to foreclose. This meant that the lender went to the equity court and asked that the right of redemption be foreclosed, such that if the borrower did not redeem (pay up) within a reasonable period of time, then the mortgage would be foreclosed.

Needless to say, the existence of Chancery as a separate, supplemental system of justice complicated procedure. Some actions had both legal and equitable characteristics, which might not become apparent until well into the pleading process. Should the action be bifurcated at this late date? Dismissed and refiled? Also, questions inevitably arose about the relative powers of law and equity courts, with periods of quite bitter turf conflicts.

The complicating aspects of the formal division between equity and law persisted for centuries. In the American federal courts, some of the problems ultimately were resolved when, in 1938, law and equity finally were merged so that one judge had power to award both equitable and legal remedies. But this is getting ahead of the story. Before turning to 1938 and its cataclysmic procedural changes, we first need to review the interim stage of pleading history—Code procedure.

## 2.   Code Procedure

Colonial legislatures in the United States sought, largely unsuccessfully, to mitigate the rigors of common law pleading and to simplify equity procedures. Judicial reforms, such as those discussed by Nelson above, were also fairly limited. Not until the mid-nineteenth century, when complaints about litigation cost, delay, and complexity became a part of Jacksonian Democratic reform agitation, was there a significant departure from the basic structure of English procedure. By that time, frustration among Democratic lawyers and laymen with the subtleties of the writ system had sharpened considerably. William Sampson, a New York lawyer and early advocate of procedural reform, derisively referred to

> those odious volumes of special pleading . . . where the suitor's story is told in twenty different ways, and answered in as many, and must be hunted for with fear and trembling in printed books . . . and made conformable to precedents composed before the party was in being, and which, in no single instance, conform to the truth: insomuch, that he who dares to tell his case according to the simple and honest truth, will for that very reason . . . fail in his suit.

William Sampson, An Anniversary Discourse, Delivered Before the Historical Society of New York, Dec. 6, 1823, in Perry Miller, The Legal Mind in America from Independence to the Civil War 132 (1962). A strong egalitarian element ran through the reform proposals—a concern, as in post-Revolutionary Massachusetts, that the writ system was inconsistent with democratic principles and biased in favor of the rich. As Henry Dwight Sedgwick, another New York lawyer, wrote:

> Americans will not long believe . . . that there is any necessity that the forms of conducting a legal controversy should be so multiplied and expensive, that the mere costs of suit . . . should be so great, that none but the rich can indulge the luxury of the law.

Henry Dwight Sedgwick, Review of Sampson's Anniversary Discourse, in Perry Miller, The Legal Mind in America from Independence to the Civil War 145-146 (1962).

The signal reform was the New York Act of 1848, drafted by David Dudley Field. The "Field Code," as it came to be known, provided "one form of action," thus abolishing the writ system and embracing all claims previously known at law and in equity. The Code also abandoned the goal of reducing the dispute to a single issue, which might require years of plead-ing. Instead, the pleadings were limited to the Complaint, the Answer, and possibly a Reply. But this streamlining did not mean that the pleadings were unimportant. To the contrary, they were the primary vehicle for con-trolling and defining the dispute. As such they served two distinct but related functions. First, the parties were supposed to learn each other's fac-tual contentions from the pleadings, so that they could be fully prepared and not surprised by developments at trial. Full disclosure through the pleadings was also intended to promote the early resolution of issues not actually in dispute. See First Report of the Commissioners on Practice and Pleadings 141-142 (1848).

In his published notes to the new Code, Field emphasized:

> The object of every suit, so far as modes of proceeding are concerned, is to place the parties, whose rights are involved in it, in a proper and convenient manner, before the tribunal by which they are to be adjudicated; to pres-ent their conflicting allegations plainly and intelligibly to each other and to the Court; to secure by adequate means a trial or hearing of the contested points; to obtain a judgment or determination adapted to the justice of the case; and to effect the enforcement of that judgment by vigorous and effi-cient means. . . . Let our Courts be hereafter confined in their adjudications to questions of substantial right, and not to the nice balancing of the ques-tion whether the party has conformed himself to the arbitrary and absurd nomenclature imposed upon him by rules, the reason of which, if they ever possessed that quality, has long since ceased to exist, and the continuance of which is a reproach to the age in which we live.

First Report, Extracts from the Notes to Title I, Part II, in 1 A.P. Sprague, Speeches, Arguments, and Misc. Papers of David Dudley Field 266-267 (1884). California adopted a version of the Field Code in 1849, and it was carried eastward from California and westward from New York until by the turn of the century more than half of the states had switched from com-mon law to Code pleading and merged law and equity.

With the hope that facts would be disclosed in the pleadings, the codi-fiers made sparing use of the costly discovery devices developed in equity. Depositions were permitted only in rare circumstances and documents were discoverable only if they were found necessary to an issue on which the moving party had the burden of producing evidence.

The plan for adversaries to disclose their cases fully in their pleadings, and thus reduce the area of dispute, proved visionary. Before the dust had settled, the liberalization of pleading created as many pitfalls for the unwary as the common law system it had revamped. A typical Code sec-tion required a statement of the facts constituting the cause of action, writ-ten in ordinary and concise language. To be avoided were "conclusions" and "evidence." But the distinction between facts and evidence, or even facts and conclusions, soon proved impossible to make. The attempt pro-duced some grand legal writing:

> The distinction between propositions of fact and conclusions of law is this: Propositions of fact are descriptive; conclusions of law are dispositive. Propositions of fact state history; conclusions of law assign legal significance to that history. But since useful propositions of fact must be relevant, and the relevancy of statements of ultimate fact depends on legal considerations, this distinction is not as easy as it seems. While statements of ultimate fact only describe, and do not decide cases, yet they must describe legally relevant aspects of the events to which they refer. A description of a totally irrelevant aspect cannot be a fact-of-the-case.

Clarence Morris, Law and Fact, 55 Harv. L. Rev. 1303, 1329 (1942). Walter Wheeler Cook was especially influential on the distinction between facts and conclusions, finding that it is one of degree only, and that no rational argument can settle the question of whether a particular allegation is too abstract. Only precedent or officially approved form books can guide the pleader. Walter Wheeler Cook, "Facts" and "Statements of Fact," 4 U. Chi. L. Rev. 233 (1937); Walter Wheeler Cook, Statements of Fact in Pleading Under the Codes, 21 Colum. L. Rev. 416 (1921).

In practice, courts developed exceptions to the Code pleading requirements by, for instance, allowing or even requiring the pleading of evidence when it was needed to give full notice to the opponent. Or, on the other hand, courts endorsed the pleading of conclusions:

> In cases of negligence, the sufferer may only know the general, the immediate, cause of the injury, and may be entirely ignorant as to the specific acts or omissions which lead up to it. The term "negligence," for the purpose of pleading, is a fact to be pleaded, an ultimate fact, which qualifies an act otherwise not wrongful. Negligence is not the act itself, but the fact which defines the character of the act, and makes it a legal wrong.

Rannard v. Lockheed Aircraft Corp., 157 P.2d 1, 5 (1945). Contra Kramer v. Kansas City Power & Light Co., 279 S.W. 43 (1925).

Such language by the California Supreme Court hardly comports with the ideal of Code pleading that "the allegations must be of dry, naked actual facts, while the rules of law applicable thereto, and the legal rights and duties arising therefrom, must be left entirely to the courts." John Norton Pomeroy, Code Remedies 640 (5th ed. 1929).

The entrenched habits of mind of judges and pleaders made them resist Code pleading. As Justice Grier opined: "The distinction between the different forms of action for different wrongs, requiring different remedies, lies in the nature of things; it is absolutely inseparable from the correct administration of justice in common law courts." McFaul v. Ramsey, 61 U.S. 523, 525 (1857). Maitland summed up all the difficulties with pleading reform when he wrote: "the forms of action we have buried, but they still rule us from their graves." Frederick William Maitland, Equity and the Forms of Action at Common Law 296 (1909).

Despite Maitland's famous bon mot, Code pleading was not a dark failure in the history of pleading reform. California and New York, as well as several other states, retain their Codes, with a decisional gloss stretching over more than a hundred years. And the rulemakers who drafted the Federal Rules of Civil Procedure in 1938 were richly informed by the experience under the Codes.

## 3.  Modern Procedure in Federal Courts

The limitations of older forms of pleading that plagued the state courts likewise plagued the federal courts, as the federal courts for many years conformed their procedure in actions arising on the law side of their jurisdiction (rather than the equity side) to that of local state courts. For actions arising in equity the federal courts had their own nationally uniform rules of procedure. Thus a federal district court in Maryland would in nonequity cases conform its civil procedure to that of Maryland state courts, though even in these cases exceptions existed to the general rule of borrowing state procedural law.

The problems with this often confusing system of borrowing state procedure, and with the anachronistic state procedures it borrowed, prompted a protracted fight for revised, uniform rules of federal procedure. The reform effort was spearheaded by Thomas Shelton, who instigated a resolution by the American Bar Association in 1911 favoring court-made rules of civil procedure for the federal courts. These efforts, however, did not bear fruit for over 20 years. It was not until 1934 that Congress finally adopted a bill that authorized the U.S. Supreme Court to promulgate rules of "pleading and practice" that would be uniform among all of the federal district courts of the United States. See Rules Enabling Act of 1934, 28 U.S.C. §§ 2071-2077.

The Rules Enabling Act of 1934 contains the caveat that no rule shall "abridge, enlarge, or modify any substantive rights." 28 U.S.C. § 2072(b); see generally Stephen B. Burbank, The Rules Enabling Act of 1934, 130 U. Pa. L. Rev. 1015 (1982) (describing the history that gave rise to the 1934 Act); Stephen N. Subrin, How Equity Conquered Common Law: The Federal Rules of Civil Procedure in Historical Perspective, 130 U. Pa. L. Rev. 909 (1982) (describing how the rules of equity, rather than common law procedure, became the model for the federal rules). The Court appointed an Advisory Committee, composed of law professors, practicing lawyers, and former judges, that was charged with responsibility for drafting uniform rules of procedure for the district courts. Charles E. Clark, Dean of Yale Law School, was named the Reporter of the Advisory Committee and became the principal draftsperson of the rules it eventually proposed. Dean Clark had for years before his appointment devoted considerable scholarly energy to denouncing the way in which procedural technicalities often stood in the way of substantive merits of disputes, and to proposals for minimizing the role of procedure in determining legal outcomes. See Subrin, supra, at 961-962.

In 1938, the first uniform rules adopted pursuant to the 1934 Act took effect. The changes affected by the rules were sweeping and massively influential, as the new streamlined rules became models for reform of state procedure in many jurisdictions. Significant among the changes were the abolition of the forms of action in favor of one form of action for all types of lawsuits, expanded discovery, greatly simplified pleading requirements, and the merger of law and equity. The overriding goal, stated with elegant simplicity in Rule 1, was "to secure the just, speedy, and inexpensive determination of every action." Two scholars have offered excellent historical and theoretical surveys of the overarching goals the rules and rulemaking procedures are intended to serve. See Brooke Coleman, Recovering Access: Rethinking the Structure of Federal Civil Rulemaking, 39 N.M. L. Rev. 261 (2009) (describing commitment of original Advisory Committee to opening access to the courts and questioning the current structure of the Advisory Committee); David Marcus, The Federal Rules of Civil Procedure and Legal Realism as a Jurisprudence of Law Reform, 44 Ga. L. Rev. 433 (2010).

The centerpiece of the new rules was Rule 8, which required only a "short and plain statement of the claim showing that the pleader is entitled to relief." Almost immediately, the shibboleth became "notice pleading": The pleader was required only to state enough of anything — facts, conclusions, law — to give the court and the opponent notice of the nature of his claim. Supplementing the limited pleadings were elaborate provisions for pretrial discovery and Rule 16, which provided for a pretrial conference to shape the issues for trial.

The new Rules were greeted with high hopes but have failed to conclude the eternal debate about the function of pleadings. In the early 1950s, one critic observed as follows:

> The conversion of Rule 8 to notice pleadings is part of a broader tendency of deferring the inevitable necessity of thinking through one's case. . . . [T]he necessary job of coming to grips with the issues is deferred with the consoling assurance to counsel that the issues can be found and framed by discovery procedures and the pretrial conference.
>
> . . . [But d]iscovery does not define the issues. It simply throws into the hopper the whole undigested mass of facts. Anything goes.
>
> . . . Discovery . . . ought not to be required until some preliminary definition of issues has occurred.

Harold Lasky, Memorandum for the Committee on Rule 8, 13 F.R.D. 275 (1952).

The tone of the debate grew increasingly sharp in the late twentieth century, and there were many ready on the fiftieth birthday of the Rules to declare them another failed procedural reform. In addition to the dissatisfaction with notice pleading, the Rules were criticized for encouraging overly adversarial behavior, unfairly advantaging rich litigants, vesting too much discretion in judges, and being subject to unpredictable application. Over the last two decades the Supreme Court and the Advisory Committee have attempted to respond to these concerns.

As the cases in section B of this chapter show, the Court has been especially proactive in its interpretation of Rule 8. And in what became the most comprehensive overhaul since the Rules were first adopted, the Advisory Committee restyled every one, from Rule 1 to Rule 86, and redesigned the practice forms in 2007. The Advisory Committee Note to each rule now contains the explicit disclaimer: "The language of Rule has been amended as a part of the general restyling of the Civil Rules to make them more easily understood. . . . These changes are intended to be stylistic only." The Supreme Court has indicated its agreement with the Advisory Committee's view that "the changes were stylistic only." Republic of Philippines v. Pimentel, 553 U.S. 851, 855-856 (2008) (interpreting the new Rule 19). Finally, in 2015 the Committee approved sweeping substantive revisions to the rules. Many of the most important modifications concern discovery practice, a subject we take up in Chapter 3. But the spirit of the 2015 reforms is reflected in edits to Rule 1 that impress upon litigants their responsibility for vindicating the purposes of the Rules and empower judges to ensure that those purposes are met. Rule 1 now provides that the Federal Rules of Civil Procedure "[s]hould be construed, administered, *and employed by the court and the parties* to secure the just, speedy, and inexpensive determination of every action and proceeding."

As you read the materials in this chapter on pleading, keep in mind the cycles of reform and reaction that are the background of the governing rules as well as the balance of power between the Advisory Committee and federal judges. Remember that the dream of the rulemakers was to simplify pretrial procedure. Is this an impossible dream?

## B. THE ALLEGATIONS: PLEADING AND RESPONDING UNDER THE FEDERAL RULES OF CIVIL PROCEDURE

### 1. The Complaint

**Problem Case: The Aggrieved Nurses**

#### IN THE UNITED STATES DISTRICT COURT
#### FOR THE NORTHERN DISTRICT OF ILLINOIS

American Nurses Association, )
              Plaintiff )
                      )
v.                    )   Civil Action
                      )   File No. xx-xxx
State of Illinois,        )
              Defendant )

This court has jurisdiction under 28 U.S.C.S. § 1331 [Federal Question Jurisdiction]. This case arises under Title VII of the Civil Rights Act of 1964, 42 U.S.C. § 2000e.

## COMPLAINT

1. Plaintiffs are two associations of nurses plus 21 individuals, mostly women, who work for the state in jobs like nursing that are mainly filled by women. They represent a class of all current women employees of the state.

2. Defendants are the State of Illinois, its departments and other Agencies subject to the State Personnel Code, and State Officials.

3. Defendants have intentionally discriminated and continue to intentionally discriminate against female state employees in the terms and conditions of their employment because of their sex and because of their employment in historically female-dominated sex-segregated job classifications.

Wherefore plaintiffs demand judgment against defendant, and the entry of such relief in damages, backpay, and such other relief as the court deems proper and the evidence supports.

Signed:_____
Attorney for the Plaintiff
45 La Salle St.
Chicago, Illinois

---

Does this complaint meet the requirements of Rule 8? Can it survive a motion to dismiss under Rule 12(b)(6)? Passing the issue of whether it meets a minimum standard, is this a good complaint? Are you impressed by the justice of the cause?

### a.   The Basic Standard: Rule 8

### *Conley v. Gibson*
355 U.S. 42 (1957)

JUSTICE BLACK delivered the opinion of the Court.

This class suit was brought in a Federal District Court in Texas by certain Negro members of the Brotherhood of Railway and Steamship Clerks, petitioners here, on behalf of themselves and other Negro employees similarly situated against the Brotherhood, its Local Union No. 28 and certain officers of both. In summary, the complaint made the following allegations relevant to our decision: Petitioners were employees of the Texas and New Orleans Railroad at its Houston Freight House. Local 28 of the Brotherhood was the designated bargaining agent under the Railway Labor Act for the bargaining unit to which petitioners belonged. A contract existed between the Union and the Railroad which gave the employees in the bargaining unit certain protection from discharge and loss of seniority. In May 1954, the Railroad purported to abolish 45 jobs held by petitioners or other Negroes all of whom were either discharged or demoted. In truth the 45 jobs were not abolished at all but instead filled by whites as the Negroes were ousted, except for a few instances where Negroes were rehired to fill their old jobs but with loss of seniority. Despite repeated pleas by petitioners, the Union, acting according to plan, did nothing to protect them against these discriminatory discharges and refused to give them protection comparable to that given white employees. The complaint then went on to allege that the Union had failed in general to represent Negro employees equally and in good faith. It charged that such discrimination constituted a violation of petitioners' rights under the Railway Labor Act to fair representation from their bargaining agent. And it concluded by asking for relief in the nature of declaratory judgment, injunction and damages.

The respondents appeared and moved to dismiss the complaint on several grounds[, including that] the complaint failed to state a claim upon which relief could be given. . . . [The District Court granted the motion to dismiss and the Fifth Circuit affirmed. 229 F.2d 436. The part of the opinion dealing with other grounds for dismissal is omitted.]

. . . In appraising the sufficiency of the complaint we follow, of course, the accepted rule that a complaint should not be dismissed for failure to state a claim unless it appears beyond doubt that the plaintiff can prove no set of facts in support of his claim which would entitle him to relief.[5] Here, the complaint alleged, in part, that petitioners were discharged wrongfully by the Railroad and that the Union, acting according to plan, refused to protect their jobs as it did those of white employees or to help them with their grievances all because they were Negroes. If these allegations are proven there has been a manifest breach of the Union's statutory duty to represent fairly and without hostile discrimination all of the employees in the bargaining unit. This Court squarely held in *Steele* and subsequent cases that discrimination in representation because of race is prohibited by the Railway Labor Act. The bargaining representative's duty not to draw "irrelevant and invidious"[6] distinctions among those it represents does not come to an abrupt end, as the respondents seem to contend, with the making of an agreement between union and employer. Collective bargaining is a continuing process. Among other things, it involves day-to-day adjustments in the contract and other working rules, resolution of new problems not covered by existing agreements, and the protection of employee rights already secured by contract. The bargaining representative can no more unfairly discriminate in carrying out these functions than it can in negotiating a collective agreement. A contract may be fair and impartial on its face yet administered in such a way, with the active or tacit consent of the union, as to be flagrantly discriminatory against some members of the bargaining unit.

The respondents also argue that the complaint failed to set forth specific facts to support its general allegations of discrimination and that its dismissal is therefore proper. The decisive answer to this is that the Federal Rules of Civil Procedure do not require a claimant to set out in detail the

5. See, e.g., Leimer v. State Mutual Life Assur. Co., 108 F.2d 302 [8th Cir. 1940]; Dioguardi v. Durning, 139 F.2d 774 [2d Cir. 1944]; Continental Collieries v. Shober, 130 F.2d 631 [3d Cir. 1942].

6. Steele v. Louisville & Nashville R. Co., 323 U.S. 192, 203 [1944].

facts upon which he bases his claim. To the contrary, all the Rules require is "a short and plain statement of the claim"[8] that will give the defendant fair notice of what the plaintiff's claim is and the grounds upon which it rests. The illustrative forms appended to the Rules plainly demonstrate this. Such simplified "notice pleading" is made possible by the liberal opportunity for discovery and the other pretrial procedures established by the Rules to disclose more precisely the basis of both claim and defense and to define more narrowly the disputed facts and issues.[9] Following the simple guide of Rule 8(f) that "all pleadings shall be so construed as to do substantial justice,"* we have no doubt that petitioners' complaint adequately set forth a claim and gave the respondents fair notice of its basis. The Federal Rules reject the approach that pleading is a game of skill in which one misstep by counsel may be decisive to the outcome and accept the principle that the purpose of pleading is to facilitate a proper decision on the merits.

The judgment is reversed and the cause is remanded to the District Court for further proceedings not inconsistent with this opinion.

*It is so ordered.*

## Notes and Questions

1. *The Ideals of Notice Pleading. Conley's* requirement that a complaint should not be dismissed "unless it appears beyond doubt that the plaintiff can prove no set of facts in support of the claim that entitle him to relief" sets an almost impossible standard, doesn't it? One reason for this wide interpretation of Rule 8's requirements was that the plaintiffs appeared particularly deserving. Look at the date of the case, well before Title VII of the Civil Rights Act of 1964 would have allowed a suit against the employer, the natural defendant, as well as providing a sure statutory basis for a suit against the union.

Moreover, the plaintiffs, black workers in the South, may have feared that they could not get a fair hearing on breach of contract claims against the employers in their state courts. They needed a federal forum, and it would certainly have been against the spirit of the rules to throw them out on a pleading technicality.

Another reason that *Conley* sets such a high standard for dismissing a complaint is that details and evidence regarding the actions charged, a conspiracy between the union and the employer to deprive African-Americans of their jobs, were peculiarly within the knowledge of the defendants.

---

8. Rule 8(a)(2).

9. See, e.g., Rule 12(e) (motion for a more definite statement); Rule 12(f) (motion to strike portions of the pleading); Rule 12(c) (motion for judgment on the pleadings); Rule 16 (pretrial procedure and formulation of issues); Rules 26-37 (depositions and discovery); Rule 56 (motion for summary judgment); Rule 15 (right to amend).

* [Rule 8(f) now appears as Rule 8(e) following the restyled federal Rules. —Eds.]

Access to information is often a consideration when courts are considering who should bear the burden of pleading or failing to plead more fully.

2. A law-trained person reading the complaint must be able to infer from it that at least one legal theory arguably would justify the request for a remedy, if the facts are as alleged. Knowing what facts to plead therefore requires some substantive knowledge. Given this interdependence of substance and procedure, many law students find this first encounter with pleading fairly abstract; after all, you are just learning the elements of torts, contracts, and other legal wrongs.

Nevertheless, some general principles about pleading should be obvious even at this early stage in your legal career. The complaint should tell the judge who did what to whom, where, how, and why what happened was illegal, and then ask for relief. Many attorneys will do more in describing the event and its consequences. A good complaint, for example, should allow journalists to readily understand the case on a single read. Also, many districts require lawyers to fill out a civil cover sheet when they file a complaint, on which they must indicate what kind of case it is by checking the appropriate box, for example, negligence or contract. This means the lawyer is expected to have a theory of the case when she files a lawsuit, even if it is only a general idea and may change as discovery dictates. Our inquiry at this point, however, is not whether more can or should be included in a complaint filed in federal court, but what—at the least—*must* be included.

3. *Pleading and Subject Matter Jurisdiction.* Recall that Rule 8 not only requires a short and plain statement of the claim, but also "a short and plain statement of the grounds for the court's jurisdiction." Rule 8(a)(1). This refers to the federal court's subject matter jurisdiction, the basic rules of which you encountered in Chapter 1, supra.

Quickly review those jurisdictional principles, and consider their pleading implications before responding to the following questions:

a. In an action based solely on diversity, brought by two plaintiffs against one defendant, what would the jurisdictional allegations need to include? See Fed. R. Civ. P. Form 7 and the materials in Chapter 1, section D(2), supra.

b. In an action based solely on a federal statute, what must the jurisdictional allegation include? See Fed. R. Civ. P. Form 7 and the materials in Chapter 1, section D(3), supra.

c. In an action based on a federal question that also asserts a related state law claim, what must the jurisdictional allegation include? See Fed. R. Civ. P. Form 7 and the materials in Chapter 6, section A(2), infra.

4. *Factual Versus Substantive Sufficiency.* Note that there are two ways in which a complaint may fail to state a claim. The first occurs when the complaint is insufficiently detailed to allege the violation of an existing, valid law. The second occurs when the complaint satisfies the "notice pleading" baseline of *Conley* but nevertheless fails to state a claim because no law

exists, at the moment, to support plaintiff's claim. In the former situation, plaintiff can attempt to amend the complaint to provide the missing details. In the latter, plaintiff cannot amend to cure the defect; her only recourse may be to appeal, should the trial judge refuse to extend existing law to fit her situation. As we will see in section C, infra, however, there are ethical and other limits on lawyers' license to file lawsuits to forge new legal paths, as opposed to following familiar ones.

5. *Responding to a Motion to Dismiss.* Once a motion to dismiss is filed under Rule 12(b)(6), plaintiff may file an opposition brief arguing why the complaint meets the plausibility standard. As we'll see shortly, another option is to amend the complaint under Rule 15.

6. *Pleading Too Much?* All that *Conley* requires is that the complaint set forth a claim and give fair notice of its basis. You would think from reading Justice Black's opinion that the complaint here was very short and unspecific. Actually, the opposite was true. The complaint was a rambling affair, with dark allegations of secret meetings and conspiratorial cover-ups. All the facts alleged did not add up to a coherent, much less a concise story, however. Justice Black artfully redrew their complaint to make it a short and plain statement, and declared that the standard for the future.

7. Although Justice Black generously reframed the complaint in the case, over the years the standard *Conley* set out produced frustration for many lower court judges. On the one hand, it failed to prevent prolixity in pleading, forcing judges to spend time sorting through lengthy allegations to determine whether any should survive a motion to dismiss. As Judge Posner put it in a controversial and frequently cited sex discrimination case, "The idea of a 'plain and short statement of the claim' has not caught on. . . . Plaintiff's lawyers, knowing that some judges read a complaint as soon as it is filed in order to get a sense of the suit, hope by pleading facts to 'educate' (that is to say, influence) the judge with regard to the nature and probable merits of the case, and also help to set the stage for an advantageous settlement by showing the defendant what a powerful case they intend to prove." American Nurses' Ass'n v. Illinois, 783 F.2d 716, 723-724 (7th Cir. 1986). In some instances, lengthy pleadings became so disorganized that judges cannot identify the relevant claims and defenses. In reviewing a race discrimination case, an exasperated Eleventh Circuit judge wrote:

> If the framers of the Federal Rules of Civil Procedure could read the record in this case — beginning with the plaintiffs' complaint and [defendant's] answer and continuing to the district court's final order granting [defendant] summary judgment — they would roll over in their graves. In fashioning the Rules, they assumed that complaints would be drafted as clearly and definitively as possible, so that the defendant could understand the cause(s) of action the plaintiff was asserting and frame a responsive pleading, and the district court, having a clear and definitive response before it, could recognize the parties' claims and defenses, identify the issues of fact to be litigated, and proceed to a just result. The framers also assumed that the lawyers appearing before the district court would adhere to the standards of professional responsibility and conduct, and that, as officers of the

court, would be aware that the federal courts constitute a scarce resource for resolving disputes and that their failure to adhere to these standards would likely yield countless untoward, and totally unacceptable, consequences.

This case confounds these assumptions. The complaint is a model of "shotgun" pleading of the sort this court has been roundly, repeatedly, and consistently condemning for years, long before this lawsuit was filed. And the defendant's answer is no better. . . .

Plaintiffs' complaint, first amended complaint, and second amended complaint are nearly identical, each containing three counts. . . . [In the 121 paragraphs of Count I] plaintiffs were contending . . . race discrimination in "pay, raises, benefits, ability to advance, and right to be free of racial discrimination, harassment and intimidation, and other terms and conditions of employment," all in violation of Title VII. This all-encompassing discrimination gave the eight named plaintiffs (and the unnamed members of their class) untold causes of action, all bunched together in one count contrary to the requirements of Federal Rule of Civil Procedure 10(b). With one exception . . . Count I failed explicitly to link a particular plaintiff to a particular cause of action. . . .

No competent lawyer . . . could compose an answer to these sweeping and multifaceted acts of discrimination that would be in keeping with what the framers of the Rules intended. Yet [defendant's] lawyers framed one. They used the same shotgun strategy plaintiffs had employed. Their answer contained fourteen defenses. . . . The second through the fourteenth defense were affirmative defenses, and except for the seventh defense, consisted of one sentence. These affirmative defenses did not respond to specific causes of action, because the drafter of the answer could not identify the specific causes of action each named plaintiff was purporting to allege. . . .

It took several rounds of pleadings . . . for the court even to begin the process of narrowing the issues. In the end, as our preceding analysis of plaintiffs' arguments discloses, the court missed some claims altogether. . . .

The unvarnished truth is that this court puts no credence in briefs written against a backdrop of a case disposed of on shotgun pleadings. . . . Had we not approached the appeal in this manner, there is no telling how many mistakes we might have made in identifying plaintiffs' claims, the district court's treatment of those claims, and the issues plaintiffs reserved for appeal.

Davis v. Coca-Cola Bottling Co., 516 F.3d 955, 979-983 (11th Cir. 2008).

On the other hand, judges complained that the *Conley* standard was so strict that even cases that would never get to trial survive motions to dismiss and thus lead to costly but needless discovery. As Judge Posner put it, "In the system created by the Federal Rules . . . a complaint 'should not be dismissed for failure to state a claim unless it appears beyond reasonable doubt that the plaintiff can prove no set of facts in support of his claim which would entitle him to relief.' *Conley*, 355 U.S. at 45-46. *This language, repeated though it has been in countless later cases . . . should not be taken literally; for taken literally it would permit dismissal only in frivolous cases.*" *American Nurses*, 783 F.2d at 727 (emphasis added).

The sex discrimination suit survived the motion to dismiss in *American Nurses*, but Judge Posner openly challenged the plausibility of the plaintiffs' case, which was based on statistical evidence in a comparable worth study showing wide disparities in the way female state employees and state employees in jobs traditionally held by women ("historically female-dominated sex-segregated job classifications" such as nursing) were paid relative to men and employees in jobs traditionally held by men. Id. at 726. Judge Posner denied the motion to dismiss, but held that the plaintiffs could not prevail at trial without showing intentional steering or sex segregation between traditionally male and female jobs. As he put it, "proof of this causality is essential and is not to be inferred merely from the results of a comparable worth study and from the refusal of the employer to implement the study's recommendations." Id. at 730. After all, Judge Posner reasoned, the wage disparities the state was paying might simply reflect general market wages for those jobs, "and of course the fact that the state knew that market wages do not always comport with the principles of comparable worth would not make a refusal to abandon the market actionable under Title VII." Id. at 726. A defendant paying market wages is not, on this view, engaged in sex discrimination just because the market itself may reflect historical discrimination against women or work traditionally performed by women. And the state may have failed to respond to the comparable worth study, not because it believed women deserved less money, but because "implementation would cost too much or lead to excess demand for some jobs and insufficient demand for others." Id. Plaintiffs could not meet this high threshold of proof so they dropped their case after Judge Posner's ruling.

Notice the series of inferences about possible innocent explanations for the defendant's conduct. The case purports to apply the *Conley* standard, but is laced with precisely the kind of skepticism about the merits of plaintiffs' case that *Conley* is supposed to prohibit. In *American Nurses* and other turn-of-the-century cases, you can see the perennial temptation on the part of judges with crowded dockets to use Rule 12(b)(6) motions to screen out cases that, while not frivolous, seem unlikely to succeed or unworthy of the court's attention.

*American Nurses*'s ambivalence toward *Conley* proved prescient. In 2007, the Supreme Court revisited *Conley* and answered the question whether the oft-cited "any set of facts" language should be taken literally.

## Problem Case: What You Don't Know Can Hurt You

The tenants of the Pinkerton Heights public housing apartments have been in a long-running dispute with Meridian Property Management and the public housing authority over conditions in their buildings. MPM is the private contractor hired by the housing authority to manage the apartments. The company pays a flat annual fee to the city in exchange for the right to collect and keep rent paid by tenants. It shares responsibility with the city for upkeep and maintenance. The tenants have brought a class action lawsuit in state court against the housing authority and MPM alleging that conditions in the buildings are so poor that they fall below the standards of state property law and the tenants should not have to pay rent until conditions improve. Several former tenants who were instrumental in organizing the tenants and finding public interest lawyers to bring the class action have recently filed a new suit in federal court. Here are the relevant allegations of the complaint:

¶ 1 Plaintiffs are former tenants of the Pinkerton Heights public housing apartments.

¶ 2 Defendants are the San Francisco Public Housing Authority, Meridian Property Management (MPM), and Harold Hartliss, an employee of MPM and director of operations for the Pinkerton Heights public housing apartments.

¶ 3 This court has subject matter jurisdiction under 28 U.S.C. § 1331 because this action arises under the Due Process Clause of the Fourteenth Amendment of the U.S. Constitution. See 42 U.S.C. § 1983.

## Count I

¶ 4 Defendant Hartliss forced dozens of tenants he deemed "undesirable" out of their apartments at Pinkerton Heights by threatening them with physical harm. Plaintiffs were among these tenants.

¶ 5 No unlawful detainer actions were filed by MPM against Plaintiffs and Plaintiffs were not in breach of their leases.

¶ 6 On January 15, 2013, "three large, armed, angry looking men showed up at the doors" of Plaintiffs' apartments and told them they had to "get out of the apartments now, or you will regret it." Hartliss ordered these men to kick plaintiffs out and the same men have been running a drug distribution ring from the vacated apartments for months.

¶ 7 These summary evictions occurred via a conspiracy in violation of the federal constitutional guarantee of due process of law under the Fourteenth Amendment. There was no notice or hearing before plaintiffs were thrown out of their homes. See Greene v. Lindsey, 456 U.S. 444 (1982).

All of the defendants moved to dismiss under Rule 12(b)(6) on the ground that the complaint nowhere identifies how the men who made threats against the plaintiffs were connected to Hartliss, MPM, or the public housing authority. MPM and Hartliss concede that if there has been a civil rights violation, they are liable to the same extent as the public housing authority because of MPM's contract with the city. But the motion to dismiss contends that the allegation of complicity on the part of either public housing officials or MPM in a drug distribution ring is completely unfounded and implausible. You are a law clerk for the judge in the federal case. Would you recommend that the motion to dismiss for failure to state a claim be granted or denied?

## Bell Atlantic Corp. v. Twombly
550 U.S. 544 (2007)

JUSTICE SOUTER delivered the opinion of the Court.

Liability under § 1 of the Sherman Act, 15 U.S.C. § 1, requires a "contract, combination . . . , or conspiracy, in restraint of trade or commerce." The question in this putative class action is whether a § 1 complaint can survive a motion to dismiss when it alleges that major telecommunications providers engaged in certain parallel conduct unfavorable to competition, absent some factual context suggesting agreement, as distinct from identical, independent action. We hold that such a complaint should be dismissed.

# I

The upshot of the 1984 divestiture of the American Telephone & Telegraph Company's (AT&T) local telephone business was a system of regional service monopolies (variously called "Regional Bell Operating Companies," "Baby Bells," or "Incumbent Local Exchange Carriers" (ILECs)), and a separate, competitive market for long-distance service from which the ILECs were excluded. More than a decade later, Congress withdrew approval of the ILECs' monopolies by enacting the Telecommunications Act of 1996 (1996 Act), 110 Stat. 56, which "fundamentally restructure[d] local telephone markets" and "subject[ed] [ILECs] to a host of duties intended to facilitate market entry." AT&T Corp. v. Iowa Utilities Bd., 525 U.S. 366, 371 (1999). In recompense, the 1996 Act set conditions for authorizing ILECs to enter the long-distance market. See 47 U.S.C. § 271.

"Central to the [new] scheme [was each ILEC's] obligation . . . to share its network with competitors," Verizon Communications Inc. v. Law Offices of Curtis V. Trinko, LLP, 540 U.S. 398, 402 (2004), which came to be known as "competitive local exchange carriers" (CLECs). A CLEC could make use of an ILEC's network in any of three ways: by (1) "purchas[ing] local telephone services at wholesale rates for resale to end users," (2) "leas[ing] elements of the [ILEC's] network 'on an unbundled basis,'" or (3) "interconnect[ing] its own facilities with the [ILEC's] network." Iowa Utilities Bd., supra, at 371 (quoting 47 U.S.C. § 251(c)). . . .

Respondents William Twombly and Lawrence Marcus (hereinafter plaintiffs) represent a putative class consisting of all "subscribers of local telephone and/or high speed internet services . . . from February 8, 1996 to present." Amended Complaint ¶ 53. In this action against petitioners, a group of ILECs,[1] plaintiffs seek treble damages and declaratory and injunctive relief for claimed violations of § 1 of the Sherman Act, 15 U.S.C. § 1, which prohibits "[e]very contract, combination in the form of trust or otherwise, or conspiracy, in restraint of trade or commerce among the several States, or with foreign nations."

---

1. The 1984 divestiture of AT&T's local telephone service created seven Regional Bell Operating Companies. Through a series of mergers and acquisitions, those seven companies were consolidated into the four ILECs named in this suit: BellSouth Corporation, Qwest Communications International, Inc., SBC Communications, Inc., and Verizon Communications, Inc. (successor-in-interest to Bell Atlantic Corporation). Complaint ¶ 21. Together, these ILECs allegedly control 90 percent or more of the market for local telephone service in the 48 contiguous States. Id., ¶ 48.

The complaint alleges that the ILECs conspired to restrain trade in two ways, each supposedly inflating charges for local telephone and high-speed Internet services. Plaintiffs say, first, that the ILECs "engaged in parallel conduct" in their respective service areas to inhibit the growth of upstart CLECs. Their actions allegedly included making unfair agreements with the CLECs for access to ILEC networks, providing inferior connections to the networks, overcharging, and billing in ways designed to sabotage the CLECs' relations with their own customers. . . .

Second, the complaint charges agreements by the ILECs to refrain from competing against one another. These are to be inferred from the ILECs' common failure "meaningfully [to] pursu[e]" "attractive business opportunit[ies]" in contiguous markets where they possessed "substantial competitive advantages," and from a statement of Richard Notebaert, chief executive officer (CEO) of the ILEC Qwest, that competing in the territory of another ILEC "'might be a good way to turn a quick dollar but that doesn't make it right.'"

The complaint couches its ultimate allegations this way:

> In the absence of any meaningful competition between the [ILECs] in one another's markets, and in light of the parallel course of conduct that each engaged in to prevent competition from CLECs within their respective local telephone and/or high speed internet services markets and the other facts and market circumstances alleged above, Plaintiffs allege upon information and belief that [the ILECs] have entered into a contract, combination or conspiracy to prevent competitive entry in their respective local telephone and/or high speed internet services markets and have agreed not to compete with one another and otherwise allocated customers and markets to one another.

The United States District Court for the Southern District of New York dismissed the complaint for failure to state a claim upon which relief can be granted. The District Court acknowledged that "plaintiffs may allege a conspiracy by citing instances of parallel business behavior that suggest an agreement," but emphasized that "while '[c]ircumstantial evidence of consciously parallel behavior may have made heavy inroads into the traditional judicial attitude toward conspiracy[, . . . ] "conscious parallelism" has not yet read conspiracy out of the Sherman Act entirely.'" 313 F. Supp. 2d 174, 179 (2003) (quoting Theatre Enterprises, Inc. v. Paramount Film Distributing Corp., 346 U.S. 537, 541 (1954)). Thus, the District Court understood that allegations of parallel business conduct, taken alone, do not state a claim under § 1; plaintiffs must allege additional facts that "ten[d] to exclude independent self-interested conduct as an explanation for defendants' parallel behavior." 313 F. Supp. 2d at 179. . . .

The Court of Appeals for the Second Circuit reversed, holding that the District Court tested the complaint by the wrong standard. . . . "[T]o rule that allegations of parallel anticompetitive conduct fail to support a plausible conspiracy claim, a court would have to conclude that there is no set of facts that would permit a plaintiff to demonstrate that the particular parallelism asserted was the product of collusion rather than coincidence." Id.

We granted certiorari to address the proper standard for pleading an antitrust conspiracy through allegations of parallel conduct and now reverse.

## II

### A

Because § 1 of the Sherman Act "does not prohibit [all] unreasonable restraints of trade . . . but only restraints effected by a contract, combination, or conspiracy," Copperweld Corp. v. Independence Tube Corp., 467 U.S. 752, 775 (1984), "[t]he crucial question" is whether the challenged anticompetitive conduct "stem[s] from independent decision or from an agreement, tacit or express," *Theatre Enterprises*, 346 U.S. at 540. While a showing of parallel "business behavior is admissible circumstantial evidence from which the fact finder may infer agreement," it falls short of "conclusively establish[ing] agreement or . . . itself constitut[ing] a Sherman Act offense." Id. at 540-541. Even "conscious parallelism," a common reaction of "firms in a concentrated market [that] recogniz[e] their shared economic interests and their interdependence with respect to price and output decisions" is "not in itself unlawful." Brooke Group Ltd. v. Brown & Williamson Tobacco Corp., 509 U.S. 209, 227 (1993); see 6 P. Areeda & H. Hovenkamp, Antitrust Law ¶ 1433a, p. 236 (2d ed. 2003) (hereinafter Areeda & Hovenkamp) ("The courts are nearly unanimous in saying that mere interdependent parallelism does not establish the contract, combination, or conspiracy required by Sherman Act § 1"). . . .

The inadequacy of showing parallel conduct or interdependence, without more, mirrors the ambiguity of the behavior: consistent with conspiracy, but just as much in line with a wide swath of rational and competitive business strategy unilaterally prompted by common perceptions of the market. Accordingly, we have previously hedged against false inferences from identical behavior at a number of points in the trial sequence. An antitrust conspiracy plaintiff with evidence showing nothing beyond parallel conduct is not entitled to a directed verdict; proof of a § 1 conspiracy must include evidence tending to exclude the possibility of independent action; and at the summary judgment stage a § 1 plaintiff's offer of conspiracy evidence must tend to rule out the possibility that the defendants were acting independently, see Matsushita Elec. Industrial Co. v. Zenith Radio Corp., 475 U.S. 574 (1986).

### B

This case presents the antecedent question of what a plaintiff must plead in order to state a claim under § 1 of the Sherman Act. Federal Rule of Civil Procedure 8(a)(2) requires only "a short and plain statement of the claim showing that the pleader is entitled to relief," in order to "give the defendant fair notice of what the . . . claim is and the grounds upon which it rests," Conley v. Gibson, 355 U.S. 41, 47 (1957). While a complaint attacked by a Rule 12(b)(6) motion to dismiss does not need detailed factual allegations, id., a plaintiff's obligation to provide the "grounds" of his "entitle[ment] to relief" requires more than labels and conclusions, and a formulaic recitation of the elements of a cause of action will not do. Factual allegations must be enough to raise a right to relief above the speculative level, see 5 C. Wright & A. Miller, Federal Practice and Procedure § 1216, pp. 235-236 (3d ed. 2004) ("[T]he pleading must contain something more . . . than . . . a statement of facts that merely creates a suspicion [of] a legally cognizable right of action"),[3] on the assumption that all the allegations in the complaint are true (even if doubtful in fact), see, e.g., Swierkiewicz v. Sorema N.A., 534 U.S. 506, 508, n.1 (2002); Neitzke v. Williams, 490 U.S. 319, 327 (1989) ("Rule 12(b)(6) does not countenance . . . dismissals based on a judge's disbelief of a complaint's factual allegations"); Scheuer v. Rhodes, 416 U.S. 232, 236 (1974) (a well-pleaded complaint may proceed even if it appears "that a recovery is very remote and unlikely").

In applying these general standards to a § 1 claim, we hold that stating such a claim requires a complaint with enough factual matter (taken as true) to suggest that an agreement was made. Asking for plausible grounds to infer an agreement does not impose a probability requirement at the pleading stage; it simply calls for enough fact to raise a reasonable expectation that discovery will reveal evidence of illegal agreement. And, of course, a well-pleaded complaint may proceed even if it strikes a savvy judge that actual proof of those facts is improbable, and "that a recovery is very remote and unlikely." Id. In identifying facts that are suggestive enough to render a § 1 conspiracy plausible, we have the benefit of the prior rulings and considered views of leading commentators, already quoted, that lawful parallel conduct fails to bespeak unlawful agreement. It makes sense to say, therefore, that an allegation of parallel conduct and a bare assertion of conspiracy will not suffice. Without more, parallel conduct does not suggest conspiracy, and a conclusory allegation of agreement at some unidentified point does not supply facts adequate to show illegality. Hence, when allegations of parallel conduct are set out in order to make

---

3. The dissent greatly oversimplifies matters by suggesting that the Federal Rules somehow dispensed with the pleading of facts altogether. See post, at 10 (opinion of Stevens, J.) (pleading standard of Federal Rules "does not require, or even invite, the pleading of facts").

While, for most types of cases, the Federal Rules eliminated the cumbersome requirement that a claimant "set out in detail the facts upon which he bases his claim," Conley v. Gibson, 355 U.S. 41, 47 (1957) (emphasis added), Rule 8(a)(2) still requires a "showing," rather than a blanket assertion, of entitlement to relief. Without some factual allegation in the complaint, it is hard to see how a claimant could satisfy the requirement of providing not only "fair notice" of the nature of the claim, but also "grounds" on which the claim rests. See 5 Wright & Miller § 1202, at 94, 95 (Rule 8(a) "contemplate[s] the statement of circumstances, occurrences, and events in support of the claim presented" and does not authorize a pleader's "bare averment that he wants relief and is entitled to it").

a § 1 claim, they must be placed in a context that raises a suggestion of a preceding agreement, not merely parallel conduct that could just as well be independent action.

The need at the pleading stage for allegations plausibly suggesting (not merely consistent with) agreement reflects the threshold requirement of Rule 8(a)(2) that the "plain statement" possess enough heft to "sho[w] that the pleader is entitled to relief." A statement of parallel conduct, even conduct consciously undertaken, needs some setting suggesting the agreement necessary to make out a § 1 claim; without that further circumstance pointing toward a meeting of the minds, an account of a defendant's commercial efforts stays in neutral territory. An allegation of parallel conduct is thus much like a naked assertion of conspiracy in a § 1 complaint: it gets the complaint close to stating a claim, but without some further factual enhancement it stops short of the line between possibility and plausibility of "entitle[ment] to relief."

We alluded to the practical significance of the Rule 8 entitlement requirement in Dura Pharmaceuticals, Inc. v. Broudo, 544 U.S. 336 (2005), when we explained that something beyond the mere possibility of loss causation must be alleged, lest a plaintiff with "'a largely groundless claim'" be allowed to "'take up the time of a number of other people, with the right to do so representing an *in terrorem* increment of the settlement value.'" Id. at 347 (quoting Blue Chip Stamps v. Manor Drug Stores, 421 U.S. 723, 741 (1975)). So, when the allegations in a complaint, however true, could not raise a claim of entitlement to relief, "'this basic deficiency should . . . be exposed at the point of minimum expenditure of time and money by the parties and the court.'" 5 Wright & Miller § 1216, at 233-234 (quoting Daves v. Hawaiian Dredging Co., 114 F. Supp. 643, 645 (D. Haw. 1953)); see also *Dura*, supra, at 346; Asahi Glass Co. v. Pentech Pharmaceuticals, Inc., 289 F. Supp. 2d 986, 995 (N.D. Ill. 2003) (Posner, J., sitting by designation) ("[S]ome threshold of plausibility must be crossed at the outset before a patent antitrust case should be permitted to go into its inevitably costly and protracted discovery phase").

Thus, it is one thing to be cautious before dismissing an antitrust complaint in advance of discovery, but quite another to forget that proceeding to antitrust discovery can be expensive. As we indicated over 20 years ago in Associated Gen. Contractors of Cal., Inc. v. Carpenters, 459 U.S. 519, 528, n.17 (1983), "a district court must retain the power to insist upon some specificity in pleading before allowing a potentially massive factual controversy to proceed." See also Car Carriers, Inc. v. Ford Motor Co., 745 F.2d 1101, 1106 (7th Cir. 1984) ("[T]he costs of modern federal antitrust litigation and the increasing caseload of the federal courts counsel against sending the parties into discovery when there is no reasonable likelihood that the plaintiffs can construct a claim from the events related in the complaint"); . . . Memorandum from Paul V. Niemeyer, Chair, Advisory Committee on Civil Rules, to Hon. Anthony J. Scirica, Chair, Committee on Rules of Practice and Procedure (May 11, 1999), 192 F.R.D. 354, 357 (2000) (reporting that discovery accounts for as much as 90 percent of litigation costs when discovery is actively employed). That potential expense is obvious enough in the present case: Plaintiffs represent a putative class of at least 90 percent of all subscribers to local telephone or high-speed Internet service in the continental United States, in an action against America's largest telecommunications firms (with many thousands of employees generating reams and gigabytes of business records) for unspecified (if any) instances of antitrust violations that allegedly occurred over a period of seven years.

It is no answer to say that a claim just shy of a plausible entitlement to relief can, if groundless, be weeded out early in the discovery process through "careful case management," post, given the common lament that the success of judicial supervision in checking discovery abuse has been on the modest side. See, e.g., Easterbrook, Discovery as Abuse, 69 B.U. L. Rev. 635, 638 (1989) ("Judges can do little about impositional discovery when parties control the legal claims to be presented and conduct the discovery themselves"). And it is self-evident that the problem of discovery abuse cannot be solved by "careful scrutiny of evidence at the summary judgment stage," much less "lucid instructions to juries," post; the threat of discovery expense will push cost-conscious defendants to settle even anemic cases before reaching those proceedings. Probably, then, it is only by taking care to require allegations that reach the level suggesting conspiracy that we can hope to avoid the potentially enormous expense of discovery in cases with no "'reasonably founded hope that the [discovery] process will reveal relevant evidence'" to support a § 1 claim. *Dura*, 544 U.S., at 347 (quoting *Blue Chip Stamps*, supra, at 741; alteration in *Dura*).[6]

---

6. The dissent takes heart in the reassurances of plaintiffs' counsel that discovery would be "phased" and "limited to the existence of the alleged conspiracy and class certification." Post. But determining whether some illegal agreement may have taken place between unspecified persons at different ILECs (each a multibillion dollar corporation with legions of management level employees) at some point over seven years is a sprawling, costly, and hugely time-consuming undertaking not easily susceptible to the kind of line drawing and case management that the dissent envisions. Perhaps the best answer to the dissent's optimism that antitrust discovery is open to effective judicial control is a more extensive quotation of the authority just cited, a judge with a background in antitrust law. Given the system that we have, the hope of effective judicial supervision is slim: "The timing is all wrong. The plaintiff files a sketchy complaint (the Rules of Civil Procedure discourage fulsome documents), and discovery is launched. A judicial officer does not know the details of the case the parties will present and in theory *cannot* know the details. Discovery is used to find the details. The judicial officer always knows less than the parties, and the parties themselves may not know very well where they are going or what they expect to find. A magistrate supervising discovery does not—cannot—know the expected productivity of a given request, because the nature of the requester's claim and the contents of the files (or head) of the adverse party are unknown. Judicial officers cannot measure the costs and benefits to the requester and so cannot isolate impositional requests. Requesters have no reason to disclose their own estimates because they gain from imposing costs on rivals (and may lose from an improvement in accuracy). The portions of the Rules of Civil Procedure calling on judges to trim back excessive demands, therefore, have been, and are doomed to be, hollow. We cannot prevent what we cannot detect; we cannot detect what we cannot define; we cannot define 'abusive' discovery except in theory, because in practice we lack essential information." Easterbrook, Discovery as Abuse, 69 B.U. L. Rev. 635, 638-639 (1989).

Plaintiffs do not, of course, dispute the requirement of plausibility and the need for something more than merely parallel behavior explained in *Theatre Enterprises, Monsanto,* and *Matsushita,* and their main argument against the plausibility standard at the pleading stage is its ostensible conflict with an early statement of ours construing Rule 8. Justice Black's opinion for the Court in Conley v. Gibson spoke not only of the need for fair notice of the grounds for entitlement to relief but of "the accepted rule that a complaint should not be dismissed for failure to state a claim unless it appears beyond doubt that the plaintiff can prove no set of facts in support of his claim which would entitle him to relief." 355 U.S. at 45-46. This "no set of facts" language can be read in isolation as saying that any statement revealing the theory of the claim will suffice unless its factual impossibility may be shown from the face of the pleadings; and the Court of Appeals appears to have read *Conley* in some such way when formulating its understanding of the proper pleading standard.

On such a focused and literal reading of *Conley's* "no set of facts," a wholly conclusory statement of claim would survive a motion to dismiss whenever the pleadings left open the possibility that a plaintiff might later establish some "set of [undisclosed] facts" to support recovery. So here, the Court of Appeals specifically found the prospect of unearthing direct evidence of conspiracy sufficient to preclude dismissal, even though the complaint does not set forth a single fact in a context that suggests an agreement. It seems fair to say that this approach to pleading would dispense with any showing of a "'reasonably founded hope'" that a plaintiff would be able to make a case, see *Dura,* 544 U.S. at 347 (quoting *Blue Chip Stamps,* 421 U.S. at 741); Mr. Micawber's optimism would be enough.*

Seeing this, a good many judges and commentators have balked at taking the literal terms of the *Conley* passage as a pleading standard. See, e.g., *Car Carriers,* 745 F.2d at 1106 ("*Conley* has never been interpreted literally" and, "[i]n practice, a complaint . . . must contain either direct or inferential allegations respecting all the material elements necessary to sustain recovery under *some* viable legal theory" (internal quotation marks omitted; emphasis and omission in original)); Ascon Properties, Inc. v. Mobil Oil Co., 866 F.2d 1149, 1155 (9th Cir. 1989) (tension between *Conley's* "no set of facts" language and its acknowledgment that a plaintiff must provide the "grounds" on which his claim rests); O'Brien v. DiGrazia, 544 F.2d 543, 546, n.3 (1st Cir. 1976) ("[W]hen a plaintiff . . . supplies facts to support his claim, we do not think that *Conley* imposes a duty on the courts to conjure up unpleaded facts that might turn a frivolous claim of unconstitutional . . . action into a substantial one"); Hazard, From Whom No Secrets Are Hid, 76 Tex. L. Rev. 1665, 1685 (1998) (describing *Conley* as having "turned Rule 8 on its head"); Marcus, The Revival of Fact Pleading Under the Federal Rules of Civil Procedure, 86 Colum. L. Rev. 433, 463-465 (1986) (noting tension between *Conley* and subsequent understandings of Rule 8).

* [A reference to a character in Charles Dickens's *David Copperfield*. — EDS.]

We could go on, but there is no need to pile up further citations to show that *Conley*'s "no set of facts" language has been questioned, criticized, and explained away long enough. To be fair to the *Conley* Court, the passage should be understood in light of the opinion's preceding summary of the complaint's concrete allegations, which the Court quite reasonably understood as amply stating a claim for relief. But the passage so often quoted fails to mention this understanding on the part of the Court, and after puzzling the profession for 50 years, this famous observation has earned its retirement. The phrase is best forgotten as an incomplete, negative gloss on an accepted pleading standard: once a claim has been stated adequately, it may be supported by showing any set of facts consistent with the allegations in the complaint. See *Sanjuan*, 40 F.3d at 251 (once a claim for relief has been stated, a plaintiff "receives the benefit of imagination, so long as the hypotheses are consistent with the complaint"); accord, *Swierkiewicz*, 534 U.S. at 514. *Conley*, then, described the breadth of opportunity to prove what an adequate complaint claims, not the minimum standard of adequate pleading to govern a complaint's survival.

## III

When we look for plausibility in this complaint, we agree with the District Court that plaintiffs' claim of conspiracy in restraint of trade comes up short. To begin with, the complaint leaves no doubt that plaintiffs rest their § 1 claim on descriptions of parallel conduct and not on any independent allegation of actual agreement among the ILECs. Supra. Although in form a few stray statements speak directly of agreement, on fair reading these are merely legal conclusions resting on the prior allegations. Thus, the complaint first takes account of the alleged "absence of any meaningful competition between [the ILECs] in one another's markets," "the parallel course of conduct that each [ILEC] engaged in to prevent competition from CLECs," "and the other facts and market circumstances alleged [earlier]"; "in light of" these, the complaint concludes "that [the ILECs] have entered into a contract, combination or conspiracy to prevent competitive entry into their . . . markets and have agreed not to compete with one another." Complaint ¶ 51.[10] The nub of the complaint, then, is the ILECs' parallel behavior, consisting of

10. If the complaint had not explained that the claim of agreement rested on the parallel conduct described, we doubt that the complaint's references to an agreement among the ILECs would have given the notice required by Rule 8. Apart from identifying a sevenyear span in which the § 1 violations were supposed to have occurred (i.e., "[b]eginning at least as early as February 6, 1996, and continuing to the present," id. ¶ 64), the pleadings mentioned no specific time, place, or person involved in the alleged conspiracies. This lack of notice contrasts sharply with the model form for pleading negligence, Form 9 [now Form 11 under the restyled Federal Rules], which the dissent says exemplifies the kind of "bare allegation" that survives a motion to dismiss. Post. Whereas the model form alleges that the defendant struck the plaintiff with his car while plaintiff was crossing a particular highway

steps to keep the CLECs out and manifest disinterest in becoming CLECs themselves, and its sufficiency turns on the suggestions raised by this conduct when viewed in light of common economic experience.

We think that nothing contained in the complaint invests either the action or inaction alleged with a plausible suggestion of conspiracy. As to the ILECs' supposed agreement to disobey the 1996 Act and thwart the CLECs' attempts to compete, we agree with the District Court that nothing in the complaint intimates that the resistance to the upstarts was anything more than the natural, unilateral reaction of each ILEC intent on keeping its regional dominance. The 1996 Act did more than just subject the ILECs to competition; it obliged them to subsidize their competitors with their own equipment at wholesale rates. The economic incentive to resist was powerful, but resisting competition is routine market conduct, and even if the ILECs flouted the 1996 Act in all the ways the plaintiffs allege, there is no reason to infer that the companies had agreed among themselves to do what was only natural anyway; so natural, in fact, that if alleging parallel decisions to resist competition were enough to imply an antitrust conspiracy, pleading a § 1 violation against almost any group of competing businesses would be a sure thing.

The complaint makes its closest pass at a predicate for conspiracy with the claim that collusion was necessary because success by even one CLEC in an ILEC's territory "would have revealed the degree to which competitive entry by CLECs would have been successful in the other territories." Id. ¶ 50. But, its logic aside, this general premise still fails to answer the point that there was just no need for joint encouragement to resist the 1996 Act; as the District Court said, "each ILEC has reason to want to avoid dealing with CLECs" and "each ILEC would attempt to keep CLECs out, regardless of the actions of the other ILECs." 313 F. Supp. 2d at 184.[12]

Plaintiffs' second conspiracy theory rests on the competitive reticence among the ILECs themselves in the wake of the 1996 Act, which was supposedly passed in the "'hop[e] that the large incumbent local monopoly companies . . . might attack their neighbors' service areas, as they are the best situated to do so.'" Complaint ¶ 38. Contrary to hope, the ILECs

---

at a specified date and time, the complaint here furnishes no clue as to which of the four ILECs (much less which of their employees) supposedly agreed, or when and where the illicit agreement took place. A defendant wishing to prepare an answer in the simple fact pattern laid out in Form 9 would know what to answer; a defendant seeking to respond to plaintiffs' conclusory allegations in the § 1 context would have little idea where to begin.

12. From the allegation that the ILECs belong to various trade associations, see Complaint ¶ 46, the dissent playfully suggests that they conspired to restrain trade, an inference said to be "buttressed by the common sense of Adam Smith." Post. If Adam Smith is peering down today, he may be surprised to learn that his tongue-in-cheek remark would be authority to force his famous pinmaker to devote financial and human capital to hire lawyers, prepare for depositions, and otherwise fend off allegations of conspiracy; all this just because he belonged to the same trade guild as one of his competitors when their pins carried the same price tag.

declined "'to enter each other's service territories in any significant way,'" Complaint ¶ 38, and the local telephone and high speed Internet market remains highly compartmentalized geographically, with minimal competition. Based on this state of affairs, and perceiving the ILECs to be blessed with "especially attractive business opportunities" in surrounding markets dominated by other ILECs, the plaintiffs assert that the ILECs' parallel conduct was "strongly suggestive of conspiracy." Id. ¶ 40.

But it was not suggestive of conspiracy, not if history teaches anything. In a traditionally unregulated industry with low barriers to entry, sparse competition among large firms dominating separate geographical segments of the market could very well signify illegal agreement, but here we have an obvious alternative explanation. In the decade preceding the 1996 Act and well before that, monopoly was the norm in telecommunications, not the exception. The ILECs were born in that world, doubtless liked the world the way it was, and surely knew the adage about him who lives by the sword. Hence, a natural explanation for the noncompetition alleged is that the former Government-sanctioned monopolists were sitting tight, expecting their neighbors to do the same thing.[13]

. . . We agree with the District Court's assessment that antitrust conspiracy was not suggested by the facts adduced under either theory of the complaint, which thus fails to state a valid § 1 claim.[14]

Plaintiffs say that our analysis runs counter to Swierkiewicz v. Sorema N.A., 534 U.S. 506, 508 (2002), which held that "a complaint in an employment discrimination lawsuit [need] not contain specific facts establishing a prima facie case of discrimination under the framework set forth in

---

13. The complaint quoted a reported statement of Qwest's CEO, Richard Notebaert, to suggest that the ILECs declined to compete against each other despite recognizing that it "'might be a good way to turn a quick dollar.'" ¶ 42 (quoting Chicago Tribune, Oct. 31, 2002, Business Section, p. 1). This was only part of what he reportedly said, however, and the District Court was entitled to take notice of the full contents of the published articles referenced in the complaint, from which the truncated quotations were drawn. See Fed. Rule Evid. 201. Notebaert was also quoted as saying that entering new markets as a CLEC would not be "a sustainable economic model" because the CLEC pricing model is "just . . . nuts." Chicago Tribune, Oct. 31, 2002, Business Section, p. 1 (cited at Complaint ¶ 42). Another source cited in the complaint quotes Notebaert as saying he thought it "unwise" to "base a business plan" on the privileges accorded to CLECs under the 1996 Act because the regulatory environment was too unstable. Chicago Tribune, Dec. 19, 2002, Business Section, p. 2 (cited at Complaint ¶ 45).

14. In reaching this conclusion, we do not apply any "heightened" pleading standard, nor do we seek to broaden the scope of Federal Rule of Civil Procedure 9, which can only be accomplished "'by the process of amending the Federal Rules, and not by judicial interpretation.'" Swierkiewicz v. Sorema N.A., 534 U.S. 506, 515 (2002) (quoting Leatherman v. Tarrant County Narcotics Intelligence and Coordination Unit, 507 U.S. 163, 168 (1993)). On certain subjects understood to raise a high risk of abusive litigation, a plaintiff must state factual allegations with greater particularity than Rule 8 requires. Fed. Rules Civ. Proc. 9(b)-(c). Here, our concern is not that the allegations in the complaint were insufficiently "particular[ized]", id.; rather, the complaint warranted dismissal because it failed *in toto* to render plaintiffs' entitlement to relief plausible.

McDonnell Douglas Corp. v. Green, 411 U.S. 792 (1973)." They argue that just as the prima facie case is a "flexible evidentiary standard" that "should not be transposed into a rigid pleading standard for discrimination cases," *Swierkiewicz*, supra, at 512, "transpos[ing] 'plus factor' summary judgment analysis woodenly into a rigid Rule 12(b)(6) pleading standard . . . would be unwise," Brief for Respondents 39. As the District Court correctly understood, however, "*Swierkiewicz* did not change the law of pleading, but simply re-emphasized . . . that the Second Circuit's use of a heightened pleading standard for Title VII cases was contrary to the Federal Rules' structure of liberal pleading requirements." 313 F. Supp. 2d at 181 (citation and footnote omitted). Even though *Swierkiewicz*'s pleadings "detailed the events leading to his termination, provided relevant dates, and included the ages and nationalities of at least some of the relevant persons involved with his termination," the Court of Appeals dismissed his complaint for failing to allege certain additional facts that Swierkiewicz would need at the trial stage to support his claim in the absence of direct evidence of discrimination. *Swierkiewicz*, 534 U.S. at 514. We reversed on the ground that the Court of Appeals had impermissibly applied what amounted to a heightened pleading requirement by insisting that Swierkiewicz allege "specific facts" beyond those necessary to state his claim and the grounds showing entitlement to relief. Id. at 508.

Here, in contrast, we do not require heightened fact pleading of specifics, but only enough facts to state a claim to relief that is plausible on its face. Because the plaintiffs here have not nudged their claims across the line from conceivable to plausible, their complaint must be dismissed.

The judgment of the Court of Appeals for the Second Circuit is reversed, and the cause is remanded for further proceedings consistent with this opinion.

*It is so ordered.*

JUSTICE STEVENS, with whom JUSTICE GINSBURG joins except as to Part IV, dissenting.

. . . [T]his is a case in which there is no dispute about the substantive law. If the defendants acted independently, their conduct was perfectly lawful. If, however, that conduct is the product of a horizontal agreement among potential competitors, it was unlawful. Plaintiffs have alleged such an agreement and, because the complaint was dismissed in advance of answer, the allegation has not even been denied. Why, then, does the case not proceed? Does a judicial opinion that the charge is not "plausible" provide a legally acceptable reason for dismissing the complaint? I think not.

Respondents' amended complaint describes a variety of circumstantial evidence and makes the straightforward allegation that petitioners

> "entered into a contract, combination or conspiracy to prevent competitive entry in their respective local telephone and/or high speed internet services markets and have agreed not to compete with one another and otherwise allocated customers and markets to one another." Complaint ¶ 51.

The complaint explains that, contrary to Congress' expectation when it enacted the 1996 Telecommunications Act, and consistent with their own economic self-interests, petitioner Incumbent Local Exchange Carriers (ILECs) have assiduously avoided infringing upon each other's markets and have refused to permit nonincumbent competitors to access their networks. The complaint quotes Richard Notebaert, the former CEO of one such ILEC, as saying that competing in a neighboring ILEC's territory "might be a good way to turn a quick dollar but that doesn't make it right." Id. ¶ 42. Moreover, respondents allege that petitioners "communicate amongst themselves" through numerous industry associations. Id. ¶ 46. In sum, respondents allege that petitioners entered into an agreement that has long been recognized as a classic *per se* violation of the Sherman Act.

Under rules of procedure that have been well settled since well before our decision in *Theatre Enterprises,* a judge ruling on a defendant's motion to dismiss a complaint, "must accept as true all of the factual allegations contained in the complaint." Swierkiewicz v. Sorema N.A., 534 U.S. 506, n.1 (2002). But instead of requiring knowledgeable executives such as Notebaert to respond to these allegations by way of sworn depositions or other limited discovery—and indeed without so much as requiring petitioners to file an answer denying that they entered into any agreement—the majority permits immediate dismissal based on the assurances of company lawyers that nothing untoward was afoot. The Court embraces the argument of those lawyers that "there is no reason to infer that the companies had agreed among themselves to do what was only natural anyway," ante; that "there was just no need for joint encouragement to resist the 1996 Act," ante; and that the "natural explanation for the noncompetition alleged is that the former Government-sanctioned monopolists were sitting tight, expecting their neighbors to do the same thing," ante.

The Court and petitioners' legal team are no doubt correct that the parallel conduct alleged is consistent with the absence of any contract, combination, or conspiracy. But that conduct is also entirely consistent with the *presence* of the illegal agreement alleged in the complaint. And the charge that petitioners "agreed not to compete with one another" is not just one of "a few stray statements," ante; it is an allegation describing unlawful conduct. As such, the Federal Rules of Civil Procedure, our longstanding precedent, and sound practice mandate that the District Court at least require some sort of response from petitioners before dismissing the case. . . .

## I

Rule 8(a)(2) of the Federal Rules requires that a complaint contain "a short and plain statement of the claim showing that the pleader is entitled to relief." The rule did not come about by happenstance and its language is not inadvertent. The English experience with Byzantine special pleading rules—illustrated by the hypertechnical Hilary rules of 1834—made obvious the appeal of a pleading standard that was easy for the common litigant to understand and sufficed to put the defendant on notice as to the nature of the claim against him and the relief sought. Stateside, David Dudley Field developed the highly influential New York Code of 1848, which required "[a] statement of the facts constituting the cause of action, in ordinary and concise language, without repetition, and in such a manner as to enable a person of common understanding to know what is intended." An Act to Simplify and Abridge the Practice, Pleadings and Proceedings of the Courts of this State, ch. 379, § 120(2), 1848 N.Y. Laws pp. 497, 521. Substantially similar language appeared in the Federal Equity Rules adopted in 1912. See Fed. Equity Rule 25 (requiring "a short and simple statement of the ultimate facts upon which the plaintiff asks relief, omitting any mere statement of evidence").

A difficulty arose, however, in that the Field Code and its progeny required a plaintiff to plead "facts" rather than "conclusions," a distinction that proved far easier to say than to apply. As commentators have noted,

> "it is virtually impossible logically to distinguish among 'ultimate facts,' 'evidence,' and 'conclusions.' Essentially any allegation in a pleading must be an assertion that certain occurrences took place. The pleading spectrum, passing from evidence through ultimate facts to conclusions, is largely a continuum varying only in the degree of particularity with which the occurrences are described." Weinstein & Distler, Comments on Procedural Reform: Drafting Pleading Rules, 57 Colum. L. Rev. 518, 520-521 (1957).

See also Cook, Statements of Fact in Pleading Under the Codes, 21 Colum. L. Rev. 416, 417 (1921) (hereinafter Cook) ("[T]here is no logical distinction between statements which are grouped by the courts under the phrases 'statements of fact' and 'conclusions of law'"). Rule 8 was directly responsive to this difficulty. Its drafters intentionally avoided any reference to "facts" or "evidence" or "conclusions." . . .

Under the relaxed pleading standards of the Federal Rules, the idea was not to keep litigants out of court but rather to keep them in. The merits of a claim would be sorted out during a flexible pretrial process and, as appropriate, through the crucible of trial. See *Swierkiewicz*, 534 U.S. at 514 ("The liberal notice pleading of Rule 8(a) is the starting point of a simplified pleading system, which was adopted to focus litigation on the merits of a claim"). Charles E. Clark, the "principal draftsman" of the Federal Rules, put it thus:

> "Experience has shown . . . that we cannot expect the proof of the case to be made through the pleadings, and that such proof is really not their function. We can expect a general statement distinguishing the case from all others, so that the manner and form of trial and remedy expected are clear, and so that a permanent judgment will result." The New Federal Rules of Civil Procedure: The Last Phase—Underlying Philosophy Embodied in Some of the Basic Provisions of the New Procedure, 23 A.B.A. J. 976, 977 (1937) (hereinafter Clark, New Federal Rules).

The pleading paradigm under the new Federal Rules was well illustrated by the inclusion in the appendix of Form 9, a complaint for negligence. As relevant, the Form 9 complaint states only: "On June 1, 1936, in a public highway called Boylston Street in Boston, Massachusetts, defendant negligently drove a motor vehicle against plaintiff who was then crossing said highway." Form 9, Complaint for Negligence, Forms App., Fed. Rules Civ. Proc., 28 U.S.C. App., p. 829 (hereinafter Form 9). The complaint then describes the plaintiff's injuries and demands judgment. The asserted ground for relief—namely, the defendant's negligent driving—would have been called a "'conclusion of law'" under the code pleading of old. See, e.g., Cook 419. But that bare allegation suffices under a system that "restrict[s] the pleadings to the task of general notice-giving and invest[s] the deposition-discovery process with a vital role in the preparation for trial." Hickman v. Taylor, 329 U.S. 495, 501 (1947); see also *Swierkiewicz*, 534 U.S. at 513, n.4 (citing Form 9 as an example of "'the simplicity and brevity of statement which the rules contemplate'"); Thomson v. Washington, 362 F.3d 969, 970 (7th Cir. 2004) (Posner, J.) ("The federal rules replaced fact pleading with notice pleading").

## II

. . . If *Conley*'s "no set of facts" language is to be interred, let it not be without a eulogy. That exact language, which the majority says has "puzzl[ed] the profession for 50 years," ibid., has been cited as authority in a dozen opinions of this Court and four separate writings. In not one of those 16 opinions was the language "questioned," "criticized," or "explained away." Indeed, today's opinion is the first by any Member of this Court to express *any* doubt as to the adequacy of the *Conley* formulation. Taking their cues from the federal courts, 26 States and the District of Columbia utilize as their standard for dismissal of a complaint the very language the majority repudiates: whether it appears "beyond doubt" that "no set of facts" in support of the claim would entitle the plaintiff to relief.[5]

---

5. See, e.g., EB Invs., LLC v. Atlantis Development, Inc., 930 So. 2d 502, 507 (Ala. 2005); Department of Health & Social Servs. v. Native Village of Curyung, 151 P.3d 388, 396 (Alaska 2006); Newman v. Maricopa Cty., 167 Ariz. 501, 503, 808 P.2d 1253, 1255 (App. 1991); Public Serv. Co. of Colo. v. Van Wyk, 27 P.3d 377, 385-386 (Colo. 2001) (en banc); Clawson v. St. Louis Post-Dispatch, LLC, 906 A.2d 308, 312 (D.C. 2006); Hillman Constr. Corp. v. Wainer, 636 So. 2d 576, 578 (Fla. App. 1994); Kaplan v. Kaplan, 266 Ga. 612, 613, 469 S.E.2d 198, 199 (1996); Wright v. Home Depot U.S.A., 111 Haw. 401, 406, 142 P.3d 265, 270 (2006); Taylor v. Maile, 142 Idaho 253, 257, 127 P.3d 156, 160 (2005); Fink v. Bryant, 2001-CC-0987, p. 4 (La. 11/28/01), 801 So. 2d 346, 349; Gagne v. Cianbro Corp., 431 A.2d 1313, 1318-1319 (Me. 1981); Gasior v. Massachusetts Gen. Hospital, 446 Mass. 645, 647, 846 N.E.2d 1133, 1135 (2006); Ralph Walker, Inc. v. Gallagher, 926 So. 2d 890, 893 (Miss. 2006); Jones v. Montana Univ. System, 337 Mont. 1, 7, 155 P.3d 1247, 1254 (2007); Johnston v. Nebraska Dept. of Correctional Servs., 270 Neb. 987, 989, 709 N.W.2d 321, 324 (2006); Blackjack Bonding v. Las Vegas Munic. Ct., 116

. . . I would not rewrite the Nation's civil procedure textbooks and call into doubt the pleading rules of most of its States without far more informed deliberation as to the costs of doing so. Congress has established a process—a rulemaking process—for revisions of that order. See 28 U.S.C. §§ 2072-2074.

Today's majority calls *Conley's* "'no set of facts'" language "an incomplete, negative gloss on an accepted pleading standard: once a claim has been stated adequately, it may be supported by showing any set of facts consistent with the allegations in the complaint." Ante. This is not and cannot be what the *Conley* Court meant. First, as I have explained, and as the *Conley* Court well knew, the pleading standard the Federal Rules meant to codify does not require, or even invite, the pleading of facts. . . . Second, it is pellucidly clear that the *Conley* Court was interested in what a complaint *must* contain, not what it *may* contain. In fact, the Court said without qualification that it was "appraising the *sufficiency* of the complaint." 355 U.S. at 45 (emphasis added). It was, to paraphrase today's majority, describing "the minimum standard of adequate pleading to govern a complaint's survival," ante.

---

Nev. 1213, 1217, 14 P.3d 1275, 1278 (2000); Shepard v. Ocwen Fed. Bank, 361 N.C. 137, 139, 638 S.E.2d 197, 199 (2006); Rose v. United Equitable Ins. Co., 2001 ND 154, ¶ 10, 632 N.W.2d 429, 434; State ex rel. Turner v. Houk, 112 Ohio St. 3d 561, 562, 2007-Ohio-814, ¶ 5, 862 N.E.2d 104, 105 (per curiam); Moneypenney v. Dawson, 2006 OK 53, ¶ 2, 141 P.3d 549, 551; Gagnon v. State, 570 A.2d 656, 659 (R.I. 1990); Osloond v. Farrier, 2003 SD 28, ¶ 4, 659 N.W.2d 20, 22 (per curiam); Smith v. Lincoln Brass Works, Inc., 712 S.W.2d 470, 471 (Tenn. 1986); Association of Haystack Property Owners v. Sprague, 145 Vt. 443, 446, 494 A.2d 122, 124 (1985); In re Coday, 156 Wash. 2d 485, 497, 130 P.3d 809, 815 (2006) (en banc); Haines v. Hampshire Cty. Comm'n, 216 W. Va. 499, 502, 607 S.E.2d 828, 831 (2004); Warren v. Hart, 747 P.2d 511, 512 (Wyo. 1987); see also Malpiede v. Townson, 780 A.2d 1075, 1082-1083 (Del. 2001) (permitting dismissal only "where the court determines with reasonable certainty that the plaintiff could prevail on no set of facts that may be inferred from the well-pleaded allegations in the complaint" (internal quotation marks omitted)); Canel v. Topinka, 212 Ill. 2d 311, 318, 818 N.E.2d 311, 317 (2004) (replacing "appears beyond doubt" in the *Conley* formulation with "is clearly apparent"); In re Young, 522 N.E.2d 386, 388 (Ind. 1988) (per curiam) (replacing "appears beyond doubt" with "appears to a certainty"); Barkema v. Williams Pipeline Co., 666 N.W.2d 612, 614 (Iowa 2003) (holding that a motion to dismiss should be sustained "only when there exists no conceivable set of facts entitling the non-moving party to relief"); Pioneer Village v. Bullitt Cty., 104 S.W.3d 757, 759 (Ky. 2003) (holding that judgment on the pleadings should be granted "if it appears beyond doubt that the nonmoving party cannot prove any set of facts that would entitle him/her to relief"); Corley v. Detroit Bd. of Ed., 470 Mich. 274, 277, 681 N.W.2d 342, 345 (2004) (per curiam) (holding that a motion for judgment on the pleadings should be granted only "'if no factual development could possibly justify recovery'"); Oberkramer v. Ellisville, 706 S.W.2d 440, 441 (Mo. 1986) (en banc) (omitting the words "beyond doubt" from the *Conley* formulation); Colman v. Utah State Land Bd., 795 P.2d 622, 624 (Utah 1990) (holding that a motion to dismiss is appropriate "only if it clearly appears that [the plaintiff] can prove no set of facts in support of his claim"); NRC Management Servs. Corp. v. First Va. Bank-Southwest, 63 Va. Cir. 68, 70 (2003) ("The Virginia standard is identical [to the *Conley* formulation], though the Supreme Court of Virginia may not have used the same words to describe it").

We can be triply sure as to *Conley's* meaning by examining the three Court of Appeals cases the *Conley* Court cited as support for the "accepted rule." . . . 355 U.S. at 45-46. In the first case, Leimer v. State Mut. Life Assur. Co. of Worcester, Mass., 108 F.2d 302 (8th Cir. 1940), the plaintiff alleged that she was the beneficiary of a life insurance plan and that the insurance company was wrongfully withholding proceeds from her. In reversing the District Court's grant of the defendant's motion to dismiss, the Eighth Circuit noted that court's own longstanding rule that, to warrant dismissal, "'it should appear from the allegations that a cause of action does not exist, rather than that a cause of action has been defectively stated.'" Id. at 305 (quoting Winget v. Rockwood, 69 F.2d 326, 329 (8th Cir. 1934).

The *Leimer* court viewed the Federal Rules—specifically Rules 8(a)(2), 12(b)(6), 12(e) (motion for a more definite statement), and 56 (motion for summary judgment)—as reinforcing the notion that "there is no justification for dismissing a complaint for insufficiency of statement, except where it appears to a certainty that the plaintiff would be entitled to no relief under any state of facts which could be proved in support of the claim." 108 F.2d at 306. The court refuted in the strongest terms any suggestion that the unlikelihood of recovery should determine the fate of a complaint: "No matter how improbable it may be that she can prove her claim, she is entitled to an opportunity to make the attempt, and is not required to accept as final a determination of her rights based upon inferences drawn in favor of the defendant from her amended complaint." Ibid.

The Third Circuit relied on *Leimer's* admonition in Continental Collieries, Inc. v. Shober, 130 F.2d 631 (1942), which the *Conley* Court also cited in support of its "no set of facts" formulation. In a diversity action the plaintiff alleged breach of contract, but the District Court dismissed the complaint on the ground that the contract appeared to be unenforceable under state law. The Court of Appeals reversed, concluding that there were facts in dispute that went to the enforceability of the contract, and that the rule at the pleading stage was as in *Leimer*: "No matter how likely it may seem that the pleader will be unable to prove his case, he is entitled, upon averring a claim, to an opportunity to try to prove it." 130 F.2d at 635.

The third case the *Conley* Court cited approvingly was written by Judge Clark himself. In Dioguardi v. Durning, 139 F.2d 774 (2d Cir. 1944), the *pro se* plaintiff, an importer of "tonics," charged the customs inspector with auctioning off the plaintiff's former merchandise for less than was bid for it . . . and complained that two cases of tonics went missing three weeks before the sale. The inference, hinted at by the averments but never stated in so many words, was that the defendant fraudulently denied the plaintiff his rightful claim to the tonics, which, if true, would have violated federal law. Writing six years after the adoption of the Federal Rules he held the lead rein in drafting, Judge Clark said that the defendant

> "could have disclosed the facts from his point of view, in advance of a trial
> if he chose, by asking for a pre-trial hearing or by moving for a summary
> judgment with supporting affidavits. But, as it stands, we do not see how the

plaintiff may properly be deprived of his day in court to show what he obviously so firmly believes and what for present purposes defendant must be taken as admitting." Id. at 775.

. . . Judge Clark's opinion disquieted the defense bar and gave rise to a movement to revise Rule 8 to require a plaintiff to plead a "'cause of action.'" See 5 Wright & Miller § 1201, at 86-87. The movement failed; *Dioguardi* was explicitly approved in *Conley*; and "[i]n retrospect the case itself seems to be a routine application of principles that are universally accepted," 5 Wright & Miller § 1220, at 284-285.

In light of *Leimer, Continental Collieries*, and *Dioguardi, Conley's* statement that a complaint is not to be dismissed unless "no set of facts" in support thereof would entitle the plaintiff to relief is hardly "puzzling." It reflects a philosophy that, unlike in the days of code pleading, separating the wheat from the chaff is a task assigned to the pretrial and trial process. *Conley's* language, in short, captures the policy choice embodied in the Federal Rules and binding on the federal courts.

We have consistently reaffirmed that basic understanding of the Federal Rules in the half century since *Conley*. For example, in *Scheuer v. Rhodes*, 416 U.S. 232 (1974), we reversed the Court of Appeals' dismissal on the pleadings when the respondents, the Governor and other officials of the State of Ohio, argued that petitioners' claims were barred by sovereign immunity. In a unanimous opinion by then-Justice Rehnquist, we emphasized that

"[w]hen a federal court reviews the sufficiency of a complaint, before the reception of any evidence either by affidavit or admissions, its task is necessarily a limited one. The issue is not whether a plaintiff will ultimately prevail but whether the claimant is entitled to offer evidence to support the claims. *Indeed it may appear on the face of the pleadings that a recovery is very remote and unlikely but that is not the test."* Id. at 236 (emphasis added).

The *Rhodes* plaintiffs had "alleged generally and in conclusory terms" that the defendants, by calling out the National Guard to suppress the Kent State University student protests, "were guilty of wanton, willful and negligent conduct." Krause v. Rhodes, 471 F.2d 430, 433 (6th Cir. 1972) . . .

We again spoke with one voice against efforts to expand pleading requirements beyond their appointed limits in Leatherman v. Tarrant County Narcotics Intelligence and Coordination Unit, 507 U.S. 163 (1993). Writing for the unanimous Court, Chief Justice Rehnquist rebuffed the Fifth Circuit's effort to craft a standard for pleading municipal liability that accounted for "the enormous expense involved today in litigation," Leatherman v. Tarrant Cty. Narcotics Intelligence and Coordination Unit, 954 F.2d 1054, 1057 (1992) (internal quotation marks omitted), by requiring a plaintiff to "state with factual detail and particularity the basis for the claim which necessarily includes why the defendant-official cannot successfully maintain the defense of immunity." *Leatherman*, 507 U.S. at 167 (internal quotation marks omitted). We found this language inconsistent with Rules 8(a)(2) and 9(b) and emphasized that motions to dismiss were not the place to combat discovery abuse: "In the absence of [an amendment to Rule 9(b)], federal courts and litigants must rely on summary judgment and control of discovery to weed out unmeritorious claims sooner rather than later." Id. at 168-169.

Most recently, in *Swierkiewicz*, 534 U.S. 506, we were faced with a case more similar to the present one than the majority will allow. In discrimination cases, our precedents require a plaintiff at the summary judgment stage to produce either direct evidence of discrimination or, if the claim is based primarily on circumstantial evidence, to meet the shifting evidentiary burdens imposed under the framework articulated in *McDonnell Douglas Corp. v. Green*, 411 U.S. 792 (1973). Swierkiewicz alleged that he had been terminated on account of national origin in violation of Title VII of the Civil Rights Act of 1964. The Second Circuit dismissed the suit on the pleadings because he had not pleaded a prima facie case of discrimination under the *McDonnell Douglas* standard.

We reversed in another unanimous opinion, holding that "under a notice pleading system, it is not appropriate to require a plaintiff to plead facts establishing a prima facie case because the *McDonnell Douglas* framework does not apply in every employment discrimination case." *Swierkiewicz*, 534 U.S. at 511. We also observed that Rule 8(a)(2) does not contemplate a court's passing on the merits of a litigant's claim at the pleading stage. Rather, the "simplified notice pleading standard" of the Federal Rules "relies on liberal discovery rules and summary judgment motions to define disputed facts and issues and to dispose of unmeritorious claims." Id. at 512. . . .

As in the discrimination context, we have developed an evidentiary framework for evaluating claims under § 1 of the Sherman Act when those claims rest on entirely circumstantial evidence of conspiracy. See Matsushita Elec. Industrial Co. v. Zenith Radio Corp., 475 U.S. 574 (1986). Under *Matsushita*, a plaintiff's allegations of an illegal conspiracy may not, at the summary judgment stage, rest solely on the inferences that may be drawn from the parallel conduct of the defendants. In order to survive a Rule 56 motion, a § 1 plaintiff "must present evidence 'that tends to exclude the possibility' that the alleged conspirators acted independently." Id. at 588 (quoting Monsanto Co. v. Spray-Rite Service Corp., 465 U.S. 752, 764 (1984)). That is, the plaintiff "must show that the inference of conspiracy is reasonable in light of the competing inferences of independent action or collusive action." 475 U.S. at 588.

Everything today's majority says would therefore make perfect sense if it were ruling on a Rule 56 motion for summary judgment and the evidence included nothing more than the Court has described. But it should go without saying in the wake of *Swierkiewicz* that a heightened production burden at the summary judgment stage does not translate into a heightened pleading burden at the complaint stage. The majority rejects the complaint in this case because—in light of the fact that the parallel conduct alleged is consistent with ordinary market behavior—the claimed conspiracy is "conceivable" but not "plausible." I have my doubts about the majority's assessment of the plausibility of this alleged conspiracy. But even if the majority's speculation is correct, its "plausibility" standard is irreconcilable with Rule 8 and with our governing precedents. . . .

The same year we decided *Conley*, Judge Clark wrote, presciently,

> "I fear that every age must learn its lesson that special pleading cannot be made to do the service of trial and that live issues between active litigants are not to be disposed of or evaded on the paper pleadings, i.e., the formalistic claims of the parties. Experience has found no quick and easy short cut for trials in cases generally *and antitrust cases in particular*." Special Pleading in the "Big Case," in Procedure—The Handmaid of Justice 147, 148 (C. Wright & H. Reasoner eds., 1965) (hereinafter Clark, Special Pleading in the Big Case) (emphasis added).

In this "Big Case," the Court succumbs to the temptation that previous Courts have steadfastly resisted. While the majority assures us that it is not applying any "'heightened'" pleading standard, see ante, n.14, I shall now explain why I have a difficult time understanding its opinion any other way.

## III

The Court does not suggest that an agreement to do what the plaintiffs allege would be permissible under the antitrust laws. Nor does the Court hold that these plaintiffs have failed to allege an injury entitling them to sue for damages under those laws. Rather, the theory on which the Court permits dismissal is that, so far as the Federal Rules are concerned, no agreement has been alleged at all. This is a mind-boggling conclusion.

As the Court explains, prior to the enactment of the Telecommunications Act of 1996 the law prohibited the defendants from competing with each other. The new statute was enacted to replace a monopolistic market with a competitive one. The Act did not merely require the regional monopolists to take affirmative steps to facilitate entry to new competitors; it also permitted the existing firms to compete with each other and to expand their operations into previously forbidden territory. See 47 U.S.C. § 271. Each of the defendants decided not to take the latter step. That was obviously an extremely important business decision, and I am willing to presume that each company acted entirely independently in reaching that decision. I am even willing to entertain the majority's belief that any agreement among the companies was unlikely. But the plaintiffs allege in three places in their complaint, ¶¶ 4, 51, 64, that the ILECs did in fact agree both to prevent competitors from entering into their local markets and to forgo competition with each other. And as the Court recognizes, at the motion to dismiss stage, a judge assumes "that all the allegations in the complaint are true (even if doubtful in fact)."

The majority circumvents this obvious obstacle to dismissal by pretending that it does not exist. The Court admits that "in form a few stray statements in the complaint speak directly of agreement," but disregards those allegations by saying that "on fair reading these are merely legal conclusions resting on the prior allegations" of parallel conduct. The Court's dichotomy between factual allegations and "legal conclusions" is the stuff of a bygone era. That distinction was a defining feature of code pleading, see generally Clark, The Complaint in Code Pleading, 35 Yale L.J. 259 (1925-1926), but was conspicuously abolished when the Federal Rules were enacted in 1938. . . .[9]

Even if I were inclined to accept the Court's anachronistic dichotomy and ignore the complaint's actual allegations, I would dispute the Court's suggestion that any inference of agreement from petitioners' parallel conduct is "implausible." Many years ago a truly great economist perceptively observed that "[p]eople of the same trade seldom meet together, even for merriment and diversion, but the conversation ends in a conspiracy against the public, or in some contrivance to raise prices." A. Smith, An Inquiry into the Nature and Causes of the Wealth of Nations, in 39 Great Books of the Western World 55 (R. Hutchins & M. Adler eds., 1952). I am not so cynical as to accept that sentiment at face value, but I need not do so here. Respondents' complaint points not only to petitioners' numerous opportunities to meet with each other, Complaint ¶ 46, but also to Notebaert's curious statement that encroaching on a fellow incumbent's territory "might be a good way to turn a quick dollar but that doesn't make it right," id. ¶ 42. What did he mean by that? One possible (indeed plausible) inference is that he meant that while it would be in his company's economic self-interest to compete with its brethren, he had agreed with his competitors not to do so. According to the complaint, that is how the Illinois Coalition for Competitive Telecom construed Notebaert's statement, id. ¶ 44, and that is how Members of Congress construed his company's behavior, id. ¶ 45.

Perhaps Notebaert meant instead that competition would be sensible in the short term but not in the long run. That's what his lawyers tell us anyway. But I would think that no one would know better what Notebaert meant than Notebaert himself. Instead of permitting respondents to ask Notebaert, however, the Court looks to other quotes from that and other articles and decides that what he meant was that entering new markets as a CLEC would not be a "'sustainable economic model.'" . . . But . . . the District Court was required at this stage of the proceedings to construe Notebaert's ambiguous statement in the plaintiffs' favor. The inference the statement supports—that simultaneous decisions by ILECs not even to attempt to poach customers from one another once the law authorized them to do so were the product of an agreement—sits comfortably within the realm of possibility. That is all the Rules require. . . .

---

9. The Court suggests that the allegation of an agreement, even if credited, might not give the notice required by Rule 8 because it lacks specificity. The remedy for an allegation lacking sufficient specificity to provide adequate notice is, of course, a Rule 12(e) motion for a more definite statement. See Swierkiewicz v. Sorema N.A., 534 U.S. 506, 514 (2002).

Respondents in this case proposed a plan of "'phased discovery'" limited to the existence of the alleged conspiracy and class certification. . . . Given the charge in the complaint—buttressed by the common sense of Adam Smith—I cannot say that the possibility that joint discussions and perhaps some agreements played a role in petitioners' decisionmaking process is so implausible that dismissing the complaint before any defendant has denied the charge is preferable to granting respondents even a minimal opportunity to prove their claims. See Clark, New Federal Rules 977 ("[T]hrough the weapons of discovery and summary judgment we have developed new devices, with more appropriate penalties to aid in matters of *proof,* and do not need to force the pleadings to their less appropriate function").[13]

I fear that the unfortunate result of the majority's new pleading rule will be to invite lawyers' debates over economic theory to conclusively resolve antitrust suits in the absence of any evidence. It is no surprise that the antitrust defense bar—among whom "lament" as to inadequate judicial supervision of discovery is most "common," see ante—should lobby for this state of affairs. But "we must recall that their primary responsibility is to win cases for their clients, not to improve law administration for the public." Clark, Special Pleading in the Big Case 152. As we did in our prior decisions, we should have instructed them that their remedy was to seek to amend the Federal Rules—not our interpretation of them. See *Swierkiewicz,* 534 U.S. at 515.

## IV

Just a few weeks ago some of my colleagues explained that a strict interpretation of the literal text of statutory language is essential to avoid judicial decisions that are not faithful to the intent of Congress. Zuni Public School Dist. No. 89 v. Department of Education, 127 S. Ct. 1534 (2007) (Scalia, J., dissenting). I happen to believe that there are cases in which other tools of construction are more reliable than text, but I agree of course

---

13. The potential for "sprawling, costly, and hugely time-consuming" discovery, ante, at 13, n.6, is no reason to throw the baby out with the bathwater. The Court vastly underestimates a district court's case-management arsenal. Before discovery even begins, the court may grant a defendant's Rule 12(e) motion; Rule 7(a) permits a trial court to order a plaintiff to reply to a defendant's answer; and Rule 23 requires "rigorous analysis" to ensure that class certification is appropriate, General Telephone Co. of Southwest v. Falcon, 457 U.S. 147, 160 (1982). Rule 16 invests a trial judge with the power, backed by sanctions, to regulate pretrial proceedings via conferences and scheduling orders . . . . Subsequently, Rule 26 confers broad discretion to control [discovery]. Indeed, Rule 26(c) specifically permits a court to take actions "to protect a party or person from annoyance, embarrassment, oppression, or undue burden or expense" by, for example, disallowing a particular discovery request, setting appropriate terms and conditions, or limiting its scope. . . . And should it become apparent over the course of litigation that a plaintiff's filings bespeak an *in terrorem suit,* the district court has at its call its own *in terrorem* device, in the form of a wide array of Rule 11 sanctions. . . .

that congressional intent should guide us in matters of statutory inter-pretation. Id. at 1534 (Stevens, J., concurring). This is a case in which the intentions of the drafters of three important sources of law—the Sherman Act, the Telecommunications Act of 1996, and the Federal Rules of Civil Procedure—all point unmistakably in the same direction, yet the Court marches resolutely the other way. . . .

The transparent policy concern that drives the decision is the interest in protecting antitrust defendants—who in this case are some of the wealthi-est corporations in our economy—from the burdens of pretrial discovery. Even if it were not apparent that the legal fees petitioners have incurred in arguing the merits of their Rule 12(b) motion have far exceeded the cost of limited discovery, or that those discovery costs would burden respon-dents as well as petitioners, that concern would not provide an adequate justification for this law-changing decision. For in the final analysis it is only a lack of confidence in the ability of trial judges to control discovery, buttressed by appellate judges' independent appraisal of the plausibility of profoundly serious factual allegations, that could account for this stark break from precedent. . . .

Accordingly, I respectfully dissent.

## Notes and Questions

1. Does *Twombly* in effect overrule *Conley*? The Court said it was merely clarifying the meaning of a sentence—though the sentence it "clarifies" is the centerpiece of the Rule 8 pleading regime *Conley* endorsed. In June 2007, when *Twombly* was decided, *Conley* had been cited 78,133 times by courts and commentators. The Court gave short shrift to the history of *Conley* and to the fact that it settled for 50 years an intense debate in American proce-dure about what due process requires of pleading. For an article predicting the erosion of the *Conley* standard, see Richard L. Marcus, The Revival of Fact Pleading Under the Federal Rules of Civil Procedure, 86 Colum. L. Rev. 433 (1986).

2. At least in cases where the plaintiff is not represented by counsel, *Twombly* appears not to demand more than notice pleading. In Erickson v. Pardus, 551 U.S. 89 (2007), issued just a few weeks after the decision in *Twombly*, the Court reversed the dismissal of a suit filed by a Colorado prisoner against prison officials alleging wrongful termination of medical treatment for hepatitis C. Erikson's complaint stated only that prison offi-cials had wrongly terminated his hepatitis treatment for at least 18 months based on an erroneous belief that plaintiff was using drugs. The district court dismissed his complaint, and the Tenth Circuit affirmed, holding that Erickson's complaint was merely "conclusory." Id. at 89. The Supreme Court reversed, stating that the Tenth Circuit's holding "departs in [a] stark . . . manner from the pleading standard mandated by the Federal Rules of Civil Procedure." Id. The Court cited *Twombly* only once, for the proposition that a complaint need only "give the defendant fair notice of what the . . . claim

is and the grounds upon which it rests." Id. at 93. *Twombly*'s "plausibility" language was entirely absent and the Court emphasized that the Tenth Circuit's "departure from the liberal pleading standards set forth by Rule 8(a)(2) is even more pronounced in this particular case because petitioner has been proceeding, from the litigation's outset, *without counsel.*" Id. at 94 (emphasis added).

3. But in cases where the plaintiff is represented, *Twombly* surely requires more than notice pleading in the sense *Conley* approved. In *Twombly* the Court declares that that *Conley*'s "no set of facts" formulation "is best forgotten as an incomplete, negative gloss on an accepted pleading standard." How must an ordinary tort victim now plead her case to show that it is "plausible"? Can she still simply state the "who, what, where, and when" of the accident? Can she state the facts of the accident and assert that the defendant was "negligent," or is that a mere conclusion unsupported by any facts?

The *Twombly* majority refers to Form 11 for pleading simple negligence. However, after amendments by the Advisory Committee, effective December 1, 2015, Form 11, along with Rule 84 and all the other forms except Forms 5 and 6, was *abrogated*. The Committee determined that the forms were not frequently used or particularly helpful to litigants:

> Many of the forms are out of date. The sample complaints, for example, embrace far fewer causes of action than now exist in federal court and illustrate a simplicity of pleading that has not been used in many years. The increased use of Rule 12(b)(6) motions to dismiss, the enhanced pleading requirements of Rule 9 and some federal statutes, the proliferation of statutory and other causes of action, and the increased complexity of most modern cases have resulted in a detailed level of pleading that is far beyond that illustrated in the forms. . . .
>
> In addition to being out of date and difficult to amend, the Committee's perception was that the forms are rarely used. . . . Many alternative sources of civil forms are available. These include forms created by private publishing companies and a set of non-pleading forms created and maintained by a Forms Working Group at the Administrative Office of the United States Courts ("AO"). . . .
>
> A May 2012 survey of the websites maintained by the 94 federal district courts around the country found that 88 of the 94 either link electronically to the AO forms or post some of the AO forms on their websites. . . . The Subcommittee ultimately recommended that the Committee get out of the forms business. . . .

Summary of the Report of the Judicial Conference, Committee on Rules of Practice and Procedure, September 2014, B-19.

4. What about the plaintiffs in *American Nurses, discussed in the notes before Twombly*—would their case survive a Rule 12(b)(6) motion under the interpretation of *Conley* given in *Twombly*? The issue Judge Posner spent so much time wrestling with—whether failure to respond to a comparable worth study revealing significant, gender-based pay disparities supports

an inference of discrimination—seems very similar to the *Twombly* plaintiffs' attempt to support a claim of conspiracy by inference from evidence of "parallel action."

In both complaints, what we might think of as the "ultimate fact" (intentional discrimination on the one hand, and conspiracy in restraint of trade on the other), is alleged generally and then supported by more specific allegations about behavior, the legality of which depends entirely on the inferences one draws. In both cases, the courts believed the general allegations of illegality were economically "implausible" because innocent explanations could be inferred. What exactly must the *Twombly* plaintiffs now plead for their suit to continue? As in *American Nurses,* plaintiffs threw in the towel after the 12(b)(6) ruling; what would they have had to plead to go forward?

5. One of the main questions the case left open was whether it applied across the board or only to antitrust cases. The Court's language suggests broad application, but one could reasonably conclude that the Court only wanted to see more detailed pleadings in antitrust cases of the *Twombly* type, and perhaps other "big cases." As you will see when we come to summary judgment in Chapter 4, there are unique reasons to worry about antitrust suits when the effect of defendant companies' conduct—whether conspiratorial or not—is to lower prices for the consumer. See Matsushita Elec. Indus. Co. v. Zenith Radio Corp., 475 U.S. 574 (1986). Does it look like this is the effect of defendants' conduct in *Twombly*?

Confusion about the scope of *Twombly* prompted the Court to intervene again in the following case. It decisively holds that "plausibility" pleading is the new standard for 12(b)(6) motions in all cases. As you read the opinion, consider whether it applies the same theory of plausibility Justice Souter announced in *Twombly.*

### *Ashcroft v. Iqbal*
556 U.S. 662 (2009)

JUSTICE KENNEDY delivered the opinion of the Court.

Respondent Javaid Iqbal is a citizen of Pakistan and a Muslim. In the wake of the September 11, 2001, terrorist attacks he was arrested in the United States on criminal charges and detained by federal officials. Respondent claims he was deprived of various constitutional protections while in federal custody. To redress the alleged deprivations, respondent filed a complaint against numerous federal officials, including John Ashcroft, the former Attorney General of the United States, and Robert Mueller, the Director of the Federal Bureau of Investigation (FBI). Ashcroft and Mueller are the petitioners in the case now before us. As to these two petitioners, the complaint alleges that they adopted an unconstitutional policy that subjected respondent to harsh conditions of confinement on account of his race, religion, or national origin.

In the District Court petitioners raised the defense of qualified immunity and moved to dismiss the suit, contending the complaint was not sufficient to state a claim against them. The District Court denied the motion to dismiss, concluding the complaint was sufficient to state a claim despite petitioners' official status at the times in question. Petitioners brought an interlocutory appeal in the Court of Appeals for the Second Circuit. The court . . . affirmed the District Court's decision.

Respondent's account of his prison ordeal could, if proved, demonstrate unconstitutional misconduct by some governmental actors. But the allegations and pleadings with respect to these actors are not before us here. This case instead turns on a narrower question: Did respondent, as the plaintiff in the District Court, plead factual matter that, if taken as true, states a claim that petitioners deprived him of his clearly established constitutional rights. We hold respondent's pleadings are insufficient.

# I

Following the 2001 attacks, the FBI and other entities within the Department of Justice began an investigation of vast reach to identify the assailants and prevent them from attacking anew. The FBI dedicated more than 4,000 special agents and 3,000 support personnel to the endeavor. By September 18 "the FBI had received more than 96,000 tips or potential leads from the public." Dept. of Justice, Office of Inspector General, The September 11 Detainees: A Review of the Treatment of Aliens Held on Immigration Charges in Connection with the Investigation of the September 11 Attacks 1, 11-12 (Apr. 2003) (hereinafter OIG Report).

In the ensuing months the FBI questioned more than 1,000 people with suspected links to the attacks in particular or to terrorism in general. Id. at 1. Of those individuals, some 762 were held on immigration charges; and a 184-member subset of that group was deemed to be "of 'high interest'" to the investigation. Id. at 111. The high-interest detainees were held under restrictive conditions designed to prevent them from communicating with the general prison population or the outside world. Id. at 112-13.

Respondent was one of the detainees. According to his complaint, in November 2001 agents of the FBI and Immigration and Naturalization Service arrested him on charges of fraud in relation to identification documents and conspiracy to defraud the United States. Iqbal v. Hasty, 490 F.3d 143, 147-48 (2d Cir. 2007). Pending trial for those crimes, respondent was housed at the Metropolitan Detention Center (MDC) in Brooklyn, New York. Respondent was designated a person "of high interest" to the September 11 investigation and in January 2002 was placed in a section of the MDC known as the Administrative Maximum Special Housing Unit (ADMAX SHU). Id. at 148. As the facility's name indicates, the ADMAX SHU incorporates the maximum security conditions allowable under Federal Bureau of Prison regulations. Id. ADMAX SHU detainees were kept in lockdown 23 hours a day, spending the remaining hour outside their cells in handcuffs and leg irons accompanied by a four-officer escort. Id.

Respondent pleaded guilty to the criminal charges, served a term of imprisonment, and was removed to his native Pakistan. Id. at 149. He then filed a *Bivens* action in the United States District Court for the Eastern District of New York against 34 current and former federal officials and 19 "John Doe" federal corrections officers. See Bivens v. Six Unknown Fed. Narcotics Agents, 403 U.S. 388 (1971). The defendants range from the correctional officers who had day-to-day contact with respondent during the term of his confinement, to the wardens of the MDC facility, all the way to petitioners—officials who were at the highest level of the federal law enforcement hierarchy. First Amended Complaint in No. 04-CV-1809 (JG) (JA), ¶¶ 10-11.

. . .

The allegations against petitioners are the only ones relevant here. The complaint contends that petitioners designated respondent a person of high interest on account of his race, religion, or national origin, in contravention of the First and Fifth Amendments to the Constitution. The complaint alleges that "the [FBI], under the direction of Defendant Mueller, arrested and detained thousands of Arab Muslim men . . . as part of its investigation of the events of September 11." Id. ¶ 47. It further alleges that "[t]he policy of holding post-September-11th detainees in highly restrictive conditions of confinement until they were 'cleared' by the FBI was approved by Defendants Ashcroft and Mueller in discussions in the weeks after September 11, 2001." Id. ¶ 69. Lastly, the complaint posits that petitioners "each knew of, condoned, and willfully and maliciously agreed to subject" respondent to harsh conditions of confinement "as a matter of policy, solely on account of [his] religion, race, and/or national origin and for no legitimate penological interest." Id. ¶ 96. The pleading names Ashcroft as the "principal architect" of the policy, id. ¶ 10, and identifies Mueller as "instrumental in [its] adoption, promulgation, and implementation." Id. ¶ 11.

Petitioners moved to dismiss the complaint for failure to state sufficient allegations to show their own involvement in clearly established unconstitutional conduct. The District Court denied their motion. Accepting all of the allegations in respondent's complaint as true, the court held that "it cannot be said that there [is] no set of facts on which [respondent] would be entitled to relief as against" petitioners. Id. (relying on Conley v. Gibson, 355 U.S. 41 (1957)). Invoking the collateral-order doctrine petitioners filed an interlocutory appeal in the United States Court of Appeals for the Second Circuit. While that appeal was pending, this Court decided Bell Atlantic Corp. v. Twombly, 550 U.S. 544 (2007), which discussed the standard for evaluating whether a complaint is sufficient to survive a motion to dismiss.

The Court of Appeals considered *Twombly*'s applicability to this case. Acknowledging that *Twombly* retired the *Conley* no-set-of-facts test relied upon by the District Court, the Court of Appeals' opinion discussed at length how to apply this Court's "standard for assessing the adequacy of pleadings." 490 F.3d, at 155. It concluded that *Twombly* called for a "flexible 'plausibility standard,' which obliges a pleader to amplify a claim with some factual allegations in those contexts where such amplification is needed to render the claim *plausible*." Id. at 157-158. The court found that petitioners' appeal did not present one of "those contexts" requiring amplification. As a consequence, it held respondent's pleading adequate to allege petitioners' personal involvement in discriminatory decisions which, if true, violated clearly established constitutional law. Id. at 174.

. . . We granted certiorari, 128 S. Ct. 2931 (2008), and now reverse.

[In Part II of the opinion, the Court concluded that it had subject matter jurisdiction over the appeal under the collateral-order doctrine. — EDS.]

## III

In *Twombly*, the Court found it necessary first to discuss the antitrust principles implicated by the complaint. Here too we begin by taking note of the elements a plaintiff must plead to state a claim of unconstitutional discrimination against officials entitled to assert the defense of qualified immunity.

. . .

In the limited settings where *Bivens* does apply, the implied cause of action is the "federal analog to suits brought against state officials under Rev. Stat. § 1979, 42 U.S.C. § 1983." *Hartman*, 547 U.S., at 254, n.2. Cf. Wilson v. Layne, 526 U.S. 603, 609 (1999). Based on the rules our precedents establish, respondent correctly concedes that Government officials may not be held liable for the unconstitutional conduct of their subordinates under a theory of respondeat superior. Iqbal Brief 46 ("[I]t is undisputed that supervisory *Bivens* liability cannot be established solely on a theory of respondeat superior"). See Monell v. New York City Dept. of Social Servs., 436 U.S. 658, 691, 98 S. Ct. 2018, 56 L. Ed. 2d 611 (1978) (finding no vicarious liability for a municipal "person" under 42 U.S.C. § 1983); see also Dunlop v. Munroe, 7 Cranch 242, 269 (1812) (a federal official's liability "will only result from his own neglect in not properly superintending the discharge" of his subordinates' duties). Because vicarious liability is inapplicable to *Bivens* and § 1983 suits, a plaintiff must plead that each Government-official defendant, through the official's own individual actions, has violated the Constitution.

The factors necessary to establish a *Bivens* violation will vary with the constitutional provision at issue. Where the claim is invidious discrimination in contravention of the First and Fifth Amendments, our decisions make clear that the plaintiff must plead and prove that the defendant acted with discriminatory purpose. Church of Lukumi Babalu Aye, Inc. v. Hialeah, 508 U.S. 520, 540-41 (1993) (First Amendment); Washington v. Davis, 426 U.S. 229, 240 (1976) (Fifth Amendment). Under extant precedent purposeful discrimination requires more than "intent as volition or intent as awareness of consequences." Personnel Administrator of Mass. v. Feeney, 442 U.S. 256, 279 (1979). It instead involves a decisionmaker's undertaking a course of action "'because of,' not merely 'in spite of,' [the action's] adverse effects upon an identifiable group." Id. It follows that, to state a claim based on a violation of a clearly established right, respondent must plead sufficient factual matter to show that petitioners adopted and implemented the detention policies at issue not for a neutral, investigative reason but for the purpose of discriminating on account of race, religion, or national origin. . . .

## IV

### A

We turn to respondent's complaint. Under Federal Rule of Civil Procedure 8(a)(2), a pleading must contain a "short and plain statement of the claim showing that the pleader is entitled to relief." As the Court held in *Twombly*, the pleading standard Rule 8 announces does not require "detailed factual allegations," but it demands more than an unadorned, the-defendant-unlawfully-harmed-me accusation. Id. at 555 (citing Papasan v. Allain, 478 U.S. 265, 286 (1986)). A pleading that offers "labels and conclusions" or "a formulaic recitation of the elements of a cause of action will not do." 550 U.S., at 555. Nor does a complaint suffice if it tenders "naked assertion[s]" devoid of "further factual enhancement." Id. at 557.

To survive a motion to dismiss, a complaint must contain sufficient factual matter, accepted as true, to "state a claim to relief that is plausible on its face." Id. at 570. A claim has facial plausibility when the plaintiff pleads factual content that allows the court to draw the reasonable inference that the defendant is liable for the misconduct alleged. Id. at 556. The plausibility standard is not akin to a "probability requirement," but it asks for more than a sheer possibility that a defendant has acted unlawfully. Id. Where a complaint pleads facts that are "merely consistent with" a defendant's liability, it "stops short of the line between possibility and plausibility of 'entitlement to relief.'" Id. at 557.

Two working principles underlie our decision in *Twombly*. First, the tenet that a court must accept as true all of the allegations contained in a complaint is inapplicable to legal conclusions. Threadbare recitals of the elements of a cause of action, supported by mere conclusory statements, do not suffice. Id. at 555 (Although for the purposes of a motion to dismiss we must take all of the factual allegations in the complaint as true, we "are not bound to accept as true a legal conclusion couched as a factual allegation"). Rule 8 marks a notable and generous departure from the hyper-technical, code-pleading regime of a prior era, but it does not unlock the doors of discovery for a plaintiff armed with nothing more than conclusions. Second, only a complaint that states a plausible claim for relief survives a motion to dismiss. Id. at 556. Determining whether a complaint states a plausible claim for relief will, as the Court of Appeals observed, be a context-specific task that requires the reviewing court to draw on its judicial experience and common sense. 490 F.3d, at 157-58. But where the well-pleaded facts do not permit the court to infer more than the mere possibility of misconduct, the complaint has alleged—but it has not "show[n]"—"that the pleader is entitled to relief." Fed. Rule Civ. Proc. 8(a)(2).

In keeping with these principles a court considering a motion to dismiss can choose to begin by identifying pleadings that, because they are no more than conclusions, are not entitled to the assumption of truth. While legal conclusions can provide the framework of a complaint, they must be supported by factual allegations. When there are well-pleaded factual allegations, a court should assume their veracity and then determine whether they plausibly give rise to an entitlement to relief.

Our decision in *Twombly* illustrates the two-pronged approach. There, we considered the sufficiency of a complaint alleging that incumbent telecommunications providers had entered an agreement not to compete and to forestall competitive entry, in violation of the Sherman Act, 15 U.S.C. § 1. Recognizing that § 1 enjoins only anticompetitive conduct "effected by a contract, combination, or conspiracy," Copperweld Corp. v. Independence Tube Corp., 467 U.S. 752, 775 (1984), the plaintiffs in *Twombly* flatly pleaded that the defendants "ha[d] entered into a contract, combination or conspiracy to prevent competitive entry . . . and ha[d] agreed not to compete with one another." 550 U.S., at 551. The complaint also alleged that the defendants' "parallel course of conduct . . . to prevent competition" and inflate prices was indicative of the unlawful agreement alleged. Id.

The Court held the plaintiffs' complaint deficient under Rule 8. In doing so it first noted that the plaintiffs' assertion of an unlawful agreement was a "legal conclusion" and, as such, was not entitled to the assumption of truth. Id. at 555. Had the Court simply credited the allegation of a conspiracy, the plaintiffs would have stated a claim for relief and been entitled to proceed perforce. The Court next addressed the "nub" of the plaintiffs' complaint—the well-pleaded, nonconclusory factual allegation of parallel behavior—to determine whether it gave rise to a "plausible suggestion of conspiracy." Id. at 565-66. Acknowledging that parallel conduct was consistent with an unlawful agreement, the Court nevertheless concluded that it did not plausibly suggest an illicit accord because it was not only compatible with, but indeed was more likely explained by, lawful, unchoreographed free-market behavior. Id. at 567. Because the well-pleaded fact of parallel conduct, accepted as true, did not plausibly suggest an unlawful agreement, the Court held the plaintiffs' complaint must be dismissed. Id. at 570.

### B

Under *Twombly*'s construction of Rule 8, we conclude that respondent's complaint has not "nudged [his] claims" of invidious discrimination "across the line from conceivable to plausible." Id.

We begin our analysis by identifying the allegations in the complaint that are not entitled to the assumption of truth. Respondent pleads that petitioners "knew of, condoned, and willfully and maliciously agreed to subject [him]" to harsh conditions of confinement "as a matter of policy, solely on account of [his] religion, race, and/or national origin and for no legitimate penological interest." Complaint ¶ 96. The complaint alleges that Ashcroft was the "principal architect" of this invidious policy, id., ¶ 10, and that Mueller was "instrumental" in adopting and executing it, id., ¶ 11. These bare assertions, much like the pleading of conspiracy in *Twombly*, amount to nothing more than a "formulaic recitation of the elements" of a constitutional discrimination claim, 550 U.S., at 555, namely, that petitioners adopted a policy "'because of,' not merely 'in spite of,' its adverse effects upon an identifiable group." *Feeney*, 442 U.S., at 279. As such, the allegations are conclusory and not entitled to be assumed true. *Twombly*, supra, 550 U.S., at 554-55. To be clear, we do not reject these bald allegations on the ground that they are unrealistic or nonsensical. We do not so characterize them any more than the Court in *Twombly* rejected the plaintiffs' express allegation of a "'contract, combination or conspiracy to prevent competitive entry,'" id. at 551, because it thought that claim too chimerical to be maintained. It is the conclusory nature of respondent's allegations, rather than their extravagantly fanciful nature, that disentitles them to the presumption of truth.

We next consider the factual allegations in respondent's complaint to determine if they plausibly suggest an entitlement to relief. The complaint alleges that "the [FBI], under the direction of Defendant Mueller, arrested and detained thousands of Arab Muslim men . . . as part of its investigation of the events of September 11." Complaint ¶ 47. It further claims that "[t]he policy of holding post-September-11th detainees in highly restrictive conditions of confinement until they were 'cleared' by the FBI was approved by Defendants Ashcroft and Mueller in discussions in the weeks after September 11, 2001." Id. ¶ 69. Taken as true, these allegations are consistent with petitioners' purposefully designating detainees "of high interest" because of their race, religion, or national origin. *But given more likely explanations, they do not plausibly establish this purpose.* [Emphasis added. EDS.]

The September 11 attacks were perpetrated by 19 Arab Muslim hijackers who counted themselves members in good standing of al Qaeda, an Islamic fundamentalist group. Al Qaeda was headed by another Arab Muslim—Osama bin Laden—and composed in large part of his Arab Muslim disciples. It should come as no surprise that a legitimate policy directing law enforcement to arrest and detain individuals because of their suspected link to the attacks would produce a disparate, incidental impact on Arab Muslims, even though the purpose of the policy was to target neither Arabs nor Muslims. On the facts respondent alleges the arrests Mueller oversaw were likely lawful and justified by his nondiscriminatory intent to detain aliens who were illegally present in the United States and who had potential connections to those who committed terrorist acts. As between that "obvious alternative explanation" for the arrests, *Twombly*, supra, at 567, and the purposeful, invidious discrimination respondent asks us to infer, discrimination is not a plausible conclusion.

But even if the complaint's well-pleaded facts give rise to a plausible inference that respondent's arrest was the result of unconstitutional discrimination, that inference alone would not entitle respondent to relief. It is important to recall that respondent's complaint challenges neither the constitutionality of his arrest nor his initial detention in the MDC. Respondent's constitutional claims against petitioners rest solely on their ostensible "policy of holding post-September-11th detainees" in the ADMAX SHU once they were categorized as "of high interest." Complaint ¶ 69. To prevail on that theory, the complaint must contain facts plausibly showing that petitioners purposefully adopted a policy of classifying post-September-11 detainees as "of high interest" because of their race, religion, or national origin.

This the complaint fails to do. Though respondent alleges that various other defendants, who are not before us, may have labeled him a person of "of high interest" for impermissible reasons, his only factual allegation against petitioners accuses them of adopting a policy approving "restrictive conditions of confinement" for post-September-11 detainees until they were "'cleared' by the FBI." Id. Accepting the truth of that allegation, the complaint does not show, or even intimate, that petitioners purposefully housed detainees in the ADMAX SHU due to their race, religion, or national origin. All it plausibly suggests is that the Nation's top law enforcement officers, in the aftermath of a devastating terrorist attack, sought to keep suspected terrorists in the most secure conditions available until the suspects could be cleared of terrorist activity. Respondent does not argue, nor can he, that such a motive would violate petitioners' constitutional obligations. He would need to allege more by way of factual content to "nudg[e]" his claim of purposeful discrimination "across the line from conceivable to plausible." *Twombly*, 550 U.S., at 570.

To be sure, respondent can attempt to draw certain contrasts between the pleadings the Court considered in *Twombly* and the pleadings at issue here. In *Twombly*, the complaint alleged general wrongdoing that extended over a period of years, id., at 551, whereas here the complaint alleges discrete wrongs—for instance, beatings—by lower level Government actors. The allegations here, if true, and if condoned by petitioners, could be the basis for some inference of wrongful intent on petitioners' part. Despite these distinctions, respondent's pleadings do not suffice to state a claim. Unlike in *Twombly*, where the doctrine of respondeat superior could bind the corporate defendant, here, as we have noted, petitioners cannot be held liable unless they themselves acted on account of a constitutionally protected characteristic. Yet respondent's complaint does not contain any factual allegation sufficient to plausibly suggest petitioners' discriminatory state of mind. His pleadings thus do not meet the standard necessary to comply with Rule 8.

It is important to note, however, that we express no opinion concerning the sufficiency of respondent's complaint against the defendants who are not before us. Respondent's account of his prison ordeal alleges serious official misconduct that we need not address here. Our decision is limited to the determination that respondent's complaint does not entitle him to relief from petitioners.

## C

Respondent offers three arguments that bear on our disposition of his case, but none is persuasive.

### 1

Respondent first says that our decision in *Twombly* should be limited to pleadings made in the context of an antitrust dispute. Iqbal Brief 37-38. This argument is not supported by *Twombly* and is incompatible with the Federal Rules of Civil Procedure. Though *Twombly* determined the sufficiency of a complaint sounding in antitrust, the decision was based on our interpretation and application of Rule 8. 550 U.S., at 554. That Rule in turn governs the pleading standard "in all civil actions and proceedings in the United States district courts." Fed. Rule Civ. Proc. 1. Our decision in *Twombly* expounded the pleading standard for "all civil actions," ibid., and it applies to antitrust and discrimination suits alike. See 550 U.S., at 555-56, and n.3.

### 2

Respondent next implies that our construction of Rule 8 should be tempered where, as here, the Court of Appeals has "instructed the district court to cabin discovery in such a way as to preserve" petitioners' defense of qualified immunity "as much as possible in anticipation of a summary judgment motion." Iqbal Brief 27. We have held, however, that the question presented by a motion to dismiss a complaint for insufficient pleadings does not turn on the controls placed upon the discovery process. *Twombly*, supra, at 559 ("It is no answer to say that a claim just shy of a plausible entitlement to relief can, if groundless, be weeded out early in the discovery process through careful case management given the common lament that the success of judicial supervision in checking discovery abuse has been on the modest side").

Our rejection of the careful-case-management approach is especially important in suits where Government-official defendants are entitled to assert the defense of qualified immunity. The basic thrust of the qualified-immunity doctrine is to free officials from the concerns of litigation, including "avoidance of disruptive discovery." Siegert v. Gilley, 500 U.S. 226, 236 (1991) (Kennedy, J., concurring in judgment). There are serious and legitimate reasons for this. If a Government official is to devote time to his or her duties, and to the formulation of sound and responsible policies, it is counterproductive to require the substantial diversion that is attendant to participating in litigation and making informed decisions as to how it should proceed. Litigation, though necessary to ensure that officials comply with the law, exacts heavy costs in terms of efficiency and expenditure of valuable time and resources that might otherwise be directed to the proper execution of the work of the Government. The costs of diversion are only magnified when Government officials are charged with responding to, as Judge Cabranes aptly put it [in his concurring opinion below], "a national and international security emergency unprecedented in the history of the American Republic." 490 F.3d, at 179. . . .

We decline respondent's invitation to relax the pleading requirements on the ground that the Court of Appeals promises petitioners minimally intrusive discovery. That promise provides especially cold comfort in this pleading context, where we are impelled to give real content to the concept of qualified immunity for high-level officials who must be neither deterred nor detracted from the vigorous performance of their duties. Because respondent's complaint is deficient under Rule 8, he is not entitled to discovery, cabined or otherwise.

### 3

Respondent finally maintains that the Federal Rules expressly allow him to allege petitioners' discriminatory intent "generally," which he equates with a conclusory allegation. Iqbal Brief 32 (citing Fed. Rule Civ. Proc. 9). . . .

But "generally" is a relative term. In the context of Rule 9, it is to be compared to the particularity requirement applicable to fraud or mistake. Rule 9 merely excuses a party from pleading discriminatory intent under an elevated pleading standard. It does not give him license to evade the less rigid—though still operative—strictures of Rule 8. . . . And Rule 8 does not empower respondent to plead the bare elements of his cause of action, affix the label "general allegation," and expect his complaint to survive a motion to dismiss.

## V

We hold that respondent's complaint fails to plead sufficient facts to state a claim for purposeful and unlawful discrimination against petitioners. The Court of Appeals should decide in the first instance whether to remand to the District Court so that respondent can seek leave to amend his deficient complaint.

The judgment of the Court of Appeals is reversed, and the case is remanded for further proceedings consistent with this opinion.

*It is so ordered.*

JUSTICE SOUTER, with whom JUSTICE STEVENS, JUSTICE GINSBURG, and JUSTICE BREYER join, dissenting.

. . . I respectfully dissent from both the rejection of supervisory liability as a cognizable claim in the face of petitioners' concession, and from the holding that the complaint fails to satisfy Rule 8(a)(2) of the Federal Rules of Civil Procedure.

## I

### A

Iqbal claims that on the day he was transferred to the special unit, prison guards, without provocation, "picked him up and threw him against the wall, kicked him in the stomach, punched him in the face, and dragged him across the room." First Amended Complaint in No. 04-CV-1809 (JG) (JA). He says that after being attacked a second time he sought medical attention but was denied care for two weeks. Id. ¶¶ 187-188. According to Iqbal's complaint, [for more than six months while he was held in the Special Housing Unit] prison staff in the special unit subjected him to unjustified strip and body cavity searches, id. ¶¶ 136-140, verbally berated him as a "'terrorist'" and "'Muslim killer,'" id. ¶ 87, refused to give him adequate food, id. ¶ 91, and intentionally turned on air conditioning during the winter and heating during the summer, id. ¶ 84. He claims that prison staff interfered with his attempts to pray and engage in religious study, id. ¶¶ 153-154, and with his access to counsel, id. ¶¶ 168, 171.

. . .

[In their briefing] Ashcroft and Mueller argued that the factual allegations in Iqbal's complaint were insufficient to overcome their claim of qualified immunity; they also contended that they could not be held liable on a theory of constructive notice. . . . [T]hey conceded, however, that they would be subject to supervisory liability if they "had actual knowledge of the assertedly discriminatory nature of the classification of suspects as being 'of high interest' and they were deliberately indifferent to that discrimination." Iqbal argued that the allegations in his complaint were sufficient under Rule 8(a)(2) and *Twombly*, and conceded that as a matter of law he could not recover under a theory of respondeat superior. Thus, the parties agreed as to a proper standard of supervisory liability, and the disputed question was whether Iqbal's complaint satisfied Rule 8(a)(2).

. . .

## B

The majority, however . . . ignore[s] the[se] concession[s]. According to the majority, because Iqbal concededly cannot recover on a theory of respondeat superior, it follows that he cannot recover under any theory of supervisory liability. . . .

The dangers of the majority's readiness to proceed without briefing and argument are apparent in its cursory analysis, which rests on the assumption that only two outcomes are possible here: respondeat superior liability, in which "an employer is subject to liability for torts committed by employees while acting within the scope of their employment," Restatement (Third) of Agency § 2.04 (2005), or no supervisory liability at all. The dichotomy is false. . . . See, e.g., Whitfield v. Melendez-Rivera, 431 F.3d 1, 14 (1st Cir. 2005) (distinguishing between respondeat superior liability and supervisory liability); . . . Hall v. Lombardi, 996 F.2d 954, 961 (8th Cir. 1993) (same).

In fact, there is quite a spectrum of possible tests for supervisory liability: it could be imposed where a supervisor has actual knowledge of a subordinate's constitutional violation and acquiesces, see, e.g., Baker v. Monroe Twp., 50 F.3d 1186, 1194 (3d Cir. 1995); Woodward v. Worland, 977 F.2d 1392, 1400 (10th Cir. 1992); or where supervisors "'know about the conduct and facilitate it, approve it, condone it, or turn a blind eye for fear of what they might see,'" International Action Center v. United States, 365 F.3d 20, 28 (D.C. Cir. 2004) (Roberts, J.) (quoting Jones v. Chicago, 856 F.2d 985, 992 (7th Cir. 1988) (Posner, J.)); or where the supervisor has no actual knowledge of the violation but was reckless in his supervision of the subordinate, see, e.g., *Hall*, supra, at 961; or where the supervisor was grossly negligent, see, e.g., Lipsett v. University of Puerto Rico, 864 F.2d 881, 902 (1st Cir. 1988).

## II

Given petitioners' concession, the complaint satisfies Rule 8(a)(2). Ashcroft and Mueller admit they are liable for their subordinates' conduct if they "had actual knowledge of the assertedly discriminatory nature of the classification of suspects as being 'of high interest' and they were deliberately indifferent to that discrimination." Brief for Petitioners 50. Iqbal alleges that after the September 11 attacks the Federal Bureau of Investigation (FBI) "arrested and detained thousands of Arab Muslim men," Complaint ¶ 47, that many of these men were designated by high-ranking FBI officials as being "'of high interest,'" id. ¶¶ 48, 50, and that in many cases, including Iqbal's, this designation was made "because of the race, religion, and national origin of the detainees, and not because of any evidence of the detainees' involvement in supporting terrorist activity," id. ¶ 49. The complaint further alleges that Ashcroft was the "principal architect of the policies and practices challenged," id. ¶ 10, and that Mueller "was instrumental in the adoption, promulgation, and implementation of the policies and practices challenged," id. ¶ 11. According to the complaint, Ashcroft and Mueller "knew of, condoned, and willfully and maliciously agreed to subject [Iqbal] to these conditions of confinement as a matter of policy, solely on account of [his] religion, race, and/or national origin and for no legitimate penological interest." Id. ¶ 96. The complaint thus alleges, at a bare minimum, that Ashcroft and Mueller knew of and condoned the discriminatory policy their subordinates carried out. Actually, the complaint goes further in alleging that Ashcroft and Muller affirmatively acted to create the discriminatory detention policy. If these factual allegations are true, Ashcroft and Mueller were, at the very least, aware of the discriminatory policy being implemented and deliberately indifferent to it.

Ashcroft and Mueller argue that these allegations fail to satisfy the "plausibility standard" of *Twombly*. They contend that Iqbal's claims are implausible because such high-ranking officials "tend not to be personally involved in the specific actions of lower-level officers down the bureaucratic chain of command." But this response bespeaks a fundamental misunderstanding of the enquiry that *Twombly* demands. *Twombly* does not require a court at the motion-to-dismiss stage to consider whether the factual allegations are probably true. We made it clear, on the contrary, that a court must take the allegations as true, no matter how skeptical the court may be. See *Twombly*, 550 U.S., at 555 (a court must proceed "on the assumption that all the allegations in the complaint are true (even if doubtful in fact)"); id. at 556 ("[A] well-pleaded complaint may proceed even if it strikes a savvy judge that actual proof of the facts alleged is improbable"). . . . The sole exception to this rule lies with allegations that are sufficiently fantastic to defy reality as we know it: claims about little green men, or the plaintiff's recent trip to Pluto, or experiences in time travel. That is not what we have here.

Under *Twombly*, the relevant question is whether, assuming the factual allegations are true, the plaintiff has stated a ground for relief that is plausible. That is, in *Twombly*'s words, a plaintiff must "allege facts" that, taken as true, are "suggestive of illegal conduct." 550 U.S., at 564, n. 8. In *Twombly*, we were faced with allegations of a conspiracy to violate § 1 of the Sherman Act through parallel conduct. The difficulty was that the conduct alleged was "consistent with conspiracy, but just as much in line with a wide swath of rational and competitive business strategy unilaterally prompted by common perceptions of the market." Id. at 554. . . . Here, by contrast, the allegations in the complaint are neither confined to naked legal conclusions nor consistent with legal conduct. The complaint alleges that FBI officials discriminated against Iqbal solely on account of his race, religion, and national origin, and it alleges the knowledge and deliberate indifference that, by Ashcroft and Mueller's own admission, are sufficient to make them liable for the illegal action. Iqbal's complaint therefore contains "enough facts to state a claim to relief that is plausible on its face." Id. at 570.

I do not understand the majority to disagree with this understanding of "plausibility" under *Twombly*. Rather, the majority discards the allegations discussed above with regard to Ashcroft and Mueller as conclusory, and is left considering only two statements in the complaint: that "the [FBI], under the direction of Defendant Mueller, arrested and detained thousands of Arab Muslim men . . . as part of its investigation of the events of September 11," Complaint ¶ 47, and that "[t]he policy of holding post-September-11th detainees in highly restrictive conditions of confinement until they were 'cleared' by the FBI was approved by Defendants Ashcroft and Mueller in discussions in the weeks after September 11, 2001," id. ¶ 69. I think the majority is right in saying that these allegations suggest only that Ashcroft and Mueller "sought to keep suspected terrorists in the most secure conditions available until the suspects could be cleared of terrorist activity," ante, and that this produced "a disparate, incidental impact on Arab Muslims," ante. And I agree that the two allegations selected by the majority, standing alone, do not state a plausible entitlement to relief for unconstitutional discrimination.

But these allegations do not stand alone as the only significant, nonconclusory statements in the complaint, for the complaint contains many allegations linking Ashcroft and Mueller to the discriminatory practices of their subordinates. See Complaint ¶ 10 (Ashcroft was the "principal architect" of the discriminatory policy); id. ¶ 11 (Mueller was "instrumental" in adopting and executing the discriminatory policy); id. ¶ 96 (Ashcroft and Mueller "knew of, condoned, and willfully and maliciously agreed to subject" Iqbal to harsh conditions "as a matter of policy, solely on account of [his] religion, race, and/or national origin and for no legitimate penological interest").

The majority says that these are "bare assertions" that, "much like the pleading of conspiracy in *Twombly*, amount to nothing more than a 'formulaic recitation of the elements' of a constitutional discrimination claim" and therefore are "not entitled to be assumed true." Ante. The fallacy of the majority's position, however, lies in looking at the relevant assertions in isolation. The complaint contains specific allegations that, in the aftermath of the September 11 attacks, the Chief of the FBI's International Terrorism Operations Section and the Assistant Special Agent in Charge for the FBI's New York Field Office implemented a policy that discriminated against Arab Muslim men, including Iqbal, solely on account of their race, religion, or national origin. See Complaint ¶¶ 47-53. Viewed in light of these subsidiary allegations, the allegations singled out by the majority as "conclusory" are no such thing. Iqbal's claim is not that Ashcroft and Mueller "knew of, condoned, and willfully and maliciously agreed to subject" him to a discriminatory practice that is left undefined; his allegation is that "they knew of, condoned, and willfully and maliciously agreed to subject" him to a particular, discrete, discriminatory policy detailed in the complaint. Iqbal does not say merely that Ashcroft was the architect of some amorphous discrimination, or that Mueller was instrumental in an ill-defined constitutional violation; he alleges that they helped to create the discriminatory policy he has described. Taking the complaint as a whole, it gives Ashcroft and Mueller "'fair notice of what the . . . claim is and the grounds upon which it rests.'" *Twombly*, 550 U.S., at 555 (quoting Conley v. Gibson, 355 U.S. 41, 47 (1957)).

That aside, the majority's holding that the statements it selects are conclusory cannot be squared with its treatment of certain other allegations in the complaint as nonconclusory. For example, the majority takes as true the statement that "[t]he policy of holding post-September-11th detainees in highly restrictive conditions of confinement until they were 'cleared' by the FBI was approved by Defendants Ashcroft and Mueller in discussions in the weeks after September 11, 2001." Complaint ¶ 69. This statement makes two points: (1) after September 11, the FBI held certain detainees in highly restrictive conditions, and (2) Ashcroft and Mueller discussed and approved these conditions. If, as the majority says, these allegations are not conclusory, then I cannot see why the majority deems it merely conclusory when Iqbal alleges that (1) after September 11, the FBI designated Arab Muslim detainees as being of "'high interest'" "because of the race, religion, and national origin of the detainees, and not because of any evidence of the detainees' involvement in supporting terrorist activity," Complaint ¶¶ 48-50, and (2) Ashcroft and Mueller "knew of, condoned, and willfully and maliciously agreed" to that discrimination, id. ¶ 96. By my lights, there is no principled basis for the majority's disregard of the allegations linking Ashcroft and Mueller to their subordinates' discrimination.

I respectfully dissent.

[JUSTICE BREYER wrote separately in dissent to emphasize that there are appropriate case-management tools in discovery to "diminish the risk of imposing unwarranted burdens upon public officials" who are eligible for qualified immunity.]

---

## Notes and Questions

1. In an important article based on detailed interviews with Iqbal, Shirin Sinnar describes Iqbal's life in America before he was detained and how he has been affected by the government's actions. Sinnar, The Lost Story of Iqbal, 105 Geo. L.J. __ (forthcoming 2017). Sinnar contends that, based on the Supreme Court's radically incomplete characterization of the facts, readers of the opinion might incorrectly assume 1) that Iqbal was a suspicious person on account of his immigration status, his national origin, and his religion, and 2) that whatever harm he suffered from his detention and deportation were "temporary and limited." Id. Among the many facts Sinnar uncovers is that Iqbal had been living and working as a cable repair technician on Long Island since 1992. For part of that time, he worked using false identity papers, as many immigrants do. At the time of his arrest he was married to an American woman and in the process of seeking a green card. He was scheduled to renew his work authorization card with immigration officials on September 11, 2001 in lower Manhattan, so he was one block away from the World Trade Center when he saw the planes strike the Twin Towers. Like all New Yorkers, he was horrified. In an interview with a local TV reporter at an exit from the subway he took back to Queens, Iqbal described "how pained he felt at the loss of innocent life." He was arrested six weeks later. Since his detention and deportation to Pakistan he has been repeatedly harassed by the government, accused by community members of being a spy for the CIA, and pressured by militants to seek revenge against the United States. Iqbal's refusal apparently led militants to accuse his son of blasphemy, a crime under Pakistan's penal code. In 2013, after religious authorities issued a death warrant, his son fled the family home. "Haunted by the loss of his son and afraid for his other children, Iqbal describes life now as 'worse than being at the MDC . . . I am free but not free.' He is anxious to raise his children without harassment or fear, and he remains wistful about the life he once had in America":

> If they asked me [my] last wish today, and if they asked me, "Would you wish to go to America?" I would [a] thousand times say, "Yes, yes, yes," but not by myself—with my kids. Take me there. And I will be working again in the street as a cable guy.

While fifteen months of confinement as a terrorist seared into Iqbal one image of the U.S. government, a decade in Long Island had exposed him to another America—of kind people, economic opportunity, relative freedom, and a legal system that offered the hope of challenging injustice. Those dueling images seem to confound him, even now.

Sinnar connects her research to the legal storytelling traditions of critical race theory, arguing that an "extended account [of Iqbal's experience] invites us to humanize the individual considered in cursory and categorical terms by the Court and rendered a procedural symbol by lawyers. The tendency to place individuals into familiar categories is a product of both the conventions of legal argument and basic cognitive processing. . . . These frames need not be replaced by an equally one-dimensional trope of the heroic, flawless immigrant to be rejected as . . . too simple." She also argues that an extended account suggests that the government and the Court relied on a casual, overinclusive association between immigration fraud and national and religious identity, on the one hand, and possible involvement in terrorism, on the other. The Court could not have had access at the pleading phase to all of the facts that Sinnar gathered about Iqbal's life in America, but it seemed caught in a set of assumptions both about Iqbal's identity and about the good intentions of the defendants. Plausibility pleading may increase the risk that courts will rely upon rather than challenge these types of background assumptions. Finally, Sinnar argues that a deeper inquiry shows that "the effects of the detentions were not nearly as limited in space or time as readers of the Supreme Court opinion might have assumed."

2. Notwithstanding the dismissal of Iqbal's complaint, the policy of rounding up Muslim and Arab men after the September 11 attacks remains the subject of ongoing litigation and continues to implicate pleading standards. A class action lawsuit was filed in 2002 by aliens who were arrested and detained on immigration charges following the attacks. Turkmen v. Hasty, 789 F.3d 218 (2015). The named plaintiffs were all detained at the Metropolitan Detention Center in Brooklyn, New York. The complaint names the Attorney General, the Director of the FBI, the Commissioner of the Immigration and Naturalization Service, the Warden, and the Associate Warden. It alleges that the plaintiffs and other similarly situated detainees were subjected to flagrantly abusive and unconstitutional conditions of confinement because of their status as Arab or Muslim or, with respect to some plaintiffs, because they were incorrectly assumed by defendants to be Arab or Muslim.

With respect to high level officials such as Attorney General Ashcroft and Director Mueller, the complaint's allegations are more detailed than Iqbal's because the plaintiffs 1) drew on information learned through discovery against lower-level defendants, and 2) attached and cited at length details of a report issued by the Department of Justice Office of Inspector General. The Report discloses important facts about what these officials knew at the time. As the *Turkmen* complaint alleges:

> Ashcroft and Mueller developed "a policy whereby any Muslim or Arab man encountered during the investigation of a tip received in the 9/11 terrorism investigation . . . and discovered to be a non-citizen who had violated the terms of his visa, was arrested." Compl. ¶ 1; see also id. ¶¶ 39-49. Ashcroft also created the related "hold-until-cleared" policy, which mandated that individuals arrested in the wake of 9/11 not be released from "custody until

[FBI Headquarters] affirmatively cleared them of terrorist ties." Id. ¶ 2; see also OIG Report at 38-39.

Within a week of 9/11, the FBI had received approximately 96,000 tips from civilians across the country. These tips varied significantly in quality and reliability. "Mueller [nonetheless] ordered that every one of these tips be investigated, even if they were implausible on their face." Compl. ¶ 40. Ultimately, 762 detainees were placed on the INS Custody List (the "INS List") that then made them subject to Ashcroft's hold-until-cleared policy.

In the months following 9/11, the DOJ Defendants "received detailed daily reports of the arrests and detentions." Id. ¶ 47. Ashcroft and Mueller also "met regularly with a small group of government officials in Washington, D.C., and mapped out ways to exert maximum pressure on the individuals arrested in connection with the terrorism investigation." Id. ¶ 61.10. This small group "discussed and decided upon a strategy to restrict the 9/11 detainees' ability to contact the outside world and delay their immigration hearings. The group also decided to spread the word among law enforcement personnel that the 9/11 detainees were suspected terrorists[ ] . . . and that they needed to be encouraged in any way possible to cooperate." Id.

Defendants moved to dismiss, with Ascroft and Muller arguing that their supervisory decisions had already been upheld as lawful in Iqbal. The district court agreed but the Second Circuit reversed, pointing to allegations in the complaint that Ashcroft and Mueller

were aware that illegal aliens were being detained in punitive conditions of confinement in New York and further knew that there was no suggestion that those detainees were tied to terrorism except for the fact that they were, or were perceived to be, Arab or Muslim. The MDC Plaintiffs further allege that while knowing these facts, the DOJ Defendants were responsible for a decision to merge the New York List with the national INS List, which contained the names of detainees whose detention was dependent not only on their illegal immigrant status and their perceived Arab or Muslim affiliation, but also a suspicion that they were connected to terrorist activities. The merger ensured that the MDC Plaintiffs would continue to be confined in punitive conditions. This is sufficient to plead a Fifth Amendment substantive due process violation. Given the lack of individualized suspicion, the decision to merge the lists was not "reasonably related to a legitimate goal." See *Wolfish*, 441 U.S. at 539, 99 S. Ct. 1861. The only reason why the MDC Plaintiffs were held as if they were suspected of terrorism was because they were, or appeared to be, Arab or Muslim.

Id. at 238-239 (noting complaint's emphasis on a DOJ report documenting defendants' knowledge of the conditions of confinement). The court reversed the dismissal of claims against Ashcroft and Mueller as well as the other defendants under the Fourth Amendment, the Fifth Amendment, the Equal Protection Clause, and § 1985 for a civil rights conspiracy. It affirmed dismissal of the First Amendment claim, claims against a former prison official, and all claims relating to a county detention facility where plaintiffs were held in the general population rather than a special housing unit like the one in federal facility in Brooklyn. The court further held that none of the officials remaining in the case were entitled to qualified immunity.

As of this writing a petition for certiorari remains pending in the U.S. Supreme Court. Assuming the facts alleged in the *Turkmen* complaint and in the attached DOJ report about what Attorney General Ashcroft and Director Mueller knew are accurate, was it appropriate for government lawyers to seek dismissal in Iqbal's case?

As the next case and the notes following show, the lower courts have not settled on a consistent approach to the new plausibility pleading standard.

## *Swanson v. Citibank*
614 F.3d 400 (7th Cir. 2010)

WOOD, CIRCUIT JUDGE.

. . . Gloria Swanson based her complaint on the following set of events, which we accept as true for purposes of this appeal. In February 2009 Citibank announced a plan to make loans using funds that it had received from the federal government's Troubled Assets Relief Program. Encouraged by this prospect, Swanson went to a Citibank branch to apply for a home-equity loan. A representative named Skertich told Swanson that she could not apply alone, because she owned her home jointly with her husband; he had to be present as well. Swanson was skeptical, suspecting that Skertich's demand was a ploy to discourage loan applications from African-Americans. She therefore asked to speak to a manager. When the manager joined the group, Swanson disclosed to both Skertich and the manager that Washington Mutual Bank previously had denied her a home-equity loan. The manager warned Swanson that, although she did not want to discourage Swanson from applying for the loan, Citibank's loan criteria were more stringent than those of other banks.

Still interested, Swanson took a loan application home and returned the next day with the necessary information. She was again assisted by Skertich, who entered the information that Swanson had furnished into the computer. When he reached a question regarding race, Skertich told Swanson that she was not required to respond. At some point during this exchange, Skertich pointed to a photograph on his desk and commented that his wife and son were part African-American.

A few days later Citibank conditionally approved Swanson for a home-equity loan of $50,000. It hired Andre Lanier, who worked for PCI Appraisal Services, to visit Swanson's home for an onsite appraisal. Although Swanson had estimated in her loan application that her house was worth $270,000, Lanier appraised it at only $170,000. The difference was critical: Citibank turned down the loan and explained that its conditional approval had been based on the higher valuation. Two months later Swanson paid for and obtained an appraisal from Midwest Valuations, which thought her home was worth $240,000.

Swanson saw coordinated action in this chain of events, and so she filed a complaint (later amended) charging that Citibank, Lanier, and PCI disfavor providing home-equity loans to African-Americans, and so they deliberately lowered the appraised value of her home far below its actual market value, so that they would have an excuse to deny her the loan. She charges that in so doing, they violated the Fair Housing Act, 42 U.S.C. § 3605, and the Equal Credit Opportunity Act. The district court granted the defendants' motions to dismiss both theories. It relied heavily on Latimore v. Citibank Fed. Savings Bank, 151 F.3d 712 (7th Cir. 1998), a case in which this court described the evidence required to defeat a defense motion for summary judgment on a credit discrimination claim. . . .

Before turning to the particulars of Swanson's case, a brief review of the standards that apply to dismissals for failure to state a claim is in order. It is by now well established that a plaintiff must do better than putting a few words on paper that, in the hands of an imaginative reader, *might* suggest that something has happened to her that *might* be redressed by the law. Cf. Conley v. Gibson, 355 U.S. 41 (1957), disapproved by Bell Atlantic Corp. v. Twombly, 550 U.S. 544, 563 (2007) ("after puzzling the profession for 50 years, this famous observation [the 'no set of facts' language] has earned its retirement"). The question with which courts are still struggling is how much higher the Supreme Court meant to set the bar, when it decided not only *Twombly*, but also Erickson v. Pardus, 551 U.S. 89 (2007), and Ashcroft v. Iqbal, 556 U.S. 662 (2009). This is not an easy question to answer, as the thoughtful dissent from this opinion demonstrates. On the one hand, the Supreme Court has adopted a "plausibility" standard, but on the other hand, it has insisted that it is not requiring fact pleading, nor is it adopting a single pleading standard to replace Rule 8, Rule 9, and specialized regimes like the one in the Private Securities Litigation Reform Act ("PSLRA"), 15 U.S.C. § 78u-4(b)(2).

Critically, in none of the three recent decisions—*Twombly*, *Erickson*, or *Iqbal*—did the Court cast any doubt on the validity of Rule 8 of the Federal Rules of Civil Procedure. To the contrary: at all times it has said that it is interpreting Rule 8, not tossing it out the window. It is therefore useful to begin with a look at the language of the rule:

> (a) Claim for Relief. A pleading that states a claim for relief must contain:
>     . . . (2) a short and plain statement of the claim showing that the pleader is entitled to relief. . . .

Fed. R. Civ. P. 8(a)(2). As one respected treatise put it in 2004,

> all that is necessary is that the claim for relief be stated with brevity, conciseness, and clarity. . . . [T]his portion of Rule 8 indicates that a basic objective of the rules is to avoid civil cases turning on technicalities and to require that the pleading discharge the function of giving the opposing party fair notice of the nature and basis or grounds of the pleader's claim and a general indication of the type of litigation that is involved. . . .

5 Charles A. Wright & Arthur R. Miller, Federal Practice and Procedure § 1215 at 165–173 (3d ed. 2004).

Nothing in the recent trio of cases has undermined these broad principles. As *Erickson* underscored, "[s]pecific facts are not necessary." 551 U.S. at 93. The Court was not engaged in a *sub rosa* campaign to reinstate the old fact-pleading system called for by the Field Code or even more modern codes. We know that because it said so in *Erickson*: "the statement need only give the defendant fair notice of what the . . . claim is and the grounds upon which it rests." . . .

This is the light in which the Court's references in *Twombly*, repeated in *Iqbal*, to the pleader's responsibility to "state a claim to relief that is plausible on its face" must be understood. See *Twombly*, 550 U.S. at 570; *Iqbal*, 129 S. Ct. at 1949. "Plausibility" in this context does not imply that the district court should decide whose version to believe, or which version is more likely than not. Indeed, the Court expressly distanced itself from the latter approach in *Iqbal*, "the plausibility standard is not akin to a probability requirement." 129 S. Ct. at 1949. As we understand it, the Court is saying instead that the plaintiff must give enough details about the subject-matter of the case to present a story that holds together. In other words, the court will ask itself *could* these things have happened, not *did* they happen. For cases governed only by Rule 8, it is not necessary to stack up inferences side by side and allow the case to go forward only if the plaintiff's inferences seem more compelling than the opposing inferences. Compare Makor Issues & Rights, Ltd. v. Tellabs Inc., 513 F.3d 702, 705 (7th Cir. 2008) (applying PSLRA standards).

The Supreme Court's explicit decision to reaffirm the validity of Swierkiewicz v. Sorema N.A., 534 U.S. 506 (2002), which was cited with approval in *Twombly*, 550 U.S. at 556, indicates that in many straightforward cases, it will not be any more difficult today for a plaintiff to meet that burden than it was before the Court's recent decisions. A plaintiff who believes that she has been passed over for a promotion because of her sex will be able to plead that she was employed by Company X, that a promotion was offered, that she applied and was qualified for it, and that the job went to someone else. That is an entirely plausible scenario, whether or not it describes what "really" went on in this plaintiff's case. A more complex case involving financial derivatives, or tax fraud that the parties tried hard to conceal, or antitrust violations, will require more detail, both to give the opposing party notice of what the case is all about and to show how, in the plaintiff's mind at least, the dots should be connected. Finally, as the Supreme Court warned in *Iqbal* and as we acknowledged later in Brooks v. Ross, 578 F.3d 574 (7th Cir. 2009), "abstract recitations of the elements of a cause of action or conclusory legal statements," 578 F.3d at 581, do nothing to distinguish the particular case that is before the court from every other hypothetically possible case in that field of law. Such statements therefore do not add to the notice that Rule 8 demands.

We realize that one powerful reason that lies behind the Supreme Court's concern about pleading standards is the cost of the discovery that will follow in any case that survives a motion to dismiss on the pleadings. The costs of discovery are often asymmetric, as the dissent points out, and one way to rein them in would be to make it more difficult to earn the right to engage in discovery. That is just what the Court did, by interring the rule that a complaint could go forward if any set of facts at all could be imagined, consistent with the statements in the complaint, that would permit the pleader to obtain relief. Too much chaff was moving ahead with the wheat. . . .

Returning to Swanson's case, we must analyze her allegations defendant-by-defendant. We begin with Citibank. On appeal, Swanson challenges only the dismissal of her Fair Housing Act and fraud claims. The Fair Housing Act prohibits businesses engaged in residential real estate transactions, including "[t]he making . . . of loans or providing other financial assistance . . . secured by residential real estate," from discriminating against any person on account of race. 42 U.S.C. § 3605(a), (b)(1)(B). Swanson's complaint identifies the type of discrimination that she thinks occurs (racial), by whom (Citibank, through Skertich, the manager, and the outside appraisers it used), and when (in connection with her effort in early 2009 to obtain a home-equity loan). This is all that she needed to put in the complaint. See *Swierkiewicz*, 534 U.S. at 511-12 (employment discrimination).

The fact that Swanson included other, largely extraneous facts in her complaint does not undermine the soundness of her pleading. She points to Citibank's announced plan to use federal money to make more loans, its refusal to follow through in her case, and Skertich's comment that he has a mixed-race family. She has not pleaded herself out of court by mentioning these facts; whether they are particularly helpful for proving her case or not is another matter that can safely be put off for another day. It was therefore error for the district court to dismiss Swanson's Fair Housing Act claim against Citibank.

Her fraud claim against Citibank stands on a different footing. . . . Swanson asserts that Citibank falsely announced plans to make federal funds available in the form of loans to all customers, when it actually intended to exclude African-American customers from those who would be eligible for the loans. Swanson relied, she says, on that false information when she applied for her home-equity loan. But she never alleged that she lost anything from the process of applying for the loan. We do not know, for example, whether there was a loan application fee, or if Citibank or she covered the cost of the appraisal. This is the kind of particular information that Rule 9 requires, and its absence means that the district court was entitled to dismiss the claim.

We now turn to Swanson's claims against Lanier and PCI. Here again, she pursues only her Fair Housing Act and fraud claims. . . .

Swanson accuses the appraisal defendants of skewing their assessment of her home because of her race. It is unclear whether she believes that they did so as part of a conspiracy with Citibank, or if she thinks that they deliberately undervalued her property on their own initiative. Once again, we find that she has pleaded enough to survive a motion under Rule 12(b)(6). The appraisal defendants knew her race, and she accuses them of discriminating against her in the specific business transaction that they had with her. When it comes to proving her case, she will need to come up with more evidence than the mere fact that PCI (through Lanier) placed a far lower value on her house than Midwest Valuations did. See *Latimore*, 151 F.3d at 715 (need more at the summary judgment stage than evidence of a discrepancy between appraisals). All we hold now is that she is entitled to take the next step in this litigation.

This does not, however, save her common-law fraud claim against Lanier and PCI. She has not adequately alleged that she relied on their appraisal, nor has she pointed to any out-of-pocket losses that she suffered because of it.

We therefore *Reverse* the judgment of the district court insofar as it dismissed Swanson's Fair Housing Act claims against all three defendants, and we *Affirm* insofar as it dismissed the common-law fraud claims against all three. Each side will bear its own costs on appeal.

POSNER, CIRCUIT JUDGE, dissenting in part.

I join the majority opinion except with respect to reversing the dismissal of the plaintiff's claim of housing discrimination. I have difficulty squaring that reversal with Ashcroft v. Iqbal, 556 U.S. 662 (2009), unless *Iqbal* is limited to cases in which there is a defense of official immunity—especially if as in that case it is asserted by very high-ranking officials (the Attorney General of the United States and the Director of the FBI)—because the defense is compromised if the defendants have to respond to discovery demands in a case unlikely to have merit. . . .

Suppose this [were] a promotion case, and several people were vying for a promotion, all were qualified, several were men and one was a woman, and one of the men received the promotion. No complexity; yet the district court would "draw on its judicial experience and common sense," *Iqbal*, 129 S. Ct. at 1950, to conclude that discrimination would not be a plausible explanation of the hiring decision, without additional allegations.

This case is even stronger for dismissal because it lacks the competitive situation—man and woman, or white and black, vying for the same job and the man, or the white, getting it. We had emphasized this distinction, long before *Twombly* and *Iqbal*, in *Latimore*, 151 F.3d 712 (7th Cir. 1998), like this a case of credit discrimination rather than promotion. "Latimore was not competing with a white person for a $51,000 loan. A bank does not announce, 'We are making a $51,000 real estate loan today; please submit your applications, and we'll choose the application that we like best and give that applicant the loan.'" Id. at 714. We held that there was no basis for an inference of discrimination. Noland v. Commerce Mortgage Corp., 122 F.3d 551, 553 (8th Cir. 1997), and Simms v. First Gibraltar Bank, 83 F.3d 1546, 1558 (5th Cir. 1996), rejected credit-discrimination claims because there was no evidence that similar applicants were treated better, and Boykin v. Bank of America Corp., 162 Fed. Appx. 837, 840 (11th Cir. 2005) (per curiam), rejected such a claim because "absent direct evidence of discrimination, there is no basis for a trier of fact to assume that a decision to deny a loan was motivated by discriminatory animus unless the plaintiff makes a showing that a pattern of lending suggests the existence of discrimination."

There is no allegation that the plaintiff in this case was competing with a white person for a loan. It was the low appraisal of her home that killed her chances for the $50,000 loan that she was seeking. The appraiser thought her home worth only $170,000, and she already owed $146,000 on it (a first mortgage of $121,000 and a home-equity loan of $25,000). A further loan of $50,000 would thus have been undersecured. We must assume that the appraisal was a mistake, and the house worth considerably more, as she alleges. But errors in appraising a house are common because "real estate appraisal is not an exact science," *Latimore*, 151 F.3d at 715—common enough to have created a market for "Real Estate Appraisers Errors & Omissions" insurance policies. See, e.g., OREP (Organization of Real Estate Professionals), "E&O Insurance," www.orep. org/appraisers-e&o.htm (visited July 11, 2010). The Supreme Court would consider error the plausible inference in this case, rather than discrimination, for it said in *Iqbal* that "as between that 'obvious alternative explanation' for the [injury of which the plaintiff is complaining] and the purposeful, invidious discrimination [the plaintiff] asks us to infer, discrimination is not a plausible conclusion." *Iqbal*, 129 S. Ct. at 1951-52, quoting *Twombly*, 550 U.S. at 567.

Even before *Twombly* and *Iqbal*, complaints were dismissed when they alleged facts that refuted the plaintiffs' claims. Under the new regime, it should be enough that the allegations render a claim implausible. The complaint alleges that Citibank was the second bank to turn down the plaintiff's application for a home-equity loan. This reinforces the inference that she was not qualified. We further learn that, subject to the appraisal, which had not yet been conducted, Citibank had approved the $50,000 home-equity loan that the plaintiff was seeking on the basis of her representation that her house was worth $270,000. But she didn't think it was worth that much when she applied for the loan. The house had been appraised at $260,000 in 2004, and the complaint alleges that home values had fallen by "only" 16 to 20 percent since. This implies that when she applied for the home-equity loan her house was worth between $208,000 and $218,400—much less than what she told Citibank it was worth.

If the house was worth $208,000, she would have owed a total of $196,000 had she gotten the loan, or just a shade under the market value of the house. If the bank had insisted that she have a 20 percent equity in the house, which would be $41,600, it would have lent her only $20,400 ($166,400—80 percent of $208,000—minus the $146,000 that she already owed on the house). The loan figure rises to $28,720 if the house was worth $218,400 rather than $208,000. In either case a $50,000 loan would have been out of the question, especially in the wake of the financial crash of September 2008, when credit, including home-equity credit, became extremely tight. E.g., Bob Tedeschi, "Opening the Tap on Home Equity," *N.Y. Times*, Nov. 7, 2008, p. RE9, www.nytimes.com/2008/11/02/realestate/02mort.html. For it was a home-equity loan that the plaintiff was seeking in early

February of 2009, at the nadir of the economic collapse—and seeking it from troubled Citibank, one of the banks that required a federal bailout in the wake of the crash. Financial reports in the weeks surrounding the plaintiff's application make clear the difficulty of obtaining credit from Citibank during that period. See Binyamin Appelbaum, "Despite Federal Aid, Many Banks Fail to Revive Lending," *Wash. Post*, Feb. 3, 2009, www.washingtonpost.com/wp-dyn/content/article/2009/02/02/AR2009020203338_pf.html ("some of the first banks to get funding, such as Citigroup and J.P. Morgan Chase, have reported the sharpest drops in lending"); Liz Moyer, "Banks Promise Loans but Hoard Cash," *Forbes.com*, Feb. 3, 2009, www.forbes.com/2009/02/03/banking-federal-reserve-business-wall-street–0203_loans.html ("'banks and other lenders have tightened access to credit and are conserving capital in order to absorb the losses that occur when borrowers default,' the company [Citibank] said: 'Citi will not and cannot take excessive risk with the capital the American public and other investors have entrusted to the company'"); Mara Der Hovanesian & David Henry, "Citi: The Losses Keep Coming," *Bloomberg BusinessWeek*, Jan. 12, 2009, www.businessweek.com/bwdaily/dnflash/content/jan2009/db20090112_136301.htm?campaign_id=rss_daily ("banks are not lending. They are using every opportunity to pull loans and force liquidations"). (All web sites were visited on July 11, 2010.)

In Erickson v. Pardus, 551 U.S. 89 (2007) (per curiam), decided two weeks after *Twombly*, the Supreme Court, without citing *Twombly*, reinstated a prisoner's civil rights suit that had been dismissed on the ground that the allegations of the complaint were "conclusory." The suit had charged deliberate indifference to the plaintiff's need for medical treatment. In the key passage in the Court's opinion, we learn that "the complaint stated that Dr. Bloor's decision to remove the petitioner [that is, the plaintiff] from his prescribed hepatitis C medication was 'endangering [his] life.' It alleged this medication was withheld 'shortly after' petitioner had commenced a treatment program that would take one year, that he was 'still in need of treatment for this disease,' and that the prison officials were in the meantime refusing to provide treatment. *This alone was enough to satisfy Rule 8(a)(2).* Petitioner, in addition, bolstered his claim by making more specific allegations in documents attached to the complaint and in later filings" (emphasis added, record citations omitted). It was reasonable to infer from these allegations, assuming their truth, that the defendants (who included Dr. Bloor, a prison doctor) had acted with deliberate indifference to the petitioner's serious medical need by refusing to provide him with any medical treatment after taking away his medication. Indeed it's difficult (again assuming the truth of the allegations) to imagine an alternative interpretation. Hepatitis C is a serious disease and the prisoner had been put in a treatment program expected to last a year. To refuse him any treatment whatsoever seemed (as the other allegations to which the Court referred confirmed) to be punitive. I think *Erickson* is good law even after *Iqbal*, but I also think it's miles away from a case in which all that's alleged (besides pure speculation about the defendants' motive) is that someone was denied a loan because her house was mistakenly appraised for less than its market value.

The majority opinion relies heavily on Swierkiewicz v. Sorema N.A., 534 U.S. 506 (2002), cited with approval in *Twombly*, see 550 U.S. at 556 (though not cited in *Iqbal*) and not overruled. Although it is regarded in some quarters as dead after *Iqbal*, e.g., Fowler v. UPMC Shadyside, 578 F.3d 203, 211 (3d Cir. 2009); Suja A. Thomas, "The New Summary Judgment Motion: The Motion to Dismiss Under *Iqbal* and *Twombly*," 14 Lewis & Clark L. Rev. 15, 35 (2010), lower-court judges are not to deem a Supreme Court decision overruled even if it is plainly inconsistent with a subsequent decision. State Oil Co. v. Khan, 522 U.S. 3 (1997). But that principle is not applicable here; *Swierkiewicz* is distinguishable.

. . . Title VII cases are not exempted by *Swierkiewicz* from the doctrine of the *Iqbal* case. *Iqbal* establishes a general requirement of "plausibility" applicable to all civil cases in federal courts.

It does so, however, in opaque language: "The plausibility standard is not akin to a 'probability requirement,' but it asks for more than a sheer possibility that a defendant has acted unlawfully." 129 S. Ct. at 1949. In statistics the range of probabilities is from 0 to 1, and therefore encompasses "sheer possibility" along with "plausibility." It seems (no stronger word is possible) that what the Court was driving at was that even if the district judge doesn't think a plaintiff's case is more likely than not to be a winner (that is, doesn't think $p > .5$), as long as it is substantially justified that's enough to avert dismissal. Cf. Equal Access to Justice Act, 28 U.S.C. § 2412(d)(1)(A). But when a bank turns down a loan applicant because the appraisal of the security for the loan indicates that the loan would not be adequately secured, the alternative hypothesis of racial discrimination does not have substantial merit; it is implausible.

Behind both *Twombly* and *Iqbal* lurks a concern with asymmetric discovery burdens and the potential for extortionate litigation (similar to that created by class actions, to which Rule 23(f) of the civil rules was a response) . . . that such an asymmetry creates. In most suits against corporations or other institutions, and in both *Twombly* and *Iqbal*—but also in the present case—the plaintiff wants or needs more discovery of the defendant than the defendant wants or needs of the plaintiff, because the plaintiff has to search the defendant's records (and, through depositions, the minds of the defendant's employees) to obtain evidence of wrongdoing. With the electronic archives of large corporations or other large organizations holding millions of emails and other electronic communications, the cost of discovery to a defendant has become in many cases astronomical. And the cost is not only monetary; it can include, as well, the disruption of the defendant's operations. If no similar costs are borne by the plaintiff in complying with the defendant's discovery demands, the costs to the defendant may induce it to agree early in the litigation to a settlement favorable to the plaintiff.

It is true, as critics of *Twombly* and *Iqbal* point out, that district courts have authority to limit discovery. But especially in busy districts, which is where complex litigation is concentrated, the judges tend to delegate that authority to magistrate judges. And because the magistrate judge to whom a case is delegated for discovery only is not responsible for the trial or the decision and can have only an imperfect sense of how widely the district judge would want the factual inquiry in the case to roam to enable him to decide it, the magistrate judge is likely to err on the permissive side. "One common form of unnecessary discovery (and therefore a ready source of threatened discovery) is delving into ten issues when one will be dispositive. A magistrate lacks the authority to carve off the nine unnecessary issues; for all the magistrate knows, the judge may want evidence on any one of them. So the magistrate stands back and lets the parties have at it. Pursuit of factual and legal issues that will not matter to the outcome of the case is a source of enormous unnecessary costs, yet it is one hard to conquer in a system of notice pleading and even harder to limit when an officer lacking the power to decide the case supervises discovery." Frank H. Easterbrook, "Discovery as Abuse," 69 B.U. L. Rev. 635, 639 (1989); see also Milton Pollack, "Discovery — Its Abuse and Correction," 80 F.R.D. 219, 223 (1979); Virginia E. Hench, "Mandatory Disclosure and Equal Access to Justice: The 1993 Federal Discovery Rules Amendments and the Just, Speedy and Inexpensive Determination of Every Action," 67 Temple L. Rev. 179, 232 (1994).

This structural flaw helps to explain and justify the Supreme Court's new approach. It requires the plaintiff to conduct a more extensive precomplaint investigation than used to be required and so creates greater symmetry between the plaintiff's and the defendant's litigation costs, and by doing so reduces the scope for extortionate discovery. If the plaintiff shows that he can't conduct an even minimally adequate investigation without limited discovery, the judge presumably can allow that discovery, meanwhile deferring ruling on the defendant's motion to dismiss. Miller v. Gammie, 335 F.3d 889, 899 (9th Cir. 2003) (en banc); Coss v. Playtex Products, LLC, No. 08 C 50222, 2009 WL 1455358 (N.D. Ill. May 21, 2009); Edward A. Hartnett, "Taming *Twombly*, Even After *Iqbal*," 158 U. Pa. L. Rev. 473, 507-14 (2010); Suzette M. Malveaux, "Front Loading and Heavy Lifting: How Pre-Dismissal Discovery Can Address the Detrimental Effect of Iqbal on Civil Rights Cases," 14 Lewis & Clark L. Rev. 65 (2010). No one has suggested such a resolution for this case.

The plaintiff has an implausible case of discrimination, but she will now be permitted to serve discovery demands that will compel elaborate document review by Citibank and require its executives to sit for many hours of depositions. (Not that the plaintiff is capable of conducting such proceedings as a pro se, but on remand she may — indeed she would be well advised to — ask the judge to help her find a lawyer.) The threat of such an imposition will induce Citibank to consider settlement even if the suit has no merit at all. That is the pattern that the Supreme Court's recent decisions are aimed at disrupting.

We should affirm the dismissal of the suit in its entirety.

## *Notes and Questions*

1. Do you agree with the majority that neither *Twombly* nor *Iqbal* altered the basic principles of notice pleading?

2. How much does the suggestion of conspiracy between the appraiser and Citibank add to the plausibility of Swanson's discrimination claim? Do you think the majority's reasoning depends on assumptions about the nature of implicit bias?

3. The dissent claims that *Iqbal* controls this case. Are there grounds to distinguish *Iqbal* other than the argument that cases against government officers entitled to immunity are unique? Perhaps a distinction can be drawn between "garden variety" discrimination claims under Title VII and the kind of purposeful discrimination the Supreme Court held must be shown in suits against government actors under § 1983.

4. It is a truism with which you are now familiar that allegations in a complaint are to be treated as true. What about inferences that can be drawn from those allegations? Under notice pleading the inferences went to the plaintiff—that was a central effect of the "any set of facts" standard. It resolved doubt, grounded in inferences, in favor of the plaintiff.

Does the same practice hold under plausibility pleading? What inferences underpin Judge Posner's analysis? Notice the wide range of sources he cites. Is it permissible to supplement the allegations of the complaint with outside fact gathering regarding, say, the financial conditions at the time Swanson applied for her loan in order to determine whether the complaint is plausible? Or is this no more than the kind of "common sense" analysis the Supreme Court invited in *Iqbal*?

5. Both the majority and the dissent emphasize the relationship between pleading and discovery. They appear to be debating the effects of pleading standards on discovery costs, just as the Supreme Court did in *Twombly* and *Iqbal*. The primary concern, highlighted by the dissent, is asymmetric costs. Neither opinion, however, has anything to say about asymmetric *information*—whether the cause of action is one as to which access to the most relevant evidence rests uniquely with the plaintiff or defendant. Would the discussion of asymmetric discovery costs proceed on different terms if asymmetries in information were made explicit? If the unique nature of asymmetries in discrimination claims were made explicit? Or is Judge Posner's point the same as Justice Souter's in *Twombly*—that discovery is broken and can only be managed through pleading rules, even in cases of information asymmetry?

6. For all the concern about complaints that fall short of the new plausibility standard by failing to include enough detail, courts still gripe about complaints that are "prolix." In UPS Store, Inc. v. Hagen, Inc., 2015 WL 1456654, at *1-2 (S.D.N.Y. 2015), for example, the court admonished both parties in the course of ruling on a 12(b)(6) motion:

A troubling trend toward prolixity in pleading is infecting court dockets in this district and elsewhere. As this case illustrates, a growing number of attorneys, from solo practitioners to 'big law' partners, are ignoring Rule 8. . . . UPS launched its relatively straightforward claims with a sprawling 175-paragraph Complaint, larded with more than 1,400 pages of exhibits. . . . [Defendants] retaliated with a 210-page, 1,020-paragraph Answer asserting twelve counterclaims and attaching voluminous exhibits. . . . Voluminous pleading is self-defeating. It chokes the docket and obscures otherwise meritorious claims and defenses. . . . Lawyers should think twice about the burden they impose on judges to wade through surfeit pleadings. . . . They should also think about their clients who presumably come to court "to secure the just, speedy, and inexpensive determination" of their claims. Fed. R. Civ. P. 1.

This may be the bitter fruit of *Twombly* and *Iqbal*—to avoid dismissal and the vagaries of different judges' conceptions of what is plausible in the exercise of "common sense," attorneys may err in the direction of prolixity.

7. Confusion and disagreement about how to apply the new plausibility pleading standard extends well beyond the Seventh Circuit. In some courts the standard is strictly applied. See, e.g., Sanders v. Grenadier Realty, Inc., 367 Fed. Appx. 173, 2010 WL 605715 (2d Cir. Feb. 22, 2010) (upholding dismissal of Fair Housing Act and First Amendment claims brought by African-American residents of a New York housing project); Nemet Chevrolet Ltd. v. Consumeraffairs.com, Inc., 591 F.3d 250, 262 (4th Cir. 2009) ("*Twombly* and *Iqbal* announced a new, stricter pleading standard"; "the present federal pleading regime is a significant change from the past"); cf. Vega v. Hempstead Union Free School Dist., 801 F.3d 72 (2d Cir. 2015) (reversing dismissal of § 1983 and Title VII employment discrimination suit).

In others, the standard is applied on terms that appear to resemble the notice pleading standard of *Conley*. Braden v. Wal-Mart Stores, 588 F.3d 585, 595-598 (8th Cir. 2009) (reversing dismissal of class action against Wal-Mart by employees asserting the company mismanaged its employee retirement plans; holding that the district court ignored reasonable inferences supported by the facts alleged in the complaint and improperly drew inferences for the defendants rather than the plaintiff; "*Rule 8 does not require a plaintiff to plead facts tending to rebut all possible lawful explanations for a defendant's conduct. . . . Not every potential lawful explanation for the defendant's conduct renders the plaintiff's theory implausible. Just as a plaintiff cannot proceed if his allegations are '"merely consistent with' a defendant's liability,*" *Iqbal*, at 1949 (quoting *Twombly*, 550 U.S. at 557), *so a defendant is not entitled to dismissal if the facts are merely consistent with lawful conduct.*") (emphasis added).

8. *Twombly* and *Iqbal* addressed the obligation of a plaintiff to plead facts showing her claims are plausible. The Supreme Court recently held that the plaintiff is under no obligation to specify the *legal theory* supporting her claim. Even if she knows the statute or cause of action under which she seeks to recover, she does not have to cite it to survive a motion to dismiss. As the Court put it:

Federal pleading rules call for a "short and plain statement of the claim showing that the pleader is entitled to relief," Fed. Rule Civ. Proc. 8(a)(2); they do not countenance dismissal of a complaint for imperfect statement of the legal theory supporting the claim asserted. . . . Our decisions in [*Twombly*] and [*Iqbal*] are not in point, for they concern the *factual* allegations a complaint must contain to survive a motion to dismiss. A plaintiff, they instruct, must plead facts sufficient to show that her claim has substantive plausibility. [Plaintiff's] complaint was not deficient in that regard.

Johnson v. City of Shelby, 135 S. Ct. 346, 346-347 (2014) (police officers alleged they were fired in retaliation for reporting criminal activities by one of the city aldermen; Fifth Circuit dismissed for failure to "expressly invoke" § 1983 in the complaint). In many state courts, however, the plaintiff will at least have to take an educated guess as to her legal theory because form pleadings require the plaintiff to check a box indicating the cause of action the case arises under. Indeed, in some courts, digital form pleading has supplanted drafting. See, for example, http://www.intresys.com (providing e-filing software to counties in California and Texas).

### Note: Plausibility Versus Probability

One of the ambiguities lingering after *Twombly* and *Iqbal, and discussed in Swanson,* is whether a complaint must contain enough factual detail to make the plaintiff's claim seem "probable" in order to meet the plausibility standard. Justice Kennedy states in *Iqbal* that "[t]he plausibility standard is not a 'probability' requirement," but he immediately adds that plaintiffs must plead facts establishing more than "a sheer possibility that the defendant has acted unlawfully." And in his substantive analysis, he twice uses the term "likely" in a way that suggests a complaint is "plausible" only when it contains facts sufficient to conclude that the inferences of liability are *more likely true* than innocent inferences. See supra, *Iqbal* Section IV.B ("given more likely explanations, [the allegations] do not plausibly establish this purpose"; "the arrests Mueller oversaw were likely lawful and justified by his nondiscriminatory intent to detain aliens who were illegally present in the United States and who had potential connections to terrorist acts"). Isn't Justice Souter's test in *Twombly* narrower? Does Judge Posner's framing strike you as correct?

A First Circuit case illustrates the challenges faced by lower courts in distinguishing plausibility and probability. In Sepúlveda-Villarini v. Department of Education of Puerto Rico, 628 F.3d 25 (1st Cir. 2010), two public school teachers sued school officials for violating the Americans with Disabilities Act and the Rehabilitation Act. The complaint alleged that school officials failed to make reasonable accommodations for their disabilities. The complaint alleged that over a four- to five-year period, school officials had reduced their class sizes in response to accommodation requests. Subsequent increases in class sizes caused deterioration in plaintiffs' emotional and physical health, requiring them to seek medical treatment.

The district court dismissed the complaint on the ground that the plaintiffs had not explained "how" increases in class size were significant or causally related to their health problems. The First Circuit reversed. It reasoned that if the complaint had been read in the light most favorable to plaintiffs, the trial court would have assumed that the change in class sizes was the sole variable, allowing a causal connection with the physical and emotional deterioration of plaintiffs' health to be inferred. The trial court's approach, by contrast, would have required plaintiffs to plead "details of medical evidence" to establish causation. That level of detail is not required by *Twombly*, which cautions against treating the plausibility standard as a requirement that plaintiffs show they are *likely* to succeed on the merits:

> ... *Twombly* cautioned against thinking of plausibility as a standard of likely success on the merits; the standard is plausibility assuming the pleaded facts to be true and read in a plaintiff's favor. . . .
>
> None of this is to deny the wisdom of the old maxim that after the fact does not necessarily mean caused by the fact, but its teaching here is not that the inference of causation is implausible (taking the facts as true), but that it is possible that other, undisclosed facts may explain the sequence better. Such a possibility does not negate plausibility, however; it is simply a reminder that plausibility of allegations may not be matched by adequacy of evidence. A plausible but inconclusive inference from pleaded facts will survive a motion to dismiss, and the fair inferences from the facts pleaded in these cases point to the essential difference between each of them and the circumstances in *Twombly*, for example, in which the same actionable conduct alleged on the defendant's part had been held in some prior cases to be lawful behavior.

628 F.3d at 30.

In In re Text Messaging Antitrust Litigation, 630 F.3d 622 (7th Cir. 2010), a putative class of subscribers to cellular telephone services brought suit against wireless service providers for allegedly conspiring to fix the pricing of text messaging services. The district court held that the first amended complaint failed to state a claim, but dismissed without prejudice. After the plaintiffs filed a second amended complaint, defendants moved to dismiss again, arguing that the complaint did not satisfy the *Twombly* pleading standard. This time the district court denied the motion.

The defendants then sought permission to file an interlocutory appeal to have the Seventh Circuit rule immediately on the denial of the motion to dismiss. The Seventh Circuit agreed to take up the appeal. After analyzing the complaint's allegations under the plausibility standard, the Seventh Circuit "agree[d] with the district judge that the complaint alleges a conspiracy with sufficient plausibility to satisfy the pleading standard of *Twombly*." As with the First Circuit's decision in *Sepúlveda-Villerini*, the court homed in on the relationship between plausibility and probability:

> The Court said in *Iqbal* that the "plausibility standard is not akin to a 'probability requirement,' but it asks for more than a sheer possibility that a defendant has acted unlawfully." 129 S. Ct. at 1949. This is a little unclear because plausibility, probability, and possibility overlap. Probability runs the gamut from a zero likelihood to a certainty. What is impossible has a zero

likelihood of occurring and what is plausible has a moderately high likelihood of occurring. The fact that the allegations undergirding a claim could be true is no longer enough to save a complaint from being dismissed; the complaint must establish a nonnegligible probability that the claim is valid; but the probability need not be as great as such terms as "preponderance of the evidence" connote.

The plaintiffs have conducted no discovery. Discovery may reveal the smoking gun or bring to light additional circumstantial evidence that further tilts the balance in favor of liability. All that we conclude at this early stage in the litigation is that the district judge was right to rule that the second amended complaint provides a sufficiently plausible case of price fixing to warrant allowing the plaintiffs to proceed to discovery.

630 F.3d at 629. On this view, plausibility pleading *is* a probabilistic inquiry, but the allegations in the complaint do not have to be more likely than not true (> .5 as Judge Posner put it in *Swanson*), to survive a motion to dismiss. As a formal, mathematical matter, that makes sense. But in practical application it seems likely that what convinces a judge that a complaint is plausible (as opposed to merely possible) is comparison between the inferences that establish liability and the inferences that cut against it. In *Swanson*, for instance, Judge Posner thinks there are simple market explanations for what Citibank did, whereas the majority treats the pervasiveness of racial discrimination as an important background fact that informs the inferences it draws about the bank's withdrawal of the loan. Once we move past judging whether a complaint states a claim on the standard set out in *Conley* there may not be any way to prevent judges from relying on (probabilistic) background assumptions about economic and social behavior.

## Note: Trans-substantivity, Information Asymmetry, and Discovery

A separate concern is that the Court in *Twombly* and *Iqbal* invited lower courts to carve out special rules for certain types of cases. This is a real departure from the trans-substantive nature of the Federal Rules, thought by the original rulemakers to be one of their greatest accomplishments and a vindication of core due process values. Recall that the Seventh Circuit appeared to reject trans-substantivity in *Swanson*. 614 F.3d at 404-405 ("[I]n many straightforward cases, it will not be any more difficult for a plaintiff to meet [the pleading] burden than it was before the Court's recent decisions . . . [but a] more complex case . . . will require more detail.").

Consider as well the tension between the due process values of efficiency and access to justice. The Court in *Twombly* decries the way in which costly discovery can yield *"in terrorem"* increases in settlement values, and *Twombly* seeks to prevent the injustice that results when defendants are forced to spend significant time and money responding to claims that later turn out to be baseless. On the other hand, in antitrust cases and discrimination cases, the "smoking gun" evidence often rests *exclusively* in the hands of defendants. It is not at all clear how plaintiffs in such cases could prevail without reaching discovery to develop the necessary proof. And there is some evidence that the new pleading standard is much easier to meet when the degree of asymmetry between what the plaintiff and defendant know is relatively small. See, e.g., Bowen v. Warden Baldwin State Prison, 2016 WL 3435501 (11th Cir. June 22, 2016) (upholding denial of motion to dismiss in 1983 and Eighth Amendment suit to recover damages where prisoner was beaten to death by a cell mate; detailed allegations regarding history of violence, mental health conditions, and threat posed by cellmate sufficient to infer that deputy warden and corrections officers were aware of and ignored substantial risk of harm to decedent); Connelly v. Lane, 809 F.3d 780 (3d Cir. 2016) (reversing dismissal of sexual harassment claim brought by female truck driver against company where complaint pled repeated incidents of harassment, retaliation for raising reporting those incidents, and being replaced by male drivers with lower union seniority). Paradoxically then, the cases that would most benefit from discovery are least likely to survive the motion to dismiss.

Part of the original purpose of the Rules was to allow easy access to court through simplified pleading, and to let the allegations be filled in through discovery. As we will see in Chapter 3, the original scope of discovery in Rule 26 was correspondingly broad; parties might seek from each other any information "relevant to the subject matter involved in the action." The nature, cost, and depth of discovery would vary among different types of civil actions according to the merits and incentives of the parties, but the overall principle was to ensure that all cases were decided on their merits after full fact development in discovery.

Amendments to Rule 26, adopted before *Twombly* and *Iqbal*, modified this regime by restricting initial mandatory disclosures among the parties to discovery of information that is *relevant to the claims or defenses of the disclosing party*, and restricting ordinary discovery to information relevant to claims and defenses of *any* party. Subsequent amendments in 2015 provide that all discovery should be limited in proportion to the size and complexity of the case. Even under a liberal notice pleading standard these new discovery rules likely would have affected pleading behavior. That is because they create incentives to plead claims and defenses with more specificity than Rule 8 would have required in order to trigger broader mandatory discovery duties for one's opponent and justify broader discovery down the road. In a plausibility pleading regime, the incentives to plead more would seem even greater. At least, that is, where one possesses the facts necessary to plead with specificity.

### Note: Public Debate and Empirics

Congress considered restoring some version of notice pleading in 2009, but legislative efforts stalled out. See S. 1504, Notice Pleading Restoration

Act of 2009. On July 22, 2009, the bill was referred to the Senate Judiciary Committee. The substantive provision of the bill provided:

> Except as otherwise expressly provided by an Act of Congress or by an amendment to the Federal Rules of Civil Procedure which takes effect after the date of enactment of this Act, a Federal court shall not dismiss a complaint under rule 12(b)(6) or (e) of the Federal Rules of Civil Procedure, except under the standards set forth by the Supreme Court of the United States in Conley v. Gibson, 355 U.S. 41 (1957).

The bill was reintroduced in 2010 but never made it out of committee. For the parallel bill in the House, see H.R. 4115, Open Access to Courts Act of 2009. The Civil Rules Advisory Committee also has considered making amendments to the Rules in response to *Twombly* and *Iqbal*. However, the Committee has indicated that it wants to study the effects of plausibility pleading in detail before taking any action. For its latest report, following a May 2010 conference, see http://www.uscourts.gov/uscourts/RulesAndPolicies/rules/Reports/CV05-2010.pdf.

Academic commentary, favorable and critical, on plausibility pleading and procedural reform is already legion. See David Marcus, The Past, Present, and Future of Trans-Substantivity in Federal Civil Procedure, 59 DePaul L. Rev. 371 (2010); Adam Steinman, The Pleading Problem, 62 Stan. L. Rev. 1293 (2010); Scott Dodson, New Pleading, New Discovery, 109 Mich. L. Rev. 53 (2010); A. Benjamin Spencer, *Iqbal* and the Slide Toward Restrictive Procedure, 14 Lewis & Clark L. Rev. 185 (2010); Richard Nagareda, 1938 All Over Again? Pre-Trial as Trial in Complex Litigation, 60 DePaul L. Rev. 647 (2011); Robert G. Bone, *Twombly*, Pleading Rules, and the Regulation of Court Access, 94 Iowa L. Rev. 873 (2009); Robert G. Bone, Plausibility Pleading Revisited and Revised: A Comment on *Ashcroft v. Iqbal*, 85 Notre Dame L. Rev. 849 (2010); Kevin M. Clermont and Stephen C. Yeazell, Inventing Tests, Destabilizing Systems, 95 Iowa L. Rev. 821 (2010); Samuel Issacharoff, Private Claims, Aggregate Rights, Sup. Ct. Rev. (2008); Kevin M. Clermont, Litigation Realities Redux, 84 Notre Dame L. Rev. 1919 (2009). See also Daniel E. Troy and John O'Tuel, A Toolkit for Change: How the Federal Civil Rules Advisory Committee Can Fix a Civil Justice System "In Serious Need of Repair," 25 Legal Backgrounder, Issue No. 19 May, 21 (2010); Denver University Law Review Symposium—Civil Justice Reform, 87 Denv. U. L. Rev. 213 (2010); Hearing on Whether the Supreme Court Has Limited Americans' Access to Court, Before the Committee on the Judiciary, United States Senate, Prepared Statement of Stephen B. Burbank, Dec. 2, 2009.

Brooke Coleman and A. Benjamin Spencer have raised especially provocative questions about the development of plausibility pleading. Professor Spencer situates plausibility pleading in the context of a more "restrictive ethos" in the jurisprudence of procedure and in the implementation of procedural rules. A. Benjamin Spencer, The Restrictive Ethos in Civil Procedure, 78 Geo. Wash. L. Rev. 353 (2010). Professor Coleman argues that "the departure from a liberal procedural regime is not just a complex response to a complex world. . . . [R]estrictive changes to procedure do not have a neutral effect. Judges, Congress, and the rulemaking bodies responsible for procedural changes are making trade-offs, and those trade-offs are made based on value judgments. . . . [T]he price of a restrictive shift in procedural doctrine is that it marginalizes particular claims, and by extension, particular people," especially those who are already economically and socially marginalized. Brooke Coleman, The Vanishing Plaintiff, 42 Seton Hall L. Rev. 501, 502-503 (2012).

Although *Twombly* and *Iqbal* have not had much time to percolate through the lower courts, empirical studies of their possible effects are already in print. As you read what follows here, consider what conclusions you would draw about amendments to Rule 8 if you were on the Civil Rules Advisory Committee.

An early study comparing post-*Twombly* cases to a control group of cases using the old *Conley* standard found that the new "plausibility" requirement had little impact on the rate of 12(b)(6) dismissals in most areas of law. However, in civil rights cases that cited *Twombly*, the plaintiffs' claims were dismissed at a statistically higher rate than under the old *Conley* framework. See Kendall W. Hannon, Note, Much Ado About *Twombly*: A Study on the Impact of *Bell Atlantic Corp. v. Twombly* on 12(b)(6) Motions, 83 Notre Dame L. Rev. 1811 (2008).

In March 2011, the Federal Judicial Center released a Report to the Advisory Committee on Civil Rules entitled Motions to Dismiss for Failure to State a Claim After *Iqbal*, authored by Joe S. Cecil, George W. Cort, Margaret S. Williams, and Jared J. Bataillon. The report casts doubt on the earlier evidence suggesting that *Twombly* and *Iqbal* were having a significant effect in the lower courts, even in civil rights cases. The executive summary states:

This report presents the findings of a Federal Judicial Center study on the filing and resolution of motions to dismiss for failure to state a claim under Rule 12(b)(6) of the Federal Rules of Civil Procedure. The study was requested by the Judicial Conference Advisory Committee on Civil Rules. The study compared motion activity in 23 federal district courts in 2006 and 2010 and included an assessment of the outcome of motions in orders that do not appear in the computerized legal reference systems such as Westlaw. Statistical models were used to control for such factors as differences in levels of motion activity in individual federal district courts and types of cases.

After excluding cases filed by prisoners and pro se parties, and after controlling for differences in motion activity across federal district courts and across types of cases and for the presence of an amended complaint, we found the following:

- There was a general increase from 2006 to 2010 in the rate of filing of motions to dismiss for failure to state a claim.
- In general, there was no increase in the rate of grants of motions to dismiss without leave to amend. There was, in particular, no increase in the rate of grants of motions to dismiss without leave to amend in civil rights cases and employment discrimination cases.

- Only in cases challenging mortgage loans on both federal and state law grounds did we find an increase in the rate of grants of motions to dismiss without leave to amend. Many of these cases were removed from state to federal court. This category of cases tripled in number during the relevant period in response to events in the housing market. There is no reason to believe that the rate of dismissals without leave to amend would have been lower in 2006 had such cases existed then.
- There was no increase from 2006 to 2010 in the rate at which a grant of a motion to dismiss terminated the case.

The report can be found at http://www.fjc.gov/public/pdf.nsf/lookup/motioniqbal.pdf/$file/motioniqbal.pdf.

In the same year the Statistics Division of the Administrative Office of the United States Courts published a data set on motions to dismiss before and after *Iqbal* based on data collected electronically from 94 district courts' docket entries. According to Professor William Janssen:

This data is amenable to a few observations. First, the raw totals of newly filed motions to dismiss jumped meaningfully in the four months following the *Iqbal* decision when compared to the filing activity in the four months immediately preceding the *Twombly* decision, but that growth in numbers has stopped and begun to ebb through the 13 months after *Iqbal*. Second, the volume of dismissal motions granted likewise jumped in the four months following *Iqbal* when compared to the four months preceding *Twombly*, but that growth, too, seems to have stalled and begun to recede. Third, when measured against new-motion filing activity, the percentage of motions to dismiss that were granted has remained essentially level. In fact, when the data for the full last 13 months is considered, the percentage of motions granted has actually fallen to a point lower now than it was during the pre-*Twombly* period. Fourth, the number of motions to dismiss that were denied also rose significantly in the period after *Iqbal* as compared to the period before *Twombly*, but that growth has likewise now ended and the numbers have begun to recede. Whether these figures represent actual trends, or mere anomalies influenced by the small volumes of data and the brief window of time, remains unclear.

Professor Janssen has also published an article examining the empirical effect of *Iqbal* on federal pharmaceutical and medical device litigation. William M. Jannsen, *Iqbal* "Plausibility" in Pharmaceutical and Medical Device Litigation, 71 La. L. Rev. 541 (2011).

Jonah B. Gelbach questions the methodology used in other studies, such as the Federal Judicial Center's study quoted above. His analysis indicates a much more significant effect in the shift to plausibility pleading. Jonah G. Gelbach, Locking the Doors to Discovery? Conceptual Challenges in and Empirical Results for Assessing the Effects of *Twombly* and *Iqbal* on Access to Discovery, 121 Yale L.J. 2270 (2012) ("*Twombly* and *Iqbal* have negatively affected plaintiffs in at least 15% to 20% of cases that faced Rule 12(b)(6) motions in the post-*Iqbal* data window. . . . [T]hese figures represent between one-fourth and two-fifths of the cases that fail to reach discovery on at least some claims."). See also Patricia Hatamyar, The Tao of Pleading: Do *Twombly* and *Iqbal* Matter Empirically?, 59 Am. U. L. Rev. 553 (2010) (concluding, "with some caution, that *Twombly* and *Iqbal* have significantly increased the rate at which 12(b)(6) motions have been granted by district courts").

An interesting study looking beyond mere filing and grant rates for Rule 12(b)(6) motions was conducted by Senior Federal Judicial Center researchers Emery G. Lee III and Thomas E. Willging. See Attorney Satisfaction with the Federal Rules of Civil Procedure: Report to the Judicial Conference Advisory Committee on Civil Rules, Federal Judicial Center, March 2010. The article provides a comparison of the results of three surveys of attorneys in the American College of Trial Lawyers, the American Bar Association Section of Litigation, and the National Employment Lawyers Association.

The results of a National Employment Lawyers Association survey attempting to evaluate the impact of "plausibility" pleading on employment law practice is of particular interest. Over 70 percent of those who responded agreed that *Iqbal* and/or *Twombly* had "affected how [they] structure complaints in employment discrimination cases." Specifically, the vast majority of responders agreed that they now "include more factual allegations in the complaint than . . . prior to *Twombly/Iqbal*" and that they "have to respond to motions to dismiss that might not have been filed prior to *Twombly/Iqbal*" (74.6 percent). Interestingly, however, fewer than 15 percent of responders agreed that they "conduct more factual investigation," that they "screen cases more carefully," or that they "raise different claims" after *Twombly/Iqbal*. Of those who had actually filed an employment discrimination case since the *Twombly* decision was released, only 7.2 percent agreed that a case had been dismissed "for failure to state a claim under the standard announced in *Twombly/Iqbal*." In Measuring the Impact of Plausibility Pleading, 101 Virginia L. Rev. 2117 (2015), Alex Reinert reviews the published and unpublished resolution of motions to dismiss in 4,200 cases from 15 different judicial districts in the years 2006, before *Twombly* was decided, and 2010. He reports that in cases in which the plaintiff had counsel, the dismissal rate rose 13 percentage points (from 40 percent to 53 percent), and in pro se cases 11 percentage points (from 75 percent to 86 percent), "nearly extinguish[ing] any chance that a pro se complaint will survive a motion to dismiss." Id. at 2143. Moreover, he reports that the vast majority of courts dismissing pro se complaints (83 percent) do so on the ground that the plausibility pleading standards announced in *Twombly* and *Iqbal* control. Finally, unlike the FJC study, which did not find a statistically significant increase in the dismissal of civil rights cases, Reinert found an 18 percent increase in the dismissal of civil rights cases. Id. See also Eisenberg & Clermont, Plaintiphobia in the Supreme Court, 100 Cornell L. Rev. 193 (2014) (examining long-term rates of pretrial disposition in constitutional tort and employment discrimination cases).

Isn't there something incurably speculative about trying to figure out how a case might have come out if the trial judge had not been bound by the plausibility pleading standard? Wouldn't one have to read the complaint and interview the lawyers and parties in the case? Isn't the most important question how many cases have *not* been filed at all because plaintiffs' lawyers conclude that the new pleading standard cannot be met? Or that it cannot be met without expending more money in pretrial investigation than the case appears to be worth? See Brooke Coleman, The Vanishing Plaintiff, 42 Seton Hall L. Rev. 501 (2012). Other scholars have tied the new plausibility pleading standard into previous procedural reforms and suggest that we have entered a new era of hostility to federal court adjudication. See, e.g., Judith Resnik, The Privatization of Process: Requiem for and Celebration of the Federal Rules of Civil Procedure at 75, 162 U. Pa. L. Rev. 1793 (2014); Stephen Subrin and Thomas O. Main, The Fourth Era of American Civil Procedure, 162 U. Pa. L. Rev. 1839 (2014).

Profound reasons for methodological skepticism regarding empirical studies of the new pleading standard are explored in David Engstrom's article, The Twiqbal Puzzle and Empirical Study of Civil Procedure, 65 Stan. L. Rev. 1203 (2013). Engstrom examines every published empirical study of the effects of *Twombly* and *Iqbal* to date and shows that *none* take account of both whether dismissals were granted with or without leave to amend and litigant "selection and settlement effects." Moreover, few rely on random samples and many fail to employ multiple regressions with statistical controls. He warns that "low-grade empirical research" resulting in "wildly divergent empirical findings" can be "counterproductive" and contradict a core purpose of empirical study — "disciplin[ing] public debate over litigation by deterring the more overheated claims made by the Chamber of Commerce, the American Tort Reform Association, or the plaintiffs' bar." Recent empirical studies of pleading appear rather to be "muddying debate and liberating public actors from any data-based accountability at all." Id. at 1236.

### b. Special Pleading Requirements: Statutory and Rule-Imposed Burdens

*Twombly* and *Iqbal* claim to be interpretations of the language in Rule 8(a)(2). One of the reasons notice pleading endured for so long is that the Supreme Court previously insisted that if Congress or the Advisory Committee believed certain cases should meet a higher pleading standard, it could simply say so in the Rules or separate legislation. For instance, in Leatherman v. Tarrant County Narcotics Intelligence & Coordination Unit, 507 U.S. 163 (1993) — a case the Court attempts to distinguish in *Twombly* — the Fifth Circuit had created a "heightened pleading requirement" for civil rights cases against municipalities under 42 U.S.C. § 1983. In a unanimous opinion, the Court reversed, emphasizing that standard principles of statutory interpretation preclude judicial expansion of heightened pleading requirements:

We think that it is impossible to square the "heightened pleading standard" applied by the Fifth Circuit in this case with the liberal system of "notice pleading" set up by the Federal Rules. Rule 8(a)(2) requires that a complaint include only "a short and plain statement of the claim showing that the pleader is entitled to relief." In Conley v. Gibson, 355 U.S. 41 (1957), we said in effect that the Rule meant what it said:

> [T]he Federal Rules of Civil Procedure do not require a claimant to set out in detail the facts upon which he bases his claim. To the contrary, all the Rules require is "a short and plain statement of the claim" that will give the defendant fair notice of what the plaintiff's claim is and the grounds upon which it rests. Id. at 47 (footnote omitted).

Rule 9(b) does impose a particularity requirement in two specific instances. It provides that "[i]n all averments of fraud or mistake, the circumstances constituting fraud or mistake shall be stated with particularity." Thus, the Federal Rules do address in Rule 9(b) the question of the need for greater particularity in pleading certain actions, but do not include among the enumerated actions any reference to complaints alleging municipal liability under § 1983. *Expressio unius est exclusio alterius.*

The phenomenon of litigation against municipal corporations based on claimed constitutional violations by their employees dates from our decision in *Monell*, where we for the first time construed § 1983 to allow such municipal liability. Perhaps if Rules 8 and 9 were rewritten today, claims against municipalities under § 1983 might be subjected to the added specificity requirement of Rule 9(b). *But that is a result which must be obtained by the process of amending the Federal Rules, and not by judicial interpretation. In the absence of such an amendment, federal courts and litigants must rely on summary judgment and control of discovery to weed out unmeritorious claims sooner rather than later.*

507 U.S. at 168-169 (emphasis added).

The details of the police misconduct alleged in the complaint in *Leatherman* received very little attention, even in Justice Rehnquist's majority opinion. Consider the following excerpt from the Fifth Circuit opinion:

> This civil rights case arose out of two separate incidents involving the execution of search warrants by law enforcement officers with the Tarrant County Narcotics Intelligence and Coordination Unit. One incident involved Charlene Leatherman, her son Travis, and her two dogs, Shakespeare and Ninja. Ms. Leatherman and Travis were driving in Fort Worth when they were suddenly stopped by police cars. Police officers surrounded the two of them, shouting instructions and threatening to shoot them. The officers informed Ms. Leatherman that other law enforcement officers were in the process of searching her residence. The officers also informed her that the search team had shot and killed their two dogs. Ms. Leatherman and Travis returned to their home to find Shakespeare lying dead some twenty-five feet from the front door. He had been shot three times, once in the stomach, once in the leg, and once in the head. Ninja was lying in a pool of blood on the bed in the master bedroom. He had been shot in the head at close range, evidently with a shotgun, and brain matter was splattered across the bed,

against the wall, and on the floor around the bed. The officers found nothing in the home relevant to their investigation. Rather than departing with dispatch, they proceeded to lounge on the front lawn of the Leatherman home for over an hour, drinking, smoking, talking, and laughing, apparently celebrating their seemingly unbridled power.

The other incident alleged in plaintiffs' amended complaint involved a police raid of the home of Gerald Andert pursuant to a search warrant. The warrant was issued on the basis that police officers had smelled odors associated with the manufacture of amphetamines emanating from the Andert home. At the time of the raid, Andert, a sixty-four year old grandfather, was at home with his family mourning the death of his wife; she had died after a three year battle with cancer. Without knocking or identifying themselves, the officers burst into the home and, without provocation, began beating Andert. First, an unidentified officer knocked him backwards. When Andert turned, he was greeted by two swift blows to the head inflicted by a club, presumably of the billy-style. His head wound would require eleven stitches. Other officers, in the meantime, shouted obscenities at the family members, who were still unaware of the intruders' identities. At gunpoint, the officer forced the family members to lie face down on the floor. The officers did not relent: they continued to insult the residents and threatened to harm them. After searching the residence for one and one-half hours and finding nothing in the residence related to narcotics activity, the officers finally left.

Leatherman v. Tarrant County Narcotics Intelligence & Coordination Unit, 954 F.2d 1054, 1055-1056 (5th Cir. 1992). Why might plaintiff's counsel want to include such detail in a complaint, even if not required to by the notice pleading standard? What *must* be included after *Twombly* and *Iqbal*? What would be necessary to meet the Fifth Circuit's heightened pleading standard?

Even after *Leatherman*, the Fifth Circuit continued to try to find ways to impose higher pleading burdens on plaintiffs in civil rights cases, via, for example, encouraging district courts to require plaintiffs to file a reply under Rule 7(a) before the case could proceed to discovery. See Schultea v. Wood, 47 F.3d 1427, 1433-1434 (5th Cir. 1995) (en banc) ("because Rule 8(a) does not list Rule 7 replies, Rule 8(a)'s 'short and plain' standard does not govern Rule 7 replies"; "a district court's discretion not to [order a reply] is narrow indeed" when the defendant pleads qualified immunity). The Fifth Circuit's Rule 7(a) practice appears to continue even after the Court raised the pleading standard in *Twombly* and *Iqbal*. See Floyd v. City of Kenner, La., 351 Fed. Appx. 890, 896 (5th Cir. 2009) (unpublished opinion) (using the plausibility pleading standard to reject allegations contained in the plaintiff's Rule 7(a) reply as insufficiently "'threadbare'" and "'conclusory'").

Concern about imposing discovery obligations on public servants was certainly relevant to the majority in *Iqbal*. See also Ashcroft v. Al-Kidd, 131 S. Ct. 2074 (2011) (reversing denial of motion to dismiss, brought on grounds of qualified immunity, where Attorney General was accused of illegally converting material witness statute into justification for detention of individuals suspected of having ties to terrorist organizations without probable cause). For an example of what might be taken as the opposite conclusion about the imposition of a lawsuit and discovery on a public official's time, see Clinton v. Jones, 520 U.S. 681 (1997).

But, until *Twombly* and *Iqbal*, no one questioned the core proposition that unless the Advisory Committee or Congress authorized heightened pleading requirements, the courts could not impose them. As the First Circuit put it prior to *Twombly*, in cases like *Swierkiewicz* and *Leatherman*, the Supreme Court "sounded the death knell for the imposition of a heightened pleading standard except in cases in which either a federal statute or specific Civil Rule requires that result." Educadores Puertorriqueños Acciòn, 367 F.3d 61, 66 (1st Cir. 2004).

### *Note: Rule 9(b)—The Securities Fraud Litigation Example*

Securities fraud is perhaps the most prominent example of an area in which plaintiffs must meet not only rule-imposed but statutory heightened pleading requirements. The federal securities laws—Securities and Exchange Act of 1934 § 10(b) and Rule 10b-5—prohibit corporate officers and directors from misleading the investing public with statements and omissions that contain material misrepresentations. Rule 9(b) lists "fraud" as one of the allegations that must be pleaded with particularity. Given that § 10(b) and Rule 10b-5 are directed at fraudulent acts, courts have long held that Rule 9(b) governs and, thus, a heightened pleading standard may be applied. See In re Glenfed, Inc. Sec. Litig., 42 F.3d 1541 (9th Cir. 1994). Yet, as the Second Circuit has explained, Rule 9(b) produces an irresolvable tension:

> On the one hand, there is the interest in deterring fraud in the securities markets and remedying it when it occurs. That interest is served by recognizing that the victims of fraud often are unable to detail their allegations until they have had some opportunity to conduct discovery of those reasonably suspected of having perpetrated a fraud. . . .
>
> On the other hand, there is the interest in deterring the use of the litigation process as a device for extracting undeserved settlements as the price of avoiding the extensive discovery costs that frequently ensue once a complaint survives dismissal, even though no recovery would occur if the suit were litigated to completion. It has never been clear how these competing interests are to be accommodated, and the adjudication process is not well suited to the formulation of a universal resolution of the tensions between them. In the absence of a more refined statutory standard than the vague contours of section 10(b) or a more detailed attempt at rulemaking than the SEC has managed in Rule 10b-5, despite 50 years of unavailed opportunity, courts must adjudicate the precise cases before them, striking the balance as best they can. . . .

In re Time Warner, Inc. Sec. Litig., 9 F.3d 259, 263-264 (2d Cir. 1993).

The tension between these two interests, along with the internal conundrum of Rule 9(b)—which demands that fraud be pleaded "with particularity" but that intent may be "averred generally"—led to conflicting results in early securities cases. Some courts read the rule to require fairly specific allegations for pleadings, while others were more liberal. Compare Ross v. A. H. Robins Co., 607 F.2d 545 (2d Cir. 1979) (requiring specific allegations of intent), with In re Glenfed, Inc., 42 F.3d 1541 (9th Cir. 1994) (en banc) (interpreting Rule 9(b) to allow general allegations of intent).

The conflict over these two approaches led to congressional hearings in 1995 that resulted in the controversial Private Securities Litigation Reform Act of 1995. Passed over the veto of President Clinton, the Act made several significant changes in securities litigation, including a modification of pleading requirements. A plaintiff now must "state with particularity facts giving rise to a strong inference that the defendant acted with the required state of mind," essentially adopting the Second Circuit position. See Elliott J. Weiss, The New Securities Fraud Pleading Requirements: Speed Bump or Road Block?, 38 Ariz. L. Rev. 675 (1996).

In 2007, the same year *Twombly* was decided, the Supreme Court attempted to clarify this new heightened pleading requirement for scienter. As you read the case, consider the differences with plausibility pleading.

### *Tellabs, Inc. v. Makor Issues & Rights, Ltd.*
551 U.S. 308 (2007)

Justice Ginsburg delivered the opinion of the Court.

This Court has long recognized that meritorious private actions to enforce federal antifraud securities laws are an essential supplement to criminal prosecutions and civil enforcement actions brought, respectively, by the Department of Justice and the Securities and Exchange Commission (SEC). Private securities fraud actions, however, if not adequately contained, can be employed abusively to impose substantial costs on companies and individuals whose conduct conforms to the law. As a check against abusive litigation by private parties, Congress enacted the Private Securities Litigation Reform Act of 1995 (PSLRA).

Exacting pleading requirements are among the control measures Congress included in the PSLRA. The PSLRA requires plaintiffs to state with particularity both the facts constituting the alleged violation, and the facts evidencing scienter, *i.e.,* the defendant's intention "to deceive, manipulate, or defraud." Ernst & Ernst v. Hochfelder, 425 U.S. 185, 194, and n.12 (1976); see 15 U.S.C. § 78u-4(b)(1), (2). This case concerns the latter requirement. As set out in § 21D(b)(2) of the PSLRA, plaintiffs must "state with particularity facts giving rise to a strong inference that the defendant acted with the required state of mind." 15 U.S.C. § 78u-4(b)(2).

Congress left the key term "strong inference" undefined, and Courts of Appeals have divided on its meaning. In the case before us, the Court of Appeals for the Seventh Circuit held that the "strong inference" standard would be met if the complaint "allege[d] facts from which, if true, a reasonable person could infer that the defendant acted with the required intent." 437 F.3d 588, 602 (2006). That formulation, we conclude, does not capture the stricter demand Congress sought to convey in § 21D(b)(2). It does not suffice that a reasonable factfinder plausibly could infer from the complaint's allegations the requisite state of mind. Rather, to determine whether a complaint's scienter allegations can survive threshold inspection for sufficiency, a court governed by § 21D(b)(2) must engage in a comparative evaluation; it must consider, not only inferences urged by the plaintiff, as the Seventh Circuit did, but also competing inferences rationally drawn from the facts alleged. An inference of fraudulent intent may be plausible, yet less cogent than other, nonculpable explanations for the defendant's conduct. To qualify as "strong" within the intendment of § 21D(b)(2), we hold, an inference of scienter must be more than merely plausible or reasonable—it must be cogent and at least as compelling as any opposing inference of nonfraudulent intent.

## I

Petitioner Tellabs, Inc., manufactures specialized equipment used in fiber optic networks. During the time period relevant to this case, petitioner Richard Notebaert was Tellabs' chief executive officer and president. Respondents (Shareholders) are persons who purchased Tellabs stock between December 11, 2000, and June 19, 2001. They accuse Tellabs and Notebaert (as well as several other Tellabs executives) of engaging in a scheme to deceive the investing public about the true value of Tellabs' stock. Beginning on December 11, 2000, the Shareholders allege, Notebaert (and by imputation Tellabs) "falsely reassured public investors, in a series of statements . . . that Tellabs was continuing to enjoy strong demand for its products and earning record revenues," when, in fact, Notebaert knew the opposite was true. From December 2000 until the spring of 2001, the Shareholders claim, Notebaert knowingly misled the public in four ways. First, he made statements indicating that demand for Tellabs' flagship networking device, the TITAN 5500, was continuing to grow, when, in fact, demand for that product was waning. Second, Notebaert made statements indicating that the TITAN 6500, Tellabs' next-generation networking device, was available for delivery, and that demand for that product was strong and growing, when in truth the product was not ready for delivery and demand was weak. Third, he falsely represented Tellabs' financial results for the fourth quarter of 2000 (and, in connection with those results, condoned the practice of "channel stuffing," under which Tellabs flooded its customers with unwanted products). Fourth, Notebaert made a series of overstated revenue projections, when demand for the TITAN 5500 was drying up and production of the TITAN 6500 was behind schedule. Based on Notebaert's sunny assessments, the Shareholders contend, market analysts recommended that investors buy Tellabs' stock.

The first public glimmer that business was not so healthy came in March 2001 when Tellabs modestly reduced its first quarter sales projections. In the next months, Tellabs made progressively more cautious statements about its projected sales. On June 19, 2001, the last day of the class period, Tellabs disclosed that demand for the TITAN 5500 had significantly dropped. Simultaneously, the company substantially lowered its revenue projections for the second quarter of 2001. The next day, the price of Tellabs stock, which had reached a high of $67 during the period, plunged to a low of $15.87.

On December 3, 2002, the Shareholders filed a class action in the District Court for the Northern District of Illinois. Their complaint stated, *inter alia,* that Tellabs and Notebaert had engaged in securities fraud in violation of § 10(b) of the Securities Exchange Act of 1934, and SEC Rule 10b-5, also that Notebaert was a "controlling person" under § 20(a) of the 1934 Act, and therefore derivatively liable for the company's fraudulent acts. Tellabs moved to dismiss the complaint on the ground that the Shareholders had failed to plead their case with the particularity the PSLRA requires. The District Court agreed, and therefore dismissed the complaint without prejudice.

The Shareholders then amended their complaint, adding references to 27 confidential sources and making further, more specific, allegations concerning Notebaert's mental state. The District Court again dismissed, this time with prejudice. The Shareholders had sufficiently pleaded that Notebaert's statements were misleading, the court determined, but they had insufficiently alleged that he acted with scienter.

The Court of Appeals for the Seventh Circuit reversed in relevant part. . . .

We granted certiorari to resolve the disagreement among the Circuits on whether, and to what extent, a court must consider competing inferences in determining whether a securities fraud complaint gives rise to a "strong inference" of scienter.

## II

. . . Section 10(b), this Court has implied from the statute's text and purpose, affords a right of action to purchasers or sellers of securities injured by its violation. To establish liability under § 10(b) and Rule 10b-5, a private plaintiff must prove that the defendant acted with scienter, "a mental state embracing intent to deceive, manipulate, or defraud." *Ernst & Ernst,* 425 U.S., at 193-194, and n.12.

In an ordinary civil action, the Federal Rules of Civil Procedure require only "a short and plain statement of the claim showing that the pleader is entitled to relief." Fed. Rule Civ. Proc. 8(a)(2). . . . Prior to the enactment of the PSLRA, the sufficiency of a complaint for securities fraud was governed not by Rule 8, but by the heightened pleading standard set forth in Rule 9(b). Rule 9(b) applies to "all averments of fraud or mistake"; it requires that "the circumstances constituting fraud . . . be stated with particularity" but provides that "[m]alice, intent, knowledge, and other condition of mind of a person may be averred generally."

Courts of Appeals diverged on the character of the Rule 9(b) inquiry in § 10(b) cases. . . . The Second Circuit's formulation was the most stringent. Securities fraud plaintiffs in that Circuit were required to "specifically plead those [facts] which they assert give rise to a *strong inference* that the defendants had" the requisite state of mind. *Ross v. A.H. Robins Co.*, 607 F.2d 545, 558 (1979) (emphasis added). The "strong inference" formulation was appropriate, the Second Circuit said, to ward off allegations of "fraud by hindsight." See, e.g., Shields v. Citytrust Bancorp, Inc., 25 F.3d 1124, 1129 (1994) (quoting Denny v. Barber, 576 F.2d 465, 470 (C.A.2 1978) (Friendly, J.)).

Setting a uniform pleading standard for § 10(b) actions was among Congress' objectives when it enacted the PSLRA. Designed to curb perceived abuses of the § 10(b) private action—"nuisance filings, targeting of deep-pocket defendants, vexatious discovery requests and manipulation by class action lawyers," *Dabit*, 547 U.S., at 81 (quoting H.R. Conf. Rep. No. 104-369, p. 31 (1995))—the PSLRA installed both substantive and procedural controls.[4] Notably, Congress prescribed new procedures for the appointment of lead plaintiffs and lead counsel. This innovation aimed to increase the likelihood that institutional investors—parties more likely to balance the interests of the class with the long-term interests of the company—would serve as lead plaintiffs. Congress also "limit[ed] recoverable damages and attorney's fees, provide[d] a 'safe harbor' for forward-looking statements, . . . mandate[d] imposition of sanctions for frivolous litigation, and authorize[d] a stay of discovery pending resolution of any motion to dismiss." *Dabit*, 547 U.S., at 81, 126 S. Ct. 1503. And in § 21D(b) of the PSLRA, Congress "impose[d] heightened pleading requirements in actions brought pursuant to § 10(b) and Rule 10b-5." Ibid. . . .

The "strong inference" standard "unequivocally raise[d] the bar for pleading scienter," 437 F.3d, at 601, and signaled Congress' purpose to promote greater uniformity among the Circuits. . . . While adopting the Second Circuit's "strong inference" standard, Congress did not codify that Circuit's case law interpreting the standard. See § 78u-4(b)(2). With no clear guide from Congress other than its "inten[tion] to strengthen existing pleading requirements," H.R. Conf. Rep., p. 41, Courts of Appeals have diverged again, this time in construing the term "strong inference." Among the uncertainties, should courts consider competing inferences in determining whether an inference of scienter is "strong"? Our task is to prescribe a workable construction of the "strong inference" standard, a reading geared to the PSLRA's twin goals: to curb frivolous, lawyer-driven litigation, while preserving investors' ability to recover on meritorious claims.

---

4. Nothing in the PSLRA, we have previously noted, casts doubt on the conclusion "that private securities litigation [i]s an indispensable tool with which defrauded investors can recover their losses"—a matter crucial to the integrity of domestic capital markets. See Merrill Lynch, Pierce, Fenner & Smith Inc. v. Dabit, 547 U.S. 71, 81 (2006).

## III

### A

We establish the following prescriptions: *First,* faced with a Rule 12(b)(6) motion to dismiss a § 10(b) action, courts must, as with any motion to dismiss for failure to plead a claim on which relief can be granted, accept all factual allegations in the complaint as true. See Leatherman v. Tarrant County Narcotics Intelligence and Coordination Unit, 507 U.S. 163, 164 (1993). . . .

*Second,* courts must consider the complaint in its entirety, as well as other sources courts ordinarily examine when ruling on Rule 12(b)(6) motions to dismiss, in particular, documents incorporated into the complaint by reference, and matters of which a court may take judicial notice. See 5B Wright & Miller § 1357 (3d ed. 2004 and Supp. 2007). The inquiry, as several Courts of Appeals have recognized, is whether *all* of the facts alleged, taken collectively, give rise to a strong inference of scienter, not whether any individual allegation, scrutinized in isolation, meets that standard.

*Third,* in determining whether the pleaded facts give rise to a "strong" inference of scienter, the court must take into account plausible opposing inferences. The Seventh Circuit expressly declined to engage in such a comparative inquiry. A complaint could survive, that court said, as long as it "alleges facts from which, if true, a reasonable person could infer that the defendant acted with the required intent"; in other words, only "[i]f a reasonable person could not draw such an inference from the alleged facts" would the defendant prevail on a motion to dismiss. 437 F.3d, at 602. But in § 21D(b)(2), Congress did not merely require plaintiffs to "provide a factual basis for [their] scienter allegations," ibid., *i.e.,* to allege facts from which an inference of scienter rationally *could* be drawn. Instead, Congress required plaintiffs to plead with particularity facts that give rise to a "strong"—*i.e.,* a powerful or cogent—inference. See American Heritage Dictionary 1717 (4th ed. 2000) (defining "strong" as "[p]ersuasive, effective, and cogent"); 16 Oxford English Dictionary 949 (2d ed. 1989) (defining "strong" as "[p]owerful to demonstrate or convince" (definition 16b)); cf. 7 *id.,* at 924 (defining "inference" as "a conclusion [drawn] from known or assumed facts or statements"; "reasoning from something known or assumed to something else which follows from it").

The strength of an inference cannot be decided in a vacuum. The inquiry is inherently comparative: How likely is it that one conclusion, as compared to others, follows from the underlying facts? To determine whether the plaintiff has alleged facts that give rise to the requisite "strong inference" of scienter, a court must consider plausible, nonculpable explanations for the defendant's conduct, as well as inferences favoring the plaintiff. The inference that the defendant acted with scienter need not be irrefutable, *i.e.,* of the "smoking-gun" genre, or even the "most plausible of competing inferences," *Fidel,* 392 F.3d, at 227. . . . Yet the inference of scienter must be more than merely "reasonable" or "permissible"—it must be cogent and compelling, thus strong in light of other explanations. A complaint will survive, we hold, only if a reasonable person would deem the inference of scienter cogent and at least as compelling as any opposing inference one could draw from the facts alleged.[5]

## B

Tellabs contends that when competing inferences are considered, Notebaert's evident lack of pecuniary motive will be dispositive. The Shareholders, Tellabs stresses, did not allege that Notebaert sold any shares during the class period. While it is true that motive can be a relevant consideration, and personal financial gain may weigh heavily in favor of a scienter inference, we agree with the Seventh Circuit that the absence of a motive allegation is not fatal. As earlier stated, allegations must be considered collectively; the significance that can be ascribed to an allegation of motive, or lack thereof, depends on the entirety of the complaint.

Tellabs also maintains that several of the Shareholders' allegations are too vague or ambiguous to contribute to a strong inference of scienter. For example, the Shareholders alleged that Tellabs flooded its customers with unwanted products, a practice known as "channel stuffing." But they failed, Tellabs argues, to specify whether the channel stuffing allegedly known to Notebaert was the illegitimate kind (e.g., writing orders for products customers had not requested) or the legitimate kind (e.g., offering customers discounts as an incentive to buy). We agree that omissions and ambiguities count against inferring scienter, for plaintiffs must "state with particularity facts giving rise to a strong inference that the defendant acted with the required state of mind." § 78u-4(b)(2). We reiterate, however, that the court's job is not to scrutinize each allegation in isolation but to assess all the allegations holistically. In sum, the reviewing court must ask: When the allegations are accepted as true and taken collectively, would a reasonable person deem the inference of scienter at least as strong as any opposing inference?

## IV

Accounting for its construction of § 21D(b)(2), the Seventh Circuit explained that the court "th[ought] it wis[e] to adopt an approach that

---

5. Justice Scalia objects to this standard on the ground that "[i]f a jade falcon were stolen from a room to which only A and B had access," it could not *possibly* be said there was a 'strong inference' that B was the thief." We suspect, however, that law enforcement officials as well as the owner of the precious falcon would find the inference of guilt as to B quite strong—certainly strong enough to warrant further investigation. Indeed, an inference at least as likely as competing inferences can, in some cases, warrant recovery. See Summers v. Tice, 33 Cal. 2d 80, 84-87, 199 P.2d 1, 3-5 (1948) (plaintiff wounded by gunshot could recover from two defendants, even though the most he could prove was that each defendant was at least as likely to have injured him as the other); Restatement (Third) of Torts § 28(b), Comment *e*, p. 504 (Proposed Final Draft No. 1, Apr. 6, 2005) ("Since the publication of the Second Restatement in 1965, courts have generally accepted the alternative-liability principle of [Summers v. Tice, adopted in] § 433B(3), while fleshing out its limits."). In any event, we disagree with Justice Scalia that the hardly stock term "strong inference" has only one invariably right ("natural" or "normal") reading—his. . . .

[could not] be misunderstood as a usurpation of the jury's role." 437 F.3d, at 602. In our view, the Seventh Circuit's concern was undue. A court's comparative assessment of plausible inferences, while constantly assuming the plaintiff's allegations to be true, we think it plain, does not impinge upon the Seventh Amendment right to jury trial.[8]

Congress, as creator of federal statutory claims, has power to prescribe what must be pleaded to state the claim, just as it has power to determine what must be proved to prevail on the merits. It is the federal lawmaker's prerogative, therefore, to allow, disallow, or shape the contours of—including the pleading and proof requirements for—§ 10(b) private actions. No decision of this Court questions that authority in general, or suggests, in particular, that the Seventh Amendment inhibits Congress from establishing whatever pleading requirements it finds appropriate for federal statutory claims. . . .[9]

Our decision in Fidelity & Deposit Co. of Md. v. United States, 187 U.S. 315 (1902), is instructive. That case concerned a rule adopted . . . in 1879 pursuant to rulemaking power delegated by Congress. The rule required defendants, in certain contract actions, to file an affidavit "specifically stating . . . , in precise and distinct terms, the grounds of his defen[s]e." Id., at 318. The defendant's affidavit was found insufficient, and judgment was entered for the plaintiff, whose declaration and supporting affidavit had been found satisfactory. This Court upheld the [District of Columbia's] rule against the contention that it violated the Seventh Amendment. Just as the purpose of § 21D(b) is to screen out frivolous complaints, the purpose of the prescription at issue in *Fidelity & Deposit Co.* was to "preserve the court from frivolous defen[s]es," ibid. Explaining why the Seventh Amendment was not implicated, this Court said that the heightened pleading rule simply "prescribes the means of making an issue," and that, when "[t]he issue [was] made as prescribed, the right of trial by jury accrues." Ibid.; accord Ex parte Peterson, 253 U.S. 300, 310 (1920) (Brandeis, J.) (citing *Fidelity & Deposit Co.*, and reiterating: "It does not infringe the constitutional right to a trial by jury [in a civil case], to require, with a view to formulating the issues, an oath by each party to the facts relied upon."). See also Walker v. New Mexico & Southern Pacific R. Co., 165 U.S. 593, 596 (1897) (Seventh Amendment "does not attempt to regulate matters of pleading").

In the instant case, provided that the Shareholders have satisfied the congressionally "prescribe[d] . . . means of making an issue," *Fidelity & Deposit Co.*, 187 U.S., at 320, the case will fall within the jury's authority to assess the

8. In numerous contexts, gatekeeping judicial determinations prevent submission of claims to a jury's judgment without violating the Seventh Amendment. See, *e.g.*, Daubert v. Merrell Dow Pharmaceuticals, Inc., 509 U.S. 579, 589 (1993) (expert testimony can be excluded based on judicial determination of reliability); Neely v. Martin K. Eby Constr. Co., 386 U.S. 317, 321 (1967) (judgment as a matter of law); Pease v. Rathbun-Jones Engineering Co., 243 U.S. 273, 278 (1917) (summary judgment).

9. Any heightened pleading rule, including Fed. Rule Civ. Proc. 9(b), could have the effect of preventing a plaintiff from getting discovery on a claim that might have gone to a jury, had discovery occurred and yielded substantial evidence. In recognizing Congress' or the Federal Rule makers' authority to adopt special pleading rules, we have detected no Seventh Amendment impediment.

credibility of witnesses, resolve any genuine issues of fact, and make the ultimate determination whether Notebaert and, by imputation, Tellabs acted with
scienter. We emphasize, as well, that under our construction of the "strong
inference" standard, a plaintiff is not forced to plead more than she would
be required to prove at trial. A plaintiff alleging fraud in a § 10(b) action, we
hold today, must plead facts rendering an inference of scienter *at least as likely
as* any plausible opposing inference. At trial, she must then prove her case by
a "preponderance of the evidence." Stated otherwise, she must demonstrate
that it is *more likely* than not that the defendant acted with scienter.

* * *

. . . Neither the District Court nor the Court of Appeals had the opportunity to consider the matter in light of the prescriptions we announce today.
We therefore vacate the Seventh Circuit's judgment so that the case may be
reexamined in accord with our construction of § 21D(b)(2).

The judgment of the Court of Appeals is vacated, and the case is remanded
for further proceedings consistent with this opinion.

*It is so ordered.*

Justice Scalia, concurring in the judgment.

I fail to see how an inference that is merely "at least as compelling as any
opposing inference," can conceivably be called what the statute here at issue
requires: a "strong inference." If a jade falcon were stolen from a room to
which only A and B had access, could it *possibly* be said there was a "strong
inference" that B was the thief? I think not, and I therefore think that the
Court's test must fail. In my view, the test should be whether the inference
of scienter (if any) is *more plausible* than the inference of innocence.

The Court's explicit rejection of this reading rests on two assertions. The
first (doubtless true) is that the statute does not require that "[t]he inference
that the defendant acted with scienter . . . be irrefutable, *i.e.,* of the 'smoking-
gun' genre," ibid. It is up to Congress, however, and not to us, to determine
what pleading standard would avoid those extremities while yet effectively
deterring baseless actions. Congress has expressed its determination in the
phrase "strong inference"; it is our job to give that phrase its normal meaning. And if we are to abandon text in favor of unexpressed purpose, as the
Court does, it is inconceivable that Congress's enactment of stringent pleading requirements in the Private Securities Litigation Reform Act of 1995
somehow manifests the purpose of giving plaintiffs the edge in close cases.

The Court's second assertion (also true) is that "an inference at least as
likely as competing inferences can, in some cases, warrant recovery." Ante,
n.5 (citing Summers v. Tice, 33 Cal. 2d 80, 84-87 (1948)). *Summers* is a famous
case, however, because it sticks out of the ordinary body of tort law like
a sore thumb. It represented "a relaxation" of "such proof as is ordinarily
required" to succeed in a negligence action. Id., at 86. There is no indication
that the statute at issue here was meant to relax the ordinary rule under
which a tie goes to the defendant. To the contrary, it explicitly strengthens
that rule by extending it to the pleading stage of a case. . . .

The Court and the dissent criticize me for suggesting that there is only one reading of the text. They are both mistaken. I assert only that mine is the natural reading of the statute (i.e., the normal reading), not that it is the only conceivable one. . . .

With the above exceptions, I am generally in agreement with the Court's analysis, and so concur in its judgment.

[The concurring opinion of Justice Alito is omitted.]

JUSTICE STEVENS, dissenting.

. . . The basic purpose of the heightened pleading requirement in the context of securities fraud litigation is to protect defendants from the costs of discovery and trial in unmeritorious cases. Because of its intrusive nature, discovery may also invade the privacy interests of the defendants and their executives. Like citizens suspected of having engaged in criminal activity, those defendants should not be required to produce their private effects unless there is probable cause to believe them guilty of misconduct.

. . . There are times when an inference can easily be deemed strong without any need to weigh competing inferences. For example, if a known drug dealer exits a building immediately after a confirmed drug transaction, carrying a suspicious looking package, a judge could draw a strong inference that the individual was involved in the aforementioned drug transaction without debating whether the suspect might have been leaving the building at that exact time for another unrelated reason.

If, using that same methodology, we assume the truth of the detailed factual allegations attributed to 27 different confidential informants described in the complaint, and view those allegations collectively, I think it clear that they establish probable cause to believe that Tellabs' chief executive officer "acted with the required intent," as the Seventh Circuit held.[2]

Accordingly, I would affirm the judgment of the Court of Appeals.

---

2. The "channel stuffing" allegations in ¶¶ 62-72 of the amended complaint are particularly persuasive. Contrary to petitioners' arguments that respondents' allegations of channel stuffing "are too vague or ambiguous to contribute to a strong inference of scienter," ante, at 2511, this portion of the complaint clearly alleges that Notebaert himself had specific knowledge of illegitimate channel stuffing during the relevant time period, see, *e.g.,* App. 111, ¶ 67 ("Defendant Notebaert worked directly with Tellabs' sales personnel to channel stuff SBC"); id., at 110-112 (alleging, in describing such channel stuffing, that Tellabs took "extraordinary" steps that amounted to "an abnormal practice in the industry"; that "distributors were upset and later returned the inventory" (and, in the case of Verizon's chairman, called Tellabs to complain); that customers "did not want" products that Tellabs sent and that Tellabs employees wrote purchase orders for; that "returns were so heavy during January and February 2001 that Tellabs had to lease extra storage space to accommodate all the returns"; and that Tellabs "backdat[ed] sales" that actually took place in 2001 to appear as having occurred in 2000). If these allegations are actually taken as true and viewed in the collective, it is hard to imagine what competing inference could effectively counteract the inference that Notebaert and Tellabs "'acted with the required state of mind.'"

### *Note:* **Tellabs** *Back in the Seventh Circuit*

Heightened pleading requires close attention to the material facts alleged in a complaint. On remand the Seventh Circuit emphasized that "[t]he critical question . . . is how likely it is that the allegedly false statements . . . were the result of merely careless mistakes at the management level based on false information fed it from below, rather than of an intent to deceive or reckless indifference to whether the statements were misleading." Makor Issues & Rights, Ltd. v. Tellabs, Inc., 513 F.3d 702, 709 (7th Cir. 2008). The court found it "exceedingly unlikely" that the false statements were simply careless mistakes of reliance on errors made by lower-level employees and it affirmed its initial decision that the complaint should have survived the motion to dismiss.

The court compared the inferences available from the facts alleged in the following manner:

> The 5500 and the 6500 were Tellabs's most important products. The 5500 was described by the company as its "flagship" product and the 6500 was the 5500's heralded successor. They were to Tellabs as Windows XP and Vista are to Microsoft. That no member of the company's senior management who was involved in authorizing or making public statements about the demand for the 5500 and 6500 knew that they were false is very hard to credit, and no plausible story has yet been told by the defendants that might dispel our incredulity. The closest is the suggestion that while "available" no doubt meant to most investors that the 6500 was ready to be shipped to customers rather than that the new product was having teething troubles that would keep it off the market for many months, this may have been a bit of corporate jargon innocently intended to indicate that the company was ready to take orders. . . . But this is highly implausible when "available" is set among the company's alleged lies about the 6500—that "customers are embracing" the 6500, that "interest in and demand for the 6500 continues to grow," that "we are satisfying very strong demand and growing customer demand [for the 6500 and] we are as confident as ever—that may be an understatement—about the 6500," and that "we should hit our full manufacturing capacity in May or June to accommodate the demand [for the 6500] we are seeing. Everything we can build, we are building and shipping. The demand is very strong."
>
> Another possible, though again very unlikely, example of innocent misunderstanding is the charge of "channel stuffing." The term refers to shipping to one's distributors more of one's product than one thinks one can sell. A certain amount of channel stuffing could be innocent and might not even mislead—a seller might have a realistic hope that stuffing the channel of distribution would incite his distributors to more vigorous efforts to sell the stuff lest it pile up in inventory. Channel stuffing becomes a form of fraud only when it is used, as the complaint alleges, to book revenues on the basis of goods shipped but not really sold because the buyer can return them. They are in effect sales on consignment, and such sales cannot be booked as revenue. . . . The huge number of returns of 5500 systems is evidence that the purpose of the stuffing was to conceal the disappointing demand for the

product rather than to prod distributors to work harder to attract new customers, and the purpose would have been formed or ratified at the highest
level of management. . . .

Against all this the defendants argue that they could have had no motive
to paint the prospects for the 5500 and 6500 systems in rosy hues because
within months they acknowledged their mistakes and disclosed the true situation of the two products, and because there is no indication that Notebaert
or anyone else who may have been in on the fraud profited from it financially. The argument confuses expected with realized benefits. Notebaert
may have thought that there was a chance that the situation regarding the
two key products would right itself. If so, the benefits of concealment might
exceed the costs. Investors do not like to think they're riding a roller coaster.
Prompt disclosure of the truth would have caused Tellabs's stock price to
plummet, as it did when the truth came out a couple of months later. Suppose
the situation had corrected itself. Still, investors would have discovered that
the stock was more volatile than they thought, and risk-averse investors
(who predominate) do not like volatility and so, unless it can be diversified
away, demand compensation in the form of a lower price; consequently the
stock might not recover to its previous level. . . .

So the inference of corporate scienter is not only as likely as its opposite,
but more likely. And is it cogent? Well, if there are only two possible inferences, and one is much more likely than the other, it must be cogent. . . .
Because the alternative hypotheses—either a cascade of innocent mistakes,
or acts of subordinate employees, either or both resulting in a series of false
statements—are far less likely than the hypothesis of scienter at the corporate level at which the statements were approved, the latter hypothesis must
be considered cogent.

. . . [A]t the top of the corporate pyramid sat Notebaert, the CEO. The 5500
and the 6500 were his company's key products. Almost all the false statements that we quoted emanated directly from him. Is it conceivable that
he was unaware of the problems of his company's two major products and
merely repeating lies fed to him by other executives of the company? It is
conceivable, yes, but it is exceedingly unlikely.

513 F.3d at 709-711.

## Note: Drawing Inferences, Plausible and Otherwise

In its analysis of scienter, the Supreme Court in *Tellabs* emphasizes that
the heightened pleading requirements of the PSLRA are met if the allegations of the complaint make the inference of intent "cogent and at least
as compelling as any opposing inference one could draw from the facts
alleged." *Tellabs*, 551 U.S. at 324. The Seventh Circuit was reversed for failing to conduct a comparison of the available inferences.

Surely this has implications for how lower courts should treat the plausibility pleading standard of *Twombly*. If we read *Tellabs* and *Twombly* together,
plausibility pleading cannot be as strict as pleading with particularity
under the PSLRA. On this view, in cases pled under Rule 8 lower courts
arguably should not require that the allegations be "at least as compelling

as any [innocent] inference one could draw from the facts alleged." *Tellabs*, 551 U.S. at 324. A complaint should be dismissed only if it is obviously implausible. See *Twombly*, 550 U.S. at 566-567 (stating that "there is no reason to infer that the companies had agreed among themselves to do what was only *natural* anyway"; "here we have an *obvious* alternative explanation") (emphasis added).

However attractive this approach may seem, and however nicely it fits the language of Justice Souter's majority opinion in *Twombly*, it is considerably more difficult to reconcile with *Iqbal*. There the Court appeared to find the complaint deficient because it did not contain facts sufficient to establish that the inference of discriminatory intent by high-level executive branch officials was as "likely" as the inference that they simply acted in the interest of national security. *Iqbal*, 556 U.S. at 681 ("*given more likely explanations*, they do not plausibly establish this purpose") (emphasis added).

The Court nevertheless insists that the standards are different, as they must be if plausibility pleading is grounded in Rule 8(a)(2) and heightened pleading derives from Rule 9(b) and statutes like the PSLRA. See Matrixx Initiatives, Inc. v. Siracusano, 131 S. Ct. 1309, 1323-1325 (2011) (scienter adequately pled where complaint described pharmaceutical company's awareness of reports that its cold remedy caused some consumers to lose their sense of smell before it issued a press release suggesting studies had confirmed that its product had no such effect; "These allegations, 'taken collectively,' give rise to a 'cogent and compelling' inference that Matrixx elected not to disclose the reports of adverse events not because it believed they were meaningless but because it understood their likely effect on the market."); see id. (applying plausibility pleading to the allegations addressing whether the allegedly false statements were "material"). Perhaps the key distinction is that in plausibility pleading inferences favoring liability need not be "compelling."

### c.  Pleading in the Alternative: How Consistent Must the Plaintiff Be?

Recall that the complaint is filed before formal discovery has begun. Sometimes the plaintiff does not know precisely what happened, yet has an adequate basis for filing a lawsuit. How should the plaintiff handle these ambiguities and fact gaps in the pleading? Should pleading alternative legal theories or alternative statements of the facts be permitted? Subject to what limits? See Fed. R. Civ. P. 8(e).

### *McCormick v. Kopmann*
161 N.E.2d 720 (Ill. Ct. App. 1959)

On the evening of November 21, 1956, Lewis McCormick was killed on Main Street in Gifford, Illinois, when a truck being operated by defendant Lorence Kopmann collided with the automobile which McCormick was driving.

This action was brought by McCormick's widow in the Circuit Court of Champaign County against Kopmann and Anna, John and Mary Huls. The complaint contains four counts; the issues raised on this appeal concern only the first and fourth counts.

Count I is brought by plaintiff as Administratrix of McCormick's Estate, against Kopmann, under the Illinois Wrongful Death Act. Plaintiff sues for the benefit of herself and her eight children, to recover for the pecuniary injury suffered by them as a result of McCormick's death. It is charged that Kopmann negligently drove his truck across the center line of Main Street and collided with McCormick's automobile. In paragraph 3 of Count I, plaintiff alleges:

> That at the time of the occurrence herein described, and for a reasonable period of time preceding it, the said decedent was in the exercise of ordinary care for his own safety and that of his property.

Count IV is brought by plaintiff as Administratrix of McCormick's Estate, against the Huls, under the Illinois Dram Shop Act. Plaintiff avers that Count IV is brought "in the alternative to Count I." She sues for the benefit of herself and her four minor children, to recover for the injury to their means of support suffered as a result of McCormick's death. It is alleged that Anna Huls operated a dramshop in Penfield, Illinois; that John and Mary Huls operated a dramshop in Gifford; that on November 21, 1956 the Huls sold alcoholic beverages to McCormick which he consumed and which rendered him intoxicated; and that "as a result of such intoxication" McCormick drove his automobile "in such a manner as to cause a collision with a truck" being driven by Kopmann on Main Street in Gifford.

Kopmann, defendant under Count I, moved to dismiss the complaint on the theory that the allegations of that Count I and Count IV were fatally repugnant and could not stand together, because McCormick could not be free from contributory negligence as alleged in Count I, if his intoxication caused the accident as alleged in Count IV. Kopmann also urged that the allegation in Count IV that McCormick's intoxication was the proximate cause of his death, is a binding judicial admission which precludes an action under the Wrongful Death Act. Kopmann's motion was denied. He raised the same defenses in his answer.

The Huls, defendants under Count IV, answered. They did not file a motion directed against Count IV.

Neither defendant sought a severance (see Civil Practice Act, Sections 44(2) and 51), and both counts came on for trial at the same time.

Plaintiff introduced proof that at the time of the collision, McCormick was proceeding North in the northbound traffic lane, and that Kopmann's truck, travelling South, crossed the center line and struck McCormick's car. Plaintiff also introduced testimony that prior to the accident McCormick drank a bottle of beer in Anna Huls' tavern in Penfield and one or two bottles of beer in John and Mary Huls' tavern in Gifford. Plaintiff's witness Roy Lowe, who was with McCormick during the afternoon and evening of November 21, and who was seated in the front seat of McCormick's car when the collision occurred, testified on cross examination that in his opinion McCormick was sober at the time of the accident.

At the close of plaintiff's evidence, all defendants moved for directed verdicts. The motions were denied.

Kopmann, the defendant under the Wrongful Death count, introduced testimony that at the time of the collision, his truck was in the proper lane; that McCormick's automobile was backed across the center line of Main Street, thus encroaching on the southbound lane, and blocking it; that the parking lights on McCormick's automobile were turned on, but not the headlights; that Kopmann tried to swerve to avoid hitting McCormick's car; and that there was an odor of alcohol on McCormick's breath immediately after the accident. Over plaintiff's objection, the trial court permitted Kopmann's counsel to read to the jury the allegations of Count IV relating to McCormick's intoxication, as an admission.

The Huls, defendants under the Dram Shop count, introduced opinion testimony of a number of witnesses that McCormick was not intoxicated at the time of the accident. Anna Huls testified that McCormick drank one bottle of beer in her tavern. Several witnesses testified that McCormick had no alcoholic beverages in John and Mary Huls' tavern.

All defendants moved for directed verdicts at the close of all the proof. The motions were denied. The jury was instructed that Count IV was an alternative to Count I; that Illinois law permits a party who is uncertain as to which state of facts is true to plead in the alternative, and that it is for the jury to determine the facts. At Kopmann's request, the court instructed the jury on the law of contributory negligence, and further:

> [I]f you find from all of the evidence in the case that (McCormick) was operating his automobile while intoxicated and that such intoxication, if any, contributed proximately to cause the collision in question, then in that case . . . you should find the defendant, Lorence Kopmann, not guilty.

The jury returned a verdict against Kopmann for $15,500 under Count I. The jury found the Huls not guilty under Count IV. Kopmann's motions for judgment notwithstanding the verdict, and in the alternative for a new trial, were denied.

Kopmann has appealed. His first contention is that the trial court erred in denying his pretrial motion to dismiss the complaint. Kopmann is correct in asserting that the complaint contains inconsistent allegations. The allegation of Count I that McCormick was free from contributory negligence, cannot be reconciled with the allegation of Count IV that McCormick's intoxication was the proximate cause of his death. Freedom from contributory negligence is a prerequisite to recovery under the Wrongful Death Act. Russell v. Richardson, 31 N.E.2d 427, at p. 434. If the jury had found that McCormick was intoxicated and that his intoxication caused the accident, it could not at the same time have found that McCormick was not contributorily negligent. The Illinois Supreme Court has held that "voluntary intoxication will not excuse a person from exercising such care as may reasonably be expected from one who is sober." Keeshan v. Elgin A. & S. Traction Co., 82 N.E. 360, 362. . . .

Counts I and IV, therefore, are mutually exclusive; plaintiff may not recover upon both counts. It does not follow, however, that these counts may not be pleaded together. Section 24(1) of the Illinois Civil Practice Act (Ill. Rev. Stat. Ch. 110, Sec. 24) authorizes joinder of defendants against whom a liability is asserted in the alternative arising out of the same transaction. Section 24(3) of the Act provides:

> If the plaintiff is in doubt as to the person from whom he is entitled to redress, he may join two or more defendants, and state his claim against them in the alternative in the same count or plead separate counts in the alternative against different defendants, to the intent that the question which, if any, of the defendants is liable, and to what extent, may be determined as between the parties.

Section 34 of the Act states in part that "Relief, whether based on one or more counts, may be asked in the alternative." Section 43(2) of the Act provides:

> When a party is in doubt as to which of two or more statements of fact is true, he may, regardless of consistency, state them in the alternative or hypothetically in the same or different counts or defenses, whether legal or equitable. A bad alternative does not affect a good one.

Thus, the Civil Practice Act expressly permits a plaintiff to plead inconsistent counts in the alternative, where he is genuinely in doubt as to what the facts are and what the evidence will show. The legal sufficiency of each count presents a separate question. It is not ground for dismissal that allegations in one count contradict those in an alternative count. . . .

The 1955 revision of Section 43(2) of the Civil Practice Act was designed to make it clear that inconsistent facts or theories could be pleaded alternatively, whether in the same or different counts. In their note respecting the revised section, the drafters of the 1955 Act, having explained why clarifying language was needed, concluded: "Under the revision the inconsistency may exist either in the statement of the facts, or in the legal theories adopted." S.H.A. ch. 110, sec. 43, p. 514. This provision was modelled after Rule 8(e)(2) of the Federal Rules of Civil Procedure, [now Rule 8(d)(2)—Eds.]. Federal courts have held that where the plaintiff in personal injury cases is uncertain as to who is liable, he may assert his claims against the several defendants alternatively. . . .

Sound policy weighs in favor of alternative pleading, so that controversies may be settled and complete justice accomplished in a single action. Illinois Civil Practice Act, Section 4; City of Nokomis v. Sullivan, 153 N.E.2d 48; Fleshner v. Copeland, 147 N.E.2d 329. If the right is abused, as where the pleader has knowledge of the true facts (viz., he knows that the facts belie the alternative) pleading in the alternative is not justified. Thus in Church v. Adler, 113 N.E.2d 327 at page 332, we said:

> [A]lternative pleading is not permitted when in the nature of things the pleader must know which of the inconsistent averments is true and which is false. Plaintiff must know whether she will be sick, sore, lame and disordered for the rest of her life or whether on the contrary she has regained her health, as alleged in Count II. She must make up her mind which is the fact, and strike the inconsistent allegation from her pleading on remand.

There is nothing in the record before us to indicate that plaintiff knew in advance of the trial, that the averments of Count I, and not Count IV, were true. In fact, at the trial, Kopmann attempted to establish the truth of the allegations of Count IV that McCormick was intoxicated at the time of the collision and that his intoxication caused his death. He can hardly be heard now to say that before the trial, plaintiff should have known that these were not the facts. Where, as in the *Church* case, the injured party is still living and able to recollect the events surrounding the accident, pleading in the alternative may not be justified, but where, as in the case at bar, the key witness is deceased, pleading alternative sets of facts is often the only feasible way to proceed. . . .

We hold that, in the absence of a severance, plaintiff had the right to go to trial on both Counts I and IV, and to adduce all the proof she had under both Count I and Count IV. . . . Plaintiff pleaded alternative counts because she was uncertain as to what the true facts were. Even assuming she introduced proof to support all essential allegations of both Count I and Count IV, she was entitled to have all the evidence submitted to the trier of fact, and to have the jury decide where the truth lay. She was not foreclosed *ipso facto* from going to the jury under Count I, merely because she submitted proof, under Count IV, tending to prove that McCormick's intoxication proximately caused his death. If this were the rule, one who in good faith tried his case on alternative theories, pursuant to the authorization, if not the encouragement of Section 43, would run the risk of having his entire case dismissed. The provisions of the Civil Practice Act authorizing alternative pleading, necessarily contemplate that the pleader adduce proof in support of both sets of allegations or legal theories, leaving to the jury the determination of the facts. . . .

What we have said is not to say that a plaintiff assumes no risks in adducing proof to support inconsistent counts. The proof in support of one inconsistent count necessarily tends to negate the proof under the other count and to have its effect upon the jury. While the fact alone of inconsistent evidence will not bar submission of the case to the jury, it may very well affect the matter of the weight of the evidence and warrant the granting of a new trial, even though, as we have held, it does not warrant *ipso facto* a directed verdict or judgment notwithstanding the verdict.

Kopmann argues that plaintiff should have been required to elect between her alternative counts before going to the jury. The doctrine known as "election of remedies" has no application to the case at bar. Here, either of two defendants may be liable to plaintiff, depending upon what the jury finds the facts to be. It has been aptly said that "truth cannot be stated until known, and, for purposes of judicial administration, cannot be known until the trier of facts decides the fact issues." McCaskill, Illinois Civil Practice Act Annotated (1933), p. 103. Plaintiff need not choose between the alternative counts. Such a requirement would, to a large extent, nullify the salutary purposes of alternative pleading. Since she could bring actions against the defendants seriatim, or at the same time in separate suits, she is entitled to join them in a single action, introduce all her proof, and submit the entire case to the jury under appropriate instructions. . . .

Kopmann contends he was prejudiced because Counts I and IV were submitted together to the jury, in that the jury was confused by plaintiff's inconsistent positions as to liability. We believe this argument is no longer open to Kopmann, since he failed to seek a separate trial pursuant to Section 51 of the Illinois Civil Practice Act. Russell v. Chicago Trust & Savings Bank, 29 N.E. 37; cf. People v. Skaggs, 76 N.E.2d 455. We also note that Kopmann's counsel repeatedly sought to establish McCormick's intoxication, indicating that this issue would have been injected into the case whether or not Count IV was presented concurrently with Count I. And, in any event, the jury was carefully instructed as to the law and the position of each party. The verdict itself shows that the instructions were understood and followed.

Kopmann argues that the practical effect of the trial court's instructions was to direct the jury to determine whether he or the Huls were liable to plaintiff, depending upon whether or not McCormick was intoxicated. The instructions given belie this contention. At Kopmann's request, the jury was repeatedly admonished that Kopmann was not liable to plaintiff if the jury found McCormick was guilty of contributory negligence, as well as if the jury found McCormick was intoxicated and his intoxication contributed proximately to cause the accident. No error was committed in this regard. . . .

Plaintiff has perfected a cross appeal, contending that the verdict is inadequate as a matter of law. We believe the jury could reasonably fix plaintiff's damages under Count I at $15,500. . . .

We conclude that the verdict and judgment below are correct and the judgment is affirmed.

## 2. Responding to the Complaint

### Problem Case: A Woman Partner

Attorney Shayes sued her former law firm partners at McKenzie, Brachman et al. for violation of Title VII of the Civil Rights Act, alleging that she was "forced out" of the partnership because of conduct and attitudes that discriminated against her on the basis of sex. She also claimed that she was fired from the partnership because she had refused to go along with the cover-up of malpractice toward an unknowing client.

McKenzie filed a timely motion to dismiss for failure to state a claim upon which relief can be granted, based on his argument that Title VII does not cover professional legal partnerships. Relying on Hishon v. King & Spalding, 467 U.S. 69 (1984), the district court rejected the motion.

Can McKenzie now:

a) move to dismiss for improper venue?
b) move to dismiss for lack of subject matter jurisdiction?
c) make a motion for a more definite statement?
d) include in its answer the defense of lack of jurisdiction over the person?

### a.   The Rules and Forms

We now consider the options available to the defendant in responding to the complaint. The alternatives may be clustered, in general, as the following types of objections, in terms coined by the late Professor Delmar Karlen:

1) "Tain't so." The defendant may deny the factual allegations of the complaint. The means for denying allegations is the answer. See Fed. R. Civ. P. 8(b) and Fed. R. Civ. P. Form 30, ¶ 2 (forms follow the text of the Rules).

2) "Yes, but." This is an affirmative defense, once called a "confession and avoidance." Here, the defendant may concede that the plaintiff's facts are true, and even that the law would entitle the plaintiff to relief under those facts, but asserts that other facts or law provide the defendant with a legal "out." For example, the plaintiff may properly allege the existence of a contract and that the contract was breached, but the defendant may have an affirmative defense because the contract was not in writing and is one for which a writing is required under the statute of frauds. See Fed. R. Civ. P. 8(c). An affirmative defense is raised in the answer, if any is filed. See Fed. R. Civ. P. Form 30, ¶ 3.

3) "So what!" The defense is the motion to dismiss for failure to state a claim in which the movant admits the facts as stated (for purposes of the motion only), but insists that the law does not support the claim. For example, the complaint may allege, in some detail, how the defendant's lawn decorations offend plaintiff's tastes, but no law may protect plaintiff from a neighbor defendant's bad taste. The defendant may raise this defense in a pre-answer motion *or* in the answer. See Fed. R. Civ. P. 12(b)(6) and Fed. R. Civ. P. Form 30, ¶4.

4) "Not here." The plaintiff may have chosen the wrong court system or the wrong court within the system—jurisdiction and venue problems. Defendant can object to these either by pre-answer

motion or in the answer, but with venue and personal jurisdiction the defendant must be careful to include the objection in whichever document is filed first. These are *waivable* defenses. Subject matter jurisdiction objections are more resilient and can be raised at any time during the proceedings, even on appeal. See Fed. R. Civ. P. 12(b)(1)-(3) and Fed. R. Civ. P. Form 40.

5) "Right back at ya." This is a counterclaim. The defendant may have an independent claim for relief against the plaintiff. If so, defendant can raise this counterclaim in the answer. See Fed. R. Civ. P. 8(c)(2), 13 and Form 30, ¶ 7 Counterclaim.

6) Other defenses—bad notice, service of process, or other defects in the complaint—may be raised either in the answer or in a pre-trial motion. Again, however, beware: some must be raised in the first document filed or else are waived. See Fed. R. Civ. P. 12(g) and (h).

In working with the materials that follow, be aware that a full explanation of some of the defenses—such as lack of subject matter jurisdiction, venue, or personal jurisdiction—appears elsewhere in the book. We focus here on the means by which these objections are made and where they fit in the defendant's arsenal of responses to the complaint.

### b.   The Pre-Answer Motion

The first option available to the attorney is to file a pre-answer motion. How does a motion differ from a pleading? Rule 7 defines the *pleadings* as the *complaint*, the *answer,* and the *reply*, if any. A *motion* is a request that the court enter an order of some kind. See, e.g., Fed. R. Civ. P. Forms 40-42.

A motion has four parts: a notice of the motion, the motion, a certificate of service, and a memorandum in support of the motion. The first part tells your opponent when the motion will be heard. The second part is the specific request that the judge enter an order. For example, you may file a motion that requests that the judge dismiss the complaint for failure to state a claim. The third part is simply your averment to the court that you served the motion on your opponent, and how. The final part is a legal brief explaining to the court why you believe the motion should be granted under the applicable facts and law. If the motion cannot be granted on the basis of the pleadings, and rests on facts that lie outside the pleadings, then you may need to add a fifth document—an affidavit that sets forth the facts on which the motion depends.

Why might an attorney elect to file a motion, rather than an answer, when the answer can include all of the pre-answer objections (except the little-used 12(e)) plus the responses that can be made only in an answer? Isn't the lawyer risking the expense of filing two sets of papers instead of one, should the pre-answer motion fail?

One answer is that there are motions that will serve to defeat a case at a very early stage, and thus save the defendant from costly investigation and discovery. Challenging subject matter or personal jurisdiction, for instance, may quickly dispose of a case.

Defendants who think the case against them is hopeless often move to dismiss under Rule 12(b)(6). Used properly, this motion asks the court to dismiss the complaint because, as written, it cannot be construed to state a claim upon which legal relief may be granted.

The modern 12(b)(6) motion is an outgrowth of the common law demurrer, a term still used in many courts. These older forms carried with them many technicalities no longer observed. For example, the distinction between a general demurrer—which went to the merits of a case—and a special demurrer—which went to defects of form—has disappeared.

As we saw in *Twombly*, to survive the modern 12(b)(6) motion, the complaint must state facts that, if true, would give rise to a legally enforceable right. The judge must not decide the facts at this stage; rather, the facts alleged in the complaint are assumed to be true. Note that the plaintiff is not required to state her legal theory in the complaint, only facts sufficient to put defendant on notice of the matter about which plaintiff is suing.

Given the bare pleading requirement of Rule 8, as interpreted in *Conley* and *Twombly*, how often do you think the 12(b)(6) motion should be granted? Also consider the possibility that your motion will educate your opponent about defects in her case. In some situations, therefore, some lawyers may elect to file a motion for summary judgment or even take a case to trial rather than use 12(b)(6) prematurely. See, e.g., Jean Maclean Snyder, Tripping at the Threshold, 17 Litig. 17, 21 (1990).

Sufficiency of a complaint refers not only to the allegations in the pleading, but also to the available legal theories. A complaint may be very detailed, yet still lose on a motion to dismiss for failure to state a claim because no law supports plaintiff's alleged right to recover. Isn't this the heart of the *American Nurses* case?

Other means by which a party may attack a claim or counterclaim that is "hopeless" are through a motion for judgment on the pleadings, Rule 12(c), and the motion for summary judgment, Rule 56. The difference between the 12(c) and 12(b)(6) motions is timing; 12(c) is the proper designation for a motion to dismiss an action for failure to state a claim that is filed *after* the pleadings are closed—that is, after the complaint and answer (and reply, if any) have been filed. The difference between the motion for summary judgment and both the 12(c) and 12(b)(6) motions is that a summary judgment motion looks outside the pleadings to discover that plaintiff's claim is hopeless. Formerly called a "speaking demurrer," the summary judgment motion presents information, usually in the form of an affidavit that demonstrates that a trial would be pointless because no material issue of fact exists. The judge therefore may rule in advance of any fact-finding, as a matter of law. You will work more closely with summary judgment in Chapter 4, infra.

## c.  The Answer

*Fuentes v. Tucker*
187 P.2d 752 (1947)

GIBSON, CHIEF JUSTICE.

The minor sons of the respective plaintiffs were killed by an automobile operated by defendant. The two actions were consolidated for trial, and in each case the verdict of the jury awarded the plaintiffs $7,500. Defendant appealed from the judgments claiming the trial court erred in permitting plaintiffs to present evidence of facts outside the issues framed by the pleadings.

On the day of the trial defendant filed an amended answer in each case which admitted "that he was and is liable for the death of the deceased . . . and the damages directly and proximately caused thereby." Plaintiffs were nevertheless permitted to prove the circumstances of the accident, including the facts that defendant was intoxicated and that the children were thrown eighty feet by the force of the impact.

It is defendant's position that the introduction of evidence as to the circumstances of the accident was error because it was not relevant or material to the amount of the damages, which was the only issue to be determined by the jury. Plaintiffs contend that defendant could not, by acknowledging legal responsibility for the deaths of the children, deprive them of the right to show the circumstances surrounding the accident, and that therefore it was not error to admit evidence of such facts. They do not claim, however, that the evidence was material to any of the facts in dispute under the pleadings as they stood at the commencement of the trial.

It is a doctrine too long established to be open to dispute that the proof must be confined to the issues in the case and that the time of the court should not be wasted, and the jury should not be confused, by the introduction of evidence which is not relevant or material to the matters to be adjudicated. This is merely one aspect of the larger problem of delay in the conduct of litigation. Every court has a responsibility to the public to see that justice is administered efficiently and expeditiously and that the facilities of the court are made available at the first possible moment to those whose cases are awaiting trial. It would be an unwarranted waste of public funds, and a manifest injustice to the many litigants seeking an early trial date, to allow counsel in a particular case to occupy substantial periods of time in the useless presentation of evidence on matters not in controversy; and we know of no well considered opinion which asserts such a right.

One of the functions of pleadings is to limit the issues and narrow the proofs. If facts alleged in the complaint are not controverted by the answer, they are not in issue, and no evidence need be offered to prove their existence. Travelers Ins. Co. v. Byers, 11 P.2d 444 [1932]; Code Civ. Proc., §§ 462, 588, 1868, 1870, subds. (1), (15); see I Wigmore on Evidence, 3d ed. 1940, p. 9, § 2. Evidence which is not pertinent to the issues raised by the pleadings is immaterial, and it is error to allow the introduction of such evidence.

It follows, therefore, if an issue has been removed from a case by an admission in the answer, that it is error to receive evidence which is material solely to the excluded matter. This, of course, does not mean that an admission of liability precludes a plaintiff from showing how an accident happened if such evidence is material to the issue of damages. In an action for personal injuries, where liability is admitted and the only issue to be tried is the amount of damage, the force of the impact and the surrounding circumstances may be relevant and material to indicate the extent of plaintiff's injuries. Johnson v. McRee, 152 P.2d 526 [1944]; Martin v. Miqueu, 98 P.2d 816 [1940]. Such evidence is admissible because it is relevant and material to an issue remaining in the case.

The defendant here by an unqualified statement in his answer admitted liability for the deaths of the children, and the sole remaining question in issue was the amount of damages suffered by the parents. In an action for wrongful death of a minor child the damages consist of the pecuniary loss to the parents in being deprived of the services, earnings, society, comfort and protection of the child. Bond v. United Railroads, 113 P. 366 [1911]. The manner in which the accident occurred, the force of the impact, or defendant's intoxication could have no bearing on these elements of damage. The evidence, therefore, was not material to any issue before the jury, and its admission was error. . . .

The introduction of evidence of admitted facts is permissible in cases where the admission is ambiguous in form or limited in scope or where, during the trial of a case, a party seeks to deprive his opponents of the legitimate force and effect of material evidence by the bald admission of a probative fact. . . .

. . . The boys involved in this accident were approximately twelve years old when they were killed. Certainly the sum of $7,500, which was awarded by the jury in each case, cannot be said to be an unreasonable amount to allow for the wrongful death of a child of that age, and the verdicts are not so large as to indicate that the jury was unduly influenced by the admission of the immaterial testimony in question. It does not appear, therefore, that the error resulted in a miscarriage of justice. . . .

*The judgments are affirmed.*

CARTER, JUSTICE (concurring). . . .

The effect of the majority holding in this case is to deny to an injured person the benefit of presenting to the trier of fact the entire factual situation surrounding the accident out of which the injury arose. It cannot be denied that either a jury or a trial judge is more disposed to award a substantial amount of damages in a case where the defendant is shown to have been guilty of gross negligence and his conduct was such as to indicate a reckless disregard for the safety of others, than where the negligence amounted to only an error in judgment. The present holding will make it possible for a defendant who has been guilty of the most heinous kind of reckless and wanton conduct, including intoxication, to conceal from the trier of fact the extent of his culpability, and thereby gain any advantage which

might flow from the absence of such disclosure. Theoretically and technically, and judged by academic standards, this practice may be justified, but
when gauged by actual experience in the administration of justice it favors
the worst offenders by permitting them to escape from a larger award of
damages which the trier of fact might feel justified in awarding if the entire
picture were presented. . . .

## *Zielinski v. Philadelphia Piers, Inc.*
139 F. Supp. 408 (E.D. Pa. 1956)

VAN DUSEN, DISTRICT JUDGE.

Plaintiff requests a ruling that, for the purposes of this case, the motor-
driven fork lift operated by Sandy Johnson on February 9, 1953, was owned
by defendant and that Sandy Johnson was its agent acting in the course
of his employment on that date. The following facts are established by the
pleadings, interrogatories, depositions and uncontradicted portions of
affidavits:

1. Plaintiff filed his complaint on April 28, 1953, for personal injuries
received on February 9, 1953, while working on Pier 96, Philadelphia, for
J. A. McCarthy, as a result of a collision of two motor-driven fork lifts.

2. Paragraph 5 of this complaint stated that "a motor-driven vehicle
known as a fork lift or chisel, owned, operated and controlled by the defendant, its agents, servants and employees, was so negligently and carelessly
managed . . . that the same . . . did come into contact with the plaintiff causing him to sustain the injuries more fully hereinafter set forth."

3. The "First Defense" of the Answer stated "Defendant . . . (c) denies the
averments of paragraph 5. . . ."

4. The motor-driven vehicle known as a fork lift or chisel, which collided
with the McCarthy fork lift on which plaintiff was riding, had on it the
initials "P.P.I."

5. On February 10, 1953, Carload Contractors, Inc. made a report of this
accident to its insurance company, whose policy No. CL 3964 insured
Carload Contractors, Inc. against potential liability for the negligence of its
employees contributing to a collision of the type described in paragraph 2
above.

6. By letter of April 29, 1953, the complaint served on defendant was forwarded to the above-mentioned insurance company. This letter read as
follows:

Gentlemen:

As per telephone conversation today with your office, we attach hereto
"Complaint in Trespass" as brought against Philadelphia Piers, Inc. by one
Frank Zielinski for supposed injuries sustained by him on February 9, 1953.

We find that a fork lift truck operated by an employee of Carload
Contractors, Inc. also insured by yourselves was involved in an accident with

another chisel truck, which, was alleged, did cause injury to Frank Zielinski, and same was reported to you by Carload Contractors, Inc. at the time, and you assigned Claim Number OL 0153-94 to this claim.

Should not this Complaint in Trespass be issued against Carload Contractors, Inc. and not Philadelphia Piers, Inc.?

We forward for your handling.

7. Interrogatories 1 to 5 and the answers thereto, which were sworn to by defendant's General Manager on June 12, 1953, and filed on June 22, 1953, read as follows:

1. State whether you have received any information of an injury sustained by the plaintiff on February 9, 1953, South Wharves. If so, state when and from whom you first received notice of such injury. A. We were first notified of this accident on or about February 9, 1953 by Thomas Wilson.

2. State whether you caused an investigation to be made of the circumstances of said injury and if so, state who made such investigation and when it was made. A. We made a very brief investigation on February 9, 1953 and turned the matter over to (our insurance company) for further investigation. . . .

8. At a deposition taken August 18, 1953, Sandy Johnson testified that he was the employee of defendant on February 9, 1953, and had been their employee for approximately fifteen years.

9. At a pretrial conference held on September 27, 1955, plaintiff first learned that over a year before February 9, 1953, the business of moving freight on piers in Philadelphia, formerly conducted by defendant, had been sold by it to Carload Contractors, Inc. and Sandy Johnson had been transferred to the payroll of this corporation without apparently realizing it, since the nature or location of his work had not changed. . . .

11. Defendant now admits that on February 9, 1953, it owned the fork lift in the custody of Sandy Johnson and that this fork lift was leased to Carload Contractors, Inc. It is also admitted that the pier on which the accident occurred was leased by defendant.

12. There is no indication of action by either party in bad faith and there is no proof of inaccurate statements being made with intent to deceive. Because defendant made a prompt investigation of the accident, its insurance company has been representing the defendant since suit was brought, and this company insures Carload Contractors, Inc. also, requiring defendant to defend this suit will not prejudice it.

Under these circumstances, and for the purposes of this action, it is ordered that the following shall be stated to the jury at the trial:

It is admitted that, on February 9, 1953, the towmotor or fork lift bearing the initials "P.P.I." was owned by defendant and that Sandy Johnson was a servant in the employ of defendant and doing its work on that date.

This ruling is based on the following principles:

1. Under the circumstances of this case, the answer contains an ineffective denial of that part of paragraph 5 of the complaint which alleges that "a motor-driven vehicle known as a fork lift or chisel (was) owned, operated and controlled by the defendant, its agents, servants and employees."

Fed. R. Civ. P. 8(b) provides:

> A party shall state in short and plain terms his defenses to each claim asserted and shall admit or deny the averments upon which the adverse party relies. . . . Denials shall fairly meet the substance of the averments denied. When a pleader intends in good faith to deny only a part or a qualification of an averment, he shall specify so much of it as is true and material and shall deny only the remainder.

For example, it is quite clear that defendant does not deny the averment in paragraph 5 that the fork lift came into contact with plaintiff, since it admits, in the answers to interrogatories, that an investigation of an occurrence of the accident had been made and that a report dated February 10, 1953, was sent to its insurance company stating "While Frank Zielinski was riding on bumper of chisel and holding rope to secure cargo, the chisel truck collided with another chisel truck operated by Sandy Johnson causing injuries to Frank Zielinski's legs and hurt head of Sandy Johnson." Compliance with the above-mentioned rule required that defendant file a more specific answer than a general denial. A specific denial of parts of this paragraph and specific admission of other parts would have warned plaintiff that he had sued the wrong defendant.

Paragraph 8.23 of Moore's Federal Practice (2nd Edition) Vol. II, p. 1680, says: "In such a case, the defendant should make clear just what he is denying and what he is admitting." This answer to paragraph 5 does not make clear to plaintiff the defenses he must be prepared to meet.

Under circumstances where an improper and ineffective answer has been filed, the Pennsylvania courts have consistently held that an allegation of agency in the complaint requires a statement to the jury that agency is admitted where an attempt to amend the answer is made after the expiration of the period of limitation. See Burns v. Joseph Flaherty Co., 1924, 278 Pa. 579, 582-583; Boles v. Federal Electric Co., 1926, 89 Pa. Super. 160, 163-164. Although the undersigned has been able to find no federal court decisions on this point, he believes the principle of these Pennsylvania appellate court decisions may be considered in view of all the facts of this case, where jurisdiction is based on diversity of citizenship, the accident occurred in Pennsylvania, and the federal district court is sitting in Pennsylvania. . . .

2. Under the circumstances of this case, principles of equity require that defendant be estopped from denying agency because, otherwise, its inaccurate statements and statements in the record, which it knew (or had the means of knowing within its control) were inaccurate, will have deprived plaintiff of his right of action.

If Interrogatory 2 had been answered accurately by saying that employees of Carload Contractors, Inc. had turned the matter over to the insurance company, it seems clear that plaintiff would have realized his mistake. The fact that if Sandy Johnson had testified accurately, the plaintiff could have brought its action against the proper party defendant within the statutory period of limitations is also a factor to be considered, since defendant was represented at the deposition and received knowledge of the inaccurate testimony.

At least one appellate court has stated that the doctrine of equitable estoppel will be applied to prevent a party from taking advantage of the statute of limitations where the plaintiff has been misled by conduct of such party. See Peters v. Public Service Corporation, 29 A.2d 189, 195 (1942). . . .

> Of course, defendants were under no duty to advise complainants' attorney of his error, other than by appropriate pleadings, but neither did defendants have a right, knowing of the mistake, to foster it by its acts of omission.

This doctrine has been held to estop a party from taking advantage of a document of record where the misleading conduct occurred after the recording, so that application of this doctrine would not necessarily be precluded in a case such as this where the misleading answers to interrogatories and depositions were subsequent to the filing of the answer, even if the denial in the answer had been sufficient. . . .

Since this is a pre-trial order, it may be modified at the trial if the trial judge determines from the facts which then appear that justice so requires.

## Notes and Questions

1. *Strategy in Pleading.* Remember that in our problem case, Shayes pleaded inconsistently about the reasons for her being fired. Why might she want to plead both theories, even though she would not proceed to trial on both at once? Defendants also plead strategically — as illustrated by *Fuentes*. Note the tactical advantages of admitting certain facts, even if untrue or possible to contest.

2. *Insufficient Denials Treated as Admissions.* Note that Rule 8(b) was thoroughly "restyled" in 2007. Harsh applications of the strictures of Rule 8(b) on the pleading of denials have generally been avoided and the sanction of Fed. R. Civ. P. 8(b)(6) has been applied sparingly. On the other hand, gross departures from the requirements of the Rule, such as those that could mislead the adversary, may be treated as admissions. For example, a denial of sufficient knowledge under Fed. R. Civ. P. 8(b) may be deemed an admission if the party denying the knowledge clearly has it, see, e.g., Mesirow v. Duggan, 240 F.2d 751 (8th Cir. 1957).

3. *The Relation Between Fed. R. Civ. P. 8(b)(6) and Fed. R. Civ. P. 9(c).* Rule 8(b)(6) may also be read with Rule 9(c). In Lumbermens Mutual Insurance Co. v. Bowman, 313 F.2d 381 (10th Cir. 1963), it was held that a general denial was

not sufficient to put in issue noncompliance with conditions precedent to liability.

4. *Failing to Respond.* What if the defendant simply fails to respond at all? See Fed. R. Civ. P. 55; see also Honda Power Equip. Mfg., Inc. v. Woodhouse, 219 F.R.D. 2, 4-5 (D.D.C. 2003) (entering default judgment against British defendants in patent litigation who, nine months after the complaint was filed and six months after seeking an extension of time to answer, "had neither filed responsive pleadings nor entered an appearance in this case"; defendants sought a stay of the motion for default judgment pending the outcome of parallel litigation in the United Kingdom between the parties as well as leave to file an answer and counterclaim, but then dropped out of contact with their lawyers in the United States).

### d.  Affirmative Defenses

### Problem Case: A Woman Partner (Part Two)

In the lawsuit by Shayes against her former partners, McKenzie intends to raise as a defense that Shayes was paid a substantial severance bonus upon leaving the partnership, and that there was an oral agreement that she would not sue the firm. Must McKenzie include this defense in his answer, or may he simply deny the allegations of her complaint? Read Rule 8(c) and consider the following cases.

### *Gomez v. Toledo*
446 U.S. 635 (1980)

JUSTICE MARSHALL delivered the opinion of the Court.

The question presented is whether, in an action brought under 42 U.S.C. § 1983 against a public official whose position might entitle him to qualified immunity, a plaintiff must allege that the official has acted in bad faith in order to state a claim for relief or, alternatively, whether the defendant must plead good faith as an affirmative defense.

### I

Petitioner Carlos Rivera Gomez brought this action against respondent, the Superintendent of the Police of the Commonwealth of Puerto Rico, contending that respondent had violated his right to procedural due process by discharging him from employment with the Police Department's Bureau of Criminal Investigation.[1] Basing jurisdiction on 28

---

1. The complaint originally named the Commonwealth of Puerto Rico and the police of the Commonwealth of Puerto Rico as additional defendants, but petitioner consented to their dismissal from the action.

U.S.C. § 1343(3),[2] petitioner alleged the following facts in his complaint.[3] Petitioner had been employed as an agent with the Puerto Rican police since 1968. In April 1975, he submitted a sworn statement to his supervisor in which he asserted that two other agents had offered false evidence for use in a criminal case under their investigation. As a result of this statement, petitioner was immediately transferred from the Criminal Investigation Corps for the Southern Area to Police Headquarters in San Juan, and a few weeks later to the Police Academy in Gurabo, where he was given no investigative authority. In the meantime respondent ordered an investigation of petitioner's claims, and the Legal Division of the Police Department concluded that all of petitioner's factual allegations were true.

In April 1976, while still stationed at the Police Academy, petitioner was subpoenaed to give testimony in a criminal case arising out of the evidence that petitioner had alleged to be false. At the trial petitioner, appearing as a defense witness, testified that the evidence was in fact false. As a result of this testimony, criminal charges, filed on the basis of information furnished by respondent, were brought against petitioner for the allegedly unlawful wiretapping of the agents' telephones. Respondent suspended petitioner in May 1976 and discharged him without a hearing in July. In October, the District Court of Puerto Rico found no probable cause to believe that petitioner was guilty of the allegedly unlawful wiretapping and, upon appeal by the prosecution, the Superior Court affirmed. Petitioner in turn sought review of his discharge before the Investigation, Prosecution, and Appeals Commission of Puerto Rico, which, after a hearing, revoked the discharge order rendered by respondent and ordered that petitioner be reinstated with backpay.

Based on the foregoing factual allegations, petitioner brought this suit for damages, contending that his discharge violated his right to procedural due process, and that it had caused him anxiety, embarrassment, and injury to his reputation in the community. In his answer, respondent denied a number of petitioner's allegations of fact and asserted several affirmative defenses. Respondent then moved to dismiss the complaint for failure to state a cause of action, see Fed. Rule Civ. Proc. 12(b)(6), and the District Court granted the motion. Observing that respondent was entitled to qualified immunity for acts done in good faith within the scope of his official duties, it concluded that petitioner was required to plead as part of his claim for relief that, in committing the actions alleged, respondent was motivated by bad faith. The absence of any such allegation, it held, required

---

2. That section grants the federal district courts jurisdiction "[t]o redress the deprivation, under color of any State law, statute, ordinance, regulation, custom or usage, of any right, privilege or immunity secured by the Constitution of the United States or by any Act of Congress providing for equal rights of citizens or of all persons within the jurisdiction of the United States."

3. At this state of proceedings, of course, all allegations of the complaint must be accepted as true.

dismissal of the complaint. The United States Court of Appeals for the First Circuit affirmed. 602 F.2d 1018 (1979).

We granted certiorari to resolve a conflict among the Courts of Appeals. We now reverse.

## II

Section 1983 provides a cause of action for "the deprivation of any rights, privileges, or immunities secured by the Constitution and laws" by any person acting "under color of any statute, ordinance, regulation, custom, or usage, of any State or Territory." 42 U.S.C. § 1983.[6] This statute, enacted to aid in "'the preservation of human liberty and human rights,'" Owen v. City of Independence, 445 U.S. 622, 636 (1980), quoting Cong. Globe, 42d Cong., 1st Sess., App. 68 (1871) (Rep. Shellabarger), reflects a congressional judgment that a "damages remedy against the offending party is a vital component of any scheme for vindicating cherished constitutional guarantees," 445 U.S. at 651. As remedial legislation, § 1983 is to be construed generously to further its primary purpose. See 445 U.S. at 636.

In certain limited circumstances, we have held that public officers are entitled to a qualified immunity from damages liability under § 1983. This conclusion has been based on an unwillingness to infer from legislative silence a congressional intention to abrogate immunities that were both "well established at common law" and "compatible with the purposes of the Civil Rights Act." 445 U.S. at 638. Findings of immunity have thus been "predicated upon a considered inquiry into the immunity historically accorded the relevant official at common law and the interests behind it." Imbler v. Pachtman, 424 U.S. 409, 421 (1976). In Pierson v. Ray, 386 U.S. 547, 555 (1967), for example, we concluded that a police officer would be "excus[ed] from liability for acting under a statute that he reasonably believed to be valid but that was later held unconstitutional, on its face or as applied." And in other contexts we have held, on the basis of "[c]ommon law tradition . . . and strong public-policy reasons," Wood v. Strickland, 420 U.S. 308, 318 (1975), that certain categories of executive officers should be allowed qualified immunity from liability for acts done on the basis of an objectively reasonable belief that those acts were lawful.

---

6. Section 1983 provides in full: "Every person who, under color of any statute, ordinance, regulation, custom, or usage, of any State or Territory, subjects, or causes to be subjected, any citizen of the United States or other person within the jurisdiction thereof to the deprivation of any rights, privileges, or immunities secured by the Constitution and laws, shall be liable to the party injured in an action at law, suit in equity, or other proper proceeding for redress."

Nothing in the language or legislative history of § 1983, however, suggests that in an action brought against a public official whose position might entitle him to immunity if he acted in good faith, a plaintiff must allege bad faith in order to state a claim for relief. By the plain terms of § 1983, two—and only two—allegations are required in order to state a cause of action under that statute. First, the plaintiff must allege that some person has deprived him of a federal right. Second, he must allege that the person who has deprived him of that right acted under color of state or territorial law. See Monroe v. Pape, 365 U.S. 167, 171 (1961). Petitioner has made both of the required allegations. He alleged that his discharge by respondent violated his right to procedural due process, see Board of Regents v. Roth, 408 U.S. 564 (1972), and that respondent acted under color of Puerto Rican law.

Moreover, this Court has never indicated that qualified immunity is relevant to the existence of the plaintiff's cause of action; instead we have described it as a defense available to the official in question. See Procunier v. Navarette, [434 U.S. 555,] 562 [1978]; Pierson v. Ray, supra, at 556, 557; Butz v. Economou, 438 U.S. 478, 508 (1978). Since qualified immunity is a defense, the burden of pleading it rests with the defendant. See Fed. Rule Civ. Proc. 8(c) (defendant must plead any "matter constituting an avoidance or affirmative defense"); 5 C. Wright & A. Miller, Federal Practice and Procedure § 1271 (1969). It is for the official to claim that his conduct was justified by an objectively reasonable belief that it was lawful. We see no basis for imposing on the plaintiff an obligation to anticipate such a defense by stating in his complaint that the defendant acted in bad faith.

Our conclusion as to the allocation of the burden of pleading is supported by the nature of the qualified immunity defense. As our decisions make clear, whether such immunity has been established depends on facts peculiarly within the knowledge and control of the defendant. Thus we have stated that "[i]t is the existence of reasonable grounds for the belief formed at the time and in light of all the circumstances, coupled with good-faith belief, that affords a basis for qualified immunity of executive officers for acts performed in the course of official conduct." Scheuer v. Rhodes, [416 U.S. 232,] at 247-248 [1974]. The applicable test focuses not only on whether the official has an objectively reasonable basis for that belief, but also on whether "[t]he official himself [is] acting sincerely and with a belief that he is doing right," Wood v. Strickland, supra, at 321. There may be no way for a plaintiff to know in advance whether the official has such a belief or, indeed, whether he will even claim that he does. The existence of a subjective belief will frequently turn on factors which a plaintiff cannot reasonably be expected to know. For example, the official's belief may be based on state or local law, advice of counsel, administrative practice, or some other factor of which the official alone is aware. To impose the pleading burden on the plaintiff would ignore this elementary fact and be contrary to the established practice in analogous areas of the law.[8]

The decision of the Court of Appeals is reversed, and the case is remanded to that court for further proceedings consistent with this opinion.

*It is so ordered.*

JUSTICE REHNQUIST joins the opinion of the Court, reading it as he does to leave open the issue of the burden of persuasion, as opposed to the burden of pleading, with respect to a defense of qualified immunity.

### Note: Pleading Clearly Established Law

Notwithstanding the more than 30-year-old precedent of *Gomez* holding that qualified immunity is an affirmative defense, the Supreme Court has recently held, without overturning or even citing *Gomez*, that a plaintiff must plead certain facts in her complaint to overcome the defense. See Wood v. Moss, 134 S. Ct. 2056, 2059 (2014) ("The doctrine of qualified immunity protects government officials from liability for civil damages 'unless a plaintiff pleads facts showing (1) that the official violated a statutory or constitutional right, and (2) that the right was "clearly established" at the time of the challenged conduct.'") (quoting Ashcroft v. al-Kidd, 131 S. Ct. 2074, 2080 (2011)); see id. at 2061 (ordering case against Secret Service for violating First Amendment rights of protesters dismissed for failure to state a claim because officers were entitled to qualified immunity; no clearly established law applied to agents' decisions about how to control protestors in response to a detour in the president's motorcade). At a minimum, the complaint in a suit against a government officer must contain facts showing that the law the defendant allegedly violated was clearly established. See Cornell v. Burke, 559 Fed. Appx. 577, 579 (7th Cir. 2014) (citing and relying on Wood v. Moss in affirming dismissal of civil rights suit on qualified immunity grounds; officers were "entitled to qualified immunity because [plaintiff's] complaint [did] not contain allegations that [the officers] violated a clearly established constitutional right").

That means qualified immunity is a unique affirmative defense. It plays a crucial role in almost all suits against individual government officers and the modern Court has become much more sensitive to the burdens of litigation on government actors as civil rights litigation has expanded. Can

---

8. As then-Dean Charles Clark stated over 40 years ago: "It seems to be considered only fair that certain types of things which in common law pleading were matters in confession and avoidance—i.e., matters which seemed more or less to admit the general complaint and yet to suggest some other reason why there was no right—must be specifically pleaded in the answer, and that has been a general rule." ABA, Proceedings Institute at Washington and Symposium at New York City on the Federal Rules of Civil Procedure 49 (1939).

you see why the clarity of the law at the time of the alleged wrongdoing is something plaintiffs can reasonably be expected to plead even though it is an element of the qualified immunity defense? For one thing, it is a legal question the answer to which will depend on precedent on the books anyone can look up. Moreover, if the law was *not* clearly established, a motion to dismiss seems like the right tool to ensure that the defendant avoids the burdens of litigation. Summary judgment, by contrast, ordinarily turns on fact discovery.

These are compelling arguments, but they are also deeply controversial because the legal question of whether the law was clearly established actually can be bound up in subtle ways with the factual question of how and why the defendant violated the plaintiff's rights. So plaintiffs will often believe that if they can establish a specific fact in discovery about what the defendant knew or did, they will be able to show that the defendant violated clearly established law.

Outside the unique context of qualified immunity plaintiffs "need not anticipate, and attempt to plead around, potential affirmative defenses." Davis v. Indiana State Police, 541 F.3d 760 (7th Cir. 2008) (citing and following *Gomez* in case involving affirmative defense provided under the Age Discrimination in Employment Act). And the factors the Court applied in *Gomez* are still the principal factors federal courts use to decide if an issue not listed in Rule 8(c) should be treated as an affirmative defense which the defendant must plead and prove. See Evankavitch v. Green Tree Servicing, LLC, 793 F.3d 355 (3d Cir. 2015) (looking to statutory text, the risk of surprise or undue prejudice, and the party likely to have knowledge of the relevant facts in concluding that an exception to the anti-harassment provisions of the Fair Debt Collection Practices Act, protecting debtor from abusive communication by debt collectors, is an affirmative defense the debt collector must prove).

### Ingraham v. United States
808 F.2d 1075 (5th Cir. 1987)

POLITZ, CIRCUIT JUDGE.

The appellees in these consolidated cases sued the United States, under the Federal Tort Claims Act, for severe injuries caused by the negligence of government physicians. In each case, after entry of adverse judgment the government moved for relief from the judgment to the extent that the damages exceeded the limit imposed on medical malpractice awards by the Medical Liability and Insurance Improvement Act of Texas, Tex. Rev. Civ. Stat. Ann. art. 4590i. The respective district courts denied these posttrial motions. Concluding that the government did not raise the issue timely before the trial courts, that the issues were not preserved for appeal, and, in the Bonds case, that the challenged awards were not otherwise excessive, we affirm both judgments.

## Background

In 1977, in response to what was perceived to be a medical malpractice crisis, the Legislature of Texas, like several other state legislatures, adopted certain limitations on damages to be awarded in actions against health care providers, for injuries caused by negligence in the rendering of medical care and treatment. Of particular significance to these appeals is the $500,000 cap placed on the *ex delicto* recovery,[1] not applicable to past and future medical expenses.[2]

On February 12, 1979, Dwight L. Ingraham was operated on by an Air Force surgeon. During the back surgery a drill was negligently used and Ingraham's spinal cord was damaged, causing severe and permanent injuries. The court awarded Ingraham judgment for $1,264,000. This total included $364,000 for lost wages and $900,000 for pain, suffering, and disability. There is no reference to the Medical Liability and Insurance Improvement Act of Texas in the pleadings, nor was any reference made to the Act during the trial. After entry of judgment the United States filed a notice of appeal. Thereafter, urging the Act's limitations, the government sought relief from judgment under Fed. R. Civ. P. 60(b). The district court denied that motion. No appeal was taken from that ruling.

Similarly, in March of 1979, Jocelyn and David Bonds, and their infant daughter Stephanie, were victims of the negligent performance by an Air Force physician. Because of the mismanagement of the 43rd week of Jocelyn Bonds's first pregnancy, and the failure to perform timely a caesarian section delivery, Stephanie suffered asphyxiation *in utero*. The loss of oxygen caused extensive brain damage, resulting in spastic quadriparesis, cortical blindness, seizures, and mental retardation. In their FTCA action the court awarded Stephanie $1,814,959.70 for medical expenses and $1,675,595.90 for the other losses. Jocelyn Bonds was awarded $750,000 for her losses, including loss of the society of her daughter. As in the Ingraham case, the government did not invoke the Texas malpractice limitation in pleading or at trial. Postjudgment the government filed a motion to amend the judgment under Fed. R. Civ. P. 59, but, again, there was no mention of the limitations Act. Subsequently, three months after entry of the judgment, the government filed a pleading entitled "Motion for Reconsideration," in which it advanced the malpractice Act. That motion was denied. The government

---

1. Tex. Rev. Civ. Stat. Ann. art. 4590i, § 11.02(a), provides:

In an action on a health care liability claim where final judgment is rendered against a physician or health care provider, the limit of civil liability for damages of the physician or health care provider shall be limited to an amount not to exceed $500,000.

2. Tex. Rev. Civ. Stat. Ann. art. 4590i, § 11.02(b), provides:

Subsection (a) of this section does not apply to the amount of damages awarded on a health care liability claim for the expenses of necessary medical, hospital, and custodial care received before judgment or required in the future for treatment of the injury.

appealed the judgment and motion to amend, but did not appeal the denial of the "motion for reconsideration."

These appeals do not challenge the courts' findings of liability, but object only to quantum, contending that damages are limited by the Medical Liability and Insurance Improvement Act and, in the case of Stephanie and Jocelyn Bonds, are otherwise excessive.

## Analysis

Appellees maintain that we should not consider the statutory limitation of liability invoked on appeal because it is an affirmative defense under Rule 8(c) of the Federal Rules of Civil Procedure, and the failure to raise it timely constitutes a waiver. We find this argument persuasive.

Rule 8(c) first lists 19 specific affirmative defenses, and concludes with the residuary clause "any other matter constituting an avoidance or affirmative defense." In the years since adoption of the rule, the residuary clause has provided the authority for a substantial number of additional defenses which must be timely and affirmatively pleaded. These include: exclusions from a policy of liability insurance; breach of warranty; concealment of an alleged prior undissolved marriage; voidable preference in bankruptcy; noncooperation of an insured; statutory limitation on liability; the claim that a written contract was incomplete; judgment against a defendant's joint tortfeasor; circuity of action; discharge of a contract obligation through novation or extension; recission or mutual abandonment of a contract; failure to mitigate damages; adhesion contract; statutory exemption; failure to exhaust state remedies; immunity from suit; good faith belief in lawfulness of action; the claim that a lender's sale of collateral was not commercially reasonable; a settlement agreement or release barring an action; and custom of trade or business. See 5 C. Wright & A. Miller, Federal Practice and Procedure: Civil, § 1271 (1969 & supp.), and 27 Fed. Proc., L. Ed. § 62. 63 (1984 & supp.), for discussion and citations.

Determining whether a given defense is "affirmative" within the ambit of Rule 8(c) is not without some difficulty. We find the salient comments of Judge Charles E. Clark, Dean of the Yale Law School, later Chief Judge of the United States Second Circuit Court of Appeals, and the principal author of the Federal Rules, to be instructive:

> [J]ust as certain disfavored allegations made by the plaintiff . . . must be set forth with the greatest particularity, so like disfavored defenses must be particularly alleged by the defendant. These may include such matters as fraud, statute of frauds . . . , statute of limitations, truth in slander and libel . . . and so on. In other cases the mere question of convenience may seem prominent, as in the case of payment, where the defendant can more easily show the affirmative payment at a certain time than the plaintiff can the negative of nonpayment over a period of time. Again it may be an issue which may be generally used for dilatory tactics, such as the question of the plaintiff's

right to sue . . . a vital question, but one usually raised by the defendant on technical grounds. These have been thought of as issues "likely to take the opposite party by surprise," which perhaps conveys the general idea of fairness or the lack thereof, though there is little real surprise where the case is well prepared in advance.

Clark, Code Pleading, 2d ed. 1947, § 96 at 609-610, quoted in 5 C. Wright & A. Miller, Federal Practice and Procedure: Civil, § 1271, p. 313 (1969).

Also pertinent to the analysis is the logical relationship between the defense and the cause of action asserted by the plaintiff. This inquiry requires a determination (1) whether the matter at issue fairly may be said to constitute a necessary or extrinsic element in the plaintiff's cause of action; (2) which party, if either, has better access to relevant evidence; and (3) policy considerations: should the matter be indulged or disfavored? See 27 Fed. Proc., L. Ed. § 62.63.

Central to requiring the pleading of affirmative defenses is the prevention of unfair surprise. A defendant should not be permitted to "lie behind a log" and ambush a plaintiff with an unexpected defense. The instant cases illustrate this consideration. Plaintiffs submit that, had they known the statute would be applied, they would have made greater efforts to prove medical damages which were not subject to the statutory limit. In addition, plaintiffs maintain that they would have had an opportunity and the incentive to introduce evidence to support their constitutional attacks on the statute.

This distinction separates the present cases from our recent decision in Lucas v. United States, 807 F.2d 414 (5th Cir. 1986). In *Lucas,* although the limitation of recovery issue was not pleaded, it was raised at trial. We held that the trial court was within its discretion to permit the defendant to effectively amend its pleadings and advance the defense. The treatment we accorded this issue in *Lucas* is consistent with long-standing precedent of this and other circuits that "'where [an affirmative defense] is raised in the trial court in a manner that does not result in unfair surprise, . . . technical failure to comply with Rule 8(c) is not fatal.'" Bull's Corner Restaurant v. Director, Federal Emergency Management Agency, 759 F.2d 500, 502 (5th Cir. 1985), quoting Allied Chemical Corp. v. Mackay, 695 F.2d 854, 855 (5th Cir. 1983).

We view the limitation on damages as an "avoidance" within the intendment of the residuary clause of 8(c). Black's Law Dictionary, 5th ed. 1979, defines an avoidance in pleadings as "the allegation or statement of new matter, in opposition to a former pleading, which, admitting the facts alleged in such former pleading, shows cause why they should not have their ordinary legal effect." Applied to the present discussion, a plaintiff pleads the traditional tort theory of malpractice and seeks full damages. The defendant responds that assuming recovery is in order under the ordinary tort principles, because of the new statutory limitation, the traditional precedents "should not have their ordinary legal effect."

Considering these factors, against the backdrop and with the illumination provided by other applications of Rule 8(c), we conclude that the Texas statutory limit on medical malpractice damages is an affirmative defense which must be pleaded timely and that in the cases at bar the defense has been waived.

## Notes and Questions

1. *Identifying an Affirmative Defense.* The line between an affirmative defense and a denial is not always easily discerned or drawn. For substantial assistance in identifying defenses that the federal courts deem "affirmative," see Fed. R. Civ. P. 8(c). Note that the list is not exhaustive. In the problem case, does the alleged settlement between Shayes and her old law firm fall within any of the named affirmative defenses? Who should logically plead it, and thus probably have to prove it?

Which issues are for the plaintiff to plead and which for the defendant continues to be a difficult question in many cases. For a typical instance where the court found that a defense need not be specially pleaded, see Sanden v. Mayo Clinic, 495 F.2d 221 (8th Cir. 1974), holding that the fraudulent pretense of injury in a malpractice action is not an affirmative defense.

2. *Unpleaded Defenses.* Rule 8 does not explicitly state that affirmative defenses not pleaded are waived. Rule 12(h) is explicit in regard to a few defenses that may be the subject of motions to dismiss. Nevertheless, a number of cases have applied Rule 8(c) to preclude untimely consideration of unpleaded defenses. Thus, in Radio Corp. of Am. v. Radio Station KYFM, Inc., 424 F.2d 14 (10th Cir. 1970), a defendant tried unsuccessfully to raise on a posttrial motion the defenses of the statute of frauds, illegality of contract, and lack of authority. An amazingly harsh case is Crawford v. Zeitler, 326 F.2d 119 (6th Cir. 1964), which imposed a waiver on a defendant who had pleaded the wrong statute of limitations. Certainly the better view is that the defendant need not identify the particular statute in his answer because the court can take notice of the correct law, e.g., Wade v. Lynn, 181 F. Supp. 361 (N.D. Ohio 1960). See also Harris v. Secretary, U.S. Dep't of Veterans Affairs, 126 F.3d 339 (D.C. Cir. 1997), which held that where no statute of limitations defense was raised in the responsive pleading, the defense cannot be raised in a motion to dismiss or motion for summary judgment, even if no prejudice to the opponent has been shown; rather, the party must file an amended pleading under Rule 15(a) to preserve the structure of notice pleading. Leave to amend should be freely granted if no prejudice would occur, but the technical requirements of Rule 8(c) cannot be elided.

3. *Affirmative Defenses Apparent on the Face of the Complaint.* Some defenses may be raised on a pre-answer motion to dismiss as well as by the answer, if the factual basis for the defense is disclosed in the complaint. See, e.g., Larter & Sons, Inc. v. Dinkler Hotels Co., 199 F.2d 854 (5th Cir. 1952). The statute of limitations is the most frequent example, but the limitations period may be extended by facts not revealed in the complaint. Perhaps the plaintiff who alleges an apparently stale claim should anticipate the defense of limitations and make the appropriate allegations that might negate it; this

is suggested in Kincheloe v. Farmer, 214 F.2d 604 (7th Cir. 1954). On the other hand, if a defendant files a general motion to dismiss for failure to state a claim that is not specifically based on the statute of limitations, the court may not view this motion as sufficient to preserve the issue of statute of limitations. Wagner v. Fawcett Publ'ns, 307 F.2d 409 (7th Cir. 1962). To be safe, therefore, a defendant who uses the pre-answer motion to attack a stale complaint should follow up with an answer that asserts "statute of limitations" as an affirmative defense, lest the defense be deemed waived.

4. *Other Causes of Waivers.* The pleading of an affirmative defense is not a guarantee against waiver. In Demsey & Assocs. v. S.S. Sea Star, 461 F.2d 1009 (2d Cir. 1972), *abrogated on other grounds by* Seguros Illimani S.A. v. M/V POPI P, 929 F.2d 89 (2d Cir. 1991), a defendant pleaded an arbitration clause as a defense, but proceeded to litigate other defenses without moving for a stay. It was held that the failure to move for a stay was an effective waiver of the arbitration clause.

5. *Should Plausibility Pleading Apply to Answers?* A question that has divided lower courts since the Supreme Court decided *Twombly* and *Iqbal* is whether the new plausibility pleading standard applies to answers as well as complaints. Rule 8(b)(1) provides that a party responding to a pleading must "state in short and plain terms its defenses to each claim asserted against it," and Rule 8(c)(1) provides that in "responding to a pleading, a party must affirmatively state any avoidance or affirmative defense." A handful of lower courts have concluded that, at least with respect to affirmative defenses, the plausibility pleading standard of *Twombly* and *Iqbal* must be met. See Dodson v. Strategic Rests. Acquisition Co. II, LLC, 289 F.R.D. 595 (E.D. Cal. 2013), (granting motion to strike affirmative defenses where defendant simply listed the names of the affirmative defenses without alleging any supporting facts; gathering and discussing divided authorities; discussing division of authority); see id. at 603 ("the Answer lacks any factual allegations demonstrating that the defenses are plausible on their face"). This approach can be justified under the traditional rule that affirmative defenses are disfavored to the extent that they defeat resolution of the case on the merits. But see Kohler v. Flava Enterprises, Inc., 779 F.3d 1016, 1019 (9th Cir. 2015) (abrogating *Dodson* by reaffirming the traditional rule that "the 'fair notice' required by the pleading standards only requires describing the defense in 'general terms'") (quoting Wright & Miller, Federal Practice and Procedure § 1274).

Other courts have held that the plausibility pleading standard does *not* apply to affirmative defenses, emphasizing textual differences between Rule 8(a) and Rule 8(c), as well as the different procedural functions of the complaint and affirmative defenses. See Tardif v. City of New York, 302 F.R.D. 31 (S.D.N.Y. 2014) (summarizing authority of district courts within the Second Circuit). The court in *Tardif* offered the following reasons to reject plausibility pleading for affirmative defenses: textual differences between Rule 8(a) and Rule 8(c); "a diminished concern that plaintiffs receive notice in light of their ability to obtain more information during discovery; the absence of concern that the defense is 'unlocking the doors of discovery;'

the limited discovery costs, in relation to the costs imposed on a defendant, since it is unlikely that either side will pursue discovery on frivolous defenses"; the limited time a defendant has to respond after service of the complaint; the potential waste of time spent litigating motions to strike given the liberal approach to requests for leave to amend under Rule 15; "the risk that a defendant will waive a defense at trial by failing to plead it at the early stage of the litigation; the lack of detail in Form 30; and the fact that a heightened pleading requirement would produce more motions to strike, which are disfavored." Id. at 33-34.

Some courts have attempted to cut a middle path, requiring less than plausibility pleading but "more than a mere rote recitation of generally available affirmative defenses without citation to any other fact or premise from which an inference may arise that the stated defense is logically related to the case in any way." See Mifflinburg Telegraph, Inc. v. Criswell, 80 F. Supp. 3d 566 (M.D. Pa. 2015).

### e.   Amending the Pleadings

### Problem Case: A Woman Partner (Part Three)

After McKenzie, Brachman had answered the complaint, Shayes learned that one of the reasons things turned sour for her at the firm was that a fellow partner, Arnie Becker, was having an affair with a woman associate he wanted to advance in her place. Becker and the woman associate have since left the firm.

How should Shayes go about amending the complaint to include this information and these parties? What if she learned this information after the statute of limitations had passed for filing a suit based on this information?

### *Note: Liberal Pleading and Liberal Amendments*

Free leave to amend pleadings as the case develops is part of the Rules' original design. Read Rule 15 carefully. Note that it progresses chronologically from the point before the defendant has answered through post-judgment amendment. Of course, the requirements vary at each stage that amendment is sought, and the judge's discretion about allowing the amendment is extremely broad. A further complication is the increasing use of the pretrial order in Rule 16 which frames the issues for trial, and has a high standard for amendment. First, read Rule 15, with special emphasis on 15(a) and (b). What do these sections suggest about the following questions:

1) Can you amend a complaint without court permission or agreement by your opponent? Under what circumstances?
2) Can you amend an answer without court permission or agreement by your opponent? Under what circumstances?

3) If the time for amending as of course (without permission) has elapsed, what must you do to amend a pleading?

4) If a party files an amended pleading to which a response must be filed, how much time does the opponent get to respond?

5) If a matter proceeds to trial and evidence is introduced that departs from the pleadings, what happens to the pleadings? Does it depend on whether an objection to the evidence is made?

6) Now read Rule 16. Does the answer to 5) change when there is a pretrial order that frames the issues for trial?

The real difficulty occurs when a party seeks to amend a pleading after the statute of limitations has run. The general rule is that the amendment will relate back to the time the original pleading was filed, provided the amended claim arises from the same transaction or occurrence as that described in the original pleading. The idea here is that the opponent had adequate notice within the applicable statute of limitations of the amended claim because it is factually related to the claim first described. Also, if the law of the jurisdiction that supplies the applicable statute of limitations would allow the amendment, it will be allowed in federal court even if the amended claim is *not* factually related to the original claim.

The most difficult amendment situation is one in which the amendment seeks to change parties, not just claims, after the statute of limitations has elapsed. This usually is impermissible *unless* the narrow requirements of Rule 15(c) are met. Essentially, this means that the case must be one of mistaken identity, and the real party must have been aware within the period described in Rule 15(c) that, but for an error, the original pleading would have named him as the defendant.

Before proceeding to questions that test your comprehension of Rule 15(c), you need to appreciate the distinction between filing a pleading and serving it on your opponent. *Filing* means carrying the papers to the courthouse and handing them to the clerk. Filing gives the court notice of your request, but not other parties to the lawsuit. *Service* means delivering the pleading to all parties of record, whether by hand-carrying it, mailing it, or other means. Only service assures that your opponents are on notice of the pleadings. To be safe, a lawyer should assure whenever possible that *both* filing *and* service occur before the statute of limitations elapses. Some states require that *both* occur within the statute of limitations. In other states, however, and in federal court actions for which federal law governs the statute of limitations, only filing must occur before the statute of limitations runs out. This *tolls* the statute of limitations. Thereafter, in federal court a lawyer has 120 days within which to serve the complaint or risk dismissal, which would mean the lawyer would have to refile the matter, thus losing any interim "tolling" time.

Now, how would you analyze the following problems?

a) The applicable statute of limitations is two years, and requires that both filing and service occur within this period. On June 1, 2004, *A* and

Company *B* are involved in an accident. On May 31, 2006, *A* files suit against *B* in federal court. Service of the complaint follows on June 15, 2006. May *B* move to dismiss on the ground that the complaint is untimely?

b) Assume instead that filing and service occur within the statute of limitations period. May *A* now move to amend the complaint to add a claim for damages in a contract matter that arose in 2003?

c) Same as b) except that *A* moves in July 2006 to amend to add a claim for physical injuries that occurred in the June 1 accident. Permissible?

d) Same as a), and *A* moves to amend the complaint in July 2006. The amendment seeks to change the name of the party against whom the complaint is filed, because the plaintiff since has learned Company *C* actually owns the vehicle involved in the June 1 collision, though the name on the vehicle read "Co. *B*." The president of Co. *B* is also the president of Co. *C*, and she read the original complaint when it was served on June 15, 2006. What result?

As we saw in *Zielinski*, one of the critical tasks for plaintiffs is determining the identity of the proper defendant. That will depend not just on who harmed the plaintiff—a sometimes difficult question now given the Byzantine structure of corporate organization—but what causes of action are available for the harm suffered, and what remedies are associated with the available causes of action. Statutes of limitation add urgency to the matter—a plaintiff may recover nothing if her lawyer gets tied up in litigation against the wrong party. Rule 15(c)(1)(C), added in 1966, well after *Zielinski* was decided, provides plaintiff's counsel some room for error in identifying the proper defendant. Just how much is the subject of the next case.

### *Krupski v. Costa Crociere S.p.A.*
560 U.S. 538 (2010)

JUSTICE SOTOMAYOR delivered the opinion of the Court.

Rule 15(c) of the Federal Rules of Civil Procedure governs when an amended pleading "relates back" to the date of a timely filed original pleading and is thus itself timely even though it was filed outside an applicable statute of limitations. Where an amended pleading changes a party or a party's name, the Rule requires, among other things, that "the party to be brought in by amendment . . . knew or should have known that the action would have been brought against it, but for a mistake concerning the proper party's identity." Rule 15(c)(1)(C). In this case, the Court of Appeals held that Rule 15(c) was not satisfied because the *plaintiff* knew or should have known of the proper defendant before filing her original complaint. The court also held that relation back was not appropriate because the plaintiff had unduly delayed in seeking to amend. We hold that relation back under Rule 15(c)(1)(C) depends on what *the party to be added* knew or should have known, not on the amending party's knowledge or its timeliness in seeking to amend the pleading. [Emphasis added. — Eds.] Accordingly, we reverse the judgment of the Court of Appeals.

## I

On February 21, 2007, petitioner, Wanda Krupski, tripped over a cable and fractured her femur while she was on board the cruise ship Costa Magica. Upon her return home, she acquired counsel and began the process of seeking compensation for her injuries. Krupski's passenger ticket — which explained that it was the sole contract between each passenger and the carrier — included a variety of requirements for obtaining damages for an injury suffered on board one of the carrier's ships. The ticket identified the carrier as

> Costa Crociere S.p.A., an Italian corporation, and all Vessels and other ships owned, chartered, operated, marketed or provided by Costa Crociere, S.p.A., and all officers, staff members, crew members, independent contractors, medical providers, concessionaires, pilots, suppliers, agents and assigns onboard said Vessels, and the manufacturers of said Vessels and all their component parts.

The ticket required an injured party to submit "written notice of the claim with full particulars . . . to the carrier or its duly authorized agent within 185 days after the date of injury." The ticket further required any lawsuit to be "filed within one year after the date of injury" and to be "served upon the carrier within 120 days after filing." For cases arising from voyages departing from or returning to a United States port in which the amount in controversy exceeded $75,000, the ticket designated the United States District Court for the Southern District of Florida in Broward County, Florida, as the exclusive forum for a lawsuit. The ticket extended the "defenses, limitations and exceptions . . . that may be invoked by the CARRIER" to "all persons who may act on behalf of the CARRIER or on whose behalf the CARRIER may act," including "the CARRIER's parents, subsidiaries, affiliates, successors, assigns, representatives, agents, employees, servants, concessionaires and contractors" as well as "Costa Cruise Lines N.V.," identified as the "sales and marketing agent for the CARRIER and the issuer of this Passage Ticket Contract." The front of the ticket listed Costa Cruise Lines' address in Florida and stated that an entity called "Costa Cruises" was "the first cruise company in the world" to obtain a certain certification of quality.

On July 2, 2007, Krupski's counsel notified Costa Cruise Lines of Krupski's claims. On July 9, 2007, the claims administrator for Costa Cruise requested additional information from Krupski "[i]n order to facilitate our future attempts to achieve a pre-litigation settlement." The parties were unable to reach a settlement, however, and on February 1, 2008 — three weeks before the 1-year limitations period expired — Krupski filed a negligence action against Costa Cruise, invoking the diversity jurisdiction of the

Federal District Court for the Southern District of Florida. The complaint alleged that Costa Cruise "owned, operated, managed, supervised and controlled" the ship on which Krupski had injured herself; that Costa Cruise had extended to its passengers an invitation to enter onto the ship; and that Costa Cruise owed Krupski a duty of care, which it breached by failing to take steps that would have prevented her accident. The complaint further stated that venue was proper under the passenger ticket's forum selection clause and averred that, by the July 2007 notice of her claims, Krupski had complied with the ticket's presuit requirements. Krupski served Costa Cruise on February 4, 2008.

Over the next several months—after the limitations period had expired—Costa Cruise brought Costa Crociere's existence to Krupski's attention three times. First, on February 25, 2008, Costa Cruise filed its answer, asserting that it was not the proper defendant, as it was merely the North American sales and marketing agent for Costa Crociere, which was the actual carrier and vessel operator. Second, on March 20, 2008, Costa Cruise listed Costa Crociere as an interested party in its corporate disclosure statement. Finally, on May 6, 2008, Costa Cruise moved for summary judgment, again stating that Costa Crociere was the proper defendant.

On June 13, 2008, Krupski responded to Costa Cruise's motion for summary judgment, arguing for limited discovery to determine whether Costa Cruise should be dismissed. According to Krupski, the following sources of information led her to believe Costa Cruise was the responsible party: The travel documents prominently identified Costa Cruise and gave its Florida address; Costa Cruise's Web site listed Costa Cruise in Florida as the United States office for the Italian company Costa Crociere; and the Web site of the Florida Department of State listed Costa Cruise as the only "Costa" company registered to do business in that State. Krupski also observed that Costa Cruise's claims administrator had responded to her claims notification without indicating that Costa Cruise was not a responsible party. With her response, Krupski simultaneously moved to amend her complaint to add Costa Crociere as a defendant.

On July 2, 2008, after oral argument, the District Court denied Costa Cruise's motion for summary judgment without prejudice and granted Krupski leave to amend, ordering that Krupski effect proper service on Costa Crociere by September 16, 2008. Complying with the court's deadline, Krupski filed an amended complaint on July 11, 2008, and served Costa Crociere on August 21, 2008. On that same date, the District Court issued an order dismissing Costa Cruise from the case pursuant to the parties' joint stipulation, Krupski apparently having concluded that Costa Cruise was correct that it bore no responsibility for her injuries.

Shortly thereafter, Costa Crociere—represented by the same counsel who had represented Costa Cruise—moved to dismiss, contending that the amended complaint did not relate back under Rule 15(c) and was therefore untimely. The District Court agreed. Rule 15(c), the court explained, imposes three requirements before an amended complaint against a newly named defendant can relate back to the original complaint. First, the claim against

the newly named defendant must have arisen "out of the conduct, transaction, or occurrence set out—or attempted to be set out—in the original
pleading." Fed. Rules Civ. Proc. 15(c)(1)(B), (C). Second, "within the period
provided by Rule 4(m) for serving the summons and complaint" (which is
ordinarily 120 days from when the complaint is filed, see Rule 4(m)), the
newly named defendant must have "received such notice of the action that it
will not be prejudiced in defending on the merits." Rule 15(c)(1)(C)(i). Finally,
the plaintiff must show that, within the Rule 4(m) period, the newly named
defendant "knew or should have known that the action would have been
brought against it, but for a mistake concerning the proper party's identity."
Rule 15(c)(1)(C)(ii).

The first two conditions posed no problem, the court explained: The
claim against Costa Crociere clearly involved the same occurrence as the
original claim against Costa Cruise, and Costa Crociere had constructive
notice of the action and had not shown that any unfair prejudice would
result from relation back. But the court found the third condition fatal to
Krupski's attempt to relate back, concluding that Krupski had not made a
mistake concerning the identity of the proper party. Relying on Eleventh
Circuit precedent, the court explained that the word "mistake" should not
be construed to encompass a deliberate decision not to sue a party whose
identity the plaintiff knew before the statute of limitations had run. Because
Costa Cruise informed Krupski that Costa Crociere was the proper defendant in its answer, corporate disclosure statement, and motion for summary judgment, and yet Krupski delayed for months in moving to amend
and then in filing an amended complaint, the court concluded that Krupski
knew of the proper defendant and made no mistake.

The Eleventh Circuit affirmed in an unpublished *per curiam* opinion. . . .

We granted certiorari to resolve tension among the Circuits over the
breadth of Rule 15(c)(1)(C)(ii), and we now reverse.


## II

. . .

In our view, neither of the Court of Appeals' reasons for denying relation back under Rule 15(c)(1)(C)(ii) finds support in the text of the Rule. We
consider each reason in turn.


## A

The Court of Appeals first decided that Krupski either knew or should
have known of the proper party's identity and thus determined that she
had made a deliberate choice instead of a mistake in not naming Costa
Crociere as a party in her original pleading. By focusing on Krupski's
knowledge, the Court of Appeals chose the wrong starting point. The question under Rule 15(c)(1)(C)(ii) is not whether Krupski knew or should have
known the identity of Costa Crociere as the proper defendant, but whether

Costa Crociere knew or should have known that it would have been named as a defendant but for an error. Rule 15(c)(1)(C)(ii) asks what the prospective *defendant* knew or should have known during the Rule 4(m) period, not what the *plaintiff* knew or should have known at the time of filing her original complaint.

Information in the plaintiff's possession is relevant only if it bears on the defendant's understanding of whether the plaintiff made a mistake regarding the proper party's identity. For purposes of that inquiry, it would be error to conflate knowledge of a party's existence with the absence of mistake. A mistake is "[a]n error, misconception, or misunderstanding; an erroneous belief." Black's Law Dictionary 1092 (9th ed. 2009). That a plaintiff knows of a party's existence does not preclude her from making a mistake with respect to that party's identity. A plaintiff may know that a prospective defendant—call him party A—exists, while erroneously believing him to have the status of party B. Similarly, a plaintiff may know generally what party A does while misunderstanding the roles that party A and party B played in the "conduct, transaction, or occurrence" giving rise to her claim. If the plaintiff sues party B instead of party A under these circumstances, she has made a "mistake concerning the proper party's identity" notwithstanding her knowledge of the existence of both parties. The only question under Rule 15(c)(1)(C)(ii), then, is whether party A knew or should have known that, absent some mistake, the action would have been brought against him. . . .

This reading is consistent with the purpose of relation back: to balance the interests of the defendant protected by the statute of limitations with the preference expressed in the Federal Rules of Civil Procedure in general, and Rule 15 in particular, for resolving disputes on their merits. A prospective defendant who legitimately believed that the limitations period had passed without any attempt to sue him has a strong interest in repose. But repose would be a windfall for a prospective defendant who understood, or who should have understood, that he escaped suit during the limitations period only because the plaintiff misunderstood a crucial fact about his identity. . . .

Our reading is also consistent with the history of Rule 15(c)(1)(C). That provision was added in 1966 to respond to a recurring problem in suits against the Federal Government, particularly in the Social Security context. Advisory Committee's 1966 Notes 122. Individuals who had filed timely lawsuits challenging the administrative denial of benefits often failed to name the party identified in the statute as the proper defendant—the current Secretary of what was then the Department of Health, Education, and Welfare—and named instead the United States; the Department of Health, Education, and Welfare itself; the nonexistent "Federal Security Administration"; or a Secretary who had recently retired from office. By the time the plaintiffs discovered their mistakes, the statute of limitations in many cases had expired, and the district courts denied the plaintiffs leave to amend on the ground that the amended complaints would not relate back. Rule 15(c) was therefore "amplified to provide a general solution" to this problem. It is conceivable that the Social Security litigants knew or reasonably should have known the identity of the proper defendant either because of documents in their administrative cases or by dint of the statute setting forth the filing requirements. Nonetheless, the Advisory Committee clearly meant their filings to qualify as mistakes under the Rule.

Respondent suggests that our decision in Nelson v. Adams USA, Inc., 529 U.S. 460 (2000), forecloses the reading of Rule 15(c)(1)(C)(ii) we adopt today. We disagree. In that case, Adams USA, Inc. (Adams), had obtained an award of attorney's fees against the corporation of which Donald Nelson was the president and sole shareholder. After Adams became concerned that the corporation did not have sufficient funds to pay the award, Adams sought to amend its pleading to add Nelson as a party and simultaneously moved to amend the judgment to hold Nelson responsible. The District Court granted both motions, and the Court of Appeals affirmed. We reversed, holding that the requirements of due process, as codified in Rules 12 and 15 of the Federal Rules of Civil Procedure, demand that an added party have the opportunity to respond before judgment is entered against him. Id., at 465-67. In a footnote explaining that relation back does not deny the added party an opportunity to respond to the amended pleading, we noted that the case did not arise under the "mistake clause" of Rule 15(c): "Respondent Adams made no such mistake. It knew of Nelson's role and existence and, until it moved to amend its pleading, chose to assert its claim for costs and fees only against [Nelson's company]." Id., at 467, n.1.

Contrary to respondent's claim, *Nelson* does not suggest that Rule 15(c)(1)(C)(ii) cannot be satisfied if a plaintiff knew of the prospective defendant's existence at the time she filed her original complaint. In that case, there was nothing in the initial pleading suggesting that Nelson was an intended party, while there was evidence in the record (of which Nelson was aware) that Adams sought to add him only after learning that the company would not be able to satisfy the judgment. This evidence countered any implication that Adams had originally failed to name Nelson because of any "mistake concerning the proper party's identity," and instead suggested that Adams decided to name Nelson only after the fact in an attempt to ensure that the fee award would be paid. The footnote merely observes that Adams had originally been under no misimpression about the function Nelson played in the underlying dispute. We said, after all, that Adams knew of Nelson's "role" as well as his existence. Read in context, the footnote in *Nelson* is entirely consistent with our understanding of the Rule. . . . This conclusion is in keeping with our rejection today of the Court of Appeals' reliance on the plaintiff's knowledge to deny relation back.

## B

The Court of Appeals offered a second reason why Krupski's amended complaint did not relate back: Krupski had unduly delayed in seeking to file, and in eventually filing, an amended complaint. The Court of Appeals offered no support for its view that a plaintiff's dilatory conduct can justify the denial of relation back under Rule 15(c)(1)(C), and we find none. The Rule plainly sets forth an exclusive list of requirements for relation back, and the amending party's diligence is not among them. Moreover, the Rule mandates relation back once the Rule's requirements are satisfied; it does not leave the decision whether to grant relation back to the district court's equitable discretion. See Rule 15(c)(1) ("An amendment . . . *relates back . . .* when" the three listed requirements are met (emphasis added)).

The mandatory nature of the inquiry for relation back under Rule 15(c) is particularly striking in contrast to the inquiry under Rule 15(a), which sets forth the circumstances in which a party may amend its pleading before trial. By its terms, Rule 15(a) gives discretion to the district court in deciding whether to grant a motion to amend a pleading to add a party or a claim. . . . We have previously explained that a court may consider a movant's "undue delay" or "dilatory motive" in deciding whether to grant leave to amend under Rule 15(a). Foman v. Davis, 371 U.S. 178, 182 (1962). As the contrast between Rule 15(a) and Rule 15(c) makes clear, however, the speed with which a plaintiff moves to amend her complaint or files an amended complaint after obtaining leave to do so has no bearing on whether the amended complaint relates back. . . .

## C

Applying these principles to the facts of this case, we think it clear that the courts below erred in denying relation back under Rule 15(c)(1)(C)(ii). The District Court held that Costa Crociere had "constructive notice" of Krupski's complaint within the Rule 4(m) period. Costa Crociere has not challenged this finding. Because the complaint made clear that Krupski meant to sue the company that "owned, operated, managed, supervised and controlled" the ship on which she was injured, and also indicated (mistakenly) that Costa Cruise performed those roles, Costa Crociere should have known, within the Rule 4(m) period, that it was not named as a defendant in that complaint only because of Krupski's misunderstanding about which "Costa" entity was in charge of the ship—clearly a "mistake concerning the proper party's identity."

. . .

It is also worth noting that Costa Cruise and Costa Crociere are related corporate entities with very similar names; "crociera" even means "cruise" in Italian. . . . In addition, Costa Crociere's own actions contributed to passenger confusion over "the proper party" for a lawsuit. The front of the ticket advertises that "Costa Cruises" has achieved a certification of quality, without clarifying whether "Costa Cruises" is Costa Cruise Lines, Costa Crociere, or some other related "Costa" company. Indeed, Costa Crociere is evidently aware that the difference between Costa Cruise and Costa Crociere can be confusing for cruise ship passengers. See, e.g., Suppa v. Costa Crociere, S.p.A., No. 07-60526-CIV, 2007 WL 4287508, *1 (S.D. Fla. Dec. 4, 2007) (denying Costa Crociere's motion to dismiss the amended complaint where the original complaint had named Costa Cruise as a defendant after "find[ing] it simply inconceivable that Defendant Costa Crociere was not on notice . . . that . . . but for the mistake in the original Complaint, Costa Crociere was the appropriate party to be named in the action").

In light of these facts, Costa Crociere should have known that Krupski's failure to name it as a defendant in her original complaint was due to a mistake concerning the proper party's identity. We therefore reverse the judgment of the Court of Appeals for the Eleventh Circuit and remand the case for further proceedings consistent with this opinion.

*It is so ordered.*

## Notes and Questions

1. You might think misnaming a party is a fairly rare event, but with the complexity of corporate ownership and the increasing use of subsidiaries and affiliates, it can happen easily. A recent case from the Seventh Circuit, *Joseph v. Elan Motorsports Technologies Racing Corp.*, 638 F.3d 555 (7th Cir. 2011), shows just how easily. The plaintiff sued Elan Motorsports Technologies Racing Corporation ("Elan Corp.") for breach of an employment contract even though the contract at issue named Elan Motorsports Technologies, Inc. ("Elan Inc.") — a legally distinct affiliate of Elan Corp. Six years went by before the plaintiff realized his error and sought leave to amend the complaint. Since the statute of limitations had expired, he had to rely on the doctrine of relation back. Citing a previous Seventh Circuit case holding that "it is the plaintiff's responsibility to determine the proper party to sue and to do so before the statute of limitations expires," *Hall v. Norfolk Southern Railway Co.*, 469 F.3d 590 (7th Cir. 2006), the district court denied leave to amend and dismissed the suit.

The Seventh Circuit reversed, noting that under *Krupski*, the district court was limited to two inquiries in determining relation back: 1) whether the new defendant knew or should have known that, but for a mistake, it would have been sued originally, and 2) whether plaintiff's delay in discovering that the wrong defendant was named in the original complaint will adversely affect defendant's ability to put on an effective defense. A plaintiff's carelessness is not an independent basis for denying relation back. As a party to the contract on which the lawsuit was based, Elan Inc. was aware that it was the intended defendant. The complaint was served on a de facto Elan Inc. employee — the person who supervised plaintiff's work. This person certainly knew, as soon as he was served, that, had it not been for an error by plaintiff, Elan Inc. would have been named the defendant. Thus, any prejudice that did result was Elan Inc.'s responsibility — and was not a basis for denying relation back.

2. Some government officials can be sued in their official capacity, which means that the state itself will answer for any liability, or in their personal

capacity, which means liability will be assessed against assets of the officer. Failure to name the defendant in her proper capacity can raise problems similar to those addressed in *Krupski*. See Sanders-Burns v. City of Plano, 594 F.3d 366 (5th Cir. 2010) (allowing an amendment filed in a section 1983 action after the statute of limitations expired to change the capacity in which the defendant was sued; amendment relates back to the date of the original pleading because the defendant received adequate notice of the action, was not prejudiced in preparing a defense, and knew or should have known that, but for plaintiff's mistake, he would have been named in his individual capacity in the original complaint).

3. Are you persuaded by the Court's effort to distinguish *Nelson* in the *Krupski* case? Though *Nelson* seems like a relatively straightforward case, the decision is significant because the Court recognizes the possibility that pleadings may be amended to add a party *after* the case has gone to judgment. That can be quite significant in cases in which corporate defendants seek to render themselves judgment proof by filing for bankruptcy or shifting assets from the corporation to its officers. The plaintiff in *Nelson* was denied leave to amend postjudgment because the defendant was given no opportunity to respond—the trial court simply swapped out the corporation for its president and sole shareholder.

> Nelson was never served with an amended pleading. Indeed, no such pleading was ever actually composed and filed in court. Nor, after the amendment naming him as a party, was Nelson accorded 10 days to state his defenses against personal liability for costs and fees. Instead, judgment was entered against him the moment permission to amend the pleading was granted.

Nelson v. Adams USA, Inc., 529 U.S. 460, 466 (2000). But if the new party *is* given an appropriate opportunity to respond, *Nelson* appears not to preclude amendment after judgment. As the Court emphasized in *Nelson*, "Our decision surely does not insulate Nelson from liability. . . . Once the amended pleading is served and Nelson's response is submitted, it will be open to Adams to urge . . . that issue preclusion (collateral estoppel) bars Nelson from contesting findings made during the litigation between OCP and Adams." Id. at 472 n.5. See also Insituform Technologies, Inc. v. Cat Contracting, Inc., 385 F.3d 1360 (Fed. Cir. 2004) (allowing amendment adding executive officer of defendant corporation postjudgment; distinguishing *Nelson* on the grounds that the officer had notice of the suit and was liable as an individual tortfeasor); Johns v. Harborage I, Ltd., 664 N.W.2d 291 (Minn. 2003) (plaintiff allowed to amend pleadings after judgment in sexual harassment suit).

4. *Krupski* involves an amendment to name the correct defendant and it expressly reaffirms the commitment of the Rules to decision on the merits. What about amendments that change the *theory* of the case, not the named parties? Do you think an amendment should relate back if, in later stages of litigation, the plaintiff seeks to change her cause of action? The Court takes up these questions in the following case.

## *Barcume v. City of Flint*
819 F. Supp. 631 (E.D. Mich. 1993)

NEWBLATT, DISTRICT JUDGE.

Before the Court is defendant City of Flint's ("City") motion for summary judgment, plaintiffs' response, and defendant City's reply. For the reasons that follow, defendant's motion is GRANTED IN PART and DENIED IN PART.

This civil rights action arises out of the alleged discriminatory hiring and promotion practices of the City of Flint and alleged discriminatory employment practices and sexually hostile working environment within the Flint Police Department ("FPD"). The thirteen plaintiffs are all female law enforcement officers employed by, or previously employed by, the FPD. This case is not a class action lawsuit, but rather consists of thirteen separate plaintiffs alleging personal discrimination and harassment at the hands of fellow male police officers, supervisory personnel, the FPD and its command staff, and the City of Flint through its alleged policy and practice of discrimination and tacit approval of the harassment that allegedly exists within the FPD.

Plaintiffs filed their original complaint on January 30, 1984. In that complaint, plaintiffs made various claims against both the City of Flint and the Flint Police Officers Association ("FPOA"). The original complaint consisted of five counts: (I) a claim of discrimination in hiring and promotion practices in violation of 42 U.S.C. § 1983 against defendant City; (II) a claim for violation of the duty of fair representation against defendant FPOA; (III) a claim of conspiracy to deprive plaintiffs of their civil rights in violation of 42 U.S.C. § 1985(3) against both defendants; (IV) a claim of discrimination in hiring and promotion practices and in terms, conditions and privileges of employment in violation of the Elliott-Larsen Civil Rights Act against defendant City; and (V) a claim against defendant FPOA for violation of the Elliott-Larsen Civil Rights Act.

On December 4, 1985, after extensive discovery had already taken place, plaintiffs moved the Court for leave to file a Second Amended Complaint. A hearing on this motion was held on June 23, 1986. At that hearing, the Court granted plaintiffs' motion to file an amended complaint, provided that the amended pleading separated plaintiffs' claims regarding the constitutionality of defendant City's Affirmative Action Plan ("AAP") from those alleging "traditional" or "garden variety" discrimination on the basis of sex. Id. at 26. The Court indicated that the AAP's exclusion of women may be evidence relevant to a classic discrimination claim, but that the determination regarding the constitutionality of the AAP is a separate claim to be filed as a separate count. Id. As noted in the Court's Memorandum Opinion and Order of January 26, 1987, leave for plaintiffs to amend their complaint had been granted at the June 23, 1986 hearing. Nevertheless, it was not until February 26, 1987 that plaintiffs filed their Second Amended Complaint and Jury Demand. The Second Amended Complaint contains six counts, two of which still remain to be adjudicated as to defendant City; count II, a claim pursuant to 42 U.S.C. § 1983 that defendant City violated plaintiffs' rights to equal protection in the terms and conditions of employment; and count VI, a claim that defendant City violated plaintiffs' rights secured by the Elliott-Larsen Civil Rights Act in the terms and conditions of employment.[1] Through their motion, defendant City seeks summary judgment to dismiss or limit plaintiffs' claims under counts II and VI.

## I.   Factual Background

The specific facts alleged by plaintiffs shall be addressed as necessary in context of discussion regarding defendant City's motion. Defendant City's arguments shall be addressed seriatim.

## II.   Statute of Limitations

Defendant's first argument is that plaintiffs' claims of alleged discriminatory conduct occurring before February 26, 1984 are barred by the statute of limitations. Plaintiffs do not dispute that the statute of limitations for both 42 U.S.C. § 1983 and the Elliott-Larsen Civil Rights Act ("Elliott-Larsen"), M.C.L. §§ 37. 2101 et seq., is three years. Conlin v. Blanchard 890 F.2d 811 (6th Cir. 1989); Browning v. Pendleton, 869 F.2d 989 (6th Cir. 1989). Thus, argues defendant City, to the extent that plaintiffs' claims are based upon conduct and events occurring more than three years before the filing of the Second Amended Complaint, these claims are time-barred. Of course, defendant City's position presumes that plaintiffs' Second Amended Complaint neither relates back to plaintiffs' original complaint, filed January 30, 1984, nor alleges a continuing violation that would allow plaintiffs to recover damages for the entire period of the continuing illegal conduct.

### A.   Relation Back

Federal Rule of Civil Procedure 15(c) provides in relevant part that:

> An amendment of a pleading relates back to the date of the original pleading when . . . the claim . . . asserted in the amended pleading arose out of the conduct, transaction, or occurrence set forth or attempted to be set forth in the original pleading. . . .

---

1. Count I was a § 1983 claim challenging the constitutionality of the AAP for its failure to include women in its remedial provisions. The Court granted summary judgment to defendants on count I, upholding the constitutionality of the AAP. Count IV of the Second Amended Complaint was a claim against defendants City and FPOA alleging conspiracy to deprive plaintiffs of their civil rights through implementation of the AAP to the exclusion of women. Because this Court has upheld the constitutionality of the AAP, plaintiffs concede that count IV is also effectively dismissed. Thus, the Court will not address defendant City's motion as it relates to count IV.

Fed. R. Civ. P. 15(c)(2) [now 15(c)(1)(B)]. The effect of this rule is that

> once litigation involving particular conduct or a given transaction or occur-
> rence has been instituted, the parties are not entitled to the protection of the
> statute of limitations against the later assertion by amendment of defenses
> or claims that arise out of the same conduct, transaction, or occurrence as set
> forth in the original pleading.

Wright, Miller & Kane, Federal Practice and Procedure: Civil 2d § 1496
(1990) at 64. The rationale behind Rule 15(c) is to allow an amendment to
relate back to the filing of the original complaint where the defendant has
been put on notice, through the pleadings or from other sources, of the
entire scope of the transaction or occurrence out of which the amended
claims arise. See id. at § 1497. Thus,

> amendments that merely correct technical deficiencies or expand or modify
> the facts alleged in the earlier pleading meet the Rule 15(c) test and will relate
> back. . . . [A]mendments that do no more than restate the original claim with
> greater particularity or amplify the details of the transaction alleged in the
> preceding pleading fall within Rule 15(c). But, if the alteration of the origi-
> nal statement is so substantial that it cannot be said that defendant [sic] was
> given adequate notice of the conduct, transaction, or occurrence that forms
> the basis of the claim or defense, then the amendment will not relate back
> and will be time barred if the limitations period has expired.

Id. at § 1497 pp. 74-79; see also Tiller v. Atlantic Coast Line R.R. Co., 323
U.S. 574, 581 (1995); Boddy v. Dean, 821 F.2d 346, 351 (6th Cir. 1987) (amendment that alleges added events leading up to same injury may relate back).
Furthermore, that the amendment changes the legal theory upon which the
action initially was brought will not automatically bar relation back. Id. at
§ 1497 p. 94. Thus,

> [t]he fact that an amendment changes the legal theory on which the action
> initially was brought is of no consequence if the factual situation upon which
> the action depends remains the same and has been brought to defendant's
> [sic] attention by the original pleading.

Id. at § 1497 pp. 94-95; see also Hageman v. Signal L.P. Gas, Inc., 486 F.2d 479,
484 (6th Cir. 1973) (added theory of liability for same occurrence may relate
back). An amendment will not relate back, however, if it asserts a new claim
for relief based on different facts than set forth in the original complaint.
Koon v. Lakeshore Contractors, 128 F.R.D. 650, 653 (W.D. Mich. 1988).

In their response brief, plaintiffs argue that defendant City was not surprised by plaintiffs' allegations made in the Second Amended Complaint.
Plaintiffs' response brief at 23. Plaintiffs argue that the original complaint
gave defendant City ample notice that plaintiffs were suffering from continuing sexual discrimination in a variety of forms by the FPD and its
agents. Id. At the very least, argue plaintiffs, the allegations of the Second

Amended Complaint were an "attempt" to raise claims of sex discrimination which merely were particularized from the more broad allegations of the original complaint. Id. Plaintiffs further argue that, apart from the notice provided by the original complaint, defendant City became aware through its deposition of plaintiffs in 1984 and 1985 "that plaintiffs' exclusion from the AAP was but one act in a long line of discriminatory events." Id. Because defendant City, through discovery, knew of the sexually discriminatory and hostile work environment at the FPD, plaintiffs assert that their sexual discrimination and sexual harassment claims relate back to the filing of the original complaint. Id. at 24.

Defendant City argues in its motion that the Second Amended Complaint does not relate back to the original complaint. Defendant City argues that the original complaint only presented a challenge to the validity of the AAP, adopted and implemented in 1984, which excluded women from its definition of minorities to receive the benefits of affirmative action. Defendant City asserts that any mention of sexually discriminatory practices was limited to creating an historical perspective upon which to justify the necessity for the inclusion of women in the AAP. No specific persons were identified in the complaint as perpetrators of sexual discrimination. Rather, plaintiffs discussed generally the historical hiring practices of the FPD and the concomitant effect this had on promotional opportunities for women. Conversely, argues defendant City, the Second Amended Complaint alleges different causes of action based upon vastly different facts not pleaded in the original complaint. Defendant City asserts that the Second Amended Complaint implicates an entirely new set of actors who allegedly engaged in inappropriate conduct independent of that alleged in the original complaint. Finally, defendant City argues that the original complaint did not provide notice of the subsequently filed claims of sexual discrimination and sexual harassment; in fact, plaintiffs will need to introduce entirely different evidence to establish their claims set forth in the Second Amended Complaint as opposed to that required to support their claims in the original complaint.

In support of their position, plaintiffs cite several cases as authority that claims based upon new legal theories may relate back to the original pleading where the facts upon which they are derived were included in the original complaint, or are similar and related to the facts set forth originally. See Maty v. Grasselli Co., 303 U.S. 197 (1938); Boddy v. Dean, 821 F.2d 346 (6th Cir. 1987); Carter v. Delta Air Lines, Inc., 441 F. Supp. 808 (S.D.N.Y. 1977); Baruan v. Young, 536 F. Supp. 356 (D. Md. 1982). Thus, the question before the Court regarding this issue is whether the claims raised in plaintiffs' Second Amended Complaint constitute different legal theories, and whether these claims arise out of the same or related occurrences or transactions as those pleaded in the original complaint.

A review of the original complaint, filed on January 30, 1984, reveals absolutely no claims of sexual harassment. Moreover, the entire complaint, consisting of eighty-four paragraphs, is devoid of any reference to conduct that could be interpreted as sexual harassment by the most reasonably prudent defense attorney. The original complaint also fails to allege a single incident of harassment or any other discrimination attributable to any individual person acting as an agent of the City of Flint. The original complaint does, however, make claims of discrimination in hiring and promotion of women in violation of their civil rights secured by 42 U.S.C. § 1983 (count I) and the Elliott-Larsen Civil Rights Act (count IV).

Plaintiffs' Second Amended Complaint, filed February 26, 1987, states much broader claims under § 1983 and Elliott-Larsen. Not only do counts II and VI allege discrimination in hiring and promotional practices of defendant City, they further allege claims of disparate treatment and harassment that were not included in the original pleading. Most notably, both counts II and VI allege that defendant City condones and ratifies sexual harassment toward women in the workplace, and that defendant City has done so with knowledge or notice of the sexually hostile environment. These claims with regard to sexual harassment and hostile work environment are new to the Second Amended Complaint. There was not an inkling of factual support for such claims in the original complaint. Therefore, defendant City did not have notice that plaintiffs were pursuing that particular type of discrimination claim in this law-suit.

Plaintiffs' original complaint alleges a violation of 42 U.S.C. § 1983 by defendant City for traditional and historical discrimination against women in hiring police officers. This historical discrimination, it is alleged, has adversely impacted women in the promotion to sergeant. The AAP's failure to include women allegedly acts to perpetuate the past discrimination against women in the FPD.

To the extent that count II of the Second Amended Complaint alleges discrimination in hiring and promotion practices, and disparate impact upon present opportunities for promotion of women to the rank of sergeant, plaintiffs' claims relate back to the original complaint for statute of limitations purposes. To the extent, however, that plaintiffs' claims under count II allege disparate treatment based upon sex, sexual harassment, and the existence of a hostile work environment within the FPD, plaintiffs' claims do not relate back to the original complaint.

The same is true with regard to count VI of the Second Amended Complaint. Although count IV of the original complaint stated a claim of discrimination against plaintiffs in the terms and conditions of employment, there was no notice to defendant City that this claim was for any violation other than discrimination in hiring and promotion practices, and in the exclusion of women from the relief prescribed by the AAP. No facts were alleged that would support, or that would indicate an attempt to support, a sexual harassment claim. Plaintiffs' view that defendant City was on notice from defendants' depositions of plaintiffs in 1984 and 1985 is rejected. Plaintiffs had ample opportunity to amend the complaint to state the expanded scope of their Elliott-Larsen and § 1983 claims—to include sexual harassment—or to notify defendant City directly that such claims were being pursued. As a result of the filing of plaintiffs' Second Amended Complaint, defendant City was required to engage extensively in further discovery, including redeposition of the thirteen plaintiffs. This would not have been the case had defendant City been made aware of the sexual harassment claim. Therefore, the Court finds that defendant City did not have notice of the added claims.

Plaintiffs' position that the Second Amended Complaint merely particularized allegations made or attempted to be raised in the original pleadings also is rejected. As stated previously, there is no indication from the original complaint that plaintiff was making a claim of sexual harassment. Therefore, to the extent that count VI alleges that defendant City discriminated against plaintiffs in hiring and promotional practices, plaintiffs' claim relates back to the original pleading. Plaintiffs' claims of sexual harassment and disparate treatment in terms and conditions of employment, other than in hiring or promotional decisions, do not relate back and, unless they constitute a continuing violation as discussed below, they are barred by the statute of limitations for those incidents occurring more than three years prior to the filing of the Second Amended Complaint.

## Notes and Questions

1. *Amending the Legal Theory.* To what extent does the ability to file an amended complaint hinge on how generally the plaintiff words the original complaint? Should a plaintiff always be allowed to amend a complaint to add a new theory of recovery based on the same facts? If so, was *Barcume* wrongly decided? Wouldn't the plaintiff in some cases be able to ascertain the proper theory (or theories) only after some discovery? Yet in *Barcume,* shouldn't the plaintiffs have known at the time they filed the complaint whether the workplace was hostile? It's not as clear a case of information asymmetry as *Twombly* or *Iqbal.*

2. *Adding Related Claims.* As the cases indicate, the test for determining whether an added claim is sufficiently related to the original claim is hardly wooden. Context matters much here, as it does in determining relatedness under Rule 13(a) (compulsory counterclaims) and under 28 U.S.C. § 1367 (supplemental jurisdiction).

3. *Some Examples.* What do you think about the following proposed amendments that were offered after the statute of limitations period had elapsed?

a. In an action against a surgeon for lack of informed consent, may the plaintiff amend the complaint to add a claim that the surgeon was negligent during and after the surgery? See Moore v. Baker, 989 F.2d 1129 (11th Cir. 1993) (concluding amendment did not relate back).

b. In an action against a union for refusal to file a grievance on behalf of an employee, may the plaintiff-employee amend the complaint to add a claim that the union refused on a second occasion to file a grievance on the employee's behalf? See Gomes v. Avco Corp., 964 F.2d 1330 (2d Cir. 1992) (concluding amendment did not relate back).

c. In a securities fraud action, may the plaintiff amend the complaint to add a claim against a defendant when the plaintiff knew the identity of the defendant but was not fully aware of the defendant's responsibility for the alleged harm? See Powers v. Graff, 148 F.3d 1223 (11th Cir. 1998) (concluding amendment did not relate back).

d. In a habeas petition challenging a criminal conviction on the ground that evidence from a witness for the prosecution was admitted in violation of the Confrontation Clause of the Sixth Amendment, may the petitioner amend the complaint to add a claim that coercive tactics were used to obtain damaging statements from him and introduced at trial in violation of his Fifth Amendment right against self-incrimination? See Mayle v. Felix, 545 U.S. 644 (2005) (concluding amendment did not relate back; the relevant underlying "conduct, transaction, or occurrence" was not petitioner's trial and conviction in state court, in which both pieces of evidence were introduced, but the circumstances surrounding the extraction of evidence from the prosecution witness before trial).

4. *Amending the Pleadings After 12(b)(6) Dismissal.* There is a manifest tendency of federal courts to be less tolerant of multiple repleadings. See, e.g., Kamsler v. H.A. Seinscheimer Co., 347 F.2d 740 (7th Cir. 1965). But there may still be a right to amend without leave of court, at least once. Note the first sentence of Fed. R. Civ. P. 15(a). It has been held that a motion under Rule 12(b)(6) is not a "responsive pleading," Breier v. N. Cal. Bowling Proprietors' Assn., 316 F.2d 787 (9th Cir. 1963). Where the plaintiff has repleaded after his first complaint had been successfully attacked, and then gone to trial on an amended complaint, the first complaint may be regarded as withdrawn; if so, the ruling on it is no longer open to appellate review. Blazer v. Black, 196 F.2d 139 (10th Cir. 1952). If dismissals for failure to state a claim increase under *Twombly* and *Iqbal* should courts be even more generous in granting leave to amend?

Note that the judge has no explicit power to dismiss a complaint *sua sponte*, and Rule 12(i) cannot be disregarded. Courts have nevertheless recognized the power to dismiss *sua sponte* without notice in limited circumstances. See, e.g., Rollins v. Wakenhut Services, Inc., 703 F.3d 122, 127 (D.C. Cir. 2012) ("The district court may *sua sponte* dismiss a claim pursuant to Rule 12(b)(6) without notice where it is 'patently obvious' that the plaintiff cannot possibly prevail based on the facts alleged in the complaint."); cf. Carroll v. Fort James Corp., 470 F.3d 1171, 1177 (5th Cir. 2006) ("As a general rule, a district court may dismiss a complaint on its own for failure to state a claim. However . . . the district court can only dismiss on its own motion as long as the procedure employed is fair. . . . [F]airness in this context requires both notice of the court's intention and an opportunity to respond.").

The Fourth Circuit and the Ninth Circuit have split on whether a plaintiff may amend a complaint as a matter of right under 15(a) even after 12(b)(6) dismissal. Compare Zachair Ltd. v. Driggs, 141 F.3d 1162 (4th Cir. 1998) (no) (unpublished opinion), with Doe v. United States, 58 F.3d 494 (9th Cir. 1995) (yes). In any case, a plaintiff must take care in seeking amendment. See In re

2007 Novastar Financial Inc., Sec. Litig., 579 F.3d 878 (8th Cir. 2009) (inserting a footnote at the end of an opposition to the defendant's motion to dismiss stating that "[t]o the extent that the court finds the Complaint's allegations insufficient, plaintiffs respectfully request an opportunity to amend their claims," is not a proper Rule 15 request for leave to amend).

5. *Adding Nondiverse Parties.* As we saw in *Krupski*, Rule 15(c) makes it relatively easy to add a party if a litigant discovers she has made a mistake in naming her opponent. More generally, Rule 15(a) suggests parties have the right to amend once as of right before an answer or other responsive pleading is filed. But using either rule to add a party is always risky where subject matter jurisdiction rests on diversity. In Am. Fiber & Finishing, Inc. v. Tyco Healthcare Group, LP, 362 F.3d 136 (1st Cir. 2004), a suit to recover the costs of cleaning up an industrial site, the plaintiff used Rule 15(a) to switch defendants when it learned that Tyco was the corporate successor to the original polluter. Three years later, after Tyco prevailed in the trial court, American Fiber moved to vacate the judgment on appeal claiming that the addition of Tyco destroyed the requisite diversity. Although the Supreme Court has held that "if jurisdiction exists at the time an action is commenced, such jurisdiction may not be divested by subsequent events," Freeport-McMoRan, Inc. v. KN Energy, Inc., 498 U.S. 426, 428 (1991), the First Circuit reasoned that plaintiff's discovery that it named the wrong defendant is not a "subsequent event" within the meaning of *Freeport-McMoRan*. The court admitted that there "is something unsettling about a party bringing a case in a federal court, taking the case to final judgment, losing, and then invoking a jurisdictional defect that it created—with the result that it escapes from the judgment and returns, albeit in a different venue, to relitigate the merits." *American Fiber*, 362 F.3d at 142. But "the shoe could have been on the other foot," the court noted, since American Fiber might have won "only to have its victory snatched away by the belated discovery of the jurisdictional snafu." Id. at 143. The court at least charged plaintiff for the costs of the appeal.

6. *Amending Other Documents.* Take another look at the text of Rule 15(c). Does the doctrine of relation back apply exclusively to "pleadings"? In Scarborough v. Principi, 541 U.S. 401 (2004), plaintiff prevailed before the Court of Appeals for Veterans Claims in an action seeking disability benefits. His lawyer then filed a timely application for attorneys' fees under the Equal Access to Justice Act, which provides that the prevailing party in an action against the federal government may recover attorneys' fees. The government opposed the application and sought to have it dismissed on the ground that it failed to include an allegation, required under the EAJA, that the government's position in the underlying case for disability benefits "was not substantially justified." Scarborough's lawyer responded right away by filing an amended application including the necessary language, but the 30-day fee application period had already expired and the court dismissed his application for that reason. The Supreme Court reversed, holding that the lawyer's amended application "related back" to his initial timely application even though an application for attorneys' fees is not a

"pleading" within the meaning of Rule 15(c). As the Court reasoned, the doctrine of relation back was applied "well before 1938, the year the Federal Rules became effective," and had "'roots in the former federal equity practice and a number of state codes.'" 541 U.S. at 1867. See also Edleman v. Lynchburg Coll., 535 U.S. 106 (2002) (failure to verify by oath a Title VII discrimination charge timely filed with the EEOC); Becker v. Montgomery, 532 U.S. 757 (2001) (failure to sign a timely notice of appeal).

## Note: Waiting Too Long to Amend

Rule 15(a) provides that a court "should freely give leave when justice so requires," and Rule 16 permits modification of scheduling orders "only for good cause and with the judge's consent." Are these standards identical? The language in both seems to reflect the liberal spirit of notice pleading—that parties should be able to adjust their claims and defenses as they learn the details of the dispute, and that cases should be decided on their merits rather than technicalities. Note that the pre-2007 Rule 1 said leave *"shall* be freely given." Is the verb change merely stylistic?

As with any discretionary standard, pleaders are at the mercy of the court deciding just what "justice requires" and just what constitutes "good cause." At a certain point, amendments jeopardize efficiency and fair notice to opponents. Recall the *Nelson* case, discussed in *Krupski*, where amendment followed the entry of judgment—an extreme example. More commonly, courts are asked to consider amendments as a case approaches trial and discovery deepens or as some claims are dismissed and plaintiffs struggle to keep their case alive. Eleventh hour amendments can affect pretrial scheduling orders, the pace and scope of discovery, and preparations for trial. See Southland Sec. Corp. v. INSpire Ins. Solutions, Inc., 365 F.3d 353, 384 (5th Cir. 2004) (affirming denial of third request for leave to amend in securities case where district court had repeatedly warned plaintiffs of deficiencies in their pleadings and offered "'one more opportunity to amend their pleadings in accordance with the requirements of Rule 9(b) and the PSLRA'"); Leary v. Daeschner, 349 F.3d 888 (6th Cir. 2003) (affirming denial of second request for leave to amend filed almost two years after the deadline set by the lower court's scheduling order for the close of discovery and dispositive motions). See also Brzozowski v. Corr. Physician Servs., Inc., 360 F.3d 173 (3d Cir. 2004) (even where there is no statute of limitations, late attempts to amend are subject to the equitable doctrine of laches; remanding to consider reasonableness of delay and prejudice to added party where plaintiff sought to add successor entity in gender discrimination suit after learning that her employer was going bankrupt and had already sold its major assets to the successor entity).

As the advisory committee notes to Rule 16 emphasize, the Rule "is designed to ensure that at some point both the parties and the pleadings will be fixed." Permitting late amendments in disregard of pretrial scheduling orders may simply "reward the indolent and the cavalier." *Johnson v. Mammoth Recreations, Inc.*, 975 F.2d 604, 611 (9th Cir. 1992). Courts are even less tolerant of attempts to modify claims mid-course by parties who do not formally request leave to amend under Rule 15. See *Gilmour v. Gates, McDonald & Co.*, 382 F.3d 1312, 1315 (11th Cir. 2004) (holding that a plaintiff cannot add a claim by raising it in a brief filed in opposition to defendant's motion for summary judgment: "Liberal pleading does not require that, at the summary judgment stage, defendants must infer all possible claims that could arise out of facts set forth in the complaint. The proper procedure for Gilmour to assert a new contract claim was to seek to amend her complaint.").

What general principles should guide lower courts in deciding whether to grant leave to amend? "Freely give" is capacious language—what else besides delay might weigh against granting leave to amend? The Supreme Court has held that several factors are relevant:

> In the absence of any apparent or declared reason—such as undue delay, bad faith, or dilatory motive on the part of the movant, repeated failure to cure deficiencies by amendments previously allowed, undue prejudice to the opposing party by virtue of allowance of the amendment, futility of the amendment, etc.—the leave sought should, as the rules require, be "freely given."

*Foman v. Davis*, 371 U.S. 178, 182 (1962). Thus, if the party seeking to amend has been diligent, and the other side can adjust to the added claims, leave should generally be granted. But where leave to amend is requested after the deadline set in a Rule 16 scheduling order, the standard is more exacting. See *Parker v. Columbia Pictures Indus.*, 204 F.3d 326, 340 (2d Cir. 2000) ("[D]espite the lenient standard of Rule 15(a), a district court does not abuse its discretion in denying leave to amend the pleadings after the deadline set in the scheduling order where the moving party has failed to establish good cause" under Rule 16).

## C. POLICING THE PLEADINGS: ETHICAL CONSTRAINTS, FRIVOLOUS CASES, AND CREATIVE ADVOCACY

### Problem Case: The Worker with the "Bad" Accent

Manuel Perfume sued the State of Hawaii in federal court for national origin discrimination in violation of Title VII of the Civil Rights Act. He claimed as well that the state's hiring procedures denied him due process of law. His suit asked for $1 million in damages.

In a lengthy complaint he made the following allegations: 1) He had immigrated from the Philippines, become a naturalized citizen, and sought work as a clerk at the Department of Motor Vehicles. 2) He had placed first among 500 people who took the Civil Service Examination, which tests, among other skills, the ability to read, write, and understand English. 3) After being interviewed for the job he was turned down because of his Filipino accent. 4) This reason was a proxy for national origin discrimination, as evidenced partly by the fact that the DMV has never hired any clerks of Filipino origin. 5) The State of Hawaii did not follow its own procedures in denying him a job, in that the ability to speak "unaccented English" was not listed as a job qualification, nor was there a rating on the official interview form for such a qualification. 6) Finally, Perfume claimed that he speaks perfectly clearly, though with an identifiable Filipino accent.

Accent discrimination is a novel claim under antidiscrimination laws. Attached as an exhibit to Perfume's original complaint was a 100-page study commissioned by the Hawaii Civil Rights Commission showing that Filipinos are heavily discriminated against in Hawaii. One example of prejudicial attitudes was that many people simply fail to listen to people of Philippine ancestry.

On the day the suit was filed there was a press conference in the offices of Perfume's lawyers, at which copies of the complaint were provided to the media and where Perfume discussed his background and decision to litigate. "Million-Dollar Discriminators" was the headline the next day in the major Honolulu newspaper.

The State moved for sanctions under Fed. R. Civ. P. 11, alleging the following as to the original complaint: 1) The job description had included the ability to deal with the public among the qualifications. 2) Clear communication with a great number of contentious and disgruntled people was a bona fide occupational qualification of the DMV clerk job (and thus a statutory exception to Title VII). 3) Perfume's accent was extremely strong, making him unintelligible to many people. 4) At the time of Perfume's application 4 out of 40 clerks at the DMV were Filipino.

The State also claims that the suit was filed in bad faith. The press conference and the "preposterous" damages are alleged as evidence of improper purpose: to force an unwarranted settlement. Moreover, the State claims that the plaintiff is continuing to generate adverse publicity, and that this excuses them from observing the 21-day waiting period, see Rule 11(c)(2), before filing the sanctions motion with the court.

If you were the district court judge, how would you rule on the State's motion for sanctions? What would you say about the failure to observe the waiting period? Suppose you feel that there are too many employment discrimination cases on your docket—can this legitimately enter your decision?

Professor Mari Matsuda has written about the actual case on which our problem is built. See Mari J. Matsuda, Voices of America: Accent, Antidiscrimination Law, and a Jurisprudence for the Last Reconstruction, 100 Yale L.J. 1329, 1333-1340 (1991).

# The History and Importance of Rule 11

Many of you, at least on first reading, might think it ridiculous that a man with a difficult accent would sue for a position that required dealing with an irascible public. Professor Matsuda's article offers some compelling evidence that in fact the perception of his accent was part of a pattern of discrimination. As a lawyer, would you have accepted Perfume's case? As a judge, would you find it professionally fulfilling to have it on your docket?

The original design of the Rules to increase access and simplify procedure also made it easier for people to file unmerited, even frivolous, cases. Rule 11, framed in terms of the lawyer's duty to the court, was intended, from the first, to deal with this problem. It provided for striking pleadings filed for "delay" or without good ground to support them. One of the shortest and least used Rules, it lay dormant for many years. In 1976, one commentator wrote that there were only eleven reported cases. Michael Risinger, Honesty in Pleading and Its Enforcement: Some "Striking" Problems with Federal Rule of Procedure 11, 61 Minn. L. Rev. 1, 36 (1976).

This all changed in 1983 when Rule 11 was amended to require that attorneys certify that they had made "a reasonable inquiry" before filing a complaint. But most significantly, the new rule made a monetary sanction, attorneys' fees, available for the amount incurred because of the filing of the "bad" pleading. By this provision, the rulemakers assured that Rule 11 would arise from its desuetude, because for defendants especially, practically everything that happened in the litigation up to and including the filing of the Rule 11 motion could be ascribed to the original "bad" pleading. Here is the relevant language from the 1983 rule:

### Rule 11. Signature of Pleadings, Motions and Other Papers; Sanctions

Every pleading, motion, and other paper of a party represented by an attorney shall be signed by at least one attorney of record in the attorney's individual name, whose address shall be stated. A party who is not represented by an attorney shall sign the party's pleading, motion, or other paper and state the party's address. Except when otherwise specifically provided by rule or statute, pleadings need not be verified or accompanied by affidavit. The rule in equity that averments of an answer under oath must be overcome by the testimony of two witnesses or of one witness sustained by corroborating circumstances is abolished. The signature of an attorney or party constitutes a certificate by the signer that the signer has read the pleading, motion, or other paper; that to the best of the signer's knowledge, information, and belief formed after reasonable inquiry it is well grounded in fact and is warranted by existing law or a good faith argument for the extension, modification, or reversal of existing law, and that it is not interposed for any improper purpose, such as to harass or to cause unnecessary delay or needless increase in the cost of litigation. If a pleading, motion, or other paper is not signed, it shall be stricken unless it is signed promptly after the omission is called to the attention of the pleader or movant. If a pleading, motion, or other paper is signed in violation of this rule, the court, upon motion or upon its own initiative, shall impose upon the person who signed it, a represented party, or both, an appropriate sanction, which may include an order to pay to the other party or parties the amount of the reasonable expenses incurred because of the filing of the pleading, motion, or other paper, including a reasonable attorney's fee.

Note that, once a court finds that the rule has been violated, it *must* impose sanctions. The prospect of automatic sanctions under the amended Rule generated "collateral disputes of unprecedented—and perhaps unanticipated—magnitude" and over 3,000 published opinions. George Cochran, Rule 11: The Road to Amendment, 2 Att'y Sanctions Newsl. 141 (1991); John Frank, Bench-Bar Proposal to Revise Civil Procedure Rule 11, 137 F.R.D. 159 (1991) (noting that courts were *"drowning in satellite litigation"* under the 1983 rule) (emphasis added). Virtually every circuit produced lengthy, often *en banc* (i.e., all judges sitting), decisions about various aspects of the Rule, dealing with such questions as the standard of review, the content and timing of a hearing on Rule 11 motions, standing to make the motion, and many other issues.

The U.S. Supreme Court decided four cases under the 1983 version of Rule 11, the first coming six years into the new regime. Though these cases shared a "get tough" tone, they offered no structure or vision for the burgeoning Rule 11 case law. Two of them have been superseded by the 1993 amendments to the Rule. In Pavelic & LeFlore v. Marvel Entm't Group, 493 U.S. 120 (1989) (superseded), the Court held that only the individual attorney who signed a pleading, and not the law firm with which she was associated, could be sanctioned. The majority opinion scanted any discussion of which method might better serve the Rule's purposes or the intent of the rulemakers.

With the same "plain meaning" approach, the Court found that a represented party could be sanctioned directly for actions her lawyer took at her behest. Bus. Guides, Inc. v. Chromatic Commc'ns Enters., 498 U.S. 533 (1991). Again, the Court showed little concern about the impact of its decision on the administration of the Rule, that is, that making the client a target for sanctions would have the effect of turning up the heat in practice. Cooter & Gell v. Hartmarx Corp., 496 U.S. 384 (1990) (superseded), held that a Rule 11 sanction motion survived the voluntary dismissal of an action by the plaintiff under Rule 41(a)(1)(A)(i). In other words, a plaintiff might not "cure" a violation by giving up his court action. Many commentators criticized this opinion for its tendency to keep litigation alive instead of streamlining it. Similarly, the Supreme Court declined to review Willy v. Coastal Corp., in which the Fifth Circuit held that sanctions imposed against a plaintiff would be upheld even though the court imposing them lacked subject matter jurisdiction over the dispute at the time of the sanctionable conduct. 504 U.S. 935 (1992), *denying cert. to* 855 F.2d 1160 (5th Cir. 1988).

In considering all of the ink spilled over the 1983 Amendments to Rule 11, remember that the published decisions may be the tip of the iceberg in terms of the impact of an active sanctions practice on lawyer's work. In an impressively designed empirical study of the Rule's operation, the authors found that 82 percent of the federal litigators in three circuits reported having been affected by the Rule. Lawrence C. Marshall, Herbert M. Kritzer, and Frances Kahn Zemans, The Use and Impact of Rule 11, 86 Nw. U. L. Rev. 943 (1992). Positive effects ranged from declining a case to withholding a claim or defense. On the negative side, a substantial number of lawyers reported that they failed to assert a claim or defenses that had merit because of sanction fears. Id. at 959-962.

The following passage became a rallying cry for those who would reform the Rule:

> Sometimes there are reasons to sue even when one cannot win. Bad court decisions must be challenged if they are to be overruled, but the early challenges are certainly hopeless. The first attorney to challenge Plessy v. Ferguson was certainly bringing a frivolous action, but his efforts and the efforts of others eventually led to Brown v. Board of Education.

Eastway Constr. Corp. v. City of New York, 637 F. Supp. 558, 575 (E.D.N.Y. 1986).

The reformers won, and a new version of Rule 11 went into effect in December 1993. It was meant to moderate the heat of the adversary practice under the previous Rule. What role the huge jurisprudence generated by the prior Rule will play in interpreting the new Rule, as well as the meaning of the Rule itself, are subjects that will continue to stir and confound proceduralists well into the twenty-first century.

Read the current Rule 11 and the Advisory Committee Notes. The major changes in the 1993 Rule were to increase the discretion of the trial judge on whether to impose sanctions and to de-emphasize monetary sanctions in administering the Rule. A 21-day "safe harbor" provision was also added in part (c). The 1993 version of Rule 11 retains the duty of investigation, and the same basic categories of disapproved pleadings: improper purpose; inadequate legal basis; inadequate factual basis.

The 1993 amendments had the desired effect of cutting down substantially the cases and commentary under. Several studies and articles indicate general satisfaction with the functioning of the new Rule 11, particularly with the safe harbor provision. See, e.g., Theodore Hirt, A Second Look at Amended Rule 11, 48 Am. U. L. Rev. 1007, 1027-1028 (1999); Laura Duncan, Sanctions Litigation Declining, A.B.A. J., Mar. 1995 (concluding on the basis of interviews with judges, lawyers, and law professors that there has been a marked decline in Rule 11 litigation). A 2005 Federal Judicial Center survey found that "the percentage of judges supporting the safe harbor has increased from 70% to 86% since 1995; the percentage of judges showing strong support has increased from 32% to 60%. The percentage of judges opposing the safe harbor has decreased from 16% to 10%." Federal Judicial Center, Report of a Survey of United States District Judges' Experiences and Views Concerning Rule 11, at 5 (2005). Likewise, "[a]pproximately 85% of the district judges view groundless litigation in [cases where the plaintiff is represented by counsel] as no more than a small problem and another 12% see such litigation as a moderate problem." Id. at 3. For supporting evidence in a more recent study, see David B. Owens, Civil Rights Foe or Frivolous Litigation Enabler? An Empirical Study of Rule 11 Practice Under the 1983 and 1993 Version (June 10, 2010), ssrn #1622061. Remarkably, beyond occasionally noting the availability of sanctions, the Supreme Court has remained largely silent on the interpretation of Rule 11 after the 1993 amendments. For a comprehensive survey on the ten-year anniversary of the 1993 amendments, see Symposium: Happy (?) Birthday Rule 11, 37 Loy. L.A. L. Rev. 515 (2004).

Still, skeptics remain. On the one hand, some have suggested that the safe harbor provision has not eliminated the chilling effect of sanctions targeted at civil rights plaintiffs. See Danielle Kie Hart, Symposium: Happy (?) Birthday Rule 11: And the Chill Goes On, 37 Loy. L.A. L. Rev. 645, 662 (2004) (arguing that courts have shifted to other sanctions tools such as the inherent power doctrine and 28 U.S.C. § 1927); Georgene Vairo, Rule 11 and the Profession, 67 Fordham L. Rev. 589, 643 (1998) (same). On the other hand, concerns about "litigation abuse" have prompted calls to do away with the safe harbor and return to the mandatory sanctions provision of the 1983 amendments. These critics worry that the safe harbor provision "actually can increase the number of frivolous actions because attorneys can file those suits with impunity, knowing that, if challenged, they can simply withdraw or amend their complaints within the twenty-one day period." Friedenthal, Kane, and Miller, Civil Procedure 269 (1999) (citing scholars who advocate eliminating the safe harbor).

As in 1983 and 1993, Rule 11 has become a focal point in the larger debate about "litigation abuse." H.R. 420, the Lawsuit Abuse Reduction Act of 2005, which would have restored 1983-style mandatory sanctions, was reported out of the House Judiciary Committee on May 25, 2005, and a similar bill was passed by the House of Representatives in 2004, though it failed in the Senate. Concerns about litigation abuse, particularly in the area of medical malpractice, also were prominent in the 2004 presidential campaign. Reviewing the broader arguments on litigation abuse and arguments for Rule 11 reform, Aaron Hiller contends that circumstances have changed since the 1990s:

> From 1992 to 2001, the overall number of civil lawsuits filed in America dropped by 47%. The number of tort suits fell by 31.8% and the number of medical malpractice claims—an area of litigation often cited by tort reformers and insurance companies for increasing abuse—declined by 14.2%.
>
> As the amount of litigation on the docket has declined, so have the jury awards so often decried as outrageous and skyrocketing by tort reformers. The median jury award in 2001 was $37,000, representing a 43.1% decrease over the previous decade. Limiting that analysis only to tort cases, the median jury award stood at $28,000, a 56% drop since 1992. Moreover, juries rarely award punitive damages at all—less than 3% of all plaintiff winners in tort trials were awarded punitive damages; the median award was $38,000.

Aaron Hiller, Rule 11 and Tort Reform: Myth, Reality, and Legislation, 18 Geo. J. Legal Ethics 809, 818 (2005).

If these are the facts on the ground, what is driving public and political debate on litigation abuse? First, there is certainly some distortion in the cases covered by the media. As Deborah Rhode puts it, "[t]he public gets anecdotal glimpses of atypical cases without a sense of their overall significance." Deborah L. Rhode, In the Interests of Justice: Reforming the Legal Profession 121 (2000). Second, politicians seeking stricter rules often offer "polemics that take considerable poetic license." Id. (quoting former California Governor Pete Wilson's comment that the "'lawyer's briefcase has become a weapon of terror,'" and then Governor George W. Bush's denunciation of "'junk lawsuits that clog our courts'"). Third, and perhaps most important, in a pluralistic society we are bound to disagree on what amounts to "abuse" of the litigation system. As Professor Rhode elaborates:

> [W]hat qualifies as a frivolous claim depends on the eye of the beholder. While a few commonly cited examples meet almost anyone's definition, the line between vindictiveness and vindication is often difficult to draw. Sexual harassment claims were once routinely dismissed as matters beneath judicial notice. In some quarters, the situation has not significantly improved. Press commentators have a field day with harassment "witch trials" and "corporate McCarthyism," which assertedly allow radical feminists to "sue anybody about anything." To some (usually male) judges, it is a mistake to allow antidiscrimination law to redress the "petty slights of the hypersensitive." Yet only through these ostensibly petty claims have Americans finally begun to recognize the real costs of harassment. Women pay the highest price in terms of direct economic and psychological injuries, but all of us pay more indirectly. Harassment costs the average Fortune 500 company an estimated $6 million annually in turnover, worker absences, and lost productivity.

"Many of the media's favorite examples of trivial claims and outrageous verdicts," she continues,

> rely on highly selective factual excerpts. A textbook illustration involves a recent multimillion dollar punitive damages award against McDonald's for serving coffee at scalding temperatures. To most journalists, this case served as an all-purpose indictment of the legal profession and legal process; an avaricious lawyer paraded a petty incident before an out-of-control jury and extracted an absurd recovery. Newspaper editorials, radio talk shows, and magazine commentaries replayed endless variations on the theme summarized by the national Chamber of Commerce: "Is it fair to get a couple of million dollars from a restaurant just because you spilled hot coffee on yourself?"
>
> On closer examination, the question no longer looks rhetorical. The plaintiff, a seventy-nine-year-old woman, suffered acutely painful third degree burns from 180 degree coffee. She spent eight days in the hospital and returned again for skin grafts. Only after McDonald's refused to reimburse her medical expenses did she bring suit. At trial, jurors learned of seven hundred other burn cases involving McDonald's coffee during the preceding

decade. Although medical experts had warned that such high temperatures were causing serious injuries, the corporation's safety consultant had viewed the number of complaints as "trivial." The jury's verdict of $2.3 million was not an arbitrary choice. Its punitive damages award represented two days of coffee sales revenues, and the judge reduced the judgment to $640,000. To avoid an appeal, the plaintiff then settled the case for a smaller, undisclosed amount. McDonald's put up warning signs, and other fast-food chains adopted similar measures. While evaluations of this final result may vary, it was not the patently "ridiculous" travesty that media critics described. . . .

All too often, anecdotes substitute for analysis and masquerade as reflective of broader trends. . . . Commentators point to dramatic growth in certain kinds of cases, such as bankruptcy and product liability suits in federal courts. But federal filings account for only 2 percent of American litigation. And in state courts, product liability suits have been declining. While business leaders raise the most complaints about legal hypochondria, disputes between businesses are the largest and fastest growing category of civil litigation. . . . Higher per capita caseloads occurred in previous centuries in some American communities [and] United States court filings are now in the same range, when adjusted for population, as those in Canada, Australia, New Zealand, England, and Denmark.

Id. at 121-123.

Media and political distortion surely play a role in framing the debate on litigation abuse along with lack of consensus on what interests we expect the legal system to serve. Are there other elements at work? Consider the following cases in thinking about the "Bad Accent" problem case, the debate on litigation abuse, and the efficacy of Rule 11 in general.

## 1. "An Inquiry Reasonable Under the Circumstances"

Although their holdings did not deal directly with the point, two of the cases to reach the U.S. Supreme Court on the 1983 version of Rule 11 were cases of inadequate investigation. In Cooter & Gell v. Hart-Marx Corp., 496 U.S. 384 (1990), the lawyers apparently filed a major antitrust case on the basis of a few phone calls to men's clothing stores in four cities, from which they determined that only one store in each place sold Hart, Schaffner & Marx suits.

The other case, Business Guides, Inc. v. Chromatic Commc'ns Enters., 498 U.S. 533 (1991), held that Rule 11 imposes an objective standard of reasonable inquiry on parties who sign pleadings, motions, or other papers. The plaintiffs in *Business Guides* filed an application for a temporary restraining order against a competitor, claiming that Chromatic was copying from Business Guides' trade directory. Id. at 535-536. To support its TRO application, Business Guides filed signed affidavits identifying ten false directory listings (called "seeds") that Chromatic had allegedly copied along with other accurate listings. The company did not, however, specify the false information it had planted in the seeds. Id. at 536. When lawyers for Business Guides were asked to specify the false data in the seeds by the law clerk for the district court judge, they contacted their clients and then promptly withdrew their claims as to three of the ten listings. This was apparently the first time the lawyers had asked anyone at Business Guides about the accuracy of the seeds. Having become suspicious, the district judge's law clerk made an independent investigation and discovered that *nine* of the ten seeds contained no inaccuracies. Id.

Unaware, the lawyers for Business Guides prepared a supplemental affidavit for a company employee identifying "false" information in the seven remaining listings. On the day of the hearing, the employee realized that at least one seed in the affidavit was accurate and crossed it out by hand. Armed with the law clerk's more comprehensive findings, the district court denied the TRO application and referred the matter to a magistrate judge to determine whether sanctions should be imposed. The magistrate recommended sanctions against the client for failing to conduct a proper prefiling inquiry, and against the client and law firm for failing to inquire into the accuracy of the listings after learning that four contained no misinformation. Id. at 537-538.

Affirming the lower courts' decision to apply a standard of objective reasonableness to both the client's and attorney's conduct, the Supreme Court observed that

> the essence of Rule 11 is that *signing is no longer a meaningless act; it denotes merit.* A signature sends a message to the district court that this document is to be taken seriously. This case is illustrative. Business Guides sought a TRO on the strength of an initial application accompanied by five signed statements to the effect that Chromatic was pirating its directory. Because these documents were filed under seal, the District Court had to determine the credibility of the allegations without the benefit of hearing the other side's view. The court might plausibly have attached some incremental significance to the fact that Business Guides itself risked being sanctioned if the factual allegations contained in these signed statements proved to be baseless. Business Guides asks that we construe Rule 11 in a way that would render the signatures on these statements risk free. Because this construction is at odds with the Rule's general admonition that signing denotes merit, we are loath to do so.

Id. at 546 (emphasis added).

*Business Guides* makes clear that it is risky business to file a complaint simply because you believe your client's story. In the case that follows, consider whether you think the lawyer did enough before filing.

### *Kraemer v. Grant County*
892 F.2d 686 (7th Cir. 1990)

PER CURIAM.

Attorney Mark D. Lawton appeals from the district court's order requiring him to pay $3,000 to William and Betty Baker, defendants below and appellees here, as a sanction under Fed. R. Civ. P. 11 for having filed a lawsuit on behalf of his client without first having made reasonable investigation into the facts of the case. We hold that under the circumstances presented here the imposition of sanctions was erroneous and we reverse.

Lawton was contacted in the late summer of 1986 by Laura Kraemer. Kraemer told him that Herbert Hottenstein, the sheriff of Grant County, Wisconsin, had conspired with the Bakers to evict her from her home and steal her belongings. Lawton asked Kraemer to write a detailed letter explaining what had happened. In her letter, Kraemer gave this account of events relevant to this appeal: She and her fiance Steven Baker had been living together for about three years. In late April 1986, they discovered that Kirk and Cindy Novinski had a house for rent in rural Grant County, and they chose to take it. The Novinskis demanded a $150 security deposit and $150 per month in rent, and Steven Baker agreed to pay it. A couple of days later Kraemer gave the Novinskis $100 and the Novinskis gave her the key. The rest of the rent was never paid because Steven Baker was killed in a work-related accident on May 8. The funeral took place on May 10. At the funeral, Steven Baker's parents, Bill and Betty Baker, asked Kraemer if they could come over to the house to pick up Steven Baker's belongings the next day. Kraemer reluctantly gave her permission. Before going home, Kraemer stopped at a friend's house. When she finally returned home she found that almost everything had been taken from the house, and she found a note from Betty Baker stating that they had taken the things they wanted. Kraemer immediately notified the sheriff's department.

The sheriff's officer on duty called the Bakers and told them to return what they had taken by 10:30 the next morning, May 11. At that time, however, Sheriff Hottenstein himself came out to Kraemer's house and said that the Bakers were within their rights. While Kraemer and the sheriff were talking, the Bakers arrived. Sheriff Hottenstein ordered Kraemer to turn her car keys and ownership papers over to the Bakers, telling her that the car was both unregistered and unsafe, and that the Bakers would make sure the car was not driven in that condition.

Kraemer went to visit her mother in another city for a few days. When she returned, she found a note on the front door, signed by a sheriff's deputy, which read: "To whom it may concern—Nothing is to be removed from the premises until you contact Grant County Sheriff's Department." The electricity had been cut off on orders of the Bakers. Kraemer went to the utility company and ordered service restored. When she got back to the house, on June 4, she met the landlord, Kirk Novinski. She tried to give him the money owing on May's rent, but Novinski refused to take it, telling her to hold off until she could straighten things out with the Bakers. At the time, someone from the utility company arrived to hook up the electricity, but Novinski objected. Kraemer convinced the man to leave the power on at least for the night. That evening, Sheriff Hottenstein returned and told Kraemer that she had to leave the house right then. The next day, the sheriff and the Bakers watched as Kraemer moved her belongings out of the house.

On July 29, when Kraemer was five months pregnant, she had another brush with the law. She was arrested by a Wisconsin State Patrol officer for driving with a defective brakelight. She was unable to produce a valid driver's license (the trooper knew the license was on file with the Wisconsin Department of Transportation), or the $33 bond required for that offense, and she was jailed for several hours until someone posted bond for her.

On the strength of this letter, Lawton made an administrative claim against the county on Kraemer's behalf for damages. When the claim was denied, Lawton hired (at his own expense) a private investigator to look into the allegations Kraemer had made. The investigator's report is not in the record, but Lawton conceded that he was unable to confirm or to discredit any part of Kraemer's story except that he had been given a statement by one of the Bakers' relatives saying that she had been with the Bakers when they took property out of Kraemer's house, and that she felt that action was "wrong." The investigator reported that the potential defendants had been "hostile."

This is all the information Lawton had been able to gather when he filed this suit against the Bakers and Hottenstein (and others not involved in this appeal) on January 29, 1987, alleging violations of Kraemer's constitutional rights and seeking damages under 42 U.S.C. § 1983 and 28 U.S.C. § 1343. Both of these statutes require the plaintiff to show state action before recovery can be had. Many of the allegations of the complaint are undisputed. The complaint stated a claim sufficient to withstand a motion for dismissal under Fed. R. Civ. P. 12(b)(6). Through discovery it was learned, among other things, that at the time of the events charged in the complaint there had been lengthy and frequent telephone conversations between the Bakers and the sheriff's office. Lawton was not able, however, to produce through discovery sufficient facts with respect to state action to defeat the defendants' motion for summary judgment. This court affirmed the grant of summary judgment in an unpublished order, Kraemer v. Grant County, 870 F.2d 659 (7th Cir. 1989), with one judge concurring specially to state that he considered the issue of state action to be a close one on summary judgment. It appeared that the sheriff played an active role in the dispute between the parties, although not necessarily an improper role.

Along with their motion for summary judgment, the Bakers requested that the court require Kraemer or Lawton to pay their legal fees in defending a frivolous or vexatious action under 42 U.S.C. § 1988. See Christiansburg Garment Co. v. EEOC, 434 U.S. 412 (1978). The district court held a hearing on the request on October 28, 1988, and found that an award of attorneys' fees was not proper in this case under § 1988 due to Kraemer's poverty, but also found that an award against Lawton personally was appropriate under Fed. R. Civ. P. 11. On November 10, 1989 the court ordered Lawton to pay $3,000 of the Bakers' total legal bill of about $8,000. The court ruled that Lawton should have known that there was no factual or legal basis for the allegation of state action at the time the complaint was filed. The award was less than the actual damages caused by his actions because Lawton is a fairly recent law school graduate, and had done some investigation before filing Kraemer's complaint. Lawton filed a motion to amend findings under Fed. R. Civ. P. 52(b), which was denied on December 14, 1988. Lawton filed a timely notice of appeal and we reverse.

Under our decision *en banc* in Mars Steel Corp. v. Continental Bank N.A., 880 F.2d 928 (7th Cir. 1989), our review of an order imposing Rule 11 sanctions (or refusing to impose them, see Tabrizi v. Village of Glen Ellyn, 883 F.2d 587 (7th Cir. 1989)) is deferential—we review only for abuse of discretion. But deferential review is different from no review at all, even when there is no controlling legal issue in the case. *Mars Steel*, 880 F.2d at 936. "Concerns for the effect on both an attorney's reputation and for the vigor and creativity of advocacy by other members of the bar necessarily require that we exercise less than total deference to the district court in its decision to impose Rule 11 sanctions." In re Ronco, Inc., 838 F.2d 212, 217 (7th Cir. 1988) (quoted with approval in *Mars Steel*). See also *Mars Steel*, 880 F.2d at 940-941 (Flaum, J., concurring) (no single abuse of discretion standard exists). In reviewing the imposition of sanctions under Rule 11, then, we will give deference to the decision of the district court, but with careful reference to the standards governing the exercise of the court's discretion and to the purposes Rule 11 is meant to serve.

In this case, our focus is on the reasonableness of Lawton's prefiling research into the facts of the case. Although the district court referred to Lawton's failure to establish a basis for the complaint in fact and in law, the legal problems drop out if his version of the facts was correct. If Sheriff Hottenstein was in fact conspiring with the Bakers to deprive Kraemer of her property, then there would be a remedy under 42 U.S.C. § 1983 for violation of Kraemer's civil rights. See Dennis v. Sparks, 449 U.S. 24, 27-28 (1980). Absent the sheriff's involvement, of course, there is no state action and no legal basis for a federal claim. But Kraemer's claim ultimately failed because she could not establish the necessary facts, not because the law did not provide a federal remedy for the wrongs she alleged in her complaint. Indeed, the complaint survived a Fed. R. Civ. P. 12(b)(6) motion for dismissal for failure to state a claim upon which relief could be granted. Therefore we need only determine whether the district court properly found that Lawton had not performed reasonable research into the facts of the case before filing the complaint.

It is not necessary that an investigation into the facts be carried to the point of absolute certainty. Nemmers v. United States, 795 F.2d 628, 632 (7th Cir. 1986). The investigation need merely be reasonable under the circumstances. S.A. Auto Lube, Inc. v. Jiffy Lube Intl., Inc., 842 F.2d 946, 948 (7th Cir. 1988). Relevant factors for the court to consider include:

> Whether the signer of the documents had sufficient time for investigation; the extent to which the attorney had to rely on his or her client for the factual foundation underlying the pleading, motion, or other paper; whether the case was accepted from another attorney; the complexity of the facts and the attorney's ability to do a sufficient pre-filing investigation; and whether discovery would have been beneficial to the development of the underlying facts.

Brown v. Federation of State Medical Bds., 830 F.2d 1429, 1435 (7th Cir. 1987). An analysis of these factors shows that it was error to conclude that Lawton's conduct in filing the complaint was sanctionable.

The key fact that Lawton and Kraemer had to establish was the sheriff's involvement in a conspiracy with the Bakers. "Because conspiracies are carried out in secret, direct proof of agreement is rare." United States v. Koenig, 856 F.2d 843, 854 (7th Cir. 1988). We cannot require an attorney to procure a confession of participation in a conspiracy from one of the prospective defendants before filing suit — if there were such a confession, no lawsuit would be necessary. Lawton did all he reasonably could have done to investigate his client's account of events before the complaint was filed. He hired a private investigator to interview the prospective defendants and to determine what had actually happened. The defendants refused to cooperate with the investigator. We cannot insist that a lawyer abandon his client's cause simply because the investigator was unable to obtain the cooperation of the prospective defendants.

When the defendants refused to cooperate voluntarily, Lawton had only two options: he could advise his client to give up, or he could file a complaint on her behalf and try to develop the necessary facts through discovery. Absent some official coercion, the defendants had proved unwilling to provide any evidence whatever relating to Kraemer's case, and their unwillingness was reflected in their hostile reactions to Lawton's investigator. No one else could be expected to have knowledge of the conspiracy. Until some other source of information became available, then, Lawton had to rely on his client for the factual foundation of the claim. There was simply no other source to which he could turn.

Once Lawton was armed with the coercive power of the federal courts to enforce the rules of discovery, he was able to get telephone records showing frequent and lengthy telephone conversations between the sheriff and the Bakers during May and June 1986, including a 22-minute conversation in the early morning of May 11, after Kraemer had reported to the sheriff's office that her house had been broken into, and just before Sheriff Hottenstein came out to the house to tell Kraemer that the Bakers had acted within their rights. Lawton was even able to get tapes of some later conversations between the sheriff and the Bakers, including one in which William Baker told the sheriff that "if we all stick together and find out she's lying then they'll call it [the lawsuit] off quick."[2] The particular facts that Lawton unearthed during discovery are irrelevant to the reasonableness of his filing the complaint, *Mars Steel*, 880 F.2d at 932 (focus of Rule 11 is on what should have been done before filing rather than on results), but the fact that he had to use discovery to learn them is relevant. If discovery is necessary to establish a claim, then it is not unreasonable to file a complaint so as to obtain the right to conduct that discovery. "Rule 11 must not bar the courthouse door to people who have some support for a complaint but need discovery to prove their case." Frantz v. United States Powerlifting Federation, 836 F.2d 1063 (7th Cir. 1987).

---

2. Apparently this tape was not available at the time summary judgment was entered, and it was not considered by the district court or by this court in affirming on the merits.

Rule 11 cannot be allowed to thoroughly undermine zealous advocacy. "The rule is not intended to chill an attorney's enthusiasm or creativity in pursuing factual or legal theories." Advisory Committee Notes to 1983 Amendment to Fed. R. Civ. P. 11. This is especially so in civil rights cases involving unpopular clients. Lawton's client is a young woman who appears to be exceedingly unpopular with the authorities in Grant County, as indicated by the fact that she was jailed for a minor traffic offense. It may on occasion take the power of the federal courts to keep state officials from harassing unpopular and powerless citizens. If that is the case, a federal forum must be available to them. We cannot allow such officials to avoid their constitutional duties simply by stonewalling an investigator.

Lawton took all the steps he reasonably could have taken before filing suit to determine the truth of Kraemer's allegations. He should not have been sanctioned for turning to the judiciary, whose function is to find truth, when his own resources failed.

*Reversed.*

## Note: The Effect of Rule 11 on Lawyers' Work

Rule 11 cases open incomparable insights into the practice of law. In these two cases, we see a large law firm and a solo practitioner fined for essentially the same conduct: filing a complaint founded on little more than what the clients told them. Why is this more justified in *Kraemer*?

The bulk of the opinion in *Business Guides* was directed to whether the client should be sanctioned, along with the law firm (for signing an affidavit supporting the TRO). Can you see why the law firm was eager to "take the rap" for the client in this case? Though *Business Guides* was decided under the 1983 version of the rule, parties may still be sanctioned under current practice, though not for mistakes about the law. See Rule 11(c)(5)(A).

Think about the sanctioned lawyer in *Kraemer.* One Stanford student called him in 1993 and found him still embittered. From his standpoint, he had worked hard on the case, perhaps devoting more effort than it required because it was early in his career and he was sympathetic to the client. In reaction to the sanctions, he claimed that he "would never, ever, file a civil rights suit in federal court again."

The present version of the Rule is meant to reduce the adversariness and anger that has resulted from the effort in the previous decade to put teeth into the requirements of nonfrivolous pleading. One major way the Rule seeks to accomplish this is to eliminate the emphasis courts gave monetary sanctions under the previous Rule. Professors Marshall, Kritzer, and Zemans in their excellent empirical study of sanctions in three federal circuits found that monetary sanctions were the norm under the 1983 rule. Yet the amount was not "as large as many media accounts of sensational cases may lead some to imagine." About 90 percent of the cases involved sanctions of $25,000 or less. The median sanction was $2,500. The authors concluded that "much of the bar's resistance to Rule 11 has its source in the stigma attached to being labelled a Rule 11 violator," rather than the amount of money paid. They acknowledged, however, a possible *in terrorem* effect of newspaper accounts of huge monetary awards. The Use and Impact of Rule 11, 86 Nw. U. L. Rev. 943, 956-957 (1992).

What are some possible nonmonetary sanctions? One that could have considerable bite is referral to the bar disciplinary committee. See Thornton v. General Motors Corp., 136 F.3d 450, 455 (5th Cir. 1998) ("[W]hen a district court finds that a disciplinary sanction more severe than admonition, reprimand, or censure under Rule 11 is warranted, it should refer the matter to the appropriate disciplinary authorities."). If the bar decides to discipline the attorney, it must first conduct its own investigation of the alleged misconduct, and otherwise follow its own rules regarding lawyer discipline. In a case of severe misconduct, the lawyer may face suspension of his license to practice law or even disbarment. But public bar sanctions are exceedingly rare. Not only do most state bar associations lack sufficient resources to investigate and prosecute complaints of misconduct, they, like other self-regulating bodies, often lack the will to aggressively pursue misconduct by their members. This means that judges bear a heavy burden in choosing sanctions that will adequately compensate for and deter misconduct. For examples of other nonmonetary sanctions, see Reinhardt v. Gulf Ins. Co., 489 F.3d 405, 417 (1st Cir. 2007) (ten hours pro bono service as sanction for refusal to negotiate over a stipulation, which "forc[ed] defendants to litigate the issue," even though the court eventually adopted language suggested by the sanctioned lawyer); Jimenez v. Madison Area Tech. College, 321 F.3d 652, 655-657 (7th Cir. 2003) (recognizing that "dismissal is a harsh sanction," but upholding district court's decision to dismiss case as a sanction after finding that plaintiff had used "obviously fraudulent documents" to bolster her discrimination claims; "it is proper for the trial court to impose a severe sanction where the sanction is sufficient to deter repetition of the misconduct or to deter similar conduct by third parties").

In the case that follows, we see a trial judge eager to bear that burden. As you read, consider the factors that provoked the judge to enter such a high sanctions award.

### *Christian v. Mattel, Inc.*
286 F.3d 1118 (9th Cir. 2002)

McKeown, Circuit Judge.

It is difficult to imagine that the Barbie doll, so perfect in her sculpture and presentation, and so comfortable in every setting, from "California girl" to "Chief Executive Officer Barbie," could spawn such acrimonious litigation and such egregious conduct on the part of her challenger. In her wildest dreams, Barbie could not have imagined herself in the middle of Rule 11 proceedings. But the intersection of copyrights on Barbie sculptures and the scope of Rule 11 is precisely what defines this case.

James Hicks appeals from a district court order requiring him, pursuant to Federal Rule of Civil Procedure 11, to pay Mattel, Inc. $501,565 in attorneys' fees that it incurred in defending against what the district court determined to be a frivolous action. Hicks brought suit on behalf of [his client] Harry Christian, claiming that Mattel's Barbie dolls infringed Christian's Claudene doll sculpture copyright. . . .

We hold that the district court did not abuse its discretion in determining that the complaint filed by Hicks was frivolous under Rule 11. In parsing the language of the district court's sanctions orders, however, we cannot determine with any degree of certainty whether the district court grounded its Rule 11 decision on Hicks' misconduct that occurred outside the pleadings, such as in oral argument, at a meeting of counsel, and at a key deposition. . . . Consequently, we vacate the district court's orders and remand for further proceedings consistent with this opinion. . . .

### Background

As context for examining the district court's determination that the underlying action was frivolous, we begin by discussing the long history of litigation between Mattel and Hicks' past and current clients: Harry Christian; Christian's daughter, Claudene; and the Collegiate Doll Company ("CDC"), Claudene's proprietorships.

### I. Prior Litigation Between Mattel and CDC

Mattel is a toy company that is perhaps best recognized as the manufacturer of the world-famous Barbie doll. Since Barbie's creation in 1959, Mattel has outfitted her in fashions and accessories that have evolved over time. In perhaps the most classic embodiment, Barbie is depicted as a slender-figured doll with long blonde hair and blue eyes. Mattel has sought to protect its intellectual property by registering various Barbie-related copyrights, including copyrights protecting the doll's head sculpture. Mattel has vigorously litigated against putative infringers.

In 1990, Claudene Christian, then an undergraduate student at the University of Southern California ("USC"), decided to create and market a collegiate cheerleader doll. The doll, which the parties refer to throughout their papers as "Claudene," had blonde hair and blue eyes and was outfitted to resemble a USC cheerleader.

Mattel soon learned about the Claudene doll. After concluding that it infringed certain Barbie copyrights, Mattel brought an administrative action before the United States Customs Service in 1996 in which it alleged that the Claudene doll, manufactured abroad, had pirated the head sculpture of the "Teen Talk" and "SuperStar" Barbies. The Customs Service ruled in CDC's favor and subsequently released a shipment of Claudene dolls. Undaunted, Mattel commenced a federal court action in 1997 in which it once again alleged that CDC infringed various of Mattel's copyrights. At the time, Claudene Christian was president of CDC and Harry Christian was listed as co-founder of the company and chief financial officer. CDC retained Hicks as its counsel. After the court dismissed CDC's multiple counterclaims, the case . . . settled. . . .

## II.   The Present Action

Seizing on a loophole in the parties' settlement agreement, within weeks of the agreement, Harry Christian, who was not a signatory to the agreement, retained Hicks as his counsel and filed a federal court action against Mattel. In the complaint . . . Christian alleged that Mattel obtained a copy of the copyrighted Claudene doll in 1996, the year of its creation, and then infringed its overall appearance, including its face paint, by developing a new Barbie line called "Cool Blue" that was substantially similar to Claudene. Christian sought damages in the amount of $2.4 billion and various forms of injunctive relief. . . . [In a letter to Mattel's counsel, Hicks claimed] that an additional doll called "Virginia Tech University Barbie" also infringed the Claudene doll copyright. Hicks, however, never amended the complaint to plead allegations about Virginia Tech Barbie.

Two months after the complaint was filed, Mattel moved for summary judgment. In support of its motion, Mattel proffered evidence that the Cool Blue Barbie doll contained a 1991 copyright notice on the back of its head, indicating that it predated Claudene's head sculpture copyright by approximately six years. Mattel . . . argued that Cool Blue Barbie could not as a matter of law infringe Claudene's head sculpture copyright. Mattel similarly contended that the copyright on the Virginia Tech Barbie's head sculpture also significantly predated the purported copyright on the Claudene head sculpture. Virginia Tech Barbie and other Barbie dolls contained a head sculpture that was copyrighted in 1976 and originally appeared on SuperStar Barbie.

At a follow-up counsel meeting required by a local rule, Mattel's counsel attempted to convince Hicks that his complaint was frivolous. During the videotaped meeting, they presented Hicks with copies of various Barbie dolls that not only had been created prior to 1996 (the date of Claudene's creation), but also had copyright designations on their heads that pre-dated Claudene's creation. Additionally, Mattel's counsel noted that the face paint on some of the earlier-created Barbie dolls was virtually identical to that used on Claudene. Hicks declined Mattel's invitation to inspect the dolls and, later during the meeting, hurled them in disgust from a conference table.

Having been unsuccessful in convincing Hicks to dismiss Christian's action voluntarily, Mattel served Hicks with a motion for Rule 11 sanctions. . . . Hicks declined to withdraw the complaint during the 21-day safe harbor period provided by Rule 11, and Mattel filed its motion.

Seemingly unfazed by Mattel's Rule 11 motion, Hicks proceeded with the litigation and filed a motion pursuant to Federal Rule of Civil Procedure 56(f) to obtain additional discovery. . . . Hicks then began filing additional papers that were characterized by frequency and volume. Following official completion of the summary judgment briefing schedule, Hicks filed what was styled as a "supplemental opposition." In those papers, Christian asserted for the first time that the head sculpture of Mattel's CEO Barbie (which was created in 1998) infringed Christian's copyright in the Claudene doll. He did not, however, move for leave to amend the complaint.

Hicks later filed additional papers alleging that several additional Barbie dolls infringed the Claudene sculpture. As with CEO Barbie, no motion for leave to amend the complaint was filed. . . .

## III.   The District Court Orders

The district court granted Mattel's motions for summary judgment and Rule 11 sanctions. The court ruled that Mattel did not infringe the 1997 Claudene copyright because it could not possibly have accessed the Claudene doll at the time it created the head sculptures of the Cool Blue (copyrighted in 1991) and Virginia Tech (copyrighted in 1976) Barbies. The court also rejected Christian's theory that the Mattel dolls had infringed the totality of Claudene's appearance, including its face paint, because the copyright is "limited in scope and extends only to 3-dimensional sculptures and not 2-dimensional artwork. . . ." Alternatively, the court found that Mattel had been using lighter-colored face paint "on dolls produced before the Claudene doll was created in 1996, such as Colonial Barbie (1994) and Pioneer Barbie (1995)," and therefore could not have infringed the later-created Claudene doll even if the Claudene copyright protected two-dimensional artwork. Finally, the court found that Mattel, as owner of various Barbie head sculpture copyrights, had "the exclusive right to prepare derivative works of its own copyrighted works. See 17 U.S.C. § 106(2). Thus, Mattel has the right to paint and repaint its own copyrighted sculptures." . . .

As for Mattel's Rule 11 motion, the district court found that Hicks had "filed a meritless claim against defendant Mattel. A reasonable investigation by Mr. Hicks would have revealed that there was no factual foundation for [Christian's] copyright claim." Indeed, the district court noted that Hicks needed to do little more than examine "the back of the heads of the Barbie dolls he claims were infringing," because such a perfunctory inquiry would have revealed "the pre-1996 copyright notices on the Cool Blue and [Virginia Tech] Barbie doll heads." . . .

The district court awarded Mattel $501,565 in attorneys' fees. At the outset of its order, the court summarized the findings in its earlier order, namely that it had "predicated its [Rule 11] decision" on Hicks' filing a frivolous complaint and "further found" that he had "'behaved boorishly, misrepresented the facts and misstated the law.'" In discussing Rule 11's purpose of deterring such conduct, the district court made further findings about Hicks' behavior during prior proceedings—some of which were completely unrelated to this case.

The district court next considered various arguments that Hicks had advanced in opposition to Mattel's fee application. Hicks first contended, without much elaboration, that a fee award would have a "ruinous" effect on his finances and ability to practice law.[4] The district court held, however, that "repeated reprimands and sanctions" imposed in prior litigations "clearly have not had the desired deterrent effect on his behavior," and it concluded that Hicks would not be punished sufficiently if the court were to impose mere "non-monetary sanctions." Hicks also argued (somewhat ironically) that Mattel's fees request was excessive in light of how simplistic it should have been to defend against Christian's action. The district court disagreed, reasoning [as] in Brandt v. Schal Assocs., Inc., 960 F.2d 640, 648 (7th Cir. 1992), [that] the judiciary has "'little sympathy for the litigant who fires a big gun, and when the adversary returns fire, complains because he was firing blanks.'"

## Discussion

### I. Standard of Review

We review the district court's decision to impose Rule 11 sanctions—and, if they are warranted, the reasonableness of the actual amount imposed—for abuse of discretion. Cooter & Gell v. Hartmarx Corp., 496 U.S. 384, 401, 405 (1990). . . .

### II. Imposition of Rule 11 Sanctions

. . .

#### A. General Rule 11 Principles

Filing a complaint in federal court is no trifling undertaking. An attorney's signature on a complaint is tantamount to a warranty that the complaint is well grounded in fact and "existing law" (or proposes a good faith extension of the existing law) and that it is not filed for an improper purpose. . . .

The attorney has a duty prior to filing a complaint not only to conduct a reasonable factual investigation, but also to perform adequate legal research that confirms whether the theoretical underpinnings of the complaint are

---

4. Hicks argues that the district court erred in failing to consider his ability to pay such considerable sanctions. Although we note language in In re Yagman, 796 F.2d 1165 (9th Cir. 1986), that appears to require the district court to make such a determination, see id. at 1185, the Yagman case pre-dated the 1993 amendments to Rule 11. The Advisory Committee's notes concerning the amendments indicate that an attorney's financial wherewithal is only one of several factors that a district court may consider in deciding the amount of sanctions. See Fed. R. Civ. P. 11, advisory committee notes, 1993 Amendments, Subdivisions (b) and (c). Here, Hicks had an opportunity to present specific financial information to the district court, but merely argued conclusorily that the sanctions would be "ruinous." The district court acknowledged this argument. Nothing in Rule 11 mandates a specific weighing of this factor, however.

"warranted by existing law or a good faith argument for an extension, modification or reversal of existing law." Golden Eagle Distrib. Corp. v. Burroughs Corp., 801 F.2d 1531, 1537 (9th Cir. 1986). One of the fundamental purposes of Rule 11 is to "reduce frivolous claims, defenses or motions and to deter costly meritless maneuvers, . . . [thereby] avoid[ing] delay and unnecessary expense in litigation." Id. at 1536. Nonetheless, a finding of significant delay or expense is not required under Rule 11. Where, as here, the complaint is the primary focus of Rule 11 proceedings, a district court must conduct a two-prong inquiry to determine (1) whether the complaint is legally or factually "baseless" from an objective perspective, and (2) if the attorney has conducted "a reasonable and competent inquiry" before signing and filing it. Buster v. Greisen, 104 F.3d 1186, 1190 (9th Cir. 1997).

## B.  The District Court's Findings Regarding the Meritless Claim

*1. Did Hicks Have an Adequate Legal or Factual Basis for Filing the Complaint?* Hicks filed a single claim of copyright infringement against Mattel. The complaint charges that the Cool Blue Barbie infringed the copyright in the Claudene doll head. In addition, in a subsequent letter to Mattel's counsel, he claimed that Virginia Tech Barbie also infringed Claudene. Hicks cannot seriously dispute the district court's conclusions that, assuming the applicability of the doctrine of prior creation, Christian's complaint was legally and factually frivolous. Indeed, as a matter of copyright law, it is well established that a prior-created work cannot infringe a later-created one. See Grubb v. KMS Patriots, L.P., 88 F.3d 1, 5 (1st Cir. 1996) (noting that "prior creation renders any conclusion of access or inference of copying illogical").

Copyright infringement requires proof that a plaintiff owns a valid copyright in the work and that the defendant copied the work. Feist Publ'n, Inc. v. Rural Tel. Serv. Co., Inc., 499 U.S. 340, 361 (1991). Proof of copying often revolves around whether the defendant had sufficient access to copy the work. Access is only a theoretical issue in this case, however. By simple logic, it is impossible to copy something that does not exist. Thus, if Mattel created its doll sculptures before CDC created Claudene in 1994, it is factually and legally impossible for Mattel to be an infringer.

The record of creation is telling and conclusive. The Cool Blue Barbie doll uses the Neptune's Daughter doll head which was created in 1991, some six years before the Claudene doll. The Virginia Tech Barbie doll uses the SuperStar sculpture which Mattel created in 1976. The SuperStar doll was the subject of the just-completed federal court litigation, and Hicks should have been well aware of the prior creation, not to mention that the copyright notice (including date of creation) appears prominently on the back of the dolls' heads.

Recognizing the futility of attacking prior creation, Hicks argues that the paint on the Claudene doll's face features a light makeup that is distinctive and that the two Barbie dolls thus infringe Claudene's overall appearance and presentation. This argument fails because, among other things, Mattel used the light face paint on the Pioneer Barbie, which was created two years before the Claudene doll, thus defeating once again any claim of copying.[7] It also bears noting that Mattel has been repainting various doll heads for decades. Under Hicks' theory, CDC's use of an infringing doll head coupled with "new" face paint would result in liability for Mattel's repainting of its prior-created Barbie doll sculptures. Neither common sense nor copyright law countenances such a result, even if the Claudene doll were deemed a derivative work. See Entm't Research Group, Inc. v. Genesis Creative Group, Inc., 122 F.3d 1211, 1220 (9th Cir. 1997) (holding that owners of copyrighted works have broad latitude to copyright derivatives thereof if they have "adequate originality").

In the face of facts and law clearly against his client, Hicks sought to resurrect the copyright claim by deluging the district court with supplemental filings, including entirely new claims regarding a different assortment of Barbie dolls and non-Barbie dolls. The dolls included, for example, the CEO doll, which used the 1991 Neptune's Daughter head with a modified mouth.

The district court did not consider any of Hicks' supplemental filings, noting that Hicks failed to comply with local rules regarding page limitations and typefaces. Given the chameleon nature of the claims and Hicks' flip-flop from the sculpture-plus-painting theory back to the sculpture-only theory, the district court was justified in putting an end to Hicks' serial filings. The district court has considerable latitude in managing the parties' motion practice and enforcing local rules that place parameters on briefing. We cannot say that the court abused its discretion by declining to consider Hicks' multitudinous efforts to circumvent the court's local rules and to expand the scope of an already frivolous suit. At some point, enough is enough. . . .

*2. Did Hicks Conduct an Adequate Factual Investigation?* The district court concluded that Hicks "filed a case without factual foundation." Hicks, having argued unsuccessfully that his failure to perform even minimal due diligence was irrelevant as a matter of copyright law, does not contest that he would have been able to discover the copyright information simply by examining the doll heads. Instead he argues that the district court did not understand certain "complex" issues. Simply saying so does not make it so. The district court well understood the legal and factual background of the case. It was Hicks' absence of investigation, not the district court's absence of analysis, that brought about his downfall.

The district court did not abuse its discretion in concluding that Hicks' failure to investigate fell below the requisite standard established by Rule 11.

---

7. When shown a Pioneer Barbie doll at his deposition, Christian claimed that it infringed the Claudene doll. This fatal admission, which was made just before Hicks whisked him from the deposition room, underscores the frivolousness of Christian's claim.

### III.   The District Court's Additional Findings Regarding Misconduct

Hicks argues that even if the district court were justified in sanction-ing him under Rule 11 based on Christian's complaint and the follow-on motions, its conclusion was tainted because it impermissibly considered other misconduct that cannot be sanctioned under Rule 11, such as dis-covery abuses, misstatements made during oral argument, and conduct in other litigation.

[This] argument has merit. While Rule 11 permits the district court to sanction an attorney for conduct regarding "pleading[s], written motion[s], and other paper[s]" that have been signed and filed in a given case, Fed. R. Civ. P. 11(a), it does not authorize sanctions for, among other things, discov-ery abuses or misstatements made to the court during an oral presentation. See Bus. Guides, Inc. v. Chromatic Communications Enter., 892 F.2d 802, 813 (9th Cir. 1989) (holding that misstatements made during oral argument can-not constitute sanctionable offenses under Rule 11); In re Yagman, 796 F.2d at 1187 (holding that discovery abuses cannot be sanctioned under Rule 11); see also Fed. R. Civ. P. 11, advisory committee notes, 1993 Amendments, Subdivisions (b) and (c) ("The rule applies only to assertions contained in papers filed with or submitted to the court. It does not cover matters arising for the first time during oral presentations to the court, when counsel may make statements that would not be made if there had been more time for study and reflection.").

In its January 5, 2000, order, the district court cited multiple bases for its Rule 11 findings:

> Mr. Hicks has filed a case without factual foundation. Moreover, while this court cannot evaluate Mr. Hicks' conduct in the litigation before Judge Matz, his conduct in this case and the related one pending before this court has fallen below the standards expected of attorneys practicing in the Central District of California. In the related case, this court has already ordered Mr. Hicks to personally pay plaintiff's attorney's fees incurred as a result of his culpable conduct. Order of July 13, 1999 in CV99-4667. In connection with the instant motion and the discovery preceding it, he has behaved boor-ishly, misrepresented the facts, and misstated the law. Accordingly, the court grants defendant's motion for Rule 11 sanctions against Mr. Hicks.

In connection with the conclusion on boorish behavior, the court cited Hicks' conduct ("tossing Barbie dolls off a table") at a meeting of counsel and his interruption of a deposition following a damaging admission by his client. The charge of misrepresentation of facts was based on a state-ment made at oral argument that he had never seen a particular catalogue while a videotape of exhibit inspections showed him "leisurely thumbing through the catalogue." Hicks' conflicting representations in pleadings as to the identity of allegedly infringing Barbie dolls was an additional example of misrepresentation noted by the court. Finally, the court deter-mined that Hicks made misrepresentations in his briefs concerning the law of joint authorship in the copyright context. . . .

The orders clearly demonstrate that the district court decided, at least in part, to sanction Hicks because he signed and filed a factually and legally meritless complaint and for misrepresentations in subsequent briefing. But the orders, coupled with the supporting examples, also strongly suggest that the court considered extra-pleadings conduct as a basis for Rule 11 sanctions. . . .

The laundry list of Hicks' outlandish conduct is a long one and raises serious questions as to his respect for the judicial process. Nonetheless, Rule 11 sanctions are limited to "paper[s]" signed in violation of the rule. Conduct in depositions, discovery meetings of counsel, oral representations at hearings, and behavior in prior proceedings do not fall within the ambit of Rule 11. Because we do not know for certain whether the district court granted Mattel's Rule 11 motion as a result of an impermissible intertwining of its conclusion about the complaint's frivolity and Hicks' extrinsic misconduct, we must vacate the district court's Rule 11 orders.

We decline Mattel's suggestion that the district court's sanctions orders could be supported in their entirety under the court's inherent authority. To impose sanctions under its inherent authority, the district court must "make an explicit finding [which it did not do here] that counsel's conduct constituted or was tantamount to bad faith." Primus Auto. Fin. Serv., Inc. v. Batarse, 115 F.3d 644, 648 (9th Cir. 1997) (internal quotation marks omitted). We acknowledge that the district court has a broad array of sanctions options at its disposal: Rule 11, 28 U.S.C. § 1927,[11] and the court's inherent authority. Each of these sanctions alternatives has its own particular requirements, and it is important that the grounds be separately articulated to assure that the conduct at issue falls within the scope of the sanctions remedy. See, e.g., B.K.B. v. Maui Police Dep't, 276 F.3d 1091, 1107 (9th Cir. 2002) (holding that misconduct committed "in an unreasonable and vexatious manner" that "multiplies the proceedings" violates § 1927); Fink v. Gomez, 239 F.3d 989, 991-992 (9th Cir. 2001) (holding that sanctions may be imposed under the court's inherent authority for "bad faith" actions by counsel, "which includes a broad range of willful improper conduct"). On remand, the district court will have an opportunity to delineate the factual and legal basis for its sanctions orders.

## IV.  The District Court's Decision to Award Attorney's Fees

. . . Because we are vacating the district court's Rule 11 orders on other legal grounds, we express no opinion at this stage about the particular reasonableness of any of the fees the district court elected to award Mattel. We do, however, encourage the district court on remand to ensure that the time spent by Mattel's attorneys was reasonably and appropriately spent in relation to both the patent frivolousness of Christian's complaint and the

---

11. Section 1927 provides for imposition of "excess costs, expenses, and attorneys' fees" on counsel who "multiplies the proceedings in any case unreasonably and vexatiously."

services directly caused by the sanctionable conduct.[12] See Fed. R. Civ. P. 11, advisory committee notes, 1993 Amendments, Subdivisions (b) and (c) (noting that attorneys' fees may only be awarded under Rule 11 for those "services directly and unavoidably caused" by the sanctionable conduct).

## Conclusion

We vacate the district court's Rule 11 orders and remand for further proceedings consistent with this opinion.

*Vacated and Remanded.*

## *Note: No-Holds-Barred Advocacy*

Counsel for Business Guides could plausibly claim to have been under time pressure to file. Counsel for Kraemer could plausibly claim to have made as diligent a prefiling inquiry as limited resources and the recalcitrance of the defendant would permit. Is there any excuse for Hicks's conduct in *Christian*, or does he seem to you like the kind of lawyer for whom Rule 11 sanctions are obviously appropriate? Should it matter that the amount of the sanctions might end his practice (see footnote 4, supra)? Is the evidence of Hicks's misconduct in other cases relevant to the question whether he should be sanctioned in this case?

Even if Hicks made a woefully inadequate prefiling inquiry, what would a reasonable lawyer have done? Would it have been enough to check the copyright stamps on the back of Barbie's head when Mattel's counsel made the dolls available for inspection? In *Kraemer*, the Seventh Circuit places a lot of weight on the fact that Lawton hired a private investigator who was stonewalled. That leaves open the question how far a lawyer should go when there is no stonewalling, when time and money permit open inquiry into the facts. Consider Intamin Ltd. v. Magnetar Tech. Corp., 483 F.3d 1328 (Fed. Cir. 2007), in which the Federal Circuit upheld a district court's decision not to impose sanctions in a patent infringement case involving competing brake systems for roller coasters. The defendant, Magnetar, argued that Intamin's prefiling inquiry was inadequate

---

12. For example, because the action was frivolous on its face, why would Mattel's attorneys need to spend 700 hours ($173,151.50 in fees) for the summary judgment motion and response? Although Hicks clearly complicated the proceedings through multiple filings, Mattel's theory and approach was stunningly simple and required little explication: (1) Mattel's Barbie dolls and face paint were prior copyright creations that could not infringe the after-created Claudene doll and (2) Christian was neither a contributor to nor owner of the copyright. This is not to say that Hicks' defense of the motion necessarily called for a timid response, but neither does it compel a bazooka approach.

because it did not obtain and physically cut open the metal casing on the magnets in Magnetar's brake system. The record shows that Magnetar's system encased the magnets in metal tubes. Accordingly, a visual inspection would not disclose the orientation of the magnets within the tubes. In Judin v. United States, 110 F.3d 780, 784 (Fed. Cir. 1997), this court held that the district court abused its discretion in not granting Rule 11 sanctions against a patentee who failed to obtain a sample of the product as part of its pre-filing investigation. However, *Judin* did not create a blanket rule that a patentee must obtain and thoroughly deconstruct a sample of a defendant's product to avoid violating Rule 11. Rather, in *Judin*, the patentee could have easily obtained a sample of the accused device (a bar code scanner) for a nominal price from the post office. In this case, the technology presented the patentee with unreasonable obstacles to any effort to obtain a sample of Magnetar's amusement ride brake system, let alone the difficulty of opening the casing.

In lieu of cutting open the casing, Intamin might have tested a Magnetar device for magnetic polarities. In *Q-Pharma*, however, this court did not impose on a patentee a Rule 11 obligation to perform a simple chemical test on a sample to determine its composition. 360 F.3d at 1302. Instead, this court found that the patentee satisfied its Rule 11 obligations with other reasonable pre-filing inquiries. Id. Here, the district court determined: "In light of the other information [Intamin] had at the time of filing . . . [its] prefiling inquiry was reasonable." Reconsideration Decision, slip op. at 7. In particular, the district court noted that Intamin "evaluated the patent portfolio, analyzed the patent's validity, determined the scope of the patent's claims, and performed an infringement analysis." Id. The district court further determined that Intamin "reviewed publicly available documents on [Magnetar's] brakes, inspected [Magnetar's] brakes as installed on a roller coaster, took photos of the brakes, and reviewed the brakes with experts." Id. Thus the district court determined that Intamin's pre-filing inquiry was reasonable under the circumstances. Id. This court discerns no abuse of discretion in the district court's determination.

483 F.3d at 1338. Cf. United Stars Ind. v. Plastech Engineered Prods., Inc., 525 F.3d 605 (7th Cir. 2008) (defendant sanctioned for filing counterclaim in commercial contract dispute with no evidentiary support); Garr v. U.S. Healthcare Inc., 22 F.3d 1274 (3d Cir. 1994) (inadequate investigation by attorney who relied on *Wall Street Journal* story and copied another attorney's complaint before filing securities fraud suit); Ideal Instruments, Inc. v. Rivard Instruments, Inc., 243 F.R.D. 322 (N.D. Iowa 2007) (awarding sanctions for reliance on bogus expert report in motion for preliminary injunction without proper prefiling investigation), 245 F.R.D. 381 (N.D. Iowa 2007) (adjusting attorney fee award downward to comport with Rule 11 focus on deterrence and to punish attorneys seeking sanctions for block billing); Guidry v. Clare, 442 F. Supp. 2d 282 (E.D. Va. 2006) (inadequate investigation in frivolous unfair debt collection practices suit arising from attempts by defendant to collect $62 bounced check for daughter's cheerleading lessons).

### Note: "Later Advocating" Written Submissions

The Ninth Circuit remanded *Christian* for a reassessment of the sanctions award in part because it worried the trial court had punished Hicks for "boorishness" and for misrepresentations made during oral argument. The opinion emphasizes that Rule 11 sanctions are "limited to '*paper*[s]' signed in violation of the rule." The 1993 Amendments, however, make sanctions available for "presenting to the court a pleading, written motion, or other paper," and "presenting" explicitly includes "signing, filing, submitting, or *later advocating*" a written submission. See Fed. R. Proc. 11, 1993 Advisory Committee Notes. Has the Ninth Circuit ignored the "later advocating" language of the rule?

Compare the reasoning in *Christian* with the analysis of the Second Circuit in O'Brien v. Alexander:

> Our review of the sanctions imposed is a more difficult and delicate task [than the review of the sufficiency of the complaint]. A lawyer fighting for his client's rights in a courtroom is expected to be as wily and resourceful as Daniel Webster was in his defense of Jabez Stone in the foreclosure action brought against him by the Devil, to whom Stone had sold his soul. Stephen Vincent Benét, The Devil and Daniel Webster, reprinted in Law in Action: An Anthology of the Law in Literature 139 (Crown Publishers 1947). Counsel must be able to think and argue on his or her feet in a courtroom, a forum where conditions change rapidly. Yet zealous oral advocacy must be conducted according to the rules and counsel may not "knowingly make a false statement of law or fact," Model Code of Professional Responsibility DR 7-102(A.5). To violate this professional standard may result in sanctions under Rule 11. Such sanctions were imposed for two oral statements made by counsel. In our view, one violated Rule 11, the other did not. . . .
>
> [T]he 1993 amendment expanded the scope of litigating lawyers' obligations in a manner directly relevant to the present case. It permits sanctions based upon the "presenting" of a paper — rather than limiting sanctions to those papers that bear an attorney's signature — and defining "presenting" broadly as "signing, filing, submitting, or later advocating." Fed. R. Civ. P. 11(b). The Advisory Committee explained the new provision as follows:
>
>> The rule applies only to assertions contained in papers filed with or submitted to the court. It does not cover matters arising for the first time during oral presentations to the court, when counsel may make statements that would not have been made if there had been more time for study and reflection. However, a litigant's obligations with respect to the contents of these papers are not measured solely as of the time they are filed with or submitted to the court, but include reaffirming to the court and advocating positions contained in those pleadings and motions after learning that they cease to have any merit. For example, an attorney who during a pretrial conference insists on a claim or defense should be viewed as "presenting to the court" that contention and would be subject to the obligations of subdivision (b) measured as of that time.

The new language and the Advisory Committee's comments make evident that although sanctions may now be based on litigants' oral representations, not all oral statements are sanctionable under Rule 11, even when they advance baseless allegations or objectively frivolous arguments. Moreover, to avoid imposing sanctions for oral statements regarding matters that do not flow directly from the signed paper—even when such new matters arise in the course of a presentation relating generally to the paper—the amended Rule 11 requires a close nexus between the oral statement and the underlying written paper. As the Advisory Committee stated, the rule applies only to "assertions" contained in the underlying paper, not to that paper generally or in the abstract.

Consequently, we are unable to accept the district court's view that Rule 11 applies to oral advocacy whenever an attorney advocates a signed paper. *O'Brien*, 898 F. Supp. at 176. Such a broad rule is completely contrary to the Advisory Committee's recognition that oral advocacy often requires lawyers to address new matters without much opportunity for study and reflection. In fact, because oral advocacy almost always relates in some way to a prior signed paper, adopting the district court's proposition would entail a significant and unintended expansion of Rule 11's scope.

That an oral statement is made in the course of advocating a pleading or motion is not enough; to be sanctionable the oral statement must relate directly to a particular representation contained in the document that the lawyer is then advocating. Thus, to be sanctionable an oral representation must meet two requirements: (1) it must violate the certification requirement of Rule 11(b), e.g., by advocating baseless allegations, and (2) it must relate directly to a matter addressed in the underlying paper and be in furtherance of that matter to constitute advocating within the meaning of subsection (b).

101 F.3d 1479 (2d Cir. 1996) (upholding sanctions for misrepresentations linked directly to frivolous complaint made by plaintiff's counsel during oral argument). See also *Bees v. Federal Emergency Management Agency*, 562 F.3d 284 (4th Cir. 2009) (holding that an oral statement is a basis for Rule 11 sanctions only if it affirms an assertion already contained in a written submission to the court; reversing *sua sponte* sanctions order where government lawyer made misstatements about comment period for FEMA decision to redraw flood maps; finding attorney's statements were "inadvertent mistakes" and not linked to any written filings).

## Note: The Standard of Review on Appeal

Recall that the Seventh Circuit in *Kraemer* reviewed the lower court's decision on what it called an "abuse of discretion" standard. At least in theory, this means that the lower court's decision should be treated with great deference. The Supreme Court endorsed this deferential standard of review for Rule 11 sanctions in Cooter & Gell v. Hartmarx Corp.:

The considerations involved in the Rule 11 context are similar to those involved in determining negligence, which is generally reviewed deferentially. . . .

Familiar with the issues and litigants, the district court is better situated than the court of appeals to marshall the pertinent facts and apply the fact-dependent legal standard mandated by Rule 11. Of course, this standard would not preclude the appellate court's correction of a district court's legal errors, e.g., . . . relying on a materially incorrect view of the relevant law in determining that a pleading was not "warranted by existing law or a good faith argument" for changing the law. An appellate court would be justified in concluding that, in making such errors, the district court abused its discretion. . . . Pierce v. Underwood, 487 U.S. 552 (1988), strongly supports applying a unitary abuse of discretion standard to all aspects of a Rule 11 proceeding. In *Pierce,* the Court held a District Court's determination under the Equal Access to Justice Act (EAJA), 28 U.S.C. § 2412(d) (1982 ed.), that "the position of the United States was substantially justified" should be reviewed for an abuse-of-discretion. As a position is "substantially justified" if it "has a reasonable basis in law and fact," 487 U.S. at 566, n.2, EAJA requires an inquiry similar to the Rule 11 inquiry as to whether a pleading is "well grounded in fact" and legally tenable. . . .

Two factors the Court found significant in *Pierce* are equally pertinent here. First, the Court indicated that "as a matter of the sound administration of justice," deference was owed to the "judicial actor . . . better positioned than another to decide the issue in question." 487 U.S. at 559-560. Because a determination whether a legal position is "substantially justified" depends greatly on factual determinations, the Court reasoned that the district court was "better positioned" to make such factual determinations. See 487 U.S. at 560. A district court's ruling that a litigant's position is factually well grounded and legally tenable for Rule 11 purposes is similarly fact specific. . . .

Second, *Pierce* noted that only deferential review gave the district court the necessary flexibility to resolve questions involving "multifarious, fleeting, special, narrow facts that utterly resist generalization." Id. at 561-562. . . . The issues involved in determining whether an attorney has violated Rule 11 likewise involve "fact-intensive, close calls." Shaffer & Sandler 15. . . . The district court is best acquainted with the local bar's litigation practices and thus best situated to determine when a sanction is warranted to serve Rule 11's goal of specific and general deterrence. Deference to the determination of courts on the front lines of litigation will enhance these courts' ability to control the litigants before them. Such deference will streamline the litigation process by freeing appellate courts from the duty of reweighing evidence and reconsidering facts already weighed and considered by the district court; it will also discourage litigants from pursuing marginal appeals, thus reducing the amount of satellite litigation.

496 U.S. 384, 402-404 (1990).

Was the Seventh Circuit appropriately deferential to the district court's decision in *Kraemer*? Isn't the district court in a better position to know the facts and circumstances supporting sanctions in the case? As you read the cases that follow, notice how the standard of review affects the way the appellate courts treat the decision to grant or deny sanctions made by the courts below.

## 2. "Improper Purpose," Frivolous Claims, and Arguments for Legal Change

*Saltany v. Reagan*
886 F.2d 438 (D.C. Cir. 1989)

BUCKLEY, D.H. GINSBURG, and SENTELLE, CIRCUIT JUDGES.
PER CURIAM.

On April 13, 1988, fifty-five Libyan citizens and residents filed suit in the district court seeking damages for injuries, death, and property loss sustained in the 1986 United States air strike on Libya. Substantial damages were sought from the United States, President Reagan, senior civilian and military officials, and from the United Kingdom and Prime Minister Thatcher as well. Plaintiffs sought to hold the British defendants liable on the basis that the Prime Minister gave the United States permission to use British air bases in the air strike. Plaintiffs asserted claims under the Federal Tort Claims Act, 28 U.S.C. § 2671, et seq., the Foreign Claims Act, 10 U.S.C. § 2734, the Alien Tort Claims Act, 28 U.S.C. § 1350, the Racketeer Influenced and Corrupt Organizations Act, 18 U.S.C. § 1961, et seq., and various constitutional and common law theories, including the "tort law of Libya."

Upon motions, the district court dismissed plaintiffs' claims as to all defendants. See Saltany v. Reagan, 702 F. Supp. 319 (D.D.C. 1988). Plaintiffs appealed and defendants have moved this court for summary affirmance: By separate order this date, we affirm the decision dismissing plaintiffs' case.

Both the United States and the British defendants also moved the district court for sanctions pursuant to Federal Rule of Civil Procedure 11, on the grounds that plaintiffs abused the judicial process and needlessly imposed upon defendants the cost of defending against an action not supported by existing law or by any good faith argument for the extension, modification, or reversal of existing law. The district court found that plaintiffs' counsel "surely knew" that the case "offered no hope whatsoever of success," but it declined to impose sanctions in the interest of keeping the courthouse door open as a forum for suits "brought as a public statement of protest of Presidential action with which counsel (and, to be sure, their clients) were in profound disagreement."

The United Kingdom has cross-appealed from, and seeks summary reversal of, the decision denying sanctions. Additionally, the United Kingdom seeks attorneys' fees and costs, pursuant to both Federal Rule of Appellate Procedure 38 and 28 U.S.C. § 1927, for the costs of defending against a frivolous appeal. For the reasons stated below, we reverse and remand the district court decision with regard to the Rule 11 sanction, and grant the United Kingdom's motion for attorneys' fees and costs on appeal pursuant to Rule 38.

## I.   Federal Rule of Civil Procedure 11

The United Kingdom asserts that the district court erred in denying its Rule 11 motion for attorneys' fees and costs, relying upon the well established principle that the court must impose a sanction "once it has found a violation of the rule." Weil v. Markowitz, 829 F.2d 166, 171 (D.C. Cir. 1987) (footnote omitted); Westmoreland v. CBS, 770 F.2d 1168, 1174-1175 (D.C. Cir. 1985). Thus, the question is whether the district court found, or should have found, that plaintiffs violated Rule 11. If so, then a sanction must be imposed.

Here, the district court observed that plaintiffs, citizens or residents of Libya, could not be "presumed to be familiar with the rules of law of the United States." *Saltany*, 702 F. Supp. at 322. The court noted, however, that "[i]t is otherwise . . . with their counsel. The case offered no hope whatsoever of success, and plaintiffs' attorneys surely knew it." Id.

The court thus found, in substance if not in terms, that plaintiffs' counsel had violated Rule 11; yet the court did not impose a sanction. Instead, the court went on to observe that because the "injuries for which the suit is brought are not insubstantial," the case is not "frivolous so much as it is audacious." Id. The seriousness of the injury, however, has no bearing upon whether a complaint is properly grounded in law and fact. We may agree with the district court that the suit is audacious—that is not sanctionable in itself—but, we do not see how filing a complaint that "plaintiffs' attorneys surely knew" had "no hope whatsoever of success" can be anything but a violation of Rule 11.

Nonetheless, surmising that the suit was brought as a public statement of protest, the district court opined that courts can "serve in some respects as a forum for making such statements, and should continue to do so." Id. (citing Talamini v. Allstate Insurance Co., 470 U.S. 1067, 1070-71 (1985) (Stevens, J., concurring in dismissal of appeal)). We do not conceive it a proper function of a federal court to serve as a forum for "protests," to the detriment of parties with serious disputes waiting to be heard. In any event, reliance upon *Talamini* was inappropriate. That opinion, representing the views of Justice Stevens and three other justices, argued in opposition to awarding sanctions against an attorney who had pursued an unmeritorious application for review in an otherwise unremarkable unfair trade practices action. It in no way speaks to the use of the courts as any sort of political or protest forum. Whether punitive sanctions should be imposed for invoking the judicial process is properly fit into the equation when considering whether a Rule 11 violation has occurred. Here, the district court had already determined in effect that a violation had occurred. Therefore, we grant the United Kingdom's motion for summary reversal and remand the matter to the district court for imposition of an appropriate sanction.

## II.   Federal Rule of Appellate Procedure 38

The United Kingdom (with the support of the United States) seeks to recover the attorneys' fees and costs it incurred by reason of plaintiffs' pursuit of a frivolous appeal. We grant attorneys' fees and costs under Rule 38, and thus do not consider the alternate claim under 28 U.S.C. § 1927.

The basis for the United Kingdom's request is that the Supreme Court's decision in Argentine Republic v. Amerada Hess Corp., 109 S. Ct. 683 (1989), which was issued about a month after the decision of the district court, utterly foreclosed plaintiff's argument that the United Kingdom is subject to the jurisdiction of the courts of the United States.

In *Amerada Hess,* the Court ruled unanimously and unequivocally that the Foreign Sovereign Immunities Act ("FSIA") provides the "sole basis for obtaining jurisdiction over a foreign state in our courts." *Amerada Hess,* 109 S. Ct. at 688. Furthermore, the Court held that a foreign state's use of military force allegedly in violation of international law fell outside any of the exceptions to sovereign immunity provided by the FSIA. . . .

. . . [W]e find that *Amerada Hess* clearly bars plaintiffs' claim against the United Kingdom, and that so much was apparent to counsel for plaintiffs before they imposed upon the United Kingdom the burden of this appeal. Accordingly, we grant the United Kingdom's motion for attorneys' fees and costs to be assessed against counsel. . . .

*So ordered.*

## Saltany v. Bush*
960 F.2d 1060 (D.C. Cir. 1992)

WALD, EDWARDS, and D.H. GINSBURG, CIRCUIT JUDGES.
PER CURIAM.
. . . Counsel challenge the award of Rule 11 and Rule 38 sanctions against them, as directed by a previous panel. The law of the case doctrine bars this challenge. See, e.g., Melong v. Micronesian Claims Commn., 643 F.2d 10, 17 (D.C. Cir. 1980). We see no clear error combined with manifest injustice, nor does Cooter & Gell v. Hartmarx Corp., 496 U.S. 384 (1990), constitute intervening law on the Rule 11 issue. The prior panel determined that the District Court had found a Rule 11 violation, see Saltany v. Reagan, and there is no basis under *Cooter* or any other precedent for us to reconsider this determination. Moreover, *Cooter* makes clear that sanctions must be imposed once a violation is found. See 100 S. Ct. at 2454, 2460.

Counsel also argue for a nonmonetary Rule 11 sanction, but the District Court considered this possibility and reasonably exercised its discretion to impose a fine instead. . . .

WALD, CIRCUIT JUDGE, dissenting.
I regretfully dissent from the majority's affirmance of the district court's imposition of Rule 11 sanctions against plaintiffs' counsel. The district

---

* President Bush is substituted for former President Reagan, insofar as the latter is sued in his official capacity. See Fed. R. App. P. 43(c).

court had originally denied appellees' motion for Rule 11 sanctions, concluding that "[i]t cannot . . . be said that the case is frivolous so much as it is audacious." Saltany v. Reagan, 702 F. Supp. 319, 322 (D.D.C. 1988).

On the first appeal, this court nonetheless concluded that, when the district judge commented in his opinion that "[t]he case offered no hope whatsoever of success, and plaintiffs' attorneys surely knew it," id., he "found, in substance if not in terms, that plaintiffs' counsel had violated Rule 11; yet the court did not impose a sanction." The prior panel remanded to the district court for the "imposition of an appropriate sanction." Id. On remand, the district judge not unreasonably interpreted the remand order "as an unequivocal direction to it" to impose Rule 11 sanctions, and he ordered plaintiffs' counsel to pay $10,000 each to the British appellees.

Under the "law of the case" doctrine, a decision on an issue of law made at one stage of a case ordinarily becomes a binding precedent to be followed in successive stages of the same case. However, this doctrine "is not an inexorable command that rigidly binds a court to its former decisions but rather is an expression of good sense and wise judicial practice." Carpa, Inc. v. Ward Foods, Inc., 567 F.2d 1316, 1320 (5th Cir. 1978). As this court has stated on several occasions, "[t]o warrant divergence from the law of the case, a court must not only be convinced that its earlier decision was erroneous; it must also be satisfied that adherence to the law of the case will work a grave injustice." Melong v. Micronesian Claims Commn., 643 F.2d 10, 17 (D.C. Cir. 1980); Laffey v. Northwest Airlines, Inc., 642 F.2d 578, 585 (D.C. Cir. 1980); see also Browning v. Navarro, 887 F.2d 553, 556 (5th Cir. 1989) ("We have the discretion to ignore a previous decision if substantially different evidence has been presented, there has been an intervening change in the law, or the prior decision was clearly erroneous and it would work a manifest injustice.").

Despite the extremely high threshold that any departure from past holdings in the same case must meet, I feel one is justified here. Cooter & Gell v. Hartmarx Corp., 496 U.S. 384 (1990), decided after the first appeal in this case, does represent an "intervening change in the law" to the extent that it establishes a "clearly erroneous" standard rather than a *de novo* review standard for a review of a decision to impose (or not to impose) Rule 11 sanctions. Although the prior panel opinion did not expressly identify its standard in reviewing the district judge's denial of Rule 11 sanctions, in my view, it did not treat his express decision not to impose sanctions with the required deference by finding that he had ruled on the factual predicates of Rule 11 but had erred in not properly applying the law to those findings.

In order to find a violation of Rule 11, the district judge must conclude that, to the best of counsel's knowledge, information, and belief formed after reasonable inquiry, the pleading was neither "well grounded in fact" nor "warranted by existing law or a good faith argument for the extension, modification, or reversal of existing law," or that the pleading was "interposed for an[] improper purpose, such as to harass or to cause unnecessary delay or needless increase in the cost of litigation." Fed. R. Civ. P. 11. The district judge here explicitly declined to make any such finding. His remark that the case "offered no hope whatsoever of success, and plain-tiffs' attorneys surely knew it" is not an appropriate substitute for the con-clusions required by Rule 11. Even if the district judge's conclusion that appellants' counsel knew that they had no hope of prevailing was cor-rect—a "fact" put in some doubt both by the enormous time and energy expended by counsel in preparation of their case and the expert opinions they were able to assemble on behalf of the legitimacy of their clients' cause of action—that conclusion is still not equivalent to a finding that counsel did not have a "good faith argument for the extension, modification, or reversal of existing law." Surely the propriety of Rule 11 sanctions should not depend on the degree of optimism with which counsel approach liti-gation. The prior panel's conclusion that the district judge had found "in substance" that appellants' counsel had violated Rule 11 was itself, in my view, "clearly erroneous," and the sanctions imposed on the basis of that substituted finding have created a "manifest injustice."

The effect of reaching beyond a district judge's clear exercise of his dis-cretion not to impose Rule 11 sanctions and not to make the specific fact findings required by Rule 11 by reconstructing that decision out of side comments about the likelihood of plaintiffs' prevailing (and counsels' knowledge thereof) cannot but chill well-founded future suits, whose time in the law may not yet have come, but whose value in exposing abuses and educating courts and the public is substantial. Cognizant that the district judge had no realistic choice but to impose sanctions on remand, I dissent from the result which our prior decision required of him.

### Note: Lawyers for Causes

One of the lawyers sanctioned in this case was Ramsey Clark, a former Attorney General of the United States. Here is his professional biography, reprinted from Martindale-Hubbell Law Directory, a selective directory of practicing lawyers:

> *RAMSEY CLARK*, born Dallas, Texas, December 18, 1927; admitted to bar, 1951, Texas; 1956, U.S. Supreme Court; 1969, District of Columbia; 1970, New York. *Education:* University of Texas (B.A., 1949); University of Chicago (M.A., 1950; J.D., 1950). Assistant Attorney General, 1961-1964, Deputy Attorney General, 1965-1966 and Attorney General of the United States, 1967-1969.
> *General Civil and Criminal Practice. Constitutional Trials and Appeals.*

Why would a man with this impeccable resume bring a case like *Saltany*, which had so little chance of success? Do you think that if the 1993 version of the Rule applied, and defendants had warned Mr. Clark of their inten-tion to seek sanctions, he would have used the so-called safe harbor and withdrawn the complaint?

Your political view of whether bombing is a "proper" response to state-sponsored terrorism influences whether you think the case was properly filed, doesn't it? Brian L. Davis, in Quaddafi, Terrorism and the Origins of the U.S. Attack on Libya (1990), argues strongly that bombing with a high risk of hitting civilian populations is misguided policy and wrong morally. Should a lawyer deciding whether to take a case read up on its moral and political implications?

Generally speaking, when you think of yourself as a lawyer deciding whether to take a case that reaches beyond disputes between individuals, what factors enter your decision? Would the fact that the clients have an arguable claim and are able to pay handsomely for representation be enough to induce you to take the case?

There is a long-standing professional norm of providing legal services without attempting to prejudge the moral, political, or ideological merits of a case. Scholars refer to this as the neutrality norm, the service norm, or, more precisely, "thin professional identity." Norman W. Spaulding, Reinterpreting Professional Identity, 74 U. Colo. L. Rev. 1 (2003). It reflects both a professional ideal of diligently serving all who require legal services (or at least all who require services for the purpose of bringing *non-frivolous* claims) and two practical considerations: First, because human judgment is fallible, lawyers are likely to misjudge a case or client, particularly at the outset when they know little about the specific facts. Second, if lawyers prejudge cases, popular, or at least well-paying and uncontroversial, clients will likely enjoy meaningful access to the law, but others will not—both the quantity of clients served and the quality of client service provided would vary according to the preferences of individual lawyers. The rules of professional conduct generally endorse the service norm, see ABA Model Rule 1.2(b), but they do not require it. A lawyer is *encouraged* to be open to take all clients she can competently serve, especially clients who cannot afford to pay, and clients whose claims are controversial and who may therefore have trouble finding another lawyer. But, excepting court-ordered appointment, a lawyer generally cannot be *sanctioned* for refusing a case. In practice, this means lawyers are free to pick and choose.

Another tradition endorses "cause lawyering"—not only allowing, but encouraging, lawyers to seek out (or refuse) cases based on moral, political, and ideological criteria or personal identification with a client and/or her cause. It too reflects the professional ideal of expanding access to legal services. Many cause lawyers have dedicated themselves to serving clients others will not, either because the clients cannot pay, or because they are members of marginalized social groups, or, as is all too often the case, both. See Austin Sarat and Stuart Scheingold, Cause Lawyering: Political Commitments and Professional Responsibilities (1998).

Anthony D'Amato argues, in The Imposition of Sanctions for Claims Arising from the U.S. Air Raid on Libya, 84 Am. J. Int'l L. 705 (1990), that the underlying claims in *Saltany* were strong ones, and that it was wrong in the face of international law precedent to dismiss the case summarily. As to the sanctions against the plaintiffs' lawyers, he notes:

It may very well be true that there was no hope of success in a case brought before these particular judges. The three-judge panel on appeal consisted of judges who had all been appointed by President Reagan. The complaint accused President Reagan of being a war criminal. It is not unreasonable to suppose that such judges would view the complaint with abhorrence and disgust.

Id. at 707. Are hopeless claims the same as frivolous ones? Are lawsuits in federal courts one way to express political opinion and dissent? Or is this an improper purpose?

Indeed, you might wonder why an "improper purpose" should matter if the underlying claim is nonfrivolous. Is this language in Rule 11 superfluous? Or does it only seem so as it applies to complaints, versus other pleadings governed by Rule 11? Compare Sussman v. Bank of Israel (Appeal of Lewin), 56 F.3d 450 (2d Cir. 1995) (holding that a party should not be sanctioned for filing a nonfrivolous complaint simply because one of his multiple motives in filing it may have been improper), with F.D.I.C. v. Maxxam, Inc., 523 F.3d 566 (5th Cir. 2008) (plaintiff "would violate Rule 11 if it filed a case that it reasonably thought had merit, but pursued it in a manner calculated to increase the costs of defense," rejecting view that "the filing of a paper for an improper purpose is immunized from Rule 11 sanctions simply because it is well grounded in fact and law"), and Szabo Food Serv., Inc. v. Canteen Corp., 823 F.2d 1073, 1083 (7th Cir. 1987) (stating that "filing a colorable suit for the purpose of imposing expense on the defendant rather than for the purpose of winning" is sanctionable under Rule 11). But see Townsend v. Holman Consulting Corp., 929 F.2d 1358, 1362 (9th Cir. 1990) (holding that "a determination of improper purpose must be supported by a determination of frivolousness when a complaint is at issue").

## Note: Post-Pleading Improper Purposes

The *Saltany* cases involve attempts to get in the courthouse door. But the obligations of Rule 11 do not end with the pleadings. The Rule covers not just pleadings, but as the O'Brien court discussed, every "written motion, and other paper" presented to the court. So sanctions can be imposed for "later advocating" any prior filing. See Rule 11(b). Consider Whitehead v. Food Max of Mississippi, Inc., 332 F.3d 796 (5th Cir. 2003) (en banc). After winning a $3.4 million jury verdict against Kmart for negligently failing to provide adequate parking lot security (the plaintiff and her daughter were abducted from a Kmart parking lot in Jackson, Mississippi), plaintiff's lawyer used a handwritten request to obtain a writ of execution from the clerk of the court before Kmart had a chance to appeal. He then notified the media and proceeded to the nearest Kmart with two federal Marshalls in order to seize money from the cash registers and store vault. Although interrupted by a stay order from the court once it learned of the lawyer's conduct, the lawyer proceeded to give statements to the media about

Kmart's "outrageous" and "arrogant" actions and claimed that Kmart had refused to pay the judgment. Id. at 800. The district court fined the lawyer $8,000 (Kmart's attorneys' fees for opposing the writ of execution) and the Fifth Circuit affirmed, reasoning that shameless self-promotion and deliberately seeking to embarrass Kmart were improper purposes within the meaning of Rule 11(b)(1). In his defense, the lawyer claimed that "almost everything an attorney in litigation does . . . is designed to embarrass an opponent in one way or another" and "establishing a reputation for success in the representation of clients is the most professional way for a lawyer to build a practice," id. at 807. The court categorically rejected this argument:

> The execution did not require Minor to accompany the two United States Marshalls to the Kmart (especially where, as here, the involved property was well-known, open, and obvious). See Fed. R. Civ. P. 69. And, the execution certainly did not require the media's presence at the Kmart or the improper comments Minor made there to the media.

Id. at 806-807. Notice that the improper purpose here is not the content of the lawyer's written application for a writ of execution, but rather the conduct incident to enforcing the writ. Cf. *Christian,* supra.

Would your view of the case change if it turned out that plaintiff was not even legally entitled to a writ of execution when her lawyer applied for it? See id. at 800, 803-804 (Kmart claimed, and the district court agreed, that Kmart was entitled to an automatic ten-day stay of execution; the Fifth Circuit held that improper purpose was sufficient ground for sanction and declined to consider, as an additional ground, whether the application for the writ was based on a reasonable inquiry into the law).

A postscript: In a separate opinion, the Fifth Circuit reversed the jury verdict and remanded for a new trial because it found that the jury was unduly influenced by the "passion and prejudice" of the plaintiff's lawyer's closing argument. See Whitehead v. Food Max of Miss., Inc., 163 F.3d 265, 276-281 (5th Cir. 1998).

## 3. "Warranted by Existing Law . . ."

### *Frantz v. U.S. Powerlifting Federation*
836 F.2d 1063 (7th Cir. 1987)

EASTERBROOK, CIRCUIT JUDGE.

The complaint charged the International Powerlifting Federation (IPF), its American affiliate the United States Powerlifting Federation (USPF), and Conrad Cotter, the president of the USPF, with conspiring to monopolize the sport of weight lifting. The plaintiffs include two weight lifters who were disqualified from participating in events sponsored by the IPF because they participated in events sponsored by the American Powerlifting Federation (APF), a rival to the USPF. . . .

The IPF did not file an appearance, and a default judgment was entered against it. The district court dismissed the complaint against the USPF and Cotter under Fed. R. Civ. P. 12(b)(6) for failure to state a claim on which relief may be granted, after plaintiffs' counsel conceded that the complaint was insufficient. The plaintiffs then filed an amended complaint against USPF, dropping Cotter as a defendant. The district court dismissed this complaint under Rule 12(b)(6), finding it dependent on a theory of conspiracy between the USPF and the IPF that could not be sustained. The court also held that Cotter is entitled to attorneys' fees as a sanction under Fed. R. Civ. P. 11 for the initial complaint against him, because the plaintiffs did not have a plausible argument about how the USPF could conspire with its officers. The court denied the USPF's request for sanctions, however, because it concluded that the plaintiffs' amended complaint had a colorable, though unsuccessful, theory.

Cotter's request for fees came to $44,700: $4,300 to obtain dismissal of the initial complaint, and $40,400 to pursue the request for fees (and ask the district court to ensure that the amended complaint did not apply to him). The size of the request surprised—shocked—the district judge. The court vacated its award under Rule 11, writing:

> Sanctions were awarded because it was extremely clear to the court that there was no legal or factual basis for naming Cotter as a defendant. Cotter's attorneys, however, contend that they have spent at least 39.535 hours drafting that portion of the motion to dismiss, memorandum in support of the motion and summary of the motion which pertained to Cotter. They have requested $4,289.48 in fees as to this activity (they also request an additional $40,401.40 in legal fees). Apparently, the issues regarding Cotter's legal and factual involvement in the case were vastly more complicated than this court had determined. . . . Therefore, the court is sua sponte reconsidering the award . . . and is hereby denying the award of attorneys' fees in toto.

Cotter appeals from the vacation of the award in his favor, and the USPF appeals the denial of its request for sanctions.

I

The suit against Cotter was frivolous, given Copperweld Corp. v. Independence Tube Corp., 467 U.S. 752 (1984), decided a year before this suit began. Rule 11 requires counsel to do legal research before filing, and to be aware of legal rules established by the Supreme Court. A party may not strike out blindly and rely on its opponent to do the research to make the case or expose its fallacies. . . .

The court vacated the sanction because the request for fees showed that counsel spent about 40 hours preparing and filing the motion to dismiss. This showed, according to the court, that the case was "vastly more complicated" than the court had believed. Perhaps this is a droll way to say that Cotter's total bill was out of line. We consider this possibility later. If the court meant the remark seriously, it is insufficient. Whether the complaint violated Rule 11 depends on what the plaintiffs and their lawyer did—whether they performed the legal and factual work necessary to avoid filing an unwarranted paper—not on what the defendants did with the complaint. That the defendants may have taken too long to find *Copperweld* does not absolve plaintiffs; the violation of Rule 11 exists at the moment the paper is filed. If Cotter's lawyers were inefficient, then Cotter must pay them (or counsel must swallow the costs, as counsel who waste time recognize when exercising billing judgment). The defendants' inefficiency does not show that the case was "vastly more complex" than the district court first thought. *Copperweld* holds that corporate officers cannot conspire with their corporations for purposes of the antitrust laws. The complaint was based on a conspiracy between officer and corporation; this was doomed after *Copperweld,* and sanctions were in order.

For what it is worth, we doubt that 40 hours is preposterous for preparing a response to this complaint. Cotter's lawyers had to find *Copperweld* and then consider the possibility that plaintiffs were trying to create an exception to that case. This might entail researching the treatment of *Copperweld* in later cases and interviewing Cotter, a resident of Florida, to discover whether there were facts (and therefore a theory) lurking behind the outline provided by the complaint. Antitrust suits are easy to file yet notoriously costly to defend, and achieving the dismissal of an antitrust case in under 40 hours is unusual.

What is even more unusual is that counsel took about 400 hours to pursue the compensation for 40 hours, a ratio of billing time to productive time that would be fatal when collecting from one's own clients. The request for sanctions was an adversarial proceeding, which eats up time that need not be spent when collecting from friendlier clients, but a ratio of ten to one still is extreme. The district court was entitled to be skeptical of this bill. . . .

The complaint in this case was frivolous, which calls at a minimum for censure of Victor D. Quilici, the plaintiffs' lawyer. Whether it calls for amercement—and, if so, whether Cotter or the Treasury is the appropriate beneficiary—is something the district court should consider as an initial matter. . . .

There is no single "right" sanction, any more than there is one "right" penalty for bank robbery. Much must be left to the good judgment of the courts of first instance. . . . Because this case involved a request for a tidy sum, the court should explain why it chose to equate the two sanctions (if that remains its disposition after reconsideration). . . . [A]n explanation need not be complex, and a judge need not pretend that there is a single right answer that can be reached by deductive logic or defended with precision. The absence of ineluctable answers does not imply the privilege to indulge an unexamined gestalt. This case must be remanded so that the district court may put its reasoning on record—a process that, by inducing critical scrutiny of one's initial reactions, often improves the quality of decisions.

## II

The district court rejected outright the USPF's request for attorneys' fees under Rule 11[, saying] only this about the USPF's request for sanctions under Rule 11:

> The allegations of seven types of anticompetitive conduct by the USPF and the IPF are largely conclusory. However, there are at least a few facts in the complaint which describe the anti-competitive conduct. Although it is difficult to determine the exact nature of the alleged anti-competitive conduct in the absence of greater specificity, the allegations on the whole appear to be based on plausible legal theories.

The court appears to be making two points. One is that if a complaint contains any formally correct statement of a legal theory, then the pleader's obligation under Rule 11 has been satisfied. This is incorrect. A claim may be sufficient in form but sanctionable because, for example, counsel failed to conduct a reasonable investigation before filing. And the inclusion of one sufficient (and adequately investigated) claim does not permit counsel to file a stream of unsubstantiated claims as riders.

Each claim takes up the time of the legal system and the opposing side. A single claim in an antitrust case may occasion the expenditure of hundreds or thousands of hours, as opposing counsel try to verify or refute the allegations and theories. Rule 18(a) permits the liberal joinder of claims, but each joined claim, potentially the basis of separate litigation, must have a foundation—the same foundation it would have needed if the claims had been pursued separately. Just as evidence that Perkins is a thief does not justify an accusation that he is a murderer, so a colorable legal theory about boycotts of weight lifters does not excuse a baseless allegation about price fixing in the television business. Rule 11 applies to all statements in papers it covers. Each claim must have sufficient support; each must be investigated and researched before filing.

The court's other point is that the complaint contains sufficient facts from which the judge may discern the legal claims. The USPF takes issue with this, arguing that the complaint was shy the necessary facts. The USPF's reply brief asserts: "This court has made clear that even if Mr. Quilici possessed sufficient information in his files to support plaintiffs' claims, his failure to include it in the complaint violated Rule 11." The USPF does not cite the cases where we "made clear" this proposition. There aren't any such cases. The USPF has confused Rule 8 with Rule 11. Rule 8 determines how much information has to be in the complaint—not much, as both the language of Rule 8 and the forms attached to the Rules show. The complaint should contain a "short and plain statement of the claim showing that the pleader is entitled to relief," Rule 8(a)(2). It is not only unnecessary but also undesirable to plead facts beyond limning the nature of the claim (with exceptions, see Rule 9, that do not concern us). Bloated, argumentative pleadings are a bane of modern practice. American Nurses' Assn. v.

Illinois, 783 F.2d 716 (7th Cir. 1986). Rule 11 requires not that counsel *plead* facts but that counsel *know* facts after conducting a reasonable investigation—and then only enough to make it reasonable to press litigation to the point of seeking discovery. Rule 11 neither modifies the "notice pleading" approach of the federal rules nor requires counsel to prove the case in advance of discovery. See also Szabo [Food Servs. v. Canteen Corp., 823 F.2d 1073 (7th Cir. 1987)] (Rule 11 requires only an "outline of a case" before filing the complaint, though it does require enough investigation to discover that outline).

This is a fine line. Rule 11 must not bar the courthouse door to people who have some support for a complaint but need discovery to prove their case, yet the need for discovery does not excuse the filing of a vacuous complaint. No matter how such inquiries come out, however, courts must ask the right question: whether the side filing the pleading knew enough at the time, not whether it spread all on the record. Rule 11 states that the signature verifies that the paper is "well grounded in fact," not that all the facts are contained in the paper.

The case is remanded for further inquiry, under the standards of [our previous cases,] into the support for each of the theories contained in the complaint.

*Reversed and Remanded.*


## Note: Nonfrivolous Arguments for Extension of the Law

Read Rule 11(b)(2) about the duty of the lawyer (and parties representing themselves) to get the law right. The pleader who wants to change or extend the law must make a "nonfrivolous" argument for doing so. Previously, the Rule tracked most professional ethics by requiring that lawyers seeking extension, modification, or reversal of existing law do so in "good faith." The Advisory Committee notes that the new wording sets a more objective standard. Do you agree?

In addition to the duty to file only meritorious claims, most codes of professional responsibility also include an injunction to reveal controlling adverse authority to the tribunal. See, e.g., Model Rule 3.3: "A lawyer shall not knowingly: . . . (2) fail to disclose to the tribunal legal authority in the controlling jurisdiction known to the lawyer to be directly adverse to the position of the client and not disclosed by opposing counsel."

For an article about the profession's standards of internal regulation and Rule 11, see Georgene Vairo, Rule 11 and the Profession, 67 Fordham L. Rev. 589 (1998) (finding that Rule 11 replaced bar discipline in many respects and that practice under the 1983 version often decreased civility and professionalism).

*Frantz* was decided under the previous version of the Rule, making the imposition of sanctions mandatory once a Rule 11 violation was found. Would the result have been different under the current version? One difference that flows from changing the mandatory nature of sanctions is the standard of review by the appellate court. When the trial judge has discretion, the appellate court usually reviews for abuse of discretion, rather than for the correctness of the decision. Are there good reasons for putting the main responsibility for administering Rule 11 in the trial judge's hands?

Judge Easterbrook is not the only judge to express surprise at a fee bill submitted by attorneys prevailing on a Rule 11 motion. See Kathrein v. Monar, 218 Fed. Appx. 530 (7th Cir. 2007) (upholding sanctions against plaintiff found to have filed suit against his ex-wife's new husband for the improper purpose of harassing and "runn[ing] up Monar's legal fees," but reversing the $56,858.15 fee award reflecting 200 hours of attorney time as unreasonable for a case dismissed on the pleadings).

## 4.  "Factual Contentions Have Evidentiary Support"

### Young v. City of Providence ex rel. Napolitano
404 F.3d 33 (1st Cir. 2005)

BOUDIN, CHIEF JUDGE.

In the course of a civil rights action, the district court determined that three attorneys for the plaintiff had violated Rule 11 of the Federal Rules of Civil Procedure. The court revoked the pro hac vice status of the two attorneys who were not members of the court's bar and formally censured one of the two. Young v. City of Providence, 301 F. Supp. 2d 187 (D.R.I. 2004). In this decision, we address appeals by all three attorneys; the merits of the civil rights action are the subject of the plaintiff's separate appeal resolved in our companion decision issued today *sub nom.*

The civil rights action grew out of a tragedy that occurred in January 2000 in Providence, Rhode Island. Two police officers (Michael Solitro and Carlos Saraiva), responding to the scene of a nighttime disturbance at a restaurant, shot and killed an off-duty officer—Cornel Young, Jr., who, with his weapon drawn, was attempting to assist them. In June 2001, Young's mother, acting on her own behalf and as executor of Young's estate, brought a civil rights action in district court asserting claims under section 1983, 42 U.S.C. § 1983 (2000), and under state law, against the city, various officials and the two officers.

The case, assigned to Judge Mary Lisi, was a complex one. This was due in part to the difficulty in reconstructing exactly what had happened in the nighttime encounter, in part to the different tiers of liability asserted against various defendants (direct, supervisory and municipal) and in part to plaintiff's aim to show a pattern or policy of incompetent hiring and inadequate training. Both Barry Scheck and Nicholas Brustin of the New York firm of Cochran, Neufeld & Scheck LLP were admitted pro hac vice to represent the plaintiff; Robert Mann of the Providence firm of Mann & Mitchell acted as local counsel. Scheck was admitted, to replace his partner Johnnie Cochran, Jr., only in September 2003—shortly before a "phase I" trial was to begin focusing on the conduct of Solitro and Saraiva.

The litigation was the subject of extensive publicity; among other facets, the officers who fired the shots were white while Cornel Young was black (and the son of a senior Providence police officer). Scheck, who acted as lead counsel after his admission, was at odds with the district judge over various matters, including the division of the trial into two phases. Yet the incident that gave rise to the Rule 11 findings, censure and revocation of pro hac vice status was narrowly focused and arose against the following background.

By September 2003, extensive discovery had been conducted. One of the issues in the discovery, and in the ensuing trial, concerned the precise movements of Cornel Young and of Solitro. The former had been inside the restaurant; Solitro and Saraiva had approached the building through the parking lot to find a man (later identified as Aldrin Diaz, who had caused an earlier disturbance) pointing a gun out of the window of a Chevrolet Camaro parked in the lot in front of the restaurant. Solitro broke cover and started toward the car. Young, moving to assist, emerged from the restaurant with his own weapon drawn and was shot by Solitro and Saraiva. Just where Young and Solitro had stood and moved had a bearing on who was at fault in the episode.

During discovery, Solitro had drawn a line indicating his own movement in relation to other physical landmarks including the Camaro; the line was drawn on a clear overlay laid atop a made-to-scale diagram prepared by the state attorney general in his own investigation. Scheck planned to rely importantly on the diagram in his opening to explain to the jury the defense version of what had happened. However, in September 2003, out-takes filmed by a local TV station on the night of the shooting became available and, from defense counsel's viewpoint, raised questions about the accuracy of the diagram—at least as to the location of the Camaro. Until then it had apparently been expected that both sides would agree to the admission of the diagram.

At the final pre-trial conference on September 19, 2003, the district court was told briefly that there was a dispute about the diagram. . . . Defense counsel then told the district judge that the defense objected to the diagram as inconsistent with photographs made from the out-takes, and the judge responded that the parties should confer to see whether they could stipulate as to the matter. The judge told plaintiff's counsel: "If you can't agree to a stipulation on that, then I'm going to have to tell you to stay away from it because you're going to need testimony to explain it to the jury."

Scheck then offered as a compromise to stipulate that the diagram conflicted with photographs made from the film out-takes, but the next morning defense counsel declined the offer. Scheck again sought unsuccessfully to persuade the judge that he ought to be allowed to refer to the diagram in the opening. Then, with the opening statements about to begin, Scheck signed a stipulation drafted by defense counsel that the diagram was inaccurate as to the location of the Camaro and that the actual alignment of the car was as described in the stipulation. On this basis, Scheck was allowed to use the diagram in the opening, but he was not allowed thereafter to elicit testimony contradicting the stipulation.

Over the next several days of trial, further examination of the photographs persuaded Scheck and his colleagues that the out-takes did not contradict the diagram. A young associate at Scheck's firm was told to draft a memorandum to support a motion seeking relief from the stipulation on grounds of mistake. The memorandum was filed with the court on October 16, 2003 in mid-trial, after being reviewed and then signed by all three counsel—Scheck, Brustin and Mann. That same morning the judge directed counsel to re-read the memorandum, saying that she was disturbed by representations made in the memorandum, "particularly as they relate to the actions of the court."

The memorandum, set forth in full at 301 F. Supp. 2d at 199-204, started with an introductory paragraph that conflated the earlier events by saying that counsel had believed prior to trial that the diagram could be used at trial and then continued:

> It was only on the eve of opening statements, once plaintiff had prepared her entire opening based on that stipulation, that defendants first said they would not stipulate to Exhibit 18, based on two new photographs they had found, Exhibits X and Y. Plaintiff, moments before her opening, was informed by the Court she had to agree to defendants' stipulation. Plaintiff was genuinely confused about the import of photographs X and Y. Plaintiff's opening relied critically on using that exhibit to explain events to the jury. In this state of confusion and uncertainty, plaintiff felt little choice but to accept any stipulation defendant provided.

Id. at 200.

Thereafter, the memorandum provided a much more detailed recitation of events, together with legal arguments to justify relief from the stipulation entered into in such circumstances. Later, the memorandum blamed defense counsel for rejecting Scheck's October 7 compromise stipulation, adding that "[u]nder the circumstances, plaintiff had no choice but to sign a stipulation without any chance to review the photographs at issue." Id. at 208. It there quoted a well known treatise that "'courts will look at the facts carefully to see that one litigant has not been coerced into the stipulation.'" Id. at 208 n.5 (quoting 22 Wright & Graham, Federal Practice and Procedure § 5194 (1978)).

After filing the motion and then hearing the judge's statement that she was disturbed by its representations, plaintiff's counsel returned to their office after the trial ended for the day and, assertedly unable to determine what had so troubled the judge, prepared a letter of general apology, which was immediately delivered to court. It apologized for any misstatement and said that "we do not seek to shift responsibility to the Court [for the stipulation], and if we have created a contrary impression, we are sorry." It did not withdraw any specific statement; plaintiff's counsel's position is that at that time they did not fully appreciate what had so concerned the district judge.

The following morning, during argument on the motion for relief from the stipulation, the judge made clear her view that "the reference [in the memorandum] to the Court instructing you that you had to stipulate is, again, a misrepresentation." Scheck now sought to explain that he had been misunderstood, but the judge denied the motion for relief from the stipulation. Later that day the court called counsel before it and ruled that, based on the memorandum's misrepresentation, the pro hac vice admissions of Scheck and Brustin were revoked. Mann was directed to proceed to represent plaintiff at the trial. The trial proceeded to its completion and to a final judgment on February 12, 2004. [One of the two officers was found to have used excessive force.]

After the trial but before final judgment was entered, the district court on November 7, 2003, issued a show cause order to the three plaintiff's counsel. The order said that all three counsel had violated Rule 11(b)(3) and directed the parties to show cause why sanctions should not be imposed. Counsel filed a memorandum and affidavits arguing that they had had no deceptive intent and that, read as a whole and in context, their memorandum asking to withdraw the stipulation had not misrepresented any facts. The Rhode Island Bar Association filed an amicus brief in support of the lawyers; the ACLU also sought unsuccessfully to do so. . . .

[T]he Rule 11 findings focused solely upon two specific "misrepresentations" in the memorandum: one was the above block-quoted language including the key statement that "[p]laintiff, moments before her opening, was informed by the Court she had to agree to defendants' stipulation." 301 F. Supp. 2d at 200. The other was the statement that defense counsel "had no choice" but to sign the stipulation without any chance to review the photographs. Id. at 208. Both statements, said the court, falsely indicated that the court had ordered the stipulation to be signed; and, the court noted, the memorandum's references to injustice and coercion gave the impression that the court was responsible for such wrongs.

The court accepted that the memorandum had been drafted by a young associate and that plaintiff's counsel had denied instructing the younger lawyer to say that the court had directed the stipulation. However, the court said that plaintiff's counsel were responsible under Rule 11 for statements made in a memorandum that they had reviewed and signed. Assessing relative responsibility, the court sanctioned Scheck by imposing "a public censure," 301 F. Supp. 2d at 198; Brustin, an associate whom the court said took direction from Scheck, was merely "admonished" to be more careful, id.; and as to Mann, whose role was ascribed to "inattention," id. at 199, the court said that his reputation in Rhode Island for integrity was well established and a sanction was unnecessary to deter repetition.

All three of plaintiff's counsel have appealed from the order determining that they committed Rule 11 violations, and Scheck and Brustin have asked that their censure and admonition be overturned and their pro hac vice status restored. . . .

Rule 11(b) is not a strict liability provision. It prohibits filings made with "any improper purpose," the offering of "frivolous" arguments, and the assertion of factual allegations without "evidentiary support" or the "likely" prospect of such support. A lawyer who makes an inaccurate factual representation must, at the very least, be culpably careless to commit a violation. See Fed. R. Civ. P. 11(b) (requiring that factual contentions have evidentiary support only "to the best of the person's knowledge, information, and belief, formed after an inquiry reasonable under the circumstances"). The question presented by plaintiff's counsel's first argument is whether something more than falsity and serious carelessness is required; counsel contend that where the court itself initiates the Rule 11 inquiry, the conduct must involve "situations that are akin to a contempt of court." The phrase is taken from an Advisory Committee's Note, to which we will return.

This distinction urged by plaintiff's counsel is at odds with the plain language of Rule 11. Rule 11(b), creating duties, sets out the substantive obligations of counsel (e.g., that factual claims must have evidentiary support or a likely prospect of it) without in any way suggesting that the substantive obligations differ depending on whether a later claim of violation is raised by opposing counsel or the court. Nor is it obvious why anyone would wish such duties governing "primary conduct" to depend on who might thereafter raise objections in a remedial proceeding. . . .

The only hint of such a distinction as to the substantive standard appears in the Advisory Committee's Note, which explains the absence of a safe harbor for court-initiated inquiries as follows: "Since show cause orders will ordinarily be issued only in situations that are akin to a contempt of court, the rule does not provide a [comparable] 'safe harbor' [to withdraw the objected-to statement]." This language has, indeed, been taken by several circuits as suggesting that only egregious conduct can be reached where the court begins the inquiry,[4] but we think mistaken any inference that this language requires malign subjective intent.

It is true that courts ought not invoke Rule 11 for slight cause; the wheels of justice would grind to a halt if lawyers everywhere were sanctioned every time they made unfounded objections, weak arguments, and dubious factual claims. However, this is an argument for requiring serious misconduct, whoever initiated the inquiry into a violation—not for distinguishing between the judge and opposing counsel. The "akin to contempt" language used by the Advisory Committee's Note may well have meant only that no safe harbor was needed because judges would act only in the face of serious misconduct.

A specific purpose of the 1993 revision of Rule 11 was to reject such a bad faith requirement. See Advisory Committee's Note saying that the amendments were "intended to eliminate any 'empty-head pure-heart' justification for patently frivolous arguments." Since then only one circuit court has read the present rule to require bad faith, In re Pennie & Edmonds LLP, 323

---

4. See Kaplan v. DaimlerChrysler, A.G., 331 F.3d 1251, 1255-56 (11th Cir. 2003); In re Pennie & Edmonds LLP, 323 F.3d 86, 90-93 (2d Cir. 2003); Hunter v. Earthgrains Co. Bakery, 281 F.3d 144, 151, 153 (4th Cir. 2002); United Nat'l Ins. Co. v. R & D Latex Corp., 242 F.3d 1102, 1115, 1118 (9th Cir. 2001).

F.3d 86, 90-93 (2d Cir. 2003), and it did so in the teeth of a strong dissent, id. at 93-102. True, judges must be especially careful where they are both prosecutor and judge; but careful appellate review is the answer to this concern, whether the charge is negligence or deliberate dishonesty and whether it is contempt or a Rule 11 violation. If anything, opposing counsel has far greater incentive than the trial judge to invoke Rule 11 for slight cause.

We come, then, to the question whether the two objected-to statements in the memorandum were false and, if so, sufficiently careless to warrant sanction. The trial judge read both statements to suggest that the court had forced plaintiff's counsel to sign the stipulation. In our view, read as a whole, the memorandum makes it clear that the judge did not require that the stipulation be signed but only said that a stipulation was a condition to use of the diagram in Scheck's opening statement—which is entirely accurate. There is some warrant for criticism of the memorandum but the central charge of falsity on which the Rule 11 findings rest cannot be sustained, so the issue of carelessness disappears.

The first paragraph of the memorandum (block-quoted above) did say that plaintiff was informed at the opening that "she had to agree to defendants' stipulation," omitting to add the phrase "in order to use the diagram in the opening argument." But the memorandum soon makes it explicitly clear that the judge required the stipulation only in the sense that it was a condition of using the diagram in the opening. Describing the events of October 8 after defense counsel rejected Scheck's stipulation, the memorandum states: "The Court instructed plaintiff again that the exhibit could be only used under stipulation."

As for the second quotation objected to by the judge—the statement that "plaintiff had no choice but to sign a stipulation"—the memorandum did not assert that the judge had directed Scheck to sign; indeed, the statement followed immediately after the memorandum's statement that defendants had rejected the Scheck stipulation "minutes before the opening" (in which, as the memorandum had already explained, the diagram was crucial to Scheck's planned presentation). "Forced" refers to these circumstances and not to any directive from the judge that Scheck sign the stipulation.

The main problem in this memorandum is that in the introductory summary the drafter took as an unexplained premise what the lawyers and the judge full well knew: that the judge had made clear, before the fatal stipulation was signed, that a disputed document could not be used in the opening argument absent a stipulation. Yet, as we have just seen, even this premise is made explicit later in the memorandum. The general rule is that statements must be taken in context, United States v. Moran, 393 F.3d 1, 16 (1st Cir. 2004), and that related parts of a document must be taken together, Nadherny v. Roseland Property Co., 390 F.3d 44, 49 (1st Cir. 2004). That a hasty reader might take the first paragraph out of context is not in the present circumstances enough to brand the memorandum as false.

We are not suggesting that a deliberate lie would be immune to sanction merely because corrective language can be found buried somewhere else in the document. But here the trial judge did not find, and in these circumstances could not have found, that plaintiff's counsel had intended to deceive. The memorandum was drafted under pressure, by a younger lawyer not admitted as counsel in the case; and it was reviewed and signed by Mann, whose established reputation and integrity the opinion praises, and by Brustin, whose trial conduct is also approved of by the judge in her decision. Nor, of course, can anyone suppose that the judge would have been misled as to what she herself had earlier directed.

As it happens, the memorandum may otherwise have been misleading or inaccurate in certain of its detail. If one accepts the account of defense counsel at the show cause hearing, the memorandum left out both the fact of prior warnings from defense counsel that they were concerned about the diagram and the fact that the photographs themselves were furnished to Brustin on September 25 or 26. By omitting such detail, the memorandum enhances the "surprise" element tincturing the memorandum's gloss on the events of October 7 and 8 ("for the first time," "last minute choice"). Further, assuming that the photographs were provided on September 25 or 26, the memorandum's statement that the stipulation was signed "without any chance to review the photographs at issue" is doubtful; perhaps Scheck meant only that he had not focused on the issue but it would have been better to say that.

However, the district court made no definitive findings as to what warnings were given and when. The basis for the Rule 11 charges was the suggestion that the judge had required the stipulation. We also do not know how far defense counsel had gone, prior to receiving the out-takes, in leading plaintiff's counsel to believe that the diagram was common ground. Nor can we tell how far Scheck was involved in trial preparations before his last-minute pro hac vice appearance. The final period before a large trial, like the trial itself, involves late nights, multiplying tasks and resulting confusions that are hard to imagine for one who has not experienced them. The burden upon the trial judge is scarcely less.

The district judge is well known for both patience and care. It is easy to imagine why, in the course of a tense and contentious trial, she was greatly displeased at a document, emblazoned with references to injustice, that could be publicly read as blaming the trial judge for what had patently been plaintiff's counsel's own miscalculation. But on a close reading and a consideration of all the circumstances, the memorandum taken as a whole did no more than say, albeit inartfully, that the trial judge had required the stipulation to be signed as a condition of using the diagram in the opening.

Accordingly, the findings that plaintiff's counsel violated Rule 11 cannot stand; and, as those findings are the only grounds for the censure, admonition and revocation of pro hac vice status, they too must be undone. The findings of Rule 11 violations are set aside, the sanction and admonition are vacated, and the pro hac vice status of Scheck and Brustin is restored. No costs.

*It is so ordered.*

## Note: Tension Between Zealous and Accurate Advocacy?

At first glance *Young* seems to be about factual assertions that took on exaggerated significance—first in the eyes of the plaintiff, then in the eyes of the trial judge. The judge appears to have become quite upset about the implication that she forced the hand of plaintiff's counsel with respect to evidence central to his case. The appellate court, from a distance, seems to have recognized that the trial was heated, that things might have gotten overblown, and that innocent mistakes (mistakes that do not bespeak *over-*zealous advocacy) can happen under the pressure of trial.

Rule 11(b)(3) cases typically concern misrepresentations about facts in the world material to the merits of the case, not misrepresentations of prior statements made by the trial judge. There is, however, a hint that what was really at stake in *Young* was concern about misrepresentations about facts in the world—indeed, the fact most material to this case: the precise location of the threat that caused the white officers to shoot their plainclothes colleague. The appellate court seems to have recognized that the ultimate difference of opinion had more to do with the accuracy of the diagram that was the subject of the contested eve-of-trial stipulation than with anything the judge said. But without specific findings on what prior representations the lawyers made to the court and to each other regarding the accuracy of the diagram, the appellate court could not get to the bottom of the matter. Hence the reversal.

It is clear that if either side knew the diagram was false, introducing it at trial would be sanctionable misconduct. But the real issue here seems to have been that defendants either knew the diagram to be accurate, as the testimony at trial tended to confirm, or they knew the diagram would be inculpating (whether accurate or not). Does their resistance to the stipulation that plaintiff's counsel initially sought trouble you? What about factual contentions about the video out-take photographs in support of that resistance? For the result on remand, see Young v. City of Providence, 396 F. Supp. 2d (D.R.I. 2005) (denying defendants motion for summary judgment on qualified immunity).

## Note: Factual Contentions Versus Inferences

Does the requirement that factual contentions have evidentiary support prohibit attorneys from on relying on inferences? In Lucas v. Duncan, 574 F.3d 772 (D.C. Cir. 2009), John Karl represented the plaintiff Theodore Lucas, an employee who claimed he was denied a promotion because of his age in violation of the Age Discrimination in Employment Act (ADEA). Defendant's summary judgment motion was referred to a magistrate judge who recommended denial of the motion. However, the magistrate judge imposed a $3,000 sanction upon Karl for failing to label his inferences as inferences and failing to present material adverse facts in his opposition to the motion for summary judgment. See Lucas v. Spellings, 408 F. Supp. 2d 8, 13 (D.D.C. 2006) (concluding that Karl's statements "obliterate again and again the distinction between drawing an inference and stating a fact").

The D.C. Circuit reversed, emphasizing that "[t]here is no basis in the text of Rule 11(b)(3) for the legal proposition that an attorney must separately identify 'fact' and 'inference.'" *Lucas*, 574 F.3d at 777. The Rule merely requires an attorney to certify that the factual contentions in a paper he presents to the court "have evidentiary support." Fed. R. Civ. P. 11(b)(3). Inferences, the court observed, are a form of circumstantial evidence, and, as the Supreme Court has explained, "'Circumstantial evidence is not only sufficient, but may also be more certain, satisfying and persuasive than direct evidence.'" Id. (quoting Rogers v. Mo. Pac. R.R. Co., 352 U.S. 500, 508 n.17 (1957)).

The D.C. Circuit also rejected the magistrate judge's conclusion that an attorney is obliged to disclose evidence contrary to any factual contentions she makes.

> . . . The pleading at issue here was an opposition to the defendant's motion for summary judgment. The defendant's motion asserted that "there is no genuine issue of material fact precluding the entry of judgment for defendant as a matter of law." Def.'s Mem. in Supp. of Its Mot. for Summ. J. at 1. Under Local Rules 7(h) and 56.1, Karl's obligation in opposing the defendant's motion was to file a separate statement "setting forth all material facts as to which it is contended there exists a genuine issue necessary to be litigated." To do that, Karl was obliged to do no more than set forth facts in contravention of the defendant's claims. The rules do not require him to rehearse the government's evidence, and nothing in Rule 11 imposes that added burden. Nor could the omission of that evidence have been misleading to the reader. Many of the facts that the magistrate judge criticized Karl for failing to disclose in his opposition were contained in the government motion to which he was responding.

Id. at 780.


## Note: De-emphasizing Monetary Sanctions — Turning Down the Heat

The current Rule 11 not only makes sanctions discretionary, even when the judge finds a violation, but also downgrades the award of monetary sanctions. Do you see how the rulemakers do this? See, for example, (c)(4) and think about deterrence as a rationale. Isn't it likely to produce fewer monetary awards than goals of punishment or compensation? What other provisions might make lawyers less likely to file Rule 11 motions?

What sorts of nonmonetary sanctions might a court impose? The advisory committee suggests some possibilities: "striking the offending paper; issuing an admonition, reprimand, or censure; requiring participation in seminars or other educational programs; ordering a fine payable to the court; referring the matter to disciplinary authorities. . . ." Again, trial courts have wide authority in fashioning sanctions. Consider for instance this shaming technique:

> Counsel is admonished about her reliance on [inapplicable case law] and is warned that her advocacy will receive strict scrutiny in future cases. . . .
>
> Counsel is hereby reprimanded for what was at the least a careless reading of the caselaw. She is ordered to show a copy of this Order and Reasons to her supervisor and to certify to this Court that she has done so.

Traina v. United States, 911 F.2d 1155, 1158 (5th Cir. 1990) (holding that this was a severe sanction even under the 1983 version of the Rule).

Note that Rule 11(c)(3) allows the court to impose sanctions on its own initiative (*sua sponte*). What kinds of sanctions may the court impose when it is acting without a motion? Courts that have considered the issue have concluded that the "plain meaning" of the pre-style change Rule 11(c)(2) is that a sanction of attorneys' fees is not permitted. A payment of sanctions may be directed to the court only. See Nuwesra v. Merrill Lynch, Fenner & Smith, Inc., 174 F.3d 87 (2d Cir. 1999); Johnson v. Wadell & Reed, Inc., 74 F.3d 147 (7th Cir. 1995). There is, however, another way for a court to award attorneys' fees in this situation. See Clark v. United Parcel Serv., Inc., 460 F.3d 1004, 1011 (8th Cir. 2006) (upholding award of attorneys' fees under 28 U.S.C. § 1927, in addition to *sua sponte* Rule 11 sanctions, where counsel's conduct was found to be vexatious by the trial court). Plaintiff's counsel in *Clark* filed a 480-page opposition brief replete with misrepresentations and misstatements in response to defendants' summary judgment motion. The Eighth Circuit agreed with the district court that counsel's filing was a deplorable form of "litigation by attrition, wherein *the practitioner's intent* was to force the opposition either to yield to its position or be crushed under a great weight of misstated factual assertions and drowned in a sea of bombast." Id. at 1010-1011.

Should a court be allowed to impose sanctions *sua sponte* when the lawyer has no opportunity to withdraw or correct her sanctionable conduct? Remember that one of the most significant changes in the 1993 Amendments is Rule 11(c)(2), providing a 21-day safe harbor in which attorneys can remedy potentially offending conduct and avoid sanctions. Parties, to be sure, cannot file for sanctions without offering the requisite safe harbor, and this means that any motion for sanctions must be filed at least 21 days before a case ends. See Brickwood Contractors Inc. v. Datanet Engineering Inc., 369 F.3d 385, 389 (4th Cir. 2004) ("Because the rule requires that the party submitting the challenged pleading be given an opportunity to withdraw the pleading, sanctions cannot be sought after summary judgment has been granted."); Barber v. Miller, 146 F.3d 707 (9th Cir. 1998) (disallowing sanctions where Rule 11 motion was filed after complaint dismissed); Ridder v. City of Springfield, 109 F.3d 288 (6th Cir. 1997) (same result where motion was filed after summary judgment granted). See also Rule 11 Advisory

Committee Notes 1993 ("Given the 'safe harbor' provisions . . . a party cannot delay serving its Rule 11 motion until conclusion of the case (or judicial rejection of the offending contention)."). What if the party who receives the sanctions motion does not object when it is deprived of the safe harbor? See *Brickwood Contractors*, 369 F.3d at 395 (noting that "the issue of whether a party has complied with the [safe harbor] rule is subject to forfeiture if not timely raised").

Should the result be different where a court imposes sanctions on its own motion? Recall the First Circuit's discussion of this in *Young*. But see In re Pennie & Edmonds LLP, 323 F.3d 86 (2d Cir. 2003) (court may impose sanctions *sua sponte* even if lawyers had no opportunity to correct their offending submission, but sanctions appropriate only where, as in findings of contempt, lawyers acted in bad faith); *Brickwood Contractors*, 369 F.3d at 389 n.2; *Clark*, 460 F.3d at 1010 (noting that whenever a court acts *sua sponte* to impose Rule 11 sanctions, the new rule should be applied with "particular strictness," but declining to expressly adopt standard set out by the Second Circuit in *In re Pennie & Edmonds LLP*).

## 5.  The Inherent Power to Sanction

Rule 11 is neither the exclusive, nor the most powerful, means for regulating the conduct of lawyers and litigants appearing before a court. In Chambers v. NASCO, Inc., the Supreme Court held that the district court had inherent power to impose a sanction for a party's bad-faith conduct. 501 U.S. 32 (1991). Plaintiff sought specific performance of a contract with Chambers according to which Chambers had agreed to sell a television facility and broadcast license for $18 million. Concerned that the property might be sold to someone else before the complaint was filed and a temporary restraining order put in place, plaintiff's counsel notified Chambers on a Friday that he planned to file a complaint and request for a TRO the following Monday. See Rule 65.

Upon receiving the notice, Chambers scrambled to create a trust in his sister's name and convey the property to the trust for $1.4 million—a fraction of its value. On Monday morning the deeds were recorded before plaintiff's counsel filed the complaint and request for TRO. However, the trustee had not signed the deeds, none of the purchase price had been paid, and Chambers's company retained possession of the facility. With plaintiff's counsel present in court for the TRO motion, the court telephoned counsel for Chambers, A.J. Gray III. When the court asked Mr. Gray whether Chambers was negotiating to sell the property to a third person, "Gray made no mention of the recordation of the deeds earlier that morning." 501 U.S. at 37.

On Tuesday, after Chambers's sister signed the trust documents and made out a $1.4 million note to Chambers's company, Gray informed the court that the property was no longer owned by Chambers and "admitted that he had intentionally withheld information from the court." Id.

at 37. Over the next few days Gray prepared an agreement that allowed Chambers's company to lease the facilities and remain in operation. The court held Chambers in contempt and assessed a fine of $25,000. Undeterred by the TRO and a subsequent preliminary injunction, Chambers continued during the pendency of the litigation to make it impossible for the plaintiff to acquire both the property and the broadcast license. For example, Chambers built a new transmission tower at a different site and applied to the FCC to have the broadcast license promised to the plaintiff transferred to the new tower. Even after the court entered judgment on the merits for plaintiff, Chambers's company filed papers with the FCC opposing transfer of the license to plaintiff and removed equipment from the facility.

Reviewing these incidents and other misconduct, the court imposed a nearly $1 million sanction to compensate plaintiff for its litigation costs. The court concluded that only some of the misconduct involved "false and frivolous" papers covered by Rule 11. Moreover, the defects in some papers did not become apparent until after the trial on the merits. The court not only found Rule 11 insufficient to capture all of Chambers's misconduct, it noted that 28 U.S.C. § 1927 was also inadequate because the statute applies to attorneys and is not broad enough to capture "acts which degrade the judicial system." Id. at 42. That meant the court had to rely on its inherent power in imposing sanctions. Chambers appealed, arguing that legislatively endorsed sanctions such as Rule 11 and § 1927 displace any inherent powers. The Supreme Court rejected this argument and affirmed the sanctions award:

> It has long been understood that "[c]ertain implied powers must necessarily result to our Courts of justice from the nature of their institution," powers "which cannot be dispensed with in a Court, because they are necessary to the exercise of all others." United States v. Hudson, 7 Cranch 32, 34 (1812); see also Roadway Express, Inc. v. Piper, 447 U.S. 752, 764 (1980) (citing *Hudson*). For this reason, "Courts of justice are universally acknowledged to be vested, by their very creation, with power to impose silence, respect, and decorum, in their presence, and submission to their lawful mandates." Anderson v. Dunn, 6 Wheat. 204, 227 (1821); see also Ex parte Robinson, 19 Wall. 505, 510 (1874). These powers are "governed not by rule or statute but by the control necessarily vested in courts to manage their own affairs so as to achieve the orderly and expeditious disposition of cases." Link v. Wabash R. Co., 370 U.S. 626, 630-631 (1962).
>
> . . . For example, the Court has held that a federal court has the power to control admission to its bar and to discipline attorneys who appear before it. See Ex parte Burr, 9 Wheat. 529, 531 (1824). While this power "ought to be exercised with great caution," it is nevertheless "incidental to all Courts." Ibid.
>
> In addition, it is firmly established that "[t]he power to punish for contempts is inherent in all courts." *Robinson*, supra, at 510. This power reaches both conduct before the court and that beyond the court's confines, for "[t]he underlying concern that gave rise to the contempt power was not . . . merely the disruption of court proceedings. Rather, it was disobedience to the orders

of the Judiciary, regardless of whether such disobedience interfered with the conduct of trial." Young v. United States ex rel. Vuitton et Fils S.A., 481 U.S. 787, 798 (1987) (citations omitted).

Of particular relevance here, the inherent power also allows a federal court to vacate its own judgment upon proof that a fraud has been perpetrated upon the court. See Hazel-Atlas Glass Co. v. Hartford-Empire Co., 322 U.S. 238 (1944). This "historic power of equity to set aside fraudulently begotten judgments," *Hazel-Atlas,* 322 U.S. at 245, is necessary to the integrity of the courts, for "tampering with the administration of justice in [this] manner . . . involves far more than an injury to a single litigant. It is a wrong against the institutions set up to protect and safeguard the public." Id. at 246. Moreover, a court has the power to conduct an independent investigation in order to determine whether it has been the victim of fraud. *Universal Oil,* supra, 328 U.S. at 580 . . . .

Because of their very potency, inherent powers must be exercised with restraint and discretion. See *Roadway Express,* supra, 447 U.S. at 764. A primary aspect of that discretion is the ability to fashion an appropriate sanction for conduct which abuses the judicial process. As we recognized in *Roadway Express,* outright dismissal of a lawsuit, which we had upheld in *Link,* is a particularly severe sanction, yet is within the court's discretion. 447 U.S. at 765. Consequently, the "less severe sanction" of an assessment of attorney's fees is undoubtedly within a court's inherent power as well. Ibid.

Indeed, "[t]here are ample grounds for recognizing . . . that in narrowly defined circumstances federal courts have inherent power to assess attorney's fees against counsel," *Roadway Express,* supra, 447 U.S. at 765, even though the so-called American Rule prohibits fee-shifting in most cases. See Alyeska Pipeline Service Co. v. Wilderness Society, 421 U.S. 240, 259 (1975). As we explained in *Alyeska,* these exceptions fall into three categories. The first, known as the "common fund exception," derives not from a court's power to control litigants, but from its historic equity jurisdiction, see Sprague v. Ticonic National Bank, 307 U.S. 161 (1939), and allows a court to award attorney's fees to a party whose litigation efforts directly benefit others. *Alyeska,* 421 U.S. at 257-258. Second, a court may assess attorney's fees as a sanction for the "'willful disobedience of a court order.'" Id. at 258 (quoting Fleischmann Distilling Corp. v. Maier Brewing Co., 386 U.S. 714, 718 (1967)). Thus, a court's discretion to determine "[t]he degree of punishment for contempt" permits the court to impose as part of the fine attorney's fees representing the entire cost of the litigation. Toledo Scale Co. v. Computing Scale Co., 261 U.S. 399, 428 (1923).

Third, and most relevant here, a court may assess attorney's fees when a party has "'acted in bad faith, vexatiously, wantonly, or for oppressive reasons.'" *Alyeska,* supra, 421 U.S. at 258-259 (quoting F.D. Rich Co. v. United States ex rel. Industrial Lumber Co., 417 U.S. 116 (1974)). In this regard, if a court finds "that fraud has been practiced upon it, or that the very temple of justice has been defiled," it may assess attorney's fees against the responsible party, *Universal Oil,* supra, 328 U.S. at 580, as it may when a party "shows bad faith by delaying or disrupting the litigation or by hampering enforcement of a court order," *Hutto,* 437 U.S. at 689, n.14. The imposition of sanctions in this instance transcends a court's equitable power concerning relations between the parties and reaches a court's inherent power to police itself, thus serving the dual purpose of "vindicat[ing] judicial authority without resort to the more drastic sanctions available for contempt of court and mak[ing] the prevailing party whole for expenses caused by his opponent's obstinacy." Id. . . .

We discern no basis for holding that the sanctioning scheme of the statute and the rules displaces the inherent power to impose sanctions for the bad-faith conduct described above. These other mechanisms, taken alone or together, are not substitutes for the inherent power, for that power is both broader and narrower than other means of imposing sanctions. First, whereas each of the other mechanisms reaches only certain individuals or conduct, the inherent power extends to a full range of litigation abuses. At the very least, the inherent power must continue to exist to fill in the interstices. . . . Second, while the narrow exceptions to the American Rule effectively limit a court's inherent power to impose attorney's fees as a sanction to cases in which a litigant has engaged in bad-faith conduct or willful disobedience of a court's orders, many of the other mechanisms permit a court to impose attorney's fees as a sanction for conduct which merely fails to meet a reasonableness standard. Rule 11, for example, imposes an objective standard of reasonable inquiry which does not mandate a finding of bad faith.[11]

It is true that the exercise of the inherent power of lower federal courts can be limited by statute and rule, for "[t]hese courts were created by act of Congress." *Robinson,* 19 Wall. at 511. Nevertheless, "we do not lightly assume that Congress has intended to depart from established principles" such as the scope of a court's inherent power. Weinberger v. Romero-Barcelo, 456 U.S. 305, 313 (1982); see also *Link,* 370 U.S. at 631-32. . . .

The Court's prior cases have indicated that the inherent power of a court can be invoked even if procedural rules exist which sanction the same conduct. In *Link,* it was recognized that a federal district court has the inherent power to dismiss a case *sua sponte* for failure to prosecute, even though the language of Federal Rule of Civil Procedure 41(b) appeared to require a motion from a party. . . .

Like the Court of Appeals, we find no abuse of discretion in resorting to the inherent power in the circumstances of this case. . . . Much of the bad-faith conduct by Chambers . . . was beyond the reach of the rules. . . . In circumstances such as these in which all of a litigant's conduct is deemed sanctionable, requiring a court first to apply rules and statutes containing sanctioning provisions to discrete occurrences before invoking inherent power to address remaining instances of sanctionable conduct would serve only to foster extensive and needless satellite litigation, which is contrary to the aim of the rules themselves. . . .

Id. at 43-51.

After *Chambers* courts are free to sanction attorneys for "bad faith" conduct. As a lower court has emphasized, "[i]t is axiomatic that courts have

---

11. Indeed, Rule 11 was amended in 1983 precisely because the subjective bad-faith standard was difficult to establish and courts were therefore reluctant to invoke it as a means of imposing sanctions. See Advisory Committee Notes on the 1983 Amendment to Rule 11, 28 U.S.C. App., pp. 575-76. Consequently, there is little risk that courts will invoke their inherent power "to chill the advocacy of litigants attempting to vindicate all other important federal rights." See [dissent]. To the extent that such a risk does exist, it is no less present when a court invokes Rule 11. See Cooter & Gell v. Hartmarx Corp., 496 U.S. 384 (1990).

the authority to impose sanctions *sua sponte* under the various sources of the sanctioning power—i.e., federal statutes, the Federal Rules of Civil Procedure, and the inherent power of the courts." Wolters Kluwer Fin. Servs. Inc. v. Scivantage, 525 F. Supp. 2d 448, 452 n.8 (S.D.N.Y. 2007), *rev'd in part and aff'd in part*, 564 F.3d 110 (2d Cir. 2008) (reversing sanctions imposed on a law firm and senior partner but affirming sanctions imposed on the junior attorney who primarily handled the case). This "axiomatic" power, however, has raised concerns. First, exercising "inherent" power in an area where Congress has already legislated procedural rules is at least potentially controversial. See John Papachristos, Comment, Inherent Power Found, Rule 11 Lost: Taking a Shortcut to Impose Sanctions in Chambers v. NASCO, 59 Brook. L. Rev. 1225, 1265 (1993); see also Danielle Kie Hart, And the Chill Goes On—Federal Civil Rights Plaintiffs Beware: Rule 11 Vis-à-Vis 28 U.S.C. § 1927 and the Court's Inherent Power, 38 Loy. L.A. L. Rev. 645 (2004); Danielle Kie Hart, Still Chilling After All These Years: Rule 11 of the Federal Rules of Civil Procedure and Its Impact on Federal Civil Rights Plaintiffs After the 1993 Amendments, 37 Val. U. L. Rev. 1 (2002).

Note as well that while Rule 11 is evaluated for objective reasonableness, a finding of subjective bad faith is required when a court imposes sanctions under its inherent power. How might this difference play out in practice? See Charles Yablon, Hindsight, Regret and Safe Harbors in Rule 11 Litigation, 37 Loy. L.A. L. Rev. 599 (2004) (arguing that amended Rule 11's safe harbor reduces the potential for hindsight bias); see also Gillette Foods Inc. v. Bayerwald-Fruchteverwertung, 977 F.2d 809, 813 (3d Cir. 1992) (holding that courts have the inherent power to sanction conduct that does not violate Rule 11 since such inherent power is necessary to "fill in the interstices" between the range of potential bad faith conduct and the scope of Rule 11 (quoting *Chambers*, 501 U.S. at 47)).

## Note: The Contempt Power

One form of the court's inherent power discussed in *Chambers*, and in more detail in Chapter 5, is the contempt sanction. The history of the contempt power of the judge lies in English equity procedure. If the Chancellor found an addressee of an injunction or other court order to be in contempt, he might impose the sanctions of *civil* or *criminal* contempt. The latter was strictly punitive in purpose and would take the form of a fine or a term of imprisonment. The former was intended to be coercive and remedial. Usually, it would take the form of an imprisonment until such time as the addressee complied with the court's order. It was said, somewhat glibly, that the defendant carries his own jail keys in his pocket. It also was said that the power exercised by the Chancellor was the minimum necessary to secure compliance. Nevertheless, there were numerous instances in which defiant litigants remained imprisoned for many years.

In some instances, it was possible that a contempt proceeding would be conducted summarily. This would occur if the contempt could be classified as direct, meaning presumably that the chancellor had direct knowledge of the defiance. This kind of proceeding had also been known to the law courts, where criminal contempt sanctions had long been applied to those who disturbed proceedings or offended the dignity of the court, but the instances of the exercise of this power were always few. A notable example of a summary contempt proceeding occurred in a law court in the eighteenth century when a subject flung an ax at the judge. Although he missed, he was executed on the spot in the courtroom.

The basic provision of modern federal law on contempt, 18 U.S.C. § 401, is representative of much similar state legislation:

> A court of the United States shall have power to punish by fine or imprisonment, at its discretion, such contempt of its authority, and none other, as:
>
> (1) Misbehavior of any person in its presence or so near thereto as to obstruct the administration of justice;
> (2) Misbehavior of any of its officers in their official transactions;
> (3) Disobedience or resistance to its lawful writ, process, order, rule, decree, or command.

Note that the basic statute does not distinguish between civil and criminal contempt. In a series of cases on contempt, culminating in United Mine Workers of America v. Bagwell, 512 U.S. 821 (1994), the Supreme Court has clarified the distinction. What follows on whether a contempt is labeled criminal or civil?

### Note: Contracting for Sanctions?

In addition to Rule 11 and the courts' inherent power to sanction, a party may be sanctioned if she has agreed to it as a penalty for disobedience. In Baella-Silva v. Hulsey, 454 F.3d 5 (1st Cir. 2006), an attorney sued co-counsel to recover fees allegedly owed according to a fee-sharing agreement. The parties entered a settlement agreement, which the court incorporated into its judgment disposing of the case. The settlement agreement contained a confidentiality clause, as almost all settlement agreements do, but this particular confidentiality clause provided liquidated damages in the amount of $50,000 for breach. When Baella-Silva filed a motion for disbursement of funds using the court's new-fangled e-filing system, he neglected to file it under seal, so it was posted live on the court's online docket.

Although Baella-Silva realized his mistake within an hour and promptly withdrew the motion, defendant Hulsey immediately filed a motion to suspend disbursement of Baella-Silva's fee and to collect the $50,000 specified in the contract as a sanction for his breach of the confidentiality clause. The First Circuit upheld the sanction, as well as an additional $20,320 sanction imposed by the district court under its inherent powers when Baella-Silva violated a separate provision of the settlement contract prohibiting contact between the parties. Baella-Silva violated the latter provision when he filed two new suits against defendants. The district court chose $20,320 because it equaled the damages sought in Baella-Silva's new suits. The First Circuit agreed that the amount was not excessive, observing that "[s]o long as a sanction is reasonably proportionate to the offending conduct, the trial court's quantification of it ought not to be disturbed." Id. at 13 (internal quotation marks omitted).

# 3   *Discovery of the Adversary's Case*

## Problem Case: The Elusive Defendant (Part Two)

Return to your client, the disappointed decorator Paulette Peinture, Chapter 1. Assume that you have managed to serve the complaint and have received in return a form answer that denies all the factual allegations of the complaint. What happens next in the case?

Read Rule 26(a) and (f).

What would you turn over voluntarily to the other side? What would you expect to get from them?

What formal discovery will you undertake? Sketch out a discovery plan.

## A.   AN OVERVIEW OF THE DISCOVERY TOOLS AND THEIR DEPLOYMENT

Discovery is the process by which parties may learn about relevant evidence that is known to or in the hands of the adversary. More Rules are devoted to discovery than to any other subject, yet the interpretive case law is not large. Can you see why this is? Part of the answer lies in the fact-specific nature of discovery fights, making it less likely that any case will serve as a far-ranging precedent. Part of the answer is that judges dislike getting caught up in discovery disputes and find ways to avoid spending too much time and energy on them. Rather than dealing with all the Rule permutations through cases, therefore, we offer instead a practicing lawyer's advice about investigating a case and planning discovery. We then turn to a more general consideration of the ambitions for and frustrations with the modern discovery regime revealed in decisional law.

*Lawrence J. Zweifach, Deposition Strategy in the Framework of an Overall Discovery Plan*
Practising Law Institute 9-20 (1998)

## I. Preliminary Considerations for the Development of a Discovery Plan

A. The attorney and the client should work together closely as a team in the development of a discovery plan.

B. Define major objectives in the litigation.

C. Evaluate alternative courses of action.

D. Formulate a "theory of the case."

1. The initial theory of the case is a working hypothesis that undoubtedly will change during the course of discovery and other pretrial proceedings.

2. At the outset of the litigation, draft a tentative outline setting forth the major points that would be made in summation after the trial of the case. This outline, which should be revised on a regular basis throughout the litigation, will be a valuable tool for ensuring that you are "litigating with a purpose."

E. The client should develop a litigation budget based on a careful analysis of the potential gains and losses involved in the litigation, as well as the client's resources.

1. The budget should be broken down to include expenses as well as pretrial, trial and post-trial activities.

2. The budget should also reflect the possibility that the litigation will give rise to activities beyond the initial claims; for example, counterclaims and third-party claims.

3. Ideally, the attorney should be directly involved in the budgeting process. At the very least, the attorney must be fully apprised of all budgetary constraints.

F. Define short-range and medium-range goals.

1. Temporary restraining order and/or preliminary injunction.

2. Motion for summary judgment.

3. Settlement goals.

G. Formulate strategies to achieve objectives.

1. The discovery plan should be based on the client's overall litigation objectives and strategies for achieving those objectives.

2. Objectives must be clearly defined. For example, if your principal goal is to set the stage for an early settlement, your strategy might be to pursue selected discovery on a fast track. Or, if your goal is to make an early summary judgment motion, you might want to focus your preliminary discovery on only those issues that will be the subject of that motion. On the other hand, if your ultimate goal is to be prepared fully to take the case to trial, your discovery plan will be directed towards maximizing your ability to prevail at trial.

3. In preparing a plan, consider the cost and potential benefits of all available discovery tools.
4. Carefully analyze alternative approaches to discovery, paying particular attention to all available discovery devices, and the timing and sequence of discovery. . . .

## II. The Primary Discovery Tools

A. Informal discovery.
   1. In some situations, informal witness interviews can be more advantageous than formal deposition testimony.
   2. An interview of a potential non-party witness can help you decide whether or not you should subpoena the witness for a deposition.
   3. Witnesses can be "locked in" to positions on the facts by having them sign written statements or by having them swear to affidavits.
   4. Before attempting to contact a potential witness, make sure that you understand the ethical proscriptions that govern whom you may contact directly. For example, you generally will not be permitted to contact (without the permission of your adversary) the opposing party or its employees. See Model Code of Professional Responsibility DR7-104(A)(1) (1980). . . .
   5. In some cases, private investigators can be valuable sources of information.
   6. It is critical to remember that the attorney-client privilege will not protect your statements to a witness during an informal interview. Moreover, the work-product doctrine, to the extent that it is applicable, will rarely afford lasting protection. Finally, you never know what a witness will ultimately claim that you said to him during an interview. In sum, be discreet and avoid conducting any one-on-one interviews.
B. Formal discovery.
   1. Interrogatories.
   2. Depositions.
   3. Notice of subpoena to produce documents and things.
   4. Requests for admissions.
   5. Physical and mental examinations.
C. In deciding which discovery devices to use, pay careful attention to all applicable procedural rules, local rules, individual judge's rules and standing orders. . . .
D. Uses and advantages of interrogatories.
   1. Determine the existence and location of documents.
   2. Learn the identity of persons with knowledge relevant to the litigation.
   3. Learn the specific contentions of the opposing party.
   4. Interrogatories are less expensive and time-consuming than depositions.

E.  Uses and advantages of requests for admissions.
    1.  Narrow issues.
    2.  Can obviate need for complicated proof regarding foundations for admissibility of documents.
    3.  Can help to avoid unnecessary areas of discovery and trial preparation.

## III.  Uses and Advantages of Depositions

A.  Secure admissions and impeachment evidence from an adverse party.
B.  Learn what adverse party and non-party witnesses know about the issues in the case and what their testimony will be at trial.
    1.  "Lock" adverse party and non-party witnesses into facts and positions so that there will be no surprises at trial.
C.  Depositions, unlike interrogatories, allow the examiner to receive spontaneous answers from the witness and to ask follow-up questions.
D.  The examiner has an opportunity to observe the demeanor of a potential trial witness.
E.  Depositions can narrow and clarify issues for trial.
F.  Determine the location, nature, and availability of documents and other physical evidence.
G.  Learn the identity of other potential witnesses.
H.  Preserve for trial the testimony of individuals who might be beyond subpoena power at the time of trial or who might otherwise be unavailable.
I.  To obtain the production of documents and other physical evidence and to lay the foundation for their admission into evidence at trial.

## IV.  The Timing and Sequence of Discovery

A.  The timing and sequence of discovery will sometimes be dictated by an individual judge's rules or by a pre-trial order issued after a pretrial conference.
B.  One traditional approach to discovery is to issue general discovery requests first, and to have subsequent discovery requests build on the previous general requests, so that the information obtained becomes increasingly detailed. This approach is particularly useful when the attorney does not have substantial knowledge about the claims and the underlying facts at the outset of the litigation. Here, the adverse party would be deposed only after all relevant documents and answers to the principal interrogatories have been received. This approach enables the attorney to maximize her ability to take a thorough deposition of the adverse party and to avoid duplicative discovery. Under this approach, the following sequence of discovery might be employed:

      1. First, issue interrogatories of a general nature to identify potential witnesses and the existence of documents. At the same time, issue an initial request for the production of documents. Also, if appropriate, issue a preliminary request to admit in order to narrow the issues.

      2. Depose secondary witnesses.

      3. Issue follow-up document requests and interrogatories.

      4. Depose key witnesses.

      5. Depose the adverse party.

      6. Issue follow-up requests to admit.

      7. Depose expert witnesses.

      8. Issue contention interrogatories.

      9. Issue final, "clean up" discovery requests.

C. In some circumstances, it is desirable to take the deposition of a plaintiff shortly after the pleadings have been filed and prior to the taking of other discovery.

    1. This approach enables defense counsel to obtain admissions before the plaintiff has had a full opportunity to learn about the defendant's theory of the case, and prior to the time that the issues have become refined. . . .

D. The sequence of discovery must be tailored to the particular circumstances of each case. In most cases, it will be extremely difficult to take a useful deposition without first having had an opportunity to examine relevant documents. However, under certain circumstances, the taking of depositions to "lock in" the testimony of witnesses at the outset of discovery can be invaluable.

## V.  Deciding Whether to Depose a Witness

A. As a general rule, always depose the adverse party.

B. Depositions are expensive and time-consuming.

C. Many of the purposes of a deposition can be accomplished with an informal interview.

D. Depositions can influence settlement valuation. . . .

E. The deposition of the "favorable" nonparty witness.

    1. The consequences of taking the deposition:

       a. You eliminate the opportunity of having a tactical advantage at trial—i.e., calling a witness to testify who has not been deposed.

       b. Your adversary gets two big bites at the apple. That is, assuming that the witness will be available for trial, your adversary can "experiment" impeachment techniques at the deposition, knowing that she will have a full opportunity to cross examine the witness at trial. This opportunity to take risks at the deposition (that one otherwise wouldn't take during their first confrontation with the witness at trial) is extremely advantageous.

        c. On the other hand, a strong performance by a key, non-party witness can facilitate the settlement of a case and save the cost of additional litigation.

   2. The consequences of not taking the deposition:

        a. You might lose the benefit of the witness's potentially favorable testimony because the witness might become unavailable to testify at trial.

        b. Even worse, today's seemingly "friendly" witness could be a hostile witness at trial. By the time of trial, the witness could have a change of heart (if not a change of recollection) and testify for your adversary. . . .

F. The deposition of the adverse non-party witness.

   1. The consequences of taking the deposition:

        a. You might direct your adversary to a witness that they did not know about.

        b. You might preserve for trial the unfavorable testimony of a witness who otherwise would be unavailable to testify at trial.

   2. The consequences of not taking the deposition:

        a. You might be called upon to cross-examine the witness at trial without having any prior knowledge of the nature of the witness's testimony.

        b. If you do not learn about the damaging nature of the witness's testimony during the discovery stage of the case, you might miss the opportunity to reach a reasonable settlement.

## VI. Determining the Sequence of Depositions

A. One popular school of thought is to take the depositions of secondary witnesses before the deposition of key witnesses and the adverse party.

   1. This approach enables the attorney to gather as much information as possible before attempting to depose the critical witnesses and the adverse party. By starting at the bottom of the pyramid, the examiner will be able to take more thorough depositions at the end of discovery.

   2. The downside is that you enable the adverse party and principal witnesses to become better-educated by the time they are deposed.

B. Taking the depositions of principal witnesses and the adverse party before the depositions of secondary witnesses.

   1. If the attorney has an understanding of the basic facts and contentions underlying the litigation, this approach might be attractive.

   2. Here, admissions can be obtained from the adverse party before he has an opportunity to learn all of the facts, issues and available defense in the case.

3. This approach contemplates a rapid pace of discovery. It can foster an early settlement and lay the groundwork for a relatively early motion for summary judgment.

## B.   DISCOVERY REFORM REDUX:* HOW THE SOLUTION BECAME THE PROBLEM

The greatest single innovation of the Federal Rules was their provision for open-handed, self-executing discovery. In one of its first major cases dealing with the Rules, the Supreme Court expressed the goal of the new order: "Mutual knowledge of all the relevant facts gathered by both parties is essential to proper litigation." Hickman v. Taylor, 329 U.S. 495, 507 (1947). The idea was that full disclosure not only would promote reasonable settlements and allow cases to be shaped for summary judgment, but also would prevent trials from becoming sporting events where each side tried to surprise the other with evidence for which it was unprepared.

As originally promulgated, and for more than four decades, Rule 26 invited all-out inquiry in terms of its scope and methods, providing for good measure that unless the court ordered otherwise, "the frequency of use" of the various discovery methods was not to be limited. The parties were expected to work together to share information without, at least in the first instance, relying on the power of the court to compel disclosure.

But starting in the 1970s, liberal discovery came under increasing attack. One of the underlying arguments against the original conception of the discovery rules was that, in combination with liberal pleading, it created a potent and unfair shift of advantage to plaintiffs in litigation. Clearing the pleading hurdle means that the plaintiff can use the discovery process to obtain evidence in support of her claims from the defendant, essentially at the defendant's expense. Indeed, some analysts assert that the 1938 Federal Rules represented an effort, "under the guise of procedural reform, . . . to gain an advantage for New Deal constituencies, particularly plaintiffs, in pursuing litigation." Jay S. Goodman, On the Fiftieth Anniversary of the Federal Rules of Civil Procedure: What Did the Drafters Intend?, 21 Suffolk U. L. Rev. 351, 352 (1987) (citing Stephen N. Subrin, The New Era in American Civil Procedure, 67 A.B.A. J. 1648, 1651 (1981)). Chief among these "New Deal constituencies" were individual consumers, employees, and shareholders who were thought to be at a disadvantage in litigation against corporate defendants. See, e.g., Harry Kalven, Jr. and Maurice Rosenfield, The Contemporary Function of the Class Suit, 8 U. Chi. L. Rev. 684 (1941). In effect, the Rules transferred power, in the form of access to information, from corporate defendants to individual plaintiffs.

A second attack, applicable to both parties but perhaps more common to corporate litigants, is the use of wide-ranging discovery not to find facts

---

* This title is taken from an article by Carl Tobias of the same name in 31 Conn. L. Rev. 1433 (1999).

but to impose transaction costs on the other side, forcing settlement to avoid the even higher costs of litigating. Judges also voiced frustration with the extent of collateral litigation over compliance with discovery obligations by parties who were "stonewalling" or engaged in so-called fishing expeditions.

The widespread sense that there was discovery abuse has led to a cascade of reforms, the most important of which occurred in 1983, 1993, 2000, and 2015. The reforms have concentrated on four dominant themes: (1) the development of a regime of sanctions for discovery abuse separate from Rule 11, see Rules 26(g) and 37; (2) the kind of information that must be turned over to adversaries at the outset of a case and without awaiting a discovery request, see Rule 26(a); (3) special rules pertaining to electronically stored information as digital storage has eclipsed all other documentary evidence in civil cases, see Rules 26(b)(2)(B) and 37(e); and (4) the standard that defines the overall scope of discoverable information, see Rule 26(b)(1). Over time, each successive wave of amendments has promised to address perceived abuses by imposing constraints on discovery practice and amplifying the supervision of judges over this phase of litigation.

With respect to electronically stored information, lawyers' "duties in discovery [are] evolv[ing] rapidly" as the means for digital data storage and modes of communication that leave a digital trail (so-called e-discovery) proliferate. Christopher D. Wall, Ethics in the Era of Electronic Evidence, 41 Trial 56 (2005). As much as "90 percent of potentially discoverable information is generated and stored electronically." Id. And as cloud technology develops and social media platforms multiply, people sometimes "store" digital information without intending to do so, without knowing the location of the files that have been stored and without being able to control access to or the disposition of those files. In addition to the new provisions for managing e-discovery, the 2015 amendments add specific sanctions under Rule 37(e) for failure to preserve electronically stored information (or "ESI").

Constraints designed to eliminate the practice of withholding obviously relevant information are most evident in the 1993 and 2000 amendments requiring parties to provide certain information to their opponents *without* awaiting a discovery request. See Rule 26(a). The mandatory disclosure option provision triggered a massive outpouring of commentary, pro and con, when it was first announced. On one side of the debate were those like Judge Schwarzer and Magistrate Judge Brazil, who have argued for years that mandatory disclosure of the type called for in the amended Rule is simply what an ethical lawyer would disclose at any rate, especially in response to skilled queries from the other side. See William W. Schwarzer, The Federal Rules, the Adversary Process, and Discovery Reform, 50 U. Pitt. L. Rev. 703 (1989); Wayne D. Brazil, The Adversary Character of Civil Discovery: A Critique and Proposals for Change, 31 Vand. L. Rev. 1295 (1978).

On the other side of the debate were many observers who felt that the mandatory disclosure provisions were a radical, dangerous incursion into the lawyer's ethical obligations of respect for a client's confidences and of zealous representation. Justice Scalia dissented from the amendments to Rule 26 in the same opinion in which he had excoriated the new Rule 11 (see Chapter 2): "[T]he new Rule would place intolerable strain upon lawyers' ethical duty to represent their clients and not to assist the opposing side. Requiring a lawyer to make a judgment as to what information is 'relevant to disputed facts' plainly requires him to use his professional skills in the service of the adversary." Justice Scalia, Dissenting Statement to Amendments to the Federal Rules of Civil Procedure, 146 F.R.D. 507, 511 (1993). Still other critics of discovery reform argued that the claim of widespread abuse was ungrounded. See, e.g., Linda S. Mullinex, Discovery in Disarray: The Pervasive Myth of Pervasive Discovery Abuse and the Consequences for Unfounded Rulemaking, 46 Stan. L. Rev. 1393 (1994).

To appease the contingent that argued that the adversary system was at stake, the 1993 amendments allowed any district to opt out of the mandatory disclosure provisions. Although opinion was divided, and nearly half the federal districts chose not to implement the Rule, studies showed that the new Rule 26(a)(1) was achieving its intended goals of cutting litigation costs and speeding case disposition. See Robert E. Oliphant, Four Years of Experience with Rule 26(a)(1): The Rule Is Alive and Well, 24 Wm. Mitchell L. Rev. 323 (1998); Thomas E. Willing et al., An Empirical Study of Discovery and Disclosure Practice Under the 1993 Federal Rule Amendments, 39 B.C. L. Rev. 525, 534-535 (1998). This encouraging empirical evidence, together with a growing sense of unease about undercutting the uniformity of practice in federal courts, prompted the Advisory Committee to remove the opt-out and make mandatory disclosure universal in all federal districts. A small class of cases that remain exempt from the mandatory disclosure obligation is enumerated in Rule 26(a)(1)(B).

Constraints designed to limit "fishing expeditions" and enhance the supervisory powers of district courts are most prominent in amendments to Rule 26(b)(1)—the crucial provision that regulates the flow of disclosures made upon request of the parties after the initial Rule 26(a) mandatory disclosures have been made. Originally, Rule 26(b) provided that either party could request any information "relevant to the subject matter." The 2000 amendments sought to narrow discovery by limiting disclosure to information "relevant to *any party's claim or defense*" (emphasis added). Information falling within the broader "relevant to the subject matter" standard was available only by court order upon a showing of good cause. The 2000 amendments further emphasized that the frequency and extent of discovery should be regulated under Rule 26(b)(2) by attention to the costs and benefits of any given discovery request.

Not satisfied with these limitations, the Advisory Committee introduced major new limitations on the scope of permissible discovery under Rule 26(b)(1) in 2015. Under the new definition a party may only obtain discovery of information "that is relevant to any party's claim or defense and *proportional to the needs of the case*, considering the importance of the issues at stake in the action, the amount in controversy, the parties' relative access to relevant information, the parties' resources, the importance of the discovery in resolving the issues, and whether the burden or expense of the proposed discovery outweighs its likely benefit" (emphasis added). The objectives of the Advisory Committee were described in the Committee's report submitted to the Judicial Conference in September 2014:

> During the advisory committee's May 2010 Conference on Civil Litigation held at Duke University School of Law, there was nearly unanimous agreement that the disposition of civil actions could be improved. Participants also agreed that this goal should be pursued by several means: education of the bench and the bar; implementation of pilot projects; and rules amendments.
>
> The advisory committee formed a subcommittee to develop rules amendments consistent with the overarching goal of improving the disposition of civil cases by reducing the costs and delays in civil litigation, increasing realistic access to the courts, and furthering the goals of Rule 1. . . .

Summary of the Report of the Judicial Conference, Committee on Rules of Practice and Procedure, Sept. 2014, 12. With respect to public comments on the proportionality requirement, the Committee stated:

> Many favored the proposal. They asserted that costs of discovery in civil litigation are too often out of proportion to the issues at stake in the litigation, resulting in cases not being filed or settlements made to avoid litigation costs regardless of the merits. They stated that disproportionate litigation costs bar many from access to federal courts and have resulted in a flight to other dispute resolution fora such as arbitration. They noted that the proportionality factors currently found in Rule 26(b)(2)(C)(iii) often are overlooked by courts and litigants. . . .
>
> Many others saw proportionality as a new limit that would favor defendants. They criticized the factors from Rule 26(b)(2)(C)(iii) as subjective and so flexible as to defy uniform application. . . . They were particularly concerned that proportionality would impose a new burden on the requesting party to justify each and every discovery request. . . .

Id. at Appendix B-5. The Committee also emphasized survey results from major national bar associations:

> Surveys of ABA Section of Litigation and [National Employment Lawyers Association] attorneys found more than 80 [percent] agreement that discovery costs are disproportionately high in small cases, with more than 40 [percent] of respondents saying they are disproportionate in large cases. In the survey of the ABA Section of Litigation, 78 [percent] of plaintiffs' attorneys, 91 [percent] of defense attorneys, and 94 [percent] of mixed practice attorneys agreed that litigation costs are not proportional to the value of small cases, with 33 [percent] of plaintiffs' lawyers, 44 [percent] of defense lawyers, and 41 [percent] of mixed-practice lawyers agreeing that litigation costs are not proportional in large cases. In the NELA survey, which included primarily plaintiffs' lawyers, more than 80 [percent] said that litigation costs are not proportional to the value of small cases, with a fairly even split on

whether they are proportional to the value of large cases. An [Institute for the Advancement of the American Legal System] survey of corporate counsel found 90 [percent] agreement with the proposition that discovery costs in federal court are not generally proportional to the needs of the case, and 80 [percent] disagreement with the suggestion that outcomes are driven more by the merits than by costs. In its report summarizing the results of some of the Duke empirical research, IAALS noted that between 61 [percent] and 76 [percent] of the respondents in the ABA, [American College of Trial Lawyers], and NELA surveys agreed that judges do not enforce the rules' existing proportionality limitations on their own.

Id. at B-6, B-7. And the Committee pointed out that previous efforts to encourage courts and litigants to make discovery proportionate to the needs of the case had failed:

[T]hree previous Civil Rules Committees in three different decades have reached the same conclusion as the current Committee—that proportionality is an important and necessary feature of civil litigation in federal courts. And yet one of the primary conclusions of comments and surveys at the 2010 Duke Conference was that proportionality is still lacking in too many cases. The previous amendments have not had their desired effect.

Id. at B-8. There is case law to support this conclusion. See, e.g., Breon v. Coca-Cola Bottling Co. of New England, 232 F.R.D. 49, 52 (D. Conn. 2005) ("The definition of relevance continues to be liberally interpreted even after changes to Rule 26 in 2000. . . . [T]here is no indication that the change in focus from relevance in relation to the subject matter, to relevance in relation to claims and defenses, 'marks a substantial departure from the traditional liberal construction of the term, which is designed to assure access to the information necessary for the achievement of justice and fair trials.'") (citation omitted); Equal Emp't Opportunity Comm'n v. Caesars Entm't, Inc., 237 F.R.D. 428, 431 (D. Nev. 2006) ("There seems to be a general consensus that the Amendments to Rule 26(b) 'do not dramatically alter the scope of discovery.'") (quoting World Wrestling Fed'n Entm't, Inc. v. William Morris Agency, Inc., 204 F.R.D. 263, 265 n.1 (S.D.N.Y. 2001)).

The Committee must also have been mindful of the Supreme Court's criticisms of discovery in *Twombly* and *Iqbal* (see Chapter 2) as well as the dramatic increase in electronically stored information over the last decade.

The new amendments to Rule 26(b)(1) are not without their critics. Hundreds of law professors submitted public comments opposing the amendments to the scope of discovery during the public comment period, emphasizing that while discovery remains a vexing problem in some cases, "evidence of system-wide, cost-multiplying abuse does not exist, and the proposed amendments are not designed to address the small subset of problematic cases . . . ." Helen Hershkoff et al., Joint Comments, Feb. 2014, http://www.regulations.gov/#!documentDetail;D=USC-RULES-CV-2013-0002-0622. See also Brooke D. Coleman, The Real Cost of Litigation Reform: Justice, Not Discovery Costs, Are at Stake, Feb. 2014, https://www.acslaw.org/acsblog/

the-real-cost-of-litigation-reform-justice-not-discovery-costs-are-at-stake (noting that empirical studies show "discovery costs are generally not too high in comparison to the stakes parties have in litigation"; citing a Federal Judicial Center report concluding that "median discovery costs in 2010 for plaintiffs were $15,000, and the median costs for defendants were $20,000"). The debate over discovery and litigation costs also raises important questions about how to define and measure the value of efficiency in federal litigation. See Brooke D. Coleman, The Efficiency Norm, 46 B.C. L. Rev. 1777 (2015) (arguing that cost and efficiency should not be defined in narrow neoclassical economic terms); Brooke D. Coleman, One Percent Procedure, 91 Wash. L. Rev. ___ (forthcoming 2016) (arguing that the 2015 amendments conflate problems associated with complex, high-stakes litigation with the needs of ordinary litigants who face barriers to "get the discovery they would need to carry their burdens of proof").

In an op-ed piece, Professor Suja Thomas has charged that corporations exercised undue influence over the Advisory Committee process in its work on the new proportionality standard for Rule 26(b)(1) and in the promulgation of separate guidelines to educate judges on how to apply the new standard. See Via Duke, Companies Are Shaping Discovery, Law360 (Nov. 4, 2015) (arguing that the Duke Center for Judicial Studies, which sponsored the conference in 2010 that prompted the new amendments, is funded by corporate sponsors who stand to gain by the limitation of the scope of discovery; claiming that the Center also hosted an "invitation only" conference on implementation with corporate representatives, judges, and lawyers, developed guidelines, and coordinated with the Federal Judicial Center for training sessions on the guidelines with federal judges), available online at http://www.law.illinois.edu/news/article/3175. For the response letter published by the Director of the Center for Judicial Studies at Duke, see https://law.duke.edu/sites/default/files/centers/judicialstudies/response_prof_thomass_opinion_piece.pdf.

As the cases and materials that follow suggest, you can see the full flowering of the adversary system, for better and for worse, in discovery practice. Our goal in this chapter is to help you understand and participate in the long-running debate about the purpose and regulation of discovery rather than to master all the discovery rules and their considerable technicalities. Full mastery will require understanding of the law of evidence, a separate course, and deep sensitivity to the nuances of human error in the areas of social action regulated by the law. We focus, therefore, on the introductory topics of scope, privilege, the use of experts, and the regulation of discovery practice by the appellate courts.

## Problem Case: The Secret Memo

You represent DiChem, a small San Diego corporation whose business is assessing air and water quality for private industries to determine compliance with environmental and occupational safety regulations. In the fall of 2012, DiChem advertised nationally to fill the position of Director of Advertising and interviewed several applicants. Charles Morris from New Mexico won the job, sold his house, and came on board in December. Shortly thereafter, the company went through hard financial times and laid him off.

Morris has sued DiChem and its president Eve Barrie, alleging that the company should have disclosed its precarious fiscal state to him and had failed to do so. Eve Barrie tells you that neither she nor anyone else said anything at all about DiChem's financial situation at the interviews. She adds, "Any management-level employee knows that the job depends on the company's continued financial viability."

When you ask for Eve Barrie's complete file on the hiring of the Director of Advertising, she gives you a meaningful look and says, "Shall I go through it first?" You smile back and say, "I need to know everything. Anything detrimental to our position will be covered by a privilege, I'm sure."

Back at your office, you go through the file and make notes on each item in it, using special firm letterhead on which is preprinted in large capital letters, "Attorney Work Product." You attach a separate sheet of this special letterhead, with your notes on it, to each item in Barrie's file.

Your heart misses a beat when you come to an undated scrawled note in what you have come to recognize as Eve Barrie's handwriting. It says, "If we ever get into a court fight, must decide how much to tell re black hole—company collapse????" You make the following note: "Item 5—looks like a possible damning admission that company knew they were in danger of collapse. Was it bad enough to verge over into fraud? Did they misrepresent? Get associate to research this if it becomes relevant. Barrie is a smart cookie, but it may be better not to ask her too many more questions until and unless we have to prepare her for deposition."

Must you turn the note over under Rule 26(a)(1)(A)? How will you respond if your opponent moves the court under Rule 26(b) for the complete file on the hiring of the new director? Suppose the court orders disclosure of everything in the file; does that include your memorandum attached to the Eve Barrie note? How will you protect your work?

In order to fully answer these questions, you will need to read through the end of this chapter. For now, you should begin to consider the urgency of these basic discovery questions: what must you disclose to an opponent, in what form, and under what circumstances?

### Chalick v. Cooper Hosp./Univ. Med. Ctr.
192 F.R.D. 145 (D.N.J. 2000)

KUGLER, UNITED STATES MAGISTRATE JUDGE.

This matter comes before the Court upon Plaintiff Conrad Chalick's Motion to Amend the Complaint. Plaintiff seeks to replace a fictitiously-named John Doe defendant with Richard Burns, M.D., pursuant to Fed. R. Civ. P. 15(c). It is uncontested that the original complaint was filed within the limitations period, but the request to add Dr. Burns as a defendant was made after the limitations period expired, and that, therefore, the question before this Court is whether the addition of Dr. Burns relates back to the filing of the original complaint under Fed. R. Civ. P. 15(c). Because, as discussed below, the court finds that defendants' violations of Fed. R. Civ. P. 26(a) preclude them from claiming that Dr. Burns did not receive notice and was unaware that he was a proper defendant, plaintiff's motion shall be granted.

## I. Background

Plaintiff initiated this medical malpractice action by filing a complaint in this court on or about March 9, 1999, claiming diversity jurisdiction under 28 U.S.C. § 1332. Plaintiff named Cooper Hospital-University Medical Center and University Radiology Services, P.A., as defendants, along with four individual physicians: Raja Salem, M.D., Chin-Wei Huang, M.D., Edward G. Moss, M.D., and Robert M. White, M.D. Plaintiff also named as defendants John Does 1-50 and Jane Does 1-50, whom plaintiff identified as [other hospital personnel whose names were presently unknown who had participated in caring for the plaintiff's son—EDS.]

Plaintiff alleged that defendants were responsible for the death of plaintiff's decedent, Michael Ellis Chalick, who was admitted to Cooper Hospital-University Medical Center on May 30, 1997, following a parachuting accident. . . .

There is no dispute that the named defendants were timely served. Defendants University Radiology and Drs. White and Moss [hereinafter referred to as the "University Radiology defendants"] filed their answer to the amended complaint on or about May 5, 1999. Defendants Cooper Hospital and Drs. Salem and Huang [hereinafter referred to as the "Cooper Hospital defendants"] filed their answer to the amended complaint on or about May 19, 1999.

### A. Rule 26(a) Disclosures

On or about June 2, 1999, the Cooper Hospital defendants served plaintiff with their Rule 26(a) disclosures. With respect to persons with relevant knowledge, defendants identified the four individual physician defendants, along with five other physicians or nurses, including Dr. Richard Burns. Defendants provided nothing other than Dr. Burns' name; they did not provide Dr. Burns' address or the basis of his knowledge, as is required under Fed. R. Civ. P. 26(a)(1)(A).

On or about June 14, 1999, the University Radiology defendants served plaintiff's counsel with their Rule 26(a) disclosures, also identifying Dr. Richard Burns as an individual with relevant knowledge. These defendants also failed to provide the information required by Rule 26(a)(1)(A), other than Dr. Burns' name.

## B.  Interrogatories and Depositions

Plaintiff's counsel then served interrogatories and deposition notices. On or about July 14, 1999, Defendant Dr. Huang responded to plaintiff's interrogatories. Form C(3) Interrogatory No. 15 stated in relevant part:

> 15. State the names and addresses of all consultants or other physicians who saw, examined and treated plaintiff at your request for the condition forming the basis of the complaint, . . . .

Defendant Huang responded: "No consultations per se, however, thoracic and lumbar spine x-rays were ordered and trauma attending Dr. Burns was notified of the change in patient's condition."

In addition, in response to Supplemental Interrogatory No. 2, which asked for the identities of all persons known to fit the description of the John Doe defendants, [any and all other individuals named in the Cooper Hospital records who may have discoverable information about the care and treatment of the decedent and history of the decedent's injury — Eds.], Defendant Huang objected to the interrogatory, but referred plaintiff to his response to Form C Interrogatory No. 4, which identified Dr. Richard Burns, among others, as persons with relevant knowledge.[3]

On or about August 18, 1999, defendant Dr. Salem served plaintiff with responses to interrogatories. In response to Form C Interrogatory No. 4, Dr. Salem also identified Dr. Richard Burns as a person with relevant knowledge. He did not, however, identify Dr. Burns in response to Form C(3) Interrogatory No. 15.

Plaintiff's counsel initially scheduled depositions of the individual doctor defendants for August 24, 1999. Those depositions were then rescheduled to October, 1999, then to November, 1999, and again to December, 1999. It was not until the deposition of Defendant Dr. Salem on December 10, 1999, that plaintiff claims he first became aware that he had a claim against Dr. Burns.

It was from Dr. Salem's testimony that plaintiff learned that Dr. Burns was a trauma surgeon at Cooper Hospital-University Medical Center who filled in as attending physician in the trauma unit for Dr. Salem during the early morning hours of May 31, 1997, while Dr. Salem was in the operating room. Salem testified that he asked Dr. Burns to check on Michael Chalick in response to his complaints of pain, tingling, and numbness, that Dr. Burns did check on Michael Chalick, made a notation of Mr. Chalick's complaints on his chart, and reviewed Mr. Chalick's x-rays with Dr. Salem. Dr. Salem further testified that Dr. Burns discussed Michael Chalick's condition with Dr. Salem on the morning of May 31, 1997.

As a result of this testimony, on or about December 27, 1999, plaintiff filed this motion to amend the amended complaint to add Richard Burns, M.D.,

---

3. . . . . There is no indication that the response did anything to explain the nature of Dr. Burns' knowledge, other than to merely identify him by name as a person with relevant knowledge.

as a defendant, conceding that the statute of limitations ran on plaintiff's claim against Dr. Burns, but claiming that the amendment relates back to the filing of the original Complaint under Fed. R. Civ. P. 15(c). In the proposed Second Amended Complaint, plaintiff identifies Dr. Burns as "an individual licensed to practice medicine in the State of New Jersey, who at all times relevant herein maintained a practice of medicine at Three Cooper Plaza, Suite 411, Camden, New Jersey." Plaintiff further alleges in the First Count that "at all relevant times defendants Salem, Huang, Moss, Burns, and White were duly authorized agents, servants, workmen or employees of defendant Cooper Hospital-University Medical Center, acting within the course and scope of their employment."

All other allegations in the proposed Second Amended Complaint remain the same.

The Cooper Hospital defendants filed a brief in opposition to plaintiff's motion. In their opposition, the Cooper Hospital defendants argue that Dr. Burns did not receive actual or constructive notice of this lawsuit, and did not have reason to know that plaintiff intended to sue him until he received plaintiff's motion to amend.

## II. Relation Back of Amendments

[Most of the Rule 15 discussion is omitted. Suffice it to say that the Magistrate started from this proposition: "The Third Circuit has shown a strong liberality in allowing amendments under Rule 15 in order to ensure that claims will be decided on the merits rather than on technicalities." *Chalick*, 192 F.R.D. at 148. It then reached the following conclusion:

> These relation back conditions are subject to equitable considerations. In Bechtel v. Robinson, 886 F.2d 644 (3d Cir. 1989), the Third Circuit held that a defendant, by virtue of misleading the plaintiff as to the proper party to sue, was equitably estopped from asserting he did not receive notice under Rule 15(c). The court examined the principles of equitable estoppel under Delaware law and found that they prevented the defendant from relying upon the statute of limitations defense.
>
> While we recognize that "the statute of limitations is important to a defendant to protect it from the unfair surprise of a stale claim," in this case any surprise to [the defendant] is not "unfair." It was through [the defendant's] own conduct, by misleading the appellants as to the proper party to sue, that appellants were forced to bring a stale claim against him. 886 F.2d at 650.

— Eds.]

## [III. Disclosure Requirements]

In medical malpractice wrongful death cases such as this, it is the defendants who possess the indisputably relevant information about who the decedent's treating physicians were during the decedent's stay in the hospital. The only information that plaintiffs often have at the time of filing a lawsuit are medical records and charts that contain undecipherable handwriting and signatures.[6] It is the obligation of defendants to provide plaintiff with the identities and roles of the decedent's treating physicians so that the case can be decided on the merits. Simply put, defendants must tell a plaintiff who did what, and when, with regard to plaintiff's care and treatment. Just as important, however, is defendants' obligation to provide this information early in the action pursuant to Rule 26(a).

Rule 26(a) obligations are clear and established in this District. . . . While some courts chose to opt-out of certain provisions of the 1993 amendments to Rule 26, this court adopted the new Rule 26(a) in its entirety. . . .

The voluntary disclosure provision of Rule 26(a) that was amended in response to the Civil Justice Reform Act of 1990 was a dramatic and unprecedented shift in federal discovery practice—a shift that was necessitated by the progressively increasing undue time and expense spent on obtaining undisputedly relevant discovery, which was a waste of the litigants' time, as well as that of the court in enforcing the federal discovery rules against recalcitrant parties. This District does not take Rule 26(a) lightly. See Local Civil Rule 26.1, comment. The purpose of voluntary disclosures is to streamline discovery and thereby avoid the practice of serving multiple, boilerplate interrogatories and document requests, which themselves bring into play a concomitant set of delays and costs. The requirement of the identification of persons with relevant knowledge in Rule 26(a)(1)(A), along with the subject matter of their knowledge, serves the important purpose of assisting the parties in deciding whom to depose. Fed. R. Civ. P. 26(a) advisory committee's note, 1993 amendments.

Particularly in medical negligence cases, Rule 26(a) disclosure requirements should eliminate what has degenerated into a ritualistic jousting over who should be a defendant. Strict enforcement of the rule leads to early identity of the proper parties so that the litigants can focus on the real issue—who, if anyone, was negligent. This aids defendants as well as plaintiffs, for consistent with the obligations under Rule 11, plaintiff's counsel will be expected to dismiss those defendants who had no role in the care and treatment of the plaintiff.

Litigants are warned not to "indulge in gamesmanship with respect to the disclosure obligations." Advisory Committee Notes, Rule 26(a). To curb such "gamesmanship," Rule 37(c)(1) provides the court with broad latitude in fashioning an appropriate sanction for failure to provide the information required under Rule 26(a). . . . This provision is self-executing; there is no

---

6. Dr. Richard Burns' notes and signature appear in Michael Chalick's medical records—specifically, a progress notation made at 4:30 A.M. on May 31, 1997, on Michael Chalick's chart—but plaintiff argues, and the court agrees, that the signature was illegible.

need for a litigant to make a motion to compel. Advisory Committee Notes, Fed. R. Civ. P. 37(c). Nor does the imposition of a sanction under this provision require a violation of a court order as a prerequisite.

The automatic enforcement power of Rule 37(c)(1) has been well documented since its revision in 1993. See, e.g., Newman v. GHS Osteopathic, Inc., 60 F.3d 153, 156 (3d Cir. 1995) ("Rule 37 is written in mandatory terms and 'is designed to provide a strong inducement for disclosure of Rule 26(a) material.'"); Vance v. United States of America, [1999 U.S. App. LEXIS 14943, at *8-*9] (6th Cir. 1999) ("It is well-established that Fed. R. Civ. P. 37(c)(1), enacted in 1993, mandates that a trial court punish a party for discovery violations in connection with Rule 26 unless the violation was harmless or is substantially justified."); Salgado v. [Gen.] Motors Corp., 150 F.3d 735, 742 and n.6 (7th Cir. 1998) (holding that Rule 37(c)(1) provides enforcement mechanism for violations of Rule 26(a) and that "the district court is not required to fire a warning shot"); Klonoski v. Mahlab, 156 F.3d 255, 269 (1st Cir. 1998) ("The new rule [37(c)(1)] clearly contemplates stricter adherence to discovery requirements, and harsher sanctions for breaches of this rule, and the required sanction in the ordinary case is mandatory preclusion.").

The sanctions available to this court under Rule 37(c)(1) are those set forth in subparagraphs (A), (B) and (C) of subdivision (b)(2). . . .

With these rules in mind, the court makes the following findings. Defendants failed to comply with their disclosure obligations under Rule 26(a)(1)(A), because they provided no information about Dr. Burns other than his name. They did not provide the basis of his knowledge, as required by the rule. Had they complied with their Rule 26(a)(1)(A) obligations, plaintiff would have been duly informed by June 2, 1999, that Dr. Burns was one of the physicians responsible for the care of Michael Chalick on the day that he died.

Defendants have not provided "substantial justification" for their failure to explain the role of Dr. Burns, nor was this failure harmless. The prejudice resulting to plaintiff is obvious. If he had received that information on June 2, 1999, plaintiff would reasonably have had the time and information necessary to add Dr. Burns as a defendant and provide notice to him before July 29, 1999. That not only would have allowed Dr. Burns to participate in the litigation from the outset, but it also would have prevented defendants from arguing now that Dr. Burns did not receive notice within the Rule 15(c) period. That prejudice also extends to the court, for defendants' refusal to provide plaintiff with the information necessary to determine who the physicians were who were responsible for the care of Michael Chalick has hindered the efficient management of the pretrial process with which the court is charged under Rule 16 and has delayed a resolution of this action on its merits. Defendants' failure to comply with Rule 26(a), along with the resulting prejudice, warrants a sanction.

The court further finds that an appropriate sanction is to refuse to allow defendants to rely on their claim that Dr. Burns, within the Rule 15(c) period, did not receive notice of the action and did not have reason to believe that he would be a named defendant.[8] See Fed. R. Civ. P. 37(b)(2)(B); Bechtel v. Robinson, 886 F.2d at 652 (applying equitable estoppel to bar defendant from claiming that he did not receive notice within the limitations period). Dr. Burns cannot claim to have suffered prejudice from his late addition to this lawsuit when the defendants, with whom Dr. Burns apparently shares an identity of interest, had reason to know as early as June, 1999, by virtue of the John Doe paragraph in the complaint, that plaintiff intended to name all of the physicians who treated Michael Chalick on the day before and morning of his death, and that Dr. Burns was one of those physicians.[9] . . .

Accordingly, the court finds that a sanction under Rule 37(c)(1) is warranted by defendants' violation of their disclosure obligations under Rule 26(a). . . .

## Notes and Questions

1. *The Rhythm of Discovery. Chalick* shows both the usual progression of discovery and how delays occur. First in line is mandatory discovery. How soon must that be made? How can it be resisted? See Rules 16 and 26(f). Next in the usual course are some interrogatories. Who answered the interrogatories that are mentioned in the case? How do you think it happened that there were discrepancies among the defendants in the answers to the interrogatories?

Notice that the interrogatories were followed by depositions of the treating doctors. That is standard—interrogatories and typically also requests

---

8. The fact that plaintiff had knowledge on July 14, 1999, of Dr. Huang's interrogatory response in which he stated that "trauma attending Dr. Burns was notified of the change in patient's condition" does not undo the prejudice that defendants caused by their earlier Rule 26(a) violation, nor does plaintiff's delay in deposing any of the defendant doctors change the sanction which this court finds is an appropriate remedy for defendants' discovery violations. See Lundy v. Adamar of New Jersey, Inc., 34 F.3d [1173, 1197 (3d Cir. 1994)] (Becker, J., concurring in part, dissenting in part) ("This Court has repeatedly stated outright that unexcused delay unaccompanied by real detriment to the defendant or to the judiciary does not constitute undue delay.").

9. Even if the Cooper Hospital defendants were allowed to rely on their claim that Dr. Burns suffered prejudice, the court finds that defendants' burden of showing actual prejudice has not been met. See Urrutia v. Harrisburg [Cty.] Police Dept., 91 F.3d [451, 461 (3d Cir. 1996)] ("The prejudice must be actual, not hypothetical."); Bechtel v. Robinson, 886 F.2d [644, 652 (3d Cir. 1989)] (defendant must show that it was unfairly denied opportunity to present facts or evidence which it would have presented had amendment been timely). Any lost opportunity of Dr. Burns to present facts or evidence was not unfair, given the Cooper Hospital defendants' knowledge of his role in Michael Chalick's care and the common interest of Dr. Burns and the Cooper Hospital defendants, who presumably have been engaged in the preparation of a defense that will not differ significantly from that which Dr. Burns will present. In any event, there has been no claim of loss of witness testimony or other evidence as a result of the delay in naming Dr. Burns, and the court will permit the parties adequate time to exchange discovery regarding Dr. Burns.

for production of documents help lawyers create a documentary foundation for oral examination in depositions.

Some of the delay in the case was the five months in which the depositions were continued again and again. Why does the magistrate not count these against the plaintiff in making his equitable assessment? If you were the lawyer for Dr. Burns, what arguments would you make about the unfairness of adding him as a defendant after the limitations period? One of the strongest arguments is that the plaintiffs had notice very early on that there was a Dr. Burns in the case; why wasn't it up to them to find out who he was?

2. *The Advantages of Mandatory Disclosure.* What are the strategic consequences of making early disclosures? Might the advantages of disclosure ever be great enough to trigger the exchange of information even without the mandatory disclosure rule? See Robert D. Cooter and Daniel L. Rubinfeld, An Economic Model of Legal Discovery, 23 J. Legal Stud. 435, 436 (1994) (noting that "[r]evealing information to correct the other side's false optimism creates an advantage in settlement bargaining for the disclosing party . . . [that] provides a strong incentive voluntarily to disclose facts correcting the other side's false optimism before trial").

Apparently, many practicing lawyers see the advantage of some mandatory disclosure. Studies done of the operation of Rule 26(a) in the places where it was first tried found substantial satisfaction with its effect on the cost of discovery and the promotion of settlement. Most significantly, the Rule did not produce the satellite litigation that many opponents predicted. See Thomas E. Willging et al., An Empirical Study of Discovery and Disclosure Practice Under the 1993 Federal Rule Amendments, 39 B.C. L. Rev. 525 (1998). In a recent study, 71 percent of respondents who held a Rule 26(f) meeting "reported that the meeting assisted them in making arrangements to make initial disclosures . . . 60 [percent] reported that it helped them to better understand the opposing side's claims and/or defenses, 40 [percent] reported that they discussed discovery of electronically stored information, and 30 [percent] reported that the meeting increased the likelihood of a prompt resolution of the . . . case." Emery G. Lee III, Early Stages of Litigation Attorney Survey, Report to the Judicial Conference Advisory Committee on Civil Rules, Fed. Judicial Ctr. 1, Mar. 2012.

Still, the risk of abuse, or "gamesmanship," as the court put it in *Chalick,* is ever present. In *Chalick* the problem was failure to fully disclose under Rule 26(a). Is it possible to defeat the purpose of the Rule by disclosing too much? Consider United States ex rel. Hunt v. Merck-Medco Managed Care, LLC, 223 F.R.D. 330, 333 (E.D. Pa. 2004), a consumer fraud action against a pharmaceutical company in which defendants objected to the plaintiffs' initial disclosures on the grounds of the sheer volume of the names provided (3,900!) and that this hefty disclosure thwarted "the purpose and intent of Rule 26(a) to provide an efficient start to relevant discovery." Defendants sought an order requiring plaintiffs, among other things, to "(1) make a qualitative judgment on the importance or relevance of each individual listed; (2) identify the twenty most significant individuals for

Plaintiffs' case in each category [including patients, physicians, as well as former and current employees of the defendant pharmaceutical company. — Eds.]; [and] (3) identify the subject of discoverable information for each individual listed. . . ." Id. at 332.

Are these demands legitimate under Rule 26(a)? Have plaintiffs abused Rule 26(a) by dumping a massive amount of information (a version of the needle-in-the-haystack approach to discovery), or are defendants abusing Rule 26(a) by forcing plaintiffs to reveal more than the Rule requires?

The district court sided with the plaintiffs, holding that the sheer volume of a party's initial disclosure statements "cannot, by itself, constitute a violation of Rule 26(a) because the self-executing disclosures are merely a starting point for the discovery process," and initial disclosures will vary in each case according to the sophistication of the claims raised in the pleadings. Id. at 333. "Logically," the court reasoned, "the more complex the case in terms of the number of parties and the scope of allegations, the larger the disclosure statements should be." Id. Looking at the facts of this case, the court continued:

> Medco Defendants are alleged to have defrauded patients, clients, and the United States by canceling and destroying prescriptions, by failing to perform needed pharmaceutical services, by switching patient's subscriptions without their knowledge and consent, by . . . billing patients for drugs never ordered, by creating false records, by soliciting and receiving inducements from [other drug companies] to favor their products, and by making false and misleading statements to the government about its conduct. These allegations encompass . . . potentially numerous Merck-Medco facilities across the country, numerous current and former Merck Medco employees, numerous physicians and patients. Given the broad language of Rule 26(a)(1) — parties must provide information concerning "each individual likely to have discoverable information" — one would expect the self-executing initial disclosures in this case to be voluminous.

Id. Finally, the court chastised defendants' counsel for trying to force plaintiffs to reveal their subjective impressions of the quality of evidence in the disclosures:

> [I]t is apparent that the Medco Defendants seek to use the self-executing disclosure statements of Rule 26(a)(1) not only as a tool for starting relevant discovery, but also as a tool to learn details of Plaintiffs' investigation and trial strategy. For example, the Medco Defendants ask this court to require Plaintiffs to make a qualitative determination of the most important witnesses in each category as part of their Amended Initial Disclosure Statement. This request clearly seeks information and analysis that goes well beyond the purpose and intent of Rule 26(a)(1).

Id. at 335.

3. *The Ethics of Nondisclosure.* In the problem case, would Eve Barrie's memorandum be subject to Rule 26(a) required disclosure? To answer

this completely, you need to know some evidence law. Is the memorandum something that the company might use to support its defense? Not likely—since it seems to undercut the defense. But who can tell what might happen at trial that might make the memorandum relevant to the defense? In the same vein, can you say with certainty that the memorandum need not be disclosed because it would be used "solely for impeachment" of Eve Barrie? That word "solely" is quite a limitation, isn't it?

The Secret Memo hypothetical also has obvious ethical implications. What do professional ethics dictate in this situation, apart from *any* rules of procedure? Consider the following discussion of this dilemma from Deborah Rhode's Professional Responsibility: Ethics by the Pervasive Method 442-444 (2d ed. 1998):

> In a well-known passage from his autobiography, Samuel Williston described an incident from practice involving a financial dispute. As counsel for the defendant, Williston had carefully reviewed his client's correspondence with the plaintiff. Opposing counsel had made no inquiries concerning certain letters relevant to the controversy, and no one mentioned them at trial. The court ruled in favor of the defendant and gave an oral explanation of its reasoning that Williston describes as follows:
>
> > In the course of his remarks the Chief Justice stated as one reason for his decision a supposed fact which I knew to be unfounded. I had in front of me a letter that showed his error. Though I have no doubt of the propriety of my behavior in keeping silent, I was somewhat uncomfortable at the time. . . . The lawyer must decide when he takes a case whether it is a suitable one for him to undertake and after this decision is made, he is not justified in turning against his client by exposing injurious evidence entrusted to him. If that evidence was unknown to him when he took the case, he may sometimes withdraw from it, but while he is engaged as counsel he is not only not obligated to disclose unfavorable evidence, but it is a violation of his duty to his client if he does so.
>
> In another often-discussed case from around the same period, the New York County Bar Ethics Committee was asked for an opinion about disclosures in tort litigation. The plaintiff was a three-year-old child, who was injured by falling off a porch, allegedly because of the defendant owner's negligence. The defendant's attorney successfully moved to dismiss the case for lack of evidence without disclosing that he had an eyewitness to the accident present in court. Neither the judge nor the plaintiff's attorney was aware that any witness existed. The Committee's entire assessment of the case was as follows: "In the opinion of the Committee the conduct of the defendant's attorney is not professionally improper. The fact of infancy does not call for a different reply."
>
> Such dead ends in the search for truth are not uncommon. . . . Nor are the costs insubstantial: consider the nondisclosure of an opponent's life-threatening disease. . . . The rationale for withholding information in such cases rests on two considerations. One involves the need to protect confidential information in order to ensure trust and candor in lawyer-client relationships. The other consideration involves the need to provide incentives in a competitive adversarial structure. If parties begin to assume that they can

rely on an opponent's disclosure of material information, they may cease to do adequate preparation themselves. The result would be inequity and inefficiency. One party could end up subsidizing both sides of a lawsuit. And the more that individuals attempted to freeload on their adversaries, the greater the risk that neither side would prepare adequately.

Are these considerations sufficient to justify the bar's current ethical rules concerning disclosure of facts? Disciplinary Rule 7-102(A) provides that a lawyer "shall not conceal or knowingly fail to disclose that which he is required by law to reveal" and "shall not knowingly make a false statement of law or fact." Model Rule 3.3(a) similarly prohibits lawyers from making a "false statement of material fact or law to a tribunal," and from failing "to disclose a material fact to a tribunal when disclosure is necessary to avoid assisting a criminal or fraudulent act by the client." In ex parte proceedings, a lawyer must "inform the tribunal of all material facts known to the lawyer which will enable the tribunal to make an informed decision, whether or not the facts are adverse."

Should the rule governing ex parte proceedings apply to all litigation? . . . A similar obligation applies to prosecutors, who must reveal exculpatory facts under Brady v. Maryland, (373 U.S. 83 (1963)), Model Rule 3.8, and DR 7-103(B). Defenders of a broader duty of disclosure in civil cases point out that these analogous provisions have worked reasonably well in criminal cases without undermining incentive structures or trusting relationships in contexts such as criminal prosecutions or securities regulation. Advocates also argue that additional disclosure requirements would not chill client confidences. . . . From this perspective:

- clients often have no realistic alternative to confiding in counsel;
- lawyers acquire much adverse information through means other than direct client communication;
- clients already are unaware of the scope of confidentiality protections; and
- the bar in many countries and in this nation historically has managed to provide adequate representation without sweeping confidentiality protections.

What is your view? Would you support an initial proposal by the Model Rules Commission that 1) would have required disclosure of adverse facts if they would "probably have a substantial effect on the determination of a material issue" and 2) would have permitted disclosure of evidence favorable to opposing parties?

## C.  THE SCOPE OF DISCOVERY

## 1.  "Relevant to Any Party's Claim or Defense"

The following case was decided under the original, broad "relevant to the subject matter" rule for the scope of permissible discovery. As you read it, consider how the new proportionality limitations of Rule 26(b)(1) might have affected the court's analysis.

## *Blank v. Sullivan & Cromwell*
16 Fair Empl. Prac. Cas. (BNA) 87 (S.D.N.Y. 1976)

MOTLEY, DISTRICT JUDGE.

[Plaintiffs were female lawyers who had unsuccessfully applied for positions as associates around 1970; they sued, alleging sex discrimination in hiring — EDS.]

Plaintiffs have moved for a rehearing and modification of so much of this court's order of May 24, 1976[,] as denied plaintiffs the discovery sought in Interrogatories 60(f) and (g), 61, 62, and 63 of their First Interrogatories[1] (filed in court on April 18, 1976). That order adopted the report of Magistrate Harold J. Raby, to whom plaintiffs' Rule 37 motion had previously been referred, but modified the report insofar as it had recommended compliance with the Interrogatories here in question. Specifically, with respect to these Interrogatories (and certain others not in issue on the motion for rehearing), the court held that "the defendant need not respond in any form to such Interrogatories since the information sought therein relates to defendant's partners and employees who became partners, and is not relevant to the subject matter of the suit before this court." However, upon reconsideration and upon careful examination of the arguments submitted by plaintiffs, defendant, and amicus Equal Employment Opportunity Commission, the court has decided to order defendants to respond to the Interrogatories here in issue. . . .

In reversing its prior ruling, this court also is mindful of the fact that a plaintiff may not sue for injuries that he or she has not suffered, and he or she may not sue on behalf of a class of which he or she is not a member. Plaintiff, therefore, cannot represent in this action those who may be aggrieved by defendant's partner selection criteria. However, defendant is incorrect in suggesting that because the individual plaintiff here has not

---

1.

60. Identify each and every female permanent associate at Sullivan & Cromwell prior to August 30, 1970 and indicate as to each . . .

(f). whether each was offered an opportunity to become a partner; and
(g). whether each became a partner.

61. State the average length of service at the firm as an associate, of all associates who were offered partnerships in the firm between 1961 and the present date.

62. If any person listed in answer to Question 60 was not offered an opportunity to become a partner within the average length of service period noted in answer to Question 61, state the reason why she was not extended such an offer.

63. State the name of each male attorney hired by the firm after the earliest date listed in answer to Question 60(b) who was offered an opportunity to become a partner at the firm, and indicate:

(a) the date when each person started work at the firm;
(b) the date on which each person was offered the opportunity to become a partner; and
(c) the area of specialization of each person.

alleged that she was denied partnership due to her sex, she is not entitled to the requested discovery.

Under Rule 26, Fed. R. Civ. P., a party is entitled to discovery, not only of material which is relevant and admissible at trial, but also of information which "appears reasonably calculated to lead to the discovery of admissible evidence."* More specifically, in Title VII cases, in which a plaintiff alleges discriminatory employment practices, both the Supreme Court, in McDonnell Douglas Corp. v. Green, 411 U.S. 792, 804-805 (1973), and the Second Circuit in Kohn v. Royall, Koegel & Wells, 496 F.2d 1094 (2d Cir. 1974), have ruled that general information on defendant's labor hierarchy may be reflective of restrictive or exclusionary hiring practices within the contemplation of the statute.

Thus, the narrow inquiry is whether the information requested is so unrelated to plaintiffs' claim that women are discriminated against by defendant on account of sex that it cannot be said to be "relevant" within the expansive meaning of that term in Rule 26. In the court's view, this connection is not nearly so tenuous as defendant suggests.

By order dated June 13, 1975, this court ruled that "the class represented by plaintiff is defined to include all women qualified to hold legal positions at the law firm of Sullivan and Cromwell who have been or would be denied employment because of their sex." Judge Lasker of this Court dealt with a plaintiff class similarly constituted in a suit against the law firm of Royall, Koegel & Wells. By order dated January 7, 1975, he granted plaintiffs in that suit similar discovery with respect to advancement to partnership, endorsing the recommendation of Magistrate, now Judge Goettel, who had commented as follows: "It is difficult to conceive of anything more telling with respect to whether or not these associates [females] are being subject to employment discrimination than whether they proceed on to partnerships in the firm in the same manner as male attorneys with similar capabilities."

The court is, of course, aware that the numerous factors, which bear upon the admission to partnership, make it impossible to equate that decision with the decision to hire an associate. However, it does not follow from that recognition that a firm's practices in advancing, or failing to advance, associates to partnership have no probative bearing upon allegations of improper discrimination in hiring associates. Even assuming, *arguendo*, that Title VII does not proscribe the use of sex as a criterion for admission to partnership, that legal conclusion does not necessarily indicate that evidence of sexually oriented discrimination at that level might not be probative of a similar pattern in the selection of associates, where it would be illegal.

Accordingly, defendant is directed to answer the Interrogatories referred to above.

---

* [This language appears in Rule 26(b)(1) — Eds.]

## Note: Relevance and Proportionality

First, note that the Federal Rules of Evidence define "relevant evidence" as evidence having "any tendency to make a fact more or less probable than it would be without the evidence; and . . . the fact is of consequence in determining the action." Fed. R. Evid. 401. Rule 26 of the Federal Rules of Civil Procedure, however, is concerned with relevant "information," not "evidence." Indeed, Rule 26(b)(1) explicitly states that "information within [the] scope of discovery *need not be admissible in evidence* to be discoverable" (emphasis added). Relevant information is therefore broader than relevant evidence. See, e.g., A.M. v. Am. School for the Deaf, 2016 WL 1117363 (D. Conn. March 22, 2016) ("Discovery, however, 'is concerned with "relevant information"—not "relevant evidence"—and . . . as a result the scope of relevance for discovery purposes is necessarily broader than trial relevance.'") (quoting Steven S. Gensler, 1 Federal Rules of Civil Procedure, Rules and Commentary Rule 26 (Feb. 2016 Update)).

The clarifying language referred to in *Blank*—that information within the scope of discovery is admissible if it appears "reasonably calculated to lead to the discovery of admissible evidence"—was deleted from the Rule in 2015. That older language prompted judges to consider whether a request for information that would be inadmissible at trial could help the party discover admissible evidence. The Advisory Committee explained that the phrase, "has been used by some, incorrectly, to define the scope of discovery." Fed. R. Civ. P. 26 Advisory Committee Notes (2015 Amendment).

Now, it appears, analysis concentrates on whether the requested information helps make a fact regarding a claim or defense more or less probable than it would be without that information, *irrespective of whether that information would be admissible at trial*. To give a simple example, discovery of statements in an email that constitute hearsay, or statements that would be more prejudicial than probative under Fed. R. Evid. 403, should be allowed if the statements make a fact regarding a claim or defense more probable than it would be without those statements. That means the party served with the request cannot refuse to produce the email on the ground that the statements it contains would not be admissible at trial or on the ground that disclosure is not "reasonably calculated to lead to the discovery of admissible evidence." So, as long as the request for the email is also "proportional to the needs of the case," it should be produced. See Arcelormittal Indiana Harbor LLC v. Amex Nooter, LLC, 2016 WL 614144 (N.D. Ind. Feb. 16, 2016) (permitting discovery of information regarding confidential settlement negotiations inadmissible as evidence in court under Fed. R. Evid. 408).

Second, as we saw at the start of the chapter, the old Rule 26(b)(1) standard, "relevance to the subject matter" of the lawsuit, which *Blank* applied, has been replaced with the new formulation: "relevant to *any party's claim or defense* and *proportional to the needs of the case*" (emphasis added). (Remember, too, that an even narrower standard applies for the Rule 26(a) mandatory disclosures: The disclosing party must turn over materials that support her *own* claims or defenses.)

The intent of the rulemakers is crystal clear, isn't it? They want to limit discovery after initial disclosures and to cut down on its excesses. Bearing that in mind, do you think the partnership information in *Blank* is discoverable by interrogatory under the new Rule 26(b)(1)? Should the burden of showing the proportionality (or disproportionality) of that discovery request fall on Blank's lawyers or the lawyers representing Sullivan & Cromwell?

The Advisory Committee Notes to the 2015 amendments state that adding "the proportionality calculation to Rule 26(b)(1) . . . does not place on the party seeking discovery the burden of addressing all proportionality considerations. Nor is the change intended to permit the opposing party to refuse discovery simply by making a boilerplate objection that it is not proportional." Instead, the "[t]he parties and the court have a collective responsibility to consider the proportionality of all discovery and consider it in resolving discovery disputes." Id. See also Chief Justice John Roberts, 2015 Year-End Report on the Federal Judiciary 10, Dec. 31, 2015 (encouraging judges "to take on a stewardship role, managing their cases from the outset rather than allowing parties alone to dictate the scope of discovery and pace of litigation").

It is too early to know how this "collective responsibility" will be shared by judges and litigants. In principle, collective responsibility with regard to proportionality should not alter the traditional obligation of the party seeking discovery to demonstrate *relevance*. But proportionality and relevance are closely intertwined. A request for discovery of material that is obviously relevant is more likely to seem proportional, isn't it? The hardest cases seem likely to be those in which the requesting party is correct to believe that an event occurred (e.g., a conspiratorial agreement or a complete recovery from injuries sustained in an accident) but uncertain about the sources necessary to establish the relevant facts. Even assuming cases of this kind survive a 12(b)(6) motion, early discovery requests by the party in the dark may appear overbroad, like a fishing expedition, and therefore disproportionate. Relevance will be harder to establish precisely because the connections between the facts one seeks to establish and the evidence one requests either will not be known or may appear attenuated.

The Advisory Committee Notes suggest that the Rule 26(f) conference can help "address[] and reduce[]" these uncertainties. Fed. R. Civ. P. 26 Advisory Committee Notes (2015 Amendment). Courts are also directed to be sensitive to cases that involve "'information asymmetry.' One party—often an individual plaintiff—may have very little discoverable information. The other party may have vast amounts of information that can be readily retrieved and information that is more difficult to retrieve. In practice these circumstances often mean that the burden of responding to discovery lies heavier on the party who has more information, and properly so." Id. One early, provisional examination of proportionality litigation suggests that while the party resisting disclosure invokes the standard more often, that resistance does not appear to be any more successful than under the prior standard. See David. F Kerr and Steven Baicker-McKee, 2015 Amendments in the Courts, 31 No. 5 Fed. Litigator NL 6 (May 2016).

Finally, consider the likely implications for pleading practice of the new proportionality standard. To ensure broad discovery, there is an incentive to draft expansive pleadings.

### Note: Unduly Burdensome or Expensive

Responding to discovery can be very burdensome. Written interrogatories, for example, can be cheap to produce and costly to answer; lengthy or numerous depositions can seriously disrupt normal business and the activities of life. Balancing the legitimate need for information against the burden and expense of producing it has proved a nearly intractable problem both for the rulemakers and for the courts.

The original tool for dealing with excessive discovery requests was a motion for a protective order from the court under Rule 26(c). Because the original scope of discovery was so broad, such orders were seldom granted. In the first round of attack on discovery abuse, the 1983 revision called for a court to place limits on the frequency of discovery if it was found "unreasonably cumulative, more readily obtainable from another source, redundant of discovery already taken, unduly burdensome or expensive taking into account the needs of the case, the amount in controversy, limitations on the parties' resources, and the importance of the issues at stake in the litigation."

The 2000 revisions went even further in providing for the court to raise the matter of limits on its own, without waiting for an aggrieved party to complain or seek a protective order. See Rule 26(b)(2)(C).

These provisions signal that parties no longer have an unquestioned right to pursue discovery until "no stone is left unturned" or their adversary collapses from exhaustion (whichever comes first). But they have been criticized on the ground that they call for an impossibly subjective inquiry; they authorize the courts to make inappropriate judgments about the relative "importance" of cases; and they require judgments about whether discovery requests are proportional before the facts that would reveal the complexity of a case are known.

### Note: Penalties for Noncompliance with Discovery Orders

Ordinarily parties comply with orders compelling production under Rule 37 and are very sensitive to the threat of sanctions for noncompliance under Rules 26(g) and 37. But what should the court do if orders compelling production are defied? In AngioDynamics, Inc. v. Biolitec AG, 780 F.3d 429 (1st Cir. 2015), *cert. denied*, 136 S. Ct. 535 (2015), after defendants repeatedly refused to produce various individuals for depositions, the plaintiff moved for and received a $75 million default judgment as a sanction under Rule 37. Although default judgment is an extraordinary sanction, the First Circuit emphasized that it rests within the sound discretion of the district court. In choosing a sanction, the First Circuit reasoned, a trial court must consider "the severity of the discovery violations, legitimacy of the party's excuse for failing to comply, repetition of violations, deliberateness of the misconduct, mitigating excuses, prejudice to the other party and to the operations of the court, and adequacy of lesser sanctions." Id. at 435. Here, despite receiving numerous admonitions,

> Defendants continued to engage in a deliberate pattern of stonewalling with the aim of frustrating effective discovery and the progress of the case. Facing repeated recalcitrance almost five years after ADI filed the instant action, the district court acted well within its discretion when it concluded that no lesser sanction could address the twin goals of penalty and deterrence.
>
> Although entry of default judgment is a drastic sanction, it nonetheless provides a useful remedy where, as here, a litigant is confronted by an obstructionist adversary.

Id. at 436 (internal quotation marks and citations omitted).

Why would the defendants risk default judgment by refusing to produce witnesses for discovery? The underlying suit was to recover on a New York judgment of $23 million arising from a supply contract dispute. ADI sought to secure payment on the judgment by suing Biolitec in Massachusetts (where it had its principal place of business), and naming the company's president and CEO, as well as its German corporate parents. The complaint alleged that defendants had conspired to loot Biolitec of $18 million in assets in order to render the company judgment proof. Id. at 432. Moreover, while the litigation was pending, not only did defendants refuse to appear for depositions or produce documents, but the corporate parent merged with an Austrian subsidiary in order to further insulate its assets from the jurisdiction of the federal court in Massachusetts. The merger occurred in direct violation of a preliminary injunction issued by the federal court for which defendants were held in contempt. See AngioDynamics, Inc. v. Biolitec AG, 946 F. Supp. 2d 205, 215 (D. Mass. 2013) (issuing an arrest warrant for the Biolitec CEO and a multimillion dollar schedule of sanctions for each month the defendants failed to "return Biolitec AG to the status quo ante"; denying motions for relief from contempt order, to vacate injunction, and to disqualify judge).

## 2. "Any Matter Not Privileged"

### Problem Case: A Literary Law Student

Donna Doolittle is a second-year student at Stamford Law School in Stamford, Connecticut. In 2008, she began publishing a book, in weekly installments, in the National Legal Gossip Journal. Entitled *Stamford Law*, the book recounts the trials and tribulations of a first-year law student.

In 2009, Evan Monson, the author of *First Year* (a best-selling book about a first-year student's experience in law school, published in the early 1990s), sued Doolittle and the National Legal Gossip Corporation for copyright infringement, claiming that her book impermissibly copied Monson's book.

Doolittle has retained you as her attorney. You have filed an answer denying that she copied any part of *First Year.* Your answer was based in part on the following:

Donna has never read *First Year.* However, a friend of hers, who read a draft of *Stamford Law,* remarked on the striking similarities between her book and Monson's. As a result, Donna retained Charlie Counsel to advise her about copyright law before she published the first installment. Charlie sent Donna a memorandum, which begins: "Based on your friend's comment that *Stamford Law* bears a 'striking resemblance' to *First Year,* I have done some legal research. . . ." The memo goes on to say that one does not infringe a copyrighted work unless one actually copied the work, and it concludes that Donna should not read *First Year.* (You check and determine that this is an accurate account of copyright law.) Donna doesn't have a copy of the memo in her possession; she recalled that she had lent it to a fellow student to assist him in preparing for a copyright exam. Rather than try to track down the student, who has since graduated, you obtained a copy of the memo directly from Charlie Counsel.

Donna says that all of the stories recounted in *Stamford Law* were based on her own experiences or those of law school classmates. There are four sets of documents relating to these experiences:

1) A diary, written during her first year at law school, that, in addition to recounting events at the school, contains much personal material, which she says would be terribly embarrassing to reveal to anyone. She has adamantly refused to let you see the diary, saying that her personal thoughts and revelations are so intertwined with descriptions of events at the school that they can't be separated.

2) Some very rough notes, in an orange notebook, of her conversations with classmates, upon which she drew to write the book.

3) After completing the book, but before the first installment was published, Donna started systematically re-interviewing her classmates to hear their stories again. Rough notes of the re-interviews are in a blue notebook. When you asked her why she did the re-interviews, Donna said that she had the impression that it was important to check out the stories "in case someone claimed they were untrue."

4) Donna was still conducting the re-interviews as the installments were being published, but she stopped when Monson filed suit. You asked her to continue re-interviewing the remainder of her classmates to get their stories. She has completed the project and given you a yellow notebook with these interview notes.

You are Donna's lawyer. Which, if any, of the four sets of documents are you required to disclose under Rule 26(a)(1)? Suppose that Monson's counsel notices Donna's deposition and asks that she bring "all correspondence, notes, interviews, drafts, and other documents relating to the writing and publication of *Stamford Law*." What will you tell her to produce?

Do you think this is an appropriate case in which to move for a protective order under Rule 26(c)? What would your argument be?

## Note: Privileges in Civil Litigation

One principle of discovery has withstood all rule revision and rethinking: privileged information is not discoverable. Some privileges are defined by the law of evidence, though analysis of them occurs in light of long-established common law privileges. A witness who successfully asserts a privilege may avoid giving relevant evidence in a case. The Fifth Amendment privilege against self-incrimination is a familiar example; it applies in civil litigation only if the witness faces a serious threat of *criminal* prosecution. Privileges designed to protect certain professional or confidential relationships—the doctor-patient, priest-penitent, and marital privileges, for example—are also established in most jurisdictions. A less established example, recognized in most but not all jurisdictions, is the journalist's privilege to protect confidential news sources, recognized by a few courts and some statutory law. See, e.g., Baker v. F & F Inv., 470 F.2d 778 (2d Cir. 1972). See also Omokehinde v. Detroit Bd. Educ., 251 F.R.D. 261, 264 (E.D. Mich. 2007) (noting that most jurisdictions have adopted some qualified privilege for journalists despite the Sixth Circuit's refusal).

In all of these areas, it is a given that recognizing the privilege may impede the search for truth by depriving the parties and the court of relevant, often highly probative evidence. The privilege represents a judgment that other social values outweigh the needs and interests of the civil litigation system. Given the strong interest in disclosure of relevant facts, all privileges generally are construed narrowly, and care must be taken not to waive the privilege inadvertently. Thus, for example, submitting an insurance form to recover medical expenses may constitute a waiver of any psychiatrist-patient privilege. Likewise, the privilege may be only as good as the professional in whom one confides. In a New Jersey criminal case that received national attention, the court held that no privilege barred a jailhouse minister from testifying that the defendant confessed to him. Although the minister could not be compelled to testify, he could do so voluntarily. See Wade Lambert, Courts Say Penitents' Secrets May Not Be Secret, Wall St. J., Jan. 13, 1994, at B1.

The privileges most common in civil litigation are the attorney-client privilege and its offshoot, the work-product privilege. Unlike all other privileges, these two are said to promote, or at least be consistent with, the underlying values of the adversary system. Thus, they are more robust and easier to maintain than other privileges. This is true even though they operate, like the others, to deprive the fact finder of relevant information. In the following cases, you will see the profound conviction expressed by the

Supreme Court over many decades that protection of the lawyer's private work is essential to the sound operation of the system as a whole.

The attorney-client privilege is mostly a creature of common law, with local variations. For analysis of the history of the privilege, see Norman W. Spaulding, The Privilege of Probity: Forgotten Foundations of the Attorney-Client Privilege, 26 Geo. J. Leg. Ethics 301 (2013). Nowhere does it mean, as laypeople tend to think, that telling something to a lawyer turns it into a protected secret. The hornbook elements of attorney-client privilege are 1) a communication 2) from the client to the lawyer 3) without the presence of others 4) for the purpose of seeking legal advice.

In the famous case of Hickman v. Taylor, the privilege argued was attorney-client. The Court found that it did not apply but fashioned a new privilege instead: work-product protection. As you read the following materials, think about the view they give of lawyers' work and of the adversary system.

## Hickman v. Taylor
329 U.S. 495 (1947)

JUSTICE MURPHY delivered the opinion of the Court.

This case presents an important problem under the Federal Rules of Civil Procedure . . . as to the extent to which a party may inquire into oral and written statements of witnesses, or other information, secured by an adverse party's counsel in the course of preparation for possible litigation after a claim has arisen. . . .

On February 7, 1943, the tug *"J. M. Taylor"* sank while engaged in helping to tow a car float of the Baltimore & Ohio Railroad across the Delaware River at Philadelphia. The accident was apparently unusual in nature, the cause of it still being unknown. Five of the nine crew members were drowned. Three days later the tug owners and the underwriters employed a law firm, of which respondent Fortenbaugh is a member, to defend them against potential suits by representatives of the deceased crew members and to sue the railroad for damages to the tug.

A public hearing was held on March 4, 1943, before the United States Steamboat Inspectors, at which the four survivors were examined. This testimony was recorded and made available to all interested parties. Shortly thereafter, Fortenbaugh privately interviewed the survivors and took statements from them with an eye toward the anticipated litigation; the survivors signed these statements on March 29. Fortenbaugh also interviewed other persons believed to have some information relating to the accident and in some cases he made memoranda of what they told him. At the time when Fortenbaugh secured the statements of the survivors, representatives of two of the deceased crew members had been in communication with him. Ultimately claims were presented by representatives of all five of the deceased; four of the claims, however, were settled without litigation. The fifth claimant, petitioner herein, brought suit in a federal court under the Jones Act on November 26, 1943, naming as defendants the two tug owners, individually and as partners, and the railroad.

One year later, petitioner filed 39 interrogatories directed to the tug owners. The 38th interrogatory read:

> State whether any statements of the members of the crews of the Tugs 'J.M. Taylor' and 'Philadelphia' or of any other vessel were taken in connection with the towing of the car float and the sinking of the Tug 'John M. Taylor'. Attach hereto exact copies of all such statements if in writing, and if oral, set forth in detail the exact provisions of any such oral statements or reports.

Supplemental interrogatories asked whether any oral or written statements, records, reports, or other memoranda had been made concerning any matter relative to the towing operation, the sinking of the tug, the salvaging and repair of the tug, and the death of the deceased. If the answer was in the affirmative, the tug owners were then requested to set forth the nature of all such records, reports, statements or other memoranda.

The tug owners, through Fortenbaugh, answered all of the interrogatories except No. 38 and the supplemental ones just described. While admitting that statements of the survivors had been taken, they declined to summarize or set forth the contents. They did so, on the ground that such requests called "for privileged matter obtained in preparation for litigation" and constituted "an attempt to obtain indirectly counsel's private files." It was claimed that answering these requests "would involve practically turning over not only the complete files, but also the telephone records and, almost, the thoughts of counsel."

In connection with the hearing on these objections, Fortenbaugh made a written statement and gave an informal oral deposition explaining the circumstances under which he had taken the statements. But he was not expressly asked in the deposition to produce the statements. The District Court for the Eastern District of Pennsylvania, sitting en banc, held that the requested matters were not privileged. 4 F.R.D. 479 [(E.D. Pa. 1945)]. The court then decreed that the tug owners and Fortenbaugh, as counsel and agent for the tug owners, forthwith

> Answer Plaintiff's 38th interrogatory and supplementary interrogatories; produce all written statements of witnesses obtained by Mr. Fortenbaugh, as counsel and agent for Defendants; state in substance any fact concerning this case which Defendants learned through oral statements made by witnesses to Mr. Fortenbaugh whether or not included in his private memoranda and produce Mr. Fortenbaugh's memoranda containing statements of fact by witnesses or to submit these memoranda to the Court for determination of those portions which should be revealed to Plaintiff.

Upon their refusal, the court adjudged them in contempt and ordered them imprisoned until they complied.

The Third Circuit Court of Appeals, also sitting en banc, reversed the judgment of the District Court. 153 F.2d 212 [(3d Cir. 1945)]. It held that the information here sought was part of the "work product of the lawyer" and hence privileged from discovery under the Federal Rules of Civil Procedure. The importance of the problem, which has engendered a great divergence of views among district courts, led us to grant certiorari. 328 U.S. 876 [(1946)].

The pretrial deposition-discovery mechanism established by Rules 26 to 37 is one of the most significant innovations of the Federal Rules of Civil Procedure. Under the prior federal practice, the pretrial functions of notice giving, issue formulation and fact revelation were performed primarily and inadequately by the pleadings. Inquiry into the issues and the facts before trial was narrowly confined and was often cumbersome in method. The new rules, however, restrict the pleadings to the task of general notice giving and invest the deposition-discovery process with a vital role in the preparation for trial. The various instruments of discovery now serve (1) as a device, along with the pretrial hearing under Rule 16, to narrow and clarify the basic issues between the parties, and (2) as a device for ascertaining the facts, or information as to the existence or whereabouts of facts relative to those issues. Thus civil trials in the federal courts no longer need be carried on in the dark. The way is now clear, consistent with recognized privileges, for the parties to obtain the fullest possible knowledge of the issues and facts before trial. . . .

In urging that he has a right to inquire into the materials secured and prepared by Fortenbaugh, petitioner emphasizes that the deposition-discovery portions of the Federal Rules of Civil Procedure are designed to enable the parties to discover the true facts and to compel their disclosure wherever they may be found. It is said that inquiry may be made under these rules, epitomized by Rule 26, as to any relevant matter which is not privileged; and since the discovery provisions are to be applied as broadly and liberally as possible, the privilege limitation must be restricted to its narrowest bounds. On the premise that the attorney-client privilege is the one involved in this case, petitioner argues that it must be strictly confined to confidential communications made by a client to his attorney. And since the materials here in issue were secured by Fortenbaugh from third persons rather than from his clients, the tug owners, the conclusion is reached that these materials are proper subjects for discovery under Rule 26.

As additional support for this result, petitioner claims that to prohibit discovery under these circumstances would give a corporate defendant a tremendous advantage in a suit by an individual plaintiff. Thus in a suit by an injured employee against a railroad or in a suit by an insured person against an insurance company the corporate defendant could pull a dark veil of secrecy over all the pertinent facts it can collect after the claim arises merely on the assertion that such facts were gathered by its large staff of attorneys and claim agents. At the same time, the individual plaintiff, who often has direct knowledge of the matter in issue and has no counsel until some time after his claim arises could be compelled to disclose all the intimate details of his case. By endowing with immunity from disclosure all that a lawyer discovers in the course of his duties, it is said, the rights of individual litigants in such cases are drained of vitality and the lawsuit becomes more of a battle of deception than a search for truth.

But framing the problem in terms of assisting individual plaintiffs in their suits against corporate defendants is unsatisfactory. Discovery concededly may work to the disadvantage as well as to the advantage of individual plaintiffs. Discovery, in other words, is not a one-way proposition. It is available in all types of cases at the behest of any party, individual or corporate, plaintiff or defendant. The problem thus far transcends the situation confronting this petitioner. And we must view that problem in light of the limitless situations where the particular kind of discovery sought by petitioner might be used.

We agree, of course, that the deposition-discovery rules are to be accorded a broad and liberal treatment. No longer can the time-honored cry of "fishing expedition" serve to preclude a party from inquiry into the facts underlying his opponent's case. Mutual knowledge of all the relevant facts gathered by both parties is essential to proper litigation. To that end, either party may compel the other to disgorge whatever facts he has in his possession. The deposition-discovery procedure simply advances the stage at which the disclosure can be compelled from the time of trial to the period preceding it, thus reducing the possibility of surprise. But discovery, like all matters of procedure, has ultimate and necessary boundaries. As indicated by [Rule 26(c)] . . . limitations inevitably arise when it can be shown that the examination is being conducted in bad faith or in such a manner as to annoy, embarrass, or oppress the person subject to the inquiry. And as Rule 26(b) provides, further limitations come into existence when the inquiry touches upon the irrelevant or encroaches upon the recognized domains of privilege.

We also agree that the memoranda, statements, and mental impressions in issue in this case fall outside the scope of the attorney-client privilege and hence are not protected from discovery on that basis. It is unnecessary here to delineate the content and scope of that privilege as recognized in the federal courts. For present purposes, it suffices to note that the protective cloak of this privilege does not extend to information which an attorney secures from a witness while acting for his client in anticipation of litigation. Nor does this privilege concern the memoranda, briefs, communications and other writings prepared by counsel for his own use in prosecuting his client's case; and it is equally unrelated to writings which reflect an attorney's mental impressions, conclusions, opinions or legal theories.

But the impropriety of invoking that privilege does not provide an answer to the problem before us. Petitioner has made more than an ordinary request for relevant, nonprivileged facts in the possession of his adversaries or their counsel. He has sought discovery as of right of oral and written statements of witnesses whose identity is well known and whose availability to petitioner appears unimpaired. He has sought production of these matters after making the most searching inquires of his opponents as to the circumstances surrounding the fatal accident, which inquiries were sworn to have been answered to the best of their information and belief. Interrogatories were directed toward all the events prior to, during and subsequent to the sinking of the tug. Full and honest answers to such broad inquiries would necessarily have included all pertinent information gleaned by Fortenbaugh through his interviews with the witnesses. Petitioner makes no suggestion, and we cannot assume, that the tug owners or Fortenbaugh were incomplete or dishonest in the framing of their answers. In addition, petitioner was free to examine the public testimony of the witnesses taken before the United States Steamboat Inspectors. We are thus dealing with an attempt to secure the production of written statements and mental impressions contained in the files and the mind of the attorney Fortenbaugh without any showing of necessity or any indication or claim that denial of such production would unduly prejudice the preparation of petitioner's case or cause him any hardship or injustice. For aught that appears, the essence of what petitioner seeks either has been revealed to him already through the interrogatories or is readily available to him direct from the witnesses for the asking.

The District Court, after hearing objections to petitioner's request, commanded Fortenbaugh to produce all written statements of witnesses and to state in substance any facts learned through oral statements of witnesses to him. Fortenbaugh was to submit any memoranda he had made of the oral statements so that the court might determine what portions should be revealed to petitioner. All of this was ordered without any showing by petitioner, or any requirement that he make a proper showing, of the necessity for the production of any of this material or any demonstration that denial of production would cause hardship or injustice. The court simply ordered production on the theory that the facts sought were material and were not privileged as constituting attorney-client communications.

In our opinion, neither Rule 26 nor any other rule dealing with discovery contemplates production under such circumstances. That is not because the subject matter is privileged or irrelevant, as those concepts are used in these rules. Here is simply an attempt, without purported necessity or justification, to secure written statements, private memoranda and personal recollections prepared or formed by an adverse party's counsel in the course of his legal duties. As such, it falls outside the arena of discovery and contravenes the public policy underlying the orderly prosecution and defense of legal claims. Not even the most liberal of discovery theories can justify unwarranted inquiries into the files and the mental impressions of an attorney.

Historically, a lawyer is an officer of the court and is bound to work for the advancement of justice while faithfully protecting the rightful interests of his clients. In performing his various duties, however, it is essential that a lawyer work with a certain degree of privacy, free from unnecessary intrusion by opposing parties and their counsel. Proper preparation of a client's case demands that he assemble information, sift what he considers to be the relevant from the irrelevant facts, prepare his legal theories and plan his strategy without undue and needless interference. That is the historical and the necessary way in which lawyers act within the framework of our system of jurisprudence to promote justice and to protect their clients' interests. This work is reflected, of course, in interviews, statements, memoranda, correspondence, briefs, mental impressions, personal beliefs, and countless other tangible and intangible ways—aptly though roughly termed by the Circuit Court of Appeals in this case as the "work product of the lawyer" (citation omitted). Were such materials open to opposing counsel on mere demand, much of what is now put down in writing would remain unwritten. An attorney's thoughts, heretofore inviolate, would not be his own. Inefficiency, unfairness, and sharp practices would inevitably develop in the giving of legal advice and in the preparation of cases for trial. The effect on the legal profession would be demoralizing. And the interests of the clients and the cause of justice would be poorly served.

We do not mean to say that all written materials obtained or prepared by an adversary's counsel with an eye toward litigation are necessarily free from discovery in all cases. Where relevant and nonprivileged facts remain hidden in an attorney's file and where production of those facts is essential to the preparation of one's case, discovery may properly be had. Such written statements and documents might, under certain circumstances, be admissible in evidence or give clues as to the existence or location of relevant facts. Or they might be useful for purposes of impeachment or corroboration. And production might be justified where the witnesses are no longer available or can be reached only with difficulty. Were production of written statements and documents to be precluded under such circumstances, the liberal ideals of the deposition-discovery portions of the Federal Rules of Civil Procedure would be stripped of much of their meaning. But the general policy against invading the privacy of an attorney's course of preparation is so well recognized and so essential to an orderly working of our system of legal procedure that a burden rests on the one who would invade that privacy to establish adequate reasons to justify production through a subpoena or court order. That burden, we believe, is necessarily implicit in the rules as now constituted.

Rule [26(c)], as presently written, gives the trial judge the requisite discretion to make a judgment as to whether discovery should be allowed as to written statements secured from witnesses. But in the instant case there was no room for that discretion to operate in favor of the petitioner. No attempt was made to establish any reason why Fortenbaugh should be forced to produce the written statements. There was only a naked, general demand for these materials as of right and a finding by the District Court that no recognizable privilege was involved. That was insufficient to justify discovery under these circumstances and the court should have sustained the refusal of the tug owners and Fortenbaugh to produce.

But as to oral statements made by witnesses to Fortenbaugh, whether presently in the form of his mental impressions or memoranda, we do not believe that any showing of necessity can be made under the circumstances of this case so as to justify production. Under ordinary conditions, forcing an attorney to repeat or write out all that witnesses have told him and to deliver the account to his adversary gives rise to grave dangers of inaccuracy and untrustworthiness. No legitimate purpose is served by such production. The practice forces the attorney to testify as to what he remembers or what he saw fit to write down regarding witnesses' remarks . . . [and] would make the attorney much less an officer of the court and much more an ordinary witness. The standards of the profession would thereby suffer.

Denial of production of this nature does not mean that any material, non-privileged facts can be hidden from the petitioner in this case. He need not be unduly hindered in the preparation of his case, in the discovery of facts or in his anticipation of his opponents' position. Searching interrogatories directed to Fortenbaugh and the tug owners, production of written documents and statements upon a proper showing and direct interviews with the witnesses themselves all serve to reveal the facts in Fortenbaugh's possession to the fullest possible extent consistent with public policy. Petitioner's counsel frankly admits that he wants the oral statements only to help prepare himself to examine witnesses and to make sure that he has overlooked nothing. That is insufficient under the circumstances to permit him an exception to the policy underlying the privacy of Fortenbaugh's professional activities. If there should be a rare situation justifying production of these matters, petitioner's case is not of that type.

We fully appreciate the wide-spread controversy among the members of the legal profession over the problem raised by this case. It is a problem that rests on what has been one of the most hazy frontiers of the discovery process. But until some rule or statute definitely prescribes otherwise, we are not justified in permitting discovery in a situation of this nature as a matter of unqualified right. When Rule 26 and the other discovery rules were adopted, this Court and the members of the bar in general certainly did not believe or contemplate that all the files and mental processes of lawyers were thereby opened to the free scrutiny of their adversaries. And we refuse to interpret the rules at this time so as to reach so harsh and unwarranted a result.

We therefore affirm the judgment of the Circuit Court of Appeals.
*Affirmed.*

JUSTICE JACKSON, concurring. . . .

The primary effect of the practice advocated here would be on the legal profession itself. But it too often is overlooked that the lawyer and the law office are indispensable parts of our administration of justice. Law-abiding people can go nowhere else to learn the ever changing and constantly multiplying rules by which they must behave and to obtain redress for their wrongs. The welfare and tone of the legal profession is therefore of prime consequence to society, which would feel the consequences of such a practice as petitioner urges secondarily but certainly. . . .

Counsel for the petitioner candidly said on argument that he wanted this information to help prepare himself to examine witnesses, to make sure he overlooked nothing. He bases his claim to it in his brief on the view that the Rules were to do away with the old situation where a law suit developed into "a battle of wits between counsel." But a common law trial is and always should be an adversary proceeding. Discovery was hardly intended to enable a learned profession to perform its functions either without wits or on wits borrowed from the adversary.

The real purpose and the probable effect of the practice ordered by the district court would be to put trials on a level even lower than a "battle of wits." I can conceive of no practice more demoralizing to the Bar than to require a lawyer to write out and deliver to his adversary an account of what witnesses have told him. Even if his recollection were perfect, the statement would be his language, permeated with his inferences. Everyone who has tried it knows that it is almost impossible so fairly to record the expressions and emphasis of a witness that when he testifies in the environment of the court and under the influence of the leading question there will not be departures in some respects. Whenever the testimony of the witness would differ from the "exact" statement the lawyer had delivered, the lawyer's statement would be whipped out to impeach the witness. Counsel producing his adversary's "inexact" statement could lose nothing by saying, "Here is a contradiction, gentlemen of the jury. I do not know whether it is my adversary or his witness who is not telling the truth, but one is not." Of course, if this practice were adopted, that scene would be repeated over and over again. The lawyer who delivers such statements often would find himself branded a deceiver afraid to take the stand to support his own version of the witness's conversation with him, or else he will have to go on the stand to defend his own credibility—perhaps against that of his chief witness, or possibly even his client. . . .

And what is the lawyer to do who has interviewed one whom he believes to be a biased, lying or hostile witness to get his unfavorable statements and know what to meet? He must record and deliver such statements even though he would not vouch for the credibility of the witness by calling him. Perhaps the other side would not want to call him either, but the attorney is open to the charge of suppressing evidence at the trial if he fails to call such a hostile witness even though he never regarded him as reliable or truthful.

Having been supplied the names of the witnesses, petitioner's lawyer gives no reason why he cannot interview them himself. If an employee-witness refuses to tell his story, he, too, may be examined under the Rules. He may be compelled on discovery, as fully as on the trial, to disclose his version of the facts. But that is his own disclosure—it can be used to impeach him if he contradicts it and such a deposition is not useful to promote an unseemly disagreement between the witness and the counsel in the case. . . .

## Note: The Necessities of Adversary Litigation

Work-product protection, as recognized by the Supreme Court in Hickman v. Taylor, has been incorporated into and extended by Rule

26(b)(3). Can you see why Rule 26(b)(3) is broader than the rule established in *Hickman*?

In 1947, *Hickman* was among the first cases to reach the Supreme Court after the Federal Rules of Civil Procedure became effective in 1938. Running through the case is the concern that the discovery rules are incompatible with the adversary system, the traditional mode of uncovering truth. Easily discernible as a subtext is the Court's fear that the harder-working, more skilled, and ingenious counsel may not win his just reward under a system of open-handed discovery. See Richard L. Marcus, The Story of *Hickman*: Preserving Adversarial Incentives While Embracing Broad Discovery, in Civil Procedure Stories 323 (Kevin M. Clermont ed., 2d ed. 2008).

In view of the Court's concerns about the adversary system in *Hickman*, which, as you will see momentarily, are just as strong in a more recent case, Upjohn Co. v. United States, 449 U.S. 383 (1981), it seems strange indeed that in some places the practice of taking formal discovery, often depositions under oath, from opposing counsel has emerged. Can you see arguments that this is inoffensive, that it is the easiest way to obtain the information, and that it does not necessarily trench on the lawyer-client relationship?

Would the mandatory disclosure provisions of Rule 26(a) obviate any argument for taking opposing counsel's deposition? Is this an argument in their favor? For a summary of cases and a good exposition on both sides of the issue of whether lawyers may, or should, be allowed to take opposing counsel's deposition, see Timothy Flynn, Jr., Note, On "Borrowed Wits": A Proposed Rule for Attorney Depositions, 93 Colum. L. Rev. 1956 (1993). For contrasting views on deposing counsel, compare Club Vista Fin. Servs. v. Dist. Ct., 276 P.3d 246, 250 (Nev. 2012) (adopting strict approach of Shelton v. Am. Motors Corp., 805 F.2d 1323 (8th Cir. 1986), and holding that depositions of counsel "should only be permitted under exceptionally limited circumstances"), with In re Subpoena Issued to Dennis Friedman, 350 F.3d 65, 72 (2d Cir. 2003) (taking a more flexible approach).

For a case in which opposing counsel were ordered to submit to deposition, due to their waiver of the attorney-client privilege by failing to object and to maintain confidentiality, see Nguyen v. Excel Corp., 197 F.3d 200 (5th Cir. 1999). For a discussion of the ethical and practical considerations an attorney may face when subpoenaed for deposition, see Daniel J. Pope and Suzanne Lee, Discovery on Wits "Borrowed from the Adversary": Deposition of the Trial Attorney, 65 Def. Couns. J. 285, 285 (1998) ("As unusual as it may seem, the practice of deposing opposing trial counsel is not an uncommon method of discovery."). In United States v. Nobles, 422 U.S. 225 (1975), a criminal case, the written report made by a defense investigator was ordered turned over to the prosecutor when the investigator was called to testify at trial. One claim was that the investigator's report was work product and thus shielded from production. The Court held that in the circumstances of this case the privilege had been waived and noted: "At its core, the work-product doctrine shelters the mental processes of the attorney, providing a privileged area within which he can analyze and prepare his client's case. But the doctrine is an intensely practical one, grounded in the realities of litigation in our adversary system." Id. at 238.

### Note: The Scope of Work Product and Anticipating Litigation

Work product is one of the most frequently litigated privileges, and the phrase "in anticipation of litigation" is often the focus of dispute. See Rule 26(b)(3). To some, almost every business decision in today's world anticipates litigation. Others interpret the words to mean that a specific claim must have been filed, or at least threatened, before the work product privilege kicks in to protect documents from disclosure.

The Second Circuit has weighed in with the broad view, holding that work-product protection extends to documents created for the primary purpose of informing a business decision where the business decision is influenced by anticipated litigation. See United States v. Adlman, 134 F.3d 1194 (2d Cir. 1998). The case involved an IRS summons to obtain a memorandum prepared by the corporate taxpayer's outside accountants at the request of the company's tax counsel. The aim was to assess the tax consequences of a proposed corporate reorganization on anticipated litigation with the IRS. The court stated that "[n]owhere does Rule 26(b)(3) state that a document must have been prepared *to aid* in the conduct of litigation in order to constitute work product, much less *primarily or exclusively* to aid in litigation. Preparing a document 'in anticipation of litigation' is sufficient. . . . Nothing in the Rules states or suggests that documents prepared 'in anticipation of litigation' with the purpose of assisting in making a business decision do not fall within its scope." Id. at 1198-1199 (emphasis in original). Accordingly, the court held that "[w]here a document is created because of the prospect of litigation, analyzing the likely outcome of that litigation, it does not lose protection . . . merely because it is created in order to assist with a business decision." Id. at 1202.

*Adlman*'s "because of" standard is now the majority rule. See United States v. Roxworthy, 457 F.3d 590, 593 (6th Cir. 2006); In re Grand Jury Subpoena (Mark Torf), 350 F.3d 1010, 1015-1016 (9th Cir. 2003), *as amended by* 357 F.3d 900 (9th Cir. 2004); PepsiCo, Inc. v. Baird, Kurtz & Dobson LLP, 305 F.3d 813, 817 (8th Cir. 2002); State of Maine v. U.S. Dep't of Interior, 298 F.3d 60, 68 (1st Cir. 2002); Montgomery Cty. v. MicroVote Corp., 175 F.3d 296, 305 (3d Cir. 1999); Logan v. Commercial Union Ins. Co., 96 F.3d 971, 977 (7th Cir. 1996); Nat'l Union Fire Ins. Co. of Pittsburgh v. Murray Sheet Metal Co., 967 F.2d 980, 984 (4th Cir. 1992). As the Ninth Circuit summarized the rule, "a document should be deemed prepared 'in anticipation of litigation' . . . if 'in light of the nature of the document and the factual situation in the particular case, the document can be fairly said to have been prepared or obtained because of the prospect of litigation.'" *Grand Jury Subpoena*, 350 F.3d at 1016 (quoting Wright and Miller, 8 Federal Practice and Procedure § 2024 (2d ed. 1994)).

The District of Columbia Circuit has followed an even broader, *motive*-based application of the "because of" test, holding that documents need not have been prepared in connection with a specific claim to be shielded by attorney work-product privilege. The sole criterion is whether they were prepared based on an actual subjective and objectively reasonable belief that litigation was an even "real possibility." See In re Sealed Case, 146 F.3d 881, 884 (D.C. Cir. 1998). Judge Tatel explains that, "[w]ithout a strong work-product privilege, lawyers would keep their thoughts to themselves, avoid communicating with other lawyers, and hesitate to take notes." Id.

> [A] contrary ruling would undermine lawyer effectiveness at a particularly critical stage of a legal representation. It is often prior to the emergence of specific claims that lawyers are best equipped either to help clients avoid litigation or to strengthen available defenses should litigation occur. For instance, lawyers routinely meet with potential grand jury targets to discuss possible charges, consider whether business decisions might result in anti-trust or securities lawsuits, analyze copyright and patent implications of new technologies or works of art, and assess the possibility that new products might give rise to tort actions. If lawyers had to wait for specific claims to arise before their writings could enjoy work-product protection, they would not likely risk taking notes about such matters or communicating in writing with colleagues, thus severely limiting their ability to advise clients effectively. A lawyer advising a potential grand jury target, for example, might be reluctant to write something like "the critical facts which could harm my client are . . ." even though it would help the lawyer organize complex thoughts, because in the government's hands, such a note could become a powerful weapon against the client. Likewise, asked by a client to evaluate the antitrust implications of a proposed merger and advised that no specific claim had yet surfaced, a lawyer knowing that work product is unprotected would not likely risk preparing an internal legal memorandum assessing the merger's weaknesses, jotting down on a yellow legal pad possible areas of vulnerability, or sending a note to a partner—"After reviewing the proposed merger, I think it's O.K., although I'm a little worried about. . . . What are your views?" Nor would the partner respond in writing, "I disagree. This merger is vulnerable because. . . ." Discouraging lawyers from engaging in the writing, note-taking, and communications so critical to effective legal thinking would, in Hickman's words, "demoraliz[e]" the legal profession, and "the interests of the clients and the cause of justice would be poorly served."

Id. at 886-887. See also Equal Emp't Opportunity Comm'n v. Lutheran Soc. Servs. 186 F.3d 959, 969 (D.C. Cir. 1999), in which the appellate court applied its test in a similar case where "evidence suggest[ed] that litigation lay just over the horizon" and found a report protected by the work-product privilege. Other appellate courts favor a narrower construction of the work-product privilege, one where the disputed document is tailored to particular litigation. See, e.g., United States v. Davis, 636 F.2d 1028 (5th Cir. 1981), *cert. denied*, 454 U.S. 862 (1981); United States v. El Paso Co., 682 F.2d 530 (5th Cir. 1982), *cert. denied*, 466 U.S. 944 (1984).

The Second Circuit in *Adlman* was quick to emphasize that "the 'because of' formulation that we adopt here withholds protection from documents that are prepared in the ordinary course of business *or that would have been created in essentially similar form irrespective of the litigation.*" 134 F.3d at 1202 (emphasis added). The accountant's tax memorandum was prepared in anticipation of litigation in *Adlman*, but also to help the company assess the business consequences of the proposed merger, so the Second Circuit remanded the case for more fact-finding. Under the Second Circuit's approach, then, close attention to the circumstances surrounding a document's preparation is often necessary to draw the line. See *Grand Jury Subpoena*, 350 F.3d at 1017-1018 (work-product protection applies to documents prepared by environmental consultant in anticipation of litigation and in efforts to comply with an EPA civil investigation and supervised cleanup where a criminal investigation later develops: "Having chosen to pursue a criminal investigation, the government now seeks to capitalize on [the paint manufacturer's] earlier cooperation and obtain all of [the consultant's] documents pertaining to the disposal of [the manufacturer's] waste material. . . . The documents are entitled to work product protection because, taking into account the facts surrounding their creation, their litigation purpose so permeates any non-litigation purpose that the two purposes cannot be discretely separated. . . ."); United States v. Textron Inc., 577 F.3d 21, 27 (1st Cir. 2009) (en banc) (holding that tax accrual work papers shared with an outside accounting firm to obtain a necessary "clean" financial opinion were not protected work product; "[a]ny experienced litigator would describe the tax accrual work papers as tax documents and not as case preparation materials"). See also United States v. Deloitte LLP, 610 F.3d 129 (D.C. Cir. 2010) (distinguishing *Textron* and remanding for in camera review where IRS sought documents concerning tax treatment of partnerships owed by Dow, for whom Deloitte served as an independent auditor).

A final issue on the scope of work-product protection: How do you think a court should treat the claim that an attorney's selection among documents produced by an adversary should qualify as protected work product? Say the adversary produces thousands of documents in response to a request for production of documents or to prepare a client's deposition. Won't it reveal mental impressions if the lawyer has to disclose which documents she has selected from the heap?

In the most commonly cited case, the Third Circuit held that an attorney's choice of documents from among those produced qualifies as protected work product "[b]ecause identification of the documents as a group will reveal defense counsel's selection process, and thus his mental impressions. . . ." Sporck v. Peil, 759 F.2d 312, 315 (3d Cir. 1985), *cert. denied*, 474 U.S. 903 (1985). The Third Circuit relied on a district court opinion from Delaware in which the court emphasized that "'[i]n selecting and ordering a few documents out of thousands counsel could not help but reveal important aspects of his understanding of the case,'" and especially in cases "'involving extensive document discovery, the process of selection and distillation is often more critical than pure legal research.'" Id. at 316 (quoting James Julian, Inc. v. Raytheon Co., 93 F.R.D. 138, 144 (D. Del. 1982)); cf. Miller v. Holzmann, 238 F.R.D. 30, 32-33 (D.D.C. 2006) (distinguishing *Sporck* on the ground that the number of documents plaintiffs scanned from defendant's production, around 20,000, was "so large that it would be difficult to conceive of [defendant] gleaning plaintiffs' trial strategy solely by virtue of plaintiffs' disclosing the identity of the documents," concluding that the information was merely fact work product, not opinion work product, and denying plaintiffs' motion for a protective order because defendant's interest in accelerating the progress of litigation qualified as a "substantial need" under Rule 26(b)(3)).

## Upjohn Co. v. United States
449 U.S. 383 (1981)

JUSTICE REHNQUIST delivered the opinion of the Court.

. . . Petitioner Upjohn manufactures and sells pharmaceuticals here and abroad. In January 1976 independent accountants conducting an audit of one of petitioner's foreign subsidiaries discovered that the subsidiary made payments to or for the benefit of foreign government officials in order to secure government business. The accountants so informed Mr. Gerard Thomas, petitioner's Vice-President, Secretary, and General Counsel. Thomas is a member of the Michigan and New York bars, and has been petitioner's General Counsel for 20 years. He consulted with outside counsel and R. T. Parfet, Jr., petitioner's Chairman of the Board. It was decided that the company would conduct an internal investigation of what were termed "questionable payments." As part of this investigation the attorneys prepared a letter containing a questionnaire which was sent to "all foreign general and area managers" over the Chairman's signature. The letter began by noting recent disclosures that several American companies made "possibly illegal" payments to foreign government officials and emphasized that the management needed full information concerning any such payments made by Upjohn. The letter indicated that the Chairman had asked Thomas, identified as "the company's General Counsel," "to conduct an investigation for the purpose of determining the nature and magnitude of any payments made by the Upjohn Company or any of its subsidiaries to any employee or official of a foreign government." The questionnaire sought detailed information concerning such payments. Managers were instructed to treat the investigation as "highly confidential" and not to discuss it with anyone other than Upjohn employees who might be helpful in providing the requested information. Responses were to be sent directly to Thomas. Thomas and outside counsel also interviewed the recipients of the questionnaire and some 33 other Upjohn officers or employees as part of the investigation.

On March 26, 1976, the company voluntarily submitted a preliminary report to the Securities and Exchange Commission on Form 8-K disclosing certain questionable payments. A copy of the report was simultaneously submitted to the Internal Revenue Service, which immediately began an investigation to determine the tax consequences of the payments. Special agents conducting the investigation were given lists by Upjohn of all those interviewed and all who had responded to the questionnaire. On November 23, 1976, the Service issued a summons pursuant to 26 U.S.C. § 7602 demanding production of:

> All files relative to the investigation conducted under the supervision of Gerard Thomas to identify payments to employees of foreign governments and any political contributions made by the Upjohn Company or any of its affiliates since January 1, 1971[,] and to determine whether any funds of the Upjohn Company had been improperly accounted for on the corporate books during the same period.
>
> The records should include but not be limited to written questionnaires sent to managers of the Upjohn Company's foreign affiliates, and memorandums or notes of the interviews conducted in the United States and abroad with officers and employees of the Upjohn Company and its subsidiaries. . . .

The company declined to produce the documents specified in the second paragraph on the grounds that they were protected from disclosure by the attorney-client privilege and constituted the work product of attorneys prepared in anticipation of litigation. On August 31, 1977, the United States filed a petition seeking enforcement of the summons under 26 U.S.C. §§ 7402(b) and 7604(a) in the United States District Court for the Western District of Michigan. That court adopted the recommendation of a Magistrate who concluded that the summons should be enforced. Petitioner appealed to the Court of Appeals for the Sixth Circuit[, which upheld the order requiring production — EDS.] . . .

Federal Rule of Evidence 501 provides that "the privilege of a witness . . . shall be governed by the principles of the common law as they may be interpreted by the courts of the United States in light of reason and experience." The attorney-client privilege is the oldest of the privileges for confidential communications known to the common law. . . . Its purpose is to encourage full and frank communication between attorneys and their clients and thereby promote broader public interests in the observance of law and administration of justice. The privilege recognizes that sound legal advice or advocacy serves public ends and that such advice or advocacy depends upon the lawyer being fully informed by the client. . . .

Admittedly complications in the application of the privilege arise when the client is a corporation, which in theory is an artificial creature of the law, and not an individual; but this Court has assumed that the privilege applies when the client is a corporation. United States v. Louisville & Nashville R. Co., 236 U.S. 318, 336 (1915), and the Government does not contest the general proposition.

The Court of Appeals, however, considered the application of the privilege in the corporate context to present a "different problem," since the client was an inanimate entity and "only the senior management, guiding and integrating the several operations, . . . can be said to possess an identity analogous to the corporation as a whole." 600 F.2d at 1226. . . .

Such a view, we think, overlooks the fact that the privilege exists to protect not only the giving of professional advice to those who can act on it but also the giving of information to the lawyer to enable him to give sound and informed advice. . . . See also Hickman v. Taylor, 329 U.S. 495, 511 (1947).

In the case of the individual client the provider of information and the person who acts on the lawyer's advice are one and the same. In the corporate context, however, it will frequently be employees beyond the control group as defined by the court below—"officers and agents . . . responsible for directing [the company's] actions in response to legal advice"—who will possess the information needed by the corporation's lawyers. Middle-level—and indeed lower-level—employees can, by actions within the scope of their employment, embroil the corporation in serious legal difficulties, and it is only natural that these employees would have the relevant information needed by corporate counsel if he is adequately to advise the client with respect to such actual or potential difficulties. . . .

The narrow scope given the attorney-client privilege by the court below not only makes it difficult for corporate attorneys to formulate sound advice when their client is faced with a specific legal problem but also threatens to limit the valuable efforts of corporate counsel to ensure their client's compliance with the law. In light of the vast and complicated array of regulatory legislation confronting the modern corporation, corporations, unlike most individuals, "constantly go to lawyers to find out how to obey the law," [Bryson B.] Burnham, The Attorney-Client Privilege in the Corporate Arena, 24 Bus. Law. 901, 913 (1969), particularly since compliance with the law in this area is hardly an instinctive matter. . . . The test adopted by the court below is difficult to apply in practice, though no abstractly formulated and unvarying "test" will necessarily enable courts to decide questions such as this with mathematical precision. But if the purpose of the attorney-client privilege is to be served, the attorney and client must be able to predict with some degree of certainty whether particular discussions will be protected. An uncertain privilege, or one which purports to be certain but results in widely varying applications by the courts, is little better than no privilege at all. . . .

The communications at issue were made by Upjohn employees to counsel for Upjohn acting as such, at the direction of corporate superiors in order to secure legal advice from counsel. As the magistrate found, "Mr. Thomas consulted with the Chairman of the Board and outside counsel and thereafter conducted a factual investigation to determine the nature and extent of the questionable payments *and to be in a position to give legal advice to the company with respect to the payments.*" (Emphasis supplied.) . . . Information, not available from upper-echelon management, was needed to supply a basis for legal advice concerning compliance with securities and tax laws, foreign laws, currency regulations, duties to shareholders, and potential litigation in each of these areas. The communications concerned matters within the scope of the employees' corporate duties, and the employees themselves were sufficiently aware that they were being questioned in order that the corporation could obtain legal advice. . . .

The Court of Appeals declined to extend the attorney-client privilege beyond the limits of the control group test for fear that doing so would entail severe burdens on discovery and create a broad "zone of silence" over corporate affairs. Application of the attorney-client privilege to communications such as those involved here, however, puts the adversary in no worse position than if the communications had never taken place. The privilege only protects disclosure of communications; it does not protect disclosure of the underlying facts by those who communicated with the attorney:

> The protection of the privilege extends only to communications and not to facts. A fact is one thing[,] and a communication concerning that fact is an entirely different thing. The client cannot be compelled to answer the question, "What did you say or write to the attorney?" but may not refuse to disclose any relevant fact within his knowledge merely because he incorporated a statement of such fact into his communication to his attorney. Philadelphia v. Westinghouse [Elec.] Corp., 205 F. Supp. 830, 831 (E.D. Pa. 1962).

See also Diversified [Indus., Inc. v. Meredith,] 572 F.2d [596,] 611 [8th Cir. 1977]; State v. Circuit Court, 34 Wis. 2d 559, 580, 150 N.W.2d 387, 399 (1967) ("the courts have noted that a party cannot conceal a fact merely by revealing it to his lawyer"). Here the Government was free to question the employees who communicated with Thomas and outside counsel. . . .

Our decision that the communications by Upjohn employees to counsel are covered by the attorney-client privilege disposes of the case so far as the responses to the questionnaires and any notes reflecting responses to interview questions are concerned. The summons reaches further, however, and Thomas has testified that his notes and memoranda of interviews go beyond recording responses to his questions. To the extent that the material subject to the summons is not protected by the attorney-client privilege as disclosing communications between an employee and counsel, we must reach the ruling by the Court of Appeals that the work-product doctrine does not apply to summonses issued under 26 U.S.C. sect. 7602. . . .

While conceding the applicability of the work-product doctrine, the Government asserts that it has made a sufficient showing of necessity to overcome its protections. The magistrate apparently so found. The Government relies on the following language in *Hickman*:

> We do not mean to say that all written materials obtained or prepared by an adversary's counsel with an eye toward litigation are necessarily free from discovery in all cases. Where relevant and non-privileged facts remain hidden in an attorney's file[,] and where production of those facts is essential to the preparation of one's case, discovery may properly be had. . . . And production might be justified where the witnesses are no longer available or may be reached only with difficulty. [Hickman v. Taylor, 329 U.S. 495, 511 (1947).]

The Government stresses that interviews are scattered across the globe and that Upjohn has forbidden its employees to answer questions it considers irrelevant. The above-quoted language from *Hickman*, however, did not apply to "oral statements made by witnesses . . . whether presently in the form of [the attorney's] mental impressions or memoranda." Id. at 512. . . . As to such material the Court did "not believe that any showing of necessity can be made under the circumstances of this case so as to justify production. . . . If there should be a rare situation justifying production of these matters petitioner's case is not of that type." Id. at 512-513. . . . Forcing an attorney to disclose notes and memoranda of witnesses' oral statements is particularly disfavored because it tends to reveal the attorney's mental processes, [id.] at 513 . . . ("what he saw fit to write down regarding witnesses' remarks"); id. at 516-517, . . . ("the statement would be his [the attorney's] language, permeated with his inferences") (Jackson, J., concurring).[8]

Rule 26 accords special protection to work product revealing the attorney's mental processes. The Rule permits disclosure of documents and tangible things constituting attorney work product upon a showing of substantial need and inability to obtain the equivalent without undue hardship. This was the standard applied by the magistrate. . . . Rule 26 goes on, however, to state that "[i]n ordering discovery of such materials when the required showing has been made, the court shall protect against disclosure of the mental impressions, conclusions, opinions or legal theories of an attorney or other representative of a party concerning the litigation." Although this language does not specifically refer to memoranda based on oral statements of witnesses, the *Hickman* court stressed the danger that compelled disclosure of such memoranda would reveal the attorney's mental processes. It is clear that this is the sort of material the draftsmen of the Rule had in mind as deserving special protection. . . .

Based on the foregoing, some courts have concluded that *no* showing of necessity can overcome protection of work product which is based on oral statements from witnesses. See, e.g., In re Grand Jury Proceedings, 473 F.2d 840, 848 (8th Cir. 1973) (personal recollections, notes and memoranda pertaining to conversation with witnesses). . . . Those courts declining to adopt an absolute rule have nonetheless recognized that such material is entitled to special protection. . . .

We do not decide the issue at this time. It is clear that the magistrate applied the wrong standard when he concluded that the Government had made a sufficient showing of necessity to overcome the protections of the work-product doctrine. The magistrate applied the "substantial need" and "without undue hardship" standard articulated in the first part of Rule 26(b)(3). The notes and memoranda sought by the Government here, however, are work product based on oral statements. If they reveal

---

8. Thomas described his notes of the interviews as containing "what I consider to be the important questions, the substance of the responses to them, my beliefs as to the importance of these, my beliefs as to how they related to the inquiry, my thoughts as to how they related to other questions. In some instances they might even suggest other questions that I would have to ask or things that I needed to find elsewhere."

communications, they are, in this case, protected by the attorney-client privilege. To the extent they do not reveal communications, they reveal the attorneys' mental processes in evaluating the communications. As Rule 26 and *Hickman* make clear, such work product cannot be disclosed simply on a showing of substantial need and inability to obtain the equivalent without undue hardship.

While we are not prepared at this juncture to say that such material is always protected by the work-product rule, we think a far stronger showing of necessity and unavailability by other means than was made by the Government or applied by the magistrate in this case would be necessary to compel disclosure. Since the Court of Appeals thought that the work-product protection was never applicable in an enforcement proceeding such as this, and since the magistrate whose recommendations the District Court adopted applied too lenient a standard of protection, we think the best procedure with respect to this aspect of the case would be to reverse the judgment of the Court of Appeals for the Sixth Circuit and remand the case to it for such further proceedings in connection with the work-product claim as are consistent with this opinion.

Accordingly, the judgment of the Court of Appeals is reversed, and the case is remanded for further proceeding.

*It is so ordered.*

### Note: The Lifetime of the Privilege:
### *Swidler & Berlin v. United States*

In *Upjohn*, both the attorney-client and the work-product privileges were invoked. This is often true, because parties would always prefer the broader, unqualified privilege to the more limited work-product exception. *Upjohn* is often cited for the importance of the attorney-client privilege, which "promotes trust in the representational relationship, thereby facilitating the provision of legal services and ultimately the administration of justice." See, e.g., Swidler & Berlin v. United States, 524 U.S. 399, 412 (1998) (Justice O'Connor, dissenting).

*Swidler & Berlin* was one of the cases growing out of the investigation of President Clinton. The Supreme Court again strongly endorsed the importance of the privilege, holding that in most circumstances, it extends even beyond the grave.

Here are the facts, as stated by Chief Justice Rehnquist for the majority:

> This dispute arises out of an investigation conducted by the Office of the Independent Counsel into whether various individuals made false statements, obstructed justice, or committed other crimes during investigations of the 1993 dismissal of employees from the White House Travel Office. Vincent W. Foster, Jr., was Deputy White House Counsel when the firing occurred. In July, 1993, Foster met with petitioner James Hamilton, an attorney at petitioner Swidler & Berlin, to seek legal representation concerning

possible congressional or other investigations of the firings. During a 2-hour meeting, Hamilton took three pages of handwritten notes. One of the first entries in the notes is the word "Privileged." Nine days later, Foster committed suicide.

In December 1995, a federal grand jury, at the request of the Independent Counsel, issued subpoenas to petitioners Hamilton and Swidler & Berlin for, *inter alia*, Hamilton's handwritten notes of his meeting with Foster. Petitioners filed a motion to quash, arguing that the notes were protected by the attorney-client privilege and by the work product privilege. The District Court, after examining the notes *in camera*, concluded they were protected from disclosure by both doctrines and denied enforcement of the subpoenas.

Id. at 401-402.

The Court of Appeals for the District of Columbia Circuit reversed, but the Supreme Court found that "the great body of . . . case law" and most commentators supported the survival of the privilege. Id. at 405. In addition, the Court discerned

weighty reasons that counsel in favor of posthumous application. Knowing that communications will remain confidential even after death encourages the client to communicate fully and frankly with counsel. While the fear of disclosure, and the consequent withholding of information from counsel, may be reduced if disclosure is limited to posthumous disclosure in a criminal context, it seems unreasonable to assume that it vanishes altogether. Clients may be concerned about reputation, civil liability or possible harm to friends or family. Posthumous disclosure of such communications may be as feared as disclosure during the client's lifetime. . . .

The Independent Counsel assumes, incorrectly we believe, that the privilege is analogous to the Fifth Amendment's protection against self-incrimination. But as suggested above, the privilege serves much broader purposes. Clients consult attorneys for a wide variety of reasons, only one of which involves possible criminal liability. Many attorneys act as counselors on personal and family matters, where, in the course of obtaining the desired advice, confidences about family members or financial problems must be revealed in order to assure sound legal advice. The same is true of owners of small businesses who may regularly consult their attorneys about a variety of problems arising in the course of the business. These confidences may not come close to any sort of admission of criminal wrongdoing, but nonetheless be matters which the client would not wish divulged. . . .

In related cases, we have said that the loss of evidence admittedly caused by the privilege is justified in part by the fact that without the privilege, the client may not have made such communications in the first place. . . . This is true of disclosure before and after the client's death. Without assurance of the privilege's posthumous application, the client may very well not have made disclosures to his attorney at all, so the loss of evidence is more apparent than real. In the case at hand, it seems quite plausible that Foster, perhaps already contemplating suicide, may not have sought legal advice from Hamilton if he had not been assured the conversation was privileged.

Id. at 407-408.

Three Justices (O'Connor, Scalia, and Thomas) dissented even though they agreed that ordinarily the privilege extends beyond the death of the client. They argued that there might be compelling reasons for disclosure in some instances, and that the case should be remanded for the district court to consider whether these existed.

## Note: Waiving the Privilege

The privilege extends beyond the grave, but while lawyer and client are alive, it is generally quite easy to waive. The rationale is simple—the privilege can be an obstacle to the search for truth in the adversary process, and waivers give meaning to the principle that the privilege should be narrowly construed. See United States v. Nixon, 418 U.S. 683, 710 (1974). Most prominently, courts have carved out an exception to the privilege where legal advice is used in furtherance of crime or fraud. As Justice Cardozo wrote: "The privilege takes flight if the relation is abused. A client who consults an attorney for advice that will serve him in the commission of a fraud will have no help from the law." Clark v. United States, 289 U.S. 1, 15 (1933).

In an important opinion for the Ninth Circuit arising from the rise and fall of Napster, Judge William Fletcher offered the following summary of the standard for determining whether the crime-fraud exception applies:

> A party seeking to vitiate the attorney-client privilege under the crime-fraud exception must satisfy a two-part test. First, the party must show that "the client was engaged in or planning a criminal or fraudulent scheme when it sought the advice of counsel to further the scheme." In re Grand Jury Proceedings, 87 F.3d [377, 381 (9th Cir. 1996)]. . . . Second, it must demonstrate that the attorney-client communications for which production is sought are "sufficiently related to" and were made "*in furtherance of* [the] intended, or present, continuing illegality. Id. at 382-83 (internal quotation marks omitted) (emphasis added)." . . .
>
> The attorney need not have been aware that the client harbored an improper purpose. Because both the legal advice and the privilege are for the benefit of the client, it is the client's knowledge and intent that are relevant. . . . The planned crime or fraud need not have succeeded for the exception to apply. The client's abuse of the attorney-client relationship, not his or her successful criminal or fraudulent act, vitiates the privilege. . . .
>
> [I]n a civil case the burden of proof that must be carried by a party seeking outright disclosure of attorney-client communications under the crime-fraud exception should be preponderance of the evidence.

In re Napster, Inc., 479 F.3d 1078, 1090-1095 (9th Cir. 2007) (holding that $85 million loan by German conglomerate to Napster, part of which was used by Napster to pay for litigation expenses against American copyright holders, was not an attempted fraud on the court sufficient to pierce attorney-client privilege between German conglomerate and its counsel), *abrogated on other grounds by* Mohawk Ind., Inc. v. Carpenter, 558 U.S. 100 (2009).

Should the attorney-client privilege cover conversations planning or otherwise encouraging implementation of a document destruction policy to eliminate evidence in anticipation of litigation? See Rambus, Inc. v. Infineon Techs. AG, 220 F.R.D. 264, 284 (E.D. Va. 2004) (holding privilege gives way where software company and its lawyers, anticipating patent litigation with a competitor, drafted and implemented a document destruction policy including "Shred Day," which "culminated in a 5:00 pm beer, pizza, and champagne 'celebration' . . . [for] morale boosting after a day of heavy sack lifting and laborious document review").

The privilege also is destroyed if confidential communications are disclosed to adversaries or other third parties—the privilege needn't protect secrets the client is careless about keeping. See In re Keeper of the Records (Grand Jury Subpoena Addressed to XYZ Corp.), 348 F.3d 16 (1st Cir. 2003) (company lost privilege as to any confidential information it shared in a conference call with its co-venturer); Clady v. County of Los Angeles, 770 F.2d 1421 (9th Cir. 1985). Traditionally, even *inadvertent* disclosure of privileged material results in waiver. Compare In re Sealed Case, 877 F.2d 976 (D.C. Cir. 1989) (inadvertence no grounds for relief from waiver), with KL Group v. Case, Kay & Lynch, 829 F.2d 909 (9th Cir. 1987) (lower court has discretion to order return of inadvertently disclosed material), and Rule 26(b)(5)(B).

Lawyers and clients must be equally cautious about making *voluntary* disclosures. Disclosing significant portions of privileged material can waive the privilege as to the remainder on the ground that the privilege should not operate both as a sword and a shield for the privilege holder—allowing her to disclose helpful information while refusing to release countervailing facts. See In re Keeper, 348 F.3d at 23-24 ("fairness concerns" justify extending the waiver "beyond the matter actually revealed"). And courts have deemed the privilege waived for failure to comply with the requirement in Rule 26(b)(5)(A) that claims of privilege be explicit and "describe the nature of the documents, communications or tangible things not disclosed . . . in a manner that . . . will enable other parties to assess the claim." See Clarke v. Am. Commerce Nat'l Bank, 974 F.2d 127, 129 (9th Cir. 1992) ("blanket assertions of the privilege are extremely disfavored") (internal quotations and citation omitted), and United States v. Constr. Prods. Research, Inc., 73 F.3d 464, 473 (2d Cir. 1996). Finally, because it puts attorney-client communications directly in issue in the litigation, the privilege can be waived if the client asserts as part of a claim or defense that she relied on the advice of counsel. See United States v. Bilzerian, 926 F.2d 1285 (2d Cir. 1991), *overruled on other grounds by* United States v. Mandanici, 205 F.3d 519 (2d Cir. 2000).

### Note: Privilege in a Corporate Context

*Upjohn* takes the attorney-client privilege, which is ordinarily conceived of in terms of an attorney advising an individual client, and applies it to a collective entity—the corporation. In what ways do individual and corporate clients differ that alter the assumptions that tend to drive the privilege? Are the costs inevitably entailed in allowing a privilege to shield information from an opponent compounded in the corporate context? The theory of the privilege the Court repeatedly emphasizes in *Upjohn* is that corporate clients go to lawyers to figure out how to comply with the law. Isn't it more likely that the decision about whether to comply with law depends on whether the costs of compliance exceed the benefits of noncompliance or minimal compliance? If advising compliance is the purpose of the attorney-client privilege, why should the crime-fraud exception be restricted to crime and fraud? For a critique of the compliance theory, see Norman W. Spaulding, Compliance, Creative Deviance, and Resistance to Law: A Theory of the Attorney-Client Privilege, 2013 ABA J. Prof'l Law. 135.

*Upjohn* tells us that communication between counsel to a corporation and lower level employees can be protected by the privilege. What about communication with independent professionals like accountants and tax experts who are not employees, but who regularly provide advice to corporations that can have important legal consequences? If a company has engaged in Enron-like fast and loose financial accounting, will conversations about the issue with outside accountants be covered by the privilege just because a lawyer working for the company is also in the room? Remember that the privilege disappears upon any voluntary disclosure of confidential information to a third party.

The general rule is that where the services of an agent are used in order to assist the lawyer in giving legal advice to the client, communications between the agent, the client, and the lawyer are covered by the privilege as long as they relate to issues on which legal advice is sought. However, the privilege is waived when privileged information is shared with an agent for purposes unrelated to seeking legal advice. In First Fed. Savings Bank of Hegeswisch v. United States, 55 Fed. Cl. 263 (2003), for instance, First Federal shared confidential minutes of its board meetings with its accounting firm KPMG on two occasions: first, to conduct a fraud audit as part of an internal investigation run by First Federal's lawyers, and second, to prepare annual audits of First Federal's financial statements. The court concluded that while the privilege covered the first disclosure of the board minutes, see id. at 268 ("Lawyers frequently experience difficulty when interpreting and applying accounting principles. . . . Given the complexity of the accounting issues [in this case], the court is persuaded that [the fraud audit] procedures were related to the rendition of legal advice."), disclosures to KPMG so it could prepare annual audits were purely for business purposes and therefore waived the privilege. Id. at 269 ("Just as documents transmitted to an agent for the preparation of a tax return are not privileged, documents transmitted to an agent for the preparation of an audited financial statement likewise are not privileged."); cf. In re Kellogg Brown & Root, Inc., 796 F.3d 137, 144 (D.C. Cir. 2015) (report prepared as part of internal investigation by non-lawyer is not subject to disclosure under Fed. R. Evid. 612, where a KBR vice president reviewed the report in preparation for his deposition; permitting disclosure in these circumstances "would allow the attorney-client privilege and work product protection covering internal investigations to be defeated routinely by a counter-party noticing a deposition on the topic of the privileged nature of the internal investigation").

The same rule regarding agents applies for individual clients, but in the corporate context covering communications with agents raises all the concerns we saw in *Upjohn* about extending the privilege beyond the control group.

## Note: "Upjohn Warnings"

According to *Upjohn*, the privilege belongs to the corporate entity. As you might expect, difficult questions can arise when corporate officers claim that an attorney for the corporation gave them personal legal advice, or that the corporate attorney received confidential information from an officer soliciting personal legal advice. For any corporate officers or employees, the line between personal legal advice and advice relevant to decisions or actions on behalf of the corporate entity can blur easily. For precisely this reason ABA Model Rule of Professional Conduct 1.13 requires corporate lawyers to advise officers and employees that their client is the corporation, not the officer or employee—a so-called *Upjohn* warning. Confusion can nevertheless arise, particularly when the interests of the officer or employee diverge from the interests of the company.

In United States v. Graf, 610 F.3d 1148 (9th Cir. 2010), the government prosecuted the founder and alleged "outside" consultant to a corporation. The corporation waived the attorney-client privilege as it applied to communications with its legal counsel, but Graf insisted that in his capacity as an "outside consultant" he had an individual attorney-client relationship with attorneys for the company. If true, that would make Graf a joint holder of the privilege as to communications with corporate counsel. The district court rejected this argument. It found that Graf was heavily involved in all facets of the company's operations, that he had never consulted the attorneys for personal legal advice, and that his subjective belief that the attorneys represented him personally as an outside consultant was neither reasonable nor manifested. Graf was found guilty on multiple charges relating to a scheme to defraud health insurance carriers. He was sentenced to nearly 30 years in jail and ordered to pay restitution of nearly $20 million.

On appeal, Graf argued once again that he was entitled to control the privilege as an outside consultant to the company. The Ninth Circuit disagreed, noting that Graf had been an active agent of the corporation authorized to communicate with its attorneys regarding legal matters affecting the corporation. Indeed, the evidence showed that he was the attorneys' primary contact within the corporation. In reaching this conclusion the court adopted the five-factor test outlined in In re Bevill, Bresler & Schulman Asset Management Corp., 805 F.2d 120 (3d Cir. 1986), for determining whether communications between a corporate officer or employee and the corporation's counsel are covered by a personal privilege.

Graf must establish: (1) he approached the attorneys for the purpose of seeking legal advice; (2) when he did so, he made it clear to the attorneys that he was seeking legal advice in his individual rather than in his representative capacity; (3) the attorneys saw fit to represent him personally, knowing a conflict could arise; (4) his conversations with the attorneys were in confidence; and (5) "the substance of [his] conversations with [the attorneys] did not concern matters within [Employers Mutual] or the general affairs of [Employers Mutual]." *Bevill*, 805 F.2d at 123.

*Graf*, 610 F.3d at 1161. The Ninth Circuit observed that

[t]here are strong policy reasons to adopt the *Bevill* test. . . . [A]ny time a corporation retains counsel, counsel will have to talk to individual employees to represent the company effectively. The *Bevill* test responds to this reality by ensuring that a corporation is free to obtain information from its officers, employees, and consultants about company matters and then control the attorney-client privilege, waiving it when necessary to serve corporate interests. The test also preserves the individual's ability to claim a personal attorney-client privilege when the individual makes clear he or she is seeking personal legal advice and the communications relate to personal legal affairs, not to the company's business. Moreover, there are reasons to look to other circuits when contemplating the proper standard in this arena. As the Supreme Court cautioned in *Upjohn*, "[a]n uncertain privilege, or one which purports to be certain but results in widely varying applications by the courts, is little better than no privilege at all." 449 U.S. at 393.

Id. at 1160-1161. The First, Second, and Tenth Circuits have also adopted the *Bevill* test. See In re Grand Jury Subpoena (Newparent, Inc.), 274 F.3d 563, 571-572 (1st Cir. 2001); In re Grand Jury Proceedings, 156 F.3d 1038, 1040-1041 (10th Cir. 1998); United States v. Int'l Bhd. Teamsters, 119 F.3d 210, 214-215 (2d Cir. 1997). The Sixth Circuit has suggested it adheres to a similar test. See Ross v. City of Memphis, 423 F.3d 596, 605 (6th Cir. 2005). The Fourth and D.C. Circuits have cited the test favorably. See In re Grand Jury Subpoena: Under Seal, 415 F.3d 333, 340 n.6 (4th Cir. 2005); In re Sealed Case, 29 F.3d 715, 719 n.5 (D.C. Cir. 1994).

## Note: The Role of Privileges in Assuring Accurate Outcomes

Assume, arguendo, that the primary and sole aim of civil litigation is accurate outcomes (as opposed to party satisfaction or other potential values of civil process we explored in Chapter 1). Can you nevertheless defend the attorney-client privilege? Work-product privilege? Does it matter whether you allow for sharing of the costs of generating the information that work-product and attorney-client privilege protect?

Consider the following scenarios and their "accurate-outcome" implications, described by Professor Elizabeth G. Thornburg in Sanctifying Secrecy: The Mythology of the Corporate Attorney-Client Privilege, 69 Notre Dame L. Rev. 157, 193-197 (1993):

[XYZ Corporation, a manufacturer of consumer widgets, is sued by a consumer who was injured by the widget and alleges that it was defective. The corporation has an employee named Smith whose job is to test new products. Eds.] Assume that Jones, the president of XYZ, instructs Green, the vice-president, to call the corporate attorney and tell him that Smith has admitted that the widget was known to be defective before it was marketed. If the plaintiff deposes Green and asks what the president said to Green or what Green said to the attorney, both Green and Jones would be held to be "representatives of the client," and the privilege would allow Green to refuse to answer the question. This direct method of learning about Smith's warning is thus closed to the plaintiff.

If the plaintiff instead deposes Jones, the president, and asks him what Smith said, the president should be required to testify about what Smith told him, because this communication went straight from employee to employee for business purposes. Unfortunately, the claims and the case law are not so clear. Many corporations would still claim a privilege, based on the attorney's need to gather information. . . .

Assume that a plaintiff/consumer has sent an interrogatory asking whether XYZ adequately tested the widget. Assume further that there are five engineers in XYZ's research and development department, including Smith. Smith has told the corporate attorney that inadequate testing was done; that some of the documentation making it appear that tests were done is actually falsified; and that the tests themselves were structured so as to avoid exposing a known problem in the widget's design. The other four engineers told the lawyer that the testing was fine. All of these conversations are privileged. XYZ answers the interrogatory merely by saying that the widget was adequately tested. If requested, it will provide the documentation on the tests. XYZ further identifies the other four engineers as persons with knowledge of the testing procedures. XYZ does *not* mention Smith's opinion.

Is this response a lie? Not really. But it is an incomplete picture of the information available to XYZ and clearly misleading to the plaintiff. The privilege contributes to the scenario by letting the lawyer and corporate entity decide which of the employees' conflicting stories to believe and to present this as the only available information. While presenting its favorite version of the facts, the corporation simultaneously claims privilege as to any document reflecting Smith's concerns (if these documents did not hit the shredder long ago) and as to any conversation between Smith and the lawyer. If documents do exist and the lawyer acts ethically, the corporation will acknowledge that documents exist, but claim privilege. Less responsible lawyers may make a "silent assertion" of the privilege. Thus the corporation makes and rules on its own privilege objection, and the plaintiff may never know that the information exists in order to pursue it in unprotected form.

In light of recent corporate accounting scandals and the mortgage-backed securities crisis, does the shield of the corporate attorney-client privilege extend too far? Has the underlying problem been that lawyers are made aware of irresponsible transactions but do nothing to prevent them, or is it that lawyers fail to seek or are not given access to information that would have required them to counsel forbearance? For an analysis of the role of lawyers and confidentiality rules in the Enron scandal, see Roger

C. Cramton, Enron and the Corporate Lawyer: A Primer on Legal and Ethical Issues, 58 Bus. Law. 143 (2002).

## Note: Administering a Claim of Privilege

In the previous note, the privilege claim itself, combined with the testing, reveals the likelihood that the results were unfavorable. How can a party make a claim of privilege without risking the revelation of the very information he is seeking to shield? How much does a court need to know in order to assess the validity of a claim of privilege? In United States v. Constr. Prods. Research, Inc., 73 F.3d 464 (2d Cir. 1996), as in *Upjohn,* the court was asked to enforce the subpoena of an administrative agency. The NRC (Nuclear Regulatory Commission) was investigating whether a government contractor had wrongfully discharged a whistleblower. Here is the description of the subpoena and the privilege claim:

> [T]he NRC issued the subpoena involved here, requiring Respondents to produce: (1) all documents related to Holub's termination; (2) Holub's personnel file; (3) all of Respondents' policies, procedures, and requirements regarding involuntary terminations; and (4) "position descriptions of jobs" held by Holub and two other employees. . . . Respondents refused to comply with it.
>
> The United States, on behalf of the NRC, filed a petition to enforce the subpoena in the United States District Court for the District of Connecticut. The district court referred the petition to a magistrate judge, who recommended that the petition be granted and that Respondents' claim of privilege be rejected as a general defense to enforcement of the subpoena. The district court adopted the magistrate judge's recommended ruling *in toto,* and issued an order of enforcement. This ruling appears not to have considered the applicability of the privilege to any particular document, though it is arguable that the district court's denial of Respondents' motion to reconsider constituted a rejection of the privilege as to all documents for which privilege had been claimed. Respondents appealed, but turned over to the NRC those documents which they conceded were not privileged, while refusing to produce allegedly privileged documents. . . .
>
> The party asserting the privilege must establish the essential elements of the privilege. United States v. Adlman, 68 F.3d 1495, 1499 (2d Cir. 1995); von Bulow by Auersperg v. von Bulow, 811 F.2d 136, 144 (2d Cir.), *cert. denied,* 481 U.S. 1015 (1987). To invoke the attorney-client privilege, a party must demonstrate that there was: (1) a communication between client and counsel, which (2) was intended to be and was in fact kept confidential, and (3) made for the purpose of obtaining or providing legal advice. Fisher v. United States, 425 U.S. 391, 403 (1976); Adlman, 68 F.3d at 1499; United States v. Abrahams, 905 F.2d 1276, 1283 (9th Cir. 1990).
>
> Respondents also assert a work-product privilege. To invoke this privilege, a party generally must show that the documents were prepared principally or exclusively to assist in anticipated or ongoing litigation. . . .
>
> To facilitate its determination of privilege, a court may require "an adequately detailed privilege log in conjunction with evidentiary submissions

to fill in any factual gaps." Bowne, 150 F.R.D. at 474; see also In re Grand Jury Investigation, 974 F.2d 1068, 1071 (9th Cir. 1992). The privilege log should:

> identify each document and the individuals who were parties to the communications, providing sufficient detail to permit a judgment as to whether the document is at least potentially protected from disclosure. Other required information, such as the relationship between . . . individuals not normally within the privileged relationship, is then typically supplied by affidavit or deposition testimony. Even under this approach, however, if the party invoking the privilege does not provide sufficient detail to demonstrate fulfillment of all the legal requirements for application of the privilege, his claim will be rejected. . . .

> We have reviewed Respondents' privilege log, and find it deficient. The log contains a cursory description of each document, the date, author, recipient, and "comments." Further, under a heading entitled "Basis of Claim," each of the documents listed is alleged to be an "Attorney-Client Communication."

> These general allegations of privilege, however, are not supported by the information provided. For example, descriptions and comments for some of the documents listed are as follows: (a) "Fax Re: DOL Findings" with comment "cover sheet;" (b) "Fax: Whistleblower article" with comment "Self-explanatory;" (c) "Letter Re: Customer Orders" with comment "Re: Five Star Products;" (d) "Summary of Enclosures" with comment "Self-explanatory;" etc. The descriptions and comments simply do not provide enough information to support the privilege claim, particularly in the glaring absence of any supporting affidavits or other documentation. See Bowne, 150 F.R.D. at 475; Allendate Mut. Ins. Co. v. Bull Data Sys., Inc., 145 F.R.D. 84, 88 (N.D. Ill. 1992) (privilege log should provide "a specific explanation of why the document is privileged").

Id. at 468-474.

Once a privilege log is filed, attorneys for the adversary must review it and decide whether to file a motion to compel. If they believe the asserted privilege has been abused in furtherance of crime or fraud (not just that the log is inadequate), there are special procedures to determine whether the privilege should be waived. Typically, in a civil case (there are different procedures when prosecutors seek to put privileged material before a grand jury), the motion to compel will include waiver as a ground for compelling production. The difficulty, of course, is that the party seeking disclosure usually does not have access to the very documents that would most clearly establish whether the attorney-client relationship has been abused. So how can a lawyer prove the crime-fraud exception applies?

Sometimes the underlying criminal or fraudulent behavior has already come to light. This makes it a lot easier to argue for waiver of the privilege, particularly in contexts such as the recent financial accounting and mortgage scandals, where it is obvious that counsel would have been involved in the decision-making. But without a proven (or at least publicly exposed) crime or fraud, and in any context where the role of counsel is unknown, establishing the elements of waiver can be exceedingly difficult. Just as thorny is the question of how to decide whether the exception applies without revealing the very information covered by the privilege—public revelation, as you have read above, is itself a form of waiver.

In United States v. Zolin, 491 U.S. 554, 572 (1989), the Supreme Court held that when the party seeking waiver makes a prima facie showing, the trial court has discretion to review the privileged documents *"in camera"* to determine whether the crime/fraud exception indeed applies. This seems reasonable because it preserves the privilege while allowing the issue of waiver to be decided, but it is subject to abuse in practice. To begin with, in order to secure *in camera* review, a party does not have to prove by a preponderance of the evidence that the attorney-client relationship was in fact abused by the other side. As the Court held in *Zolin*, the party seeking waiver need only present "a factual basis adequate to support a good faith belief by a reasonable person . . . that *in camera* review of the materials may reveal evidence to establish the claim that the crime-fraud exception applies." Id. (internal quotations and citation omitted). Perhaps more troublingly, seeking waiver offers a chance to have the judge who will adjudicate the merits of the case see evidence of criminal or fraudulent conduct by an opponent and her lawyer. Even if the material the judge reviews is not bad enough to result in waiver, it may nonetheless color the judge's view of the case. All of which is just to say that abuse of waiver, not just abuse of the privilege, is possible.

This is not the only approach, though. A party may bypass *in camera* review and move for outright disclosure. But if she does, the Third, Seventh, Eighth, and Ninth Circuits have held that the court must allow the party seeking to preserve the attorney-client privilege an opportunity to present countervailing evidence in support of its claim of privilege. See In re Napster, 479 F.3d 1078, 1093 (9th Cir. 2007), *abrogated on other grounds by* Mohawk Ind., Inc. v. Carpenter, 558 U.S. 100 (2009); In re Gen. Motors Corp., 153 F.3d 714, 716 (8th Cir. 1998); Haines v. Liggett Group Inc., 975 F.2d 81, 96-97 (3d Cir. 1992); In re Feldberg, 862 F.2d 622, 625-626 (7th Cir. 1988).

Finally, recall that in *Hickman*, the attorney Fortenbaugh was held in contempt. That means he could have been imprisoned for refusing to produce the statements of the witnesses he had obtained. The contempt order was immediately appealable; indeed, it appears the trial court agreed to find him in contempt in order to allow an immediate appeal. Not all trial judges may be so accommodating—the decision to commit contempt is ordinarily fraught with peril for the lawyer. But if you think the trial court has erroneously compelled production of material you believe is privileged, you have limited alternatives. The Supreme Court has held that disclosure orders adverse to the attorney-client privilege do not qualify for immediate appeal under the collateral-order doctrine. Mohawk Industries, Inc. v. Carpenter, 558 U.S. 100 (2009). The collateral-order doctrine provides an exception to the general rule that decisions of the trial court are not reviewable on appeal until final judgment is entered. See 28 U.S.C. § 1291.

As you can imagine, a client's desire to maintain confidentiality may induce it to settle rather than disclose embarrassing facts or trade secrets. And discovery disputes often become moot once a case settles or goes to trial, making appellate review for error infrequent notwithstanding the importance of discovery to pretrial and trial outcomes. But you can also imagine the delay and inefficiency produced by appeals of discovery orders. The defendant in *Mohawk* argued that even though general pretrial discovery orders cannot be immediately appealed, "rulings implicating the attorney-client privilege differ in kind from the run-of-the-mill discovery orders because of the important institutional interests at stake. According to *Mohawk*, the right to maintain attorney-client confidences—the *sine qua non* of a meaningful attorney-client relationship—is 'irreparably destroyed absent immediate appeal' of adverse privilege rulings." 558 U.S. at 108 (citation omitted). The Supreme Court brushed aside these concerns, emphasizing that it "routinely require[s] litigants to wait until after final judgment to vindicate valuable rights, including rights central to our adversary system." Id. at 108-109 (citing rule that orders disqualifying counsel in civil and criminal cases do not qualify for immediate appeal under the collateral-order doctrine).

The Court also noted that parties have other options for obtaining immediate review in exceptional cases: 1) "a party may ask the district court to certify, and the court of appeals to accept, an interlocutory appeal pursuant to 28 U.S.C. § 1292(b)"; 2) "in extraordinary circumstances—*i.e.*, when a disclosure order 'amounts to a judicial usurpation of power or a clear abuse of discretion,' or otherwise works a manifest injustice—a party may petition the court of appeals for a writ of mandamus"; and 3) "[a]nother long-recognized option is for a party to defy a disclosure order and incur court-imposed sanctions. [citing Rule 37(b)(2)(i)-(iii)—EDS.]... Such sanctions allow a party to obtain post-judgment review without having to reveal its privileged information." Id. at 110-111 (citation omitted). Finally, "a district court may hold a noncomplying party in contempt. The party can then appeal directly from that ruling, at least when the contempt citation can be characterized as a criminal punishment." Id. "Permitting parties to undertake successive, piecemeal appeals of all adverse attorney-client rulings would unduly delay the resolution of district court litigation and needlessly burden the Courts of Appeals." Id. at 112.

### Note: The Privilege as Applied to Government Attorneys

Should government employees enjoy the benefits of the attorney-client privilege in their communications with government counsel? On the one hand, we certainly want public servants to engage in full and frank communication with lawyers about how to comply with law. On the other hand, government lawyers and the government officials they represent ultimately work for the public, and we deeply value transparency in government affairs. A government shrouded in secrecy is not a democracy, and an informed electorate and accountability to the public cannot be achieved without transparency.

In the nongovernmental setting, once a court determines that the elements of the privilege have been met, the privilege applies even if it means other societal values are undermined. Indeed, we knowingly diminish the truth-finding function of the adversary process to protect the privilege because, as the Court argued in *Upjohn*, full and frank communication promotes compliance with law. When the communication occurs between government lawyer and government client, however, the Seventh, Eighth, and D.C. Circuit Courts of Appeals have endorsed a balancing test, holding that the privilege should give way to further a criminal investigation because the true client of the government lawyer is a public entity, and the public interest is served by transparency in government affairs. See In re: A Witness Before the Special Grand Jury 2000-02, 288 F.3d 289 (7th Cir. 2002); In re Lindsey (Grand Jury Testimony), 158 F.3d 1263 (D.C. Cir. 1998); In re Grand Jury Subpoena Duces Tecum, 112 F.3d 910 (8th Cir. 1997).

The Second Circuit, by contrast, rejected the balancing test in a case in which federal prosecutors sought to compel the testimony of the former chief legal counsel to the Office of the Governor of Connecticut. In re Grand Jury Investigation, 399 F.3d 527 (2d Cir. 2005). The governor was under investigation for receiving gifts in exchange for public favors, including lucrative state contracts. On several occasions the chief legal counsel discussed the receipt of gifts and related state ethics law with the governor and his staff. She also discussed the governor's practice of personally approving state contracts.

The district court entered an order compelling her to testify on the ground that, unlike the private attorney-client relationship, a government lawyer owes loyalty not only to the government official she serves, but also to the public. As the district court put it, "any governmental attorney-client privilege must yield because the interests served by the grand jury's fact-finding process clearly outweigh the interests served by the privilege." 399 F.3d at 530. The Second Circuit reversed, holding that weighing the public interest against the interest in confidentiality is inappropriate even for government attorneys. "If anything," the court stated,

> the traditional rationale for the privilege applies with special force in the government context. It is crucial that government officials, who are expected to uphold and execute the law and who may face criminal prosecution for failing to do so, be encouraged to seek out and receive fully informed legal advice. Upholding the privilege furthers a culture in which consultation with government lawyers is accepted as a normal, desirable, and even indispensable part of conducting public business. Abrogating the privilege undermines that culture and thereby impairs the public interest.

Id. at 534. Which rule best serves the public interest?

A government official's conversations with a private attorney she retains for her own protection are privileged under the traditional rule. Why provide another privilege for conversations with government lawyers as well? For one thing, the government lawyer has an interest in getting a full picture of the facts so she can discharge her duties. (Recall that *Upjohn* spoke not only of the client's need for advice, but the lawyer's need for a full understanding of the facts to which advice will be tailored.)

Another answer is that there are two entities involved—the office and the office-holder. When the public official seeks legal advice from a government lawyer, she speaks in her capacity as an office-holder. That would imply that the privilege for communications between office-holders and government lawyers "belongs" to the office. If that is right, shouldn't a future occupant of the office be allowed to waive the privilege as to the conversations of earlier office-holders? And if future office-holders can waive the privilege, doesn't that diminish the concern about excessive secrecy in recognizing a governmental attorney-client privilege? For discussion of this issue, see id. at 534-535.

## Note: Opinion Work Product

At the end of *Upjohn*, the Supreme Court briefly considered work-product protection for documents relating to Gerard Thomas's internal investigation. Note that Rule 26(b)(3) distinguishes between ordinary work product and "opinion work product." See Rule 26(b)(3)(B). Distinctions between the two are not easily made, and this has prompted court struggles and decisions that Professor Waits describes as "almost as big a mess as [the case law on] ordinary work product." See Kathleen Waits, Opinion Work Product: A Critical Analysis of Current Law and a New Analytical Framework, 73 Or. L. Rev. 385, 386 (1994).

*Upjohn*, Rule 26(b)(3)(B), and *Hickman* all indicate that opinion work product is entitled to special protection. Is it *ever* discoverable? Consider Holmgren v. State Farm Mutual Auto. Ins. Co., 976 F.2d 573 (9th Cir. 1992). Plaintiff sought and obtained production of a memorandum prepared during a personal injury suit by the insurer's adjuster, in which the adjuster set forth a range of potential liability for plaintiff's claims. The insurer argued that the memo was "opinion work product" under Rule 26(b)(3) and thus entitled to absolute protection. The court held that no absolute privilege exists for opinion work product:

> State Farm contends that the district court erred in compelling it to produce and admitting as evidence plaintiff's exhibits 92 and 93. These items are handwritten memoranda drafted during the litigation of the Cannon suit by a State Farm adjuster. They contain a range of values for Holmgren's claims, including aggravation, medical expenses, lost earnings, pain and suffering, loss of course of life and loss of home, fixing the range of potential liability as from $78,000 to $145,000. State Farm argues that these items are opinion work product and protected under Fed. R. Civ. P. 26(b)(3).
>
> . . . Exhibits 92 and 93 meet the threshold requirements for qualification as work product: both are (a) documents sought by Holmgren that were (b)

prepared for trial (c) by a representative of State Farm. They reflect the opinion of a State Farm adjuster on the range of potential liability. See Reavis v. Metropolitan Property & Liability Ins. Co., 117 F.R.D. 160, 164 (S.D. Cal. 1987) (recognizing opinion work product of adjusters handling claim).

We need not decide whether Rule 26(b)(3) provides any protection for material prepared for litigation that has terminated. For even if it does, *the rule permits discovery when mental impressions are the pivotal issue in the current litigation and the need for the material is compelling.*

A party seeking opinion work product must make a showing beyond the substantial need/undue hardship test required under Rule 26(b)(3) for non-opinion work product. Upjohn Co. v. United States, 449 U.S. 383, 401-02 (1981). The Supreme Court, however, has so far declined to decide whether opinion work product is absolutely protected from discovery. Id. at 401.

The leading case denying all discovery of opinion work product is Duplan Corp. v. Moulinage et Retorderie de Chavanoz, 509 F.2d 730, 734 (4th Cir. 1974) (*Duplan II*). The *Duplan II* court reasoned, "[i]n our view, no showing of relevance, substantial need or undue hardship should justify compelled disclosure of an attorney's mental impressions, conclusions, opinions or legal theories. This is made clear by the Rule's use of the term 'shall' as opposed to 'may.'" Id. at 734. This argument ignores the Advisory Committee notes to the 1970 amendment to Rule 26(b)(3) which state that the Rule "conform[s] to the holdings of the cases, when viewed in light of their facts." In Hickman [v. Taylor, 329 U.S. 495 (1947)], the Court stated that "[i]f there should be a rare situation justifying production of [work product], petitioner's case is not of that type." 329 U.S. at 513.

The Supreme Court, in 1946, rejected a proposed amendment to Rule 30(b) that would have given opinion work product absolute protection. See Report of Proposed Amendments to Rules of Civil Procedure, 5 F.R.D. 433, 456-57 (1946); Order dated December 27, 1946, 329 U.S. 843 (1946) (omitting reference to Rule 30(b) amendment in enumeration of amendments to rules adopted). That rejection, followed closely by the *Hickman* decision, which ordained a case-by-case approach to work product questions, suggests that the Court did not view the mandatory language of Rule 26(b)(3) as demanding absolute protection of opinion work product.

We agree with the several courts and commentators that have concluded that opinion work product may be discovered and admitted when mental impressions are *at issue* in a case and the need for the material is compelling. . . .

Both elements are met here. In a bad faith insurance claim settlement case, the "strategy, mental impressions and opinion of [the insurer's] agents concerning the handling of the claim are directly at issue." *Reavis,* 117 F.R.D. at 164. Further, Holmgren's need for the exhibits was compelling. Montana permits insureds and third party claimants to proceed under § 33-18-201 against an insurer for bad faith in the settlement process. See Mont. Code Ann. § 33-18-242 (1979) (applicable to claims arising after July 1, 1987); Klaudt v. Flink, 658 P.2d 1065, 1067 (1983), *overruled on other grounds [sub nom.]* Fode v. Farmers Ins. Exch., 719 P.2d 414 (1986). Unless the information is available elsewhere, a plaintiff may be able to establish a compelling need for evidence in the insurer's claim file regarding the insurer's opinion of the viability and value of the claim. We review the question on a case-by-case basis. . . .

In *Handgards,* "the lawyers who managed and supervised the former litigation for the defendants [were] being called as witnesses to express their opinions as to the merits of the prior suits." Handgards[, Inc. v. Johnson & Johnson,] 413 F. Supp [926,] 931 [(N.D. Cal. 1976)]. This comment, and others like it in "at issue" cases, is a practical acknowledgment of the fact that, in bad faith settlement cases, insurers may call their adjusters to testify to their opinions as to the lack of viability of the underlying claim. When an insurer chooses to remain mute on the subject, the plaintiff is not foreclosed from developing the same evidence.

976 F.2d at 576-578 (emphasis added). See also Logan v. Commercial Union Ins. Co., 96 F.3d 971, 977 (7th Cir. 1996) ("[A] naked claim of bad faith cannot, without more, authorize a fishing expedition into privileged communications. . . . The plaintiff must demonstrate some likelihood or probability that the documents sought may contain evidence of bad faith."); In re Sealed Case, 676 F.2d 793, 809-810 (D.C. Cir. 1982) (requiring "extraordinary justification" to overcome protection of opinion work product).

### Note: Spoliation and the Duty to Preserve Evidence

Both work-product protection and the attorney-client privilege insulate facts from disclosure in litigation. However, lawyers and their clients have an affirmative obligation to preserve documents and other things that may be relevant to pending and anticipated litigation. Nothing can be turned over in discovery if it has not been preserved. Willful destruction of evidence is called "spoliation," and in addition to potential criminal liability for obstruction of justice, courts have inherent power to impose sanctions against parties who commit spoliation. See Haeger v. Goodyear Tire & Rubber Co., 813 F.3d 1233 (9th Cir. 2016) (en banc) (affirming district court's exercise of inherent power to award monetary sanctions of $548,240 against one defense lawyer as well as $2.1 million jointly against another defense lawyer and Goodyear in tire failure personal injury case where plaintiffs learned, after entering into a settlement agreement, that Goodyear withheld relevant evidence). Sanctions can range from shifting the costs of discovery to the party who has destroyed evidence to instructing the jury that it can draw an adverse inference against the offending party that the evidence destroyed was harmful to that party and favorable to the adversary.

Consider Zubulake v. UBS Warburg LLC, 220 F.R.D. 212 (S.D.N.Y. 2003). Laura Zubulake, an equities trader for UBS earning $650,000 a year, sued the company for gender discrimination. Although lawyers for UBS instructed it to preserve all relevant documents once Zubulake filed an administrative charge with the EEOC, UBS employees (possibly fearful for their own jobs if Zubulake's charges proved true) lost or failed to retain backup records of e-mail correspondence between Zubulake, Human Resources, and others in her working group. Claiming that evidence essential to proving her case was in the lost e-mails, Zubulake filed a motion for sanctions.

The court reasoned that UBS had a duty to preserve relevant evidence once it reasonably anticipated that Zubulake might sue:

> Documents create a paper reality we call proof. The absence of such documentary proof may stymie the search for the truth. . . . Electronic evidence only complicates matters. . . . [I]t has become easier to delete or tamper with evidence (both intentionally and inadvertently) and more difficult for litigants to craft policies that ensure all relevant documents are preserved.

Id. at 214. Once a party recognizes that litigation is possible, the court continued, "it must suspend its routine document retention/destruction policy and put in place a 'litigation hold' to ensure the preservation of relevant documents." Id. at 218. Although UBS failed to take these steps, the court concluded that the *"in terrorem* effect" of an adverse inference sanction would be too harsh and instead shifted the costs of additional discovery to UBS: "In practice, an adverse inference instruction often ends litigation — it is too difficult a hurdle for the spoliator to overcome." Id. at 219-220.

When UBS employees involved in the document destruction were re-deposed two years into the litigation, plaintiff learned that additional e-mails harmful to UBS's defense had been deleted and that other potentially detrimental e-mail correspondence on active UBS servers had never been disclosed in response to valid requests. Plaintiff again moved for sanctions, and this time around the court agreed that UBS's conduct was willful, warranting an adverse inference instruction to the jury:

> [A] major consideration in choosing an appropriate sanction — along with punishing UBS and deterring future misconduct — is to restore Zubulake to the position that she would have been in had UBS faithfully discharged its discovery obligations. . . . [T]he jury empanelled to hear this case will be given an adverse inference instruction with respect to e-mails deleted after August 2001, and in particular, with respect to e-mails that were irretrievably lost when UBS's backup tapes were recycled. No one can ever know precisely what was on those tapes, but the content of e-mails recovered from other sources — along with the fact that UBS employees willfully deleted e-mails — is sufficiently favorable to Zubulake that I am convinced that the contents of the lost tapes would have been similarly, if not more, favorable.

Zubulake v. UBS Warburg LLC, 229 F.R.D. 422, 437 (S.D.N.Y. 2004) (also forcing UBS to pay the costs incurred by plaintiff as a result of UBS's tardy compliance with discovery requests, including the costs of moving for sanctions). See also Coleman (Parent) Holdings, Inc. v. Morgan, Stanley & Co., 2005 WL 679071, at *7 (Fla. Cir. Ct. Mar. 1, 2005) (shifting burden of proof at trial and reading description of discovery misconduct to jury).

At trial, the jury found UBS liable and awarded $29.3 million dollars in damages. A court's power to choose among different sanctions for spoliation thus carries with it the power to determine the outcome of the case. See also United States v. Philip Morris USA, Inc., 327 F. Supp. 2d 21, 23 (D.D.C. 2004) (declining to impose adverse inference as sanction where at least 11 high-level corporate officers at Philip Morris deleted numerous e-mails in violation of the company's document retention policy and the court's Case Management Order "requiring preservation of 'all documents and other records containing information which could be . . . relevant to the subject matter of this litigation'") (citation omitted); see also id. at 26 (approving exclusion of testimony by any employees who engaged in document destruction and imposing a $2,750,000 penalty as sanctions for the defendants' "reckless disregard and gross indifference . . . toward their discovery and document preservation obligations").

While laying most of the blame on UBS and its employees, the *Zubulake* court also emphasized that lawyers are bound, ethically and by Rule 26(e), to help ensure that their clients appropriately supplement their initial disclosures and avoid spoliation:

> *First*, counsel must issue a "litigation hold" at the outset of litigation or whenever litigation is reasonably anticipated. The litigation hold should be periodically reissued so that new employees are aware of it, and so that it is fresh in the minds of all employees.
>
> *Second*, counsel should communicate directly with the "key players" in the litigation, i.e., the parties identified in a party's initial disclosure and any subsequent supplementation thereto. . . . As with the litigation hold, the key players should be periodically reminded that the preservation duty is still in place.
>
> *Finally*, counsel should instruct all employees to produce electronic copies of their relevant active files. Counsel must also make sure that all backup media which the party is required to retain is identified and stored in a safe place. . . . One of the primary reasons that electronic data is lost is ineffective communication with information technology personnel.

Id. at 433-434. In this case, the court found that "counsel failed to properly oversee UBS in a number of important ways, both in terms of its duty to locate relevant information and its duty to preserve and timely produce that information." Id. at 435. Cf. Cedars-Sinai Med. Ctr. v. Sup. Ct., 18 Cal. 4th 1 (1998) (rejecting separate tort liability for intentional spoliation discovered before trial); Temple Cmty. Hosp. v. Sup. Ct., 20 Cal. 4th 464 (1999) (rejecting tort liability for intentional spoliation by third party); Emery G. Lee III, Early Stages of Litigation Attorney Survey, Report to the Judicial Conference Advisory Committee on Civil Rules, Federal Judicial Center, Mar. 2012, 1 (reporting that of the 40 percent of lawyers who said they discuss discovery of electronically stored information in their Rule 26(f) conferences, only "60 [percent] reported discussing preservation obligations").

*Zubulake* held that the duty to preserve potentially relevant evidence is triggered once litigation is possible. Other courts have held that an ongoing agency investigation is sufficient to trigger the duty. Abdulahi v. Wal-Mart, 2014 WL 7448533 (N.D. Ga. Dec. 18, 2014) (granting adverse jury instruction as sanction against defendant for failure to preserve video footage relevant to employment discrimination dispute prior to litigation but during EEOC investigation).

In 2005 an unpublished order in a state case involving electronic discovery and spoliation attracted national attention. See Coleman Holdings v. Morgan Stanley & Co., Inc., 2005 WL 679071 (Fla. Cir. Ct. Mar. 1, 2005) (defendant in fraud suit preserved some documents once it anticipated litigation but it continued to overwrite emails after 12 months despite an SEC order that such material be preserved for two years; defendant also failed to locate and produce relevant backup files; adverse jury instruction granted). The ABA journal Law Practice noted that *Coleman Holdings* "caused a ripple of dread throughout the litigation realm," as lawyers scramble to keep pace with the complexities of storage, management, and discovery of electronically stored information. Sharon Nelson and John Simek, Hot Buttons, ABA Law Practice, http://www.americanbar.org/publications/law_practice_home/law_practice_archive/lpm_magazine_articles_v32_is8_an7.html.

## 3.   Digital Data and the Problem of Electronic Discovery

As *Zubulake* and *Coleman Holdings* demonstrate, modern discovery disputes increasingly involve digital data. This new form of data is both a blessing and a curse. Unlike work that used to be done orally, or communication that takes place exclusively by phone or in live meetings, digital communication leaves a record. And we are becoming increasingly reliant on digital methods of work and communication. The amount of raw information generated and stored on computers and other electronic media is huge and growing fast. A 2003 study found that in 2002 alone, nearly five "exabytes" of new data were created. Five exabytes of data are equivalent to the contents of 37,000 libraries, each with a book collection the size of the Library of Congress. Ninety-two percent of that data is stored on magnetic media such as hard disks, 7 percent on film, just 0.01 percent on paper, and 0.002 percent on optical media. See How Much Information? 2003, Executive Summary, Oct. 27, 2003, www.sims.berkeley.edu/research/projects/how-much-info-2003/execsum.htm#summary. More than two-thirds of electronically stored data is never printed. Tricia Bishop, Electronic Records Open Up Fertile Legal Research Field, L.A. Times, Dec. 27, 2004, at C3.

We are now in the era of "big data." Massive amounts of digital data can now be stored in tiny, high-volume memory devices, on massive off-site servers, and in the cloud. And individuals now produce, disseminate, and store enormous amounts of digital data on personal electronic devices (iPhones, iPads, MP3 players, GoPro portable video cameras, etc.). The sheer amount of communication occurring in digital form is staggering. By the end of 2016, one study predicted, there will be more than 4.3 billion e-mail accounts worldwide, up from 3.3 billion in 2012. In 2012, consumer e-mail accounts made up 75 percent of e-mail inboxes worldwide, but in the remaining 25 percent of corporate e-mail accounts, *89 billion e-mails* were sent and received *each day*. This figure was predicted to reach over 143 billion per day by the end of 2016. Over 2.7 billion instant messaging accounts existed in 2012, along with a similar number of social networking sites. Sara Radicati, Email Statistics Report, 2012-2106, The Radicati Group, http://www.radicati.com/wp/wp-content/uploads/2012/04/Email-Statistics-Report-2012-2016-Executive-Summary.pdf.

Apart from the relative ease of digital file generation and destruction, can you see some of the unique problems this new format for data storage creates for discovery in civil litigation? As you read the case below, consider whether any of the issues that give rise to sanctions are distinctive because of the type of information Qualcomm tried to conceal, or whether the case reflects problems all too familiar in traditional discovery practice.

## *Qualcomm Inc. v. Broadcom Corp.*
2008 WL 66932 (S.D. Cal. Jan. 7, 2008)

BARBARA L. MAJOR, UNITED STATES MAGISTRATE JUDGE.

## Background

### A. *The Patent Infringement Case*

Qualcomm initiated this patent infringement action on October 14, 2005, alleging Broadcom's infringement of Qualcomm patent numbers 5,452,104 ("the 104 patent") and 5,576,767 ("the 767 patent") based on its manufacture, sale, and offers to sell H.264-compliant products. Qualcomm sought injunctive relief, compensatory damages, attorneys' fees and costs.

On December 8, 2006, Broadcom filed a First Amended Answer and Counterclaims in which it alleged (1) a counterclaim that the '104 patent is unenforceable due to inequitable conduct, and (2) an affirmative defense that both patents are unenforceable due to waiver. Broadcom's waiver defense was predicated on Qualcomm's participation in the Joint Video Team ("JVT") in 2002 and early 2003. The JVT is the [international] standards-setting body that created the H.264 standard, which was released in May 2003 and governs video coding.*

### B. *Evidence of Qualcomm's Participation in the JVT*

Over the course of discovery, Broadcom sought information concerning Qualcomm's participation in and communications with the JVT through

---

* [The patents at issue cover methods for compressing video image data. H.264/MPEGAVC creates a global, uniform standard specification that enables High Definition (HD) images to be efficiently stored and delivered over satellite, broadcast, and cable television, as well as Blu-ray disc, mobile phones, and Internet-based television. Since 2001, through the JVT, prominent video technology companies, including Microsoft and Sony, collaborated with others in the development of the H.264 standard for their mutual benefit. The goal was a standard that would allow efficient product creation centered around a single coding mechanism. H.264 has been a substantial breakthrough in HD development—even winning a Primetime Emmy Engineering Award from the U.S. Academy of Television Arts & Science. For more information on H.264, see http://images.apple.com/br/quicktime/pdf/H264_Technology_Brief.pdf. EDs.]

a variety of discovery devices. For example, as early as January 23, 2006, Broadcom served its First Set of Requests for the Production of Documents and Things (Nos. 1-88), in which it requested:

> [a]ll documents given to or received from a standards setting body or group that concern any standard relating to the processing of digital video signals that pertains in any way to any Qualcomm Patent, including without limitation communications, proposals, presentations, agreements, commitments, or contracts to or from such bodies. . . . [and]
>
> [a]ll documents concerning any Qualcomm membership, participation, interaction, and/or involvement in setting any standard relating to the processing of digital video signals that pertains in any way to any Qualcomm Patent. This request also covers all proposed or potential standards, whether or not actually adopted. . . .
>
> [a]ll documents referring to or evidencing any participation by Qualcomm in the proceedings of the JVT, the ISO, the IEC, and/or the ITU-T; and
>
> [a]ll documents constituting, referring to, or evidencing any disclosure by any party to the JVT, the ISO, the IEC, and/or the ITU-T of any Qualcomm Patent and/or any Related Qualcomm Patent.

Id. Broadcom also requested similar information via interrogatories and multiple Rule 30(b)(6) deposition notices.

On their face, Qualcomm's written discovery responses did not appear unusual. In response to Broadcom's request for JVT documents, Qualcomm, in a discovery response signed by attorney Kevin Leung, stated, "Qualcomm will produce non-privileged relevant and responsive documents describing Qualcomm's participation in the JVT, if any, which can be located after a reasonable search." Similarly, Qualcomm committed to producing "responsive non-privileged documents that were given to or received from standards-setting body responsible for the [H.264] standard, and which concern any Qualcomm participation in setting the [H.264] standard." When asked for "the facts and circumstances of any and all communications between Qualcomm and any standards setting body relating to video technology, including . . . the JVT . . . ," Qualcomm responded that it first attended a JVT meeting in December 2003 and that it first submitted a JVT proposal in January 2006. . . . Qualcomm stated that it submitted four proposals to the JVT in 2006 but had no earlier involvement. . . . Kevin Leung signed both of these interrogatory responses.

Qualcomm's responses to Broadcom's Rule 30(b)(6) deposition notices were more troubling. Initially, Qualcomm designated Christine Irvine as the corporation's most knowledgeable person on the issue of Qualcomm's involvement in the JVT. Although attorney Leung prepared Irvine for her deposition, Qualcomm did not search her computer for any relevant documents or emails or provide her with any information to review. Irvine testified falsely that Qualcomm had never been involved in the JVT. Broadcom impeached Irvine with documents showing that Qualcomm had participated in the JVT in late 2003. Qualcomm ultimately agreed to provide another Rule 30(b)(6) witness.

Qualcomm designated Scott Ludwin as the new representative to testify about Qualcomm's knowledge of and involvement in the JVT. Leung prepared and defended Ludwin at his deposition. Qualcomm did not search Ludwin's computer for any relevant documents nor take any other action to prepare him. Ludwin testified falsely that Qualcomm only began participating in the JVT in late 2003, after the H.264 standard had been published. In an effort to impeach him (and extract the truth), Broadcom showed Ludwin a December 2002 email reflector list from the Advanced Video Coding ("AVC") Ad Hoc Group that listed the email address viji@qualcomm.com.[2] Although Ludwin did not recognize the document, Broadcom utilized the document throughout the litigation to argue that Qualcomm had participated in the JVT during the development of the H.264 standard.

As the case progressed, Qualcomm became increasingly aggressive in its argument that it did not participate in the JVT during the time the JVT was creating the H.264 standard.[3] This argument was vital to Qualcomm's success in this litigation because if Qualcomm had participated in the creation of the H.264 standard, it would have been required to identify its patents that reasonably may be essential to the practice of the H.264 standard, including the '104 and '767 patents, and to license them royalty-free or under non-discriminatory, reasonable terms. Thus, participation in the JVT in 2002 or early 2003 during the creation of the H.264 standard would have prohibited Qualcomm from suing companies, including Broadcom, that utilized the H.264 standard. . . .

### C. Trial and Decision Not to Produce avc_ce Emails

Trial commenced on January 9, 2007, and throughout trial, Qualcomm argued that it had not participated in the JVT in 2002 and early 2003 when the H.264 standard was being created. In his opening statement, Qualcomm's lead attorney, James Batchelder, stated:

2. The document is an "Input Document to JVT" entitled "Ad Hoc Report on AVC Verification Test." The Report discusses a meeting to take place among JVT members. The Annex A to the document is entitled a "list of Ad Hoc Members." It includes Raveendran's email address, viji@qualcomm.com, and identifies her as a member of list avc_ce. Id. While the document is not an email sent to or from Raveendran, it indicates that a Qualcomm employee was receiving JVT/AVC reports in 2002. This document became critical to Broadcom as it was the only evidence in Broadcom's possession indicating the truth—that Qualcomm had been actively involved in the JVT and the development of the H.264 standard in 2002.

3. For example, on September 1, 2006, Qualcomm submitted an expert declaration confirming the absence of any corporate records indicating Qualcomm's participation in the JVT. The declaration was prepared by the Heller Ehrman lawyers and reviewed by numerous Day Casebeer and Qualcomm in-house attorneys. . . . Numerous in-house and outside counsel also [prepared and reviewed other motions, including a motion for summary judgment and motions in limine denying any involvement by Qualcomm with the JVT while the H.264 standard was being created].

Later, in May of '03, the standard is approved and published. And then Qualcomm, in the fall of 2003, it begins to participate not in JVT because it's done. H.264 is approved and published. Qualcomm begins to participate in what are called professional extensions, things that sit on top of the standard, additional improvements.

While preparing Qualcomm witness Viji Raveendran to testify at trial, attorney Adam Bier discovered an August 6, 2002[,] email to viji@qual-comm.com welcoming her to the avc_ce mailing list. Several days later, on January 14, 2007, Raveendran searched her laptop computer using the search term "avc_ce" and discovered 21 separate emails, none of which Qualcomm had produced in discovery. The email chains bore several dates in November 2002 and the authors discussed various issues relating to the H.264 standard. While Raveendran was not a named author or recipient, the emails were sent to all members of two JVT email groups (jvt-experts and avc_ce) and Raveendran maintained them on her computer for more than four years. The Qualcomm trial team decided not to produce these newly discovered emails to Broadcom, claiming they were not responsive to Broadcom's discovery requests. The attorneys ignored the fact that the presence of the emails on Raveendran's computer undercut Qualcomm's premier argument that it had not participated in the JVT in 2002. The Qualcomm trial team failed to conduct any investigation to determine whether there were more emails that also had not been produced.

Four days later, during a sidebar discussion, Stanley Young argued against the admission of the December 2002 avc_ce email reflector list declaring: "Actually, there are no emails—there are no emails . . . there's no evidence that any email was actually sent to this list. This is just a list of email . . . addresses. There's no evidence of anything being sent." None of the Qualcomm attorneys who were present during the sidebar mentioned the 21 avc_ce emails found on Raveendran's computer a few days earlier.

During Raveendran's direct testimony on January 24th, attorney Lee Patch pointedly did not ask her any questions that would reveal the fact that she had received the 21 emails from the avc_ce mailing list; instead, he asked whether she had "any knowledge of having read" any emails from the avc_ce mailing list. But on cross-examination, Broadcom asked the right question and Raveendran was forced to admit that she had received emails from the avc_ce mailing list. Immediately following this admission, in response to Broadcom's request for the emails, and despite the fact that he had participated in the decision three days earlier not to produce them, Patch told the Court at sidebar:

> [I]t's not clear to me [the emails are] responsive to anything. So that's something that needs to be determined before they would be produced. . . . I'm talking about whether they were actually requested in discovery. . . . I'm simply representing that I haven't seen [the emails], and [whether Broadcom requested them] hasn't been determined.

Over the lunch recess that same day, Qualcomm's counsel produced the 21 emails they previously had retrieved from Raveendran's email archive.

On January 26, 2007, the jury returned unanimous verdicts in favor of Broadcom regarding the non-infringement of the '104 and '767 patents, and in favor of Qualcomm regarding the validity and non-obviousness of the same. The jury also returned a unanimous advisory verdict in favor of Broadcom that the '104 patent is unenforceable due to inequitable conduct and the '104 and '767 patents are unenforceable due to waiver.

On March 21, 2007, Judge Brewster found (1) in favor of Qualcomm on Broadcom's inequitable conduct counterclaim regarding the '104 patent, and (2) in favor of Broadcom on Broadcom's waiver defense regarding the '104 and '767 patents. Judge Brewster issued a comprehensive order detailing the appropriate remedy for Qualcomm's waiver. After a thorough overview of the JVT, the JVT's policies and guidelines, and Qualcomm's knowledge of the JVT and evidence of Qualcomm's involvement therein, Judge Brewster found:

> by clear and convincing evidence that Qualcomm, its employees, and its witnesses actively organized and/or participated in a plan to profit heavily by (1) wrongfully concealing the patents-in-suit while participating in the JVT and then (2) actively hiding this concealment from the Court, the jury, and opposing counsel during the present litigation.

*Id.* at 22. Judge Brewster further found that Qualcomm's "counsel participated in an organized program of litigation misconduct and concealment throughout discovery, trial, and post-trial before new counsel took over lead role in the case on April 27, 2007." Based on "the totality of the evidence produced both before and after the jury verdict," and in light of these findings, Judge Brewster concluded that "Qualcomm has waived its rights to enforce the '104 and '767 patents and their continuations, continuations-in-part, divisions, reissues, or any other derivatives of either patent."

Also on August 6, 2007, Judge Brewster granted Broadcom's Motion for an Award of Attorneys' Fees pursuant to 35 U.S.C. § 285. Judge Brewster found clear and convincing evidence that Qualcomm's litigation misconduct, as set forth in his Waiver Order, justified Qualcomm's payment of all "attorneys' fees, court costs, expert witness fees, travel expenses, and any other litigation costs reasonably incurred by Broadcom" in the defense of this case. On December 11, 2007, Judge Brewster adopted this court's recommendation and ordered Qualcomm to pay Broadcom $9,259,985.09 in attorneys' fees and related costs, as well as post-judgment interest on the final fee award of $8,568,633.24 at 4.91 percent accruing from August 6, 2007.

### D. Qualcomm's Post-Trial Misconduct

Following trial, Qualcomm continued to dispute the relevancy and responsiveness of the 21 Raveendran emails. Qualcomm also resisted Broadcom's efforts to determine the scope of Qualcomm's discovery violation. . . .

But, on April 9, 2007, James Batchelder and Louis Lupin, Qualcomm's General Counsel, submitted correspondence to Judge Brewster in which they admitted Qualcomm had thousands of relevant unproduced documents and that their review of these documents "revealed facts that appear to be inconsistent with certain arguments that [outside counsel] made on Qualcomm's behalf at trial and in the equitable hearing following trial." Batchelder further apologized "for not having discovered these documents sooner and for asserting positions that [they] would not have taken had [they] known of the existence of these documents."

As of June 29, 2007, Qualcomm had searched the email archives of twenty-one employees and located more than forty-six thousand documents (totaling more than three hundred thousand pages), which had been requested but not produced in discovery. Qualcomm continued to produce additional responsive documents throughout the summer.

## Discussion

As summarized above, and as found by Judge Brewster, there is clear and convincing evidence that Qualcomm intentionally engaged in conduct designed to prevent Broadcom from learning that Qualcomm had participated in the JVT during the time period when the H.264 standard was being developed. To this end, Qualcomm withheld tens of thousands of emails showing that it actively participated in the JVT in 2002 and 2003 and then utilized Broadcom's lack of access to the suppressed evidence to repeatedly and falsely aver that there was "no evidence" that it had participated in the JVT prior to September 2003. Qualcomm's misconduct in hiding the emails and electronic documents prevented Broadcom from correcting the false statements and countering the misleading arguments.

### A.  Legal Standard

The Federal Civil Rules authorize federal courts to impose sanctions on parties and their attorneys who fail to comply with discovery obligations and court orders. Rule 37 authorizes a party to file a motion to compel an opponent to comply with a discovery request or obligation when the opponent fails to do so initially. Fed. R. Civ. P. 37(a). If such a motion is filed, the rule requires the court to award reasonable attorney's fees to the prevailing party unless the court finds the losing party's position was "substantially justified" or other circumstances make such an award unjust. . . . There is no requirement under this rule that the failure be willful or reckless; "sanctions may be imposed even for negligent failures to provide discovery." Fjelstad v. Am. Honda Motor Co., Inc., 762 F.2d 1334, 1343 (9th Cir. 1985).

The Federal Rules also provide for sanctions against individual attorneys who are remiss in complying with their discovery obligations. . . . Fed. R. Civ. P. 26(g)(2). . . . "[W]hat is reasonable is a matter for the court to decide on the totality of the circumstances." Fed. R. Civ. P. 26 Advisory Committee Notes (1983 Amendment). The Committee explained that:

> Rule 26(g) imposes an affirmative duty to engage in pretrial discovery in a responsible manner that is consistent with the spirit and purposes of Rules 26 through 37. In addition, Rule 26(g) is designed to curb discovery abuse by explicitly encouraging the imposition of sanctions. This subdivision provides a deterrent to both excessive discovery and evasion by imposing a certification requirement that obliges each attorney to stop and think about the legitimacy of a discovery request, a response thereto, or an objection. . . . If primary responsibility for conducting discovery is to continue to rest with the litigants, they must be obliged to act responsibly and avoid abuse. . . .

Id. . . . In addition to this rule-based authority, federal courts have the inherent power to sanction litigants to prevent abuse of the judicial process. See Chambers v. NASCO, Inc., 501 U.S. [32, 44-46 (1991)]. . . .

### B. *Broadcom Did Not File a Motion to Compel Discovery*

As summarized above, Broadcom served interrogatories and requested documents relating to Qualcomm's participation in the JVT. Qualcomm responded that "Qualcomm will produce non-privileged relevant and responsive documents describing QUALCOMM's participation in the JVT, if any, which can be located after a reasonable search." Qualcomm also committed to producing "responsive non-privileged documents that were given to or received from the standards-setting body responsible for the [H.264] standard, and which concern any Qualcomm participation in setting the [H.264] standard."

Despite these responses, Qualcomm did not produce over 46,000 responsive documents, many of which directly contradict the non-participation argument that Qualcomm repeatedly made to the court and jury. Because Qualcomm agreed to produce the documents and answered the interrogatories (even though falsely), Broadcom had no reason to file a motion to compel. . . .

This dilemma highlights another problem with Qualcomm's conduct in this case. The Federal Rules of Civil Procedure require parties to respond to discovery in good faith; the rules do not require or anticipate judicial involvement unless or until an actual dispute is discovered. As the Advisory Committee explained, "[i]f primary responsibility for conducting discovery is to continue to rest with the litigants, they must be obliged to act responsibly and avoid abuse." Fed. R. Civ. P. 26(g) Advisory Committee Notes (1983 Amendment). The Committee's concerns are heightened in this age of electronic discovery when attorneys may not physically touch and read every document within the client's custody and control. For the current "good faith" discovery system to function in the electronic age, attorneys and clients must work together to ensure that both understand how and where electronic documents, records and emails are maintained and to determine how best to locate, review, and produce responsive documents. Attorneys must take responsibility for ensuring that their clients conduct a comprehensive and appropriate document search. Producing 1.2 million pages of marginally relevant documents while hiding 46,000 critically important ones does not constitute good faith and does not satisfy either the client's or attorney's discovery obligations. Similarly, agreeing to produce certain categories of documents and then not producing all of the documents that fit within such a category is unacceptable. Qualcomm's conduct warrants sanctions.

## C. Sanctions

. . .

### 1. Misconduct by Qualcomm

Qualcomm violated its discovery obligations by failing to produce more than 46,000 emails and documents that were requested in discovery and that Qualcomm agreed to produce. . . .

Qualcomm has not established "substantial justification" for its failure to produce the documents. In fact, Qualcomm has not presented any evidence attempting to explain or justify its failure to produce the documents. Despite the fact that it maintains detailed records showing whose computers were searched and which search terms were used, Qualcomm has not presented any evidence establishing that it searched for pre-September 2003 JVT, avc_ce, or H.264 records or emails on its computer system or email databases. Qualcomm also has not established that it searched the computers or email databases of the individuals who testified on Qualcomm's behalf at trial or in depositions as Qualcomm's most knowledgeable corporate witnesses; in fact, it indicates that it did not conduct any such search. The fact that Qualcomm did not perform these basic searches at any time before the completion of trial indicates that Qualcomm intentionally withheld the documents. This conclusion is bolstered by the fact that when Qualcomm "discovered" the 21 Raveendran emails, it did not produce them and did not engage in any type of review to determine whether there were additional relevant, responsive, and unproduced documents. The conclusion is further supported by the fact that after trial Qualcomm did not conduct an internal investigation to determine if there were additional unproduced documents, but, rather, spent its time opposing Broadcom's efforts to force such a search and insisting, without any factual basis, that Qualcomm's search was reasonable.

Qualcomm's claim that it inadvertently failed to find and produce these documents also is negated by the massive volume and direct relevance of the hidden documents. As Judge Brewster noted, it is inexplicable that Qualcomm was able to locate the post-September 2003 JVT documents that either supported, or did not harm, Qualcomm's arguments but were unable to locate the pre-September 2003 JVT documents that hurt its arguments. Similarly, the inadvertence argument is undercut by Qualcomm's ability to easily locate the suppressed documents using fundamental JVT and avc_ce search terms when forced to do so by Broadcom's threat to return to court. Finally, the inadvertence argument also is belied by the number of Qualcomm employees and consultants who received the emails, attended the JVT meetings, and otherwise knew about the information set forth in the undisclosed emails. It is inconceivable that Qualcomm was unaware of its involvement in the JVT and of the existence of these documents.

Assuming *arguendo*, that Qualcomm did not know about the suppressed emails, Qualcomm failed to heed several warning signs that should have alerted it to the fact that its document search and production were inadequate. The first significant concern should have been raised in connection with the Rule 30(b)(6) depositions of Christine Irvine and Scott Ludwin. Both individuals testified as the Qualcomm employee most knowledgeable about Qualcomm's involvement in the JVT. But Qualcomm did not search either person's computer for JVT documents, did not provide either person with relevant JVT documents to review, and did not make any other efforts to ensure each person was in fact knowledgeable about Qualcomm's JVT involvement. These omissions are especially incriminating because many of the suppressed emails were to or from Irvine. If a witness is testifying as an organization's most knowledgeable person on a specific subject, the organization has an obligation to conduct a reasonable investigation and review to ensure that the witness does possess the organization's knowledge.[6] Fed. R. Civ. P. 30(b)(6); In re JDS Uniphase Corp. Sec. Litig., 2007 WL 219857, *1 (N.D. Cal. Jan. 29, 2007) (the corporation "must prepare the designee to the extent matters are reasonably available, whether from documents, past employees, or other sources"). An adequate investigation should include an analysis of the sufficiency of the document search and, when electronic documents are involved, an analysis of the sufficiency of the search terms and locations. In the instant case, a reasonable inquiry should have included using the JVT, avc_ce, and H.264 search terms and searching the computers of Raveendran, Irvine, Ludwin (and other Qualcomm employees identified in the emails discovered on the computers of these witnesses). This minimal inquiry would have revealed the existence of the suppressed documents. . . .

Another ignored warning flag was the December 2002 avc_ce email reflector containing Raveendran's email address. Broadcom utilized

---

6. . . . Qualcomm also has not presented any evidence that outside counsel knew enough about Qualcomm's organization and operation to identify all of the individuals whose computers should be searched and determine the most knowledgeable witness. And, more importantly, Qualcomm is a large corporation with an extensive legal staff; it clearly had the ability to identify the correct witnesses and determine the correct computers to search and search terms to use. Qualcomm just lacked the desire to do so.

this document in several ways to argue that Qualcomm was involved in the JVT prior to September 2003. Even though this document indicated that in December 2002, a Qualcomm employee was a member of the avc_ce email group, which related to the JVT and the development of the H.264 standard, there is no evidence that its presence triggered a search by Qualcomm for "avc_ce," "JVT," or any other relevant term on Raveendran's computer or any other Qualcomm database. Again, if Qualcomm had performed this search, it would have located the suppressed emails. The fact that Qualcomm chose not to investigate this document supports the conclusion that Qualcomm intentionally withheld the 46,000 emails. This conclusion is reinforced by the fact that, without any investigation, Qualcomm repeatedly tried to discredit the document and Broadcom's reliance on it.

Qualcomm had the ability to identify its employees and consultants who were involved in the JVT, to access and review their computers, databases and emails, to talk with the involved employees and to refresh their recollections if necessary. . . . Qualcomm chose not to do so and therefore must be sanctioned.

### 2. Attorneys' Misconduct

The next question is what, if any, role did Qualcomm's retained lawyers play in withholding the documents? The Court envisions four scenarios. First, Qualcomm intentionally hid the documents from its retained lawyers and did so so effectively that the lawyers did not know or suspect that the suppressed documents existed. Second, the retained lawyers failed to discover the intentionally hidden documents or suspect their existence due to their complete ineptitude and disorganization. Third, Qualcomm shared the damaging documents with its retained lawyers (or at least some of them) and the knowledgeable lawyers worked with Qualcomm to hide the documents and all evidence of Qualcomm's early involvement in the JVT. Or, fourth, while Qualcomm did not tell the retained lawyers about the damaging documents and evidence, the lawyers suspected there was additional evidence or information but chose to ignore the evidence and warning signs and accept Qualcomm's incredible assertions regarding the adequacy of the document search and witness investigation.

Given the impressive education and extensive experience of Qualcomm's retained lawyers, the Court rejects the first and second possibilities. It is inconceivable that these talented, well-educated, and experienced lawyers failed to discover through their interactions with Qualcomm any facts or issues that caused (or should have caused) them to question the sufficiency of Qualcomm's document search and production. Qualcomm did not fail to produce a document or two; it withheld over 46,000 critical documents that extinguished Qualcomm's primary argument of nonparticipation in the JVT. In addition, the suppressed documents did not belong to one employee, or a couple of employees who had since left the company; they belonged to (or were shared with) numerous, current

Qualcomm employees, several of whom testified (falsely) at trial and in depositions. . . .

The Court finds no direct evidence establishing option three. Neither party nor the attorneys have presented evidence that Qualcomm told one or more of its retained attorneys about the damaging emails or that an attorney learned about the emails and that the knowledgeable attorney(s) then helped Qualcomm hide the emails. While knowledge may be inferred from the attorneys' conduct, evidence on this issue is limited due to Qualcomm's assertion of the attorney-client privilege.[8]

Thus, the Court finds it likely that some variation of option four occurred; that is, one or more of the retained lawyers chose not to look in the correct locations for the correct documents, to accept the unsubstantiated assurances of an important client that its search was sufficient, to ignore the warning signs that the document search and production were inadequate, not to press Qualcomm employees for the truth, and/or to encourage employees to provide the information (or lack of information) that Qualcomm needed to assert its non-participation argument and to succeed in this lawsuit. These choices enabled Qualcomm to withhold hundreds of thousands of pages of relevant discovery and to assert numerous false and misleading arguments to the court and jury. This conduct warrants the imposition of sanctions.

### a. Identity of Sanctioned Attorneys

The Court finds that each of the following attorneys contributed to Qualcomm's monumental discovery violation and is personally responsible: James Batchelder, Adam Bier, Kevin Leung, Christopher Mammen, Lee Patch, and Stanley Young ("Sanctioned Attorneys").

[Day Casebeer a]ttorneys Leung, Mammen and Batchelder are responsible for the initial discovery failure because they handled or supervised Qualcomm's discovery responses and production of documents. . . . Had Leung, Mammen, Batchelder, or any of the other attorneys insisted on reviewing Qualcomm's records regarding the locations searched and terms utilized, they would have discovered the inadequacy of the search and

---

8. Qualcomm asserted the attorney-client privilege and decreed that its retained attorneys could not reveal any communications protected by the privilege. Several attorneys complained that the assertion of the privilege prevented them from providing additional information regarding their conduct. This concern was heightened when Qualcomm submitted its self-serving declarations describing the failings of its retained lawyers. Recognizing that a client has a right to maintain this privilege and that no adverse inference should be made based upon the assertion, the Court accepted Qualcomm's assertion of the privilege and has not drawn any adverse inferences from it. However, the fact remains that the Court does not have access to all of the information necessary to reach an informed decision regarding the actual knowledge of the attorneys. As a result, the Court concludes for purposes of this Order that there is insufficient evidence establishing option three.

the suppressed documents.[10] Similarly, Leung's difficulties with the Rule 30(b)(6) witnesses, Irvine and Ludwin, should have alerted him (and the supervising or senior attorneys) to the inadequacy of Qualcomm's document production and to the fact that they needed to review whose computers and databases had been searched and for what. . . .

[Day Casebeer a]ttorneys Bier, Mammen and Patch are responsible for the discovery violation because they also did not perform a reasonable inquiry to determine whether Qualcomm had complied with its discovery obligations. When Bier reviewed the August 6, 2002 email welcoming Raveendran to the avc_ce email group, he knew or should have known that it contradicted Qualcomm's trial arguments and he had an obligation to verify that it had been produced in discovery or to immediately produce it. If Bier, as a junior lawyer, lacked the experience to recognize the significance of the document, then a more senior or knowledgeable attorney should have assisted him. To the extent that Patch was supervising Bier in this endeavor, Patch certainly knew or should have recognized the importance of the document from his involvement in Qualcomm's motion practice and trial strategy sessions.

Similarly, when Bier found the 21 emails on Raveendran's computer that had not been produced in discovery, he took the appropriate action and informed his supervisors, Mammen and Patch. Patch discussed the discovery and production issue with Young and Batchelder. While all of these attorneys assert that there was a plausible argument that Broadcom did not request these documents, only Bier and Mammen actually read the emails. Moreover, all of the attorneys missed the critical inquiry: was Qualcomm's document search adequate? If these 21 emails were not discovered during Qualcomm's document search, how many more might exist? The answer, obviously, was tens of thousands. . . . And, these experienced attorneys should have realized that the presence on Raveendran's computer of 21

---

10. Leung's attorney represented during the OSC hearing that Leung requested a more thorough document search but that Qualcomm refused to do so. If Leung was unable to get Qualcomm to conduct the type of search he deemed necessary to verify the adequacy of the document search and production, then he should have obtained the assistance of supervising or senior attorneys. If Mammen and Batchelder were unable to get Qualcomm to conduct a competent and thorough document search, they should have withdrawn from the case or taken other action to ensure production of the evidence. See The State Bar of California, Rules of Professional Conduct, Rule 5-220 (a lawyer shall not suppress evidence that the lawyer or the lawyer's client has a legal obligation to reveal); Rule 3-700 (a lawyer shall withdraw from employment if the lawyer knows or should know that continued employment will result in a violation of these rules or the client insists that the lawyer pursue a course of conduct prohibited under these rules). Attorneys' ethical obligations do not permit them to participate in an inadequate document search and then provide misleading and incomplete information to their opponents and false arguments to the court. Id.; Rule 5-200 (a lawyer shall not seek to mislead the judge or jury by a false statement of fact or law); see also In re Marriage of Gong and Kwong, 157 Cal. App. 4th 939, 951 (1st Dist. 2007) ("[a]n attorney in a civil case is not a hired gun required to carry out every direction given by the client"; he must act like the professional he is).

JVT/avc_ce emails from 2002 contradicted Qualcomm's numerous arguments that it had not participated in the JVT during that same time period. This fact, alone, should have prompted the attorneys to immediately produce the emails and to conduct a comprehensive document search.

Finally, [Heller Ehrman attorney] Young, [and Day Casebeer attorneys] Patch and Batchelder bear responsibility for the discovery failure because they did not conduct a reasonable inquiry into Qualcomm's discovery production before making specific factual and legal arguments to the court. Young decided that Qualcomm should file a motion for summary adjudication premised on the fact that Qualcomm had not participated in the JVT until after the H.264 standard was adopted in May 2003. Given that non-participation was vital to the motion, Young had a duty to conduct a reasonable inquiry into whether that fact was true. And, again, had Young conducted such a search, he would have discovered the inadequacy of Qualcomm's document search and production and learned that his argument was false. Similarly, Young had a duty to conduct a reasonable inquiry into the accuracy of his statement before affirmatively telling the court that no emails were sent to Raveendran from the avc_ce email group. Young also did not conduct a reasonable (or any) inquiry during the following days before he approved the factually incorrect JMOL.[12] A reasonable investigation would have prevented the false filing.

Patch was an integral part of the trial team—familiar with Qualcomm's arguments, theories and strategies. He knew on January 14th that 21 avc_ce emails had been discovered on Raveendran's computer. Without reading or reviewing the emails, Patch participated in the decision not to produce them. Several days later, Patch carefully tailored his questions to ensure that Raveendran did not testify about the unproduced emails. And, after Broadcom stumbled into the email testimony, Patch affirmatively misled the Court by claiming that he did not know whether the emails were responsive to Broadcom's discovery requests. This conduct is unacceptable and, considering the totality of the circumstances, it is unrealistic to think that Patch did not know or believe that Qualcomm's document search was inadequate and that Qualcomm possessed numerous, similar and unproduced documents.

Batchelder also is responsible because he was the lead trial attorney and, as such, he was most familiar with Qualcomm's important arguments and

---

12. While the Court recognizes that the Day Casebeer attorneys were primarily responsible for discovery in this case, the Heller Ehrman attorneys took on the task of preparing witnesses and briefing regarding the JVT and, thus, were in a position to evaluate during this process whether the underlying discovery upon which they relied was adequate. Young, unlike [other, unsanctioned Heller Ehrman attorneys] Venkatesan and Robertson, was the primary liaison with Day Casebeer and also was privy to the evolving theories of the case. As such, he was made aware of some of the red flags such as the discovery of the JVT emails on Raveendran's computer and was in the best position both to understand their significance and to communicate any concerns to the Day Casebeer attorneys or Qualcomm in-house counsel.

witnesses. Batchelder stated in his opening statement that Qualcomm had not participated in the JVT before late 2003. Despite this statement and his complete knowledge of Qualcomm's legal theories, Batchelder did not take any action when he was informed that JVT documents that Qualcomm had not produced in discovery were found on Raveendran's computer. He did not read the emails, ask about their substance, nor inquire as to why they were not located during discovery. And, he stood mute when four days later, Young falsely stated that no emails had been sent to Raveendran from the avc_ce email group. Finally, all of the pleadings containing the lie that Qualcomm had not participated in the JVT in 2002 or early 2003 were sent to Batchelder for review and he approved or ignored all of them. The totality of the circumstances, including all of the previously-discussed warning signs, demanded that Batchelder conduct an investigation to verify the adequacy of Qualcomm's document search and production. His failure to do so enabled Qualcomm to withhold the documents. . . .

### 3. Imposed Sanctions

. . . The remaining issue, then, is what are the appropriate sanctions.

#### a. Monetary Sanctions Against Qualcomm

. . .

Because Broadcom prevailed at trial and in the post-trial hearings despite the suppressed evidence, it is reasonable to infer that had Qualcomm intended to produce the 46,000 incriminating emails (and thereby acknowledge its early involvement in the JVT and its accompanying need to disclose its intellectual property), the instant case may never have been filed. Even if Qualcomm did file this case, the hidden evidence would have dramatically undermined Qualcomm's arguments and likely resulted in an adverse pretrial adjudication, much as it caused the adverse post-trial rulings. Accordingly, Qualcomm's failure to produce the massive number of critical documents at issue in this case significantly increased the scope, complexity and length of the litigation and justifies a significant monetary award.

The Court therefore awards Broadcom all of its attorneys' fees and costs incurred in the instant litigation. Because Judge Brewster already has awarded these costs and fees to Broadcom [under fee-shifting provisions of the patent statute] and a double recovery would be improper, this Court directs that Qualcomm receive credit toward this penalty. . . . Accordingly, for its monumental and intentional discovery violation, Qualcomm is ordered to pay $8,568,633.24 to Broadcom; this figure will be reduced by the amount actually paid by Qualcomm to Broadcom to satisfy the exceptional case award.[17]

---

17. Because the attorneys' fees sanction is so large, the Court declines to fine Qualcomm. If the imposition of an $8.5 million dollar sanction does not change Qualcomm's conduct, the Court doubts that an additional fine would do so.

### b. *Referral to the California State Bar*

As set forth above, the Sanctioned Attorneys assisted Qualcomm in committing this incredible discovery violation by intentionally hiding or recklessly ignoring relevant documents, ignoring or rejecting numerous warning signs that Qualcomm's document search was inadequate, and blindly accepting Qualcomm's unsupported assurances that its document search was adequate. The Sanctioned Attorneys then used the lack of evidence to repeatedly and forcefully make false statements and arguments to the court and jury. As such, the Sanctioned Attorneys violated their discovery obligations and also may have violated their ethical duties. See e.g., The State Bar of California, Rules of Professional Conduct, Rule 5-200 (a lawyer shall not seek to mislead the judge or jury by a false statement of fact or law), Rule 5-220 (a lawyer shall not suppress evidence that the lawyer or the lawyer's client has a legal obligation to reveal or to produce). To address the potential ethical violations, the Court refers the Sanctioned Attorneys to The State Bar of California for an appropriate investigation and possible imposition of sanctions. Within ten days of the date of this Order, each of the Sanctioned Attorneys must forward a copy of this Order and Judge Brewster's Waiver Order to the Intake Unit, The State Bar of California, 1149 South Hill Street, Los Angeles, California 90015 for appropriate investigation.

### c. *Case Review and Enforcement of Discovery Obligations*

The Court also orders Qualcomm and the Sanctioned Attorneys to participate in a comprehensive Case Review and Enforcement of Discovery Obligations ("CREDO") program. . . .

At a minimum, the CREDO protocol must include a ***detailed analysis*** (1) identifying the factors that contributed to the discovery violation . . . , (2) creating and evaluating proposals, procedures, and processes that will correct the deficiencies identified in subsection (1), (3) developing and finalizing a comprehensive protocol that will prevent future discovery violations (e.g., determining the depth and breadth of case management and discovery plans that should be adopted; identifying by experience or authority the attorney from the retained counsel's office who should interface with the corporate counsel and on which issues; describing the frequency the attorneys should meet and whether other individuals should participate in the communications; identifying who should participate in the development of the case management and discovery plans; describing and evaluating various methods of resolving conflicts and disputes between the client and retained counsel, especially relating to the adequacy of discovery searches; describing the type, nature, frequency, and participants in case management and discovery meetings; and, suggesting required ethical and discovery training; etc.), (4) applying the protocol that was developed in subsection (3) to other factual situations, such as when the client does not have corporate counsel, when the client has a single in-house lawyer, when the client has a large legal staff, and when there are two law firms representing one client, (5) identifying and evaluating data tracking systems, software, or procedures that corporations could implement to better enable inside and outside counsel to identify potential sources of discoverable documents (e.g., the correct databases, archives, etc.), and (6) any other information or suggestions that will help prevent discovery violations. . . .

*It is so ordered.*

## Note: A Problem of Divided Responsibility?

*Qualcomm* sent shockwaves through the legal community and remains, in many ways, a wake-up call for attorneys regarding the potential uses and abuses of e-discovery. Electronically stored information vastly multiplies the number of potentially relevant documents and, concomitantly, the responsibilities of lawyers to manage them before and during litigation. For an analysis of some of these issues, see Hon. Paul W. Grimm, Ethical Issues Associated with Preserving, Accessing, Discovering, and Using Electronically Stored Information, SP003 ALI-ABA 693 (2008) (discussing Rule of Professional Responsibility 3.4 (Fairness to Opposing Party and Counsel) and using *Qualcomm* as a case in point for its ethical discussion); see id. at 718-719 ("There are many lessons to be learned from *Qualcomm*, but chief among them is that lawyers can expect that courts will require them to live up to their obligations under Rule 26(g), and that blind reliance on a client's representations that it adequately searched for and produced all responsive ESI will not insulate a lawyer from sanctions or charges of ethical misconduct when the lawyer knows or should suspect the client's response is inadequate."); Kristine L. Roberts, ABA Section of Litigation, Qualcomm Fined for "Monumental" E-Discovery Violations—Possible Sanctions Against Counsel Remain Pending (May 2008), http://www. abanet.org/litigation/litigationnews/2008/may/0508_article_qualcomm. html (discussing steps attorneys should take to "avoid Qualcomm's fate" by making e-discovery checklists). For the post-trial order that got the sanctions ball rolling, see Qualcomm Inc. v. Broadcom Corp., 539 F. Supp. 2d 1214 (S.D. Cal. 2007).

The trial court's separate attorneys' fee award against Qualcomm has been upheld. See Qualcomm Inc. v. Broadcom Corp., 548 F.3d 1004, 1004 (Fed. Cir. 2008) (upholding attorneys' fee award under the federal patent statute's fee-shifting provision for inequitable conduct). However, the district court vacated the sanctions order against Qualcomm's outside counsel and remanded to the magistrate judge. Qualcomm, Inc. v. Broadcom, Inc., 2008 WL 638108 (S.D. Cal. Mar. 5, 2008). The court determined that the magistrate judge had erred by not allowing the attorneys to assert the self-defense exception to the attorney-client privilege and disclose confidential communications with Qualcomm. Those communications, the attorneys argued, proved that any omissions in discovery were caused by Qualcomm itself. On remand, and after reviewing the privileged communications, the magistrate judge agreed with the outside attorneys, declined to impose any sanctions upon them, and dissolved the order to show cause that initiated the sanctions proceedings. Here is how the judge summarized the errors with e-discovery that led to the debacle at trial:

Over a period of roughly fifteen months, the parties undertook a massive discovery effort. Qualcomm searched for, uploaded to its internal review database, and had its outside counsel review for responsiveness and privilege, over 1.6 million documents. It ultimately produced approximately 22,500 documents (totaling well over 100,000 pages) to Responding Attorneys. The Day Casebeer firm produced approximately 31,000 pages of hard copy documents and 39,000 electronic documents to attorney Young in response to his document requests. These documents were reviewed by Day Casebeer's outside counsel, Young's outside counsel, and Qualcomm's outside counsel prior to use in these proceedings. . . . [A]ll of the parties producing documents prepared and provided extensive privilege logs and, where appropriate, redacted responsive documents. They then culled this universe of documents down to the subset to be used for depositions. All told, Responding Attorneys deposed seven Qualcomm engineers, three of Qualcomm's in-house attorneys, two of Qualcomm's in-house paralegals, and one fellow Responding Attorney during the remand proceedings. Excerpts from all of these depositions, as well as three depositions of Qualcomm engineers from the underlying proceedings (depositions taken by Broadcom), were presented via video at the three-day evidentiary hearing before this Court. . . .

The fundamental problem in this case was an incredible breakdown in communication. The lack of meaningful communication permeated all of the relationships (amongst Qualcomm employees—including between Qualcomm engineers and in-house legal staff—between Qualcomm employees and outside legal counsel, and amongst outside counsel) and contributed to all of the other failures. The Court was not presented with any evidence establishing that either in-house lawyers or outside counsel met in person with the appropriate Qualcomm engineers (those who were likely to have been involved in the conduct at issue and who were likely to be witnesses) at the beginning of the case to explain the legal issues and discuss appropriate document collection. Moreover, outside counsel did not obtain sufficient information from any source to understand how Qualcomm's computer system is organized: where emails are stored, how often and to what location laptops and personal computers are backed up, whether, when and under what circumstances data from laptops are copied into repositories, what type of information is contained within the various databases and repositories, what records are maintained regarding the search for, and collection of, documents for litigation, etc. Finally, no attorney took supervisory responsibility for verifying that the necessary discovery had been conducted (including ensuring that all of the correct locations, servers, databases, repositories, and computers were correctly searched for potentially relevant documents) and that the resulting discovery supported the important legal arguments, claims, and defenses being presented to the court. These fundamental failures led to the discovery violations.

Another factor that contributed to the discovery failure was a lack of agreement amongst the participants regarding responsibility for document collection and production. Batchelder delegated discovery responsibility to Leung and Mammen, assuming they would be assisted by capable and trustworthy in-house lawyers and paralegals. Leung and Mammen testified that they followed the procedure set forth in the memorandum entitled "Overview of Document Collection at Qualcomm" ("Overview Memo") in which Qualcomm legal staff dictates which databases and computers are searched. In contrast, in-house legal personnel apparently were unaware of the Overview Memo. Morever, contrary to the guidelines set forth in the Overview Memo, the paralegals understood that while they might suggest potential search locations or custodians, it was outside counsel's role to direct them to documents and to instruct them as to what to collect.

With regard to the Rule 30(b)(6) deponents, in-house attorneys provided guidance on the appropriate witnesses. Leung followed the advice and then specifically requested that the designated individuals' files be collected. In response, Qualcomm paralegals advised Leung that they believed there was no need to search the witnesses' individual files or laptops because the information was likely to duplicate information and documents contained in other corporate repositories that already were being searched. Moreover, the paralegals represented that this procedure had been utilized successfully in other litigation against Broadcom proceeding in the International Trade Commission ("ITC"). Leung and Mammen acquiesced to this suggestion even though they had not reviewed any of the witnesses' individual files, did not know what information was contained in the databases or repositories that were being searched, and had not been involved in the ITC litigation and did not know how documents were collected for it. Leung then sent an email to the trial team explaining that they were not going to search individual computers or files of deponents because "none of the document requests propounded by Broadcom call for documents uniquely in the possession of these individuals[,]" and "it was determined that anything responsive in their possession would be cumulative of documents otherwise collected and produced." Apparently no one, including in-house attorneys or more experienced outside counsel, responded to the email or otherwise advised Leung that the proposed method of collecting documents was inadequate.

These failures were exacerbated by an incredible lack of candor on the part of the principal Qualcomm employees. For example, Viji Raveendran repeatedly told Responding Attorneys, other outside counsel, and Qualcomm employees that she had not participated in, and had no involvement with, the JVT during development of the H.264 standard[,] and she testified to those facts under oath. In fact, when directly asked whether a consultant working for Qualcomm had attended the JVT meetings, Raveendran replied "I don't know," despite having personally exchanged approximately 118 emails with Qualcomm's paid JVT consultant, Jordan Isailovic. While Raveendran provided a nuanced explanation for her statements during the remand proceedings, the fact remains that she did not provide any of these facts to Responding Attorneys, even when asked. Unfortunately, this lack of candor was not limited to her JVT attendance nor was it unique to Raveendran, or even to just the Qualcomm engineers . . . and yet no one informed Responding Attorneys.

While they did not adequately search for documents, Responding Attorneys did repeatedly try to determine whether Qualcomm had participated in the JVT proceedings during the time the H.264 standard was being developed. . . . Moreover, five third-parties, including the chair of the JVT and a Broadcom employee involved in the JVT proceedings, confirmed their belief that Qualcomm was not involved with JVT during development of the H.264 standard. As Batchelder's counsel concisely summed it up, Responding Attorneys received confirmation by fifteen Qualcomm employees, including lawyers, on thirty-one occasions that Qualcomm did not participate in JVT or that the same was probably or almost certainly correct.

The problems created by this pervasive miscommunication and incomplete document search were compounded by an inadequate follow-up in response to contradictory, or potentially contradictory evidence. Although numerous Qualcomm employees indicated that the same employees, including Raveendran and Garudadri, were the employees most likely to have been involved in the JVT process, neither in-house nor outside counsel ensured that the identified employees' computers were searched for relevant documents and emails. Similarly, no one checked the standards group's travel records to verify which employees went to the locations where JVT meetings were held. Even when the avc_ce reflector list with Raveendran's email address on it was discovered, Raveendran's personal computer and emails were not searched for similar documents. Finally, when the twenty-one emails were found on Raveendran's computer during trial, none of the attorneys considered the fact that the discovery of the "new" emails proved Qualcomm's document collection and production had been inadequate, reviewed the discovery production log to determine the scope of the document collection and production, or otherwise reflected on the state of the discovery or its application to trial arguments.

Qualcomm Inc. v. Broadcom Corp., 2010 WL 1336937, at *2-*5 (S.D. Cal. Apr. 2, 2010).

Can you discern from this opinion and the original one imposing sanctions what the division of labor was among the lawyers representing Qualcomm? There were two outside law firms, Heller Ehrman and Day Casebeer, and Qualcomm is a large enough company that it has a substantial in-house counsel's office. The company is also regularly involved in litigation with high-tech industry competitors. In part to save costs, it appears to have divided up its litigation work among outside firms and in-house counsel not only between cases, but also *within* cases. In this case, Day Casebeer appears to have been in charge of pleading and discovery, but lawyers from Heller Ehrman were brought in for trial. Doesn't this division of labor inherently increase the risk that lawyers accountable under procedural and ethical rules for the accuracy of their representations may not know or be in a position to verify the truth of what they tell the judge, jury, and opposing counsel? See David Luban, The Ethics of Wrongful Obedience, in Luban, Legal Ethics and Human Dignity 237 (2007) (discussing the problem of divided responsibility in large organizations, especially large law firms); David Luban, Contrived Ignorance, 87 Geo. L.J. 957 (1999) (arguing that lawyers often face incentives to remain deliberately ignorant of client misdeeds even when directly confronted with evidence of such wrongdoing).

What about the lawyers for defendants? Are you troubled that they had the August 6, 2002, e-mail to Viji Raveendran from the JVT avc_ce mailing list in their possession but did not use it as the basis for a motion to compel or for pressing Qualcomm's lawyers for more information about why an employee had such an e-mail if the company was not involved with JVT before late 2003? Could more effective use of discovery tools by the defendant have avoided the debacle of a last-minute revelation on cross-examination at trial, or do you think filing proper requests in the first place was enough? Discovery is supposed to avoid surprise, but that only happens if both sides act both ethically *and* diligently.

*Qualcomm* is not the only case involving professional misconduct in e-discovery. In Doe v. Norwalk Cmty. Coll., 248 F.R.D. 372 (D. Conn. 2007), for instance, the district court had to decide on an appropriate sanction against defendants who scrubbed their hard drive of the names of key witnesses in a sexual harassment case. The court ultimately decided to issue an adverse inference based on the spoliation of evidence. See also Krumwiede v. Brighton Assocs., 2006 WL 1308629, at *9 (N.D. Ill. May 8, 2006) (unreported) (imposing the "harsh sanction" of a default judgment against a party that altered, modified, and deleted documents on a laptop computer before surrendering it during discovery). For a general survey of case law touching on e-discovery ethics issues, see Dale M. Cendali et al., Potential Ethical Pitfalls in Electronic Discovery, in Ethics in Context 2007, at 105 (PLI/NY Practice Skills, Course Handbook Series No. 10960, 2007), available at 171 PLI/NY 105 (Westlaw). See also Joseph Gallagher, Note, E-Ethics: The Ethical Dimension of the Electronic Discovery Amendments to the Federal Rules of Civil Procedure, 20 Geo. J. Legal Ethics 613, 626 (2007) (concluding that the e-discovery rules represent a "general movement away from boilerplate discovery mechanisms and towards the private resolution of conflicts," making it all the more important for lawyers to act ethically).

### Note: E-Discovery Amendments

Notice the sheer scale of electronically stored information in *Qualcomm.* The amount of ESI withheld is itself astonishing—46,000 emails! People charged with managing data in large organizations are struggling to keep up with the volume of ESI. According to a 2012 survey,

> more than one out of 10 data managers now have in excess of a petabyte of data within their organizations, and a majority of respondents report their levels of unstructured data are growing. Fewer than one out of five respondents feel their IT infrastructure will be ready to handle this incoming surge of data.

2012 IOUG Big Data Strategies Survey Report Now Available, Database Trends and Applications, September 26, 2012, http://www.dbta.com/Editorial/News-Flashes/2012-IOUG-Big-Data-Strategies-Survey-Report-

Now-Available-85193.aspx. Organizations as big as the federal government and as small as individual users of social networking sites have struggled not only with how to optimize use of the data at their disposal, but how to prevent security breaches and protect privacy.

As importantly for our purposes, the proliferation of ESI and transformations in the way that large firms negotiate to represent corporations have reshaped the landscape of modern discovery practice. It is no longer logistically feasible or cost effective to pay junior lawyers to review every document potentially relevant to a discovery request to determine whether it is relevant and privileged. Instead, elaborate software has been created to take advantage of Boolean search algorithms, and large firms frequently outsource the development of the technology as well as the actual review process. The global market for e-discovery software and services is projected to reach $11.6 billion by 2020. See MPC-7017: E-Discovery (Software and Services)—A Global Strategic Industry Report, Global Industry Analysts, Inc. (May 28, 2015), http://www.strategyr.com/pressMCP-7017. asp. Dozens of software companies concentrating on e-discovery—not law firms(!)—dominate the market. The standard approach in software for e-discovery is called Technology-Assisted Review (TAR), defined as

> [a] process for Prioritizing or Coding a Collection of Documents using a computerized system that harnesses human judgments of one or more Subject Matter Expert(s) on a smaller set of Documents and then extrapolates those judgments to the remaining Document Collection. Some TAR methods use Machine Learning Algorithms to distinguish Relevant from NonRelevant Documents, based on Training Examples Coded as Relevant or Non-Relevant by the Subject Matter Experts(s), while other TAR methods derive systematic Rules that emulate the expert(s)' decisionmaking process. TAR processes generally incorporate Statistical Models and/or Sampling techniques to guide the process and to measure overall system effectiveness.

Paul Burns & Mindy Morton, Technology-Assisted Review: The Judicial Pioneers, The Sedona Conference Institute 3 (Mar. 2014). One of the most common TAR methods is "predictive coding," a machine learning algorithm that separates relevant from nonrelevant documents by relying on a subject matter expert's coding on a "training set" of documents. Id.

Courts have explicitly approved the use of TAR in appropriate cases so that lawyers can rely on the software. The leading opinion is Da Silva Moore v. Publicis Groupe & MSL Grp., 287 F.R.D. 182 (S.D.N.Y. 2012); see also Rio Tinto PLC v. Vale S.A., 306 F.R.D. 125, 126, 127 n.1 (S.D.N.Y. 2015) ("In the three years since *Da Silva Moore*, the case law has developed to the point that it is now black letter law that where the producing party wants to utilize TAR for document review, courts will permit it"; noting case in which court refused to approve TAR where the requesting party sought to force the producing party to use it and the producing parties had already spent over $1 million on keyword search and keyword culling technology); id. at 128-129 (discussing the degree of cooperation and transparency between opposing counsel necessary to create an effective "training set" and disclose associated documents; emphasizing that "it is inappropriate to hold TAR to a higher standard than keywords or manual review").

As *Qualcomm* shows, lawyers have a professional duty to their clients to understand how their clients produce and manage digital data, as well as the mechanics of e-discovery technologies, such as TAR, on which their third-party software service providers are relying. See ABA Commission on Ethics 20/20, Report and Resolution (2012) ("Technology has irrevocably changed and continues to alter the practice of law in fundamental ways"; amending Comment to lawyer's duty of competence in ABA Model Rule 1.1 to include duty to "keep abreast of changes in the law and its practice, including the benefits and risks associated with relevant technology").

Concerns about the differences between digital data and traditional materials subject to discovery led the Advisory Committee to propose amendments to the discovery rules in 2004. The amendments, which took effect January 1, 2006, addressed the need to meet and confer about discovery of electronic data early in the litigation, Fed. R. Civ. P. 26(f)(3)(C); the form in which electronic data should be produced, Rules 33(d), 34, 45(d)(1); how to deal with privileged information (whether digital or not) that is inadvertently disclosed, Rules 26(b)(5)(B), 26(f)(3)(C); how to manage discovery of data that are not stored in readily accessible formats, Rule 26(b)(2)(B); and protection against sanctions for failing to produce information where a party can make a good faith showing that the data have been destroyed or made inaccessible as a result of the routine operation of an electronic information management system, Rule 37(f). ESI is also now formally recognized as a separate category of discovery along with the traditional categories of "documents" and "things." For an overview of some of the early case law applying these amendments, see Kenneth J. Withers, Federal Court Decisions Involving Electronic Discovery December 1, 2006–June 15, 2007, SN009 ALI-ABA 1725 (Westlaw). See also Bar v. Lowe's Home Ctrs., Inc., 2007 WL 1299180 (W.D.N.C. May 2, 2007) (model discovery plan to facilitate discovery of electronically stored information under new F.R.C.P. 26(f)).

Cases like *Zubulake* and *Qualcomm* heightened the attention of the bench and the bar on sanctions related to ESI. Circuit courts were divided, for instance, over whether bad faith must be shown to impose sanctions for failure to preserve ESI. Compare Rimkus Consulting Grp., Inc. v. Cammarata, 688 F. Supp. 2d 598 (S.D. Tex. 2010) (following Fifth Circuit precedent requiring bad faith to impose a sanction for spoliation) with Residential Funding Corp. v. DeGeorge Fin. Corp., 306 F.3d 99, 108 (2d Cir. 2002) (requiring only knowing or negligent destruction of evidence).

The Advisory Committee concluded that confusion among the circuit courts "caused litigants to expend excessive effort and money on preservation in order to avoid the risk of severe sanctions if a court finds they did not do enough." Rule 37(e) Advisory Committee Notes (2015 Amendment). The Committee also recognized the "serious problems resulting from the continued exponential growth in the volume of [ESI]." Id. The 2015 amendments to Rule 37(e) specify the kinds of sanctions that may be ordered for spoliation of ESI and the standard of culpability that must be proved to warrant sanctions:

> **Rule 37(e) Failure to Preserve Electronically Stored Information.**
>
> If electronically stored information that should have been preserved in the anticipation or conduct of litigation is lost because a party failed to take reasonable steps to preserve it, and it cannot be restored or replaced through additional discovery, the court:
>
> (1) upon finding prejudice to another party from loss of the information, may order measures no greater than necessary to cure the prejudice; or
>
> (2) only upon finding that the party acted with the intent to deprive another party of the information's use in the litigation may:
>
> (A) presume that the lost information was unfavorable to the party;
>
> (B) instruct the jury that it may or must presume the information was unfavorable to the party; or
>
> (C) dismiss the action or enter a default judgment.

The Rule's reference to "intent to deprive" squarely rejects the holding of *Residential Funding Corp.* insofar as the case permitted sanctions on a finding of mere negligence or gross negligence. Does the Rule preclude a district court from relying on its inherent authority or borrowing from state law to impose a sanction? The Committee thought so. Its Note states that the new rule "forecloses reliance on inherent authority or state law to determine when certain measures should be used." Rule 37(e) Advisory Committee Notes (2015 Amendment).

## Note: The Discovery of "Metadata"

"Metadata" refers to electronically stored information that is created any time a digital file is made, used, or altered. A simple example is the "track changes" function in a word processing program and information regarding the computer and user who generated the file. Courts and commentators have been divided over whether metadata must be produced whenever electronically stored information is requested in discovery. Debate has centered on the questions of whether metadata is in fact part of the "document" subject to discovery and whether electronically stored information can be "scrubbed" of its metadata before production. In an employment dispute, for instance, a trail of tracked changes may be the only information revealing workforce changes that were planned or imposed by the employer. Can an employer scrub such metadata from its spreadsheets prior to disclosure? See Williams v. Sprint/United Mgmt. Co., 230 F.R.D. 640 (D. Kan. 1995) (holding metadata in employment spreadsheets was relevant and should not have been scrubbed; withholding sanctions but imposing a waiver of privileges and work-product protection as to metadata).

Rule 34 provides that metadata are discoverable, "subject to the relevance limit under Rule 26(b)(1) and the proportionality limits under Rule 26(b)(2)(C) that apply to all discovery." Hon. Lee H. Rosenthal, A Few Thoughts on Electronic Discovery After December 1, 2006, 116 Yale L.J. Pocket Part 167, 185-189 (2006) (discussing *Williams*); see also W. Lawrence Wescott II, The Increasing Importance of Metadata in Electronic Discovery, 14 Rich. J.L. & Tech. 10, 10 (2008) (surveying trends in recent case law and concluding that practitioners should make a "regular practice" of preserving metadata). The Advisory Committee Notes to the 2006 amendments to Rule 26 encourage discussion of metadata in the Rule 26(f) conference.

> Parties may attempt to minimize . . . costs and delays by agreeing to protocols that minimize the risk of waiver. They may agree that the responding party will provide certain requested materials for initial examination without waiving any privilege or protection—sometimes known as a "quick peek." The requesting party then designates the documents it wishes to have actually produced. This designation is the Rule 34 request. The responding party then responds in the usual course, screening only those documents actually requested for formal production and asserting privilege claims as provided in Rule 26(b)(5)(A). On other occasions, parties enter agreements—sometimes called "clawback agreements"—that production without intent to waive privilege or protection should not be a waiver so long as the responding party identifies the documents mistakenly produced, and that the documents should be returned under those circumstances. Other voluntary arrangements may be appropriate depending on the circumstances of each litigation. In most circumstances, a party who receives information under such an arrangement cannot assert that production of the information waived a claim of privilege or of protection as trial-preparation material.

These agreements do not, however, offer protection against claims of waiver made by *third parties*. See Hon. Lee H. Rosenthal, A Few Thoughts on Electronic Discovery After December 1, 2006, 116 Yale L.J. Pocket Part 167, 183 (2006) ("The Civil Rules cannot . . . change substantive privilege law, including the law of privilege waiver, without an affirmative act of Congress. Under current law, depending on the jurisdiction, even if the parties agree to various protocols under which disclosure will not waive a privilege or protection, and the court includes their agreement in an order, neither the agreement nor the order assures that the agreement will bind *third parties*. . . . The risk of waiver and of disclosure will lead some parties, particularly those who are frequently sued, to continue to insist on extensive, time-consuming, and costly preproduction privilege reviews, even with a nonwaiver agreement in place between the parties.") (emphasis added).

Finally, the format in which digital data are stored may seem a trivial issue, but it is not. Typically, a business keeps records it regularly uses in digital files that are readily accessible. Computer memory of this sort is costly, though, so as data become less useful, businesses will often either destroy them as part of a document management program or arrange for storage in compressed files that can retain massive amounts of data.

Compressed data, however, are functionally inaccessible without payment for their retrieval; the data cannot be searched electronically in compressed format, and restoring them to a searchable format is both time-consuming and very expensive. Rule 26(b)(2)(B) provides that, absent a showing of good cause, "[a] party need not provide discovery of electronically stored information from sources that the party identifies as not reasonably accessible because of undue burden or cost."

Does this Rule create an incentive for parties to move information that may be relevant to litigation into compressed data files? Normally, the producing party pays the costs of production, see Oppenheimer Fund, Inc. v. Sanders, 437 U.S. 340, 358 (1978), though trial courts have authority under Rule 26(c) to condition discovery on payment of costs by the requesting party if the request would otherwise impose "undue burden or expense." Should a defendant have to bear all the costs of restoring compressed data even when the plaintiff has submitted overbroad discovery requests?

In a sex discrimination suit, Quinby v. WestLB AG, 245 F.R.D. 94 (S.D.N.Y. 2006), the court adopted a seven-factor test first articulated in Zubulake v. UBS Warburg, LLC, 217 F.R.D. 309, 322 (S.D.N.Y. 2003), for determining whether the plaintiff was obliged to share production costs for data stored in inaccessible formats. In shifting 30 percent of the $181,013.28 retrieval tab to the plaintiff, the *Quinby* court placed heavy emphasis on the fact that the plaintiff had initially requested "to search nineteen current and former WestLB employees' e-mails for over 170 search terms for approximately a five year period" in order to find references to plaintiff, terms that were "potentially sexist," information "relating to discrimination against other women at WestLB," and "e-mails showing that men were more highly compensated than women." *Quinby*, 245 F.R.D. at 98-99. After reviewing a sample of the data produced and finding little relevant information, the court agreed with defendant that plaintiff's request was overbroad.

Still, the court refused to order cost sharing as to information that defendant improperly converted into an inaccessible format after it knew, or should have known, plaintiff would likely file suit. Id. at 104 ("[I]f a party creates its own burden or expense by converting into an inaccessible format data that it should have reasonably foreseen would be discoverable material at a time when it should have anticipated litigation, then it should not be entitled to shift the costs of restoring and searching the data."). The court grounded this portion of its order on defendant's duty to avoid spoliation, noting that "the downgrading of data to a less accessible form—which systematically hinders future discovery by making the recovery of the information more costly and burdensome—is a violation of the preservation obligation." Id. at 103 n.12 (internal quotation marks and citation omitted).

Similarly, consider PSEG Power N.Y., Inc. v. Alberici Constructors, Inc., 2007 WL 2687670 (N.D.N.Y. Sept. 7, 2007) (unreported), where the court adopted a variant of the seven-factor *Zubulake* test to determine whether plaintiffs should exclusively bear the costs of reproducing data already transmitted to defendants in an unusable form. Because of a technical glitch, plaintiff's production of some 3,000 e-mails divorced messages from attachments in a manner that made it impossible to tether them back. Since the controversy would not exist "but for PSEG's vendor creating [the] email attachment fiasco," the court concluded that PSEG should bear the entire costs of production: "Whether created by a software incompatibility or malfunction, such deficiency does not provide a sufficient excuse from presenting an important aspect of discovery in a convoluted fashion. . . . Alberici should not be resigned to accept a flawed discovery process." Id. at *12. See also In re Bristol-Myers Squibb Secs. Litig., 205 F.R.D. 437 (D.N.J. 2002) (plaintiffs agreed to pay the cost of copying documents requested before learning the data were available in electronic form; plaintiffs obtained production in electronic form but were forced to pay just over $300,000 for the paper copying already completed); Zubulake v. UBS Warburg LLC, 217 F.R.D. 309 (S.D.N.Y. 2003) (dispute over obligation to produce documents from difficult-to-access backup tapes and who should bear costs of such production); Zubulake v. UBS Warburg LLC, 216 F.R.D. 280 (S.D.N.Y. 2003) (same).

Are these results consistent with amended Rule 26(b)(2)(B)?

### Note: Privilege Logs and Inadvertent Disclosure in E-Discovery

Privilege logs have long been a burdensome and time-consuming affair, often consuming thousands of hours in complex cases. Many a junior associate can recount memories of long hours spent in windowless rooms surrounded by boxes of documents to be sorted for relevance and privileges. The practice (and the temptation to take shortcuts) has become even more burdensome with electronically stored information. At least one court has threatened waiver as a sanction where attorneys for AT&T improperly listed an entire e-mail strand, consisting of 29 separate e-mails, as privileged in its log when only one e-mail in the strand was privileged. In re Universal Serv. Fund Tel. Billing Practices Litig., 232 F.R.D. 669 (D. Kan. 2005). AT&T contended that an e-mail strand is analogous to minutes of a meeting, or a transcript of a conversation, such that individual e-mails should not be separated for purposes of a privilege claim. Id. at 672. The court disagreed, emphasizing the risk of "stealth claims of privilege" and that e-mail strands, unlike meetings and conversations, often span several days and involve different sending and receiving individuals for separate parts of the strand. Id. at 673.

AT&T averted the sanction of waiver only by agreeing to produce the unprivileged portions of the strands it had withheld. The judge observed that

> [t]he undersigned . . . is only five years removed from private practice. He is acutely sensitive to the fact that, as a practical matter, requiring each e-mail within a strand to be listed separately on a privilege log is a laborious,

time-intensive task for counsel. And, of course, that task adds considerable expense for the clients involved; even for very well-financed corporate defendants such as those in the case at a bar. . . . But the court finds that adherence to such a procedure is essential to ensuring that privilege is asserted only where necessary to achieve its purpose. . . .

Id. at 674.

The risk of inadvertent disclosure is also far greater with electronically stored information. In Marrero Hernandez v. Esso Standard Oil Co., 2006 WL 1967364 (D.P.R. July 11, 2006), for example, the defendant inadvertently produced information it claimed was privileged after someone accidentally merged two electronic files (one privileged, the other not) through "an errant mouse click." Id. at *1. The court held that disclosure to an adversary, whether privileged or not, waives privilege even though the claim might be valid. Id. at *4-*5.

## Note: Social Networking Sites, Discovery, and Privacy

The complications of electronic discovery now extend to content posted on social networking sites. As anyone with a Facebook account knows, social networking sites can include a tremendous amount of personal information, some of which one would be reluctant (to say the least) to see exposed in litigation. See, e.g., Equal Emp't Opportunity Comm'n v. Simply Storage Mgmt., Inc., 270 F.R.D. 430 (S.D. Ill. 2010) (setting out detailed guidelines for the disclosure of plaintiffs' personal information from Facebook and MySpace accounts—including all photographs or videos posted, all updates changes or modifications, all status updates, wall comments, causes and groups joined, activity streams, blog entries, blurbs, etc.—in workplace sexual harassment suit where defendant claimed the information was relevant to the "emotional health" of the plaintiffs and their allegations of emotional distress in the complaint).

Tactical use of discovery to force sexual harassment plaintiffs to disclose personal information as cost of pursuing a claim is unfortunately common. Debrai G. Haile and Sara Leitenberger cite the following cases in an article discussing other forms of discovery abuse in civil rights cases:

Macklin v. Mendenhall, 257 F.R.D. 596, 602 (E.D. Cal. 2009) (expressing concern about "[t]he possibility that discovery tactics such as that used by the defendant herein [in requesting information about plaintiff's sexual past] might intimidate, inhibit, or discourage Title VII plaintiffs . . . from pursuing their claims . . .") (quoting Priest v. Rotary, 98 F.R.D. 755, 761 (N.D. Cal. 1983)) (internal quotation marks omitted); Williams v. Bd. of Cnty. Comm'rs, 192 F.R.D. 698, 701-03 (D. Kan. 2000) (denying defendant's motion to compel interrogatory in sex harassment case when interrogatory sought information about plaintiff's sexual history because the potential harm to the plaintiff outweighed the marginal relevance); *Priest,* 98 F.R.D. at 761 (N.D. Cal.

1983) ("This Court is deeply concerned that civil complaints based on sexual harassment in the workplace will be similarly inhibited, if discovery tactics such as the one used by defendant herein are allowed to flourish.").

Haile and Leitenberger, Improper and Abusive Written Discovery Requests in Single- and Multiple-Plaintiff Employment Cases, 27 ABA J. Lab. & Empl. L. 397, 414 n.88 (2012). See also Ellen E. Schultz and Junda Woo, The Bedroom Ploy: Plaintiffs' Sex Lives Are Being Laid Bare in Harassment Cases, Wall St. J., Sept. 19, 1994, at A1. Did the court strike the correct balance between the need for disclosure of relevant facts and the interests of privacy and preventing a repetition of the injury during discovery in *Simply Storage*?

## 4. The Adversary's Experts

### Problem Case: XRT and the SafeTeeTot

The XRT Corporation, which manufacturers the SafeTeeTot infant car seat, has been sued in federal court by a consumer who claims that the seat design is defective. XRT's in-house counsel, Lucy Lee, hired two engineers, Tony McGee, a university professor, and Mickey Wayne, a private consultant, to render their expert opinions about the design. Pursuant to Lee's instructions each expert made an oral report of his finding to XRT's managing officers, which Lee then reduced to writing.

McGee concluded, based on experiments conducted in his university laboratory, that the SafeTeeTot is "the safest infant seat on the market due to XRT's use of what are known in the trade as 'extra-secure' buckles, which are buckles commonly used in commercial airplanes." Wayne's conclusion, on the other hand, is highly critical of XRT's design, particularly XRT's improper use of "extra-secure" buckles. Wayne bases his conclusion on industry-generated safety reports.

Lee paid Wayne for the preliminary consultation and told him no further work would be required. She then informed McGee that XRT intended to call him as an expert witness at trial and requested a formal written report, which he duly produced.

In response to properly framed requests by the plaintiff, must XRT:

1) disclose Wayne's and McGee's names?
2) produce Lee's memorandum summarizing Wayne's and McGee's oral reports?
3) disclose the substance of Wayne's and McGee's opinions?
4) produce a copy of McGee's written report?
5) May the plaintiff in the case now retain Wayne? If the plaintiff tried to retain Wayne, what would you do procedurally to try to stop her from using him as an expert? What arguments would you make?

## *Note: Berkey Photo, Inc. v. Eastman Kodak Co.,*
### *603 F.2d 263 (2d Cir. 1979)*

In "one of the largest and most significant private antitrust suits in history," Kodak relied upon a single expert witness, Professor Peck of Yale, to explain its view of the relevant markets and the reason for Kodak's persistently high market shares in the film processing industry. Several weeks before trial, this expert was deposed; in connection with this deposition, a number of documents were supplied to Berkey by Perkins, a lawyer for Kodak. Perkins represented that these documents included all those supplied to Peck by Kodak and all reports made by Peck to Kodak. In the course of the deposition, Peck stated that he had sent his own notes and work papers to Perkins because they were confidential and because he lacked storage. Perkins stated that all of these work papers had been destroyed; Peck said that he did not remember when he learned that Perkins was destroying the material but that he had continued to send material to Perkins after learning that the destruction was happening.

Peck was the last witness at the trial. He testified that Kodak had done well because it was innovative, not because it was predatory. On the 110th day of trial, Berkey counsel, Stein, was allowed to cross-examine Peck on the nature of the materials sent to Perkins that were destroyed. He started by asking whether his memorandum of April 21, 1975, the earliest supplied by Perkins at the time of the deposition, was, indeed, the earliest report prepared by Peck for Kodak. Peck acknowledged that it was not. Kodak then produced a letter of November 25, 1974, in which Peck acknowledged to Kodak that he had no persuasive answers as yet to two troublesome economic questions. Kodak had not supplied the document earlier because it thought it was a "letter," not a "report." Stein was then permitted to question Peck as to why at the time of the deposition he had failed to remember and discuss his letter of November 1974. The judge also asked Kodak to search its files again for any other relevant documents. At the beginning of the next week, the trial counsel for Kodak, Doar, acknowledged that all of the documents previously said to have been destroyed were still in Kodak's possession. Moreover, Peck, who had claimed to have no files, had discovered his copy of the letter of November 1974.

Perhaps as a result of these revelations, the jury found in favor of Berkey on every disputed issue. Judgment was accordingly entered in its favor in an amount exceeding $87 million. Among the contentions made on appeal by Kodak was that the trial judge, Marvin Frankel, had allowed Stein to make too much of the revelations of the missing documents, thus destroying the force of Peck's testimony. The Court of Appeals complimented the judge on his restraint:

> We are also of the view that the cross-examination of Peck remained within permissible channels, particularly in light of the extraordinary revelations that preceded it. Peck conceded at his deposition that he continued to forward research materials to Kodak's lawyers after learning they were

destroyed upon receipt, thereby providing more than a sufficient threshold showing of relevance to permit further inquiry on cross-examination. Suspicion could only have been increased by the sudden appearance of PX 666, a letter of great importance to Berkey's efforts to impeach Peck, which the writer claimed to have forgotten existed. And when Peck revealed on Monday that his files had contained a copy of this letter from the outset, deeper inquiry was certainly justified. As each new fact came to light, Judge Frankel carefully reassessed its relevance to Peck's credibility and gradually enlarged the scope of permissible inquiry into the witness's actions.

Mr. Stein's questions, therefore, far from consisting of the mere compendium of inflammatory rhetoric that Kodak describes, were legitimate challenges to Peck's credibility and to the independence of his judgment. Indeed, Judge Frankel, who throughout the unusual disclosures described here maintained an attitude of cautious restraint, noted in a colloquy with the attorneys that Peck's credibility had, in his judgment, been destroyed on the witness stand. To be sure, the jury need not have believed Berkey's argument that Peck had deliberately collaborated with Perkins in an effort to destroy or conceal documents unfavorable to Kodak's cause. But there was certainly more than an adequate basis to permit Berkey to contend that this inference was justified, and that, at best, Peck was a willing tool of Kodak.

We are not unmindful that the incidents described, as presented to the jury, led to the unfortunate consequence of casting Kodak's attorneys, and the defendant itself, in a highly unfavorable light. It is no less true, however, that the cross-examination elicited information that was highly relevant to an assessment of the independence of judgment and probity of one of Kodak's principal witnesses. Where the trial judge has taken great care to balance the probative value of the evidence against the prejudice that may accrue from its introduction, we think it inappropriate to substitute our judgment for his. . . .

603 F.2d at 308.


## David Margolick, The Long Road Back for a Disgraced Patrician
N.Y. Times, Jan. 19, 1990, at B6

At the Center for Constitutional Rights, Mahlon F. Perkins Jr. is something of an oddball. Among its young, polyglot legal staff, he is a 71-year-old patrician, who looks and speaks like Robert Frost. His colleagues wear beards or blue jeans; he favors herringbone trousers. They like rock music; he watches birds. They come to work by subway; he takes the train from Greenwich.

But incongruity is not his chief distinction. Ten years ago, in a scandal that rocked the Wall Street bar, Mr. Perkins, then counsel for Kodak, admitted lying in a major antitrust case brought against his client by Berkey Photo.

After almost 30 years at Donovan, Leisure, Newton & Irvine, one of Manhattan's most prominent law firms, he left in disgrace. Then he was sentenced to a month in prison, an extraordinary punishment for a lawyer of his stature and reputation.

In sentencing Perkins, federal District Judge Robert Ward—a Harvard Law School classmate of his—mourned a career ended and a reputation destroyed.

That assessment, it turns out, was quite premature. In an ending that is not only happy but also quite unforeseeable, Perkins has come back, reincarnated as a civil liberties lawyer.

Three days each week, Perkins volunteers his services at the center, which handles primarily civil rights, First Amendment and criminal justice cases. In his former life, he represented institutions like the American Association of Advertising Agencies and Hughes Tool Co., and earned $200,000 a year doing it. Now, his clients include Corazon Aquino, president of the Philippines; the White Earth Band of Chippewa Indians, and Harvard alumni seeking South African divestiture—and he serves them without pay, living off past earnings.

Where once he occupied a stately office on the 34th floor of 30 Rockefeller Plaza, with a panoramic view of Central Park, Perkins now works out of a tiny 7th-floor rectangle overlooking the discount houses of lower Broadway. . . .

All of the perquisites of corporate law practice—the secretaries, the tea cart, the lunch clubs—are gone, but so, too, are the time sheets, the pressures and the Brooks Brothers suits, a change that especially pleases him. "I've hated jackets and ties for years," he said. "I thought they were ridiculous."

Mr. Perkins' stop at the center is only the most recent leg of an extraordinary journey that has taken him from Shanghai, where he was born the son of a diplomat and lived until he was 13, to Phillips Exeter, to Harvard to the Office of Strategic Services to corporate law to the Metropolitan Correctional Facility, a place he had previously seen only on his way to court. This last transition was not easy.

After prison, he fought off disbarment with the support of friends. . . . Then Mr. Perkins found himself, a onetime editor of the Harvard Law Review, unable to sell or even give away his services. Skeptics at the center wondered whether they were getting damaged goods, or if a strait-laced type could ever passionately represent clients who were black or Hispanic or poor, let alone move from the hierarchy of Wall Street to the anarchy of public-interest work.

Their fears have long since been allayed. In more than five years at the center, Perkins has earned a reputation for productivity, effectiveness, dedication, and modesty. He has also become a treasured colleague. . . .

"For a Protestant WASP type coming in from the corporate world, particularly with my history, it was really something for them to let me come here in the first place," said Mr. Perkins. In some ways, he said, his ordeal was a blessing in disguise, forcing him into a career change he had considered but might never have had the courage to make.

"Intellectually, the work here is every bit as satisfying as what I did before," he said. "And politically, I derive a lot more satisfaction than I did at Donovan, Leisure. I'm helping in causes I believe in very deeply. This wasn't a very good way to have gotten out, but at this point, I'm very happy not to be there, and very happy to be here."

Mr. Perkins was on the legal team defending Kodak against antitrust charges brought by Berkey in 1973. At one point, he informed opposing counsel that some documents it sought had been destroyed. In fact, they were in a suitcase back in his office, and he knew it. He came forward in January 1978 and acknowledged his misstatement to the court. Quickly, he was suspended from the firm. By March, he had resigned.

For Mr. Perkins, a man with a heretofore unblemished record, it was a crushing blow. Dozens of times over the next few months, he was asked—and asked himself—why he had lied. None of the withheld documents was crucial; virtually all had been duplicated and were given to the other side anyway. "It was sort of an impromptu kind of thing, and then I sort of got stuck with it," he once said.

Eventually, he pleaded guilty to contempt of court, an offense somewhere in the never-never land between misdemeanors and felonies. . . .

Mr. Perkins, who had always been interested in prison reform—he had contributed to the Fortune Society, which helps find jobs for former convicts—soon tasted the humiliations of jail firsthand: . . . the lockups, the strip searches before and after every visitation.

But there were compensations. "I met a lot of very interesting, wonderful people," he said. "I began to feel that many of the inmates were better than a lot of the guards." . . .

Upon his release, he resolved to go into public interest law, and he began looking for work the following spring, after a court-appointed referee ruled that he be censured rather than disbarred.

"I had a lot of interviews, at the NAACP, the [New York Civil Liberties Union], the New York Legal Aid Society, but I got no offers," he recalled. "They didn't think I was their type. At the Civil Liberties Union, they told me they were looking for women and blacks. I interviewed with Ramsey Clark for an hour, then never heard any more from him."

In the meantime, Perkins worked part time for a small Manhattan law firm and plunged himself into volunteer activities in Greenwich, Conn., for the symphony orchestra, the library, the United Way, the National Association for the Advancement of Colored People, the Audubon Society. But while his community rallied around him, his old law firm did not. It was his rude introduction to the harsh new realities of large firm practice.

Few of his former partners visited him in prison. Younger, career-conscious lawyers, many of whom he had hired, were told to keep their distance. He was gently told he was no longer welcome to visit his old offices or even to enter its reception area.

"The only place that I felt shunned was my old law firm, and I resented that," he said. "But to be fair to Donovan, Leisure, this was a very traumatic thing for them. One of my regrets is that what I had done, really unwittingly, had done great harm to the people there." . . .

## Note: The Temptations of Expert Witnesses

How did it happen that lawyers as skilled and as concerned with their reputations as Kodak's counsel could have concealed the documents in the *Berkey-Kodak* case? In thinking about that question, never really answered in the decision, consider the organization of many firms into different branches. It may be that the corporate lawyer who was in charge of working with the expert to develop his opinion thought that the litigation branch had lower standards than the rest of the firm ("it's a jungle out there" mentality).

Another explanation could be that the expert and his lawyers had a sense of having a right to work in private and to express doubts and questions, without these being turned over to the other side. Note also, though, that in the hands of a skilled lawyer, the facts that Professor Peck had initial doubts and then changed his mind and that he had thought of all the possibilities could add to his credibility. Good tactics and good ethics are often entwined.

Finally, the importance of expert testimony may posit an irresistible temptation to some lawyers. In most civil cases these days, experts are hired by each side, even in cases where their utility is not immediately apparent, as it is, for instance, in medical or legal malpractice cases. Two aviation lawyers probably spoke for many of their colleagues when they wrote:

> We all have horror stories involving expert witnesses. Cases where too many experts have been used, where experts have been harassed by opposing counsel, and where experts have been qualified on the most mundane or off-the-wall issues, to name a few of the gripes.

William G. Burd and Madelyn Simon Lozano, Experts: Is the End Near for Their Use?, 59 J. Air L. & Com. 77, 77 (1993).

Expert witnesses have become so common in civil litigation that Rule 26 deals with disclosures regarding their research and testimony explicitly and at length. First, under Rule 26(a)(2)(A), a party must disclose the identity of any witnesses it may use at trial to present expert testimony. The expert must also prepare a written report setting out her opinions, the "facts or data" providing foundation for them, any exhibits, her qualifications, her other service as an expert, and her compensation package. That report has to be disclosed under Rule 26(a)(2)(B). Experts who consult on a case but are not retained to testify need not produce a report, though they are required by amendments made in 2010 to provide a short summary. Rule 26(a)(2)(C).

Testifying experts may be deposed but specific work product rules prevent disclosure of draft reports and communication between the party's attorney and the testifying witness. Rule 26(b)(4)(C). However, the personal notes of a testifying expert and communications among testifying experts are not entitled to work product protection. See Republic of Ecuador v.

Hinchee, 741 F.3d 1185 (11th Cir. 2013) (ordering production under 28 U.S.C. § 1782 of testifying expert's notes and communications with other experts working for Chevron in long-running litigation and treaty arbitration regarding environmental pollution by oil company in Ecuador; expert is not a "representative" of a party under Rule 26(b)(3)); see also Republic of Ecuador v. Mackay, 742 F.3d 860 (9th Cir. 2014); Republic of Ecuador v. For Issuance of Subpoena Under 28 U.S.C. Sec. 1782(a), 735 F.3d 1179 (10th Cir. 2013) (same). Ordinarily, litigation opponents have much more restricted access to "facts known or opinions held" by consulting experts not expected to be called as witnesses at trial. Rule 26(b)(4)(D).

The following cases deal with these provisions and the inherent power of courts to regulate experts' conflicts of interest.

### Cordy v. The Sherwin-Williams Co.
156 F.R.D. 575 (D.N.J. 1994)

KUGLER, UNITED STATES MAGISTRATE JUDGE.

In this day of divided and shifting loyalties, when it is not unknown for lawyers to change firms in the middle of litigation, we are faced with the phenomenon of an expert essentially doing the same thing by changing sides in the litigation. The question for the Court is whether he should get away with it.

The underlying lawsuit involves a claim by plaintiff Sterling Cordy for damages for massive injuries he suffered while riding his bicycle over a railroad track crossing in Lindenwold, New Jersey, on August 30, 1991. Plaintiff alleges that defendant Sherwin-Williams Company owns the crossing and is liable to him for damages.

Before the Court are cross-motions. Defendant first moved for an Order compelling Plaintiff's counsel to produce the bicycle for examination and testing by their expert, James Marley Green. Plaintiff moved for an Order barring Defendant from using Green as their expert, and further to disqualify the law firm of Marshall, Dennehey, Warner, Coleman & Goggin, from further representing Sherwin-Williams Company in this case. Plaintiff contends that he had first retained Green to work on his behalf, and that Green changed sides in the middle of this litigation. . . .

Any analysis properly begins with a recognition of the Court's inherent power to disqualify experts. . . .

Some jurisdictions have established a two-step inquiry to determine whether to disqualify an expert who had prior relationship with a party. [Paul v. Rawlings Sporting Goods Co., 123 F.R.D. 271, 279 (S.D. Ohio 1988).] First, was it objectively reasonable for the first party who retained the expert to believe that a confidential relationship existed? Second, did that party disclose any confidential information to the expert? . . .

In addition to the above analysis, the Court should balance the competing policy objectives in determining expert disqualification. . . . The policy objectives favoring disqualification include preventing conflicts of interest and maintaining the integrity of the judicial process. . . . The main policy objectives militating against disqualification are ensuring access to expert witnesses who possess specialized knowledge and allowing experts to pursue their professional calling. *English Feedlot,* 833 F. Supp 1498, 1505 (D. Colo. 1993). . . . Courts have also expressed concern that if experts are too easily subjected to disqualification, unscrupulous attorneys and clients[ may attempt to create an inexpensive relationship with potentially harmful experts solely to keep them from the opposing party. Id.

Under Federal Rule of Civil Procedure 26, the opposition is entitled to obtain information upon which a testifying expert intends to rely in formulating his or her opinions. Generally, when an expert obtains information from Plaintiff's attorneys, who in turn have obtained that information from the client, the attorney-client privilege applies, subject to a variety of qualifications. . . .

Defendant contends that one reason the Court should not disqualify Green is because Brown & Connery never "retained" him. This argument is based in part on Green's conduct in returning the original retainer payment after he resigned in July, 1993.

Nonsense. Green accepted a retainer from Plaintiff, and later returned it. The fact that he returned it cannot erase his acceptance of it, the significance of it, or the implications arising from it when he later accepted a retainer from Defendant.

Defendant also contends that Green only had "minimal contacts" with Brown & Connery. However, there is no question that Green performed services for Brown & Connery. He entered into a written contract. He was paid. He learned their litigation strategy and reviewed their investigation. He billed for 28 hours of work. He rendered some kind of oral opinion. There was extensive contact between Green and Brown & Connery. Their relationship was clearly not a preliminary interview or consultation in order to determine whether an attorney desired to enter into a relationship with an expert. . . .

Clearly Brown & Connery retained Green. . . .

Defendant contends that Brown & Connery never shared any confidential information with Green. Counsel points to the lack of any "Confidentiality Agreement" or commitment that Green would not work for any other party involved in the lawsuit, relying on Wang [Labs.], Inc. v. Toshiba [Corp.], 762 F. Supp. 1246, 1250 (E.D. Va. 1991) (suggesting the steps that an attorney should take to make sure the expert knows that confidentiality is expected) and English Feedlot[, Inc. v. Norden Lab,] 833 F. Supp. [1498,] 1505 [D. Colo. 1993] (". . . a lawyer seeking to retain an expert and establish a confidential relationship should make this intention unmistakably clear and should confirm it in writing").

But there is no "right" way for an attorney to retain an expert for purposes of litigation. *Paul,* 123 F.R.D. at 270. No case in New Jersey has held that an attorney must go through the formalistic rituals suggested in *Wang* [*Labs.*], and this Court declines the invitation to be the first.

The real question is whether Brown & Connery acted reasonably in assuming that a confidential or fiduciary relationship existed with Green. Palmer v. Ozbek, 144 F.R.D. 66, 67 (D. Md. 1992). The answer is yes.

Some of the contents of P-10 (the three-ring binder sent by Brown & Connery to Green) are clearly confidential and not subject to disclosure. The selection process used to assemble P-10, and the grouping of the photographs and documents represent the mental impressions of Plaintiff's counsel and are protected work product. Sporck [v. Peil, 759 F.2 312, 315 (3d Cir. 1985)]. Green acknowledges that Plaintiff's firm informed him of their theory of the case and their targeted defendants. This also was protected work product. Conforti [& Eisele, Inc. v. Div. of Bldg. and Constr., 170 N.J. Super. 64, 73 (L. Div. 1979)]. . . . . Plaintiff's counsel had every reason to assume that it had entered into a confidential relationship with Green. Plaintiff's counsel passed confidential information to Green. It is simply not possible for Green to ignore what he learned from Brown & Connery. At the very least, his engagement with Brown & Connery has to "subliminally affect his testimony and assessment of facts." Michelson v. Merrill Lynch Pierce Fenner & Smith, Inc., 83 Civ. 8898, 1989 WL 31514, *3 (S.D.N.Y.). . . .

Defendant, however, raises additional issues. First, counsel seems to imply that Plaintiff's counsel engaged Green simply to disqualify him from serving as an expert for the other side. That kind of odious practice is roundly condemned. See Paul, 123 F.R.D. at 281-82. . . . However, there is no evidence this was Plaintiff's purpose, and the Court will not impute such motives to one of its own officers. W.R. Grace & Co. v. Gracecare, Inc., 152 F.R.D. 61, 63 n.4 (D. Md. 1993). . . .

Moreover, there is no evidence that either side is unable to secure another expert. Although counsel may feel Green is a "world respected expert on the subject of bicycle accident reconstruction and railroad grade crossing accident[s]," Db-19, there is no evidence of anything unique about his services. See Wang [Labs.], 762 F. Supp. at 1249 n.6 ("a different result might be warranted if the consultant involved were unique in some relevant sense"). The business of being an expert has become a cottage industry. . . .

This Court need not impute any evil motive to either Green or Defendant's law firm. This analysis does not seek out intentional wrongdoing but addresses an issue of fairness. Any party to a law-suit who retains an expert should not have to worry that the expert will change sides in the middle of the proceeding. To hold otherwise would adversely affect the confidence parties place in this system of justice. As noted in American [Prot. Ins.] Co. v. MGM Grand Hotel-Las Vegas, Inc., CV-LV 82-26 (HDM), 1986 WL 57464 [, at *6 (D. Nev. Mar. 11, 1986)]:

> Were the most important witness' assistance in the litigation to be sold to the highest bidder, the court's integrity would be discredited. In addition, the public estimation of the judicial system would be diminished.

Accordingly, plaintiff's Motion to Disqualify James Marley Green from serving as an expert for defendant Sherwin-Williams shall be granted. The

Order shall also provide that any work done to date so far by Green shall not inure to the benefit of defendant Sherwin-Williams. . . .

## *Coates v. AC & S, Inc.*
133 F.R.D. 109 (E.D. La. 1990)

CHARLES SCHWARTZ, JR., DISTRICT JUDGE.

This matter is before the Court on the motion of plaintiff to compel discovery of experts consulted by defendants. . . .

Plaintiff in this matter, Charles Coates, recently died, allegedly of peritoneal mesothelioma. After his death, tissue samples were taken and sent to both plaintiff's and defendant's experts. Defendants have sent the samples to certain experts whom they have designated pursuant to Rule 26(b)(4)[(D)]* as experts who have been retained in anticipation of litigation but who will not testify at trial. Plaintiff now seeks to depose these experts or to obtain copies of any written reports including the results of all tests made and all conclusions of these experts. . . . The Court finds that the exceptional circumstances contemplated by Rule 26(b)(4)[(D)(ii)] are present in this situation. Moreover, the Court finds that a pathologist's or other expert's examination of tissue samples taken from the body of a person who is now deceased is sufficiently analogous to an examination under Rule 35(b) so that all parties have a right to the type of information set forth in that rule.

The Court issued its original ruling on August 8, 1990, in an effort to curtail the "shopping" of tissue samples by requiring all parties to file into the record the names and addresses of all persons or entities to whom such tissue samples were sent. In that order, the Court stated that it "was of the opinion that without this Order, there is the possibility of 'shopping' of tissue samples and this creates an 'exceptional circumstance.'" The Court is still of the opinion that "shopping" continues to take place and that such "shopping" is sufficient to fall within the Rule's exceptional circumstances exception.

Defendants oppose the instant motion and make much of their "right" to determine their trial strategy, arguing that allowing plaintiffs to depose or to obtain the written reports of experts who will not be called at trial will significantly undermine this "right." Defendants have apparently forgotten, however, that the goal of litigation is not for the side with the best strategy to win; rather the goal should be to seek the ultimate truth at issue in the matter. Hickman v. Taylor, 329 U.S. 495 (1947).

Defendants contend that the fact that they may send tissue samples to more than one doctor does not necessarily mean shopping for a favorable

* [The case originally referred to Rule 26(b)(4)(B). That provision became Rule 26(b)(4)(D) in the 2007 style changes to the Rules and the text of the opinion has been amended to reflect this style change—EDS.]

opinion, but only demonstrates the difficulty of making a definitive diagnosis of mesothelioma. If not for this order, both sides may continue to seek for an expert who can render a definitive diagnosis favorable to their position in the case, and at trial, then, it would appear to the jury that the experts in support of each side's position are divided evenly. Those experienced in litigation know that for the most part experts, if they can in good conscience, tend to testify favorably for those who employ them. In my experience I have never known a party to call an expert it knows would testify contrary to its interests. The reality of the situation is that if a number of other experts have been consulted herein, but who could not make a definitive diagnosis, and these experts are not called as witnesses, then the jury could be mislead [*sic*] regarding the truth of plaintiff's condition. Considering the difficulty in diagnosing mesothelioma, the fact finder is entitled to know the extent of any disagreement of those whom a plaintiff or defendant employed, unless we adopt the theory that in a civil case, as part of its trial tactics, a party has the right to suppress the truth. Absent this Order, it is impracticable for either side to obtain this information by other means, and it thus falls within the exceptional circumstances contemplated by Rule 26(b)(4)[(D)].[1]

Rule 35(b), while not directly on point, is sufficiently analogous to provide support for the Court's decision to permit the discovery sought. In In re Certain Asbestos Cases, 112 F.R.D. 427 (N.D. Tex. 1986), the defendants sought an order permitting an autopsy "for the purpose of determining the exact cause of death." Id. at 429. The defendants also requested that the court regulate the taking and preserving of tissue samples. In that case, the court held that Rule 35(a) permitted the autopsy upon a showing that the physical condition of the party was at issue and there was good cause shown for the examination. The court also noted that "[i]t would be incongruous to terminate at death the search for the true state of a person's physical condition when the precise controversy is his condition at death." Id. at 433. In the instant matter, the tissue samples have already been taken, the only question is how many doctors or other experts will examine them and whether they must disclose their findings. It is clear that if an autopsy had been performed in this matter pursuant to Rule 35(a), then under Rule 35(b), each doctor so participating would be required to disclose his conclusions. The Court finds no logical distinction between that result and the one plaintiffs seek. The fact that discovery in this matter is conducted by the sending of tissue samples rather than by autopsy should not dictate whether the findings of the doctors participating should be revealed. Accordingly,

*IT IS ORDERED* that when any party sends a tissue sample to any expert for review, then any other party may discover the result of that review,

---

1. The Court has considered appointing an additional expert pursuant to Rule 706 of the Federal Rules of Evidence and charging his expenses and costs, but feels that the approach herein obviates the necessity of such an appointment.

including obtaining any written report, diagnosis, or test result, or may take the deposition of such expert upon payment of his time and expenses when deposed and if he is not to be called as a witness at trial, also upon payment of his fee and expenses in connection with the preparation of his report.

## Notes and Questions

1. *Testing the Limits.* As a powerful example of the expert making the case, consider Haley v. Pan Am. World Airways, Inc., 746 F.2d 311 (5th Cir. 1984), in which the parents of an adult passenger recovered damages for their son's pre-impact fear in a crash that killed everyone. They proved his fear through a psychiatrist who had treated survivors of aircraft accidents and who testified to the five levels of stress, culminating in panic, that most, if not all, people experience in crisis. Does this seem to you to be an "extreme" reliance on experts? Would your opinion change once you knew that the jury, while finding for the plaintiff, awarded only $15,000 in damages?

2. *Disclosing the Strength of the Experts.* Whether an expert will be allowed to testify, based on how she will look on the stand and how she will stand up under cross-examination, is central to the decision of each side about whether to settle in advance of trial and for how much. In fact, many a settlement has followed from the deposition performance of the expert for one side or the other. The 1993 version of the Rules reflects what had long been the practice in many places, which was to depose the adversary's experts on the eve of trial. Note that in Rule 26(a)(2)(D) there is a special provision for turning over in advance of trial the expert's report and other matters relating to his testimony. Read this provision carefully. Can you see the reasons why the Rules provide that one side give the other so much in the way of background information on the experts who will testify?

3. *The History of Rule 26(a)(2).* In light of the importance of experts in today's practice, it may seem surprising that the original Federal Rules had no provision for their discovery by the adversary. For an excellent history of the present Rule that posits that it still may not adequately reflect the actual practice where the care, feeding, and discovery of experts is a huge part of the litigation, see Douglas Alan Emerick, Note, Discovery of the Nontestifying Expert Witness's Identity Under the Federal Rules of Civil Procedure: You Can't Tell the Players Without a Program, 37 Hastings L.J. 201 (1985).

4. *Nontestifying Experts.* Notice the distinction drawn between two kinds of experts in Rule 26, experts who are likely to testify at trial and those "retained or specially employed in anticipation of litigation" but who are *not* likely to be called as witnesses. The reasons for the different treatment are obvious, but as *Cordy* and *Coates* demonstrate, there may be costs associated with prohibiting routine discovery of experts who are specially retained but won't be called as a witness at trial. Does the "exceptional circumstances"

escape hatch in Rule 26(b)(4)(D) respond fully to this concern? Does it apply not only to the opinions of nontestifying experts, but also to their *identities*? Courts have divided on this last issue. For a thorough discussion of the conflict in an opinion written by Magistrate Judge Wayne D. Brazil—who is widely respected for his knowledge of procedure—see In re Pizza Time Theatre Secs. Litig., 113 F.R.D. 94, 96-98 (N.D. Cal. 1986) (concluding that the discovery of the identities of nontestifying experts should be subject to the "exceptional circumstances" standard).

Lawyers may, of course, change their minds about whether a designated expert should testify; that decision is often influenced by the quality of the report the expert produces. But redesignating an expert as nontestifying to avoid disclosure of the report and deposition by an opponent can be sticky—the redesignation itself can send a signal that the case is weak. In Plymovent Corp. v. Air Tech Sols., Inc., 243 F.R.D. 139 (D.N.J. 2007), plaintiffs moved for a preliminary injunction in their false advertising claim relying predominantly on a retained expert's videotape and report purporting to show that Air Tech's product for removing exhaust fumes from closed garages did not work as advertised.

At the hearing, however, before Plymovent called its expert, the following colloquy occurred between the judge and counsel for Plymovent:

> THE COURT:   [A]re you going to rely on that tape and the report that's based on that tape, or are you going to ignore it and proceed without it—. . . You think that helps your case?
> MR. O'NEILL:   Absolutely, your Honor. For the purposes of today, it provides—
> THE COURT:   You don't want to reconsider that position[?]
> MR. O'NEILL:   Your Honor, what it does—
> THE COURT:   I will give you a chance.
> MR. O'NEILL:   What it does, your Honor, is it provides the court with a visual representation.—
> THE COURT:   It's a travesty of the scientific method, it's a travesty. It's the only word I can think of. I'm not saying that if it's done right you might not reach the same results, but who knows. It's a travesty. . . . I don't have to be much of a scientist to know that that report has about 35 different variables in there, none of which are harmonized. I mean it's a travesty. So, I just want to know if you want to rely on it, or you think you have a good case without it.
> MR. O'NEILL:   I have a very good case without it.
> THE COURT:   All right.

Id. at 141-142. The court denied preliminary injunctive relief and the case proceeded to discovery. Plymovent produced the report and videotape, but (probably due to the judge's admonition) it did not designate its expert as a witness for trial. Defendant nonetheless filed a *subpoena duces tecum* seeking all documents "referring or relating to" the expert report and videotape. Id. at 142. Against Plymovent's motion to quash the subpoena, defendant argued that Plymovent's expert could not be redesignated as nontestifying under Rule 26(b)(4)(B) because Plymovent attempted to rely on the expert at the preliminary injunction hearing. That attempt, defendant contended, along with disclosure of the report and videotape, waived the protections of Rule 26(b)(4)(B) for any remaining documents related to the expert's work on the case.

The court rejected the argument and granted the motion to quash, emphasizing that Rule 26(b)(4)(B) "creates a safe harbor whereby facts and opinions of non-testifying, consulting experts are shielded from discovery except upon a showing of exceptional circumstances." Id. at 143. The court found "a common theme . . . apparent throughout the cases reviewed from various jurisdictions—the conversion of an expert designated for trial purposes under Rule 26(b)(4)(A), to a consulting expert, under Rule 26(b)(4)[(D)], is allowed and results in insulating that expert from discovery. . . ." Id. at 144 (citation omitted). Here, the court found that Plymovent had never formally designated its expert as a trial witness, no relief had been granted on the basis of the expert's submitted materials, and Plymovent had functionally withdrawn its expert at the preliminary injunction hearing. Id. at 145-146 (following Intervet, Inc. v. Merial Ltd., 2007 WL 1797643 (D. Neb. June 20, 2007)).

Other courts have held that relying on or disclosing a nontestifying expert's report does waive the protection of Rule 26(b)(4)(D). See Atari Corp. v. Sega of America, 161 F.R.D. 417, 418-420 (N.D. Cal. 1994); United States v. Hooker Chems. & Plastics Corp., 112 F.R.D. 333, 338 (W.D.N.Y. 1987); but see Akamai Techs., Inc. v. Dig. Island, Inc., 2002 WL 1285126 (N.D. Cal. May 30, 2002) (upholding a contract between the parties that disclosure would *not* waive the protection of Rule 26(b)(4)(D) and explaining that Atari Corp. stood only for the proposition that "disclosure during settlement negotiations *may* give rise to waiver, so long as there is not an explicit agreement to the contrary among the parties").

5. *Applying Rule 26(b)(4).* Assume that a research scientist who works for a corporation happens to witness an industrial accident while walking to the corporation's cafeteria for lunch. The injured employee sues the company and seeks to depose the scientist. Do any of the restrictions in Rule 26(b)(4) regarding deposing an expert apply? Must the employee pay the expert a reasonable fee for time spent in responding to this discovery?

Assume instead that a consumer of the company's product seeks to depose the research scientist to determine whether the company's research department had knowledge of the alleged defect. Do any of the restrictions in Rule 26(b)(4) regarding deposing an expert apply in this situation? See In re Shell Oil Refinery, 132 F.R.D. 437 (E.D. La. 1990), *clarified by* In re Shell Oil Refinery, 134 F.R.D. 148, 151 (E.D. La. 1990); Ager v. Jane C. Stormont Hosp. & Training School for Nurses, 622 F.2d 496 (10th Cir. 1980). See also David S. Day, Discovery Standards for the Testimonial Expert Under Federal Rule of Civil Procedure 26(b)(4): A Twentieth Anniversary Assessment, 133 F.R.D. 209 (1990); Marjorie Press Lindblom, Note, Compelling Experts to Testify: A Proposal, 44 U. Chi. L. Rev. 851 (1977). In analyzing these questions of proper rule interpretation, consider the following excerpt from In re Shell Oil Refinery, 132 F.R.D. at 441-442:

The court finds that the persuasive authority favors application of Rule 26(b)(4)(B) to non-testifying in-house experts. To rule otherwise would encourage economic waste by requiring an employer to hire independent experts to obtain the protection of Rule 26(b)(4). Protection of an in-house expert's opinion's [*sic*] supports improved public safety and other social benefits of self-analysis. That the work of an in-house expert is used not only to defend a lawsuit but also to improve a company's operations or product design does not remove him from the parameters of Rule 26(b)(4)(B). See Hermsdorfer v. [Am.] Motors Corp., 96 F.R.D. 13, 15 (W.D.N.Y. 1982).

Not all in-house experts fall within the parameters of the retained or specially employed language of Rule 26(b)(4)(B). The Advisory Committee Notes exclude from the scope of Rule 26(b)(4)(B) "an expert who is simply a general employee of the party not specially employed on the case." Those in-house experts who are not retained or specially employed should be treated as ordinary witnesses under Rule 26(b)(1), and if their work was in anticipation of litigation or preparation of trial, then discovery must be analyzed under the work product doctrine, Rule 26(b)(3).

Neither the Rule nor the Notes explain when a general employee may become retained or specially employed. Some courts have found that the terms retained or specially employed mean "something more than simply the assignment of a current employee to a particular problem raised by current litigation." See Kansas-Nebraska [Nat.] Gas Co. [v. Marathon Oil Co,] 109 F.R.D. [12,] 16 [D. Neb. 1983]. To the contrary, other authority suggests that "a regular employee may become specially employed when he is designated and assigned by a party to apply his expertise to a particular matter in anticipation of litigation or for trial." See [James R.] Pielemeier, Discovery of Non-Testifying In-House Experts, 58 Ind. L.J. [597,] 602 [(1983)] (citing [Michael H.] Graham, Discovery of Experts Under Rule 26(b)(4) of the Federal Rules of Civil Procedure: Part One, An Analytical Study, 1976 U. Ill. L.F. [895, 942 (1976)]).

Whether an in-house expert is retained or specially employed must be decided case-by-case.

6. *Experts and the Attorney-Client Privilege.* Lawyers have to be very careful about what information they share with expert witnesses and whether they are confident they want an expert to testify. Giving privileged information to an expert designated to testify under Rule 26(b)(4)(A) may work a waiver of the privilege that cannot be undone by redesignating the expert as a nontestifying witness. See CP Kelco U.S. Inc. v. Pharmacia Corp., 213 F.R.D. 176 (D. Del. 2003) (privilege waived as to documents reviewed by testifying defense expert but not produced to plaintiff; holding unchanged by redesignation of expert as nontestifying after his deposition).

7. *Litigation Consultants.* Experts on depositions, trials, juries, and the tactics of testimony are increasingly hired to help lawyers and litigants "frame" their evidence in the most persuasive way to the jury. Some worry that these consultants do more than merely "frame" testimony. Should conversations between lawyers, clients, and litigation consultants be covered by the work product doctrine?

In litigation over securities fraud liability between Cendant Corporation and its outside accounting firm, Ernst & Young, Cendant sought discovery of communications between Ernst & Young and its trial consultant about the case, and, more specifically, about how to handle the deposition of Ernst & Young's audit team manager. The Third Circuit held that communications with the litigation consultant should be covered as opinion work product. It rejected Cendant's argument that "a non-attorney's advice regarding witness testimony" should not be covered because "the jury is entitled to know the consultant's communications with the witness . . . in the same way it is entitled to know and assess all other factors that may have informed the witness's testimony and may affect credibility." In re Cendant Corp. Secs. Litig., 343 F.3d 658, 666 (3d Cir. 2003). The court observed that Rule 26 expressly covers work by an attorney's agents in anticipation of litigation and that the communications with the trial consultant "focused on those issues that counsel [and the consultant] perceived to be central to the case," including "counsel's view of the important facts of the case, the contentions of the parties, and Ernst & Young's trial themes, theories and strategies." Id. at 667.

The court went out of its way to note that Cendant "conceded that it was not accusing Ernst & Young of fabricating false testimony in the meetings [with the consultant]," and that "[t]he protection afforded opinion or core work product may be breached when there is a charge of false testimony." Id. at 666-667 n.8. Still, if communications with a trial consultant are covered as opinion work product in the first instance, how can anyone know if advice from a consultant crosses the line from friendly assistance and "spin" to suborning perjury?

8. *Court-Appointed Experts.* Note that Rule 706 of the Federal Rules of Evidence authorizes judges to appoint an expert witness on its motion, even without the parties' agreement to the appointment. Fed. R. Evid. 706(a). The Rule states that an expert witness so appointed "must advise the parties of the witness's findings," if any; the witness's deposition may be taken by any party; and the witness "may be called to testify by the court on any party." Fed. R. Evid. 706(b). Consider the following description of judges' use of 706:

> The typical expert appointed under Rule 706 is called for opinion testimony on a difficult scientific or technical issue . . . most often for their medical, engineering, or accounting expertise. The medical experts tended to be appointed in personal injury cases where the party experts offered diametrically opposed views on either the proper standard of care and treatment or the causation of the injury. Engineering experts (a category that included those with knowledge of computer technology) were appointed most often for bench trials that involved technical patent or trade secret issues when the judge felt the need for assistance in understanding the technology. Accountants were typically appointed to offer an opinion on the value of complex financial claims in contract disputes or commercial failures. In addition to these areas of expertise that are most in demand, a wide variety of expert witnesses have been appointed by the trial courts to render opinions. They have testified on issues ranging from whether dwellings the Army Corps of Engineers sought to remove from navigable waters were

"houseboats" or "floating homes" to the authenticity of a signature designating a beneficiary under a pension plan.

Ellen E. Deason, Managing the Managerial Expert, 1998 U. Ill. L. Rev. 341, 348 (1998) (footnotes omitted). Does this power adequately respond to concerns about partisan experts?

## D.  INTERROGATORIES AND THE ADVERSARIAL ADVOCATE

### Problem Case: Rozier v. Ford Motor Co.

You represent defendant Ford Motor Company in a wrongful death action alleging that the defective design and placement of the fuel tank on a 1980 Ford Galaxie 500 caused a fatal explosion and fire when the car was struck from behind by another car. You have received a set of interrogatories and document requests from plaintiff's counsel that includes the following:

> Interrogatory No. 19: Over the last ten years, has Ford Motor Company prepared any written reports or analyses of the comparative advantages or disadvantages of alternate locations (e.g., on top of the rear axle or in front of the rear axle) for fuel tanks in full-sized sedans and hardtops, including the 1980 Galaxie 500?
>
> Document Request No. 19: If your answer to Interrogatory 19 is in the affirmative, produce all such written reports or analyses.

Read Rules 33-34 and Rule 60.

How would you respond to these requests? What would you have to do before deciding how to respond? Where, within a structure that resembles that of the chart in the next case, would you expect to find responsive information?

You will recall that interrogatories were at the center of the discovery litigation in *Blank*. They are traditionally used early on in discovery after the pleadings, mandatory Rule 26(a) disclosures, and Rule 26(f) conference, and give the parties a basic picture of the case and likely sources of relevant information. Skillful crafting of interrogatories is essential to proper fact development.

### *Rozier v. Ford Motor Co.*
573 F.2d 1332 (5th Cir. 1978)

SIMPSON, CIRCUIT JUDGE.
[The plaintiff, Martha Rozier, was the widow of William Rozier, who died when his 1969 Ford Galaxie 500 was struck from behind and the

fuel tank exploded. After a one-week trial, the jury returned a verdict for Ford. Approximately ten months thereafter, Mrs. Rozier moved for a new trial on the ground that Ford had failed to disclose a document covered by plaintiffs' interrogatories and that the failure to disclose constituted fraud that entitled Mrs. Rozier to relief under Rule 60(b)(3). The trial judge denied the motion, and the plaintiff appealed. On appeal, the court ruled for Mrs. Rozier, concluding that her motion was timely, that the interrogatories did cover the undisclosed document, and that Ford's failure to disclose the document prevented her from fully and fairly presenting her case—Eds.]

The facts relevant to Mrs. Rozier's 60(b)(3) motion are as follows.

On August 25, 1975, counsel for Mrs. Rozier served her fourth set of interrogatories upon counsel for defendant Ford. Interrogatories 8, 10, 12, and 16 asked whether Ford had conducted "any cost/benefit analyses" with respect to four possible design modifications of fuel tanks for passenger cars, including full-sized sedans and hard-tops. Interrogatory 19 requested similar information not limited to "cost/benefit analyses":

> 19. In conducting "its own in-house research and development work on . . . alternate fuel tank locations" over the last ten years (Stenning Deposition Vol. II, p. 32), has Ford Motor Company prepared any written reports or analyses of the comparative advantages or disadvantages of alternate locations, (e. g. on top of the rear axle or in front of the rear axle) for fuel tanks in full-sized sedans and hard-tops, including the 1969 Galaxie 500?

The interrogatories also asked whether, in the event such documents exist, Ford would make them available for inspection and copying without the necessity of a request for production.

In response, Ford objected to these and other interrogatories on the grounds that "the information sought therein does not relate to vehicles of the same size, chassis and fuel system as the 1969 Ford Galaxie 500." On December 11, 1975, counsel for Mrs. Rozier moved in writing to compel Ford to answer the fourth set of interrogatories. On January 6, 1976, the district court entered an order directing in part, as follows:

> Defendant shall file with the Court and serve upon Plaintiff's counsel, no later than January 21, 1976, answers to questions numbered 4, 5, 6, 7, 8, 9, 10, 11, 12, 13, 14, 15, 16, 17, 19, and 20 of Plaintiff's Fourth Interrogatories; *provided, however*, that the aforesaid questions are limited to such written requirements, cost/benefit analyses, and written reports or analyses which are applicable to the 1969 Ford Galaxie 500. The fact that a written requirement, cost/benefit analysis or written report may also be applicable to vehicles *other than* the 1969 Ford Galaxie 500 does *not* render it beyond the scope of the aforesaid interrogatory and must be disclosed in response to the aforesaid interrogatories. (emphasis in original).

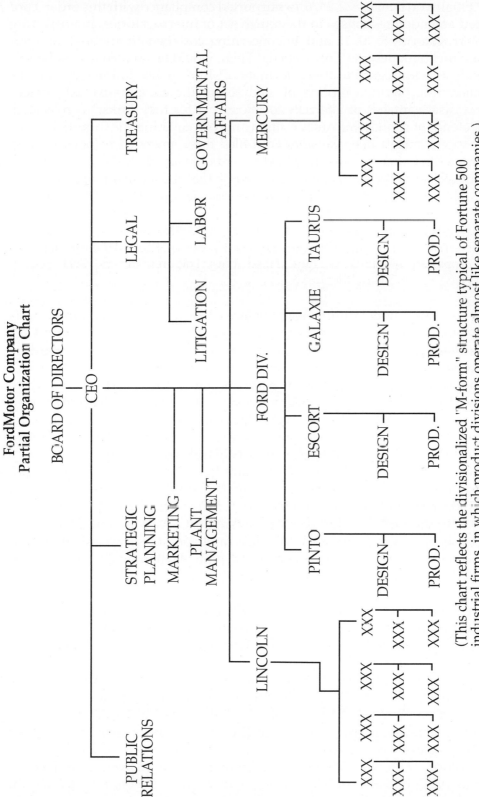

**FordMotor Company**
**Partial Organization Chart**

(This chart reflects the divisionalized "M-form" structure typical of Fortune 500 industrial firms, in which product divisions operate almost like separate companies.)

Finally, on January 22, 1976, in purported compliance with this order, Ford filed amended responses to the fourth set of interrogatories. In answering interrogatories 8, 10, 12 and 16 concerning cost/benefit analyses of alternate fuel tank designs, Ford stated: "There would be no formal cost-benefit analysis with regard to this information." In response to interrogatory 19, concerning "written reports of analyses of the comparative advantages and disadvantages of alternate locations . . . for fuel tanks," Ford stated: "Defendant cannot find such written analysis covering the inquiry."

Approximately one year after Ford filed these amended responses—and ten months after the jury returned a verdict favorable to Ford—plaintiff's counsel learned of the document from Ford's files at issue in this appeal. Dated "2/9/71," this "Confidential Cost Engineering Report" states as its subject:

> Trend Cost Estimate—Fuel Tank Proposals (30 MPH Safety Std.)—Prop[osal] I—Tank Over Rear Axle Surrounded by Body Sheet Metal Barrier & Prop[osal] II—Tank in Tank Filled With Polyurethane vs. 1971 Ford Design—1975 Ford/Mercury.

So far as we can determine from the face of the document and on the basis of remarks by counsel for Ford during oral argument, this "Trend Cost Estimate" was prepared in anticipation of a revised National Highway Traffic Safety Administration safety standard of 30 m.p.h. for rear end collisions. It compares the costs of parts and labor associated with two proposed alternate fuel tank designs based on the design of a 1971 full-sized Ford. Without dispute the 1969 Galaxie 500 model was a full-sized Ford car. Apparently, Ford planned to begin using a new fuel tank design sufficient to satisfy the 30 m.p.h. standard in its 1975 full-sized models.

In her motion for a new trial pursuant to Rule 60(b)(3), Mrs. Rozier contended that the 1971 Trend Cost Estimate should have been produced in response to the district court's January 6, 1976, order because it was "applicable to the 1969 Ford Galaxie 500." In support of her motion, Mrs. Rozier filed affidavits by Frederick E. Arndt, a safety engineering consultant, and Byron Bloch, a product safety consultant, both of whom had testified on her behalf at the trial. Each affidavit stated:

> [T]he 1969 Ford Galaxie 500 is so similar in size, design, and fuel tank location to the 1971 Ford that the subject "Confidential Cost Engineering Report" is as applicable and valid for the 1969 Ford Galaxie 500 as it is for the 1971 Ford.

In response to Mrs. Rozier's motion to vacate, Ford produced an affidavit by Thomas G. Grubba, an attorney on the house legal staff of Ford Motor Company, who "was involved in" the case. Mr. Grubba swore that he was unaware of the Trend Cost Estimate when the answers to plaintiff's interrogatories were prepared, but that he became aware of the document on February 25, 1976. We note that although Ford's answers were filed on January 22, 1976, the trial did not begin until March 1, 1976, a week after Mr. Grubba discovered the document.

By any fair reading, the district court's January 6, 1976, discovery order called for production of this Trend Cost Estimate. Ford, in response to the motion to vacate and in this appeal, has urged that, as a term of art, a "trend cost estimate" is not a "cost/benefit analysis." Whether the document in question technically is or is not a cost/benefit analysis—to our non-expert eyes, the terms are synonymous, as alike as "Tweedledum and Tweedledee"—is largely irrelevant in this case because plaintiff's interrogatories were not limited to "cost/benefit analyses." Interrogatory 19 asked whether Ford had "prepared *any* written reports or analyses of the comparative advantages or disadvantages of alternate locations . . . for fuel tanks" (emphasis added); the court's January 6 order compelled production of all such "written reports or analyses which are applicable to the 1969 Ford Galaxie 500," specifically noting that written reports also applicable to vehicles other than the 1969 Ford Galaxie 500 were not beyond the scope of the discovery order "and must be disclosed in response to the aforesaid interrogatories." Undeniably, the Trend Cost Estimate is a report "of the comparative advantages or disadvantages" of alternate fuel tank locations, since the alternative which could satisfy the safety standard for the least cost would, in terms of Ford's interests, be the most advantageous. Also, in light of the unchallenged assertions made in the Arndt and Bloch affidavits, this estimate based on the design of a 1971 full-sized Ford is applicable to a 1969 full-sized Ford. We recognize that the Trend Cost Estimate does not purport to estimate the cost of installing new fuel tanks on automobiles already manufactured, such as a 1969 Galaxie 500; however, neither the interrogatory nor the court order limited discovery to reports of that description.

We conclude that Mrs. Rozier has proved by clear and convincing evidence that Ford engaged in misrepresentation and other misconduct. Plaintiff's interrogatory 19, as limited by the district court's order, called for production of the Trend Cost Estimate. In its written response, Ford stated that it could find no such report. A month later, an in-house attorney for Ford involved in this case discovered the Trend Cost Estimate but failed to disclose it or to amend the inaccurate response to interrogatory 19.[10] If Ford

---

10. Ford's duty to amend its inaccurate response is based on Rule 26(e)(2), Fed. R. Civ. P.:A party is under a duty seasonably to amend a prior response if he obtains information upon the basis of which (A) he knows that the response was incorrect when made, or (B) he knows that the response though correct when made is no longer true and the circumstances are such that a failure to amend the response is in substance a knowing concealment. See Havenfied Corp. v. H & R Block, Inc., 509 F.2d 1263 (8th Cir. 1975), *cert. denied,* 421 U.S. 999 [1975]. [Note that the Rule has been restyled as Rule 26(e)(1) and now provides that "A party who has made a disclosure . . . must supplement or correct its disclosure . . . in a timely manner if the party learns that in some material respect the disclosure . . . is incomplete or incorrect, and if the additional or corrective information has not otherwise been made known to the other parties during the discovery process."—Eds.]

Although we are unaware of the precise nature of Mr. Grubba's involvement in this case, he did not participate in the trial itself or in the appeal. The attorneys retained by Ford to represent the company at trial and in the appeal have assured this Court that they were personally unaware of the Trend Cost Estimate until Mrs. Rozier filed her motion to vacate almost a year after the trial. We accept their statements.

in good faith believed that the district court's order was not intended to compel production of this document, the appropriate remedy was to seek a ruling by the district court at that point and not a year after the trial and then only when, by chance, the plaintiff learned of it.

The more vexing question is whether nondisclosure of the Trend Cost Estimate prevented Mrs. Rozier from fully and fairly presenting her case. At trial, Mrs. Rozier contended that Ford was negligent in designing a fuel tank that could not withstand an impact such as that involved in the accident which took her husband's life. Prior to trial, she expressed an intention to rely on 14 theories to explain how Ford deviated from the appropriate standard of care. Inevitably, information developed in the discovery stages of the case influenced the decision as to which theories would be emphasized at trial. We are left with the firm conviction that disclosure of the Trend Cost Estimate would "have made a difference in the way plaintiff's counsel approached the case or prepared for trial," Rock Island Bank & Trust Co. v. Ford Motor Co., 54 Mich. App. 278, [280] N.W.2d 799 (1974), and that Mrs. Rozier was prejudiced by Ford's nondisclosure. See Seaboldt v. Pennsylvania R.R. Co., 290 F.2d 296, 299-300 (3d Cir. 1961).

Although Ford does not specifically dispute this conclusion, it has argued, in a related context, that the Trend Cost Estimate, if admissible in trial, would merely have been cumulative because plaintiff's experts testified at length as to the feasibility of alternative fuel tank designs. Additionally, Ford contends that the document would have been inadmissible by virtue of Rule 407, Fed. R. Evid. We think that these arguments misconstrue the significance of the withheld document.

The admissibility of evidence is irrelevant in the discovery process so long as "the information sought appears reasonably calculated to lead to the discovery of admissible evidence." Fed. R. Civ. P. 26(b)(1). The Trend Cost Estimate clearly satisfies this test. It was not an isolated document, but rather one in a series; some of the other documents, also not produced by Ford during discovery, are referred to in the estimate itself: "Request from J. M. Chiara," "Layouts LA-901277 and 901278," "our report dated February 4, 1971," "A proposal for a fuel tank installation over the rear axle is illustrated in the attached drawing." At a minimum, production of the Trend Cost Estimate could have led to discovery of these other documents. . . .

We cannot know what use, if any, plaintiff's counsel would have made of the Trend Cost Estimate had it been produced by Ford prior to trial. However, consideration of one likely use reveals the prejudice that Mrs. Rozier may have suffered as a consequence of Ford's misconduct.

The negligence alleged by Mrs. Rozier may have taken place in one or both of two time frames: (1) up to and including the production of the 1969 Ford Galaxie 500, and (2) between the time of production in 1969 and the time of the fatal collision in 1973. Under the facts of this case, the task of proving negligence in the pre-production period was the most difficult. Given the industry practices and standards in 1969, the jury was less likely to find that Ford's conduct fell below that to be expected from an ordinarily prudent manufacturer in designing the fuel system for a full-sized sedan.

In the post-production period, however, Ford may have had a duty to warn consumers of a latent danger such as a defectively designed fuel tank. Here the plaintiff need not have been hamstrung by the less sophisticated state of the art in 1969, and may have been able to make a convincing case based on the Trend Cost Estimate.

Georgia courts[12] recognize a cause of action against automobile manufacturers for negligence in failing to warn of latent dangers arising from defective design. Friend v. General Motors Corp., [165 S.E.2d 734, 737 (Ga. Ct. App. 1968)]. And, as the Eighth Circuit has explained in discussing this duty to warn:

> The failure to use reasonable care in design *or knowledge* of a defective design gives rise to the reasonable duty on the manufacturer to warn of this condition. Larsen v. General Motors Corp., 391 F.2d 495, 505 (8th Cir. 1968) (emphasis added).

Here, arguably, the Trend Cost Estimate furnishes evidence that Ford, in 1971, had knowledge that the fuel tanks on those models with designs comparable to the 1969 Galaxie 500 could not withstand rear-end collisions at 30 m.p.h. or greater and that a design to correct this condition was both economically and structurally feasible. If a jury were persuaded that the fuel tank of the 1969 Galaxie was latently but not negligently defective *at the time of production*, it might still have found that once Ford acquired the knowledge evidenced by the Trend Cost Estimate it negligently failed to warn Galaxie users of the defect.

By a peculiar turn of events, the jury in this case was foreclosed at the last minute from considering Ford's failure to warn as a possible negligent omission. At least as early as December 10, 1975, when the parties filed a "Consolidated Proposed Pre-Trial Order," Mrs. Rozier indicated that one "act of negligence" upon which she intended to rely was "[f]ailure to warn owners and users of the vehicle of the risk of injury or death due to fire in the event of a collision." The trial judge so instructed the jury, noting that although several acts of negligence were alleged, the plaintiff "is merely required to prove one such act. . . ." Counsel for Ford objected to the warning instruction because it did not specify that the duty to warn extended only to unreasonable risks of injury. The exchange which followed this objection suggests that plaintiff's counsel, in the light of the information then available to him, viewed the duty to warn as an inconsequential part of the case:

THE COURT:   What do you say about the last exception?
MR. DEVINE *(For Plaintiff):*   Your Honor, I think it might do well to clarify that. The Jury has to find that there is a danger before the Defendant has a duty to

---

12. In this diversity case, we are of course *"Erie*-bound" to apply the law of Georgia, both the forum state and the state where Mr. Rozier's fatal injury occurred. Erie R.R. Co. v. Tompkins, 304 U.S. 64 (1938).

warn of that danger. I believe that there is plenty of evidence to support that
there is a danger.
*THE COURT:*     Nevertheless, what do you say. . . .
*MR. DEVINE:*    I think it should be clear.
*THE COURT:*     . . . You concede that I should withdraw then that charge from the
Jury's consideration?
*MR. DEVINE:*    I have no objection, Your Honor.

The Court thereupon further charged the Jury as follows:

*THE COURT:*     Members of the Jury, I had charged you that the Plaintiff claimed
that the Defendant was negligent in failing to warn owners and passengers
of the 1969 Ford Galaxie 500 of the risk of burn injury attendant to occupying
that vehicle. I now withdraw that charge, and you will not give that charge
any weight whatsoever in your deliberations.

The following colloquy ensued out of the presence of the jury:

*THE COURT:*     Any exceptions to that?
*MR. WEINBERG:*   No, sir.
*MR. DEVINE:*     No, sir.

It is apparent, then, that the Trend Cost Estimate, far from being a cumulative tidbit of evidence already subsumed in the case presented to the jury,
might have been the catalyst for an entirely different approach to the case
on a theory that the plaintiff, lacking the document, let die before it reached
the jury. Under these circumstances, we hold that Ford's wrongful withholding of information prevented Mrs. Rozier from fully and fairly presenting her case.

## 2. Policy Considerations

Our system of civil litigation cannot function if parties, in violation of
court orders, suppress information called for upon discovery. "Mutual
knowledge of all the relevant facts gathered by both parties is essential to
proper litigation. To that end, either party may compel the other to disgorge
whatever facts he has in his possession." Hickman v. Taylor, 329 U.S. 495,
507 (1947). The Federal Rules of Civil Procedure substitute the discovery
process for the earlier—and inadequate—reliance on pleadings for notice-
giving, issue-formulation, and fact-revelation. As the Supreme Court stated
in Hickman v. Taylor, supra, "civil trials in the federal courts no longer need
be carried on in the dark. The way is now clear, consistent with recognized
privileges, for the parties to obtain the fullest possible knowledge of the
issues and facts before trial." 329 U.S. at 501. The aim of these liberal discovery rules is to "make a trial less a game of blind man's bluff and more
a fair contest with the basic issues and facts disclosed to the fullest practicable extent." United States v. Procter & Gamble Co., 356 U.S. 677 (1958). It

is axiomatic that "[d]iscovery by interrogatory requires candor in responding." Dollar v. Long Mfg., N.C., Inc., 561 F.2d 613, 616 (5th Cir. 1977).

Through its misconduct in this case, Ford completely sabotaged the federal trial machinery, precluding the "fair contest" which the Federal Rules of Civil Procedure are intended to assure. Instead of serving as a vehicle for ascertainment of the truth, the trial in this case accomplished little more than the adjudication of a hypothetical fact situation imposed by Ford's selective disclosure of information. The policy protecting the finality of judgments is not so broad as to require protection of judgments obtained in this manner. . . .

We hold that the district court abused its discretion in denying plaintiff's Rule 60(b)(3) motion and that a new trial is required.

### Note: Discovery Against Complex Organizations

The court in *Rozier* implicitly assumes that Ford's lawyers at some point made a conscious decision not to disclose the Trend Cost Estimate. In fact, however, the document was never picked up in the search for information responsive to the plaintiff's discovery requests. It was part of a patent application that a lawyer on Ford's legal staff, who had some involvement with the case, became "aware" of about a week before trial, but only in connection with an entirely unrelated matter. Neither he nor anyone else involved in the *Rozier* case ever made an adversarial determination to withhold the document, because it never found its way into the *Rozier* information loop. In order to understand how this might have happened, consider the number of decisions and judgments, each presenting an opportunity for miscue, that go into the design, execution, and management of a responsive search effort.

The obvious place to begin the search is in the department responsible for designing the Galaxie itself, presumably a research and development or design unit within the Ford product division. But the order clearly extends to the R&D and design departments responsible for other "similar" sedans as well, which may well include Lincoln or Mercury products. Since the product divisions in an M-form structure typically compete with each other for the firm's resources, however, they stand in an almost adversarial relationship that may impede the search effort. And since R&D and design departments are often organized in an informal or "organic" rather than "mechanistic" structure, their information structures are especially difficult for an outsider to penetrate.

Certain nonproduction departments might also have responsive information. The Trend Cost Estimate was part of a patent application, which might have been found in the files of the legal department. And it had apparently been prepared "in anticipation of a revised National Highway Traffic Safety Administration safety standard of 30 M.P.H. for rear end collisions," id. at 1340, which suggests that the unit responsible for regulatory matters, probably Intergovernmental Affairs, might also be an unexpected source. Finally, consider the effect of changes in the organization over time: people who passed through Ford R&D during the relevant period but have since moved on to other jobs within the company, taking their personal files with them, and subunits reorganized out of existence long ago, whose files are languishing in some forgotten warehouse. When discovery spans a period of 10 or 20 years, as is not uncommon in product liability cases, there are few employees with long enough institutional memories to be of assistance, and document "retention" (i.e., destruction) schedules wreak havoc on the paper record.

In short, designing a search structure requires an understanding of the formal and informal structure of the organization, a form of "local knowledge" that exists only within the organization itself, if indeed it exists at all. The decentralization and mobility of personnel typical of large American corporations often mean that there is literally no single person who has all the necessary information.

Moreover, good design alone does not guarantee a thorough search. Executing the search is equally important, and equally problematic, for several reasons.

Responding to discovery entails real work: work that is outside the normal responsibilities of the employees who must do it, contrary to their institutional interests, and not rewarded within the company's regular compensation and incentive structure. Ford Motor Company builds cars, not lawsuits, and hours devoted to litigation rather than car production will not be rewarded in performance evaluations. When you ask busy people to do something as boring, time consuming, and literally unrewarding as producing documents for litigation, the initial reaction is not likely to be enthusiastic.

One of Ford's responses in *Rozier* hints at the problem: "There *would be* no formal cost benefit analysis with respect to such information," id. at 1340 (emphasis added). The peculiar subjunctive evokes a kind of phone conversation that is all too familiar to litigators trying to track down information: "We just don't do that sort of thing—believe me, there's no point in looking any further; I've been here for 25 years, and there's never been a cost-benefit analysis done." Motivating employees to go beyond the easy and the obvious in responding to discovery requests requires both a policy leadership and tangible assurances that the effort is not a wasted one. Litigators often worry about motivational problems when a case actually goes to trial, and they want their star witnesses to put in the work necessary for adequate preparation. A word of praise from a supervisor or a letter of commendation in the personnel file can help matters considerably, but it is probably the unusual litigator or client who exerts that sort of effort in responding to the opponent's discovery.

Even if the corporation does support the discovery effort in both word and deed, however, that still does not guarantee that individual employees will find it in their interests to comply. Since the people with the most information about the case are also the ones whose actions are being attacked in the litigation, self-protection provides a strong motivation for concealment even, and perhaps especially, when the organization is committed to ferreting out the truth.

And even if both management and employees are willing participants in the discovery process, there is an enormous problem of communication. Left to their own devices, employees will respond to a discovery request as laypeople, making their own judgments about the meaning of the request and the nature of the search they are supposed to do. Terms like "cost-benefit analysis," which was at issue in *Rozier,* might have a technical meaning to a design engineer that is far narrower than what the requesting, or even responding, lawyer would assume.

Another common reaction among clients is to think only in terms of formal files or official documents. Ford's response is again suggestive: "There would be no *formal* cost benefit analysis" (emphasis added), implying that the search might have been limited to central files. Trying to convince client employees that a request for "documents" includes their personal, informal notes, even (especially!) those labeled "confidential," is often a major exercise in reeducation. Ensuring that all copies of a responsive document are produced poses a related problem. It is entirely natural for an employee to assume that one final copy of a report or memorandum will be sufficient, as it is for most substantive purposes; but for purposes of discovery each draft and copy, complete with unexpurgated marginal notes, is a distinct document.

Characterizing Ford's failure to produce the Trend Cost Estimate as a failure of the search process, rather than a conscious decision to withhold the document, does not exonerate its behavior. To the contrary, the respondent's first obligation in discovery is to conduct a search reasonably designed to produce all responsive information and to monitor results so as to ensure compliance by all participants. Ford's failure to demonstrate, or even argue, that it had conducted a reasonable search that reasonably failed to pick up the Trend Cost Estimate is a more persuasive reason for the result in *Rozier* than the court's glib assertion that the Trend Cost Estimate was "clearly" called for.

Thus far we have considered the difficulties inherent in organizational discovery only from the respondent's point of view. For the requesting party, however, the problems are compounded by the constraints of the adversary system. The adversary system forces the requesting lawyer to rely on her opponent to do the real work of ferreting information out of the organization, a task that entails the exercise of subjective judgment on matters of interpretation, emphasis, and effort at every turn. The responding lawyer therefore enjoys a huge area of essentially unmonitored discretion that, according to the traditional rules of the game, will be exercised to promote her own client's interests, rather than her opponent's.

Moreover, the assumption that the requesting lawyer can protect her client's interests through follow-up and enforcement is rendered implausible by the complexity and expense of the tasks. The organizational party has far more complete knowledge about the discovery transaction than the requester can obtain at reasonable expense through arm's-length adversarial interaction. More often than not, the follow-up effort is abandoned well short of fruition.

In *Rozier*, for example, after four sets of interrogatories, a series of depositions, and a motion and order compelling production, plaintiff had not received a shred of information on the cost of alternative fuel tank designs. In theory, it was up to plaintiff's lawyer to keep on pushing if he was not satisfied. And all the weasel words in Ford's responses—that "there would be no formal cost-benefit analysis" and that it could "not find" information responsive to the request—strongly suggested the possibility of organizational failure; that is, they hadn't found any documents because they hadn't looked very far. But with only a month remaining before trial, there was probably not enough time for the laborious ritual of deposing everyone involved in the search effort. And even if there were time on the calendar, it would be difficult to justify the considerable expense in order to chase down a phantom. The most persistent reality of organizational discovery is that time, money, and inertia are on the side of the organization.

A striking example of just how hard the requesting lawyer may have to push to prevail over a savvy, recalcitrant party is provided in Network Computing Sys. v. Cisco Sys., Inc., 223 F.R.D. 392 (D.S.C. 2004).

## E.   DEPOSITIONS AND THE ADVERSARIAL ADVOCATE

### Problem Case: The Secret Memo (Part Two)

Return to the problem case in which you are representing the president of the company, Eve Barrie. You have decided to turn over the "the smoking gun" memorandum according to the voluntary disclosure provisions of Rule 26.

Your adversaries have now moved to depose Eve Barrie. How do you prepare her, in general and particularly, to answer questions about the memorandum? What would be the most helpful thing she might say about the meaning of the memorandum? What are the ethical and other restraints on putting these words into her mouth?

Assume that at the deposition, the lawyer for the other side presses her very hard in what seems to you an obvious attempt to make her lose her temper and perhaps the benefits of her careful preparation. What is your recourse when this happens? How can you protect your witness?

Remember that interrogatories and, of course, requests to admit may be addressed only to parties. But the deposition of anyone with information about the case may be taken under Rules 30 and 31. Look back also to the material on deposition strategy at the beginning of this chapter.

Usually such depositions are taken in a lawyer's office, with a court reporter who swears the witnesses. There is no judicial officer on hand to rule on objections, and particularly when the client is present, or is being deposed, lawyers sometimes become overly zealous, to put the problem mildly. To give you some idea of the possibilities for abuse, we print the following case. How would you defend the conduct of the famous lawyer in this case, were you called upon to do so before a Bar Disciplinary Committee? The press? A court considering his disbarment?

The Northern California and San Diego Chapters of the Association of Business Trial Lawyers adopted a guide to legal etiquette that includes admonitions such as: "A lawyer should take depositions only when actually needed to learn facts or preserve testimony, and should not engage in any conduct during a deposition that would not be appropriate in the presence of a judge," and "A lawyer should not behave in an offensive, derogatory or discourteous manner even when his or her client so desires." It might seem that such suggestions would be obvious, yet codes of civility in addition to codes of professional responsibility are becoming increasingly common. Ethics, Professionalism and Civility Guidelines, Association of Business Trial Lawyers, http://www.abtl.org/civilityguidelines.htm.

### Paramount Communic'ns Inc. v. QVC Network Inc.
637 A.2d 34 (Del. 1993)

### Addendum

The record in this case is extensive. The appendix filed in this Court comprises 15 volumes, totaling some 7,251 pages. It includes substantial deposition testimony which forms part of the factual record before the Court of Chancery and before this Court. . . . As noted, the Court has commended the parties for their professionalism in conducting expedited discovery, assembling and organizing the record, and preparing and presenting very helpful briefs, a joint appendix, and oral argument.

The Court is constrained, however, to add this Addendum. Although this Addendum has no bearing on the outcome of the case, it relates to a serious issue of professionalism involving deposition practice in proceedings in Delaware trial courts.[23]

The issue of discovery abuse, including lack of civility and professional misconduct during depositions, is a matter of considerable concern to

---

23. We raise this matter *sua sponte* as part of our exclusive supervisory responsibility to regulate and enforce appropriate conduct of lawyers appearing in Delaware proceedings. . . .

Delaware courts and courts around the nation.[24] One particular instance of misconduct during a deposition in this case demonstrates such an astonishing lack of professionalism and civility that it is worthy of special note here as a lesson for the future—a lesson of conduct not to be tolerated or repeated.

On November 10, 1993, an expedited deposition of Paramount, through one of its directors, J. Hugh Liedtke, was taken in the state of Texas. The deposition was taken by Delaware counsel for QVC. Mr. Liedtke was individually represented at this deposition by Joseph D. Jamail, Esquire, of the Texas Bar. Peter C. Thomas, Esquire, of the New York Bar appeared and defended on behalf of the Paramount defendants. . . .

Mr. Jamail did not otherwise appear in this Delaware proceeding representing any party, and he was not admitted *pro hac vice.* Under the rules of the Court of Chancery and this Court, lawyers who are admitted *pro hac vice* to represent a party in Delaware proceedings are subject to Delaware Disciplinary Rules, and are required to review the Delaware State Bar Association Statement of Principles of Lawyer Conduct (the "Statement of Principles").[29] During the Liedtke deposition, Mr. Jamail abused the

24. Justice Sandra Day O'Connor recently highlighted the national concern about the deterioration in civility in a speech delivered on December 14, 1993, to an American Bar Association Group on "Civil Justice Improvements":

> I believe that the justice system cannot function effectively when the professionals charged with administering it cannot even be polite to one another. Stress and frustration drive down productivity and make the process more time-consuming and expensive. Many of the best people get driven away from the field. The profession and the system itself lose esteem in the public's eyes.
>
>     . . . In my view, incivility disserves the client because it wastes time and energy—time that is billed to the client at hundreds of dollars an hour, and energy that is better spent working on the case than working over the opponent.

The Honorable Sandra Day O'Connor, "Civil Justice System Improvements," ABA at 5 (Dec. 14, 1993) (footnotes omitted).

29. The following are a few pertinent excerpts from the Statement of Principles:

> The Delaware State Bar Association, for the Guidance of Delaware lawyers, *and those lawyers from other jurisdictions who may be associated with them,* adopted the following Statement of Principles of Lawyer Conduct on [November 15, 1991]. . . . The purpose of adopting these Principles is to promote and foster the ideals of *professional courtesy, conduct and cooperation.* . . . A lawyer should develop and maintain the qualities of integrity, compassion, learning, civility, diligence and public service that mark the most admired members of our profession. . . . [A] lawyer . . . *should treat* all persons, including *adverse lawyers* and parties, *fairly and equitably . . . Professional civility is conduct that shows respect not only for the courts and colleagues, but also for all people encountered in practice* . . . Respect for the court requires . . . emotional self-control; [and] the absence of scorn and superiority in words of demeanor . . . A lawyer should use pre-trial procedures, including discovery, solely to develop a case for settlement or trial. *No pre-trial procedure should be used to harass an opponent or delay a case . . . Questions and objections at deposition should be restricted to conduct appropriate* [sic] *in the presence of a judge* . . . Before moving the admission of a lawyer from another jurisdiction, a Delaware lawyer should make such investigation as is required to form an informed conviction that the lawyer to be admitted is ethical and competent, and should furnish the candidate for admission with a copy of this Statement.

(Emphasis supplied).

privilege of representing a witness in a Delaware proceeding, in that he: (a) improperly directed the witness not to answer certain questions; (b) was extraordinarily rude, uncivil, and vulgar; and (c) obstructed the ability of the questioner to elicit testimony to assist the Court in this matter.

To illustrate, a few excerpts from the latter stages of the Liedtke deposition follow:

A.  [Mr. Liedtke] I vaguely recall [Mr. Oresman's letter]. . . . I think I did read it, probably. . . .

Q.  (By Mr. Johnston [Delaware counsel for QVC]) Okay. Do you have any idea why Mr. Oresman was calling that material to your attention?

MR. JAMAIL:  Don't answer that. How would he know what was going on in Mr. Oresman's mind? Don't answer it. Go on to your next question.

MR. JOHNSTON:  No, Joe—.

MR. JAMAIL:  He's not going to answer that. Certify it. I'm going to shut it down if you don't go to your next question.

MR. JOHNSTON:  No. Joe, Joe—

MR. JAMAIL:  Don't "Joe" me, asshole. You can ask some questions, but get off of that. I'm tired of you. You could gag a maggot off a meat wagon. Now, we've helped you every way we can.

MR. JOHNSTON:  Let's just take it easy.

MR. JAMAIL:  No, we're not going to take it easy. Get done with this.

MR. JOHNSTON:  We will go on to the next question.

MR. JAMAIL:  Do it now.

MR. JOHNSTON:  We will go on to the next question. We're not trying to excite anyone.

MR. JAMAIL:  Come on. Quit talking. Ask the question. Nobody wants to socialize with you.

MR. JOHNSTON:  I'm not trying to socialize. We'll go on to another question. We're continuing the deposition.

MR. JAMAIL:  Well, go on and shut up.

MR. JOHNSTON:  Are you finished?

MR. JAMAIL:  Yeah, you—

MR. JOHNSTON:  Are you finished?

MR. JAMAIL:  I may be and you may be. Now, you want to sit here and talk to me, fine. This deposition is going to be over with. You don't know what you're doing. Obviously someone wrote out a long outline of stuff for you to ask. You have no concept of what you're doing. Now, I've tolerated you for three hours. If you've got another question, get on with it. This is going to stop one hour from now, period. Go.

MR. JOHNSTON:  Are you finished?

MR. THOMAS:  Come on, Mr. Johnston, move it.

MR. JOHNSTON:  I don't need this kind of abuse.

MR. THOMAS:  Then just ask the next question.

Q.  (By Mr. Johnston) All right. To try to move forward, Mr. Liedtke, . . . I'll show you what's been marked as Liedtke 14 and it is a covering letter dated October 29 from Steven Cohen of Wachtell, Lipton, Rosen & Katz including QVC's Amendment Number 1 to its Schedule 14D-1, and my question—

A.  No.

Q.  —to you, sir, is whether you've seen that?

*A.* No. Look, I don't know what your intent in asking all these questions is, but, my God, I am not going to play boy lawyer.

*Q.* Mr. Liedtke—

*A.* Okay. Go ahead and ask your question.

*Q.* —I'm trying to move forward in this deposition that we are entitled to take. I'm trying to streamline it.

*MR. JAMAIL:* Come on with your next question. Don't even talk with this witness.

*MR. JOHNSTON:* I'm trying to move forward with it.

*MR. JAMAIL:* You understand me? Don't talk to this witness except by question. Did you hear me?

*MR. JOHNSTON:* I heard you fine.

*MR. JAMAIL:* You fee makers think you can come here and sit in somebody's office, get your meter running, get your full day's fee by asking stupid questions. Let's go with it.

(JA 6002-06).[30]

Staunch advocacy on behalf of a client is proper and fully consistent with the finest effectuation of skill and professionalism. Indeed, it is a mark of professionalism, not weakness, for a lawyer zealously and firmly to protect and pursue a client's legitimate interests by a professional, courteous, and civil attitude toward all persons involved in the litigation process. A lawyer who engages in the type of behavior exemplified by Mr. Jamail on the record of the Liedtke deposition is not properly representing his client, and the client's cause is not advanced by a lawyer who engages in unprofessional conduct of this nature. It happens that in this case there was no application to the Court, and the parties and the witness do not appear to have been prejudiced by this misconduct.[31]

Nevertheless, the Court finds this unprofessional behavior to be outrageous and unacceptable. If a Delaware lawyer had engaged in the kind of misconduct committed by Mr. Jamail on this record, that lawyer would have been subject to censure or more serious sanctions.[32] While the specter

---

30. Joint Appendix of the parties on appeal.

31. We recognize the practicalities of litigation practice in our trial courts, particularly in expedited proceedings such as this preliminary injunction motion, where simultaneous depositions are often taken in far-flung locations, and counsel have only a few hours to question each witness. Understandably, counsel may be reluctant to take the time to stop a deposition and call the trial judge for relief. Trial courts are extremely busy and overburdened. Avoidance of this kind of misconduct is essential. If such misconduct should occur, the aggrieved party should recess the deposition and engage in a dialogue with the offending lawyer to obviate the need to call the trial judge. If all else fails and it is necessary to call the trial judge, sanctions may be appropriate against the offending lawyer or party, or against the complaining lawyer or party if the request for court relief is unjustified. See Ch. Ct. R. 37. It should also be noted that discovery abuse sometimes is the fault of the questioner, not the lawyer defending the deposition. These admonitions should be read as applying to both sides.

32. See In re Ramunno, Del. Supr., 625 A.2d 248, 250 (1993) (Delaware lawyer held to have violated Rule 3.5 of the Rules of Professional Conduct, and therefore subject to public reprimand and warning for use of profanity similar to that involved here and "insulting conduct toward opposing counsel [found] . . . unacceptable by any standard").

of disciplinary proceedings should not be used by the parties as a litigation tactic, conduct such as that involved here goes to the heart of the trial court proceedings themselves. As such, it cries out for relief under the trial court's rules, including Ch. Ct. R. 37. Under some circumstances, the use of the trial court's inherent summary contempt powers may be appropriate. See In re Butler, Del. Supr., 609 A.2d 1080, 1082 (1992).

Although busy and overburdened, Delaware trial courts are "but a phone call away" and would be responsive to the plight of a party and its counsel bearing the brunt of such misconduct.[34] It is not appropriate for this Court to prescribe in the abstract any particular remedy or to provide an exclusive list of remedies under such circumstances. We assume that the trial courts of this State would consider protective orders and the sanctions permitted by the discovery rules. Sanctions could include exclusion of obstreperous counsel from attending the deposition (whether or not he or she has been admitted *pro hac vice*), ordering the deposition recessed and reconvened promptly in Delaware, or the appointment of a master to preside at the deposition. Costs and counsel fees should follow.

As noted, this was a deposition of Paramount through one of its directors. Mr. Liedtke was a Paramount witness in every respect. He was not there either as an individual defendant or as a third party witness. Pursuant to Ch. Ct. R. 170(d), the Paramount defendants should have been represented at the deposition by a Delaware lawyer or a lawyer admitted *pro hac vice*. A Delaware lawyer who moves the admission *pro hac vice* of an out-of-state lawyer is not relieved of responsibility, is required to appear at all court proceedings (except depositions when a lawyer admitted *pro hac vice* is present), shall certify that the lawyer appearing *pro hac vice* is reputable and competent, and that the Delaware lawyer is in a position to recommend the out-of-state lawyer. Thus, one of the principal purposes of the *pro hac vice* rules is to assure that, if a Delaware lawyer is not to be present at a deposition, the lawyer admitted *pro hac vice* will be there. As such, he is an officer of the Delaware Court, subject to control of the Court to ensure the integrity of the proceeding.

Counsel attending the Liedtke deposition on behalf of the Paramount defendants had an obligation to ensure the integrity of that proceeding.

34. See Hall v. Clifton Precision, E.D. Pa., 150 F.R.D. 525 (1993) (ruling on "coaching," conferences between deposed witnesses and their lawyers, and obstructive tactics):

> Depositions are the factual battleground where the vast majority of litigation actually takes place. . . . Thus, it is particularly important that this discovery device not be abused. Counsel should never forget that even though the deposition may be taking place far from a real courtroom, with no black-robed overseer peering down upon them, as long as the deposition is conducted under the caption of this court and proceeding under the authority of the rules of this court, counsel are operating as officers of this court. They should comport themselves accordingly; should they be tempted to stray, they should remember that this judge is but a phone call away.

150 F.R.D. at 531.

The record of the deposition as a whole (JA 5916-6054) demonstrates that, not only Mr. Jamail, but also Mr. Thomas (representing the Paramount defendants), continually interrupted the questioning, engaged in colloquies and objections which sometimes suggested answers to questions,[36] and constantly pressed the questioner for time throughout the deposition.[37] As to Mr. Jamail's tactic quoted above, Mr. Thomas passively let matters proceed as they did, and at times even added his own voice to support the behavior of Mr. Jamail. A Delaware lawyer or a lawyer admitted *pro hac vice* would have been expected to put an end to the misconduct in the Liedtke deposition.

This kind of misconduct is not to be tolerated in any Delaware court proceeding, including depositions taken in other states in which witnesses appear represented by their own counsel other than counsel for a party in the proceeding. Yet, there is no clear mechanism for this Court to deal with this matter in terms of sanctions or disciplinary remedies at this time in the context of this case. Nevertheless, consideration will be given to the following issues for the future: (a) whether or not it is appropriate and fair to take into account the behavior of Mr. Jamail in this case in the event application is made by him in the future to appear *pro hac vice* in any Delaware proceeding;[38] and (b) what rules or standards should be adopted to deal effectively with misconduct by out-of-state lawyers in depositions in proceedings pending in Delaware courts.

As to (a), this Court will welcome a voluntary appearance by Mr. Jamail if a request is received from him by the Clerk of this Court within thirty days of the date of this Opinion and Addendum. The purpose of such voluntary appearance will be to explain the questioned conduct and to show cause why such conduct should not be considered as a bar to any future

---

36. Rule 30(d)(1) of the revised Federal Rules of Civil Procedure, which became effective on December 1, 1993, requires objections during depositions to be "stated concisely and in a non-argumentative and non-suggestive manner." The Delaware trial courts and this Court are evaluating the desirability of adopting certain of the new Federal Rules, or modifications thereof, and other possible rule changes.

37. While we do not necessarily endorse everything set forth in the *Hall* case, we share Judge Gawthrop's view not only of the impropriety of coaching witnesses on and off the record of the deposition (see supra note 34), but also the impropriety of objections and colloquy which "tend to disrupt the question-and-answer rhythm of a deposition and obstruct the witness's testimony." See 150 F.R.D. at 530. To be sure, there are also occasions when the questioner is abusive or otherwise acts improperly and should be sanctioned. See supra note 31. Although the questioning in the *Liedtke* deposition could have proceeded more crisply, this was not a case where it was the questioner who abused the process.

38. The Court does not condone the conduct of Mr. Thomas in this deposition. Although the Court does not view his conduct with the gravity and revulsion with which it views Mr. Jamail's conduct, in the future the Court expects that counsel in Mr. Thomas's position will have been admitted *pro hac vice* before participating in a deposition. As an officer of the Delaware Court, counsel admitted *pro hac vice* are now clearly on notice that they are expected to put an end to conduct such as that perpetrated by Mr. Jamail on this record.

appearance by Mr. Jamail in a Delaware proceeding. As to (b), this Court and the trial courts of this State will undertake to strengthen the existing mechanisms for dealing with the type of misconduct referred to in this Addendum and the practices relating to admissions *pro hac vice.*

## Notes and Questions

1. *Deposition Details: Attendance, Location, Limitations.* How do you compel attendance at a deposition if the deponent is

a) a nonparty? See Rules 30(a), 37(b), 37(d), 45(a), (c).
b) a party? See Rules 30(a), 37(d).
c) a corporate entity? See Rules 30(b)(6), 37(d).

Where may a deposition be taken

a) of a party? Any limits on this? See Rule 26(c).
b) of a nonparty? See Rules 45(b)(2), 45(c).

2. *Recourse for Deposition Misconduct.* What is the function of the lawyer who "defends" a deposition? Can she object to a question on the ground that it calls for inadmissible hearsay? That it calls for revelation of privileged information? That it is irrelevant to the issues raised by the pleadings? That it already has been asked and answered twice? Eight times? See Rules 26, 30(d), 32(b). Can the defending lawyer ask the deponent questions? (Who pays for this time on the record?) Why might the lawyer insist on asking follow-up questions to clarify the deponent's testimony? See Rule 32. If the defending lawyer becomes overly protective of the deponent and orders her not to answer questions that are *not* beyond the scope of permissible inquiry, what may the deposing lawyer do? Review the Zweifach guide to discovery practice at the beginning of Section A of this chapter for assistance. The Guide also outlines other misconduct at depositions — such as failing to show — and its consequences. See also A Report on the Conduct of Depositions, Federal Bar Council, Committee on Second Circuit Courts, 131 F.R.D. 613 (1990) (discussing various obstructionist deposition practices, including instructing a witness not to answer, and their consequences).

3. *Video Depositions.* Rule 30(b)(3) allows for video depositions, portions of which may be introduced at trial subject to the same conditions that apply to all depositions. What are the potential benefits of video depositions? The pitfalls? Consider the following advice about use of video depositions:

Do not think that video depositions are necessarily better than readings or reenactments. A one-camera deposition can be deadly — particularly if it lasts more than an hour. Few things are more boring than watching a video screen that shows a talking head answering questions from a disembodied voice that comes from off screen.

So if you are going to use a video deposition, there are some important things to do:

a. Use two cameras—one for the lawyers and one for the witness. It does not take great technical expertise, fancy equipment, or extra people. The operator just switches back and forth from one camera to the other, depending on who is talking. That way you won't be stuck with just a talking head.

b. Keep the deposition under an hour—under a half hour is better, if you can. Short and simple is almost always better than long and pedantic.

c. Use a different piece of real or demonstrative evidence every 10 or 15 minutes. Have charts, maps, pictures, or medical illustrations blown up and mounted on an easel so the witness can point out important details that will show up on the video screen. Then when you replay the deposition for the jury, have those same exhibits on the same easel—right next to the video screen. It provides an alternate point of interest for the jury as well as giving a link of reality between the trial and the deposition.

James W. McElhaney, Nine Ways to Use Depositions, 19 No. 2 Litig. 45, 48 (1993). See also Mark A. Neubauer, Videotaping Depositions, 19 No. 4 Litig. 60 (1993); Michael J. Henke, The Taking and Use of Videotaped Depositions, 16 Am. J. Trial Advoc. 151 (1992) (reprinted with permission of the American Bar Association).

4. *Preparing Clients for Deposition.* As much may hinge on the testimony generated at a deposition, lawyers typically prepare their clients for the experience. Most lawyers likely would agree with the following description of basic client preparation for a deposition:

*Q.*   What five basic rules should a lawyer give a witness?
*A.*    1. Witnesses are under oath and are obliged to tell the truth.
       2. Witnesses are not required to answer questions that have not been asked, should not respond to a questioner's tone and should not argue with a questioner.
       3. Witnesses should not volunteer information, guess, speculate or assume.
       4. Witnesses should make certain that they understand the question that has been asked.
       5. A question that calls for a narrative response (*Q:* What happened then?) may be difficult to answer in full. The witness should be advised to preface the answer with "As I recall" or "My current recollection is" so that if something else comes to mind later, the witness will be able to testify to the additional facts without embarrassment.

Steven A. Meyerowitz, Preparing Your Clients for Depositions, 15-JUL Pa. Law. 20 (July 1993). Are there other rules you would add to this list?

### Note: The Appealability of Discovery Orders

In this chapter, you have read a number of appellate cases, including cases from the United States Supreme Court, that turned on discovery issues. Yet as a general matter, discovery rulings are not "final district court orders," within the meaning of 28 U.S.C. § 1291, which sets the jurisdiction of the courts of appeal. Nor in most cases do discovery orders fit within the requirements of 28 U.S.C. § 1292, which provides for an interlocutory appeal of some nonfinal orders.

Yet many discovery orders are, at least in the minds of the parties, dispositive of the issues in a case. Parties may settle or suffer dismissal rather than disclose under what they view as a wrong but ruinous discovery order.

One rather extreme method for getting an appeal is the one pioneered in Hickman v. Taylor. In that case, the lawyer, Samuel B. Fortenbaugh, who refused to turn over the interview notes, underwent a contempt citation, presumably criminal, which is appealable, to bring the issue to a higher court. In an interview years after the case, Fortenbaugh termed the contempt order "a deal" between the judge, opposing counsel, and himself. "We were a pretty clubby group here in Philadelphia, the Admiralty bar," Fortenbaugh remarked. Paul Coady, Dredging the Depths of Hickman v. Taylor, Harv. L. Rec., May 6, 1977, at 2. The opposing lawyer, Abraham Freedman, told an interviewer that in retrospect it was a mistake to agree to the contempt citation because that "created 'sympathy' for Fortenbaugh in some quarters." Id. at 6.

Sometimes the failure to produce some important piece of evidence becomes an issue on appeal after final judgment, as was true in Rozier v. Ford Motor Co., 573 F.2d 1332 (5th Cir. 1978). And at other times, the sanction for discovery violations may be dismissal of the lawsuit, which is most certainly a final order. See Nat'l Hockey League v. Metro. Hockey Club, 427 U.S. 639, 643 (1976) (upholding dismissal of the action for failure to answer interrogatories, "not merely to penalize those whose conduct may be deemed to warrant such a sanction, but to deter those who might be tempted to such conduct in the absence of such a deterrent").

*Upjohn,* and the note case on administering the privilege, both were appeals from judgments about the enforcement of administrative subpoenas. Neither was technically a final order. Here is what the Second Circuit said about appealability in United States v. Constr. Prods. Research, Inc., 73 F.3d 464, 468-469 (2d Cir. 1996):

> The general rule is that orders enforcing subpoenas issued in connection with civil and criminal actions, or grand jury proceedings, are *not* final, and therefore *not* appealable. United States v. Ryan, 402 U.S. 530, 532-33 (1971); Cobbledick v. United States, 309 U.S. 323, 328, (1940); Reich v. National Eng'g & Contracting Co., 13 F.3d 93, 95 (4th Cir. 1993); Kemp v. Gay, 947 F.2d 1493, 1495 (D.C. Cir. 1991). To obtain appellate review, the subpoenaed party must defy the district court's enforcement order, be held in contempt, and then appeal the contempt order, which is regarded as final under § 1291. *Ryan*, 402 U.S. at 532; *Cobbledick*, 309 U.S. at 328; *National Eng'g*, 13 F.3d at 95; *Kemp*, 947 F.2d at 1495. "The purpose of this rule is to discourage parties from pursuing appeals from orders enforcing these subpoenas, which would temporarily halt the district court's litigation process or the grand jury process." *National Eng'g*, 13 F.3d at 95.

There is a different rule, however, in administrative proceedings. A district court order enforcing a subpoena issued by a government agency in connection with an administrative investigation may be appealed immediately without first performing the ritual of obtaining a contempt order (citations omitted). The rationale is that, at least from the district court's perspective, the court's enforcement of an agency subpoena arises out of a proceeding that "may be deemed self-contained, so far as the judiciary is concerned. . . . [T]here is not, as in the case of a grand jury or trial, any further judicial inquiry which would be halted were the offending [subpoenaed party] permitted to appeal." *Cobbledick*, 309 U.S. at 330.

Finally, consider the opinion in *Cordy*. It was rendered by a magistrate judge originally. In many district courts, these subjudicial officers take on major litigation matters, like the pretrial motion to disqualify both the other side's experts, as well as their law firm.

In *Cordy*, supra, Magistrate Kugler disqualified not only the expert, but also the lawyers who had worked with him and their law firm as well. Though he found no wrongdoing or bad faith, his concern was with a certain carelessness on the part of the lawyers in dealing with the expert, as well as the appearance of impropriety.

A magistrate judge's opinion is appealable to the district court under whose direction the magistrate is working. But thenceforth, a motion to disqualify a law firm, like all other discovery matters, may not be appealed before there is a final judgment in the case. In a matter of disqualification of counsel, however, or even of an expert (given his centrality to the case), it is difficult to conceive how the point that the judge made an error might be preserved for appeal. Must the counsel or experts actually involved do a bad job, or worse job than the prior firm or expert would have done to preserve the point? Should they make a record at every major juncture of how much better the previous firm would have handled the matter?

Only extraordinary paths are available to gain review of discovery orders, and it is rare for discovery issues to survive beyond a final order in the case. Can you see why this is? Most civil cases settle without an appealable order of any kind, and among these is a subset of those that settle because of an adverse discovery ruling. For an interesting account of the experience in Texas of allowing parties seriously aggrieved by a discovery order to appeal through an extraordinary writ, see Elizabeth G. Thornburg, Interlocutory Review of Discovery Orders: An Idea Whose Time Has Come, 44 Sw. L.J. 1045 (1990).

## F.   DISCOVERY IN INTERNATIONAL LITIGATION

The Restatement of Foreign Relations asserts that "[n]o aspect of the extension of the American legal system beyond the territorial frontier of the United States has given rise to so much friction as the requests for documents in investigation and litigation in the United States." Restatement (Third) of Foreign Relations Law § 442, Reporters' Notes 1 (1987). In an increasingly global economy, litigation in the United States more and more involves parties and conduct that stretch well beyond the borders of the United States, and foreign litigation increasingly implicates parties and evidence in the United States. As one court recently put it, "transactions involving participants from many lands have become common fare. This world economic interdependence has highlighted the importance of comity, as international commerce depends to a large extent on the ability of merchants to predict the likely consequences of their conduct in overseas markets (citation omitted). This predictability, in turn, depends on cooperation, reciprocity, and respect among nations." Quaak v. KPMG-Belgium, 361 F.3d 11, 19 (1st Cir. 2004).

Rule 26 and the other federal rules we have covered in this chapter regulate discovery in federal courts but they say little about how discovery should proceed in international litigation. How, for instance, should discovery proceed in litigation before foreign tribunals when parties or witnesses with relevant evidence reside in the United States? For nearly 150 years, federal courts have provided assistance to foreign tribunals in gathering evidence in the United States. The traditional mechanism was called a "letter rogatory"—a request from one court to another, delivered through diplomatic channels, to take evidence from a witness within the jurisdiction of the receiving court. But letters rogatory were of strictly limited use. Until Congress passed amendments to the underlying statute in 1948, courts could only meet a request for evidence in a letter rogatory where the government of a foreign country was a party to, or had some interest in, the foreign litigation. And until 1964, the evidence sought had to be testimonial (documentary and other tangible evidence was excluded), the foreign proceeding had to be "judicial," thereby excluding adjudications by administrative and quasi-judicial bodies, and the litigation had to be pending before the courts of a foreign country, making it unclear whether proceedings before international tribunals were covered. On the history of letters rogatory, see Harry Leroy Jones, International Judicial Assistance: Procedural Chaos and a Program for Reform, 62 Yale L.J. 515 (1953); Hans Smit, International Litigation Under the United States Code, 65 Colum. L. Rev. 1015, 1027 (1965). See also 28 U.S.C. §§ 1781-1782.

The statute as it now stands is quite broad, see 28 U.S.C. § 1782, and it has become a centerpiece of global litigation practice particularly in cases involving U.S.-based multinational corporations. In the most significant modern case interpreting the statute, printed below, the Supreme Court addressed the statute's application to a discovery request in federal court arising out of proceedings before a multinational commission that regulates antitrust in the European Union.

### *Intel Corp. v. Advanced Micro Devices, Inc.*
542 U.S. 241 (2004)

Justice Ginsburg delivered the opinion of the Court.

This case concerns the authority of federal district courts to assist in the production of evidence for use in a foreign or international tribunal. In the matter before us, respondent Advanced Micro Devices, Inc. (AMD), filed an antitrust complaint against petitioner Intel Corporation (Intel) with the Directorate-General for Competition (DG-Competition) of the Commission of the European Communities (European Commission or Commission). In pursuit of that complaint, AMD applied to the United States District Court for the Northern District of California, invoking 28 U.S.C. § 1782(a), for an order requiring Intel to produce potentially relevant documents. Section 1782(a) provides that a federal district court "may order" a person "resid[ing]" or "found" in the district to give testimony or produce documents "for use in a proceeding in a foreign or international tribunal . . . upon the application of any interested person."

Concluding that § 1782(a) did not authorize the requested discovery, the District Court denied AMD's application. The Court of Appeals for the Ninth Circuit reversed that determination and remanded the case, instructing the District Court to rule on the merits of AMD's application. In accord with the Court of Appeals, we hold that the District Court had authority under § 1782(a) to entertain AMD's discovery request. . . .

# I

## A

Section 1782 is the product of congressional efforts, over the span of nearly 150 years, to provide federal-court assistance in gathering evidence for use in foreign tribunals. Congress first provided for federal-court aid to foreign tribunals in 1855; requests for aid took the form of letters rogatory forwarded through diplomatic channels. See Act of Mar. 2, 1855, ch. 140, § 2, 10 Stat. 630 (circuit court may appoint "a United States commissioner designated . . . to make the examination of witnesses" on receipt of a letter rogatory from a foreign court); Act of Mar. 3, 1863, ch. 95, § 1, 12 Stat. 769 (authorizing district courts to respond to letters rogatory by compelling witnesses here to provide testimony for use abroad in "suit[s] for the recovery of money or property"). In 1948, Congress substantially broadened the scope of assistance federal courts could provide for foreign proceedings. That legislation, codified as § 1782, eliminated the prior requirement that the government of a foreign country be a party or have an interest in the proceeding. The measure allowed district courts to designate persons to preside at depositions "to be used in *any civil action* pending in any court in a foreign country with which the United States is at peace." Act of June 25, 1948, ch. 646, § 1782, 62 Stat. 949 (emphasis added). The next year, Congress deleted "civil action" from § 1782's text and inserted "judicial proceeding." Act of May 24, 1949, ch. 139, § 93, 63 Stat. 103.

In 1958, prompted by the growth of international commerce, Congress created a Commission on International Rules of Judicial Procedure (Rules Commission) to "investigate and study existing practices of judicial assistance and cooperation between the United States and foreign countries with a view to achieving improvements." Act of Sept. 2, Pub. L. 85-906, § 2 (1958). . . .

As recast in 1964, § 1782 provided for assistance in obtaining documentary and other tangible evidence as well as testimony. Notably, Congress deleted the words "in any judicial proceeding pending in any court in a foreign country," and replaced them with the phrase "in a proceeding in a foreign or international tribunal." . . . Section 1782(a)'s current text reads:

> "The district court of the district in which a person resides or is found may order him to give his testimony or statement or to produce a document or other thing for use in a proceeding in a foreign or international tribunal, including criminal investigations conducted before formal accusation. The order may be made pursuant to a letter rogatory issued, or request made, by a foreign or international tribunal or upon the application of any interested person. . . . The order may prescribe the practice and procedure, which may be in whole or part the practice and procedure of the foreign country or the international tribunal, for taking the testimony or statement or producing the document or other thing . . . [or may be] the Federal Rules of Civil Procedure."
>
> "A person may not be compelled to give his testimony or statement or to produce a document or other thing in violation of any legally applicable privilege."

## B

AMD and Intel are "worldwide competitors in the microprocessor industry." 292 F.3d 664, 665 (9th Cir. 2002). In October 2000, AMD filed an antitrust complaint with the DG-Competition of the European Commission. . . . The Commission exercises responsibility over the wide range of subject areas covered by the European Union treaty; those areas include the treaty provisions, and regulations thereunder, governing competition. The DG-Competition, operating under the Commission's aegis, is the European Union's primary antitrust law enforcer. Within the DG-Competition's domain are anticompetitive agreements (Art. 81) and abuse of dominant market position (Art. 82). Ibid.; EC Treaty 64-65.

AMD's complaint alleged that Intel, in violation of European competition law, had abused its dominant position in the European market through loyalty rebates, exclusive purchasing agreements with manufacturers and retailers, price discrimination, and standard-setting cartels. AMD recommended that the DG-Competition seek discovery of documents Intel had produced in a private antitrust suit, titled Intergraph Corp. v. Intel Corp., brought in a Federal District Court in Alabama.[4] After the

---

4. The Alabama federal court granted summary judgment in Intel's favor in the Intergraph litigation, and the Court of Appeals for the Federal Circuit affirmed. See 253 F.3d 695, [699 (2001)]. A protective order, imposed by the Alabama federal court, governs the confidentiality of all discovery in that case.

DG-Competition declined to seek judicial assistance in the United States, AMD, pursuant to § 1782(a), petitioned the District Court for the Northern District of California [where both companies are headquartered] for an order directing Intel to produce documents discovered in the Intergraph litigation and on file in the federal court in Alabama. AMD asserted that it sought the materials in connection with the complaint it had filed with the European Commission. Ibid.[6]

The District Court denied the application as "[un]supported by applicable authority." Reversing that determination, the Court of Appeals for the Ninth Circuit remanded the case for disposition on the merits. 292 F.3d [at] 669. The Court of Appeals noted two points significant to its decision: § 1782(a) includes matters before "'bodies of a quasi-judicial or administrative nature,'" id., at 667; and, since 1964, the statute's text has contained "[no] requirement that the proceeding be 'pending,'" 292 F.3d, at 667. . . .

On remand, a Magistrate Judge found AMD's application "overbroad," and recommended an order directing AMD to submit a more specific discovery request confined to documents directly relevant to the European Commission investigation. The District Court has stayed further proceedings pending disposition of the questions presented by Intel's petition for certiorari.

We granted certiorari, (citation omitted), in view of the division among the Circuits on the question whether § 1782(a) contains a foreign-discoverability requirement. We now hold that § 1782(a) does not impose such a requirement. We also granted review on two other questions. First, does § 1782(a) make discovery available to complainants, such as AMD, who do not have the status of private "litigants" and are not sovereign agents? Second, must a "proceeding" before a foreign "tribunal" be "pending" or at least "imminent" for an applicant to invoke § 1782(a) successfully? Answering "yes" to the first question and "no" to the second, we affirm the Ninth Circuit's judgment.


## II


To place this case in context, we sketch briefly how the European Commission, acting through the DG-Competition, enforces European competition laws and regulations. The DG-Competition's "overriding responsibility" is to conduct investigations into alleged violations of the European Union's competition prescriptions. On receipt of a complaint or *sua sponte*, the DG-Competition conducts a preliminary investigation. Ibid. In

---

6. AMD's complaint to the Commission alleges, *inter alia*, "that Intel has monopolized the worldwide market for Windows-capable *i.e.* x86, microprocessors." Id., at 55-56. The documents from the *Intergraph* litigation relate to: "(a) the market within which Intel x86 microprocessors compete; (b) the power that Intel enjoys within that market; (c) actions taken by Intel to preserve and enhance its position in the market; and (d) the impact of the actions taken by Intel to preserve and enhance its market position."

that investigation, the DG-Competition "may take into account information provided by a complainant, and it may seek information directly from the target of the complaint." Ibid. "Ultimately, DG Competition's preliminary investigation results in a formal written decision whether to pursue the complaint. If [the DG-Competition] declines to proceed, that decision is subject to judicial review" by the Court of First Instance and, ultimately, by the court of last resort for European Union matters, the Court of Justice for the European Communities (European Court of Justice) (citations omitted).

If the DG-Competition decides to pursue the complaint, it typically serves the target of the investigation with a formal "statement of objections" and advises the target of its intention to recommend a decision finding that the target has violated European competition law. The target is entitled to a hearing before an independent officer, who provides a report to the DG-Competition. Once the DG-Competition has made its recommendation, the European Commission may "dismis[s] the complaint, or issu[e] a decision finding infringement and imposing penalties." The Commission's final action dismissing the complaint or holding the target liable is subject to review in the Court of First Instance and the European Court of Justice.

Although lacking formal "party" or "litigant" status in Commission proceedings, the complainant has significant procedural rights. Most prominently, the complainant may submit to the DG-Competition information in support of its allegations, and may seek judicial review of the Commission's disposition of a complaint (citations omitted).

## III

As "in all statutory construction cases, we begin [our examination of § 1782] with the language of the statute." Barnhart v. Sigmon Coal Co., 534 U.S. 438 (2002). The language of § 1782(a), confirmed by its context, our examination satisfies us, warrants this conclusion: The statute authorizes, but does not require, a federal district court to provide assistance to a complainant in a European Commission proceeding that leads to a dispositive ruling, i.e., a final administrative action both responsive to the complaint and reviewable in court. Accordingly, we reject the categorical limitations Intel would place on the statute's reach.

## A

We turn first to Intel's contention that the catalog of "interested person[s]" authorized to apply for judicial assistance under § 1782(a) includes only "litigants, foreign sovereigns, and the designated agents of those sovereigns," and excludes AMD, a mere complainant before the Commission, accorded only "limited rights." Highlighting § 1782's caption, "[a]ssistance to foreign and international tribunals and to *litigants* before such tribunals," Intel urges that the statutory phrase "any interested person" should be read, correspondingly, to reach only "litigants."

The caption of a statute, this Court has cautioned, "cannot undo or limit that which the [statute's] text makes plain." Trainmen v. Baltimore & Ohio R. Co., 331 U.S. 519, 529 (1947). The text of § 1782(a), "upon the application of any interested person," plainly reaches beyond the universe of persons designated "litigant." No doubt litigants are included among, and may be the most common example of, the "interested person[s]" who may invoke § 1782; we read § 1782's caption to convey no more (citation omitted).

The complainant who triggers a European Commission investigation has a significant role in the process. As earlier observed, in addition to prompting an investigation, the complainant has the right to submit information for the DG-Competition's consideration, and may proceed to court if the Commission discontinues the investigation or dismisses the complaint. Given these participation rights, a complainant "possess[es] a reasonable interest in obtaining [judicial] assistance," and therefore qualifies as an "interested person" within any fair construction of that term. See [Hans] Smit, International Litigation [Under the United States Code, 65 Colum. L. Rev. 1015,] 1027 [(1965)] ("any interested person" is "intended to include not only litigants before foreign or international tribunals, but also foreign and international officials as well as any other person whether he be designated by foreign law or international convention or merely possess a reasonable interest in obtaining the assistance").

### B

We next consider whether the assistance in obtaining documents here sought by an "interested person" meets the specification "for use in a foreign or international tribunal." Beyond question the reviewing authorities, both the Court of First Instance and the European Court of Justice, qualify as tribunals. But those courts are not proof-taking instances. Their review is limited to the record before the Commission. Hence, AMD could "use" evidence in the reviewing courts only by submitting it to the Commission in the current, investigative stage.

Moreover, when Congress established the Commission on International Rules of Judicial Procedure in 1958, it instructed the Rules Commission to recommend procedural revisions "for the rendering of assistance to foreign courts and *quasi-judicial agencies.*" § 2, 72 Stat. 1743 (emphasis added). . . . We have no warrant to exclude the European Commission, to the extent that it acts as a first-instance decisionmaker, from § 1782(a)'s ambit (citations omitted).

### C

Intel also urges that AMD's complaint has not progressed beyond the investigative stage; therefore, no adjudicative action is currently or even imminently on the Commission's agenda.

Section 1782(a) does not limit the provision of judicial assistance to "pending" adjudicative proceedings. In 1964, when Congress eliminated the requirement that a proceeding be "judicial," Congress also deleted the requirement that a proceeding be "pending." . . .

[W]e hold that § 1782(a) requires only that a dispositive ruling by the Commission, reviewable by the European courts, be within reasonable contemplation. . . . Smit, International Litigation[, supra at] 1026 ("It is not necessary . . . for the [adjudicative] proceeding to be pending at the time the evidence is sought, but only that the evidence is eventually to be used in such a proceeding.").

## D

We take up next the foreign-discoverability rule on which lower courts have divided: Does § 1782(a) categorically bar a district court from ordering production of documents when the foreign tribunal or the "interested person" would not be able to obtain the documents if they were located in the foreign jurisdiction?

We note at the outset, and count it significant, that § 1782(a) expressly shields privileged material: "A person may not be compelled to give his testimony or statement or to produce a document or other thing in violation of any legally applicable privilege" (citation omitted). Beyond shielding material safeguarded by an applicable privilege, however, nothing in the text of § 1782 limits a district court's production-order authority to materials that could be discovered in the foreign jurisdiction if the materials were located there. "If Congress had intended to impose such a sweeping restriction on the district court's discretion, at a time when it was enacting liberalizing amendments to the statute, it would have included statutory language to that effect." In re Application of Gianoli Aldunate, 3 F.3d 54, 59 ([2d Cir.] 1993) (citations omitted).[11]

Nor does § 1782(a)'s legislative history suggest that Congress intended to impose a blanket foreign-discoverability rule on the provision of assistance under § 1782(a). The Senate Report observes in this regard that § 1782(a) "leaves the issuance of an appropriate order to the discretion of the court which, in proper cases, may refuse to issue an order or may impose conditions it deems desirable." S. Rep. No. 1580, at 7, U.S. Code Cong. & Admin. News 1964, pp. 3782, 3788.

Intel raises two policy concerns in support of a foreign-discoverability limitation on § 1782(a) aid—avoiding offense to foreign governments, and maintaining parity between litigants. See In re Application of Asta Medica, S. A., 981 F.2d 1, 6 ([1st Cir.] 1992) ("Congress did not seek to place itself on

---

11. Section 1782(a) instructs that a district court's discovery order "may prescribe the practice and procedure, which may be in whole or part the practice and procedure of the foreign country or the international tribunal, for taking the testimony or statement or producing the document or other thing . . . [or may be] the Federal Rules of Civil Procedure." This mode-of-proof-taking instruction imposes no substantive limitation on the discovery to be had.

a collision course with foreign tribunals and legislatures, which have carefully chosen the procedures and laws best suited to their concepts of litigation."). While comity and parity concerns may be important as touchstones for a district court's exercise of discretion in particular cases, they do not permit our insertion of a generally applicable foreign-discoverability rule into the text of § 1782(a).

We question whether foreign governments would in fact be offended by a domestic prescription permitting, but not requiring, judicial assistance. A foreign nation may limit discovery within its domain for reasons peculiar to its own legal practices, culture, or traditions—reasons that do not necessarily signal objection to aid from United States federal courts. See [In re] Bayer [AG], 146 F.3d [188, 194 (3d Cir. 1998)] ("[T]here is no reason to assume that because a country has not adopted a particular discovery procedure, it would take offense at its use.") (citation omitted).[12] A foreign tribunal's reluctance to order production of materials present in the United States similarly may signal no resistance to the receipt of evidence gathered pursuant to § 1782(a). See South Carolina Ins. Co. v. Assurantie Maatschappij "De Zeven Provincien" N.V., [1987] 1 App. Cas. 24 (House of Lords ruled that nondiscoverability under English law did not stand in the way of a litigant in English proceedings seeking assistance in the United States under § 1782). When the foreign tribunal would readily accept relevant information discovered in the United States, application of a foreign-discoverability rule would be senseless. The rule in that situation would serve only to thwart § 1782(a)'s objective to assist foreign tribunals in obtaining relevant information that the tribunals may find useful but, for reasons having no bearing on international comity, they cannot obtain under their own laws.

Concerns about maintaining parity among adversaries in litigation likewise do not provide a sound basis for a cross-the-board foreign-discoverability rule. When information is sought by an "interested person," a district court could condition relief upon that person's reciprocal exchange of information. See Euromepa, S.A. v. R. Esmerian, Inc., 51 F.3d 1095, 1102 (2d Cir. 1995). Moreover, the foreign tribunal can place conditions on its

---

12. Most civil-law systems lack procedures analogous to the pretrial discovery regime operative under the Federal Rules of Civil Procedure. See ALI, ALI/Unidroit Principles and Rules of Transnational Civil Procedure, Proposed Final Draft, Rule 22, Comment R–22E, p. 118 (2004) ("Disclosure and exchange of evidence under the civil-law systems are generally more restricted, or nonexistent."); Hazard, Discovery and the Role of the Judge in Civil Law Jurisdictions, 73 Notre Dame L. Rev. 1017, 1018-1019 (1998) (same). See also [Hans] Smit, Recent Developments [in International Litigation, 35 S. Tex. L. Rev. 215,] 235, n. 93 ("The drafters [of § 1782] were quite aware of the circumstance that civil law systems generally do not have American type pretrial discovery, and do not compel the production of documentary evidence.").

14. A civil-law court, furthermore, might attend to litigant-parity concerns in its merits determination: "In civil law countries, documentary evidence is generally submitted as an attachment to the pleadings or as part of a report by an expert. . . . A civil law court generally rules upon the question of whether particular documentary evidence may be relied upon only in its decision on the merits." Smit, Recent Developments[, supra at] 235-236, n. 94.

acceptance of the information to maintain whatever measure of parity it concludes is appropriate. See *Euromepa*, 51 F.3d, at 1101.[14]

We also reject Intel's suggestion that a § 1782(a) applicant must show that United States law would allow discovery in domestic litigation analogous to the foreign proceeding. Brief for Petitioner 19-20 ("[I]f AMD were pursuing this matter in the United States, U.S. law would preclude it from obtaining discovery of Intel's documents."). Section 1782 is a provision for assistance to tribunals abroad. It does not direct United States courts to engage in comparative analysis to determine whether analogous proceedings exist here. Comparisons of that order can be fraught with danger. For example, we have in the United States no close analogue to the European Commission regime under which AMD is not free to mount its own case in the Court of First Instance or the European Court of Justice, but can participate only as complainant, an "interested person," in Commission-steered proceedings. See L. Ritter, W. Braun, & F. Rawlinson, European Competition Law: A Practitioner's Guide 824-826 (2d ed. 2000) (describing a complaint as a potentially "more certain (and cheaper) alternative to private enforcement through the [European Union's member states'] courts").[16]

## IV

As earlier emphasized, a district court is not required to grant a § 1782(a) discovery application simply because it has the authority to do so (citation omitted). We note below factors that bear consideration in ruling on a § 1782(a) request.

First, when the person from whom discovery is sought is a participant in the foreign proceeding (as Intel is here), the need for § 1782(a) aid generally is not as apparent as it ordinarily is when evidence is sought from a nonparticipant in the matter arising abroad. A foreign tribunal has jurisdiction over those appearing before it, and can itself order them to produce evidence. In contrast, nonparticipants in the foreign proceeding may be outside the foreign tribunal's jurisdictional reach; hence, their evidence, available in the United States, may be unobtainable absent § 1782(a) aid.

Second, as the 1964 Senate Report suggests, a court presented with a § 1782(a) request may take into account the nature of the foreign tribunal, the character of the proceedings underway abroad, and the receptivity of the foreign government or the court or agency abroad to U.S. federal-court judicial assistance. Further, the grounds Intel urged for categorical limitations on § 1782(a)'s scope may be relevant in determining whether a discovery order should be granted in a particular case. Specifically, a district court could consider whether the § 1782(a) request conceals an attempt to

---

16. At oral argument, counsel for AMD observed: "In the United States, we could have brought a private action in the district court for these very same violations. In Europe, our only Europe-wide remedy was to go to the [European Commission]." Tr. of Oral Arg. 33.

circumvent foreign proof-gathering restrictions or other policies of a foreign country or the United States. Also, unduly intrusive or burdensome requests may be rejected or trimmed. See Bayer, 146 F.3d, at 196 (remanding for district-court consideration of "appropriate measures, if needed, to protect the confidentiality of materials"); In re Application of Esses, 101 F.3d 873, 876 ([2d Cir.] 1996) (affirming limited discovery that is neither "burdensome [n]or duplicative").

Intel maintains that, if we do not accept the categorical limitations it proposes, then, at least, we should exercise our supervisory authority to adopt rules barring § 1782(a) discovery here (citations omitted). We decline, at this juncture, to adopt supervisory rules. Any such endeavor at least should await further experience with § 1782(a) applications in the lower courts.[17] The European Commission has stated in *amicus curiae* briefs to this Court that it does not need or want the District Court's assistance. It is not altogether clear, however, whether the Commission, which may itself invoke § 1782(a) aid, means to say "never" or "hardly ever" to judicial assistance from United States courts. Nor do we know whether the European Commission's views on § 1782(a)'s utility are widely shared in the international community by entities with similarly blended adjudicative and prosecutorial functions.

Several facets of this case remain largely unexplored. Intel and its amici have expressed concerns that AMD's application, if granted in any part, may yield disclosure of confidential information, encourage "fishing expeditions," and undermine the European Commission's Leniency Program. Yet no one has suggested that AMD's complaint to the Commission is pretextual. Nor has it been shown that § 1782(a)'s preservation of legally applicable privileges, and the controls on discovery available to the District Court, see, e.g., Fed. Rule Civ. Proc. 26(b)(2) and (c), would be ineffective to prevent discovery of Intel's business secrets and other confidential information.

On the merits, this case bears closer scrutiny than it has received to date. Having held that § 1782(a) authorizes, but does not require, discovery

---

17. The dissent sees a need for "categorical limits" to ward off "expensive, time-consuming battles about discovery." Post, at 2485. That concern seems more imaginary than real. There is no evidence whatsoever, in the 40 years since § 1782(a)'s adoption, see supra, at 2473-2474, of the costs, delays, and forced settlements the dissent hypothesizes. See [Hans] Smit, American Assistance [to Litigation in Foreign and International Tribunals: Section 1782 of Title 28 of the U.S.C. Revisited, 25 Syracuse J. Int'l L. & Comm. 1, 19-20) (1998)] ("The revised section 1782 . . . has been applied in scores of cases. . . . All in all, Section 1782 has largely served the purposes for which it was enacted. . . . [T]here appears to be no reason for seriously considering, at this time, any statutory amendments.").

The Commission, we note, is not obliged to respond to a discovery request of the kind AMD has made. The party targeted in the complaint and in the § 1782(a) application would no doubt wield the laboring oar in opposing discovery, as Intel did here. Not only was there no "need for the Commission to respond," the Commission in fact made no submission at all in the instant matter before it reached this Court.

assistance, we leave it to the courts below to ensure an airing adequate to determine what, if any, assistance is appropriate.

\* \* \*

For the reasons stated, the judgment of the Court of Appeals for the Ninth Circuit is
*Affirmed.*

JUSTICE O'CONNOR took no part in the consideration or decision of this case.

JUSTICE SCALIA, concurring in the judgment.
. . . [T]he Court's disposition is required by the text of the statute. None of the limitations urged by petitioner finds support in the categorical language of 28 U.S.C. § 1782(a). That being so, it is not only (as I think) improper but also quite unnecessary to seek repeated support in the words of a Senate Committee Report—which, as far as we know, not even the full committee, much less the full Senate, much much less the House, and much much much less the President who signed the bill, agreed with. . . .
. . . [B]ecause the statute—the only sure expression of the will of Congress—says what the Court says it says, I join in the judgment.

JUSTICE BREYER, dissenting.
The Court reads the scope of 28 U.S.C. § 1782 to extend beyond what I believe Congress might reasonably have intended. Some countries allow a private citizen to ask a court to review a criminal prosecutor's decision not to prosecute. On the majority's reading, that foreign private citizen could ask an American court to help the citizen obtain information, even if the foreign prosecutor were indifferent or unreceptive (citation omitted). Many countries allow court review of decisions made by any of a wide variety of nonprosecutorial, nonadjudicative bodies. On the majority's reading, a British developer, hoping to persuade the British Housing Corporation to grant it funding to build a low-income housing development, could ask an American court to demand that an American firm produce information designed to help the developer obtain the British grant. (citation omitted). This case itself suggests that an American firm, hoping to obtain information from a competitor, might file an antitrust complaint with the European antitrust authorities, thereby opening up the possibility of broad American discovery—contrary to the antitrust authorities' desires.
One might ask why it is wrong to read the statute as permitting the use of America's court processes to obtain information in such circumstances. One might also ask why American courts should not deal case by case with any problems of the sort mentioned. The answer to both of these questions is that discovery and discovery-related judicial proceedings take time, they are expensive, and cost and delay, or threats of cost and delay, can themselves force parties to settle underlying disputes. See The Brookings Institution, Justice For All: Reducing Costs and Delay in Civil Litigation,

Report of a Task Force 6-7 (1989) (lawyers surveyed estimated that 60% of litigation costs in a typical federal case are attributable to discovery and agreed that high litigation costs are often attributable to abuse of the discovery process) (citation omitted). To the extent that expensive, time-consuming battles about discovery proliferate, they deflect the attention of foreign authorities from other matters those authorities consider more important; they can lead to results contrary to those that foreign authorities desire; and they can promote disharmony among national and international authorities, rather than the harmony that § 1782 seeks to achieve. They also use up domestic judicial resources and crowd our dockets.

That is why I believe the statute, while granting district courts broad authority to order discovery, nonetheless must be read as subject to some categorical limits, at least at the outer bounds — a matter that today's decision makes even more important. Those limits should rule out instances in which it is virtually certain that discovery (if considered case by case) would prove unjustified.

This case does not require us to find a comprehensive set of limits. But it does suggest two categorical limitations, which I would adopt. First, when a foreign entity possesses few tribunal-like characteristics, so that the applicability of the statute's word "tribunal" is in serious doubt, then a court should pay close attention to the foreign entity's own view of its "tribunal"-like or non-"tribunal"-like status. By paying particular attention to the views of the very foreign nations that Congress sought to help, courts would better achieve Congress' basic cooperative objectives in enacting the statute (citation omitted).

The concept of paying special attention to administrative views is well established in American law. Cf. Chevron U.S.A. Inc. v. [Nat. Res. Def.] Council, Inc., 467 U.S. 837, 843 (1984). Like American administrators, foreign administrators are likely to understand better than American courts their own job and, for example, how discovery rights might affect their ability to carry out their responsibilities. I can think of no reason why Congress would have intended a court to pay less attention to the foreign entity's view of the matter than courts ordinarily pay to a domestic agency's understanding of the workings of its own statute.

Second, a court should not permit discovery where both of the following are true: (1) A private person seeking discovery would not be entitled to that discovery under foreign law, and (2) the discovery would not be available under domestic law in analogous circumstances. The Federal Rules of Civil Procedure, for example, make only limited provisions for nonlitigants to obtain certain discovery. See Fed. Rule Civ. Proc. 27. The limitations contained in the Rules help to avoid discovery battles launched by firms simply seeking information from competitors. Where there is benefit in permitting such discovery, and the benefit outweighs the cost of allowing it, one would expect either domestic law or foreign law to authorize it. If, notwithstanding the fact that it would not be allowed under either domestic or foreign law, there is some special need for the discovery in a particular instance, one would expect to find foreign governmental or intergovernmental authorities making the case for that need. Where *none* of these circumstances is present, what benefit could offset the obvious costs to the competitor and to our courts? I cannot think of any.

Application of either of these limiting principles would require dismissal of this discovery proceeding. First, the Commission of the European Communities' (Commission) antitrust authority's status as a "tribunal" is questionable. In many respects, the Commission more closely resembles a prosecuting authority, say, the Department of Justice's Antitrust Division, than an administrative agency that adjudicates cases, say, the Federal Trade Commission. To my knowledge, those who decide whether to bring an antitrust prosecution on the Commission's behalf are not judges. See [Wouter P.J.] Wils, The Combination of the Investigative and Prosecutorial Function and the Adjudicative Function in EC Antitrust Enforcement: A Legal and Economic Analysis, 27 World Competition Law and [Econ. Rev.] 201, 207 (June 2004) (explaining, in an article written by a member of the Commission's Legal Service, that "in European Commission proceedings there is no independent initial adjudicator . . . and the Commissioners do not sit as judges hearing directly both sides of the case"). They do not adjudicate adversary proceedings on the basis of proofs and argument. Nor, as the majority appears to recognize, does the later availability of a reviewing court matter where "review is limited to the record before the Commission," and "AMD could 'use' evidence in the reviewing courts only by submitting it to the Commission in the current, investigative stage." At a minimum, then, the question whether the Commission is a "tribunal" is unclear. See Wils, supra, at 207-209 (noting the scholarly and legal debate as to whether the Commission's antitrust investigation and enforcement activities qualify it as an "'independent and impartial tribunal'" for purposes of the European Convention on Human Rights).

At the same time, the Commission has told this Court that it is not a "tribunal" under the Act. It has added that, should it be considered, against its will, a "tribunal," its "ability to carry out its governmental responsibilities" will be seriously threatened. Brief for Commission of the European Communities as Amicus Curiae 2. Given the potential need for the Commission to respond when a private firm (including an American company) files a complaint with the Commission and seeks discovery in an American court (say, from a competitor), its concerns are understandable.

The Commission's characterization of its own functions is, in my view, entitled to deference. The majority disregards the Commission's opinion and states categorically that "the Commission is a § 1782(a) 'tribunal' when it acts as a first-instance decisionmaker." In so ignoring the Commission, the majority undermines the comity interests § 1782 was designed to serve and disregards the maxim that we construe statutes so as to "hel[p] the potentially conflicting laws of different nations work together in harmony—a harmony particularly needed in today's highly interdependent commercial world." F. Hoffmann-LaRoche Ltd. v. Empagran S. A., [542 U.S. 155, 164-165 (2004)].

The second limiting factor is also present. Neither Advanced Micro Devices, Inc. (AMD), nor any comparable private party would be able to obtain the kind of discovery AMD seeks, either in Europe or in the United States. In respect to Europe, the Commission has told us that any person in the world is free to file a complaint with the Commission, but it is the Commission that then investigates. The private complainant lacks any authority to obtain discovery of business secrets and commercial information. In respect to the United States, AMD is a nonlitigant, apart from this discovery proceeding. Conditions under which a nonlitigant may obtain discovery are limited. AMD does not suggest that it meets those conditions, or that it is comparable in any other way to one who might obtain discovery under roughly analogous circumstances. In addition, the material it seeks is under a protective order.

What is the legal source of these limiting principles? In my view, they, and perhaps others, are implicit in the statute itself, given its purpose and use of the terms "tribunal" and "interested person." § 1782(a). But even if they are not, this Court's "supervisory powers . . . permit, at the least, the promulgation of procedural rules governing the management of litigation," not to mention "'procedures deemed desirable from the viewpoint of sound judicial practice although in nowise commanded by statute or by the Constitution.'" Thomas v. Arn, 474 U.S. 140, 146-147 (1985) (quoting Cupp v. Naughten, 414 U.S. 141, 146 (1973)). See also Dickerson v. United States, 530 U.S. 428, 437 (2000) ("This Court has supervisory authority over the federal courts, and we may use that authority to prescribe rules of evidence and procedure that are binding in those tribunals"). Intel Corp. has asked us to exercise those powers in this case. We should do so along the lines that I suggest; consequently, we should reverse the judgment below and order the complaint in this case dismissed.

I respectfully dissent from the Court's contrary determination.

## Notes and Questions

1. As the Court emphasized in Intel, production under § 1782 is *not* automatic. The Court noted that a district court has discretion in whether to grant a § 1782 request. Factors relevant to the exercise of that discretion include 1) whether the applicant seeks information from individuals who are not party to the foreign proceeding and thus not subject to the discovery powers of the foreign tribunal, 2) whether the requests are "unduly intrusive or burdensome," 3) "the nature of the foreign tribunal," 4) "the character of the proceedings underway abroad," 5) "the receptivity of the foreign government or the court or agency abroad to U.S. federal-court judicial assistance," and 6) "whether the § 1782 request conceals an attempt to circumvent foreign proof-gathering restrictions or other policies of a foreign country or the United States." Id. at 244-245.

Notice that, apart from the limitation covering privileged material, there is no requirement that district courts consider whether "United States law would allow discovery in domestic litigation analogous to the foreign proceeding." Id. at 263. That means Intel can be forced to disclose information to the European Commission, with the aid of the federal courts, which a federal court could not order disclosed in domestic litigation. Isn't Justice Breyer correct to worry that this can invite abuse of § 1782 for "fishing expeditions"?

2. What is the risk in allowing a party to obtain discovery beyond the limits of the discovery laws of both the foreign and domestic jurisdictions in an antitrust case like this? Certainly there is a question about whether district courts, which already have overcrowded dockets, should be drawn into discovery of this kind. At the limit, moreover, this type of discovery risks becoming untethered from the legal systems whose substantive and procedural law would be applied to any evidence produced. On the other hand, if Intel is not engaged in anti-competitive behavior in the EU market, why should it fear open discovery?

3. Federal courts can also be drawn into disputes involving discovery requests for evidence and information *held overseas* to aid in litigation in the United States. Consider Quaak v. KPMG-Belgium, 361 F.3d 11 (1st Cir. 2004). *Quaak* is a consolidation of several class actions and numerous other suits against the Belgian accounting firm KPMG-B alleging securities fraud in the firm's role as the auditor for a publicly traded company that collapsed under financial mismanagement. The cases were consolidated in Massachusetts federal district court. When the case reached pretrial discovery, plaintiffs moved to compel production of relevant auditing records and other work papers located in Belgium. KPMG-B refused to produce, arguing that Article 458 of the Belgian Criminal Code prohibits auditors from disclosing confidential client information. When the district court nevertheless granted plaintiffs' motion to compel, KPMG-B filed an *ex parte* action with a Belgian court in Brussels "seeking to enjoin the securities fraud plaintiffs from 'taking any step' to proceed with the requested discovery. To ensure compliance, they asked the Belgian court to impose a fine of one million Euros for each violation of the proposed injunction." Id. at 15. The Belgian court declined to proceed *ex parte*, directed notice to the U.S. plaintiffs, and scheduled a hearing on the injunction. Plaintiffs responded by immediately seeking an injunction from the Massachusetts district court against KPMG-B to prevent it from proceeding with its suit in Belgium. The court granted the "anti-suit injunction," ordering KPMG-B "to withdraw forthwith its writ in the Court of First Instance in Brussels and . . . not to proceed with the hearing . . . [and to] file proof of compliance with this order." Id. The court also refused to stay its order compelling production of the requested documents.

KPMG-B appealed to the First Circuit, arguing that the international anti-suit injunction was inconsistent with principles of comity and the presumption in favor of concurrent jurisdiction. In a carefully reasoned opinion the First Circuit followed the Second, Third, Sixth, and D.C. Circuits in endorsing a "conservative approach for gauging the propriety of international anti-suit injunctions." Id. at 17 (citing cases). According to this approach, "considerations of international comity must be given substantial weight—and those considerations ordinarily establish a rebuttable presumption against the issuance of an order that has the effect of halting foreign judicial proceedings." Id. at 18. See also Goss Int'l Corp. v. Man Roland Druckmaschinen Aktiengesellschaft, 491 F.3d 355 (8th Cir. 2007).

The Fifth, Seventh, and Ninth Circuits have adopted a more permissive approach toward granting international anti-suit injunctions whenever, as the *Quaak* court put it, parallel international proceedings "would frustrate the speedy and efficient determination of the [local] case." *Quaak* at 17 (citing Kaepa, Inc. v. Achilles Corp., 76 F.3d 624, 627 (5th Cir. 1996); Philips Med. Sys. Int'l B.V. v. Bruetman, 8 F.3d 600, 605 (7th Cir. 1993); and Seattle Totems Hockey Club, Inc. v. Nat'l Hockey League, 652 F.2d 852, 855-856 (9th Cir. 1981)); cf. Canon Latin Am., Inc. v. Lantech, S.A., 508 F.3d 597 (11th Cir. 2007).

Even applying its conservative approach, however, the court upheld the international anti-suit injunction against KPMG-B. Characterizing KPMG-B's Belgian action as an "attempt to chill legitimate discovery by in terrorem tactics [and to] quash the practical power of the United States courts," the court reasoned that "[w]here, as here, a party institutes a foreign action in a blatant attempt to evade the rightful authority of the forum court, the need for an antisuit injunction crests." *Quaak* at 20 (internal quotations and citation omitted).

Assuming Article 458 of the Belgian Criminal Code is valid, and that none of the exceptions to the confidentiality rule it creates apply to this case, is it right to say that KPMG-B is trying to quash or evade the authority of the federal court in Massachusetts? Isn't it just trying to assure that the federal court does not negate its rights and duties under Belgian law? What other options did KPMG-B have facing the court's order compelling production of the documents? The First Circuit admonishes that KPMG-B could have "exhaust[ed] its position in the federal judicial system before attempting to sidetrack that system." Id. at 21. It also might have "sought clarification from the Belgian courts without raising the stakes to a level that necessarily precipitated a direct conflict with the pending securities fraud action." Id. Would either course have been effective? Wouldn't both have favored the U.S. plaintiffs proceeding against KPMG-B in U.S. courts?

# 4 *Dispositions and Adjudications*

Approximately 98 percent of cases filed in federal court drop out of the system before trial—most often by settlement, but sometimes by rulings on motions to dismiss or to enter summary judgment. Leonidas Ralph Mecham, Judicial Business of the Federal Courts: 2001 Annual Report of the Director 154 (2001); Stephen C. Yeazell, The Misunderstood Consequences of Modern Civil Process, 1994 Wis. L. Rev. 631, 633 & n.6 (1996) (reporting a settlement rate of 95 percent). As Professor Yeazell has observed, "[w]e have moved from a trial-based procedure to one centered on the events that occur instead of trial and which typically head off trial." Id. at 639. He explains:

> Specific procedural changes achieved this reallocation of judicial resources. In 1938, the Federal Rules reoriented the trial process of the federal courts. They did not eliminate trial. But they interposed a number of new steps between the commencement of litigation and trial, each of which could yield a judicial ruling and thus require judicial time. As a consequence, trial, once the center of judicial attention, became one among many tasks. Even more significant, these other tasks often produced enough information or sufficiently exhausted resources that the parties settled. Courts now devote the bulk of their civil work to such pretrial tasks—ruling on discovery disputes, deciding joinder issues, conducting pretrial and settlement conferences, and, sadly, punishing lawyers for misbehavior during this phase of proceedings. This work is important, required, and often practically dispositive. But it does not, by itself, produce a judgment that finally disposes of the case in the way that a trial, successful summary judgment motion, or a dismissal on the pleadings does. Instead, these judicial decisions provide a framework within which the parties decide how to evaluate settlement or abandonment of the underlying lawsuits. These developments suggest a quiet revolution in the process of civil litigation in the United States.

Id. The same quiet revolution has occurred in state courts. A 2003 study of 21 states conducted by the National Center for State Courts reports that only 8 percent of civil cases ended in a jury or bench trial. Brian J. Ostrom et al., Examining the Work of State Courts, 2003: A National Perspective from the Court Statistics Project 22 (2004). The remaining 92 percent of the caseload was disposed of either by settlement, voluntary dismissal, default judgment, or summary judgment. Id. See also Paula Hannaford Agor et al., The Landscape of Civil Litigation in State Courts, Nat'l Ctr. for State Cts. (2015).

What are the consequences of this quiet revolution for the balance of power between judges and juries? Why, as a society, do we constantly re-imagine jury trials in television, film, and fiction, when they are no longer occurring very much in fact? As the following excerpt describes, the actual administration of justice is becoming "enclosed":

American trials have always been popular forms of public entertainment. Court days were widely attended well into the nineteenth century, and the trial scene has been, and is now, endlessly reproduced in popular culture. Law, as Tocqueville put it, has become our "vulgar tongue," channeling all manner of social interests and disputes into adversarial space (both real and imagined) and into the discourse of rights. A camera shot of the wood-paneled witness box adjacent to and below the judge's bench; the standard reverse shot from over the shoulder of a testifying witness to the litigants whose case her testimony helps or hurts and interested community members sitting behind the bar; the movement and sound of the judge's gavel; jurors seated in double rows at right angles to the judge's bench in a larger wood paneled box near the witness stand—each of these images not only operates as a common synecdoche for trial in popular consciousness, but for the local practice of justice as well.

Due process thus has a readily identifiable spatial structure with deep historical and cultural resonance. It is the trial courtroom. And notwithstanding perennial accusations that due process of law is a guarantee of "wide, varied, and indefinite content,"[1] courts and legal commentators have systematically relied upon the courtroom trial as an organizing metaphor. In one of the few U.S. Supreme Court cases dealing with the procedural incidents of the federal right before the Civil War, Murray's Lessee v. Hoboken Land and Improvement Co., the Court directly identified "due process of law" with the "by the law of the land" clause in Magna Carta.[2] It did so on the premise that "'due process of law' generally implies an actor, reus, judex, regular allegations, opportunity to answer, and a trial according to some settled course of judicial proceeding."[3] . . . We know what due process of law is by looking to traditions established in the local practice of justice.

As in many cases decided by antebellum state courts, this interpretive method canonized trial by jury as the touchstone. Even the recognition of exceptions to trial by jury helped to define the rule as procedural innovations were measured for their degree of deviance from the incidents of jury trial. Modern caselaw is in accord. Indeed, modern courts are constantly imagining the adversarial space of the trial courtroom as they decide what procedures should govern pre-trial procedures, alternative forms of dispute resolution, and the operation of the modern administrative state.[4] Moreover,

[1.] Rodney Mott, Due Process of Law: A Historical and Analytical Treatise 123 (1926).

[2.] 59 U.S. 272, 276 (1855).

[3.] Id. at 280.

[4.] See Turner v. Rogers, 131 S. Ct. 2507 (2011); Hamdi v. Rumsfeld, 542 U.S. 507 (2004); United Mine Workers v. Bagwell, 512 U.S. 821 (1994); Cleveland Bd. of Educ. v. Loudermill, 470 U.S. 532 (1984); Mathews v. Eldridge, 424 U.S. 319 (1976); Goldberg v. Kelly, 397 U.S. 254 (1970); see also Jerry Mashaw, Due Process in the Administrative State (1985); Richard C. Reuben, Constitutional Gravity: A Unitary Theory of Alternative Dispute Resolution and Public Civil Justice, 47 UCLA L. Rev. 949 (2000).

because due process is a constitutional guarantee, legislators, administrators, and others engaged in designing private alternatives to adversary adjudication are bound by the same metaphor. The adversarial space of the trial courtroom thus suffuses both popular and legal conceptions of what it means for justice to be done. . . .

What then are we to make of the fact that the actual use of space from which the metaphor derives is diminishing? Lawyers and laypeople speak the vernacular of courtroom trial, and we are constantly imagining adversarial space and displacing it onto other public, private, and fictional venues for decision making, but actual trials are rare indeed. *What are the consequences of the touchstone of due process existing only as metaphor?* Not all metaphors are conceits, of course, and dead metaphors are among the most powerful. Moreover, as long as other procedures provide reliable evidence, accurate decision making, and efficient resolution, it is not obvious that the practice of justice, local and otherwise, is threatened by the disappearance of courtroom trial.

But there are reasons to worry. To begin with, private systems of dispute resolution rely parasitically on courtroom trial. Existing systems are literally and figuratively "court-annexed." Even systems that operate independently of the courts rely heavily on the expertise of a now-diminishing class of the legal profession — lawyers with extensive jury trial experience. . . . Settlement is surely possible beyond the shadow of the courthouse, and without trial lawyers, but, for the most part, we have not constructed alternative dispute resolution systems on alternative expertise.

Second, although trial is not cheap, the social costs associated with systems of dispute resolution that occupy no public space are considerable. Sealed settlements allow repeat offenders to persist in malfeasance for years without public scrutiny or accountability;[5] confidentiality rules in alternative dispute resolution promote open internal deliberation but also conceal coercion and bias;[6] and even when courts do decide cases, unpublished dispositions and de-publication of decisions . . . challenge the most basic rule-of-law values. One noteworthy study has shown that the plaintiff win rate in employment discrimination cases at the federal district court level "is four times higher in published than in unpublished opinions."[7] There is thus an already massive and steadily expanding body of subterranean law.

Third, as courtroom trial becomes mere metaphor, the substantive rights trial used to define have become mere modes of declamation in well-funded, high profile, fully litigated cases increasingly dissociated from the action of courts and dispute resolution practitioners in run-of-the-mill cases. This is

[5.] On confidential settlements and sealed records in the Catholic priest sexual abuse scandals, see Walter V. Robinson et al., Scores of Priests Involved in Sex Abuse Cases, Bos. Globe, Jan. 31, 2002, at A1; Catholic Church Mishandled Reports of Sex Abuse, Nat'l Pub. Radio (Aug. 11, 2010), http://www.npr.org/templates/story/story.php?storyId=126390884. See also Symposium, Secrecy in Litigation, 81 Chi.-Kent L. Rev. 301 (2006).

[6.] Timothy Hedeen, Coercion and Self-Determination in Court-Connected Mediation, 26 Just. Sys. J. 1 (2005).

[7.] Ruth Colker, The Americans with Disabilities Act: A Windfall for Defendants, 34 Harv. C.R.-C.L. L. Rev. 99, 99-100, 104, 105 (1999) (citations omitted).

not a tension between law on the books or the glittering generalities of rights talk, on the one hand, and law in action, on the other; but a problem of law off the books altogether, law operating in fully enclosed spaces. With run-of-the-mill cases increasingly decided in private, confidential, and sealed spaces, the discursive habits, the legal and cultural practices, and, above all, the rules of decision governing their resolution, are rendered opaque—in some instances, unknowable. The displacement and private enclosure of adjudicative space thus alters the very epistemology of justice.

Finally, outside the courtroom, and increasingly within it, the right to a meaningful hearing is more honored in the breach. . . . [R]ules permitting trial judges to take cases away from juries before and after trial have steadily expanded;[8] . . . the constitutional standard for the right to effective assistance of counsel in criminal cases is now so strict that a jurisprudence has developed to specify precisely how long an attorney must be asleep during trial to warrant reversal;[9] in civil cases, counsel is rarely provided by the state and beyond the means of most poor and middle-income litigants;[10] and in administrative settings, massive caseloads and inadequate judicial review have led to wide variation in outcomes and shockingly inadequate attention to the factual record in individual cases.[11] Not only the epistemology of justice but the basic practices that ensure decision on the merits are shifting. . . .

[Security concerns have also hindered basic physical access to courthouses and the courtrooms within. —Eds.] [T]rials have continued to rely upon *viva voce* testimony, but the perceived need for enclosure—a need present in even the earliest [courthouses]—has intensified. Metal detectors, permanent identification checkpoints supervised by armed sheriffs or federal marshals, diversion from traditional public entrances, glass walls and even closed-circuit television dividing public from the adversarial space of courtrooms, are all regularly employed in the name of enhancing courthouse security, increasing efficiency, and preventing disruption. Even for parties to litigation, security measures have become more elaborate. A line of cases now delimits the degree of state force that can be deployed to ensure courtroom security without undermining the presumption of innocence in criminal trials. Finally, a gradual but steady shift of authority from juries to judges and

[8.] See Ashcroft v. Iqbal, 556 U.S. 662 (2009); Bell Atlantic Corp. v. Twombly, 550 U.S. 544 (2007); Celotex v. Catrett, 477 U.S. 317 (1986); see also Suja A. Thomas, Why Summary Judgment Is Unconstitutional, 93 Va. L. Rev. 139 (2007). On increased judicial discretion after verdict, see Galloway v. United States, 319 U.S. 372 (1943).

[9.] See Burdine v. Johnson, 262 F.3d 336, 349 (5th Cir. 2001) (en banc) (reversing panel decision that upheld capital sentence where defense lawyer was asleep during trial but expressly "declin[ing] to adopt a per se rule that any dozing by defense counsel during trial merits a presumption of prejudice"); *see also* Tippins v. Walker, 77 F.3d 682, 685-90 (2d Cir. 1996); Javor v. United States, 724 F.2d 831, 832-35 (9th Cir. 1984).

[10.] Deborah Rhode, Access to Justice (2004); David Luban, Taking Out the Adversary: The Assault on Progressive Public Interest Lawyers, 91 Calif. L. Rev. 209 (2003); see also Lassiter v. Dept. of Social Services, 452 U.S. 18 (1981).

[11.] For a recent example drawn from asylum cases, see Iao v. Gonzales, 450 F.3d 530, 533-35 (7th Cir. 2005); see also Immigration Judges, TRAC Immigration (July 31, 2006), http://trac.syr.edu/immigration/reports/160/.

from judges to dispute resolution "neutrals" has moved the site of adjudication from courtrooms to the more enclosed spaces of judges' chambers and private conference rooms.

Enclosure offers control, efficiency, and rationality in the administration of justice. By specializing the use of space and restricting access, disruption and surprise can be avoided, deference can be enforced in participants and observers, extraneous or prejudicial information and events can be excluded from the perceptual range of decisionmakers, and the ungovernable passions social and legal conflict provoke can be minimized to promote rational deliberation. No system of dispute resolution can function without enclosure; all depend on it to prevent vigilance from descending into vigilantism.

But the enclosure of justice should not be conflated with justice itself; nor should the desire for enclosure be conflated with the desire that justice be done. To enclose justice is not, in the end, to do justice, or to ensure that it will be done.

Norman W. Spaulding, The Enclosure of Justice: Courthouse Architecture, Due Process, and the Dead Metaphor of Trial, 24 Yale J.L. & Human. 311, 332-340 (2012) (emphasis added).

In the materials that follow in this chapter and the next, we take up some of the specific procedural rules that have produced greater enclosure in the administration of justice. In section A, we discuss some of the technically nondispositive judicial activities and procedures that have a great impact on the outcome in the immediate case, as well as succeeding ones. Keep in mind what you know about discovery and motions on the pleadings—other pretrial activities that may result in a final disposition of the case. Settled cases are never reviewed by an appellate court, even though the impetus for settlement may have been an incorrect ruling. One of the results of the new emphasis on the pretrial period is a tremendous increase in the trial judge's power, and in private ordering by the parties also.

In section B, we deal with pretrial dispositions that include judgment—in particular, summary judgment—and in sections C and D we briefly introduce the procedural mechanics involved when a case goes to trial. The burgeoning universe of *alternatives* to traditional adversarial litigation, broadly referred to as "alternative dispute resolution" procedures, is covered in Chapter 5.

## A. ENDING LITIGATION WITHOUT JUDGMENT: SETTLEMENTS, PRETRIAL CONFERENCES, AND OTHER MANEUVERS

### Problem Case: Pressured to Settle

You are a lawyer member of the Advisory Committee considering the following Rule changes designed to promote settlement:

Rule 16: Change to make at least one pretrial conference mandatory, at which the possibility of settlement and the use of extrajudicial procedures to resolve the dispute must be discussed.

Rule 68: Change to provide for an offer of settlement from either party, and for sanctions, including attorneys' fees, to be imposed for the rejection of any reasonable offer, regardless of which party prevails.

What would be your position on making settlement discussion mandatory and its rejection costly? Would you feel differently about it if you were a judge?

## 1.   Settlement

Settlement—often actively encouraged by trial judges—deflects many cases from the trial stage and insulates resolutions from searching appellate review. Professor Yeazell describes this process as follows:

> Judges have long asked parties informally whether they wish to settle. Under the original version of the Rules, judges who were so inclined used the pretrial conference, authorized but not required by Rule 16, as an occasion for doing so. In 1983, and again in 1993, Rule 16 was revised to make explicit the propriety of such efforts. Congress has further encouraged judges to direct more attention to this area. One can therefore expect to see more judges encouraging settlement. Some have applauded, while others have criticized this tendency. But the debate has focused on the inherent desirability of such a rule for judges, rather than on the redistribution of power the rule entails.
>
> For the litigants, the summary jury trial and settlement discussions provide another stage of the pretrial process on which time and professional effort must be focused. This stage differs from discovery and joinder motions because it is controlled by the judge rather than the parties; parties can suggest that settlement would be useful, but the judge has almost unbounded discretion to conduct such proceedings whether or not the parties think it useful. Moreover, the amount of such effort lies within the judge's discretion: an enthusiastic judge may order a summary jury trial, a minitrial, arbitration, *and* a settlement conference. The aim of such process is, of course, to avoid a trial. If the judge succeeds, he incidentally removes his prior rulings from appellate scrutiny.

Yeazell, supra, 1994 Wis. L. Rev. at 657.

Of course, settlement may also serve other purposes. The most commonly cited advantages are that it avoids the expense of protracted proceedings and may increase party satisfaction (and thus compliance) with the outcome. The preference for settlement over trial is so strong that it prompted at least one judge to quip that "a bad settlement is almost always better than a good trial." In re Warner Commc'ns Sec. Litig., 618 F. Supp. 735, 740 (S.D.N.Y. 1985), *aff'd*, 798 F.2d 35 (2d Cir. 1986). The following case addresses Fed. R. Civ. P. 68, which promotes settlement (and its efficiencies) by making it potentially costly to decline a settlement offer. Is the Rule unduly coercive, or is it a reasonable inducement to take all serious settlement offers seriously?

### *Marek v. Chesny*
473 U.S. 1 (1985)

CHIEF JUSTICE BURGER delivered the opinion of the Court.

We granted certiorari to decide whether attorney's fees incurred by a plaintiff subsequent to an offer of settlement under Federal Rule of Civil Procedure 68 must be paid by the defendant under 42 U.S.C. § 1988, when the plaintiff recovers a judgment less than the offer.

### I

Petitioners, three police officers, in answering a call on a domestic disturbance, shot and killed respondent's adult son. Respondent, in his own behalf and as administrator of his son's estate, filed suit against the officers in the United States District Court under 42 U.S.C. § 1983 and state tort law.

Prior to trial, petitioners made a timely offer of settlement "for a sum, including costs now accrued and attorney's fees, of ONE HUNDRED THOUSAND ($100,000) DOLLARS." Respondent did not accept the offer. The case went to trial and respondent was awarded $5,000 on the state-law "wrongful death" claim, $52,000 for the § 1983 violation, and $3,000 in punitive damages.

Respondent filed a request for $171,692.47 in costs, including attorney's fees. This amount included costs incurred after the settlement offer. Petitioners opposed the claim for postoffer costs, relying on Federal Rule of Civil Procedure 68, which shifts to the plaintiff all "costs" incurred subsequent to an offer of judgment not exceeded by the ultimate recovery at trial. Petitioners argued that attorney's fees are part of the "costs" covered by Rule 68. The District Court agreed with petitioners and declined to award respondent "costs, including attorney's fees, incurred after the offer of judgment." 547 F. Supp. 542, 547 (N.D. Ill. 1982). The parties subsequently agreed that $32,000 fairly represented the allowable costs, including attorney's fees, accrued prior to petitioners' offer of settlement. Respondent appealed the denial of postoffer costs.

The Court of Appeals reversed. . . .

### II

. . . The plain purpose of Rule 68 is to encourage settlement and avoid litigation. Advisory Committee Note on Rules of Civil Procedure, Report of Proposed Amendments, 5 F.R.D. 433, 483 n.1 (1946), 28 U.S.C. App., p. 637;

Delta Air Lines, Inc. v. August, 450 U.S. 346, 352 (1981). The Rule prompts both parties to a suit to evaluate the risks and costs of litigation, and to balance them against the likelihood of success upon trial on the merits. This case requires us to decide whether the offer in this case was a proper one under Rule 68, and whether the term "costs" as used in Rule 68 includes attorney's fees awardable under 42 U.S.C. § 1988.

## A

The first question we address is whether petitioners' offer was valid under Rule 68. Respondent contends that the offer was invalid because it lumped petitioners' proposal for damages with their proposal for costs. Respondent argues that Rule 68 requires that an offer must separately recite the amount that the defendant is offering in settlement of the substantive claim and the amount he is offering to cover accrued costs. Only if the offer is bifurcated, he contends, so that it is clear how much the defendant is offering for the substantive claim, can a plaintiff possibly assess whether it would be wise to accept the offer. He apparently bases this argument on the language of the Rule providing that the defendant "may serve upon the adverse party an offer to allow judgment to be taken against him for the money or property or to the effect specified in his offer, *with costs then accrued*" (emphasis added).

The Court of Appeals rejected respondent's claim, holding that "an offer of the money or property or to the specified effect is, by force of the rule itself, 'with'—that is, plus 'costs then accrued,' whatever the amount of those costs is." 720 F.2d at 476. We, too, reject respondent's argument. We do not read Rule 68 to require that a defendant's offer itemize the respective amounts being tendered for settlement of the underlying substantive claim and for costs.

The critical feature of this portion of the Rule is that the offer be one that allows *judgment to be taken against the defendant for both the damages caused by the challenged conduct and the costs then accrued*. In other words, the drafters' concern was not so much with the particular components of offers, but with the *judgments* to be allowed against defendants. If an offer recites that costs are included or specifies an amount for costs, and the plaintiff accepts the offer, the judgment will necessarily include costs; if the offer does not state that costs are included and an amount for costs is not specified, the court will be obliged by the terms of the Rule to include in its judgment an additional amount which in its discretion, see Delta Air Lines, Inc. v. August, supra, at 362, 365 (Powell, J., concurring), it determines to be sufficient to cover the costs. In either case, however, the offer has *allowed* judgment to be entered against the defendant both for damages caused by the challenged conduct and for costs. Accordingly, it is immaterial whether the offer recites that costs are included, whether it specifies the amount the defendant is allowing for costs, or, for that matter, whether it refers to costs at all. As long as the offer does not implicitly or explicitly provide that the judgment not include costs, a timely offer will be valid.

This construction of the Rule best furthers the objective of the Rule, which is to encourage settlements. If defendants are not allowed to make lump-sum offers that would, if accepted, represent their total liability, they would understandably be reluctant to make settlement offers. As the Court of Appeals observed, "many a defendant would be unwilling to make a binding settlement offer on terms that left it exposed to liability for attorney's fees in whatever amount the court might fix on motion of the plaintiff." 720 F.2d at 477.

Contrary to respondent's suggestion, reading the Rule in this way does not frustrate plaintiffs' efforts to determine whether defendants' offers are adequate. At the time an offer is made, the plaintiff knows the amount in damages caused by the challenged conduct. The plaintiff also knows, or can ascertain, the costs then accrued. A reasonable determination whether to accept the offer can be made by simply adding these two figures and comparing the sum to the amount offered. Respondent is troubled that a plaintiff will not know whether the offer on the substantive claim would be exceeded at trial, but this is so whenever an offer of settlement is made. In any event, requiring itemization of damages separate from costs would not in any way help plaintiffs know in advance whether the judgment at trial will exceed a defendant's offer.

Curiously, respondent also maintains that petitioners' settlement offer did not exceed the judgment obtained by respondent. In this regard, respondent notes that the $100,000 offer is not as great as the sum of the $60,000 in damages, $32,000 in preoffer costs, and $139,692.47 in claimed postoffer costs. This argument assumes, however, that postoffer costs should be included in the comparison. The Court of Appeals correctly recognized that postoffer costs merely offset part of the expense of continuing the litigation to trial, and should not be included in the calculus. Id., at 476.

## B

The second question we address is whether the term "costs" in Rule 68 includes attorney's fees awardable under 42 U.S.C. § 1988. By the time the Federal Rules of Civil Procedure were adopted in 1938, federal statutes had authorized and defined awards of costs to prevailing parties for more than 85 years. See Act of Feb. 26, 1853, 10 Stat. 161; see generally Alyeska Pipeline Service Co. v. Wilderness Society, 421 U.S. 240 (1975). Unlike in England, such "costs" generally had not included attorney's fees; under the "American Rule," each party had been required to bear its own attorney's fees. The "American Rule" as applied in federal courts, however, had become subject to certain exceptions by the late 1930's. Some of these exceptions had evolved as a product of the "inherent power in the courts to allow attorney's fees in particular situations." Alyeska, supra, at 259. But most of the exceptions were found in federal statutes that directed courts to award attorney's fees as part of costs in particular cases. 421 U.S. at 260-262.

Section 407 of the Communications Act of 1934, for example, provided in relevant part that, "[i]f the petitioner shall finally prevail, he shall be allowed a reasonable attorney's fee, to be taxed and collected as a part of the costs of the suit." 47 U.S.C. § 407. There was identical language in § 3(p) of the Railway Labor Act, 45 U.S.C. § 153(p) (1934 ed.). Section 40 of the Copyright Act of 1909, 17 U.S.C. § 40 (1934 ed.), allowed a court to "award to the prevailing party a reasonable attorney's fee as part of the costs." And other statutes contained similar provisions that included attorney's fees as part of awardable "costs." See, e.g., the Clayton Act, 15 U.S.C. § 15 (1934 ed.); the Securities Act of 1933, 15 U.S.C. § 77k(e) (1934 ed.); the Securities Exchange Act of 1934, 15 U.S.C. §§ 78i(e), 78r(a) (1934 ed.).

The authors of Federal Rule of Civil Procedure 68 were fully aware of these exceptions to the American Rule. The Advisory Committee's Note to Rule 54(d), 28 U.S.C. App., p.621, contains an extensive list of the federal statutes which allowed for costs in particular cases; of the 35 "statutes as to costs" set forth in the final paragraph of the Note, no fewer than 11 allowed for attorney's fees as part of costs. Against this background of varying definitions of "costs," the drafters of Rule 68 did not define the term; nor is there any explanation whatever as to its intended meaning in the history of the Rule.

In this setting, given the importance of "costs" to the Rule, it is very unlikely that this omission was mere oversight; on the contrary, the most reasonable inference is that the term "costs" in Rule 68 was intended to refer to all costs properly awardable under the relevant substantive statute or other authority. In other words, all costs properly awardable in an action are to be considered within the scope of Rule 68 "costs." Thus, absent congressional expressions to the contrary, where the underlying statute defines "costs" to include attorney's fees, we are satisfied such fees are to be included as costs for purposes of Rule 68 (citations omitted).

Here, respondent sued under 42 U.S.C. § 1983. Pursuant to the Civil Rights Attorney's Fees Awards Act of 1976, 90 Stat. 2641, as amended, 42 U.S.C. § 1988, a prevailing party in a § 1983 action may be awarded attorney's fees "as part of the costs." Since Congress expressly included attorney's fees as "costs" available to a plaintiff in a § 1983 suit, such fees are subject to the cost-shifting provision of Rule 68. This "plain meaning" interpretation of the interplay between Rule 68 and § 1988 is the only construction that gives meaning to each word in both Rule 68 and § 1988.

Unlike the Court of Appeals, we do not believe that this "plain meaning" construction of the statute and the Rule will frustrate Congress' objective in § 1988 of ensuring that civil rights plaintiffs obtain "'effective access to the judicial process.'" Hensley v. Eckerhart, 461 U.S. 424, 429 (1983), quoting H.R. Rep. No. 94-1558, p. 1 (1976). Merely subjecting civil rights plaintiffs to the settlement provision of Rule 68 does not curtail their access to the courts, or significantly deter them from bringing suit. Application of Rule 68 will serve as a disincentive for the plaintiff's attorney to continue litigation after the defendant makes a settlement offer. There is no evidence, however, that Congress, in considering § 1988, had any thought that civil rights claims were to be on any different footing from other civil claims insofar as settlement is concerned. Indeed, Congress made clear its concern that civil rights plaintiffs not be penalized for "helping to lessen docket congestion" by settling their cases out of court. See H.R. Rep. No. 94-1558, supra, at 7.

Moreover, Rule 68's policy of encouraging settlements is neutral, favoring neither plaintiffs nor defendants; it expresses a clear policy of favoring settlement of all lawsuits. Civil rights plaintiffs—along with other plaintiffs—who reject an offer more favorable than what is thereafter recovered at trial will not recover attorney's fees for services performed after the offer is rejected. But, since the Rule is neutral, many civil rights plaintiffs will benefit from the offers of settlement encouraged by Rule 68. Some plaintiffs will receive compensation in settlement where, on trial, they might not have recovered, or would have recovered less than what was offered. And, even for those who would prevail at trial, settlement will provide them with compensation at an earlier date without the burdens, stress, and time of litigation. In short, settlements rather than litigation will serve the interests of plaintiffs as well as defendants.

To be sure, application of Rule 68 will require plaintiffs to "think very hard" about whether continued litigation is worthwhile; that is precisely what Rule 68 contemplates. This effect of Rule 68, however, is in no sense inconsistent with the congressional policies underlying § 1983 and § 1988. Section 1988 authorizes courts to award only "reasonable" attorney's fees to prevailing parties. In Hensley v. Eckerhart, supra, we held that "the most critical factor" in determining a reasonable fee "is the degree of success obtained." Id. at 436. We specifically noted that prevailing at trial "may say little about whether the expenditure of counsel's time was reasonable in relation to the success achieved." Ibid. In a case where a rejected settlement offer exceeds the ultimate recovery, the plaintiff—although technically the prevailing party—has not received any monetary benefits from the postoffer services of his attorney. This case presents a good example: the $139,692 in postoffer legal services resulted in a recovery $8,000 less than petitioners' settlement offer. Given Congress' focus on the success achieved, we are not persuaded that shifting the postoffer costs to respondent in these circumstances would in any sense thwart its intent under § 1988.

Rather than "cutting against the grain" of § 1988, as the Court of Appeals held, we are convinced that applying Rule 68 in the context of a § 1983 action is consistent with the policies and objectives of § 1988. Section 1988 encourages plaintiffs to bring meritorious civil rights suits; Rule 68 simply encourages settlements. There is nothing incompatible in these two objectives.

## III

Congress, of course, was well aware of Rule 68 when it enacted § 1988, and included attorney's fees as part of recoverable costs. The plain language of Rule 68 and § 1988 subjects such fees to the cost-shifting provision of Rule 68. Nothing revealed in our review of the policies underlying § 1988 constitutes "the necessary clear expression of congressional intent" required "to exempt . . . [the] statute from the operation of" Rule 68. Califano v. Yamasaki, 442 U.S. 682, 700 (1979). We hold that petitioners are not liable for costs of $139,692 incurred by respondent after petitioners' offer of settlement.

The judgment of the Court of Appeals is

*Reversed.*

JUSTICE POWELL, concurring.

In Delta Airlines, Inc. v. August, 450 U.S. 346 (1981), the offer under Rule 68 stated that it was *"in the amount of $450, which shall include attorney's fees,* together with costs accrued to date." Id. at 365. In a brief concurring opinion, I expressed the view that this offer did not comport with the Rule's requirements. It seemed to me that an offer of judgment should consist of two identified components: (i) the substantive relief proposed, and (ii) costs, including a reasonable attorney's fee. The amount of the fee ultimately should be within the discretion of the court if the offer is accepted. In questioning the form of the offer in *Delta*, I was influenced in part by the fact that it was a Title VII case. I concluded that the "'costs' component of a Rule 68 offer of judgment in a Title VII case must include reasonable attorney's fees accrued to the date of the offer." Id. at 363. My view, however, as to the specificity of the "substantive relief" component of the offer did not depend solely on the fact that *Delta* was a Title VII case.

No other Justice joined my *Delta* concurrence. The Court's decision was upon a different ground. Although I think it the better practice for the offer of judgment expressly to identify the components, it is important to have a Court for a clear interpretation of Rule 68. I noted in *Delta* that "parties to litigation and the public as a whole have an interest—often an overriding one—in settlement rather than exhaustion of protracted court proceedings." Ibid. The purpose of Rule 68 is to "facilitat[e] the early resolution of marginal suits in which the defendant perceives the claim to be without merit, and the plaintiff recognizes its speculative nature." Ibid. See also id. at 363, n.1. We have now agreed as to what specifically is required by Rule 68.

Accordingly, I join the opinion of the Court.

JUSTICE REHNQUIST, concurring.

In Delta Airlines, Inc. v. August, 450 U.S. 346 (1981), I expressed in dissent the view that the term "costs" in Rule 68 did not include attorney's fees. Further examination of the question has convinced me that this view was wrong, and I therefore join the opinion of the Chief Justice. Cf. McGrath v. Kristensen, 340 U.S. 162, 176 (1950) (Jackson, J., concurring).

JUSTICE BRENNAN, with whom JUSTICE MARSHALL and JUSTICE BLACKMUN join, dissenting.

. . . The Court's reasoning is wholly inconsistent with the history and structure of the Federal Rules, and its application to the over 100 attorney's fees statutes enacted by Congress will produce absurd variations in Rule 68's operation based on nothing more than picayune differences in statutory phraseology. Neither Congress nor the drafters of the Rules could possibly have intended such inexplicable variations in settlement incentives. Moreover, the Court's interpretation will "seriously undermine the purposes behind the attorney's fees provisions" of the civil rights laws, Delta Air Lines, Inc. v. August, 450 U.S. 346, 378 (1981) (Rehnquist, J., dissenting) — provisions imposed by Congress pursuant to § 5 of the Fourteenth Amendment. Today's decision therefore violates the most basic limitations on our rulemaking authority as set forth in the Rules Enabling Act, 28 U.S.C. § 2072, and as summarized in Alyeska Pipeline Co. v. Wilderness Society, 421 U.S. 240 (1975). Finally, both Congress and the Judicial Conference of the United States have been engaged for years in considering possible amendments to Rule 68 that would bring attorney's fees within the operation of the Rule. That process strongly suggests that Rule 68 has not previously been viewed as governing fee awards, and it illustrates the wisdom of deferring to other avenues of amending Rule 68 rather than ourselves engaging in "standardless judicial lawmaking." Delta Air Lines, Inc. v. August, supra, at 378 (Rehnquist, J., dissenting). . . .

## I

. . .

For a number of reasons, "costs" as that term is used in the Federal Rules should be interpreted uniformly in accordance with the definition of costs set forth in § 1920:

*First.* The limited history of the costs provisions in the Federal Rules suggests that the drafters intended "costs" to mean only taxable costs traditionally allowed under the common law or pursuant to the statutory predecessor of § 1920. . . .

*Second.* The rules provide that "costs" may automatically be taxed by the clerk of the court on one day's notice, Fed. Rule Civ. Proc. 54(d) — strongly suggesting that "costs" were intended to refer only to those routine, readily determinable charges that could appropriately be left to a clerk, and as to which a single day's notice of settlement would be appropriate. Attorney's fees, which are awardable only by the *court* and which frequently entail lengthy disputes and hearings, obviously do not fall within that category.

*Third.* When particular provisions of the Federal Rules are *intended* to encompass attorney's fees, they do so *explicitly.* Eleven different provisions of the Rules authorize a court to award attorney's fees as "expenses" in particular circumstances, demonstrating that the drafters knew the difference, and intended a difference, between "costs," "expenses," and "attorney's fees."

*Fourth.* With the exception of one recent Court of Appeals opinion and two recent District Court opinions, the Court can point to no authority suggesting that courts or attorneys have ever viewed the cost-shifting provisions of Rule 68 as including attorney's fees. . . .

*Fifth.* We previously have held that words and phrases in the Federal Rules must be given a consistent usage and be read *in pari materia*, reasoning that to do otherwise would "attribute a schizophrenic intent to the drafters." Id. at 353. Applying the Court's "plain language" approach consistently throughout the Rules, however, would produce absurd results that would turn statutes like § 1988 on their heads and plainly violate the restraints imposed on judicial rulemaking by the Rules Enabling Act. . . .

*Sixth.* As with all of the Federal Rules, the drafters intended Rule 68 to have a uniform, consistent application in *all* proceedings in federal court (citation omitted). In accordance with this intent, Rule 68 should be interpreted to provide uniform, consistent incentives "to encourage the settlement of litigation." Delta Air Lines, Inc. v. August, supra, at 352. Yet today's decision will lead to dramatically different settlement incentives depending on minor variations in the phraseology of the underlying fees-award statutes — distinctions that would appear to be nothing short of irrational and for which the Court has no plausible explanation.

Congress has enacted well over 100 attorney's fees statutes, many of which would appear to be affected by today's decision. As the Appendix to this dissent illustrates, Congress has employed a variety of slightly different wordings in these statutes. It sometimes has referred to the awarding of "attorney's fees *as part of* the costs," to "costs *including* attorney's fees," and to "attorney's fees and *other* litigation costs." Under the "plain language" approach of today's decision, Rule 68 will operate to *include* the potential loss of otherwise recoverable attorney's fees as an incentive to settlement in litigation under these statutes. But Congress frequently has referred in other statutes to the awarding of "costs *and* a reasonable attorney's fee," of "costs *together* with a reasonable attorney's fee," or simply of "attorney's fees" without reference to costs. Under the Court's "plain language" analysis, Rule 68 obviously will *not* include the potential loss of otherwise recoverable attorney's fees as a settlement incentive in litigation under these statutes because they do not refer to fees "as" costs.

The result is to sanction a senseless patchwork of fee shifting that flies in the face of the fundamental purpose of the Federal Rules — the provision of uniform and consistent procedure in federal courts. . . .

. . . [M]any statutes contain several fees-award provisions governing actions arising under different subsections, and the phraseology of these provisions sometimes differs slightly from section to section. It is simply preposterous to think that Congress or the drafters of the Rules intended to sanction differing applications of Rule 68 depending on which particular subsection of, *inter alia*, the Privacy Act of 1974, the Home Owners' Loan Act of 1933, the Outer Continental Shelf Lands Act Amendments of 1978, or the Interstate Commerce Act the plaintiff happened to invoke. . . .

## A

. . .

Rule 68 . . . is not "sensitive" at all to the merits of an action and to antidiscrimination policy. It is a mechanical *per se* provision automatically shifting "costs" incurred after an offer is rejected, and it deprives a district court of *all* discretion with respect to the matter by using "the strongest verb of its type known to the English language—'must.'" Delta Air Lines, Inc. v. August, supra, at 369. The potential for conflict between § 1988 and Rule 68 could not be more apparent.

Of course, a civil rights plaintiff who *unreasonably* fails to accept a settlement offer, and who thereafter recovers less than the proffered amount in settlement, is barred under § 1988 itself from recovering fees for unproductive work performed in the wake of the rejection. This is because "the extent of a plaintiff's success is *a* crucial factor in determining the proper amount of an award of attorney's fees," 461 U.S. at 440 (emphasis added). . . .

But the results under § 1988 and Rule 68 will *not* always be congruent, because § 1988 mandates the careful consideration of a broad range of other factors and accords appropriate leeway to the district court's informed discretion. . . .

The Court argues, however, that its interpretation of Rule 68 "is neutral, favoring neither plaintiffs nor defendants." This contention is also plainly wrong. As the Judicial Conference Advisory Committee on the Federal Rules of Civil Procedure has noted twice in recent years, Rule 68 "is a 'one-way street,' available only to those defending against claims and not to claimants." Interpreting Rule 68 in its current version to include attorney's fees will lead to a number of skewed settlement incentives that squarely conflict with Congress' intent. To discuss but one example, Rule 68 allows an offer to be made any time after the complaint is filed and gives the plaintiff only 10 days to accept or reject. The Court's decision inevitably will encourage defendants who know they have violated the law to make "low-ball" offers immediately after suit is filed and before plaintiffs have been able to obtain the information they are entitled to by way of discovery to assess the strength of their claims and the reasonableness of the offers. The result will put severe pressure on plaintiffs to settle on the basis of inadequate information in order to avoid the risk of bearing all of their fees even if reasonable discovery might reveal that the defendants were subject to far greater liability. Indeed, because Rule 68 offers may be made recurrently without limitation, defendants will be well advised to make ever-slightly larger offers throughout the discovery process and before plaintiffs have conducted all reasonably necessary discovery.

This sort of so-called "incentive" is fundamentally incompatible with Congress' goals. Congress intended for "private citizens . . . to be able to assert their civil rights" and for "those who violate the Nation's fundamental laws" not to be able "to proceed with impunity." Accordingly, civil rights plaintiffs "'appear before the court cloaked in a mantle of public interest'"; to promote the *"vigorous* enforcement of modern civil rights legislation," Congress has directed that such "private attorneys general" shall not "be deterred from bringing good faith actions to vindicate the fundamental rights here involved." Yet requiring plaintiffs to make wholly uninformed decisions on settlement offers, at the risk of *automatically* losing all of their postoffer fees no matter what the circumstances and notwithstanding the "excellent" results they might achieve after the full picture emerges, will work just such a deterrent effect.

Other difficulties will follow from the Court's decision. For example, if a plaintiff recovers less money than was offered before trial but obtains potentially far-reaching injunctive or declaratory relief, it is altogether unclear how the Court intends judges to go about quantifying the "value" of the plaintiff's success. . . .

## B

Indeed, the judgment of the Court of Appeals below turned on its determination that an interpretation of Rule 68 to include attorney's fees is beyond the pale of the judiciary's rulemaking authority. Congress has delegated its authority to this Court "to prescribe by general rules . . . the practice and procedure of the district courts and courts of appeals of the United States in civil actions." 28 U.S.C. § 2072. This grant is limited, however, by the condition that "[s]uch rules shall not abridge, enlarge or modify any substantive right." Ibid. The right to attorney's fees is "substantive" under any reasonable definition of that term. Section 1988 was enacted pursuant to § 5 of the Fourteenth Amendment, and the House and Senate Reports recurrently emphasized that "fee awards are an integral part of the *remedies* necessary to obtain . . . compliance" with the civil rights laws and to redress violations. Statutory attorney's fees remedies such as that set forth in § 1988 "are far more like new causes of action tied to specific rights than like background procedural rules governing any and all litigation." Hensley v. Eckerhart, 461 U.S. at 443, n.2 (Brennan, J., concurring in part and dissenting in part). See also 720 F.2d, at 479 (§ 1988 "does not make the litigation process more accurate and efficient for both parties; even more clearly than the statute of limitations [at issue in Ragan v. Merchants Transfer & Warehouse Co., 337 U.S. 530 (1949)], it is designed instead to achieve a substantive objective—compliance with the civil rights laws").

As construed by the Court today, Rule 68 surely will operate to "abridge" and to "modify" this statutory right to reasonable attorney's fees. "The test must be whether a rule really regulates *procedure*—the judicial process for enforcing rights and duties recognized by substantive law and for justly administering remedy and redress for disregard or infraction of them," or instead operates to abridge a substantive right "in the guise of regulating procedure." Sibbach v. Wilson & Co., 312 U.S. 1, 10, 14 (1941) (emphasis added); see also Hanna v. Plumer, 380 U.S. 460, 464-465 (1965). Unlike those provisions of the Federal Rules that explicitly authorize an award of attorney's fees, Rule 68 is not addressed to bad-faith or unreasonable litigation conduct. The courts always have had inherent authority to assess fees against parties who act "in bad faith, vexatiously, wantonly, or for oppressive reasons," Alyeska Pipeline Service Co. v. Wilderness Society, 421 U.S., at 258-259, and the assessment of fees against parties whose *unreasonable* conduct has violated the rules of litigation falls comfortably into the courts' authority to administer "remedy and redress for disregard or infraction" of those rules, Sibbach v. Wilson & Co., supra, at 14.

Rule 68, on the other hand, contains no reasonableness component (citation omitted). As interpreted by the Court, it will operate to divest a prevailing plaintiff of fees to which he otherwise might be entitled under the reasonableness standard simply because he guessed wrong, or because he did not have all information reasonably necessary to evaluate the offer, or because of unforeseen changes in the law or evidence after the offer. The Court's interpretation of Rule 68 therefore clearly collides with the congressionally prescribed substantive standards of § 1988, and the Rules Enabling Act requires that the Court's interpretation give way. . . .

## Note: Evans v. Jeff D., 475 U.S. 717 (1986)

A legal services lawyer filed a class action against Idaho officials responsible for the education and treatment of children who suffer emotional and mental handicaps, alleging deficiencies in both the educational and health facilities for these children. The complaint sought injunctive relief and costs and attorneys' fees.

One week before trial, the defendants offered a settlement giving the plaintiffs "virtually all" the injunctive relief they sought. 475 U.S. at 722. The offer was conditioned on a waiver of any claim for fees and costs. Holding that approval of a settlement with this condition was within the trial court's discretion, the Supreme Court relied specifically on Marek v. Chesny:

> [W]e believe that a general proscription against negotiated waiver of attorney's fees in exchange for a settlement on the merits would itself impede vindication of civil rights, at least in some cases, by reducing the attractiveness of settlement. Of particular relevance in this regard is our recent decision in Marek v. Chesny, 473 U.S. 1 (1985). . . .
>
> To promote both settlement and civil rights, we implicitly acknowledged in Marek v. Chesny the possibility of a tradeoff between merits relief and attorney's fees when we upheld the defendant's lump-sum offer to settle the entire civil rights action, including any liability for fees and costs.
>
> In approving the package offer in Marek v. Chesny we recognized that a rule prohibiting the comprehensive negotiation of all outstanding issues in a pending case might well preclude the settlement of a substantial number of cases:
>
>> If defendants are not allowed to make lump-sum offers that would, if accepted, represent their total liability, they would understandably be reluctant to make settlement offers. As the Court of Appeals observed, "many a defendant would be unwilling to make a binding settlement offer on terms that left it exposed to liability for attorney's fees in whatever amount the court might fix on motion of the plaintiff." [Chesny v. Marek,] 720 F.2d [474, 477 (7th Cir. 1983). Id., at 6-7.
>
> . . . Most defendants are unlikely to settle unless the cost of the predicted judgment, discounted by its probability, plus the transaction costs of further litigation, are greater than the cost of the settlement package. If fee waivers cannot be negotiated, the settlement package must either contain

an attorney's fee component of potentially large and typically uncertain magnitude, or else the parties must agree to have the fee fixed by the court. Although either of these alternatives may well be acceptable in many cases, there surely is a significant number in which neither alternative will be as satisfactory as a decision to try the entire case.[23]

The adverse impact of removing attorney's fees and costs from bargaining might be tolerable if the uncertainty introduced into settlement negotiations were small. But it is not. The defendants' potential liability for fees in this kind of litigation can be as significant as, and sometimes even more significant than, their potential liability on the merits. This proposition is most dramatically illustrated by the fee awards of district courts in actions seeking only monetary relief.[24] Although it is more difficult to compare fee awards with the cost of injunctive relief, in part because the cost of such relief is seldom reported in written opinions, here too attorney's fees awarded by district courts have "frequently outrun the economic benefits ultimately obtained by successful litigants." 122 Cong. Rec. 31472 (1976) (remarks of Sen. Kennedy).[25] Indeed, in this very case "[c]ounsel for defendants view[ed] the risk of an attorney's fees award as the most significant liability in the case." Brief for Defendants in Support of Approval of Compromise in Jeff D. v. Evans, No. 80-4091 (D. Idaho), p.5. Undoubtedly there are many other civil rights actions in which potential liability for attorney's fees may overshadow the potential cost of relief on the merits and darken prospects for settlement if fees cannot be negotiated.

475 U.S. at 732-735.

23. It is unrealistic to assume that the defendant's offer on the merits would be unchanged by redaction of the provision waiving fees. If it were, the defendant's incentive to settle would be diminished because of the risk that attorney's fees, when added to the original merits offer, will exceed the discounted value of the expected judgment plus litigation costs. If, as is more likely, the defendant lowered the value of its offer on the merits to provide a cushion against the possibility of a large fee award, the defendant's offer on the merits will in many cases be less than the amount to which the plaintiff feels himself entitled, thereby inclining him to reject the settlement. Of course, to the extent that the merits offer is somewhere between these two extremes the incentive of both sides to settle is dampened, albeit to a lesser degree with respect to each party.

24. See, e.g., Rivera v. Riverside, 763 F.2d 1580, 1581-1583 (9th Cir. 1985) (city ordered to pay victorious civil rights plaintiffs $245,456.25 following a trial in which they recovered a total of $33,350 in damages), cert. granted, 474 U.S. 917 (1985); Cunningham v. City of McKeesport, 753 F.2d 262, 269 (3d Cir. 1985) (city ordered to pay some $35,000 in attorney's fees in a case in which judgment for the plaintiff was entered in the amount of $17,000) [vacated by 478 U.S. 1015 (1986)]; Copeland v. Marshall, 641 F.2d 880, 891 (1980) (en banc) ($160,000 attorney's fees awarded for obtaining $33,000 judgment); Skoda v. Fontani, 646 F.2d 1193, 1194 (7th Cir.), remanded to 519 F. Supp. 309, 310 (N.D. Ill. 1981) ($6,086.12 attorney's fees awarded to obtain $1 recovery). Cf. Marek v. Chesny, 473 U.S., at 7 ($171,692.47 in claimed attorney's fees and costs to obtain $60,000 damages judgment).

25. See, e.g., Grendel's Den, Inc. v. Larkin, 749 F.2d 945, 960 (1st Cir. 1984) (awarding $113,640.85 in fees and expenses for successful challenge to law zoning liquor establishments in Larkin v. Grendel's Den, 459 U.S. 116 (1982)).

In dissent, Justices Brennan, Marshall, and Blackmun argued:

... As summed up by the Legal Ethics Committee of the District of Columbia
Bar:

> Defense counsel . . . are in a uniquely favorable position when they
> condition settlement on the waiver of the statutory fee: They make a
> demand for a benefit that the plaintiff's lawyer cannot resist as a mat-
> ter of ethics and one in which the plaintiff has no interest and there-
> fore will not resist. [Op. No. 147, reprinted in 113 Daily Washington
> Reporter, at 394.]

. . .

And, of course, once fee waivers are permitted, defendants will seek them
as a matter of course, since this is a logical way to minimize liability. Indeed,
defense counsel would be remiss *not* to demand that the plaintiff waive statutory attorney's fees. A lawyer who proposes to have his client pay more
than is necessary to end litigation has failed to fulfill his fundamental duty
zealously to represent the best interests of his client. Because waiver of fees
does not affect the plaintiff, a settlement offer is not made less attractive to
the plaintiff if it includes a demand that statutory fees be waived. Thus, in
the future, we must expect settlement offers routinely to contain demands
for waivers of statutory fees.

The cumulative effect this practice will have on the civil rights bar is evident. It does not denigrate the high ideals that motivate many civil rights
practitioners to recognize that lawyers are in the business of practicing
law, and that, like other business people, they are and must be concerned
with earning a living.[13] The conclusion that permitting fee waivers will seriously impair the ability of civil rights plaintiffs to obtain legal assistance
is Following extract, insert the following line as text, no indent: 475 U.S. at
757-59.

## Notes and Questions

1. *The Catalyst Theory of Prevailing Parties.* In *Evans*, the settlement offer
was conditioned on the waiver of any claim to attorneys' fees. Can a party
obtain attorneys' fees when a civil rights case settles and the settlement
agreement does not include a fee waiver clause? In Roberson v. Giuliani,
346 F.3d 75 (2d Cir. 2003), plaintiffs challenged the legality of various policies for the handling of applications for food stamps, Medicaid, and public
assistance in New York City. The City agreed to a settlement implementing

---

13. See [Earl Johnson, Jr.], Lawyers' Choice: A Theoretical Appraisal of Litigation
Investment Decisions, 15 Law & Soc. Rev. 567 (1980-1981) (concluding that "fee for service"
lawyers will withdraw resources from a given case when total expected costs exceed total
expected benefits); Kraus, 29 Vill. L. Rev., at 637 ("No matter how sophisticated the analysis of attorney responses becomes, the conclusion remains that the more we decrease the
reasonable expectation of Fees Act awards, the less likely it is that Fees Act cases will be
initiated.").

a variety of improvements in its procedures and the order dismissing the case provided that the court would "retain jurisdiction over the settlement agreement for enforcement purposes." Id. at 78. Plaintiffs subsequently moved for over $140,000 in attorneys' fees and costs as "prevailing parties" under 42 U.S.C. § 1988 on the theory that their lawsuit was the "catalyst" in forcing the City to change its procedures.

This was a bold move coming in the wake of the Supreme Court's decision in Buckhannon Bd. & Care Home, Inc. v. W. Va. Dep't of Health & Human Res., 532 U.S. 598, 605 (2001) (rejecting "catalyst theory" of defining prevailing parties under § 1988 and holding that to "prevail" requires a "judicially sanctioned change in the legal relationship of the parties . . . [a] *judicial imprimatur*"). Citing *Buckhannon*, the district court rejected the request for attorneys' fees. However, the Second Circuit reversed, holding that retaining jurisdiction to enforce a settlement agreement is a sufficient judicial imprimatur to confer prevailing party status on the plaintiffs. *Roberson*, 346 F.3d at 82-83. The court joined five other circuits "in concluding that judicial action other than a judgment on the merits or a consent decree can support an award of attorneys' fees, so long as such action carries with it sufficient judicial imprimatur." Id. at 81 (citing cases). Cf. Bell v. Bd. of County Comm'rs of Jefferson County, 451 F.3d 1097, 1103 (10th Cir. 2006) ("A court's mere involvement in the settlement, however, is not enough. There must be some official judicial approval of the settlement and some level of continuing judicial oversight.") (internal quotation marks and citation omitted); Torres v. Walker, 356 F.3d 238, 244-245 (2d Cir. 2004) (stipulated dismissal containing no provision reserving jurisdiction for court to monitor compliance with settlement lacked "sufficient judicial imprimatur" to warrant application of Prison Litigation Reform Act's fee cap for prevailing parties); Christina A. ex rel. Jennifer A. v. Bloomberg, 315 F.3d 990, 993 (8th Cir. 2003) ("*Buckhannon* . . . makes it clear that a party prevails only if it receives either an enforceable judgment on the merits or a consent decree.").

Still, public interest lawyers had reason to worry following the Court's rejection of the "catalyst theory" in *Buckhannon*. As an amicus brief filed in the case observed:

> The abolition of the catalyst rule would be particularly severe since the attorneys may lose their fees and expenses by action of the defendant at any time during the litigation. The case can be litigated for years. If the defendant then moots the case by granting relief, even when the case is on appeal or in this Court, the abolition of the catalyst rule would mean all the fees and expenses would be lost. Few attorneys would be willing or able to take such a risk.
>
> Many of the cases brought under fee-shifting statutes, such as environmental cases, involve major, complex litigation requiring substantial resources. The clients in this type of litigation rarely can pay any significant portion of the fees or costs. Hundreds or thousands of hours and tens or hundreds of thousands of dollars may need to be expended.

The *Laidlaw* case is a good example. [Friends of the Earth v. Laidlaw Envtl. Servs. (TOC), Inc., 528 U.S. 167 (2000).] *Laidlaw*, a Clean Water Act case against a private polluter, was brought in June 1992. Since the beginning of this case, over eight years ago, plaintiffs' attorneys' have expended approximately 9,000 hours and $230,000 in expenses on this case. While the case was in this Court, the defendant claimed that the case had become moot because the incinerator had been dismantled. This Court remanded the issue of mootness to the lower courts for resolution. If the case is found moot, and the catalyst rule is abolished, plaintiffs' counsel would be denied fees over eight years after the case was brought.

2000 WL 1701809. See also *Buckhannon*, 532 U.S. at 622-623 (Ginsburg, J., dissenting) ("[T]he Court's constricted definition of 'prevailing party,' and consequent rejection of the 'catalyst theory,' [will] impede access to court for the less well heeled, and shrink the incentive Congress created for the enforcement of federal law by private attorneys general.").

In 2007, Congress passed the OPEN Government Act. According to this new law, at least with respect to actions to force disclosure of government records under the Freedom of Information Act, the catalyst theory has been revived. The statute provides:

(i) The court may assess against the United States reasonable attorney fees and other litigation costs reasonably incurred in any case under this section in which the complainant has substantially prevailed. (ii) For purposes of this subparagraph, a complainant has substantially prevailed if the complainant has obtained relief through either—

(I) a judicial order, or an enforceable written agreement or consent decree; or

(II) a voluntary or unilateral change in position by the agency, if the complainant's claim is not insubstantial.

5 U.S.C. § 552(a)(4)(E). See also Wildlands CPR v. U.S. Forest Serv., 558 F. Supp. 2d 1096, 1097-1098 (D. Mont. 2008) (analyzing the new statute).

2. *The Defendant/Offeror's Attorneys' Fees.* In *Marek*, the Court was not presented with the question of whether Rule 68 requires a plaintiff to pay *defendant's* attorneys' fees, in addition to paying defendant's costs and losing the right to recover his own attorneys' fees under 42 U.S.C. § 1988. The question has resurfaced in cases similar to *Marek*, where prevailing party fee-shifting statutes define attorneys' fees as "costs." The majority position is that Rule 68 does not require a plaintiff to pay the defendant's attorneys' fees. As the Ninth Circuit has held:

*Marek* holds that "the term 'costs' in Rule 68 was intended to refer to all costs *properly awardable* under the relevant substantive statute or other authority." *Marek*, 473 U.S. at 9 (emphasis added). Where the substantive statute permits a "prevailing party" to recover attorneys' fees as costs, a defendant who has not "prevailed" may not recover attorneys' fees pursuant to Rule 68. Such costs are not "properly awardable" under the relevant statute.

Champion Produce, Inc. v. Ruby Robinson Co., Inc., 342 F.3d 1016, 1029 (9th Cir. 2003). See also Hescott v. City of Saginaw, 757 F.3d 518, 528 (6th Cir. 2014) (same); Le v. Univ. of Pa., 321 F.3d 403, 411 (3d Cir. 2003) (same); Harbor Motor Co. v. Arnell Chevrolet-Geo, Inc., 265 F.3d 638 (7th Cir. 2001) (same); EEOC v. Bailey Ford, Inc., 26 F.3d 570, 571 (5th Cir. 1994) (same); Crossman v. Marcoccio, 806 F.2d 329 (1st Cir. 1986) (same); O'Brien v. City of Greers Ferry, 873 F.2d 1115 (8th Cir. 1989). But see Jordan v. Time, Inc., 111 F.3d 102, 105 (11th Cir. 1997) (because plaintiff "did not obtain a judgment more favorable than the ones contained in Time's offers of judgment, Jordan must pay Time's attorneys' fees and costs" where the underlying statute allowed prevailing party fees "as part of the costs," 17 U.S.C. § 505). The Defendant/ Offeror's other post-offer costs may be recovered. See Stanczyk v. City of New York, 752 F.3d 273, 281 (2d. Cir. 2014) ("Rule 68, when applicable requires a prevailing plaintiff to pay defendant's post-offer costs, excluding attorney's fees.").

Outside the context of Rule 68 the Supreme Court has repeatedly confirmed that prevailing defendants may recover attorneys' fees if the district court finds that plaintiff's case was frivolous. See Fox v. Vice, 563 U.S. 826 (2011) (in civil rights case between two candidates for chief of police, where plaintiff conceded at summary judgment that his federal claims were invalid, the Court upheld the award of defendant's attorneys' fees under § 1988 for work necessary to rebut plaintiff's frivolous claims); Christiansburg Garment Co. v. Equal Emp't Opportunity Comm'n, 434 U.S. 412, 421 (1978) (recognizing that prevailing defendants are entitled to § 1988 fees only "upon a finding that the plaintiff's action was frivolous, unreasonable, or without foundation").

3. *A Lawyer's Competence: Negotiation and Litigation.* The Rule-driven encouragement of settlement surely reflects some ambivalence toward the adversary system and elaborate due process. Does the prevalence of settlement as an alternative to trial modify your image of the lawyer who chooses litigation as a career? To what degree are the skills of a negotiator different from those of a trial advocate? Consider these words of advice in a practice manual, directed toward mediation, but generally applicable to settlement negotiations:

> Practice Tip: For settlement to occur at a mediation conference, litigators have to abandon their well-developed confrontational mode of courtroom behavior and speech. Instead, it is essential that counsel open lines of effective communication with the opposing party. . . . Negotiation entails a totally different focus than the historical objective of "winning."
>
> Adroit negotiators know, or have learned to use non-blaming language when speaking to the opposing counsel or principal. To the contrary, a wise negotiator knows to discuss the mutual dependencies and common interests of the ostensibly hostile interests that are present at the bargaining table.

Jerome S. Levy and Robert C. Prather, Sr., Texas Practice Guide, ADR Strategies 3:13 (1998).

On the other hand, another practice tip in the same section advises coming to the negotiation with a carefully prepared game plan, a "thorough understanding of the undisputed facts," and "an appreciation of where the parties are in terms of their perceptions on the disputed facts and law." Id. This sounds a lot like what litigators do.

4. *Controversy over Rule 68.* As explained in Gudenkauf v. Stauffer Commc'ns Inc., 158 F.3d 1074, 1083-1084 (10th Cir. 1998), a Title VII case, *Marek* has been at least partially superseded by law:

> [T]he Supreme Court held in Marek v. Chesny, 473 U.S. 1 (1985), that under Rule 68, a successful civil rights plaintiff could be denied attorney's fees otherwise available under subsection (k). The legislative history of the [Civil Rights Act of 1991] specifically disapproved of the *Marek* decision and proposed to amend subsection (k) to avoid its application. "*Marek* is particularly problematic in the context of Title VII, because it may impede private actions, which Congress has relied upon for enforcement of the statute's guarantees and advancement of the public's interest." H.R. Rep. No. 102-40(I) at 82. Although subsection (k) ultimately remained unchanged in this regard, the proposed amendment was adopted in the language of subsection (g)(2)(B). Congress therefore clearly did not intend a district court to reduce a mixed motives plaintiff's fee award on the basis of a rejected pretrial settlement.

For an argument that current Rule 68 actually is an ineffective inducement to settle, and that it may increase the likelihood of trial or have an ambiguous result, see David A. Anderson, Improving Settlement Devices: Rule 68 and Beyond, 23 J. Legal Stud. 225 (1994).

One potential harshness of Rule 68 lies in its mandatory nature. For example, in Webb v. James, 147 F.3d 617 (7th Cir. 1998), the court held that a Rule 68 offer is not an ordinary contract and that the contract doctrine of rescission is inappropriate with respect to Rule 68 offers. The Rule requires that once an offer is accepted and properly filed, the clerk "shall enter judgment," thereby foreclosing any exercise of discretion to allow rescission. The sole remedy available would be to pursue relief from judgment under Rule 60(b). Given this strict construction of Rule 68, it may not be surprising that the same court also held that a defendant could not take advantage of Rule 68's cost-shifting requirement where the defendant's $10,000 settlement offer, "to be divided among all three plaintiffs," was not apportioned on an individualized basis. Gavoni v. Dobbs House, Inc., 164 F.3d 1071, 1074 (7th Cir. 1999). The jury had awarded a total of $6,500 to the plaintiffs, apportioning $2,000, $2,000, and $2,500 among them. Plaintiffs had requested $825,000 ($230,000; $320,000; $275,000). Id. at 1074. For an interesting discussion of the duty to specifically apportion Rule 68 offers in multidefendant, multi-claim actions, see Le v. Univ. of Pa., 321 F.3d 403 (3d Cir. 2003) (holding apportionment not always necessary in suit for national origin discrimination and retaliation).

In *Webb*, the parties disagreed about the meaning of the settlement. What if the defendant's Rule 68 settlement offer contains an error—can the offer be revoked before plaintiff accepts? Courts remain divided on this question. Compare Perkins v. U.S. West Commc'ns, 138 F.3d 336, 339 (8th Cir. 1998) (offer is irrevocable during ten-day acceptance period provided by Rule 68 even if trial court grants summary judgment), and Richardson v. Nat'l R.R. Passenger Corp., 49 F.3d 760 (D.C. Cir. 1995) (Rule 68 offer is irrevocable during ten-day acceptance period, but if the offer is induced by misconduct on the part of plaintiff, judgment may be modified or withdrawn under Rule 60(b)), with Colonial Penn Ins. Co. v. Coil, 887 F.2d 1236 (4th Cir. 1989) (permitting revocation of offer induced by fraud), and Cesar v. Rubie's Costume Co., 219 F.R.D. 257 (E.D.N.Y. 2004) (permitting revocation where defendant's offer contained a clerical error affecting the amount and scope of the settlement) (citing and following Fisher v. Stolaruk Corp., 110 F.R.D. 74 (E.D. Mich. 1986) (articulating test for revocation where mistake in offer is substantial, material to acceptance, not the result of negligent conduct by defendant, and where revocation will still leave plaintiff in the same position prior to the mistake).

What about vague offers—especially offers that fail to quantify damages? Are they valid if plaintiff accepts? The Fifth Circuit has upheld a district court's refusal to enter judgment on an offer specifying that the attorneys would confer and agree "upon reasonable compensation for Plaintiff's claimed 'actual damages,' and that said amount is added to this Offer of Judgment." Basha v. Mitsubishi Motor Credit of Am., Inc., 336 F.3d 451, 455 (5th Cir. 2003) (mutual assent is absent and "such a vague offer of judgment did not provide Basha with a clear baseline to evaluate the risks of continued litigation"); see also Steiner v. Lewmar, Inc., 816 F.3d 26, 32 (2d Cir. 2016) ("Where an offer is silent on attorney's fees there may be a question as to whether fees are included and whether claims for fees will be extinguished (citation omitted). Courts have generally held that such ambiguities will be construed against the offeror."); Warren v. Sessoms & Rogers, P.A., 676 F.3d 365, 372 (4th Cir. 2012, ("Defendants' offer was not unequivocal but 'conditional,' predicated on what the district court as fact finder might or might not [award in damages]."), *abrogated on other grounds by* Campbell-Ewald Co. v. Gomez, 136 S. Ct. 663, 669 (2016).

5. *Settlement in Complex Litigation.* Settlement may be a more complicated prospect when there are multiple parties with interlocking interests. For an interesting analysis of the impact of joint and several liability on settlement—especially of rules giving a right of contribution to a settling defendant—in cases involving multiple defendants, see Lewis A. Kornhauser and Richard L. Revesz, Settlements Under Joint and Several Liability, 68 N.Y.U. L. Rev. 427 (1993). For a fuller discussion of the issue of settlement in the class action context, see Chapter 6.

6. *Enforcement of Settlement Agreements and Federal Court Jurisdiction.* To understand the enforcement of a settlement agreement, one must consider that the agreement is a private contract between the parties, enforceable under the applicable law of contract. As such, a federal court lacks subject matter jurisdiction over any dispute that may arise over the enforcement of the settlement agreement, unless there is an independent basis of federal

jurisdiction over that dispute. See Kokkonen v. Guardian Life Ins. Co. of Am., 511 U.S. 375 (1994). If the settlement produces a dismissal of the action under Rule 41(a)(2), however, the court may make the parties' compliance with the settlement agreement part of its order, and thereby retain jurisdiction over the enforcement. If dismissal occurs pursuant to Rule 41(a)(1)(A)(ii), the court can, with consent of the parties, incorporate the settlement agreement in the order, and thereby retain jurisdiction over the enforcement. Otherwise, the parties must go to state court to enforce the settlement agreement, even if the settlement is of a suit pending in federal court.

7. *Conflicts of Interest in Settlement Negotiations.* An obvious potential problem is that settlement may in some cases prove more attractive to plaintiffs' lawyers than to their clients. Particularly in class action suits, or in other cases in which the lawyers are compensated under a contingency fee arrangement, the temptation to settle early rather than pursue the litigation may be overwhelming. Can you see why? If the lawyer gives in to the temptation, however, the settlement may be vulnerable to subsequent attack, as the disappointed plaintiffs challenge the fairness of the settlement and the adequacy of representation. In egregious cases, it also may expose the lawyers who negotiated the settlement to malpractice suits. But see Nicolet Instrument Corp. v. Lindquist & Vennum, 34 F.3d 453, 455 (7th Cir. 1994) (Posner, C.J.) (noting difficulty of proving attorney malpractice in settlement negotiations because while "there is a correct outcome to most lawsuits, there is no 'correct' outcome to a negotiation," where "much depend[s] on the relative bargaining skills of the negotiators, on the likely consequences to each party if the negotiations fall through, and on luck"). See also John C. Coffee, Jr., Class Action Accountability: Reconciling Exit, Voice, and Loyalty in Representative Litigation, 100 Colum. L. Rev. 370, 371-372 (2000) ("[W]here the plaintiff's attorney was once seen as a public-regarding private attorney general, increasingly the more standard depiction is a profit-seeking entrepreneur, capable of opportunistic actions and often willing to subordinate the interests of class members to the attorney's own economic self-interest").

8. *Settlement and Sentiment.* Most discussions of settlement incentives tend to assume that the parties' settlement decisions are based primarily on rational assessments of the expected value of trial, of the likely litigation costs, and of the likely outcome of trial. Might parties also weigh other factors not captured by this economic model? See Russell Korobkin and Chris Guthrie, Psychological Barriers to Litigation Settlement: An Experimental Approach, 93 Mich. L. Rev. 107 (1994) (concluding that individuals do not always behave in the rational way that economic models assume, insofar as psychological processes affect how they perceive, understand, and respond to settlement offers).

The Texas Practice Guide makes the following recommendations:

PRACTICE TIP: Most litigators have experienced an instance in which a client never advised the attorney of a hidden agenda, such as wanting a portion of the defendant's stock or wishing to "punish" the miscreant. The easiest (and most obvious) manner of clarifying such matters is to ask the following two pointed questions:

1. "Is the amount of money the only issue in this case?"
2. "Is there anything other than financial recovery that you want to achieve as a result of this lawsuit?"

If the answer to either of these questions is vague or ambivalent, it is incumbent upon counsel to cross-examine one's own client. The wise lawyer knows to use counseling and interviewing techniques to draw out the client's real objective in the case.

"I understand how important this matter is to you, but at the same time. . . ."

. . . "If we are not talking only about money, what would be the best way of settling this case from your point of view?"

"I recognize that you feel strongly about this particular point, but let me ask you if you would feel differently if the other side was willing to compensate you fairly for giving up this point?"

In short, the client should be encouraged not to take a hard and fast bargaining position on points that may come up during the negotiations. . . . This enables counsel to explore possible alternatives. Be creative.

. . . As stated previously, it is incumbent on counsel to be sure that the client understands the critical distinction between "wants" and "needs." Emotion is the driving force at the "wants" level of discussion. Reality is injected into the equation at the "needs" level. It is a perilous undertaking for an attorney to fail to be sure that the client has a realistic understanding of what is to be reasonably expected as an outcome. . . .

PRACTICE TIP: The client's level of expectation plays a major part in the process. If the client's non-negotiable goal is a result at the "want" level, the attorney at some future date may be faced with a State Bar grievance complaint filed by this same client, due to the disparity between the client's expectation and the attorney's expectation of the most likely result at trial. If the attorney cannot convince the client as to the trial value of the case, it may be in the lawyer's best interest to promptly withdraw from this particular representation.

To state the obvious, plaintiffs routinely believe that they were the losers in some tragic situation. A corollary to that belief is the misperception that no one else in the history of civilization has ever suffered that type of loss or injury. A threshold consideration is whether a given situation is a tragedy or merely an inconvenience.

Jerome S. Levy and Robert C. Prather Sr., Texas Practice Guide, ADR Strategies 3:10 (1998).

## 2. The Pretrial Conference—Helpful Judicial Oversight or Unwelcome Coercion?

The pretrial conference is perhaps the only major feature of the federal rules that is an American invention, although even this innovation had an English ancestor in the early oral pleadings, in which the judge joined in the formulation of the issues. Apparently an idea of Judge Edson Sunderland, the pretrial conference was first used in 1929 in the Wayne County Circuit Court in Detroit. William Laurens Walker and John W. Thibaut, An Experimental Examination of Pretrial Conference Techniques, 55 Minn. L. Rev. 1113 (1970). When the Federal Rules were drafted in 1938, the pretrial conference under Rule 16 was seen as the culmination of the revised pretrial process. With pleadings assuming the minor role of giving notice of the dispute, and discovery assuming major importance in exploring and developing factual issues, the pretrial conference was the point at which issues were finally to be defined and limited for trial.

The pretrial conference has not been uniformly popular with lawyers, partly because of resistance to possible settlement pressure from the judge and partly because of the additional work it entails. But the Supreme Court upheld the power of a district judge to render a default judgment against a plaintiff for failure of his counsel to attend a pretrial conference. Link v. Wabash R.R. Co., 370 U.S. 626 (1962).

From the first promulgation of the Rules, the practice under Rule 16 has varied enormously from district to district and even among judges in the same courthouse. In 1983, amid concern about abusive discovery, overworked courts, and the role of the passive, impartial judge, the rulemakers overhauled Rule 16 to make it a tool for streamlining the process. Most significantly, the new Rule included the discussion of settlement in the matters to be covered at a pretrial conference (Rule 16(c)).

The 1993 Amendments to Rule 16 went even further in designating the pretrial conference as a major step in the process and as an important settlement moment. Note, for instance, the suggestion in part (c) that "the court may require that a party or its representative be present or reasonably available by telephone in order to consider possible settlement." New amendments in 2015 require the judge to issue the scheduling order faster: 90 rather than 120 days "after any defendant has been served with the complaint," and 60 rather than 90 days after any defendant has made an appearance in the case. Rule 16(b)(2). The judge is also encouraged to include any directions regarding the preservation of electronically stored information. See Rule 16(b)(3)(B)(iii); see also Summary of the Report of the Judicial Conference, Committee on Rules of Practice and Procedure, Sept. 2014, B-12. The amendments also eliminate conference via mail and telephone to encourage "direct exchange."

In a classic article, Professor Judith Resnik made a case against the increased activity of judges in shaping the case and promoting settlement:

> I believe that the role of judges before adjudication is undergoing a change as substantial as has been recognized in the posttrial phase of public law cases. Today, federal district judges are assigned a case at the time of its filing and assume responsibility for shepherding the case to completion. Judges have described their new tasks as "case management"—hence my term "managerial judges." As managers, judges learn more about cases much earlier than they did in the past. They negotiate with parties about the course, timing, and scope of both pretrial and posttrial litigation. These managerial

responsibilities give judges greater power. Yet the restraints that formerly circumscribed judicial authority are conspicuously absent. Managerial judges frequently work beyond the public view, off the record, with no obligation to provide written, reasoned opinions, and out of reach of appellate review.

This new managerial role has emerged for several reasons. One is the creation of pretrial discovery rights. The 1938 Federal Rules of Civil Procedure embodied contradictory mandates: a discovery system ("give your opponent all information relevant to the litigation") was grafted onto American adversarial norms ("protect your client zealously" and therefore "withhold what you can"). In some cases, parties argued about their obligations under the discovery rules; such disputes generated a need for someone to decide pretrial conflicts. Trial judges accepted the assignment and have become mediators, negotiators, and planners — as well as adjudicators. Moreover, once involved in pretrial discovery, many judges became convinced that their presence at other points in a lawsuit's development would be beneficial; supervision of discovery became a conduit for judicial control over all phases of litigation and thus infused lawsuits with the continual presence of the judge-overseer.

Partly because of their new oversight role and partly because of increasing case loads, many judges have become concerned with the volume of their work. To reduce the pressure, judges have turned to efficiency experts who promise "calendar control." Under the experts' guidance, judges have begun to experiment with schemes for speeding the resolution of cases and for persuading litigants to settle rather than try cases whenever possible. During the past decade, enthusiasm for the "managerial movement" has become widespread; what began as an experiment is likely soon to become obligatory. . . .

In the rush to conquer the mountain of work, no one — neither judges, court administrators, nor legal commentators — has assessed whether relying on trial judges for informal dispute resolution and for case management, either before or after trial, is good, bad, or neutral. Little empirical evidence supports the claim that judicial management "works" either to settle cases or to provide cheaper, quicker, or fairer dispositions. Proponents of judicial management have also failed to consider the systemic effects of the shift in judicial role. Management is a new form of "judicial activism," a behavior that usually attracts substantial criticism. Moreover, judicial management may be teaching judges to value their statistics, such as the number of case dispositions, more than they value the quality of their dispositions. Finally, because managerial judging is less visible and usually unreviewable, it gives trial courts more authority and at the same time provides litigants with fewer procedural safeguards to protect them from abuse of that authority. In short, managerial judging may be redefining *sub silentio* our standards of what constitutes rational, fair, and impartial adjudication.

Judith Resnik, Managerial Judges, 96 Harv. L. Rev. 374, 378-380 (1982). But see Steven Flanders, Blind Umpires — A Response to Professor Resnik, 35 Hastings L.J. 505 (1984), for a strident disagreement with her cautions about the pretrial conference.

Judge Robert Zampano, after 30 years on the federal bench, described his approach to settlement in an ABA magazine for practitioners. He agreed with Professor Resnik that trial judges should not be case managers, but he thought they should instead become more actively involved in settling cases ("or" support court-annexed ADR). Most of the article is devoted to the subject of its title: Settlement Strategies for Trial Judges. As you read his suggestions, think about the qualities of personality and intellect that the judge is reflecting. Are these the same qualities that make a good trial judge?

### Robert Zampano, Settlement Strategies for Trial Judges
22 Litigation 3-4, 69 (1995). Reprinted with permission of the American Bar Association.

Despite the fact that settlement terminates over 90 percent of civil litigation, many trial judges do not conduct meaningful settlement conferences, but instead rely on superficial formulas or simplistic compromises. I am astonished when judges say to me: "If the lawyers refuse to settle the case between themselves, why should I bother?" I am further horrified when I hear that some judges schedule 10 or 15 settlement conferences in a day with the following stereotypical approach to the settlement of most cases: "Ms. Plaintiff's Counsel, what is your demand?" After receiving the answer, the judge turns to opposing counsel and inquires: "Mr. Defense Attorney, what is your offer?" Then with an amazing display of wisdom and mathematical dexterity, the judge announces his decision that a certain figure, usually exactly in the middle, is the proper settlement. This approach, or one similarly inflexible and passive, does not foster effective and efficient settlement conferences.

The trial judge should play an active, dynamic, and creative role in the settlement process. This may mean injecting herself personally and directly into the settlement negotiations, or it may involve a referral, with specific and well-defined guidelines set by the judge, to a special master or a panel of experts who possess a particular expertise in the subject matter of the lawsuit. . . .

The settlement judge must have the patience, open-mindedness, and skill to fashion a settlement that is fair and reasonable under all circumstances. Sometimes, a method of settlement that neither party has considered opens the door to a satisfactory resolution of the lawsuit. Thus, no particular formula for settlements is available. In effect, each case must be tailored for settlement according to its own characteristics.

Nevertheless, every case on the court docket has a potential for settlement: negligence, contract, trade secret, civil rights, anti-trust, shareholders' derivative actions, patent infringement, and so forth. Almost all cases should be assigned for settlement conferences.

This is not to say that all cases can be, or should be, settled. Public policy may require that a case be litigated rather than settled. Novel legal questions may call for definitive precedential rulings by a court. For example, certain products-liability cases, where public disclosure will benefit hundreds or even thousands of potential claimants, may not be suited for private, undisclosed settlements. . . .

Lawyers, on their own, do manage to settle a fair percentage of civil cases. However, for several reasons, we cannot depend on lawyers to resolve their clients' differences in many of the cases on the trial docket without judicial intervention.

First, law schools have seriously neglected to train students in the art of settlement techniques. "Black letter" law is taught, not the practicalities of lawyering as a business in which people resolve their disputes by negotiation and mediation.

Second, the trial attorney is a professional advocate and not a professional negotiator or decision-maker. His primary role is to advance the client's cause with skill, determination, and diligence. The lawyer earns a fee to win a case, not to compromise it.

Third, lawyers usually settle a case on their own only after following an expensive, cumbersome, awkward route in an adversarial atmosphere. Most lawyers fear that if they initiate settlement discussions, it indicates a sign of weakness to their opponents and portrays a lack of confidence to their clients. . . .

The clients' personal participation in settlement conferences is crucial to success. I can count on the fingers of one hand the cases in which I conducted a settlement conference without the individual parties or the chief executive officer of a corporation being present. If an insurance company was involved, the adjuster was required to attend and the claims manager was asked to be readily available to speak to me by phone. In-house counsel of corporations were also urged to take part in settlement discussions. I conducted no settlement conference unless counsel and their clients expressly consented beforehand to the ground rules.

Although my practices varied depending on the nature of the case, I first met with all counsel and their clients; then I usually saw and spoke with plaintiff and plaintiff's counsel privately. As a general rule, I chatted with the plaintiff about his background and prior experience with litigation. Sooner or later, I asked the person just to sit back and "tell me about your case." Many times we engaged in lively, interesting, and engaging colloquy with respect to the merits of the case. Sometimes I played the devil's advocate; other times I did not.

The most important feature of the discussion was to give the plaintiff a full opportunity to be heard, in his own way. I tried to put myself in the shoes of the party to understand exactly the source of the grievance and what type of settlement he believed would be just and fair. Generally, there was an open and frank discussion of attorneys' fees; the availability of witnesses and documents to support the case; the inconvenience of a trial; and the rock-bottom settlement terms, beyond which the individual would not give in even one degree. . . .

---

Judge Zampano's view of active judicial intervention is extremely benign. There are many examples of cases in which the parties did not desire or appreciate the judge's activism. Once the judge has everyone before him, what can he make them do? Rule 16(c)(2)(I) provides that a judge may take appropriate action with respect to "settling the case and using special procedures to assist in resolving the dispute when authorized by statute or rule."

## In re Atlantic Pipe Corp.
304 F.3d 135 (1st Cir. 2002)

SELYA, Circuit Judge.

This mandamus proceeding requires us to resolve an issue of importance to judges and practitioners alike: Does a district court possess the authority to compel an unwilling party to participate in, and share the costs of, nonbinding mediation conducted by a private mediator? We hold that a court may order mandatory mediation pursuant to an explicit statutory provision or local rule. We further hold that where, as here, no such authorizing medium exists, a court nonetheless may order mandatory mediation through the use of its inherent powers as long as the case is an appropriate one and the order contains adequate safeguards. Because the mediation order here at issue lacks such safeguards (although it does not fall far short), we vacate it and remand the matter for further proceedings.

## I. Background

In January 1996, Thames-Dick Superaqueduct Partners (Thames-Dick) entered into a master agreement with the Puerto Rico Aqueduct and Sewer Authority (PRASA) to construct, operate, and maintain the North Coast Superaqueduct Project (the Project). Thames-Dick granted subcontracts for various portions of the work, including a subcontract for construction management to Dick Corp. of Puerto Rico (Dick-PR), a subcontract for the operation and maintenance of the Project to Thames Water International, Ltd. (Thames Water), and a subcontract for the fabrication of pipe to Atlantic Pipe Corp. (APC). After the Project had been built, a segment of the pipeline burst. Thames-Dick incurred significant costs in repairing the damage. Not surprisingly, it sought to recover those costs from other parties. . . .

On April 25, 2001, the hostilities spilled over into federal court. Two entities beneficially interested in the master agreement—CPA Group International and Chiang, Patel & Yerby, Inc. (collectively CPA)—sued Thames-Dick, Dick-PR, Thames Water, and various insurers in the United States District Court for the District of Puerto Rico, seeking remuneration for consulting services rendered in connection with repairs to the Project. A googol of claims, counterclaims, cross-claims, and third-party complaints followed. Some of these were brought against APC (the petitioner here). . . .

. . . Thames-Dick asked that the case be referred to mediation and suggested Professor Eric Green as a suitable mediator. The district court

granted the motion over APC's objection and ordered non-binding mediation to proceed before Professor Green. The court pronounced mediation
likely to conserve judicial resources; directed all parties to undertake mediation in good faith; stayed discovery pending completion of the mediation;
and declared that participation in the mediation would not prejudice the
parties' positions vis-à-vis the pending motion or the litigation as a whole.
The court also stated that if mediation failed to produce a global settlement,
the case would proceed to trial.

After moving unsuccessfully for reconsideration of the mediation order,
APC sought relief by way of mandamus. . . .

## II. Jurisdiction

. . .

We believe that this case is fit for advisory mandamus because the extent
of a trial court's power to order mandatory mediation presents a systemi-
cally important issue as to which this court has not yet spoken. Moreover,
that issue is capable of significant repetition prior to effective review. . . . We
turn, then, to the merits.

## III. The Merits

There are four potential sources of judicial authority for ordering mandatory non-binding mediation of pending cases, namely, (a) the court's local
rules, (b) an applicable statute, (c) the Federal Rules of Civil Procedure, and
(d) the court's inherent powers. Because the district court did not identify
the basis of its assumed authority, we consider each of these sources.

### A. *The Local Rules*

A district court's local rules may provide an appropriate source of authority for ordering parties to participate in mediation. See Rhea v. Masey-
Ferguson, Inc., 767 F.2d 266, 268-269 (6th Cir. 1985) (per curiam). In Puerto
Rico, however, the local rules contain only a single reference to any form
of alternative dispute resolution (ADR). That reference is embodied in the
district court's Amended Civil Justice Expense and Delay Reduction Plan
(CJR Plan). See D.P.R. R. app. III.

The district court adopted the CJR Plan on June 14, 1993, in response to
the directive contained in the Civil Justice Reform Act of 1990 (CJRA), 28
U.S.C. §§ 471-482. Rule V of the CJR Plan states:

> Pursuant to 28 U.S.C. § 473(b)(4), this Court shall adopt a method of Alternative
> Dispute Resolution ("ADR") through mediation by a judicial officer.
>     Such a program would allow litigants to obtain from an impartial third
> party—the judicial officer as mediator—a flexible non-binding, dispute

resolution process to facilitate negotiations among the parties to help them reach settlement.

D.P.R. R. app. III (R. V.). . . .

The respondents concede that the mediation order in this case falls outside the boundaries of the mediation program envisioned by Rule V. It does so most noticeably because it involves mediation before a private mediator, not a judicial officer. . . .

### B. The ADR Act

There is only one potential source of statutory authority for ordering mandatory non-binding mediation here: the Alternative Dispute Resolution Act of 1998 (ADR Act), 28 U.S.C. §§ 651-658. Congress passed the ADR Act to promote the utilization of alternative dispute resolution methods in the federal courts and to set appropriate guidelines for their use. The Act lists mediation as an appropriate ADR process. Id. § 651(a). Moreover, it sanctions the participation of "professional neutrals from the private sector" as mediators. Id. § 653(b). Finally, the Act requires district courts to obtain litigants' consent only when they order arbitration, id. § 652(a), not when they order the use of other ADR mechanisms (such as non-binding mediation).

Despite the broad sweep of these provisions, the Act is quite clear that some form of the ADR procedures it endorses must be adopted in each judicial district by local rule. *See id.* § 651(b) (directing each district court to "devise and implement its own alternative dispute resolution program, by local rule adopted under [28 U.S.C.] section 2071(a), to encourage and promote the use of alternative dispute resolution in its district"). In the absence of such local rules, the ADR Act itself does not authorize any specific court to use a particular ADR mechanism. Because the District of Puerto Rico has not yet complied with the Act's mandate, the mediation order here at issue cannot be justified under the ADR Act.

. . . To say that the Act authorized each district judge to disregard a district-wide ADR plan (or the absence of one) and fashion innovative procedures for use in specific cases is simply too much of a stretch.

We add, however, that although the respondents cannot use the ADR Act as a justification, neither can APC use it as a nullification. Noting that the Act requires the adoption of local rules establishing a formal ADR program, APC equates the absence of such rules with the absence of power to employ an ADR procedure (say, mediation) in a specific case. But that is wishful thinking: if one assumes that district judges possessed the power to require mediation prior to the passage of the ADR Act, there is nothing in the Act that strips them of that power. After all, even the adoption of a federal procedural rule does not implicitly abrogate a district court's inherent power to act merely because the rule touches upon the same subject matter. . . .

## C. The Civil Rules

The respondents next argue that the district court possessed the authority to require mediation by virtue of the Federal Rules of Civil Procedure. They concentrate their attention on Fed. R. Civ. P. 16, which states in pertinent part that "the court may take appropriate action[ ] with respect to . . . (9) settlement and the use of special procedures to assist in resolving the dispute when authorized by statute or local rule. . . ." Fed. R. Civ. P. 16(c)(9).* But the words "when authorized by statute or local rule" are a frank limitation on the district courts' authority to order mediation thereunder, and we must adhere to that circumscription. Because there is no statute or local rule authorizing mandatory private mediation in the District of Puerto Rico, Rule 16(c)(9) does not assist the respondents' cause.[4]

## D. Inherent Powers

Even apart from positive law, district courts have substantial inherent power to manage and control their calendars. See Link [v. Wabash R.R. Co., 370 U.S. 626, 630 (1963) (explaining that neither the permissive language of Fed. R. Civ. P. 41(b) nor the policy behind it justified a conclusion that it was meant to limit the district courts' inherent power to dismiss a case for want of prosecution)]; see generally Brockton Sav. Bank v. Peat, Marwick, Mitchell & Co., 771 F.2d 5, 11 (1st Cir. 1985) (explaining that "the rules of civil procedure do not completely describe and limit the power of district courts"). This inherent power takes many forms. *See* Fed. R. Civ. P. 83(b) (providing that judges may regulate practice in any manner consistent with federal law and applicable rules). By way of illustration, a district court may use its inherent power to compel represented clients to attend pretrial settlement conferences, even though such a practice is not specifically authorized in the Civil Rules. See G. Heileman Brewing Co. v. Joseph Oat Corp., 871 F.2d 648, 650 (7th Cir. 1989) (en banc).

Of course, a district court's inherent powers are not infinite. There are at least four limiting principles. First, inherent powers must be used in a way reasonably suited to the enhancement of the court's processes, including the orderly and expeditious disposition of pending cases. Coyante v. P.R. Ports Auth., 105 F.3d 17, 23 (1st Cir. 1997). Second, inherent powers cannot be exercised in a manner that contradicts an applicable statute or rule. *Chambers*

---

* [Rule 16(c)(9) now appears as Rule 16(c)(2)(I) in the restyled rules. — Eds.]

4. The cases that the respondents cite for the proposition that Rule 16 sanctions mandatory ADR procedures even in the absence of an enabling statute or local rule are inapposite. All of them predate the 1993 amendments, which added the pertinent language to Rule 16. See, e.g., Fed. Reserve Bank v. Carey-Canada, Inc., 123 F.R.D. 603, 606 (D. Minn. 1988); Arabian Am. Oil Co. v. Scarfone, 119 F.R.D. 448, 448-49 (M.D. Fla. 1988).

*[v. NASCO, Inc.]*, 501 U.S. [32, 47 (1991)].** Third, the use of inherent powers must comport with procedural fairness. *Id.* at 50. And, finally, inherent powers "must be exercised with restraint and discretion." *Id.* at 44.

At one time, the inherent power of judges to compel unwilling parties to participate in ADR procedures was a hot-button issue for legal scholars. Compare, *e.g.*, [Jennifer] O'Hearne, [Comment, Compelled Participation in Innovative Trial Proceedings, 84 Nw. U.L. Rev. 290, 317 (1989),] *supra* at 320 (arguing that inherent power should not be used to compel participation in pretrial settlement proceedings), with Lucille M. Ponte, Putting Mandatory Summary Jury Trial Back on the Docket: Recommendations on the Exercise of Judicial Authority, 63 Fordham L. Rev. 1069, 1094 (1995) (urging the opposite conclusion). Although many federal district courts have forestalled further debate by adopting local rules that authorize specific ADR procedures and outlaw others, e.g., D.N.H. R. 53.1 (permitting mandatory mediation); D. Me. R. 83.11 (permitting only voluntary mediation); D. Mass. R. 16.4 (permitting mandatory summary jury trials but only voluntary mediation), the District of Puerto Rico is not among them. Thus, we have no choice but to address the question head-on.

We begin our inquiry by examining the case law. In Strandell v. Jackson County, 838 F.2d 884 (7th Cir. 1987), the Seventh Circuit held that a district court does not possess inherent power to compel participation in a summary jury trial.[5] In the court's view, Fed. R. Civ. P. 16 occupied the field and prevented a district court from forcing "an unwilling litigant [to] be sidetracked from the normal course of litigation." Id. at 887. But the group that spearheaded the subsequent revision of Rule 16 explicitly rejected that interpretation. *See* Fed. R. Civ. P. 16, advisory committee's note (1993 Amendment) ("The [amended] rule does not attempt to resolve questions as to the extent a court would be authorized to require [ADR] proceedings as an exercise of its inherent powers."). Thus, we do not find *Strandell* persuasive on this point.

The *Strandell* court also expressed concern that summary jury trials would undermine traditional discovery and privilege rules by requiring certain disclosures prior to an actual trial. 838 F.2d at 888. We find this concern unwarranted. Because a summary jury trial (like a non-binding mediation) does not require any disclosures beyond what would be required in the ordinary course of discovery, its principal disadvantage to the litigants is that it may prevent them from saving surprises for the time of trial. Since trial by

---

** [In Chambers v. NASCO, Inc., the Supreme Court rejected the argument that the adoption of various provisions of the Civil Rules eliminated the district court's inherent power to impose other sanctions. 501 U.S. 32, 42-43 (1991). It also described traditional limits on the exercise of inherent power to impose sanctions. — EDS.]

5. A summary jury trial is an ADR technique in which the opposing attorneys present their case, in abbreviated form, to a mock jury, which proceeds to render a nonbinding verdict. See In re NLO, Inc., 5 F.3d 154, 156 (6th Cir. 1993); see generally Thomas D. Lambros, The Summary Jury Trial Report to the Judicial Conference of the United States, 103 F.R.D. 461 (1984).

ambush is no longer in vogue, that interest does not deserve protection. See Fed. Reserve Bank v. Carey-Canada, Inc., 123 F.R.D. 603, 606 (D. Minn. 1988).

Relying on policy arguments, the Sixth Circuit also has found that district courts do not possess inherent power to compel participation in summary jury trials. See In re NLO, Inc., 5 F.3d 154, 157-58 (6th Cir. 1993). The court thought the value of a summary jury trial questionable when parties do not engage in the process voluntarily, and it worried that "too broad an interpretation of the federal courts' inherent power to regulate their procedure . . . encourages judicial high-handedness. . . ." Id. at 158 (citation and internal quotation marks omitted).

The concerns articulated by these two respected courts plainly apply to mandatory mediation orders. When mediation is forced upon unwilling litigants, it stands to reason that the likelihood of settlement is diminished. Requiring parties to invest substantial amounts of time and money in mediation under such circumstances may well be inefficient. Cf. Richard A. Posner, The Summary Jury Trial and Other Methods of Alternative Dispute Resolution: Some Cautionary Observations, 53 U. Chi. L. Rev. 366, 369-72 (1986) (offering a model to evaluate ADR techniques in terms of their capacity to encourage settlements).

The fact remains, however, that none of these considerations establishes that mandatory mediation is always inappropriate. There may well be specific cases in which such a protocol is likely to conserve judicial resources without significantly burdening the objectors' rights to a full, fair, and speedy trial. Much depends on the idiosyncracies of the particular case and the details of the mediation order.

In some cases, a court may be warranted in believing that compulsory mediation could yield significant benefits even if one or more parties object. After all, a party may resist mediation simply out of unfamiliarity with the process or out of fear that a willingness to submit would be perceived as a lack of confidence in her legal position. See Campbell C. Hutchinson, The Case for Mandatory Mediation, 42 Loy. L. Rev. 85, 89-90 (1996). In such an instance, the party's initial reservations are likely to evaporate as the mediation progresses, and negotiations could well produce a beneficial outcome, at reduced cost and greater speed, than would a trial. While the possibility that parties will fail to reach agreement remains ever present, the boon of settlement can be worth the risk.

. . . Mindful of these potential advantages, we hold that it is within a district court's inherent power to order non-consensual mediation in those cases in which that step seems reasonably likely to serve the interests of justice. Cf. Reilly v. United States, 863 F.2d 149, 156-57 (1st Cir. 1988) (finding that district courts have inherent power to appoint technical advisors in especially complex cases).

### E. *The Mediation Order*

Our determination that the district courts have inherent power to refer cases to non-binding mediation is made with a recognition that any such order must be crafted in a manner that preserves procedural fairness and shields objecting parties from undue burdens. We thus turn to the specifics of the mediation order entered in this case. As with any exercise of a district court's inherent powers, we review the entry of that order for abuse of discretion. See *Chambers*, 501 U.S. at 50; *Reilly*, 863 F.2d at 156.

As an initial matter, we agree with the lower court that the complexity of this case militates in favor of ordering mediation. At last count, the suit involves twelve parties, asserting a welter of claims, counterclaims, cross-claims, and third-party claims predicated on a wide variety of theories. The pendency of nearly parallel litigation in the Puerto Rican courts, which features a slightly different cast of characters and claims that are related to but not completely congruent with those asserted here, further complicates the matter. Untangling the intricate web of relationships among the parties, along with the difficult and fact-intensive arguments made by each, will be time-consuming and will impose significant costs on the parties and the court. Against this backdrop, mediation holds out the dual prospect of advantaging the litigants and conserving scarce judicial resources.

. . . APC posits that the appointment of a private mediator proposed by one of the parties is per se improper (and, thus, invalidates the order). We do not agree. The district court has inherent power to "appoint persons unconnected with the court to aid judges in the performance of specific judicial duties." Ex parte Peterson, 253 U.S. 300, 312 (1920). In the context of non-binding mediation, the mediator does not decide the merits of the case and has no authority to coerce settlement. Thus, in the absence of a contrary statute or rule, it is perfectly acceptable for the district court to appoint a qualified and neutral private party as a mediator. The mere fact that the mediator was proposed by one of the parties is insufficient to establish bias in favor of that party. Cf. TechSearch, L.L.C. v. Intel Corp., 286 F.3d 1360, 1379 n.3 (Fed. Cir. 2002) (noting that technical advisors typically would be selected from a list of candidates submitted by the parties).

We hasten to add that the litigants are free to challenge the qualifications or neutrality of any suggested mediator (whether or not nominated by a party to the case). APC, for example, had a full opportunity to present its views about the suggested mediator both in its opposition to the motion for mediation and in its motion for reconsideration of the mediation order. Despite these opportunities, APC offered no convincing reason to spark a belief that Professor Green, a nationally recognized mediator with significant experience in sprawling cases, is an unacceptable choice. . . .

APC also grouses that it should not be forced to share the costs of an unwanted mediation. We have held, however, that courts have the power under Fed. R. Civ. P. 26(f) to issue pretrial cost-sharing orders in complex litigation. See In re San Juan Dupont Plaza Hotel Fire Litig., 994 F.2d 956, 965 (1st Cir. 1993). Given the difficulties facing trial courts in cases involving multiple parties and multiple claims, we are hesitant to limit that power to the traditional discovery context. This is especially true in complicated cases, where the potential value of mediation lies not only in promoting settlement but also in clarifying the issues remaining for trial.

The short of the matter is that, without default cost-sharing rules, the use of valuable ADR techniques (like mediation) becomes hostage to the parties' ability to agree on the concomitant financial arrangements. . . . To avoid this pitfall, we hold that the district court, in an appropriate case, is empowered to order the sharing of reasonable costs and expenses associated with mandatory non-binding mediation.

. . . Even when generically appropriate, a mediation order must contain procedural and substantive safeguards to ensure fairness to all parties involved. The mediation order in this case does not quite meet that test. In particular, the order does not set limits on the duration of the mediation or the expense associated therewith.

. . . As entered, the order simply requires the parties to mediate; it does not set forth either a timetable for the mediation or a cap on the fees that the mediator may charge. The figures that have been bandied about in the briefs—$900 per hour or $9,000 per mediation day—are quite large and should not be left to the mediator's whim. Relatedly, because the mediator is to be paid an hourly rate, the court should have set an outside limit on the number of hours to be devoted to mediation. Equally as important, it is trite but often true that justice delayed is justice denied. An unsuccessful mediation will postpone the ultimate resolution of the case—indeed, the district court has stayed all discovery pending the completion of the mediation—and, thus, prolong the litigation. For these reasons, the district court should have set a definite time frame for the mediation.

. . .

A court intent on ordering non-consensual mediation should take other precautions as well. For example, the court should make it clear (as did the able district court in this case) that participation in mediation will not be taken as a waiver of any litigation position. The important point is that the protections we have mentioned are not intended to comprise an exhaustive list, but, rather, to illustrate that when a district court orders a party to participate in mediation, it should take care to assuage legitimate concerns about the possible negative consequences of such an order. . . .

## IV. Conclusion

We admire the district court's pragmatic and innovative approach to this massive litigation. . . .

That said, the need of the district judge in this case to construct his own mediation regime ad hoc underscores the greater need of the district court as an institution to adopt an ADR program and memorialize it in its local rules. In the ADR Act, Congress directed that "[e]ach United States district court shall authorize, by local rule under section 2071(a), the use of alternative dispute resolution processes in all civil actions. . . ." 28 U.S.C. § 651(b). While Congress did not set a firm deadline for compliance with this directive, the statute was enacted four years ago. This omission having been noted, we are confident that the district court will move expediently to bring the District of Puerto Rico into compliance. . . .

*Vacated and remanded. Costs shall be taxed in favor of the petitioner.*

## Note: Special Procedures to Encourage Settlement

Does the rise of these low-visibility alternatives to trial compromise our collective interest in observing civil process? What is that collective interest? Can it be described as a right, or simply a procedure preference? Aren't the parties in *Atlantic Pipe* now required to pay twice over for dispute resolution if the mandatory mediation fails? They may not have to pay for the public costs of litigation, but they'll have to pay their attorneys' fees and they may have to pay the cost of other parties.

Mandatory mediation and nonbinding summary jury trials are only two of the special procedures to which a court might resort; arbitration is another prominent example (see Chapter 5). Consider Judge Zampano's description of one of his settlement-promotion strategies, and think about where he gets the authority to do this.

When a case had difficult technical aspects, I at times requested the parties to agree upon the selection of a neutral advisor or panel of experts to sit in on the settlement talks; to listen to the contentions of the parties; and to assist in formulating a settlement plan. Many times, outside experts point out overlooked features in a case, proffer impartial analyses, and advance creative and attractive terms for a reasonable settlement.

The key ingredient to the successful use of special masters or a panel of experts is that all the parties and counsel must agree upon the individuals selected. Several methods for the appointment of neutral advisors have proven acceptable in practice. The usual procedure is for the court to submit to each party a list of 15 or 20 specialists in the field. Peremptory challenges are exercised privately by each party. When the lists are returned, the court appoints a special master or panel from those names acceptable to both sides. Another method is to have the parties provide the court with names. It is surprisingly common for the parties to submit one or more of the same names. On occasion, I have merely called in the parties, their counsel, and trial experts and openly discussed the appointment of a renowned individual from the faculty of a local university or from the staff of a business or utility company in the state, and so forth.

I have followed a few other ground rules: (1) The advisors were permitted to confer with the parties privately and separately, or together; they could make on-site inspections; they could ask questions of the parties, counsel, or the retained experts who were scheduled to testify at trial; and they could confer with me privately. (2) The predetermined charges for the experts were divided equally between the parties. (3) The recommendations of the advisors for settlement were not binding; however, if the case did not settle, any party could call the experts as witnesses, identify them as "court-appointed experts," and submit their "findings" and "opinions" to the jury within the scope permissible under the Federal Rules of Evidence.

I once employed a panel of experts to help resolve a class action civil rights case brought by a group of women to challenge the validity of the physical agility tests being given to applicants for positions on a municipality's police department. These tests had been developed years ago and had been uniformly adopted by most cities and towns in Connecticut. At the time of the settlement conference, each side had retained the services of experts, extensive discovery was scheduled, and the parties predicted the case would take several weeks to try. The issues attracted wide-scale media attention.

With the agreement of the parties, a three-person panel of experts was selected to meet and hear the parties and their experts; to view the administration of the tests; and to report their findings and recommendations to the court. The panel consisted of a Yale law professor, who was a recognized civil rights scholar; the director of women's athletic activities at Yale University; and a medical doctor, who had considerable experience in treating sports-related injuries and who had written several articles on physical agility training for male and female athletes.

Two full days were set aside for the panel to complete their assignment. They unanimously determined that, in some respects, the municipality's tests were not job-related. They designed a new series of tests that they believed would be fair and reasonable to determine the physical qualifications of the applicants, both female and male.

I reviewed the report of the panel, carefully considered its contents, and made a few minor changes to conform to several valid suggestions by the parties. I then met with the parties who agreed to the conditions of the settlement I proposed. Because it was a class action, I scheduled a formal hearing on the matter, with due notice to the class, and eventually entered judgment. I am now informed that almost every city and town in Connecticut has revised its physical entrance examinations for police and fire departments to conform to the decree entered in this case.

Robert Zampano, Settlement Strategies for Trial Judges, 22 Litigation 3, 70-71 (Fall 1995).

As you read in *Atlantic Pipe*, under the Alternative Dispute Resolution Act of 1998, 28 U.S.C. § 651(b), each federal district court is obliged to adopt local rules implementing its own ADR program with formal mechanisms for promoting settlement. A 2011 study reveals that 63 percent of courts authorize mediation, 36 percent authorize settlement conferences, 23 percent authorize arbitration, 23 percent authorize "early neutral evaluation," and 12 percent simply authorize the use of ADR in general. Summary of Selected Features of ADR Procedures in Federal Courts, Conference on Court ADR Research at the Federal Judicial Center (Nov. 17, 2011). See also John Lande, How Much Justice Can We Afford?: Defining the Courts' Roles and Deciding the Appropriate Number of Trials, Settlement Signals, and Other Elements Needed to Administer Justice, 2006 J. Disp. Resol. 213. In recent years, federal district courts appear to have shifted away from authorizing a specific form of ADR to multiple forms. See Donna Stienstra, ADR in the Federal District Courts: An Initial Report, Federal Judicial Center, Nov. 16, 2011. See also Yishai Boyarin, Court-Connected ADR—A Time of Crisis, A Time of Change, 50 Fam. Ct. Rev. 377 (2012); Jacqueline

Nolan-Haley, Mediation: The "New Arbitration," 17 Harv. Negotiation L. Rev. 61 (2012).

## *Note: "Litigotiation"*

Marc Galanter and Mia Cahill describe modern civil litigation as "a single process of pursuing remedies in the presence of courts. For mnemonic purposes, we attach to it the fanciful neologism 'litigotiation.'" "Most Cases Settle": Judicial Promotion and Regulation of Settlements, 46 Stan. L. Rev. 1339, 1341-1342 (1994). The authors question whether this growing enthusiasm for judicial promotion of settlement is a good thing by carefully analyzing many arguments that have been advanced in support of settlement in general and of judicial encouragement of settlement in particular. They express their conclusions as follows:

> What do we know of the effects of judicial intervention on the number or quality of settlements? As to number, the available studies provide no basis for thinking judicial promotion leads to a number of settlements that is sufficiently higher than would otherwise occur to compensate for the opportunity costs of the judicial attention diverted from litigation. . . . As to the effects of judicial promotion on the quality of settlements, we simply do not know. . . . Are settlements arranged by judges less variable, more principled, more reflective of the merits? No one knows.

Id. at 1388-1389. See also Carrie Menkel-Meadow, For and Against Settlement: Uses and Abuses of the Mandatory Settlement Conference, 33 UCLA L. Rev. 485 (1985).

What do you imagine are the problems that researchers encounter when attempting to answer the questions raised by Galanter and Cahill? If the questions are unanswerable, then why do so many reformers seem sold on expanding (and formalizing through Rules amendments) judicial power to encourage settlements? What is the empirical basis for this movement?

Professor Janet Cooper Alexander offers the following summary of the potential advantages of settlement over trial. What do they imply about the foregoing materials on judicial promotion of settlement?

> Settlement has many positive aspects, to be sure. For example, it may cost the parties less than trial; it avoids all-or-nothing results and allows parties to assure themselves an "average" outcome based on the expected value of the case; it permits consideration of interests that cannot be taken into account in adjudication; it allows innovative "pie-enlarging" solutions that are not possible through remedies available from adjudication; and it produces consensual, rather than coerced, outcomes. Adjudication, however, also serves important public and private interests. . . . [A]djudication produces precedents, which are a public good. Adjudication serves other public interests as well, such as enforcing the substantive law, providing a yardstick for evaluating settlements, assuring public access to information about disputes

affecting the public interest, preserving public confidence in the administration of justice, and affording citizen participation in democratic government through jury service. And adjudication advances private interests such as individual dignity and the interest in securing private rights.

Janet Cooper Alexander, Judges' Self-Interest and Procedural Rules: Comment on *Macey*, 23 J. Legal Stud. 647, 650 (1994). For recent empirical evidence regarding the disposition of state cases before trial, see Paula Hannaford-Agor et al., National Center for State Courts, The Landscape of Civil Litigation in State Courts 20 (2015) (reporting that 35 percent of filings are dismissed, 20 percent end in default judgment, while just 10 percent are explicitly recorded as settlements, and summary judgment is used in just 1 percent of cases); id. at iv, 31 (noting precipitous decline in the number of cases in which both parties are represented by counsel).

## Note: Motions in Limine

A number of the subjects for discussion at pretrial conferences deal with matters of evidence. See, e.g., Fed. R. Civ. P. 16(c)(2). It is not uncommon for the court and the parties to resolve difficult points of evidence before the trial starts, either at conference or on a motion in limine, a process that allows the parties to raise evidentiary objections before there is any trial testimony. Although these motions may seem more glamorous in criminal suits, where they deal with heightened last minute constitutional rights, motions in limine are likewise important in civil suits. If, for example, a case seems to hinge on the admissibility of certain documentary evidence, then a pretrial ruling on its admissibility could be practically dispositive, either by inducing settlement or paving the way to a successful motion for summary judgment. Pretrial rulings on the admissibility of evidence therefore serve an important role in resolving at least some suits at an early stage. Fuller comprehension of the rules that govern such motions will come from your courses in evidence, constitutional criminal procedure, and trial practice.

## B.   SUMMARY JUDGMENT

### Problem Case: A Literary Law Student (Part Two)

Return to the problem case in Chapter 3, section C(2) and assume that you are still Donna's lawyer. She has suggested that you file a motion for summary judgment, appending her affidavit stating that she has never read or heard anyone recount any part of *First Year*. Assuming that the plaintiff has no direct evidence to the contrary, what are your chances of prevailing, and why?

# 1.   The Development of Modern Summary Judgment Doctrine

## a.   Piercing the Pleadings: Historical Perspectives

The historic antecedents of Rule 56 lie in the nineteenth-century British demurrer's inadequacy in weeding out the spurious defenses raised by obligors on bills of exchange. On the surface the pleadings of these particular debtors looked good enough to escape demurrer, but the whole world knew that they were interposed only for delay. Accordingly, in 1855, Parliament enacted legislation to enable the courts to "pierce the pleadings" in such cases in order to render prompt decisions.

In the same period, American codes were enacted to provide for the striking of "sham" pleadings. Rule 56 was originally conceived in reaction to both the English and American experience. Its intention is to allow judges to dismiss cases where there is not enough evidence to justify the time and expense of trial. At the same time, it does not incorporate the condemnation of the pleading as a "sham."

Rule 56 has never been significantly amended. Practice under it has been described in these terms by a judge from the United States District Court for the Northern District of California:

> [It] is plagued by confusion and uncertainty. It suffers from misuse by those lawyers who insist on making a motion in the face of obvious fact issues; from neglect by others who, fearful of judicial hostility to the procedure, refrain from moving even where summary judgment would be appropriate; and from the failure of trial and appellate courts to define clearly what is a genuine issue of material fact.

William W. Schwarzer, Summary Judgment Under the Federal Rules: Defining Genuine Issues of Material Fact, 99 F.R.D. 465, 465 (1984).

In 1986, the Supreme Court decided three summary judgment cases in a single term, with the apparent purpose of clarifying the practice and encouraging its use. This, in turn, produced an avalanche of commentary about summary judgment. Here is a sampling of some of the best articles: Daniel P. Collins, Summary Judgment and Circumstantial Evidence, 40 Stan. L. Rev. 491 (1988); D. Michael Risinger, Another Step in the Counter Revolution: A Summary Judgment on the Supreme Court's New Approach to Summary Judgment, 54 Brook. L. Rev. 35 (1988); Melissa L. Nelken, One Step Forward, Two Steps Back: Summary Judgment After *Celotex*, 40 Hastings L.J. 53 (1988); Linda S. Mullinex, Summary Judgment: Taming the Beast of Burdens, 10 Am. J. Trial Advoc. 433 (1987); Robert K. Smits, Note, Federal Summary Judgment: The "New" Workhorse for an Overburdened Federal Court System, 20 U.C. Davis L. Rev. 955 (1987); David P. Currie, Thoughts on Directed Verdicts and Summary Judgments, 45 U. Chi. L. Rev. 72 (1977); Martin B. Louis, Federal Summary Judgment Doctrine: A Critical Analysis, 83 Yale L.J. 745 (1974).

The proponents of summary judgment tend to be the same people who urge that the pleading stage be more meaningful generally. Summary judgment is, however, a more drastic event than dismissal of a pleading, at least in the usual case; it raises, as well, the specter of denying the right to a jury trial. Excerpts from the major precedent in the path of expanding summary judgment and from the 1986 Supreme Court trilogy appear below.

### *Adickes v. S.H. Kress & Co.*
398 U.S. 144 (1970)

JUSTICE HARLAN delivered the opinion of the Court.

Petitioner, Sandra Adickes, a white school teacher from New York, brought this suit in the United States District Court for the Southern District of New York against respondent S.H. Kress & Co. ("Kress") to recover damages under 42 U.S.C. § 1983[1] for an alleged violation of her constitutional rights under the Equal Protection Clause of the Fourteenth Amendment. The suit arises out of Kress' refusal to serve lunch to Miss Adickes at its restaurant facilities in its Hattiesburg, Mississippi, store on August 14, 1964, and Miss Adickes' subsequent arrest upon her departure from the store by the Hattiesburg police on a charge of vagrancy. At the time of both the refusal to serve and the arrest, Miss Adickes was with six young people, all Negroes, who were her students in a Mississippi "Freedom School" where she was teaching that summer. Unlike Miss Adickes, the students were offered service, and were not arrested.

Petitioner's complaint had two counts, each bottomed on § 1983, and each alleging that Kress had deprived her of the right under the Equal Protection Clause of the Fourteenth Amendment not to be discriminated against on the basis of race. The first count charged that Miss Adickes had been refused service by Kress because she was a "Caucasian in the company of Negroes." Petitioner sought, *inter alia*, to prove that the refusal to serve her was pursuant to a "custom of the community to segregate the races in public eating places." However, in a pretrial decision, 252 F. Supp. 140 ([S.D.N.Y.] 1966), the District Court ruled that to recover under this count, Miss Adickes would have to prove that at the time she was refused service, there was a specific "custom . . . of refusing service to whites in the company of Negroes" and that this custom was "enforced by the State" under

---

1. Rev. Stat. § 1979, 42 U.S.C. § 1983 provides:

Every person who, under color of any statute, ordinance, regulation, custom, or usage, of any State or Territory, subjects, or causes to be subjected, any citizen of the United States or other person within the jurisdiction thereof to the deprivation of any rights, privileges, or immunities secured by the Constitution and laws, shall be liable to the party injured in an action at law, suit in equity, or other proper proceeding for redress.

Mississippi's criminal trespass statute. Because petitioner was unable to prove at the trial that there were other instances in Hattiesburg of a white person having been refused service while in the company of Negroes, the District Court directed a verdict in favor of respondent. A divided panel of the Court of Appeals affirmed on this ground, also holding that § 1983 "requires that the discriminatory custom or usage be proved to exist in the locale where the discrimination took place, and in the State generally," and that petitioner's "proof on both points was deficient," 409 F.2d 121, 124 ([2d Cir.] 1968).

The second count of her complaint, alleging that both the refusal of service and her subsequent arrest were the product of a conspiracy between Kress and the Hattiesburg police, was dismissed before trial on a motion for summary judgment. The District Court ruled that petitioner had "failed to allege any facts from which a conspiracy might be inferred." 252 F. Supp. at 144. This determination was unanimously affirmed by the Court of Appeals, 409 F.2d at 126-127.

Miss Adickes, in seeking review here, claims that the District Court erred both in directing a verdict on the substantive count, and in granting summary judgment on the conspiracy count. Last Term we granted certiorari, 394 U.S. 1011 (1969), and we now reverse and remand for further proceedings on each of the two counts. . . .

We now proceed to consider whether the District Court erred in granting summary judgment on the conspiracy count. In granting respondent's motion, the District Court simply stated that there was "no evidence in the complaint or in the affidavits and other papers from which a 'reasonably-minded person' might draw an inference of conspiracy," 252 F. Supp. at 144, *aff'd*, 409 F.2d, at 126-127. Our own scrutiny of the factual allegations of petitioner's complaint, as well as the material found in the affidavits and depositions presented by Kress to the District Court, however, convinces us that summary judgment was improper here, for we think respondent failed to carry its burden of showing the absence of any genuine issue of fact. Before explaining why this is so, it is useful to state the factual arguments, made by the parties concerning summary judgment, and the reasoning of the courts below.

In moving for summary judgment, Kress argued that "uncontested facts" established that no conspiracy existed between any Kress employee and the police. To support this assertion, Kress pointed first to the statements in the deposition of the store manager (Mr. Powell) that (a) he had not communicated with the police,[8] and that (b) he had, by a prearranged

8. In his deposition, Powell admitted knowing Hugh Herring, chief of police of Hattiesburg, and said that he had seen and talked to him on two occasions in 1964 prior to the incident with Miss Adickes. When asked how often the arresting officer, Ralph Hillman, came into the store, Powell stated that he didn't know precisely but "Maybe every day." However, Powell said that on August 14 he didn't recall seeing any policemen either inside or outside the store, and he denied (1) that he had called the police, (2) that he had agreed with any public official to deny Miss Adickes the use of the library, (3) that he had agreed with any public official to refuse Miss Adickes service in the Kress store on the day in question, or (4) that he had asked any public official to have Miss Adickes arrested.

tacit signal,[9] ordered the food counter supervisor to see that Miss Adickes was refused service only because he was fearful of a riot in the store by customers angered at seeing a "mixed group" of whites and blacks eating together.[10] Kress also relied on affidavits from the Hattiesburg chief

9. The signal, according to Powell, was a nod of his head. Powell claimed that at a meeting about a month earlier with Miss Baggett, the food counter supervisor, he "told her not to serve the white person in the group if I . . . shook my head no. But, if I didn't give her any sign, to go ahead and serve anybody."

Powell stated that he had prearranged this tacit signal with Miss Baggett because "there was quite a lot of violence . . . in Hattiesburg" directed towards whites "with colored people, in what you call a mixed group."

10. Powell described the circumstances of his refusal as follows:

> On this particular day, just shortly after 12 o'clock, I estimate there was 75 to 100 people in the store, and the lunch counter was pretty—was pretty well to capacity there, full, and I was going up towards the front of the store in one of the aisles, and looking towards the front of the store, and there was a group of colored girls, and a white woman who came into the north door, which was next to the lunch counter.
>
> And the one thing that really stopped me and called my attention to this group, was the fact that they were dressed alike. They all had on, what looked like a light blue denim skirt. And the best I can remember is that they were—they were almost identical, all of them. And they came into the door, and people coming in stopped to look, and they went on to the booths. And there happened to be two empty there. And one group of them and the white woman sat down in one, and the rest of them sat in the second group.
>
> And, almost immediately there—I mean this, it didn't take just a few seconds from the time they came into the door to sit down, but, already the people began to mill around the store and started coming over towards the lunch counter. And, by that time I was up close to the candy counter, and I had a wide open view there. And the people had real sour looks on their faces, nobody was joking, or being corny, or carrying on. They looked like a frightened mob. They really did. I have seen mobs before. I was in Korea during the riots in 1954 and 1955. And I know what they are. And this actually got me.
>
> I looked out towards the front, and we have what they call see-through windows. There is no backs to them. You can look out of the store right into the street. And the north window, it looks right into the lunch counter, 25 or 30 people were standing there looking in, and across the street even, in a jewelry store, people were standing there, and it looked really bad to me. It looked like one person could have yelled "Let's get them," which has happened before, and cause this group to turn into a mob. And, so, quickly I just made up my mind to avoid the riot, and protect the people that were in the store, and my employees, as far as the people in the mob who were going to get hurt themselves. I just knew that something was going to break loose there.

of police,[11] and the two arresting officers,[12] to the effect that store manager Powell had not requested that petitioner be arrested. Finally, Kress pointed to the statements in petitioner's own deposition that she had no knowledge of any communication between any Kress employee and any member of the Hattiesburg police, and was relying on circumstantial evidence to support her contention that there was an arrangement between Kress and the police.

Petitioner, in opposing summary judgment, pointed out that respondent had failed in its moving papers to dispute the allegation in petitioner's complaint, a statement at her deposition,[13] and an unsworn statement by a Kress employee,[14]

11. The affidavit of the chief of police, who it appears was not present at the arrest, states in relevant part:

> Mr. Powell had made no request of me to arrest Miss Sandra Adickes or any other person, in fact, I did not know Mr. Powell personally until the day of this statement. [But cf. Powell's statement at his deposition, n.8, supra.] Mr. Powell and I had not discussed the arrest of this person until the day of this statement and we had never previously discussed her in any way.

12. The affidavits of Sergeant Boone and Officer Hillman each state, in identical language:

> I was contacted on this date by Mr. John H. Williams, Jr., a representative of Genesco, owners of S.H. Kress and Company, who requested that I make a statement concerning alleged conspiracy in connection with the aforesaid arrest.
>
> This arrest was made on the public streets of Hattiesburg, Mississippi, and was an officers discretion arrest. I had not consulted with Mr. G.T. Powell, Manager of S.H. Kress and Company in Hattiesburg, and did not know his name until this date. No one at the Kress store asked that the arrest be made and I did not consult with anyone prior to the arrest.

13. When asked whether she saw any policeman in the store up to the time of the refusal of service, Miss Adickes answered: "My back was to the door, but one of my students saw a policeman come in." She went on to identify the student as "Carolyn." At the trial, Carolyn Moncure, one of the students who was with petitioner, testified that "about five minutes" after the group had sat down and while they were still waiting for service, she saw a policeman come in the store. She stated: "[H]e came in the store, my face was facing the front of the store, and he came in the store and he passed, and he stopped right at the end of our booth, and he stood up and he looked around and he smiled, and he went to the back of the store, he came right back and he left out." This testimony was corroborated by that of Dianne Moncure, Carolyn's sister, who was also part of the group. She testified that while the group was waiting for service, a policeman entered the store, stood "for a while" looking at the group, and then "walked to the back of the store."

14. During discovery, respondent gave to petitioner an unsworn statement by Miss Irene Sullivan, a check-out girl. In this statement Miss Sullivan said that she had seen Patrolman Hillman come into the store "[s]hortly after 12:00 noon," while petitioner's group was in the store. She said that he had traded a "hello greeting" with her, and then walked past her check-out counter toward the back of the store "out of [her] line of vision." She went on: "A few minutes later Patrolman Hillman left our store by the northerly front door just slightly ahead of a group composed of several Negroes accompanied by a white woman. As Hillman stepped onto the sidewalk outside our store the police car pulled across the street and into an alley that is alongside our store. The police car stopped and Patrolman Hillman escorted the white woman away from the Negroes and into the police car."

all to the effect that there was a policeman in the store at the time of the refusal to serve her, and that this was the policeman who subsequently arrested her. Petitioner argued that although she had no knowledge of an agreement between Kress and the police, the sequence of events created a substantial enough possibility of a conspiracy to allow her to proceed to trial, especially given the fact that the noncircumstantial evidence of the conspiracy could only come from adverse witnesses. Further, she submitted an affidavit specifically disputing the manager's assertion that the situation in the store at the time of the refusal was "explosive," thus creating an issue of fact as to what his motives might have been in ordering the refusal of service.

We think that on the basis of this record, it was error to grant summary judgment. As the moving party, respondent had the burden of showing the absence of a genuine issue as to any material fact, and for these purposes the material it lodged must be viewed in the light most favorable to the opposing party. Respondent here did not carry its burden because of its failure to foreclose the possibility that there was a policeman in the Kress store while petitioner was awaiting service, and that this policeman reached an understanding with some Kress employee that petitioner not be served. . . .

. . . If a policeman were present, we think it would be open to a jury, in light of the sequence that followed, to infer from the circumstances that the policeman and a Kress employee had a "meeting of the minds" and thus reached an understanding that petitioner should be refused service. Because "[o]n summary judgment the inferences to be drawn from the underlying facts contained in [the moving party's] materials must be viewed in the light most favorable to the party opposing the motion," United States v. Diebold, Inc., 369 U.S. 654, 655 (1962), we think respondent's failure to show there was no policeman in the store requires reversal.

Pointing to Rule 56(e), as amended in 1963, respondent argues that it was incumbent on petitioner to come forward with an affidavit properly asserting the presence of the policeman in the store, if she were to rely on that fact to avoid summary judgment.* Respondent notes in this regard that none of the materials upon which petitioner relied met the requirements of Rule 56(e).[19]

This argument does not withstand scrutiny, however, for both the commentary on and background of the 1963 amendment conclusively show that it was not intended to modify the burden of the moving party under Rule 56(c) to show initially the absence of a genuine issue concerning any material fact. The Advisory Committee note on the amendment states that

---

* [The portion of Rule 56(e) referred to in the text now appears as Rule 56(e)(2) in the restyled Rules. — Eds.]

19. Petitioner's statement at her deposition, see n.13, supra, was, of course, hearsay; and the statement of Miss Sullivan, see n.14, supra, was unsworn. And, the rule specifies that reliance on allegations in the complaint is not sufficient. See Fed. Rule Civ. Proc. 56(e).

the changes were not designed to "affect the ordinary standards applicable to the summary judgment." And, in a comment directed specifically to a contention like respondent's, the Committee stated that "[w]here the evidentiary matter in support of the motion does not establish the absence of a genuine issue, summary judgment must be denied *even if no opposing evidentiary matter is presented.*" Because respondent did not meet its initial burden of establishing the absence of a policeman in the store, petitioner here was not required to come forward with suitable opposing affidavits.

If respondent had met its initial burden by, for example, submitting affidavits from the policemen denying their presence in the store at the time in question, Rule 56(e) would then have required petitioner to have done more than simply rely on the contrary allegation in her complaint. To have avoided conceding this fact for purposes of summary judgment, petitioner would have had to come forward with either (1) the affidavit of someone who saw the policeman in the store or (2) an affidavit under Rule 56(f) explaining why at that time it was impractical to do so. Even though not essential here to defeat respondent's motion, the submission of such an affidavit would have been the preferable course for petitioner's counsel to have followed. As one commentator has said:

> It has always been perilous for the opposing party neither to proffer any countering evidentiary materials nor file a 56(f) affidavit. And the peril rightly continues [after the amendment to Rule 56(e)]. Yet the party moving for summary judgment has the burden to show that he is entitled to judgment under established principles; and if he does not discharge that burden then he is not entitled to judgment. No defense to an insufficient showing is required.

6 J. Moore, Federal Practice ¶56.22 [2], pp. 2824-2825 (2d ed. 1966). . . .

## Notes and Questions

*Adickes* bears indicia of its proximity to the height of the civil rights movement—the Court seems reluctant to give an interpretation of Rule 56 that would sanction judicial indifference to the powerful social forces at play in the restaurant that day. The decision also reflects traditional skepticism toward summary judgment and toward the enhanced role for trial judges Rule 56 implies. It is perhaps not surprising then that *Adickes* was read broadly in the lower courts for the principle that the movant bears a heavy burden to establish the absence of genuine issues for trial. Critics complained that this unduly limited the role of summary judgment as a tool for weeding out cases unworthy of a full blown trial.

In 1986, the Supreme Court intervened, reframing the standard governing summary judgment decisions in three separate cases. As you read these cases, consider what assumptions about summary judgment and pretrial litigation lie behind the Court's analysis, and consider whether and to what extent the standard articulated in *Adickes* is altered by the trilogy.

## b.   The Supreme Court Trilogy

*Celotex Corp. v. Catrett*
477 U.S. 317 (1986)

JUSTICE REHNQUIST delivered the opinion of the Court.

Respondent commenced this lawsuit in September 1980, alleging that the death in 1979 of her husband, Louis H. Catrett, resulted from his exposure to products containing asbestos manufactured or distributed by 15 named corporations. Respondent's complaint sounded in negligence, breach of warranty, and strict liability.... [Thirteen defendants], including petitioner, filed motions for summary judgment. Petitioner's motion ... argued that summary judgment was proper because respondent had "failed to produce evidence that any [Celotex] product ... was the proximate cause of the injuries alleged...."... In response to petitioner's summary judgment motion, respondent then produced three documents which she claimed "demonstrate that there is a genuine material factual dispute" as to whether the decedent had ever been exposed to petitioner's asbestos products. The three documents included a transcript of a deposition of the decedent, a letter from an official of one of the decedent's former employers whom petitioner planned to call as a trial witness, and a letter from an insurance company to respondent's attorney, all tending to establish that the decedent had been exposed to petitioner's asbestos products in Chicago during 1970-1971. Petitioner, in turn, argued that the three documents were inadmissible hearsay and thus could not be considered in opposition to the summary judgment motion.

... [T]he District Court granted all of the motions filed by the various defendants. The court explained that it was granting petitioner's summary judgment motion because "there [was] no showing that the plaintiff was exposed to the defendant Celotex's product...." Respondent appealed only the grant of summary judgment in favor of petitioner, and a divided panel of the District of Columbia Circuit reversed. The majority of the Court of Appeals held that petitioner's summary judgment motion was rendered "fatally defective" by the fact that petitioner "made no effort to adduce *any* evidence, in the form of affidavits or otherwise, to support its motion." [Catrett v. Johns-Manville Sales Corp., 756 F.2d 181, 184 (D.C. Cir. 1985)] (emphasis in original). According to the majority, Rule 56(e) of the Federal Rules of Civil Procedure, and this Court's decision in Adickes v. S.H. Kress & Co., 398 U.S. 144, 159 (1970), establish that "the party opposing the motion for summary judgment bears the burden of responding *only after* the moving party has met its burden of coming forward with proof of the absence of any genuine issues of material fact." 756 F.2d, at 184....

We think that the position taken by the majority of the Court of Appeals is inconsistent with the standard for summary judgment set forth in Rule 56(c) of the Federal Rules of Civil Procedure. Under Rule 56(c), summary judgment is proper "if the pleadings, depositions, answers to interrogatories, and admissions on file, together with the affidavits, if any, show that there is no genuine issue as to any material fact and that the moving party is entitled to a judgment as a matter of law." In our view, the plain language of Rule 56(c) mandates the entry of summary judgment, after adequate time for discovery and upon motion, against a party who fails to make a show-ing sufficient to establish the existence of an element essential to that party's case, and on which that party will bear the burden of proof at trial. In such a situation, there can be "no genuine issue as to any material fact," since a complete failure of proof concerning an essential element of the nonmov-ing party's case necessarily renders all other facts immaterial. The moving party is "entitled to a judgment as a matter of law" because the nonmoving party has failed to make a sufficient showing on an essential element of her case with respect to which she has the burden of proof. "[The] standard [for granting summary judgment] mirrors the standard for a directed ver-dict under Federal Rule of Civil Procedure 50(a). . . ." Anderson v. Liberty Lobby, Inc., 477 U.S. 242, 250 (1986).

Of course, a party seeking summary judgment always bears the initial responsibility of informing the district court of the basis for its motion, and identifying those portions of "the pleadings, depositions, answers to interrogatories, and admissions on file, together with the affidavits, if any," which it believes demonstrate the absence of a genuine issue of material fact. But unlike the Court of Appeals, we find no express or implied require-ment in Rule 56 that the moving party support its motion with affidavits or other similar materials *negating* the opponent's claim. On the contrary, Rule 56(c), which refers to "the affidavits, *if any*" (emphasis added), sug-gests the absence of such a requirement. And if there were any doubt about the meaning of Rule 56(c) in this regard, such doubt is clearly removed by Rules 56(a) and (b), which provide that claimants and defendants, respec-tively, may move for summary judgment *"with or without supporting affida-vits"* (emphasis added). The import of these subsections is that, regardless of whether the moving party accompanies its summary judgment motion with affidavits, the motion may, and should, be granted so long as whatever is before the district court demonstrates that the standard for the entry of summary judgment, as set forth in Rule 56(c), is satisfied. One of the prin-cipal purposes of the summary judgment rule is to isolate and dispose of factually unsupported claims or defenses, and we think it should be inter-preted in a way that allows it to accomplish this purpose.[5]

Respondent argues, however, that Rule 56(e), by its terms, places on the nonmoving party the burden of coming forward with rebuttal affidavits, or other specified kinds of materials, only in response to a motion for sum-mary judgment "made and supported as provided in this rule." According to respondent's argument, since petitioner did not "support" its motion with

---

5. See [Martin B.] Louis, Federal Summary Judgment Doctrine: A Critical Analysis, 83 Yale L.J. 745, 752 (1974); David P. Currie, Thoughts on Directed Verdicts and Summary Judgments, 45 U. Chi. L. Rev. 72, 79 (1977).

affidavits, summary judgment was improper in this case. But as we have already explained, a motion for summary judgment may be made pursuant to Rule 56 "with or without supporting affidavits." In cases like the instant one, where the nonmoving party will bear the burden of proof at trial on a dispositive issue, a summary judgment motion may properly be made in reliance solely on the "pleadings, depositions, answers to interrogatories, and admissions on file." Such a motion, whether or not accompanied by affidavits, will be "made and supported as provided in this rule," and Rule 56(e) therefore requires the nonmoving party to go beyond the pleadings and by her own affidavits, or by the "depositions, answers to interrogatories, and admissions on file," designate "specific facts showing that there is a genuine issue for trial."

. . . Obviously, Rule 56 does not require the nonmoving party to depose her own witnesses. Rule 56(e) permits a proper summary judgment motion to be opposed by any of the kinds of evidentiary materials listed in Rule 56(c), except the mere pleadings themselves, and it is from this list that one would normally expect the nonmoving party to make the showing to which we have referred.

The Court of Appeals in this case felt itself constrained, however, by language in our decision in Adickes v. S.H. Kress & Co., 398 U.S. 144 (1970). There we held that summary judgment had been improperly entered in favor of the defendant restaurant in an action brought under 42 U.S.C. § 1983. In the course of its opinion, the *Adickes* Court said that "both the commentary on and the background of the 1963 amendment conclusively show that it was not intended to modify the burden of the moving party . . . to show initially the absence of a genuine issue concerning any material fact." Id. at 159. We think that this statement is accurate in a literal sense, since we fully agree with the *Adickes* Court that the 1963 amendment to Rule 56(e) was not designed to modify the burden of making the showing generally required by Rule 56(c). It also appears to us that, on the basis of the showing before the Court in *Adickes*, the motion for summary judgment in that case should have been denied. But we do not think the *Adickes* language quoted above should be construed to mean that the burden is on the party moving for summary judgment to produce evidence showing the absence of a genuine issue of material fact, even with respect to an issue on which the nonmoving party bears the burden of proof. Instead, as we have explained, the burden on the moving party may be discharged by "showing" — that is, pointing out to the district court — that there is an absence of evidence to support the nonmoving party's case.

The last two sentences of Rule 56(e) were added, as this Court indicated in *Adickes*, to disapprove a line of cases allowing a party opposing summary judgment to resist a properly made motion by reference only to its pleadings. While the *Adickes* Court was undoubtedly correct in concluding that these two sentences were not intended to *reduce* the burden of the moving party, it is also obvious that they were not adopted to *add to* that burden. Yet that is exactly the result which the reasoning of the Court of Appeals would produce. . . .

Respondent commenced this action in September 1980, and petitioner's motion was filed in September 1981. The parties had conducted discovery, and no serious claim can be made that respondent was in any sense "railroaded" by a premature motion for summary judgment. Any potential problem with such premature motions can be adequately dealt with under Rule 56(f), which allows a summary judgment motion to be denied, or the hearing on the motion to be continued, if the nonmoving party has not had an opportunity to make full discovery.

In this Court, respondent's brief and oral argument have been devoted as much to the proposition that an adequate showing of exposure to petitioner's asbestos products was made as to the proposition that no such showing should have been required. But the Court of Appeals declined to address either the adequacy of the showing made by respondent in opposition to petitioner's motion for summary judgment, or the question whether such a showing, if reduced to admissible evidence, would be sufficient to carry respondent's burden of proof at trial. We think the Court of Appeals with its superior knowledge of local law is better suited than we are to make these determinations in the first instance.

The Federal Rules of Civil Procedure have for almost 50 years authorized motions for summary judgment upon proper showings of the lack of a genuine, triable issue of material fact. Summary judgment procedure is properly regarded not as a disfavored procedural shortcut, but rather as an integral part of the Federal Rules as a whole, which are designed "to secure the just, speedy and inexpensive determination of every action." Fed. R. Civ. Proc. 1; see Schwarzer, Summary Judgment Under the Federal Rules: Defining Genuine Issues of Material Fact, 99 F.R.D. 465, 467 (1984). Before the shift to "notice pleading" accomplished by the Federal Rules, motions to dismiss a complaint or to strike a defense were the principal tools by which factually insufficient claims or defenses could be isolated and prevented from going to trial with the attendant unwarranted consumption of public and private resources. But with the advent of "notice pleading," the motion to dismiss seldom fulfills this function any more, and its place has been taken by the motion for summary judgment. Rule 56 must be construed with due regard not only for the rights of persons asserting claims and defenses that are adequately based in fact to have those claims and defenses tried to a jury, but also for the rights of persons opposing such claims and defenses to demonstrate in the manner provided by the Rule, prior to trial, that the claims and defenses have no factual basis.

The judgment of the Court of Appeals is accordingly reversed, and the case is remanded for further proceedings consistent with this opinion.

*It is so ordered.*

JUSTICE WHITE, concurring.

I agree that the Court of Appeals was wrong in holding that the moving defendant must always support his motion with evidence or affidavits showing the absence of a genuine dispute about a material fact. . . . But the movant must discharge the burden the Rules place upon him: It is not enough to move for summary judgment without supporting the motion in any way or with a conclusory assertion that the plaintiff has no evidence to prove his case.

A plaintiff need not initiate any discovery or reveal his witnesses or evidence unless required to do so under the discovery Rules or by court order. Of course, he must respond if required to do so; but he need not also depose his witnesses or obtain their affidavits to defeat a summary judgment motion asserting only that he has failed to produce any support for his case. It is the defendant's task to negate, if he can, the claimed basis for the suit. . . .

JUSTICE BRENNAN, with whom THE CHIEF JUSTICE and JUSTICE BLACKMUN join, dissenting.

. . . [T]he Court has not clearly explained what is required of a moving party seeking summary judgment on the ground that the nonmoving party cannot prove its case. This lack of clarity is unfortunate: district courts must routinely decide summary judgment motions, and the Court's opinion will very likely create confusion. For this reason, even if I agreed with the Court's result, I would have written separately to explain more clearly the law in this area. However, because I believe that Celotex did not meet its burden of production under Federal Rule of Civil Procedure 56, I respectfully dissent from the Court's judgment.

# I

. . . The burden of establishing the nonexistence of a "genuine issue" is on the party moving for summary judgment (citations omitted). This burden has two distinct components: an initial burden of production, which shifts to the nonmoving party if satisfied by the moving party; and an ultimate burden of persuasion, which always remains on the moving party (citation omitted). The court need not decide whether the moving party has satisfied its ultimate burden of persuasion[2] unless and until the court finds that the moving party has discharged its initial burden of production. Adickes v. S.H. Kress & Co., 398 U.S. 144, 157-61 (1970); 1963 Advisory Committee's Notes on Fed. Rule Civ. Proc. 56(e), 28 U.S.C. App., p. 626.

The burden of production imposed by Rule 56 requires the moving party to make a prima facie showing that it is entitled to summary judgment (citation omitted). The manner in which this showing can be

---

2. The burden of persuasion imposed on a moving party by Rule 56 is a stringent one (citations omitted). Summary judgment should not be granted unless it is clear that a trial is unnecessary, Anderson v. Liberty Lobby, Inc., 477 U.S. 242, 255 (1986), and any doubt as to the existence of a genuine issue for trial should be resolved against the moving party, *Adickes,* 398 U.S. at 158-59. . . .

made depends upon which party will bear the burden of persuasion on the challenged claim at trial. If the *moving* party will bear the burden of persuasion at trial, that party must support its motion with credible evidence — using any of the materials specified in Rule 56(c) — that would entitle it to a directed verdict if not controverted at trial. (citation omitted). Such an affirmative showing shifts the burden of production to the party opposing the motion and requires that party either to produce evidentiary materials that demonstrate the existence of a "genuine issue" for trial or to submit an affidavit requesting additional time for discovery. Ibid.; Fed. Rules Civ. Proc. 56(e), (f).

If the burden of persuasion at trial would be on the *nonmoving* party, the party moving for summary judgment may satisfy Rule 56's burden of production in either of two ways. First, the moving party may submit affirmative evidence that negates an essential element of the nonmoving party's claim. Second, the moving party may demonstrate to the court that the nonmoving party's evidence is insufficient to establish an essential element of the nonmoving party's claim (citations omitted). If the nonmoving party cannot muster sufficient evidence to make out its claim, a trial would be useless and the moving party is entitled to summary judgment as a matter of law. Anderson v. Liberty Lobby, Inc., 477 U.S. 242, 249 (1986).

Where the moving party adopts this second option and seeks summary judgment on the ground that the nonmoving party — who will bear the burden of persuasion at trial — has no evidence, the mechanics of discharging Rule 56's burden of production are somewhat trickier. Plainly, a conclusory assertion that the nonmoving party has no evidence is insufficient (citation omitted). Such a "burden" of production is no burden at all and would simply permit summary judgment procedure to be converted into a tool for harassment (citation omitted). Rather, as the Court confirms, a party who moves for summary judgment on the ground that the nonmoving party has no evidence must affirmatively show the absence of evidence in the record (citation omitted). This may require the moving party to depose the nonmoving party's witnesses or to establish the inadequacy of documentary evidence. If there is literally no evidence in the record, the moving party may demonstrate this by reviewing for the court the admissions, interrogatories, and other exchanges between the parties that are in the record. Either way, however, the moving party must affirmatively demonstrate that there is no evidence in the record to support a judgment for the nonmoving party.

If the moving party has not fully discharged this initial burden of production, its motion for summary judgment must be denied, and the court need not consider whether the moving party has met its ultimate burden of persuasion. Accordingly, the nonmoving party may defeat a motion for summary judgment that asserts that the nonmoving party has no evidence by calling the court's attention to supporting evidence already in the record that was overlooked or ignored by the moving party. In that event, the moving party must respond by making an attempt to demonstrate the inadequacy of this evidence, for it is only by attacking all the record evidence allegedly supporting the nonmoving party that a party seeking summary judgment satisfies Rule 56's burden of production.[3] . . .

The result in *Adickes*, is fully consistent with these principles. In that case, petitioner was refused service in respondent's lunchroom and then was arrested for vagrancy by a local policeman as she left. Petitioner brought an action under 42 U.S.C. § 1983 claiming that the refusal of service and subsequent arrest were the product of a conspiracy between respondent and the police; as proof of this conspiracy, petitioner's complaint alleged that the arresting officer was in respondent's store at the time service was refused. Respondent subsequently moved for summary judgment on the ground that there was no actual evidence in the record from which a jury could draw an inference of conspiracy. In response, petitioner pointed to a statement from her own deposition and an unsworn statement by a Kress employee, both already in the record and both ignored by respondent, that the policeman who arrested petitioner was in the store at the time she was refused service. We agreed that "[if] a policeman were present, . . . it would be open to a jury, in light of the sequence that followed, to infer from the circumstances that the policeman and Kress employee had a 'meeting of the minds' and thus reached an understanding that petitioner should be refused service." 398 U.S., at 158. Consequently, we held that it was error to grant summary judgment "on the basis of this record" because respondent had "failed to fulfill its initial burden" of demonstrating that there was no evidence that there was a policeman in the store. Id. at 157-58.

The opinion in *Adickes* has sometimes been read to hold that summary judgment was inappropriate because the respondent had not submitted affirmative evidence to negate the possibility that there was a policeman in the store. The Court of Appeals apparently read *Adickes* this way and therefore required Celotex to submit evidence establishing that plaintiff's decedent had not been exposed to Celotex asbestos. I agree with the Court that this reading of *Adickes* was erroneous and that Celotex could seek summary judgment on the ground that plaintiff could not prove exposure to Celotex asbestos at trial. However, Celotex was still required to satisfy its initial burden of production.

---

3. Once the moving party has attacked whatever record evidence—if any—the non-moving party purports to rely upon, the burden of production shifts to the nonmoving party, who must either (1) rehabilitate the evidence attacked in the moving party's papers, (2) produce additional evidence showing the existence of a genuine issue for trial as provided in Rule 56(e), or (3) submit an affidavit explaining why further discovery is necessary as provided in Rule 56(f). See 10A C. Wright, A. Miller & M. Kane, Federal Practice and Procedure § 2727, pp. 138-43 (2d ed. 1983). Summary judgment should be granted if the nonmoving party fails to respond in one or more of these ways, or if, after the nonmoving party responds, the court determines that the moving party has met its ultimate burden of persuading the court that there is no genuine issue of material fact for trial. See, e.g., First [Nat'l] Bank of Arizona v. Cities [Serv.] Co., 391 U.S. 253, 289 (1968).

## II

I do not read the Court's opinion to say anything inconsistent with or different than the preceding discussion. My disagreement with the Court concerns the application of these principles to the facts of this case.

Defendant Celotex sought summary judgment on the ground that plaintiff had "failed to produce" any evidence that her decedent had ever been exposed to Celotex asbestos. Celotex supported this motion with a two-page "Statement of Material Facts as to Which There is No Genuine Issue" and a three-page "Memorandum of Points and Authorities" which asserted that the plaintiff had failed to identify any evidence in responding to two sets of interrogatories propounded by Celotex and that therefore the record was "totally devoid" of evidence to support plaintiff's claim.

Approximately three months earlier, Celotex had filed an essentially identical motion. Plaintiff responded to this earlier motion by producing three pieces of evidence which she claimed "[at] the very least . . . demonstrate that there is a genuine factual dispute for trial": (1) a letter from an insurance representative of another defendant describing asbestos products to which plaintiff's decedent had been exposed; (2) a letter from T.R. Hoff, a former supervisor of decedent, describing asbestos products to which decedent had been exposed, and (3) a copy of decedent's deposition from earlier workmen's compensation proceedings. Plaintiff also apparently indicated at that time that she intended to call Mr. Hoff as a witness at trial.

Celotex subsequently withdrew its first motion for summary judgment. However, as a result of this motion, when Celotex filed its second summary judgment motion, the record *did* contain evidence—including at least one witness—supporting plaintiff's claim. . . .

On these facts, there is simply no question that Celotex failed to discharge its initial burden of production. Having chosen to base its motion on the argument that there was no evidence in the record to support plaintiff's claim, Celotex was not free to ignore supporting evidence that the record clearly contained. Rather, Celotex was required, as an initial matter, to attack the adequacy of this evidence. Celotex'[s] failure to fulfill this simple requirement constituted a failure to discharge its initial burden of production under Rule 56, and thereby rendered summary judgment improper.

This case is indistinguishable from *Adickes*. Here, as there, the defendant moved for summary judgment on the ground that the record contained no evidence to support an essential element of the plaintiff's claim. Here, as there, the plaintiff responded by drawing the court's attention to evidence that was already in the record and that had been ignored by the moving party. Consequently, here, as there, summary judgment should be denied on the ground that the moving party failed to satisfy its initial burden of production.

[The dissenting opinion of Justice Stevens is omitted.]

## Notes and Questions

On remand, the D.C. Circuit still refused to grant Celotex's motion. As you read the decision, consider why each appellate court to rule on *Celotex* was so sharply divided. Does it have to do with the specific facts of this case, or the implications for summary judgment in future decisions?

### Catrett, Administratrix of the Estate of Louis H. Catrett, Deceased v. Johns-Manville Sales Corp.
826 F.2d 33 (D.C. Cir. 1987)

STARR, CIRCUIT JUDGE.

This case is before us on remand from the Supreme Court. The sole question is whether the District Court properly granted summary judgment in favor of an asbestos manufacturer in a suit brought by the survivor of a victim of asbestosis. . . .

The Supreme Court . . . instructed . . . [this court] to address questions we had previously found unnecessary to consider, namely

> the adequacy of the showing made by [Mrs. Catrett] in opposition to [Celotex's] motion for summary judgment, or . . . whether such a showing, if reduced to admissible evidence, would be sufficient to carry [Mrs. Catrett's] burden of proof at trial.

(citation omitted). We thus are called upon to determine whether Mrs. Catrett's showing was sufficient to avoid summary judgment under Federal Rule of Civil Procedure 56(e). . . .

## II

Upon review, we discern several items pointing to the existence of a genuine issue concerning Mr. Catrett's alleged exposure to Celotex products. First, Mrs. Catrett (twice) submitted the letter from Mr. Hoff, the Anning-Johnson executive. This letter chronicles Mr. Catrett's work for Anning-Johnson, reporting that he worked for the company for "one calendar year ending, 12/22/71." According to the Hoff letter, Mr. Catrett's "duties were to supervise and train crews in the application of Firebar Fireproofing." Thus, on its face, the letter reflects knowledge by a specific Anning-Johnson official of the deceased employee's exposure to Firebar fireproofing. The letter further relates an "understanding" that the manufacturer of Firebar was now owned by Celotex.

Confronted with this potentially damning piece of evidence, Celotex argues that the Hoff letter should be ignored by virtue of its asserted inadmissibility at trial. *See* 10A C. Wright, A. Miller & M. Kane, Federal Practice and Procedure § 2721 (2d ed. 1983) (In passing on a summary judgment motion, a court may consider materials specified in Federal Rule of Civil Procedure 56(c) as well as "any material *that would be admissible or usable at trial.*") (emphasis added).

In the circumstances of this case, we believe that the Hoff letter should be considered. . . . Mrs. Catrett argues that the letter is admissible, asserting that the Hoff letter is admissible as falling within the business records exception to the hearsay rule. See Fed. R. Evid. 803(6). *More importantly, Celotex never objected to the District Court's consideration of the Hoff letter.* . . .

In this situation, it could scarcely be clearer that the letter was before the District Court. . . . [I]t is well established that "inadmissible documents may be considered by the court if not challenged," 10A C. Wright, A. Miller & M. Kane, Federal Practice and Procedure, § 2722, at 60 (2d ed. 1983). . . .

The second item also relates to Mr. Hoff. In her supplemental interrogatory responses, Mrs. Catrett listed Hoff as a witness. There can, of course, be no doubt that this response is properly considered in ruling on a summary judgment motion. See Fed. R. Civ. P. 56(c) (specifically listing "answers to interrogatories" as items that may be considered). Taking this response together with the Hoff letter, the record, dispassionately viewed, reflects the existence of a witness who can testify with respect to Mr. Catrett's exposure to Firebar. Thus, even if the Hoff letter itself would not be admissible at trial, Mrs. Catrett has gone on to indicate that the substance of the letter is reducible to admissible evidence in the form of trial testimony.

Third, . . . the record contains several documents, *submitted by Celotex*, recording the sale of Firebar to Anning-Johnson during the period when Mr. Catrett worked there. These [purchase orders] operate to put Firebar and Mr. Catrett in the same place at the same time. Since Mrs. Catrett's interrogatory responses make it abundantly clear that Mr. Catrett's particular vocation was the application of fireproofing, these documents go a long way toward creating a genuine issue with respect to Mr. Catrett's exposure to Firebar.

Fourth, the record reflects a direct link among the three corporate entities or divisions of relevance, namely Carey-Canadian Asbestos, Panacon Corporation, and Celotex. Carey-Canadian is identified in the sales records furnished by Celotex as the entity selling Firebar to Anning-Johnson, Mr. Catrett's employer. Those sales records describe Carey-Canadian as "A Division of Panacon Corporation." Celotex's interrogatory responses, in turn, relate that Panacon was merged into Celotex in 1972 (thus corroborating the more general statements as to corporate ownership found in the Hoff letter). The responses stated, in addition, that "this merger was . . . statutory, and The Celotex Corporation assumed the assets and ordinary liabilities of Panacon Corporation." Thus . . . the record before the District Court evinces a clear link between Carey-Canadian and Celotex, and thus between Celotex and Firebar. . . .

## III

. . . Considering the record before the District Court when it granted summary judgment—in particular, the four items discussed above—we believe that the issue of exposure was not so one-sided that Celotex was entitled to judgment as a matter of law. The record contains sufficient evidence to create a genuine issue of material fact with respect to Mr. Catrett's exposure to the asbestos product Firebar while working for Anning-Johnson. While the four items taken individually provide less than over-powering support for Mrs. Catrett's position, their cumulative effect is, we believe, sufficient to defeat the summary judgment motion. . . .

On this record, therefore, an unbroken chain links Mr. Catrett to Firebar, and Firebar to Celotex. . . . Accordingly, the District Court's grant of summary judgment was, on the basis of the record then before it, in error. We therefore reverse the judgment and remand the case for further proceedings not inconsistent with this opinion.

*It is so ordered.*

BORK, CIRCUIT JUDGE, dissenting.

. . . The central issue here on motion for summary judgment is causation. Defendant alleges that plaintiff has made no showing that anyone can offer personal knowledge that any exposure to asbestos occurred in this case. I agree that plaintiff has not identified "specific facts" that would indicate such exposure occurred, and I certainly think that plaintiff has not made the kind of showing necessary to defeat a directed verdict motion. I would therefore grant defendant's motion for summary judgment.

Plaintiff has identified two items that may bear on whether anyone has personal knowledge of exposure to asbestos in this case. . . .

It would seem apparent that the mere listing of a potential witness, without more, does not constitute setting forth specific facts. Here plaintiff has never claimed that Mr. Hoff has any personal knowledge that her husband was exposed to asbestos during his year of work at this company, and indeed did not specify the grounds of his possible testimony at all, except to say that he would be able to testify about "facts relevant to the subject matter of this lawsuit." . . .

The majority concludes, however, that we should interpret plaintiff's listing of Mr. Hoff as a witness in light of his letter to the insurance company, thereby finding enough evidence to stave off the equivalent of a motion for directed verdict on causation. . . . [But], the sum total of all this "evidence" falls far short of showing, or even suggesting, that anyone has been identified who can testify from personal knowledge about any asbestos exposure. That lack alone requires that defendant's motion for summary judgment be granted. . . .

For these reasons, I think plaintiff has not carried her burden in resisting summary judgment. . . . [D]espite more than two years for discovery, she has been unable to present the district court with any "specific facts" beyond the vague listing of a potential witness not claimed to have any personal knowledge about exposure. My concern is that the majority's view may make decisions on summary judgment both more difficult and more uncertain because the majority's rationale suggests that trial judges must consider various permutations of vague and inadmissible evidence in reaching those decisions. . . . This approach represents a departure from the Supreme Court's admonition [in *Celotex*] that "summary judgment procedure is properly regarded not as a disfavored procedural shortcut, but rather as an integral part of the Federal Rules as a whole, which are designed 'to secure the just, speedy, and inexpensive determination of every action'" (citation omitted). I respectfully dissent.

## Note: Burdens of Proof, Pleading, and Production

Reread Justice Brennan's dissent in *Celotex*, in which he describes the burdens of production and proof (persuasion) by a party moving for summary judgment and the interplay between these burdens and the more general burden of persuasion in the case. To understand the opinion, you need to distinguish among three concepts: burdens of proof and persuasion, burdens of pleading, and burdens of production. For good measure, we also add *presumptions* to this list, as they can modify the burdens.

The *burden of proof* is the burden of persuading the fact finder—jury or judge—of a material issue. In a civil case, if the evidence on an issue is in equipoise at the end of the case, then the party with the burden of proof on the issue *loses*, because the burden in most civil cases is the "preponderance of the evidence" standard. A motion for summary judgment is, in effect, an early argument by one party that because her opponent lacks sufficient evidence on an essential element of her case, she could not prevail at trial. Indeed, the party moving for summary judgment (the "movant") must establish that no reasonable fact finder could—were a trial to occur—rule for her opponent, such that the trial judge would be obliged to enter a judgment in favor of the movant as a matter of law. Thus, to evaluate whether a party is entitled to summary judgment one must consider the burden of proof that will govern the matter at trial, as well as all of the available evidence that has been, or might be, uncovered. The burden of prevailing on the *motion*, in other words, hinges in part on the burden of proof at *trial*, which may or may not rest with the party moving for summary judgment.

In allocating burdens of proof, judges are guided by precedent and, on occasion, by statutes. As Professor Morgan has observed, several factors tend to influence decisions about who has the burden:

> In reaching its determination to put this burden upon plaintiff or defendant, [the court] is influenced by substantially the same considerations as those which obtain in the determination of any question of substantive law. . . . These respectively make it fall upon (1) the party having the affirmative of the issues, (2) the party to whose case the fact in question is essential,

(3) the party having peculiar means of knowing the fact, and (4) the party who has the burden of pleading it.

Edmund M. Morgan, Some Observations Concerning Presumptions, 44 Harv. L. Rev. 906, 910-911 (1931).

As factor four of Morgan's list suggests, the party with the *burden of pleading* an issue usually—but not always—has the burden of *proving* that issue. Thus the burden of pleading is not necessarily the same as the burden of proof, and one must take care to distinguish between these two concepts, just as one must distinguish between the burden of production and the burden of proof.

Finally, there is the *burden of production*. This is the threshold burden of presenting at least *some* evidence to fulfill the obligation of taking an issue to the jury or judge so they can decide if the burden of proof is satisfied. If the issue is debatable, then the burden of production is met and the fact finder can then weigh the evidence to determine whether the party with the burden of proof should win or lose. If a party fails to meet her burden of production at trial, then her opponent is entitled to judgment as a matter of law. Again, the summary judgment motion is an early, pretrial allegation that the movant's opponent will be unable to satisfy the burden of production at trial. Hence, no trial is necessary and summary judgment is proper.

Put another way, when the plaintiff has the burden of proof, the division of labor is as follows:

*Pretrial*

1) Plaintiff moves for summary judgment. Plaintiff must persuade judge that *defendant* will be unable to produce sufficient evidence at trial to survive plaintiff's motion for judgment as a matter of law. Essentially, this means plaintiff has such weighty or uncontradicted evidence to support each element of her prima facie case that no reasonable fact finder could find for defendant—a difficult standard to meet. (This is the pretrial motion that parallels the trial motion in paragraph 3 below.)

2) Defendant moves for summary judgment. Defendant must show that *plaintiff* will be unable to produce sufficient evidence at trial to satisfy her burden of production, such that defendant would succeed on a motion for judgment as a matter of law. (This is the *Celotex*-type pretrial motion that parallels the trial motion in paragraph 1 below.)

*Trial*

1) Plaintiff presents her case. If, at the close of plaintiff's evidence, there is insufficient evidence of an essential element of the prima facie case to make it debatable, then plaintiff has *not* met the burden of production. Defendant can now move for judgment as a matter of law. (This is the trial motion that parallels the defendant's summary judgment motion in paragraph 2 above.)

2) Assuming plaintiff meets her burden of production, the case proceeds.

3) Defendant presents her case. If, at the close of defendant's evidence, there is insufficient evidence to *rebut* an essential element of plaintiff's case to make it debatable, then defendant has *not* met the burden of production. Plaintiff can now move for judgment as a matter of law. (This is the trial motion that parallels the plaintiff's summary judgment motion in pretrial paragraph 1 above.)

4) Close of evidence. Assuming the burdens of production are met, the case goes to the fact finder, who weighs the evidence and decides whether the party with the burden of proof—usually the plaintiff—has satisfied the applicable standard.

One final evidentiary concept must be added to this collection. In some areas of law, rebuttable *presumptions* operate to ease a party's burden of proof. For example, a court may presume that a child born to a married woman is the offspring of the woman's legal husband. This presumption, which is based on public policy, must be taken as true once the basic facts are shown (birth of a child, valid marriage) in the absence of adequate rebuttal of either the basic facts or the presumed fact (paternity by the legal husband).

One of the major lingering questions after *Celotex* has been just how little a movant can put in the record to support a motion for summary judgment when the nonmovant has the burden of proof on the issue at trial. In a personal injury case, for instance, may the defendant simply "point out" that the plaintiff's proof of causation is weak? Is that sufficient to shift the burden of production, or must the defendant do more? Do you think the showing in *Celotex* was sufficient? For an excellent study of how *Celotex*'s change in the moving party's initial burden on summary judgment has affected practice, see Brooke D. Coleman, The *Celotex* Initial Burden Standard and an Opportunity to "Revivify" Rule 56, 32 S. Ill. U. L.J. 295, 309-314 (2008) (surveying district court opinions and finding that a majority of summary judgment decisions come on cross-motions, not an early motion by defendant; that defendants tend to file extensive motions, not the one-page motions theoretically possible under *Celotex*; and that most motions come after significant discovery, not when plaintiff has not had a chance to gather evidence)

In addition to the burden-shifting standard of Rule 56, note that parties must take care to follow any local rules in the jurisdiction in which the case is filed. See Flint v. City of Belvidere, 791 F.3d 764, 767 (7th Cir. 2015) ("This Court has consistently upheld district judges' discretion to require strict compliance with Local Rule 56.1," which guides parties on how to present evidence "at the summary judgment stage"; upholding district court's decision to deem most defendant's factual assertions admitted, to ignore additional facts presented by plaintiff, and grant summary judgment against plaintiff).

In the second summary judgment case decided in the 1986 term, the Supreme Court reversed the Third Circuit's finding that summary judgment was improper in a complex antitrust suit between Japanese and American television manufacturers. Like the other two cases in the 1986 trilogy, this one provoked a heated dissent. In the past, the Supreme Court has indicated that "summary judgment should be used sparingly in complex antitrust litigation where motive and intent play leading roles, the proof is largely in the hands of the alleged conspirators, and hostile witnesses thicken the plot." Poller v. Columbia Broad. Sys., Inc., 368 U.S. 464, 473 (1962).

In *Matsushita*, the majority apparently adhered to the idea that antitrust cases require special analysis on summary judgment, but it found that this analysis cut against the American television manufacturers, who opposed the motion.

### *Matsushita Elec. Indus. Co. v. Zenith Radio Corp.*
475 U.S. 574 (1986)

JUSTICE POWELL delivered the opinion of the Court.

This case requires that we again consider the standard district courts must apply when deciding whether to grant summary judgment in an antitrust conspiracy case.

### I

Stating the facts of this case is a daunting task. The opinion of the Court of Appeals for the Third Circuit runs to 69 pages; the primary opinion of the District Court is more than three times as long. In re Japanese Electronic Products Antitrust Litigation, 723 F.2d 238, ([3d Cir.] 1983); 513 F. Supp. 1100 (E.D. Pa. 1981). Two respected District Judges each have authored a number of opinions in this case; the published ones alone would fill an entire volume of the Federal Supplement. In addition, the parties have filed a 40-volume appendix in this court that is said to contain the essence of the evidence on which the [lower courts] based their respective decisions. . . .

. . . What follows is a summary of this case's long history.

### A

Petitioners, defendants below, are 21 corporations that manufacture or sell "consumer electronic products" (CEPs)—for the most part, television sets. Petitioners include both Japanese manufacturers of CEPs and American firms, controlled by Japanese parents, that sell the Japanese-manufactured products. Respondents, plaintiffs below, are Zenith Radio Corporation (Zenith) and National Union Electric Corporation (NUE). Zenith is an American firm that manufactures and sells television sets. NUE is the corporate successor to Emerson Radio Company, an American firm that manufactured and sold television sets until 1970, when it withdrew from the market after sustaining substantial losses. Zenith and NUE began this lawsuit in 1974, claiming that petitioners had illegally conspired to drive American firms from the American CEP market. According to respondents, the gist of this conspiracy was a scheme to raise, fix and maintain artificially *high* prices for television receivers sold by [petitioners] in Japan and, at the same time, to fix and maintain *low* prices for television receivers exported to and sold in the United States (internal quotation marks and citation omitted). These "low prices" were allegedly at levels that produced substantial losses for petitioners (citation omitted). The conspiracy allegedly began as early as 1953, and according to respondents was in full operation by sometime in the late 1960's. Respondents claimed that various portions of this scheme violated §§ 1 and 2 of the Sherman Act, § 2(a) of the Robinson-Patman Act, § 73 of the Wilson Tariff Act, and the Antidumping Act of 1916. . . .

## B

. . . [The district court granted petitioners' motion for summary judgment. The Court of Appeals reversed on the ground] that a factfinder reasonably could draw the following conclusions:

1. The Japanese market for CEPs was characterized by oligopolistic behavior, with a small number of producers meeting regularly and exchanging information on price and other matters. This created the opportunity for a stable combination to raise both prices and profits in Japan. American firms could not attack such a combination because the Japanese Government imposed significant barriers to entry.
2. Petitioners had relatively higher fixed costs than their American counterparts, and therefore needed to operate at something approaching full capacity in order to make a profit.
3. Petitioners' plant capacity exceeded the needs of the Japanese market.
4. By formal agreements arranged in cooperation with Japan's Ministry of International Trade and Industry (MITI), petitioners fixed minimum prices for CEPs exported to the American market. The parties refer to these prices as the "check prices," and to the agreements that require them as the "check price agreements."
5. Petitioners agreed to distribute their products in the United States according to a "five company rule": each Japanese producer was permitted to sell only to five American distributors.
6. Petitioners undercut their own check prices by a variety of rebate schemes. Petitioners sought to conceal these rebate schemes both from the United States Customs Service and from MITI, the former to avoid various customs regulations as well as action under the antidumping laws, and the latter to cover up petitioners' violations of the check-price agreements (citations omitted).

Based on inferences from the foregoing conclusions,[5] the Court of Appeals concluded that a reasonable facfinder could find a conspiracy to depress prices in the American market in order to drive out American competitors, which conspiracy was funded by excess profits obtained in the Japanese market. The court apparently did not consider whether it was as plausible to conclude that petitioners' price-cutting behavior was independent and not conspiratorial. . . .

## II

We begin by emphasizing what respondents' claim is *not*. Respondents cannot recover antitrust damages based solely on an alleged cartelization of the Japanese market, because American antitrust laws do not regulate the competitive conditions of other nations' economies (citations omitted). Nor can respondents recover damages for any conspiracy by petitioners to charge higher than competitive prices in the American market. Such conduct would indeed violate the Sherman Act, (citations omitted), but it could not injure respondents: as petitioners' competitors, respondents stand to gain from any conspiracy to raise the market price in CEPs (citation omitted). Finally, for the same reason, respondents cannot recover for a conspiracy to impose nonprice restraints that have the effect of either raising market price or limiting output. Such restrictions, though harmful to competition, actually *benefit* competitors by making supracompetitive pricing more attractive. Thus, neither petitioners' alleged supracompetitive pricing in Japan, nor the five company rule that limited distribution in this country, nor the check prices insofar as they established minimum prices in this country, can by themselves give respondents a cognizable claim against petitioners for antitrust damages. The Court of Appeals therefore erred to the extent that it found evidence of these alleged conspiracies to be "direct evidence" of a conspiracy that injured respondents (citation omitted).

Respondents nevertheless argue that these supposed conspiracies, if not themselves grounds for recovery of antitrust damages, are circumstantial evidence of another conspiracy that *is* cognizable: a conspiracy to monopolize the American market by means of pricing below the market level. The thrust of respondents' argument is that petitioners used their monopoly profits from the Japanese market to fund a concerted campaign to price predatorily and thereby drive respondents and other American manufacturers of CEPs out of business. Once successful, according to respondents, petitioners would cartelize the American CEP market, restricting output

---

5. In addition to these inferences, the court noted that there was expert opinion evidence that petitioners' export sales "generally were at prices which produced losses, often as high as twenty-five percent on sales." 723 F.2d, at 311. The court did not identify any direct evidence of below-cost pricing; nor did it place particularly heavy reliance on this aspect of the expert evidence.

and raising prices above the level that fair competition would produce. The resulting monopoly profits, respondents contend, would more than compensate petitioners for the losses they incurred through years of pricing below market level.

The Court of Appeals found that respondents' allegation of a horizontal conspiracy to engage in predatory pricing,[8] if proved, would be a *per se* violation of § 1 of the Sherman Act (citation omitted). Petitioners did not appeal from that conclusion. The issue in this case thus becomes whether respondents adduced sufficient evidence in support of their theory to survive summary judgment. . . .

## III

To survive petitioners' motion for summary judgment, respondents must establish that there is a genuine issue of material fact as to whether petitioners entered into an illegal conspiracy that caused respondents to suffer a cognizable injury. Fed. Rule Civ. Proc. 56(e); First National Bank of Arizona v. Cities [Serv.] Co., 391 U.S. 253, 288-289 (1968). This showing has two components. First, respondents must show more than a conspiracy in violation of the antitrust laws; they must show an injury to them resulting from the illegal conduct. Respondents charge petitioners with a whole host of conspiracies in restraint of trade. . . . [However], unless, in context, evidence of these "other" conspiracies raises a genuine issue concerning the existence of a predatory pricing conspiracy, that evidence cannot defeat petitioners' summary judgment motion.

Second, the issue of fact must be "genuine." Fed. Rules Civ. Proc. 56(c), (e). When the moving party has carried its burden under Rule 56(c), its opponent must do more than simply show that there is some metaphysical doubt as to the material facts (citations omitted); Clark, Special Problems in Drafting and Interpreting Procedural Codes and Rules, 3 Vand. L. Rev. 493, 504-505 (1950). In the language of the Rule, the nonmoving party must come forward with "specific facts showing that there is a *genuine issue for trial*." Fed. Rule Civ. Proc. 56(e) (emphasis added). See also Advisory Committee Note to 1963 Amendment of Fed. Rule Civ. Proc. 56(e), 28 U.S.C. App., p.626 (purpose of summary judgment is to "pierce the pleadings and to assess the proof in order to see whether there is a genuine need for trial"). Where the record taken as a whole could not lead a rational trier of fact to find for the nonmoving party, there is no "genuine issue for trial." *Cities* [*Serv.*], 391 U.S. at 289.

8. Throughout this opinion, we refer to the asserted conspiracy as one to price "predatorily." This term has been used chiefly in cases in which a single firm, having a dominant share of the relevant market, cuts its prices in order to force competitors out of the market, or perhaps to deter potential entrants from coming in (citations omitted). In such cases, "predatory pricing" means pricing below some appropriate measure of cost. . . .

It follows from these settled principles that if the factual context renders respondents' claim implausible—if the claim is one that simply makes no economic sense—respondents must come forward with more persuasive evidence to support their claim than would otherwise be necessary. . . .

Respondents correctly note that "[on] summary judgment the inferences to be drawn from the underlying facts . . . must be viewed in the light most favorable to the party opposing the motion." United States v. Diebold, Inc., 369 U.S. 654, 655 (1962). But antitrust law limits the range of permissible inferences from ambiguous evidence in a § 1 case. Thus, in Monsanto Co. v. Spray-Rite [Serv.] Corp., 465 U.S. 752 (1984), we held that conduct as consistent with permissible competition as with illegal conspiracy does not, standing alone, support an inference of antitrust conspiracy. Id., at 764. See also *Cities [Serv.]*, 391 U.S., at 280. To survive a motion for summary judgment or for a directed verdict, a plaintiff seeking damages for a violation of § 1 must present evidence "that tends to exclude the possibility" that the alleged conspirators acted independently. 465 U.S., at 764. Respondents in this case, in other words, must show that the inference of conspiracy is reasonable in light of the competing inferences of independent action or collusive action that could not have harmed respondents. See *Cities [Serv.]*, 391 U.S., at 280.

Petitioners argue that these principles apply fully to this case. According to petitioners, the alleged conspiracy is one that is economically irrational and practically infeasible. Consequently, petitioners contend, they had no motive to engage in the alleged predatory pricing conspiracy; indeed, they had a strong motive *not* to conspire in the manner respondents allege. . . . This argument requires us to consider the nature of the alleged conspiracy and the practical obstacles to its implementation.

## IV

### A

A predatory pricing conspiracy is by nature speculative. Any agreement to price below the competitive level requires the conspirators to forgo profits that free competition would offer them. The forgone profits may be considered an investment in the future. For the investment to be rational, the conspirators must have a reasonable expectation of recovering, in the form of later monopoly profits, more than the losses suffered. As then-Professor Bork, discussing predatory pricing by a single firm, explained:

> Any realistic theory of predation recognizes that the predator as well as his victims will incur losses during the fighting, but such a theory supposes it may be a rational calculation for the predator to view the losses as an investment in future monopoly profits (where rivals are to be killed) or in future undisturbed profits (where rivals are to be disciplined). The future flow of profits, appropriately discounted, must then exceed the present size of the losses. R. Bork, The Antitrust Paradox 145 (1978).

See also McGee, Predatory Pricing Revisited, 23 J. Law & Econ. 289, 295-97 (1980). As this explanation shows, the success of such schemes is inherently uncertain: the short-run loss is definite, but the long-run gain depends on successfully neutralizing the competition. Moreover, it is not enough simply to achieve monopoly power, as monopoly pricing may breed quick entry by new competitors eager to share in the excess profits. The success of any predatory scheme depends on *maintaining* monopoly power for long enough both to recoup the predator's losses and to harvest some additional gain. Absent some assurance that the hoped-for monopoly will materialize, *and* that it can be sustained for a significant period of time, "[t]he preda-tor must make a substantial investment with no assurance that it will pay off." [Frank H.] Easterbrook, Predatory Strategies and Counterstrategies, 48 U. Chi. L. Rev. 263, 268 (1981). For this reason, there is a consensus among commentators that predatory pricing schemes are rarely tried, and even more rarely successful (citations omitted).

These observations apply even to predatory pricing by a *single firm* seek-ing monopoly power. In this case, respondents allege that a large number of firms have conspired over a period of many years to charge below-mar-ket prices in order to stifle competition. Such a conspiracy is incalculably more difficult to execute than an analogous plan undertaken by a single predator. The conspirators must allocate the losses to be sustained during the conspiracy's operation, and must also allocate any gains to be realized from its success. Precisely because success is speculative and depends on a willingness to endure losses for an indefinite period, each conspirator has a strong incentive to cheat, letting its partners suffer the losses necessary to destroy the competition while sharing in any gains if the conspiracy suc-ceeds. The necessary allocation is therefore difficult to accomplish. . . .

Finally, if predatory pricing conspiracies are generally unlikely to occur, they are especially so where, as here, the prospects of attaining monopoly power seem slight. In order to recoup their losses, petitioners must obtain enough market power to set higher than competitive prices, and then must sustain those prices long enough to earn in excess profits what they earlier gave up in below-cost prices (citations omitted). Two decades after their conspiracy is alleged to have commenced, petitioners appear to be far from achieving this goal: the two largest shares of the retail market in televi-sion sets are held by RCA and respondent Zenith, not by any of petition-ers. Moreover, those shares, which together approximate 40% of sales, did not decline appreciably during the 1970's. Petitioners' collective share rose rapidly during this period, from one-fifth or less of the relevant markets to close to 50% (citation omitted). Neither the District Court nor the Court of Appeals found, however, that petitioners' share presently allows them to charge monopoly prices; to the contrary, respondents contend that the conspiracy is ongoing—that petitioners are still artificially *depressing* the market price in order to drive Zenith out of the market. The data in the record strongly suggest that that goal is yet far distant.

The alleged conspiracy's failure to achieve its ends in the two decades of its asserted operation is strong evidence that the conspiracy does not in fact exist. Since the losses in such a conspiracy accrue before the gains, they must be "repaid" with interest. . . . If the losses have been substantial—as would likely be necessary in order to drive out the competition—petitioners would most likely have to sustain their cartel for years simply to break even.

Nor does the possibility that petitioners have obtained supracompetitive profits in the Japanese market change this calculation. Whether or not petitioners have the *means* to sustain substantial losses in this country over a long period of time, they have no *motive* to sustain such losses absent some strong likelihood that the alleged conspiracy in this country will eventually pay off. The courts below found no evidence of any such success, and—as indicated above—the facts actually are to the contrary: RCA and Zenith, not any of the petitioners, continue to hold the largest share of the American retail market in color television sets. . . .

### B

In *Monsanto*, we emphasized that courts should not permit factfinders to infer conspiracies when such inferences are implausible, because the effect of such practices is often to deter procompetitive conduct. *Monsanto*, 465 U.S., at 762-64. Respondents, petitioners' competitors, seek to hold petitioners liable for damages caused by the alleged conspiracy to cut prices. Moreover, they seek to establish this conspiracy indirectly, through evidence of other combinations (such as the check-price agreements and the five company rule) whose natural tendency is to raise prices, and through evidence of rebates and other price-cutting activities that respondents argue tend to prove a combination to suppress prices. But cutting prices in order to increase business often is the very essence of competition. Thus, mistaken inferences in cases such as this one are especially costly, because they chill the very conduct the antitrust laws are designed to protect. See [id.], at 763-64. "[We] must be concerned lest a rule or precedent that authorizes a search for a particular type of undesirable pricing behavior end up by discouraging legitimate price competition." Barry Wright Corp. v. ITT Grinnell Corp., 724 F.2d 227, 234 ([1st Cir.] 1983).

In most cases, this concern must be balanced against the desire that illegal conspiracies be identified and punished. That balance is, however, unusually one-sided in cases such as this one. As we earlier explained, predatory pricing schemes require conspirators to suffer losses in order eventually to realize their illegal gains; moreover, the gains depend on a host of uncertainties, making such schemes more likely to fail than to succeed. These economic realities tend to make predatory pricing conspiracies self-deterring: unlike most other conduct that violates the antitrust laws, failed predatory pricing schemes are costly to the conspirators. See [Frank H.] Easterbrook, The Limits of Antitrust, 63 Texas L. Rev. 1, 26 (1984). Finally, unlike predatory pricing by a single firm, *successful* predatory pricing conspiracies involving a large number of firms can be identified and punished once they succeed, since some form of minimum price-fixing agreement would be necessary in order to reap the benefits of predation. Thus, there is little reason to be concerned that by granting summary judgment in cases where the evidence of conspiracy is speculative or ambiguous, courts will encourage such conspiracies.

## V

. . . [P]etitioners had no motive to enter into the alleged conspiracy. To the contrary, as presumably rational businesses, petitioners had every incentive *not* to engage in the conduct with which they are charged, for its likely effect would be to generate losses for petitioners with no corresponding gains (citation omitted). The Court of Appeals did not take account of the absence of a plausible motive to enter into the alleged predatory pricing conspiracy. . . .

The "direct evidence" on which the court relied was evidence of *other* combinations, not of a predatory pricing conspiracy. Evidence that petitioners conspired to raise prices in Japan provides little, if any, support for respondents' claims: a conspiracy to increase profits in one market does not tend to show a conspiracy to sustain losses in another. Evidence that petitioners agreed to fix *minimum* prices (through the check-price agreements) for the American market actually works in petitioners' favor, because it suggests that petitioners were seeking to place a floor under prices rather than to lower them. The same is true of evidence that petitioners agreed to limit the number of distributors of their products in the American market—the so-called five company rule. That practice may have facilitated a horizontal territorial allocation (citation omitted), but its natural effect would be to raise market prices rather than reduce them. Evidence that tends to support any of these collateral conspiracies thus says little, if anything, about the existence of a conspiracy to charge below market prices in the American market over a period of two decades.

That being the case, the absence of any plausible motive to engage in the conduct charged is highly relevant to whether a "genuine issue for trial" exists within the meaning of Rule 56(e). Lack of motive bears on the range of permissible conclusions that might be drawn from ambiguous evidence: if petitioners had no rational economic motive to conspire, and if their conduct is consistent with other, equally plausible explanations, the conduct does not give rise to an inference of conspiracy (citation omitted). . . .

The decision of the Court of Appeals is reversed, and the case is remanded for further proceedings consistent with this opinion.

*It is so ordered.*

JUSTICE WHITE, with whom JUSTICE BRENNAN, JUSTICE BLACKMUN, and JUSTICE STEVENS join, dissenting.

. . . In defining what respondents must show in order to recover, the Court makes assumptions that invade the factfinder's province. The Court states with very little discussion that respondents can recover under § 1 of the Sherman Act only if they prove that "petitioners conspired to drive respondents out of the relevant markets by (i) pricing below the level necessary to sell their products, or (ii) pricing below some appropriate measure of cost." This statement is premised on the assumption that "[an] agreement without these features would either leave respondents in the same position as would market forces or would actually benefit respondents by raising market prices." In making this assumption, the Court ignores the contrary conclusions of respondents' expert DePodwin, whose report in very relevant part was erroneously excluded by the District Court.

The DePodwin Report, on which the Court of Appeals relied along with other material, indicates that respondents were harmed in two ways that are independent of whether petitioners priced their products below "the level necessary to sell their products or . . . some appropriate measure of cost." First, the Report explains that the price-raising scheme in Japan resulted in lower consumption of petitioners' goods in that country and the exporting of more of petitioners' goods to this country than would have occurred had prices in Japan been at the competitive level. Increasing exports to this country resulted in depressed prices here, which harmed respondents.[2] Second, the DePodwin Report indicates that petitioners exchanged confidential proprietary information and entered into agreements such as the five company rule with the goal of avoiding intragroup competition in the

2. Dr. DePodwin summarizes his view of the harm caused by Japanese cartelization as follows:

When we consider the injuries inflicted on United States producers, we must again look at the Japanese television manufacturers' export agreement as part of a generally collusive scheme embracing the Japanese domestic market as well. This scheme increased the supply of television receivers to the United States market while restricting supply in the Japanese market. If Japanese manufacturers had competed in both domestic and export markets, they would have sold more in the domestic market and less in the United States. A greater proportion of Japanese production capacity would have been devoted to domestic sales. Domestic prices would have been lower and export prices would have been higher. The size of the price differential between domestic and export markets would have diminished practically to the vanishing point. Consequently, competition among Japanese producers in both markets would have resulted in reducing exports to the United States and United States prices would have risen. In addition, investment by the United States industry would have increased. As it was, however, the influx of sets at depressed prices cut the rates of return on television receiver production facilities in the United States to so low a level as to make such investment uneconomic.

We can therefore conclude that the American manufacturers of television receivers would have made larger sales at higher prices in the absence of the Japanese cartel agreements. Thus, the collusive behavior of Japanese television manufacturers resulted in a very severe injury to those American television manufacturers, particularly to National Union Electric Corporation, which produced a preponderance of television sets with screen sizes of nineteen inches and lower, especially those in the lower range of prices.

United States market. The Report explains that petitioners' restrictions on intragroup competition caused respondents to lose business that they would not have lost had petitioners competed with one another.[3]

The DePodwin Report alone creates a genuine factual issue regarding the harm to respondents caused by Japanese cartelization and by agreements restricting competition among petitioners in this country. No doubt the Court prefers its own economic theorizing to Dr. DePodwin's, but that is not a reason to deny the factfinder an opportunity to consider Dr. DePodwin's views on how petitioners' alleged collusion harmed respondents.

The Court, in discussing the unlikelihood of a predatory conspiracy, also consistently assumes that petitioners valued profit-maximization over growth. In light of the evidence that petitioners sold their goods in this country at substantial losses over a long period of time, I believe that this is an assumption that should be argued to the factfinder, not decided by the Court.

## Notes and Questions

The majority relies on a lot of scholarly commentary about the economics of anti-competitive behavior. Is relying on this commentary still viewing

---

3. The DePodwin Report has this, among other things, to say in summarizing the harm to respondents caused by the five company rule, exchange of production data, price coordination, and other allegedly anti-competitive practices of petitioners:

> The impact of Japanese anti-competitive practices on United States manufacturers is evident when one considers the nature of competition. When a market is fully competitive, firms pit their resources against one another in an attempt to secure the business of individual customers. However, when firms collude, they violate a basic tenet of competitive behavior, i.e., that they act independently. United States firms were confronted with Japanese competitors who collusively were seeking to destroy their established customer relationships. Each Japanese company had targeted customers which it could service with reasonable assurance that its fellow Japanese cartel members would not become involved. But just as importantly, each Japanese firm would be assured that what was already a low price level for Japanese television receivers in the United States market would not be further depressed by the actions of its Japanese associates.
>
> The result was a phenomenal growth in exports, particularly to the United States. Concurrently, Japanese manufacturers, and the defendants in particular, made large investments in new plant and equipment and expanded production capacity. It is obvious, therefore, that the effect of the Japanese cartel's concerted actions was to generate a larger volume of investment in the Japanese television industry than would otherwise have been the case. This added capacity both enabled and encouraged the Japanese to penetrate the United States market more deeply than they would have had they competed lawfully.

the evidence in the light most favorable to the nonmovant? What value does the evidence of additional conspiracies have for the material issue of whether a predatory pricing conspiracy existed in the U.S. market? Is the Court's analysis limited to antitrust cases, or does it have broader implications for summary judgment in all cases?

## Note: *Anderson v. Liberty Lobby, Inc.,* 477 U.S. 242 (1986)

In *Anderson*, the final case in the 1986 trilogy, the Court made summary judgment more readily available in libel cases. The Court, in an opinion by Justice White, explained its view of the relationship between a motion for summary judgment under Rule 56 and one for a directed verdict under Rule 50(a) as follows:

> [T]he "genuine issue" summary judgment standard is "very close" to the "reasonable jury" directed verdict standard: "The primary difference between the two motions is procedural; summary judgment motions are usually made before trial and decided on documentary evidence, while directed verdict motions are made at trial and decided on the evidence that has been admitted." Bill Johnson's Restaurants, Inc. v. NLRB, 461 U.S. 731, 745, n.11 (1983). In essence, though, the inquiry under each is the same: whether the evidence presents a sufficient disagreement to require submission to a jury or whether it is so one-sided that one party must prevail as a matter of law.
>
> Progressing to the specific issue in this case, we are convinced that the inquiry involved in a ruling on a motion for summary judgment or for a directed verdict necessarily implicates the substantive evidentiary standard of proof that would apply at the trial on the merits. If the defendant in a run-of-the-mill civil case moves for summary judgment or for a directed verdict based on the lack of proof of a material fact, the judge must ask himself not whether he thinks the evidence unmistakably favors one side or the other but whether a fair-minded jury could return a verdict for the plaintiff on the evidence presented. The mere existence of a scintilla of evidence in support of the plaintiff's position will be insufficient; there must be evidence on which the jury could reasonably find for the plaintiff. The judge's inquiry, therefore, unavoidably asks whether reasonable jurors could find by a preponderance of the evidence that the plaintiff is entitled to a verdict — "whether there is [evidence] upon which a jury can properly proceed to find a verdict for the party producing it, upon whom the *onus* of proof is imposed." [Improvement Co. v. Munson, 81 U.S. (14 Wall.) 442, 448 (1872).]
>
> In terms of the nature of the inquiry, this is no different from the consideration of a motion for acquittal in a criminal case, where the beyond-a-reasonable-doubt standard applies and where the trial judge asks whether a reasonable jury could find guilt beyond a reasonable doubt. See Jackson v. Virginia, 443 U.S. 307, 318-19 (1979). Similarly, where the First Amendment mandates a "clear and convincing" standard, the trial judge in disposing of a directed verdict motion should consider whether a reasonable factfinder could conclude, for example, that the plaintiff had shown actual malice with convincing clarity. . . .

In sum, we conclude that the determination of whether a given factual dispute requires submission to a jury must be guided by the substantive evidentiary standards that apply to the case. This is true at both the directed verdict and summary judgment stages. Consequently, where the *New York Times* [376 U.S. 254, 285 (1964)] "clear and convincing" evidence requirement applies, the trial judge's summary judgment inquiry as to whether a genuine issue exists will be whether the evidence presented is such that a jury applying that evidentiary standard could reasonably find for either the plaintiff or the defendant. Thus, where the factual dispute concerns actual malice, clearly a material issue in a *New York Times* case, the appropriate summary judgment question will be whether the evidence in the record could support a reasonable jury finding either that the plaintiff has shown actual malice by clear and convincing evidence or that the plaintiff has not. . . .

. . . Because the Court of Appeals did not apply the correct standard in reviewing the District Court's grant of summary judgment, we vacate its decision and remand the case for further proceedings consistent with this opinion.

477 U.S. at 251-257.

Justice Brennan dissented on the following grounds:

I simply cannot square the direction that the judge "is not himself to weigh the evidence" with the direction that the judge also bear in mind the "quantum" of proof required and consider whether the evidence is of sufficient "caliber or quantity" to meet that "quantum." I would have thought that a determination of the "caliber and quantity," i.e., the importance and value, of the evidence in light of the "quantum," i.e., amount "required," could *only* be performed by weighing the evidence.

If in fact, this is what the Court would, under today's decision, require of district courts, then I am fearful that this new rule—for this surely would be a brand new procedure—will transform what is meant to provide an expedited "summary" procedure into a full-blown paper trial on the merits. It is hard for me to imagine that a responsible counsel, aware that the judge will be assessing the "quantum" of the evidence he is presenting, will risk either moving for or responding to a summary judgment motion without coming forth with *all* of the evidence he can muster in support of his client's case. Moreover, if the judge on motion for summary judgment really is to weigh the evidence, then in my view grave concerns are raised concerning the constitutional right of civil litigants to a jury trial. . . .

In my view, if a plaintiff presents evidence which either directly or by permissible inference (and these inferences are a product of the substantive law of the underlying claim) supports all of the elements he needs to prove in order to prevail on his legal claim, the plaintiff has made out a prima facie case and a defendant's motion for summary judgment must fail regardless of the burden of proof that the plaintiff must meet. In other words, whether evidence is "clear and convincing," or proves a point by a mere preponderance, is for the factfinder to determine. As I read the case law, this is how it has been, and because of my concern that today's decision may erode the constitutionally enshrined role of the jury, and also undermine the usefulness of summary judgment procedure, this is how I believe it should remain.

477 U.S. at 266-268.

Justice Rehnquist, joined by Chief Justice Burger, also dissented. A study by the Libel Defense Resource Center reports that media defendants' ultimate success rate on summary judgment motions reached 82.3 percent during 1995-1996. This marks an increase in success rate that is likely attributable to Anderson v. Liberty Lobby, 477 U.S. 242 (1986). See Mass Media — Defamation: Study Finds Media Success in Summary Judgments at Peak, 66 U.S.L.W. 2186 (Sept. 30, 1997) (reporting increase in success rate on summary judgment from 74.6 percent to 77.9 percent).

## Notes and Questions

1. *Appeal.* When a district court grants summary judgment on all claims in a case, this creates a final judgment that can be appealed. But what if summary judgment is denied, the case goes to trial, and the movant loses before the jury as well? Can the movant raise the denial of summary judgment on appeal? In Ortiz v. Jordan, the Supreme Court held that a party may not appeal the denial of summary judgment after the case has gone to trial. 562 U.S. 180 (2011). Ortiz was a former inmate in an Ohio prison for women. She sued several prison officers for violating her civil rights by failing to respond properly to her complaints that she was repeatedly sexually assaulted by a male corrections officer. Two defendants moved for summary judgment on the ground of qualified immunity. The district court denied the motions after concluding that there were multiple, material factual disputes regarding the conduct of the officers. At trial the jury returned six-figure verdicts against the defendants who had requested summary judgment. The defendants made no motion for a new trial and no request to renew their motions for judgment as a matter of law, made during the trial. On appeal they argued that the trial court erred in denying summary judgment.

The Supreme Court held that after trial in such a case, "the full record developed in court supersedes the record existing at the time of the summary judgment motion. . . . The plea [of qualified immunity] remains available . . . but . . . the defense must be evaluated in the light of the character and quality of the evidence received in court." Id. at 184.

One issue left unresolved by *Ortiz* is whether a party who loses on summary judgment *for purely legal reasons* (i.e., not because the court concludes there are genuine issues as to any material fact) may appeal the denial of summary judgment after trial. The circuit courts have entertained these appeals. See Fencorp Co. v. Ohio Kentucky Oil Corp., 675 F.3d 933, 940 (6th Cir. 2012) (gathering cases).

Prior to *Ortiz*, the majority of circuit courts had allowed such appeals. As one court describes the general rule:

> [A] denial of summary judgment is a prediction that the evidence will be sufficient to support a verdict in favor of the nonmovant. Once the trial has taken place, our focus is on the evidence actually admitted and not on the earlier

summary judgment record. After the trial, the merits should be judged in relation to the fully-developed record emerging from trial. . . . We will not at that point step back in time to determine whether a different judgment may have been warranted on the record at summary judgment. . . .

But when, as in this case, the court's denial of summary judgment is not based on the adequacy of the evidence, the justification we just described does not apply.

Chemetall GMBH v. ZR Energy, Inc., 320 F.3d 714, 718-719 (7th Cir. 2003) (citations omitted). Reviewing the denial of summary judgment on a question of law after the jury trial would not put the court in the position of re-judging the case on incomplete proof. The Seventh Circuit's position is consistent with eight other circuits, see id. at 719; see also Feld v. Feld, 688 F.3d 779, 783 (D.C. Cir. 2012); Rothstein v. Carriere, 373 F.3d 275 (2d Cir. 2004), and widened the split with the Fourth Circuit, which held in Chesapeake Paper Prods. Co. v. Stone & Webster Eng'g Corp., 51 F.3d 1229, 1236 (4th Cir. 1995), that summary judgment denials are unreviewable because it is often difficult to separate legal and factual grounds and because any legal issue can be preserved for appeal by making a motion for judgment as a matter of law under Rule 50 at the close of evidence at trial. In *Chemetall*, the appealability of a denial of summary judgment was presented precisely because counsel for plaintiff failed to make a proper Rule 50 motion challenging once again the validity of the confidentiality agreement. See 320 F.3d at 719-720.

In *Ortiz*, the Supreme Court appeared sympathetic to the *Chemetall* approach *if* an issue such as qualified immunity is decided on purely legal grounds at the summary judgment stage. 562 U.S. at 188 ("Because a plea of qualified immunity can spare an official not only from liability but from trial, we have recognized a limited exception to the categorization of summary judgment denials as nonappealable orders"); see also Fed. R. App. P. 4(a)(1)(A).

2. *Partial Summary Judgment*. Read Rules 56(a) and 54(b). Particularly in complex cases with multiple parties and claims, these rules permit the judge to dispose of portions of the case as to which no factual dispute exists. The result is a better-defined, simpler lawsuit at trial than would be possible without partial summary judgment.

3. Sua Sponte *Summary Judgment*. As *Celotex* noted, a motion by a party is not necessary for a judge to award summary judgment *sua sponte*, but due process requires notice and an opportunity to be heard when a judge acts on her own to dispose of a claim or the entire case. See also DL Res., Inc. v. FirstEnergy Solutions Corp., 506 F.3d 209, 223 (3d Cir. 2007) ("District courts may grant summary judgment *sua sponte* in appropriate circumstances. However, a district court may not generally grant summary judgment *sua sponte* unless it gives prior notice and an opportunity to oppose summary judgment."). That means a judge cannot isolate weak claims and throw them out just because the parties have filed for summary judgment on other aspects of the case. See *DL Res.*, 506 F.3d at 223. The parties must

be informed that the court is considering granting summary judgment *sua sponte* on that claim and given a chance to respond.

A recognized exception to the notice requirement is where "(1) the point at issue is purely legal; (2) the record was fully developed[;] and (3) the failure to give notice does not prejudice the party." Gibson v. Mayor & Council of Wilmington, 355 F.3d 215, 219 (3d Cir. 2004).

### c.   A New Standard for Summary Judgment?

Plainly, the Supreme Court hoped its reframing of the Rule 56 standard in the 1986 trilogy would enhance the role of summary judgment. In an early commentary, Professor Jack H. Friedenthal suggested that the ultimate effect of the cases was actually "uncertain and could prove to be limited, in part because a number of the Justices dissented in each of these cases, and in part because the Court has somewhat of a history of deciding one summary judgment case one way, only to return later with an opinion leaning the other way." Cases on Summary Judgment: Has There Been a Material Change in Standards?, 63 Notre Dame L. Rev. 770, 771 (1988). Other commentators took a less sanguine view; see, for instance, Jeffrey W. Stempel, A Distorted Mirror: The Supreme Court's Shimmering View of Summary Judgment, Directed Verdict, and the Adjudication Process, 49 Ohio St. L.J. 95, 161 (1988) (warning against the unfairness to plaintiffs of a regime in which summary judgment is freely granted).

Some, however, hailed the three cases as harbingers of a new day when the "summary judgment motion is a viable and welcome alternative to needless and extended litigation in federal courts." Judge Lawrence W. Pierce, Summary Judgment: A Favored Means of Summarily Resolving Disputes, 53 Brook. L. Rev. 279, 286 (1987). One study found a "widespread and dramatic recasting of summary judgment doctrine by the lower courts" since the 1986 trilogy, with many such motions freely granted at the district court level. Samuel Issacharoff and George Loewenstein, Second Thoughts About Summary Judgment, 100 Yale L.J. 73, 88 (1990).

Judge Patricia M. Wald, one of the circuit judges in *Celotex* who insisted on remand from the Supreme Court that summary judgment could not stand, Catrett v. Johns-Manville Sales Corp., 826 F.2d 33 (D.C. Cir. 1987), *cert. denied*, 484 U.S. 1066 (1988), has written of the course of summary judgment practice since the trilogy:

> [W]e are now at a stage where the focus should be on ensuring that summary judgment stays within its proper boundaries, rather than on encouraging its unimpeded growth. Its expansion across subject matter boundaries and its frequent conversion from a careful calculus of factual disputes (or the lack thereof) to something more like a gestalt verdict based on an early snapshot of the case have turned it into a potential juggernaut which, if not carefully monitored, could threaten the relatively small residue of civil trials that remain.

Patricia M. Wald, Summary Judgment at Sixty, 76 Tex. L. Rev. 1897, 1917 (1998).

More recent studies indicate that summary judgment is both more frequently sought, and more frequently granted, but the data also show these trends beginning well before the 1986 trilogy. See, e.g., Joe S. Cecil et al., Trends in Summary Judgment Practice: A Preliminary Analysis, Federal Judicial Center 1-3 (2001); see also Stephen B. Burbank, Vanishing Trials and Summary Judgment in Federal Civil Cases: Drifting Towards Bethlehem or Gomorrah?, 1 J. Empirical Legal Stud. 591 (2004); Stephen B. Burbank, Keeping Our Ambition Under Control: The Limits of Data and Inference in Searching for the Causes and Consequences of Vanishing Trials in Federal Court, 1 J. Empirical Legal Stud. 571 (2004). For arguments that the trilogy has indeed made an impact, see Martin H. Redish, Summary Judgment and the Vanishing Trial: Implications of the Litigation Matrix, 57 Stan. L. Rev. 1329 (2005) (arguing that liberalized summary judgment is one of the main reasons why a lower percentage of cases go to trial today); Marc Galanter, The Vanishing Trial: An Examination of Trials and Related Matters in Federal and State Courts, 1 J. Empirical Legal Stud. 459 (2004); Arthur R. Miller, The Pretrial Rush to Judgment: Are the "Litigation Explosion," "Liability Crisis," and Efficiency Clichés Eroding Our Day in Court and Jury Trial Commitments?, 78 N.Y.U. L. Rev. 982 (2003). No one disputes that fewer cases are going to trial, but the underlying reasons are difficult to isolate and measure. See Marc Galanter, The Hundred-Year Decline of Trials and the Thirty Years War, 57 Stan. L. Rev. 1255, 1257-1260 (2005) (reporting that federal civil trials fell "from a high of 12,570 in 1985 to 4,206 in 2003" and a gradual decline in state trials, but also pointing to evidence of a "steady downward trend . . . in progress for more than a century, marking a long historic movement away from trial as a mode of disposing of civil cases").

The rate of summary judgment grants is one way to assess the effect of the trilogy on the distribution of labor between judge and jury. Another aspect of that distribution of labor, whether a judge has crossed the line from the judicial role of reviewing undisputed facts to intrude upon the jury's role of weighing the evidence, is much more difficult to measure. In the following case, the Supreme Court struggled with how to evaluate facts in a summary judgment motion where the high-speed chase at issue had been recorded on video—a medium that tends to imply objectivity.

### Scott v. Harris
550 U.S. 372 (2007)

JUSTICE SCALIA delivered the opinion of the Court.

We consider whether a law enforcement official can, consistent with the Fourth Amendment, attempt to stop a fleeing motorist from continuing his public-endangering flight by ramming the motorist's car from behind. Put another way: Can an officer take actions that place a fleeing motorist at risk of serious injury or death in order to stop the motorist's flight from endangering the lives of innocent bystanders?

**I**

In March 2001, a Georgia county deputy clocked respondent's vehicle traveling at 73 miles per hour on a road with a 55-mile-per-hour speed limit. The deputy activated his blue flashing lights indicating that respondent should pull over. Instead, respondent sped away, initiating a chase down what is in most portions a two-lane road, at speeds exceeding 85 miles per hour. The deputy radioed his dispatch to report that he was pursuing a fleeing vehicle, and broadcast its license plate number. Petitioner, Deputy Timothy Scott, heard the radio communication and joined the pursuit along with other officers. In the midst of the chase, respondent pulled into the parking lot of a shopping center and was nearly boxed in by the various police vehicles. Respondent evaded the trap by making a sharp turn, colliding with Scott's police car, exiting the parking lot, and speeding off once again down a two-lane highway.

Following respondent's shopping center maneuvering, which resulted in slight damage to Scott's police car, Scott took over as the lead pursuit vehicle. Six minutes and nearly 10 miles after the chase had begun, Scott decided to attempt to terminate the episode by employing a "Precision Intervention Technique ('PIT') maneuver, which causes the fleeing vehicle to spin to a stop." Having radioed his supervisor for permission, Scott was told to "'[g]o ahead and take him out.'" Harris v. Coweta Cty., 433 F.3d 807, 811 ([11th Cir.] 2005). Instead, Scott applied his push bumper to the rear of respondent's vehicle.[1] As a result, respondent lost control of his vehicle, which left the roadway, ran down an embankment, overturned, and crashed. Respondent was badly injured and was rendered a quadriplegic.

Respondent filed suit against Deputy Scott and others under Rev. Stat. § 1979, 42 U.S.C. § 1983, alleging, inter alia, a violation of his federal constitutional rights, viz. use of excessive force resulting in an unreasonable seizure under the Fourth Amendment. In response, Scott filed a motion for summary judgment based on an assertion of qualified immunity. The District Court denied the motion, finding that "there are material issues of fact on which the issue of qualified immunity turns which present sufficient disagreement to require submission to a jury." Harris v. Coweta Cty., No. 3:01-CV-148-WBH, 2003 WL 25419527 (N.D. Ga. Sept. 23, 2003). On interlocutory appeal,[2] the United States Court of Appeals for the Eleventh

---

1. Scott says he decided not to employ the PIT maneuver because he was "concerned that the vehicles were moving too quickly to safely execute the maneuver." Respondent agrees that the PIT maneuver could not have been safely employed.

2. Qualified immunity is "an *immunity from suit* rather than a mere defense to liability; and like an absolute immunity, it is effectively lost if a case is erroneously permitted to go to trial." Mitchell v. Forsyth, 472 U.S. 511, 526 (1985). Thus, we have held that an order denying qualified immunity is immediately appealable even though it is interlocutory; otherwise, it would be "effectively unreviewable." Id., at 527. Further, "we repeatedly have stressed the importance of resolving immunity questions at the earliest possible stage in litigation." Hunter v. Bryant, 502 U.S. 224, 227 (1991) (*per curiam*).

Circuit affirmed the District Court's decision to allow respondent's Fourth Amendment claim against Scott to proceed to trial. Taking respondent's view of the facts as given, the Court of Appeals concluded that Scott's actions could constitute "deadly force" under Tennessee v. Garner, 471 U.S. 1 (1985), and that the use of such force in this context "would violate [respondent's] constitutional right to be free from excessive force during a seizure. Accordingly, a reasonable jury could find that Scott violated [respondent's] Fourth Amendment rights." 433 F.3d, at 816. The Court of Appeals further concluded that "the law as it existed [at the time of the incident], was sufficiently clear to give reasonable law enforcement officers 'fair notice' that ramming a vehicle under these circumstances was unlawful." Id., at 817. The Court of Appeals thus concluded that Scott was not entitled to qualified immunity. We granted certiorari and now reverse.

## II

In resolving questions of qualified immunity, courts are required to resolve a "threshold question: Taken in the light most favorable to the party asserting the injury, do the facts alleged show the officer's conduct violated a constitutional right? This must be the initial inquiry." Saucier v. Katz, 533 U.S. 194, 201 (2001). If, and only if, the court finds a violation of a constitutional right, "the next, sequential step is to ask whether the right was clearly established . . . in light of the specific context of the case." Ibid. Although this ordering contradicts "[o]ur policy of avoiding unnecessary adjudication of constitutional issues," United States v. Treasury Employees, 513 U.S. 454, 478 (1995) (citing [case]), we have said that such a departure from practice is "necessary to set forth principles which will become the basis for a [future] holding that a right is clearly established," Saucier, supra, at 201. We therefore turn to the threshold inquiry: whether Deputy Scott's actions violated the Fourth Amendment.

## III

### A

The first step in assessing the constitutionality of Scott's actions is to determine the relevant facts. As this case was decided on summary judgment, there have not yet been factual findings by a judge or jury, and respondent's version of events (unsurprisingly) differs substantially from Scott's version. When things are in such a posture, courts are required to view the facts and draw reasonable inferences "in the light most favorable to the party opposing the [summary judgment] motion." United States v. Diebold, Inc., 369 U.S. 654, 655 (1962) (*per curiam*). In qualified immunity cases, this usually means adopting (as the Court of Appeals did here) the plaintiff's version of the facts.

There is, however, an added wrinkle in this case: existence in the record of a videotape capturing the events in question. There are no allegations or indications that this videotape was doctored or altered in any way, nor any contention that what it depicts differs from what actually happened. The videotape quite clearly contradicts the version of the story told by respondent and adopted by the Court of Appeals. For example, the Court of Appeals adopted respondent's assertions that, during the chase, "there was little, if any, actual threat to pedestrians or other motorists, as the roads were mostly empty and [respondent] remained in control of his vehicle." 433 F.3d, at 815. Indeed, reading the lower court's opinion, one gets the impression that respondent, rather than fleeing from police, was attempting to pass his driving test:

> [T]aking the facts from the non-movant's viewpoint, [respondent] remained in control of his vehicle, slowed for turns and intersections, and typically used his indicators for turns. He did not run any motorists off the road. Nor was he a threat to pedestrians in the shopping center parking lot, which was free from pedestrian and vehicular traffic as the center was closed. Significantly, by the time the parties were back on the highway and Scott rammed [respondent], the motorway had been cleared of motorists and pedestrians allegedly because of police blockades of the nearby intersections.

Id., at 815-16 (citations omitted).

The videotape tells quite a different story. There we see respondent's vehicle racing down narrow, two-lane roads in the dead of night at speeds that are shockingly fast. We see it swerve around more than a dozen other cars, cross the double-yellow line, and force cars traveling in both directions to their respective shoulders to avoid being hit.[6] We see it run multiple red lights and travel for considerable periods of time in the occasional center left-turn-only lane, chased by numerous police cars forced to engage in the same hazardous maneuvers just to keep up. Far from being the cautious and controlled driver the lower court depicts, what we see on the video more closely resembles a Hollywood-style car chase of the most frightening

---

6. Justice Stevens hypothesizes that these cars "had already pulled to the side of the road or were driving along the shoulder because they heard the police sirens or saw the flashing lights," so that "[a] jury could certainly conclude that those motorists were exposed to no greater risk than persons who take the same action in response to a speeding ambulance." Post, at 1782. It is not our experience that ambulances and fire engines careen down two-lane roads at 85-plus miles per hour, with an unmarked scout car out in front of them. The risk they pose to the public is vastly less than what respondent created here. But even if that were not so, it would in no way lead to the conclusion that it was unreasonable to eliminate the threat to life that respondent posed. Society accepts the risk of speeding ambulances and fire engines in order to save life and property; it need not (and assuredly does not) accept a similar risk posed by a reckless motorist fleeing the police.

sort, placing police officers and innocent bystanders alike at great risk of serious injury.

At the summary judgment stage, facts must be viewed in the light most favorable to the nonmoving party only if there is a "genuine" dispute as to those facts. Fed. Rule Civ. Proc. 56(c). As we have emphasized, "[w]hen the moving party has carried its burden under Rule 56(c), its opponent must do more than simply show that there is some metaphysical doubt as to the material facts. . . . Where the record taken as a whole could not lead a rational trier of fact to find for the nonmoving party, there is no 'genuine issue for trial.'" Matsushita Elec. Indus. Co. v. Zenith Radio Corp., 475 U.S. 574, 586-87 (1986) (footnote omitted). "[T]he mere existence of some alleged factual dispute between the parties will not defeat an otherwise properly supported motion for summary judgment; the requirement is that there be no genuine issue of material fact." Anderson v. Liberty Lobby, Inc., 477 U.S. 242, 247-48 (1986). When opposing parties tell two different stories, one of which is blatantly contradicted by the record, so that no reasonable jury could believe it, a court should not adopt that version of the facts for purposes of ruling on a motion for summary judgment.

That was the case here with regard to the factual issue whether respondent was driving in such fashion as to endanger human life. Respondent's version of events is so utterly discredited by the record that no reasonable jury could have believed him. The Court of Appeals should not have relied on such visible fiction; it should have viewed the facts in the light depicted by the videotape.

## B

Judging the matter on that basis, we think it is quite clear that Deputy Scott did not violate the Fourth Amendment. Scott does not contest that his decision to terminate the car chase by ramming his bumper into respondent's vehicle constituted a "seizure." "[A] Fourth Amendment seizure [occurs] . . . when there is a governmental termination of freedom of movement through means intentionally applied." Brower v. County of Inyo, 489 U.S. 593, 596-97 (emphasis deleted). See also id., at 597 ("If . . . the police cruiser had pulled alongside the fleeing car and sideswiped it, producing the crash, then the termination of the suspect's freedom of movement would have been a seizure"). It is also conceded, by both sides, that a claim of "excessive force in the course of making [a] . . . 'seizure' of [the] person . . . [is] properly analyzed under the Fourth Amendment's 'objective reasonableness' standard." Graham v. Connor, 490 U.S. 386, 388 (1989). The question we need to answer is whether Scott's actions were objectively reasonable.[8]

8. Justice Stevens incorrectly declares this to be "a question of fact best reserved for a jury," and complains we are "usurp[ing] the jury's factfinding function." At the summary judgment stage, however, once we have determined the relevant set of facts and drawn all inferences in favor of the nonmoving party to the extent supportable by the record, the reasonableness of Scott's actions . . . is a pure question of law.

**1**

Respondent urges us to analyze this case as we analyzed *Garner*, 471 U.S. 1. . . .

Respondent's argument falters at its first step; *Garner* did not establish a magical on/off switch that triggers rigid preconditions whenever an officer's actions constitute "deadly force." *Garner* was simply an application of the Fourth Amendment's "reasonableness" test (citation omitted), to the use of a particular type of force in a particular situation. *Garner* held that it was unreasonable to kill a "young, slight, and unarmed" burglary suspect, 471 U.S., at 21, by shooting him "in the back of the head" while he was running away on foot, id., at 4, and when the officer "could not reasonably have believed that [the suspect] . . . posed any threat," and "never attempted to justify his actions on any basis other than the need to prevent an escape," id., at 21. Whatever *Garner* said about the factors that might have justified shooting the suspect in that case, such "preconditions" have scant applicability to this case, which has vastly different facts. "*Garner* had nothing to do with one car striking another or even with car chases in general. . . . A police car's bumping a fleeing car is, in fact, not much like a policeman's shooting a gun so as to hit a person." Adams v. St. Lucie County Sheriff's Dept., 962 F.2d 1563, 1577 (C.A.11 1992) (Edmondson, J., dissenting), adopted by 998 F.2d 923 (C.A.11 1993) (en banc) (*per curiam*). Nor is the threat posed by the flight on foot of an unarmed suspect even remotely comparable to the extreme danger to human life posed by respondent in this case. Although respondent's attempt to craft an easy-to-apply legal test in the Fourth Amendment context is admirable, in the end we must still slosh our way through the factbound morass of "reasonableness." Whether or not Scott's actions constituted application of "deadly force," all that matters is whether Scott's actions were reasonable.

**2**

In determining the reasonableness of the manner in which a seizure is effected, "[w]e must balance the nature and quality of the intrusion on the individual's Fourth Amendment interests against the importance of the governmental interests alleged to justify the intrusion." United States v. Place, 462 U.S. 696, 703 (1983). Scott defends his actions by pointing to the paramount governmental interest in ensuring public safety, and respondent nowhere suggests this was not the purpose motivating Scott's behavior. Thus, in judging whether Scott's actions were reasonable, we must consider the risk of bodily harm that Scott's actions posed to respondent in light of the threat to the public that Scott was trying to eliminate. Although there is no obvious way to quantify the risks on either side, it is clear from the videotape that respondent posed an actual and imminent threat to the lives of any pedestrians who might have been present, to other civilian motorists, and to the officers involved in the chase. It is equally clear that Scott's actions posed a high likelihood of serious injury or death to respondent—though not the near certainty of death posed by, say, shooting a fleeing felon in the back of the head, see *Garner*, supra, at 4, or pulling alongside a fleeing motorist's car and shooting the motorist, cf. Vaughan v. Cox, 343

F.3d 1323, 1326-27 ([11th Cir.] 2003). So how does a court go about weighing the perhaps lesser probability of injuring or killing numerous bystanders against the perhaps larger probability of injuring or killing a single person? We think it appropriate in this process to take into account not only the number of lives at risk, but also their relative culpability. It was respondent, after all, who intentionally placed himself and the public in danger by unlawfully engaging in the reckless, high-speed flight that ultimately produced the choice between two evils that Scott confronted. Multiple police cars, with blue lights flashing and sirens blaring, had been chasing respondent for nearly 10 miles, but he ignored their warning to stop. By contrast, those who might have been harmed had Scott not taken the action he did were entirely innocent. We have little difficulty in concluding it was reasonable for Scott to take the action that he did.

But wait, says respondent: Couldn't the innocent public equally have been protected, and the tragic accident entirely avoided, if the police had simply ceased their pursuit? We think the police need not have taken that chance and hoped for the best. Whereas Scott's action—ramming respondent off the road—was *certain* to eliminate the risk that respondent posed to the public, ceasing pursuit was not. First of all, there would have been no way to convey convincingly to respondent that the chase was off, and that he was free to go. Had respondent looked in his rearview mirror and seen the police cars deactivate their flashing lights and turn around, he would have had no idea whether they were truly letting him get away, or simply devising a new strategy for capture. Perhaps the police knew a shortcut he didn't know, and would reappear down the road to intercept him; or perhaps they were setting up a roadblock in his path (citation omitted). Given such uncertainty, respondent might have been just as likely to respond by continuing to drive recklessly as by slowing down and wiping his brow.

Second, we are loath to lay down a rule requiring the police to allow fleeing suspects to get away whenever they drive so recklessly that they put other people's lives in danger. It is obvious the perverse incentives such a rule would create: Every fleeing motorist would know that escape is within his grasp, if only he accelerates to 90 miles per hour, crosses the double-yellow line a few times, and runs a few red lights. The Constitution assuredly does not impose this invitation to impunity-earned-by-recklessness. Instead, we lay down a more sensible rule: A police officer's attempt to terminate a dangerous high-speed car chase that threatens the lives of innocent bystanders does not violate the Fourth Amendment, even when it places the fleeing motorist at risk of serious injury or death.

\* \* \*

The car chase that respondent initiated in this case posed a substantial and immediate risk of serious physical injury to others; no reasonable jury could conclude otherwise. Scott's attempt to terminate the chase by forcing respondent off the road was reasonable, and Scott is entitled to summary judgment. The Court of Appeals' judgment to the contrary is reversed.

*It is so ordered.*

JUSTICE GINSBURG, concurring.

I join the Court's opinion and would underscore two points. First, I do not read today's decision as articulating a mechanical, per se rule. Cf. post, at 1781 (Breyer, J., concurring). . . . Among relevant considerations: Were the lives and well-being of others (motorists, pedestrians, police officers) at risk? Was there a safer way, given the time, place, and circumstances, to stop the fleeing vehicle? "[A]dmirable" as "[an] attempt to craft an easy-to-apply legal test in the Fourth Amendment context [may be]," the Court explains, "in the end we must still slosh our way through the factbound morass of 'reasonableness.'" . . .

JUSTICE BREYER, concurring.

. . . Because watching the video footage of the car chase made a difference to my own view of the case, I suggest that the interested reader take advantage of the link in the Court's opinion, and watch it. Having done so, I do not believe a reasonable jury could, in this instance, find that Officer Timothy Scott (who joined the chase late in the day and did not know the specific reason why the respondent was being pursued) acted in violation of the Constitution.

. . . I disagree with the Court insofar as it articulates a *per se* rule. The majority states: "A police officer's attempt to terminate a dangerous high-speed car chase that threatens the lives of innocent bystanders does not violate the Fourth Amendment, even when it places the fleeing motorist at risk of serious injury or death." This statement is too absolute. . . .

JUSTICE STEVENS, dissenting.

. . . Relying on a de novo review of a videotape of a portion of a night-time chase on a lightly traveled road in Georgia where no pedestrians or other "bystanders" were present, buttressed by uninformed speculation about the possible consequences of discontinuing the chase, eight of the jurors on this Court reach a verdict that differs from the views of the judges on both the District Court and the Court of Appeals who are surely more familiar with the hazards of driving on Georgia roads than we are. The Court's justification for this unprecedented departure from our well-settled standard of review of factual determinations made by a district court and affirmed by a court of appeals is based on its mistaken view that the Court of Appeals' description of the facts was "blatantly contradicted by the record" and that respondent's version of the events was "so utterly discredited by the record that no reasonable jury could have believed him."

Rather than supporting the conclusion that what we see on the video "resembles a Hollywood-style car chase of the most frightening sort," the tape actually confirms, rather than contradicts, the lower courts' appraisal of the factual questions at issue. More importantly, it surely does not provide a principled basis for depriving the respondent of his right to have a jury evaluate the question whether the police officers' decision to use deadly force to bring the chase to an end was reasonable.

Omitted from the Court's description of the initial speeding violation is the fact that respondent was on a four-lane portion of Highway 34 when the officer clocked his speed at 73 miles per hour and initiated the chase. More significantly—and contrary to the Court's assumption that respondent's vehicle "force[d] cars traveling in both directions to their respective shoulders to avoid being hit," ibid.—a fact unmentioned in the text of the opinion explains why those cars pulled over prior to being passed by respondent. The sirens and flashing lights on the police cars following respondent gave the same warning that a speeding ambulance or fire engine would have provided. The 13 cars that respondent passed on his side of the road before entering the shopping center, and both of the cars that he passed on the right after leaving the center, no doubt had already pulled to the side of the road or were driving along the shoulder because they heard the police sirens or saw the flashing lights before respondent or the police cruisers approached.[4] A jury could certainly conclude that those motorists were exposed to no greater risk than persons who take the same action in response to a speeding ambulance, and that their reactions were fully consistent with the evidence that respondent, though speeding, retained full control of his vehicle.

The police sirens also minimized any risk that may have arisen from running "multiple red lights," ibid. In fact, respondent and his pursuers went through only two intersections with stop lights and in both cases all other vehicles in sight were stationary, presumably because they had been warned of the approaching speeders. Incidentally, the videos do show that the lights were red when the police cars passed through them but, because the cameras were farther away when respondent did so and it is difficult to discern the color of the signal at that point, it is not entirely clear that he ran either or both of the red lights. In any event, the risk of harm to the stationary vehicles was minimized by the sirens, and there is no reason to believe that respondent would have disobeyed the signals if he were not being pursued.

My colleagues on the jury saw respondent "swerve around more than a dozen other cars," and "force cars traveling in both directions to their respective shoulders," ibid., but they apparently discounted the possibility that those cars were already out of the pursuit's path as a result of hearing the sirens. Even if that were not so, passing a slower vehicle on a two-lane road always involves some degree of swerving and is not especially dangerous if there are no cars coming from the opposite direction. At no point during the chase did respondent pull into the opposite lane other than to pass a car in front of him; he did the latter no more than five times and, on most of those occasions, used his turn signal. On none of these occasions

4. Although perhaps understandable, because their volume on the sound recording is low (possibly due to sound proofing in the officer's vehicle), the Court appears to minimize the significance of the sirens audible throughout the tape recording of the pursuit.

was there a car traveling in the opposite direction. In fact, at one point, when respondent found himself behind a car in his own lane and there were cars traveling in the other direction, he slowed and waited for the cars traveling in the other direction to pass before overtaking the car in front of him while using his turn signal to do so. This is hardly the stuff of Hollywood. To the contrary, the video does not reveal any incidents that could even be remotely characterized as "close calls."

In sum, the factual statements by the Court of Appeals quoted by the Court, were entirely accurate. That court did not describe respondent as a "cautious" driver as my colleagues imply, but it did correctly conclude that there is no evidence that he ever lost control of his vehicle. That court also correctly pointed out that the incident in the shopping center parking lot did not create any risk to pedestrians or other vehicles because the chase occurred just before 11 p.m. on a weekday night and the center was closed. It is apparent from the record (including the videotape) that local police had blocked off intersections to keep respondent from entering residential neighborhoods and possibly endangering other motorists. I would add that the videos also show that no pedestrians, parked cars, sidewalks, or residences were visible at any time during the chase. The only "innocent bystanders" who were placed "at great risk of serious injury," ibid., were the drivers who either pulled off the road in response to the sirens or passed respondent in the opposite direction when he was driving on his side of the road.

I recognize, of course, that even though respondent's original speeding violation on a four-lane highway was rather ordinary, his refusal to stop and subsequent flight was a serious offense that merited severe punishment. It was not, however, a capital offense, or even an offense that justified the use of deadly force rather than an abandonment of the chase. The Court's concern about the "imminent threat to the lives of any pedestrians who might have been present," while surely valid in an appropriate case, should be discounted in a case involving a nighttime chase in an area where no pedestrians were present.

What would have happened if the police had decided to abandon the chase? We now know that they could have apprehended respondent later because they had his license plate number. Even if that were not true, and even if he would have escaped any punishment at all, the use of deadly force in this case was no more appropriate than the use of a deadly weapon against a fleeing felon in Tennessee v. Garner, 471 U.S. 1 (1985). In any event, any uncertainty about the result of abandoning the pursuit has not prevented the Court from basing its conclusions on its own factual assumptions. The Court attempts to avoid the conclusion that deadly force was unnecessary by speculating that if the officers had let him go, respondent might have been "just as likely" to continue to drive recklessly as to slow down and wipe his brow. That speculation is unconvincing as a matter of common sense and improper as a matter of law. Our duty to view the evidence in the light most favorable to the nonmoving party would foreclose such speculation if the Court had not used its observation of the video as an excuse for replacing the rule of law with its ad hoc judgment. There is no evidentiary basis for an assumption that dangers caused by flight from a police pursuit will continue after the pursuit ends. Indeed, rules adopted by countless police departments throughout the country are based on a judgment that differs from the Court's. See, e.g., App. to Brief for Georgia Association of Chiefs of Police, Inc., as Amicus Curiae A-52 ("During a pursuit, the need to apprehend the suspect should always outweigh the level of danger created by the pursuit. When the immediate danger to the public created by the pursuit is greater than the immediate or potential danger to the public should the suspect remain at large, then the pursuit should be discontinued or terminated. . . . [P]ursuits should usually be discontinued when the violator's identity has been established to the point that later apprehension can be accomplished without danger to the public").

Although *Garner* may not, as the Court suggests, "establish a magical on/off switch that triggers rigid preconditions" for the use of deadly force, it did set a threshold under which the use of deadly force would be considered constitutionally unreasonable:

> "Where the officer has probable cause to believe that the suspect poses a threat of serious physical harm, either to the officer or to others, it is not constitutionally unreasonable to prevent escape by using deadly force. Thus, if the suspect threatens the officer with a weapon or there is probable cause to believe that he has committed a crime involving the infliction or threatened infliction of serious physical harm, deadly force may be used if necessary to prevent escape, and if, where feasible, some warning has been given." 471 U.S., at 11-12.

Whether a person's actions have risen to a level warranting deadly force is a question of fact best reserved for a jury. Here, the Court has usurped the jury's factfinding function and, in doing so, implicitly labeled the four other judges to review the case unreasonable. It chastises the Court of Appeals for failing to "vie[w] the facts in the light depicted by the videotape" and implies that no reasonable person could view the videotape and come to the conclusion that deadly force was unjustified. However, the three judges on the Court of Appeals panel apparently did view the videotapes entered into evidence[7] and described a very different version of events:

> At the time of the ramming, apart from speeding and running two red lights, Harris was driving in a non-aggressive fashion (i.e., without trying to ram or run into the officers). Moreover, . . . Scott's path on the open highway was largely clear. The videos introduced into evidence show little to no vehicular (or pedestrian) traffic, allegedly because of the late hour and the police blockade of the nearby intersections. Finally, Scott issued absolutely no warning (e.g., over the loudspeaker or otherwise) prior to using deadly force.

433 F.3d 807, 819, n.14 ([11th Cir.] 2005).

---

7. In total, there are four police tapes which captured portions of the pursuit, all recorded from different officers' vehicles.

If two groups of judges can disagree so vehemently about the nature of the pursuit and the circumstances surrounding that pursuit, it seems eminently likely that a reasonable juror could disagree with this Court's characterization of events. Moreover, under the standard set forth in *Garner*, it is certainly possible that "a jury could conclude that Scott unreasonably used deadly force to seize Harris by ramming him off the road under the instant circumstances." 433 F.3d, at 821.

The Court today sets forth a per se rule that presumes its own version of the facts. . . . Not only does that rule fly in the face of the flexible and case-by-case "reasonableness" approach applied in *Garner* and Graham v. Connor, 490 U.S. 386 (1989), but it is also arguably inapplicable to the case at hand, given that it is not clear that this chase threatened the life of any "innocent bystande[r]." In my view, the risks inherent in justifying unwarranted police conduct on the basis of unfounded assumptions are unacceptable, particularly when less drastic measures—in this case, the use of stop sticks or a simple warning issued from a loudspeaker—could have avoided such a tragic result. In my judgment, jurors in Georgia should be allowed to evaluate the reasonableness of the decision to ram respondent's speeding vehicle in a manner that created an obvious risk of death and has in fact made him a quadriplegic at the age of 19.

I respectfully dissent.

## *Notes and Questions*

1. The video that so moved the majority in Scott v. Harris can be viewed at http://www.supremecourt.gov/media/media.aspx. Do you think the reasonableness of the officer's conduct is appropriate for jury resolution, or does the video render the facts indisputable and therefore an appropriate question for summary judgment? See United States v. Jones, 762 F. Supp. 2d 270, 273 n.2 (D. Mass. 2010) (lamenting that, after *Scott*, "it is now all the rage for appellate courts to review . . . primary evidence [from videotape] and draw their own conclusions"); Tobias Barrington Wolff, Scott v. Harris and the Future of Summary Judgment, 15 Nev. L.J. 1351, 1359 (2015) (arguing that the case has weakened the traditional presumption that the evidence must be viewed in the light most favorable to the nonmoving party; focusing on passage of decision stating that "facts must be viewed in the light most favorable to the nonmoving party only if there is a 'genuine' dispute as to those facts"); id. at 1365-1367 (offering examples from lower court applications of Scott v. Harris); cf. Amelia G. Yowell, Race to Judgment, An Empirical Study of Scott v. Harris and Summary Judgment, 85 Notre Dame L. Rev. 1759, 1761 (2010) (finding that *Scott* "has had little to no substantive impact on summary judgment rates overall," but that where courts cite *Scott*, they are more likely to grant summary judgment).

2. In their article Whose Eyes Are You Going to Believe: Scott v. Harris and the Perils of Cognitive Illiberalism, Dan M. Kahan, David A. Hoffman and Donald Braman contend that well-documented "social psychological

mechanisms" explain how group identity and different cultural experiences "influence cognition of facts." 122 Harv. L. Rev. 837, 851 (2009). For example, "people are much more disposed to perceive voluntariness, action, causation, and harm (as well as other conditions of blaming) when the putatively blameworthy agent is behaving in ways that defy social norms . . . including norms contested across distinct subcommunities." Id. at 852. Second, because "[i]ndividual well-being, material and emotional, is bound up with membership in various self-defining groups . . . [r]ejecting factual beliefs widespread within such a group can undermine individual well-being. . . . As a means of psychological self-defense, then, people tend to process information in a selective fashion that bolsters beliefs dominant within their self-defining groups." Id. Third, "as a result of various cognitive mechanisms, people are motivated to believe that behavior they find noble is also socially beneficial (or at least benign) and behavior they find base is also socially harmful. For example, people who hold individualist values discount claims that commerce and industry harm the environment because they value markets and other forms of private ordering. People who hold egalitarian values, in contrast, readily credit claims of environmental risk. . . . [And] people who subscribe to hierarchical values impute risk to homosexuality, drug use, abortion, subversive speech, and other behaviors that defy authority . . . whereas egalitarians and individualists reject these risk claims as specious." Id. at 852-853.

What do these social psychology insights have to do with Scott v. Harris? The authors state that "[c]ombined, *these theories furnish strong grounds to expect individuals of diverse identities and commitments . . . to form different perceptions of the facts revealed by the* Scott *[video] tape.*" Id. at 853 (emphasis added). In particular, "[b]eliefs about the extent to which the police in general abuse their authority (particularly against minorities), and correspondingly the relative preponderance of licit and illicit reasons for attempting to avoid police encounters, vary across socio-demographic and political groups." Id. Does the possibility of cognitive bias in assessing the conduct in *Scott* make the case more or less appropriate for resolution by a jury? The authors believe the case is more appropriate for jury resolution. "By insisting that a case like *Scott* be decided summarily, the Court not only denied those citizens an opportunity, in the context of jury deliberations, to inform and possibly *change* the views of citizens endowed with a different perspective. It also needlessly bound the result in the case to a process of decisionmaking that deprived the decision of any prospect of legitimacy in the eyes of that subcommunity whose members saw the facts differently." Id. at 841 (emphasis in original).

For extensions of the author's argument, see Rory K. Schneider, Illiberal Construction of Pro Se Pleadings, 159 U. Pa. L. Rev. 585 (2011); Adam N. Steinman, The Pleading Problem, 62 Stan. L. Rev. 1293 (2010) (relating cognitive illiberalism argument to the new pleading standards); Arthur R. Miller, From *Conley* to *Twombly* to *Iqbal*: A Double Play on the Federal Rules of Civil Procedure, 60 Duke L.J. 1 (2010) (same); Howard M. Wasserman, Orwell's Vision: Video and the Future of Civil Rights Enforcement, 68 Md. L. Rev.

600 (2009); Adam Benforado, Frames of Injustice: The Bias We Overlook, 85 Ind. L.J. 1333, 1336 (2010) (noting that while Kahan, et al., are correct about differences in perception among social groups, its also true that *"the same person* can . . . see different things depending on how information is presented and the broader context in which it is perceived") (emphasis added).

3. Research also shows that humans respond in very distinctive ways to the presentation of visual evidence. See Richard Howells and Robert Matson, Using Visual Evidence (2009); E. Bruce Goldstein, Sensation and Perception 140 (8th ed. 2010) (discussing viewers' misperceptions of basic changes in the content of video as a "blindness to change in films"); Miles Orvell, The Real Thing: Imitation and Authenticity in American Culture 198 (1989) ("[T]o the twentieth century, the fact that the camera was a machine became its most exalted characteristic, *guaranteeing the authenticity of its productions* and forming the basis of its appeal . . . as a model for the synthesis of science and art") (emphasis added). Whether the video should have been admitted in Scott v. Harris is a question of the law of evidence, but the law is fairly well settled and the practice is long-standing. See Gregory P. Joseph, Modern Visual Evidence § 4.02[1] (2005) ("Videotape evidence of all sorts is today commonly offered and admitted into evidence. . . . The fundamental rule . . . is that the admission or exclusion of videotape evidence is a matter committed to the sound discretion of the trial court. . . ."); Christian Delage, La Vérite par l'image: de Nuremberg au procès Milosevic (2006) (describing famed American director John Ford's editing of films of concentration camps for use in trials of Nazi war criminals). Although this is an evidentiary issue, the admissibility of visual evidence, particularly video of the disputed event, is tied closely to procedural questions about whether a judge or jury is best suited to decide whether the officers in *Scott* acted reasonably.

4. Even in summary judgment decisions where there is no video, aren't decisions about whether a material fact is disputed and what inferences can reasonably be drawn from any undisputed facts *quintessential* questions for the jury? That is, aren't they questions deeply factual in nature? Professor Suja Thomas contends that modern summary judgment procedure is unconstitutional because it denies civil litigants their Seventh Amendment right to a jury trial. See Suja A. Thomas, Why Summary Judgment Is Unconstitutional, 93 Va. L. Rev. 139 (2007). The Seventh Amendment guarantees litigants the right to a jury trial in all legal actions that would have been tried to a jury at English common law. Professor Thomas contends that "no procedure similar to summary judgment existed under the English common law" and that summary judgment in fact "violates the core principles or 'substance' of the English common law," id. at 139-140. She adds:

> the substance of the common law is surprisingly clear. First, under the common law, the jury or the parties determined the facts. . . . A court itself never decided the case without such a determination by the jury or the parties, however improbable the evidence might be. Second, only after the parties presented evidence at trial and only after a jury rendered a verdict, would a

court ever determine whether the evidence was sufficient to support a jury verdict. If the court decided that the evidence was insufficient to support the verdict, it would order a new trial. Another jury would determine the facts and decide which party won. In other words, if the court itself believed the evidence was insufficient, it would never determine who should win. Third, a jury would decide every case in which there was any evidence, however improbable the evidence was, unless the moving party admitted the facts and conclusions of the nonmoving party, including the improbable facts and conclusions.

These core principles of the common law reveal that summary judgment is unconstitutional. Under summary judgment, a court decides whether a "genuine issue as to any material fact" exists or, in other words, whether "a reasonable jury could return a verdict for the nonmoving party." Under this standard, in contrast to under the common law, the court decides whether factual inferences from the evidence are reasonable, applies the law to any "reasonable" factual inferences, and as a result makes the determination as to whether a claim could exist. In other words, the court decides whether the case should be dismissed before a jury hears the case. Under the common law, a court would never engage in this determination. Cases that would have been decided by a jury under the common law are now dismissed by a judge under summary judgment.

Id. at 143. See also Brooke D. Coleman, Summary Judgment: What We Think We Know Versus What We Ought to Know, 43 Loy. U. Chi. L.J. 705 (2012) (discussing the importance of the deterrent effect the trilogy may have on the filing of meritorious cases and other gaps in empirical study of summary judgment); John Bronsteen, Against Summary Judgment, 75 Geo. Wash. L. Rev. 522 (2007) (noting strong evidence that summary judgment violates the Seventh Amendment and arguing that the civil justice system would be both fairer and more efficient without it).

Professor Thomas's article provoked a stir both on the bench and in legal journals. Several federal court judges cited the article and commented on its conclusions in their opinions. See In re Zyprexa Prods. Liab. Litig., 489 F. Supp. 2d 230, 263 (E.D.N.Y. 2007) (noting that the increasing use of early dismissal procedures like summary judgment "poses a threat to the continued viability of the Seventh Amendment jury trial"); In re One Star Class Sloop Sailboat Built in 1930 with Hull No. 721, Named "Flash II," 517 F. Supp. 2d 546, 555 (D. Mass. 2007) ("[F]ederal courts overuse summary judgment as a case management tool."). See also Cook v. McPherson, No. 07-5552, 2008 WL 904736, at *3 (6th Cir. Apr. 2, 2008) (noting that the "historical examination [in the article] . . . is interesting," but ultimately rejecting the plaintiff's argument that summary judgment is unconstitutional).

Other scholars have defended the use of Rule 56 as a constitutional and necessary expedient to resolve modern cases. See William E. Nelson, Summary Judgment and the Progressive Constitution, 93 Iowa L. Rev. 1653 (2008) (largely agreeing with Thomas's historical findings, but arguing that the Constitution should not be tied to anachronistic, centuries-old law and instead should be capable of evolution in response to changing societal needs); Edward Brunet, Summary Judgment Is Constitutional, 93 Iowa L. Rev. 1625 (2008) (arguing that modern summary judgment is consistent with the Seventh Amendment and that two historical antecedents used by common law courts, trial by inspection and demurrer to the evidence, justify its use). But see Suja Thomas, Why Summary Judgment Is Still Unconstitutional: A Reply to Professors Brunet and Nelson, 93 Iowa L. Rev. 1667 (2008) (rejecting the analogies to trial by inspection and demurrer to the evidence and arguing that the substance of common law jury trials should continue to control the question of summary judgment's constitutionality); see also Suja Thomas, Why the Motion to Dismiss Is Now Unconstitutional, 92 Minn. L. Rev. 1851 (2008) (extending her analysis to 12(b)(6) motions).

5. Prior to Scott v. Harris, full-dress opinions on the summary judgment standard were rare. The first since the trilogy was Cleveland v. Policy Management System Corp., 526 U.S. 795 (1999). Cleveland swore that she was totally disabled in her application for Social Security benefits after a stroke. Later she went back to work, but was fired. She brought suit under the Americans with Disabilities Act (ADA), alleging that the employer had failed to make a reasonable accommodation to her disability, which would have enabled her to "perform the essential functions of her job." The lower courts found that she was judicially estopped from bringing a claim under the ADA because of her prior sworn statement and granted summary judgment. The Supreme Court reversed, holding that the prior statement raised only a rebuttable presumption against her:

> Summary judgment for a defendant is appropriate when the plaintiff "fails to make a showing sufficient to establish the existence of an element essential to [her] case, and on which [she] will bear the burden of proof at trial." *Celotex Corp. v. Catrett*, 477 U.S. 317, 322 (1986). An ADA plaintiff bears the burden of proving that she is a "qualified individual with a disability"—that is, a person "who, with or without reasonable accommodation, can perform the essential functions" of her job. . . . And a plaintiff's sworn assertion in an application for disability benefits that she is, for example, "unable to work" will appear to negate an essential element of her ADA case—at least if she does not offer a sufficient explanation. For that reason, we hold that an ADA plaintiff cannot simply ignore the apparent contradiction that arises out of the earlier SSDI total disability claim. Rather, she must proffer a sufficient explanation. . . . To defeat summary judgment that explanation must be sufficient to warrant a reasonable juror's concluding that, assuming the truth of, or the plaintiff's good faith belief in, the earlier statement, the plaintiff could nonetheless "perform the essential functions" of her job, with or without "reasonable accommodation."

562 U.S. at 805-806. What might the plaintiff be able to show, by way of explanation, to overcome her sworn statement in her application for Social Security benefits?

Since Scott v. Harris, however, the Court has been more active, particularly in the Fourth Amendment context. Indeed, the conflict between substantive Fourth Amendment law (which favors officers in excessive use of force cases) and the procedural standard for summary judgment (which requires courts to view the evidence in the light most favorable to the non-movant) continues. In Plumhoff v. Rickard, 134 S. Ct. 2012 (2014), the Court reversed the denial of a police officer's summary judgment motion in a suit for excessive use of force. The case involved a traffic stop that turned into a high-speed car chase and ended when officers fired fifteen shots at the escaping car, killing both occupants. The Supreme Court held that the case was controlled by Scott v. Harris:

> We see no basis for reaching a different conclusion [than we did in Scott v. Harris]. . . . [T]he chase in this case exceeded 100 miles per hour and lasted over five minutes. During that chase, Rickard passed more than two dozen other vehicles, several of which were forced to alter course. Rickard's outrageously reckless driving posed a grave public safety risk. And while it is true that Rickard's car eventually collided with a police car and came temporarily to a near standstill, that did not end the chase. Less than three seconds later, Rickard resumed maneuvering his car. Just before the shots were fired, when the front bumper of his car was flush with that of one of the police cruisers, Rickard was obviously pushing down on the accelerator because the car's wheels were spinning, and then Rickard threw the car into reverse "in an attempt to escape." Thus, the record conclusively disproves respondent's claim that the chase in the present case was already over when petitioners began shooting. Under the circumstances at the moment when the shots were fired, all that a reasonable police officer could have concluded was that Rickard was intent on resuming his flight and that, if he was allowed to do so, he would once again pose a deadly threat for others on the road. Rickard's conduct even after the shots were fired — as noted, he managed to drive away despite the efforts of the police to block his path — underscores the point.
>
> In light of the circumstances we have discussed, it is beyond serious dispute that Rickard's flight posed a grave public safety risk, and here, as in *Scott*, the police acted reasonably in using deadly force to end that risk.
>
> We now consider respondent's contention that, even if the use of deadly force was permissible, petitioners acted unreasonably in firing a total of 15 shots. We reject that argument. It stands to reason that, if police officers are justified in firing at a suspect in order to end a severe threat to public safety, the officers need not stop shooting until the threat has ended. As petitioners noted below, "if lethal force is justified, officers are taught to keep shooting until the threat is over" (citation omitted).
>
> Here, during the 10-second span when all the shots were fired, Rickard never abandoned his attempt to flee. Indeed, even after all the shots had been fired, he managed to drive away and to continue driving until he crashed. This would be a different case if petitioners had initiated a second round of shots after an initial round had clearly incapacitated Rickard and had ended any threat of continued flight, or if Rickard had clearly given himself up. But that is not what happened.

Id. at 2021-2022.

The substance/procedure tension was not taken up in explicit terms by the Court, but it is worth carefully considering. On the one hand, under the Fourth Amendment, courts analyze the "reasonableness" of the officer's conduct "from the perspective of a reasonable officer on the scene, rather than with the 20/20 vision of hindsight. [They] thus allow for the fact that police officers are often forced to make split-second judgments—in circumstances that are tense, uncertain, and rapidly evolving—about the amount of force that is necessary in a particular situation." Id. at 2020. On the other hand, on a police officer's motion for summary judgment in an excessive use of force case, the evidence is supposed to be viewed in the light most favorable to the plaintiff. It is possible to reconcile these competing demands by taking the evidence regarding what occurred in the light most favorable to the plaintiff, and then assessing whether the officer's response was reasonable, but it is easy for the substantive standard to dominate the procedural one. Put differently, it may be difficult to view the facts in the light most favorable to the plaintiff when substantive law (both the Fourth Amendment and qualified immunity doctrine) demands so much deference to the judgment of the police officer.

Compare the analysis in *Plumhoff* with that in Tolan v. Cotton, a case in which the lower courts *flagrantly* disregard the mandate of Rule 56 that the evidence be viewed in the light most favorable to the nonmovant. In Tolan v. Cotton, 134 S. Ct. 1861 (2014), a police officer in Bellaire, Texas shot Robert Tolan in the early morning hours after New Year's Eve, 2008. Tolan, a 23-year-old black man, was unarmed on his parents' front porch about 15 to 20 feet from police sergeant Jeffrey Cotton when the shooting occurred.

After a quick turn onto a residential street in an SUV aroused the suspicion of a police officer on patrol, the officer incorrectly typed the license plate number of Tolan's SUV into his police computer. The incorrect entry matched a stolen vehicle of the same make and color so the officer pulled up behind the parked car, drew his pistol, ordered Tolan and his companion to the ground, and accused them of having stolen the car. Tolan and his companion tried to explain that the car was Tolan's. His parents, hearing the commotion, came out of the house in their pajamas. They instructed Tolan and his companion to remain on the ground and say nothing. They then began to remonstrate with the police officer, explaining that this was their house, that Tolan was their son, and that the car belonged to the family.

The officer radioed for assistance and Cotton arrived on the scene. Tolan's mother reiterated that the car was not stolen and that this was their home. Cotton then instructed her to stand against the garage door. She responded "'Are you kidding me? We've lived her[e] for 15 years. We've never had anything like this happen before.'" Id. at 1864. Testimony diverged regarding what happened next. The family testified that Cotton grabbed the arm of Tolan's mother and slammed her against the garage door with so much force that she fell. Cotton testified in his deposition that Tolan's mother "flipped her arm up and told him to get his hands off." Id. The parties agreed that Tolan responded to the incident between his mother and Cotton by exclaiming, "Get your fucking hands off my mom." Id. The parties also agreed that Cotton then turned and fired at Tolan three times, striking him once in the chest and puncturing his lung and piercing his liver. The testimony diverged over whether and to what extend Tolan made a threatening movement to intervene in Cotton's handling of his mother. Cotton and his fellow police officer testified that Tolan rose to his feet. Tolan testified that he only rose to his knees.

Tolan survived the shooting, but the injury was "life-altering . . . disrupt[ing] his budding professional baseball career and caus[ing] him to experience pain on a daily basis." Id. The trial court granted Cotton's motion for summary judgment on the theory that Cotton's use of force was not unreasonable. The Fifth Circuit affirmed on a different theory. It concluded that even if Cotton's conduct was unreasonable, he was entitled to qualified immunity because his conduct did not violate a clearly established right. An officer in Cotton's position, the Fifth Circuit reasoned, "could have believed that Tolan presented an immediate threat to the safety of the officers. In support of this conclusion, the court relied on the following facts: the front porch had been 'dimly-lit'; Tolan's mother had 'refus[ed] orders to remain quiet and calm'; and Tolan's words had amounted to a 'verba[l] threa[t].' Id. at 1865. Most critically, the court also relied on the purported fact that Tolan was 'moving to intervene in Cotton's handling of his mother,' and that Cotton therefore could reasonably have feared for his life. Id. Accordingly, the court held, Cotton did not violate clearly established law in shooting Tolan." Id. In unanimously reversing the grant of summary judgment, the Supreme Court emphasized that the Fifth Circuit had adopted Cotton's view of the facts, not Tolan's:

> By failing to credit evidence that contradicted some of its key factual conclusions, the court improperly "weigh[ed] the evidence" and resolved disputed issues in favor of the moving party, *Anderson*, 477 U.S., at 249.
>
> First, the court relied on its view that at the time of the shooting, the Tolans' front porch was "dimly-lit." The court appears to have drawn this assessment from Cotton's statements in a deposition that when he fired at Tolan, the porch was "'fairly dark,'" and lit by a gas lamp that was "'decorative.'" In his own deposition, however, Tolan's father was asked whether the gas lamp was in fact "more decorative than illuminating." He said that it was not. Moreover, Tolan stated in his deposition that two floodlights shone on the driveway during the incident, and Cotton acknowledged that there were two motion-activated lights in front of the house. And Tolan confirmed that at the time of the shooting, he was "not in darkness."
>
> Second, the Fifth Circuit stated that Tolan's mother "refus[ed] orders to remain quiet and calm," thereby "compound[ing]" Cotton's belief that Tolan "presented an immediate threat to the safety of the officers." But here, too, the court did not credit directly contradictory evidence. Although the parties agree that Tolan's mother repeatedly informed officers that Tolan was her son, that she lived in the home in front of which he had parked, and that the vehicle he had been driving belonged to her and her husband, there is a dispute as to how calmly she provided this information. Cotton stated during his deposition that Tolan's mother was "very agitated" when she spoke

to the officers. By contrast, Tolan's mother testified at Cotton's criminal trial that she was neither "aggravated" nor "agitated."

Third, the Court concluded that Tolan was "shouting," and "verbally threatening" the officer, in the moments before the shooting. The court noted, and the parties agree, that while Cotton was grabbing the arm of his mother, Tolan told Cotton, "[G]et your fucking hands off my mom." But Tolan testified that he "was not screaming." And a jury could reasonably infer that his words, in context, did not amount to a statement of intent to inflict harm. Cf. United States v. White, 258 F.3d 374, 383 (5th Cir. 2001) ("A threat imports '[a] communicated intent to inflict physical or other harm'" (quoting Black's Law Dictionary 1480 (6th ed. 1990))); Morris v. Noe, 672 F.3d 1185, 1196 (10th Cir. 2012) (inferring that the words "Why was you talking to Mama that way" did not constitute an "overt threa[t]"). Tolan's mother testified in Cotton's criminal trial that he slammed her against a garage door with enough force to cause bruising that lasted for days. A jury could well have concluded that a reasonable officer would have heard Tolan's words not as a threat, but as a son's plea not to continue any assault of his mother.

Fourth, the Fifth Circuit inferred that at the time of the shooting, Tolan was "moving to intervene in Sergeant Cotton's" interaction with his mother. See also id. (characterizing Tolan's behavior as "abruptly attempting to approach Sergeant Cotton," thereby "inflam[ing] an already tense situation"). The court appears to have credited Edwards' account that at the time of the shooting, Tolan was on both feet "[i]n a crouch" or a "charging position" looking as if he was going to move forward. Tolan testified at trial, however, that he was on his knees when Cotton shot him, a fact corroborated by his mother. Tolan also testified in his deposition that he "wasn't going anywhere," and emphasized that he did not "jump up."

Considered together, these facts lead to the inescapable conclusion that the court below credited the evidence of the party seeking summary judgment and failed properly to acknowledge key evidence offered by the party opposing that motion. And while "this Court is not equipped to correct every perceived error coming from the lower federal courts," Boag v. MacDougall, 454 U.S. 364, 366 (1982) (O'Connor, J., concurring), we intervene here because the opinion below reflects a clear misapprehension of summary judgment standards in light of our precedents. Cf. [Brosseau v. Haugen], 543 U.S. [194,] 197-98 [(2004)] (summarily reversing decision in a Fourth Amendment excessive force case "to correct a clear misapprehension of the qualified immunity standard"); see also Florida Dept. of Health and Rehabilitative Servs. v. Florida Nursing Home Assn., 450 U.S. 147, 150 (1981) (per curiam ) (summarily reversing an opinion that could not "be reconciled with the principles set out" in this Court's sovereign immunity jurisprudence).

The witnesses on both sides come to this case with their own perceptions, recollections, and even potential biases. It is in part for that reason that genuine disputes are generally resolved by juries in our adversarial system. By weighing the evidence and reaching factual inferences contrary to Tolan's competent evidence, the court below neglected to adhere to the fundamental principle that at the summary judgment stage, reasonable inferences should be drawn in favor of the nonmoving party.

Id. at 1866-1868. *Plumhoff* makes no mention of *Tolan* whatsoever. Has the Court in *Plumhoff* committed the same error it accuses the Fifth Circuit of making in *Tolan*? See also Lash v. Lemke, 786 F.3d 1, 6 (D.C. Cir. 2015) (distinguishing *Tolan* and declining to draw all reasonable inferences in favor of the nonmovant given the "clear evidence provided by a videorecording," leading the court to conclude that "[n]o matter what [plaintiff] claims now, we know to a certainty that he resisted arrest because we can see him doing so;" holding officers were entitled to qualified immunity from an excessive force claim); see also Ani-Deng v. Jeffboat, LLC, 777 F.3d 452 (7th Cir. 2015) (discounting plaintiff's affidavit); Harrison v. City of Dallas, No 3:14-CV-3585-N, at 5 (N.D. Tex. 2016) (granting summary judgment on the basis of video evidence in favor of police officers who fatally shot a man wielding a screwdriver; relying on Scott v. Harris to conclude that even though the "viewing angle was not always ideal . . . disposition of the motion begins and ends with [the video]" notwithstanding contrary evidence in affidavit submitted by the decedent's mother).

## 2. Summary Judgment Problems

*Sample Issues*

Based on the foregoing materials on summary judgment, how would you answer the following questions?

a. Assume that a corporation is sued for employment discrimination in hiring. One person, a supervisor, was solely responsible for hiring for the open position. He denies intent to discriminate. Can the plaintiff survive a motion for summary judgment on the ground that the fact finder might disbelieve the supervisor?

b. Assume instead that a plaintiff sues the city for negligence in failure to repair a large pothole, which she claims caused her to swerve into a parked car on the side of the road. There is only one witness, who says plaintiff's car did not swerve; rather, plaintiff drove straight into the back of the parked car while plaintiff seemed to be distracted. Evidence at the scene indicates that plaintiff had a cup of hot coffee in the car, which she had just purchased at a drive-through restaurant, and that an opened but half-full container of cream was on the front seat next to her. Should the city's motion for summary judgment be granted?

c. Assume that 90 percent of all taxicabs in Dodge City are owned by defendant Orange Cab Co. Plaintiff was injured in a hit-and-run accident in the early morning hours. Plaintiff sues Orange Cab Co. She states at her deposition that the vehicle that hit her was a taxicab, but she can recall nothing more specific. The only other taxicab company in town is the Yellow Cab Co., whose cabs look very similar to Orange Cab Co.'s though they are a slightly lighter color. Their records indicate that only one of their drivers was out that morning, and he claims that he was in a different part of town that morning.

Plaintiff and defendant Orange Cab Co. file cross-motions for summary judgment. Should either one be granted?

d. Plaintiff, a lawyer, sues defendant, her law partner, for defamation, claiming that defendant had made false statements that plaintiff was padding clients' bills for personal profit. Defendant denies making the statements. Defendant deposes the three people to whom the defamatory statements allegedly were made, all of whom deny that defendant made the statements. Defendant then moves for summary judgment. Should it be granted? See Dyer v. MacDougall, 201 F.2d 265 (2d Cir. 1952).

Consider in this regard the following language from Colosi v. Electri-Flex Co., 965 F.2d 500, 503 (7th Cir. 1992), in an opinion by Judge Posner:

If a party presents multiple affidavits on summary judgment, covering the same ground, and some are shown to be unworthy of belief but others are not, do those others entitle the party to summary judgment or can the falsity of some support a negative inference about the others? We should think the latter, at least in extreme cases. If (to choose a number at random) a party presents nine affidavits each saying the same thing, and eight are shown to be perjurious, we would doubt that the party was entitled to summary judgment merely because the last stood uncontradicted.

# 5   Decision Makers and Decision Models

It matters who decides. Lawyers invest much skill and energy in efforts to reach the "right" decision maker. The legal system invests at least as much effort and expense in trying to prevent the identity of the decision maker from assuming significance. The effort to reach the same result, no matter who decides, is the essence of the rule of law.

Although our ideal is that all litigants are treated the same, regardless of their own, or the decision maker's, identity, we know that ideals are never fully attained, so that lawyers will continue to worry about the procedures for determining who decides. In an adversary system, moreover, one side's choice of decision maker is constantly subject to the charge of bias, incompetence, or inconvenience by the other side. You have already seen in our study of jurisdiction how the issue of who decides is a question that can itself prompt great litigation battles.

This chapter will examine some of the bimodal choices that confront lawyers in their quest for an understanding tribunal in a particular case: judge or jury; litigation or an alternative. We look first at how judges are chosen and at the great powers they wield. Then we consider the jury, how it is chosen, and its powers (which we study through the efforts of the trial judge and the appellate courts to manage the jury). Finally, we introduce you to some of the leading methods of alternative dispute resolution.

## A.   THE JUDGE

### Problem Case: Judicial Positioning

Many lawyers regard a judicial appointment, especially to the federal bench, as the crown atop a successful legal career. If you were to begin now in shaping your professional life so as to be in the best position for a judgeship sometime in the future, what steps would you take? What law school or other activities would you pursue? What jobs, post–law school? What professional and personal contacts would you cultivate?

Why would a person want to become a judge? Why might someone *not* want such a job? To what sorts of people is such a position likely to be most appealing? Are they likely to be the best ones for the job?

## 1.   Judicial Selection: Appointment and Election

### a.   Selection of Federal Judges

Article II of the Constitution provides that the president shall nominate and appoint federal judges, with the "Advice and Consent" of the Senate. For Supreme Court Justices, the president has often nominated candidates without significant senatorial consultation. Although most Supreme Court nominations have been approved by the Senate, on occasion this practice has resulted in heated confirmation fights within the Senate, and some nominations have been rejected or withdrawn in the face of likely rejection.

By contrast, the traditional practice for nominating federal district court judges has been for the nomination to originate with the senior senator of the president's political party from the nominee's state. If there is no senator of the president's political party then in office, the president generally may rely on other sources to decide on a nominee.

Federal court of appeals judges have traditionally been selected through a joint effort of the executive and legislative branches. The president has more power with regard to these appointments because the circuits include multiple states; a president having difficulty with a senator on a court of appeals appointment has the option of appointing a judge from a different state.

The procedures to be observed by the president in selecting judicial candidates and the Senate in considering nominees are not specified in any constitutional or statutory provisions. As objectives have shifted over the years, the process has taken on a variety of forms. See Judith Resnik, Judicial Selection and Democratic Theory: Demand, Supply, and Life Tenure, 26 Cardozo L. Rev. 579 (2005); Symposium: Federal Judicial Selection, 39 U. Rich. L. Rev. 793 (2004).

As the chart on the following page depicts, regardless of selection procedures, presidential priorities can dramatically shape the profile of federal judicial nominees.

### b.   Federal Magistrates and Special Masters

In 1968, Congress created the office of United States Magistrate to replace a former system of U.S. Commissioners. Unlike the commissioner, the magistrate was to be paid a fixed salary, to be an attorney if at all possible, to serve a fixed term of eight years, and to be subject to removal from office only for cause. 28 U.S.C. § 636; Fed. R. Civ. P. 72-76. Section 636 provided that any district court "may establish rules pursuant to which any full-time United States magistrate . . . may be assigned . . . such additional duties as

Percentage of Female and Minority Appointees by President Obama Compared to Prior Presidents

| President/Term | Total appointments | Male | Female | White | African American | Latino | Asian American | Native American | Arab American |
|---|---|---|---|---|---|---|---|---|---|
| Barack Obama 2008– | 329 | 191 (58.05%) | 138 (41.95%) | 211 (64.13%) | 62 (13.84%) | 36 (10.94%) | 21 (6.38%) | 2 | N/A |
| George W. Bush 2001-2008 | 327 | 256 (78.2%) | 71 (21.80%) | 269 (82.2%) | 24 (7.3%)* | 30 (9.1%) | 4 (1.2%) | 0 | 0 |
| Clinton 1993-2000 | 378 | 267 (70.6%) | 111 (29.4%) | 285 (75.4%) | 62 (16.4%) | 24 (6.3%) | 5 (1.3%) | 1 (0.26%) | 1 (0.26%) |
| Bush 1989-1992 | 192 | 156 (81.2%) | 36 (18.8%) | 172 (89.6%) | 11 (5.7%) | 8 (4.2%) | 1 (0.5%) | 0 | 0 |
| Reagan 1981-1988 | 378 | 347 (91.8%) | 31 (8.2%) | 356 (94.2%) | 7 (1.9%) | 13 (3.4%) | 2 (0.5%) | 0 | 0 |
| Carter 1977-1980 | 258 | 217 (84.1%) | 41 (15.9%) | 202 (78.3%) | 37 (14.3%) | 16 (6.2%) | 2 (0.8%) | 1 (0.4%) | 0 |
| Ford 1974-1976 | 65 | 64 (98.5%) | 1 (1.5%) | 59 (90.8%) | 3 (4.6%) | 1 (1.5%) | 2 (3.1%) | 0 | 0 |
| Nixon 1969-1974 | 227 | 226 (99.6%) | 1 (0.4%) | 218 (96.0%) | 6 (2.6%) | 2 (0.9%) | 1 (0.4%) | 0 | 0 |

* Of the twenty-four, one was Roger Gregory, President Clinton's recess appointment to the Fourth Circuit.
*Sources:* Alliance for Justice, Judicial Selection Project, http://www.afj.org/wp-content/uploads/2015/04/Judicial_Selection_Snapshot.pdf; Judicial Selection During the Bush Administration (2008); Alliance for Justice Judicial Selection Project 2001-02 Biennial Report.

are not inconsistent with the Constitution and laws of the United States." Magistrates are appointed by the district courts that they serve, and these courts determine their duties.

Congressional concern about the increased burdens on federal trial judges motivated the creation of the magistrate position. In the decades since the statute's passage, the legislature's goal of diverting to magistrates many matters that would otherwise consume judicial time has been realized. Since 1968, there has been a steady increase in both the number and complexity of matters referred to magistrates.

Magistrates are not appointed by the president in the manner prescribed by Article III of the Constitution, but are appointed by the judges to whom they are subordinate. They also do not enjoy life tenure. This arrangement has led many to argue—so far unsuccessfully—that delegating federal judicial authority to magistrates violates Article III. In a criminal case, United States v. Raddatz, 447 U.S. 667, 681 (1980), the Supreme Court rejected the argument that Article III was violated when an evidentiary ruling was referred to a magistrate:

> Congress made clear that the district court has plenary discretion whether to authorize a magistrate to hold an evidentiary hearing and that the magistrate acts subsidiary to and only in aid of the district court. Thereafter, the entire process takes place under the district court's total control and jurisdiction.
>
> We need not decide whether . . . Congress could constitutionally have delegated the task of rendering a final decision on a suppression motion to a non-Art. III officer . . . . Congress has not sought to make any such delegation.

Pressures to increase the authority of magistrate judges remain strong. Citing the "mounting queue of civil cases" in the district courts and a desire to "improve access to the courts for all groups," Congress substantially expanded the power of magistrate judges to conduct jury trials, decide dispositive motions, and enter final judgment in the Federal Magistrate Act of 1979. S. Rep. No. 96-74, at 4 (1979). Under the statute, magistrates can now handle "any or all proceedings in a jury or nonjury civil matter and order the entry of judgment in the case" if the parties consent to disposition by the magistrate and if the judge has been "specially designated to exercise such jurisdiction" by the district court. 28 U.S.C. § 636(c)(1). Significantly, § 636(c)(1) proceedings conducted by magistrate judges occur without any supervision or review by district courts and a judgment entered by the magistrate judge pursuant to § 636(c)(1) is treated as a final judgment of the district court. This means magistrate judges now routinely handle not only a wide range of nondispositive matters (especially Rule 11 and discovery disputes) but also dispositive matters such as motions for summary judgment.

The parties' consent is the only effective way to prevent busy or biased district courts from coercing certain litigants into trials before magistrate judges. Nonetheless, Congress amended the Act in 1990 to permit district courts to "again advise the parties of the availability of the magistrate" even after they have declined referral. Judicial Improvements Act, 28 U.S.C. § 636(c)(2). And more recently, the Supreme Court has held that consent to case-dispositive authority for a magistrate judge need not be express if the circumstances indicate that the parties "clearly implied their consent." Roell v. Withrow, 538 U.S. 580, 586 (2003) (finding implied consent where defendants appeared before the magistrate judge and did not express any reservation after being notified of their right to refuse the judge's exercise of case-dispositive authority). Defendants prevailed before the magistrate judge and the plaintiff attempted to use their failure to expressly consent as grounds for vacating the judgment. The Court observed that its implied consent rule would "check[] the risk of gamesmanship by depriving parties of the luxury of waiting for the outcome before denying the magistrate judge's authority. Judicial efficiency is served; the Article III right is substantially honored." Id. at 590. Four Justices dissented, emphasizing that express consent "ensures that the parties knowingly and voluntarily waive their right to an Article III judge." Id. at 595.

Under Rule 53, district court judges also have the power to appoint special masters in exceptional, complex cases. The powers and compensation of the master are subject to the judge's discretion. The master is to assist the judge or jury, as directed, but the master's factual findings are accepted unless clearly erroneous in nonjury cases, and may be admissible as evidence in jury cases. Fed. R. Civ. P. 53(f). Special masters have become particularly important in the supervision of compliance with structural injunctions. See, e.g., Brown v. Plata, 563 U.S. 493 (2011) (citing and relying heavily on findings of special master regarding overcrowding of California prisons and failure of state to provide prisoners adequate access to health care; upholding injunction ordering reduction in the state's prison population).

As a practical matter, the sub-judiciary is indispensable. Federal judges likely could not manage their caseloads effectively without delegating some tasks to magistrates and special masters. The question, therefore, is not whether to deploy these assistants, but how, and according to what system of appointment, compensation, and judicial review. See Mark A. Fellows and Roger S. Haydock, Federal Court Special Masters: A Vital Resource in the Era of Complex Litigation, 31 Wm. Mitchell L. Rev. 1269 (2005); 2004 Special Masters Conference: Transcript of Proceedings, 31 Wm. Mitchell L. Rev. 1193 (2005).

Amendments to Rule 53 in 2003 confirm the indispensability of and increasingly extensive reliance on special masters. It also reaffirms that the "core of the original Rule 53 remains," but the language of section (b) that "[a] reference to a master shall be the exception and not the rule," Fed. R. Civ. P. 53(b) (1993), is gone. The new Rule also explicitly permits special masters to "address pretrial and posttrial matters that cannot be effectively and timely addressed by an available district judge or magistrate judge of the district." Rule 53(a)(1)(C). Before the amendments, the Rule only discussed "trial" masters, implying that special masters should not be assigned to handle pre- and post-trial issues. The amendment recognizes facts on the ground, since special masters have long been assigned nontrial matters.

### c.  Selection of State Judges

The judges who serve in the judicial systems of the states are selected by diverse methods. The history and extent of this variety are summarized in the following article.

## Glenn Winters, Selection of Judges—An Historical Introduction
44 Tex. L. Rev. 1081, 1082-1086 (1966)

The early years of our national existence probably stand without parallel in the intensity of popular interest in government. The hardships of emigration from the comfortable, settled life of the old country and the struggle for survival in the new world placed a premium on self-reliance and independence which found expression in all aspects of life, including government. The new nation as a whole was a grand experiment in popular self-government, and the spirit of experimentation did not cease with the adoption of the federal and state constitutions. There had never been an elected judiciary, but with the new concept of sovereignty in the populace as a whole, it was inevitable that someone would propose popular election of judges, since governors and legislators were already being elected. This was not particularly designed for improving justice but was simply another manifestation of the populism movement. However, there is some indication that it was inspired in part by a feeling that judges were being appointed too frequently from the ranks of the wealthy and privileged. Apparently the first elected judges were lower court judges in Georgia, elected as early as 1812. Mississippi, in 1832, was the first state to adopt a completely elective judiciary. New York, however, by action of its constitutional convention in 1846, led the switch from legislative and gubernatorial appointment to election. All states entering the Union from then until the entrance of Alaska in 1958 came in with an elected judiciary, and even the colonial states of Georgia, Maryland, Virginia, and Pennsylvania joined in the switch from appointment to election. New Hampshire, Massachusetts, Connecticut, Rhode Island, New Jersey, Delaware, and South Carolina resisted and to this day have never had elected judges.

Dissatisfaction began to develop almost immediately after election of the judiciary came into vogue in the mid-1800's. In the 1860's, the Tammany Hall organization in New York City seized control of the elected judiciary and aroused public indignation by ousting able judges and putting in incompetent ones. As a result, the question of a return to the appointment method was submitted to the people by referendum in 1873 but was defeated. Tammany control of the judiciary continued, and similar conditions in other states led to a revulsion against the elective system soon after it was established. Virginia went back to legislative selection after fourteen years of judicial elections. Vermont elected minor court judges for twenty years but abandoned this method in 1870. Even Mississippi went back to appointment in 1868 and retained it until 1910. Furthermore, states which retained the elective system became increasingly concerned about the adverse effects of political selection on the quality of judicial personnel and developed the nonpartisan ballot as a means of "taking the judges out of politics."

The nonpartisan-ballot system gained its greatest acceptance around the turn of the century in the states of the Northwest, from Ohio and Michigan to the Pacific coast, but it was also adopted in others such as Arizona and Tennessee. It soon became clear, however, that this was not the answer. As early as 1913, William Howard Taft, then ex-President of the United States and destined to be Chief Justice of the United States Supreme Court, told the American Bar Association that the nonpartisan ballot was a failure. He asserted that the system would only further lower the quality of judicial personnel by making it possible for unqualified persons who could not even get political support to run entirely on their own and to get elected by means of aggressive campaigning.

The early years of the twentieth century were times of activity, interest, and progress in judicial administration. In 1906, Roscoe Pound, a youthful professor at the University of Nebraska, delivered his historic address before the American Bar Association on "Causes of Popular Dissatisfaction with the Administration of Justice," in which he declared that popular election of judges had almost destroyed the traditional respect for the bench. In 1913, the same year that Taft addressed the American Bar Association, the American Judicature Society was founded by Pound, John H. Wigmore, Herbert Harley, and others as an instrumentality through which persons interested in the administration of justice might work together for its improvement.

. . . The system which . . . the American Judicature Society took up and promoted consisted of appointment and election with the addition of a third element—a nonpolitical nominating commission. Under this plan, judicial vacancies would be filled through appointment by a high elected official from a list of names submitted by the commission, which would have an affirmative responsibility to seek out the best available judicial talent. The judges nominated and appointed would thereafter go before the voters, without competing candidates, on the sole question of their retention in office. In the event of a rejection, the resulting vacancy would be filled as before by nomination and appointment.

In 1937, nearly twenty-five years after its formulation, this plan was given the endorsement of the American Bar Association. Three years later it was voted into the constitution of Missouri and has since been commonly known as the Missouri Plan. . . .

During the twenty-five years since adoption of the Missouri Plan in 1940, some or all of its features have been adopted for use in selecting some or all of the judges of a dozen states. . . .

The nominating-commission plan has also been used on a voluntary basis, without a constitutional or statutory mandate, in several other states.

In recent years, campaign battles over judgeships have grown intense and costly, sometimes inducing opponents to spend millions of dollars. Hot button political issues including abortion, tort reform, same-sex marriage, and school financing and reform have made the races more contentious, increasingly high profile, and often more dependent on the support of political parties. Those who favor the election of judges argue that campaigning forces judges to be accountable to those who live under the law and requires them to be responsive to and represent a wider array of views. Critics allege that leaving judicial selection to political whims forces judges and their opponents to shape their views according to public opinion rather than their interpretation of the law and to abdicate the impartiality that justice requires. Currently, 42 states choose at least some of their judges through political elections. Over 80 percent of state appeals court judges retain their power through the electoral process. William Glaberson, Fierce Campaigns Signal a New Era for State Courts, N.Y. Times, June 5, 2000, at A1.

In 2012, the New York Times reported that 31 states held elections for seats on their top court—"multicandidate races and 'retention' votes for a total of 73 judgeships nationwide." Editorial, No Way to Choose a Judge, N.Y. Times, Mar. 15, 2012. In a hotly contested Alabama race, the top contender, Roy Moore, had previously lost the job "in 2003 when a special ethics court removed him from the bench after he defied a court order to remove a Ten Commandments monument from the lobby of the state judicial building in Montgomery." Id. For 2012, the primary races in the state raised "roughly $2 million. In 2006, candidates for five Supreme Court seats spent a total of $13.4 million in both the primary and general election." Id. The Times predicted that less money would be spent overall in 2012, but only because current members of the court were elected with such "strong business backing" that "the plaintiff's bar and other opposing interests with their own deep pockets decided it was not worth competing." Id. Moore won reelection in November 2012 and has "vowed not to return the monument to the judicial building." Sebastian Kitchen, The Montgomery Advertiser, Nov. 7, 2012.

Nationwide, "[c]andidates in state supreme court races from 2000 to 2009 raised around $211 million—two and a half times more than in the previous decade." Billy Corriher, Merit Selection and Retention Elections Keep Judges out of Politics, Center for American Progress, Nov. 1, 2012. In Iowa in 2010, three state supreme court justices were voted out of office after joining a unanimous opinion holding that the Constitution protects the rights of same-sex couples to marry. And in 2011 "a record-breaking number of bills were filed to impeach or remove judges." Bert Brandenburg, Beating Back the War on Judges, Slate, Nov. 12, 2012. In the 2012 elections, "spending on television advertisements in state Supreme Court races set an all-time record . . . totaling an estimated $27.8 million . . . . More than 50% of all TV ads came from non-candidate groups. . . ." Seth Hoy and Eeva Moore, Judicial Election TV Spending Sets New Record, Justice at Stake, Nov. 7, 2012.

## 2. Judicial Qualifications

In America there is no formal, extended training program for judges beyond those required for certification as a lawyer. This is not true of all systems. In many European countries, for example, it is usual to establish a separate career track for judges who undergo longer educational programs and meet somewhat more rigorous academic standards than other members of the legal profession. One possible consequence is reduced social mobility, since those who are willing and able to undergo the longer and more rigorous program will tend to be from a more privileged socioeconomic class. This may mean, in turn, that the degree to which the judicial establishment reflects the politics and values of minorities and the disadvantaged is lessened. If these consequences are real, are there offsetting advantages? It may depend on the extent to which the attributes required for judicial work can be inculcated by formal training. In the absence of convincing data, is it intuitively reasonable to suppose that those who have undergone more rigorous academic training will be more courageous, decisive, fair, patient, or sane? Or is it reasonable to suppose that those who invested more in their judicial careers will be more likely to manifest the desired traits?

As an alternative to the separate track approach, the idea that judges should continue their education after attaining judicial office has gained credence in recent decades. While a substantial effort to move in this direction has been made by various public agencies and private institutions, the appropriate subjects of on-the-job training for judges have not yet been settled.

What about the candidate's philosophy regarding judicial authority? To what extent should the candidate's belief in *stare decisis*, statutory language, or the "plain meaning" of constitutional provisions as restraints on judicial discretion be relevant?

Catherine Pierce Wells has described two basic strands of judicial philosophy — formalism and realism — as follows:

> In analyzing the judicial task, legal theorists have generally divided into two camps. On the one hand, there are formalists who argue that legal decision making is a matter of applying preexisting rules or theories to the facts of a given case. On the other hand, there are realists who reject this idea and argue that substantive legal theories do not decide concrete cases. Not surprisingly, these two camps possess different attitudes towards judicial selection. The formalist places the emphasis on substantive law and normative theory, beginning the process with assumptions about the correctness of certain legal views and proceeding to make an evaluation by examining the candidate's grasp of and commitment to these views. The realist, by contrast, focuses on character and background, asking whether the prospective judge has the kind of character and background that would produce sound intuitions for resolving legal controversies. . . .

Catherine Pierce Wells, Clarence Thomas: The Invisible Man, 67 S. Cal. L. Rev. 117, 119-120 (1993); see also Gregory C. Sisk and Michael Heise, Judges and Ideology: Public and Academic Debates About Statistical Measures, 99 Nw. U. L. Rev. 743 (2005).

Controversy over the issue of judicial philosophy and over the extent to which inquiries into the candidate's position on particular legal disputes are fair game was fever-pitched during the failed confirmation hearings of Judge Robert Bork. These hearings, during which the nominee underwent intense and specific questioning on a range of legal issues, gave rise to a new verb: "Borking" a nominee. The disappointed candidate thereafter penned a work in which he angrily denounced the process that led to his defeat and the legal philosophy of his detractors. Robert H. Bork, The Tempting of America: The Political Seduction of the Law (1990).

What about race, ethnicity, or gender? Some commentators have argued that a judge should decide a case "from the bottom up," which means, among other things, that the judge should be "sensitive to a diverse range of interests." See Wells, supra, 67 S. Cal. L. Rev. at 128-131. Does this imply the further step of assuring that the bench as a whole be diverse, in order to improve its overall ability to hear a wide range of voices? If it does, what kind of diversity will further this end? Of particular, sometimes divisive, concern is whether a candidate's race, ethnicity, or gender should be relevant factors in judicial appointments. Here again, Supreme Court nominations have been the most visible example of how these factors can bear on judicial selections.

In a letter published in the New York Times, Judge A. Leon Higginbotham made the following argument in favor of treating racial diversity as a relevant factor in making judicial appointments:

> Since Justice Thomas moved from the Court of Appeals to the Supreme Court, *no* African-Americans appointed by President Bush remain on the Courts of Appeals. As Judge Reinhardt has said: "In President Bush's view, Clarence Thomas is apparently all there is out there. Clarence Thomas *is* black America to our President."
>
> By 1993, six of the 10 African-Americans sitting on the Courts of Appeals will be eligible for retirement. As the African-American judges appointed by President Carter have retired, Presidents Reagan and Bush have replaced them largely with white judges in their 30's and early 40's. Why is it important for the Federal bench to be pluralistic? Pluralism, more often than not, creates a milieu in which the judiciary, the litigants — indeed, our democratic system — benefit from the experience of those whose backgrounds reflect the breadth of the American experience.
>
> I do not want to be misunderstood. Pluralism does not mean that only a judge of the same race as a litigant will be able to adjudicate the case fairly. Rather, by creating a pluralistic court, we make sure judges will reflect a broad perspective. For example, speaking of Justice Thurgood Marshall, Justice Sandra Day O'Connor said: "At oral arguments and conference meetings, in opinions and dissents, Justice Marshall imparted not only his legal acumen but also his life experiences, pushing and prodding us to respond not only to the persuasiveness of legal argument but also to the power of moral truth."

Judicial pluralism is important for another reason. It is difficult to have a court that in the long run has the respect of most segments of the population if the court has no or minuscule pluralistic strands. Of course, pluralism does not absolutely and forever guarantee an effective and fair judiciary. Nothing really does. However, pluralism is a sine qua non in building a court that is both substantively excellent *and* respected by the general population. In other words, judicial pluralism breeds judicial legitimacy. Judicial homogeneity, by contrast, is more often than not a deterrent to, rather than a promoter of, equal justice for all.

A. Leon Higginbotham, The Case of the Missing Black Judges, N.Y. Times, July 29, 1992, at A21.

Others have argued that gender diversity should likewise be relevant to judicial appointment decisions. Like people of color, women of all races have been underrepresented on the judiciary. See, e.g., Judith Resnik, Revising the Canon: Feminist Help in Teaching Procedure, 61 U. Cin. L. Rev. 1181, 1191 (1993).

Both Judge Higginbotham and Professor Resnik regard the absence of members of certain groups within the judiciary as troublesome. But in what ways, exactly, is that absence potentially problematic? Is the matter similar to the problem produced by a jury that is not cross-representative of the community? If so, what *is* that problem? Does it go to the appearance of justice, its content, or both?

The extent to which one regards racial, gender, and ethnic pluralism on the bench as important also may depend on the extent to which one regards law as open-ended and judges as properly filling in the interstices. As such, the realist versus formalist discussion also may have a bearing on the diversity issue.

## 3.  Disqualification of Judges in Individual Cases

### Problem Case: The Prejudiced Judge

Graham Buchanan, the lawyer for the plaintiff in a personal injury case that is in federal court because the parties are diverse, believes that the federal district judge, Rosemary McArthur, is biased against him to such a degree that she cannot fairly try any case in which he appears. His evidence of bias is as follows:

1) That, while in law school in 1995-1998, he and McArthur were academic rivals and that McArthur is biased against Buchanan because he was chosen as editor-in-chief of the law review rather than McArthur; McArthur at that time stated to the law school newspaper that the sole reason he was chosen instead of her was that he was male, which Buchanan told the newspaper was "feminist fantasy."

2) That McArthur is biased against Buchanan for political reasons. He was the head of the law student chapter of the Federalist Society, a politically conservative organization, and she headed the student chapter of the American Constitution Society, a politically liberal organization. During an argument between them over welfare, in spring of 1998, McArthur called Buchanan's position "fascist fantasy."

3) That, before McArthur became a federal judge in 2009, she and Buchanan served together on a state bar committee charged with investigating allegations of ethical violations. During their joint tenure, Buchanan brought a complaint against McArthur, accusing her of refusing to pursue claims brought against women or minorities. McArthur denied the charge and warned Buchanan that such accusations were slanderous, but filed no action against him. The complaint against her was dismissed for lack of evidence.

4) That, in 2008, Buchanan and McArthur were opposing counsel in a personal injury suit, and McArthur told Buchanan that she would "mop the courtroom floor with him." Her client prevailed in the suit. No other, similar courtroom incidents between them occurred after 2008. They opposed each other in four subsequent lawsuits without problems.

5) That, shortly after McArthur was appointed to the federal bench in 2009, Buchanan saw McArthur at a bar function and said to her, in a joking tone, "Well, now we're even, Rose. You think I got editor-in-chief because I'm a male, and I think you got a federal judgeship because you're a female." McArthur made no response to Buchanan's quip.

Buchanan since has appeared before Judge McArthur in three matters. In the first, his client prevailed when the opponent defaulted. The second is currently in discovery. The third matter is the one at hand.

## Statutes and Precedents

Two statutes, 28 U.S.C. §§ 144 and 455, govern the disqualification of judges in federal cases. Section 144 permits a party to file a "timely and sufficient affidavit" alleging either that the judge is biased against that party or that the judge is biased in favor of an opponent. Such a challenge may be made only once in each case, with the judge retaining the power to deny the motion and remain on the case. Section 455 mandates that a judge "shall disqualify himself in any proceeding in which his impartiality might reasonably be questioned," and further may not continue to preside over a case if any of a series of specific circumstances obtain.

Virtually every state code has some process by which lawyers may challenge the impartiality of the judge assigned to hear a case. Many state codes, unlike the federal statutes, give each side one free strike—similar to a peremptory challenge to a juror—which may be exercised to excuse a judge without offering a reason. Section 144, by contrast, requires the challenging party to state reasons for alleging bias and leaves it in the judge's discretion to remain on the case despite the challenge.

The following scenarios, drawn from actual federal cases, involve judges accused of being "too partial" to hear the particular disputes before them. As you read them, consider whether you think the judges exhibited bias and whether you believe the challenges were well founded.

### *United States v. Hatahley*

In this case, the district court judge was deemed too partial to hear an action filed by Native Americans in southeastern Utah for losses of horses and burros that were seized and destroyed by the U.S. government in pursuance of its range clearance program. Evidence of the judge's bias was thought to lie in his statements describing the range clearance program, with its instances of brutal handling and slaughter of the Native Americans' livestock, as "'horrible,' 'monstrous,' 'atrocious,' 'cruel,' 'coldblooded depredation,' and 'without a sense of decency.'" United States v. Hatahley, 257 F.2d 920 (10th Cir. 1958). The district judge also suggested that Congress or the president should conduct investigations to determine the tribe's aboriginal rights, and threatened to conduct one himself. A public appeal on behalf of the plaintiffs was made for funds and supplies to be cleared through the judge's chambers.

### *Haines v. Liggett Group, Inc.*

In the second case, the district judge was held to have compromised the appearance of impartiality by making the following statements—which were widely publicized in the media—in a case brought against the tobacco industry:

> In the light of the current controversy surrounding breast implants, one wonders when all industries will recognize their obligation to voluntarily disclose risks from the use of their products. All too often in the choice between the physical health of consumers and the financial well being of business, concealment is chosen over disclosure, sales over safety, and money over morality. Who are these persons who knowingly and secretly decide to put the buying public at risk solely for the purpose of making profits and who believe that illness and death of consumers is an appropriate cost of their own prosperity!
>
> . . . [D]espite some rising pretenders, the tobacco industry may be the king of concealment and disinformation.

Haines v. Liggett Group, Inc., 975 F.2d 81 (3d Cir. 1992).

*Pennsylvania v. Local Union 542, International Union of Operating Engineers*

The third case involved a petition for disqualification of Judge Higginbotham, on the ground that his involvement in racial justice issues made him too partial to hear a race discrimination case. He said that the evidence of his alleged personal bias included the following:

1) That the instant case is a class action, brought under the Civil Rights Act of 1964 and other civil rights statutes, charging that defendants have discriminated against the twelve black plaintiffs and the class they represent on the basis of race, and seeking extensive equitable and legal remedies for the alleged discrimination;

2) That I will try the instant case without a jury, and that I am black;

3) That on Friday, October 25, 1974, I addressed a luncheon meeting of the Association for the Study of Afro-American Life and History, during the 59th Annual Meeting of that organization, "a group composed of black historians";

4) That in the course of that speech I criticized two recent Supreme Court decisions which involved alleged racial discrimination, and said, *inter alia,* that:

> (a) "I do not see the [Supreme] Court of the 1970's or envision the Court of the 1980's as the major instrument for significant change and improvement in the quality of race relations in America";
>
> (b) "The message of these recent decisions is that if we are to deal with the concept of integration, we must probably make our major efforts in another forum";
>
> (c) "As I see it, we must make major efforts in other forums without exclusive reliance on the federal legal process."

5) That I used the pronoun "we" several times in the course of the speech, and that my use of this pronoun evidences my "intimate tie with and emotional attachment to the advancement of black civil rights";

6) That by my agreement to deliver the speech I presented myself as "a leader in the future course of the black civil rights movement";

7) That my speech took place in "an extra-judicial and community context," and not in the course of this litigation;

8) That the following day, Saturday, October 26, 1974, *The Philadelphia Inquirer* published "an article appearing under a predominant headline on the first page of the metropolitan news section . . . describing the October 25th meeting and publishing the aforementioned quotes";

9) That approximately 450,000 copies of *The Philadelphia Inquirer* containing this account were distributed publicly on or about October 26, 1974;

10) That this account made "the community at large" aware of my "significant role as a spokesman, scholar and active supporter of the advancement of the causes of integration";

11) That I believe "that there has been social injustice to blacks in the United States"; "that these injustices must be corrected and remedied"; and "that they must be remedied by extra-judicial efforts by blacks, including [myself]";

12) That "the very invitation to speak," "the content of [my] remarks" and my "posing for photographs" after the address identify me as "a leader for and among blacks," and "one of the country's leading civil rights proponents";

13) That I am a "celebrity" within the black community;

14) That "I [have] identified, and [do] identify, [myself] with causes of blacks, including the cause of correction of social injustices which [I believe] have been caused to blacks"; that I have made myself "a participant in those causes, including the cause of correction of social injustices which [I believe] have been caused to blacks";

15) That "in view of the applicable federal law," and by reason of my "personal and emotional commitments to civil rights causes of the black community, the black community expectation as to [my] leadership and spokesmanship therein, and the basic tenet of our legal system requiring both actual and apparent impartiality in the federal courts," my "continuation . . . as trier of fact, molder of remedy and arbiter of all issues constitutes judicial impropriety."

Pennsylvania v. Local Union 542, International Union of Operating Engineers, 388 F. Supp. 155 (E.D. Pa. 1974).

### Blank v. Sullivan & Cromwell

The fourth case involved a petition requesting Judge Constance Motley to disqualify herself in an action brought by a female plaintiff against a prominent New York law firm alleging that the law firm discriminated in the employment of lawyers on the basis of sex. The basis of the petition was that Judge Motley, who is African-American, "strongly identified with those who suffered discrimination in employment because of sex or race." Blank v. Sullivan & Cromwell, 418 F. Supp. 1 (S.D.N.Y. 1975). Support for this claim was thought to lie in a quote, attributed to the judge, on the crippling effects of discrimination.

Responding to the accusation of bias, Judge Motley had this to say:

It is beyond dispute that for much of my legal career I worked on behalf of blacks who suffered race discrimination. I am a woman, and before being elevated to the bench, was a woman lawyer. These obvious facts, however, clearly do not, *ipso facto*, indicate or even suggest the personal bias or prejudice required by [28 U.S.C.] § 144. The assertion, without more, that a judge who engaged in civil rights litigation and who happens to be of the same sex as a plaintiff in a suit alleging sex discrimination on the part of a law firm, is, therefore, so biased that he or she could not hear the case, comes nowhere near the standards required for recusal. Indeed, if background or sex or race of each judge were, by definition, sufficient grounds for removal, no judge on this court could hear this case, or many others, by virtue of the fact that all of them were attorneys, of a sex, often with distinguished law firm or public service backgrounds. . . .

Nowhere in their affidavits do defense counsel or defendant indicate that I have any relationship or personal association or interest in this litigation. They merely point to my general background and the obvious facts of my race and sex as evidence of extrajudicial prejudice.

Blank v. Sullivan & Cromwell, 418 F. Supp. 1, 4 (S.D.N.Y. 1975).

## Note: Liteky v. United States, 510 U.S. 540 (1994)

In 1994, the United States Supreme Court had occasion to consider the nature of judicial bias and the circumstances under which it renders a judge unable to be impartial. Before and during the defendants' 1991 trial on federal criminal charges, the district judge denied defense motions that he recuse himself pursuant to 28 U.S.C. § 455(a) (the companion statute to that involved in the Higginbotham case, supra), which requires a federal judge to "disqualify himself in any proceeding in which his impartiality might reasonably be questioned." These motions were based first on rulings and statements this same judge made, which allegedly displayed impatience, disregard, and animosity toward the defense, and second on the judge's admonishment of the defendants' counsel and codefendants in front of the jury at the 1991 trial. The court of appeals confirmed the defendants' convictions, concluding that matters arising from judicial proceedings are not a proper basis for recusal, and the Supreme Court agreed.

In the opinion for the Court, Justice Scalia wrote:

> [T]he pejorative connotation of the terms "bias" and "prejudice" demands that they be applied only to judicial predispositions that go beyond what is normal and acceptable. We think there is an equivalent pejorative connotation, with equivalent consequences, to the term "partiality." See American Heritage Dictionary 1319 (3d ed. 1992) ("partiality" defined as "[f]avorable prejudice or bias"). A prospective juror in an insurance-claim case may be stricken as partial if he always votes for insurance companies; but not if he always votes for the party whom the terms of the contract support. "Partiality" does not refer to all favoritism, but only to such as is, for some reason, wrongful or inappropriate. Impartiality is not gullibility....
>
> ... First, judicial rulings alone almost never constitute valid basis for a bias or partiality motion. See United States v. Grinnell Corp., 384 U.S. 563, 583 (1966). In and of themselves (i.e., apart from surrounding comments or accompanying opinion), they cannot possibly show reliance upon an extrajudicial source; and can only in the rarest circumstances evidence the degree of favoritism or antagonism required (as discussed below) when no extrajudicial source is involved. Almost invariably, they are proper grounds for appeal, not for recusal. Second, opinions formed by the judge on the basis of facts introduced or events occurring in the course of the current proceedings, or of prior proceedings, do not constitute a basis for a bias or partiality motion unless they display a deep-seated favoritism or antagonism that would make fair judgment impossible. Thus, judicial remarks during the course of a trial that are critical or disapproving of, or even hostile to, counsel, the parties, or their cases, ordinarily do not support a bias or partiality challenge. They *may* do so if they reveal an opinion that derives from an extrajudicial source; and they *will* do so if they reveal such a high degree of favoritism or antagonism as to make fair judgment impossible. An example of the latter (and perhaps of the former as well) is the statement that was alleged to have been made by the District Judge in Berger v. United States, 255 U.S. 22 (1921), a World War I espionage case against German-American defendants: "One must have a very judicial mind, indeed, not [to be] prejudiced against the German

Americans" because their "hearts are reeking with disloyalty." Id., at 28. *Not* establishing bias or partiality, however, are expressions of impatience, dissatisfaction, annoyance, and even anger, that are within the bounds of what imperfect men and women, even after having been confirmed as federal judges, sometimes display. A judge's ordinary efforts at courtroom administration—even a stern and short-tempered judge's ordinary efforts at courtroom administration—remain immune.

510 U.S. at 552-556.

## Note: Caperton v. A.T. Massey Coal Co., 556 U.S. 868 (2009)

The Court addressed the constitutional standard for determining impermissible bias in Caperton v. A.T. Massey Coal Co. Attempts to influence judicial elections are not uncommon in states that allow popular election and recall, but the facts of *Caperton* are rather extraordinary:

A West Virginia jury returned a verdict that found Massey liable for fraudulent misrepresentation, concealment, and tortious interference with existing contractual relations. The jury awarded plaintiffs $50 million in compensatory and punitive damages.

. . . After the verdict but before the appeal, West Virginia held its 2004 judicial elections. Knowing the Supreme Court of Appeals of West Virginia would consider the appeal in the case, Massey's chairman, chief executive officer, and president, Don Blankenship, decided to support an attorney who sought to replace Justice McGraw . . . . The attorney who sought to replace him was Brent Benjamin.

In addition to contributing the $1,000 statutory maximum to Benjamin's campaign committee, Blankenship donated almost $2.5 million to "And For The Sake Of The Kids," a political organization formed under 26 U.S.C. § 527 [that] supported Benjamin. Blankenship's donations accounted for more than two-thirds of the total funds it raised. Blankenship also spent more than $500,000 on independent expenditures—for direct mailings and letters soliciting donations as well as television and newspaper advertisements—"'to support . . . Brent Benjamin.'"

Blankenship's $3 million in contributions were more than the total amount spent by all other Benjamin supporters, three times the amount spent by Benjamin's own committee, and $1 million more than the total amount spent by the campaign committees of both candidates combined.

Benjamin won . . . .

In October 2005, before Massey filed its petition for appeal in West Virginia's highest court, Caperton moved to disqualify now-Justice Benjamin under the Due Process Clause and the West Virginia Code of Judicial Conduct, based on the conflict caused by Blankenship's campaign involvement. Justice Benjamin denied the motion . . . and Massey filed its appeal.

A year later that court reversed the $50 million verdict against Massey [on procedural grounds] . . . . Justice Starcher dissented, stating that the "majority's opinion is morally and legally wrong." Justice Albright also dissented, accusing the majority of "misapplying the law and introducing sweeping 'new law' into our jurisprudence that may well come back to haunt us."

Caperton sought rehearing, and the parties moved for disqualification of three of the five justices who decided the appeal. Photos had surfaced of Justice Maynard vacationing with Blankenship in the French Riviera while the case was pending. Justice Maynard granted Caperton's recusal motion. On the other side Justice Starcher granted Massey's recusal motion, apparently based on his public criticism of Blankenship's role in the 2004 elections. In his recusal memorandum Justice Starcher urged Justice Benjamin to recuse himself as well. He noted that "Blankenship's bestowal of his personal wealth, political tactics, and 'friendship' have created a cancer in the affairs of this Court." Justice Benjamin declined Justice Starcher's suggestion and denied Caperton's recusal motion.

The court granted rehearing. Justice Benjamin, now in the capacity of acting chief justice, selected Judges Cookman and Fox to replace the recused justices. Caperton moved a third time for disqualification, arguing that Justice Benjamin had failed to apply the correct standard under West Virginia law — i.e., whether "a reasonable and prudent person, knowing these objective facts, would harbor doubts about Justice Benjamin's ability to be fair and impartial." Caperton also included the results of a public opinion poll, which indicated that over 67% of West Virginians doubted Justice Benjamin would be fair and impartial. Justice Benjamin again refused to withdraw, noting that the "push poll" was "neither credible nor sufficiently reliable to serve as the basis for an elected judge's disqualification."

In April 2008 a divided court again reversed the jury verdict, and again it was a 3-to-2 decision. . . .

Four months later—a month after the petition for writ of certiorari was filed in this Court—Justice Benjamin filed a concurring opinion. He defended the merits of the majority opinion as well as his decision not to recuse. He rejected Caperton's challenge to his participation in the case under both the Due Process Clause and West Virginia law. Justice Benjamin reiterated that he had no "'direct, personal, substantial, pecuniary interest'" in this case." Adopting "a standard merely of 'appearances,'" he concluded, "seems little more than an invitation to subject West Virginia's justice system to the vagaries of the day—a framework in which predictability and stability yield to supposition, innuendo, half-truths, and partisan manipulations."

556 U.S. at 872-876.

Justice Kennedy, writing for a 5-4 majority of the Court, reversed on federal due process grounds. The Due Process Clause incorporates the common law rule that requires recusal if a judge has "a direct, personal, substantial, pecuniary interest" in a case. Tumey v. Ohio, 273 U.S. 510 (1927). And in a line of cases that developed in the context of criminal contempt, due process also requires recusal where "the probability of actual bias on the part of the judge or decisionmaker is too high to be constitutionally tolerable." Withrow v. Larkin, 421 U.S. 35 (1975). Applying these principles, Justice Kennedy concluded that the possibility of temptation for Justice Benjamin was dispositive even without proof of actual bias:

Not every campaign contribution by a litigant or attorney creates a probability of bias that requires a judge's recusal, but this is an exceptional case. We conclude that there is a serious risk of actual bias—based on objective and reasonable perceptions—when a person with a personal stake in a particular case had a significant and disproportionate influence in placing the judge on the case by raising funds or directing the judge's election campaign when the case was pending or imminent. The inquiry centers on the contribution's relative size in comparison to the total amount of money contributed to the campaign, the total amount spent in the election, and the apparent effect such contribution had on the outcome of the election.

Applying this principle, we conclude that Blankenship's campaign efforts had a significant and disproportionate influence in placing Justice Benjamin on the case. Blankenship contributed some $3 million to unseat the incumbent and replace him with Benjamin. His contributions eclipsed the total amount spent by all other Benjamin supporters and exceeded by 300% the amount spent by Benjamin's campaign committee.

Massey responds that Blankenship's support, while significant, did not cause Benjamin's victory. In the end the people of West Virginia elected him, and they did so based on many reasons other than Blankenship's efforts. Massey points out that every major state newspaper, but one, endorsed Benjamin. . . .

Due process requires an objective inquiry into whether the contributor's influence on the election under all the circumstances "would offer a possible temptation to the average . . . judge to . . . lead him not to hold the balance nice, clear and true." *Tumey*, supra, at 532. In an election decided by fewer than 50,000 votes (382,036 to 334,301), Blankenship's campaign contributions—in comparison to the total amount contributed to the campaign, as well as the total amount spent in the election—had a significant and disproportionate influence on the electoral outcome. And the risk that Blankenship's influence engendered actual bias is sufficiently substantial that it "must be forbidden if the guarantee of due process is to be adequately implemented." *Withrow*, supra, at 47.

The temporal relationship between the campaign contributions, the justice's election, and the pendency of the case is also critical. It was reasonably foreseeable, when the campaign contributions were made, that the pending case would be before the newly elected justice. . . . Although there is no allegation of a quid pro quo agreement, the fact remains that Blankenship's extraordinary contributions were made at a time when he had a vested stake in the outcome. Just as no man is allowed to be a judge in his own cause, similar fears of bias can arise when—without the consent of the other parties—a man chooses the judge in his own cause. And applying this principle to the judicial election process, there was here a serious, objective risk of actual bias that required Justice Benjamin's recusal.

Justice Benjamin did undertake an extensive search for actual bias. But, as we have indicated, that is just one step in the judicial process; objective standards may also require recusal whether or not actual bias exists or can be proved. Due process "may sometimes bar trial by judges who have no actual bias and who would do their very best to weigh the scales of justice equally between contending parties." *Murchison*, 349 U.S., at 136. . . . We find that Blankenship's significant and disproportionate influence—coupled with the temporal relationship between the election and the pending case—"offer a possible temptation to the average . . . judge to . . . lead him not to hold the balance nice, clear and true." *Lavoie*, 475 U.S., at 825. On these extreme facts the probability of actual bias rises to an unconstitutional level. . . .

Because the codes of judicial conduct provide more protection than due process requires, most disputes over disqualification will be resolved without resort to the Constitution. Application of the constitutional standard implicated in this case will thus be confined to rare instances.

Id. at 884-890.

Chief Justice Roberts and Justice Scalia filed vigorous dissents bemoaning the intrusion of federal due process standards into a matter of state concern and predicting that the courts will be deluged with *"Caperton"* motions to disqualify judges. A year after the decision, one study found just 26 cases that involved "in-depth" analysis of *Caperton*, and only 33 referencing the decision. See Catherine Stone & Wendy Martinez, Caperton v. A.T. Massey Coal Co., 41 St. Mary's L.J. 621, 634 (2010).

### Problem Case: The Prejudiced Judge, Revisited

Revisit the problem case at the beginning of this section. Answer the following questions:

1. In your opinion, is Judge McArthur biased against Graham Buchanan within the meaning of §§ 144 and 455? Can she be fair in any matter involving Buchanan?
2. How should Buchanan raise his bias claim? How should McArthur respond?
3. What legal, practical, and policy issues are at stake? Think about the qualities of an ideal judge, the role the judge plays in fair procedure, and the extent to which McArthur may or may not match that ideal.
4. Would Buchanan have a stronger motion if he sought to disqualify McArthur in a sex discrimination case where he represented the male employer?
5. If past experience is relevant to a judge's qualifications, at what point does it imperil her ability to be impartial? When does perspective become bias?

## B.　THE JUDGE'S POWERS

### 1.　Injunctions and Contempt

A recurrent theme in our study is the huge power of the trial judge. She is guided by rules that leave much to discretion, she possesses certain inherent powers, and she issues orders that are often dispositive without being appealable. We have seen, moreover, that judges may take an activist (and unsupervised) role in the settlement of cases without trial. In addition to this kind of daily exercise of power, there are two related situations in which the trial judge's authority is at its peak. One is the issuance of preliminary injunctive relief, and the second is the power to hold in contempt one who disobeys a court order. Both of these extraordinary powers, exercised in the most heated circumstances, can be observed in the following cases.

## Walker v. City of Birmingham
388 U.S. 307 (1967)

JUSTICE STEWART delivered the opinion of the Court.

On Wednesday, April 10, 1963, officials of Birmingham, Alabama, filed a bill of complaint in a state circuit court asking for injunctive relief against 139 individuals and two organizations. The bill and accompanying affidavits stated that during the preceding seven days:

> [R]espondents had sponsored and/or participated in and/or conspired to commit and/or to encourage and/or to participate in certain movements, plans or projects commonly called "sit-in" demonstrations, "kneel-in" demonstrations, mass street parades, trespasses on private property after being warned to leave the premises by the owners of said property, congregating in mobs upon the public streets and other public places, unlawfully picketing private places of business in the City of Birmingham, Alabama; violation of numerous ordinances and statutes of the City of Birmingham and State of Alabama. . . .

It was alleged that this conduct was "calculated to provoke breaches of the peace," "threaten(ed) the safety, peace and tranquility of the City," and placed "an undue burden and strain upon the manpower of the Police Department."

The bill stated that these infractions of the law were expected to continue and would "lead to further imminent danger to the lives, safety, peace, tranquility and general welfare of the people of the City of Birmingham," and that the "remedy by law (was) inadequate." The circuit judge granted a temporary injunction as prayed in the bill, enjoining the petitioners from, among other things, participating in or encouraging mass street parades or mass processions without a permit as required by a Birmingham ordinance.[1]

Five of the eight petitioners were served with copies of the writ early the next morning. Several hours later four of them held a press conference.

---

1. The text of the injunction is reproduced as Appendix A to this opinion. The Birmingham parade ordinance, § 1159 of the Birmingham City Code, provides that:

> It shall be unlawful to organize or hold, or to assist in organizing or holding, or to take part or participate in, any parade or procession or other public demonstration on the streets or other public ways of the city, unless a permit therefor has been secured from the commission.
>
> To secure such permit, written application shall be made to the commission, setting forth the probable number of persons, vehicles and animals which will be engaged in such parade, procession or other public demonstration, the purpose for which it is to be held or had, and the streets or other public ways over, along or in which it is desired to have or hold such parade, procession or other public demonstration. The commission shall grant a written permit for such parade, procession or other public demonstration, prescribing the streets or other public ways which may be used therefor, unless in its judgment the public welfare, peace, safety, health, decency, good order, morals or convenience require that it be refused. It shall be unlawful to use for such purposes any other streets or public ways than those set out in said permit.
>
> The two preceding paragraphs, however, shall not apply to funeral processions.

There a statement was distributed, declaring their intention to disobey the injunction because it was "raw tyranny under the guise of maintaining law and order."[2] At this press conference one of the petitioners stated: "That they had respect for the Federal Courts, or Federal Injunctions, but in the past the State Courts had favored local law enforcement, and if the police couldn't handle it, the mob would."

That night a meeting took place at which one of the petitioners announced that "[i]njunction or no injunction we are going to march tomorrow." The next afternoon, Good Friday, a large crowd gathered in the vicinity of Sixteenth Street and Sixth Avenue North in Birmingham. A group of about 50 or 60 proceeded to parade along the sidewalk while a crowd of 1,000 to 1,500 onlookers stood by, "clapping, and hollering, and [w]hooping." Some of the crowd followed the marchers and spilled out into the street. At least three of the petitioners participated in this march.

Meetings sponsored by some of the petitioners were held that night and the following night, where calls for volunteers to "walk" and go to jail were made. On Easter Sunday, April 14, a crowd of between 1,500 and 2,000 people congregated in the midafternoon in the vicinity of Seventh Avenue and Eleventh Street North in Birmingham. One of the petitioners was seen organizing members of the crowd in formation. A group of about 50, headed by three other petitioners, started down the sidewalk two abreast. At least one other petitioner was among the marchers. Some 300 or 400 people from among the onlookers followed in a crowd that occupied the entire width of the street and overflowed onto the sidewalks. Violence occurred. Members of the crowd threw rocks that injured a newspaperman and damaged a police motorcycle.

The next day the city officials who had requested the injunction applied to the state circuit court for an order to show cause why the petitioners should not be held in contempt for violating it. At the ensuing hearing the petitioners sought to attack the constitutionality of the injunction on the ground that it was vague and overbroad, and restrained free speech. They also sought to attack the Birmingham parade ordinance upon similar grounds, and upon the further ground that the ordinance had previously been administered in an arbitrary and discriminatory manner.

The circuit judge refused to consider any of these contentions, pointing out that there had been neither a motion to dissolve the injunction, nor an effort to comply with it by applying for a permit from the city commission before engaging in the Good Friday and Easter Sunday parades. Consequently, the court held that the only issues before it were whether it had jurisdiction to issue the temporary injunction, and whether thereafter the petitioners had knowingly violated it. Upon these issues the court found against the petitioners, and imposed upon each of them a sentence of five days in jail and a $50 fine, in accord with an Alabama statute.[3]

---

2. The full statement is reproduced as Appendix B to this opinion.

3. "The circuit court, or judges thereof when exercising equity jurisdiction and powers may punish for contempt by fine not exceeding fifty dollars, and by imprisonment, not exceeding five days, one or both." Ala. Code, Tit. 13, § 143; see also id., §§ 4-5, 126.

The Supreme Court of Alabama affirmed.[4] That court, too, declined to consider the petitioners' constitutional attacks upon the injunction and the underlying Birmingham parade ordinance:

> It is to be remembered that petitioners are charged with violating a temporary injunction. We are not reviewing a denial of a motion to dissolve or discharge a temporary injunction. Petitioners did not file any motion to vacate the temporary injunction until after the Friday and Sunday parades. Instead, petitioners deliberately defied the order of the court and did engage in and incite others to engage in mass street parades without a permit.
>
> We hold that the circuit court had the duty and authority, in the first instance, to determine the validity of the ordinance, and, until the decision of the circuit court is reversed for error by orderly review, either by the circuit court or a higher court, the orders of the circuit court based on its decision are to be respected and disobedience of them is contempt of its lawful authority, to be punished. Howat v. State of Kansas, 258 U.S. 181.

Howat v. State of Kansas, 258 U.S. 181 [1922], was decided by this Court almost 50 years ago. That was a case in which people had been punished by a Kansas trial court for refusing to obey an antistrike injunction issued under the state industrial relations act. They had claimed a right to disobey the court's order upon the ground that the state statute and the injunction based upon it were invalid under the Federal Constitution. The Supreme Court of Kansas had affirmed the judgment, holding that the trial court "had general power to issue injunctions in equity, and that even if its exercise of the power was erroneous, the injunction was not void, and the defendants were precluded from attacking it in this collateral proceeding . . . that, if the injunction was erroneous, jurisdiction was not thereby forfeited, that the error was subject to correction only by the ordinary method of appeal, and disobedience to the order constituted contempt." 258 U.S. at 189.

This Court, in dismissing the writ of error, not only unanimously accepted but fully approved the validity of the rule of state law upon which the judgment of the Kansas court was grounded:

> An injunction duly issuing out of a court of general jurisdiction with equity powers, upon pleadings properly invoking its action, and served upon persons made parties therein and within the jurisdiction, must be obeyed by them, however erroneous the action of the court may be, even if the error be in the assumption of the validity of a seeming, but void law going to the merits of the case. It is for the court of first instance to determine the question of the validity of the law, and until its decision is reversed for error by orderly review, either by itself or by a higher court, its orders based on its decision are to be respected, and disobedience of them is contempt of its lawful authority, to be punished.

258 U.S. at 189-190.

---

4. The Alabama Supreme Court quashed the conviction of one defendant because of insufficient proof that he knew of the injunction before violating it, and the convictions of two others because there was no showing that they had disobeyed the order. 279 Ala. 53, 64 (1965).

The rule of state law accepted and approved in Howat v. State of Kansas is consistent with the rule of law followed by the federal courts.

In the present case, however, we are asked to hold that this rule of law, upon which the Alabama courts relied, was constitutionally impermissible. We are asked to say that the Constitution compelled Alabama to allow the petitioners to violate this injunction, to organize and engage in these mass street parades and demonstrations, without any previous effort on their part to have the injunction dissolved or modified, or any attempt to secure a parade permit in accordance with its terms. Whatever the limits of Howat v. State of Kansas,[6] we cannot accept the petitioners' contentions in the circumstances of this case.

Without question the state court that issued the injunction had, as a court of equity, jurisdiction over the petitioners and over the subject matter of the controversy. And this is not a case where the injunction was transparently invalid or had only a frivolous pretense to validity. We have consistently recognized the strong interest of state and local governments in regulating the use of their streets and other public places. When protest takes the form of mass demonstrations, parades, or picketing on public streets and sidewalks, the free passage of traffic and the prevention of public disorder and violence become important objects of legitimate state concern. As the Court stated, in Cox v. State of Louisiana, "We emphatically reject the notion . . . that the First and Fourteenth Amendments afford the same kind of freedom to those who would communicate ideas by conduct such as patrolling, marching, and picketing on streets and highways, as these amendments afford to those who communicate ideas by pure speech." 379 U.S. 536, 555 [1965]. And as a unanimous Court stated in Cox v. State of New Hampshire:

> Civil liberties, as guaranteed by the Constitution, imply the existence of an organized society maintaining public order without which liberty itself would be lost in the excesses of unrestrained abuses. The authority of a municipality to impose regulations in order to assure the safety and convenience of the people in the use of public highways has never been regarded as inconsistent with civil liberties but rather as one of the means of safeguarding the good order upon which they ultimately depend. 312 U.S. 569, 574 [1941].

6. In In re Green, 369 U.S. 689 [1962], the petitioner was convicted of criminal contempt for violating a labor injunction issued by an Ohio court. Relying on the pre-emptive command of the federal labor law, the Court held that the state courts were required to hear Green's claim that the state court was without jurisdiction to issue the injunction. The petitioner in *Green*, unlike the petitioners here, had attempted to challenge the validity of the injunction before violating it by promptly applying to the issuing court for an order vacating the injunction. The petitioner in *Green* had further offered to prove that the court issuing the injunction had agreed to its violation as an appropriate means of testing its validity.

The generality of the language contained in the Birmingham parade ordinance upon which the injunction was based would unquestionably raise substantial constitutional issues concerning some of its provisions. The petitioners, however, did not even attempt to apply to the Alabama courts for an authoritative construction of the ordinance. Had they done so, those courts might have given the licensing authority granted in the ordinance a narrow and precise scope, as did the New Hampshire courts in Cox v. State of New Hampshire and Poulos v. State of New Hampshire, both supra. Cf. Shuttlesworth v. City of Birmingham, 382 U.S. 87, 91 [1965]; City of Darlington v. Stanley, 239 S.C. 139 [1961]. Here, just as in *Cox* and *Poulos*, it could not be assumed that this ordinance was void on its face.

The breadth and vagueness of the injunction itself would also unquestionably be subject to substantial constitutional question. But the way to raise that question was to apply to the Alabama courts to have the injunction modified or dissolved. The injunction in all events clearly prohibited mass parading without a permit, and the evidence shows that the petitioners fully understood that prohibition when they violated it.

The petitioners also claim that they were free to disobey the injunction because the parade ordinance on which it was based had been administered in the past in an arbitrary and discriminatory fashion. In support of this claim they sought to introduce evidence that, a few days before the injunction issued, requests for permits to picket had been made to a member of the city commission. One request had been rudely rebuffed,[9] and this same official had later made clear that he was without power to grant the permit alone, since the issuance of such permits was the responsibility of the entire city commission.[10] Assuming the truth of this proffered evidence, it does not follow that the parade ordinance was void on its face. The petitioners, moreover, did not apply for a permit either to the commission itself or to any commissioner after the injunction issued. Had they done so, and

---

9. Mrs. Lola Hendricks, not a petitioner in this case, testified that on April 3:

"I went to Mr. Connor's office, the Commissioner's office at the City Hall Building. We went up and Commissioner Connor met us at the door. He asked, 'May I help you?' I told him, 'Yes, sir, we came up to apply or see about getting a permit for picketing, parading, demonstrating.'" . . .

"I asked Commissioner Connor for the permit, and asked if he could issue the permit, or other persons who would refer me to, persons who would issue a permit. He said, 'No, you will not get a permit in Birmingham, Alabama, to picket. I will picket you over to the City Jail,' and he repeated that twice."

10. Commissioner Connor sent the following telegram to one of the petitioners on April 5:

"Under the provisions of the city code of the City of Birmingham, a permit to picket as requested by you cannot be granted by me individually but is the responsibility (sic) of the entire commission. I insist that you and your people do not start any picketing on the streets in Birmingham, Alabama."

Eugene "Bull" Connor, Commissioner of Public Safety.

had the permit been refused, it is clear that their claim of arbitrary or discriminatory administration of the ordinance would have been considered by the state circuit court upon a motion to dissolve the injunction.

This case would arise in quite a different constitutional posture if the petitioners, before disobeying the injunction, had challenged it in the Alabama courts, and had been met with delay or frustration of their constitutional claims. But there is no showing that such would have been the fate of a timely motion to modify or dissolve the injunction. There was an interim of two days between the issuance of the injunction and the Good Friday march. The petitioners give absolutely no explanation of why they did not make some application to the state court during that period. The injunction had issued *ex parte*; if the court had been presented with the petitioners' contentions, it might well have dissolved or at least modified its order in some respects. If it had not done so, Alabama procedure would have provided for an expedited process of appellate review. It cannot be presumed that the Alabama courts would have ignored the petitioners' constitutional claims. Indeed, these contentions were accepted in another case by an Alabama appellate court that struck down on direct review the conviction under this very ordinance of one of these same petitioners.[13]

The rule of law upon which the Alabama courts relied in this case was one firmly established by previous precedents. We do not deal here, therefore, with a situation where a state court has followed a regular past practice of entertaining claims in a given procedural mode, and without notice has abandoned that practice to the detriment of a litigant who finds his claim foreclosed by a novel procedural bar. Barr v. City of Columbia, 378 U.S. 1466 [1964]. This is not a case where a procedural requirement has been sprung upon an unwary litigant when prior practice did not give him fair notice of its existence. Wright v. State of Georgia, 373 U.S. 284, 291 [1963].

The Alabama Supreme Court has apparently never in any criminal contempt case entertained a claim of nonjurisdictional error. In Fields v. City of Fairfield, 273 Ala. 588 [1962], decided just three years before the present case, the defendants, members of a "White Supremacy" organization who had disobeyed an injunction, sought to challenge the constitutional validity of a permit ordinance upon which the injunction was based. The Supreme Court of Alabama, finding that the trial court had jurisdiction, applied the same rule of law which was followed here:

> As a general rule, an unconstitutional statute is an absolute nullity and may not form the basis of any legal right or legal proceedings, yet until its unconstitutionality has been judicially declared in appropriate proceedings, no person charged with its observance under an order or decree may disregard or violate the order or the decree with immunity from a charge of contempt of court; and he may not raise the question of its unconstitutionality in

---

13. Shuttlesworth v. City of Birmingham, 43 Ala. App. 68 [1965]. The case is presently pending on certiorari review in the Alabama Supreme Court.

collateral proceedings on appeal from a judgment of conviction for contempt of the order or decree. . . . 273 Ala. at 590.

These precedents clearly put the petitioners on notice that they could not by-pass orderly judicial review of the injunction before disobeying it. Any claim that they were entrapped or misled is wholly unfounded, a conclusion confirmed by evidence in the record showing that when the petitioners deliberately violated the injunction they expected to go to jail.

The rule of law that Alabama followed in this case reflects a belief that in the fair administration of justice no man can be judge in his own case, however exalted his station, however righteous his motives, and irrespective of his race, color, politics, or religion.[16] This Court cannot hold that the petitioners were constitutionally free to ignore all the procedures of the law and carry their battle to the streets. One may sympathize with the petitioners' impatient commitment to their cause. But respect for judicial process is a small price to pay for the civilizing hand of law, which alone can give abiding meaning to constitutional freedom.

*Affirmed.*

*Appendix A to the Opinion of the Court*
*Temporary Injunction—April 10, 1963*

A verified Bill of Complaint in the above styled cause having been presented to me on this the 10th of April 1963 at 9:00 o'clock P.M. in the City of Birmingham, Alabama.

Upon consideration of said verified Bill of Complaint and the affidavits of Captain G. V. Evans and Captain George Wall, and the public welfare, peace and safety requiring it, it is hereby considered, ordered, adjudged and decreed that a peremptory or a temporary writ of injunction be and the same is hereby issued in accordance with the prayer of said petition.

It is therefore ordered, adjudged and decreed by the Court that upon the complainant entering into a good and sufficient bond conditioned as provided by law, in the sum of Twenty five Hundred Dollars ($2500.00), same to be approved by the Register of this Court that the Register issue a peremptory or temporary writ of injunction that the respondents and the

16. The same rule of law was followed in Kasper v. Brittain, 245 F.2d 92 [6th Cir. 1957]. There, a federal court had ordered the public high school in Clinton, Tennessee, to desegregate. Kasper "arrived from somewhere in the East," and organized a campaign "to run the Negroes out of the school." The federal court issued an ex parte restraining order enjoining Kasper from interfering with desegregation. Relying upon the First Amendment, Kasper harangued a crowd "to the effect that although he had been served with the restraining order, it did not mean anything. . . ." His conviction for criminal contempt was affirmed by the Court of Appeals for the Sixth Circuit. That court concluded that "an injunctional order issued by a court must be obeyed," whatever its seeming invalidity, citing Howat v. State of Kansas, 258 U.S. 181. This Court denied certiorari, 355 U.S. 834.

others identified in said Bill of Complaint, their agents, members, employees, servants, followers, attorneys, successors and all other persons in active concert or participation with the respondents and all persons having notice of said order from continuing any act hereinabove designated particularly: engaging in, sponsoring, inciting or encouraging mass street parades or mass processions or like demonstrations without a permit, trespass on private property after being warned to leave the premises by the owner or person in possession of said private property, congregating on the street or public places into mobs, and unlawfully picketing business establishments or public buildings in the City of Birmingham, Jefferson County, State of Alabama or performing acts calculated to cause breaches of the peace in the City of Birmingham, Jefferson County, in the State of Alabama or from conspiring to engage in unlawful street parades, unlawful processions, unlawful demonstrations, unlawful boycotts, unlawful trespasses, and unlawful picketing or other like unlawful conduct or from violating the ordinances of the City of Birmingham and the Statutes of the State of Alabama or from doing any acts designed to consummate conspiracies to engage in said unlawful acts of parading, demonstrating, boycotting, trespassing and picketing or other unlawful acts, or from engaging in acts and conduct customarily known as "kneel-ins" in churches in violation of the wishes and desires of said churches.

W. A. Jenkins, Jr., As Circuit Judge of the Tenth Judicial Circuit of Alabama, In Equity Sitting.

### *Appendix B to the Opinion of the Court*

In our struggle for freedom we have anchored our faith and hope in the rightness of the Constitution and the moral laws of the universe.

Again and again the Federal judiciary has made it clear that the privileges (sic) guaranteed under the First and the Fourteenth Amendments are to (sic) sacred to be trampled upon by the machinery of state government and police power. In the past we have abided by Federal injunctions out of respect for the forthright and consistent leadership that the Federal judiciary has given in establishing the principle of integration as the law of the land.

However we are now confronted with recalcitrant forces in the Deep South that will use the courts to perpetuate the unjust and illegal system of racial separation.

Alabama has made clear its determination to defy the law of the land. Most of its public officials, its legislative body and many of its law enforcement agents have openly defied the desegregation decision of the Supreme Court. We would feel morally and legal (sic) responsible to obey the injunction if the courts of Alabama applied equal justice to all of its citizens. This would be sameness made legal. However the issuance (sic) of this injunction is a blatant of difference made legal.

Southern law enforcement agencies have demonstrated now and again that they will utilize the force of law to misuse the judicial process.

This is raw tyranny under the guise of maintaining law and order. We cannot in all good conscience obey such an injunction which is an unjust, undemocratic and unconstitutional misuse of the legal process.

We do this not out of any desrespect (sic) for the law but out of the highest respect for the law. This is not an attempt to evade or defy the law or engage in chaotic anarchy. Just as in all good conscience we cannot obey unjust laws, neither can we respect the unjust use of the courts.

We believe in a system of law based on justice and morality. Out of our great love for the Constitution of the U.S. and our desire to purify the judicial system of the state of Alabama, we risk this critical move with an awareness of the possible consequences involved.

CHIEF JUSTICE WARREN, whom JUSTICE BRENNAN and JUSTICE FORTAS join, dissenting.

Petitioners in this case contend that they were convicted under an ordinance that is unconstitutional on its face because it submits their First and Fourteenth Amendment rights to free speech and peaceful assembly to the unfettered discretion of local officials. They further contend that the ordinance was unconstitutionally applied to them because the local officials used their discretion to prohibit peaceful demonstrations by a group whose political viewpoint the officials opposed. The Court does not dispute these contentions, but holds that petitioners may nonetheless be convicted and sent to jail because the patently unconstitutional ordinance was copied into an injunction—issued *ex parte* without prior notice or hearing on the request of the Commissioner of Public Safety—forbidding all persons having notice of the injunction to violate the ordinance without any limitation of time. I dissent because I do not believe that the fundamental protections of the Constitution were meant to be so easily evaded, or that "the civilizing hand of law" would be hampered in the slightest by enforcing the First Amendment in this case.

The salient facts can be stated very briefly. Petitioners are Negro ministers who sought to express their concern about racial discrimination in Birmingham, Alabama, by holding peaceful protest demonstrations in that city on Good Friday and Easter Sunday 1963. For obvious reasons, it was important for the significance of the demonstrations that they be held on those particular dates. A representative of petitioners' organization went to the City Hall and asked "to see the person or persons in charge to issue permits, permits for parading, picketing, and demonstrating." She was directed to Public Safety Commissioner Connor, who denied her request for a permit in terms that left no doubt that petitioners were not going to be issued a permit under any circumstances. "He said, 'No you will not get a permit in Birmingham, Alabama to picket. I will picket you over to the City Jail,' and he repeated that twice." A second, telegraphic request was also summarily denied, in a telegram signed by "Eugene 'Bull' Connor," with the added information that permits could be issued only by the full City Commission, a three-man body consisting of Commissioner Connor and two others.[1] According to petitioners' offer of proof, the truth of which is assumed for purposes of this case, parade permits had uniformly been issued for all other groups by the city clerk on the request of the traffic bureau of the police department, which was under Commissioner Connor's direction. The requirement that the approval of the full Commission be obtained was applied only to this one group.

Understandably convinced that the City of Birmingham was not going to authorize their demonstrations under any circumstances, petitioners proceeded with their plans despite Commissioner Connor's orders. On Wednesday, April 10, at 9 in the evening, the city filed in a state circuit court a bill of complaint seeking an *ex parte* injunction. The complaint recited that petitioners were engaging in a series of demonstrations as "part of a massive effort . . . to forcibly integrate all business establishments, churches, and other institutions" in the city, with the result that the police department was strained in its resources and the safety, peace, and tranquility were threatened. It was alleged as particularly menacing that petitioners were planning to conduct "kneel-in" demonstrations at churches where their presence was not wanted. The city's police dogs were said to be in danger of their lives. Faced with these recitals, the Circuit Court issued the injunction in the form requested, and in effect ordered petitioners and all other persons having notice of the order to refrain for an unlimited time from carrying on any demonstrations without a permit. A permit, of course, was clearly unobtainable; the city would not have sought this injunction if it had any intention of issuing one.

Petitioners were served with copies of the injunction at various times on Thursday and on Good Friday. Unable to believe that such a blatant

---

1. The uncontradicted testimony relating to the rebuffs of petitioners' attempts to obtain a permit is set out in footnotes 9 and 10 of the majority opinion. Petitioners were prevented by a ruling of the trial court from introducing further proof of the intransigence of Commissioner Connor and the other city officials toward any effort by Negroes to protest segregation and racial injustice. The attitude of the city administration in general and of its Public Safety Commissioner in particular are a matter of public record, of course, and are familiar to this Court from previous litigation. See Shuttlesworth v. City of Birmingham, 382 U.S. 87 (1965); Shuttlesworth v. City of Birmingham, 376 U.S. 339 (1964); Shuttlesworth v. City of Birmingham, 373 U.S. 262 (1963); Gober v. City of Birmingham, 373 U.S. 374 (1963); In re Shuttlesworth, 369 U.S. 35 (1962). The United States Commission on Civil Rights found continuing abuse of civil rights protesters by the Birmingham police, including use of dogs, clubs, and firehoses. 1963 Report of the United States Commission on Civil Rights 114 (Government Printing Office, 1963). Commissioner Eugene "Bull" Connor, a self-proclaimed white supremacist (see Congress and the Nation 1945-1964: A Review of Government and Politics in the Postwar Years 1604 (Congressional Quarterly Service, 1965)) made no secret of his personal attitude toward the rights of Negroes and the decisions of this Court. He vowed that racial integration would never come to Birmingham, and wore a button inscribed "Never" to advertise that vow. Yet the Court indulges in speculation that these civil rights protesters might have obtained a permit from this city and this man had they made enough repeated applications.

and broadly drawn prior restraint on their First Amendment rights could be valid, they announced their intention to defy it and went ahead with the planned peaceful demonstrations on Easter weekend. On the following Monday, when they promptly filed a motion to dissolve the injunction, the court found them in contempt, holding that they had waived all their First Amendment rights by disobeying the court order.

These facts lend no support to the court's charges that petitioners were presuming to act as judges in their own case, or that they had a disregard for the judicial process. They did not flee the jurisdiction or refuse to appear in the Alabama courts. Having violated the injunction, they promptly submitted themselves to the courts to test the constitutionality of the injunction and the ordinance it parroted. They were in essentially the same position as persons who challenge the constitutionality of a statute by violating it, and then defend the ensuing criminal prosecution on constitutional grounds. It has never been thought that violation of a statute indicated such a disrespect for the legislature that the violator always must be punished even if the statute was unconstitutional. On the contrary, some cases have required that persons seeking to challenge the constitutionality of a statute first violate it to establish their standing to sue. Indeed, it shows no disrespect for law to violate a statute on the ground that it is unconstitutional and then to submit one's case to the courts with the willingness to accept the penalty if the statute is held to be valid.

The Court concedes that "(t)he generality of the language contained in the Birmingham parade ordinance upon which the injunction was based would unquestionably raise substantial constitutional issues concerning some of its provisions." That concession is well-founded but minimal. I believe it is patently unconstitutional on its face. Our decisions have consistently held that picketing and parading are means of expression protected by the First Amendment, and that the right to picket or parade may not be subjected to the unfettered discretion of local officials. Although a city may regulate the manner of use of its streets and sidewalks in the interest of keeping them open for the movement of traffic, it may not allow local officials unbridled discretion to decide who shall be allowed to parade or picket and who shall not. "Wherever the title of streets and parks may rest, they have immemorially been held in trust for the use of the public and, time out of mind, have been used for purposes of assembly, communicating thoughts between citizens, and discussing public questions. Such use of the streets and public places has, from ancient times, been a part of the privileges, immunities, rights, and liberties of citizens. The privilege of a citizen of the United States to use the street and parks for communication of views on national questions may be regulated in the interest of all; it is not absolute, but relative, and must be exercised in subordination to the general comfort and convenience, and in consonance with peace and good order; but it must not, in the guise of regulation, be abridged or denied." Hague v. C.I.O., 307 U.S. 496, 515-516 (1939) (opinion of Mr. Justice Roberts). When local officials are given totally unfettered discretion to decide whether a proposed demonstration is consistent with "public welfare, peace, safety, health, decency, good order, morals or convenience," as they were in this case, they are invited to act as censors over the views that may be presented to the public. The unconstitutionality of the ordinance is compounded, of course, when there is convincing evidence that the officials have in fact used their power to deny permits to organizations whose views they dislike. The record in this case hardly suggests that Commissioner Connor and the other city officials were motivated in prohibiting civil rights picketing only by their overwhelming concern for particular traffic problems. Petitioners were given to understand that under no circumstances would they be permitted to demonstrate in Birmingham, not that a demonstration would be approved if a time and place were selected that would minimize the traffic difficulties. The only circumstance that the court can find to justify anything other than a per curiam reversal is that Commissioner Connor had the foresight to have the unconstitutional ordinance included in an ex parte injunction issued without notice or hearing or any showing that it was impossible to have notice or a hearing, forbidding the world at large (insofar as it knew of the order) to conduct demonstrations in Birmingham without the consent of the city officials. This injunction was such potent magic that it transformed the command of an unconstitutional statute into an impregnable barrier, challengeable only in what likely would have been protracted legal proceedings and entirely superior in the meantime even to the United States Constitution.

I do not believe that giving this Court's seal of approval to such a gross misuse of the judicial process is likely to lead to greater respect for the law any more than it is likely to lead to greater protection for First Amendment freedoms. The *ex parte* temporary injunction has a long and odious history in this country, and its susceptibility to misuse is all too apparent from the facts of the case. As a weapon against strikes, it proved so effective in the hands of judges friendly to employers that Congress was forced to take the drastic step of removing from federal district courts the jurisdiction to issue injunctions in labor disputes.[6] The labor injunction fell into disrepute largely because it was abused in precisely the same way that the injunctive power was abused in this case. Judges who were not sympathetic to the union cause commonly issued, without notice or hearing, broad restraining orders addressed to large numbers of persons of forbidding them to engage in acts that were either legally permissible or, if illegal, that could better have been left to the regular course of criminal prosecution. The injunctions might later be dissolved, but in the meantime strikes would be crippled because the occasion on which concerted activity might have been effective had passed.[7] Such injunctions so long discredited as

---

6. The Norris-LaGuardia Act, 1932, 47 Stat. 70, 29 U.S.C. §§ 101-115.

7. Frankfurter & Greene, The Labor Injunction 47-48 (1930); Cox & Bok, Cases and Materials on Labor Law 101-107 (1962).

weapons against concerted labor activities, have now been given new life by this Court as weapons against the exercise of First Amendment freedoms. Respect for the courts and for judicial process was not increased by the history of the labor injunction.[8]

Nothing in our prior decisions, or in the doctrine that a party subject to a temporary injunction issued by a court of competent jurisdiction with power to decide a dispute properly before it must normally challenge the injunction in the courts rather than by violating it, requires that we affirm the convictions in this case. The majority opinion in this case rests essentially on a single precedent, and that a case the authority of which has clearly been undermined by subsequent decisions. Howat v. State of Kansas, 258 U.S. 181 (1922), was decided in the days when the labor injunction was in fashion. Kansas had adopted an Industrial Relations Act, the purpose of which in effect was to provide for compulsory arbitration of labor disputes by a neutral administrative tribunal, the "Court of Industrial Relations." Pursuant to its jurisdiction to investigate and perhaps improve labor conditions in the coal mining industry, the "Court" subpoenaed union leaders to appear and testify. In addition, the State obtained an injunction to prevent a strike while the matter was before the "Court." The union leaders disobeyed both the subpoena and the injunction, and sought to challenge the constitutionality of the Industrial Relations Act in the ensuing contempt proceeding. The Kansas Supreme Court held that the constitutionality of the Act could not be challenged in a contempt proceeding, and this Court upheld that determination.

Insofar as Howat v. State of Kansas might be interpreted to approve an absolute rule that any violation of a void court order is punishable as contempt, it has been greatly modified by later decisions. In In re Green, 369 U.S. 689 (1962), we reversed a conviction for contempt of a state injunction forbidding labor picketing because the petitioner was not allowed to present evidence that the labor dispute was arguably subject to the jurisdiction of the National Labor Relations Board and hence not subject to state regulation. If an injunction can be challenged on the ground that it deals with a matter arguably subject to the jurisdiction of the National Labor

---

8. "The history of the labor injunction in action puts some matters beyond question. In large part, dissatisfaction and resentment are caused, first, by the refusal of courts to recognize that breaches of the peace may be redressed through criminal prosecution and civil action for damages, and, second, by the expansion of a simple, judicial device to an enveloping code of prohibited conduct, absorbing, en masse, executive and police functions and affecting the livelihood, and even lives, of multitudes. Especially those zealous for the unimpaired prestige of our courts have observed how the administration of law by decrees which through vast and vague phrases surmount law, undermines the esteem of courts upon which our reign of law depends. Not government, but 'government by injunction,' characterized by the consequences of a criminal prosecution without its safeguards, has been challenged." Frankfurter & Greene, supra, at 200.

Relations Board, then *a fortiori* it can be challenged on First Amendment grounds.[9]

It is not necessary to question the continuing validity of the holding in Howat v. State of Kansas, however, to demonstrate that neither it nor the *Mine Workers*[10] case supports the holding of the majority in this case. In Howat the subpoena and injunction were issued to enable the Kansas Court of Industrial Relations to determine an underlying labor dispute. In the *Mine Workers* case, the District Court issued a temporary anti-strike injunction to preserve existing conditions during the time it took to decide whether it had authority to grant the Government relief in a complex and difficult action of enormous importance to the national economy. In both cases the orders were of questionable legality, but in both cases they were reasonably necessary to enable the court or administrative tribunal to decide an underlying controversy of considerable importance before it at the time. This case involves an entirely different situation. The Alabama Circuit Court did not issue this temporary injunction to preserve existing conditions while it proceeded to decide some underlying dispute. There was no underlying dispute before it, and the court in practical effect merely added a judicial signature to a preexisting criminal ordinance. Just as the court had no need to issue the injunction to preserve its ability to decide some underlying dispute, the city had no need of an injunction to impose a criminal penalty for demonstrating on the streets without a permit. The ordinance already accomplished that. In point of fact, there is only one apparent reason why the city sought this injunction and why the court issued it: to make it possible to punish petitioners for contempt rather than for violating the ordinance, and thus to immunize the unconstitutional statute and its unconstitutional application from any attack. I regret that this strategy has been so successful.

It is not necessary in this case to decide precisely what limits should be set to the *Mine Workers* doctrine in cases involving violations of the First Amendment. Whatever the scope of that doctrine, it plainly was not intended to give a State the power to nullify the United States Constitution by the simple process of incorporating its unconstitutional criminal statutes into judicial decrees. I respectfully dissent.

---

9. The attempt in footnote 6 of the majority opinion to distinguish In re Green is nothing but an attempt to alter the holding of that case. The opinion of the Court states flatly that "a state court is without power to hold one in contempt for violating an injunction that the state court had no power to enter by reason of federal pre-emption." 369 U.S. at 692 (footnote omitted). The alleged circumstance that the court issuing the injunction had agreed to its violation as an appropriate means of testing its validity was considered only a concurring opinion. Although the petitioner in *Green* had attempted to challenge the order in court before violating it, we did not rely on that fact in holding that the order was void. Nor is it clear to me why the Court regards this fact as important, unless it means to imply that the petitioners in this case would have been free to violate the court order if they had first made a motion to dissolve in the trial court.

10. United States v. United Mine Workers, 330 U.S. 258 (1947).

JUSTICE DOUGLAS, with whom THE CHIEF JUSTICE, JUSTICE BRENNAN, and JUSTICE FORTAS join, dissenting.

We sit as a court of law functioning primarily as a referee in the federal system. Our function in cases coming to us from state courts is to make sure that state tribunals and agencies work within the limits of the Constitution. Since the Alabama courts have flouted the First Amendment, I would reverse the judgment.

Picketing and parading are methods of expression protected by the First Amendment against both state and federal abridgment. Edwards v. South Carolina, 372 U.S. 229, 235-36 [1963]; Cox v. State of Louisiana, 379 U.S. 536, 546-48 [1965]. Since they involve more than speech itself and implicate street traffic, the accommodation of the public and the like, they may be regulated as to the times and places of the demonstrations. But a State cannot deny the right to use streets or parks or other public grounds for the purpose of petitioning for the redress of grievances. See Hague v. C.I.O., 307 U.S. 496, 515-16 [1939].

The rich can buy advertisements in newspapers, purchase radio or television time, and rent billboard space. Those less affluent are restricted to the use of handbills, Murdock v. Commonwealth of Pennsylvania, 319 U.S. 105, 108 [1943], or petitions, or parades, or mass meetings. This "right of the people peaceably to assemble, and to petition the Government for a redress of grievance," guaranteed by the First Amendment, applicable to the States by reason of the Fourteenth, Edwards v. South Carolina, supra, 372 U.S. at 235, was flouted here.

The evidence shows that a permit was applied for. Mrs. Lola Hendricks, a member of the Alabama Christian Movement for Human Rights, authorized by its president, Reverend Shuttlesworth, on April 3, went to the police department and asked to see the person in charge of issuing permits. She then went to the office of Commissioner Eugene "Bull" Connor and told him that "we came up to apply or see about getting a permit for picketing, parading, demonstrating." She asked Connor for the permit, "asked if he could issue the permit, or other persons who would refer me to, persons who would issue a permit." Commissioner Connor replied, "No, you will not get a permit in Birmingham, Alabama to picket. I will picket you over to the City Jail." On April 5, petitioner Shuttlesworth sent a telegram to Commissioner Connor requesting a permit to picket on designated sidewalks on April 5 and 6. The message stated that "the normal rules of picketing" would be observed. The same day, Connor wired back a reply stating that he could not individually grant a permit, that it was the responsibility of the entire Commission and that he "insist[ed] that you and your people do not start any picketing on the streets in Birmingham, Alabama." Petitioners' efforts to show that the City Commission did not grant permits, but that they were granted by the city clerk at the request of the traffic division were cut off.

The record shows that petitioners did not deliberately attempt to circumvent the permit requirement. Rather they diligently attempted to obtain a permit and were rudely rebuffed and then reasonably concluded that any further attempts would be fruitless.

The right to defy an unconstitutional statute is basic in our scheme. Even when an ordinance requires a permit to make a speech, to deliver a sermon, to picket, to parade, or to assemble, it need not be honored when it is invalid on its face. Lovell v. City of Griffin, 303 U.S. 444, 452-53 [1938].

By like reason, where a permit has been arbitrarily denied one need not pursue the long and expensive route to this Court to obtain a remedy. The reason is the same in both cases. For if a person must pursue his judicial remedy before he may speak, parade, or assemble, the occasion when protest is desired or needed will have become history and any later speech, parade, or assembly will be futile or pointless.

Howat v. State of Kansas, states the general rule that court injunctions are to be obeyed until error is found by normal and orderly review procedures. See United States v. United Mine Workers, 330 U.S. 258, 293-94 [1947]. But there is an exception where "the question of jurisdiction" is "frivolous and not substantial." Id. at 293. Moreover, a state court injunction is not per se sacred where federal constitutional questions are involved. In re Green, 369 U.S. 689 [1962], held that contempt could not be imposed without a hearing where the state decree bordered the federal domain in labor relations and only a hearing could determine whether there was federal pre-emption. In the present case the collision between this state court decree and the First Amendment is so obvious that no hearing is needed to determine the issue.

As already related, petitioners made two applications to Commissioner "Bull" Connor for a permit and were turned down. At the trial, counsel for petitioners offered to prove through the city clerk that the Commission never has granted a permit, the issuing authority being the city clerk who acts at the request of the traffic division. But he was not allowed to answer the question. And when asked to describe the practice for granting permits an objection was raised and sustained.

It is clear that there are no published rules or regulations governing the manner of applying for permits, and it is clear from the record that some permits are issued. One who reads this record will have, I think, the abiding conviction that these people were denied a permit solely because their skin was not of the right color and their cause was not popular.

A court does not have *jurisdiction* to do what a city or other agency of a State lacks *jurisdiction* to do. The command of the Fourteenth Amendment, through which the First Amendment is made applicable to the States, is that no "State" shall deprive any person of "liberty" without due process of law. The decree of a state court is "state" action in the constitutional sense, Shelley v. Kraemer, 334 U.S. 1, 14-18 [1948], as much as the action of the state police, the state prosecutor, the state legislature, or the Governor himself. An ordinance—unconstitutional on its face or patently unconstitutional as applied—is not made sacred by an unconstitutional injunction that enforces it. It can and should be flouted in the manner of the ordinance itself. Courts as well as citizens are not free "to ignore all the procedures of the law," to use the Court's language. The "constitutional freedom" of which the Court speaks can be won only if judges honor the Constitution.

[The dissenting opinion of Justice Brennan is omitted].

## Notes and Questions

1. *The Temporary Restraining Order.* In *Walker,* the litigants on both sides are implacable and their world views seemingly irreconcilable. Each side is also well represented by lawyers who share their clients' goals. Pyrotechnical procedure usually accompanies such a clash, and that is certainly true here.

Note that in federal litigation, Rule 65 contemplates the possibility that a TRO may issue ex parte, as well as in advance of any adjudication of the merits. This is truly the outer limits of due process—a powerful remedy *before* a proven wrong. Why is this kind of remedy sometimes necessary? Can you identify the provisions of Rule 65 that serve to protect due process values in this unusual context?

Issuance of such a pre-merits order evolved from equity practice in the fourteenth century, and there were never hard and fast rules about when such an order was appropriate. Rule 65, you will note, includes no standards for the issuance of preliminary relief. Instead there is a large body of common law that dictates that a court must find a substantial likelihood of success on the merits, irreparable injury, and that the balance of hardships tips in favor of the party seeking relief before entering a TRO or a preliminary injunction. See Dan B. Dobbs, 1 Law of Remedies § 2.11, at 21 (2d ed. 1993).

Dr. King and the others decided to violate the state trial court's order and march on the appointed days because they felt that the momentum of their weeks of demonstrations and months of planning would otherwise be lost. See David Benjamin Oppenheimer, Martin Luther King, Walker v. City of Birmingham, and the Letter from the Birmingham Jail, 26 U.C. Davis L. Rev. 791 (1993), for a stirring account of the background of the case. In the Supreme Court, a majority of five found that the civil rights leaders were wrong to disobey the order without making some effort to gain its reconsideration, or to appeal it. Was it the protestors who showed disrespect for the law and the courts, or was it the city officials?

Despite *Walker,* the question of whether to obey a court order that almost certainly violates due process (and sometimes other constitutional rights as well) is far from settled.

2. *Another Heated Case: A & M Records v. Napster.* The sweeping equity powers of a single judge were vividly displayed when Judge Marilyn Hall Patel commanded Napster, an Internet company, to remove all links to the plaintiffs' copyrighted material from its online directory by midnight July 28, 2000. The plaintiff companies and the Recording Industry of America sought a preliminary injunction as part of their copyright-infringement suit against Napster. In defense, Napster claimed that it was not storing songs on its own computer servers, but merely facilitating peer swapping of music. It argued, moreover, that the recording industry was not harmed by but actually profited from Napster's online activities because peer swapping increased record sales.

Unimpressed by Napster's defenses, Judge Patel ruled from the bench that "to prevail on a preliminary injunction, plaintiffs must demonstrate a combination of probable success on the merits—and the possibility of irreparable harm and a balance of hardships tipping in plaintiff's favor." She went on to hold that plaintiffs had shown a strong likelihood of ultimate success on the merits, and that in a copyright case, this showing actually melded with the showing of irreparable injury. Urging that the preliminary injunction would destroy their business overnight without a full hearing on novel issues raised by new technology, Napster went to the Ninth Circuit and obtained a stay of the preliminary injunction, pending an expedited appeal. A & M Records Inc. v. Napster, Inc. No. C 99-5183 MHP, 2000 WL 1009483 (N.D. Cal.); A & M Records Inc. v. Napster, Inc., 114 F. Supp. 2d 896 (N.D. Cal. 2000), *aff'd in part*, 239 F.3d 1004 (9th Cir. 2001) (remanding with instructions to narrow scope of injunction regarding Napster's contributory liability), *reaffirmed*, 284 F.3d 1091 (9th Cir. 2002).

For an interesting case involving the use of injunctions in the increasingly controversial laws governing elections, see Purcell v. Gonzalez, 549 U.S. 1 (2006) (per curiam) (vacating an injunction issued a month before statewide elections that barred Arizona from enforcing a ballot initiative requiring voters to present proof of citizenship when they register to vote and identification when they vote).

## C.   THE JURY: THE SEVENTH AMENDMENT RIGHT

### Problem Case: The Harassed Student*

Christine Faulkner sued the Mitchell County Public Schools alleging that over a four-year period while she was a student in high school, Thomas Wolfe, a sports coach and teacher, continually sexually harassed her. Among other allegations, Faulkner avers that Wolfe engaged her in sexually oriented conversations in which he asked her about her sexual practices with her boyfriend and about whether she would consider sex with an older man; that he forcibly kissed her on the mouth in the parking lot; and that on three occasions he interrupted a class, requested that the teacher excuse Faulkner, and took her to a private office where he subjected her to coercive intercourse.

She further alleges that though school officials knew that Wolfe was harassing Faulkner and others, and opened an investigation, they took no action to halt it and, in fact, discouraged her from pressing criminal

---

* The facts of the problem case are based on Franklin v. Gwinnett Public Schools, 503 U.S. 60 (1992), and have not been significantly altered. Originally, the district court dismissed the complaint on the ground that Title IX of the Education Amendments of 1972, 20 U.S.C. §§ 1681-1688, did not provide a damages remedy. Franklin took her case to the United States Supreme Court, which reversed, holding that there was a right of action for money damages implied in the statute.

charges. Ultimately, Wolfe resigned on condition that all matters pending against him be dropped, and the school closed its investigation.

Faulkner seeks money damages for the cost of therapy, the loss of educational advantage, and emotional distress. She also wants to enjoin the school from operating in an ad hoc and secret fashion when investigating future sexual harassment claims.

As Faulkner's lawyer, would you file a jury demand under Rule 38? What would you tell your client about the advantages and disadvantages of a jury trial?

As the district judge assigned to this case, how would you decide whether it is jury-triable?

## 1.   The Jury Trial Advantage

The right to a jury trial is "preserved" in federal courts by the Seventh Amendment, as reflected in Rule 38. Note that for a fundamental right, jury trial is rather easily waived. See, e.g., Lutz v. Glendale Union High School, 403 F.3d 1061, 1065 (9th Cir. 2005) (holding that because complaint requested, albeit vaguely, jury trial on some issues, plaintiff waived right to jury trial on others, including the question of liability). Why might Faulkner prefer a jury trial?

What about the school board? Do they want a jury trial? In civil cases, the defendant as well as the plaintiff has a jury trial right. (This contrasts with the criminal system in which the constitutional right to jury trial is guaranteed to the defendant.) Often, if one party strongly prefers a judge, the other side will want a jury for mirror image reasons. Think about the problem case in light of the following, from Professor Steven A. Saltzburg, Improving the Quality of Jury Decision Making, in Verdict: Assessing the Civil Jury System 343-345 (Robert E. Litan ed., 1993):

> The trial system in the United States essentially affords two choices, trial by judge or trial by jury. The advantages of trial by judge are many:
>
> - the judge is presumed to know the law, which may eliminate some of the need for trial attorneys to devote part of their opening statements and closing arguments to legal matters and to submit proposed jury instructions;
> - the judge is a single decision maker who can indicate more readily than a jury whether he or she is confused and can ask questions with knowledge as to what questioning is permissible and impermissible and what evidence is admissible;
> - the judge can deliberate alone, eliminating the possibility of a hung jury;
> - the judge often has experience sifting through evidence, which may help in resolving disputed issues of fact; and
> - the judge is likely to be more consistent in deciding cases than a group of juries.

The advantages of a jury are perhaps more numerous:

- jurors, who come to each case without the baggage of having heard similar cases, are more likely than a judge to keep open minds and not prejudge a case simply because it bears some resemblance to earlier cases;
- the jury has the benefit of input from a number of people, all of whom have heard the same evidence and analyzed it from their different perspectives, while the judge deliberates alone;
- the jury hears only the evidence the judge has ruled admissible, whereas a judge in a bench trial often hears inadmissible evidence and must perform the difficult task of ignoring that evidence;
- jurors do not speak directly to lawyers, and thus any hostility that might develop in a case between lawyers and the judge will not prejudice the jury's fact-finding;
- a jury selected from a cross-section of the community is likely to have members whose biases or prejudices cancel or neutralize each other, but nothing cancels or neutralizes those of a judge;
- a representative jury offers the possibility that at least some of its members will be from a social class which a litigant can view as a peer group, while a judge may not be perceived as a peer; and
- a jury is by definition drawn from all parts of a community and therefore is in touch with community standards, but a judge may have experience with only a small part of the community.

There is a final aspect of trial by jury that makes the jury preferable to a judge in many cases. Federal judges are appointed for life and are, therefore, totally independent. Such independence is essential if they are to make difficult judgments on important questions, particularly those involving sensitive constitutional issues. But it does create a unique problem: independent judges may take on a regal air that makes litigants feel that judges do not think about things the way "ordinary people" do. Moreover, this independence means that, even if lawyers and litigants have little confidence in the decision-making ability of a presiding judge, they have no remedy for questionable decisions other than appeal. Appeals are costly, and the deference appellate courts show to trial court decisions means that truly questionable decisions may be affirmed.

Few state court judges have life tenure. Some are appointed; others are elected. Those who are elected may face opposition in future elections, or they may run on their records. Thus, the danger exists that they may be inclined to make decisions that may help them continue in office.

## 2. Incidents of Jury Trial: Size and Unanimity

What does the jury look like in a civil case such as that of the harassed student? See Fed. R. Civ. P. 47, 48. By local rule in many federal courts, six-, eight-, or ten-person juries are customary. The Supreme Court upheld this practice in Colgrove v. Battin, 413 U.S. 149 (1973).

Although a prior ruling upholding a six-person jury in a criminal case, Williams v. Florida, 399 U.S. 78 (1970), made the outcome in *Colgrove* inevitable, Justice Marshall was vehement in his dissent:

> [M]y brethren mount a frontal assault on the very nature of the civil jury as that concept has been understood for some seven hundred years. No one need be fooled by reference to the six-man trier of fact utilized in the District Court for the District of Montana as a "jury." This six-man mutation is no more a "jury" than the panel of three judges condemned in Baldwin v. New York, 399 U.S. 66 (1970), or the 12 laymen instructed by a justice of the peace outlawed in Capital Traction Co. v. Hof, [174 U.S. 1 (1899)]. We deal there not with some minor tinkering with the role of the civil jury, but with its wholesale abolition and replacement with a different institution which functions differently, produces different results, and was wholly unknown to the Framers of the Seventh Amendment.
>
> In my judgment, if such a radical restructuring of the judicial process is deemed wise or necessary, it should be accomplished by constitutional amendment. See, e.g., Tamm, The Five-Man Civil Jury: A Proposed Constitutional Amendment, 51 Geo. L.J. 120 (1962). It appears, however, that the common law jury is destined to expire not with a bang, but a whimper. The proponents of the six-man jury have not secured the approval of two-thirds of both Houses of Congress and three-fourths of the state legislatures for their proposal. Indeed, they have not even secured the passage of simple legislation to accomplish their goal. Instead, they have relied upon the interstitial rulemaking power of the majority of the district court judges sitting in a particular district to rewrite the ancient definition of a civil jury. . . .

Id. at 166-168.

Finally, in Ballew v. Georgia, 435 U.S. 223 (1978), it was held to be a denial of due process of law for the state to convict on the basis of a verdict rendered by only five jurors. The Court justified this result on the basis of scholarship published in the aftermath of *Williams* and *Colgrove* that suggests that progressively smaller juries are less likely to foster effective group deliberation, which "[a]t some point . . . leads to inaccurate fact finding and inaccurate application of the common sense of the community to the facts. Generally, a positive correlation exists between group size and both the quality of group performance and group productivity." Id. at 232-233. But see Sanford v. United States, 586 F.3d 28 (D.C. Cir. 2009) (refusing to apply *Ballew* to trial by court martial of a sergeant in the Marine Corps).

Should Colgrove v. Battin be overruled? Much contemporary social-science research, of the type the Court credited (but, critics claim, misinterpreted) in *Ballew,* suggests that juries of 6 and 12 people do not function in the same ways. Among the advantages ascribed to larger juries are more consistent and reliable verdicts due to more vigorous debate, greater capacity to remember evidence presented during a trial, and the improved ability of jurors with minority views to resist peer pressure when they have allies.

A survey of this scholarship can be found in Robert H. Miller, Six of One Is Not a Dozen of the Other: A Reexamination of *Williams v. Florida* and the Size of State Criminal Juries, 146 U. Pa. L. Rev. 621 (1998). Miller concludes: "The consistent findings delivered by these studies probing the differences in the 'essential features' of the jury as cited in *Williams* now clearly establish the functional superiority of the twelve-person jury." Id. at 662.

Shortly after validating smaller juries, the Court ruled in Apodaca v. Oregon, 406 U.S. 404 (1972), that unanimity is not a constitutional requirement, finding a nine-to-three conviction sufficient for state criminal trials. For a mathematical analysis supporting this conclusion, see Robert Timothy Reagan, Supreme Court Decisions and Probability Theory: Getting the Analysis Right, 76 U. Det. Mercy L. Rev. 991, 1019 (1999).

While it may comport with probability theory, elimination of the unanimity requirement might take away the voting power of jurors with minority viewpoints. See Kim Taylor-Thompson, Empty Votes in Jury Deliberations, 113 Harv. L. Rev. 1261 (2000). These silenced voices are likely to belong to women and people of color, who only recently won meaningful access to jury service. According to Professor Taylor-Thompson, non-unanimous voting tends to inhibit inclusion, truncating or even eliminating jury deliberations:

> By discouraging meaningful examination of opposing viewpoints, majority rule decision making impoverishes deliberations. . . . Given that people of color tend to form the numerical minority on juries, the majority could ignore minority views by simply outvoting dissenters. Equally troubling is the fact that studies examining the participation rates of women in a group setting, coupled with jury research on the impact of non-unanimous voting, suggest that a majority of jurors could reach a verdict without ever hearing from women on the jury. Thus, despite the simplistic appeal of making the jury system more "democratic," non-unanimity threatens to eliminate the voices of those who have only recently secured the right to participate in the democratic process.

Id. at 1264.

If you are the counsel for Faulkner in her suit against Mitchell County Public Schools, what would you consider the optimal size of a jury in your case? Would you be concerned about the elimination of the unanimity requirement for the reasons Taylor-Thompson suggests?

## 3. Interpreting the Seventh Amendment: The Historical Test

Because the Seventh Amendment speaks in terms of "preserving" the jury trial, the Court has tended to rely on history in deciding when the right applies. Simply stated, the test is whether the claim being asserted is one that was tried on the law, versus equity, side of the English courts of law. But the rule is much easier to state than to apply, especially to modern claims that bear little relation to anything known to either law or equity.

The Seventh Amendment does not apply to state courts. Unlike many of the other protections in the first ten amendments, the civil jury trial right has not been incorporated into due process and guaranteed against state encroachment by the Fourteenth Amendment, as illustrated by the historic case of Walker v. Sauvinet, 92 U.S. 90 (1875). Sauvinet charged that a Louisiana statute deprived him of a jury trial in his action against Walker, a licensed keeper of a coffeehouse in New Orleans, for refusing him refreshments when called for, on the ground that he was a man of color. The United States Supreme Court held:

> A State cannot deprive a person of his property without due process of law; but this does not necessarily imply that all trials in the State courts affecting the property of persons must be by jury. This requirement of the Constitution is met if the trial is had according to the settled course of judicial proceedings.

92 U.S. at 92-93. Despite the fact that the Seventh Amendment does not apply, most state courts have faced issues of interpretation about the reach of the jury trial right under state constitutions or statutes.

The following case and notes will help you understand the interpretive moves involved in the historical test.

### Curtis v. Loether
115 U.S. 189 (1974)

JUSTICE MARSHALL delivered the opinion of the Court.

Section 812 of the Civil Rights Act of 1968, 82 Stat. 88, 42 U.S.C. § 3612, authorizes private plaintiffs to bring civil actions to redress violations of Title VIII, the fair housing provisions of the Act, and provides that "[t]he court may grant as relief, as it deems appropriate, any permanent or temporary injunction, temporary restraining order, or other order, and may award to the plaintiff actual damages and not more than $1,000 punitive damages, together with court costs and reasonable attorney fees. . . ." The question presented in this case is whether the Civil Rights Act or the Seventh Amendment requires a jury trial upon demand by one of the parties in an action for damages and injunctive relief under this section.

Petitioner, a Negro woman, brought this action under § 812, claiming that respondents, who are white, had refused to rent an apartment to her because of her race, in violation of § 804(a) of the Act, 42 U.S.C. § 3604(a). In her complaint she sought only injunctive relief and punitive damages; a claim for compensatory damages was later added. After an evidentiary hearing, the District Court granted preliminary injunctive relief, enjoining the respondents from renting the apartment in question to anyone else pending the trial on the merits. This injunction was dissolved some five months later with the petitioner's consent, after she had finally obtained other housing, and the case went to trial on the issues of actual and punitive damages.

Respondents made a timely demand for jury trial in their answer. The District Court, however, held that jury trial was neither authorized by Title VIII nor required by the Seventh Amendment, and denied the jury request. . . . After trial on the merits, the District Judge found that respondents had in fact discriminated against petitioner on account of her race. Although he found no actual damages, he awarded $250 in punitive damages, denying petitioner's request for attorney's fees and court costs.

The Court of Appeals reversed on the jury trial issue. Rogers v. Loether, 467 F.2d 1110 (7th Cir. 1972). After an extended analysis, the court concluded essentially that the Seventh Amendment gave respondents the right to a jury trial in this action, and therefore interpreted the statute to authorize jury trials so as to eliminate any question of its constitutionality. In view of the importance of the jury trial issue in the administration and enforcement of Title VIII and the diversity of views in the lower courts on the question, we granted certiorari, 412 U.S. 937 (1973). We affirm.

The legislative history on the jury trial question is sparse, and what little is available is ambiguous. There seems to be some indication that supporters of Title VIII were concerned that the possibility of racial prejudice on juries might reduce the effectiveness of civil rights damages actions. On the other hand, one bit of testimony during committee hearings indicates an awareness that jury trials would have to be afforded in damages actions under Title VIII. Both petitioner and respondents have presented plausible arguments from the wording and construction of § 812. We see no point to giving extended consideration to these arguments, however, for we think it is clear that the Seventh Amendment entitles either party to demand a jury trial in an action for damages in the federal courts under § 812.

The Seventh Amendment provides that "[i]n suits at common law, where the value in controversy shall exceed twenty dollars, the right of trial by jury shall be preserved." Although the thrust of the Amendment was to preserve the right to jury trial as it existed in 1791, it has long been settled that the right extends beyond the common-law forms of action recognized at that time. Mr. Justice Story established the basic principle in 1830:

> The phrase "common law," found in this clause, is used in contradistinction to equity, and admiralty, and maritime jurisprudence. . . . By *common law,* [the Framers of the Amendment] meant . . . not merely suits, which the *common* law recognized among its old and settled proceedings, but suits in which *legal* rights were to be ascertained and determined, in contradistinction to those where equitable rights alone were recognized, and equitable remedies were administered. . . . In a just sense, the amendment then may well be construed to embrace all suits which are not of equity and admiralty jurisdiction, whatever might be the peculiar form which they may assume to settle legal rights.

Parsons v. Bedford, 3 Pet. 433, 446-447 (1830) (emphasis in original).

Petitioner nevertheless argues that the Amendment is inapplicable to new causes of action created by congressional enactment. As the Court of Appeals observed, however, we have considered the applicability of the constitutional right to jury trial in actions enforcing statutory rights "as a matter too obvious to be doubted." 467 F.2d at 1114. Although the Court has apparently never discussed the issue at any length, we have often found the Seventh Amendment applicable to causes of action based on statutes. See, e.g., Dairy Queen, Inc. v. Wood, 369 U.S. 469, 477 (1962) (trademark laws); Hepner v. United States, 213 U.S. 103, 115 (1909) (immigration laws); cf. Fleitmann v. Welsbach Street Lighting Co., 240 U.S. 27 (1916) (antitrust laws), and the discussion of *Fleitmann* in Ross v. Bernhard, 396 U.S. 531, 535-536 (1970). Whatever doubt may have existed should now be dispelled. The Seventh Amendment does apply to actions enforcing statutory rights, and requires a jury trial upon demand, if the statute creates legal rights and remedies, enforceable in an action for damages in the ordinary courts of law.

NLRB v. Jones & Laughlin Steel Corp., 301 U.S. 1 (1937), relied on by petitioner, lends no support to her statutory-rights argument. The Court there upheld the award of backpay without jury trial in an NLRB unfair labor practice proceeding, rejecting a Seventh Amendment claim on the ground that the case involved a "statutory proceeding" and "not a suit at common law or in the nature of such a suit." Id. at 48. *Jones & Laughlin* merely stands for the proposition that the Seventh Amendment is generally inapplicable in administrative proceedings, where jury trials would be incompatible with the whole concept of administrative adjudication and would substantially interfere with the NLRB's role in the statutory scheme. Katchen v. Landy, 382 U.S. 323 (1966), also relied upon by petitioner, is to like effect. There the Court upheld, over a Seventh Amendment challenge, the Bankruptcy Act's grant of summary jurisdiction to the bankruptcy court over the trustee's action to compel a claimant to surrender a voidable preference; the Court recognized that a bankruptcy court has been traditionally viewed as a court of equity, and that jury trials would "dismember" the statutory scheme of the Bankruptcy Act. Id. at 339. See also Guthrie National Bank v. Guthrie, 173 U.S. 528 (1899). These cases uphold congressional power to entrust enforcement of statutory rights to an administrative process or specialized court of equity free from the strictures of the Seventh Amendment. But when Congress provides for enforcement of statutory rights in an ordinary civil action in the district courts, where there is obviously no functional justification for denying the jury trial right, a jury trial must be available if the action involves rights and remedies of the sort typically enforced in an action at law.

We think it is clear that a damages action under § 812 is an action to enforce "legal rights" within the meaning of our Seventh Amendment decisions. A damages action under the statute sounds basically in tort — the statute merely defines a new legal duty, and authorizes the courts to compensate a plaintiff for the injury caused by the defendant's wrongful breach. As the Court of Appeals noted, this cause of action is analogous to a number of tort actions recognized at common law.[10] More important, the relief sought here—actual and punitive damages—is the traditional form of relief offered in the courts of law.

We need not, and do not, go so far as to say that any award of monetary relief must necessarily be "legal" relief. A comparison of Title VIII with Title VII of the Civil Rights Act of 1964, where the courts of appeals have held that jury trial is not required in an action for reinstatement and backpay, is instructive, although we of course express no view on the jury trial issue in that context. In Title VII cases the courts of appeals have characterized backpay as an integral part of an equitable remedy, a form of restitution. But the statutory language on which this characterization is based—"[T]he court may enjoin the respondent from engaging in such unlawful employment practice, and order such affirmative action as may be appropriate, which may include, but is not limited to, reinstatement or hiring of employees, with or without back pay . . . , or any other equitable relief as the court deems appropriate," 42 U.S.C. § 2000e-5(g) (1970 ed., Supp. II)—contrasts sharply with § 812's simple authorization of an action for actual and punitive damages. In Title VII cases, also, the courts have relied on the fact that the decision whether to award backpay is committed to the discretion of the trial judge. There is no comparable discretion here: if a plaintiff proves unlawful discrimination and actual damages, he is entitled to judgment for that amount. Nor is there any sense in which the award here can be viewed as requiring the defendant to disgorge funds wrongfully withheld from the plaintiff. Whatever may be the merit of the "equitable" characterization in Title VII cases, there is surely no basis for characterizing the award of compensatory and punitive damages here as equitable relief.

We are not oblivious to the force of petitioner's policy arguments. Jury trials may delay to some extent the disposition of Title VIII damages actions. But Title VIII actions seeking only equitable relief will be unaffected, and preliminary injunctive relief remains available without a jury trial even in damages actions. Dairy Queen, Inc. v. Wood, 369 U.S., at 479 n.20. Moreover, the statutory requirement of expedition of § 812 actions, 42 U.S.C. § 3614, applies equally to jury and non-jury trials. We recognize, too, the possibility that jury prejudice may deprive a victim of discrimination of the verdict to which he or she is entitled. Of course, the trial judge's power to direct a verdict, to grant judgment notwithstanding the verdict, or to grant a new trial provides substantial protection against this risk, and respondents'

---

10. For example, the Court of Appeals recognized that Title VIII could be viewed as an extension of the common-law duty of innkeepers not to refuse temporary lodging to a traveler without justification, a duty enforceable in a damages action triable to a jury, to those who rent apartments on a long-term basis. An action to redress racial discrimination may also be likened to an action for defamation or intentional infliction of mental distress. Indeed, the contours of the latter tort are still developing, and it has been suggested that "under the logic of the common-law development of a law of insult and indignity, racial discrimination might be treated as a dignitary tort." C. Gregory & H. Kalven, Cases and Materials on Torts 961 (2d ed. 1969).

suggestion that jury trials will expose a broader segment of the populace to the example of the federal civil rights laws in operation has some force. More fundamentally, however, these considerations are insufficient to overcome the clear command of the Seventh Amendment. The decision of the Court of Appeals must be affirmed.

*Affirmed.*

## Note: Other Applications of the Historical Test

Generally, the Supreme Court in modern times has liberally construed the Seventh Amendment, often, as in *Curtis*, finding the right in new statutes. Tull v. United States, 481 U.S. 412 (1987), is another example of the historical test in action. The U.S. government charged Tull with dumping fill in wetlands in violation of the Clean Water Act, which authorizes both an injunction and a civil penalty of up to $10,000 per day while the violation is occurring. Tull demanded a jury trial, which was refused. After a 15-day bench trial, the judge found violations of the Act and fined Tull $75,000, with further fines to follow unless Tull undertook extremely expensive restoration efforts.

The Court held that Tull had a right to jury trial on the question of liability—whether he had violated the Act—but that the amount of the civil penalties was up to the judge. Recall that one of the historical differences between law and equity is trial by jury in legal actions. Here is how Justice Brennan characterized the historical arguments in *Tull:*

> The petitioner analogizes this Government suit . . . to an action in debt within the jurisdiction of English courts of law. Prior to the enactment of the Seventh Amendment, English courts had held that a civil penalty suit was a particular species of an action in debt that was within the jurisdiction of the courts of law. . . .
>
> The Government argues, however, that—rather than an action in debt—the closer historical analog is an action to abate a public nuisance. . . .
>
> Whether, as the Government argues, a public nuisance action is a better analogy than an action in debt is debatable. But we need not decide the question. As Pernell v. Southall Realty[, 416 U.S. 363 (1974),] cautioned, the fact that the subject matter of a modern statutory action and an 18th century English action are close equivalents "is irrelevant for Seventh Amendment purposes," because "that Amendment requires trial by jury in actions unheard of at common law." It suffices that we conclude that both the public nuisance action and the action in debt are appropriate analogies to the instant statutory action. . . .
>
> A civil penalty was a type of remedy at common law that could only be enforced in courts of law. Remedies intended to punish culpable individuals, as opposed to those intended simply to extract compensation or restore the status quo, were issued by courts of law, not courts of equity. [This] action . . . is of this character. [The Act] does not direct that the "civil penalty" imposed be calculated solely on the basis of equitable determinations,

such as the profits gained from violations of the statute, but simply imposes a maximum penalty of $10,000 per day of violation. . . . [The Act's] authorization of punishment to further retribution and deterrence clearly evidences that this subsection reflects more than a concern to provide equitable relief. . . . Because the nature of the relief authorized by [the Act] was traditionally available only in a court of law, the petitioner in this present action is entitled to jury trial on demand.

The punitive nature of the relief sought in the present case is made apparent by a comparison with the relief sought in an action to abate a public nuisance. A public nuisance action was a classic example of the kind of suit that relied on the injunctive relief provided by courts of equity. . . .

Id. at 418-423. The Court went on, however, to hold that there was no right to jury determination of the amount of civil penalties.

In another case applying the historical test, Chauffeurs Local No. 391 v. Terry, 494 U.S. 558 (1990), the Court addressed the question of whether a duty of fair representation suit was jury-triable. The plaintiffs in the case were employees of a trucking company who were represented by the chauffeurs' union. When the union declined to refer to a grievance committee the plaintiffs' charges concerning the company's layoff and recall policies, the employees sought injunctive relief and money damages for the alleged breach of the union's duty of fair representation under Section 301 of the Labor Management Relations Act of 1947. The damage sought was compensation for lost wages and health benefits; all claims for injunctive relief were dismissed when the company filed for bankruptcy. The employees demanded a jury trial.

The Court's opinion applied the *Curtis* two-part test to determine whether the suit would resolve legal—rather than equitable—rights, thereby making the plaintiffs entitled to a jury trial. First, the Court compared the breach of fair representation claim to eighteenth-century causes of action brought in courts of England before the merger of courts of law and equity to determine whether at common law the claim would have been legal or equitable. Because the plaintiff's claim in *Terry* was comparable both to an action by a trust beneficiary for breach of fiduciary duty—an equitable action—and to a breach of contract claim—a legal issue—the Court found that this prong left the jury trial question "in equipoise." Second, the Court analyzed the type of remedy sought. Because plaintiffs sought compensatory damages, which is essentially legal relief, the Court held that they were entitled to a jury trial on all issues. In reaching this conclusion, the Court distinguished the damages sought in this case from those under other statutes where Congress has specifically characterized the damages as equitable relief. Moreover, the Court found the money damages were central to the claim, rather than being simply incidental to a demand for injunctive relief.

The Court held in Feltner v. Columbia Pictures Television, Inc., 523 U.S. 340 (1998), that there is no *statutory* right to a jury trial when a copyright owner elects to recover statutory damages under § 504(c) of the Copyright Act, in lieu of actual damages. There nevertheless is a *Seventh Amendment* right to jury trial on all issues pertinent to the award of damages under § 504(c), given close eighteenth-century analogues that were tried before juries. See also City of Monterey v. Del Monte Dunes at Monterey, Ltd., 526 U.S. 687 (1999) (discussing issues properly submitted to a jury in a regulatory takings cases brought under 42 U.S.C. § 1983).

### Note: Jury Trials and Civil Rights

*Curtis* was one of the first of a series of late twentieth-century cases dealing with the right to a jury trial, many of which, like *Curtis*, were brought under civil rights statutes. Even those brought under other laws — *Terry*, for instance — often have civil rights undertones.

Title VII of the Civil Rights Act of 1964, which forbids discrimination in employment on the basis of race, sex, religion, and national origin, did not originally address the jury trial issue, with dicta in *Curtis* and *Terry* indicating that such a right would not be available. In its section on remedies, Title VII provides that a "court may enjoin the respondent" and "order such affirmative action as may be appropriate, which may include, but is not limited to, reinstatement for hiring of employees, with or without back pay . . . , or any other *equitable* relief as the court deems appropriate" (emphasis added).

The 1991 Civil Rights Act, 42 U.S.C. § 1981a(a), however, which amends the 1964 Act, adds that a Title VII plaintiff might seek "compensatory and punitive damages," and that if a "complaining party seeks compensatory or punitive damages . . . any party may demand a trial by jury. . . ." Section 102(c). Damages are a classic legal remedy, so this addendum clearly made some cases of employment discrimination, just like housing discrimination, jury-triable.

Determining jury-triability under Title VII can be complicated, however, because the statute provides for several different methods of proving discrimination — mixed motive, intentional, or disparate impact. In disparate impact cases, plaintiffs are not entitled to monetary damages. Thus, those plaintiffs are presumptively not entitled to a jury trial. The opposite is true of mixed motive and intentional discrimination cases, which allow monetary damages as a remedy and thus permit a jury trial. What, if any, implications do these decisions involving jury trials and civil rights suits have for our case of the harassed student?

When plaintiffs sue as a class, matters can be even more complex. We take up this final issue in Chapter 6 through the Supreme Court's decision in Wal-Mart Stores, Inc. v. Dukes, 564 U.S. 338, 360-367 (2011).

## 4.   Preserving the Right: The Order of Trial

In the problem case, as often happens, the plaintiff is seeking more than one form of relief: money damages, the hallmark of a legal action; and an injunction, the chancellor's tool. Also, remember the extremely loose approach of the Rules to joinder, and to the allowance of counter- and cross-claims. This can result in a case where legal and equitable issues are mixed together. The following case shows how a court may sort out the issues for trial.

## *Beacon Theatres, Inc. v. Westover*
359 U.S. 500 (1959)

JUSTICE BLACK delivered the opinion of the Court.

[Petitioner Beacon Theatres claimed that it had been wrongfully deprived of a jury trial in a suit brought against it by Fox West Coast Theatres, Inc. The theater companies were disputing the issue of "clearances," or contracts giving a theater exclusive rights to show "first-run" movies in its geographical area. After building a drive-in theater near San Bernardino, California, Beacon notified Fox — which operated a "first-run" movie theater there — that it believed clearances violated antitrust laws. In response, Fox claimed that Beacon's threats deprived Fox of a valuable property right: the right to negotiate for exclusive first-run contracts. Fox filed a "Complaint for Declaratory Relief," asking for a declaration that clearances did not violate the antitrust laws and for an injunction preventing Beacon from bringing any antitrust action until the controversy was resolved. Beacon filed a counterclaim, seeking treble damages under the Sherman Antitrust Act, and demanded a jury trial under Rule 38(b). — EDS.]

Beacon demanded a jury trial of the factual issues in the case as provided by Federal Rules of Civil Procedure 38(b). The District Court, however, viewed the issues raised by the "Complaint for Declaratory Relief," including the question of competition between the two theatres, as essentially equitable. Acting under the purported authority of Rules 42(b) and 57, it directed that these issues be tried to the court before jury determination of the validity of the charges of antitrust violations made in the counterclaim and cross-claim. A common issue of the "Complaint for Declaratory Relief," the counterclaim, and the cross-claim was the reasonableness of the clearances granted to Fox, which depended, in part, on the existence of competition between the two theatres. Thus the effect of the action of the District Court could be, as the Court of Appeals believed, "to limit the petitioner's opportunity fully to try to a jury every issue which has a bearing upon its treble damage suit," for determination of the issue of clearances by the judge might "operate either by way of res judicata or collateral estoppel so as to conclude both parties with respect thereto at the subsequent trial of the treble damage claim." 252 F.2d at 874.

The District Court's finding that the Complaint for Declaratory Relief presented basically equitable issues draws no support from the Declaratory Judgment Act, 28 U.S.C. §§ 2201, 2202; Fed. R. Civ. Proc. 57. See also 48 Stat. 955, 28 U.S.C. (1940 ed.) § 400. That statute, while allowing prospective defendants to sue to establish their non-liability, specifically preserves the right to jury trial for both parties. It follows that if Beacon would have been entitled to a jury trial in a treble damage suit against Fox it cannot be deprived of that right merely because Fox took advantage of the availability of declaratory relief to sue Beacon first. Since the right to trial by jury applies to treble damage suits under the antitrust laws, and is, in fact, an essential part of the congressional plan for making competition rather than monopoly the rule of trade, see Fleitmann v. Welsbach Street Lighting Co., 240 U.S. 27, 29 [1916], the Sherman and Clayton Act issues on which Fox sought a declaration were essentially jury questions.

Nevertheless the Court of Appeals [for the Ninth Circuit] refused to upset the order of the district judge. It held that the question of whether a right to jury trial existed was to be judged by Fox's complaint read as a whole. In addition to seeking a declaratory judgment, the court said, Fox's complaint can be read as making out a valid plea for injunctive relief, thus stating a claim traditionally cognizable in equity. . . .

Beacon takes issue with the holding of the Court of Appeals that the complaint stated a claim upon which equitable relief could be granted. . . . Assuming that . . . the complaint can be read as alleging the kind of harassment by a multiplicity of lawsuits which would *traditionally* have justified equity to take jurisdiction and settle the case in one suit we are nevertheless of the opinion that, under the Declaratory Judgment Act and the Federal Rules of Civil Procedure, neither claim can justify denying Beacon a trial by jury of all the issues in the antitrust controversy.

The basis of injunctive relief in the federal courts has always been irreparable harm and inadequacy of legal remedies. At least as much is required to justify a trial court in using its discretion under the Federal Rules to allow claims of equitable origins to be tried ahead of legal ones, since this has the same effect as an equitable injunction of the legal claims. . . .

Viewed in this manner, the use of discretion by the trial court under Rule 42(b) to deprive Beacon of a full jury trial on its counterclaim and cross-claim, as well as on Fox's plea for declaratory relief, cannot be justified. Under the Federal Rules the same court may try both legal and equitable causes in the same action. Fed. R. Civ. P. 1, 2, 18. Thus any defenses, equitable or legal, Fox may have to charges of antitrust violations can be raised either in its suit for declaratory relief or in answer to Beacon's counterclaim. On proper showing, harassment by threats of other suits, or other suits actually brought, involving the issues being tried in this case, could be temporarily enjoined pending the outcome of this litigation. Whatever permanent injunctive relief Fox might be entitled to on the basis of the decision in this case could, of course, be given by the court after the jury renders its verdict. In this way the issues between these parties could be settled in one suit giving Beacon a full jury trial of every antitrust issue. Cf. Ring v. Spina, 166 F.2d 546 [2d Cir. 1948]. By contrast, the holding of the court below while granting Fox no additional protection unless the avoidance of jury trial be considered as such, would compel Beacon to split his antitrust case, trying part to a judge and part to a jury. Such a result, which involves the postponement and subordination of Fox's own legal claim for declaratory relief as well as of the counterclaim which Beacon was compelled by the Federal Rules to bring is not permissible.

Our decision is consistent with the plan of the Federal Rules and the Declaratory Judgment Act to effect substantial procedural reform while retaining a distinction between jury and nonjury issues and leaving substantive rights unchanged. Since in the federal courts equity has always acted only when legal remedies were inadequate, the expansion of adequate legal remedies provided by the Declaratory Judgment Act and the Federal Rules necessarily affects the scope of equity. Thus, the justification for equity's deciding legal issues once it obtains jurisdiction, and refusing to dismiss a case, merely because subsequently a legal remedy becomes available, must be reevaluated in the light of the liberal joinder provisions of the Federal Rules which allow legal and equitable causes to be brought and resolved in one civil action. Similarly the need for, and therefore, the availability of such equitable remedies as Bills of Peace, Quia Timet and Injunction must be reconsidered in view of the existence of the Declaratory Judgment Act as well as the liberal joinder provision of the Rules. This is not only in accord with the spirit of the Rules and the Act but is required by the provision in the Rules that "[t]he right to trial by jury as declared by the Seventh Amendment to the Constitution or as given by a statute of the United States shall be preserved . . . inviolate."

If there should be cases where the availability of declaratory judgment or joinder in one suit of legal and equitable causes would not in all respects protect the plaintiff seeking equitable relief from irreparable harm while affording a jury trial in the legal cause, the trial court will necessarily have to use its discretion in deciding whether the legal or equitable cause should be tried first. Since the right to jury trial is a constitutional one, however, while no similar requirement protects trials by the court, that discretion is very narrowly limited and must, wherever possible, be exercised to preserve jury trial. . . .

Respondent claims mandamus is not available under the All Writs Act, 28 U.S.C. § 1651. Whatever differences of opinion there may be in other types of cases, we think the right to grant mandamus to require jury trial where it has been improperly denied is settled.

The judgment of the Court of Appeals is
*Reversed.*


Justice Stewart, with whom Justice Harlan and Justice Whittaker join, dissenting.

There can be no doubt that a litigant is entitled to a writ of mandamus to protect a clear constitutional or statutory right to a jury trial. But there was no denial of such a right here. The district judge simply exercised his inherent discretion, now explicitly confirmed by the Federal Rules of Civil Procedure, to schedule the trial of an equitable claim in advance of an action at law. Even an abuse of such discretion could not, I think, be attacked by the extraordinary writ of mandamus. In any event no abuse of discretion is apparent in this case.

The complaint filed by Fox stated a claim traditionally cognizable in equity. That claim, in brief, was that Beacon had wrongfully interfered with the right of Fox to compete freely with Beacon and other distributors for the licensing of films for first-run exhibition in the San Bernardino area. The complaint alleged that the plaintiff was without an adequate remedy at law and would be irreparably harmed unless the defendant were restrained from continuing to interfere—by coercion and threats of litigation—with the plaintiff's lawful business relationships.

The Court of Appeals found that the complaint, although inartistically drawn, contained allegations entitling the petitioner to equitable relief. That finding is accepted in the prevailing opinion today. If the complaint had been answered simply by a general denial, therefore, the issues would under traditional principles have been triable as a proceeding in equity. Instead of just putting in issue the allegations of the complaint, however, Beacon filed pleadings which affirmatively alleged the existence of a broad conspiracy among the plaintiff and other theatre owners to monopolize the first-run exhibition of films in the San Bernardino area, to refrain from competing among themselves, and to discriminate against Beacon in granting film licenses. Based upon these allegations, Beacon asked damages in the amount of $300,000. Clearly these conspiracy allegations stated a cause of action triable as of right by a jury. What was demanded by Beacon, however, was a jury trial not only of this cause of action, but also of the issues presented by the original complaint.

Upon motion of Fox the trial judge ordered the original action for declaratory and equitable relief to be tried separately to the court and in advance of the trial of the defendant's counterclaim and cross-claim for damages. The court's order, which carefully preserved the right to trial by jury upon the conspiracy and damage issues raised by the counterclaim and cross-claim, was in conformity with the specific provisions of the Federal Rules of Civil Procedure. Yet it is decided today that the Court of Appeals must compel the district judge to rescind it.

Assuming the existence of a factual issue common both to the plaintiff's original action and the defendant's counterclaim for damages, I cannot agree that the District Court must be compelled to try the counterclaim first. It is, of course, a matter of no great moment in what order the issues between the parties in the present litigation are tried. What is disturbing is the process by which the Court arrives at its decision—a process which appears to disregard the historic relationship between equity and law.

The Court suggests that "the expansion of adequate legal remedies provided by the Declaratory Judgment Act . . . necessarily affects the scope of equity." Does the Court mean to say that the mere availability of an action for a declaratory judgment operates to furnish "an adequate remedy at law" so as to deprive a court of equity of the power to act? That novel line of reasoning is at least implied in the Court's opinion. But the Declaratory Judgment Act did not "expand" the substantive law. That Act merely provided a new statutory remedy, neither legal nor equitable, but available in the areas of both equity and law. . . .

The availability of a declaratory judgment did not, therefore, operate to confer upon Beacon the right to trial by jury with respect to the issues raised by the complaint.

The Court's opinion does not, of course, hold or even suggest that a court of equity may never determine "legal rights." For indeed it is precisely such rights which the Chancellor, when his jurisdiction has been properly invoked, has often been called upon to decide. Issues of fact are rarely either "legal" or "equitable." All depends upon the context in which they arise. . . .

The Court today sweeps away these basic principles as "precedents decided under discarded procedures." It suggests that the Federal Rules of Civil Procedure have somehow worked an "expansion of adequate legal remedies" so as to oust the District Courts of equitable jurisdiction, as well as to deprive them of their traditional power to control their own dockets. But obviously the Federal Rules could not and did not "expand" the substantive law one whit.

Like the Declaratory Judgment Act, the Federal Rules preserve inviolate the right to trial by jury in actions historically cognizable at common law, as under the Constitution they must. They do not create a right of trial by jury where that right "does not exist under the Constitution or statutes of the United States." Rule 39(a). Since Beacon's counterclaim was compulsory under the Rules, see Rule 13(a), it is apparent that by filing it Beacon could not be held to have waived its jury rights. Compare American Mills Co. v. American Surety Co., 260 U.S. 360 [1922]. But neither can the counterclaim be held to have transformed Fox's original complaint into an action at law. See Bendix Aviation Corp. v. Glass, (D.C. Pa.) 81 F. Supp. 645 [1922].

The Rules make possible the trial of legal and equitable claims in the same proceeding, but they expressly affirm the power of a trial judge to determine the order in which claims shall be heard. Rule 42(b). Certainly the Federal Rules were not intended to undermine the basic structure of equity jurisprudence, developed over the centuries and explicitly recognized in the United States Constitution.

For these reasons I think the petition for a writ of mandamus should have been dismissed.

### Note: What Facts a Judge May Decide

*Beacon* emphasized that a trial court's discretion to sever or sequence the adjudication of legal and equitable claims is limited by the Seventh Amendment. But even where the plaintiff has a right to a jury trial, there are many mixed questions of law and fact that the judge can decide herself. When a dispute arises regarding the court's subject matter jurisdiction, for instance, facts about diversity of citizenship and the amount in controversy are resolved by the judge. Indeed, the judge may conduct an evidentiary hearing to resolve disputed facts. The same goes for facts about a defendant's contacts with the forum state in personal jurisdiction analysis, and facts related to a decision about the exercise of supplemental jurisdiction under 28 U.S.C. § 1367. What unifies these factual questions is that they pertain to decisions about the proper forum for adjudication. As the Seventh Circuit described, "[j]uries decide cases, not issues of judicial traffic control." Pavey v. Conley, 544 F.3d 739, 741 (7th Cir. 2008). The Seventh Circuit applied that principle to hold that a prisoner challenging excessive use of force by corrections officers was not entitled to a jury trial on the defense that the prisoner had failed to exhaust any state administrative remedies for his injuries:

> The alternative of trying the merits before exhaustion, as under the *Beacon Theatres* line of cases, is unsatisfactory in the present setting because it would thwart Congress's effort to bar trials of prisoner cases in which the prisoner has failed to exhaust his administrative remedies. . . . A jury might decide the merits of a case that should never have gotten to the merits stage because the judge should have found that the prisoner had failed to exhaust his administrative remedies.

544 F.3d at 742 (distinguishing Wyatt v. Terhune, 315 F.3d 1108, 1119-1120 (9th Cir. 2003)); see also Drippe v. Tobelinski, 604 F.3d 778, 782 (3d Cir. 2010) (following *Pavey*'s rule on a judge's authority to decide exhaustion in prison conditions cases). But see Begolli v. Home Depot, U.S.A., Inc., 701 F.3d 1158, 1161 (7th Cir. 2012) (distinguishing *Pavey* in a Title VII case where factual question related to compliance with a filing deadline because a filing deadline is not a rule distributing adjudication among different courts; noting that, unlike the exhaustion requirement of the Prison Litigation Reform Act, which was meant to make access to federal court more difficult, Title VII was designed "to expand opportunities for bringing employment-discrimination suits in federal court").

## 5.   The Jury's Competence: A Functional Analysis

Think about the issues in the problem case. What if Wolfe denies that the sexual incidents happened at all, or happened in the way the plaintiff alleges? We think a jury is especially capable of resolving credibility conflicts. Does it have other special competencies?

Generally, in the division of trial labor between the judge and the jury, we say that the judge decides the law, and the jury the facts. Sometimes, however, facts and law merge together, and sometimes the facts are very complicated for a group of laypeople to understand. Consider the following case in thinking about the modern role of the civil jury.

### *Markman v. Westview Instruments, Inc.*
517 U.S. 370 (1996)

JUSTICE SOUTER delivered the opinion of the Court.

The question here is whether the interpretation of a so-called patent claim, the portion of the patent document that defines the scope of the patentee's rights, is a matter of law reserved entirely for the court, or subject to a Seventh Amendment guarantee that a jury will determine the meaning of any disputed term of art about which expert testimony is offered. We hold that the construction of a patent, including terms of art within its claim, is exclusively within the province of the court. . . .

The Seventh Amendment provides that "[i]n Suits at common law, where the value in controversy shall exceed twenty dollars, the right of trial by jury shall be preserved. . . ." U.S. Const., Amdt. 7. Since Justice Story's day, United States v. Wonson, 28 F. Cas. 745, 750 (No. 16,750) (CC Mass. 1812), we have understood that "[t]he right of trial by jury thus preserved is the right which existed under the English common law when the Amendment was adopted." Baltimore & Carolina Line, Inc. v. Redman, 295 U.S. 654, 657 (1935). In keeping with our long-standing adherence to this "historical test," Wolfram, The Constitutional History of the Seventh Amendment, 57 Minn. L. Rev. 639, 640-643 (1973), we ask, first, whether we are dealing with a cause of action that either was tried at law at the time of the Founding or is at least analogous to one that was, see, e.g., Tull v. United States, 481 U.S. 412, 417 (1987). If the action in question belongs in the law category, we then ask whether the particular trial decision must fall to the jury in order to preserve the substance of the common-law right as it existed in 1791.[3]

### A

As to the first issue, going to the character of the cause of action, "[t]he form of our analysis is familiar. 'First we compare the statutory action to 18th century actions brought in the courts of England prior to the merger of the courts of law and equity.'" Granfinanciera, S.A. v. Nordberg, 492 U.S. 33, 42 (1989) (citation omitted). Equally familiar is the descent of today's patent infringement action from the infringement actions tried at law in the 18th century, and there is no dispute that infringement cases today must be tried to a jury, as their predecessors were more than two centuries ago.

### B

This conclusion raises the second question, whether a particular issue occurring within a jury trial (here the construction of a patent claim) is itself necessarily a jury issue, the guarantee being essential to preserve the right to a jury's resolution of the ultimate dispute. In some instances the answer to this second question may be easy because of clear historical evidence that the very subsidiary question was so regarded under the English practice of leaving the issue for a jury. But when, as here, the old

---

3. Our formulations of the historical test do not deal with the possibility of conflict between actual English common-law practice and American assumptions about what that practice was, or between English and American practices at the relevant time. No such complications arise in this case.

practice provides no clear answer, we are forced to make a judgment about the scope of the Seventh Amendment guarantee without the benefit of any fool-proof test.

The Court has repeatedly said that the answer to the second question "must depend on whether the jury must shoulder this responsibility as *necessary to preserve the 'substance of the common-law right of trial by jury.'*" Tull v. United States, supra, at 426 (emphasis added) (quoting Colgrove v. Battin, 413 U.S. 149, 156 (1973)). . . .

The "substance of the common-law right" is, however, a pretty blunt instrument for drawing distinctions. We have tried to sharpen it, to be sure, by reference to the distinction between substance and procedure. We have also spoken of the line as one between issues of fact and law.

But the sounder course, when available, is to classify a mongrel practice (like construing a term of art following receipt of evidence) by using the historical method, much as we do in characterizing the suits and actions within which they arise. Where there is no exact antecedent, the best hope lies in comparing the modern practice to earlier ones whose allocation to court or jury we do know, seeking the best analogy we can draw between an old and the new.

## C

"Prior to 1790 nothing in the nature of a claim had appeared either in British patent practice or in that of the American states," Lutz, Evolution of the Claims of U.S. Patents, 20 J. Pat. Off. Soc. 134 (1938), and we have accordingly found no direct antecedent of modern claim construction in the historical sources. . . .

## III

Since evidence of common-law practice at the time of the Framing does not entail application of the Seventh Amendment's jury guarantee to the construction of the claim document, we must look elsewhere to characterize this determination of meaning in order to allocate it as between court or jury. We accordingly consult existing precedent and consider both the relative interpretive skills of judges and juries and the statutory policies that ought to be furthered by the allocation. . . .

## B

Where history and precedent provide no clear answers, functional considerations also play their part in the choice between judge and jury to define terms of art. We said in Miller v. Fenton, 474 U.S. 104, 114 (1985), that when an issue "falls somewhere between a pristine legal standard and a simple historical fact, the fact/law distinction at times has turned on a determination that, as a matter of the sound administration of justice, one judicial actor is better positioned than another to decide the issue in question." So it turns out here, for judges, not juries, are the better suited to find the acquired meaning of patent terms.

The construction of written instruments is one of those things that judges often do and are likely to do better than jurors unburdened by training in exegesis. Patent construction in particular "is a special occupation, requiring, like all others, special training and practice. The judge, from his training and discipline, is more likely to give a proper interpretation to such instruments than a jury; and he is, therefore, more likely to be right, in performing such a duty, than a jury can be expected to be." Parker v. Hulme, 18 F. Cas. at 1140 [(1849)]. Such was the understanding nearly a century and a half ago, and there is no reason to weigh the respective strengths of judge and jury differently in relation to the modern claim; quite the contrary, for "the claims of patents have become highly technical in many respects as the result of special doctrines relating to the proper form and scope of claims that have been developed by the courts and the Patent Office." Woodward, Definiteness and Particularity in Patent Claims, 46 Mich. L. Rev. 755, 765 (1948).

Markman would trump these considerations with his argument that a jury should decide a question of meaning peculiar to a trade or profession simply because the question is a subject of testimony requiring credibility determinations, which are the jury's forte. It is, of course, true that credibility judgments have to be made about the experts who testify in patent cases, and in theory there could be a case in which a simple credibility judgment would suffice to choose between experts whose testimony was equally consistent with a patent's internal logic. But our own experience with document construction leaves us doubtful that trial courts will run into many cases like that. In the main, we expect, any credibility determinations will be subsumed within the necessarily sophisticated analysis of the whole document, required by the standard construction rule that a term can be defined only in a way that comports with the instrument as a whole. Thus, in these cases a jury's capabilities to evaluate demeanor, to sense the "mainsprings of human conduct," Commissioner of Internal Revenue v. Duberstein, 363 U.S. 278, 289 (1960), or to reflect community standards, United States v. McConney, 728 F.2d 1195, 1204 (9th Cir. 1984) (en banc), are much less significant than a trained ability to evaluate the testimony in relation to the overall structure of the patent. The decisionmaker vested with the task of construing the patent is in the better position to ascertain whether an expert's proposed definition fully comports with the specification and claims and so will preserve the patent's internal coherence. We accordingly think there is sufficient reason to treat construction of terms of art like many other responsibilities that we cede to a judge in the normal course of trial, notwithstanding its evidentiary underpinnings.

## C

. . . Finally, we see the importance of uniformity in the treatment of a given patent as an independent reason to allocate all issue of construction to the court. As we noted in General Elec. Co. v. Wabash Appliance Corp., 304 U.S. 364, 369 (1938), "[t]he limits of a patent must be known for the protection of the patentee, the encouragement of the inventive genius of others and the assurance that the subject of the patent will be dedicated ultimately to the public." Otherwise, a "zone of uncertainty which enterprise and experimentation may enter only at the risk of infringement claims would discourage invention only a little less than unequivocal foreclosure of the field," United Carbon Co. v. Binney & Smith Co., 317 U.S. 228, 236 (1942), and "[t]he public [would] be deprived of rights supposed to belong to it, without being clearly told what it is that limits these rights." Merrill v. Yeomans, 94 U.S. 568, 573 (1876). It was just for the sake of such desirable uniformity that Congress created the Court of Appeals for the Federal Circuit as an exclusive appellate court for patent cases, H.R. Rep. No. 97-312, pp. 20-23 (1981), observing that increased uniformity would "strengthen the United States patent system in such a way as to foster technological growth and industrial innovation." Id. at 20.

Uniformity would, however, be ill served by submitting issues of document construction to juries. Making them jury issues would not, to be sure, necessarily leave evidentiary questions of meaning wide open in every new court in which a patent might be litigated, for principles of issue preclusion would ordinarily foster uniformity. . . .

Accordingly, we hold that the interpretation of the word "inventory" in this case is an issue for the judge, not the jury, and affirm the decision of the Court of Appeals for the Federal Circuit.

## Notes and Questions

1. *Fairness and Complexity.* Does *Markman* endorse a complexity exception to the Seventh Amendment? At least one commentator thinks so. See Dana C. Butzer, Markman v. Westview: Juries and Patent Infringement Suits (Or Why Is That Jury in the Courtroom Anyway?), 58 Ohio St. L.J. 271 (1997). What is the Court saying about jury competence in patent infringement cases? Does it apply to other highly technical lawsuits, such as antitrust cases, which may turn on sophisticated economic analysis? To mass tort cases, in which difficult scientific evidence is often central?

*Markman* does not directly address a complexity exception to the jury trial right, though the Court's functional approach was presaged in Ross v. Bernhard, 396 U.S. 531 (1970). In *Ross*, the Court upheld the jury trial right in a stockholder derivative suit, but noted: "As our cases indicate, the 'legal' nature of an issue is determined by considering, first, the premerger custom with reference to such questions; second, the remedy sought; and, third, the practical abilities and limitations of juries." Id. at 538 n.10. The Court arguably built on the third prong — "the practical abilities and limitations of juries" — in its ruling in *Markman*, in which the Court stated that "functional considerations" play a part in choosing whether a judge or a jury defines terms of art.

The circuits disagree on whether there should be a "complexity exception" to the jury trial right. The Third Circuit upheld such an exception in an important case, In re Japanese Electronic Products Antitrust Litigation, 631 F.2d 1069 (3d Cir. 1980). The court first noted that the purpose of due process in fact finding was to "minimize the risk of erroneous decisions," and then declared:

> A jury that cannot understand the evidence and the legal rules to be applied provides no reliable safeguard against erroneous decisions. Moreover, in the context of a completely adversarial proceeding like a civil trial, due process requires that "the decision maker's conclusion rest solely on the legal rules and evidence adduced at the hearing." Goldberg v. Kelly, 397 U.S. 254, 271 (1970). Unless the jury can understand the legal rules and evidence, we cannot realistically expect that the jury will rest its decision on them.

Id. at 1084.

In dissent, one judge noted values other than accuracy in decision making that are served by the civil jury:

> Part of my difficulty with the majority's position probably results from a perception of the nature of the judicial process and the role of juries in that process. It is often said that the judicial process involves the search for objective truth. We have no real assurance, however, of objective truth whether the trial is to the court or to a jury. The judicial process can do no more than legitimize the imposition of sanctions by requiring that some minimum standards of fair play, which we call due process, are adhered to. In this legitimizing process, the seventh amendment is not a useless appendage to the Bill of Rights, but an important resource in maintaining the authority of the rule of law. In the process of gaining public acceptance for the imposition of sanctions, the role of the jury is highly significant. The jury is a sort of ad hoc parliament convened from the citizenry at large to lend respectability and authority to the process. Judges are often prone to believe that they, alone, can bear the full weight of this legitimizing function. I doubt that they can. Any erosion of citizen participation in the sanctioning system is in the long run likely, in my view, to result in a reduction in the moral authority that supports the process.

Id. at 1093 (Gibbons, J., dissenting).

Both the Ninth Circuit and the Federal Circuit have rejected these due process arguments. The Ninth Circuit did so in In re U.S. Financial Securities Litigation, 609 F.2d 411 (9th Cir. 1979), *cert. denied sub nom.* Gant v. Union Bank, 446 U.S. 929 (1980). Notably, the Federal Circuit, which hears appeals from district court cases involving patents, rejected a "complexity exception" to the jury trial right in patent infringement cases in SRI International v. Matsushita Electric Corp. of America, 775 F.2d 1107 (Fed. Cir. 1985). The court found that "[t]here is no peculiar cachet which removes 'technical' subject matter from the competency of a jury when competent counsel have carefully marshaled and presented the evidence of that subject matter and a competent judge has supplied carefully prepared instructions." Id. at 1130. The Federal Circuit wrote that the argument that a jury that is "incapable" of understanding evidence could return an "erroneous" result "confuses the route with the destination, for 'due process' is just that, a process. It is an important and constitutionally required process. It is not a result." Id. at 1128. The court added in a footnote: "The requirement is that trials be fair, not perfect. . . . [N]umerous safeguards exist against a clearly 'erroneous result' following a jury trial." Id. at n.6. Cf. Monolithic Power Systems, Inc. v. O2 Micro Int'l Ltd., 558 F.3d 1341, 1347 (Fed. Cir. 2009) (rejecting defendant/counterclaimant's argument that appointment of an independent expert unduly burdened its Seventh Amendment right to a jury trial; holding that the appointment of an independent expert does not create a "'complexity exception' to a litigant's Seventh Amendment rights"). See also Phillips v. Kaplus, 764 F.2d 807 (1985) (noting that "[w]hile at least one circuit has suggested that mere complexity of facts alone can provide the basis for equitable jurisdiction and the denial of a jury trial . . . we have not done so, and we do not do so here"); Kian v. Mirro Aluminum Co., 88 F.R.D. 351, 355 (E.D. Mich. 1980) ("This Court rejects the rationale of the Third Circuit in In re Japanese Electronic Products, and elects to follow the Ninth Circuit's decision in In re U.S. Financial Securities Litigations").

Commentators have weighed in on all sides of the debate over whether jurors are competent to decide cases believed to reflect the increasing complexity of our society. See, e.g., Amy Tindell, Toward a More Reliable Fact-Finder in Patent Litigation, Marq. Intell. Prop. L. Rev. 309, 310 (2009) (noting that the Federal Circuit "has narrowed the role of the jury in patent trials . . . [and] the Supreme Court has for the most part affirmed these . . . decisions"); Joseph A. Miron Jr., Note, The Constitutionality of a Complexity Exception to the Seventh Amendment, 73 Chi.-Kent L. Rev. 865 (1998) (arguing that a complexity exception is constitutional under the Seventh Amendment because it is consistent with English common law); The Jury's Capacity to Decide Complex Civil Cases, 110 Harv. L. Rev. 1489 (1997) (urging that juries should be empowered to make better decisions in some complex cases, not discarded).

2. *Effects of* Markman *on the Trial and Appellate Processes.* In *Markman v. Westview* and the Sophistry of Judicial Claim Construction: An Economic Approach (paper on file with the editors), David Berl argues that the *Markman* decision has had the disturbing short-term impact of reducing settlements in patent litigation while increasing costs. Berl writes that the decision has increased uncertainty in the patent litigation process—the opposite of the result the Federal Circuit intended when it made claim construction the province of the judge rather than the jury. "Judicial claim construction has engendered confusion and uncertainty, thus diminishing the incentive for settlement." In part, this is because *Markman* instituted de novo appellate review of judicial claim construction, and the reversal rate has hovered around 40 percent. The *Markman* claim construction procedure

also has increased the costs of patent litigation because it generally involves an expensive pretrial hearing, followed by an expensive jury trial. No pretrial appeal of the claim construction is allowed, leading to more waste. Post-*Markman*, "[a]s a result of the uncertainty, the patent litigation process is characterized by less settlement and enormous expenditures—two signs," he concludes, "of the current system's suboptimality."

3. *Reforms to Improve Jury Performance.* As public perception of problems with juror performance has risen, particularly in the wake of the O.J. Simpson and Rodney King trials of the 1990s, a number of states have studied and experimented with a variety of reforms intended to improve jury performance. Perhaps the most ambitious has been Arizona, which instituted a number of changes in its jury system in 1995. Many of these reforms are aimed at making jurors more active. They include simplifying jury instructions into "plain English"; allowing counsel to make "mini-opening statements" to the entire venire before juror selection; telling jurors that they may take notes; permitting jurors to submit questions to the judge during the trial; providing each juror with copies of the jury instructions and notebooks of trial materials; and, most controversial, permitting jurors to discuss the evidence during trial. See Jacqueline A. Connor, Jury Reform: Notes on the Arizona Seminar, 1 J. Legal Advoc. & Prac. 25, 26 (1999); see also Randall T. Shepard, State Court Reform of the American Jury, 117 Yale L.J. Pocket Part 166 (2008); Lewis Maltby, Jury Duty Reform: Arizona Leads the Way, 18:22 Legal Backgrounder, June 20, 2003.

Lawyers, judges, social scientists, and jurors participating in a recent symposium on jury reform also agreed that the most urgent need is increased juror involvement:

> [M]any of the proposed reforms are designed to transform jurors from passive sponges to active participants: allowing them to take notes and to ask questions, and providing them with the information they need, when they need it, to make the right decision. The goals are to increase attention and a sense of continuous engagement, and to reduce confusion. They range from relatively uncontroversial suggestions, such as providing jurors with written copies of the instructions, to more radical reforms, such as allowing jurors to question witnesses or to discuss the case among themselves before the trial is over.

Phoebe C. Ellsworth, Introduction: Jury Reform at the End of the Century: Real Agreement, Real Changes, 32 U. Mich. J.L. Reform 213, 224 (1999). For other discussions and innovations in jury reform, see generally Symposium: The American Civil Jury, 48 DePaul L. Rev. 197 (1998); J. Clark Kelso, Final Report of the Blue Ribbon Commission on Jury System Improvement, 47 Hastings L.J. 1433 (1996); Council for Court Excellence, for the Year 2000 and Beyond: Proposals to Improve the Jury System in Washington, D.C. (setting forth 32 Recommendations for Changes to jury service).

## D.   CHOOSING A JURY

### Problem Case: The Harassed Student (Part Two)

You represent Christine Faulkner, who has sued the school board on the facts recounted at the beginning of Section C above. She seeks money damages for the cost of therapy, the loss of educational advantage, and emotional distress. You have demanded a jury trial, and the day of trial has come.

Your task now is to pick a jury. Those available for selection in your case, called the venire, are pictured below. The larger pool from which this venire was drawn was chosen from the voter registration lists, which in this district are 60 percent male and 10 percent minority. Census data reveal that men and women are about evenly divided and that minorities compose about 20 percent of the population.

In order to reduce the amount of information you would have to assimilate to participate in the task, we will select only a three-person jury from a venire of nine. Each side has one peremptory to supplement the unlimited challenges for cause.

1) Think first about the ideal juror for the plaintiff. What qualities and background should that person have? Who is the ideal juror for the defense? Does anyone in the venire meet your ideal requirements?
2) What else would you like to know about these potential jurors? What nonroutine voir dire questions would each side want to ask?
3) In many places, the practice of designing a questionnaire tailored to the facts of the case and submitting it to the jury beforehand has emerged. What are the advantages and disadvantages of this procedure? Would you want to seek its use in this case?

Start with the first row, and think about whether any of these jurors should be struck for cause. What arguments would you make that one or more of these jurors should be eliminated?

As you look at the total of nine, is there anyone else who might be eliminated for cause? Against whom would you exercise your peremptory challenge for the plaintiff? Against whom for the defense?

As you engage in this exercise, think about the stereotypes you are using and the assumptions you are making. Students are sometimes discomfited by how natural this kind of thinking proves to be. Might it be better to do away with the peremptory challenge altogether, and simply put the first 6 to 12 people in the jury box?

### 1.   The Law of Jury Selection

The jurors who ultimately stand and swear to "do justice in this cause" between Faulkner and the school board will have survived four possible

## The Venire for Faulkner v. Mitchell County

(1)

Mikhail Pavlovski
Age 39
Unmarried
1 child
Risk arbitrageur
M.B.A.

(2)

Aisha Jackson
Age 33
Married
1 child
School teacher
B.A.

(3)

Adam Michaels
Age 33
Married
2 children
Contractor
12th grade

(4)

Helen Hardy
Age 58
Unmarried
No children
University professor
Ph.D.

(5)

Jennifer Carmichael
Age 29
Unmarried
No children
Secretary
High school equivalent

(6)

Tony Silver
Age 53
Divorced
Three children
Labor organizer
1 year college

(7)

Randall Li
Age 21
Unmarried
No children
College student
2 years college

(8)

Rose Ibarra
Age 27
Married
1 child
Real estate broker
12th grade

(9)

Jack Prentiss
Age 66
Married
5 children
Retired psychiatrist
M.D.

elimination points. Originally summoned from lists that typically do not include, for example, the convicted felon, the unregistered voter, and the homeless (see the Federal Jury Selection Act of 1968, 28 U.S.C. §§ 1861-1878), each potential juror then had a chance to offer a personal excuse (a sick child, busy time at work). Some of those who remained were later called to the courtroom for trial and questioned by the judge or by counsel about their fitness to serve in the Faulkner case.

After this "voir dire" examination, the judge might have removed some potential jurors for cause—friendship with one of the litigants, or the lawyers, for instance. Finally, lawyers for each side struck others without giving a reason—peremptorily.

The first case deals with the summoning of jurors for the pool, before the selection for an individual case. As you read this venerable precedent, think about its historical context, its doctrinal base, and the remedy the court imposes.

## *Thiel v. Southern Pacific Co.*
328 U.S. 217 (1946)

JUSTICE MURPHY delivered the opinion of the Court.

Petitioner, a passenger, jumped out of the window of a moving train operated by the respondent, the Southern Pacific Company. He filed a complaint in a California state court to recover damages, alleging that the respondent's agents knew that he was "out of his normal mind" and should not be accepted as a passenger or else should be guarded and that, having accepted him as a passenger, they left him unguarded and failed to stop the train before he finally fell to the ground. At respondent's request the case was removed to the federal district court at San Francisco on the ground of diversity of citizenship, respondent being a Kentucky corporation. . . .

After demanding a jury trial, petitioner moved to strike out the entire jury panel, alleging inter alia that

> mostly business executives or those having the employer's viewpoint are purposely selected on said panel, thus giving a majority representation to one class or occupation and discriminating against other occupations and classes, particularly the employees and those in the poorer classes who constitute, by far, the great majority of citizens eligible for jury service.

Following a hearing at which testimony was taken, the motion was denied. Petitioner then attempted to withdraw his demand for a jury trial but the respondent refused to consent. A jury of 12 was chosen. Petitioner thereupon challenged these jurors upon the same grounds previously urged in relation to the entire jury panel and upon the further ground that 6 of the 12 jurors were closely affiliated and connected with the respondent. The court denied this challenge. The trial proceeded and the jury returned a verdict for the respondent.

Petitioner renewed his objections in his motion to set aside the verdict or, in the alternative, to grant a new trial. In denying this motion the court orally found that 5 of the 12 jurors "belong more closely and intimately with the working man and employee class than they do with any other class" and that they might be expected to be "sympathetic with the experiences in life, the affairs of life, and with the economic views, of people who belong to the working or employee class." The Ninth Circuit Court of Appeals affirmed the judgment in its entirety, 149 F.2d 783, and we brought the case here on certiorari "limited to the question whether petitioner's motion to strike the jury panel was properly denied."

The American tradition of trial by jury, considered in connection with either criminal or civil proceedings, necessarily contemplates an impartial jury drawn from a cross-section of the community. Smith v. Texas, 311 U.S. 128, 130 [1940]; Glasser v. United States, 315 U.S. 60, 85 [1942]. This does not mean, of course, that every jury must contain representatives of all the economic, social, religious, racial, political and geographical groups of the community; frequently such complete representation would be impossible. But it does mean that prospective jurors shall be selected by court officials without systematic and intentional exclusion of any of these groups. Recognition must be given to the fact that those eligible for jury service are to be found in every stratum of society. Jury competence is an individual rather than a group or class matter. That fact lies at the very heart of the jury system. To disregard it is to open the door to class distinctions and discriminations which are abhorrent to the democratic ideals of trial by jury.

The undisputed evidence in this case demonstrates a failure to abide by the proper rules and principles of jury selection. Both the clerk of the court and the jury commissioner testified that they deliberately and intentionally excluded from the jury lists all persons who work for a daily wage. They generally used the city directory as the source of names of prospective jurors. In the words of the clerk,

> If I see in the directory the name of John Jones and it says he is a longshore-man, I do not put his name in, because I have found by experience that that man will not serve as a juror, and I will not get people who will qualify. . . . Where I thought the designation indicated that they were day laborers, I mean they were people who were compensated solely when they were working by the day, I leave them out.

The evidence indicated, however, that laborers who were paid weekly or monthly wages were placed on the jury lists, as well as the wives of daily wage earners.

It was further admitted that business men and their wives constituted at least 50 percent of the jury lists, although both the clerk and the commissioner denied that they consciously chose according to wealth or occupation. Thus the admitted discrimination was limited to those who worked for a daily wage, many of whom might suffer financial loss by serving on juries at the rate of $4 a day and would be excused for that reason.

This exclusion of all those who earn a daily wage cannot be justified by federal or state law. Certainly nothing in the federal statutes warrants such an exclusion. And the California statutes are equally devoid of justification for the practice.

Moreover, the general principles underlying proper jury selection clearly outlaw the exclusion practice in this instance. Jury competence is not limited to those who earn their livelihood on other than a daily basis. Wage earners, including those who are paid by the day, constitute a very substantial portion of the community, a portion that cannot be intentionally and systematically excluded in whole or in part without doing violence to the democratic nature of the jury system. Were we to sanction an exclusion of this nature we would encourage whatever desires those responsible for the selection of jury panels may have to discriminate against persons of low economic and social status. We would breathe life into any latent tendencies to establish the jury as the instrument of the economically and socially privileged. That we refuse to do.

It is clear that a federal judge would be justified in excusing a daily wage earner for whom jury service would entail an undue financial hardship. But that fact cannot support the complete exclusion of all daily wage earners regardless of whether there is actual hardship involved. Here there was no effort, no intention, to determine in advance which individual members of the daily wage earning class would suffer an undue hardship by serving on a jury at the rate of $4 a day. All were systematically and automatically excluded. In this connection it should be noted that the mere fact that a person earns more than $4 a day would not serve as an excuse. Jury service is a duty as well as a privilege of citizenship; it is a duty that cannot be shirked on a plea of inconvenience or decreased earning power. Only when the financial embarrassment is such as to impose a real burden and hardship does a valid excuse of this nature appear.

It follows that we cannot sanction the method by which the jury panel was formed in this case. The trial court should have granted petitioner's motion to strike the panel. That conclusion requires us to reverse the judgment below in the exercise of our power of supervision over the administration of justice in the federal courts. See McNabb v. United States, 318 U.S. 332, 340 [(1943)]. On that basis it becomes unnecessary to determine whether the petitioner was in any way prejudiced by the wrongful exclusion or whether he was one of the excluded class. It is likewise immaterial that the jury which actually decided the factual issue in the case was found to contain at least five members of the laboring class. The evil lies in the admitted wholesale exclusion of a large class of wage earners in disregard of the high standards of jury selection. To reassert those standards, to guard against the subtle undermining of the jury system, requires a new trial by a jury drawn from a panel properly and fairly chosen.

*Reversed.*

[The dissenting opinion of Justice Frankfurter, who is joined by Justice Reed, is omitted.—Eds.]

## *Note: Reversal as the Remedy for Improper Jury Selection*

Thiel argued on appeal that there should have been more daily wage earners in the pool (that is, among all those summoned to serve), though he did not urge that members of this class were more likely to respond to his claim. Indeed, there had been five apparently unsympathetic daily wage earners actually among the jurors who decided against him.

Yet the Court reversed the judgment in the exercise of its supervisory power in order to "reassert . . . high standards of jury selection." 328 U.S. at 225. Decided the year after World War II ended, *Thiel* rings with affirmations of the jury as fundamental to a democratic society. Selection procedures should draw "every stratum of society into jury service" and treat "jury competence" as "individual rather than a group or class matter." Id. It finds essential to the jury's (somewhat mysterious) functioning that it be inclusive of all elements of the community. When some identifiable group has been excluded, reversal, according to *Thiel,* is the only remedy that will "guard against the subtle undermining of the jury system." Id. at 227. (The quote is from Justice Frankfurter's dissent, who, though he agreed about the importance of maintaining the "broad representative character of the jury . . . as assurance of a diffuse impartiality," thought the remedy of reversal too extreme. Id.)

The fact that reversal is the only remedy for a "mistake" in jury selection puts tremendous pressure on the system for choosing jurors.

In *Thiel,* the challenge was to the entire system of summoning jurors—to the methods used to assemble the pool. The following case deals with another point of selection: when the individual accepted for the pool is rejected from participating in a specific trial. At the end of the twentieth century, the Supreme Court issued an extraordinary series of cases dealing with the peremptory challenge. Keep in mind the extremity of the remedy—reversed verdicts—as you read the following case. Think also of what these cases reveal about our conception of juries, and their place in modern adjudication.

What other remedies might there be? What could the trial judge do at the time if he thought jurors were being wrongly excluded?

## *Edmonson v. Leesville Concrete Co.*
500 U.S. 614 (1991)

JUSTICE KENNEDY delivered the opinion of the Court.

We must decide in the case before us whether a private litigant in a civil case may use peremptory challenges to exclude jurors on account of their race. Recognizing the impropriety of racial bias in the courtroom, we hold the race-based exclusion violates the equal protection rights of the challenged jurors. This civil case originated in a United States District Court, and we apply the equal protection component of the Fifth Amendment's Due Process Clause. See Bolling v. Sharpe, 347 U.S. 497 (1954).

## I

Thaddeus Donald Edmonson, a construction worker, was injured in a jobsite accident at Fort Polk, Louisiana, a federal enclave. Edmonson sued Leesville Concrete Company for negligence in the United States District Court for the Western District of Louisiana, claiming that a Leesville employee permitted one of the company's trucks to roll backward and pin him against some construction equipment. Edmonson invoked his Seventh Amendment right to a trial by jury.

During voir dire, Leesville used two of its three peremptory challenges authorized by statute to remove black persons from the prospective jury. Citing our decision in Batson v. Kentucky, 476 U.S. 79 (1986), Edmonson, who is himself black, requested that the District Court require Leesville to articulate a race-neutral explanation for striking the two jurors. The District Court denied the request on the ground that Batson does not apply in civil proceedings. As empaneled, the jury included 11 white persons and 1 black person. The jury rendered a verdict for Edmonson, assessing his total damages at $90,000. It also attributed 80% of the fault to Edmonson's contributory negligence, however, and awarded him the sum of $18,000.

Edmonson appealed, and a divided panel of the Court of Appeals for the Fifth Circuit reversed, holding that our opinion in Batson applies to a private attorney representing a private litigant and that peremptory challenges may not be used in a civil trial for the purpose of excluding jurors on the basis of race. 860 F.2d 1308 (1989). The Court of Appeals panel held that private parties become state actors when they exercise peremptory challenges and that to limit Batson to criminal cases "would betray Batson's fundamental principle [that] the state's use, toleration, and approval of peremptory challenges based on race violates the equal protection clause." Id. at 1314. The panel remanded to the trial court to consider whether Edmonson had established a prima facie case of racial discrimination under Batson.

The full court then ordered rehearing en banc. A divided en banc panel affirmed the judgment of the District Court, holding that a private litigant in a civil case can exercise peremptory challenges without accountability for alleged racial classifications. 895 F.2d 218 (5th Cir. 1990). The court concluded that the use of peremptories by private litigants does not constitute state action and, as a result, does not implicate constitutional guarantees. The dissent reiterated the arguments of the vacated panel opinion. The Courts of Appeals have divided on the issue. We granted certiorari, 498 U.S. 809 (1990), and now reverse the Court of Appeals.

## II

### A

In Powers v. Ohio, 499 U.S. 400 (1991), we held that a criminal defendant, regardless of his or her race, may object to a prosecutor's race-based exclusion of persons from the petit jury. Our conclusion rested on a two-part analysis. First, following our opinions in *Batson* and in Carter v. Jury Commission of Greene County, 396 U.S. 320 (1970), we made clear that a prosecutor's race-based peremptory challenge violates the equal protection rights of those excluded from jury service. 499 U.S. at 407-409. Second, we relied on well-established rules of third-party standing to hold that a defendant may raise the excluded jurors' equal protection rights. Id., at 410-415.

*Powers* relied upon over a century of jurisprudence dedicated to the elimination of race prejudice within the jury selection process. While these decisions were for the most part directed at discrimination by a prosecutor or other government officials in the context of criminal proceedings, we have not intimated that race discrimination is permissible in civil proceedings. See Thiel v. Southern Pacific Co., 328 U.S. 217, 220-221 (1946). Indeed, discrimination on the basis of race in selecting a jury in a civil proceeding harms the excluded juror no less than discrimination in a criminal trial. See id. at 220. In either case, race is the sole reason for denying the excluded venireperson the honor and privilege of participating in our system of justice.

That an act violates the Constitution when committed by a government official, however, does not answer the question whether the same act offends constitutional guarantees if committed by a private litigant or his attorney. The Constitution's protections of individual liberty and equal protection apply in general only to action by the government. National Collegiate Athletic Assn. v. Tarkanian, 488 U.S. 179, 191 (1988). Racial discrimination, though invidious in all contexts, violates the Constitution only when it may be attributed to state action. Moose Lodge No. 107 v. Irvis, 407 U.S. 163, 172 (1972). Thus, the legality of the exclusion at issue here turns on the extent to which a litigant in a civil case may be subject to the Constitution's restrictions. . . .

The trial judge exercises substantial control over *voir dire* in the federal system. See Fed. Rule Civ. Proc. 47. The judge determines the range of information that may be discovered about a prospective juror, and so affects the exercise of both challenges for cause and peremptory challenges. In some cases, judges may even conduct the entire *voir dire* by themselves, a common practice in the District Court where the instant case was tried. See Louisiana Rules of Court, Local Rule 13.02 (W.D. La. 1990). The judge oversees the exclusion of jurors for cause, in this way determining which jurors remain eligible for the exercise of peremptory strikes. In cases involving multiple parties, the trial judge decides how peremptory challenges shall be allocated among them. 28 U.S.C. § 1870. When a lawyer exercises a peremptory challenge, the judge advises the juror he or she has been excused. . . .

The principle that the selection of state officials, other than through election by all qualified voters, may constitute state action applies with even greater force in the context of jury selection through the use of peremptory challenges. Though the motive of a peremptory challenge may be to protect a private interest, the objective of jury selection proceedings is to determine representation on a governmental body. Were it not for peremptory challenges, there would be no question that the entire process of determining who will serve on the jury constitutes state action. The fact that the government delegates some portion of this power to private litigants does not change the governmental character of the power exercised. . . . Here, as in most civil cases, the initial decision whether to sue at all, the selection of counsel, and any number of ensuing tactical choices in the course of discovery and trial may be without the requisite governmental character to be deemed state action. That cannot be said of the exercise of peremptory challenges, however; when private litigants participate in the selection of jurors, they serve an important function within the government and act with its substantial assistance. If peremptory challenges based on race were permitted, persons could be required by summons to be put at risk of open and public discrimination as a condition of their participation in the justice system. The injury to excluded jurors would be the direct result of governmental delegation and participation.

Finally, we note that the injury caused by the discrimination is made more severe because the government permits it to occur within the courthouse itself. Few places are a more real expression of the constitutional authority of the government than a courtroom, where the law itself unfolds. Within the courtroom, the government invokes its laws to determine the rights of those who stand before it. In full view of the public, litigants press their cases, witnesses give testimony, juries render verdicts, and judges act with the utmost care to ensure that justice is done.

Race discrimination within the courtroom raises serious questions as to the fairness of the proceedings conducted there. Racial bias mars the integrity of the judicial system and prevents the idea of democratic government from becoming a reality. Rose v. Mitchell, 443 U.S. 545, 556 (1979); Smith v. Texas, 311 U.S. 128, 130 (1940). In the many times we have addressed the problem of racial bias in our system of justice, we have not "questioned the premise that racial discrimination in the qualification or selection of jurors offends the dignity of persons and the integrity of the courts." *Powers,* 499 U.S. at 402. To permit racial exclusion in this official forum compounds the racial insult inherent in judging a citizen by the color of his or her skin. . . .

We believe the only issue that warrants further consideration in this case is whether a civil litigant can demonstrate a sufficient interest in challenging the exclusion of jurors on account of race. In *Powers,* we held:

> The discriminatory use of peremptory challenges by the prosecution causes a criminal defendant cognizable injury, and the defendant has a concrete interest in challenging the practice. See Allen v. Hardy, 478 U.S. [255,] 259 [(1986)] (recognizing a defendant's interest in "neutral jury selection procedures"). This is not because the individual jurors dismissed by the prosecution may have been predisposed to favor the defendant; if that were true, the jurors might have been excused for cause. Rather, it is because racial discrimination in the selection of jurors "casts doubt on the integrity of the judicial process," Rose v. Mitchell, [supra, at 556], and places the fairness of a criminal proceeding in doubt.

Id. at 411.

The harms we recognized in *Powers* are not limited to the criminal sphere. A civil proceeding often implicates significant rights and interests. Civil juries, no less than their criminal counterparts, must follow the law and act as impartial factfinders. And, as we have observed, their verdicts, no less than those of their criminal counterparts, become binding judgments of the court. Racial discrimination has no place in the courtroom, whether the proceeding is civil or criminal. See Thiel v. Southern Pacific Co., 328 U.S., at 220. Congress has so mandated by prohibiting various discriminatory acts in the context of both civil and criminal trials. See 18 U.S.C. § 243; 28 U.S.C. §§ 1861, 1862. The Constitution demands nothing less. We conclude that courts must entertain a challenge to a private litigant's racially discriminatory use of peremptory challenges in a civil trial.

It may be true that the role of litigants in determining the jury's composition provides one reason for wide acceptance of the jury system and of its verdicts. But if race stereotypes are the price for acceptance of a jury panel as fair, the price is too high to meet the standard of the Constitution. Other means exist for litigants to satisfy themselves of a jury's impartiality without using skin color as a test. If our society is to continue to progress as a multiracial democracy, it must recognize that the automatic invocation of race stereotypes retards that progress and causes continued hurt and injury. By the dispassionate analysis which is its special distinction, the law dispels fears and preconceptions respecting racial attitudes. The quiet rationality of the courtroom makes it an appropriate place to confront race-based fears or hostility by means other than the use of offensive stereotypes. Whether the race generality employed by litigants to challenge a potential juror derives from open hostility or from some hidden and unarticulated fear, neither motive entitles the litigant to cause injury to the excused juror. And if a litigant believes that the prospective juror harbors the same biases or instincts, the issue can be explored in a rational way that consists with respect for the dignity of persons, without the use of classifications based on ancestry or skin color.

[JUSTICE O'CONNOR, joined by CHIEF JUSTICE REHNQUIST and JUSTICE SCALIA, wrote a dissenting opinion. JUSTICE SCALIA also wrote a separate dissent. — EDS.]

### Note: The Right of the Individual Potential Juror

*Edmonson* began the shift to a focus on the right of the individual juror, rather than on the other interests served by a diverse jury. What are some of these other interests? See Toni M. Massaro, Peremptories or Peers? — Rethinking Sixth Amendment Doctrine, Images, and Procedures, 64 N.C. L. Rev. 501, 517-518 (1986).

In J.E.B. v. Alabama ex rel. T.B., 511 U.S. 127 (1994), the state used peremptory challenges to remove all but one male juror in a paternity and child support proceeding. The resulting jury was all female after the father/

defendant exercised his peremptories. The defendant objected to the state's peremptory challenges on the ground that *Batson*'s anti-discrimination principle applies to gender as well as race. The trial court overruled the objection. After the trial, the all-female jury found that the defendant was the father and the court entered an order for child support. The Supreme Court reversed, concluding that "[i]ntentional discrimination on the basis of gender by state actors violates the Equal Protection Clause, particularly where, as here, the discrimination serves to ratify and perpetuate invidious, archaic, and overbroad stereotypes about the relative abilities of men and women." 511 U.S. at 130-131.

*J.E.B.* is important because it finally established that women have a constitutional right to serve on juries, which the Court had never before formally declared, despite the long struggle by women's rights advocates.

For a discussion of this disparate treatment and related issues, see Joanna L. Grossman, Women's Jury Rights: Right of Citizenship or Privilege of Difference?, 46 Stan. L. Rev. 601 (1994). A year before the decision, Professor Babcock argued that *Batson* must be extended to women in order to prevent gender from becoming an improper proxy for race:

### Barbara Allen Babcock, A Place in the Palladium: Women's Rights and Jury Service
61 U. Cin. L. Rev. 1139, 1175-1180 (1993)

. . . Aside from the difficulty of accomplishing it, total elimination of the peremptory challenge is ill-advised as it would focus jury selection entirely on the challenge for cause. The judge alone—in a series of highly discretionary, practically unreviewable decisions—would then be permitted to shape the jury in every case. But under the Constitution, the jury trial is guaranteed precisely because our tradition is not to trust the unilateral actions of judges. In particular, the jury is meant to offset the class bias and elitism that characterizes the judiciary, yet we can hardly expect judges to find "cause"—i.e., incipient bias—in jurors who reflect their own image in background or outlook.

Not only would the increased importance of the cause challenge heighten the judge's power, but abolition of the peremptory would make it more difficult for the litigant to lay the groundwork for a cause challenge, as vigorous questioning may antagonize and hence prejudice a potential juror. The peremptory challenge is the insurance that makes genuine inquiry into juror bias possible.

Most important, the peremptory endows the litigant with a role in the process, thus promoting in Blackstone's words "a good opinion of the jury the want of which might totally disconcert him." Although the Supreme Court disallows race as a reason for striking jurors, and should forbid female gender as an explanation also, it does not follow that litigants must relinquish all sense of choice over their shared juries.

The peremptory is important enough that instead of urging our legis-latures to abolish it, we should seize the occasion of the Supreme Court's intervention in jury selection to enact modern statutes that will aid our "progress toward a multiracial democracy."[122] This essay concludes by out-lining some of the elements such a statute might include, though many of the suggestions could easily be implemented by trial judges or by appellate courts through their respective supervisory powers.

A comprehensive statute would begin by broadening the juror pool beyond voter registration lists to include licensed drivers, utility users, and residents listed in the city directory. Jurors to be summoned should each receive (on the back of the summons), as they now often do, a questionnaire covering items relevant to their basic fitness to serve. . . .

The voir dire process can also be changed to facilitate the exercise of peremptory challenges on a basis other than race or gender. Juror ques-tionnaires can be supplemented by questions, tailored to individual cases designed to probe the attitudes of potential jurors toward sensitive issues that are likely to arise.

Such tailored questionnaires can help the parties base their arguments for cause challenges and their exercise of peremptories on actual suspicion of race prejudice rather than simply on the color of the potential juror's skin. And though they cannot substitute for some public procedures—to see and to hear is, after all, the point of voir dire—the questionnaires can provide grounds for open inquiry that neither humiliates the potential juror nor rouses the ire of the others in the venire.

In order to explore prejudiced attitudes more effectively and efficiently, the parties might give their opening statements to the whole venire and then make inquiries afterward for both cause and peremptory challenges. Potential jurors would then understand how and where their answers fit into the theory of the case and the evidence that will be presented. Once procedures are in place allowing parties to act on intimations of actual bias, rather than on the crude proxy of race or gender, then the requirement for making a prima facie case by letting one or two strikes pass before object-ing would no longer be necessary.

Expanding the information available from voir dire responds to the concerns of those who fear that modifying the peremptory challenge will destroy the mystique—or science—of jury selection. Automatic strikes of white women and people of color are not only unnecessary to the art, but they detract from it. When the legendary jury lawyer Clarence Darrow spoke in a much-cited passage of "the knowledge of life, human nature, psychology and the reactions of the human emotions," that a lawyer must bring to jury selection, he was looking at juries that contained no racial minorities and few women.[130] Rather, in shaping the jury he examined

---

122. Edmonson v. Leesville Concrete Co., 111 S. Ct. 2077, 2088 (1991).
130. Clarence Darrow, Attorney for the Defense, Esquire, May 1936, at 35.

"nationality, business, religion, politics, social standing, family ties, friends, habits of life and thought; the books and newspapers he likes and reads and many more matters that combine to make a man."[131] These qualities will still be open for consideration after the *Batson* line of inquiry is complete.

Litigants should be able to point to attitudes that, when held by an individual, would make for bias in a particular case, and to devise procedures for uncovering these. Recently, for instance, professional football players sued to terminate a contractual system in which they allegedly could not market their services freely. They submitted affidavits from sports psychologists about the biases of "highly identified sports fans" and sought a tailored questionnaire, individual voir dire and extra peremptory challenges to identify and eliminate such fans. Special procedures for exploring attitudes and experience might also be appropriate to sexual harassment cases, for another example, rather than the present crude system in which one side strikes women and the other, men.

Finally, the actual routine of exercising challenges can be revised to ease the stigma of rejection. One attractive suggestion is a form of "affirmative selection," in which, after voir dire and cause strikes, each party designates, in preferential order, those venire persons who should sit on the jury. Jurors who appear on both lists are seated, and then, alternating between lists until the number of peremptories is reached for each side, the Court will either seat or strike a juror who appears on only one list. If the juror is a white woman or a person of color, a neutral explanation would be required. At the very least, courts should insist, as many already do, that the explanations for strikes are offered out of the potential juror's presence.

The *Batson* doctrine establishes three kinds of challenges: cause; peremptory; and modified peremptory, i.e., those for which some explanation is required. In many jurisdictions, practices regulating and enabling a modified peremptory are already in effect and can serve as models for statutory, as well as discretionary procedural change. Although its administration takes time at the jury selection stage, and still generates new issues for appeal, *Batson* has not, by any account, created the chaos some critics warned it would. And, less than a decade has passed since the case was decided—not very long in law time. There is, finally, much we can do procedurally to ease the burden of making jury selection actually and symbolically representative of our best collective selves.

---

The Supreme Court has not applied its equal protection analysis to peremptory challenges based on categories other than race and sex. Shortly

---

131. Id. Darrow did not use the male pronoun generically, since he advised striking any women who might be called.

after its decision in *J.E.B.*, the Court declined an invitation to extend *Batson* to religion by denying certiorari in Davis v. Minnesota, 511 U.S. 1115 (1994). Lower courts have divided over whether to ban religion-based peremptories. In early 2000, a California appellate court apparently became the nation's first to decide that gays and lesbians constitute a cognizable class who cannot be excluded from juries based on group bias. See People v. Garcia, 92 Cal. Rptr. 2d 339 (Cal. Ct. App. 2000). The court decided that using peremptory strikes to exclude gays would violate the defendant's right to a jury chosen from a cross-section of the community, under both the California constitution and the Sixth Amendment to the U.S. Constitution. Federal courts had not addressed the question head-on until the Ninth Circuit decision in SmithKline Beecham Corp. v. Abbott Labs., 740 F.3d 471 (9th Cir. 2014) (holding that striking a potential juror on the basis of the juror's sexual orientation violates Equal Protection Clause, in the context of a lawsuit over licensing agreement and the pricing of HIV medications during which defendant used its first peremptory challenge to strike the only self-identified gay member of the venire). The D.C. Circuit has refused to extend *Batson* and *J.E.B.* to disability. See United States v. Watson, 483 F.3d 828 (D.C. Cir. 2007) (declining to apply heightened scrutiny to peremptory challenges of blind jurors).

There was a tremendous outpouring of scholarly attention to the Supreme Court cases on jury selection and composition at the turn of the century; here is a sample of articles that are especially good: Mary M. Albright, Equal Protection and Peremptory Challenges: Reconciling the Irreconcilable, 25 Cap. U. L. Rev. 425 (1996); Beth A. Deverman, Fourteenth Amendment — Equal Protection: The Supreme Court's Prohibition of Gender-Based Peremptory Challenges, 85 J. Crim. L. & Criminology 1028 (1995); Lance Koonce, J.E.B. v. Alabama ex rel. T.B. and the Fate of the Peremptory Challenge, 73 N.C. L. Rev. 525, 555 (1995); Jason Laeser, Jurors and Litigants Beware — Savvy Attorneys Are Prepared to Strike: Has Purkett v. Elem Signaled the Demise of the Peremptory Challenge at the Federal and State Levels?, 52 U. Miami L. Rev. 635 (1998); Kevin J. Melilli, *Batson* in Practice: What We Have Learned About *Batson* and Peremptory Challenges, 71 Notre Dame L. Rev. 447 (1996); Charles J. Ogletree, Just Say No!: A Proposal to Eliminate Racially Discriminatory Uses of Peremptory Challenges, 31 Am. Crim. L. Rev. 1099 (1994); Barbara D. Underwood, Ending Race Discrimination in Jury Selection: Whose Right Is It, Anyway?, 92 Colum. L. Rev. 725 (1992). See also Susan Hightower, Sex and the Peremptory Strike: An Empirical Analysis of *J.E.B. v. Alabama*'s First Five Years, 52 Stan. L. Rev. 895 (2000), in which the author studied *J.E.B.*'s impact on the state and federal court systems. In the five years following the Supreme Court's 1994 decision, fewer than two dozen cases were reversed and a comparable number remanded due to violations of *J.E.B.*, for peremptory challenges improperly based on gender. Nearly half of the cases deciding a *J.E.B.* claim involved murder trials.

# E.   MANAGING THE JURY

## Problem Case: The Bereaved Widow

Wylie, a Nebraskan, was killed instantly in a one-car crash in Kansas. His widow brought a wrongful-death survivor action in the Nebraska federal court against Ford, the manufacturer of the automobile, alleging that Ford had sold Wylie an unfit automobile. She demanded a jury.

At trial, the plaintiff offered first the testimony of the Kansas state trooper who testified that Wylie's car had left a country road and hit an oak tree 80 feet from the road. He also testified that there were no signs of brake or skid marks.

She next presented the testimony of McCoy, an auto mechanic, who testified that the upper ball joint in the control arm of the left front wheel of Wylie's car was defectively soft and, because of this softness, the arm had fallen out of the socket. With the arm out of its socket, Wylie could not have controlled the direction of travel.

In a hard-charging cross-examination, Ford's counsel, Christian, forced McCoy to acknowledge that he had been paid only a statutory witness fee for his testimony, but that he had been promised more and that the larger fee could be paid by the widow only after she won. He also acknowledged that the joint could have been knocked out of its socket by the impact of the tree. He then reluctantly admitted that he had made no hardness tests on the metal, nor had he examined the grease in the joints for bits of worn metal. At this point, McCoy tearfully asked the judge for a recess, and Christian terminated her cross-examination. Christian then moved to strike McCoy's testimony as inherently incredible and unworthy of belief. The judge denied this motion.

The plaintiff then testified on damages; she said that Wylie was 60 years old, a public school teacher earning $35,000 a year, and her sole support. On cross-examination, she asserted that she knew of no reason why her husband might have been suicidal at the time of his death.

Ford offered two witnesses. The first was Jarvis, an employee of the parts manufacturer that supplied Ford with the steering assembly, including the control arm of which the joint was part. Jarvis testified that the marks on the assembly placed there by his employer dated the assembly as one manufactured six months after Wylie bought his car; it thus could not have been part of the car sold to him.

Ford's second witness, a police officer, testified that on the evening prior to the accident, he had arrested Wylie for sexually molesting a child.

After all evidence was presented, both parties moved for judgment as a matter of law. The case was then presented to the jury. Plaintiff's counsel argued to the jury that a company that had so brutally attacked both witness McCoy and the reputation of the deceased probably made a bad car. Defense counsel Christian then apologized to the jury for her aggression, but explained that she had a duty to show that McCoy's testimony was unworthy of belief, that Wylie may well have committed suicide and that, in any case, he was probably out of a job and thus that plaintiff was not damaged financially by his death.

The jury was instructed that the plaintiff, in order to establish her claim, had the burden of proving that there was a defect in the car at the time that it was sold, and that the defect caused an injury resulting in harm to the plaintiff. If she could prove those elements of her prima facie case, then she could be compensated for the harm, including the economic value of the life of Wylie, and the psychological harm associated with the loss of consortium. The court refused the plaintiff's request for an instruction on punitive damages, to which the plaintiff objected as error under Fed. R. Civ. P. 51.

The jury deliberated briefly and returned a verdict for the plaintiff in the amount of $800,000. The judge, finding the damages grossly excessive as a matter of law, ordered remittitur, reducing the award to $300,000.

Within the week, Christian filed a motion for judgment notwithstanding the verdict, or, in the alternative, for new trial. Attached to her motion was a letter she received from Juror Number 7, which read: "You are one mean witch and it really cost your client. I persuaded the jury that that bad assembly was put in the car by Ford when it was in for repairs, and that Wylie was a great lover. It serves you right." Christian argued on behalf of her motion that there was no evidence to support the verdict. She also contended that the jury had been misinstructed, because the judge omitted one of the elements of the plaintiff's case under Kansas law, to wit that plaintiff also had to prove that the car was being used for its intended purpose at the time of the injury.

What ruling should the district judge make?

If the district judge enters judgment on the verdict, what are the likely grounds, if any, for a successful appeal?

The following materials should help you understand how the court system will deal with the bereaved widow's case.

## 1. Guiding Jury Deliberations: Instructions and the Form of the Verdict

### *Gallick v. Baltimore & Ohio R.R. Co.*
372 U.S. 108 (1963)

JUSTICE WHITE delivered the opinion of the Court.

Upon a special verdict of the jury, the Common Pleas Court of Cuyahoga County, Ohio, entered judgment awarding damages to petitioner in this Federal Employers' Liability Act suit. The Court of Appeals reversed, 173 N.E.2d 382, and the Ohio Supreme Court refused further appellate review, 172 Ohio St. 488, 178 N.E.2d 597, making the decision of the intermediate appellate court the final judgment rendered by the state courts. This Court granted certiorari, 369 U.S. 848, to consider the question whether the decision below improperly invaded the jury's function. We have concluded that the decision below is erroneous and must be reversed.

Petitioner was a spotting crew foreman working on or about August 10, 1954, along the respondent railroad's right of way in the Cuyahoga River "flats" section of Cleveland, Ohio. At the particular stretch of road-bed where petitioner was working on that afternoon, there had been for many years a pool of stagnant water, in and about which were dead and decayed rats and pigeons, or portions thereof. Insects had been seen on, over, and about this stagnant pool, and the evidence showed, as the Court of Appeals stated, that respondent had long been aware of the fetid condition of this pool. 173 N.E.2d at 383. While he was temporarily working near the pool, petitioner experienced a bite on his left leg just above the knee. He grasped the spot with his hand and felt an object under his trousers which seemed to be a large insect and which, when he crushed it, dropped out of his trouser leg. The wound subsequently became infected. The infection failed to respond to medical treatment, and worsened progressively until it spread throughout petitioner's body, creating pus-forming lesions and eventually necessitating the amputation of both his legs. None of the doctors who treated and studied petitioner's case could explain the etiology of his present condition, although some of them diagnosed or characterized it as "pyodermagangrenosa, secondary to insect bite." See id. at 384. . . .

After a lengthy trial, the court, pursuant to the State's special verdict statute, Ohio Rev. Code, § 2315.15, under which no general verdict is rendered by the jury, submitted some two dozen interrogatories to the jury and charged them as to what it deemed the applicable law of negligence. The special verdict of the jury, to the extent that it is relevant here, follows (answers italicized):

10. On approximately August 10, 1954, was plaintiff bitten by an insect? *Yes.* . . .

13. Did the defendant B & O provide the plaintiff Mr. Gallick a reasonably safe place to work under the facts and circumstances existing at the time? *Jury can't decide on this question.*

14. [D]id the defendant B & O know that by permitting the accumulation of said pool of stagnant water, dead pigeons, dead rats, bugs, and vermin would be attracted to said area? *Yes.*

15. If the answer to 14 is yes, did the defendant B & O know that its employees would have to work in this area? *Yes.*

16. Was the defendant negligent in one or more of the particulars alleged in the petition? *Yes.*

17. If the answer to Question 16 is yes, indicate in the words of the petition the acts or omissions which constitute defendant's negligence. *There existed a pool of stagnant water on the premises in the possession of and under the control of defendant into which was accumulated dead pigeons, rats, and various forms of bugs and vermin.*

18. Was the illness or diseases from which Mr. Gallick now suffers caused in whole or in part by an insect bite sustained by him on defendant B & O's premises? *Yes.*

19. Were the injuries to the plaintiff proximately caused . . . by . . . the acts or omissions of the defendant? *Yes.*
20. [W]as there any reason for the defendant B & O to anticipate that such [maintaining stagnant, infested pool] would or might probably result in a mishap or an injury? *No.*
21. Is there a proximate causal relationship to the stagnant water, the dead rats, the dead pigeons, the insect bite, and the present physical condition of the plaintiff? *Yes.*
22. If the answer to Question 21 is yes, was it within the realm of reasonable probability or foreseeability of the defendant B & O to appreciate this proximate causal relationship between the stagnant water, the dead rats, the dead pigeons, the insect bite and the present physical condition of the plaintiff? *No.* . . .

We think that the Court of Appeals improperly invaded the function and province of the jury in this Federal Employers' Liability Act case. According to the Court of Appeals, the break in the causal chain that turned it into a mere "series of guesses and speculations" was the want of evidence from which the jury could properly conclude that respondent's fetid pool had had something to do with the insect that bit petitioner. The only question was whether or not the insect was from or had been attracted by the pool. We hold that the record shows sufficient evidence to warrant the jury's conclusion that petitioner's injuries were caused by the acts or omissions of respondent.

As the Court of Appeals stated, "insects were seen on, over and about this stagnant pool." According to petitioner's undisputed testimony, he stood near the pool for about a half a minute; then he started to walk away and was bitten on the leg after he took a few steps, perhaps one or two seconds later. Petitioner also testified, on cross-examination, that he had at times seen insects of about the same size as that which bit him crawling over the dead rats and pigeons in the stagnant pool. And on cross-examination by respondent two medical witnesses testified that stagnant, rat-infested pools breed and attract insects.[3] Moreover, the jury specifically found that the pool accumulated and attracted bugs and vermin. . . .

Although we have concluded that the jury could properly find that there was a causal relationship between the railroad's negligence and petitioner's injuries, that does not end the case. Respondent makes the further argument that the judgment under review may be sustained on the alternative ground, not accepted by the Court of Appeals, that the injury was not reasonably foreseeable, and that therefore there was no negligence.

---

3. The Court of Appeals emphasized the fact that no similar bite was ever complained about, as a factor in gauging the probability that the actual causal chain corresponded to petitioner's theory of the case, 173 N.E.2d at 387; it accepted as supported by "sufficient credible evidence" the finding that an insect bit petitioner, but it disagreed with the finding that pool and insect bite were related. Although the record does not show that any complaint was ever made to respondent about insect bites, petitioner testified that he had complained to the section foreman about the vermin-infested pool several times and another witness testified that he was bitten by an insect near it in or about September 1954.

We agree with respondent that reasonable foreseeability of harm is an essential ingredient of Federal Employers' Liability Act negligence. Inman v. Baltimore & O.R. Co., 361 U.S. 138, 140. . . . But this requirement has been satisfied in the present case by the jury's findings (Nos. 10, 14-19, 21) of negligence in maintaining the filthy pool of water. The jury had been instructed that negligence is the failure to observe that degree of care which people of ordinary prudence and sagacity would use under the same or similar circumstances; and that defendant's duty was measured by what a reasonably prudent person would anticipate as resulting from a particular condition—"defendant's duties are measured by what is reasonably foreseeable under like circumstances"—by what "in the light of the facts then known, should or could reasonably have been anticipated." Thus when the jury found these facts: petitioner was bitten by an insect; the insect bite caused illness or disease and led to petitioner's present physical condition; the stagnant pool attracted bugs and vermin and was responsible for the insect bite and the injuries to petitioner; and respondent knew that the accumulation of the pool of water would attract bugs and vermin to the area—it is clear that the jury concluded that respondent should have realized the increased likelihood of an insect's biting petitioner while he was working in the vicinity of the pool.

Respondent places reliance, however, upon two special interrogatories returned by the jury. In one, No. 22, the jury found that respondent could not foresee that the stagnant pool would set into being a chain of events that would culminate in petitioner's present physical condition—loss of two limbs, widespread ulcerations, and permanent disability. In the other, No. 20, the jury found that respondent did not have reason to anticipate that its maintenance of the pool "would or might probably result in a mishap or an injury." It is said that interrogatories Nos. 20 and 22 are findings of no foreseeability, and that there is therefore a fatal inconsistency among the jury's findings and that they cancel one another out, necessitating a judgment for the defendant, or at least a new trial. . . . But it is the duty of the courts to attempt to harmonize the answers, if it is possible under a fair reading of them: "Where there is a view of the case that makes the jury's answers to special interrogatories consistent, they must be resolved that way." Atlantic & Gulf Stevedores, Inc. v. Ellerman Lines, Ltd., 369 U.S. 355, 364 [1962]. We therefore must attempt to reconcile the jury's findings, by exegesis if necessary, as in Arnold v. Panhandle & S.F.R. Co., 353 U.S. 360 [1957]; McVey v. Phillips Co., 288 F.2d 53 (5th Cir. [1961]); Morris v. Pennsylvania R. Co., 187 F.2d 837 (2d Cir. [1951]) (collecting authorities), before we are free to disregard the jury's special verdict and remand the case for a new trial.

We do not believe that the conclusion of fatal inconsistency is compelled by these findings. In the first place, the jury might not have equated a foreseeable insect bite with a mishap or injury. The trial judge more than once in his instructions separated an "insect bite" from "injury," "infection," "illness" or "disease." The answer to Question 20 thus might mean simply that while an insect bite was foreseeable, there was no reason to anticipate a "mishap" or "injury" from such a bite. This answer therefore falls in the same category as the jury's response to Question 22, where the jury found that there was no reasonably foreseeable causal relationship between the insect bite and the present physical condition of the plaintiff. It is widely held that for a defendant to be liable for consequential damages he need not foresee the particular consequences of his negligent acts: assuming the existence of a threshold tort against the person, then whatever damages flow from it are recoverable. . . . And we have no doubt that under a statute where the tortfeasor is liable for death or injuries in producing which his "negligence played any part, even the slightest" (Rogers v. Missouri Pac. R. Co., 352 U.S. 500, 506 [1957]) such a tortfeasor must compensate his victim for even the improbable or unexpectedly severe consequences of his wrongful act. . . . The answers to these two interrogatories are therefore not controlling for Federal Employers' Liability Act purposes.

In the second place, in deciding whether respondent had reason to anticipate and foresee any harm to petitioner, the trial court instructed the jury to take into account "the past experience respecting the location and conditions in question" and the fact "that no occurrence of the kind here alleged either occurred, or was known by the defendant to have occurred, at or near this place before August of 1954." The jury thus might have determined that, since there had been no similar incidents at this pool in the past, the respondent had no specific "reason" for anticipating a mishap or injury to petitioner—a far too narrow a concept of foreseeable harm to negative negligence under the Federal Employers' Liability Act. Thus there is a second and independent ground for the court to have put aside No. 20 as immaterial. Looking at No. 20 in the context of the charge and the total context of the special verdict, see McVey v. Phillips Co., 288 F.2d 53, 59 (C.A. 5th Cir. [1961]); Halprin v. Mora, 231 F.2d 197, 201 (C.A. 3d Cir. [1956]), we cannot assign it sufficient weight to warrant overturning the judgment of the trial court entered pursuant to the jury's special verdict. . . .

*Reversed.*

JUSTICE HARLAN, dissenting.

Heartrending as the petitioner's accident has turned out to be, I think this case should not have been brought here. It involves no unsettled questions of federal law calling for decision by this Court, nor, in any acceptable sense, a departure by the state courts from legal principles already decided requiring this Court's intervention. The case thus does not qualify for review under Rule 19.* See the dissenting opinion of Mr. Justice Frankfurter

---

* The Supreme Court Rule to which Justice Harlan referred then read, in pertinent part:

1. A review on writ of certiorari is not a matter of right, but of sound judicial discretion, and will be granted only where there are special and important reasons therefor. The following, while neither controlling nor fully measuring the court's discretion, indicate the character of reasons which will be considered:

(a) Where a state court has decided a federal question of substance not theretofore determined by this court, or has decided it in a way probably not in accord with applicable decisions of this court. . . .

372 U.S. at 123. [The current version of the Supreme Court Rules includes a similar provision in Rule 10(c). — EDS.]

in Rogers v. Missouri Pacific R. Co., 352 U.S. 500, 524 [1957], and the separate opinion of this writer, p. 559. The case has necessarily required an inordinate amount of time, which the Court can ill afford in the present state of its docket. . . .

JUSTICE STEWART and JUSTICE GOLDBERG, dissenting.

We cannot agree with the Court's disposition of this case, in view of the jury's explicit finding that injury to the petitioner was not reasonably foreseeable. As the Court correctly states, "foreseeability of harm is an essential ingredient of Federal Employers' Liability Act negligence." Interrogatory No. 20 was unambiguous: "[W]as there any reason for the defendant B & O to anticipate that such [maintenance of a stagnant, infested pool] would or might probably result in a mishap or an injury?" In our view the jury's answer to this interrogatory, finding that the railroad had no reason here to anticipate mishap or injury, was irreconcilably inconsistent with its finding of negligence in answer to Interrogatory No. 16, and a new trial should have been ordered.

The Court agrees that the answer to Interrogatory No. 20 was inconsistent with the jury's answer to Interrogatory No. 16. But instead of concluding that this inconsistency cancels out the several findings involved and thus voids the entire verdict, the Court undertakes to search for an alternative meaning to be given to Interrogatory No. 20 in order to bring it into line with the special finding which favors the petitioner. The Court seeks support for this Procrustean exercise in the often-repeated admonition that courts should make every effort "to reconcile the jury's findings, by exegesis, if necessary, . . . before we are free to disregard the jury's special verdict and remand the case for a new trial." We think this generally sound guideline is misapplied in the present case.

The duty of courts to attempt to reconcile inconsistent jury findings has emerged from cases in which the jury answered special interrogatories *and also* returned a general verdict. See, e.g., Arnold v. Panhandle & S.F.R. Co., 353 U.S. 360 [1957].

The inconsistencies which the courts have dealt with in these cases were inconsistencies between a general verdict for one of the parties and seemingly conflicting special findings in answer to added interrogatories. The purpose of such an effort has been to preserve, if possible, the integrity of the jury's general verdict. As one leading commentator has explained, in the context of Federal Rule 49(b),

> [t]he power to enter judgment on findings consistent with each other but inconsistent with the general verdict is a constitutional one and does not violate the Seventh Amendment since the jury's findings of fact are not being reexamined but, as a reasonable regulation of practice, their more specific findings of fact are allowed to control over their general conclusion embodied in the general verdict. Every reasonable intendment should, however, be indulged in favor of the general verdict in an effort to harmonize it with the answers to the interrogatories, and the latter should be held controlling only

"where the conflict on a material question is beyond reconciliation on any reasonable theory consistent with the evidence and its fair inferences." Of course, if the answers are inconsistent with each other, and one or more with the general verdict, the court cannot enter judgment upon the basis of any of the findings, and as provided by the Rule, should not direct the entry of judgment at all, but should return the jury for further deliberation or should order a new trial. [5 Moore, Federal Practice, § 49.04]. . . .

. . . Because the jury in answer to No. 16 found that the railroad was negligent, and yet at the same time specifically found in answer to No. 20 that the mishap was unforeseeable, it is, in our view, impossible to enter a judgment for either party based on these findings. By undertaking to reconcile irretrievably conflicting findings of the jury, the Court, we think, has made the same error that it correctly attributes to the Ohio Court of Appeals — it has invaded the province of the jury under this federal statute. We would avoid such an intrusion by ordering that the cause be put to another jury.

For these reasons we would set aside the judgment and remand this case for a new trial.

## Notes and Questions

1. *"Little" Cases.* You might wonder why the United States Supreme Court is reviewing a judgment of the intermediate court of appeals of Ohio, in a case about a bug bite. The Frankfurter dissent mentioned by Justice Harlan rails against the practice of the Court to grant certiorari in such cases (requiring only four votes). Justice Frankfurter also pointedly observes that the Court almost always restored jury verdicts to employee-plaintiffs. He was talking not only about the liberalized rights of tort recovery for railroad employees (covered by the Federal Employers Liability Act) but also about similar statutes for seamen (the Jones Act, 41 Stat. 1007) and other special plaintiffs. See Ferguson v. Moore-McCormack Lines, Inc., 352 U.S. 521, 525 n.2 (1957).

Whatever the merits of the prudential debate over the Court's resources, the practice of reviewing these cases over a number of years has given us a rich jury trial lore.

2. *Instructions.* The usual device for compelling the jury to follow the law is the judge's instructions at the end of all the evidence. Because the accuracy of these instructions is often the main point on appeal — as may be true in our problem case about the bereaved widow — most trial judges are reluctant to deviate from the standard forms in the jurisdiction.

Fed. R. Civ. P. 51 on jury instructions places no limitations on what a judge may say to the jury and envisions a collaborative process between the judge and the advocates on the design of the instructions. Although Rule 51 is silent on this, the cases establish that district court judges may even comment on the evidence in their instructions to the jury. Here, for instance, is an instruction that was upheld, though not as a model:

> Now it is rather clear in this case that the defendant is negligent and her negligence was responsible for the accident—the Court believes that the facts indicate that . . . but, out of fairness, you may disagree with the Court. . . . I think the question of liability is clearly against the defendant but I am submitting it to you in the event that you wish to disagree with the Court, and you have that right, of course, because you are the triers of the fact.

*Trezza v. Dame*, 370 F.2d 1006, 1008-1009 (5th Cir. 1967). The Fifth Circuit concluded that "[a]lthough the comments under consideration would have been better left unsaid, we hold that they did not constitute prejudicial error in light of the facts of this case." Id. at 1009.

What if the jury seeks additional guidance from the judge during its deliberations, or is confused by the initial instructions? A judge should be careful how she frames any supplemental instructions, especially instructions that "clarify" her initial charge to the jury. In Boyd v. Illinois State Police, the Seventh Circuit held that the trial judge erred in advising a jury that race had to be a "significant reason" under anti-discrimination law for the state police's salary decisions after transferring plaintiffs. 384 F.3d 888, 893 (7th Cir. 2004). After beginning deliberations, the jury had asked whether race had to be "a" factor or "the" factor. The Seventh Circuit admonished that the proper standard is whether race is a "motivating factor," but deemed the trial court's error harmless because, in its view, the record established inadequate evidence of racial motive.

3. *Special Verdicts.* Instructions do not fully serve to hold juries to the law because there is no way to know whether they have been followed. The jury is a "black box" from which emerges a general verdict—often said to be inscrutable. The special verdict is a way out of the black box. Fed. R. Civ. P. 49 covers special verdicts. Note that the Rule makes the use of the device a matter of the trial judge's discretion. What would a special verdict look like in our problem case? Which side might want one?

In Skidmore v. Baltimore & Ohio R.R. Co., 167 F.2d 54 (2d Cir. 1948), the appellant sought a reversal on the ground that the trial court improperly denied its motion for a special verdict under Fed. R. Civ. P. 49, which provides for different jury verdict forms in federal cases. The judgment was affirmed by the court of appeals, which held that the use of Fed. R. Civ. P. 49 is discretionary with the trial judge. Judge Jerome Frank took the occasion, however, to make an effective statement of the case for the use of the Rule:

> Undeniably, the verdict affords no satisfactory information about the jury's findings. But almost every general verdict sheds similar or even greater darkness. Such verdicts account for much (not all) of the criticism of the civil jury. Some reevaluation of the jury system seems not unjustified in the light of the fact that ours is the only country in the world where it is still highly prized. Lauded as essential to individual liberty and democracy, and imported in the late eighteenth and nineteenth centuries from England and the United States, trial by jury was adopted in criminal cases on the European continent, but subsequently ceased there, in pre-Hitler days, to maintain its popularity. Nor can that attitude be explained as a symptom

of decreased interest in democracy and individualism. For Scotland, surely long a land of liberty-loving individualists, having in the sixteenth century virtually rejected the civil jury, readopted it in 1815, and, still later, all but gave it up. In England, whence trial by jury came to us, it is now seldom employed in civil suits, has been abandoned in criminal prosecutions other than for major crimes, and even there is used decreasingly. In the United States, the number of jury waivers indicates the jury's slowly waning popularity. But here, especially in the federal courts, the civil jury, in many cases, cannot be eliminated except by constitutional amendments. We must, then, as to some kind of cases, assume that it will long be with us.

But what many persons regard as its major defects can be mitigated. One device which will help to achieve that end is the special or fact verdict. Those who resent any reform which invades the jury's province should be reassured by the historians who teach that the special verdict is no newfangled idea, but one almost as old as the jury itself, older indeed than the modern jury. . . .

"Competent observers," writes Judge Rossman, "who have interviewed the jurors in scores of jury trials, declare that, in many cases where the general verdict was employed, principal issues received no consideration whatever from the jury." The general verdict, then, has some strange characteristics. As Sunderland puts it: "The peculiarity of the general verdict is the merger into a single indivisible residuum of all matters, however numerous, whether of law or fact. It is a compound made by the jury which is incapable of being broken up into its constituent parts. No judicial reagents exist for either a qualitative or a quantitative analysis. The law supplies the means for determining neither what facts were found, nor what principles of law were applied, nor how the application was made." There are therefore three unknown elements which enter into the general verdict: (a) the facts; (b) the law; (c) the application of the law to the facts. And it is clear that the verdict is liable to three sources of error, corresponding to these three elements. It is also clear that if error does occur in any of these matters it cannot be discovered, for the constituents of the compound cannot be ascertained. No one but the jurors can tell what was put into it and the jurors will not be heard to say. The general verdict is as inscrutable and essentially mysterious as the judgment which issued from the ancient oracle of Delphi. Both stand on the same foundation—a presumption of wisdom. . . .

The general verdict enhances, to the maximum, the power of appeals to the biases and prejudices of the jurors, and usually converts into a futile ritual the use of stock phrases about dispassionateness almost always included in judges' charges. . . .

Perhaps the least desirable feature of the general verdict, a feature which the fact verdict wipes out, is this: The theory of the general verdict involves the assumption that the jury fully comprehends the judge's instructions concerning the applicable substantive legal rules. Yet, often the judge must state those rules to the jury with such niceties that many lawyers do not comprehend them, and it is impossible that the jury can. Judge Bok noted that "juries have the disadvantage . . . of being treated like children while the testimony is going on, but then being doused with a kettleful of law during the charge that would make a third-year law-student blanch. . . ."

167 F.2d at 56-64. A powerful statement against Rule 49 was made by Justices Black and Douglas in their dissent from the adoption of the 1963 Rule amendments:

Rule 49 should be repealed. . . . Such devices are used to impair or totally take away the power of the jury to render a general verdict. One of the ancient fundamental reasons for having general jury verdicts was to preserve the right of trial by jury as an indispensable part of a free government. . . . Some English jurors had to go to jail because they insisted on their right to render general verdicts over the repeated commands of tyrannical judges not to do so.

Amendments to Rules of Civil Procedure, 31 F.R.D. 587, 618-619 (1963) (dissenting statement of Justices Black and Douglas).

4. *The Right to Be Informed of the Jury Instructions.* In DeCaro v. Hasbro, Inc., 580 F.3d 55 (1st Cir. 2009), one of Hasbro's longtime employees sought to return to work after a several-year bout with multiple sclerosis. He sued for disability discrimination when the company refused to give him his job back. At the end of the trial, the judge held a "charge conference," at which counsel for both sides were heard on proposed instructions for the jury and objections. The next day the judge read the instructions to the jury, but before the jury retired to begin deliberations, the court directed counsel to a sidebar conference where it queried counsel about objections to the instructions it had just read. Plaintiff's counsel objected that the judge had misstated the law. The court denied these objections and the jury entered a defense verdict.

On appeal, plaintiff argued that the district court did not follow the proper procedure for jury instructions. Plaintiff argued that the 2003 revisions to Rule 51 require that a court "inform the parties of its proposed instructions and proposed action on the[ir] requests before instructing the jury and before final jury arguments." See Rule 51(b)(1). Plaintiff contended that this means a court must provide counsel with the exact text of its intended jury instructions *at the charge conference.*

The First Circuit disagreed. Although it recognized that "[t]he strictures of Rule 51 are not to be taken lightly," the court stated that Rule 51 does not require the trial judge to provide litigants a written copy of the jury instructions before charging the jury. 580 F.3d at 60. The court found no evidence that the revisions were intended to alter the traditional manner of conducting the charge conference. The court cited opinions from the Second, Third, Fifth, and Eighth Circuits, all of which concluded that the earlier rule "did not require the delivery of written jury instructions to the parties before the court actually delivered the charge." Id. at 64.

## 2.  Taking the Case Away: Judgment as a Matter of Law

*Galloway v. United States*
319 U.S. 372 (1943)

[Galloway, by his wife as next friend, brought this action to recover benefits for a total disability alleged to have occurred during his military service in France in 1918. He was insured by the United States for disability occurring before May 31, 1919.

It was not disputed that Galloway was in good health at the time of his enlistment in the Army in 1917: He had been a Philadelphia longshoreman. He served as a battalion cook in France. Two members of the battalion testified that his behavior on some occasions in France was memorably "disturbed."

He was discharged in 1919. His boyhood friend, O'Neill, testified that he was a "wreck" in 1919 compared to his state in 1917.

He enlisted in the Navy in January 1920. Commander Platt testified that Galloway had been discharged after six months for disobedience and being absent without leave.

He re-enlisted in the Army in December 1920. Colonel Matthews testified that Galloway was at times a very good soldier but not dependable, having alternate periods of gaiety and depression and sometimes talking incoherently. He finally deserted in 1922, and he was still listed as a deserter by the Army.

In 1930, Galloway consulted the Veterans Administration and was diagnosed as a moron. The government did not dispute that he was disabled by 1930, or that he was disabled at the time of trial in 1941. In 1931, the Veterans Administration did change its diagnosis and described him as psychotic-manic.

Galloway's physician first saw him about 1940; on the basis of his examination and his familiarity with the medical history, he gave his opinion that Galloway was born with an inherent instability, had "gone to pieces" in France, and had been insane ever since.

At the close of this evidence, the district court granted the motion of the United States for a directed verdict. The court of appeals affirmed. — Eds.]

Justice Rutledge delivered the opinion of the Court.

. . . [I]f the record is taken to show that some form of mental disability existed in 1930, which later became total and permanent, petitioner's problem remains to demonstrate by more than speculative inference that this condition itself began on or before May 31, 1919 and continuously existed or progressed through the intervening years to 1930.

To show origin before the crucial date, he gives evidence of two abnormal incidents occurring while he was in France, one creating the disturbance before he came near the fighting front, the other yelling that the Germans were coming when he was on guard duty at the Marne. There is no other evidence of abnormal behavior during his entire service of more than a year abroad.

O'Neill's testimony apparently takes no account of petitioner's having spent 101 days in a hospital in France with influenza just before he came home. But, given the utmost credence, as is required, it does no more than show that petitioner was subject to alternating periods of gaiety and depression for some indefinite period after his return, extending perhaps as late as 1922. But because of its vagueness as to time, dates, frequency of opportunity for observation, and specific incident, O'Neill's testimony concerning the period from 1922 to 1925 is hardly more than speculative.

We have then the two incidents in France followed by O'Neill's testimony of petitioner's changed condition in 1919 and its continuance to 1922. There is also the testimony of Commander Platt and Lt. Col. James E. Matthews as to his service in the Navy and the Army, respectively, during 1920-1922. Neither thought petitioner was insane or that his conduct indicated insanity. Then follows a chasm of eight years. . . .

This period was eight years of continuous insanity, according to the inference petitioner would be allowed to have drawn. If so, he should have no need of inference. Insanity so long and continuously sustained does not hide itself from the eyes and ears of witnesses. The assiduity which produced the evidence of two "crazy" incidents during a year and a half in France should produce one during eight years or, for that matter, five years in the United States.

Inference is capable of bridging many gaps. But not, in these circumstances, one so wide and deep as this. Knowledge of petitioner's activities and behavior from 1922 or 1925 to 1930 was peculiarly within his ken and that of his wife, who has litigated this cause in his and presumably, though indirectly, in her own behalf. His was the burden to show continuous disability. What he did in this time, or did not do, was vital to his case. Apart from the mere fact of his marriage, the record is blank for five years and almost blank for eight. For all that appears, he may have worked full time and continuously for five and perhaps for eight, with only a possible single interruption.

No favorable inference can be drawn from the omission. It was not one of oversight or inability to secure proof. That is shown by the thoroughness with which the record was prepared for all other periods, before and after this one, and by the fact petitioner's wife, though she married him during the period and was available, did not testify. The only reasonable conclusion is that petitioner, or those who acted for him, deliberately chose, for reasons no doubt considered sufficient (and which we do not criticize, since such matters including tactical ones, are for the judgment of counsel) to present no evidence or perhaps to withhold evidence readily available concerning this long interval, and to trust to the genius of expert medical inference and judicial laxity to bridge this canyon.

In the circumstances exhibited, the former is not equal to the feat, and the latter will not permit it. No case has been cited and none has been found in which inference, however expert, has been permitted to make so broad a leap and take the place of evidence which, according to all reason, must have been at hand. To allow this would permit the substitution of inference, tenuous at best, not merely for evidence absent because impossible or difficult to secure, but for evidence disclosed to be available and not produced. This would substitute speculation for proof. . . .

What has been said disposes of the case as the parties have made it. For that reason perhaps nothing more need be said. But objection has been advanced that, in some manner not wholly clear, the directed verdict practice offends the Seventh Amendment.

It may be noted, first, that the Amendment has no application of its own force to this case. The suit is one to enforce a monetary claim against the United States. It hardly can be maintained that under the common law in 1791 jury trial was a matter of right for persons asserting claims against the sovereign. Whatever force the Amendment has therefore is derived because Congress . . . has made it applicable. Even so, the objection made on the score of its requirements is untenable.

If the intention is to claim generally that the Amendment deprives the federal courts of power to direct a verdict for insufficiency of evidence, the short answer is the contention has been foreclosed by repeated decisions made here consistently for nearly a century. More recently the practice has been approved explicitly in the promulgation of the Federal Rules of Civil Procedure. . . . The objection therefore comes too late.

Furthermore, the argument from history is not convincing. It is not that "the rules of common law" in 1791 deprived trial courts of power to withdraw cases from the jury, because not made out, or appellate courts of power to review such determinations. The jury was not absolute master of fact in 1791. Then as now courts excluded evidence for irrelevancy and relevant proof for other reasons. The argument concedes they weighed the evidence, not only piece-meal but in toto for submission to the jury, by at least two procedures, the demurrer to the evidence and the motion for a new trial. The objection is not therefore to the basic thing, which is the power of the court to withhold cases from the jury or set aside the verdict for insufficiency of the evidence. It is rather to incidental or collateral effects, namely, that the directed verdict as now administered differs from both those procedures because, on the one hand, allegedly higher standards of proof are required and, on the other, different consequences follow as to further maintenance of the litigation. Apart from the standards of proof, the argument appears to urge that in 1791, a litigant could challenge his opponent's evidence, either by the demurrer, which when determined ended the litigation, or by motion for a new trial which if successful, gave the adversary another chance to prove his case; and therefore the Amendment excluded any challenge to which one or the other of these consequences does not attach.

The Amendment did not bind the federal courts to the exact procedural incidents or details of jury trial according to the common law in 1791, any more than it tied them to the common-law system of pleading or the specific rules of evidence then prevailing. Nor were "the rules of the common law" then prevalent, including those relating to the procedure by which the judge regulated the jury's role on questions of fact, crystallized in a fixed and immutable system. On the contrary, they were constantly changing and developing during the late eighteenth and early nineteenth centuries.[23]

___

23. E.g., during the eighteenth and nineteenth centuries, the nonsuit was being transformed in practice from a device by which a plaintiff voluntarily discontinued his action in order to try again another day into a procedure by which a defendant could put in issue the sufficiency of the plaintiff's evidence to go to the jury, differing from the directed verdict in that respect only in form. . . . The nonsuit, of course, differed in consequence from the directed verdict, for it left the plaintiff free to try again. . . . Similarly, the demurrer to the evidence practice was not static during this period as a comparison of Cocksedge v. Fanshaw, 1779, 1 Doug. 118, with Gibson v. Hunter, 1793, 2 H. Bl. 187, and the American practice on the demurrer to the evidence reveals. . . . Nor was the conception of directing a verdict entirely unknown to the eighteenth century common law. . . . While there is no reason to believe that the notion at that time even approximated in character the present directed verdict, the cases serve further to show the plastic and developing character of these procedural devices during the eighteenth and nineteenth centuries.

In 1791 this process already had resulted in widely divergent common-law rules on procedural matters among the states, and between them and England. . . .

This difficulty, no doubt, accounts for the amorphous character of the objection now advanced, which insists, not that any single one of the features criticized, but that the cumulative total or the alternative effect of all, was embodied in the Amendment. The more logical conclusion, we think, and the one which both history and the previous decisions here support, is that the Amendment was designed to preserve the basic institution of jury trial in only its most fundamental elements, not the great mass of procedural forms and details, varying even then so widely among common-law jurisdictions.

Apart from the uncertainty and the variety of conclusion which follows from an effort at purely historical accuracy, the consequences flowing from the view asserted are sufficient to refute it. It may be doubted that the Amendment requires challenge to an opponent's case to be made without reference to the merits of one's own and at the price of all opportunity to have it considered. On the other hand, there is equal room for disbelieving it compels endless repetition of litigation and unlimited chance, by education gained at the opposing party's expense, for perfecting a case at other trials. The essential inconsistency of these alternatives would seem sufficient to refute that either or both, to the exclusion of all others, received constitutional sanctity by the Amendment's force. The first alternative, drawn from the demurrer to the evidence, attributes to the Amendment the effect of forcing one admission because another and an entirely different one is made, and thereby compels conclusion of the litigation once and for all. The true effect of imposing such a risk would not be to guarantee the plaintiff a jury trial. It would be rather to deprive the defendant (or the plaintiff if he were the challenger) of that right; or, if not that, then of the right to challenge the legal sufficiency of the opposing case. The Amendment was not framed or adopted to deprive either party of either right. It is impartial in its guaranty of both. To posit assertion of one upon sacrifice of the other would dilute and distort the full protection intended. The admitted validity of the practice on the motion for a new trial goes far to demonstrate this. It negatives any idea that the challenge must be made at such a risk as the demurrer imposed. As for the other alternative, it is not urged that the Amendment guarantees another trial whenever challenge to the sufficiency of evidence is sustained. . . . That argument, in turn, is precluded by the practice on demurrer to the evidence. . . .

. . . Whatever may be the general formulation, the essential requirement is that mere speculation be not allowed to do duty for probative facts, after making due allowance for all reasonably possible inferences favoring the party whose case is attacked. The mere difference in labels used to describe this standard . . . cannot amount to a departure from "the rules of the common law" which the Amendment requires to be followed. . . .

Judged by this requirement, or by any standard other than sheer speculation, we are unable to conclude that one whose burden, by the nature of his claim, is to show continuing and total disability for nearly twenty years supplies the essential proof of continuity when he wholly omits to show his whereabouts, activities or condition for five years, although the record discloses evidence must have been available, and, further, throws no light upon three additional years, except for one vaguely described and dated visit to his former home. . . . The words "total and permanent" are the statute's, not our own. They mean something more than incipient or occasional disability. We hardly need add that we give full credence to all of the testimony. But that cannot cure its inherent vagueness or supply essential elements omitted or withheld.

Accordingly, the judgment is

*Affirmed.*

JUSTICE BLACK, with whom JUSTICE DOUGLAS and JUSTICE MURPHY concur, dissenting.

. . . The Court here re-examines testimony offered in a common law suit, weighs conflicting evidence, and holds that the litigant may never take this case to a jury. . . . Today's decision marks a continuation of the gradual process of judicial erosion which in one hundred fifty years has slowly worn away a major portion of the essential guarantee of the Seventh Amendment. . . .

Alexander Hamilton in The Federalist emphasized his loyalty to the jury system in civil cases and declared that jury verdicts should be reexamined, if at all, only "by a second jury, either by remanding the cause to the court below for a second trial of the fact, or by directing an issue immediately out of the Supreme Court."

The first Congress expected the Seventh Amendment to meet the objections of men like Patrick Henry to the Constitution itself. Henry, speaking in the Virginia Constitutional Convention, had expressed the general conviction of the people of the Thirteen States when he said, "We are told that we are to part with that trial by jury with which our ancestors secured their lives and property. . . . I hope we shall never be induced, by such arguments, to part with that excellent mode of trial. No appeal can now be made as to fact in common law suits. *The unanimous verdict of impartial men cannot be reversed.*" . . .

In 1789, juries occupied the principal place in the administration of justice. They were frequently in both criminal and civil cases the arbiters not only of fact but of law. Less than three years after the ratification of the Seventh Amendment, this Court called a jury in a civil case brought under our original jurisdiction. There was no disagreement as to the facts of the case. Chief Justice Jay, charging the jury for a unanimous Court, three of whose members had sat in the Constitutional Convention, said: "For as, on the one hand, it is presumed, that juries are the best judges of facts; it is, on the other hand, presumable, that the court[s] are the best judges of law. But still, both objects are lawfully within your power of decision." State of Georgia v. Brailsford, 3 Dall. 1, 4. . . . The principal method by which judges prevented cases from going to the jury in the Seventeenth and Eighteenth

Centuries was by the demurrer to the evidence. . . . This practice fell into disuse in England in 1793, Gibson v. Hunter, 2 H. Bl. 187, and in the United States federal courts in 1826, Fowle v. Alexandria, 11 Wheat. 320. . . . The power of federal judges to comment to the jury on the evidence gave them additional influence. . . . The right of involuntary nonsuit of a plaintiff, which might have been used to expand judicial power at jury expense was at first denied federal courts. . . .

As Hamilton had declared in The Federalist, the basic judicial control of the jury function was in the court's power to order a new trial. In 1830, this Court said: "The only modes known to the common law to re-examine such facts, are the granting of a new trial by the court where the issue was tried, or to which the record was properly returnable; or the award of a venire facias de novo, by an appellate court, for some error of law which intervened in the proceedings." Parsons v. Bedford, 3 Pet. at page 448. . . .

A long step toward the determination of fact by judges instead of by juries was the invention of the directed verdict. In 1850, what seems to have been the first directed verdict case considered by this Court, Parks v. Ross, 11 How. 362, 374, . . . was presented for decision. The Court held that the directed verdict serves the same purpose as the demurrer to the evidence, and that since there was "no evidence whatever" on the critical issue in the case, the directed verdict was approved. The decision was an innovation, a departure from the traditional rule restated only fifteen years before in Greenleaf v. Birth, 1835, 9 Pet. 292, 299 . . . in which this Court had said: "Where there is no evidence tending to prove a particular fact, the court[s] are bound so to instruct the jury, when requested; but they cannot legally give any instruction which shall take from the jury the right of weighing the evidence and determining what effect it shall have."

This new device contained potentialities for judicial control of the jury which had not existed in the demurrer to the evidence. In the first place, demurring to the evidence was risky business, for in so doing the party not only admitted the truth of all the testimony against him but also all reasonable inferences which might be drawn from it; and upon joinder in demurrer the case was withdrawn from the jury while the court proceeded to give final judgment either for or against the demurrant. . . . Imposition of this risk was no mere technicality; for by making withdrawal of a case from the jury dangerous to the moving litigant's cause, the early law went far to assure that facts would never be examined except by a jury. . . . The litigant not only takes no risk by a motion for a directed verdict, but in making such a motion gives himself two opportunities to avoid the jury's decision; for under the federal variant of judgment notwithstanding the verdict, the judge may reserve opinion on the motion for a directed verdict and then give judgment for the moving party after the jury has formally found against him. In the second place, under the directed verdict practice the courts soon abandoned the "admission of all facts and reasonable inferences" standard referred to, and created the so-called "substantial evidence" rule which permitted directed verdicts even though there was far more evidence in the case than a plaintiff would have needed to withstand a demurrer. The substantial evidence rule did not spring into existence immediately upon the adoption of the directed verdict device. For a few more years federal judges held to the traditional rule that juries might pass finally on facts if there was "any evidence" to support a party's contention. The rule that a case must go to the jury unless there was "no evidence" was completely repudiated in Schuylkill and Dauphin Improvement Co. v. Munson, 1871, 14 Wall. 442, 447, 448, . . . upon which the Court today relies in part. There the Court declared that "some" evidence was not enough—there must be evidence sufficiently persuasive to the judge so that he thinks "a jury can properly proceed." The traditional rule was given an ugly name, "the scintilla rule," to hasten its demise. . . . The same transition from jury supremacy to jury subordination through judicial decisions took place in State courts.

Later cases permitted the development of added judicial control. . . . [J]ury verdicts on disputed facts have been set aside or directed verdicts authorized so regularly as to make the practice commonplace while the motion for directed verdict itself has become routine. . . . Today the Court comes dangerously close to weighing the credibility of a witness and rejecting his testimony because the majority do not believe it.

The call for the true application of the Seventh Amendment is not to words, but to the spirit of honest desire to see that Constitutional right preserved. Either the judge or the jury must decide facts and to the extent that we take this responsibility, we lessen the jury function. Our duty to preserve this one of the Bill of Rights may be peculiarly difficult, for here it is our own power which we must restrain. . . . As for myself, I believe that a verdict should be directed, if at all, only when, without weighing the credibility of the witnesses, there is in the evidence no room whatever for honest difference of opinion over the factual issue in controversy. . . .

. . . It is undisputed that the petitioner's health was sound in 1918, and it is evidently conceded that he was disabled at least since 1930. When in the intervening period, did the disability take place?

. . . There is substantial testimony from which reasonable men might conclude that the petitioner was insane from the date claimed.

Two witnesses testify as to the petitioner's mental irresponsibility while he was in France. . . . The Court disposes of this testimony, which obviously indicates some degree of mental unbalance, by saying no more than that it "does not prove he was insane." No reason is given, nor can I imagine any, why a jury should not be entitled to consider this evidence and draw its own conclusions. . . .

The Court analyzes O'Neill's testimony for internal consistency, criticizes his failure to remember the details of his association with the petitioner fifteen years before his appearance in this case, and concludes that O'Neill's evidence shows no more than that "petitioner was subject to alternating periods of gaiety and depression for some indefinite period." This extreme emotional instability is an accepted symptom of the disease from which the petitioner suffers. If he exhibited the same symptoms in 1922, it is, at the minimum, probable that the condition has been continuous since an origin during the war. O'Neill's testimony coupled with the petitioner's present condition presents precisely the type of question which a jury should resolve.

. . . The testimony of his Commanding Officer while he was in the Army, Col. Matthews, is that the petitioner had "periods of gaiety and exhilaration" and was then "depressed as if he had a hangover"; that petitioner tried to create disturbances and dissatisfy the men; that he suffered from a belief that he was being treated unfairly; and that generally his actions "were not those of a normal man." The Colonel was not a doctor and might well not have recognized insanity had he seen it; as it was, he concluded that the petitioner was an alcoholic and a narcotic addict. However, the officer was unable, upon repeated investigations, to discover any actual use of narcotics. A jury fitting this information into the general pattern of the testimony might well have been driven to the conclusion that the petitioner was insane at the time the Colonel had him under observation.

All of this evidence, if believed, showed a man healthy and normal before he went to the war suffering for several years after he came back from a disease which had the symptoms attributed to schizophrenia and who was insane from 1930 until his trial. Under these circumstances, I think that the physician's testimony of total and permanent disability by reason of continuous insanity from 1918 to 1938 was reasonable. The fact that there was no direct testimony for a period of five years, while it might be the basis of fair argument to the jury by the government, does not, as the Court seems to believe, create a presumption against the petitioner so strong that his case must be excluded from the jury entirely. Even if during these five years the petitioner was spasmodically employed, we could not conclude that he was not totally and permanently disabled. . . . It is not doubted that schizophrenia is permanent even though there may be a momentary appearance of recovery. . . .

This case graphically illustrates the injustice resulting from permitting judges to direct verdicts instead of requiring them to await a jury decision and then, if necessary, allow a new trial. The chief reason given for approving a directed verdict against this petitioner is that no evidence except expert medical testimony was offered for a five to eight year period. Perhaps, now that the petitioner knows he has insufficient evidence to satisfy a judge even though he may have enough to satisfy a jury, he would be able to fill this time gap to meet any judge's demand. . . . If, as the Court believes, insufficient evidence has been offered to sustain a jury verdict for the petitioner, we should at least authorize a new trial. . . .

### Notes and Questions

1. *The Standard for Judgment as a Matter of Law.* The "directed verdict" in *Galloway* is the prior term for what is now called judgment as a matter of law (JMOL). See Fed. R. Civ. P. 50. The same motion made after the verdict, formerly called a motion for judgment notwithstanding the verdict (JNOV), is now called a renewed JMOL.

The motion for judgment as a matter of law and the renewed motion for judgment as a matter of law are both directed toward the sufficiency of the evidence, not to procedural irregularities at the trial (such as incorrect evidentiary rulings or attorney misconduct). The notion underlying both motions is that a jury should not be allowed to enter an arbitrary verdict or one that is against the great weight of the evidence. These motions are, in essence, delayed motions for summary judgment, though unlike Rule 56 motions, these trial motions are made after the parties have had a full chance to establish a question of fact through the presentation of evidence. As such, the judge has a more informed look at the nonmovant's case than she has at the pretrial, summary judgment stage.

The cases demonstrate that some confusion exists regarding the precise standard for granting a motion for judgment as a matter of law. A frequently quoted articulation of the test for both motions is Boeing Co. v. Shipman, 411 F.2d 365, 374-375 (5th Cir. 1969) (en banc):

> On motions for directed verdict and for judgment notwithstanding the verdict the Court should consider all of the evidence—not just that evidence which supports the nonmover's case—but in the light and with all reasonable inferences most favorable to the party opposed to the motion. If the facts and inferences point so strongly and overwhelmingly in favor of one party that the Court believes that reasonable men could not arrive at a contrary verdict, granting of the motions is proper. On the other hand, if there is such substantial evidence opposed to the motions, that is, evidence of such quality and weight that reasonable and fair-minded men in the exercise of impartial judgment might reach different conclusions, the motion should be denied, and the case submitted to the jury. A mere scintilla of evidence is insufficient to present a question for the jury. The motions for directed verdict and judgment n.o.v. should not be decided by which side has the better of the case, nor should they be granted only when there is a complete absence of probative facts to support a jury verdict. There must be a conflict in substantial evidence to create a jury question. However, it is the function of the jury as the traditional finder of the facts, and not the Court, to weigh conflicting evidence and inferences, and determine the credibility of witnesses.

Generally speaking, the standard is correctly expressed as follows: The motion should be granted in favor of the movant when, viewing all the evidence in the light most favorable to the nonmovant, there is no evidence upon which a reasonable juror could find for the nonmovant. The judge's role in ruling on the motion therefore is not to weigh the evidence, in the sense of passing on the credibility of witnesses or otherwise ruling on the quality of the evidence; rather, the judge should determine the *existence* of the required standard of evidence. Even on a *renewed* motion for judgment as a matter of law, after the jury renders a verdict the judge cannot look to the jury's findings. See Chaney v. City of Orlando, 483 F.3d 1221, 1228 (11th Cir. 2007) (reversing renewed judgment as a matter of law and remanding for reconsideration in civil rights suit for excessive use of force where trial judge relied on the jury's finding that officer had probable cause to arrest to conclude that officer used reasonable force to effect the arrest: "The jury's findings should be excluded from the decision-making calculus on a Rule 50(b) motion, other than to ask whether there was sufficient evidence, as a legal matter, from which a reasonable jury could find for the party which prevailed at trial."). But the concerns expressed by Justice Black in *Galloway*, and by Justice Brennan in *Celotex*, that standards such as this allow judges to impose their views regarding the weight of the evidence, are very real.

It is considerably more difficult for the party with the burden of proof to prevail on a motion for judgment as a matter of law. Can you explain why this is so? Recall the previous discussions of burdens of proof, production, and pleading. How do these different concepts and the pretrial motion for summary judgment tie together?

What shall a court do when the evidence is in perfect balance? Consider an old chestnut, Reid v. San Pedro, Los Angeles & Salt Lake R.R., 118 P. 1009 (1911). In that case, a young heifer strayed onto a railroad track and was hit by an oncoming train. The applicable law absolved the railroad of responsibility if the cow entered the area through an open gate on private property. But the railroad would be held responsible if the cow entered through the railroad's fence, which was in disrepair at the time of the incident. The owner of the cow sued the railroad for the value of the heifer. Undisputed evidence was presented that demonstrated both that the fence was down and that the gate was open. The defendant railroad moved for judgment as a matter of law. What result? Does it matter whether the heifer died closer to the down fence than to the open gate? The Supreme Court of Utah overturned a jury verdict for the plaintiff-respondent, holding that

> in order to entitle respondent to recover it was essential for her to show by a preponderance of the evidence that the cow entered upon the right of way through the broken down fence. This the respondent failed to do.
>
> We are of the opinion that the verdict . . . is not supported by the evidence, and that the trial court should have directed a verdict for appellant on that cause of action in accordance with appellant's request.

In the problem case, what evidence must the plaintiff widow enter in order to survive a motion for judgment as a matter of law by Ford? What must Ford show in order to defeat a motion for JMOL by Wylie? Is it necessary for Wylie to call auto mechanic McCoy or another expert witness? Would doing so be a reasonable expense for her? What other witnesses and documents might be necessary and admissible in this case? What kind of evidence will persuade the jury? The judge? Is there any evidence you think the plaintiff could have submitted to avoid the judge's order of remittitur?

2. *The Jury and Credibility.* In deciding the JMOL, the judge is to leave issues of credibility to the jury, unless no reasonable jury could believe one side of contested testimony.

Is plaintiff Karnes entitled to JMOL in the following case? He sues a police officer for stopping him and searching his car in violation of the Fourth Amendment; the police officer, Skrutski, says that he thought certain vegetable matter observed in the car was marijuana. Unless no jury could possibly believe the officer, the plaintiff is not entitled to JMOL. The appellate court gave this account of the testimony:

Q:    [on examination by Karnes's attorney] Let's talk a little bit about this green and brown vegetable matter. This was on various spots—over the floor of the car, isn't that right?

A:    [Skrutski] That's correct.

Q:    And it was quite obvious as you looked in the window you could see it, isn't that true?

A:    It was—it was there. It was visible. I don't know how obvious it was, sir.

Q:    Would you please take a look at page 21 of your deposition Mr. Skrutski—line 6. Question, "Well, are you saying you saw a couple of leaves or did you see it all over the interior of the car?" Answer, "It was in various spots on the vehicle floor." Question, "Quite obvious?" Answer, "Yes, it was."

App. at 382-383.

Q:    [on examination by Skrutski and Kowalski's attorney] And there was some discussion in your testimony [earlier] about a green/brown vegetable matter. Could you describe that?

A:    [Skrutski] It was—a green/brown vegetable matter that was—pulverized. There were very small pieces of it.

Q:    Based upon your training and experience, did you have any belief [at the time you were searching the bags Karnes consented to having you search] as to what it may have been?

A:    I suspected that it may have been marijuana.

App. At 407.

Karnes's testimony presents a different picture of the appearance of this "vegetable matter":

Q:    [on examination by Karnes's attorney] Okay. Let's talk about these leaves for a second. Because there is some mention in the police report of a green brown vegetable matter in your car. What was that exactly?

A:    [Karnes] . . . There wasn't just a little bit of leaves, there were leaves everywhere in there. We've driven around all weekend after doing this with the windows down in a state park. And there were—the only place in my car where there wasn't some of these leaves, was where I had been sitting in the seat.

App. at 189-190.

We believe this contradictory testimony creates a genuine issue of material fact, and we cannot say that a reasonable jury could never believe Skrutski's description and credit only Karnes's. The presence of drugs in plain view in an automobile creates probable cause to search, United States v. Burnett, 791 F.2d 64, 67 (6th Cir. 1986), and can support reasonable suspicion to conduct a further investigation. While the troopers were mistaken about the presence of marijuana, on the basis of this record we cannot say their mistake was unreasonable as a matter of law.

Karnes v. Skrutski, 62 F.3d 485, 498-499 (3d Cir. 1995); see also Valazquez v. City of Long Beach, 793 F.3d 1010, 1021 (9th Cir. 2015) (reversing grant of judgment as a matter of law to police officer where evidence at trial was sufficient for a jury to conclude that arrestee did not resist; district court improperly "disregarded evidence supporting Valazquez's version of events; improperly chose to credit the defense's witnesses over Valazquez's; made adverse credibility findings about Valazquez and his supporting witness; and refused to draw all reasonable inferences in Valazquez's favor"); but see Curley v. Klem, 499 F.3d 199, 209 (3d Cir. 2007) ("Our recent precedents say that the court, not a jury, should decide whether there is immunity in any given case.").

## Note: The Procedure for Moving for JMOL

In the problem case, the defendant moved early and often for judgment as a matter of law. This is the common practice, and indeed the legal point is often made on a motion for summary judgment before the trial even begins. It was held in Slocum v. New York Life Insurance Co., 228 U.S. 364 (1913), that the Seventh Amendment forbade the entry of a judgment contrary to a jury verdict. But in Baltimore & Carolina Line v. Redman, 295 U.S. 654 (1935), it was held that a ruling on a motion for a directed verdict could be postponed until after the jury had delivered its verdict. The language of Fed. R. Civ. P. 50(b) is written to use *Redman* for the purpose of overruling *Slocum*. It remains true, however, that a motion for a judgment as a matter of law made prior to the jury's deliberation is an indispensable prerequisite to the making of a successful renewed motion for judgment as a matter of law. See Starling v. Gulf Life Ins. Co., 382 F.2d 701 (5th Cir. 1967).

The points at which one may make a motion for judgment as a matter of law are outlined in the following chart:

Trial Begins

Opening Statements (a)

Plaintiff's Case Presented (b)

Defendant's Case Presented (c)

Rebuttal, If Any

Close of the Evidence (d)

    (a)  Rare, but parties can move after opening statements.
    (b)  Defendant may move at close of plaintiff's case. Plaintiff may also, but rarely does so, and even more rarely is such a motion granted.
    (c)  Either or both parties may move after the close of defendant's case.
    (d)  After presentation of all of the evidence, either or both parties may move or renew motions made earlier in the trial.

Indeed, the rule in many jurisdictions is that the parties *must renew* the motion at the close of the evidence, or they cannot make the renewed motion for judgment as a matter of law later, and cannot attack the sufficiency of the evidence on appeal.

Note that the judge can reserve ruling on the motion until after the jury has returned with its verdict. The judge almost always will do so, for efficiency reasons. If the jury returns a verdict that the judge considers against the great weight of the evidence, and the judge overturns the verdict by granting the JMOL, then there is a jury verdict to reinstate, should an appellate court disagree with the trial judge's ruling. If the jury never deliberates because the judge has granted a motion for judgment as a matter of law, then there is no verdict to reinstate, and a new trial will be necessary to correct for the trial judge's mistake—an avoidable expense.

The procedure for making a renewed motion for judgment as a matter of law (JNOV) in federal court is quite simple. First, the movant must have made or renewed a motion for judgment as a matter of law at the close of the evidence. Second, the renewed motion must be made within ten days after entry of the judgment. The judge who agrees that the evidence is insufficient to support the verdict has three options, however, when ruling on a renewed motion. She can: 1) direct entry of judgment in favor of the movant; 2) order a new trial; or 3) order a dismissal without prejudice under Fed. R. Civ. P. 41.

A party should always renew the motion for judgment as a matter of law if she wishes to appeal the denial of an earlier motion for judgment as a matter of law or the award of an opponent's motion. See Cone v. West Virginia Pulp & Paper, 330 U.S. 212 (1947).

## 3.   Starting Over: The New Trial Motion

### *Sanders-El v. Wencewicz*
987 F.2d 483 (8th Cir. 1993)

HEANEY, SENIOR CIRCUIT JUDGE.

In the morning of 19 May 1989 City of St. Louis police officers stopped the car driven by 22-year-old Sorkis Sanders-El pursuant to a warrant for his arrest. The officers arrested Sanders-El, handcuffed him, and put him in the back seat of a police vehicle. As one of the officers was closing the door of the vehicle, Sanders-El kicked it open and fled. The officers gave chase. When the officers reapprehended Sanders-El—who was still handcuffed—a struggle ensued during which Sanders-El sustained injuries to his eye, face, and head.

Sanders-El filed this action against the officers pursuant to 42 U.S.C. § 1983, alleging the officers used excessive force, depriving him of constitutional rights. A jury first heard the dispute in August 1991, but the magistrate judge declared a mistrial when the jury could not agree on a verdict. A second trial in December 1991 ended with a verdict in favor of the defendant police officers. Sanders-El appeals from the judgment entered on that verdict. We reverse and remand for a new trial.

Sanders-El argues there were numerous prejudicial errors in the trial below, including faulty evidentiary rulings, incomplete instructions to the jury, and racially biased peremptory challenges to members of the venire. What most troubles us, however, was the intentionally prejudicial conduct of defense counsel—particularly an incident in which defense counsel, when cross-examining the plaintiff about prior criminal convictions, dramatically dropped a lengthy computer printout in front of the jury.

The manifest intent of the conduct was to arouse the prejudices of the jury by leading it to believe Sanders-El had the conviction record of a veteran vocational criminal. Counsel conducted this piece of theatrics despite pretrial discussions in which the court indicated its intention not to admit such evidence. After objections by both the plaintiff and his counsel, the court excused the jury and admonished defense counsel against a repetition of the display:

> [T]he record should reflect that defense counsel . . . beginning to question the witness about his prior record dramatically dropped in front of the jury a computer printout of some approximately—what looks like about 10 feet of paper[—]then beginning to question the witness from it. That I think is uncalled for. It's not been shown to me that he has convictions which would warrant that kind of a display in front of the jury and I will caution you not to engage in such displays again in this lawsuit.

Vol. I Noce Trial Transcript at 142 (No. 89-1710-C(2)). Plaintiff also moved the court for sanctions and a mistrial, and the court denied the motion.

The standard of review applicable to a trial court's denial of a motion for mistrial is abuse of discretion. United States v. Muza, 788 F.2d 1309, 1312 (8th Cir. 1986). In appraising the trial court's exercise of its discretion, we bear in mind that "[i]mproper questioning by counsel 'generally entitles the aggrieved party to a new trial' if such questioning 'conveys improper information to the jury and [ . . . ] prejudices the opposing litigant.'" Williams v. Mensey, 785 F.2d 631, 637 (8th Cir. 1986) (quoting Harris v. Zurich Ins. Co., 527 F.2d 528, 531 (8th Cir. 1975)). . . .

Defendants cite 88 C.J.S. Trial § 199 (1955) for the proposition that improper conduct by counsel ordinarily is cured by rebuke or reprimand of counsel if the conduct is not repeated. The same authority, however, states in black letter that "[i]t is highly improper for counsel, acting in bad faith, to make statements or ask questions or engage in other conduct as to witnesses merely to prejudice his opponent's case before the jury." Id. § 162(b). Further, "[t]he misconduct of counsel may be such that its effect cannot be overcome by an admonition to the jury . . . [or] by rebuke or admonition of counsel . . . and in such case the court should grant a discontinuance, mistrial, withdrawal of a juror, discharge of the jury, or a new trial." Id. § 202.

It is not only the conscious impropriety of counsel here that we find troubling, but also the nature of the information counsel improperly intended to convey to the jury. Before the second trial commenced, the judge indicated that Sanders-El's prior felony convictions were admissible for impeachment purposes, but that it was his intention not to allow evidence of prior arrests or probation violations. This sound evidentiary ruling conforms to "[t]he long-standing rule in this circuit . . . that the credibility of a witness may not be impeached by showing that he has been accused of, charged with, or arrested for a crime which has not culminated in a conviction." United States v. Kirk, 496 F.2d 947, 949 (8th Cir. 1974). "This rule is based upon a clear recognition of the fact that the probative value of such evidence is so overwhelmingly outweighed by its inevitable tendency to inflame or prejudice the jury. . . ." United States v. Ling, 581 F.2d 1118, 1121 (4th Cir. 1978). Counsel nonetheless attempted to present the arrest record to the jury first by asking Sanders-El on cross-examination *which* arrest he had been referring to in Sanders-El's response to a prior question. After a sustained objection terminated this line of questioning, counsel continued his cross-examination until it culminated in the computer printout fiasco.

Whether errors had a significant prejudicial influence on the jury in a particular case admittedly is a fine question of judgment in which precedents give little guidance, for what may be harmless in a case where the evidence strongly favors one party may be fatally prejudicial in a close case. Fortunato v. Ford Motor Co., 464 F.2d 962, 976 (2d Cir. [1972]) (Mansfield, J., concurring and dissenting), *cert. denied,* 409 U.S. 1038 (1972). In appraising prejudicial remarks and conduct such as involved here, the court must consider "the climate of the contest in which it occurred." Westchester Fire Ins. Co. v. Hanley, 284 F.2d 409, 416 (6th Cir. 1960), *cert. denied,* 365 U.S. 869 (1961).

Even out of context we are dismayed at defense counsel's impertinence, and agree with the trial judge that the conduct was "uncalled for." If this were an isolated incident in a case in which the disputes were not as close, we might have difficulty finding prejudice. In this case, however, we encounter no such difficulty. First, the case was exceedingly close—so close that once already a jury could not agree. Second, the incident was neither isolated nor accidental. Counsel, knowing that such evidence was irrelevant and prejudicial, once already had alluded to the plaintiff's arrest record in front of the jury. After the court sustained the objection to that tactic, counsel resorted to the less candid but equally prejudicial theatrical display at issue. Third, the record does not reveal that the jury received any curative instruction. Left with the distinct impression that the plaintiff was a hardened criminal with a long history of arrests, the jury retired to consider its verdict without an instruction from the court to disregard such evidence in its deliberations. Fourth, as the case law instructs, the nature of this irrelevant evidence is especially prejudicial. Fifth, considering the climate of the contest, we note that this claim by a black plaintiff against white police officers rests largely on the word of Sanders-El against that of the police. Such a case, of necessity, brings the credibility of the witnesses sharply into focus — thus highlighting the significance of the resulting prejudice. See United States v. Pennix, 313 F.2d 524, 531 (4th Cir. 1963).

Considering all the circumstances of the case, we find prejudicial error in defense counsel's courtroom misconduct, and abuse of discretion in the trial court's denial of plaintiff's motion for a mistrial. The other alleged errors we do not reach. Accordingly, based on the foregoing, we reverse and remand for a new trial.

BOWMAN, CIRCUIT JUDGE, dissenting.

The ruling of a trial court on a motion for mistrial is subject to a deferential standard of review. United States v. Huff, 959 F.2d 731, 735 (8th Cir.), *cert. denied,* 113 S. Ct. 162 (1992). Such rulings are within the broad discretion of the trial court, and we will reverse the trial court only where an abuse of that discretion is shown. United States v. Culver, 929 F.2d 389, 391 (8th Cir. 1991).

Here, the trial court rebuked counsel for dropping the computer printout in front of the jury, and the offending conduct was not repeated. The jury was entitled to weigh plaintiff's prior convictions in assessing his credibility, and aside from anything improperly communicated to the jury about plaintiff's prior arrests, the jury knew by his own admission that he had not led a saintly life. The trial court was in a far better position than we are to make a well-informed judgment as to whether misconduct by the defendants' counsel had unfairly prejudiced the jury's attitude toward the plaintiff. The finding that it had not comes to us from an experienced and respected trial judge, and I see no compelling reason for this Court to disturb that finding.

It is all too easy for this Court, working from a cold record and applying broad principles of trial practice, to assign to events occurring during the course of trial a significance they did not actually have. That is precisely why a reviewing court should give broad deference to the ruling made by the trial court in matters of this sort. As I am unable to conclude that the trial court abused its discretion in denying plaintiff's motion for a mistrial, I would affirm the judgment entered on the jury verdict.

## Notes and Questions

1. *Problems Warranting Retrial.* Parties may move for a new trial for a range of reasons, including attorney or juror misconduct, prejudicial errors

in evidentiary rulings or jury instructions, or even that the verdict was contrary to the weight of the evidence (more on this below). The trial judge has great discretion in ruling on the motion and may even order a new trial *sua sponte.*

*Sanders-El* illustrates one of the grounds—attorney misconduct or mistakes—that may cause a judge to grant a new trial. Should attorneys be subject to personal discipline for these errors, regardless of the ruling on the new trial motion? Below, Professor Deborah Rhode summarizes several ethical norms that govern attorneys' trial behavior. Did defense counsel in *Sanders-El* violate any of these? What about the lawyer in the bereaved widow problem case?

Formal prohibitions include a ban on:

- engaging in conduct intended to disrupt a tribunal or to influence a juror by means prohibited by law (Model Rule [of Professional Responsibility] 3.5);
- engaging in undignified or discourteous conduct which is degrading to a tribunal (DR [Disciplinary Rule] 7-106(C)(6));
- communicating with a juror concerning a case at trial except in official proceedings (DR 7-108(A));
- alluding to any matter that the lawyer does not reasonably believe is relevant or that will not be supported by admissible evidence, asserting personal knowledge of facts in issue except when testifying as a witness, or stating a personal opinion as to the justness of a case, the credibility of a witness, the culpability of a civil litigant or the guilt or innocence of an accused (Model Rule 3.4(e) and DR 7-106(C));
- engaging in conduct involving dishonesty, fraud, deceit, misrepresentation, or conduct prejudicial to the administration of justice (DR 1-102).

In addition, other standards not codified as disciplinary rules provide that a lawyer:

- should not ask a witness a question "solely for the purpose of harassing or embarrassing him . . . and should not by subterfuge put before a jury matters which it cannot properly consider" (EC [Ethical Consideration] 7-25);
- should refrain from argument "calculated to inflame the passions or prejudices of the jury" or "divert the jury from its duty to decide the case on the evidence, by injecting issues broader than the guilt or innocence of the accused under the controlling law, or by making predictions of the consequences of the jury's verdict" (ABA Standards Relating to the Administration of Criminal Justice, The Prosecution Function, Standard 3-5.8).

Deborah L. Rhode, Professional Responsibility: Ethics by the Pervasive Method 710 (1994).

2. *Judges Versus Juries.* The judge may grant a new trial if she believes that the verdict was against the weight of the evidence. It seems fairly clear, moreover, that a new trial may be granted on this basis, even though the

evidence would withstand the JMOL motion. In other words, the judge could hold that a reasonable jury could find as it did, but that nonetheless, the verdict is against the weight of the evidence.

This gets tricky when a party argues that the reason the evidence is insufficient is that it is not worthy of belief. We have seen the deference the judge must give to the jury's credibility assessment on the motion for JMOL. What about a new trial motion on the ground that because the evidence is unbelievable, it is insufficient to support the verdict? Most courts hold that the trial judge may disbelieve the evidence and grant a new trial in the interest of justice. See, e.g., White v. Pence, 961 F.2d 776 (8th Cir. 1991) (reversing a trial judge who doubted his power to order a new trial even though he was dissatisfied with the defendant's evidence). On the other hand, the Second Circuit upheld a trial judge who refused a new trial even though he felt the defendant's evidence was "overwhelming," but the jury sided with the plaintiff. See Compton v. Luckenbach Overseas Corp., 425 F.2d 1130 (2d Cir. 1970) (upholding the trial judge's denial of the motion for a new trial).

3. *Deadlocked Juries.* Recall our discussion of the importance of the unanimity requirement. Juries sometimes stumble on the way to a verdict — clashing viewpoints and personalities can lead to stalemates in jury deliberation. Sometimes juries reach out to the judge for help, often by sending out a note indicating that they are deadlocked, unable to reach a verdict. A judge must be very careful in handling these situations — she cannot cross the line between reminding the jury of its charge and encouraging it to continue deliberating, on the one hand, and coercing jurors to agree on a verdict it would not otherwise have reached. Especially in criminal cases, courts are divided about using "modified *Allen* charges" — supplemental instructions read to deadlocked jurors to urge them to continue deliberations — because of concerns about judicial coercion of jurors. See Allen v. United States, 164 U.S. 492 (1896); see also United States v. Fioravanti, 412 F.2d 407, 419 (3d Cir. 1969) (describing use of *Allen* charge in criminal cases as a "supplemental or 'dynamite charge' to blast a hung jury into a verdict"; use of such a charge can be reversible error), *followed in* United States v. Eastern Medical Billing, Inc., 230 F.3d 600 (3d Cir. 2000). Controversy is considerably less sharp in civil trials. See Cary v. Allegheny Technologies Inc., 267 F. Supp. 2d 442, 447 (W.D. Pa. 2003) (denying motion for new trial in gender discrimination suit where judge read modified *Allen* instructions to break deadlocked jury; noting that plaintiff would be "disproportionately burdened by having to bear the expense of a retrial" and that, unlike criminal defendants, "[a] civil defendant does not face the loss of his liberty and is not entitled to the presumption of innocence").

4. *Appellate Review of the Grant of a New Trial.* If the trial judge grants a new trial, does the party opposing the motion have to go through the whole thing again before appealing? Yes, said the Court in Allied Chemical Corp. v. Daiflon, Inc., 449 U.S. 33 (1980). Note also that the motion for new trial, like the motion for JMOL, can be a use-it-or-lose-it motion. The Fifth Circuit

has construed Rule 50(c) to require that a party who wins on a motion for judgment as a matter of law but who does not press for a contemporaneous ruling on its alternative motion for a new trial waives any right to seek a new trial after any appellate reversal on the merits. The rationale is that requiring the party to seek a ruling on both motions assures that the appellate court can review both rulings in one appeal, thereby avoiding piecemeal litigation. See Arenson v. Southern University Law Center, 43 F.3d 194 (5th Cir. 1995).

Traditionally the granting of a new trial is a chance for the trial judge to correct his own errors, or those of the lawyers or the jury, while they are fresh in his mind, and without involving the appellate court. The denial of a new trial is, on the other hand, often grounds for appeal. If the appellate court finds the evidence insufficient, can it order a new trial, or must the appellate court remand for the trial judge to reconsider the Rule 50 motion? The next case answers that question, at least as to the appellate court's power to rule.

## 4. Appellate Review of Jury Verdicts

### *Weisgram v. Marley Co.*
528 U.S. 440 (2000)

Justice Ginsburg delivered the opinion for a unanimous Court.

This case concerns the respective authority of federal trial and appellate courts to decide whether, as a matter of law, judgment should be entered in favor of a verdict loser. The pattern we confront is this. Plaintiff in a product liability action gains a jury verdict. Defendant urges, unsuccessfully before the federal district court but successfully on appeal, that expert testimony plaintiff introduced was unreliable, and therefore inadmissible, under the analysis required by Daubert v. Merrell Dow Pharmaceuticals, Inc., 509 U.S. 579 (1993). Shorn of the erroneously admitted expert testimony, the record evidence is insufficient to justify a plaintiff's verdict. May the court of appeals then instruct the entry of judgment as a matter of law for defendant, or must that tribunal remand the case, leaving to the district court's discretion the choice between final judgment for defendant or a new trial of plaintiff's case?

Our decision is guided by Federal Rule of Civil Procedure 50, which governs the entry of judgment as a matter of law, and by the Court's pathmarking opinion in Neely v. Martin K. Eby Construction Co., 386 U.S. 317 (1967). As *Neely* teaches, courts of appeals should "be constantly alert" to "the trial judge's first-hand knowledge of witnesses, testimony, and issues"; in other words, appellate courts should give due consideration to the first-instance decision maker's "'feel' for the overall case." Id. at 325. But the court of appeals has authority to render the final decision. If, in the particular case, the appellate tribunal determines that the district court is better positioned to decide whether a new trial, rather than judgment for defendant, should be ordered, the court of appeals should return the case to the trial court for such an assessment. But if, as in the instant case, the court of appeals concludes that further proceedings are unwarranted because the loser on appeal has had a full and fair opportunity to present the case, including arguments for a new trial, the appellate court may appropriately instruct the district court to enter judgment against the jury-verdict winner. Appellate authority to make this determination is no less when the evidence is rendered insufficient by the removal of erroneously admitted testimony than it is when the evidence, without any deletion, is insufficient.

# I

Firefighters arrived at the home of Bonnie Weisgram on December 30, 1993, to discover flames around the front entrance. Upon entering the home, they found Weisgram in an upstairs bathroom, dead of carbon monoxide poisoning. Her son, petitioner Chad Weisgram, individually and on behalf of Bonnie Weisgram's heirs, brought a diversity action in the United States District Court for the District of North Dakota seeking wrongful death damages. He alleged that a defect in an electric baseboard heater, manufactured by defendant (now respondent) Marley Company and located inside the door to Bonnie Weisgram's home, caused both the fire and his mother's death.[1]

At trial, Weisgram introduced the testimony of three witnesses, proffered as experts, in an endeavor to prove the alleged defect in the heater and its causal connection to the fire. The District Court overruled defendant Marley's objections, lodged both before and during the trial, that this testimony was unreliable and therefore inadmissible under Federal Rule of Evidence 702 as elucidated by *Daubert*. At the close of Weisgram's evidence, and again at the close of all the evidence, Marley unsuccessfully moved under Federal Rule of Civil Procedure 50(a) for judgment as a matter of law on the ground that plaintiffs had failed to meet their burden of proof on the issues of defect and causation. The jury returned a verdict for Weisgram. Marley again requested judgment as a matter of law, and additionally requested, in the alternative, a new trial, pursuant to Rules 50 and 59; among arguments in support of its post-trial motions, Marley reasserted that the expert testimony essential to prove Weisgram's case was unreliable and therefore inadmissible. The District Court denied the motions and entered judgment for Weisgram. Marley appealed.

---

1. At trial and on appeal, the suit of the Weisgram heirs was consolidated with an action brought against Marley Company by State Farm Fire and Casualty Company, insurer of the Weisgram home, to recover benefits State Farm paid for the damage to the Weisgram townhouse and an adjoining townhouse. State Farm was dismissed from the appeal after certiorari was granted. For purposes of this opinion, we generally refer to the plaintiffs below, and to the petitioners before us, simply as "Weisgram."

The Court of Appeals for the Eighth Circuit held that Marley's motion for judgment as a matter of law should have been granted. Writing for the panel majority, Chief Judge Bowman first examined the testimony of Weisgram's expert witnesses, the sole evidence supporting plaintiffs' product defect charge. Concluding that the testimony was speculative and not shown to be scientifically sound, the majority held the expert evidence incompetent to prove Weisgram's case. The court then considered the remaining evidence in the light most favorable to Weisgram, found it insufficient to support the jury verdict, and directed judgment as a matter of law for Marley. In a footnote, the majority "reject[ed] any contention that [it was] required to remand for a new trial." It recognized its discretion to do so under Rule 50(d), but stated: "[W]e can discern no reason to give the plaintiffs a second chance to make out a case of strict liability. . . . This is not a close case. The plaintiffs had a fair opportunity to prove their claim and they failed to do so" (internal citations omitted). The dissenting judge disagreed on both points, concluding that the expert evidence was properly admitted and that the appropriate remedy for improper admission of expert testimony is the award of a new trial, not judgment as a matter of law (citing Midcontinent Broadcasting Co. v. North Central Airlines, Inc., 471 F.2d 357 (8th Cir. 1973)).

Courts of appeals have divided on the question whether Federal Rule of Civil Procedure 50 permits an appellate court to direct the entry of judgment as a matter of law when it determines that evidence was erroneously admitted at trial and that the remaining, properly admitted evidence is insufficient to constitute a submissible case.[2] We granted certiorari to resolve the conflict, 527 U.S. 1069 (1999),[3] and we now affirm the Eighth Circuit's judgment.

## II

Federal Rule of Civil Procedure 50 governs motions for judgment as a matter of law in jury trials. It allows the trial court to remove cases or issues from the

2. The Tenth Circuit has held it inappropriate for an appellate court to direct the entry of judgment as a matter of law based on the trial court's erroneous admission of evidence, because to do so would be unfair to a party who relied on the trial court's evidentiary rulings. See Kinser v. Gehl Co., 184 F.3d 1259, 1267, 1269 (10th Cir. 1999). The Fourth, Sixth, and Eighth Circuits recently have issued decisions, in accord with the position earlier advanced by the Third Circuit, directing the entry of judgment as a matter of law based on proof rendered insufficient by the deletion of improperly admitted evidence. See Redman v. John D. Brush & Co., 111 F.3d 1174, 1178-1179 (4th Cir. 1997); Smelser v. Norfolk Southern R. Co., 105 F.3d 299, 301, 306 (6th Cir. 1997); Wright v. Willamette Industries, Inc., 91 F.3d 1105, 1108 (8th Cir. 1996); *accord,* Aloe Coal Co. v. Clark Equipment Co., 816 F.2d 110, 115-116 (3d Cir. 1987).

3. We agreed to decide only the issue of the authority of a court of appeals to direct the entry of judgment as a matter of law, and accordingly accept as final the decision of the Eighth Circuit holding the testimony of Weisgram's experts unreliable, and therefore inadmissible under Federal Rule of Evidence 702, as explicated in Daubert v. Merrell Dow Pharmaceuticals, Inc., 509 U.S. 579 (1993). We also accept as final the Eighth Circuit's determination that the remaining, properly admitted, evidence was insufficient to make a submissible case under state law.

jury's consideration "when the facts are sufficiently clear that the law requires a particular result." 9A C. Wright & A. Miller, Federal Practice and Procedure § 2521, p. 240 (2d ed. 1995) (hereinafter Wright & Miller). Subdivision (d) [now at Rule 50(e).—EDs.] controls when, as here, the verdict loser appeals from the trial court's denial of a motion for judgment as a matter of law:

> [T]he party who prevailed on that motion may, as appellee, assert grounds entitling the party to a new trial in the event the appellate court concludes that the trial court erred in denying the motion for judgment. If the appellate court reverses the judgment, nothing in this rule precludes it from determining that the appellee is entitled to a new trial, or from directing the trial court to determine whether a new trial shall be granted.

Under this Rule, Weisgram urges, when a court of appeals determines that a jury verdict cannot be sustained due to an error in the admission of evidence, the appellate court may not order the entry of judgment for the verdict loser, but must instead remand the case to the trial court for a new trial determination. Nothing in Rule 50 expressly addresses this question.[5]

In a series of pre-1967 decisions, this Court refrained from deciding the question, while emphasizing the importance of giving the party deprived of a verdict the opportunity to invoke the discretion of the trial judge to grant a new trial. See Cone v. West Virginia Pulp & Paper Co., 330 U.S. 212, 216-218 (1947); Globe Liquor Co. v. San Roman, 332 U.S. 571, 573-574 (1948); Johnson v. New York, N.H. & H.R. Co., 344 U.S. 48, 54 n.3 (1952); see also 9A Wright & Miller, § 2540, at 370. Then, in *Neely*, the Court reviewed its prior jurisprudence and ruled definitively that if a motion for judgment as a matter of law is erroneously denied by the district court, the appellate court does have the power to order the entry of judgment for the moving party. 386 U.S. at 326; see also Louis, Post-Verdict Rulings on the Sufficiency of the Evidence. Neely v. Martin K. Eby Construction Co. Revisited, 1975 Wis. L. Rev. 503 (surveying chronologically Court's decisions bearing on appellate direction of judgment as a matter of law).

*Neely* first addressed the compatibility of appellate direction of judgment as a matter of law (then styled "judgment n.o.v.") with the Seventh Amendment's jury trial guarantee. It was settled, the Court pointed out, that a trial court, pursuant to Rule 50(b), could enter judgment for the verdict loser without offense to the Seventh Amendment. 386 U.S. at 321 (citing Montgomery Ward & Co. v. Duncan, 311 U.S. 243 (1940)). "As far as the

---

5. According to the Advisory Committee Notes to the 1963 Rule 50 amendments, this "omission" was not inadvertent:

> Subdivision (d) does not attempt a regulation of all aspects of the procedure where the motion for judgment n.o.v. and any accompanying motion for a new trial are denied, since the problems have not been fully canvassed in the decisions and the procedure is in some respects still in a formative stage. It is, however, designed to give guidance on certain important features of the practice.

Advisory Committee's Notes on Fed. Rule Civ. Proc. 50(d), 28 U.S.C. App., p. 769.

Seventh Amendment's right to jury trial is concerned," the Court reasoned, "there is no greater restriction on the province of the jury when an appellate court enters judgment n.o.v. than when a trial court does"; accordingly, the Court concluded, "there is no constitutional bar to an appellate court granting judgment n.o.v." 386 U.S. at 322 (citing Baltimore & Carolina Line v. Redman, 295 U.S. 654 (1935)). The Court next turned to "the statutory grant of appellate jurisdiction to the courts of appeals [in 28 U.S.C. § 2106],"[6] which it found "certainly broad enough to include the power to direct entry of judgment n.o.v. on appeal." 386 U.S. 322. The remainder of the *Neely* opinion effectively complements Rules 50(c) and 50(d), providing guidance on the appropriate exercise of the appellate court's discretion when it reverses the trial court's denial of a defendant's Rule 50(b) motion for judgment as a matter of law. Id. at 322-330; cf. supra, note 5 (1963 observation of Advisory Committee that, as of that year, "problems [concerning motions for judgment coupled with new trial motions] ha[d] not been fully canvassed").

*Neely* represents no volte-face in the Court's understanding of the respective competences of trial and appellate forums. Immediately after declaring that appellate courts have the power to order the entry of judgment for a verdict loser, the Court cautioned:

> "Part of the Court's concern has been to protect the rights of the party whose jury verdict has been set aside on appeal and who may have valid grounds for a new trial, some or all of which should be passed upon by the district court, rather than the court of appeals, because of the trial judge's first-hand knowledge of witnesses, testimony, and issues—because of his 'feel' for the overall case. These are very valid concerns to which the court of appeals should be constantly alert." 386 U.S. at 325.[7]

Nevertheless, the Court in *Neely* continued, due consideration of the rights of the verdict winner and the closeness of the trial court to the case "do[es] not justify an ironclad rule that the court of appeals should never order dismissal or judgment for the defendant when the plaintiff's verdict has been set aside on appeal." Id. at 326. "Such a rule," the Court concluded, "would

---

6. Section 2106 reads:

The Supreme Court or any other court of appellate jurisdiction may affirm, modify, vacate, set aside or reverse any judgment, decree, or order of a court lawfully brought before it for review, and may remand the cause and direct the entry of such appropriate judgment, decree, or order, or require such further proceedings to be had as may be just under the circumstances.

7. Iacurci v. Lummus Co., 387 U.S. 86 (1967) (per curiam), decided shortly after *Neely,* is illustrative. There, the Court reversed the appellate court's direction of the entry of judgment as a matter of law for the defendant and instructed the appeals court to remand the case to the trial court for a new trial determination; the Court pointed to the jury's failure to respond to four out of five special interrogatories, which left issues of negligence unresolved, and concluded that in the particular circumstances, the trial judge "was in the best position to pass upon the question of a new trial in light of the evidence, his charge to the jury, and the jury's verdict and interrogatory answers." Id. at 88.

not serve the purpose of Rule 50 to speed litigation and to avoid unnecessary retrials." Ibid. *Neely* ultimately clarified that if a court of appeals determines that the district court erroneously denied a motion for judgment as a matter of law, the appellate court may (1) order a new trial at the verdict winner's request or on its own motion, (2) remand the case for the trial court to decide whether a new trial or entry of judgment for the defendant is warranted, or (3) direct the entry of judgment as a matter of law for the defendant. Id. at 327-30; see also 9A Wright & Miller § 2540, at 371-72.

## III

The parties before us—and court of appeals opinions—diverge regarding *Neely*'s scope. Weisgram, in line with some appellate decisions, posits a distinction between cases in which judgment as a matter of law is requested based on plaintiff's failure to produce enough evidence to warrant a jury verdict, as in *Neely*, and cases in which the proof introduced becomes insufficient because the court of appeals determines that certain evidence should not have been admitted, as in the instant case. Insufficiency caused by deletion of evidence, Weisgram contends, requires an "automatic remand" to the district court for consideration whether a new trial is warranted.

Weisgram relies on cases holding that, in fairness to a verdict winner who may have relied on erroneously admitted evidence, courts confronting questions of judgment as a matter of law should rule on the record as it went to the jury, without excising evidence inadmissible under Federal Rule of Evidence 702. See, e.g., Kinser v. Gehl Co., 184 F.3d 1259, 1267, 1269 (10th Cir. 1999); Schudel v. General Electric Co., 120 F.3d 991, 995-96 (9th Cir. 1997); Jackson v. Pleasant Grove Health Care Center, 980 F.2d 692, 695-96 (11th Cir. 1993); Midcontinent Broadcasting, 471 F.2d, at 358. But see Lightning Lube, Inc. v. Witco Corp., 4 F.3d 1153, 1198-1200 (3d Cir. 1993). These decisions are of questionable consistency with Rule 50(a)(1), which states that in ruling on a motion for judgment as a matter of law, the court is to inquire whether there is any "legally sufficient evidentiary basis for a reasonable jury to find for [the opponent of the motion]." Inadmissible evidence contributes nothing to a "legally sufficient evidentiary basis." See Brooke Group Ltd. v. Brown & Williamson Tobacco Corp., 509 U.S. 209, 242 (1993) ("When an expert opinion is not supported by sufficient facts to validate it in the eyes of the law, or when indisputable record facts contradict or otherwise render the opinion unreasonable, it cannot support a jury's verdict.").[10]

---

10. Weisgram additionally urges that the Seventh Amendment prohibits a court of appeals from directing judgment as a matter of law on a record different from the one considered by the jury. *Neely* made clear that a court of appeals may order entry of judgment as a matter of law on sufficiency-of-the-evidence grounds without violating the Seventh Amendment. 386 U.S. at 321-322. Entering judgment for the verdict loser when all of the evidence was properly before the jury is scarcely less destructive of the jury's verdict than is entry of such a judgment based on a record made insufficient by the removal of evidence the jury should not have had before it.

As *Neely* recognized, appellate rulings on post-trial pleas for judgment as a matter of law call for the exercise of "informed discretion," 386 U.S. at 329, and fairness to the parties is surely key to the exercise of that discretion. But fairness concerns should loom as large when the verdict winner, in the appellate court's judgment, failed to present sufficient evidence as when the appellate court declares inadmissible record evidence essential to the verdict winner's case. In both situations, the party whose verdict is set aside on appeal will have had notice, before the close of evidence, of the alleged evidentiary deficiency. See Fed. Rule Civ. Proc. 50(a)(2) (motion for judgment as a matter of law "shall specify . . . the law and facts on which the moving party is entitled to the judgment"). On appeal, both will have the opportunity to argue in support of the jury's verdict or, alternatively, for a new trial. And if judgment is instructed for the verdict loser, both will have a further chance to urge a new trial in a rehearing petition.

Since *Daubert*, moreover, parties relying on expert evidence have had notice of the exacting standards of reliability such evidence must meet. 509 U.S. 579; see also Kumho Tire Co. v. Carmichael, 526 U.S. 137 (1999) (rendered shortly after the Eighth Circuit's decision in Weisgram's case); General Electric Co. v. Joiner, 522 U.S. 136 (1997). It is implausible to suggest, post-*Daubert*, that parties will initially present less than their best expert evidence in the expectation of a second chance should their first try fail. We therefore find unconvincing Weisgram's fears that allowing courts of appeals to direct the entry of judgment for defendants will punish plaintiffs who could have shored up their cases by other means had they known their expert testimony would be found inadmissible. In this case, for example, although Weisgram was on notice every step of the way that Marley was challenging his experts, he made no attempt to add or substitute other evidence. See Lujan v. National Wildlife Federation, 497 U.S. 871, 897 (1990) ("[A] litigant's failure to buttress its position because of confidence in the strength of that position is always indulged in at the litigant's own risk.").

After holding Weisgram's expert testimony inadmissible, the Court of Appeals evaluated the evidence presented at trial, viewing it in the light most favorable to Weisgram, and found the properly admitted evidence insufficient to support the verdict. 169 F.3d at 516-517. Weisgram offered no specific grounds for a new trial to the Eighth Circuit.[13] Even in the petition for rehearing, Weisgram argued only that the appellate court had misapplied state law, did not have the authority to direct judgment, and had failed to give adequate deference to the trial court's evidentiary rulings. The Eighth Circuit concluded that this was "not a close case." 169 F.3d at 517 n.2. In these circumstances, the Eighth Circuit did not abuse its discretion

13. Cf. Neely v. Martin K. Eby Constr. Co., 386 U.S. 317, 327 (1967) (observing that it would not be clear that litigation should be terminated for evidentiary insufficiency when, for example, the trial court excluded evidence that would have strengthened the verdict winner's case or "itself caused the insufficiency . . . by erroneously [imposing] too high a burden of proof").

by directing entry of judgment for Marley, instead of returning the case to the District Court for further proceedings. . . .

*Neely* recognized that there are myriad situations in which the determination whether a new trial is in order is best made by the trial judge. 386 U.S. at 325-326. *Neely* held, however, that there are also cases in which a court of appeals may appropriately instruct the district court to enter judgment as a matter of law against the jury-verdict winner. Id. at 326. We adhere to *Neely's* holding and rationale, and today hold that the authority of courts of appeals to direct the entry of judgment as a matter of law extends to cases in which, on excision of testimony erroneously admitted, there remains insufficient evidence to support the jury's verdict.

For the reasons stated, the judgment of the Court of Appeals for the Eighth Circuit is affirmed.

### Notes and Questions

1. Weisgram *Versus* Neely: *The Path to Greater Control of Juries?* The Court in *Weisgram* relied on its holding in Neely v. Eby Construction Co., 386 U.S. 317 (1967). But there are significant differences between the two cases. *Neely* affirmatively answered the question of whether, faced with insufficient evidence to support a jury verdict, an appellate court could enter judgment as a matter of law without remanding the case to the district court. In *Weisgram*, the Court went a step further. Here, the Court held that an appellate court can enter judgment as a matter of law when expert testimony was admitted into evidence but was later judged unreliable and therefore inadmissible, and the plaintiff had no other evidence to support a verdict. Thus, the plaintiff loses the chance to present her case differently, as she presumably would have had she known at trial that her preferred expert evidence was inadmissible.

Does *Weisgram* lead to more control of juries, if the trial judge's evaluation of expert evidence can now be taken over by the appellate court? What could the bereaved widow have done in the problem case had an appellate court rejected the expert testimony admitted by the trial judge and ordered that she take nothing?

In Unitherm Food Systems, Inc. v. Swift-Eckrich, Inc., 546 U.S. 394 (2006), the Supreme Court held that a party loses its chance to challenge the sufficiency of the evidence on appeal if it fails to renew its motion for judgment as a matter of law or request a new trial after the verdict. The appellate court has no power to take up the sufficiency of the evidence just because there was a proper Rule 50(a) motion during trial.

2. *The Special Role of Experts.* As we have seen, judges have a special duty to assess the credibility of scientific testimony before allowing the witness to testify as an expert. Daubert v. Merrell Dow Pharmaceuticals, Inc., 509 U.S. 579 (1993). Is the holding in *Weisgram* limited to such scientific experts? Even if it is so limited, it would still affect a great number of cases because the use of experts is so widespread. What latitude should the trial judge

be given to second-guess the jury's view of expert witness credibility in granting a motion for a new trial? This question is complicated by the fact that the trial judge is, in a sense, second-guessing his earlier ruling that the witness was qualified under *Daubert*.

The Supreme Court rejected de novo review of the trial court's application of *Daubert* in General Electric Co. v. Joiner, 522 U.S. 136 (1997), reaffirming the general rule that "abuse of discretion" applies to decisions to admit or exclude expert scientific evidence. For a discussion of *Joiner* and *Daubert*, see Michael H. Gottesman, From *Barefoot* to *Daubert* to *Joiner*: Triple Play or Double Error?, 40 Ariz. L. Rev. 753 (1998). Note that *Daubert* raises a difficult definitional problem: whether the evidence in question is "scientific" versus "nonscientific." The applicability of *Daubert* to the latter category of expert testimony was addressed by the Court in Kumho Tire Co. v. Carmichael, 526 U.S. 137 (1999). The Court concluded that where a mechanical engineer's expert testimony was grounded in personal experience working for a tire manufacturer, the *Daubert* factors—the disputed theory's testability, publication, rate of error, and general acceptance among experts in the relevant field—did apply. But see Marron v. Stromstad, 123 P.3d 992 (Alaska 2005); CSX Transp., Inc. v. Miller, 858 A.2d 1025 (Md. 2004); Watson v. INCO Alloys Int'l, Inc., 545 S.E.2d 294 (2001); West Virginia Div. of Highways v. Butler, 516 S.E.2d 769 (1999).

The ambiguities created by *Daubert* have prompted changes to Federal Rule of Evidence 702, "Testimony by Experts." The amended rule provides as follows:

> If scientific, technical, or other specialized knowledge will assist the trier of fact to understand the evidence or to determine a fact in issue, a witness qualified as an expert by knowledge, skill, experience or training, or education, may testify thereto in the form of an opinion or otherwise if *(1) the testimony is based upon sufficient facts or data, (2) the testimony is the product of reliable principles and methods, and (3) the witness has applied the principles and methods reliably to the facts of the case.*

(New language in italics.)

The Advisory Committee Notes to the amendment indicate that the amendment is designed to resolve the issue presented in *Kumho Tire Co.* as follows:

> The amendment does not distinguish between scientific and other forms of expert testimony. The trial court's gatekeeping function applies to testimony by any expert. . . . While the relevant factors for determining reliability will vary from expertise to expertise, the amendment rejects the premise that an expert's testimony should be treated more permissively simply because it is outside the realm of science. An opinion from an expert who is not a scientist should receive the same degree of scrutiny for reliability as an opinion from an expert who purports to be a scientist.

In *Weisgram*, the lower courts concluded that the expert testimony admitted was not reliable. Moreover, no other grounds had been offered to support a new trial, so the Eighth Circuit directed the entry of judgment. What if the district court fails to make findings of relevance and reliability as required by *Daubert* before admitting expert evidence? In Estate of Barabin v. AstenJohnson, Inc., 740 F.3d 457 (9th Cir. 2013) (en banc), the Ninth Circuit concluded that the proper remedy is a new trial. Plaintiff sued AstenJohnson for injuries arising from exposure to asbestos while working with dryer felts in a paper mill. The district court failed to make appropriate findings of relevance and reliability as to two plaintiff experts called to establish that plaintiff's exposure was the result of working with the paper felts. The jury awarded plaintiff more than $10 million. On appeal, the Ninth Circuit held that it was an abuse of discretion to admit the expert testimony without the findings required by *Daubert*. It remanded the case for a new trial, following the traditional rule favoring a new trial when a district court has "erroneously admitted or excluded prejudicial evidence." Id. at 466. The Ninth Circuit would have directed the entry of judgment only if the trial record had been detailed enough to make informed decisions about admissibility and the sufficiency of the remaining evidence.

Five judges of the en banc panel dissented, arguing that the proper procedure would be to remand for a *Daubert* hearing and reinstate the verdict if the expert evidence, upon full *Daubert* review, is deemed admissible. Id. at 471. Only if a *Daubert* hearing established that the expert testimony should have been excluded would a new trial be warranted.

## 5.   Excessive Verdicts

### a.   Prejudice, Passion, and Punitive Damages

#### *Curtis Publishing Co. v. Butts*
351 F.2d 702 (5th Cir. 1965)

SPEARS, CIRCUIT JUDGE.

This is a libel suit. Curtis Publishing Company published an article in the March 23, 1963 issue of the Saturday Evening Post entitled "The Story of a College Football Fix," characterized by the Post in the subtitle as "A Shocking Report of How Wally Butts and 'Bear' Bryant Rigged a Game Last Fall."

On March 25, 1963, Wally Butts, former Athletic Director of the University of Georgia, instituted this action against Curtis. In August, 1963, the case was heard before a jury, which returned a verdict against Curtis for $60,000 general and $3,000,000 punitive damages. Conditioned upon the failure of Butts to remit that portion of the award for punitive damages in excess of $400,000, the trial court granted Curtis' motion for new trial. At the same time, Curtis' motion for judgment notwithstanding the verdict was denied. On January 22, 1964, after Butts had filed a remittitur, Curtis' motion for new trial was denied, and judgment for Butts in the amount of $460,000 was entered. Thereafter, Curtis filed motions for new trial under Rule 60(b),

F. R. Civ. P., which were denied on April 7, 1964. This appeal is taken from the judgment of January 22, 1964, and from the trial court's denial of Curtis' motions for judgment notwithstanding the verdict and for new trial. We affirm.

Curtis publishes various magazines including the Post. Prior to the publication of the story in question, the editor-in-chief, undoubtedly hoping to attract more readers, had decided to "change the image" of the magazine by making it an "exposé" type, and embarking upon a policy of "sophisticated muckraking," in order "to provoke people" and "make them mad."

The article involved was based upon a claim by one George Burnett that on September 13, 1962 he had accidentally overheard, and made notes of, a long-distance telephone conversation between Butts and "Bear" Bryant, football coach at the University of Alabama, in which Butts divulged certain information about football plays the University of Georgia would use in its opening game against Alabama. Georgia was subsequently defeated 35-0.

About four months after the alleged telephone conversation Burnett contacted various people, including Georgia football coach Johnny Griffith, and then decided to tell his story to the Post. A writer, Frank Graham, Jr., was assigned by the Post to investigate and write the story, and an Atlanta sports editor was retained to advise him. Graham never saw Burnett's notes, as they were at the time in the possession of Georgia school officials; he did not interview a witness known by him to have allegedly discussed the notes with Burnett on the same day the telephone conversation purportedly took place; he never viewed the game films; and neither he nor anyone else on behalf of the Post ever contacted Butts or Bryant. He agreed that both he and Curtis knew publication of the article "would ruin Coach Butts' career."

On March 11, 1963, eleven days before the article was published, Curtis was informed by telegram and letter, both sent by Butts' counsel, of the "absolute falsity of the charges" contained in the proposed story. The record does not disclose that any additional investigation was initiated, and the telegram and letter went unanswered. In addition, a long-distance telephone appeal that the article not be published, made by Butts' daughter prior to publication, was rejected. After the article was published, Curtis refused a demand that it publish a retraction.

The Post took the position from the beginning that the statements made in the article concerning Butts were true, and that because of their nature it had exercised great care by thoroughly checking every significant source of information as to their truthfulness and accuracy, in advance of publication.

Curtis chose not to use as a witness either the author of the article or any of its editors who had made contributions to the article after it had been submitted. Nor did it use the Atlanta sports editor who had assisted in the preparation of the story. As one of its principal witnesses it called upon George Burnett, who was known by Curtis to have been convicted of writing bad checks, and to be on probation at the time he claimed to have listened in on the conversation.

Both Butts and Bryant testified. Each emphatically denied the charges contained in the article and stated that there was never any conversation between them having as its purpose the fixing or rigging of any football game. Several football players, past and present, expressed their opinions to the effect that the outcome of a football game cannot be rigged or fixed without participation by the players themselves, and that there is no way in which two coaches can rig or fix the outcome of a football game without the players' knowledge. Other "experts" stated their opinion that the information contained in the "so-called" Burnett notes would not be of any assistance at all to the University of Alabama in preparing for its game with the University of Georgia. In several instances Butts' witnesses denied direct quotations attributed to them in the article. . . .

Curtis submits twenty-eight specifications of error. . . . The issues involved are: . . . (3) Did the arguments of Butts' counsel, not objected to at the trial, require a new trial? . . .

The trial judge gave his reasons for requiring the remittitur of all punitive damages in excess of $400,000. There is not the slightest suggestion that he thought, or even intimated, that the larger award was based on passion or prejudice. On the contrary, fully aware of the distinction between a verdict excessive in amount which may be reduced by remittitur, and one resulting from improper influences such as passion and prejudice which may not be corrected in this way, the judge necessarily rejected the idea that this verdict had been infected by such destructive elements. . . .

The trial judge had the duty of determining whether as a matter of law (a) any allowance for punitive damages could be made, and (b) what the maximum would be. As to (a), the trial court not only expressed the opinion that the article was extremely defamatory, and that the jury had no choice other than to find Curtis liable, but he also thought that there was "ample evidence from which a jury could have concluded that there was reckless disregard by defendant of whether the article was false or not." Upon determining (b) he had then to decide whether to grant a new trial or require a remittitur as to the excess. The latter is a permissible course and does not infringe upon the Seventh Amendment's guaranty of a jury trial. In making his determination as to (b), he pursued the correct standard of keeping the verdict "within reasonable bounds considering the purpose to be achieved as well as the corporate defendant's wanton or reckless indifference to the plaintiff's rights." Obviously, in deciding the matter the judge had to pick a dollar figure beyond which the law would not go. He selected the sum of $400,000 as the maximum which the law would accept to deter Curtis from repeating the trespass or to compensate the wounded feelings of Butts. Although the reduction required, and the sum remaining, were each substantial, there was ample basis for the trial court's judgment.

To have granted a new trial might appear to have been an easier way out. But that is really no solution. On a retrial, the judge could not instruct the next jury as to the dollar maximum of any such verdict. So that jury would be pretty much on its own, under the unavoidably vague, elastic standards prescribed in the Code, as measured by the enlightened conscience of an impartial jury. The trial judge, on the second trial, would then be forced to repeat the process of testing for (a) and (b). If, as urged by Curtis, the determination by the judge that the amount is too much, necessarily means a new trial, it is quite possible that the case would never end. Georgia has prescribed the "punishment" for aggravated willful torts. The law ought not to frustrate the vindication of that policy by an unrealistic procedure. The jury verdict, as reviewed and reduced by the trial judge, is the tortfeasor's assurance that such damages will not exceed that which the law would tolerate to achieve the Georgia objective of deterring repetition or compensating wounded feelings.

This is no ordinary libel case. The publication of the article by the Post, in the face of several specific appeals that it refrain from doing so, was part and parcel of a general policy of callousness, which recognized from the start that Butts' career would be ruined. The trial judge's appraisal of the evidence, with which we are in complete accord, was that it was sufficiently strong to justify the jury in concluding that what the Post did was done with reckless disregard of whether the article was false or not.

The case was fully developed during extensive pretrials, and in a jury trial lasting two weeks. The record itself comprises 1613 pages. We have given full consideration to the entire record, as well as to the more than 650 pages of briefs submitted by both parties, the numerous authorities cited therein, and the oral arguments of counsel. We think that Curtis has had its day in court. It apparently thought so too until the jury verdict was returned. This is attested by the fact that practically all of its present complaints were not even raised until after the trial.

Believing and so finding that the trial was fair, and that the judgment of the trial court was correct and proper in all respects, it is

*Affirmed.*

RIVES, CIRCUIT JUDGE (dissenting). . . .

The punitive damages, either as found by the jury or as fixed by the court, are many times greater in amount than the general damages. Under the court's instructions to the jury, the general damages included compensation "for the mental anguish, pain, mortification, and humiliation he has experienced as a result of the publication." . . . The punitive damages included no element to which the plaintiff was entitled by way of compensation, but, according to the court's instruction to the jury, "the purpose of punitive damages is to deter the defendant from a repetition of the offense and is a warning to others not to commit a like offense. It is intended to protect the community and has an expression of ethical indignation, although the plaintiff receives the award." . . .

For yet another reason the award of $3,000,000 by the jury, or of $400,000 by the court, as punitive damages is unconstitutional and void. There was no semblance of definite standard or controlling guide to govern the award. Can any standard be more vague or arbitrary than "an expression of ethical indignation" first on the part of the jury and then on the part of the trial judge? It must be remembered that stricter standards of permissible vagueness are applicable to a rule having a potentially inhibiting effect on freedom of the press than are applicable to rules relating to less important subjects.

Still further, I submit that the remittitur violates the defendant's rights under the Seventh Amendment. The trial judge concluded "that the award for punitive damages in this case was grossly excessive. It is the court's considered opinion that the maximum sum for punitive damages that should have been awarded against Curtis Publishing Company should be $400,000.00." . . . In another part of his opinion on motion for new trial, the district judge commented: "The award for punitive damages in the case under consideration is more than seventeen times larger than the highest award for punitive damages ever sustained." The district judge's opinion is silent as to the underlying reason for such a grossly excessive verdict. The majority opinion says that ". . . the judge necessarily rejected the idea that the verdict had been infected by such destructive elements [as passion or prejudice]." With deference, I submit that that conclusion is not based on the record or on anything said by the trial judge. . . .

. . . [I]t seems to me that "[t]he public interest requires that the court of its own motion, as is its power and duty, protect suitors in their right to a verdict, uninfluenced by the appeals of counsel to passion or prejudice." New York Central R.R. Co. v. Johnson, 1929, 279 U.S. 310, 318. That would be true even if the prejudicial argument had not been followed by a grossly excessive verdict. I submit that the $3,000,000 punitive damage verdict was so clearly the result of passion and prejudice that it could not be cured by remittitur. . . .

## b. Additur and Remittitur

Both the problem case and *Curtis Publishing* are examples of remittitur, in which a judge trims a jury verdict that is grossly excessive as a matter of law. The judge may condition the denial of a new trial motion on the plaintiff remitting a portion of the award. The flip side of remittitur is additur, in which the court increases an inadequate verdict.

In Dimick v. Schiedt, 293 U.S. 474 (1934), it was held that the practice of sustaining inadequate verdicts if the defendant should agree to pay a somewhat larger sum was violative of the Seventh Amendment. Is there a plausible distinction between additur and remittitur in the degree to which they offend the right to jury trial? A difference may be said to exist that results from the unanimity requirement; inadequate damages may reflect a compromise. The Court in the *Dimick* case also conceded that remittitur practice was too well established to be repudiated at so late a time. Nevertheless, additurs have been employed in a few exceptional federal cases. See, e.g., Rocky Mountain Tool & Machine Co. v. Tecon Corp., 371 F.2d 589 (10th Cir. 1966). Many state courts regularly employ additurs as well as remittiturs. Indeed, the Wisconsin practice rules once condoned new trial orders that were doubly conditional. If the defendant did not exercise the option of paying a sum deemed by the trial judge to be a reasonable maximum, then the plaintiff was given the option of accepting a reasonable minimum; if both refused the court's proposals, a new trial resulted. This practice was abandoned in Powers v. Allstate Insurance Co., 102 N.W. 393 (1960).

## c.  The Role of the Appellate Court in Administering Remittitur

### *Donovan v. Penn Shipping Co.*
429 U.S. 648 (1977)

PER CURIAM.

The petitioner, while employed by the respondents as a seaman on the SS *Penn Sailor,* slipped on wet paint, injuring his right wrist and elbow. He sued the respondents under the Jones Act, 46 U.S.C. § 688, and obtained a $90,000 verdict at his jury trial. The respondents moved to set aside the verdict as excessive. Fed. Rules Civ. Proc. 50, 59. The District Court granted the motion, and ordered a new trial on damages unless the petitioner agreed to remit $25,000 of the $90,000 award.

After some time the petitioner submitted to the District Court a proposed order stating that he accepted "under protest" the reduced verdict of $65,000, but reserving nonetheless "his right to appeal therefrom." This language was adopted by the District Court in entering a judgment for the petitioner in the amount of $65,000.

The petitioner sought appellate review of the District Court's decision to order a conditional new trial. In so doing he asked the Court of Appeals for the Second Circuit to discard the settled rule that a plaintiff who has accepted a remittitur may not appeal to seek reinstatement of the original verdict. The Court of Appeals refused the petitioner's invitation, and dismissed the appeal. 536 F.2d 536.

The Court of Appeals properly followed our precedents in holding that a plaintiff cannot "protest" a remittitur he has accepted in an attempt to open it to challenge on appeal. A line of decisions stretching back to 1889 has firmly established that a plaintiff cannot appeal the propriety of a remittitur order to which he has agreed.

There are decisions in the Federal Courts of Appeals that depart from these unbroken precedents. Those decisions held or intimated that a plaintiff who accepts a remittitur "under protest" may challenge on appeal the correctness of the remittitur order. Other decisions have suggested that when entertaining cases pursuant to its diversity jurisdiction, a federal court should look to state practice to determine whether such an appeal is permitted.

The proper role of the trial and appellate courts in the federal system in reviewing the size of jury verdicts is, however, a matter of federal law, see Hanna v. Plumer, 380 U.S. 460, 466-469 (1965); Byrd v. Blue Ridge Rural Electric Coop., 356 U.S. 525 (1958), and that law has always prohibited appeals in the situation at bar. The Court of Appeals for the Second Circuit correctly adhered to the consistent rule established by this Court's decisions. In order to clarify whatever uncertainty might exist, we now reaffirm the longstanding rule that a plaintiff in federal court, whether prosecuting a state or federal cause of action, may not appeal from a remittitur order he has accepted.

The petition for a writ of certiorari is granted, and the judgment is *affirmed*.

THE CHIEF JUSTICE and JUSTICE BLACKMUN would grant the petition for certiorari but would have the case argued and given plenary consideration rather than disposed of summarily.

### d.   Excessive Verdicts and Due Process

An issue that has been at the forefront of proposed civil litigation reforms is that of allegedly excessive jury verdicts. Thus far, proposed federal legislation that would cap punitive damages awards has not been adopted. The legislative murmurings, though, are an important backdrop to a trilogy of U.S. Supreme Court cases in the 1990s that addressed the due process limits on punitive damages awards, and that displayed sharp divisions among the Justices about federal constitutional limits on these awards.

In the first of these cases, Pacific Mutual Life Insurance Co. v. Haslip, 499 U.S. 1 (1991), the Court concluded that the common-law method for assessing punitive damages did not in itself violate due process, but that this was "not the end of the matter." Id. at 18. The instructions to the jury must make clear the purpose of punitive damages, which is not to compensate the plaintiff but to punish the defendant and deter the defendant and others from engaging in similar misconduct. While juries have discretion in making these awards, their discretion must be exercised within reasonable constraints. Posttrial and appellate review of such awards helps to assure that the awards do not exceed the bounds of reason. Indeed, the Court noted, the Alabama Supreme Court had weighed several factors in determining whether the punitive damage award in *Haslip* was excessive:

> (a) whether there is a reasonable relationship between the punitive damages award and the harm likely to result from the defendant's conduct as well as the harm that actually has occurred; (b) the degree of reprehensibility of the defendant's conduct, the duration of that conduct, the defendant's awareness, any concealment, and the existence and frequency of similar past conduct; (c) the profitability to the defendant of the wrongful conduct and the desirability of removing that profit and of having the defendant also sustain a loss; (d) the "financial position" of the defendant; (e) all the costs of litigation; (f) the imposition of criminal sanctions on the defendant for its conduct, these to be taken in mitigation; and (g) the existence of other civil awards against the defendant for the same conduct, these also to be taken in mitigation.

The application of these standards, we conclude, imposes a sufficiently definite and meaningful constraint on the discretion of Alabama fact finders in awarding punitive damages. The Alabama Supreme Court's post-verdict review ensures that punitive damages awards are not grossly out of proportion to the severity of the offense and have some understandable relationship to compensatory damages. . . .

Id. at 21-22.

The Court returned to the constitutionality of punitive damages in TXO Production Corp. v. Alliance Resources Corp., 509 U.S. 443 (1993). *TXO* involved a deal between TXO and Alliance Resources over a potentially lucrative tract of land in West Virginia, which TXO hoped to mine for gas and oil. Shortly after concluding the deal, TXO discovered that a previous owner of the site had severed and sold the right to mine coal there. There was no claim made by any of the owners of the coal rights that their interest extended to gas or oil. TXO nevertheless took a quitclaim deed from one of them. It then challenged Alliance's title, finally bringing an action in a West Virginia court for a declaratory judgment against Alliance. Alliance counterclaimed for slander of title.

The court decided the claim adversely to TXO, holding that the Alliance title to the oil and gas was clear. It submitted the counterclaim to trial by jury. Finding that it had cost Alliance $19,000 to defend the declaratory judgment action, it awarded compensatory damages in that amount. It also awarded Alliance punitive damages in the amount of $10,000,000. Judgment entered on that amount was affirmed by the West Virginia Supreme Court of Errors.

Certiorari was granted and the judgment was affirmed. The Court was too divided on the merits to produce an opinion of the Court. Justices Stevens, Blackmun, and Rehnquist held that the amount of the verdict was not so gross as to offend standards of due process, given the evidence that TXO was striving to renegotiate a mineral lease that had been very generous, and could have profited substantially had its tactic worked. They also concluded that it was not constitutionally objectionable for the jury to be allowed to consider the wealth of the defendant in setting the proper amount of the punishment to be imposed. And they held that the following instruction was not unconstitutionally vague:

> In addition to actual or compensatory damages, the law permits the jury, under certain circumstances, to make an award of punitive damages, in order to punish the wrongdoer for his misconduct, to serve as an example or warning to others not to engage in such conduct and to provide additional compensation for the conduct to which the injured parties have been subjected.
>
> If you find from a preponderance of the evidence that TXO Production Corp. is guilty of wanton, wilful, malicious or reckless conduct which shows an indifference to the right of others, then you may make an award of punitive damages in this case.
>
> In assessing punitive damages, if any, you should take into consideration all of the circumstances surrounding the particular occurrence, including the nature of the wrongdoing, the extent of the harm inflicted, the intent of the party committing the act, the wealth of the perpetrator, as well as any

mitigating circumstances which may operate to reduce the amount of the damages. The object of such punishment is to deter TXO Production Corp. and others from committing like offenses in the future. Therefore the law recognizes that to in fact deter such conduct may require a larger fine upon one of large means than it would upon one of ordinary means under the same or similar circumstances.

Id. at 464 n.29.

Justice Kennedy concurred in the result:

To ask whether a particular award of punitive damages is grossly excessive begs the question: excessive in relation to what? The answer excessive in relation to the conduct of the tortfeasor may be correct, but it is unhelpful, for we are still bereft of any standard by which to compare the punishment to the malefaction that gave rise to it. A reviewing court employing this formulation comes close to relying upon nothing more than its own subjective reaction to a particular punitive damages award in deciding whether the award violates the Constitution. This type of review, far from imposing meaningful, law-like restraints on jury excess, could become as fickle as the process it is designed to superintend. Furthermore, it might give the illusion of judicial certainty where none in fact exists, and, in so doing, discourage legislative intervention that might prevent unjust punitive awards.

Id. at 466-467.

Justices Scalia and Thomas concurred in the judgment, holding that the Fourteenth Amendment cannot be read to limit punitive damages. It is not "the secret repository of all sorts of other, unenumerated, substantive rights." Id. at 470.

Justices White and Souter joined in Justice O'Connor's dissent:

In my view, due process at least requires judges to engage in searching review where the verdict discloses such great disproportions as to suggest the possibility of bias, caprice, or passion. . . .

A comparison of this award and prior ones in West Virginia confirms its unusual nature: It is 20 times larger than the highest punitive damages award *ever* upheld in West Virginia history for any misconduct. . . . Although TXO's conduct was clearly wrongful, calculated, and improper, the award in this case cannot be upheld as a reasoned retributive response. Not only is it greatly in excess of the actual harm caused, but it is 10 times greater than the largest punitive damages award for the same tort in any jurisdiction. . . .

Id. at 481-482.

Finally, the Court in 1996 decided BMW of North America, Inc. v. Gore, 517 U.S. 559 (1996), a case involving a national car distributor's failure to disclose that certain automobiles had been repainted. Dr. Ira Gore purchased a black BMW sports sedan for $40,750.88 from an authorized BMW dealer. He later learned that the car had been repainted, and sued the American distributor of BMW automobiles for $500,000 in compensatory and punitive damages, and costs.

Dr. Gore's actual damage estimate was $4,000. He argued at trial that a punitive award of $4 million would be an appropriate penalty given that the distributor allegedly sold approximately 1,000 cars without disclosing that they had been repainted.

The jury agreed, and assessed BMW $4,000 in compensatory damages and $4 million in punitive damages, on the ground that the nondisclosure policy of BMW constituted fraud under Alabama law. The trial judge denied BMW's posttrial motion to set aside the punitive damages award as excessive. The Alabama Supreme Court upheld that determination, though it reduced the award to $2 million on the ground that the jury improperly computed the punitive damages.

The United States Supreme Court reversed, holding that the $2 million award was grossly excessive and therefore violated due process. Justice Stevens, writing for the majority, concluded as follows:

> Elementary notions of fairness enshrined in our constitutional jurisprudence dictate that a person receive fair notice not only of the conduct that will subject him to punishment but also of the severity of the penalty that a State may impose. Three guideposts, each of which indicates that BMW did not receive adequate notice of the magnitude of the sanction that Alabama might impose for adhering to the nondisclosure policy adopted in 1983, lead us to the conclusion that the $2 million award against BMW is grossly excessive: the degree of reprehensibility of the nondisclosure; the disparity between the harm or potential harm suffered by Dr. Gore and his punitive damages award; and the difference between this remedy and the civil penalties authorized or imposed in comparable cases. . . .
>
> The $2 million in punitive damages awarded to Dr. Gore by the Alabama Supreme Court is 500 times the amount of his actual harm as determined by the jury. Moreover, there is no suggestion that Dr. Gore or any other BMW purchaser was threatened with any additional potential harm by BMW's nondisclosure policy. The disparity in this case is thus dramatically greater than those considered in *Haslip* and *TXO.*
>
> Of course, we have consistently rejected the notion that the constitutional line is marked by a simple mathematical formula, even one that compares actual *and potential* damages to the punitive award. *TXO,* 509 U.S., at 458. Indeed, low awards of compensatory damages may properly support a higher ratio than high compensatory awards, if, for example, a particularly egregious act has resulted in only a small amount of economic damages. A higher ratio may also be justified in cases in which the injury is hard to detect or the monetary value of noneconomic harm might have been difficult to determine. It is appropriate, therefore, to reiterate our rejection of a categorical approach. Once again, "we return to what we said . . . in *Haslip*: 'We need not, and indeed we cannot, draw a mathematical bright line between the constitutionally acceptable and the constitutionally unacceptable that would fit every case. We can say, however, that [a] general concer[n] of reasonableness . . . properly enter[s] into the constitutional calculus.'" *TXO,* 509 U.S., at 458 (quoting *Haslip,* 499 U.S., at 18). In most cases, the ratio will be within a constitutionally acceptable range, and remittitur will not be justified on this basis. When the ratio is a breathtaking 500 to 1, however, the award must

surely "raise a suspicious judicial eyebrow." *TXO,* 509 U.S., at 482 (O'Connor, J., dissenting).

Id. at 574-575, 582-583.

In a concurring opinion joined by Justices O'Connor and Souter, Justice Breyer observed that the due process protection against excessive verdicts not only provides citizens notice of what actions might subject them to punishment; "it also helps to assure the uniform, general treatment of similarly situated persons that is the essence of the law itself." He continued:

> Legal standards need not be precise in order to satisfy this constitutional concern. But they must offer some kind of constraint upon a jury or court's discretion, and thus protection against purely arbitrary behavior. The standards the Alabama courts applied here are vague and open-ended to the point where they risk arbitrary results. In my view, although the vagueness of those standards does not, by itself, violate due process, it does invite the kind of scrutiny the Court has given the particular verdict before us. This is because the standards, as the Alabama Supreme Court authoritatively interpreted them here, provided no significant constraints or protection against arbitrary results.

Id. at 587-588 (Breyer, J., concurring).

Justice Scalia, joined by Justice Thomas, dissented on the ground that concern about punitive damages run wild was not of constitutional moment, and that "the Court's activities in this area are an unjustified incursion into the province of state governments." Id. at 598 (Scalia, J., dissenting). Even if it were the Court's concern, however, Justice Scalia would have objected to the imposition of a standard as vague and manipulative as the "three guideposts" standard offered by the majority.

Justice Ginsburg likewise dissented, in a separate opinion joined by Chief Justice Rehnquist. She agreed with Justice Scalia that the majority had "venture[d] into territory traditionally within the States' domain, and . . . in the face of reform measures recently adopted or currently under consideration in legislative arenas." Id. at 607 (Ginsburg, J., dissenting). In her view, the Alabama Supreme Court had faithfully applied *Haslip* and *TXO;* the United States Supreme Court thus should have let its judgment stand, in deference to "the Court's longstanding reluctance to countenance review, even by courts of appeals, of the size of verdicts returned by juries in federal district court proceedings." Id. at 613.

On remand, after considering awards in comparable cases involving fraud in the sale of an automobile, the Alabama Supreme Court recalculated the punitive damages at $50,000. The court held that a new trial was warranted unless the plaintiff filed a remittitur of the remainder of the damages. Dr. Gore accepted the remittitur in September 1997. See BMW of N.A. Inc. v. Gore, 701 So. 2d 507 (Ala. 1997); see also State Farm Mutual Auto. Ins. Co. v. Campbell, 538 U.S. 408 (2003) (applying the three-part test of *Gore* to strike down a punitive damages award of $145 million against an insurer for bad faith refusal to settle, fraud, and intentional infliction of emotional distress). The United States Supreme Court returned to the issue of appellate review of punitive damages awards in Cooper Industries, Inc. v. Leatherman Tool Group, Inc., 532 U.S. 424 (2001). It held that the United States Constitution requires de novo appellate review of the "three guideposts" of *Gore.* This is in contrast to the usual appellate deference to lower court findings of fact.

More recently, the Supreme Court invalidated a $79.5 million state court punitive damages verdict in a case brought by a smoker against the cigarette manufacturer Philip Morris, alleging fraud and deceit. Philip Morris USA v. Williams, 549 U.S. 346 (2007) (although juries may consider harm to third parties in deciding how "reprehensible" defendant's conduct was, a punitive damages award is unconstitutional to the extent that it is based on the jury's desire to punish defendant for harm to persons other than the plaintiff). The Court also reduced the $4.5 billion in punitive damages awarded for the Exxon Valdez oil spill to an amount equal to the $507.5 million compensatory damages award. Exxon Shipping Co. v. Baker, 554 U.S. 471 (2008) (purporting to follow maritime common law in adopting a 1:1 ratio of punitive to compensatory damages). Justice Breyer wrote separately to emphasize his disagreement with the way the Court applied its new standard:

> In my view, a limited exception to the Court's 1:1 ratio is warranted here. As the facts set forth in Part I of the Court's opinion make clear, this was no mine-run case of reckless behavior. The jury could reasonably have believed that Exxon knowingly allowed a relapsed alcoholic repeatedly to pilot a vessel filled with millions of gallons of oil through waters that provided the livelihood for the many plaintiffs in this case. Given that conduct, it was only a matter of time before a crash and spill like this occurred. And as Justice Ginsburg points out, the damage easily could have been much worse.

Id. at 525 (Breyer, J., concurring in part and dissenting in part).

How would you describe the competing interests in these due process cases? Has the Court offered an intelligible standard for due process review of punitive damages awards? Is it any less vague than the other due process standards that you encountered in Chapter 1?

For an empirical analysis of jury awards and the difference between awards in judge-tried and jury-tried cases, see Theodore Eisenberg et al., Juries, Judges, and Punitive Damages: An Empirical Study, 87 Cornell L. Rev. 743 (2002) (showing no substantial difference in the rate at which judges and juries award punitive damages or in the relationship between sizes of punitive and compensatory awards); Seth A. Seabury et al., Forty Years of Jury Verdicts, 1 J. Empirical Legal Stud. 1, 22-23 (2004) (finding that the rate of increase in average jury awards since 1960 is less than the growth in real GDP over the same period: "Our results suggest little evidence to support the hypothesis that juries are awarding substantially higher awards on average. . . . On the surface, it seems difficult to reconcile this statement with the kind of headline-grabbing awards that have occurred over the past decade. One explanation for this is that, away from the headlines, the awards in some cases have declined and offset the growth in the larger and more highly publicized awards."); see also Aaron Hiller, Rule 11 and Tort Reform: Myth, Reality, and Legislation, 18 Geo. J. Legal Ethics 809, 818 (2005) ("As the amount of litigation on the docket has declined, so have the jury awards so often decried as outrageous and skyrocketing by tort reformers. The median jury award in 2001 was $37,000, representing a 43.1% decrease over the previous decade. Limiting that analysis only to tort cases, the median jury award stood at $28,000, a 56.3% drop since 1992. Moreover, juries rarely award punitive damages at all—less than 3% of all plaintiff winners in tort trials were awarded punitive damages; the median award was $38,000.").

If the findings of these studies are correct, why have courts constitutionalized their worries over excessive verdicts? On the other hand, if judge-tried cases result in similar awards, why do plaintiffs' lawyers so often balk at bench trials?

In the *Baker* case, Justice Souter offered the following survey of the empirics on punitive damages:

American punitive damages have been the target of audible criticism in recent decades, see, e.g., Note, Developments, The Paths of Civil Litigation, 113 Harv. L. Rev. 1783, 1784-88 (2000) (surveying criticism), but the most recent studies tend to undercut much of it. A survey of the literature reveals that discretion to award punitive damages has not mass-produced runaway awards, and although some studies show the dollar amounts of punitive-damages awards growing over time, even in real terms, by most accounts the median ratio of punitive to compensatory awards has remained less than 1:1. Nor do the data substantiate a marked increase in the percentage of cases with punitive awards over the past several decades. The figures thus show an overall restraint and suggest that in many instances a high ratio of punitive to compensatory damages is substantially greater than necessary to punish or deter.

The real problem, it seems, is the stark unpredictability of punitive awards. Courts of law are concerned with fairness as consistency, and evidence that the median ratio of punitive to compensatory awards falls within a reasonable zone, or that punitive awards are infrequent, fails to tell us whether the spread between high and low individual awards is acceptable. The available data suggest it is not. A recent comprehensive study of punitive damages awarded by juries in state civil trials found a median ratio of punitive to compensatory awards of just 0.62:1, but a mean ratio of 2.90:1 and a standard deviation of 13.81. Juries, Judges, and Punitive Damages 269. Even to those of us unsophisticated in statistics, the thrust of these figures is clear: the spread is great, and the outlier cases subject defendants to punitive damages that dwarf the corresponding compensatories. The distribution of awards is narrower, but still remarkable, among punitive damages assessed by judges: the median ratio is 0.66:1, the mean ratio is 1.60:1, and the standard deviation is 4.54. Ibid. Other studies of some of the same data show that fully 14% of punitive awards in 2001 were greater than four times the compensatory damages, see Cohen 5, with 18% of punitives in the 1990s more than trebling the compensatory damages, see Ostrom, Rottman, & Goerdt, A Step Above Anecdote: A Profile of the Civil Jury in the 1990s, 79 Judicature 233, 240 (1996). And a study of "financial injury" cases using a different data set found that 34% of the punitive awards were greater than three times the corresponding compensatory damages. Financial Injury Jury Verdicts 333.

544 U.S. at 500.

Assuming Justice Souter has properly described "the real problem," are you convinced that the Constitution requires the Court to intervene and correct jury verdicts? Does the risk of an unpredictably high punitive damages award have its own deterrent effect on defendants accustomed to pricing harm so as to internalize it as part of the cost of doing business?

## 6. Anticipating Jury Verdicts

Given the large dollar values at stake in much civil litigation, it is not surprising that parties and lawyers invest time and money to determine the likely action of a jury in an individual case. Jury research firms compile statistical data on the quantifiable factors involved in jury trials, notably the verdict and the likely monetary award. Well-heeled individual litigants such as large corporations may also choose to conduct mock trials with mock juries in order to predict how a jury might receive certain facts or styles of presentation. A plethora of research has also been conducted on the selection of jurors, in an attempt to predict the verdict likely to be reached by juries of different racial, ethnic, and sexual compositions. This information, in turn, is used by parties to negotiate settlements with insurance companies and other defendants, to plan the presentation of a trial, or to choose between a bench or jury trial.

In the problem case, the bereaved widow, the corporate defendant would be more likely to have the resources to consult jury research firms and possibly conduct a mock trial. What kind of jurors might Ford have sought in hopes of a take-nothing verdict, or at least one lower than $800,000? Could a mock trial have helped Ford choose what evidence to present? Might Christian, the defense counsel, have chosen to alter her style of questioning if mock jurors reacted as unfavorably to her as did Juror 7?

Jury Verdict Research, a legal publishing company, has compiled a database analyzing 90,000 jury verdicts in personal injury cases nationwide, with which, they claim, the statistical likelihood of a plaintiff's winning, as well as the amount of money a jury will award, can be predicted. A snapshot of the results, reported in the New York Times, follows.

**Gauging the Chances of Winning**

Factors that determine the outcome of typical cases.

- *The size of a jury award varies by location.*

CASE 1:   A 35-year-old man falls on the ice in a department store parking lot in Berks Country, Pa. He fractures his ankle and hurts his wrist. His medical expenses are $5,000.
PROBABILITY OF WINNING: 67 percent
LIKELY AWARD: $51,404

CASE 2:   The same individual has the same type of accident and the same medical expenses, but the accident occurs in Manhattan.
PROBABILITY OF WINNING: 67 percent
LIKELY AWARD: $56,120

- *The probability of winning a personal injury suit varies with the type of accident and ranges from a little over 30 percent to a little over 90 percent. Medical malpractice suits are the hardest to win, but the awards are more generous.*

CASE 1:   A man, 35, fractures his forearm in a boating accident. His medical costs are $5,000. He sues the Berks County, Pa., retail store that sold him the boat.
PROBABILITY OF WINNING: 92 percent
LIKELY AWARD: $51,884

CASE 2:   Same circumstances, but the 35-year-old man sues his doctor for not properly setting the fracture.
PROBABILITY OF WINNING: 33 percent
LIKELY AWARD: $59,500

- *In wrongful death suits (and in cases involving severely disabling injuries) juries place a higher cash value on female victims than they do on male victims.*

CASE 1:   A married woman, 30, with no children, is killed when a construction company ladder falls on her in Berks County. Her yearly salary was $25,000.
PROBABILITY OF WINNING: 35 percent
LIKELY AWARD: $1,198,208

CASE 2:   Same circumstances, but the victim is a man.
PROBABILITY OF WINNING: 35 percent
LIKELY AWARD: $678,700

- *Young adults and middle-aged people tend to receive much larger awards than elderly people, primarily because the younger ones suffer greater loss of wages and, in some cases, because they have to live longer with the pain and suffering from an accident.*

CASE 1:   An 18-year-old man becomes a quadriplegic by diving into [a] partly filled swimming pool.

PROBABILITY OF WINNING: 55 percent
LIKELY AWARD: $3,369,251

CASE 2:    A 60-year-old becomes a quadriplegic in the same kind of swimming pool accident.
PROBABILITY OF WINNING: 55 percent
LIKELY AWARD: $2,817,885

Compiling Data, and Giving Odds, on Jury Awards, N.Y. Times, Jan. 21, 1994, at B12.

## 7. Trials in the Courtroom of the Future

Discussions of the trial process evoke images of a judge and jury presiding over a trial presented by live lawyers, with live witnesses and immediate cross-examination. Technological advances are already changing that picture. Electronic images—the "virtual courtroom"—are complementing, and may even supplant, the traditional courtroom scene. Parties already are submitting some claims to "virtual juries" for adjudication online and taking part in online settlement initiatives. See, e.g., Michael Liedtke, New Online Niche: Settling Complaints, Patriot Ledger (Quincy, Mass.), May 1, 2000, at 27; Carolyn Said, Net Services Referee Disputes Between Online Sellers, Buyers, S.F. Chron., June 12, 2000, at C1.

Even in brick-and-mortar courthouses, witnesses can now testify from a distance, thus reducing expensive scheduling conflicts. Documents can be displayed in ways that may enhance their effectiveness, and courtroom computers help trial attorneys organize and present evidence. Rather than reading back testimony, the increasingly popular use of videotaped depositions allows an attorney to impeach a witness with his own image at the touch of a button. Litigators in high-stakes patent cases commission extremely expensive graphics, such as animations intended to demonstrate mechanical processes to judges and jurors.

For explorations of the impact of computer technology on litigation, including the speculation that "[a] trial will normally be a movie presentation," see Paul D. Carrington, Virtual Civil Litigation: A Visit to John Bunyan's Celestial City, 98 Colum. L. Rev. 1516, 1525 (1998). Consider, in this respect, a court's decision to grant a motion to conduct an entire trial via video conferencing. See Edwards v. Logan, 38 F. Supp. 2d 463 (W.D. Va. 1999), discussed at 67 U.S.L.W. 1489 (Feb. 12, 1999). In this case, Michael S. Edwards filed a § 1983 excessive force civil rights lawsuit against officials of a Virginia prison where he was an inmate, claiming he had been forced to take part in a fistfight against a guard. Meanwhile, Edwards was transferred from Virginia to New Mexico to serve out the rest of his sentence. The court decided to conduct the trial by video conference for security reasons and to save the estimated $8,652 it would cost to bring Edwards to Virginia for trial.

Visual evidence in the form of video re-enactment, PowerPoint graphics, and other interactive digital video displays now profoundly influence the ways in which judges and juries interact with and synthesize facts. See N. Feigenson, Visual Evidence, 17 Psyconomic Bulletin and Review 149 (2010); Gregory P. Joseph, Modern Visual Evidence (2005).

## F. ALTERNATIVE DECISION MAKERS

### Problem Case: An Injured Quarterback

You are consulted by Sam Wyoming, a professional football quarterback and member of a health maintenance organization (HMO), who has suffered the loss of use of his throwing arm, perhaps as the result of a negligent diagnosis by one of the group doctors. Although nearing the end of his playing life, Sam might well have had several more good seasons. At the time Sam joined the health care group he signed a standard form contract that contained the following clause:

#### Arbitration of Claims

Any claim arising from the violation of a legal duty incident to this Agreement shall be submitted to binding arbitration if said claim is made on account of death or bodily injury arising out of the rendition or failure to render services under this Agreement, irrespective of the legal theory on which the claim is asserted.

In the event of arbitration, the Member will designate one arbitrator, the Group will designate another, and the two arbitrators thus named will select a third who shall be the chair of the board of arbitration. If the two arbitrators named by the parties are unable to agree on a third arbitrator, the office will be filled by appointment by the American Arbitration Association.

Sam, who is a popular figure in the area, would much prefer a jury trial. Although he had the services of a "sports lawyer" at the time he joined the HMO, he did not ask her to read the contract, nor was he aware of the presence of the clause.

Would you advise him to proceed with the arbitration or to go ahead and file suit? What considerations would enter into your decision?

Thus far, we have been dealing with the resolution of disputes in traditional public settings, where the government pays the judge, or the judge and jury, to make individual decisions in furtherance of the public's broad interest in the administration of justice. But this process is breaking down in many areas, particularly because of the costs of delay, of emotional trauma to the litigants, and of justice no longer recognizable.

The late 1980s and early 1990s saw an unprecedented rise of alternative dispute resolution (ADR) in public and private spheres at both the state and federal levels. The arbitration caseload of the American Arbitration Association, the largest provider of arbitration services in the United States, grew from

92,000 in 1988 to 136,000 in 1999. The caseload of another major ADR provider grew 2,300 percent from 1987 to 1993, averaging 1,200 cases a month in 1993 alone. See Cameron L. Sabin, The Adjudicatory Boat Without a Keel: Private Arbitration and the Need for Public Oversight of Arbitrators, 87 Iowa L. Rev. 1337, 1339-1340 (2002). This movement toward more informal methods of dispute resolution has continued and is now one of the most significant modern civil justice developments. See Thomas J. Stipanovich, Arbitration: The "New Litigation," 2010 U. Ill. L.J. 1. While there are many permutations of ADR, a few basic questions focus our study: What kind of process is being called for? Is participation mandatory or voluntary? Is the decision to use alternative processes purely private, or is it mandated by a court ("court-annexed")?

Given the expansion of private systems for resolving disputes, it is important to understand ADR's contours and to think critically about its consequences. In what kinds of cases would it be preferable to resolve a dispute through more traditional litigation? By what standards should a trade-off in values be measured in a given case? Does a given ADR procedure implicate constitutional rights to due process, equal protection, the right to a jury trial, or other constitutional guarantees? Does the emphasis on developing alternative processes inhibit the development of the traditional public system?

Although we will deal in this chapter only with the two most widely used alternative dispute resolution systems — arbitration and mediation — there are many other formats for deciding disputes without judges or juries. The concluding portion of this section deals with these other methods, and also offers a critique of ADR.

After you have completed these materials, you should return to the opening problem of the book ("The Due Process Game"). Would ADR satisfy your procedural desires in this scenario? If so, what form of ADR would you prefer and why?

## 1. Arbitration

### *Gilmer v. Interstate/Johnson Lane Corp.*
500 U.S. 20 (1991)

JUSTICE WHITE delivered the opinion of the Court.

The question presented in this case is whether a claim under the Age Discrimination in Employment Act of 1967 (ADEA), 81 Stat. 602, as amended, 29 U.S.C. §§ 621 et seq., can be subjected to compulsory arbitration pursuant to an arbitration agreement in a securities registration application. The Court of Appeals held that it could, 895 F.2d 195 (C.A.4 1990), and we affirm.

### I

Respondent Interstate/Johnson Lane Corporation (Interstate) hired petitioner Robert Gilmer as a Manager of Financial Services in May 1981. As required by his employment, Gilmer registered as a securities representative with several stock exchanges, including the New York Stock Exchange (NYSE). His registration application, entitled "Uniform Application for Securities Industry Registration or Transfer," provided, among other things, that Gilmer "agree[d] to arbitrate any dispute, claim or controversy" arising between him and Interstate "that is required to be arbitrated under the rules, constitutions or by-laws of the organizations with which I register." Of relevance to this case, NYSE Rule 347 provides for arbitration of "[a]ny controversy between a registered representative and any member or member organization arising out of the employment or termination of employment of such registered representative."

Interstate terminated Gilmer's employment in 1987, at which time Gilmer was 62 years of age. After first filing an age discrimination charge with the Equal Employment Opportunity Commission (EEOC), Gilmer subsequently brought suit in the United States District Court for the Western District of North Carolina.

In response to Gilmer's complaint, Interstate filed in the District Court a motion to compel arbitration of the ADEA claim.

The District Court denied Interstate's motion, based on this Court's decision in Alexander v. Gardner-Denver Co., 415 U.S. 36 (1974), and because it concluded that "Congress intended to protect ADEA claimants from the waiver of a judicial forum." The United States Court of Appeals for the Fourth Circuit reversed, finding "nothing in the text, legislative history, or underlying purposes of the ADEA indicating a congressional intent to preclude enforcement of arbitration agreements." 895 F.2d at 197. We granted certiorari, 498 U.S. 809 (1990), to resolve a conflict among the Courts of Appeals regarding the arbitrability of ADEA claims.[1]

## II

The FAA [Federal Arbitration Act] was originally enacted in 1925, 43 Stat. 883, and then reenacted and codified in 1947 as Title 9 of the U.S. Code. Its purpose was to reverse the longstanding judicial hostility to arbitration agreements that had existed at English common law and had been adopted by American courts, and to place arbitration agreements upon the same footing as other contracts. Dean Witter Reynolds Inc. v. Byrd, 470 U.S. 213, 219-220, and n.6 (1985); Scherk v. Alberto-Culver Co., 417 U.S. 506, 510, n.4 (1974). Its primary substantive provision states that "[a] written provision in any maritime transaction or a contract evidencing a transaction involving commerce to settle by arbitration a controversy thereafter arising out of such contract or transaction . . . shall be valid, irrevocable, and enforceable, save upon such grounds as exist at law or in equity for the revocation of any contract." 9 U.S.C. § 2. The FAA also provides for stays of proceedings

---

1. Compare the decision below with Nicholson v. CPC Int'l Inc., 877 F.2d 221 (C.A.3 1989).

in federal district courts when an issue in the proceeding is referable to arbitration, § 3, and for orders compelling arbitration when one party has failed, neglected, or refused to comply with an arbitration agreement, § 4. These provisions manifest a "liberal federal policy favoring arbitration agreements." Moses H. Cone Memorial Hospital v. Mercury Construction Corp., 460 U.S. 1, 24 (1983).

It is by now clear that statutory claims may be the subject of an arbitration agreement, enforceable pursuant to the FAA. Indeed, in recent years we have held enforceable arbitration agreements relating to claims arising under the Sherman Act, 15 U.S.C. §§ 1-7; § 10(b) of the Securities Exchange Act of 1934, 15 U.S.C. § 78j(b); the civil provisions of the Racketeer Influenced and Corrupt Organizations Act (RICO), 18 U.S.C. §§ 1961 et seq.; and § 12(2) of the Securities Act of 1933, 15 U.S.C. § 77l(2). See Mitsubishi Motors Corp. v. Soler Chrysler-Plymouth, Inc., 473 U.S. 614 (1985); Shearson/American Express Inc. v. McMahon, 482 U.S. 220 (1987); Rodriguez de Quijas v. Shearson/American Express, Inc., 490 U.S. 477 (1989). In these cases we recognized that "[b]y agreeing to arbitrate a statutory claim, a party does not forgo the substantive rights afforded by the statute; it only submits to their resolution in an arbitral, rather than a judicial, forum." *Mitsubishi,* 473 U.S. at 628.

Although all statutory claims may not be appropriate for arbitration, "[h]aving made the bargain to arbitrate, the party should be held to it unless Congress itself has evinced an intention to preclude a waiver of judicial remedies for the statutory rights at issue." Ibid. In this regard, we note that the burden is on Gilmer to show that Congress intended to preclude a waiver of a judicial forum for ADEA claims. See *McMahon,* 482 U.S. at 227. If such an intention exists, it will be discoverable in the text of the ADEA, its legislative history, or an "inherent conflict" between arbitration and the ADEA's underlying purposes. See ibid. Throughout such an inquiry, it should be kept in mind that "questions of arbitrability must be addressed with a healthy regard for the federal policy favoring arbitration." *Moses H. Cone,* 460 U.S. at 24.

## III

Gilmer concedes that nothing in the text of the ADEA or its legislative history explicitly precludes arbitration. He argues, however, that compulsory arbitration of ADEA claims pursuant to arbitration agreements would be inconsistent with the statutory framework and purposes of the ADEA. Like the Court of Appeals, we disagree.

### A

Congress enacted the ADEA in 1967 "to promote employment of older persons based on their ability rather than age; to prohibit arbitrary age discrimination in employment; [and] to help employers and workers find ways of meeting problems arising from the impact of age on employment."

29 U.S.C. § 621(b). To achieve those goals, the ADEA, among other things, makes it unlawful for an employer "to fail or refuse to hire or to discharge any individual or otherwise discriminate against any individual with respect to his compensation, terms, conditions, or privileges of employ- ment, because of such individual's age." § 623(a)(1). This proscription is enforced both by private suits and by the EEOC. In order for an aggrieved individual to bring suit under the ADEA, he or she must first file a charge with the EEOC and then wait at least 60 days. § 626(d). An individual's right to sue is extinguished, however, if the EEOC institutes an action against the employer. § 626(c)(1). Before the EEOC can bring such an action, though, it must "attempt to eliminate the discriminatory practice or practices alleged, and to effect voluntary compliance with the requirements of this chapter through informal methods of conciliation, conference, and persuasion." § 626(b); see also 29 C.F.R. § 1626.15 (1990).

As Gilmer contends, the ADEA is designed not only to address indi- vidual grievances, but also to further important social policies. See, e.g., EEOC v. Wyoming, 460 U.S. 226, 231 (1983). We do not perceive any inherent inconsistency between those policies, however, and enforcing agreements to arbitrate age discrimination claims. It is true that arbitration focuses on specific disputes between the parties involved. The same can be said, however, of judicial resolution of claims. Both of these dispute resolution mechanisms nevertheless also can further broader social purposes. The Sherman Act, the Securities Exchange Act of 1934, RICO, and the Securities Act of 1933 all are designed to advance important public policies, but, as noted above, claims under those statutes are appropriate for arbitration. "[S]o long as the prospective litigant effectively may vindicate [his or her] statutory cause of action in the arbitral forum, the statute will continue to serve both its remedial and deterrent function." *Mitsubishi*, supra, at 637.

We also are unpersuaded by the argument that arbitration will under- mine the role of the EEOC in enforcing the ADEA. An individual ADEA claimant subject to an arbitration agreement will still be free to file a charge with the EEOC, even though the claimant is not able to institute a private judicial action. Indeed, Gilmer filed a charge with the EEOC in this case. In any event, the EEOC's role in combating age discrimination is not depen- dent on the filing of a charge; the agency may receive information concern- ing alleged violations of the ADEA "from any source," and it has indepen- dent authority to investigate age discrimination. . . .

Gilmer also argues that compulsory arbitration is improper because it deprives claimants of the judicial forum provided for by the ADEA. Congress, however, did not explicitly preclude arbitration or other nonjudicial resolu- tion of claims, even in its recent amendments to the ADEA. "[I]f Congress intended the substantive protection afforded [by the ADEA] to include pro- tection against waiver of the right to a judicial forum, that intention will be deducible from text or legislative history." *Mitsubishi*, 473 U.S. at 628. Moreover, Gilmer's argument ignores the ADEA's flexible approach to resolution of claims. The EEOC, for example, is directed to pursue "informal methods of conciliation, conference, and persuasion," 29 U.S.C. § 626(b), which suggests that out-of-court dispute resolution, such as arbitration, is consistent with the statutory scheme established by Congress. . . .

## B

In arguing that arbitration is inconsistent with the ADEA, Gilmer also raises a host of challenges to the adequacy of arbitration procedures. Initially, we note that in our recent arbitration cases we have already rejected most of these arguments as insufficient to preclude arbitration of statutory claims. . . .

Gilmer first speculates that arbitration panels will be biased. However, "[w]e decline to indulge the presumption that the parties and arbitral body conducting a proceeding will be unable or unwilling to retain competent, conscientious and impartial arbitrators." *Mitsubishi,* supra, at 634. In any event, we note that the NYSE arbitration rules, which are applicable to the dispute in this case, provide protections against biased panels. The rules require, for example, that the parties be informed of the employment histories of the arbitrators, and that they be allowed to make further inquiries into the arbitrators' backgrounds. In addition, each party is allowed one peremptory challenge and unlimited challenges for cause. Moreover, the arbitrators are required to disclose "any circumstances which might preclude [them] from rendering an objective and impartial determination." . . .

Gilmer also complains that the discovery allowed in arbitration is more limited than in the federal courts, which he contends will make it difficult to prove discrimination. It is unlikely, however, that age discrimination claims require more extensive discovery than other claims that we have found to be arbitrable, such as RICO and antitrust claims. Moreover, there has been no showing in this case that the NYSE discovery provisions, which allow for document production, information requests, depositions, and subpoenas, will prove insufficient to allow ADEA claimants such as Gilmer a fair opportunity to present their claims. Although those procedures might not be as extensive as in the federal courts, by agreeing to arbitrate, a party "trades the procedures and opportunity for review of the courtroom for the simplicity, informality, and expedition of arbitration." *Mitsubishi,* supra, at 628. Indeed, an important counterweight to the reduced discovery in NYSE arbitration is that arbitrators are not bound by the rules of evidence.

A further alleged deficiency of arbitration is that arbitrators often will not issue written opinions, resulting, Gilmer contends, in a lack of public knowledge of employers' discriminatory policies, an inability to obtain effective appellate review, and a stifling of the development of the law. The NYSE rules, however, do require that all arbitration awards be in writing, and that the awards contain the names of the parties, a summary of the issues in controversy, and a description of the award issued. In addition, the award decisions are made available to the public. Furthermore, judicial decisions addressing ADEA claims will continue to be issued because it is unlikely that all or even most ADEA claimants will be subject to arbitration agreements. Finally, Gilmer's concerns apply equally to settlements of ADEA claims, which, as noted above, are clearly allowed.

It is also argued that arbitration procedures cannot adequately further the purposes of the ADEA because they do not provide for broad equitable relief and class actions. As the court below noted, however, arbitrators do have the power to fashion equitable relief. 895 F.2d, at 199-200. Indeed, the NYSE rules applicable here do not restrict the types of relief an arbitrator may award, but merely refer to "damages and/or other relief." The NYSE rules also provide for collective proceedings. But "even if the arbitration could not go forward as a class action or class relief could not be granted by the arbitrator, the fact that the [ADEA] provides for the possibility of bringing a collective action does not mean that individual attempts at conciliation were intended to be barred." Nicholson v. CPC Intl. Inc., 877 F.2d 221, 241 (3d Cir. 1989) (Becker, J., dissenting). Finally, it should be remembered that arbitration agreements will not preclude the EEOC from bringing actions seeking classwide and equitable relief.

## C

An additional reason advanced by Gilmer for refusing to enforce arbitration agreements relating to ADEA claims is his contention that there often will be unequal bargaining power between employers and employees. Mere inequality in bargaining power, however, is not a sufficient reason to hold that arbitration agreements are never enforceable in the employment context. Relationships between securities dealers and investors, for example, may involve unequal bargaining power, but we nevertheless held in *Rodriguez de Quijas* and *McMahon* that agreements to arbitrate in that context are enforceable. See 490 U.S. at 484; 482 U.S. at 230. As discussed above, the FAA's purpose was to place arbitration agreements on the same footing as other contracts. Thus, arbitration agreements are enforceable "save upon such grounds as exist at law or in equity for the revocation of any contract." 9 U.S.C. § 2. "Of course, courts should remain attuned to well-supported claims that the agreement to arbitrate resulted from the sort of fraud or overwhelming economic power that would provide grounds 'for the revocation of any contract.'" *Mitsubishi*, 473 U.S. at 627. There is no indication in this case, however, that Gilmer, an experienced businessman, was coerced or defrauded into agreeing to the arbitration clause in his registration application. As with the claimed procedural inadequacies discussed above, this claim of unequal bargaining power is best left for resolution in specific cases. . . .

## V

We conclude that Gilmer has not met his burden of showing that Congress, in enacting the ADEA, intended to preclude arbitration of claims under that Act. Accordingly, the judgment of the Court of Appeals is
*Affirmed.*

JUSTICE STEVENS, with whom JUSTICE MARSHALL joins, dissenting. Section 1 of the Federal Arbitration Act (FAA) states:

> [N]othing herein contained shall apply to contracts of employment of seamen, railroad employees, or any other class of workers engaged in foreign or interstate commerce.

9 U.S.C. § 1. The Court today, in holding that the FAA compels enforcement of arbitration clauses even when claims of age discrimination are at issue, skirts the antecedent question whether the coverage of the Act even extends to arbitration clauses contained in employment contracts, regardless of the subject matter of the claim at issue. In my opinion, arbitration clauses contained in employment agreements are specifically exempt from coverage of the FAA, and for that reason respondent Interstate/Johnson Lane Corporation cannot, pursuant to the FAA, compel petitioner to submit his claims arising under the Age Discrimination in Employment Act to binding arbitration. . . .

There is little dispute that the primary concern animating the FAA was the perceived need by the business community to overturn the common-law rule that denied specific enforcement of agreements to arbitrate in contracts between business entities. The Act was drafted by a committee of the American Bar Association (ABA), acting upon instructions from the ABA to consider and report upon "the further extension of the principle of commercial arbitration." Report of the Forty-third Annual Meeting of the ABA, 45 A.B.A. Rep. 75 (1920). At the Senate Judiciary Subcommittee hearings on the proposed bill, the chairman of the ABA committee responsible for drafting the bill assured the Senators that the bill "is not intended [to] be an act referring to labor disputes, at all. It is purely an act to give the merchants the right or the privilege of sitting down and agreeing with each other as to what their damages are, if they want to do it. Now that is all there is in this." Hearing on S. 4213 and S. 4214 before a Subcommittee of the Senate Committee on the Judiciary, 67th Cong., 4th Sess., 9 (1923). At the same hearing, Senator Walsh stated:

> The trouble about the matter is that a great many of these contracts that are entered into are really not [voluntary] things at all. Take an insurance policy; there is a blank in it. You can take that or you can leave it. The agent has no power at all to decide it. Either you can make that contract or you can not make any contract. It is the same with a good many contracts of employment. A man says, "These are our terms. All right, take it or leave it." Well, there is nothing for the man to do except to sign it; and then he surrenders his right to have his case tried by the court, and has to have it tried before a tribunal in which he has no confidence at all.

Ibid. . . .

Not only would I find that the FAA does not apply to employment-related disputes between employers and employees in general, but also I would hold that compulsory arbitration conflicts with the congressional purpose animating the ADEA, in particular. As this Court previously has noted, authorizing the courts to issue broad injunctive relief is the cornerstone to eliminating discrimination in society. Albemarle Paper Co. v. Moody, 422 U.S. 405, 415 (1975). The ADEA, like Title VII of the Civil Rights Act of 1964, authorizes courts to award broad, class-based injunctive relief to achieve the purposes of the Act. 29 U.S.C. § 626(b). Because commercial arbitration is typically limited to a specific dispute between the particular parties and because the available remedies in arbitral forums generally do not provide for class-wide injunctive relief, see Shell, ERISA and Other Federal Employment Statutes: When Is Commercial Arbitration an "Adequate Substitute" for the Courts?, 68 Texas L. Rev. 509, 568 (1990), I would conclude that an essential purpose of the ADEA is frustrated by compulsory arbitration of employment discrimination claims. Moreover, as Chief Justice Burger explained:

> Plainly, it would not comport with the congressional objectives behind a statute seeking to enforce civil rights protected by Title VII to allow the very forces that had practiced discrimination to contract away the right to enforce civil rights in the courts. For federal courts to defer to arbitral decisions reached by the same combination of forces that had long perpetuated invidious discrimination would have made the foxes guardians of the chickens.

Barrentine v. Arkansas-Best Freight System, Inc., 450 U.S. 728, 750 (1981) (dissenting opinion). In my opinion the same concerns expressed by Chief Justice Burger with regard to compulsory arbitration of Title VII claims may be said of claims arising under the ADEA. The Court's holding today clearly eviscerates the important role played by an independent judiciary in eradicating employment discrimination.

### Note: Arbitration Procedure

Although there are many different types of arbitration, they have in common informal procedures that are less adversarial than the usual civil trial. Parties may choose not to be represented by counsel, and though both sides have an opportunity to present witnesses, physical evidence, and documents, and to challenge the other side's presentation, the rules of evidence and of civil procedure (particularly elaborate discovery) are largely abandoned. As a result, the arbitrator's decision, called an "award," may be rendered quickly on the basis of the arbitrator's general sense of fairness under the circumstances rather than on legal norms.

Choosing arbitration is generally up to the parties at the time of contracting. However, many contracts, like our problem case, provide for procedures in accordance with the American Arbitration Association rules. Compare, for example, the tone of the following excerpt from the Association's Commercial Arbitration Rules to the general tone of the Federal Rules of Civil Procedure:

It cannot be denied that a large part of what goes on in hearings is people getting things off their chests, and this, of course, bears on your attitude toward evidentiary problems as they arise. The arbitrator's basic problem is to find out as much as possible about what really happened.

Am. Arbitration Ass'n R. 29.

Many arbitration clauses specify the venue for the event, for example, where the plaintiff lives or where the claim arose, while others may set venue in the location of the defendant's home office. What are the practical reasons for settling the place of arbitration in advance?

## *Note: Post-**Gilmer** Developments for Employees and Unions*

The United States Supreme Court has held that a union cannot bind non-member, nonunion employees to arbitration over a union's agency fees if the employees have not agreed to arbitration. Arbitration is inappropriate where one party has not agreed to that remedy. See Air Line Pilots Ass'n v. Miller, 523 U.S. 866 (1998).

The Court also decided Wright v. Universal Maritime Service Corp., 525 U.S. 70 (1998). The Court in *Wright* was asked to consider whether arbitration is mandatory where the union negotiated for arbitration, but an individual seeks to pursue a judicial remedy for an Americans with Disabilities Act (ADA) claim. Wright had argued that because the collective bargaining agreement did not specifically address ADA claims, the Fourth Circuit precedent that treats collective bargaining agreements to arbitrate employment disputes as binding upon individual employees was inapplicable. The Fourth Circuit disagreed, on the grounds that the arbitration clause was particularly broad (covering "all matters affecting wages, hours, and other terms and conditions of employment") and that "[a]n employer need not provide a laundry list of potential disputes in order for them to be covered by an arbitration clause." 121 F.3d 702 (4th Cir. 1997) (unpublished opinion).

The United States Supreme Court reversed the Fourth Circuit in a unanimous opinion written by Justice Scalia. 525 U.S. 70 (1998). The Court concluded that it was unnecessary to resolve a union-negotiated waiver of employees' statutory right to a federal forum, because no such waiver had occurred in this case. The collective bargaining agreement in question had not clearly and unmistakably waived the employees' right to litigate claims under the ADA. Id. at 79-82.

The Court in *Wright* did not resolve the implications and limits of its holding that federal statutory claims may in certain circumstances be submitted to arbitration where a party so contracts, and where the *Gilmer* conditions are met. For example, in Pryner v. Tractor Supply Co., 109 F.3d 354 (7th Cir.), *cert. denied,* 572 U.S. 912 (1997), the Seventh Circuit held that a collective bargaining agreement cannot compel arbitration of a federal anti-discrimination claim by an individual employee. The court noted that the worker has not necessarily agreed to arbitration in this situation simply because the union has. See also Air Line Pilots Ass'n v. Northwest Airlines, Inc., 199 F.3d 477, 484 (D.C. Cir. 1999) ("an individual may prospectively waive his own statutory right to a judicial forum, but his union may not prospectively waive that right for him"); Nelson v. Cyprus Bagdad Copper Corp., 119 F.3d 756 (9th Cir. 1997), *cert. denied*, 523 U.S. 1072 (1998) (holding that by signing a form acknowledging that he had read the employee handbook that contained an arbitration provision employee did not waive right to sue under the ADA). For the alternative position, see Austin v. Owens-Brockway Glass Container, Inc., 78 F.3d 875 (4th Cir. 1996), *cert. denied*, 519 U.S. 980 (1996) (holding that employees can be compelled to submit Title VII and ADA claims to binding arbitration pursuant to a collective bargaining agreement); Miller v. Public Storage Mgmt., Inc., 121 F.3d 215 (5th Cir. 1997) (enforcing arbitration provision in employment contract with nonunion employee). Outside the employment setting, see Bercovitch v. Baldwin School, Inc., 133 F.3d 141 (1st Cir. 1998) (holding that plaintiffs may be compelled to arbitrate ADA claims pursuant to voluntary, pre-dispute agreement for child's enrollment in school).

The Court also has held that employee-employer agreements to arbitrate employment-related disputes do not bar the federal Equal Employment Opportunity Commission from pursuing judicial relief, including damages, against an employer who violates federal employment laws. See EEOC v. Waffle House, Inc., 534 U.S. 279 (2002).

Finally, the Court held in a unanimous opinion that the proper course was to compel arbitration of a claim where an arbitration agreement imposed remedial limits on such a claim, but the limits were ambiguous. The arbitrator should have been given an opportunity to construe the ambiguous terms of the agreement. PacifiCare Health Sys., Inc. v. Book, 538 U.S. 401 (2003).

### Note: Who Decides Whether a Dispute Is Subject to Arbitration?

Along with the foregoing conflict over whether unions may bargain away employees' rights to litigate federal statutory claims is a broader debate over the scope of the Federal Arbitration Act. In Circuit City Stores, Inc. v. Adams, 532 U.S. 105 (2001), the Court held that the Act applies to most employment contracts, and exempts only contracts involving interstate transportation workers. A key aspect of the decision was the Court's conclusion that an arbitration agreement can cover both an employee's federal and state employment law claims. In Howsam v. Dean Witter Reynolds, Inc., the Court held that in suits to compel arbitration under the Federal Arbitration Act, the question whether the dispute was subject to arbitration is ordinarily for the courts rather than the arbitrator to decide. 537 U.S. 79, 83 (2002) ("The question whether the parties have submitted a particular dispute to arbitration, i.e., the '*question of arbitrability*,' is an issue for judicial determination unless the parties clearly and unmistakably provide otherwise.").

In the wake of these decisions, employees have sought, with mixed success, to avoid arbitration by arguing that no contract was formed. Compare Campbell v. Gen. Dynamics Gov't Sys. Corp., 407 F.3d 546 (1st Cir. 2005) (mass e-mail regarding arbitration policy not enforceable contract), with Gold v. Deutsche AG, 365 F.3d 144 (2d Cir. 2004) (arbitration agreement enforceable where employee signed but did not read form). Alternatively, employees have argued that the arbitration agreement was unconscionable. See, e.g., Alexander v. Anthony Int'l, L.P., 341 F.3d 256 (3d Cir. 2003) (invalidating agreement that imposed a 30-day limitations period on employee but not employer claims, and shifted fees to the loser); Circuit City Stores Inc. v. Adams, 279 F.3d 889 (9th Cir. 2002) (invalidating adhesion contract that required employee, but not employer, to arbitrate disputes, shifted fees, and severely limited remedies); Gannon v. Circuit City Stores Inc., 262 F.3d 677 (8th Cir. 2001) (remanding when severing clause limited punitive damages to $5,000).

In response, employers have taken up the invitation in *Howsam* to specify in employment contracts that basic challenges to the enforceability of an arbitration contract—so-called threshold or gateway issues of arbitrability—shall be delegated to the arbitrator. In Rent-A-Center, West, Inc. v. Jackson, 561 U.S. 63 (2010), the Supreme Court reaffirmed the validity of delegation provisions. The delegation provision at issue in the case stated that "[t]he Arbitrator, and not any federal, state, or local court or agency, shall have exclusive authority to resolve any dispute relating to the . . . enforceability or formation of this Agreement including, but not limited to any claim that all or any part of this Agreement is void or voidable." 561 U.S. at 66. The employee filed a federal suit alleging discrimination and the employer moved to compel arbitration. In response to the motion to compel arbitration, the employee claimed the entire arbitration agreement was unconscionable. The employer invoked the delegation clause, arguing that any claim of unconscionability was for the arbitrator to decide.

The Court sided with the employer. Borrowing from a line of cases in which the Court concluded that an arbitration clause in a general contract is severable and will therefore be enforced even if a party has raised a challenge to the general contract, the Court held that a delegation clause is severable from a challenge to an overall arbitration contract and will be enforced even if a party challenges the contract as a whole. Thus the employee could not litigate the validity of a delegation clause in court unless the delegation clause itself was specifically alleged to be unconscionable. Because the employee failed to do so in the trial court, the Court ordered the employee's federal suit dismissed and the motion to compel arbitration granted.

Four Justices dissented. They argued that "[q]uintessential gateway matters include whether the parties have a valid arbitration agreement at all, whether the parties are bound by a given arbitration clause, and whether an arbitration clause in a concededly binding contract applies to a particular type of controversy. It would be bizarre to send these types of gateway matters to the arbitrator as a matter of course, because they raise a 'question of arbitrability.'" Id. at 77-78. In prior cases, the Court had always insisted that although delegation is an option, questions of arbitrability are only delegable if there is "clear and unmistakable evidence" that the parties agreed to "arbitrate arbitrability." Id. at 79. That, the dissenters emphasized, was a presumption "in favor of a judicial, rather than an arbitral forum." Id. The majority's approach reverses that presumption.

The dissent also argued that the Court's reading of the employment contract and the employee's challenge to it was unduly cramped. Even if an arbitration agreement can be rescued from an unenforceable contract (a notion the dissent characterized as "difficult for any lawyer—or any person—to accept"), that rule was created for a specific purpose. Id. at 87. It prevents a court from deciding the merits of the underlying dispute in the course of deciding arbitrability. "In this case, however, resolution of the unconscionability question will have no bearing on the merits of the underlying employment dispute . . . which involves a claim of employment discrimination." Id. at 87-88. The Ninth Circuit, which was reversed in *Jackson*, continues to resist the implications of the case. Compare Bridge Fund Capital Corp. v. Fastbucks Franchise Corp., 622 F.3d 996 (9th Cir. 2010), with M.A. Mortenson Co. v. Saunders Concrete Co., 676 F.3d 1153 (8th Cir. 2012).

As *Gilmer*, *Adams*, *Howsam*, and *Jackson* show, the United States Supreme Court has entered a period of favoring arbitration. Southland Corp. v. Keating, 465 U.S. 1 (1984), was the first extremely broad-based Supreme Court case supporting arbitration. See also Allied-Bruce Terminix Companies, Inc. v. Dobson, 513 U.S. 265 (1995). The Court also has held that the Federal Arbitration Act compels enforcement of private agreements to arbitrate statutory claims arising under antitrust, securities, and racketeering laws. Mitsubishi Motors Corp. v. Soler Chrysler-Plymouth, Inc., 473 U.S. 614 (1985); Shearson Am. Express, Inc. v. McNulty, 482 U.S. 220 (1987); see also Tenaska Washington Partners II v. United States, 34 Fed. Cl. 434 (1995) (holding that there is no constitutional impediment to allowing federal agencies to enter into agreements to submit to binding arbitration, provided a given agency has the statutory authority to do so).

In 2011, the Court decided another major arbitration case. AT&T Mobile LLC v. Concepcion, 563 U.S. 333 (2011) (holding that states cannot condition the enforceability of arbitration agreements on the availability of arbitration procedures for aggregating individual claims into a class). We take up this decision in Chapter 6 after introducing the rules for certifying class actions in court.

### Note: Paying for Private Justice

Still another issue raised by mandatory arbitration is who pays for it. The Court of Appeals for the District of Columbia has concluded that where arbitration occurs solely because it is mandated by an employer as a condition of employment, the employer must bear the expense of the arbitrator's fees, given that the employee otherwise could have pursued his or her claims in court without having to pay for the judge's services. Cole v. Burns

Int'l Sec. Servs., 105 F.3d 1465 (D.C. Cir. 1997); see also Shankle v. B-G Maint. Mgmt. of Colo., Inc., 163 F.3d 1230, 1235 (10th Cir. 1999) (arbitration agreement requiring litigant to pay half of arbitration costs "failed to provide an accessible forum in which [litigant] could resolve his statutory rights"); Paladino v. Avnet Computer Tech., Inc., 134 F.3d 1054, 1062 (11th Cir. 1999); Armendariz v. Found. Health Psychcare Servs., 6 P.3d 669 (Cal. 2000). But see Williams v. Cigna Financial Advisors, Inc., 197 F.3d 752, 763-764 (5th Cir. 1999) (taking a case-by-case approach); Rosenberg v. Merrill Lynch, Pierce, Fenner & Smith, Inc., 170 F.3d 1 (1st Cir. 1999) (upholding arbitration requirement that charged plaintiffs forum fees); Koveleskie v. SBC Capital Markets, Inc., 167 F.3d 361, 366 (7th Cir. 1999).

The Supreme Court reached a similar issue in a nonemployment context, suggesting, without deciding, that large arbitration costs foisted on a consumer by virtue of her contract with a mobile home dealer could invalidate the arbitration clause:

> It may well be that the existence of large arbitration costs could preclude a litigant such as Randolph from effectively vindicating her rights in the arbitral forum.

Green Tree Fin. Corp. v. Randolph, 531 U.S. 79, 90 (2000). The Court remanded the case because the plaintiff had not offered any proof on the likely costs of arbitration that she would face.

After *Green Tree*, circuit courts have agreed that fee-splitting clauses, which require employees to share the costs of arbitration, "can render an arbitration agreement unenforceable where the arbitration fees and costs are so prohibitive as to effectively deny the employee access to the arbitral forum," but there is division between the few courts that struck down such provisions per se, as in *Cole*, and the majority that now read *Green Tree* to require case-by-case review of the burdens imposed by such provisions. See, e.g., Bradford v. Rockwell Semiconductor Sys., Inc., 238 F.3d 549, 554 (4th Cir. 2001) (rejecting *Cole*'s per se rule against fee splitting and adopting a case-by-case approach). In *Bradford*, for example, the Fourth Circuit upheld the arbitration agreement at issue, reasoning that the employee failed to prove that he was unable to pay the $4,470 in arbitration costs he was billed:

> Indeed, this case presents a paradigmatic example of why fee-splitting should not be deemed to automatically render an arbitration agreement unenforceable because Bradford was in no way deterred from attempting to vindicate his rights by means of a full and fair arbitration proceeding. Invalidating the arbitration provision now, after the arbitrator has ruled upon his claim, would simply give Bradford a second bite at the apple under circumstances in which there is no evidence that allowing him to pursue his litigation in court would cost him any less than the amount of money that he has already spent in arbitration.

238 F.3d at 558 (suggesting that individuals who object to fee splitting must raise their objection prior to the beginning of arbitration); see also LaPrade

v. Kidder, Peabody & Co., 246 F.3d 702, 708 (D.C. Cir. 2001) (upholding arbitration award where plaintiff was required to pay $8,376 in forum fees).

As you might expect, results have varied among courts following the case-by-case approach. In contrast to *Bradford*, the Sixth Circuit, sitting en banc, adopted a broader test for assessing the burdens imposed on litigants, holding that "[a] cost-splitting provision should be held unenforceable whenever it would have the 'chilling effect' of deterring a substantial number of potential litigants from seeking to vindicate their statutory rights." Morrison v. Circuit City Stores, Inc., 317 F.3d 646, 661 (6th Cir. 2003). Although Morrison would have had to pay, at most, only $1,622, the court pointed to studies showing that:

> [A] plaintiff forced to arbitrate a typical $60,000 employment discrimination claim will incur costs . . . that range from three to nearly *fifty* times the basic costs of litigating in a judicial, rather than an arbitral, forum . . . [, that] the average arbitrator fee was $700 per day and that an average employment case incurred a total of $3,750 to $14,000 in arbitration expenses.

Id. at 669. The court rejected the cost-splitting provision on those grounds. As the court reasoned:

> We believe that the following propositions of law can be derived from *Green Tree*. First, in some cases, the potential of incurring large arbitration costs and fees will deter potential litigants from seeking to vindicate their rights in the arbitral forum. Under *Gilmer*, the arbitral forum must provide litigants with an effective substitute for the judicial forum; if the fees and costs of the arbitral forum deter potential litigants, then that forum is clearly not an effective, or even adequate, substitute for the judicial forum. Second, where that prospect deters potential litigants, the arbitration agreement, or at minimum, the cost-splitting provision contained within it, is unenforceable under *Gilmer*. Third, the burden of demonstrating that incurring such costs is likely under a given set of circumstances rests, at least initially, with the party opposing arbitration. . . .
>
> In analyzing this issue, reviewing courts should consider the costs of litigation as the alternative to arbitration, as in *Bradford*, but they must weigh the potential costs of litigation in a realistic manner. In many, if not most, cases, employees (and former employees) bringing discrimination claims will be represented by attorneys on a contingency-fee basis. Thus, many litigants will face minimal costs in the judicial forum, as the attorney will cover most of the fees of litigation and advance the expenses incurred in discovery. . . . In the arbitral forum, the litigant faces an additional expense—the arbitrator's fees and costs—which are never incurred in the judicial forum. Reviewing courts must consider whether the litigant will incur this additional expense and whether that expense, taken together with the other costs and expenses of the differing fora, would deter potential litigants from bringing their statutory claims in the arbitral forum. . . .
>
> In the abstract [the costs of the arbitral forum] may not appear prohibitive, but it must be considered from the vantage point of the potential litigant in a case such as this. Recently terminated, the potential litigant must continue

to pay for housing, utilities, transportation, food, and the other necessities of life in contemporary society despite losing her primary, and most likely only, source of income. Unless she is exceedingly fortunate, the potential litigant will experience at least a brief period of unemployment. Turning to the arbitration agreement with her employer, the potential litigant finds that, as the default rule, she will be obligated to pay half the costs of any arbitration which she initiates.

Minimal research will reveal that the potential costs of arbitrating the dispute easily reach thousands, if not tens of thousands, of dollars, far exceeding the costs that a plaintiff would incur in court. Courts charge plaintiffs initial filing fees, but they do not charge extra for in-person hearings, discovery requests, routine motions, or written decisions, costs that are all common in the world of private arbitrators.

Id. at 659-660, 664, 669. The court rejected fee splitting notwithstanding the fact that the arbitration agreement included a provision limiting the employee's exposure to arbitration costs to the greater of $500 or 3 percent of her annual compensation. Such a clause, the court reasoned, "really boils down to risking one's scarce resources in the hopes of an uncertain benefit—it appears to us that a substantial number of similarly situated persons would be deterred from seeking to vindicate their statutory rights under these circumstances." Id. at 670. See also Ingle v. Circuit City Stores, Inc., 328 F.3d 1165, 1177-1178 (9th Cir. 2003) (finding fee-splitting agreement unconscionable on grounds that it gave discretion to the arbitrator to require employee to pay total costs of arbitration if employer prevailed, while employer would only have to pay half if employee prevailed).

Although the holdings vary, you can see from these cases that employers and retailers have continued to insist on arbitration clauses, and, where possible, fee splitting. The growing trend toward pre-dispute, compelled arbitration and its potential abuses made front-page news in March of 1997. See Barry Meier, In Fine Print, Customers Lose Ability to Sue, N.Y. Times, Mar. 10, 1997, at A1 (noting that "[o]n many occasions, companies have unilaterally wiped out customers' rights to sue by sending out notices of new arbitration requirements in the form of envelope stuffers"). Courts likewise have concluded that arbitration agreements can contain unfairly one-sided terms. See Hooters of Am., Inc. v. Phillips, 173 F.3d 933 (4th Cir. 1999) (finding arbitration terms egregiously unfair to employees).

### *Note: Justifying Private Justice*

For a critique of the trend toward arbitration, see Jean R. Sternlight, Panacea or Corporate Tool?: Debunking the Supreme Court's Preference for Binding Arbitration, 74 Wash. U. L.Q. 637 (1996); Jean R. Sternlight and Elizabeth J. Jensen, Using Arbitration to Eliminate Consumer Class Actions: Efficient Business Practice or Unconscionable Abuse?, 67 Law & Contemp. Probs. 75 (2004).

The data on the impact of arbitration are mixed. In an empirical examination of employment arbitration supporting the process, Sherwyn, Estreicher, and Heise summarized the findings of prior studies as follows:

> First, there is no evidence that plaintiffs fare significantly better in litigation. In fact, the opposite may be true. Second, arbitration is faster. Because employment dispute resolution can be both heart wrenching and financially crippling, a quicker resolution is a positive. Third, the question of damages is too difficult to determine based on the available data. While the strongest consensus exists with respect to disposition time, further research is warranted on all three factors, especially on the questions of win/loss records and damages. Of course . . . data will not answer the critical nonempirical questions that greatly influence the debate.

Assessing the Case for Employment Arbitration, 57 Stan. L. Rev. 1557, 1578 (2005); see also id. at 1573-1577 (discussing studies showing *lower* awards generated by arbitration relative to litigation).

The authors further contend that mandatory arbitration is particularly attractive to employers "with a high volume of low-value claims" because 1) quick, efficient resolution minimizes costs and 2) employers "are tired of what we call 'de facto severance' and wish to limit the value and incidence of nuisance settlements":

> Because it costs employers (1) between $4000 and $10,000 to defend an EEOC charge, (2) at least $75,000 to take a case to summary judgment, and (3) at least $125,000 and possibly over $500,000 to defend a case at trial, it almost always makes good business sense to settle a case for $4000. In other words, it makes economic sense to pay an employee with a salary of $48,000 per year . . . what amounts to one month's severance pay if the employee simply files an EEOC charge. . . . Mandatory arbitration arguably ends de facto severance because arbitration lowers the costs of defense, including potentially adverse publicity. Instead, employers can defend those claims that they believe are baseless.
>
> At the same time that arbitration reduces employers' incentive to settle baseless claims, arbitration programs reduce employers' ability to defeat meritorious claims by delaying or "big firming" the employee into a withdrawal or substandard settlement.

Id. at 1579-1580.

On the other hand, a July 4, 2008, article published in *Business Week* cited evidence that banks won 99.8 percent of arbitrations of credit card disputes conducted by the National Arbitration Forum in California. Robert Berner, Banks v. Consumers (Guess Who Wins?), July 4, 2008. The article cited evidence that NAF, then the primary arbitrator for consumer credit disputes in the country, marketed its services to banks by promising "'marked increase in recovery rates over existing collection methods.'" Id. "The firm goes out of its way to tell creditors they probably won't have to tussle with debtors in arbitration. The September, 2007, NAF presentation [to banks] informs companies that in cases in which an award or order is granted, 93.7% are decided without consumers ever responding." Id. Some arbitration files "lacked any evidence that the consumer had been notified." Id. One arbitrator admitted to spending only a few minutes on each arbitration, completing "'10 to 12 in an hour.' She is paid $300 an hour by NAF. If she worked more slowly, she suspects the company would assign her fewer cases." Id.

The article also quoted former NAF arbitrators who had quit on the ground that its procedures were corrupt. One former arbitrator testified that the company ran "an unfair, biased process." Id. After she "awarded a consumer $48,000 in damages in a collections case, the firm removed her from 11 other cases. 'NAF ran a process that systematically serviced the interest of credit card companies,' she said in a [subsequent] interview." Id. Another arbitrator, a former state supreme court justice, complained that the company "provided him with an award form with the amount sought by the creditor already filled in. This encourages the arbitrator 'to give creditors everything they wanted without having to think about it.'" Id. He also objected to the fees he was encouraged to charge debtors. In "three NAF cases he decided . . . he granted the credit-card companies the balances and interest they claimed but denied them administrative fees, which totaled about $300 per case. [He] says such fees wouldn't be available to creditors who filed suit in court. 'It's a system set up to squeeze small sums of money out of desperately poor people,' he asserts." Id.

NAF was sued by the City Attorney of San Francisco and exited consumer credit arbitration altogether in 2009 to settle a separate suit filed by the Attorney General of Minnesota, NAF's home state. The Minnesota complaint alleged that the company had committed consumer fraud, false advertising, and engaged in deceptive trade practices. See Robert Berner, Big Arbitration Firm Pulls Out of Credit Card Business, Business Week, July 19, 2009.

Against this backdrop, we may today consider support for arbitration as primarily conservative or corporate. But in an important review of the history of the FAA, Amalia D. Kessler describes the work of progressive lawyers in developing arbitration and conciliation as alternatives to litigation. Arbitration and Americanization: The Paternalism of Progressive Procedural Reform, 124 Yale L.J. 2940 (2015).

Scholarship expressing skepticism about arbitration includes the following: Developments in the Law, Employment Discrimination, Mandatory Arbitration of Statutory Employment Disputes, 109 Harv. L. Rev. 1568, 1670, 1692 (1996); Stephan Landsman, ADR and the Costs of Compulsion, 57 Stan. L. Rev. 1593 (2005); Carrie Menkel-Meadow, What Will We Do When Adjudication Ends?, 44 UCLA L. Rev. 1613 (1997); Frank E. Sander, H. William Allen, and Deborah Hensler, Judicial (Mis)use of ADR: A Debate, 27 U. Tol. L. Rev. 885 (1996); Jean R. Sternlight, Compelling Arbitration of Claims Under the Civil Rights Act of 1866: What Congress Could Not Have Intended, 47 U. Kan. L. Rev. 273 (1999); Jean R. Sternlight, Creeping Mandatory Arbitration: Is it Just?, 57 Stan. L. Rev. 1631 (2005); Jean R. Sternlight, Rethinking the Constitutionality of the Supreme Court's Preference for Binding Arbitration: A Fresh Assessment of Jury Trial,

Separation of Powers, and Due Process Concerns, 72 Tul. L. Rev. 1 (1997); Thomas J. Stipanovich, Arbitration: The "New Litigation," 2010 Ill. U. L.J. 1.

For data from a recent survey of the cost, speed, outcomes, and due process compliance of consumer arbitration, see Searle Center on Law, Regulation and Economic Growth, Northwestern University Law School, Consumer Arbitration Before the American Arbitration Association Preliminary Report, March 2009.

Deborah Hensler insists that "there are . . . important political values that derive from widespread access to, and use of, the public justice system" that are missing in ADR systems:

> The public spectacle of civil litigation gives life to the "rule of law." To demonstrate that the law's authority can be mobilized by the least powerful as well as the most powerful in society, we need to observe employees and consumers successfully suing large corporations and government agencies, minority group members successfully suing majority group members, and persons engaged in unpopular activities establishing their legal rights to continue those activities. Dispute resolution behind closed doors precludes such observation. In a democracy where many people are shut out of legislative power either because they are too few in number, or too dispersed to elect representatives, or because they do not have the financial resources to influence legislators, collective litigation in class or other mass form provides an alternative strategy for group action. Private individualized dispute resolution extinguishes the possibility of such collective litigation. Conciliation has much to recommend it. But the visible presence of institutionalized and legitimized conflict, channeled productively, teaches citizens that it is not always better to compromise and accept the status quo because, sometimes, great gains are to be had by peaceful contest.

Deborah R. Hensler, Our Courts, Ourselves: How the Alternative Dispute Resolution Movement Is Re Shaping Our Legal System, 108 Penn. St. L. Rev. 165, 196-197 (2003). ADR, she adds, often does not significantly reduce the average time or average transaction costs of dispute resolution. Id. at 179-180, 188. See also Kenneth S. Abraham and J.W. Montgomery III, The Lawlessness of Arbitration, 9 Conn. Ins. L.J. 355 (2003); Thomas E. Carbonneau, Arbitral Justice: The Demise of Due Process in American Law, 70 Tul. L. Rev. 1945 (1996); Bryant G. Garth, Tilting the Justice System: From ADR as Idealistic Movement to a Segmented Market in Dispute Resolution, 18 Ga. St. U. L. Rev. 927, 950-951 (2002) (arguing that by emphasizing ADR, "[w]e have created a segmented and hierarchical system skewed dramatically toward business litigants and a few other players—notably a few sectors of the personal injury bar"); Michael Z. Green, Tackling Employment Discrimination with ADR: Does Mediation Offer a Shield for the Haves or Real Opportunity for the Have-Nots?, 26 Berkeley J. Emp. & Lab. L. 321 (2005); Rex R. Perschbacher and Debra Lyn Bassett, The End of Law, 84 B.U. L. Rev. 1 (2004); Jean R. Sternlight, Is Alternative Dispute Resolution Consistent with the Rule of Law? Lessons from Abroad, 56 DePaul L. Rev. 569, 570-572 (2007) (summarizing scholarship critical of ADR).

What about a state allowing its judges and courthouses to be "rented" out for private arbitration? In 2009, Delaware passed a law permitting wealthy litigants to do just that. If the dispute exceeded $1 million and the parties were willing to pay a $12,000 filing fee and $6,000 for each day of litigation, they could have secret access to the famed Chancery judges of Delaware. Judith Resnik, Op-Ed: Renting Judges for Secret Rulings, N.Y. Times, Feb., 28, 2014. A group of news organizations challenged the constitutionality of the statute on the ground that it "violates the public's right of access to civil proceedings under the First Amendment." Id. The Third Circuit affirmed the district court's determination that Delaware's "government sponsored arbitration proceedings violated the First Amendment . . . right of public access to trials." Delaware Coalition for Open Government v. Strine, 733 F.3d 510 (3d Cir. 2013).

Quite apart from arbitration is the growth of so-called claims resolution facilities, described by Deborah Hensler as "privately designed, financed, and administered organizations for giving away money, established as a result of the settlement of mass litigation in trial or bankruptcy courts." Deborah Hensler, Alternative Courts? Litigation-Induced Claims Resolution Facilities, 57 Stan. L. Rev. 1429 (2005). She notes that, in the class action mass tort context, the "increasing resort to private claims resolution facilities to determine the eligibility for and amount of compensation for civil plaintiffs raises efficiency, equity, and due process questions that deserve broad public policy attention," but the information necessary to support broad public debate is "generally unavailable," in part because the outcomes of claims resolution facilities are "often protected from public scrutiny." Id. at 1429-1430, 1431 (listing as examples the Dalkon Shield Claimants' Trust, the asbestos-related Manville Personal Injury Trust, and the Dow Corning Silicone Gel Implant Trust). See also Samuel Issacharoff and D. Theodore Rave, The BP Oil Spill Settlement and the Paradox of Public Litigation, 74 La. L. Rev. 397 (2014) (describing the administrative claims processing program BP set up to pay claims arising out of the Deepwater Horizon oil spill).

## Note: The Appealability of Arbitration Awards

One of the most common features of arbitration clauses in contracts is the nonappealability of the awards. Arbitration awards do show up in the public court system, where they may be entered as a judgment of the court to bolster their enforceability. Most arbitrations are subject to a limited right of review in the form of a motion to modify or set aside the award, but only on the grounds of the arbitrator's bias, fraud, misconduct, or abuse of discretion. In a particularly striking case, the California Supreme Court upheld an award that showed on its face an error in the law. Moncharsh v. Heily & Blase, 3 Cal. 4th 1 (1992); see also E. Assoc. Coal Corp. v. United Mine Workers of Am., Dist. 17, 531 U.S. 57, 62 (2000) ("'as long as [an honest] arbitrator is even arguably construing or applying the contract and acting within the scope of his authority,' the fact that 'a court is convinced he committed serious error does not suffice to overturn his decision'"; refusing to vacate arbitrator's award where employer challenged order reinstating employee on ground that reinstatement violated public policy against operation of dangerous machinery by workers who test positive for drugs).

Either party to an arbitration agreement may claim in court that the issue before the court is not subject to arbitration under the terms of the agreement. Under the Federal Arbitration Act, the other side may request an order compelling arbitration and dismissing the underlying litigation. When a court grants or denies such an order, the Supreme Court has held that the decision is immediately appealable. Thus, the aggrieved party need not await the outcome of arbitration before appealing the order compelling arbitration. See Green Tree Financial Corp. v. Randolph, 531 U.S. 79, 86-87 (2000).

Actions to vacate an unfavorable arbitration award are not, however, to be filed lightly. In the Seventh Circuit, for instance, a long line of cases "[has] discouraged parties from challenging arbitration awards and has upheld Rule 11 sanctions in cases where the challenge to the award was substantially without merit." CUNA Mut. Ins. Soc. v. Office & Prof'l Employees Int'l Union, Local 39, 443 F.3d 556, 561 (7th Cir. 2006). In upholding sanctions against the employer who appealed an arbitration award favoring the union, the court emphasized the following policy grounds against such appeals:

> A company dissatisfied with the decisions of labor arbitrators need not include an arbitration clause in its collective bargaining contracts, but having agreed to include such a clause it will not be permitted to nullify the advantages to the union by spinning out the arbitral process unconscionably through the filing of meritless suits and appeals. For such conduct the law authorizes sanctions that this court will not hesitate to impose. . . . Lawyers practicing in the Seventh Circuit, take heed!

Id. (quoting Dreis & Krump Mfg. Co. v. Int'l Ass'n of Machinists, Dist. No. 8, 802 F.2d 247, 255-256 (7th Cir. 1986)).

"Unconscionable" and "meritless" motions to vacate resonate with the language of Rule 11, but is an appeal that is "substantially without merit" the same as a frivolous motion under Rule 11? It may be easier to get sanctioned for appealing an arbitration award in the Seventh Circuit than for other conduct that might fall under Rule 11.

### Note: Court-Annexed ADR

Thus far we have looked at private decisions to arbitrate disputes. The 1980s saw significant growth in state and federal experimentation with court-mandated, also known as "court-annexed," arbitration, often as a condition of trial. As of 1999, 33 states and 22 federal district courts provided for court-annexed arbitration by statute or local rule. See Developments: The Paths of Civil Litigation—VI. ADR, the Judiciary, and Justice: Coming to Terms with the Alternatives, 113 Harv. L. Rev. 1851 (2000). See generally Susan Keilitz, Court-Annexed Arbitration, National Symposium on Court-Connected Dispute Resolution Research, National Center for State Courts 35 (1994); Deborah R. Hensler, What We Know and What We Don't Know About Court Administered Arbitration, 60 Judicature 270 (1986).

While the goals of court-annexed arbitration are similar to those of private arbitration, court-annexed arbitration is unique in that it operates under the authority of a public court and results in an enforceable decision by that court. State statutes or court rules that provide for court-annexed arbitration generally require certain types of cases (defined primarily by subject matter or the amount in controversy) to be arbitrated before they may be tried in court. California, for example, requires pretrial arbitration of all civil disputes involving claims valued at less than $50,000, while Hawaii requires pretrial arbitration only for personal injury claims valued at less than $150,000. Cal. Civ. P. Code § 1141.11; Haw. Rev. Stat. § 20.

Constitutional challenges to such procedures generally have been rejected, see Kimbrough v. Holiday Inn, 478 F. Supp. 566 (E.D. Pa. 1979); Davis v. Gaona, 260 Ga. 450 (1990); Firelock, Inc. v. Dist. Court of the 20th Judicial Dist., 776 P.2d 1090 (Colo. 1989), and the popularity of ADR has resulted in federal legislation encouraging its use. The Alternative Dispute Resolution Act of 1998, 28 U.S.C. § 652, requires each federal district court to develop procedures for using alternative dispute resolution in all civil actions including, but not limited to, those involving federal contracts. The Act does not mandate a uniform set of procedures, but leaves it to each district court to develop its own local ADR rules. An exception to the mandate is that judges cannot order arbitration in actions based on alleged violations of constitutional law, or where more than $150,000 in damages is requested.

Each court is required to:

- designate a knowledgeable employee to implement the ADR program;
- require that litigants in all civil cases consider the use of an ADR process;
- offer litigants a choice of ADR processes, including mediation, early neutral evaluation, mini-trial, and arbitration;
- maintain a panel of neutrals available for each category of process offered; and
- provide for the confidentiality of ADR processes.

Although the bill, as introduced, would have provided for fee shifting if a party demanded a trial de novo after arbitration and then failed to obtain a "substantially more favorable" result, this language was deleted when the bill was approved by the House Judiciary Committee. See 66 U.S.L.W. 2584. Another provision deleted by the committee would have required the use of arbitration in certain cases. As passed, the bill merely provides that if a court elects to require the use of ADR, it may only require the use of mediation or early neutral evaluation. For further discussion of the federal Alternative Dispute Resolution Act and its practical implications, see Eileen Barkas Hoffman, The Impact of the ADR Act of 1998, 6/1/99 Trial-Mag. 35.

Do the efficiency benefits to the justice system outweigh the burdens to individual litigants of another layer of procedure? The costs of these processes, including the neutral parties' time, are generally borne by the individual litigants. Do such mandatory procedures discourage low-income litigants from pursuing just claims? Consider, too, that ADR is a process that has both public and private decision makers. Are their motivations the same? Should judges be permitted to work in both the public and private spheres? See Kirk Johnson, Public Judges as Private Contractors: A Legal Frontier, N.Y. Times, Dec. 10, 1994, at B11.

A related development in both state and federal courts is the delegation of decision-making power over all or part of a case, such as discovery or calculation of damages, to a collateral authority. In the federal courts, these authorities are known as "special masters" and are authorized by Fed. R. Civ. P. 53. See Wayne Brazil, Special Masters in Complex Cases: Extending the Judiciary or Reshaping Adjudication?, 53 U. Chi. L. Rev. 394 (1986). California has been aggressive in using what it terms "references" to aid courts in the management of cases, frequently permitting, for example, courts to assign discovery to a private judge who will be paid by the parties. While this may help in case management, what are the implications for the parties?

Similarly, federal courts have been encouraged to experiment with different ADR devices. One source of authority is Fed. R. Civ. P. 16, which includes the possibility of the use of "special procedures to assist in resolving the dispute" as a proper topic for pretrial conferences. Another source was the Civil Justice Reform Act of 1990, which gave federal courts "authorization to refer appropriate cases to alternative dispute resolution programs that . . . have been designated for use in a district court; or . . . [that] the court may make available, including mediation, mini-trial, and summary jury trial." 28 U.S.C. § 473(a)(6) (Supp. IV 1992).

### Note: The Rise of International Arbitration

Globalization has brought many businesses, not just multinational corporations, into contact with foreign partners and competitors. For a variety of reasons, some having to do with the costs of litigation and others with the complexities of jurisdiction and forum selection, arbitration has become a prominent feature of international economic dispute resolution. For a survey of the procedural aspects of international arbitration, see Alan Scott Rau and Edward F. Sherman, Tradition and Innovation in International Arbitration Procedure, 30 Tex. Int'l L.J. 89 (1995). On the enforcement of international arbitration awards in U.S. courts, see William W. Park and Alexander A. Yanos, Treaty Obligations and National Law: Emerging Conflicts in International Arbitration, 58 Hastings L.J. 251 (2006); Stephen

R. Swanson, Antisuit Injunctions in Support of International Arbitration, 81 Tul. L. Rev. 395 (2006).

## 2.   Mediation

### Problem Case: An Injured Quarterback (Part Two)

Return to the problem case at the outset of this section, and suppose that Sam Wyoming did not belong to an HMO (he couldn't stand the long waits for a doctor's care). But when he is injured, arguably by malpractice, he finds that rather than filing his suit, he must first, by state statute, submit to court-annexed mediation.

He feels that mediation is not only a pothole on the road to justice, but that this sort of procedure is a further invasion of his privacy and that it will be personally distasteful to deal with the doctor "who ruined my career" under these circumstances.

Do you advise him to proceed with the mediation? If so, how do you prepare him to participate in it?

Arbitration should be distinguished from mediation. A mediator has no power to decide; he must secure mutual assent to the resolution of the dispute. Mediation is widely used in the family law context. For example, a number of states provide for "conciliation courts" in which the parties must meet with a mediator before formal divorce and custody proceedings can be started or concluded. See, e.g., Cal. Fam. Code §§ 1800-1842. The purposes of mediation go beyond (or, some would argue, rise above) the determination of rights or the effecting of a compromise. Professor Fuller has written that the central quality of mediation is "its capacity to reorient the parties toward each other, not by imposing rules on them, but by helping them to achieve a new and shared perception of their relationship." Lon Fuller, Mediation—Its Forms and Functions, 44 S. Cal. L. Rev. 305, 327 (1971). Professor Fuller argues that mediation is most appropriate and successful in dyadic relationships such as marriage, employer-employee, and occasionally doctor-patient.

A strong preference for mediation is embedded in certain cultures. The Confucian approach is described in Jerome Alan Cohen, Chinese Mediation on the Eve of Modernization, 54 Cal. L. Rev. 1201, 1206-1208 (1966):

> According to Confucianists, the legal process was not one of the highest achievements of Chinese civilization but was, rather, a regrettable necessity. Indeed, it was usually considered disreputable to become involved in the law courts, even as a party with a legitimate grievance. A lawsuit symbolized disruption of the natural harmony that was thought to exist in human affairs. Law was backed by coercion, and therefore tainted in the eyes of Confucianists. Their view was that the optimum resolution of most disputes was to be achieved not by the exercise of sovereign force but by moral persuasion. Moreover, litigation led to litigiousness and to shameless concern for one's own interest to the detriment of the interests of society.

Confucian values emphasized not the rights of the individual but the functioning of the social order, the maintenance of the group. "[I]deas of order, responsibility, hierarchy and harmony" were enshrined in the prevailing social norms, the *li,* which were approved patterns of behavior prescribed in accordance with one's status and the particular social context. Harmony was preeminent among these ideas. Once it had been disturbed it could best be restored through compromise. If one felt he had been wronged, the Confucian ethic taught that it was better to "suffer a little" and smooth the matter over rather than make a fuss over it and create further dissension. If one was recognized as being clearly in the right in a dispute, it was better to be merciful to the offending party and set an example of the kind of cooperation that fostered group solidarity rather than exact one's pound of flesh and further alienate the offender from the group. As Jean Escarra has written: "To take advantage of one's position, to invoke one's 'rights,' has always been looked at askance in China. The great art is to give way (*jang*) on certain points, and thus accumulate an invisible fund of merit whereby one can later obtain advantages in other directions."

This attitude toward dispute settlement reflected the spirit of self-criticism that Confucian ideology sought to inculcate. When the model Confucian gentleman was treated by another in an unreasonable manner, he was supposed to attribute the difficulty to his own personal failings and to examine his own behavior to find the source of the problem. It was expected that by improving his own conduct he would evoke a positive response from the other party and thereby put an end to the matter. Moral men did not insist on their "rights" or on the exclusive correctness of their own position, but settled a dispute through mutual concessions that permitted each to save "face." A lawsuit caused one to lose "face" since it implied either some falling from virtue on one's own part through obstinacy or lack of moderation or, what was also embarrassing, the failure to elicit an appropriate concession from another as a matter of respect for one's own "face." Thus, Confucianism highly prized the art of compromise and, with it, the role of the persuasive intermediary.

### *Woods v. Holy Cross Hospital*
591 F.2d 1164 (5th Cir. 1979)

TJOFLAT, CIRCUIT JUDGE.

In this case we are called upon to examine portions of Florida's Medical Malpractice Law and determine whether its mandate that a medical malpractice claimant participate in a mediation process prior to bringing an action in court must be enforced by a federal district court in a diversity case. For the reasons set forth below, we find that this requirement meets federal constitutional standards and must be applied in such an action.

### I

On July 21, 1975, Nellie Woods, a citizen of Ohio and the administratrix of the estate of her late husband, John N. Woods, filed an action in federal

district court in which she claimed damages pursuant to Florida's Wrongful
Death Act for Mr. Woods's death. The alleged cause of death was medical malpractice committed by two physicians and a hospital, all named as
defendants. Their malpractice insurers were later added as parties-defen-
dant. Jurisdiction was based upon diversity of citizenship, 28 U.S.C. § 1332
(1976). The defendants separately moved to dismiss Mrs. Woods's complaint, alleging that her failure to abide by the mediation panel requirement
of Florida Statutes section 768.44 precluded her action. The district court
granted the motions to dismiss on the ground that Mrs. Woods had failed
to perform a condition precedent to her suit by not proceeding before a
Florida malpractice mediation panel. This appeal was taken by Mrs. Woods
from the final judgment dismissing her complaint. . . .

[The genesis of the mediation requirement were in these 1975 findings of
the Florida Legislature:]

> WHEREAS, the cost of purchasing medical professional liability insur-
> ance for doctors and other health care providers has skyrocketed in the past
> few months; and
> WHEREAS, it is not uncommon to find physicians in high-risk categories
> paying premiums in excess of $20,000 annually; and
> WHEREAS, the consumer ultimately must bear the financial burdens cre-
> ated by the high cost of insurance; and
> WHEREAS, without some legislative relief, doctors will be forced to cur-
> tail their practices, retire, or practice defensive medicine at increased cost to
> the citizens of Florida; and
> WHEREAS, the problem has reached crisis proportion in Florida. . . .

Florida Statutes section 768.44 creates a system under which prior to
bringing an action against a medical or osteopathic physician, podiatrist,
hospital or health maintenance organization in any court of the state[,] a
medical malpractice claimant must submit his claim to a medical liability
mediation panel by filing the claim on special forms with the clerk of a state
circuit court. If he fails so to file he is precluded from bringing any action
based on medical malpractice in "any court of [the state of Florida]."
After a claim is properly filed all defendants must answer within twenty
days or else a claimant may proceed in court. If answers are timely filed a
claim is heard by a mediation panel consisting of a state circuit judge, an
attorney, and a licensed physician. The circuit judge is chosen in a "blind"
system; the attorney and physician are chosen from lists compiled by the
chief judge of each judicial circuit in Florida. The attorney and physician
panel members are each paid one hundred dollars for each day they spend
on the panel; both parties to a claim are assessed equally for the payment
of these fees. A hearing must be held within ten months of the filing of
a claim with the circuit court clerk or else the mediation panel's jurisdiction terminates and a normal lawsuit may be filed; any applicable statute
of limitations is tolled from the filing of a claim until at least sixty days
after a mediation panel either mails its decision to the parties or has its

jurisdiction otherwise terminated. Discovery rules of the Florida Rules of Civil Procedure are applied at panel hearings, and procedural and evidentiary rules are less formal than in ordinary civil litigation. Parties may subpoena and cross-examine witnesses at hearings; counsel for the parties may make opening and closing statements. The judge presiding over a hearing is precluded from presiding over any subsequent judicial proceedings arising out of the claim at issue, and other panel members may act as neither counsel nor witnesses at any subsequent trial of the claim.

Within thirty days of the completion of any hearing a panel files a written decision in which, using specified language, it finds the defendant was or was not negligent and accordingly is or is not liable to the plaintiff. A panel member may concur or dissent to the decision in writing. If liability is found and the parties so agree the panel may proceed to help the parties reach a settlement. In this regard, the panel may recommend a reasonable range of damages, but may not recommend punitive damages. Any damage recommendation is not admissible into evidence at any subsequent trial.

Section 768.47 provides that if any party rejects the decision of a mediation panel he may institute litigation based on his claim in an appropriate court. The panel findings are admissible into evidence in any subsequent litigation, but specific findings of fact are inadmissible. Parties may comment upon panel findings in opening statement or closing argument just as on any other evidence introduced at trial. If there was a dissenting opinion to the panel's decision the numerical vote of the panel is also admissible into evidence. If a defendant fails to participate in the mediation panel process the plaintiff may disclose this fact in any subsequent civil action. Carter v. Sparkman, 335 So. 2d 802, 805 (Fla. 1976). Panel members may not be called to testify as witnesses concerning the merits of a case. The jury is instructed that a panel's finding is not binding upon it but should be accorded such weight as the jury chooses to ascribe to it.

Sections 768.44 and .47 are important parts of Florida's Medical Malpractice Law. They successfully weathered both state and federal constitutional challenges in Carter v. Sparkman. We now turn to Mrs. Woods's various attacks on these provisions in the case before us.

Mrs. Woods's most troublesome argument is that sections 768.44 and .47 are procedural rather than substantive and thus should be inapplicable in a district court diversity case. As a general rule, in a federal diversity case the district court applies the substantive law of the forum state. Erie Railroad Co. v. Tompkins[, 304 U.S. 64 (1938)]. . . . Under any of the relevant tests we are convinced that Florida Statutes sections 768.44 and .47 must be applied in federal court. Our opinion on this matter is heightened by the fact that we are guided by "the policies underlying the *Erie* rule." See Hanna v. Plumer, 380 U.S. [460,] 467-68 [1965].

Section 768.44 provides that a plaintiff whose claim is based on an injury or death allegedly caused by medical malpractice must submit his claim to a medical liability mediation panel before he files an action in court; section 768.47 requires the admission into evidence of the panel's findings at any subsequent trial of such a claim. If federal courts sitting in diversity cases refuse to apply sections 768.44 and .47, Florida's medical malpractice statutory scheme will be inequitably administered. Nonresident plaintiffs will have a substantial advantage over resident ones, as non-resident suitors may avoid the mediation panel provision simply by bringing their actions in federal court; consequently, the worst form of forum-shopping will be encouraged. As we have observed, the Florida Legislature acted in 1975 to avert what it viewed as an impending crisis in the health care field. An integral part of its action was to require malpractice claimants to submit their claims to mediation, "thereby reducing the cost of medical malpractice insurance and ultimately medical expenses." Carter v. Sparkman, 335 So. 2d at 806. We would do grave damage to the legislative response evidenced by Florida's Medical Malpractice Law if we refused to apply the mediation requirement in diversity cases. We decline to take such a step. . . .

[A] constitutional challenge Mrs. Woods raises against sections 768.44 and .47 is a claimed denial of due process. . . . Her contention that these provisions violate due process by requiring arbitration of malpractice claims reflects a confusion between *arbitration* and *mediation*. While arbitration generally implies that parties are bound by an arbitrator's decision, Florida merely requires a mediation, or screening, process after which a party is free to proceed to court and file his claim. State required non-consensual arbitration of medical malpractice claims might present constitutional problems, but no such problems are evident when only mediation is required. As we discuss more fully below, the admissibility of mediation panel findings at a subsequent trial does not unduly affect the fairness of that trial and therefore does not constitute a due process violation. Finally, Mrs. Woods's contention that the method for the selection of mediation panel members violates due process puzzles us. Section 768.44(2)(g) provides that the parties to a malpractice dispute may agree upon a physician and attorney to serve upon the mediation panel, and if they do not so agree they are sent the names of five attorneys and physicians. These names are randomly selected from a list prepared by the chief judge of a Florida judicial circuit. The parties have ten days in which they may challenge the named attorneys and physicians for cause, and if a challenge for cause succeeds the challenged name is stricken and a new name is added to those already under consideration. The actual panel members are chosen when the parties alternately strike names from those provided them until the names of only one attorney and one physician remain. After the panel is chosen the parties may question the physician and attorney to determine if either of them has a state of mind regarding the subject matter at issue, the case at hand, or any parties directly or indirectly involved in said case, that will prevent him from acting with impartiality. Upon a determination by the judicial referee that either panelist cannot act with complete impartiality, the judicial referee shall remove said panelist. We find that this selection process fully comports with due process standards.

Mrs. Woods's final attack against sections 768.44 and .47 is her contention that they combine unconstitutionally to restrict her seventh amendment right to a jury trial. Two seventh amendment questions are presented: (1) does making screening a condition precedent to a jury trial unduly burden the right to such a trial; and (2) does the admission into evidence of a mediation panel's finding on liability usurp the function of a jury.

Mrs. Woods argues that the delay incident to the mediation prerequisite unconstitutionally infringes upon her seventh amendment right. This contention is without merit. The seventh amendment "does not prescribe at what stage of an action a trial by jury must, if demanded, be had, or what conditions may be imposed upon the demand of such a trial, consistently with preserving the right to it." Capital Traction Co. v. Hof, 174 U.S. 1, 23 (1899). Nothing in the seventh amendment requires that a jury make its findings at the earliest possible moment in the course of civil litigation; the requirement is only that the jury *ultimately* determine the issues of fact if they cannot be settled by the parties or determined as a matter of law. As stated by the Florida Supreme Court in Carter v. Sparkman, [335 So. 2d 802, 805 (Fla. 1976), *cert. denied*, 429 U.S. 1041 (1977),]

> [a]lthough courts are generally opposed to any burden being placed on the rights of aggrieved persons to enter the courts . . . there may be reasonable restrictions prescribed by law. Typical examples are the fixing of a time within which suit must be brought, payment of reasonable cost deposits, pursuit of certain administrative relief such as zoning matters or workmen's compensation claims, or the requirement that newspapers be given the right of retraction before an action for libel may be filed.

If a federal court may constitutionally refer a complicated matter to an auditor or special master, it may certainly utilize a medical liability mediation panel without violating the dictates of the seventh amendment. Once the panel has considered the evidence and rendered its decision either party to the claim is free to proceed to a jury trial; the jury will remain the ultimate arbiter of the case. So long as Mrs. Woods's right to have her claim fully and finally determined by a jury is preserved, she cannot be heard to complain that her right to a jury trial has been unconstitutionally restricted.

Mrs. Woods maintains that the presentation of panel findings on liability at a subsequent jury trial will so influence the jury that it will be unable independently to examine the question of liability, particularly since section 768.47 precludes the calling of panel members to testify regarding the merits of the case. We are unable to accept this contention. Section 768.47(2) specifically provides that "[t]he jury shall be instructed that the conclusion of the hearing panel shall not be binding, but shall be accorded such weight as they choose to ascribe to it." The panel finding is a particularly relevant, but not conclusive, form of evidence. The parties to a malpractice dispute are free to present the same witnesses and exhibits before the trial jury that they presented to the mediation panel, and the jury may draw its own conclusions from their testimony, even if in so doing it rejects the panel's finding.

## *Notes and Questions*

1. What are the mediator's obligations—simply encouraging the parties to talk and maintaining order, or carrying messages between the parties and persuading them to accept a particular solution? Is true neutrality possible? Is the mediator legally or morally responsible for the parties' agreement? Compare Lawrence Susskind, Environmental Mediation and the Accountability Problem, 6 Vt. L. Rev. 1 (1981), with Joseph B. Stulberg, The Theory and Practice of Mediation: A Reply to Professor Susskind, 6 Vt. L. Rev. 85 (1981); see also Robert A. Baruch Bush, Efficiency and Protection, or Empowerment and Recognition?: The Mediator's Role and Ethical Standards in Mediation, 41 U. Fla. L. Rev. 253 (1989).

2. What is the role of law and of lawyers in mediation? Does the lawyer-mediator have an obligation to disclose relevant law or to take other steps that would level the parties' power imbalance? A spectrum of views has emerged, ranging from prohibitions on tendering such advice or information to full disclosure. See generally Craig A. McEwen, Nancy H. Rogers, and Richard J. Maiman, Bring in the Lawyers: Challenging the Dominant Approaches to Ensuring Fairness in Divorce Mediation, 79 Minn. L. Rev. 1317 (1995); Leonard Riskin, Toward New Standards for the Neutral Lawyer in Mediation, 26 Ariz. L. Rev. 329 (1984). Many national, state, and local bar associations have developed formal opinions on the subject. See Model Rules of Professional Conduct, Rule 2.2; Model Code of Professional Responsibility, Ethical Consideration 5-20. See also Robert Mnookin and Lewis Kornhauser, Bargaining in the Shadow of the Law: The Case of Divorce, 88 Yale L.J. 950 (1979).

3. Does the mediation option put the lawyer at odds with her client? By what standards should an attorney measure the legitimacy of a client's mediated settlement? Sandra E. Purnell, Comment, The Attorney as Mediator: Inherent Conflict of Interest?, 32 UCLA L. Rev. 986 (1985).

One consequence of the rise of mediation has been a fast-growing industry of mediators who compete with the judiciary for the "business" of dispute settlement. Some judges in Connecticut are getting a piece of that action by working as private, paid mediators settling lawsuits for a nonprofit mediation service. See Kirk Johnson, Public Judges as Private Contractors: A Legal Frontier, N.Y. Times, Dec. 10, 1994, at B11. An architect of the program, which is called "Sta-Fed," explained that one of its premises is to avoid the drain on the judiciary created by large, private mediation firms that have wooed top judges off the bench with the promise of salaries far higher than those in the public sector. Senior judges who work for Sta-Fed may do so only if they agree not to leave the bench. Is there cause for alarm in the idea of civil justice going private?

## 3.   Other Forms of ADR

Here is a brief description of other forms of dispute resolution. Some of these types build on concepts previously discussed in the sections on arbitration and mediation; others have developed independently.

*a. Negotiation.* This is probably the most common form of dispute resolution, in which two or more disputing parties try to work out their differences without intervention. While it is easy to overlook negotiation as a means of dispute resolution, recent scholarship has more fully developed its principles and applications, and has emphasized its usefulness for fundamental problem-solving that can avoid many of the other dispute resolution techniques. See, e.g., Roger Fisher and William Ury, Getting to Yes (1991).

*b. Med-Arb.* This form of private dispute resolution combines mediation and arbitration into a single process. The dispute is first mediated, and if that proves unsuccessful, the dispute moves into arbitration. This form of dispute resolution is found in labor-management agreements and, increasingly, in consumer banking. See generally Thomas J. Brewer and Lawrence R. Mills, Combining Mediation & Arbitration, 54 Disp. Resol. J. 32 (1999); Stephen B. Goldberg, The Mediation of Grievances Under a Collective Bargaining Contract: An Alternative to Arbitration, 77 Nw. U. L. Rev. 270 (1982). Should the same neutral party who handled the mediation be allowed to handle the arbitration?

*c. Mini-trials.* This form of private dispute resolution is best thought of as an aid to settlement. Although forms vary, the concept is that the parties each present their cases in truncated form to a neutral third party who renders an opinion. The opinion generally is not binding, but provides the basis for settlement discussions between the parties, which may or may not include the neutral party. See generally Texas Young Lawyers' Association Committees on ADR, State Bar of Texas, Mini-trials: Opportunities for Compromise, 51 Tex. B.J. 34 (1988).

*d. Summary Jury Trials.* Pioneered by U.S. District Judge Thomas Lambros, the summary jury trial (SJT) is a form of court-ordered mini-trial in which the neutral party rendering an opinion is a jury drawn from the same population as would be used in a real trial. Again, the SJT should be seen as an aid to settlement. See generally Thomas Lambros, The Summary Jury Trial, 103 F.R.D. 461 (1984); Richard Posner, The Summary Jury Trial and Other Alternative Methods of Dispute Resolution: Some Cautionary Observations, 53 U. Chi. L. Rev. 366 (1986).

*e. Early Neutral Evaluation.* The Northern District Court of California is among the courts that have experimented with a dispute resolution mechanism known as early neutral evaluation (ENE), under which an evaluator—not the trial judge—is assigned by the judge to meet with the parties to eyeball the case, discuss disputed issues, explore settlement possibilities, and evaluate the parties' relative chances of prevailing. See Joshua D. Rosenberg and H. Jay Folberg, Alternative Dispute Resolution: An Empirical Analysis, 46 Stan. L. Rev. 1487, 1487-1491 (1994).

*f. Multidisciplinary Practice.* Following on the heels of their European counterparts, American lawyers in growing numbers are weighing the virtues of multidisciplinary practice, in which attorneys partner with non-lawyers to provide a range of corporate services, eschewing the traditional role of lawyers as "firemen," called only in times of trouble. See, e.g., Michael Jonathan Grinfeld, What's Law Got to Do with It?, Cal. Lawyer, June 2000, at 34. The American Bar Association has been wrestling with the ethical and competitive issues raised by such previously prohibited arrangements. An ABA committee has recommended that lawyers "be permitted to share fees and join with nonlawyer professionals in a practice that delivers both legal and nonlegal professional services . . . provided that the lawyers have the control and authority necessary to assure lawyer independence in the rendering of legal services." ABA Commission on Multidisciplinary Practice, Report to the House of Delegates, http://www.abanet.org/cpr/mdp/mdpfinalrep2000.html (last visited Sept. 23, 2016).

## 4.   Critical Perspectives on ADR

Not everyone has been enthusiastic about alternatives to adversarial procedures. One concern, raised by Paul Carrington, is that by tailoring procedure to particular types of disputes we risk reproducing the arcane system of code pleading that the modern rules were intended to eliminate. The advantage of the modern system, some think, is that lawyers need not master the intricacies of multiple procedural devices; rather there is only one form of action that applies to all civil cases. See Paul Carrington, Civil Procedure and Alternative Dispute Resolution, 34 J. Legal Educ. 298 (1984).

Another potential drawback of some forms of ADR is that they may favor informal, discretionary decision making over more formal and bounded methods. This can lead to more impressionistic, idiosyncratic, or standardless decision making, which may result in bias against some litigants or arbitrary outcomes. See, e.g., John Conley and William O'Barr, Fundamentals of Jurisprudence: An Ethnography of Judicial Decision Making in Informal Courts, 66 N.C. L. Rev. 467 (1988); Richard Delgado et al., Fairness and Formality, Minimizing the Risk of Prejudice in Alternative Dispute Resolution, 1985 Wis. L. Rev. 1359; William O'Barr and John Conley, Litigant Satisfaction Versus Legal Adequacy in Small Claims Court Narratives, 19 Law & Soc'y Rev. 661 (1985). See generally 1-2 The Politics of Informal Justice (Richard L. Abel ed., 1982).

In the specific context of domestic disputes, some observers worry that mediation or other nonadversarial techniques may tend to favor the economically or emotionally stronger party over the one who can least tolerate conflict or who most values a harmonious resolution. See, e.g., Martha Fineman, Dominant Discourse, Professional Language, and Legal Change in Child Custody Decision Making, 101 Harv. L. Rev. 727, 765 (1988); Carol Lefcourt, Women, Mediation and Family Law, 18 Clearinghouse Rev. 266, 269 (1984); Lisa Lerman, Mediation of Wife Abuse Cases: The Adverse Impact of Informal Dispute Resolution on Women, 7 Harv. Women's L.J.

57 (1984). This may inspire some parties to settle for far less than they might obtain before a judge in a traditional adversarial proceeding. As one writer has put it, "compromise only is an equitable solution between equals; between unequals, it 'inevitably reproduces inequality.'" Jerold S. Auerbach, Justice Without Law? 136 (1983); see also Owen M. Fiss, Against Settlement, 93 Yale L.J. 1073 (1984).

Other critics of the informalization of procedure insist that it may "neutralize conflict that could threaten state or capital." Richard L. Abel, The Contradictions of Informal Justice, in 1 The Politics of Informal Justice, supra, at 267, 280. As Abel argues, "[i]nformal institutions neutralize conflict by denying its existence, by simulating a society in which conflict is less frequent and less threatening, and by choosing to recognize and handle only those forms of conflict that do not challenge the basic structures. Informal processes moderate the antagonistic adversarial posture of the parties. This is a difficult task because people involved in conflict usually want to win; they seek vindication." Id. at 283.

For a skeptical look at unbounded claims of a litigation explosion in the United States, see Aaron Hiller, Rule 11 and Tort Reform: Myth, Reality, and Legislation, 18 Geo. J. Legal Ethics, 809 (2005); Deborah Rhode, In the Interests of Justice (2000); Marc Galanter, Reading the Landscape of Disputes: What We Know and Don't Know (and Think We Know) About Our Allegedly Contentious and Litigious Society, 31 UCLA L. Rev. 4 (1983). To the extent that ADR is inspired by the sense that the number of claims litigated under traditional methods has skyrocketed and the attendant costs have become too expensive, Galanter's research obviously is highly relevant to the ADR movement. Indeed, many of the arguments for ADR have been met with rebuttals and surrebuttals, as the debate about ADR measures continues. See, e.g., Owen M. Fiss, Out of Eden, 94 Yale L.J. 1669 (1985); Andrew McThenia and Thomas Shaffer, For Reconciliation, 94 Yale L.J. 1660 (1985).

A very thoughtful analysis of the arguments for and against making civil justice more informal is found in William Simon, Legal Informality and Redistributive Politics, 19 Clearinghouse Rev. 384 (1985). Simon concludes that the matter is more complex than some arguments against informality admit. For example, he argues that informal procedures in welfare hearing systems, while far from perfect,

> facilitate a far more meaningful degree of participation by unrepresented claimants than any other formal system I can think of, and sympathetic and competent official performances are not uncommon. The most serious problems with welfare administration concern, not the hearing procedures, but the frontline bureaucracy and most problems arise from the tendency of increasing *formality* in administration to encumber claimant access to the system.

Id. at 386 (emphasis in original).

To what extent do the alternatives to adversarial procedure sound attractive? Workable? Efficient? On what do your responses to these questions depend?

Obviously, at this early stage in your legal career you may feel unable to judge some of the arguments about the current system's shortcomings and strengths because you have not yet worked within it. But surely you are able—some might say more able than a career-worn veteran lawyer—to judge how the various alternatives might suit the needs of laypeople who must use the civil justice system. In this respect, perhaps the most important of the foregoing materials are those that describe what process "feels fair" to people in various cultures and subcultural contexts. One of the most significant findings of this literature seems to be that people regard procedure as fair when they feel they have some control over it, in the specific sense that they are allowed to participate and *feel* as though they have been heard. Given that the vast majority of legal disputes are handled without a full-blown trial, all lawyers would do well to heed this psychological insight. For even in the nonadversarial, extrajudicial context of the lawyer's office, clients often may need to be heard, and their lawyers often will be the only audience for their grievances. As such, the emerging evidence about what kinds of hearings seem to satisfy laypeople's sense of just treatment may be as relevant to client counseling as it is to proposals for changes in formal judicial procedures.

# 6 *More Complex Litigation*

We turn now to elaborations of the basic procedural framework. In the area of federal subject matter jurisdiction, we study first the law to be applied in diversity cases: the jurisprudence of Erie R.R. Co. v. Tompkins, 304 U.S. 64 (1938). Then we turn to issues of when federal courts may hear state claims, as well as take cases from state courts, and allocate business among themselves. Finally, we move beyond the bimodal lawsuit to joinder, aggregation, and class actions.

The complexities of litigation explored in this chapter strain the transsubstantive nature of the rules and the capacities of judges and juries. Nowhere is this more apparent than in the class action device.

## A. SUBJECT MATTER JURISDICTION IN A DUAL COURT SYSTEM: A SECOND LOOK

### 1. The Governing Law in a Diversity Case

#### Problem Case: Having It Whose Way?

Recall the facts of *Burger King* in Chapter 1, which involved the franchise agreement dispute between the Miami-based Burger King Corporation and the two businessmen from Michigan. The plaintiff filed the action in a federal district court in Florida.

Yet the plaintiff corporation invoked state law only — trademark infringement and breach of contract — so that jurisdiction was based solely on diversity. (Note that there is also federal law that governs trademark, but it does not preempt all state law in this area.) How is it that a federal court comes to review matters of state substantive law? Which state's law would govern the contract and trademark infringement action — Michigan's or Florida's? Remember that there was a choice of law provision in the franchise agreement. Does that affect your answer?

#### a. From *Erie* to *Hanna*

Assume that an action is filed in federal district court based solely on diversity; that is, no federal question appears on the face of the well-pleaded complaint. What law should govern this dispute?

The Rules of Decision Act, today found at 28 U.S.C. § 1652, reads as follows:

> The laws of the several states, except where the Constitution or treaties of the United States or Acts of Congress otherwise require or provide, shall be regarded as rules of decision in civil actions in the courts of the United States in cases where they apply.

The key interpretive issue in this clause is: What are "the laws of the several states"? Do they include both substantive and procedural rules? Both statutory and decisional law?

The modern answer, which dates from the famous case of Erie R.R. Co. v. Tompkins, 304 U.S. 64 (1938), is that the Federal Rules govern procedural matters while state law (statutory and decisional) covers substantive issues. You might quickly see that this is necessarily so in a diversity case because, by definition, the case does not involve federal law. But of course, the point is more complicated.

Before *Erie*, decided in the same year that the Federal Rules of Civil Procedure took effect, the situation was just the opposite. So-called federal common law governed the substance of diversity cases whenever no state statute (versus state decisional law) on point existed, and the federal courts (lacking general procedural rules of their own) used the procedure of the state in which the district court was located, except in matters arising in equity. (The equity side versus the law side of federal court jurisdiction is discussed in Chapter 2, supra.)

This pre-*Erie* approach to choice of law in diversity suits was called the *Swift* doctrine, named after the 1842 decision Swift v. Tyson, 41 U.S. (16 Pet.) 1 (1842). Under *Swift*, the "laws of the several states" that federal courts were bound to follow included only state constitutions, statutes, and state judicial opinions interpreting statutes. Federal courts were not bound by other state common law or precedent, but were instead left to develop a body of substantive federal common law to address matters of "general"—as opposed to local—concern.

## Edward A. Purcell Jr., Litigation and Inequality: Federal Diversity Jurisdiction in Industrial America, 1870-1958
Pages 226-230 (1992)

*Erie* was an unusually dramatic case, and its New Deal context and the fact that Brandeis wrote for the majority highlighted its political and intellectual origins. Since the late nineteenth century legal writers had criticized *Swift* on the various grounds that the Court discussed, and the dissents of Field and Holmes had convinced many that *Swift* was unsound in theory as well as in practice. Southerners and westerners, and political progressives generally, had charged for more than half a century that the federal common law favored business interests, encouraged corporate forum shopping, and denigrated the authority of the states. The context of the Court's decision in *Erie,* however, blending easily into the context of both earlier criticisms and the New Deal revolution, tended to obscure the extent to which the challenges of escalating litigation tactics helped move the Court toward abolishing the federal common law by forcing the Justices to recognize its anomalous and discordant nature.

Litigation between individuals and corporations had become increasingly arbitrary and unstable after 1910. The growing arbitrariness—the fact that the value of a case could be determined largely by the tactical possibilities open to the parties, not by its merits—was apparent across the board. The arbitrariness no longer related merely to the basic questions of whether plaintiff lived in a town that was distant from the nearest federal court, or in an area where the federal court had a particularly heavy backlog, or in a state where the local and federal common law conflicted. Instead, litigation tactics had generated new and multiple levels on which arbitrary differences wholly unrelated to the merits of a suit could prove significant or even dispositive. . . .

The use of specialized procedural tactics and counter-tactics made litigation increasingly volatile and unpredictable. As parties and their attorneys grew more sophisticated, they created an ever-growing number of tactics to squeeze out an advantage. As the methods of transportation and communications improved, they yielded ready access to courts across the nation. As social subgroups organized and gained in experience and as the bar grew more specialized, they opened up for larger numbers of litigants the tactical possibilities that their predecessors had discovered. "For every weapon there is a counter weapon," an attorney for the Brotherhood of Railroad Trainmen explained. "For every form of attack a defense is developed." Tactical inventiveness and organizational development combined to intensify the pressures that pushed against the limits of both doctrine and court structure.

Equally important, the arbitrariness and volatility were becoming more visible to the formal law. Until World War I, the problem of distance had been irrelevant as a legal factor, and the problem of delay merely one of administration. The doctrines of the formal law ignored both. The new characteristics of the system, however, were different. The formal law could not ignore the persistence and frequency of certain types of jurisdictional disputes, the widening scope of interstate forum shopping, the pressures for expanded equitable remedies in state and federal courts, and the need to answer increasingly complex questions about personal jurisdiction, choice of law, the full faith and credit clause, the role of *forum non conveniens,* the availability and conditions of declaratory relief, and the scope of the constitutional right to trial by jury. . . .

Indeed, diversity litigation in the system and actions under the FELA [Federal Employers' Liability Act] were not the only areas where tactical escalation was developing or threatened. Diversity jurisdiction could offer advantages in other types of litigation as well. Given their greater resources and the much larger amounts at stake, corporations and wealthy individuals were likely to prove even more inventive in disputes involving real estate or commercial transactions. Intracorporate conflicts and shareholder derivative suits could also spur the most determined and byzantine of litigations.

When Congress passed the Rules Enabling Act in 1934, it symbolized and accelerated the changes that the twentieth century was bringing to litigation practice. The act conferred on the Supreme Court the authority to prepare and promulgate, subject to congressional approval, rules of procedure for the federal courts, and it provided for the repeal of the Conformity Act. The new Federal Rules of Civil Procedure were promulgated and went into effect in 1938. The enabling act and the new rules gave further institutional support to the idea that the federal courts constituted a national system of courts, and they in effect recognized that large corporations and a national economy were making twentieth-century corporate legal practice into an interstate enterprise. Separating federal from state practice, the new Federal Rules at once freed the national courts from state procedural rules, confirmed implicitly the higher professional status of federal practice, and facilitated the development by large urban law firms of a national practice in support of the nationwide operations of their corporate clients.

Those nationwide operations were visible in the 1930s when a number of corporations mounted elaborate legal campaigns to stall the New Deal. Companies shopped across the country for the judges and circuits that were most willing to block government agencies, and they cleverly employed shareholder derivative suits to obtain injunctions prohibiting company compliance with the laws. The latter tactic allowed suspiciously "friendly" suits with minimal opposition or agreed-upon facts, and it often prevented the government from even participating in the defense of the challenged laws or administrative actions. Justice Jackson, who had fought many of the New Deal's legal battles when he was Assistant Attorney General, noted the clever uses that the New Deal's opponents made of shareholder derivative suits. The "apparent adversaries were not in real controversy," he explained. "They framed the issues to suit themselves." Small wonder, then, that in his concurrence in Miles [v. Illinois Central R.R. Co., 315 U.S. 698 (1942),] Jackson readily appreciated the "realistic" significance of venue choice under the FELA. "There is nothing which requires a plaintiff to whom such a choice is given," Jackson had remarked, "to exercise it in a self-denying or large-hearted manner." . . .

As the Court tried to grapple with interstate forum shopping, the tactical escalation in insurance litigation, and similar developments in other areas, it began gradually to moderate the federal common law in the 1930s. To the extent that differences between the common law of the states and the federal courts could be effectively minimized, the incentives for forum shopping and other tactical maneuvers could be lessened. In 1933 the Court limited the *Swift* doctrine in insurance cases by introducing the principle that the federal courts should accept state common law if the issue was "balanced with doubt." In the mid-1930s it applied the same principle to other common law areas and seemed to defer more often to state courts for the determination of local policies and laws. The fact that the Court itself continued on occasion to apply *Swift* only highlighted the apparent unpredictability of the doctrine. . . .

If the old Supreme Court struggled with the federal common law and the challenges of tactical escalation, however, it still refused to abolish *Swift*. That drastic step required a new Court. When *Erie* came down, six Justices voted to overturn *Swift*: Brandeis and Justice Harlan F. Stone, members of the Court's so-called progressive wing who had joined Holmes's dissent in the *Taxicab* case [Black & White Taxicab & Transfer Co. v. Brown & Yellow Taxicab & Transfer Co., 276 U.S. 518 (1928)]; Chief Justice Charles Evans Hughes and Justice Owen J. Roberts, the two Justices who had apparently switched their positions in 1936-1937; and Justices Hugo L. Black and Stanley Reed, the first two Roosevelt appointees who had recently joined the Court. The remaining Justices, members of the Court's anti–New Deal wing who had been with the majority in the *Taxicab* case, dissented.

Although *Erie* eliminated the wild card of the federal common law, it arguably had some potential to increase incentives for interstate forum shopping. By abolishing the relative interstate uniformity of the federal common law, *Erie* raised the possibility that parties, knowing that the common law applied in the federal courts would no longer be uniform, might be encouraged to seek more favorable substantive law in distant states. The Roosevelt Court discounted that possibility for two reasons. First, it was more hypothetical than real. Choice-of-law rules and the full faith and credit clause restricted forum shopping for more favorable substantive state law. Indeed, interstate forum shopping was inspired in relatively few cases by differences in the states' substantive laws. Rather, it arose for the most part from the advantages offered by different procedural rules and judicial practices or by such extralegal factors as the specialized abilities of local importers, the lure of de facto larger verdicts, and the leverage gained by imposing practical burdens on adversaries. Second, and more important, the Roosevelt Court knowingly made a fundamental value choice. *Erie* protected the 95 percent of individual plaintiffs who sued, usually out of necessity, in their home states. For those plaintiffs intrastate uniformity between state and federal court was infinitely more important than whatever degree of uniformity *Swift* engendered in the common law applied nationally in the federal courts. Whatever instabilities and arbitrariness existed in the legal system, *Erie* would minimize them for the vast majority of individuals.

Although *Erie* was a product of the early Roosevelt Court, the later Roosevelt Court enforced it broadly. The New Deal Justices who subsequently joined the Court shared *Erie*'s hostility to forum shopping but doubted its constitutional language. Although the constitutional basis of the decision was not clear, many of them assumed that it rested on the Tenth Amendment. As good New Dealers, they were suspicious of the Tenth Amendment which, under the old Court, had served as a substantive limitation on the powers of Congress. Accordingly, they simply ignored *Erie*'s constitutional language, embraced it as establishing a broad anti-forum shopping policy, and transformed that policy into a major principle of federal law.

In a series of cases handed down during the 1940s, the Court enforced *Erie* to minimize the legal incentives for intrastate forum shopping. In 1940 it held that the federal courts were bound not just by the decisions of a state's "highest court" but, in the absence of such decisions, also by the rulings of intermediate state appellate courts and even by the rulings of state trial courts. The following year in Klaxon v. Stentor-Electric Manufacturing Co.[, 313 U.S. 487 (1941),] it held that *Erie*'s "prohibition" against "independent determinations" of state laws by federal courts "extends to the field of conflict of laws," even though the field was traditionally classified as an area of "procedural" law. In diversity cases involving state law issues, *Klaxon* held, federal courts were bound to apply the choice-of-law rules of the state in which they sat. In 1945 in Guaranty Trust Co. v. York[, 326 U.S. 99 (1945),] the Roosevelt Court handed down its most far-reaching elaboration of *Erie,* holding that it required federal courts to apply state "procedural" rules if they would "significantly affect the result of a litigation." The "nub of the policy that underlies *Erie*," *York* declared, was that the "accident" of diverse citizenship should not lead to a different result in a federal court than would occur in a state court.

Together *Klaxon, York,* and the Court's other decisions in the 1940s implemented *Erie* broadly and reduced to a minimum the differences in the formal law that state and federal courts in the same state would apply. By the end of the decade the federal courts applied not only the common law rules of the state in which they sat but also some of the "procedural" rules that the local state courts followed. Though differences in procedure and institutional structure between state and federal courts remained, the divergent general federal common law had been thoroughly rooted out and the law applied in state and federal courts sitting in the same state brought closely into line.

---

A workable definition of a "substantive" rule is one that characteristically and reasonably affects people's conduct at the stage of primary activity outside the context of litigation. It is a rule with a purpose other than that of assuring the fairness and/or efficiency of litigation. Rules of liability are a clear example of substantive rules, because they influence conduct (e.g., reasonable care, safety precautions) outside the courtroom.

A "procedural" rule, generally speaking, is one that is designed to make the process of dispute resolution a fair and efficient mechanism for resolving legal controversies. Rules regarding the filing of a complaint are a clear example.

With these definitions and this simple statement of the *Erie* rule in mind, we now turn to the case itself. When reading it, ask yourself how it was that the federal courts had for nearly 150 years managed to "misread" their rulemaking power. If *Erie* is constitutionally required, what do you make of the Court's failure to recognize its error for so many years? Is there another explanation for the Court's 1938 dramatic reversal?

## *Erie R.R. Co. v. Tompkins*
304 U.S. 64 (1938)

JUSTICE BRANDEIS delivered the opinion of the Court.

The question for decision is whether the oft-challenged doctrine of Swift v. Tyson[, 16 Pet. 1, 18 (1842),] shall now be disapproved.

Tompkins, a citizen of Pennsylvania, was injured on a dark night by a passing freight train of the Erie Railroad Company while walking along its right of way at Hughestown in that State. He claimed that the accident occurred through negligence in the operation, or maintenance, of the train; that he was rightfully on the premises as licensee because on a commonly used beaten footpath which ran for a short distance alongside the tracks; and that he was struck by something which looked like a door projecting from one of the moving cars. To enforce that claim he brought an action in the federal court for southern New York, which had jurisdiction because the company is a corporation of that State. It denied liability; and the case was tried by a jury.

The Erie insisted that its duty to Tompkins was no greater than that owed to a trespasser. It contended, among other things, that its duty to Tompkins, and hence its liability, should be determined in accordance with the Pennsylvania law; that under the law of Pennsylvania, as declared by its highest court, persons who use pathways along the railroad right of way—that is a longitudinal pathway as distinguished from a crossing—are to be deemed trespassers; and that the railroad is not liable for injuries to undiscovered trespassers resulting from its negligence, unless it be wanton or willful. Tompkins denied that any such rule had been established by the decisions of the Pennsylvania courts; and contended that, since there was no statute of the State on the subject, the railroad's duty and liability is to be determined in federal courts as a matter of general law.

The trial judge refused to rule that the applicable law precluded recovery. The jury brought in a verdict of $30,000; and the judgment entered thereon was affirmed by the Circuit Court of Appeals, which held, 90 F.2d 603, 604, that it was unnecessary to consider whether the law of Pennsylvania was as contended, because the question was one not of local, but of general, law and that

> upon questions of general law the federal courts are free, in absence of a local statute, to exercise their independent judgment as to what the law is; and it is well settled that the question of the responsibility of a railroad for injuries caused by its servants is one of general law. . . . Where the public has made open and notorious use of a railroad right of way for a long period of time and without objection, the company owes to persons on such permissive pathway a duty of care in the operation of its trains. . . . It is likewise

generally recognized law that a jury may find that negligence exists toward a pedestrian using a permissive path on the railroad right of way if he is hit by some object projecting from the side of the train.

The Erie had contended that application of the Pennsylvania rule was required, among other things, by § 34 of the Federal Judiciary Act of September 24, 1789, chap. 20, 28 U.S.C.A. § 725, which provides: "The laws of the several States, except where the Constitution, treaties, or statutes of the United States otherwise require or provide, shall be regarded as rules of decision in trials at common law, in the courts of the United States, in cases where they apply."

Because of the importance of the question whether the federal court was free to disregard the alleged rule of the Pennsylvania common law, we granted certiorari.

First. Swift v. Tyson . . . held that federal courts exercising jurisdiction on the ground of diversity of citizenship need not, in matters of general jurisprudence, apply the unwritten law of the State as declared by its highest court; that they are free to exercise an independent judgment as to what the common law of the State is—or should be; and that, as there stated by Mr. Justice Story:

> The true interpretation of the thirty-fourth section limited its application to State laws strictly local, that is to say, to the positive statutes of the state, and the construction thereof adopted by the local tribunals, and to rights and titles to things having a permanent locality, such as the rights and titles to real estate, and other matters immovable and intraterritorial in their nature and character. It never has been supposed by us, that the section did apply, or was designed to apply, to questions of more general nature, not at all dependent upon local statutes or local usages of a fixed and permanent operation, as, for example, to the construction of ordinary contracts or other written instruments, and especially to questions of general commercial law, where the State tribunals are called upon to perform the like functions as ourselves, that is, to ascertain upon general reasoning and legal analogies, what is the true exposition of the contract or instrument, or what is the just rule furnished by the principles of commercial law to govern the case.

The Court in applying the rule of § 34 to equity cases, in Mason v. United States, 260 U.S. 545, 559 [(1923)], said: "The statute, however, is merely declarative of the rule which would exist in the absence of the statute." The federal courts assumed, in the broad field of "general law," the power to declare rules of decision which Congress was confessedly without power to enact as statutes. Doubt was repeatedly expressed as to the correctness of the construction given § 34, and as to the soundness of the rule which it introduced. But it was the more recent research of a competent scholar, who examined the original document, which established that the construction given to it by the Court was erroneous; and that the purpose of the section was merely to make certain that, in all matters except those in which some federal law is controlling, the federal courts exercising jurisdiction in diversity of citizenship cases would apply as their rules of decision the law of the State, unwritten as well as written.[5]

Criticism of the doctrine became widespread after the decision of Black & W. Taxicab & Transfer Co. v. Brown & Y. Taxicab & Transfer Co., 276 U.S. 518 [(1928)]. There, Brown and Yellow, a Kentucky corporation owned by Kentuckians, and the Louisville and Nashville Railroad, also a Kentucky corporation, wished that the former should have the exclusive privilege of soliciting passenger and baggage transportation at the Bowling Green, Kentucky, railroad station; and that the Black and White, a competing Kentucky corporation, should be prevented from interfering with that privilege. Knowing that such a contract would be void under the common law of Kentucky, it was arranged that the Brown and Yellow reincorporate under the law of Tennessee, and that the contract with the railroad should be executed there. The suit was then brought by the Tennessee corporation in the federal court for western Kentucky to enjoin competition by the Black and White; an injunction issued by the district court was sustained by the Court of Appeals; and this court, citing many decisions in which the doctrine of Swift v. Tyson had been applied, affirmed the decree.

Second. Experience in applying the doctrine of Swift v. Tyson had revealed its defects, political and social; and the benefits expected to flow from the rule did not accrue. Persistence of state courts in their own opinions on questions of common law prevented uniformity; and the impossibility of discovering a satisfactory line of demarcation between the province of general law and that of local law developed a new well of uncertainties.

On the other hand, the mischievous results of the doctrine had become apparent. Diversity of citizenship jurisdiction was conferred in order to prevent apprehended discrimination in state courts against those not citizens of the State. Swift v. Tyson introduced grave discrimination by noncitizens against citizens. It made rights enjoyed under the unwritten "general law" vary according to whether enforcement was sought in the state or in the federal court; and the privilege of selecting the court in which the right should be determined was conferred upon the noncitizen. Thus, the doctrine rendered impossible equal protection of the law. In attempting to promote uniformity of law throughout the United States, the doctrine had prevented uniformity in the administration of the law of the State.

The discrimination resulting became in practice far-reaching. This resulted in part from the broad province accorded to the so-called "general law" as to which federal courts exercised an independent judgment. In addition to questions of purely commercial law, "general law" was held to include the obligations under contracts entered into and to be performed within the State, the extent to which a carrier operating within a State may stipulate for exemption from liability for his own negligence or that of his employee; the liability for torts committed within the State upon persons

---

5. Charles Warren, New Light on the History of the Federal Judiciary Act of 1789 (1923), 37 Harv. L. Rev. 49, 51-52, 81-88, 108.

resident or property located there, even where the question of liability depended upon the scope of a property right conferred by the State; and the right to exemplary or punitive damages. Furthermore, state decisions construing local deeds, mineral conveyances, and even devises of real estate were disregarded.

In part the discrimination resulted from the wide range of persons held entitled to avail themselves of the federal rule by resort to the diversity of citizenship jurisdiction. Through this jurisdiction, individual citizens willing to remove from their own State and become citizens of another might avail themselves of the federal rule. And, without even change of residence, a corporate citizen of the State could avail itself of the federal rule by reincorporating under the laws of another state, as was done in the *Taxicab* case.

The injustice and confusion incident to the doctrine of Swift v. Tyson have been repeatedly urged as reasons for abolishing or limiting diversity of citizenship jurisdiction. Other legislative relief has been proposed. If only a question of statutory construction were involved, we should not be prepared to abandon a doctrine so widely applied throughout nearly a century. But the unconstitutionality of the course pursued has now been made clear and compels us to do so.

Third. Except in matters governed by the Federal Constitution or by Acts of Congress, the law to be applied in any case is the law of the State. And whether the law of the State shall be declared by its Legislature in a statute or by its highest court in a decision is not a matter of federal concern. There is no federal general common law. Congress has no power to declare substantive rules of common law applicable in a State whether they be local in their nature or "general," be they commercial law or a part of the law of torts. And no clause in the Constitution purports to confer such a power upon the federal courts. . . .

The fallacy underlying the rule declared in Swift v. Tyson is made clear by Mr. Justice Holmes. The doctrine rests upon the assumption that there is "a transcendental body of law outside of any particular State but obligatory within it unless and until changed by statute," that federal courts have the power to use their judgment as to what the rules of common law are; and that in the federal courts "the parties are entitled to an independent judgment on matters of general law":

> [B]ut law in the sense in which courts speak of it today does not exist without some definite authority behind it. The common law so far as it is enforced in a State, whether called common law or not, is not the common law generally but the law of that State existing by the authority of that State without regard to what it may have been in England or anywhere else. . . . The authority and only authority is the state, and if that be so, the voice adopted by the State as its own [whether it be of its Legislature or of its Supreme Court] should utter the last word.

Thus the doctrine of Swift v. Tyson is, as Mr. Justice Holmes said, "an unconstitutional assumption of power by courts of the United States which no lapse of time or respectable array of opinion should make us hesitate to correct." In disapproving that doctrine we do not hold unconstitutional § 34 of the Federal Judiciary Act of 1789, or any other Act of Congress. We merely declare that in applying the doctrine this Court and the lower courts have invaded rights which in our opinion are reserved by the Constitution to the several States. . . .

*Reversed.*

JUSTICE CARDOZO took no part in the consideration or decision of this case.

---

In *Erie,* the Court held that there was no general federal common law upon which federal courts could draw for substantive decisions and mandated that state law apply in diversity suits.

The puzzle is whether this result was constitutionally required, as Justice Brandeis suggested, or if this was merely a statutory requirement. After all, the Constitution gives Congress the power to establish federal courts and to afford these courts power to hear actions arising between citizens of different states. Why, some scholars have asked, does the congressional power to establish these courts not include the power to create courts that may determine both the procedure and the substance of diversity actions?

Regardless of whether the Constitution requires it, however, the Court has interpreted the applicable congressional acts to mean that federal courts sitting in diversity must apply state substantive law. The relevant statutes are the Rules of Decision Act, 28 U.S.C. § 1652, and the Rules Enabling Act, 28 U.S.C. §§ 2072-2077.

The Rules Enabling Act, the current version of which is found at 28 U.S.C. § 2072, provides that the "Supreme Court shall have the power to prescribe general rules of practice and procedure and rules of evidence for cases in the United States district courts" and that "these rules shall not abridge, enlarge, or modify any substantive right." Taken together and grossly simplified, the two acts mean that federal courts apply their own procedure and state substantive law in diversity suits. But see Wilfred J. Ritz, Rewriting the History of the Judiciary Act of 1789, at 134 (Wythe Holt and Lewis LaRue eds., 1990) (arguing that the Judiciary Act of 1789, currently codified at 28 U.S.C. § 1652, directed the federal courts to apply U.S. law rather than English law, and was not intended to compel the application of state law in diversity proceedings); see also Patrick J. Borchers, The Origins of Diversity Jurisdiction, the Rise of Legal Positivism, and a Brave New World for *Erie* and *Klaxon,* 72 Tex. L. Rev. 79 (1993) (arguing that the weight of historical evidence does not support the conclusion that state substantive law must apply in diversity suits); Julius Goebel Jr., History of the Supreme Court of the United States: Antecedents and Beginnings to 1801, at 457-508 (Paul Freund ed., 1971) (recounting the history of the Judiciary Act).

## Note: The Personal and Political Aspects of *Erie*

Professor Purcell, quoted at length before *Erie*, writes about Justice Brandeis's role in shaping the great case:

> Justice Louis D. Brandeis wrote the Court's opinion. Seizing on an otherwise wholly unremarkable common law tort suit, he persuaded a somewhat hesitant majority to use it as the vehicle to overrule *Swift*. His opinion for the Court, in turn, brought together most of the major themes of his judicial career. In broad constitutional terms, *Erie* expanded the power of the states to control their own common law and at the same time restricted the nonconstitutional lawmaking power of the federal judiciary to those areas over which Congress held the ultimate constitutional authority to legislate. With respect to limiting the scope of federal jurisdiction, *Erie* indirectly restricted both diversity and removal by eliminating one of the major incentives for their use. In terms of rationalizing the nation's judicial system, it sought to eliminate the arbitrariness inherent in a rule that made the applicable substantive law vary depending on the forum that heard an action and—as had Brandeis's opinion in Davis [v. Farmer's Coop. Equity Co., 262 U.S. 312 (1923),] initiating the commerce clause venue doctrine—to discourage jurisdictional manipulation and bring greater order and predictability to litigation practice. In political and social terms, *Erie* deprived corporations of the favorable rules of the federal common law and remedied one of the major disadvantages that plaintiffs faced in the system of corporate diversity litigation. Finally, in quite personal terms, *Erie* allowed Brandeis to pay public homage to Holmes, his departed friend and colleague, who for more than a quarter-century had been recognized as the major intellectual and constitutional antagonist of *Swift* and the federal common law.

## b.   Substance and Procedure—Illustrative Cases

After 1938, federal courts sitting in diversity were to follow their own procedure and the substantive laws of the states in which they sat. Perhaps you can imagine the cases that arose next and the existential questions they raised about what is (or is not) a procedural rule. Less than a decade after *Erie*, the Court decided Guaranty Trust Co. v. York, 326 U.S. 99 (1945), which offered this famous guide to interpretation:

> Erie R.R. Co. v. Tompkins was not an endeavor to formulate scientific legal terminology. It expressed a policy that touches vitally the proper distribution of judicial power between State and federal courts. In essence, the intent of that decision was to insure that, in all cases where a federal court is exercising jurisdiction solely because of the diversity of citizenship of the parties, the outcome of the litigation in the federal court should be substantially the same, so far as legal rules determine the outcome of a litigation, as it would be if tried in a State court. The nub of the policy that underlies Erie R.R. Co. v. Tompkins is that for the same transaction the accident of a suit by a nonresident litigant in a federal court instead of in a State court a block away should not lead to a substantially different result.

Id. at 109.

Inevitably, the holding in *Guaranty Trust* was reduced to the following, ultimately unworkable bromide: If a rule is "outcome determinative," it is substantive and state law must govern. The obvious problem with the standard is that even the most relentlessly procedural rules, such as the size and color of the paper used for a complaint, may become "outcome determinative" if a court refuses to accept a complaint that does not comply with the rules.

The following cases highlight the Court's struggle with *Guaranty Trust* and with the distinction between substance and procedure. They remain more important for their results than for their reasoning, and are useful guidelines for the kinds of rules the Court has found to be "substantive."

### i.   *Cohen v. Beneficial Indus. Loan Corp.,* 337 U.S. 541 (1949)

This case held that a federal court in New Jersey was bound by a statute of that state that imposes on the plaintiff in a derivative shareholder's suit liability for the cost of the defense if he is unsuccessful, and requires security for the payment of this cost to be given by plaintiff as a condition of maintaining the suit. The Court said that the statute could not be disregarded "as a mere procedural device." Id. at 556.

Justice Rutledge, in dissent, said:

[I]n many situations procedure and substance are so interwoven that rational separation becomes well-nigh impossible. But, even so, this fact cannot dispense with the necessity of making a distinction. For as the matter stands, it is Congress which has power to govern the procedure of the federal courts in diversity cases, and the states which have that power over matters clearly substantive in nature.

Id. at 559.

### ii.   *Ragan v. Merch. Transfer & Warehouse Co.,* 337 U.S. 530 (1949)

The Court held that the Kansas statute of limitations was not tolled by a filing of a complaint in federal court despite the language of Rule 3, because the federal court was bound to apply the Kansas law that the statute was not tolled until the complaint was served on the defendant. The Court, commenting on Guaranty Trust Co. v. York, said:

We can draw no distinction in this case because local law brought the cause of action to an end after, rather than before, suit was started in the federal court. In both cases local law created the right which the federal court was asked to enforce. In both cases local law undertook to determine the life of the cause of action. We cannot give it longer life in the federal court than it would have had in the state court without adding something to the cause of action.

Id. at 553.

### iii.   *Woods v. Interstate Realty Co.,*
### *337 U.S. 535 (1949)*

The Court held that the federal court in Mississippi must dismiss an action brought by a Tennessee corporation that had violated the Mississippi law by doing business without properly qualifying and that it was therefore barred from maintaining a suit in the courts of Mississippi. The Court explained at 538:

> The *York* case was premised on the theory that a right which local law creates but which it does not supply with a remedy is no right at all for purposes of enforcement in a federal court in a diversity case; that where in such cases one is barred from recovery in the state court, he should likewise be barred in the federal court. The contrary result would create discriminations against citizens of the state in favor of those authorized to invoke the diversity jurisdiction of the federal court. It was that element of discrimination that Erie R. R. Co. v. Tompkins was designed to eliminate.

Justice Jackson, who had written the opinion in *Cohen,* decided the same day, dissented vigorously at 539-40:

> The state statute as now interpreted by this Court is a harsh, capricious and vindictive measure. It either refuses to entertain a cause of action, not impaired by state law, or it holds it invalid with unknown effects on amounts already collected. In either case the amount of this punishment bears no relation to the amount of the wrong done the State in failure to qualify and pay its taxes. The penalty thus suffered does not go to the State, which sustained the injury, but results in unjust enrichment of the debtor, who has suffered no injury from the creditor's default in qualification. If the state court had held its statute to have this effect, I should agree that federal courts should so apply it; but the whole basis of our decision is contrary to that of the state courts.

### iv.   *Byrd v. Blue Ridge Rural Elec. Coop., Inc.,*
### *356 U.S. 525 (1958)*

Courts quickly realized that strict application of the *York* outcome-determinative test was untenable. Taken to its logical extreme, nearly any rule might conceivably alter the outcome of litigation. In light of the practical difficulties courts encountered with the *York* test, the Supreme Court again took up the *Erie* doctrine in Byrd v. Blue Ridge Rural Elec. Coop., Inc.,

356 U.S. 525 (1958). *Byrd* involved a negligence action by a North Carolina worker on a construction job being performed in South Carolina for the defendant, a South Carolina utility. The defendant pleaded as a defense that the plaintiff was covered by the local worker's compensation act. It was the practice of South Carolina courts to decide the issue raised by this defense by means of judicial findings, there being no right to trial by jury of the issue of coverage. The Supreme Court nevertheless held that the issue was triable by jury in a federal court:

> We find nothing to suggest that this rule was announced as an integral part of the special relationship created by the statute. Thus the requirement appears to be merely a form and mode of enforcing the immunity, Guaranty Trust Co. v. York, 326 U.S. 99, 108 [(1945)], and not a rule intended to be bound up with the definition of the rights and obligations of the parties. . . .
>
> . . . But cases following *Erie* have evinced a broader policy to the effect that the federal courts should conform as near as may be—in the absence of other considerations—to state rules even of form and mode where the state rules may bear substantially on the question whether the litigation would come out one way in the federal court and another way in the state court if the federal court failed to apply a particular local rule. E.g., Guaranty Trust Co. v. York, supra; Bernhardt v. Polygraphic Co., 350 U.S. 198 [(1956)]. Concededly the nature of the tribunal which tries issues may be important in the enforcement of the parcel of rights making up a cause of action or defense, and bear significantly upon achievement of uniform enforcement of the right. It may well be that in the instant personal injury case the outcome would be substantially affected by whether the issue of immunity is decided by a judge or a jury. Therefore, were "outcome" the only consideration, a strong case might appear for saying that the federal court should follow the state practice.
>
> But there are affirmative countervailing considerations at work here. The federal system is an independent system for administering justice to litigants who properly invoke its jurisdiction. An essential characteristic of that system is the manner in which, in civil common-law actions, it distributes trial functions between judge and jury and, under the influence—if not the command—of the Seventh Amendment, assigns the decisions of disputed questions of fact to the jury. Jacob v. New York, 315 U.S. 752 (1942). The policy of uniform enforcement of state created rights and obligations, see, e.g., Guaranty Trust Co. v. York, supra, cannot in every case exact compliance with a state rule—not bound up with rights and obligations—which disrupts the federal system of allocating functions between judge and jury. Herron v. Southern Pacific Co., 283 U.S. 91 (1931). Thus the inquiry here is whether the federal policy favoring jury decisions of disputed fact questions should yield to the state rule in the interest of furthering the objective that the litigation should not come out one way in the federal court and another way in the state court.
>
> We think that in the circumstances of this case the federal court should not follow the state rule. It cannot be gainsaid that there is a strong federal policy against allowing state rules to disrupt the judge-jury relationship in the federal courts. . . .

Id. at 536-38.

The Court in *Byrd* thus rejected a rigid application of *York*'s outcome-determinative test, instead calling on courts to balance competing state and federal policies, particularly where, as in *Byrd*, any difference in outcome was purely speculative. Applying its balancing test, the *Byrd* Court concluded that South Carolina's weak interest in judicial determination of *Byrd*'s employment status was outweighed by the strong federal preference for jury trials, as embodied in the Seventh Amendment.

### c. The *Hanna* Presumption

The Court further refined *York*'s outcome-determinative test and clarified the *Erie* doctrine in Hanna v. Plumer, which established a powerful presumption in favor of the federal courts' power to use the Federal Rules of Civil Procedure in diversity actions. *Hanna* established that the Federal Rules are presumed to fall within the Supreme Court's statutory power under the Rules Enabling Act (28 U.S.C. § 2072) to prescribe rules of procedure that do not "abridge, enlarge or modify any substantive right."

## Hanna v. Plumer
380 U.S. 460 (1965)

CHIEF JUSTICE WARREN delivered the opinion of the Court.

The question to be decided is whether, in a civil action where the jurisdiction of the United States district court is based upon diversity of citizenship between the parties, service of process shall be made in the manner prescribed by state law or that set forth in Rule 4(d)(1)* of the Federal Rules of Civil Procedure.

On February 6, 1963, petitioner, a citizen of Ohio, filed her complaint in the District Court for the District of Massachusetts, claiming damages in excess of $10,000 for personal injuries resulting from an automobile accident in South Carolina, allegedly caused by the negligence of one Louise Plumer Osgood, a Massachusetts citizen deceased at the time of the filing of the complaint. Respondent, Mrs. Osgood's executor and also a Massachusetts citizen, was named as defendant. On February 8, service was made by leaving copies of the summons and the complaint with respondent's wife at his residence, concededly in compliance with Rule 4(d)(1). . . . Respondent filed his answer on February 26, alleging, *inter alia,* that the action could not be maintained because it had been brought "contrary to and in violation of the provisions of Massachusetts General Laws (Ter. Ed.) Chapter 197, Section 9." That section provides:

> Except as provided in this chapter, an executor or administrator shall not be held to answer to an action by a creditor of the deceased which is not

---

* [Rule 4(d)(1) now appears as Rule 4(e)(2)(B). — EDS.]

commenced within one year from the time of his giving bond for the performance of his trust, or to such an action which is commenced within said year
unless before the expiration thereof the writ in such action has been served
by delivery in hand upon such executor or administrator. . . .

On October 17, 1963, the District Court granted respondent's motion for
summary judgment, citing Ragan v. Merchants Transfer Co., 337 U.S. 530
[(1949)], and Guaranty Trust Co. v. York, 326 U.S. 99 [(1945)], in support of its
conclusion that the adequacy of the service was to be measured by § 9, with
which, the court held, petitioner had not complied. On appeal, petitioner
admitted noncompliance with § 9, but argued that Rule 4(d)(1) defines the
method by which service of process is to be effected in diversity actions.
The Court of Appeals for the First Circuit, finding that "[r]elatively recent
amendments [to § 9] evince a clear legislative purpose to require personal
notification within the year," concluded that the conflict of state and federal
rules was over "a substantive rather than a procedural matter," and unanimously affirmed. 331 F.2d 157 [(1964)]. Because of the threat to the goal of
uniformity of federal procedure posed by the decision below, we granted
certiorari, 379 U.S. 813 [(1964)].

We conclude that the adoption of Rule 4(d)(1), designed to control service
of process in diversity actions, neither exceeded the congressional mandate
embodied in the Rules Enabling Act nor transgressed constitutional bounds,
and that the Rule is therefore the standard against which the District Court
should have measured the adequacy of the service. Accordingly, we reverse
the decision of the Court of Appeals.

[The Rules Enabling Act] provides, in pertinent part:

> The Supreme Court shall have the power to prescribe, by general rules, forms
> of process, writs, pleadings, and motions, and the practice and procedure of
> the district courts of the United States in civil actions.
>
> Such rules shall not abridge, enlarge or modify any substantive right and
> shall preserve the right of trial by jury. . . .

Under the cases construing the scope of the Enabling Act, Rule (4)(d)(1)
clearly passes muster. Prescribing the manner in which a defendant is to be
notified that a suit has been instituted against him, it relates to the "practice
and procedure of the district courts." . . .

> The test must be whether a rule really regulates procedure—the judicial
> process for enforcing rights and duties recognized by substantive law and
> for justly administering remedy and redress for disregard or infraction of
> them.

Sibbach v. Wilson & Co, 312 U.S. 1 [(1991)]. . . .

Thus were there no conflicting state procedures, Rule 4(d)(1) would
clearly control. National Equip. Rental v. Szukhent, 375 U.S. 311, 316 [(1964)].
However, respondent, focusing on the contrary Massachusetts rule, calls to

the Court's attention another line of cases, a line which—like the Federal Rules—had its birth in 1938. Erie R.R. Co. v. Tompkins, 304 U.S. 64 [(1938)], overruling Swift v. Tyson, 16 Pet. 1 [(1842)], held that federal courts sitting in diversity cases, when deciding questions of "substantive" law, are bound by state court decisions as well as state statutes. The broad command of *Erie* was therefore identical to that of the Enabling Act: federal courts are to apply state substantive law and federal procedural law. However, as subsequent cases sharpened the distinction between substance and procedure, the line of cases following *Erie* diverged markedly from the line construing the Enabling Act. Guaranty Trust Co. v. York, 326 U.S. 99 [(1945)], made it clear the *Erie*-type problems were not to be solved by reference to any traditional or common-sense substance-procedure distinction:

> And so the question is not whether a statute of limitations is deemed a matter of "procedure" in some sense. The question is . . . does it significantly affect the result of a litigation for a federal court to disregard a law of a State that would be controlling in an action upon the same claim by the same parties in a State court?

326 U.S., at 109.

Respondent, by placing primary reliance on *York* and *Ragan,* suggests that the *Erie* doctrine acts as a check on the Federal Rules of Civil Procedure, that despite the clear command of Rule 4(d)(1), *Erie* and its progeny demand the application of the Massachusetts rule. Reduced to essentials, the argument is: (1) *Erie,* as refined in *York,* demands that federal courts apply state law whenever application of federal law in its stead will alter the outcome of the case. (2) In this case, a determination that the Massachusetts service requirements obtain will result in immediate victory for respondent. If, on the other hand, it should be held that Rule 4(d)(1) is applicable, the litigation will continue, with possible victory for petitioner. (3) Therefore, *Erie* demands application of the Massachusetts rule. The syllogism possesses an appealing simplicity, but is for several reasons invalid.

In the first place, it is doubtful that, even if there were no Federal Rule making it clear that in-hand service is not required in diversity actions, the *Erie* rule would have obligated the District Court to follow the Massachusetts procedure. "Outcome-determination" analysis was never intended to serve as a talisman. Byrd v. Blue Ridge Cooperative, 356 U.S. 525, 537 [(1958)]. Indeed, the message of *York* itself is that choices between state and federal law are to be made not by application of any automatic, "litmus paper" criterion, but rather by reference to the policies underlying the *Erie* rule. Guaranty Trust Co. v. York, supra, at 108-112.

The *Erie* rule is rooted in part in a realization that it would be unfair for the character or result of a litigation materially to differ because the suit had been brought in a federal court.

> Diversity of citizenship jurisdiction was conferred in order to prevent apprehended discrimination in state courts against those not citizens of the State.

Swift v. Tyson (16 Pet. 1) introduced grave discrimination by non-citizens against citizens. It made rights enjoyed under the unwritten "general law" vary according to whether enforcement was sought in the state or in the federal court; and the privilege of selecting the court in which the right should be determined was conferred upon the non-citizen. Thus, the doctrine rendered impossible equal protection of the law.

Erie R.R. Co. v. Tompkins, supra, at 74-75. The decision was also in part a reaction to the practice of "forum-shopping," which had grown up in response to the rule of Swift v. Tyson, 304 U.S. at 73-74. That the *York* test was an attempt to effectuate these policies is demonstrated by the fact that the opinion framed the inquiry in terms of "substantial" variations between state and federal litigation. 326 U.S., at 109. Not only are nonsubstantial, or trivial, variations not likely to raise the sort of equal protection problems which troubled the Court in *Erie*; they are also unlikely to influence the choice of a forum. The "outcome-determination" test therefore cannot be read without reference to the twin aims of the *Erie* rule: discouragement of forum-shopping and avoidance of inequitable administration of the laws.

The difference between the conclusion that the Massachusetts rule is applicable, and the conclusion that it is not, is of course at this point "outcome-determinative" in the sense that if we hold the state rule to apply, respondent prevails, whereas if we hold that Rule 4(d)(1) governs, the litigation will continue. But in this sense *every* procedural variation is "outcome-determinative." For example, having brought suit in a federal court, a plaintiff cannot then insist on the right to file subsequent pleadings in accord with the time limits applicable in the state courts, even though enforcement of the federal timetable will, if he continues to insist that he must meet only the state time limit, result in determination of the controversy against him. So it is here. Though choice of the federal or state rule will at this point have a marked effect upon the outcome of the litigation, the difference between the two rules would be of scant, if any, relevance to the choice of a forum. Petitioner, in choosing her forum, was not presented with a situation where application of the state rule would wholly bar recovery; rather, adherence to the state rule would have resulted only in altering the way in which process was served. Moreover, it is difficult to argue that permitting service of defendant's wife to take the place of in-hand service of defendant himself alters the mode of enforcement of state-created rights in a fashion sufficiently "substantial" to raise the sort of equal protection problems to which the *Erie* opinion alluded.

There is, however, a more fundamental flaw in respondent's syllogism: the incorrect assumption that the rule of Erie R.R. Co. v. Tompkins constitutes the appropriate test of the validity and therefore the applicability of a Federal Rule of Civil Procedure. The *Erie* rule has never been invoked to void a Federal Rule. It is true that there have been cases where this Court has held applicable a state rule in the face of an argument that the situation was governed by one of the Federal Rules. But the holding of each such case was not that *Erie* commanded displacement of a Federal Rule by an inconsistent state rule, but rather that the scope of the Federal Rule was not as broad as the losing party urged, and therefore, there being no Federal Rule which covered the point in dispute, *Erie* commanded the enforcement of state law. . . .

We are reminded by the *Erie* opinion that neither Congress nor the federal courts can, under the guise of formulating rules of decision for federal courts, fashion rules which are not supported by a grant of federal authority contained in Article I or some other section of the Constitution; in such areas state law must govern because there can be no other law. But the opinion in *Erie*, which involved no Federal Rule and dealt with a question which was "substantive" in every traditional sense (whether the railroad owed a duty of care to Tompkins as a trespasser or a licensee), surely neither said nor implied that measures like Rule 4(d)(1) are unconstitutional. For the constitutional provision for a federal court system (augmented by the Necessary and Proper Clause) carries with it congressional power to make rules governing the practice and pleading in those courts, which in turn includes a power to regulate matters which, though falling within the uncertain area between substance and procedure, are rationally capable of classification as either. Cf. McCulloch v. State of Maryland, 4 Wheat. 316, 421, 4 L. Ed. 579 [(1819)]. Neither *York* nor the cases following it ever suggested that the rule there laid down for coping with situations where no Federal Rule applies is coextensive with the limitation on Congress to which *Erie* had adverted. Although this Court has never before been confronted with a case where the applicable Federal Rule is in direct collision with the law of the relevant State, courts of appeals faced with such clashes have rightly discerned the implications of our decisions.

> One of the shaping purposes of the Federal Rules is to bring about uniformity in the federal courts by getting away from local rules. This is especially true of matters which relate to the administration of legal proceedings, an area in which federal courts have traditionally exerted strong inherent power, completely aside from the powers Congress expressly conferred in the Rules. The purpose of the *Erie* doctrine, even as extended in *York* and *Ragan*, was never to bottle-up federal courts with "outcome-determinative" and "integral-relations" stoppers—when there are "affirmative countervailing (federal) considerations" and when there is a Congressional mandate (the Rules) supported by constitutional authority. Lumbermen's [Mut. Cas.] Co. v. Wright, 322 F.2d 759, 764 ([]5th Cir. 1963).

*Erie* and its offspring cast no doubt on the long-recognized power of Congress to prescribe housekeeping rules for federal courts even though some of those rules will inevitably differ from comparable state rules. Cf. Herron v. Southern Pacific Co., 283 U.S. 91 [(1931)]. "When, because the plaintiff happens to be a non-resident, such a right is enforceable in a federal as well as in a State court, the forms and mode of enforcing the right may at times, naturally enough, vary because the two judicial systems are not identical." Guaranty Trust Co. v. York, supra, at 108; Cohen v. Beneficial

Loan Corp., 337 U.S. 541, 555 [(1949)]. Thus, though a court, in measuring a Federal Rule against the standards contained in the Enabling Act and the Constitution, need not wholly blind itself to the degree to which the Rule makes the character and result of the federal litigation stray from the course it would follow in state courts, Sibbach v. Wilson & Co., 312 U.S. 1, 13-14 (1941), it cannot be forgotten that the *Erie* rule, and the guidelines suggested in *York*, were created to serve another purpose altogether. To hold that a Federal Rule of Civil Procedure must cease to function whenever it alters the mode of enforcing state-created rights would be to disembowel either the Constitution's grant of power over federal procedure or Congress' attempt to exercise that power in the Enabling Act. Rule 4(d)(1) is valid and controls the instant case.

*Reversed.*

JUSTICE HARLAN, concurring.

It is unquestionably true that up to now *Erie* and the cases following it have not succeeded in articulating a workable doctrine governing choice of law in diversity actions. I respect the Court's effort to clarify the situation in today's opinion. However, in doing so I think it has misconceived the constitutional premises of *Erie* and has failed to deal adequately with those past decisions upon which the courts below relied.

*Erie* was something more than an opinion which worried about "forum-shopping and avoidance of inequitable administration of the laws," ante, p. 1142, although to be sure these were important elements of the decision. I have always regarded that decision as one of the modern cornerstones of our federalism, expressing policies that profoundly touch the allocation of judicial power between the state and federal systems. *Erie* recognized that there should not be two conflicting systems of law controlling the primary activity of citizens, for such alternative governing authority must necessarily give rise to a debilitating uncertainty in the planning of everyday affairs. And it recognized that the scheme of our Constitution envisions an allocation of law-making functions between state and federal legislative processes which is undercut if the federal judiciary can make substantive law affecting state affairs beyond the bounds of congressional legislative powers in this regard. Thus, in diversity cases *Erie* commands that it be the state law governing primary private activity which prevails.

The shorthand formulations which have appeared in some past decisions are prone to carry untoward results that frequently arise from over-simplification. The Court is quite right in stating that the "outcome-determinative" test of Guaranty Trust Co. v. York, 326 U.S. 99 [(1945)], if taken literally, proves too much, for any rule, no matter how clearly "procedural," can affect the outcome of litigation if it is not obeyed. In turning from the "outcome" test of *York* back to the unadorned forum-shopping rationale of *Erie*, however, the Court falls prey to like oversimplification, for a simple forum-shopping rule also proves too much; litigants often choose a federal forum merely to obtain what they consider the advantages of the Federal Rules of Civil Procedure or to try their cases before a supposedly more favorable judge. To my mind the proper line of approach in determining whether to apply a state or a federal rule, whether "substantive" or "procedural," is to stay close to basic principles by inquiring if the choice of rule would substantially affect those primary decisions respecting human conduct which our constitutional system leaves to state regulation. If so, *Erie* and the Constitution require that the state rule prevail, even in the face of a conflicting federal rule.

The Court weakens, if indeed it does not submerge, this basic principle by finding, in effect, a grant of substantive legislative power in the constitutional provision for a federal court system (compare Swift v. Tyson, 16 Pet. 1 [(1842)]), and through it, setting up the Federal Rules as a body of law inviolate.

> [T]he constitutional provision for a federal court system . . . carries with it congressional power . . . to regulate matters which, though falling within the uncertain area between substance and procedure, *are rationally capable of classification as either.*

Ante, p. 1144. (Emphasis supplied.) So long as a reasonable man could characterize any duly adopted federal rule as "procedural," the Court, unless I misapprehend what is said, would have it apply no matter how seriously it frustrated a State's substantive regulation of the primary conduct and affairs of its citizens. Since the members of the Advisory Committee, the Judicial Conference, and this Court who formulated the Federal Rules are presumably reasonable men, it follows that the integrity of the Federal Rules is absolute. Whereas the unadulterated outcome and forum-shopping tests may err too far toward honoring state rules, I submit that the Court's "arguably procedural, *ergo* constitutional" test moves too fast and far in the other direction. . . .

## Notes and Questions

1. *Arguing State Versus Federal Law.* Post-*Hanna*, when is a debatable *Erie* question likely to arise? *Hanna* makes it very difficult to argue against application of a Federal Rule of Civil Procedure that has been adopted pursuant to the Supreme Court's rulemaking procedure. But federal courts follow many other, non-Fed. R. Civ. P. rules that are arguably "procedural." When these rules conflict with relevant state rules on point, the court must confront the classic *Erie* dilemma: should federal or state rules apply? To argue for application of federal over state law, the lawyer must emphasize the procedural characteristics of the rule, characterize the rule as affecting the fairness and efficiency of litigation (rather than primary human behavior beyond the courtroom), stress the federal court system's interest in applying its own rule, and minimize concerns about outcome determinativeness and forum shopping. Her opponent, of course, will attempt to counter each of these arguments as part of a more general effort to color the rule in question "substantive."

Part of both lawyers' strategies is likely to be analogical reasoning. The lawyers will argue that the rule in question is "just like" a rule that the Court already has deemed "substantive" or "procedural." The following chart is a handy guide for making such arguments.

| Rule | Choice of law | Authority |
|---|---|---|
| Standard of care | State law | Erie R.R. Co. v. Tompkins, 304 U.S. 64 (1938) |
| Conflict of laws | State law | Klaxon Co. v. Stentor Elec., 313 U.S. 487 (1941) |
| Statute of limitations | State law | Guaranty Trust Co. v. York, 326 U.S. 99 (1945) |
| Burden of proof | State law | Cities Service Oil v. Dunlap, 308 U.S. 208 (1939) |
| Burden of pleading | Federal | Palmer v. Hoffman, 318 U.S. 109 (1943) |
| Discovery, Physical examinations | Federal | Sibbach v. Wilson & Co., 312 U.S. 1 (1941) |
| Venue transfers and effect of forum selection clause | Federal | Stewart Org. v. Ricoh Corp., 487 U.S. 22 (1988) |
| Agreement to arbitrate | State law | Bernhardt v. Polygraphic Co., 350 U.S. 198 (1956) |

2. *Determining State Law.* To say that state law applies to an issue leads to another sometimes complex question: What is the controlling state law? State law on point may be sparse, conflicting, or very old. In general, the federal court's job is to forecast what the applicable state's supreme court would say on the matter. In making this forecast, the court will rely on the supreme court's opinions, unless it is fairly confident that the court would not apply its own precedent. In the absence of controlling supreme court decisions, the federal court may consider opinions of state intermediate appellate courts, scholarly articles, the Restatement of Law, and treatises. See generally Bernhardt v. Polygraphic Co. of Am., 350 U.S. 198 (1956); Comm'r v. Estate of Bosch, 387 U.S. 456 (1967).

3. *Applying* Erie *and* Hanna. How would *Erie* and *Hanna* play out in the following cases? Before learning what the Court actually did in them, see if you can generate the best arguments for each side.

a. Rule 3 of Fed. R. Civ. P. provides that "[a] civil action is commenced by filing a complaint with the court." Plaintiff files a diversity suit in federal court one day before the applicable statute of limitations elapses. Two weeks later, plaintiff serves defendant with the complaint. Federal law grants plaintiff 120 days after filing a complaint to complete service. State law in this case requires that both filing and service must occur within the applicable statute of limitations. Defendant moves for summary judgment on the ground that the action is barred by the statute of limitations. What result?

See Ragan v. Merch. Transfer & Warehouse Co., 337 U.S. 530 (1949); Walker v. Armco Steel Corp., 446 U.S. 740 (1980).

b. Plaintiff secures a jury verdict against defendant in a federal diversity suit. After the verdict is affirmed on appeal without modification, the appellate court assesses a penalty of 10 percent of the damages, as pre-scribed by state law, for an unsuccessful appeal of a money judgment. Rule 38 of the Federal Rules of Appellate Procedure holds that "[i]f a court of appeals shall determine that an appeal is frivolous, it may award just dam-ages and single or double costs to the appellee." Defendant objects to the penalty on the ground that Rule 38 governs, and permits penalties to be imposed only when an appeal is frivolous. What result?

See Burlington N. R.R. Co. v. Woods, 480 U.S. 1 (1987).

c. Plaintiff files a diversity suit against defendant in federal court. State law permits admission into evidence of out-of-court settlements. Fed. R. Evid. 408 provides as follows:

> Evidence of (1) furnishing or offering or promising to furnish, or (2) accept-ing or offering or promising to accept, a valuable consideration in compro-mising or attempting to compromise a claim which was disputed as to either validity or amount, is not admissible to prove liability for or invalidity of the claim or its amount.

Plaintiff offers into evidence (to prove liability) out-of-court settlements between defendant and third parties. Defendant objects, invoking Rule 408. What result?

For a similar issue regarding the application of evidentiary rules, see Carota v. Johns Manville Corp., 893 F.2d 448 (1st Cir. 1990).

In any of these cases, would application of the federal rule (versus the state rule) affect primary behavior outside the courtroom? Produce forum shopping? Promote the integrity and efficiency of the federal courts? Are the federal and state rules in any of them compatible, such that no real conflict exists?

4. *Court-Imposed Sanctions and* Erie. Consider the following excerpt from Chambers v. NASCO, Inc., 501 U.S. 32, 52-53 (1991), previously encountered in Chapter 2, in which the Court held that a federal district judge in a diver-sity case has "inherent power" to sanction a party for bad-faith conduct:

> Only when there is a conflict between state and federal substantive law are the concerns of Erie R.R. Co. v. Tompkins, 304 U.S. 64 (1938), at issue. As we explained in Hanna v. Plumer, 380 U.S. 460, 468 (1965), the "outcome determi-native" test of *Erie* and Guaranty Trust Co. v. York, 326 U.S. 99 (1945), "cannot be read without reference to the twin aims of the *Erie* rule: discouragement of forum-shopping and avoidance of inequitable administration of the laws". . . . [N]either of these twin aims is implicated by the assessment of attorney's fees as a sanction for bad-faith conduct before the court which involved disobedi-ence of the court's orders and the attempt to defraud the court itself. . . . [T]he imposition of sanctions under the bad-faith exception depends not on which party wins the lawsuit, but on how the parties conduct themselves during the litigation. Consequently, there is no risk that the exception will lead to forum shopping. Nor is it inequitable to apply the exception to citizens and nonciti-zens alike, when the party, by controlling his or her conduct in litigation, has the power to determine whether sanctions will be assessed.

5. *Forum Selection Clauses and* Erie. Is a federal court sitting in diversity obliged to respect state law on the enforceability of forum selection clauses in contracts between the parties, or may it follow its own policy?

In Stewart Org., Inc. v. Ricoh Corp., 487 U.S. 22 (1988), the Court held that a federal court could enforce a forum selection clause even when the state whose substantive law applies to the matter would not. When *Ricoh* is read together with Carnival Cruise Lines, Inc. v. Shute, 499 U.S. 585 (1991) (Chapter 1, supra), which upheld the enforcement of a forum selection clause in a form ticket contract, doesn't this give the drafting party considerable control over the location of the lawsuit? For a critical analysis of *Ricoh,* see Richard D. Freer, *Erie's* Mid-Life Crisis, 63 Tul. L. Rev. 1087, 1113-31 (1989). Still undecided is the issue of whether state or federal law governs the interpretation of a forum selection clause with respect to personal jurisdiction. In Preferred Capital, Inc. v. Sarasota Kennel Club, Inc., 489 F.3d 303 (6th Cir. 2007), the Sixth Circuit held that state law controls this decision since it is a "substantive" one under *Hanna.* The Seventh and Eleventh Circuits have suggested the same, see IFC Credit Corp. v. Aliano Bros. Gen. Contractors, 437 F.3d 606 (7th Cir. 2006); Alexander Proudfoot Co. World Headquarters v. Thayer, 877 F.2d 912 (11th Cir. 1989), but the Supreme Court has not yet offered a definitive answer.

### d.  Separating Substance from Procedure, Balancing State and Federal Interests, and Other Nagging Questions of *Erie-Hanna* Jurisprudence

In Gasperini v. Center for Humanities, Inc., the Court conceded that "[c]lassification of a law as 'substantive' or 'procedural' for *Erie* purposes is sometimes a challenging endeavor." 518 U.S. 415, 427 (1996). That may be an understatement. *Hanna* clarified that when a federal procedural rule of decision has been created by Congress, it is generally controlling by virtue of the Supremacy Clause. Two major questions remain open and the Supreme Court is badly divided about how to answer them. The first question is what test to apply when there is *no* legislatively authorized federal procedural rule—that is, when a state rule of decision conflicts with judge-made federal procedural law. The second question is how to go about determining whether there is a conflict between a state and federal rule of decision.

In *Gasperini,* the Court considered a New York state law that provided a standard for reviewing jury verdicts for excessiveness. That standard granted judges more discretion to reverse arguably excessive verdicts than the applicable federal procedural rule. The federal rule reflected constraints imposed by the Seventh Amendment on federal judicial review of jury verdicts. By a 5-4 vote, the Court distinguished *Byrd* and held that federal trial courts sitting in diversity must apply the broader state standard for determining excessiveness. Looking to the "twin aims of *Erie,*" the majority reasoned that application of the federal standard would encourage forum shopping because there would be both a perceived and a real difference in the size of recoveries on jury verdicts. Moreover, New York citizens would be subjected to unchecked damages in the federal courts when they would be protected in their own courts. This would constitute inequitable administration of the laws.

In a dissenting opinion, Justice Scalia accused the majority of committing "the classic *Erie* mistake of regarding whatever changes the outcome as substantive," and reminded the majority of the admonition in *Hanna* that outcome determination "'was never intended to serve as a talisman.'" *Gasperini,* 518 U.S. at 465. He also emphasized that the Court should not have reached *Erie* analysis because Rule 59 of the Federal Rules, which sets the standard for granting a new trial in federal court, is controlling under *Hanna.* Rule 59 is the product of "Congress's 'power to regulate matters which, though falling within the uncertain area between substance and procedure, are rationally capable of classification as either.'" Id. at 468. For the District Court's decision on remand, see Gasperini v. Center for Humanities, Inc., 972 F. Supp. 765 (S.D.N.Y. 1997), *aff'd by* 149 F.3d 137 (2d Cir. 1998).

Many commentators and practitioners read *Hanna* as creating an understanding, even a presumption, that when a Federal Rule was implicated, it would trump other possible rules or standards—all the more so when, under *Byrd,* the federal rule protects a constitutional right. At the very least, *Gasperini* destabilized that understanding by brushing aside Rule 59. This may account for some of the hostility with which the decision was received. See, e.g., C. Douglas Floyd, *Erie* Awry: A Comment on Gasperini v. Center for Humanities, Inc., 1997 BYU L. Rev. 267 (1997); Richard Freer, Some Thoughts on the State of *Erie* After *Gasperini,* 76 Tex. L. Rev. 1637 (1998). The case also had its defenders. See Thomas Rowe, Not Bad for Government Work: Does Anyone Else Think the Supreme Court Is Doing a Halfway Decent Job in Its *Erie-Hanna* Jurisprudence?, 73 Notre Dame L. Rev. 963, 1014 (1998).

In Semtek Int'l Inc. v. Lockheed Martin Corp., 531 U.S. 497 (2001), the Court continued to interpret potential federal-state procedural conflicts in a manner that accommodates state procedural practices. The Court unanimously held that the claim-preclusive effect of a federal judgment dismissing a diversity action on statute-of-limitations grounds is determined by the law of the state in which the federal court sits.

The Court relied in part upon an 1875 case, Dupasseur v. Rochereau, 21 Wall. 130 (1875), which held that the res judicata effect of a federal diversity judgment "is such as would belong to judgments of state courts rendered under similar circumstances." The respondent argued that *Dupasseur* was not controlling because it was decided in an era in which federal courts were required by the Conformity Act of 1872 to apply the *procedural* law of the forum state in *non-equity* cases. Moreover, respondent maintained that Rule 41(b) was controlling, because the order of dismissal did not "otherwise specify[]" that the dismissal would "operate[] as an adjudication upon the merits."

The Court disagreed, and concluded that Rule 41(b)'s phrase "on the merits" did not necessarily mean "entitled to claim preclusive effect." Indeed, such an operation of the rule might violate the Rules Enabling Act, insofar as it might "abridge, enlarge or modify [a] substantive right." 28 U.S.C. § 2072(b). "[T]he traditional rule is that expiration of the applicable statute of limitations merely bars the remedy and does not extinguish the substantive right, so that dismissal on that ground does not have claim-preclusive effect in other jurisdictions with longer, unexpired limitations periods." *Semtek*, 531 U.S. at 504. If federal court dismissals on statute-of-limitations grounds would bar suit everywhere, this could lead to forum shopping: "[o]ut-of-state defendants sued on stale claims . . . in . . . States adhering to this traditional rule would systematically remove state-law suits brought against them to federal court. . . ." Id.

Given that Rule 41(b) did not determine the outcome, and given these competing federalism principles, the Court concluded that federal common law should incorporate state law regarding the claim-preclusive effect of dismissals, *except* "in situations in which the state law is incompatible with federal interests." *Semtek*, 531 U.S. at 504. Finding no such incompatibility in *Semtek*, the Court held that the state law of preclusion should control. See also Brereton v. Bountiful City Corp., 434 F.3d 1213 (10th Cir. 2006).

Whatever factors prompted the Court to speak with one voice in *Semtek* disappeared a decade later when the Court took up the following case. As you will see, Justice Scalia cobbles together a majority for the proposition that Fed. R. Civ. P. 23 is controlling, but he has only a plurality for the rest of his analysis. That means the Court still has not settled on a method for distinguishing substantive and procedural rules of decision or a method for determining whether state and federal rules of decision conflict.

### *Shady Grove Orthopedic Assocs. P.A. v. Allstate Ins. Co.*
559 U.S. 393 (2010)

JUSTICE SCALIA announced the judgment of the Court and delivered the opinion of the Court with respect to Parts I and II-A, an opinion with respect to Parts II-B and II-D, in which THE CHIEF JUSTICE, JUSTICE THOMAS, and JUSTICE SOTOMAYOR join, and an opinion with respect to Part II-C, in which THE CHIEF JUSTICE and JUSTICE THOMAS join.

New York law prohibits class actions in suits seeking penalties or statutory minimum damages.[1] We consider whether this precludes a federal

---

1. N.Y. Civ. Prac. Law Ann. § 901 (West 2006) provides:

(a) One or more members of a class may sue or be sued as representative parties on behalf of all if: 1. the class is so numerous that joinder of all members, whether otherwise required or permitted, is impracticable; 2. there are questions of law or fact common to the class which predominate over any questions affecting only individual members; 3. the claims or defenses of the representative parties are typical of the claims or defenses of the class; 4. the representative parties will fairly and adequately protect the interests of the class; and 5. a class action is superior to other available methods for the fair and efficient adjudication of the controversy.

(b) Unless a statute creating or imposing a penalty, or a minimum measure of recovery specifically authorizes the recovery thereof in a class action, an action to recover a penalty, or minimum measure of recovery created or imposed by statute may not be maintained as a class action.

district court sitting in diversity from entertaining a class action under Federal Rule of Civil Procedure 23.

## I

The petitioner's complaint alleged the following: Shady Grove Orthopedic Associates, P.A., provided medical care to Sonia E. Galvez for injuries she suffered in an automobile accident. As partial payment for that care, Galvez assigned to Shady Grove her rights to insurance benefits under a policy issued in New York by Allstate Insurance Co. Shady Grove tendered a claim for the assigned benefits to Allstate, which under New York law had 30 days to pay the claim or deny it. . . . Allstate apparently paid, but not on time, and it refused to pay the statutory interest that accrued on the overdue benefits (at two percent per month).

Shady Grove filed this diversity suit in the Eastern District of New York to recover the unpaid statutory interest. Alleging that Allstate routinely refuses to pay interest on overdue benefits, Shady Grove sought relief on behalf of itself and a class of all others to whom Allstate owes interest. The District Court dismissed the suit for lack of jurisdiction. . . . It reasoned that N.Y. Civ. Prac. Law Ann. § 901(b), which precludes a suit to recover a "penalty" from proceeding as a class action, applies in diversity suits in federal court, despite Federal Rule of Civil Procedure 23. Concluding that statutory interest is a "penalty" under New York law, it held that § 901(b) prohibited the proposed class action. And, since Shady Grove conceded that its individual claim (worth roughly $500) fell far short of the amount-in-controversy requirement for individual suits under 28 U.S.C. § 1332(a), the suit did not belong in federal court.[3]

The Second Circuit affirmed. . . .

## II

The framework for our decision is familiar. We must first determine whether Rule 23 answers the question in dispute. Burlington Northern R. Co. v. Woods, 480 U.S. 1, 4-5 (1987). If it does, it governs—New York's law notwithstanding—unless it exceeds statutory authorization or Congress's rulemaking power. Id. at 5, 107 S. Ct. 967; see Hanna v. Plumer, 380 U.S. 460, 463-64 (1965). We do not wade into *Erie*'s murky waters unless the federal rule is inapplicable or invalid. See 380 U.S. at 469-71.

___

3. Shady Grove had asserted jurisdiction under 28 U.S.C. § 1332(d)(2), which relaxes, for class actions seeking at least $5 million, the rule against aggregating separate claims for calculation of the amount in controversy. See Exxon Mobil Corp. v. Allapattah Services, Inc., 545 U.S. 546, 571 (2005).

*A*

The question in dispute is whether Shady Grove's suit may proceed as a class action. Rule 23 provides an answer. It states that "[a] class action may be maintained" if two conditions are met: The suit must satisfy the criteria set forth in subdivision (a) (i.e., numerosity, commonality, typicality, and adequacy of representation), and it also must fit into one of the three categories described in subdivision (b). By its terms this creates a categorical rule entitling a plaintiff whose suit meets the specified criteria to pursue his claim as a class action. (The Federal Rules regularly use "may" to confer categorical permission, see, e.g., Fed. Rules Civ. Proc. 8(d)(2)-(3), 14(a)(1), 18(a)-(b), 20(a)(1)-(2), 27(a)(1), 30(a)(1), as do federal statutes that establish procedural entitlements, see, e.g., 29 U.S.C. § 626(c)(1); 42 U.S.C. § 2000e-5(f)(1).) Thus, Rule 23 provides a one-size-fits-all formula for deciding the class-action question. Because § 901(b) attempts to answer the same question—i.e., it states that Shady Grove's suit "may *not* be maintained as a class action" (emphasis added) because of the relief it seeks—it cannot apply in diversity suits unless Rule 23 is *ultra vires*.

The Second Circuit believed that § 901(b) and Rule 23 do not conflict because they address different issues. Rule 23, it said, concerns only the criteria for determining whether a given class can and should be certified; section 901(b), on the other hand, addresses an antecedent question: whether the particular type of claim is eligible for class treatment in the first place—a question on which Rule 23 is silent. Allstate embraces this analysis. . . .

We disagree. To begin with, the line between eligibility and certifiability is entirely artificial. Both are preconditions for maintaining a class action. Allstate suggests that eligibility must depend on the "particular cause of action" asserted, instead of some other attribute of the suit. But that is not so. Congress could, for example, provide that only claims involving more than a certain number of plaintiffs are "eligible" for class treatment in federal court. In other words, relabeling Rule 23(a)'s prerequisites "eligibility criteria" would obviate Allstate's objection—a sure sign that its eligibility-certifiability distinction is made-to-order. . . .

Allstate points out that Congress has carved out some federal claims from Rule 23's reach, see, e.g., 8 U.S.C. § 1252(e)(1)(B)—which shows, Allstate contends, that Rule 23 does not authorize class actions for all claims, but rather leaves room for laws like § 901(b). But Congress, unlike New York, has ultimate authority over the Federal Rules of Civil Procedure; it can create exceptions to an individual rule as it sees fit—either by directly amending the rule or by enacting a separate statute overriding it in certain instances. . . . The fact that Congress has created specific exceptions to Rule 23 hardly proves that the Rule does not apply generally. In fact, it proves the opposite. If Rule 23 did *not* authorize class actions across the board, the statutory exceptions would be unnecessary.

Allstate next suggests that the structure of § 901 shows that Rule 23 addresses only certifiability. Section 901(a), it notes, establishes class certification criteria roughly analogous to those in Rule 23 (wherefore it agrees *that* subsection is pre-empted). But § 901(b)'s rule barring class actions for certain claims is set off as its own subsection, and where it applies § 901(a) does not. . . . Rule 23 permits all class actions that meet its requirements, and a State cannot limit that permission by structuring one part of its statute to track Rule 23 and enacting another part that imposes additional requirements. Both of § 901's subsections undeniably answer the same question as Rule 23: whether a class action may proceed for a given suit. Cf. *Burlington*, 480 U.S. at 7-8.

The dissent argues that § 901(b) has nothing to do with whether Shady Grove may maintain its suit as a class action, but affects only the *remedy* it may obtain if it wins. . . . Whereas "Rule 23 governs procedural aspects of class litigation" by "prescrib[ing] the considerations relevant to class certification and postcertification proceedings," § 901(b) addresses only "the size of a monetary award a class plaintiff may pursue." Post at 1465-1466. Accordingly, the dissent says, Rule 23 and New York's law may coexist in peace. . . .

. . . Unlike a law that sets a ceiling on damages (or puts other remedies out of reach) in properly filed class actions, § 901(b) says nothing about what remedies a court may award; it prevents the class actions it covers from coming into existence at all. Consequently, a court bound by § 901(b) could not certify a class action seeking both statutory penalties and other remedies even if it announces in advance that it will refuse to award the penalties in the event the plaintiffs prevail; to do so would violate the statute's clear prohibition on "maintain[ing]" such suits as class actions . . . .

The evidence of the New York Legislature's purpose is pretty sparse. But even accepting the dissent's account of the Legislature's objective at face value, it cannot override the statute's clear text. Even if its aim is to restrict the remedy a plaintiff can obtain, § 901(b) achieves that end by limiting a plaintiff's power to maintain a class action. The manner in which the law "could have been written," has no bearing; what matters is the law the Legislature *did* enact. We cannot rewrite that to reflect our perception of legislative purpose . . . .

But while the dissent does indeed artificially narrow the scope of § 901(b) by finding that it pursues only substantive policies, that is not the central difficulty of the dissent's position. The central difficulty is that even artificial narrowing cannot render § 901(b) compatible with Rule 23. *Whatever* the policies they pursue, they flatly contradict each other. Allstate asserts (and the dissent implies) that we can (and must) *interpret* Rule 23 in a manner that avoids overstepping its authorizing statute. If the Rule were susceptible of two meanings—one that would violate § 2072(b) and another that would not—we would agree. See Ortiz v. Fibreboard Corp., 527 U.S. 815, 842, 845 (1999); cf. Semtek Int'l Inc. v. Lockheed Martin Corp., 531 U.S. 497, 503-504 (2001). But it is not. Rule 23 unambiguously authorizes *any* plaintiff, in *any* federal civil proceeding, to maintain a class action if the Rule's prerequisites are met. We cannot contort its text, even to avert a collision with state law that might render it invalid. See Walker v. Armco Steel Corp., 446 U.S. 740, 750 n.9 (1980). What the dissent's approach achieves is not the avoiding of a "conflict between Rule 23 and § 901(b)," but rather the invalidation of Rule 23 (pursuant to § 2072(b) of the Rules Enabling Act) to the extent that it conflicts with the substantive policies of § 901. There is no other way to reach the dissent's destination. We must therefore confront head-on whether Rule 23 falls within the statutory authorization.

### B

*Erie* involved the constitutional power of federal courts to supplant state law with judge-made rules. In that context, it made no difference whether the rule was technically one of substance or procedure; the touchstone was whether it "significantly affect[s] the result of a litigation." Guaranty Trust Co. v. York, 326 U.S. 99, 109 (1945). That is not the test for either the constitutionality or the statutory validity of a Federal Rule of Procedure. Congress has undoubted power to supplant state law, and undoubted power to prescribe rules for the courts it has created, so long as those rules regulate matters "rationally capable of classification" as procedure. *Hanna*, 380 U.S., at 472. In the Rules Enabling Act, Congress authorized this Court to promulgate rules of procedure subject to its review, 28 U.S.C. § 2072(a), but with the limitation that those rules "shall not abridge, enlarge or modify any substantive right," § 2072(b).

We have long held that this limitation means that the Rule must "really regulat[e] procedure, the judicial process for enforcing rights and duties recognized by substantive law and for justly administering remedy and redress for disregard or infraction of them," *Sibbach*, 312 U.S., at 14. . . . The test is not whether the rule affects a litigant's substantive rights; most procedural rules do. Mississippi Publishing Corp. v. Murphree, 326 U.S. 438, 445 (1946). What matters is what the rule itself regulates: If it governs only "the manner and the means" by which the litigants' rights are "enforced," it is valid; if it alters "the rules of decision by which [the] court will adjudicate [those] rights," it is not. Id. at 446 (internal quotation marks omitted).

Applying that test, we have rejected every statutory challenge to a Federal Rule that has come before us. We have found to be in compliance with § 2072(b) rules prescribing methods for serving process, see . . . *Hanna*, supra at 463-465, . . . and requiring litigants whose mental or physical condition is in dispute to submit to examinations, see *Sibbach* (Fed. Rule Civ. Proc. 35); Schlagenhauf v. Holder, 379 U.S. 104, 113-114 (1964) (same). Likewise, we have upheld rules authorizing imposition of sanctions upon those who file frivolous appeals, see *Burlington* (Fed. Rule App. Proc. 38), or who sign court papers without a reasonable inquiry into the facts asserted, see Business Guides, Inc. v. Chromatic Communications Enterprises, Inc., 498 U.S. 533, 551-554 (1991) (Fed. Rule Civ. Proc. 11). Each of these rules had some practical effect on the parties' rights, but each undeniably regulated only the process for enforcing those rights; none altered the rights themselves, the available remedies, or the rules of decision by which the court adjudicated either.

Applying that criterion, we think it obvious that rules allowing multiple claims (and claims by or against multiple parties) to be litigated together are also valid. See, e.g., Fed. Rules Civ. Proc. 18 (joinder of claims), 20 (joinder of parties), 42(a) (consolidation of actions). Such rules neither change plaintiffs' separate entitlements to relief nor abridge defendants' rights; they alter only how the claims are processed. For the same reason, Rule 23—at least insofar as it allows willing plaintiffs to join their separate claims against the same defendants in a class action—falls within § 2072(b)'s authorization. A class action, no less than traditional joinder (of which it is a species), merely enables a federal court to adjudicate claims of multiple parties at once, instead of in separate suits. And like traditional joinder, it leaves the parties' legal rights and duties intact and the rules of decision unchanged.

Allstate contends that the authorization of class actions is not substantively neutral: Allowing Shady Grove to sue on behalf of a class "transform[s] [the] dispute over a five *hundred* dollar penalty into a dispute over a five *million* dollar penalty." Allstate's aggregate liability, however, does not depend on whether the suit proceeds as a class action. Each of the 1,000-plus members of the putative class could (as Allstate acknowledges) bring a freestanding suit asserting his individual claim. It is undoubtedly true that some plaintiffs who would not bring individual suits for the relatively small sums involved will choose to join a class action. That has no bearing, however, on Allstate's or the plaintiffs' legal rights. The likelihood that some (even many) plaintiffs will be induced to sue by the availability of a class action is just the sort of "incidental effec[t]" we have long held does not violate § 2072(b), *Mississippi Publishing*, 326 U.S. at 445.

Allstate argues that Rule 23 violates § 2072(b) because the state law it displaces, § 901(b), creates a right that the Federal Rule abridges—namely, a "substantive right . . . not to be subjected to aggregated class-action liability" in a single suit. To begin with, we doubt that that is so. Nothing in the text of § 901(b) (which is to be found in New York's procedural code) confines it to claims under New York law; and of course New York has no power to alter substantive rights and duties created by other sovereigns. As we have said, the *consequence* of excluding certain class actions may be to cap the damages a defendant can face in a single suit, but the law itself alters only procedure. In that respect, § 901(b) is no different from a state law forbidding simple joinder. As a fallback argument, Allstate argues that even if § 901(b) is a procedural provision, it was enacted "for *substantive* reasons," id. at 24. Its end was not to improve "the conduct of the litigation process itself" but to alter "the outcome of that process." Id. at 26.

The fundamental difficulty with both these arguments is that the substantive nature of New York's law, or its substantive purpose, *makes no difference*. A Federal Rule of Procedure is not valid in some jurisdictions and invalid in others—or valid in some cases and invalid in others—depending upon whether its effect is to frustrate a state substantive law (or a state procedural law enacted for substantive purposes). . . . *Hanna* unmistakably expressed the same understanding that compliance of a Federal Rule with the Enabling Act is to be assessed by consulting the Rule itself, and not its effects in individual applications . . . .

In sum, it is not the substantive or procedural nature or purpose of the affected state law that matters, but the substantive or procedural nature of the Federal Rule. We have held since *Sibbach*, and reaffirmed repeatedly, that the validity of a Federal Rule depends entirely upon whether it regulates procedure. . . . If it does, it is authorized by § 2072 and is valid in all jurisdictions, with respect to all claims, regardless of its incidental effect upon state-created rights.

## C

. . . The concurrence would decide this case on the basis, not that Rule 23 is procedural, but that the state law it displaces is procedural, in the sense that it does not "function as a part of the State's definition of substantive rights and remedies." A state procedural rule is not preempted, according to the concurrence, so long as it is "so bound up with," or "sufficiently intertwined with," a substantive state law right or remedy "that it defines the scope of that substantive right or remedy."

This analysis squarely conflicts with *Sibbach*, which established the rule we apply. . . .

## D

We must acknowledge the reality that keeping the federal-court door open to class actions that cannot proceed in state court will produce forum shopping. That is unacceptable when it comes as the consequence of judge-made rules created to fill supposed "gaps" in positive federal law. See *Hanna*, 380 U.S., at 471-472. For where neither the Constitution, a treaty, nor a statute provides the rule of decision or authorizes a federal court to supply one, "state law must govern because there can be no other law." Ibid.; see Clark, Erie's Constitutional Source, 95 Cal. L. Rev. 1289, 1302, 1311 (2007). But divergence from state law, with the attendant consequence of forum shopping, is the inevitable (indeed, one might say the intended) result of a uniform system of federal procedure. Congress itself has created the possibility that the same case may follow a different course if filed in federal instead of state court. . . . The short of the matter is that a Federal Rule governing procedure is valid whether or not it alters the outcome of the case in a way that induces forum shopping. To hold otherwise would be to "disembowel either the Constitution's grant of power over federal procedure" or Congress's exercise of it. [*Hanna*, 380 U.S.,] at 473-474.

\* \* \*

The judgment of the Court of Appeals is reversed, and the case is remanded for further proceedings.

*It is so ordered.*

JUSTICE STEVENS, concurring in part and concurring in the judgment.

The New York law at issue, N.Y. Civ. Prac. Law Ann. (CPLR) § 901(b), is a procedural rule that is not part of New York's substantive law. Accordingly, I agree with Justice Scalia that Federal Rule of Civil Procedure 23 must apply in this case and join Parts I and II-A of the Court's opinion. But I also agree with Justice Ginsburg that there are some state procedural rules that federal courts must apply in diversity cases because they function as a part of the State's definition of substantive rights and remedies.

# I

. . . Congress has thus struck a balance: "[H]ousekeeping rules for federal courts" will generally apply in diversity cases, notwithstanding that some federal rules "will inevitably differ" from state rules. *Hanna,* 380 U.S. at 473. But not every federal "rul[e] of practice or procedure," § 2072(a), will displace state law. To the contrary, federal rules must be interpreted with some degree of "sensitivity to important state interests and regulatory policies," Gasperini v. Center for Humanities, Inc., 518 U.S. 415, 427 n.7 (1996), and applied to diversity cases against the background of Congress' command that such rules not alter substantive rights and with consideration of "the degree to which the Rule makes the character and result of the federal litigation stray from the course it would follow in state courts," *Hanna,* 380 U.S. at 473. This can be a tricky balance to implement.

It is important to observe that the balance Congress has struck turns, in part, on the nature of the state law that is being displaced by a federal rule. . . .

Applying this balance, therefore, requires careful interpretation of the state and federal provisions at issue. . . . A "state procedural rule, though undeniably 'procedural' in the ordinary sense of the term," may exist "to influence substantive outcomes," S.A. Healy Co. v. Milwaukee Metropolitan Sewerage Dist., 60 F.3d 305, 310 (C.A.7 1995) (Posner, J.), and may in some instances become so bound up with the state-created right or remedy that it defines the scope of that substantive right or remedy. Such laws, for example, may be seemingly procedural rules that make it significantly more difficult to bring or to prove a claim, thus serving to limit the scope of that claim. See, e.g., *Cohen,* 337 U.S. at 555 (state "procedure" that required plaintiffs to post bond before suing); *Guaranty Trust Co.,* 326 U.S. 99 (state statute of limitations). Such "procedural rules" may also define the amount of recovery. See, e.g., *Gasperini,* 518 U.S. at 427 (state procedure for examining jury verdicts as means of capping the available remedy); Moore § 124.07[3][a] (listing examples of federal courts' applying state laws that affect the amount of a judgment).

. . . When a State chooses to use a traditionally procedural vehicle as a means of defining the scope of substantive rights or remedies, federal courts must recognize and respect that choice. Cf. Ragan v. Merch. Transfer & Warehouse Co., 337 U.S. 530, 533 (1949) ("Since th[e] cause of action is created by local law, the measure of it is to be found only in local law . . . . Where local law qualifies or abridges it, the federal court must follow suit").

## II

When both a federal rule and a state law appear to govern a question before a federal court sitting in diversity, our precedents have set out a two-step framework for federal courts to negotiate this thorny area. At both steps of the inquiry, there is a critical question about what the state law and the federal rule mean.

. . . Congress may have the constitutional power "to supplant state law" with rules that are "rationally capable of classification as procedure," but we should generally presume that it has not done so. Cf. Wyeth v. Levine, 129 S. Ct. 1187, 1194-1195 (2009) (observing that "we start with the assumption" that a federal statute does not displace a State's law "unless that was the clear and manifest purpose of Congress" (internal quotation marks omitted)). Indeed, the mandate that federal rules "shall not abridge, enlarge or modify any substantive right" evinces the opposite intent, as does Congress' decision to delegate the creation of rules to this Court rather than to a political branch. . . .

Thus, the second step of the inquiry may well bleed back into the first. When a federal rule appears to abridge, enlarge, or modify a substantive right, federal courts must consider whether the rule can reasonably be interpreted to avoid that impermissible result. See, e.g., Semtek Int'l Inc. v. Lockheed Martin Corp., 531 U.S. 497, 503 (2001) (avoiding an interpretation of Federal Rule of Civil Procedure 41(b) that "would arguably violate the jurisdictional limitation of the Rules Enabling Act" contained in § 2072(b)). And when such a "saving" construction is not possible and the rule would violate the Enabling Act, federal courts cannot apply the rule. See 28 U.S.C. § 2072(b) (mandating that federal rules "shall not" alter "*any* substantive right" (emphasis added)); *Hanna*, 380 U.S. at 473. . . . A federal rule, therefore, cannot govern a particular case in which the rule would displace a state law that is procedural in the ordinary use of the term but is so intertwined with a state right or remedy that it functions to define the scope of the state-created right. . . .

Justice Scalia believes that the sole Enabling Act question is whether the federal rule "really regulates procedure," which means, apparently, whether it regulates "the manner and the means by which the litigants' rights are enforced." . . . I respectfully disagree.[7] This interpretation of the Enabling Act is consonant with the Act's first limitation to "general rules of practice and procedure," § 2072(a). But it ignores the second limitation that such rules also "not abridge, enlarge or modify any substantive right," § 2072(b) (emphasis added), and in so doing ignores the balance that Congress struck between uniform rules of federal procedure and respect for a State's construction of its own rights and remedies. It also ignores the separation-of-powers presumption, and federalism presumption, that counsel against judicially created rules displacing state substantive law. . . .

Although the plurality appears to agree with much of my interpretation of § 2072, it nonetheless rejects that approach for two reasons, both of which are mistaken. First, Justice Scalia worries that if federal courts inquire into the effect of federal rules on state law, it will enmesh federal courts in difficult determinations about whether application of a given rule would displace a state determination about substantive rights. I do not see why an Enabling Act inquiry that looks to state law necessarily is more taxing than Justice Scalia's. But in any event, that inquiry is what the Enabling Act requires: While it may not be easy to decide what is actually a "substantive right," "the designations substantive and procedural become important, for the Enabling Act has made them so." Ely 723; see also Wright § 4509, at 266. . . . Although Justice Scalia may generally prefer easily administrable, bright-line rules, his preference does not give us license to adopt a second-best interpretation of the Rules Enabling Act. Courts cannot ignore text and context in the service of simplicity.

Second, the plurality argues that its interpretation of the Enabling Act is dictated by this Court's decision in *Sibbach*, which applied a Federal Rule about when parties must submit to medical examinations. But the plurality misreads that opinion. As Justice Harlan observed in *Hanna*, "shorthand formulations which have appeared in earlier opinions are prone to carry untoward results that frequently arise from oversimplification." 380 U.S. at 475 (concurring opinion). To understand *Sibbach*, it is first necessary to understand the issue that was before the Court. The petitioner raised only the facial question whether "Rules 35 and 37 [of the Federal Rules of Civil Procedure] are . . . within the mandate of Congress to this court" and not the specific question of "the obligation of federal courts to apply the substantive law of a state." 312 U.S. at 9. The Court, therefore, had no occasion to consider whether the particular application of the Federal Rules in question would offend the Enabling Act.

Nor, in *Sibbach*, was any further analysis necessary to the resolution of the case because the matter at issue, requiring medical exams for litigants, did

---

7. This understanding of the Enabling Act has been the subject of substantial academic criticism, and rightfully so. See, e.g., Wright § 4509, at 264, 269-270, 272; Ely, The Irrepressible Myth of Erie, 87 Harv. L. Rev. 693, 719 (1974) (hereinafter Ely); see also R. Fallon, J. Manning, D. Meltzer, & D. Shapiro, Hart and Wechsler's, The Federal Courts and the Federal System 593, n.6 (6th ed. 2009) (discussing Ely).

not pertain to "substantive rights" under the Enabling Act. Although most state rules bearing on the litigation process are adopted for some policy reason, few seemingly "procedural" rules define the scope of a substantive right or remedy. The matter at issue in *Sibbach* reflected competing federal and state judgments about privacy interests. Those privacy concerns may have been weighty and in some sense substantive; but they did not pertain to the scope of any state right or remedy at issue in the litigation. . . .

Accordingly, I concur in part and concur in the judgment.

JUSTICE GINSBURG, with whom JUSTICE KENNEDY, JUSTICE BREYER, and JUSTICE ALITO join, dissenting.

The Court today approves Shady Grove's attempt to transform a $500 case into a $5,000,000 award, although the State creating the right to recover has proscribed this alchemy. If Shady Grove had filed suit in New York state court, the 2% interest payment authorized by New York Ins. Law Ann. § 5106(a), as a penalty for overdue benefits would, by Shady Grove's own measure, amount to no more than $500. By instead filing in federal court based on the parties' diverse citizenship and requesting class certification, Shady Grove hopes to recover, for the class, statutory damages of more than $5,000,000. The New York Legislature has barred this remedy . . . .

The Court reads Rule 23 relentlessly to override New York's restriction on the availability of statutory damages. Our decisions, however, caution us to ask, before undermining state legislation: Is this conflict really necessary? Cf. Traynor, Is This Conflict Really Necessary? 37 Tex. L. Rev. 657 (1959). . . .

## I

. . .

## B

In our prior decisions in point, many of them not mentioned in the Court's opinion, we have avoided immoderate interpretations of the Federal Rules that would trench on state prerogatives without serving any countervailing federal interest. "Application of the *Hanna* analysis," we have said, "is premised on a 'direct collision' between the Federal Rule and the state law." Walker v. Armco Steel Corp., 446 U.S. 740, 749-750 (1980) (quoting *Hanna*, 380 U.S. at 472). To displace state law, a Federal Rule, "when fairly construed," must be "'sufficiently broad'" so as "to 'control the issue' before the court, thereby leaving no room for the operation of that law." Burlington Northern R. Co. v. Woods, 480 U.S. 1, 4-5 (1987) (quoting *Walker*, 446 U.S. at 749-50, and n.9) . . . .

In pre-*Hanna* decisions, the Court vigilantly read the Federal Rules to avoid conflict with state laws. . . .

In all of these cases, the Court stated in *Hanna*, "the scope of the Federal Rule was not as broad as the losing party urged, and therefore, there being no Federal Rule which covered the point in dispute, *Erie* commanded the enforcement of state law." 380 U.S. at 470. In *Hanna* itself, the Court found the clash "unavoidable," ibid.; the petitioner had effected service of process as prescribed by Federal Rule 4(d)(1), but that "how-to" method did not satisfy the special Massachusetts law applicable to service on an executor or administrator. . . .

Following *Hanna*, we continued to "interpre[t] the federal rules to avoid conflict with important state regulatory policies." . . .

Most recently, in *Semtek*, we addressed the claim-preclusive effect of a federal-court judgment dismissing a diversity action on the basis of a California statute of limitations. The case came to us after the same plaintiff renewed the same fray against the same defendant in a Maryland state court. (Plaintiff chose Maryland because that State's limitations period had not yet run.) We held that Federal Rule 41(b), which provided that an involuntary dismissal "operate[d] as an adjudication on the merits," did not bar maintenance of the renewed action in Maryland. To hold that Rule 41(b) precluded the Maryland courts from entertaining the case, we said, "would arguably violate the jurisdictional limitation of the Rules Enabling Act," 531 U.S. at 503, and "would in many cases violate [*Erie*'s] federalism principle," id. at 504.

In sum, both before and after *Hanna*, the above-described decisions show, federal courts have been cautioned by this Court to "interpre[t] the Federal Rules . . . with sensitivity to important state interests," *Gasperini*, 518 U.S. at 427, n.7, and a will "to avoid conflict with important state regulatory policies," id. at 438, n.22 (internal quotation marks omitted). The Court veers away from that approach—and conspicuously, its most recent reiteration in *Gasperini*, in favor of a mechanical reading of Federal Rules, insensitive to state interests and productive of discord.

## C

. . . The limitation [of Section 901(b)] was not designed with the fair conduct or efficiency of litigation in mind. Indeed, suits seeking statutory damages are arguably best suited to the class device because individual proof of actual damages is unnecessary. New York's decision instead to block class-action proceedings for statutory damages therefore makes scant sense, except as a means to a manifestly substantive end: Limiting a defendant's liability in a single lawsuit in order to prevent the exorbitant inflation of penalties—remedies the New York Legislature created with individual suits in mind.

## D

. . . As the Second Circuit well understood, Rule 23 prescribes the considerations relevant to class certification and post-certification proceedings—but it does not command that a particular remedy be available when a party sues in a representative capacity. Section 901(b), in contrast, trains on that latter issue. Sensibly read, Rule 23 governs procedural aspects of class litigation, but allows state law to control the size of a monetary award a class plaintiff may pursue.

In other words, Rule 23 describes a method of enforcing a claim for relief, while § 901(b) defines the dimensions of the claim itself. In this regard, it is immaterial that § 901(b) bars statutory penalties in wholesale, rather than retail, fashion. The New York Legislature could have embedded the limitation in every provision creating a cause of action for which a penalty is authorized; § 901(b) operates as shorthand to the same effect. It is as much a part of the delineation of the claim for relief as it would be were it included claim by claim in the New York Code.

. . . The fair and efficient *conduct* of class litigation is the legitimate concern of Rule 23; the *remedy* for an infraction of state law, however, is the legitimate concern of the State's lawmakers and not of the federal rulemakers. Cf. Ely, The Irrepressible Myth of *Erie*, 87 Harv. L. Rev. 693, 722 (1974) (It is relevant "whether the state provision embodies a substantive policy or represents only a procedural disagreement with the federal rulemakers respecting the fairest and most efficient way of conducting litigation."). . . .

The absence of an inevitable collision between Rule 23 and § 901(b) becomes evident once it is comprehended that a federal court sitting in diversity can accord due respect to both state and federal prescriptions. Plaintiffs seeking to vindicate claims for which the State has provided a statutory penalty may pursue relief through a class action if they forgo statutory damages and instead seek actual damages or injunctive or declaratory relief; any putative class member who objects can opt out and pursue actual damages, if available, and the statutory penalty in an individual action. . . . In this manner, the Second Circuit explained, "Rule 23's procedural requirements for class actions can be applied along with the substantive requirement of CPLR 901(b)." 549 F.3d, at 144. In sum, while phrased as responsive to the question whether certain class actions may begin, § 901(b) is unmistakably aimed at controlling how those actions must end. On that remedial issue, Rule 23 is silent.

Any doubt whether Rule 23 leaves § 901(b) in control of the remedial issue at the core of this case should be dispelled by our *Erie* jurisprudence, including *Hanna*, which counsels us to read Federal Rules moderately and cautions against stretching a rule to cover every situation it could conceivably reach. The Court states that "[t]here is no reason . . . to read Rule 23 as addressing only whether claims made eligible for class treatment by some other law should be certified as class actions." To the contrary, *Palmer, Ragan, Cohen, Walker, Gasperini,* and *Semtek* provide good reason to look to the law that creates the right to recover. That is plainly so on a more accurate statement of what is at stake: Is there any reason to read Rule 23 as authorizing a claim for relief when the State that created the remedy disallows its pursuit on behalf of a class? None at all is the answer our federal system should give. . . .

By finding a conflict without considering whether Rule 23 rationally should be read to avoid any collision, the Court unwisely and unnecessarily retreats from the federalism principles undergirding *Erie*. . . .

## II

Because I perceive no unavoidable conflict between Rule 23 and § 901(b), I would decide this case by inquiring "whether application of the [state] rule would have so important an effect upon the fortunes of one or both of the litigants that failure to [apply] it would be likely to cause a plaintiff to choose the federal court." *Hanna*, 380 U.S. at 468, n.9. See *Gasperini*, 518 U.S. at 428. . . .

. . . [S]tatutes qualify as "substantive" for *Erie* purposes even when they have "procedural" thrusts as well. See, e.g., *Cohen*, 337 U.S., at 555; cf. Woods v. Interstate Realty Co., 337 U.S. 535, 536-538, and n.1 (1949) (holding diversity case must be dismissed based on state statute that, by its terms, governed only proceedings in state court). Statutes of limitations are, again, exemplary. They supply "substantive" law in diversity suits, see *York*, 326 U.S. at 109-112, even though, as Shady Grove acknowledges, state courts often apply the forum's limitations period as a "procedural" bar to claims arising under the law of another State. Similarly, federal courts sitting in diversity give effect to state laws governing the burden of proving contributory negligence, see Palmer v. Hoffman, 318 U.S. 109, 117 (1943), yet state courts adjudicating foreign causes of action often apply their own local law to this issue. See Restatement § 133 and Reporter's Note.

In short, Shady Grove's effort to characterize § 901(b) as simply "procedural" cannot successfully elide this fundamental norm: When no federal law or rule is dispositive of an issue, and a state statute is outcome affective in the sense our cases on *Erie* (pre and post-*Hanna*) develop, the Rules of Decision Act commands application of the State's law in diversity suits. *Gasperini*, 518 U.S. at 428; *Hanna*, 380 U.S. at 468, n.9; *York*, 326 U.S. at 109. As this case starkly demonstrates, if federal courts exercising diversity jurisdiction are compelled by Rule 23 to award statutory penalties in class actions while New York courts are bound by § 901(b)'s proscription, "substantial variations between state and federal [money judgments] may be expected." *Gasperini*, 518 U.S. at 430 (quoting *Hanna*, 380 U.S. at 467-468). The "variation" here is indeed "substantial." Shady Grove seeks class relief that is *ten thousand times* greater than the individual remedy available to it in state court. As the plurality acknowledges, forum shopping will undoubtedly result if a plaintiff need only file in federal instead of state court to seek a massive monetary award explicitly barred by state law. See *Gasperini*, 518 U.S. at 431 ("*Erie* precludes a recovery in federal court significantly larger than the recovery that would have been tolerated in state court."). . . . The "accident of diversity of citizenship," Klaxon Co. v. Stentor Elec. Mfg. Co., 313 U.S. 487, 496 (1941), should not subject a defendant to such augmented liability. See *Hanna*, 380 U.S. at 467 ("The *Erie* rule is rooted in part in a realization that it would be unfair for the character or result of a litigation materially to differ because the suit had been brought in a federal court."). . . .

*Gasperini*'s observations apply with full force in this case. By barring the recovery of statutory damages in a class action, § 901(b) controls a defendant's maximum liability in a suit seeking such a remedy. The remedial provision could have been written as an explicit cap: "In any class action seeking statutory damages, relief is limited to the amount the named plaintiff would have recovered in an individual suit." That New York's Legislature used other words to express the very same meaning should be inconsequential.

We have long recognized the impropriety of displacing, in a diversity action, state-law limitations on state-created remedies. See *Woods*, 337 U.S. at 538 (in a diversity case, a plaintiff "barred from recovery in the state court . . . should likewise be barred in the federal court"); *York*, 326 U.S. at 108-109 (federal court sitting in diversity "cannot afford recovery if the right to recover is made unavailable by the State nor can it substantively affect the enforcement of the right as given by the State"). Just as *Erie* precludes a federal court from entering a deficiency judgment when a State has "authoritatively announced that [such] judgments cannot be secured within its borders," *Angel v. Bullington*, 330 U.S. 183, 191 (1947), so too *Erie* should prevent a federal court from awarding statutory penalties aggregated through a class action when New York prohibits this recovery. . . .

## III

The Court's erosion of *Erie*'s federalism grounding impels me to point out the large irony in today's judgment. Shady Grove is able to pursue its claim in federal court only by virtue of the recent enactment of the Class Action Fairness Act of 2005 (CAFA), 28 U.S.C. § 1332(d). In CAFA, Congress opened federal-court doors to state-law-based class actions so long as there is minimal diversity, at least 100 class members, and at least $5,000,000 in controversy. Ibid. By providing a federal forum, Congress sought to check what it considered to be the over-readiness of some state courts to certify class actions. See, e.g., S. Rep. No. 109-114, p. 4 (2005) (CAFA prevents lawyers from "gam[ing] the procedural rules [to] keep nationwide or multistate class actions in state courts whose judges have reputations for readily certifying classes."); id. at 22 (disapproving "the 'I never met a class action I didn't like' approach to class certification" that "is prevalent in state courts in some localities"). In other words, Congress envisioned fewer—not more—class actions overall. Congress surely never anticipated that CAFA would make federal courts a mecca for suits of the kind Shady Grove has launched: class actions seeking state-created penalties for claims arising under state law-claims that would be barred from class treatment in the State's own courts. . . .

\* \* \*

I would continue to approach *Erie* questions in a manner mindful of the purposes underlying the Rules of Decision Act and the Rules Enabling Act, faithful to precedent, and respectful of important state interests. I would therefore hold that the New York Legislature's limitation on the recovery of statutory damages applies in this case, and would affirm the Second Circuit's judgment.

## Notes and Questions

1. Some of the nuances of *Shady Grove* require understanding the effect of aggregating claims in a class action, a subject we treat in detail later in this chapter. For now it is sufficient to recognize that very few attorneys would be interested in representing an individual client with a claim for statutory damages of just $500. The contingency fee would barely cover the costs of filing the suit. So even if thousands of people suffered comparable injury as a result of an insurer's refusal to pay interest on overdue benefits, the insurer is unlikely to be held liable unless a class action can be filed. Aggregating the claims not only creates an attractive contingency fee, it establishes a remedy for injuries that would otherwise go uncompensated.

The central issue in *Shady Grove* is whether creating a feasible procedural mechanism to provide a remedy is the same thing as creating substantive liability. In Justice Scalia's view, if Allstate owes the penalty on the interest to each member of the class, its substantive liability has not been expanded by virtue of Rule 23. All Rule 23 does is make recovery on that liability more feasible. In Justice Ginsburg's view, the procedural device allowing for class litigation in federal court expands Allstate's substantive liability in contravention of New York state law. Both are reasonable conclusions, aren't they?

*Shady Grove* proves, in its own muddled way, that substance and procedure are deeply intertwined. We have to worry about, and lawyers have to litigate, the difference. But surely it's a mistake to begin from the assumption that what distinguishes substance and procedure is categorical in nature.

2. Justices Scalia, Stevens, and Ginsburg take very different routes to determining whether there is a conflict between state and federal rules of decision. How would you describe their methods of analysis? What reasons support making an effort to interpret the state and federal rules of decision to avoid any conflict? Justice Stevens's approach to determining whether state and federal rules of decision conflict is somewhat more exacting than Justice Scalia's. Can you see why? Some lower courts have treated Justice Stevens's opinion as controlling on this point. See Garman v. Campbell County Sch. Dist. No. 1, 630 F.3d 977, 983 n.6 (10th Cir. 2010).

3. Take a look at Federal Rule of Civil Procedure 8. How should a federal court sitting in diversity treat a state law that requires the plaintiff in any malpractice action to provide the defendant, within 60 days after the defendant files an answer, an affidavit of an expert stating "that there

exists a reasonable probability that the care, skill or knowledge exercised or exhibited in the treatment, practice or work that is the subject of the complaint, fell outside acceptable professional or occupational standards or treatment practices"? Under state law, failure to file such an affidavit "shall be deemed a failure to state a cause of action," resulting in dismissal with prejudice. Must a federal court grant a motion to dismiss if the plaintiff in a malpractice case fails to file the necessary affidavit? Does it matter that obtaining such an expert opinion can be costly? See Nuveen Mun. Trust ex rel. Nuveen High Yield Mun. Bond Fund v. WithumSmith Brown, P.C., 692 F.3d 283, 303-04, n.13 (3d Cir. 2012) (holding that neither *Twomby*, nor *Iqbal*, nor *Shady Grove* altered the circuit's prior conclusion that New Jersey's expert affidavit requirement is substantive and "can be applied by a federal court without violating any Federal Rules" because "the affidavit is not a pleading requirement").

## 2.  Supplemental Jurisdiction of the Federal Courts

### Problem Case: Suing the HMO

Plaintiffs Narensky, Chin, and O'Brien sue their health maintenance organization under both federal RICO and ERISA claims and state law claims arising out of the HMO's refusal to provide them treatment. All claims arise out of the same set of facts.

1. A federal district court would have jurisdiction over the RICO and ERISA claims, but what about the state law issues? Must plaintiffs pursue their state law claims in a separate proceeding in state court, assuming federal diversity jurisdiction does not exist?

2. Assume instead that there are no federal claims and federal jurisdiction over all of the original state law claims is based on diversity under 28 U.S.C. § 1332. The HMO impleads the doctors who treated the plaintiffs under Rule 14, thereby making the doctors parties to the litigation. (Impleader under Rule 14 is discussed more thoroughly later in this chapter.) Plaintiffs seek to make additional state law claims against the doctors, who are not diverse from plaintiffs. May the federal court adjudicate these additional claims, or must plaintiffs sue the doctors separately in state court?

3. The doctors, now third-party defendants, counterclaim against the plaintiffs, alleging slander under state law. May the federal court hear these claims?

4. Instead of suing as individuals, assume the plaintiffs are the named plaintiffs in a class action. Jurisdiction is still based on diversity, which is proper because each of the named plaintiffs alleges over $75,000 in damages. Other class members' claims, however, do not meet the amount in controversy requirements of § 1332. May the

federal court take jurisdiction over the class claims of the unnamed parties nonetheless?

### a.  Background to the Statute (28 U.S.C. § 1367)

Complexities such as those in Narensky et al. v. HMO are common in federal litigation. Multiple claims frequently arise out of the same nucleus of facts and involve at least some of the same parties. How should a federal court proceed when it does not have subject matter jurisdiction over some of the claims? On one hand are fairness and efficiency concerns for the parties, and avoidance of inconsistent outcomes in the federal and state courts. On the other hand, state courts are better at adjudicating state claims, and in many places the federal docket is overloaded (in recent times with criminal cases).

Not unlike the "clean up" doctrine in equity, common law developed over the years allowing state law claims in federal courts under certain conditions. In 1990, Congress passed a statute, intended to codify the best of the common law and to give the federal courts supplemental jurisdiction over some state law claims. 28 U.S.C. § 1367. One advantage of the statute is that it abandons the judge-made distinction between pendent and ancillary jurisdiction—calling all these exercises simply "supplemental jurisdiction." In order, however, to understand the aims of the statute as well as the older case law that still influences its interpretation, you must learn something of the history of supplemental jurisdiction.

### i.  *The* Gibbs *Test*

The most important case under the common law regime was United Mine Workers v. Gibbs, 383 U.S. 715 (1966). The Supreme Court stated the basic test for tacking on claims as well as explaining the power to do so:

> Pendent jurisdiction, in the sense of judicial power, exists whenever there is a claim "arising under [the] Constitution, the Laws of the United States, and Treaties made or which shall be made, under their Authority . . . ," U.S. Const., Art. III, § 2, and the relationship between that claim and the state claim permits the conclusion that the entire action before the court comprises but one constitutional "case." The federal claim must have substance sufficient to confer subject matter jurisdiction on the court. The state and federal claims must derive from a common nucleus of operative fact. But if, considered without regard to their federal or state character, a plaintiff's claims are such that he would ordinarily be expected to try them all in one judicial proceeding, then, assuming substantiality of the federal issues, there is power in federal courts to hear the whole.
>
> That power need not be exercised in every case in which it is found to exist. It has consistently been recognized that pendent jurisdiction is a doctrine of discretion, not of plaintiff's right. Its jurisdiction lies in considerations of

judicial economy, convenience and fairness to litigants; if these are not present a federal court should hesitate to exercise jurisdiction over state claims, even though bound to apply state law to them . . . .

Id. at 725-26.

In operation, the *Gibbs* test resulted in the following principles for joining state law "branch" claims to a federal "trunk." First, if the plaintiff asserted a claim based on federal law against the defendant, then she could add as a pendent claim any additional state law claims that arose from the same nucleus of operative facts as the trunk federal law claim. This is the formulation:

P v. D

*federal claim*

*state claim*
*(pendent claim)*

The test was one of factual relatedness, and took into account 1) whether the jury would be unduly confused; and 2) other factors that might weigh against hearing the state claim in federal court, such as whether the federal claim is insubstantial, and whether the claims would ordinarily be tried together.

Second, if the defendant (or unwilling party to a claim) wished to assert a counterclaim against the plaintiff that arose from the same transaction or occurrence as the plaintiff's claim against her, this fell within the ancillary jurisdiction of the court. Thus, compulsory counterclaims could be heard in federal court even if they did not satisfy 28 U.S.C. § 1331 or § 1332.

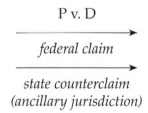

P v. D

*federal claim*

*state counterclaim*
*(ancillary jurisdiction)*

Again, the question was one of factual relatedness—matters that logically should be tried together could be tried together.

### ii.   Post-**Gibbs** *Developments*

The doctrine of ancillary jurisdiction was extended to allow a party to implead a third-party defendant (see Fed. R. Civ. P. 14) and to assert a factually related cross-claim (see Fed. R. Civ. P. 13) against a codefendant without concern for the statutory jurisdiction demands of § 1331 or § 1332. In all of these cases, the party seeking to add the claim was in a defensive posture, and the claim grew out of the original dispute against her.

In later cases, however, the Supreme Court refused to extend ancillary or pendent jurisdiction principles to other claims that, while factually related to a root federal claim, involved the addition of a new *pendent party*. Thus, for example, supplemental jurisdiction was held not to apply to a plaintiff's claim against a third-party defendant, even though the claim was factually related to the underlying cause of action against the original defendant. See Owen Equip. Co. v. Kroger, 437 U.S. 365 (1978). The Court also upheld a district court's rejection of pendent jurisdiction over state law claims against a nondiverse defendant, even though they were factually related to the underlying federal claims against the original defendants. See Aldinger v. Howard, 427 U.S. 1 (1976), *superseded by statute*, 28 U.S.C. § 1367.

Most remarkable was a case in which the Court held that a federal court lacked power to hear the factually related state claim against D(2) even when the federal claim against D(1) fell within the *exclusive* jurisdiction of the federal courts. This meant that the plaintiff would have to file two lawsuits, one in federal court against D(1) and another in state court against D(2), because neither forum could hear both claims. See Finley v. United States, 490 U.S. 545 (1989).

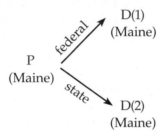

## b.   The Modern Approach

Shortly after *Finley* was decided, Congress drafted the federal supplemental jurisdiction statute, which codified much of the decisional law regarding ancillary and pendent jurisdiction and changed the hardhearted approach to pendent party jurisdiction followed by the Court in *Finley*. Read 28 U.S.C. § 1367, and keep it before you as we work through some of the statute's complexities.

The residual ambiguities of the supplemental jurisdiction statute have prompted several decisions. For example, in City of Chicago v. Int'l College of Surgeons, 522 U.S. 156 (1997), the Supreme Court held that the federal district court properly exercised supplemental jurisdiction over state law claims, including claims for on-the-record review of a municipal agency's denial of a permit to demolish certain facades of designated landmarks in Chicago. Although judicial review was on the agency's record—not de novo—the court ruled that supplemental jurisdiction was appropriate, notwithstanding objections that permitting jurisdiction in such cases could render the federal courts the superintendents of local agencies.

Justice Ginsburg, in an opinion joined by Justice Stevens, dissented, relying on Chicago, R.I. & P.R. Co. v. Stude, 346 U.S. 574 (1954), and Rooker v. Fid. Trust Co., 263 U.S. 413 (1923), which in her view preclude federal courts of first instance from exercising authority under §§ 1331 and 1332 to displace state courts as forums for on-the-record review of state and local agency actions.

The broad grant of supplemental jurisdiction authority contained in § 1367(a) and then limited with respect to diversity cases in § 1367(b) has also proved ambiguous. Section 1367(b) instructs courts not to exercise supplemental jurisdiction in diversity cases over claims by plaintiffs against persons made parties under Rule 14 (impleader), 19 (compulsory joinder), 20 (permissive joinder), or 24 (intervention), or over claims by persons proposed to be joined as plaintiffs under Rule 19, or seeking to intervene as plaintiffs under Rule 24, where exercising such jurisdiction would be inconsistent with the jurisdictional requirements of § 1332 (e.g., complete diversity). (The interplay between joinder, impleader, and intervention and supplemental jurisdiction in diversity cases can give rise to very complex procedural situations that will be somewhat clearer after you study more advanced joinder later in this chapter.)

The complexities and likely unintentional consequences of supplemental jurisdiction under § 1367 are underscored by cases like Shanaghan v. Cahill, 58 F.3d 106 (4th Cir. 1995), which noted as follows:

> [Section] 1367(a) is broadly phrased to provide for supplemental jurisdiction over claims appended to "any civil action" over which the court has "original jurisdiction." . . . [Section] 1367(b) imposes specific limits on the use of supplemental jurisdiction in diversity cases in order to prevent the addition of parties that would destroy complete diversity as required by § 1332, but otherwise plainly contemplates the use of supplemental jurisdiction in that context. . . . The only possible interpretation of this language is that state law claims between diverse parties that do not, however, satisfy the jurisdictional amount requirements appended to diversity actions are cognizable under supplemental jurisdiction.

Id. at 109. But see Carter v. Tennant Co., 585 F.3d 673 (7th Cir. 2004) (declining to adopt *Shanaghan*'s approach to Section 1367).

### c.  Solving the Problem Case

Armed with § 1367, return to the problem case. Though we supply answers below, keep in mind the fact-charged nature of the inquiry, and the discretionary aspects of the exercise of supplemental jurisdiction.

1. May the federal court exercise supplemental jurisdiction over the state law claims where it has original jurisdiction over federal claims under 28 U.S.C. § 1331, or must plaintiffs sue separately in state court?

*Answer*: Because federal jurisdiction is based on claims arising under federal laws, § 1367(a) governs. Assuming that none of the issues discussed in § 1367(c) is present, the court may exercise supplemental jurisdiction over the state law claims because they "are so related to claims in the action within [the court's] original jurisdiction that they form part of the same case or controversy." See 28 U.S.C. § 1367(a).*

2. Where original jurisdiction was based on diversity under § 1332 and the doctors are impleaded under Rule 14, may the court hear plaintiffs' claims against the third-party defendant doctors?

   *Answer*: Where original jurisdiction is based solely on diversity, federal courts may not exercise supplemental jurisdiction over claims that do not satisfy federal subject matter jurisdiction requirements if the claim is one so specified in § 1367(b). Here, the doctors were made parties to the case by means of impleader under Rule 14. Under § 1367(b), courts may not exercise supplemental jurisdiction over claims made by plaintiffs against persons made parties to a suit under Rule 14. Thus the court may not hear plaintiffs' state law claims against the doctors because federal subject matter jurisdiction is lacking and § 1367 prohibits supplemental jurisdiction over the claims. The same answer holds for parties who intervene in a diversity case where the intervenors' claims are below the amount in controversy and/or the intervenors are not of diverse citizenship. See Griffin v. Lee, 621 F.3d 380 (5th Cir. 2010).

3. May the federal court hear the claims alleged by the third-party defendant doctors against plaintiffs?

   *Answer*: Section 1367(b) carves out exceptions to § 1367(a)'s broad grant of supplemental jurisdiction authority only for claims made by plaintiffs against persons added as parties through various rules. Section 1367(b) does not cover claims made by added parties, such as the third-party defendant doctors, against plaintiffs. Thus,

---

* If the federal claims are dismissed, a court has discretion under § 1367(c)(3) either to continue exercising supplemental jurisdiction over the remaining state law claims, or dismiss the case altogether. What if the plaintiff *amends* her complaint and drops the federal claims? Should the plaintiff's choice affect the discretion of the court regarding the exercise of supplemental jurisdiction? The Eleventh Circuit has held that it should. In Pintando v. Miami-Dade Hous. Agency, the court held that because an amended pleading supersedes the former pleading, "once the amended complaint [dropping plaintiff's federal Title VII claims] was accepted by the district court . . . there was no longer a federal claim on which the district court could exercise supplemental jurisdiction for the remaining state law claims." 501 F.3d 1241, 1243 (11th Cir. 2007). The court relied upon the Supreme Court's decision in Rockwell Int'l Corp. v. United States, which held that "'when a plaintiff voluntarily amends the complaint, courts look to the amended complaint to determine jurisdiction.'" *Pintando*, 501 F.3d at 1243 (quoting and following *Rockwell*, 549 U.S. 457, 473-74 (2007), Wellness Cmty. Nat'l v. Wellness House, 70 F.3d 46, 48-49 (7th Cir. 1995), and Boelens v. Redman Homes, Inc., 759 F.3d 504, 506-08 (5th Cir. 1985)).

the court may exercise supplemental jurisdiction over the doctors' claims against the plaintiffs under § 1367(a).

4. In the class action context where federal jurisdiction is based on diversity, may the federal court adjudicate the claims of unnamed class members whose individual claims would not satisfy the amount in controversy requirement of § 1332?

*Answer*: This issue has engendered considerable debate since § 1367 was enacted. One answer is that since Rule 23 class actions are not listed among the exclusions in § 1367(b), then § 1367(a) applies and supplemental jurisdiction is proper. Read on.

### d. Operation of § 1367 in the Class Action Context

Interpreting and applying § 1367 has proven particularly problematic in the class action context. Courts and commentators have differed considerably over whether § 1367(b), by omitting class actions under Rule 23 from the list of exceptions to § 1367(a)'s broad grant of supplemental jurisdiction, was meant to overrule Zahn v. Int'l Paper Co., 414 U.S. 291 (1973). *Zahn* prohibited the exercise of supplemental jurisdiction in diversity cases over claims of unnamed class members for less than the jurisdictional amount. (In 1998, the American Law Institute recommended amending § 1367 to make clear that supplemental jurisdiction would be appropriate over such class claims; the amendments have not been adopted.)

Prompted by a sharp split in the circuit courts, the Supreme Court finally addressed the issue in the following decision. Unfortunately, as you will see, the Court itself is badly divided (5-4), so we cannot be certain that its reading of § 1367 will endure. Notice too that the case consolidates two appeals from the circuit courts, one a class action in which the claims of some class members did not meet the amount-in-controversy requirement, another a standard multi-plaintiff personal injury case in which only one plaintiff met the amount-in-controversy requirement.

### *Exxon Mobil Corp. v. Allapattah Services, Inc.*
545 U.S. 546 (2005)

JUSTICE KENNEDY delivered the opinion of the Court.

These consolidated cases present the question whether a federal court in a diversity action may exercise supplemental jurisdiction over additional plaintiffs whose claims do not satisfy the minimum amount-in-controversy requirement, provided the claims are part of the same case or controversy as the claims of plaintiffs who do allege a sufficient amount in controversy. Our decision turns on the correct interpretation of 28 U.S.C. § 1367. The question has divided the Courts of Appeals, and we granted certiorari to resolve the conflict. . . .

We hold that, where the other elements of jurisdiction are present and at least one named plaintiff in the action satisfies the amount-in-controversy requirement, § 1367 does authorize supplemental jurisdiction over the claims of other plaintiffs in the same Article III case or controversy, even if those claims are for less than the jurisdictional amount specified in the statute setting forth the requirements for diversity jurisdiction. We affirm the judgment of the Court of Appeals for the Eleventh Circuit in *[Allapattah],* and we reverse the judgment of the Court of Appeals for the First Circuit in *[Star-Kist].*

## I

In 1991, about 10,000 Exxon dealers filed a class-action suit against the Exxon Corporation in the United States District Court for the Northern District of Florida. The dealers alleged an intentional and systematic scheme by Exxon under which they were overcharged for fuel purchased from Exxon. The plaintiffs invoked the District Court's § 1332(a) diversity jurisdiction. After a unanimous jury verdict in favor of the plaintiffs, the District Court certified the case for interlocutory review, asking whether it had properly exercised § 1367 supplemental jurisdiction over the claims of class members who did not meet the jurisdictional minimum amount in controversy.

The Court of Appeals for the Eleventh Circuit upheld the District Court's extension of supplemental jurisdiction to these class members. . . . This decision accords with the views of the Courts of Appeals for the Fourth, Sixth, and Seventh Circuits. . . . The Courts of Appeals for the Fifth and Ninth Circuits, adopting a similar analysis of the statute, have held that in a diversity class action the unnamed class members need not meet the amount-in-controversy requirement, provided the named class members do. These decisions, however, are unclear on whether all the named plaintiffs must satisfy this requirement. . . .

In the other case now before us the Court of Appeals for the First Circuit took a different position on the meaning of § 1367(a). 370 F.3d 124 (2004). In that case, a 9-year-old girl sued Star-Kist in a diversity action in the United States District Court for the District of Puerto Rico, seeking damages for unusually severe injuries she received when she sliced her finger on a tuna can. Her family joined in the suit, seeking damages for emotional distress and certain medical expenses. The District Court granted summary judgment to Star-Kist, finding that none of the plaintiffs met the minimum amount-in-controversy requirement. The Court of Appeals for the First Circuit, however, ruled that the injured girl, but not her family members, had made allegations of damages in the requisite amount.

The Court of Appeals then addressed whether, in light of the fact that one plaintiff met the requirements for original jurisdiction, supplemental jurisdiction over the remaining plaintiffs' claims was proper under § 1367. The court held that § 1367 authorizes supplemental jurisdiction only when the district court has original jurisdiction over the action, and that in a diversity case original jurisdiction is lacking if one plaintiff fails to satisfy the amount-in-controversy requirement. Although the Court of Appeals claimed to "express no view" on whether the result would be the same in a class action, id., at 143 n.19, its analysis is inconsistent with that of the Court of Appeals for the Eleventh Circuit. The Court of Appeals for the First Circuit's view of § 1367 is, however, shared by the Courts of Appeal for the Third, Eighth, and Tenth Circuits, and the latter two Courts of Appeals have expressly applied this rule to class actions. . . .

## II

### A

The district courts of the United States, as we have said many times, are "courts of limited jurisdiction. They possess only that power authorized by Constitution and statute." Kokkonen v. Guardian Life Ins. Co. of America, 511 U.S. 375, 377 (1994). In order to provide a federal forum for plaintiffs who seek to vindicate federal rights, Congress has conferred on the district courts original jurisdiction in federal-question cases—civil actions that arise under the Constitution, laws, or treaties of the United States. 28 U.S.C. § 1331. In order to provide a neutral forum for what have come to be known as diversity cases, Congress also has granted district courts original jurisdiction in civil actions between citizens of different States, between U.S. citizens and foreign citizens, or by foreign states against U.S. citizens. § 1332. To ensure that diversity jurisdiction does not flood the federal courts with minor disputes, § 1332(a) requires that the matter in controversy in a diversity case exceed a specified amount, currently $75,000.

Although the district courts may not exercise jurisdiction absent a statutory basis, it is well established—in certain classes of cases—that, once a court has original jurisdiction over some claims in the action, it may exercise supplemental jurisdiction over additional claims that are part of the same case or controversy. The leading modern case for this principle is Mine Workers v. Gibbs, 383 U.S. 715 (1966). In *Gibbs*, the plaintiff alleged the defendant's conduct violated both federal and state law. The District Court, *Gibbs* held, had original jurisdiction over the action based on the federal claims. *Gibbs* confirmed that the District Court had the additional power (though not the obligation) to exercise supplemental jurisdiction over related state claims that arose from the same Article III case or controversy. Id. at 725 ("The federal claim must have substance sufficient to confer subject matter jurisdiction on the court. . . . [A]ssuming substantiality of the federal issues, there is *power* in federal courts to hear the whole.").

As we later noted, the decision allowing jurisdiction over pendent state claims in *Gibbs* did not mention, let alone come to grips with, the text of the jurisdictional statutes and the bedrock principle that federal courts have no jurisdiction without statutory authorization. Finley v. United States, 490 U.S. 545, 548 (1989). In *Finley*, we nonetheless reaffirmed and rationalized *Gibbs* and its progeny by inferring from it the interpretive principle that, in cases involving supplemental jurisdiction over additional claims between parties properly in federal court, the jurisdictional statutes should be read broadly, on the assumption that in this context Congress intended to authorize courts to exercise their full Article III power to dispose of an "'entire action before the court [which] comprises but one constitutional case.'" 490 U.S. at 549 (quoting *Gibbs*, supra, at 725).

We have not, however, applied *Gibbs'* expansive interpretive approach to other aspects of the jurisdictional statutes. For instance, we have consistently interpreted § 1332 as requiring complete diversity: In a case with multiple plaintiffs and multiple defendants, the presence in the action of a single plaintiff from the same State as a single defendant deprives the district court of original diversity jurisdiction over the entire action. Strawbridge v. Curtiss, 3 Cranch 267 (1806); Owen Equipment & Erection Co. v. Kroger, 437 U.S. 365, 375 (1978). The complete diversity requirement is not mandated by the Constitution, State Farm Fire & Casualty Co. v. Tashire, 386 U.S. 523, 530-531 (1967), or by the plain text of § 1332(a). The Court, nonetheless, has adhered to the complete diversity rule in light of the purpose of the diversity requirement, which is to provide a federal forum for important disputes where state courts might favor, or be perceived as favoring, home-state litigants. The presence of parties from the same State on both sides of a case dispels this concern, eliminating a principal reason for conferring § 1332 jurisdiction over any of the claims in the action. See Wisconsin Dept. of Corrections v. Schacht, 524 U.S. 381, 389 (1998); Newman-Green, Inc. v. Alfonzo-Larrain, 490 U.S. 826, 829 (1989). The specific purpose of the complete diversity rule explains both why we have not adopted *Gibbs'* expansive interpretive approach to this aspect of the jurisdictional statute and why *Gibbs* does not undermine the complete diversity rule. In order for a federal court to invoke supplemental jurisdiction under *Gibbs*, it must first have original jurisdiction over at least one claim in the action. Incomplete diversity destroys original jurisdiction with respect to all claims, so there is nothing to which supplemental jurisdiction can adhere.

In contrast to the diversity requirement, most of the other statutory prerequisites for federal jurisdiction, including the federal-question and amount-in-controversy requirements, can be analyzed claim by claim. True, it does not follow by necessity from this that a district court has authority to exercise supplemental jurisdiction over all claims provided there is original jurisdiction over just one. Before the enactment of § 1367, the Court declined in contexts other than the pendent-claim instance to follow *Gibbs'* expansive approach to interpretation of the jurisdictional statutes. The Court took a more restrictive view of the proper interpretation of these statutes in so-called pendent-party cases involving supplemental jurisdiction over claims involving additional parties—plaintiffs or defendants—where the district courts would lack original jurisdiction over claims by each of the parties standing alone.

Thus, with respect to plaintiff-specific jurisdictional requirements, the Court held in Clark v. Paul Gray, Inc., 306 U.S. 583 (1939), that every plaintiff must separately satisfy the amount-in-controversy requirement. Though

*Clark* was a federal-question case, at that time federal-question jurisdiction had an amount-in-controversy requirement analogous to the amount-in-controversy requirement for diversity cases. "Proper practice," *Clark* held, "requires that where each of several plaintiffs is bound to establish the jurisdictional amount with respect to his own claim, the suit should be dismissed as to those who fail to show that the requisite amount is involved." Id. at 590. The Court reaffirmed this rule, in the context of a class action brought invoking § 1332(a) diversity jurisdiction, in Zahn v. International Paper Co., 414 U.S. 291 (1973). It follows "inescapably" from *Clark*, the Court held in *Zahn*, that "any plaintiff without the jurisdictional amount must be dismissed from the case, even though others allege jurisdictionally sufficient claims." 414 U.S. at 300.

The Court took a similar approach with respect to supplemental jurisdiction over claims against additional defendants that fall outside the district courts' original jurisdiction. In Aldinger v. Howard, 427 U.S. 1 (1976), the plaintiff brought a 42 U.S.C. § 1983 action against county officials in district court pursuant to the statutory grant of jurisdiction in 28 U.S.C. § 1343(3) (1976 ed.). The plaintiff further alleged the court had supplemental jurisdiction over her related state-law claims against the county, even though the county was not suable under § 1983 and so was not subject to § 1343(3)'s original jurisdiction. The Court held that supplemental jurisdiction could not be exercised because Congress, in enacting § 1343(3), had declined (albeit implicitly) to extend federal jurisdiction over any party who could not be sued under the federal civil rights statutes. 427 U.S. at 16-19. "Before it can be concluded that [supplemental] jurisdiction [over additional parties] exists," *Aldinger* held, "a federal court must satisfy itself not only that Art[icle] III permits it, but that Congress in the statutes conferring jurisdiction has not expressly or by implication negated its existence." Id. at 18.

In Finley v. United States, 490 U.S. 545 (1989), we confronted a similar issue in a different statutory context. The plaintiff in *Finley* brought a Federal Tort Claims Act negligence suit against the Federal Aviation Administration in District Court, which had original jurisdiction under § 1346(b). The plaintiff tried to add related claims against other defendants, invoking the District Court's supplemental jurisdiction over so-called pendent parties. We held that the District Court lacked a sufficient statutory basis for exercising supplemental jurisdiction over these claims. Relying primarily on *Zahn*, *Aldinger*, and *Kroger*, we held in *Finley* that "a grant of jurisdiction over claims involving particular parties does not itself confer jurisdiction over additional claims by or against different parties." 490 U.S. at 556. While *Finley* did not "limit or impair" *Gibbs'* liberal approach to interpreting the jurisdictional statutes in the context of supplemental jurisdiction over additional claims involving the same parties, 490 U.S. at 556, *Finley* nevertheless declined to extend that interpretive assumption to claims involving additional parties. *Finley* held that in the context of parties, in contrast to claims, "we will not assume that the full constitutional power has been congressionally authorized, and will not read jurisdictional statutes broadly." Id. at 549.

As the jurisdictional statutes existed in 1989, then, here is how matters stood: First, the diversity requirement in § 1332(a) required complete diversity; absent complete diversity, the district court lacked original jurisdiction over all of the claims in the action. *Strawbridge*, 3 Cranch, at 267-268; *Kroger*, 437 U.S. at 373-374. Second, if the district court had original jurisdiction over at least one claim, the jurisdictional statutes implicitly authorized supplemental jurisdiction over all other claims between the same parties arising out of the same Article III case or controversy. *Gibbs*, 383 U.S. at 725. Third, even when the district court had original jurisdiction over one or more claims between particular parties, the jurisdictional statutes did not authorize supplemental jurisdiction over additional claims involving other parties. *Clark*, supra, at 590; *Zahn*, supra, at 300-301; *Finley*, supra, at 556.

## B

In *Finley* we emphasized that "[w]hatever we say regarding the scope of jurisdiction conferred by a particular statute can of course be changed by Congress." 490 U.S. at 556. In 1990, Congress accepted the invitation. It passed the Judicial Improvements Act, 104 Stat. 5089, which enacted § 1367, the provision which controls these cases.

Section 1367 provides, in relevant part:

(a) Except as provided in subsections (b) and (c) or as expressly provided otherwise by Federal statute, in any civil action of which the district courts have original jurisdiction, the district courts shall have supplemental jurisdiction over all other claims that are so related to claims in the action within such original jurisdiction that they form part of the same case or controversy under Article III of the United States Constitution. Such supplemental jurisdiction shall include claims that involve the joinder or intervention of additional parties.

(b) In any civil action of which the district courts have original jurisdiction founded solely on section 1332 of this title, the district courts shall not have supplemental jurisdiction under subsection (a) over claims by plaintiffs against persons made parties under Rule 14, 19, 20, or 24 of the Federal Rules of Civil Procedure, or over claims by persons proposed to be joined as plaintiffs under Rule 19 of such rules, or seeking to intervene as plaintiffs under Rule 24 of such rules, when exercising supplemental jurisdiction over such claims would be inconsistent with the jurisdictional requirements of section 1332.

All parties to this litigation and all courts to consider the question agree that § 1367 overturned the result in *Finley*. There is no warrant, however, for assuming that § 1367 did no more than to overrule *Finley* and otherwise to codify the existing state of the law of supplemental jurisdiction. We must not give jurisdictional statutes a more expansive interpretation than their text warrants, 490 U.S. at 549, 556; but it is just as important not to adopt an artificial construction that is narrower than what the text provides. No sound canon of interpretation requires Congress to speak with extraordinary clarity in order to modify the rules of federal jurisdiction within appropriate constitutional bounds. Ordinary principles of statutory construction apply. In order to determine the scope of supplemental jurisdiction authorized by § 1367, then, we must examine the statute's text in light of context, structure, and related statutory provisions.

Section 1367(a) is a broad grant of supplemental jurisdiction over other claims within the same case or controversy, as long as the action is one in which the district courts would have original jurisdiction. The last sentence of § 1367(a) makes it clear that the grant of supplemental jurisdiction extends to claims involving joinder or intervention of additional parties. The single question before us, therefore, is whether a diversity case in which the claims of some plaintiffs satisfy the amount-in-controversy requirement, but the claims of others plaintiffs do not, presents a "civil action of which the district courts have original jurisdiction." . . .

We now conclude the answer must be yes. When the well-pleaded complaint contains at least one claim that satisfies the amount-in-controversy requirement, and there are no other relevant jurisdictional defects, the district court, beyond all question, has original jurisdiction over that claim. The presence of other claims in the complaint, over which the district court may lack original jurisdiction, is of no moment. If the court has original jurisdiction over a single claim in the complaint, it has original jurisdiction over a "civil action" within the meaning of § 1367(a), even if the civil action over which it has jurisdiction comprises fewer claims than were included in the complaint. Once the court determines it has original jurisdiction over the civil action, it can turn to the question whether it has a constitutional and statutory basis for exercising supplemental jurisdiction over the other claims in the action.

Section 1367(a) commences with the direction that §§ 1367(b) and (c), or other relevant statutes, may provide specific exceptions, but otherwise § 1367(a) is a broad jurisdictional grant, with no distinction drawn between pendent-claim and pendent-party cases. In fact, the last sentence of § 1367(a) makes clear that the provision grants supplemental jurisdiction over claims involving joinder or intervention of additional parties. The terms of § 1367 do not acknowledge any distinction between pendent jurisdiction and the doctrine of so-called ancillary jurisdiction. Though the doctrines of pendent and ancillary jurisdiction developed separately as a historical matter, the Court has recognized that the doctrines are "two species of the same generic problem," *Kroger*, 437 U.S., at 370. Nothing in § 1367 indicates a congressional intent to recognize, preserve, or create some meaningful, substantive distinction between the jurisdictional categories we have historically labeled pendent and ancillary.

If § 1367(a) were the sum total of the relevant statutory language, our holding would rest on that language alone. The statute, of course, instructs us to examine § 1367(b) to determine if any of its exceptions apply, so we proceed to that section. While § 1367(b) qualifies the broad rule of § 1367(a), it does not withdraw supplemental jurisdiction over the claims of the additional parties at issue here. The specific exceptions to § 1367(a) contained in § 1367(b), moreover, provide additional support for our conclusion that § 1367(a) confers supplemental jurisdiction over these claims. Section 1367(b), which applies only to diversity cases, withholds supplemental jurisdiction over the claims of plaintiffs proposed to be joined as indispensable parties under Federal Rule of Civil Procedure 19, or who seek to intervene pursuant to Rule 24. Nothing in the text of § 1367(b), however, withholds supplemental jurisdiction over the claims of plaintiffs permissively joined under Rule 20 (like the additional plaintiffs in [*Star-Kist*]) or certified as class-action members pursuant to Rule 23 (like the additional plaintiffs in [*Allapattah*]). The natural, indeed the necessary, inference is that § 1367 confers supplemental jurisdiction over claims by Rule 20 and Rule 23 plaintiffs. This inference, at least with respect to Rule 20 plaintiffs, is strengthened by the fact that § 1367(b) explicitly excludes supplemental jurisdiction over claims against defendants joined under Rule 20.

We cannot accept the view, urged by some of the parties, commentators, and Courts of Appeals, that a district court lacks original jurisdiction over a civil action unless the court has original jurisdiction over every claim in the complaint. As we understand this position, it requires assuming either that all claims in the complaint must stand or fall as a single, indivisible "civil action" as a matter of definitional necessity—what we will refer to as the "indivisibility theory"—or else that the inclusion of a claim or party falling outside the district court's original jurisdiction somehow contaminates every other claim in the complaint, depriving the court of original jurisdiction over any of these claims—what we will refer to as the "contamination theory."

The indivisibility theory is easily dismissed, as it is inconsistent with the whole notion of supplemental jurisdiction. If a district court must have original jurisdiction over every claim in the complaint in order to have "original jurisdiction" over a "civil action," then in *Gibbs* there was no civil action of which the district court could assume original jurisdiction under § 1331, and so no basis for exercising supplemental jurisdiction over any of the claims. The indivisibility theory is further belied by our practice—in both federal-question and diversity cases—of allowing federal courts to cure jurisdictional defects by dismissing the offending parties rather than dismissing the entire action. . . .

The contamination theory, as we have noted, can make some sense in the special context of the complete diversity requirement because the presence of nondiverse parties on both sides of a lawsuit eliminates the justification for providing a federal forum. The theory, however, makes little sense with respect to the amount-in-controversy requirement, which is meant to ensure that a dispute is sufficiently important to warrant federal-court attention. The presence of a single nondiverse party may eliminate the fear of bias with respect to all claims, but the presence of a claim that falls short of the minimum amount in controversy does nothing to reduce the importance of the claims that do meet this requirement.

It is fallacious to suppose, simply from the proposition that § 1332 imposes both the diversity requirement and the amount-in-controversy requirement, that the contamination theory germane to the former is also relevant to the latter. There is no inherent logical connection between the amount-in-controversy requirement and § 1332 diversity jurisdiction. After all, federal-question jurisdiction once had an amount-in-controversy requirement as well. If such a requirement were revived under § 1331, it is clear beyond peradventure that § 1367(a) provides supplemental jurisdiction over federal-question cases where some, but not all, of the federal-law claims involve a sufficient amount in controversy. In other words, § 1367(a) unambiguously overrules the holding and the result in *Clark*. If that is so, however, it would be quite extraordinary to say that § 1367 did not also overrule *Zahn*, a case that was premised in substantial part on the holding in *Clark*.

In addition to the theoretical difficulties with the argument that a district court has original jurisdiction over a civil action only if it has original jurisdiction over each individual claim in the complaint, we have already considered and rejected a virtually identical argument in the closely analogous context of removal jurisdiction. In Chicago v. International College of Surgeons, 522 U.S. 156 (1997), the plaintiff brought federal- and state-law claims in state court. The defendant removed to federal court. The plaintiff objected to removal, citing the text of the removal statute, § 1441(a). That statutory provision, which bears a striking similarity to the relevant portion of § 1367, authorizes removal of "any civil action . . . of which the district courts of the United States have original jurisdiction. . . ." The *College of Surgeons* plaintiff urged that, because its state-law claims were not within the District Court's original jurisdiction, § 1441(a) did not authorize removal. We disagreed. The federal law claims, we held, "suffice to make the actions 'civil actions' within the 'original jurisdiction' of the district courts. . . . Nothing in the jurisdictional statutes suggests that the presence of related state law claims somehow alters the fact that [the plaintiff's] complaints, by virtue of their federal claims, were 'civil actions' within the federal courts' 'original jurisdiction.'" Id. at 166. Once the case was removed, the District Court had original jurisdiction over the federal law claims and supplemental jurisdiction under § 1367(a) over the state-law claims. Id. at 165.

. . . More importantly for present purposes, *College of Surgeons* stressed that a district court has original jurisdiction of a civil action for purposes of § 1441(a) as long as it has original jurisdiction over a subset of the claims constituting the action. Even the *College of Surgeons* dissent, which took issue with the Court's interpretation of § 1367, did not appear to contest this view of § 1441(a).

Although *College of Surgeons* involved additional claims between the same parties, its interpretation of § 1441(a) applies equally to cases involving additional parties whose claims fall short of the jurisdictional amount. If we were to adopt the contrary view that the presence of additional parties means there is no "civil action . . . of which the district courts . . . have original jurisdiction," those cases simply would not be removable. To our knowledge, no court has issued a reasoned opinion adopting this view of the removal statute. It is settled, of course, that absent complete diversity a case is not removable because the district court would lack original jurisdiction. Caterpillar Inc. v. Lewis, 519 U.S. 61, 73 (1996). This, however, is altogether consistent with our view of § 1441(a). A failure of complete diversity, unlike the failure of some claims to meet the requisite amount in controversy, contaminates every claim in the action.

We also reject the argument, similar to the attempted distinction of *College of Surgeons* discussed above, that while the presence of additional claims over which the district court lacks jurisdiction does not mean the civil action is outside the purview of § 1367(a), the presence of additional parties does. The basis for this distinction is not altogether clear, and it is in considerable tension with statutory text. Section 1367(a) applies by its terms to any civil action of which the district courts have original jurisdiction, and the last sentence of § 1367(a) expressly contemplates that the court may have supplemental jurisdiction over additional parties. So it cannot be the case that the presence of those parties destroys the court's original jurisdiction, within the meaning of § 1367(a), over a civil action otherwise properly before it. Also, § 1367(b) expressly withholds supplemental jurisdiction in diversity cases over claims by plaintiffs joined as indispensable parties under Rule 19. If joinder of such parties were sufficient to deprive the district court of original jurisdiction over the civil action within the meaning of § 1367(a), this specific limitation on supplemental jurisdiction in § 1367(b) would be superfluous. . . .

Finally, it is suggested that our interpretation of § 1367(a) creates an anomaly regarding the exceptions listed in § 1367(b): It is not immediately obvious why Congress would withhold supplemental jurisdiction over plaintiffs joined as parties "needed for just adjudication" under Rule 19 but would allow supplemental jurisdiction over plaintiffs permissively joined under Rule 20. The omission of Rule 20 plaintiffs from the list of exceptions in § 1367(b) may have been an "unintentional drafting gap," *Meritcare*, 166 F.3d at 221 and n.6. If that is the case, it is up to Congress rather than the courts to fix it. The omission may seem odd, but it is not absurd. An alternative explanation for the different treatment of Rule 19 and Rule 20 is that Congress was concerned that extending supplemental jurisdiction to Rule 19 plaintiffs would allow circumvention of the complete diversity rule: A nondiverse plaintiff might be omitted intentionally from the original action, but joined later under Rule 19 as a necessary party. See Stromberg Metal Works[, Inc. v. Press Mechanical, Inc., 77 F.3d 928, 932 (C.A.7 1996)]. The contamination theory described above, if applicable, means this ruse would fail, but Congress may have wanted to make assurance double sure. More generally, Congress may have concluded that federal jurisdiction is only appropriate if the district court would have original jurisdiction over the claims of all those plaintiffs who are so essential to the action that they could be joined under Rule 19. . . .

And so we circle back to the original question. When the well-pleaded complaint in district court includes multiple claims, all part of the same case or controversy, and some, but not all, of the claims are within the court's original jurisdiction, does the court have before it "any civil action of which the district courts have original jurisdiction"? It does. Under § 1367, the court has original jurisdiction over the civil action comprising the claims for which there is no jurisdictional defect. No other reading of § 1367 is plausible in light of the text and structure of the jurisdictional statute. Though the special nature and purpose of the diversity requirement mean that a single nondiverse party can contaminate every other claim in the lawsuit, the contamination does not occur with respect to jurisdictional defects that go only to the substantive importance of individual claims.

It follows from this conclusion that the threshold requirement of § 1367(a) is satisfied in cases, like those now before us, where some, but not all, of the plaintiffs in a diversity action allege a sufficient amount in controversy. We hold that § 1367 by its plain text overruled *Clark* and *Zahn* and authorized supplemental jurisdiction over all claims by diverse parties arising out of the same Article III case or controversy, subject only to enumerated exceptions not applicable in the cases now before us.

## C

The proponents of the alternative view of § 1367 insist that the statute is at least ambiguous and that we should look to other interpretive tools, including the legislative history of § 1367, which supposedly demonstrate Congress did not intend § 1367 to overrule *Zahn*. . . .

Those who urge that the legislative history refutes our interpretation rely primarily on the House Judiciary Committee Report on the Judicial Improvements Act. H.R. Rep. No. 101-734 (1990) (House Report or Report). This Report explained that § 1367 would "authorize jurisdiction in a case like *Finley*, as well as essentially restore the pre-*Finley* understandings of the authorization for and limits on other forms of supplemental jurisdiction." [House Report], at 28. . . . The Report then remarked that § 1367(b) "is not intended to affect the jurisdictional requirements of [§ 1332] in diversity-only class actions, as those requirements were interpreted prior to *Finley*," citing, without further elaboration, *Zahn* and Supreme Tribe of Ben-Hur v. Cauble, 255 U.S. 356 (1921). House Report, at 29, and n.17. . . .

As we have repeatedly held, the authoritative statement is the statutory text, not the legislative history or any other extrinsic material. . . . Judicial investigation of legislative history has a tendency to become, to borrow Judge Leventhal's memorable phrase, an exercise in "'looking over a crowd and picking out your friends.'" See Wald, Some Observations on the Use of Legislative History in the 1981 Supreme Court Term, 68 Iowa L. Rev. 195, 214 (1983). Second, judicial reliance on legislative materials like committee reports, which are not themselves subject to the requirements of Article I, may give unrepresentative committee members—or, worse yet, unelected staffers and lobbyists—both the power and the incentive to attempt strategic manipulations of legislative history to secure results they were unable to achieve through the statutory text. . . .

. . . [E]ven if we believed resort to legislative history were appropriate in these cases—a point we do not concede—we would not give significant weight to the House Report. The distinguished jurists who drafted the Subcommittee Working Paper, along with three of the participants in the drafting of § 1367, agree that this provision, on its face, overrules *Zahn.* This accords with the best reading of the statute's text, and nothing in the legislative history indicates directly and explicitly that Congress understood the phrase "civil action of which the district courts have original jurisdiction" to exclude cases in which some but not all of the diversity plaintiffs meet the amount in controversy requirement. . . .

## D

Finally, we note that the Class Action Fairness Act (CAFA), Pub. L. 109-2, 119 Stat. 4, enacted this year, has no bearing on our analysis of these cases. Subject to certain limitations, the CAFA confers federal diversity jurisdiction over class actions where the aggregate amount in controversy exceeds $5 million. It abrogates the rule against aggregating claims, a rule this Court recognized in *Ben-Hur* and reaffirmed in *Zahn.* The CAFA, however, is not retroactive, and the views of the 2005 Congress are not relevant to our interpretation of a text enacted by Congress in 1990. The CAFA, moreover, does not moot the significance of our interpretation of § 1367, as many proposed exercises of supplemental jurisdiction, even in the class-action context, might not fall within the CAFA's ambit. The CAFA, then, has no impact, one way or the other, on our interpretation of § 1367.

\* \* \*

The judgment of the Court of Appeals for the Eleventh Circuit is affirmed. The judgment of the Court of Appeals for the First Circuit is reversed, and the case is remanded for proceedings consistent with this opinion.

*It is so ordered.*

Justice Ginsburg, with whom Justice Stevens, Justice O'Connor, and Justice Breyer join, dissenting.

. . . Section 1367, all agree, was designed to overturn this Court's decision in Finley v. United States, 490 U.S. 545 (1989). *Finley* concerned not diversity-of-citizenship jurisdiction (28 U.S.C. § 1332), but original federal-court jurisdiction in cases arising under federal law (28 U.S.C. § 1331). . . .

What more § 1367 wrought is an issue on which courts of appeals have sharply divided. . . .

The Court adopts a plausibly broad reading of § 1367, a measure that is hardly a model of the careful drafter's art. There is another plausible reading, however, one less disruptive of our jurisprudence regarding supplemental jurisdiction. If one reads § 1367(a) to instruct, as the statute's text suggests, that the district court must first have "original jurisdiction" over a "civil action" before supplemental jurisdiction can attach, then *Clark* and *Zahn* are preserved, and supplemental jurisdiction does not open the way for joinder of plaintiffs, or inclusion of class members, who do not independently meet the amount-in-controversy requirement. For the reasons that follow, I conclude that this narrower construction is the better reading of § 1367.

# I

. . .

# II

## A

   . . . This Court has long held that, in determining whether the amount-in-controversy requirement has been satisfied, a single plaintiff may aggregate two or more claims against a single defendant, even if the claims are unrelated. See, e.g., Edwards v. Bates County, 163 U.S. 269, 273 (1896). But in multiparty cases, including class actions, we have unyieldingly adhered to the nonaggregation rule stated in *Troy Bank*. See *Clark*, 306 U.S., at 589 (reaffirming the "familiar rule that when several plaintiffs assert separate and distinct demands in a single suit, the amount involved in each separate controversy must be of the requisite amount to be within the jurisdiction of the district court, and that those amounts cannot be added together to satisfy jurisdictional requirements"); Snyder v. Harris, 394 U.S. 332, 339-40 (1969) (abandonment of the nonaggregation rule in class actions would undercut the congressional "purpose . . . to check, to some degree, the rising caseload of the federal courts"). . . .

## B

   . . . As explained by the First Circuit in *Ortega*, and applied to class actions by the Tenth Circuit in *Leonhardt*, see supra, § 1367(a) addresses "civil action[s] of which the district courts have original jurisdiction," a formulation that, in diversity cases, is sensibly read to incorporate the rules on joinder and aggregation tightly tied to § 1332 at the time of § 1367's enactment. On this reading, a complaint must first meet that "original jurisdiction" measurement. If it does not, no supplemental jurisdiction is authorized. If it does, § 1367(a) authorizes "supplemental jurisdiction" over related claims. In other words, § 1367(a) would preserve undiminished, as part and parcel of § 1332 "original jurisdiction" determinations, both the "complete diversity" rule and the decisions restricting aggregation to arrive at the amount in controversy. Section 1367(b)'s office, then, would be "to prevent the erosion of the complete diversity [and amount-in-controversy] requirement[s] that might otherwise result from an expansive application of what was once termed the doctrine of ancillary jurisdiction." See Pfander, Supplemental Jurisdiction and Section 1367: The Case for a Sympathetic Textualism, 148 U. Pa. L. Rev. 109, 114 (1999); infra, at 17-18. In contrast to the Court's construction of § 1367, which draws a sharp line between the diversity and amount-in-controversy components of § 1332, see ante, the interpretation presented here does not sever the two jurisdictional requirements.

The more restrained reading of § 1367 just outlined would yield affirmance of the First Circuit's judgment in *Ortega,* and reversal of the Eleventh Circuit's judgment in *Exxon.* It would not discard entirely, as the Court does, the judicially developed doctrines of pendent and ancillary jurisdiction as they existed when *Finley* was decided. Instead, it would recognize § 1367 essentially as a codification of those doctrines, placing them under a single heading, but largely retaining their substance, with overriding *Finley* the only basic change: Supplemental jurisdiction, once the district court has original jurisdiction, would now include "claims that involve the joinder or intervention of additional parties." § 1367(a). . . .

Not only would the reading I find persuasive "alig[n] statutory supplemental jurisdiction with the judicially developed doctrines of pendent and ancillary jurisdiction," id., it would also synchronize § 1367 with the removal statute, 28 U.S.C. § 1441. As the First Circuit carefully explained:

> Section 1441, like § 1367, applies only if the "civil action" in question is one "of which the district courts . . . have original jurisdiction." § 1441(a). Relying on that language, the Supreme Court has interpreted § 1441 to prohibit removal unless the entire action, as it stands at the time of removal, could have been filed in federal court in the first instance. See, e.g., Syngenta Crop Protection, Inc. v. Henson, 537 U.S. 28, 33 (2002); Okla. Tax Comm'n v. Graham, 489 U.S. 838, 840 (1989) (per curiam). Section 1441 has thus been held to incorporate the well-pleaded complaint rule, see City of Chicago [v. Int'l College of Surgeons, 522 U.S. 156, 163 (1997)] . . . ; the complete diversity rule, see Caterpillar, Inc. v. Lewis, 519 U.S. 61, 73 (1996); and rules for calculating the amount in controversy, see St. Paul Mercury Indem. Co. v. Red Cab Co., 303 U.S. 283, 291-92 (1938). *Ortega,* 370 F.3d at 138 (citations omitted).

The less disruptive view I take of § 1367 also accounts for the omission of Rule 20 plaintiffs and Rule 23 class actions in § 1367(b)'s text. If one reads § 1367(a) as a plenary grant of supplemental jurisdiction to federal courts sitting in diversity, one would indeed look for exceptions in § 1367(b). Finding none for permissive joinder of parties or class actions, one would conclude that Congress effectively, even if unintentionally, overruled *Clark* and *Zahn.* But if one recognizes that the nonaggregation rule delineated in *Clark* and *Zahn* forms part of the determination whether "original jurisdiction" exists in a diversity case, then plaintiffs who do not meet the amount-in-controversy requirement would fail at the § 1367(a) threshold. Congress would have no reason to resort to a § 1367(b) exception to turn such plaintiffs away from federal court, given that their claims, from the start, would fall outside the court's § 1332 jurisdiction. See Pfander, supra, at 148. . . .

What is the utility of § 1367(b) under my reading of § 1367(a)? Section 1367(a) allows parties other than the plaintiff to assert *reactive* claims once entertained under the heading ancillary jurisdiction. See supra, at 2633 (listing claims, including compulsory counterclaims and impleader claims, over which federal courts routinely exercised ancillary jurisdiction). As earlier observed, § 1367(b) stops plaintiffs from circumventing § 1332's jurisdictional requirements by using another's claim as a hook to add a claim that the plaintiff could not have brought in the first instance. *Kroger* is the paradigm case. See, supra, at 2633. There, the Court held that ancillary jurisdiction did not extend to a plaintiff's claim against a nondiverse party who had been impleaded by the defendant under Rule 14. Section 1367(b), then, is corroborative of § 1367(a)'s coverage of claims formerly called ancillary, but provides exceptions to assure that accommodation of added claims would not fundamentally alter "the jurisdictional requirements of section 1332." See Pfander, supra, at 135-137.

While § 1367's enigmatic text defies flawless interpretation, . . . the precedent-preservative reading, I am persuaded, better accords with the historical and legal context of Congress' enactment of the supplemental jurisdiction statute, . . . and the established limits on pendent and ancillary jurisdiction. . . . It does not attribute to Congress a jurisdictional enlargement broader than the one to which the legislators adverted, cf. *Finley*, 490 U.S., at 549, and it follows the sound counsel that "close questions of [statutory] construction should be resolved in favor of continuity and against change." Shapiro, Continuity and Change in Statutory Interpretation, 67 N.Y.U. L. Rev. 921, 925 (1992).

* * *

For the reasons stated, I would hold that § 1367 does not overrule *Clark* and *Zahn*. I would therefore affirm the judgment of the Court of Appeals for the First Circuit and reverse the judgment of the Court of Appeals for the Eleventh Circuit.

[A separate dissenting opinion of JUSTICE STEVENS, joined by JUSTICE BREYER, is omitted.]

## Note: Efficiency and Institutional Competence

Put to one side, for a moment, the minutiae of statutory interpretation and the rather Byzantine set of terms and rules for supplemental jurisdiction created by the Court (pendent-claim, pendent-party, and ancillary jurisdiction). Congress and the Court have wrestled with supplemental jurisdiction and created these seemingly over-subtle distinctions for two principal reasons: on the one hand, it is typically most efficient to have one court decide an entire case or controversy; on the other hand, federal courts are courts of limited jurisdiction best suited to hear claims grounded in federal law. As litigation has become more complex (not just because there are multiple parties and multiple claims, but because injuries increasingly cross state and national boundaries), it has become more difficult to define what constitutes a whole case, or, as § 1367 puts it, a "civil action" and "all other claims that are so related . . . that they form part of the same case or controversy." It is also harder to say whether any specific court, state or federal, possesses superior competence to handle the vast array of mixed federal and state law claims these cases present. Assuming the *Allapattah* majority has the correct reading of what Congress intended to accomplish in § 1367, do you think it strikes the right balance between promoting efficiency, respecting federalism, and ensuring institutional competence?

## Note: The Class Action Fairness Act of 2005

The majority opinion ends by emphasizing that the Class Action Fairness Act of 2005 had "no bearing" on its decision. Nonetheless, as you may recall from *Shady Grove,* the new statute substantially expands the subject matter jurisdiction of the federal courts. If money damages are sought by 100 or more people, at least one plaintiff class member is diverse from any defendant, and the amount in controversy exceeds $5 million, the case may be brought in or removed to federal court. See 28 U.S.C. §§ 1332, 1453. The statute also allows aggregation of plaintiffs' claims: "[T]he claims of the individual class members shall be aggregated to determine whether the matter in controversy exceeds the sum or value of $5,000,000, exclusive of interest and costs." See 28 U.S.C. § 1332(d)(6). CAFA does not apply, however, where a state sues on behalf of injured consumers. See Miss. ex. rel. Hood v. AU Optronics Corp., 134 S. Ct. 736 (2014).

The most important exception to the new grant of jurisdiction is for class actions in which there is a substantial connection to a single state. For instance, if more than two-thirds of the class members are all citizens of the state in which the action is originally filed, a key defendant is a citizen of that state, and the principal injuries underlying the claim occurred there, federal courts cannot exercise jurisdiction. See 28 U.S.C. § 1332(d)(4). Moreover, district courts have discretion to decline jurisdiction over class actions in which the primary defendants and between one-third and two-thirds of the plaintiff class members are citizens of the same state. See 28 U.S.C. § 1332(d)(3); In re Sprint Nextel Corp., 593 F.3d 669 (7th Cir. 2010) (class action limited to residents of Kansas alleging Sprint conspired with other wireless companies to inflate text messaging rates; rejecting Sprint's claim that the denominator in the two-thirds number should be all possible plaintiffs in a nationwide class, rather than all members of the class in Kansas); Villapando v. Exel Direct, Inc., 2012 WL 5464620 (N.D. Cal. Nov. 8, 2012) (discussing "home state" exception). See also Nan S. Ellis, The Class Action Fairness Act of 2005: The Story Behind the Statute, 35 J. Legis. 76 (2009); Guyon Knight, Note, The CAFA Mass Action Numerosity Requirement: Three Problems with Counting to 100, 78 Fordham L. Rev. 1875 (2010).

The net effect of CAFA is to place large-stakes, national class actions within the original jurisdiction of the federal courts. The statute passed with a groundswell of support from legislators generally hostile to class actions and concerned about abuse of the procedure, but its effect on the number and outcome of class action cases remains to be seen. (Class actions are discussed in further detail in section C of this chapter.)

One issue worth tracking closely is how the removal provisions of the statute are operating, since removal is the linchpin. The circuit courts have almost uniformly followed the traditional rule that the party seeking to remove a case to federal court bears the burden of proving that the case belongs there. See, e.g., Amoche v. Guarantee Trust Life Ins. Co., 556 F.3d 41, 48 (1st Cir. 2009); Strawn v. AT & T Mobility LLC, 530 F.3d 293, 298 (4th Cir. 2008); Smith v. Nationwide Prop. & Cas. Ins. Co., 505 F.3d 401, 404-405 (6th Cir. 2007).

However, H. Hunter Twiford III, Anthony Rollo, and John T. Rouse contend that the legislative history of CAFA supports a presumption in favor of federal jurisdiction, with the burden of proof on the party *opposing* federal removal. H. Hunter Twiford III et al., CAFA's New "Minimal Diversity" Standard for Interstate Class Actions Creates a Presumption That Jurisdiction Exists, with the Burden of Proof Assigned to the Party Opposing Jurisdiction, 25 Miss. C. L. Rev. 7 (2005) (arguing that various district court opinions shifting the burden to the party opposing removal are more faithful to CAFA); see also McGlinchey Stafford, CAFA Law Blog (http://www.cafalawblog.com). The Fifth Circuit has held that once the party seeking removal makes a prima facie showing of federal jurisdiction, the burden of proof shifts to the party seeking to invoke one of CAFA's exceptions to federal jurisdiction. See Frazier v. Pioneer Americas LLC, 455 F.3d 542 (5th Cir. 2006). In Burdens of Jurisdictional Proof, 59 Ala. L. Rev. 409 (2008), Lonny Shienkopf Hoffman argues that the Fifth Circuit's position is based on flawed assumptions, and that the removing party should carry the burden of proving that these jurisdictional "exceptions" should not apply. Stephen J. Shapiro, Applying the Jurisdictional Provisions of the Class Action Fairness Act of 2005: In Search of a Sensible Judicial Approach, 59 Baylor L. Rev. 77, 88 (2007) (analyzing the split in the courts and arguing that the removing party bears the burden of proof).

As you might imagine, plaintiffs have a strong incentive to plead damages below $5 million if they want to remain in state court. If the complaint demands monetary relief of a specific sum in good faith, that sum is "deemed to be the amount in controversy." 18 U.S.C. § 1446(c)(2). What if the plaintiff enters a stipulation that the amount in controversy will be below $5 million?

Ordinarily, an *individual* plaintiff can enter a stipulation regarding the amount in controversy in order to avoid removal to federal court—that means making a binding promise not to seek more than a specific amount in damages. In Standard Fire Ins. Co. v. Knowles, the Supreme Court addressed the question whether a named plaintiff in a class action may do this to avoid removal under CAFA. 133 S. Ct. 1345 (2013). Greg Knowles filed a class action suit against Standard Fire Insurance for failing to include certain fees in its payments to insured homeowners for losses suffered. The complaint stated that the class would seek "to recover total aggregate damages of less than $5 million." Id. at 1348. Knowles also attached an affidavit to the complaint stipulating that he would "not at any time during this case . . . seek damages for the class . . . in excess of $5,000,000 in the aggregate." Id. Defendants removed the case to federal court. In a hearing on Knowles' motion to remand, defendant offered evidence that damages would likely just exceed $5 million. However, the district court remanded, pointing to the stipulation. The Eighth Circuit declined to hear defendants' appeal and the Supreme Court reversed. The Court reasoned that for a stipulation to be effective it must be binding, and that Knowles could not speak for unnamed class members whom he hopes to represent if the class is certified.

> Because his precertification stipulation does not bind anyone but himself, Knowles has not reduced the value of the putative class members' claims. For jurisdictional purposes, our inquiry is limited to examining the case "as of the time it was filed in state court," Wisconsin Dept. of Corrections v. Schacht, 524 U.S. 381, 390 (1998). At that point, Knowles lacked the authority to concede the amount-in-controversy issue for the absent class members.

Id. at 1349. With respect to the standard district courts must use in determining the amount in controversy, the Court held that, when the complaint alleges damages falling below the jurisdictional minimum, district courts must "look beyond the four corners of the complaint" and "add[] up the value of the claim of each person who falls within the definition of [the] proposed class." Id. at 1348-50.

In some circumstances, a class plaintiff fails to plead a specific monetary sum. When this occurs, the defendant may state what she takes to be the amount in controversy in her notice of removal. See 18 U.S.C. § 1446(c)(2)(A). The Supreme Court has held that the defendant's statement of the amount in controversy need not incorporate supporting evidence. Dart Cherokee Basin Operating Co., LLC v. Owens, 135 S. Ct. 547 (2014). It need only "plausibly" allege an amount exceeding the jurisdictional threshold. If the plaintiff challenges that allegation, both sides submit proof and the court decides, "by a preponderance of the evidence, whether the amount-in-controversy requirement has been satisfied." Id. at 554.

A 2008 study by the Federal Judicial Center found that CAFA's enactment has led to an increase in the number of class actions filed in or removed to the federal courts based on diversity jurisdiction; however, in "the last months of the study period, diversity removals were at levels similar to those in the pre-CAFA period." Thomas E. Willging & Emery G. Lee III, Federal Judicial Center, The Impact of the Class Action Fairness Act of 2005 on the Federal Courts (2008), available at http://www.fjc.gov/public/pdf.nsf/lookup/cafa1108.pdf/$file/cafa1108.pdf. The observed increase was primarily associated with consumer class actions. The study also found that much of the increase in diversity class actions has been driven by an increase in original filings in federal courts, suggesting (contrary to the expectations of many) that plaintiffs' attorneys are choosing the federal forum, rather than leaving it to defense counsel to remove cases to federal court. See also Emery G. Lee III and Thomas Willging, The Impact of the Class Action Fairness Act on the Federal Courts: An Empirical Analysis of Filings and Removals, 156 U. Pa. L. Rev. 1723 (2008) (summarizing some of the same findings, and noting that the monthly average number of diversity class actions filed in or removed to federal courts approximately doubled after CAFA's passage).

## Note: The Multiparty, Multiforum
## Trial Jurisdiction Act of 2002

In another context, Congress has intervened to expand the subject matter jurisdiction of the lower federal courts to deal with complex litigation. The Multiparty, Multiforum Trial Jurisdiction Act (MMTJA) was passed in the wake of the terrorist attacks on September 11, 2001, as a means of centralizing litigation arising from large-scale accidents and disasters involving significant loss of life. See 28 U.S.C. § 1369. The statute grants federal district courts original and removal jurisdiction over "any civil action involving minimal diversity between adverse parties that arises from a single accident, where at least 75 natural persons have died in the accident at a discrete location," and where more than one state is involved because the accident took place in multiple locations, or because of the defendants' place of residence. § 1369(a). Abstention is required if the claims are primarily local, i.e., where the "substantial majority" of the plaintiffs are citizens of a single state "of which the primary defendants are also citizens," and where "the claims asserted will be primarily governed by the laws of that State." § 1369(b).

The first occasion to apply the statute arose out of a tragic fire at a Rhode Island nightclub called "The Station" in 2003. See Passa v. Derderian, 308 F. Supp. 2d 43 (D.R.I. 2004). A rock band well known for using pyrotechnics to enhance its musical performance took the stage at The Station while the band's manager ignited a series of pyrotechnic devices. The fireworks caused an explosion behind the stage area, and within three minutes the entire nightclub was ablaze. Of the 412 people inside the building, 100 died and more than 200 were injured.

A spate of lawsuits were filed in state and federal courts throughout southern New England by fire victims, their estates, and surviving family members, alleging various state law tort claims against a group of defendants including the band members, their agent, their record company and management company, as well as the nightclub owners, the companies that manufactured the insulation in the nightclub, the manufacturer of the fireworks, the corporate event sponsors, and a host of state and local government entities responsible for fire protection. In five such cases before the federal district court of Rhode Island, certain defendants filed motions to dismiss or remand the cases to state court on the theory that the federal court lacked jurisdiction. A "steering committee" of lawyers representing over 180 potential plaintiffs who had not yet sued anyone filed an amicus brief supporting the defendants seeking remand.

The parties seeking dismissal/remand argued that § 1369(b) requires abstention because a substantial majority of the plaintiffs and the defendants were citizens of Rhode Island. The court rejected this claim and retained jurisdiction over the cases. The court first held that § 1369(b) is a mandatory abstention provision, not a limit on the court's subject matter jurisdiction, even though the section heading reads, "Limitation of Jurisdiction of District Courts." This distinction matters because a court is obliged to dismiss a case at any stage if there is a defect in subject matter jurisdiction, but "once a court has determined that abstention is not required, this question is not typically revisited during later stages of the litigation." 308 F. Supp. 2d at 56. On the merits, the court concluded that abstention was not necessary because a substantial majority of the plaintiffs were not from Rhode Island.

The court reached this conclusion by including the citizenship of approximately 335 "potential plaintiffs" who had not yet filed suit. Id. at 59-60. As the court reasoned, "[s]uch an interpretation is consistent with Congress's desire to consolidate all cases arising from one major disaster in one federal court, as it conditions abstention on the citizenship of all potential claimants rather than considering only those who are first to file." Id. at 60.

There is no question that Congress wanted to streamline multidistrict disaster litigation. As the House Conference Report stated:

> It is common after a serious accident to have many lawsuits filed in several states, in both state and federal courts, with many different sets of plaintiffs' lawyers and several different defendants. Despite this multiplicity of suits, the principal issue that must be resolved first in each suit is virtually identical: Is one or more of the defendants liable? . . . The waste of judicial resources—and the costs to both plaintiffs and defendants—of litigating the same liability question several times over in separate lawsuits can be extreme.

Id. at 53. But the MMTJA unambiguously refers to "plaintiffs," in § 1369(b), not to "plaintiffs and potential plaintiffs." Has the court strayed from plain meaning? What if most of the potential plaintiffs, and especially plaintiffs from outside Rhode Island, settle without filing suit or decide not to sue?

The Class Action Fairness Act and the MMTJA hardly bespeak a trend toward the constitutional limit of federal subject matter jurisdiction, but the statutes do suggest that Congress sees the value of letting federal courts shoulder more of the litigation load in certain complex cases. Is efficiency the only concern, or are there reasons to think state courts are inferior forums for these cases?

### e.   Declining to Exercise Supplemental Jurisdiction

Where supplemental jurisdiction is permissible, a court may nonetheless decline to exercise it. Section 1367(c) describes the grounds upon which courts may refuse to exercise supplemental jurisdiction. The United States Supreme Court construed § 1367(c)'s relationship to United Mine Workers of America v. Gibbs, 383 U.S. 715 (1966), and to abstention doctrine, in City of Chicago v. Int'l College of Surgeons, 522 U.S. 156 (1997). The Court described these relationships as follows:

> [T]o say that the terms of § 1367(a) authorize the district courts to exercise supplemental jurisdiction over state law claims . . . does not mean that the

jurisdiction *must* be exercised in all cases. Our decisions have established that pendent jurisdiction is a doctrine of discretion, not of plaintiff's right, *Gibbs*, 383 U.S. at 726, and that district courts can decline to exercise jurisdiction over pendent claims for a number of valid reasons, id. at 726-727. . . . Accordingly, we have indicated that district courts [should] deal with cases involving pendent claims in the manner that best serves the principles of economy, convenience, fairness, and comity which underlie the pendent jurisdiction doctrine, [Carnegie-Mellon Univ. v. Cohill, 484 U.S. 343, 357 (1988)].

The supplemental jurisdiction statute codifies these principles. After establishing that supplemental jurisdiction encompasses other claims, in the same case or controversy as a claim within the district court original jurisdiction, § 1367(a), the statute confirms the discretionary nature of supplemental jurisdiction by enumerating the circumstances in which district courts can refuse its exercise:

> (c) The district courts may decline to exercise supplemental jurisdiction over a claim under subsection (a) if
> (1) the claim raises a novel or complex issue of State law,
> (2) the claim substantially predominates over the claim or claims over which the district court has original jurisdiction
> (3) the district court has dismissed all claims over which it has original jurisdiction, or
> (4) in exceptional circumstances, there are other compelling reasons for declining jurisdiction. 28 U.S.C. § 1367(c).

Depending on a host of factors, then—including the circumstances of the particular case, the nature of the state law claims, the character of the governing state law, and the relationship between the state and federal claims—district courts may decline to exercise jurisdiction over supplemental state law claims. The statute thereby reflects the understanding that, when deciding whether to exercise supplemental jurisdiction, 'a federal court should consider and weigh in each case, and at every stage of the litigation, the values of judicial economy, convenience, fairness, and comity.' *Cohill*, supra, at 350. In this case, the District Court decided that those interests would be best served by exercising jurisdiction over ICS state law claims.

In addition to their discretion under § 1367(c), district courts may be obligated not to decide state law claims (or to stay their adjudication) where one of the abstention doctrines articulated by this Court applies. Those doctrines embody the general notion that federal courts may decline to exercise their jurisdiction, in otherwise exceptional circumstances, where denying a federal forum would clearly serve an important countervailing interest, for example where abstention is warranted by considerations of proper constitutional adjudication, regard for federal-state relations, or wise judicial administration. Quackenbush v. Allstate Ins. Co., 517 U.S. 706, 716 (1996) (citations and internal quotation marks omitted).

522 U.S. at 172-74. See also Ameritox, Ltd. v. Millennium Labs., Inc., 803 F.3d 518, 520, 540 (11th Cir. 2015) (abuse of discretion to retain supplemental jurisdiction over "novel and complex state-law claims hailing from nine different states"; exercise of jurisdiction in these circumstances would

"contravene *Gibb*'s bedrock teaching that courts should not unnecessarily decide questions of state law. . . while a needless decision of law in one state is bad, creating law in nine states is beyond the pale").

### f. Tolling of Statutes of Limitation and Supplemental Jurisdiction

In a case involving 28 U.S.C. § 1367(d) and principles of federalism, the United States Supreme Court upheld the tolling provision of the federal jurisdiction statute. This provision suspends the running of the statute of limitations on state claims while they are pending in federal court. A unanimous court concluded that the tolling process was within Congress's power under the Necessary and Proper Clause of the United States Constitution. U.S. Const. Art. I, section 8, cl. 18. The Court did not regard the provision as an undue intrusion into state sovereignty. Jinks v. Richland County, 538 U.S. 456 (2003).

Assume, however, that a plaintiff brings an action in federal court against a state defendant that alleges both a federal claim and a related state law claim, but the federal action is dismissed on the ground that the state's Eleventh Amendment immunity bars the federal statutory claim. The plaintiff then refiles the state law claim in state court, after the applicable statute of limitations has elapsed. The plaintiff argues that the statute of limitations on the state law claim was tolled by the filing of the original suit in federal court, and that 28 U.S.C. § 1367(d) rescues this state law claim. What result? In Raygor v. Regents of the University of Minnesota, 534 U.S. 533 (2002), the United States Supreme Court held that the statute of limitations is *not* tolled under these circumstances. The dismissals covered by § 1367(d) do not include dismissals based upon the Eleventh Amendment. Rather, a court in such cases should compute the statute of limitations as if the first action had not been filed at all.

### Note: Pendent Personal Jurisdiction

In addition to curing problems of subject matter jurisdiction over supplemental claims, some courts have concluded that personal jurisdiction deficiencies may also be cured by "pendent personal jurisdiction." Assume, for example, that a plaintiff asserts two claims against a defendant in an action filed in federal court. The first claim is based on federal law, and is one for which federal law provides for nationwide service of process. The second claim is based on state law and is factually tied to the first, but involves matters that would not justify assertion of jurisdiction over the defendant on that claim in the forum chosen by the plaintiff. Does the court have personal jurisdiction over the defendant as to both claims?

Some courts that have addressed such circumstances have concluded that there is pendent personal jurisdiction. As stated by the court in IUE AFL-CIO Pension Fund v. Herrmann, 9 F.3d 1049, 1056 (2d Cir. 1993):

[U]nder the doctrine of pendent personal jurisdiction, where a federal statute authorized nationwide service of process, and the federal and state claims "derive from a common nucleus of operative fact," see United Mine Workers v. Gibbs, 383 U.S. 715, 725 (1996), the district court may assert personal jurisdiction over the parties to the related state law claims even if personal jurisdiction is not otherwise available.

A contrary rule would produce obvious inefficiencies that the supplemental jurisdiction statute as well as the case law it codifies were designed to avoid. Yet is the casual assumption that pendent personal jurisdiction exists persuasive as a matter of due process? Does the factual relatedness required for supplemental subject matter jurisdiction necessarily provide the minimum contact required for due process? See Action Embroidery Corp. v. Atlantic Embroidery, Inc., 368 F.3d 1174, 1180 (9th Cir. 2004); United States v. Botefuhr, 309 F.3d 1263, 1272-1275 (10th Cir. 2002); ESAB Group, Inc. v. Centricut, LLC, 126 F.3d 617 (4th Cir. 1997), *cert. denied*, 523 U.S. 1048 (1998).

## 3. Federal Removal Jurisdiction

### a. Introduction

When an action that is filed in state court could have been brought in federal court, the defendant may be entitled to remove the action from state court to federal court, provided the requirements of the federal removal statute (28 U.S.C. § 1441) are met. The federal court to which the defendant may remove is the federal court that embraces the jurisdiction of the state court in which the original action is filed. Thus, for example, if an action is filed in a state court located in Tucson, Arizona, removal would be to the nearest federal district court, which sits in Tucson.

The most important of the removal statute requirements are as follows:

a) The action could originally have been brought in federal court. Removal jurisdiction is no greater than original jurisdiction.
b) All defendants must join in the petition for removal, unless the narrow requirements of § 1441(c) are satisfied.
c) The defendant cannot remove if the basis for federal court jurisdiction is diversity and the defendant is a citizen of the state in which the original action was filed. This rule is based on the notion that a resident defendant has no reason to fear bias by her own home courts. The rule applies only to diversity-based removal. See Lincoln Prop. Co. v. Roche, 546 U.S. 81 (2005) (holding that a removing defendant is not obliged to inform federal court of local affiliates who are potential defendants and whose presence, if joined, would defeat removal).
d) The defendant must remove before taking substantial steps to defend the action in the state court. A nontimely petition will be denied.

## b. Remand

Once a case has been removed to federal court, the federal judge may remand the case only under the conditions set forth in the removal statutes. Construing these statutes, the U.S. Supreme Court held in Thermtron Products, Inc. v. Hermansdorfer, that a judge could not remand a case merely because of a crowded federal court docket. 423 U.S. 336 (1976). Since the removal statutes do not list "overcrowded docket" as a basis for remanding a case, the court lacked power to remand on this basis. Id., *abrogated on other grounds by* Quackenbush v. Allstate Ins. Co., 517 U.S. 706 (1996).

Despite *Thermtron*, the Court in Carnegie-Mellon University v. Cohill, 484 U.S. 343 (1988), held that a federal court could remand a case when, after removal, the federal claims in the case were dismissed and only the pendent state law claims remained. Three Justices dissented on the ground that because the removal statutes did not expressly provide for remand in such circumstances, they should be construed to disallow remand of residual pendent state law claims. The majority position seems correct, however, especially in light of the federal judiciary's longstanding practice, now codified in the supplemental jurisdiction statute, of declining jurisdiction over pendent state law claims once the anchoring federal claims have been dismissed. 28 U.S.C. § 1367(c)(3). See also 28 U.S.C. § 1447(c).

Motions to remove and to remand are subject to elaborate gaming in which the merits of the case are sometimes buried beneath its procedure. In the following case, which shows you the workings of the removal practice, the U.S. Supreme Court unanimously put considerations of finality and efficiency ahead of technicalities.

## *Caterpillar Inc. v. Lewis*
519 U.S. 61 (1996)

JUSTICE GINSBURG delivered the opinion of the Court.

This case, commenced in a state court, involves personal jury claims arising under state law. The case was removed to a federal court at a time when, the Court of Appeals concluded, complete diversity of citizenship did not exist among the parties. Promptly after the removal, the plaintiff moved to remand the case to the state court, but the District Court denied that motion. Before trial of the case, however, all claims involving the nondiverse defendant were settled, and that defendant was dismissed as a party to the action. Complete diversity thereafter existed. The case proceeded to trial, jury verdict, and judgment for the removing defendant. The Court of Appeals vacated the judgment, concluding that, absent complete diversity at the time of removal, the District Court lacked subject-matter jurisdiction.

The question presented is whether the absence of complete diversity at the time of removal is fatal to federal-court adjudication. We hold that a district court's error in failing to remand a case improperly removed is not fatal to the ensuing adjudication if federal jurisdictional requirements are met at the time judgment is entered.

## I

Respondent James David Lewis, a resident of Kentucky, filed this lawsuit in Kentucky state court on June 22, 1989, after sustaining injuries while operating a bulldozer. Asserting state-law claims based on defective manufacture, negligent maintenance, failure to warn, and breach of warranty, Lewis named as defendants both the manufacturer of the bulldozer—petitioner Caterpillar Inc., a Delaware corporation with its principal place of business in Illinois—and the company that serviced the bulldozer—Whayne Supply Company, a Kentucky corporation with its principal place of business in Kentucky.

Several months later, Liberty Mutual Insurance Group, the insurance carrier for Lewis' employer, intervened in the lawsuit as a plaintiff. A Massachusetts corporation with its principal place of business in that State, Liberty Mutual asserted subrogation claims against both Caterpillar and Whayne Supply for workers' compensation benefits Liberty Mutual had paid to Lewis on behalf of his employer.

Lewis entered into a settlement agreement with defendant Whayne Supply less than a year after filing his complaint. Shortly after learning of this agreement, Caterpillar filed a notice of removal, on June 21, 1990, in the United States District Court for the Eastern District of Kentucky. Grounding federal jurisdiction on diversity of citizenship, see 28 U.S.C. § 1332, Caterpillar satisfied with only a day to spare the statutory requirement that a diversity-based removal take place within one year of a lawsuit's commencement, see 28 U.S.C. § 1446(b). Caterpillar's notice of removal explained that the case was nonremovable at the lawsuit's start: Complete diversity was absent then because plaintiff Lewis and defendant Whayne Supply shared Kentucky citizenship. Proceeding on the understanding that the settlement agreement between these two Kentucky parties would result in the dismissal of Whayne Supply from the lawsuit, Caterpillar stated that the settlement rendered the case removable.

Lewis objected to the removal and moved to remand the case to state court. Lewis acknowledged that he had settled his own claims against Whayne Supply. But Liberty Mutual had not yet settled its subrogation claim against Whayne Supply, Lewis asserted. Whayne Supply's presence as a defendant in the lawsuit, Lewis urged, defeated diversity of citizenship. Without addressing this argument, the District Court denied Lewis' motion to remand on September 24, 1990, treating as dispositive Lewis' admission that he had settled his own claims against Whayne Supply.

Discovery, begun in state court, continued in the now federal lawsuit, and the parties filed pretrial conference papers beginning in July 1991. In June 1993, plaintiff Liberty Mutual and defendant Whayne Supply entered into a settlement of Liberty Mutual's subrogation claim, and the District

Court dismissed Whayne Supply from the lawsuit. With Caterpillar as the sole defendant adverse to Lewis, the case proceeded to a six-day jury trial in November 1993, ending in a unanimous verdict for Caterpillar. The District Court entered judgment for Caterpillar on November 23, 1993, and denied Lewis' motion for a new trial on February 1, 1994.

On appeal, the Court of Appeals for the Sixth Circuit accepted Lewis' argument that, at the time of removal, Whayne Supply remained a defendant in the case due to Liberty Mutual's subrogation claim against it. Because the party lineup, on removal, included Kentucky plaintiff Lewis and Kentucky defendant Whayne Supply, the Court of Appeals observed that diversity was not complete when Caterpillar took the case from state court to federal court. Consequently, the Court of Appeals concluded, the District Court "erred in denying [Lewis'] motion to remand this case to the state court for lack of subject matter jurisdiction." That error, according to the Court of Appeals, made it necessary to vacate the District Court's judgment.

Caterpillar petitioned for this Court's review. Caterpillar stressed that the nondiverse defendant, Whayne Supply, had been dismissed from the lawsuit prior to trial. It was therefore improper, Caterpillar urged, for the Court of Appeals to vacate the District Court's judgment—entered after several years of litigation and a six-day trial—on account of a jurisdictional defect cured, all agreed, by the time of trial and judgment. We granted certiorari, 517 U.S. 1133 (1996), and now reverse.

## II

The Constitution provides, in Article III, § 2, that "[t]he judicial Power [of the United States] shall extend . . . to Controversies . . . between Citizens of different States." Commencing with the Judiciary Act of 1789, ch. 20, § 11, 1 Stat. 78, Congress has constantly authorized the federal courts to exercise jurisdiction based on the diverse citizenship of parties. In Strawbridge v. Curtiss, 3 Cranch 267 (1806), this Court construed the original Judiciary Act's diversity provision to require complete diversity of citizenship. Id., at 267. We have adhered to that statutory interpretation ever since. See Carden v. Arkoma Associates, 494 U.S. 185, 187 (1990). The current general-diversity statute, permitting federal district court jurisdiction over suits for more than $50,000 "between . . . citizens of different States," 28 U.S.C. § 1332(a), thus applies only to cases in which the citizenship of each plaintiff is diverse from the citizenship of each defendant.

When a plaintiff files in state court a civil action over which the federal district courts would have original jurisdiction based on diversity of citizenship, the defendant or defendants may remove the action to federal court, 28 U.S.C. § 1441(a), provided that no defendant "is a citizen of the State in which such action is brought," § 1441(b). In a case not originally removable, a defendant who receives a pleading or other paper indicating the post-commencement satisfaction of federal jurisdictional requirements—for example, by reason of the dismissal of a nondiverse party—may remove the case to federal court within 30 days of receiving such information. § 1446(b). No case, however, may be removed from state to federal court based on diversity of citizenship "more than 1 year after commencement of the action." Ibid.

Once a defendant has filed a notice of removal in the federal district court, a plaintiff objecting to removal "on the basis of any defect in removal procedure" may, within 30 days, file a motion asking the district court to remand the case to state court. § 1447(c). This 30-day limit does not apply, however, to jurisdictional defects: "If at any time before final judgment it appears that the district court lacks subject matter jurisdiction, the case shall be remanded." Ibid.

# III

We note, initially, two "givens" in this case as we have accepted it for review. First, the District Court, in its decision denying Lewis' timely motion to remand, incorrectly treated Whayne Supply, the nondiverse defendant, as effectively dropped from the case prior to removal. Second, the Sixth Circuit correctly determined that the complete diversity requirement was not satisfied at the time of removal. We accordingly home in on this question: Does the District Court's initial misjudgment still burden and run with the case, or is it overcome by the eventual dismissal of the nondiverse defendant?

Petitioner Caterpillar relies heavily on our decisions in American Fire & Casualty Co. v. Finn, 341 U.S. 6 (1951), and Grubbs v. General Elec. Credit Corp., 405 U.S. 699 (1972), urging that these decisions "long ago settled the proposition that remand to the state court is unnecessary even if jurisdiction did not exist at the time of removal, so long as the district court had subject matter jurisdiction at the time of judgment." Caterpillar is right that Finn and Grubbs are key cases in point and tend in Caterpillar's favor. Each suggests that the existence of subject-matter jurisdiction at time of judgment may shield a judgment against later jurisdictional attack. But neither decision resolves dispositively a controversy of the kind we face, for neither involved a plaintiff who moved promptly, but unsuccessfully, to remand a case improperly removed from state court to federal court, and then challenged on appeal a judgment entered by the federal court.

In Finn, two defendants removed a case to federal court on the basis of diversity of citizenship. 341 U.S. at 7-8. Eventually, final judgment was entered for the plaintiff against one of the removing defendants. Id., at 8. The losing defendant urged on appeal, and before this Court, that the judgment could not stand because the requisite diversity jurisdiction, it turned out, existed neither at the time of removal nor at the time of judgment. Agreeing with the defendant, we held that the absence of federal jurisdiction at the time of judgment required the Court of Appeals to vacate the District Court's judgment. Id. at 17-18.[8]

*Finn*'s holding does not speak to the situation here, where the requirement of complete diversity was satisfied at the time of judgment. But Caterpillar points to well-known dicta in *Finn* more helpful to its cause. "There are cases," the Court observed, "which uphold judgments in the district courts even though there was no right to removal." Id., at 16.[9] "In those cases," the *Finn* Court explained, "the federal trial court would have had original jurisdiction of the controversy had it been brought in the federal court in the posture it had at the time of the actual trial of the cause or of the entry of the judgment." Ibid.

The discussion in *Finn* concentrated on cases in which courts held *removing defendants* estopped from challenging final judgments on the basis of removal errors. See id. at 17. The *Finn* Court did not address the situation of a plaintiff such as Lewis, who chose a state court as the forum for his lawsuit, timely objected to removal before the District Court, and then challenged the removal on appeal from an adverse judgment.

In *Grubbs,* a civil action filed in state court was removed to federal court on the petition of the United States, which had been named as a party defendant in a "cross-action" filed by the original defendant. 405 U.S. at 700-701; see 28 U.S.C. § 1444 (authorizing removal of actions brought against the United States, pursuant to 28 U.S.C. § 2410, with respect to property on which the United States has or claims a lien). No party objected to the removal before trial or judgment. See *Grubbs,* 405 U.S. at 701. The Court of Appeals nonetheless held, on its own motion, that the "interpleader" of the United States was spurious, and that removal had therefore been improper under 28 U.S.C. § 1444. See *Grubbs,* 405 U.S. at 702. On this basis, the Court of Appeals concluded that the District Court's judgment should be vacated and the case remanded to state court. See ibid.

This Court reversed. Id. at 700. We explained:

> "Longstanding decisions of this Court make clear . . . that where after removal a case is tried on the merits without objection and the federal court enters judgment, the issue in subsequent proceedings on appeal is not whether the case was properly removed, but whether the federal district

8. The Court left open in *Finn* the question whether, on remand to the District Court, "a new judgment [could] be entered on the old verdict without a new trial" if the nondiverse defendant were dismissed from the case. 341 U.S. at 18, n.18. In the litigation's second round, the District Court allowed the plaintiff to dismiss all claims against the nondiverse defendant. See Finn v. American Fire & Casualty Co., 207 F.2d 113, 114 (C.A.5 1953), *cert. denied,* 347 U.S. 912 (1954). Thereafter, the District Court granted a new trial, on the assumption that the original judgment could not stand for lack of jurisdiction. See 207 F.2d, at 114. Ultimately, the Court of Appeals for the Fifth Circuit set aside the judgment entered after the second trial and ordered the original judgment reinstated. Id., at 117.

9. The Court cited Baggs v. Martin, 179 U.S. 206 (1900), and three lower federal-court cases. *Finn,* 341 U.S. at 16, n.14.

court would have had original jurisdiction of the case had it been filed in that court." Id. at 702.

We concluded that, "whether or not the case was properly removed, the District Court did have jurisdiction of the parties at the time it entered judgment." Id. at 700. "Under such circumstances," we held, "the validity of the removal procedure followed *may not be raised for the first time on appeal*." Id. (emphasis added). *Grubbs* instructs that an erroneous removal need not cause the destruction of a final judgment, if the requirements of federal subject-matter jurisdiction are met at the time the judgment is entered. *Grubbs*, however, dealt with a case removed without objection. The decision is not dispositive of the question whether a plaintiff, who timely objects to removal, may later successfully challenge an adverse judgment on the ground that the removal did not comply with statutory prescriptions.

Beyond question, as Lewis acknowledges, there was in this case complete diversity, and therefore federal subject-matter jurisdiction, at the time of trial and judgment. . . . The case had by then become, essentially, a two-party law-suit: Lewis, a citizen of Kentucky, was the sole plaintiff; Caterpillar, incorporated in Delaware with its principal place of business in Illinois, was the sole defendant Lewis confronted. Caterpillar maintains that this change cured the threshold *statutory* misstep, i.e., the removal of a case when diversity was incomplete.

Caterpillar moves too quickly over the terrain we must cover. The *jurisdictional* defect was cured, i.e., complete diversity was established before the trial commenced. Therefore, the Sixth Circuit erred in resting its decision on the absence of subject-matter jurisdiction. But a statutory flaw—Caterpillar's failure to meet the § 1441(a) requirement that the case be fit for federal adjudication at the time the removal petition is filed—remained in the unerasable history of the case.

And Lewis, by timely moving for remand, did all that was required to preserve his objection to removal. An order denying a motion to remand, "standing alone," is "[o]bviously . . . not final and [immediately] appealable" as of right. Chicago, R.I. & P.R. Co. v. Stude, 346 U.S. 574, 578 (1954). Nor is a plaintiff required to seek permission to take an interlocutory appeal pursuant to 28 U.S.C. § 1292(b)[10] in order to avoid waiving whatever ultimate appeal right he may have.[11] Indeed, if a party had to invoke § 1292(b) in order to preserve an objection to an interlocutory ruling, litigants would be obliged to seek § 1292(b) certifications constantly. Routine resort to

10. Section 1292(b) provides for interlocutory appeals from otherwise not immediately appealable orders, if conditions specified in the section are met, the district court so certifies, and the court of appeals exercises its discretion to take up the request for review.

11. On brief, Caterpillar argued that "Lewis effectively waived his objection to removal by failing to seek an immediate appeal of the district court's refusal to remand." We reject this waiver argument, though we recognize that it has attracted some support in Court of Appeals opinions. See, e.g., Able v. Upjohn Co., 829 F.2d 1330, 1333-1334 (4th Cir. 1987), *cert. denied*, 485 U.S. 963 (1988).

§ 1292(b) requests would hardly comport with Congress' design to reserve interlocutory review for "'exceptional'" cases while generally retaining for the federal courts a firm final judgment rule. Coopers & Lybrand v. Livesay, 437 U.S. 463, 475 (1978) (quoting Fisons, Ltd. v. United States, 458 F.2d 1241, 1248 (7th Cir.), *cert. denied,* 405 U.S. 1041 (1972)).

Having preserved his objection to an improper removal, Lewis urges that an "all's well that ends well" approach is inappropriate here. He maintains that ultimate satisfaction of the subject-matter jurisdiction requirement ought not swallow up antecedent statutory violations. The course Caterpillar advocates, Lewis observes, would disfavor diligent plaintiffs who timely, but unsuccessfully, move to check improper removals in district court. Further, that course would allow improperly removing defendants to profit from their disregard of Congress' instructions, and their ability to lead district judges into error.

Concretely, in this very case, Lewis emphasizes, adherence to the rules Congress prescribed for removal would have kept the case in state court. Only by removing prematurely was Caterpillar able to get to federal court inside the one-year limitation set in § 1446(b).[12] Had Caterpillar waited until the case was ripe for removal, i.e., until Whayne Supply was dismissed as a defendant, the one-year limitation would have barred the way, . . . and plaintiff's choice of forum would have been preserved.[14]

These arguments are hardly meritless, but they run up against an overriding consideration. Once a diversity case has been tried in federal court, with rules of decision supplied by state law under the regime of Erie R.R. Co. v. Tompkins, 304 U.S. 64 (1938), considerations of finality, efficiency, and economy become overwhelming.

Our decision in Newman-Green, Inc. v. Alfonzo-Larrain, 490 U.S. 826 (1989), is instructive in this regard. *Newman-Green* did not involve removal, but it did involve the federal courts' diversity jurisdiction and a party defendant whose presence, like Whayne Supply's in this case, blocked complete diversity. *Newman-Green* proceeded to summary judgment with the jurisdictional flaw—the absence of complete diversity—undetected. See id. at 828-829. The Court of Appeals noticed the flaw, invited the parties to address it, and, en banc, returned the case to the District Court "to determine whether it would be prudent to drop [the jurisdiction spoiler] from the litigation." Id. at 830. We held that the Court of Appeals itself had authority "to dismiss a dispensable nondiverse party," although we recognized that, ordinarily, district courts are better positioned to make such judgments. Id. at 837-838. "[R]equiring dismissal after years of litigation," the Court stressed in *Newman-Green,* "would impose unnecessary

---

12. Congress amended § 1446(b) in 1988 to include the one-year limitation in order to "reduc[e] the opportunity for removal after substantial progress has been made in state court." H.R. Rep. No. 100-889, p. 72 (1988).

14. Lewis preferred state court to federal court based on differences he perceived in, *inter alia,* the state and federal jury systems and rules of evidence.

and wasteful burdens on the parties, judges, and other litigants waiting for judicial attention." Id. at 836. The same may be said of the remand to state court Lewis seeks here. Cf. Knop v. McMahan, 872 F.2d 1132, 1139, n.16 (3d Cir. 1989) ("To permit a case in which there is complete diversity through-out trial to proceed to judgment and then cancel the effect of that judgment and relegate the parties to a new trial in a state court because of a brief lack of complete diversity at the beginning of the case would be a waste of judicial resources.").

Our view is in harmony with a main theme of the removal scheme Congress devised. Congress ordered a procedure calling for expeditious superintendence by district courts. The lawmakers specified a short time, 30 days, for motions to remand for defects in removal procedure, 28 U.S.C. § 1447(c), and district court orders remanding cases to state courts gener-ally are "not reviewable on appeal or otherwise," § 1447(d). Congress did not similarly exclude appellate review of refusals to remand. But an evi-dent concern that may explain the lack of symmetry relates to the federal courts' subject-matter jurisdiction. Despite a federal trial court's threshold denial of a motion to remand, if, at the end of the day and case, a *jurisdic-tional* defect remains uncured, the judgment must be vacated. See Fed. Rule Civ. Proc. 12(h)(3) ("Whenever it appears by suggestion of the parties or otherwise that the court lacks jurisdiction of the subject matter, the court shall dismiss the action."); *Finn*, 341 U.S. at 18. In this case, however, no jurisdictional defect lingered through judgment in the District Court. To wipe out the adjudication postjudgment, and return to state court a case now satisfying all federal jurisdictional requirements, would impose an exorbitant cost on our dual court system, a cost incompatible with the fair and unprotracted administration of justice.

Lewis ultimately argues that, if the final judgment against him is allowed to stand, "all of the various procedural requirements for removal will become unenforceable", therefore, "defendants will have an enormous incentive to attempt wrongful removals." In particular, Lewis suggests that defendants will remove prematurely "in the hope that some subsequent developments, such as the eventual dismissal of nondiverse defendants, will permit th[e] case to be kept in federal court." We do not anticipate the dire consequences Lewis forecasts.

The procedural requirements for removal remain enforceable by the fed-eral trial court judges to whom those requirements are directly addressed. Lewis' prediction that rejection of his petition will "encourag[e] state court defendants to remove cases improperly," rests on an assumption we do not indulge—that district courts generally will not comprehend, or will balk at applying, the rules on removal Congress has prescribed. The pre-diction furthermore assumes defendants' readiness to gamble that any jurisdictional defect, for example, the absence of complete diversity, will first escape detection, then disappear prior to judgment. The well-advised defendant, we are satisfied, will foresee the likely outcome of an unwar-ranted removal—a swift and nonreviewable remand order, see 28 U.S.C. §§ 1447(c), (d), attended by the displeasure of a district court whose authority has been improperly invoked. The odds against any gain from a wrongful removal, in sum, render improbable Lewis' projection of increased resort to the maneuver.

* * *

For the reasons stated, the judgment of the Court of Appeals is reversed, and the case is remanded for proceedings consistent with this opinion.

*It is so ordered.*

## *Notes and Questions*

1. *Why Removal?* Why did Caterpillar want to be in federal court? Those reasons are driving this case, yet they could not be gathered or even guessed from the Supreme Court opinion. Nor do we know from the opinion anything about the injuries Mr. Lewis sustained or what caused them. Is it possible that Lewis made Whayne Supply Company a defendant only for purposes of defeating diversity and preventing removal? If so, it was a big tactical error to settle with the nondiverse defendant before the year limitation period ran on removal, wasn't it? Conversely, Caterpillar's lawyers were on the ball to file so quickly for removal, once it was possible. Perhaps they had their petition ready for just such an eventuality.

2. *Appealability.* The Supreme Court assumes that the district court made a mistake on Lewis's motion to remand: that the presence of Liberty Mutual's claim against Whayne did destroy diversity. What were Lewis's options at the point that the federal court denied his motion to remand? It was not appealable as such, since a decision about jurisdiction is a "first" rather than a "final" order. 28 U.S.C. § 1291 (only final orders are appealable).

He also might have tried to get the federal district court to certify this case for an interlocutory appeal under 28 U.S.C. § 1292. The Supreme Court, however, refuses to make an effort to appeal a condition of raising improper removal at the conclusion of the case. Yet the message for practice of this case is that parties had better contest removal in every way possible. Gone are the days when the absence of subject matter jurisdiction (at least as to diversity) was an automatic winner "whenever" it was raised. Fed. R. Civ. P. 12(h)(3).

Another route for correcting a clearly erroneous district court decision about removal or remand might be an extraordinary writ of mandamus. This was the route taken when the case was tossed back to the state court in Carnegie-Mellon Univ. v. Cohill, 484 U.S. 343 (1988) (discussed in the introductory note above). Generally speaking, however, there is no effective appeal from an order granting a remand to state court, no matter how clearly wrong the decision may be. See, e.g., Cook v. Wikler, 320 F.3d 431 (3d Cir. 2003) (refusing to review remand order under 28 U.S.C. § 1447(d); district court remanded case on ground that removal by third party defendant is improper). There are a few exceptions to the blanket rule against appeals, such as certain civil rights cases, and exercises of discretion under the supplemental jurisdiction statute, 28 U.S.C. § 1367(c), as well as certain class action lawsuits falling under the recently enacted Class Action Fairness Act. See 28 U.S.C. § 1453(c)(1). See also Weber v. Mobil Oil Corp., 506 F.3d 1311 (5th Cir. 2007) (§ 1453(c)(1) does not allow review of remand order where class action was filed before CAFA; post-CAFA intervention of new parties does not alter date upon which action commenced; distinguishing Prime Care, LLC v. Humana Ins. Co., 447 F.3d 1284 (10th Cir. 2006) (post-CAFA amendment adding new defendants renders remand order appealable as long as the amendment does not relate back to the pre-CAFA pleading); Amalgamated Transit Union Local 1309 v. Laidlaw Transit Servs., Inc., 435 F.3d 1140 (9th Cir. 2006) (discussing and applying § 1453(c)(1)).

The Supreme Court's recent interpretations of § 1447(d) have not produced greater clarity on when a remand can be appealed. On the one hand, the Court decisively rejected the claim that either the Private Securities Litigation Reform Act of 1995 (PSLRA) or the Securities Litigation Uniform Standards Act of 1998 creates an exception to the § 1447(d) ban on appealing remands for lack of subject matter jurisdiction. See Kircher v. Putnam Funds Trust, 547 U.S. 633 (2006). Congress passed the second act when it became clear that securities fraud plaintiffs were simply pursuing litigation in state court rather than meet the heightened requirements of federal litigation under the PSLRA. The 1998 Act precludes certain kinds of class actions altogether and it authorizes removal of such suits to federal court so that the preclusion provision can be applied.

Arguing that eight state law class actions were precluded by the 1998 Act, defendants removed the cases to federal district court, but the district court remanded once it found that plaintiffs' cases were not in fact covered by the preclusion provision. Defendants appealed and the Court held that neither it nor the circuit court had authority to entertain the appeal due to § 1447(d). Defendants sought to escape the effect of § 1447(d) by arguing that a decision on coverage by the preclusion provision is not "jurisdictional," and therefore the district court's remand was not for lack of subject matter jurisdiction. The Court flatly rejected this argument, holding that coverage by the preclusion provision is a condition of removal jurisdiction, and emphasizing that

> [t]he policy of Congress opposes "interruption of the litigation of the merits of a removed cause by prolonged litigation of questions of jurisdiction of the district court to which the cause is removed," United States v. Rice, 327 U.S. 742, 751 (1946), and nearly three years of jurisdictional advocacy in the cases before us confirm the congressional wisdom. For over a century now, statutes have accordingly limited the power of federal appellate courts to review orders remanding cases removed by defendants from state to federal court. . . . [W]e have relentlessly repeated that "any remand order issued on the grounds specified in § 1447(c) [is immunized from all forms of appellate review], whether or not that order might be deemed erroneous by an

appellate court." [Thermtron Products, Inc. v. Hermansdorfer, 423 U.S. 336, 351 (1976)].

Kircher, 547 U.S. at 640.

Although eight Justices signed the majority opinion (Justice Scalia concurred separately), *Kircher* may be less decisive than it seems. Six months later, the Court recognized an exception to the § 1447(d) ban on appeals where a federal employee is sued for wrongful or negligent conduct and the Attorney General substitutes the United States as the defendant by certifying that the employee was acting within the scope of his official duties. Osborn v. Haley, 549 U.S. 225 (2007). The Court held that § 1447(d) is trumped by the Federal Employees Liability Reform and Tort Compensation Act of 1988, which provides that the Attorney General's certification is "conclusiv[e] . . . for purposes of removal." 28 U.S.C. § 2679(d)(2). That provision both prevents the district court from reassessing the grounds for certification (whether the employee in fact acted within the scope of her duties when the injury occurred) and gives the government the right to appeal when the district court refuses to recognize the Attorney General's certification. 549 U.S. at 244. The Court so held notwithstanding the fact that the government contended that the incident causing plaintiff's injuries never even took place. Id. at 245-46.

Justice Scalia, exasperated by the majority's disregard for the plain meaning of § 1447(d), decried the Court's gradual, continued erosion of § 1447(d)'s mandate. Id. at 262-63. "How," he asked,

> can a statute explicitly eliminating appellate jurisdiction to review a remand order not "contro[l]" whether an appellate court has jurisdiction to review a remand order? The Court says the answer to this riddle lies in 28 U.S.C. § 2679(d)(2). But that section says only that the Attorney General's certification is "conclusiv[e] . . . for purposes of *removal*" (emphasis added); it says absolutely nothing about the reviewability of remand orders. Thus, the most § 2679(d)(2) can prove is that the District Court should not have remanded the case; that its remand order was erroneous. . . . Just last Term we acknowledged that "a remand premised on an erroneous conclusion of no jurisdiction is unappealable." Today's opinion repudiates that principle. . . . This utterly novel proposition, that a remand order can be set aside when it is contrary to law, leaves nothing remaining of § 1447(d).

Id. at 264-65 (citations omitted). On the scope of the federal officer removal statute, see Watson v. Philip Morris Cos., 551 U.S. 142 (2007) (regulated industry is not, by virtue of its compliance activities, an agent or officer of the federal government within the meaning of 28 U.S.C. § 1442(a)(1)).

The Court returned to the issue, this time with Justice Scalia writing for a 7-2 majority, in Powerex Corp. v. Reliant Energy Servs., 551 U.S. 224 (2007). *Powerex* was a suit brought by the State of California against a range of companies accused of fixing prices in the California energy market. The suit was filed in California state court and promptly removed by certain defendants under the Foreign Sovereign Immunities Act of 1976, which permits removal by a foreign state. See 28 U.S.C. § 1603(b)(2); see also 28 U.S.C. §§ 1441(d), 1442(a). Plaintiff moved to remand, arguing that Powerex was not a foreign state. The district court agreed and granted remand after concluding that other defendants were entitled to sovereign immunity. Powerex appealed and plaintiff invoked the § 1447(d) bar, but the Ninth Circuit decided it was not precluded from reviewing the appeal. The Supreme Court reversed, holding that "when a district court remands a properly removed case because it nonetheless lacks subject matter jurisdiction, the remand is covered by § 1447(c) and thus shielded from review by § 1447(d)." Id. at 232. Because the district court here remanded on the express ground that it had no subject matter jurisdiction under the FSIA removal provisions when the defendant is not a foreign state, the decision was unreviewable. Id.

Although acknowledging the division of authority, Justice Scalia reasoned that:

> [t]here is only one *plausible* explanation of what legal ground the District Court actually relied upon for its remand in the present case. . . . [I]t was the court's lack of *power* to adjudicate the claims against petitioner once it concluded both that petitioner was not a foreign state capable of independently removing and that the claims against other removing cross-defendants were barred by sovereign immunity.

*Powerex*, 551 U.S. at 233 (emphasis supplied).

Even though the Court itself has never decided the issue of whether there is subject matter jurisdiction to entertain claims when sovereign immunity bars the claims against the only parties capable of removing the case, Justice Scalia emphasized that § 1447(d) serves important purposes: It "reflects Congress's longstanding policy of not permitting interruption of the litigation of the merits of a removed case by prolonging litigation of questions of jurisdiction of the district court to which the cause is removed. Appellate courts must take that jurisdictional prescription seriously, however pressing the merits of the appeal might seem." *Powerex*, 551 U.S. at 238.

The language about the purposes of § 1447(d) seems to have been written with the dissent in mind. Justice Breyer, joined by Justice Stevens, analogized Powerex's appeal to the exception recognized in Osborn v. Haley, 549 U.S. 225 (2007). If, as in *Osborn*, a district court should not be permitted to trump the Attorney General's statutorily authorized determination of "action within the scope of federal employment," a fortiori a district court should not, by an erroneous remand, be allowed to trump the guarantee in the FSIA that foreign state defendants will enjoy immunity from suit.

> [L]ike *Osborn*, the removing party will have lost considerably more than a choice of forum. The removing party will have lost that which a *different* portion of the special statute sought to provide, namely, the immunity from suit that the FSIA sought to secure. . . . [A] state court [receiving the case on

remand] will likely feel bound by the federal court's prior judgment on the lack of immunity (under the state law-of-the-case doctrine) and this Court's review (of an adverse state-court judgment) will come too late.

*Powerex*, 551 U.S. at 241-42. This utterly defeats the purpose of sovereign immunity, "which is to avoid subjecting a foreign sovereign to the rigors and inconvenience of suit." Id. at 242 (internal quotations omitted).

Can you square *Kircher, Osborn,* and *Powerex*? Perhaps at least *Osborn* is explained by the distinctive federal interests involved, or by the explicit congressional directive that district courts are not to mess with the certification decisions that render this type of case removable.

The circuit courts often seem equally intent on finding ways around § 1447(d)'s ban on appellate review of remand orders. See, e.g., Wallace v. La. Citizens Prop. Ins. Co., 444 F.3d 697, 700-01 (5th Cir. 2006) (reviewing district court's remand of case removed under the Multiparty, Multiforum Trial Jurisdiction Act (MMTJA) where Hurricane Katrina victims had filed a class action in state court against their insurers; holding that a district court's decision that it was obliged to abstain under 28 U.S.C. § 1369(b) of the MMTJA is not covered by § 1447(d)).

Once the Fifth Circuit established an exception to § 1447(d) in *Wallace*, it held that the mandatory abstention provision of the MMTJA, 28 U.S.C. § 1369(b), did not in fact require remand to the state court even though the terms of § 1369(b) were met (most of the plaintiffs were from Louisiana, as were defendants, and Louisiana law applied to the case). The court reasoned, rather counterintuitively, that § 1369(b) abstention does not apply to the MMTJA's removal provision, 28 U.S.C. § 1441(e)(1)(B), notwithstanding the Act's explicit directive that "[a]n action removed under this subsection shall be deemed to be an action under section 1369 and an action in which jurisdiction is based on section 1369. . . ." 28 U.S.C. § 1441(e)(5). The Fifth Circuit simply brushed § 1441(e)(5) aside. See *Wallace*, 444 F.3d at 702.

Perhaps *Powerex* will be a strong enough signal to bring the circuit courts into line. See Alvarez v. Uniroyal Tire Co., 508 F.3d 639, 640-41 (11th Cir. 2007) (appellate court cannot review remand for lack of subject matter jurisdiction where remand occurred after plaintiff added a nondiverse party by amendment; citing and following *Powerex*).

In Carlsbad Technology, Inc. v. HIF Bio, Inc., 556 U.S. 635 (2009), the Court held that § 1446(d) does not preclude appellate review of a remand order where the district court dismisses a federal law claim and concludes that it lacks supplemental jurisdiction over remaining state law claims. Declining to exercise supplemental jurisdiction is discretionary, the Court emphasized, so the decision is not an unreviewable remand for lack of subject matter jurisdiction under § 1446(c). Four Justices wrote to emphasize that the Court's reading of § 1446(d) cuts against plain meaning and produces anomalous results.

What lies behind the desire to review and reverse remands? Is it distrust of state courts? Is it the same kind of distrust that provoked Congress to expand removal jurisdiction during the Reconstruction? See William M. Wiecek, The Reconstruction of Federal Judicial Power, 1863-1875, 13 Am. J. Legal Hist. 333 (1969). The risk that state courts will disregard federal rights can't be a concern in *Wallace*—after all, the case is grounded in Louisiana law.

3. *Removal and the Amount in Controversy in Diversity Cases.* Diversity cases filed in federal court must state the amount in controversy. But cases that are removed from state court may or may not include any statement of the amount in controversy. Pleading rules in many states do not require the plaintiff to make a specific demand for monetary relief, and in some states the rules forbid making such a demand. See Alice M. Noble-Allgire, Removal of Diversity Actions When the Amount in Controversy Cannot Be Determined from the Face of the Plaintiff's Complaint, 62 Mo. L. Rev. 681 (1997). And as you can imagine, plaintiffs content to be in state court may avoid stating a figure, or state a low figure, in an effort to prevent removal. Over the years the lower federal courts developed conflicting standards for determining the amount in controversy in such cases. In 2011, Congress passed the Jurisdiction and Venue Clarification Act. The new statute provides that an amount stated "in good faith" in the complaint "shall be deemed to be the amount in controversy," but the defendant can state a different amount in controversy in a notice of removal under certain circumstances—if, for example, the complaint requests nonmonetary relief or if "State practice either does not permit a demand for a specific sum or permits recovery of damages in excess of the amount demanded," and the ground of jurisdiction is § 1332(a). 28 U.S.C. § 1446(c)(2). The district court must then "find, by a preponderance of the evidence, that the amount in controversy exceeds" $75,000 in order to exercise jurisdiction. Id. For criticism of the statute for, among other things, failing to explain how the preponderance standard should operate, see William Baude, Clarification Needed: Fixing the Jurisdiction and Venue Clarification Act, 110 Mich L. Rev. First Impressions 33 (2012). The statute also makes changes to the procedures for removal. See 28 U.S.C. §§ 1446(b)(2) & (c).

4. *Removal and Federal Question Jurisdiction.* Litigation over removal and remand of cases under federal question jurisdiction can also raise considerable complications. We meet, for instance, our old friend from Chapter 1, the well-pleaded complaint rule. In Rivet v. Regions Bank of Louisiana, 522 U.S. 470 (1998), the Court summarized the relationship of removal to this rule:

> A state court action may be removed to federal court if it qualifies as a "civil action . . . of which the district courts of the United States have original jurisdiction," unless Congress expressly provides otherwise. 28 U.S.C. § 1441(a). In this case, respondents invoked, in support of removal, the district court's original federal-question jurisdiction over "[a]ny civil action . . . founded on a claim or right arising under the Constitution, treaties or laws of the United States." 28 U.S.C. § 1441(b); see also 28 U.S.C. § 1331.

We have long held that "[t]he presence or absence of federal-question jurisdiction is governed by the 'well-pleaded complaint rule,' which provides
that federal jurisdiction exists only when a federal question is presented
on the face of the plaintiff's properly pleaded complaint." Caterpillar Inc. v.
Williams, 482 U.S. 386, 392 (1987); see also Louisville & Nashville R. R. Co. v.
Mottley, 211 U.S. 149, 152 (1908). A defense is not part of a plaintiff's properly
pleaded statement of his or her claim. See Metropolitan Life Ins. Co. v. Taylor,
481 U.S. 58, 63 (1987); Gully v. First Nat. Bank in Meridian, 299 U.S. 109, 112
(1936) ("To bring a case within the [federal-question removal] statute, a right
or immunity created by the Constitution or laws of the United States must
be an element, and an essential one, of the plaintiff's cause of action"). Thus,
"a case may not be removed to federal court on the basis of a federal defense,
. . . even if the defense is anticipated in the plaintiff's complaint, and even if
both parties admit that the defense is the only question truly at issue in the
case." Franchise Tax Bd. of California v. Constr. Laborers Vacation Trust for
Southern Cal., 463 U.S. 1, 14 (1983).

Allied as an "independent corollary" to the well-pleaded complaint rule
is the further principle that "a plaintiff may not defeat removal by omitting
to plead necessary federal questions." Id. at 22. If a court concludes that a
plaintiff has "artfully pleaded" claims in this fashion, it may uphold removal
even though no federal question appears on the face of the plaintiff's complaint. The artful pleading doctrine allows removal where federal law completely preempts a plaintiff's state-law claim. Although federal preemption
is ordinarily a defense, "[o]nce an area of state law has been completely pre-
empted, any claim purportedly based on that pre-empted state-law claim is
considered, from its inception, a federal claim, and therefore arises under
federal law." *Caterpillar,* 482 U.S. at 393.

Id. at 474-76.

The United States Supreme Court also decided Wisconsin Dep't of
Corrections v. Schacht, 524 U.S. 381 (1998), in which the issue was whether
a federal district court to which 42 U.S.C. § 1983 claims were removed,
without objection by plaintiff, should have remanded the case to state
court, instead of dismissing claims that were barred by sovereign immunity and then granting summary judgment to the defendants on the
remaining claims. The Seventh Circuit had held that the presence of an
Eleventh Amendment-barred issue deprived the federal court of jurisdiction over the entire case and required remand of the whole case to state
court. Schacht v. Wisconsin Dep't of Corrections, 116 F.3d 1151 (7th Cir.
1997). See also McKay v. Boyd Constr. Co., 769 F.2d 1084 (5th Cir. 1985)
(accord). Other circuits had held that the federal court should remand only
the Eleventh Amendment–barred claims. See Kruse v. Hawaii, 68 F.3d 331
(9th Cir. 1995); Henry v. Metro. Sewer Dist., 922 F.2d 332 (6th Cir. 1990).
The Court took the latter view and vacated and remanded the Seventh
Circuit case. The Court relied in part on the facts that the state can waive
the Eleventh Amendment defense, and that a court may ignore the defect
unless raised by the state. The Court further noted that § 1447(c) did not
require remand of the entire case, because it refers only to cases in which

the federal court lacks subject matter jurisdiction over a "case," not over one claim within the case.

Questions of supplemental jurisdiction resurface in removal of federal question cases as well. What should a federal court do with a notice of removal where part of the case arises under federal law but there are separate, pure state law claims? Under the Jurisdiction and Venue Clarification Act of 2011, a case removable under § 1331 which contains claims that are not "within the original or supplemental jurisdiction of the district court or a claim that has been made nonremovable by statute" may nevertheless be removed to the federal courts. 28 U.S.C. § 1441(c)(1). However, the district court must sever and remand the claims outside its original and supplemental jurisdiction. § 1441(c)(2).

Another subtle issue of removal jurisdiction's requirement of "original" federal court jurisdiction arose in Syngenta Crop Protection, Inc. v. Henson, 537 U.S. 28 (2002). The Court held that 28 U.S.C. § 1441(a) does not authorize removal when federal jurisdiction is based on the "All Writs Act," 28 U.S.C. § 1651, and 28 U.S.C. § 1367. The "All Writs Act" authorizes writs in aid of a court's jurisdiction; it provides no federal subject matter jurisdiction in its own right.

5. *Removal and Forum Shopping.* Section 1446(b) provides a one-year limit for motions to remove "on the basis of jurisdiction conferred by section 1332 of this title," measured from the date the complaint is filed. Can a plaintiff seeking to avoid removal join a nondiverse defendant for 366 days in order to defeat removal based on diversity jurisdiction?

In a case of first impression, the Fifth Circuit held that the one-year limit is subject to equitable exceptions where a plaintiff engages in manipulative conduct designed to defeat removal and preserve the state forum of her choice. See Tedford v. Warner-Lambert Co., 327 F.3d 423 (5th Cir. 2003). Jeretta Kay Tedford filed suit in Texas state court alleging that Warner-Lambert's diabetes drug caused her liver to fail. The only nondiverse defendant in the original complaint was a doctor who treated a coplaintiff. When the trial court severed the two cases, Warner Lambert informed Tedford of its intent to remove. "A mere three hours later, Tedford amended her petition to name her treating physician . . . [a Texas resident] as a defendant." Id. at 425. Exactly one year after the complaint was filed, Tedford signed a Notice of Nonsuit voluntarily dismissing her doctor from the case. Ten days later, as soon as it learned of the nonsuit, Warner-Lambert removed the case to federal court.

In affirming the district court's denial of remand, the Fifth Circuit noted that "[t]ime requirements in lawsuits between private litigants are customarily subject to equitable tolling," and concluded that "Tedford's forum manipulation justifies application of an equitable exception in the form of estoppel." *Tedford*, 327 F.3d at 426-27 (quoting Irwin v. Dep't of Veterans Affairs, 498 U.S. 89, 95 (1990)). The court acknowledged that the one-year limit was designed to protect state proceedings from disruption once substantial progress has been reached, but it reasoned that "[s]trict application of the one-year limit would encourage plaintiffs to join nondiverse defendants for 366 days simply to avoid federal court, thereby undermining the very purpose of diversity jurisdiction." Id. at 427.

Is this holding consistent with Congress's intent to limit diversity jurisdiction? See Burns v. Windsor Ins. Co., 31 F.3d 1092, 1097 n.12 (11th Cir. 1994) ("Congress knew when it passed the one year bar on removal that some plaintiffs would attempt to defeat diversity jurisdiction by fraudulently (and temporarily) joining a non-diverse party. . . . *Congress has recognized and accepted that, in some circumstances, plaintiff can and will intentionally avoid federal jurisdiction.*") (emphasis added). And compare the Fifth Circuit's generous treatment of the one-year limit on *removal* with the Third Circuit's strict approach toward an untimely motion for *remand*. See Ariel Land Owners, Inc. v. Dring, 351 F.3d 611, 615 (3d Cir. 2003) (reversing district court's grant of plaintiff's motion for remand filed more than 30 days after the notice of removal; "delay and disruption [caused by removal] is only compounded by permitting federal proceedings to carry on at length (nearly two years in the instant case), only to have the case interrupted again and sent back to the state court"). Interestingly, the motion for remand in Ariel Land Owners was based on defendant's untimely removal.

6. *Exceptions to Removal Jurisdiction.* The United States Supreme Court has held that state court suits under the Fair Labor Standards Act may be removed to federal court, even though the statute gives plaintiffs the right to sue in state *or* federal court. Breuer v. Jim's Concrete of Brevard, Inc., 538 U.S. 691 (2003). Language in the FLSA that a lawsuit "may be maintained . . . in any Federal or State court of competent jurisdiction," did not constitute the unequivocal language needed to overcome the right to removal under 28 U.S.C. § 1441.

## 4. Venue Transfers Within the Federal Court System

If an action is filed in a federal district court that is the improper venue or that is a substantially less convenient venue than another federal court, the action may be transferred to another district. See 28 U.S.C. §§ 1404 and 1406.

The transferee court must be one in which the defendants would have been subject to personal jurisdiction and where venue would have been proper had the action been filed there originally.

When a party requests a transfer based on inconvenience, rather than because the venue is improper, the court will apply 28 U.S.C. § 1404(a) and will give considerable weight to the plaintiff's choice of forum, among other factors. That means that, as between venues equally inconvenient to each party, the plaintiff's choice should prevail. As the Seventh Circuit has stated: "When plaintiff and defendant are in different states there is no choice of forum that will avoid imposing inconvenience; and when the inconvenience of the alternative venues is comparable there is no basis for a change of venue; the tie is awarded to the plaintiff. . . ." In re National Presto Indus., Inc., 347 F.3d 662, 665 (7th Cir. 2003) (denying defendant's motion for change of venue to home state despite inconvenience of defending action brought by SEC in state where the district court lacked subpoena power over key witnesses).

Section 1406 applies when the reason for the transfer is that the transferor court is the improper forum, rather than merely an inconvenient forum.

Although the venue transfer statutes appear to apply only to transfers based on improper or inconvenient venues, courts have permitted transfers based on personal jurisdiction defects. Thus, if an action is filed in a federal district court that lacks personal jurisdiction over the defendant, the court may use the transfer statutes to send the action to a federal district court where personal jurisdiction and venue requirements are met. The courts disagree, however, about whether the proper statute to cite in this situation is § 1404, § 1406, or a "gloss" on both.

Of great significance to litigants is the effect of a transfer on the law applied to the controversy. If the action is based on a federal statute, then the transfer makes little difference because federal law applies in either forum, though complex questions arise when the federal circuits are in conflict over a question of federal law. See Robert A. Ragazzo, *Transfer and Choice of Federal Law: The Appellate Model*, 93 Mich. L. Rev. 703 (1995). In a diversity case, however, the transfer may have a bearing on which state's law the federal court will apply to the case. As you learned in the materials on the *Erie* doctrine, federal courts sitting in diversity must apply the substantive law of the applicable state, not federal law, to the controversy. In general, this means that the federal court will apply whatever law a state court would apply. The relevant state court, for diversity purposes, is the state court for the state in which the federal court sits. See Klaxon Co. v. Stentor Electric Mfr. Co., 313 U.S. 487 (1941). Thus, a federal court in the northern district of Arizona would apply whatever state law that the Arizona court would apply to a similar action.

Each state has a set of laws, called conflicts laws, that determines which state's laws apply to a particular type of controversy. If all of the relevant events took place within the state, then the state's own laws will apply. But if the lawsuit has multistate features, the conflicts laws typically direct the state court to apply the law of the state that is the "center of gravity" of the controversy. Thus, if an Arizona resident files an action in Arizona regarding a car accident that occurred in California, then the Arizona court may apply California law to the controversy, depending on Arizona's conflicts laws.

These rules of diversity jurisdiction, conflicts, and transfers may enable cagey counsel to forum shop through complex strategic moves. A plaintiff could — in theory — file an action in a federal district court in Arizona that counsel knows is inconvenient, though proper. Then, counsel could move (or wait until opposing counsel moves) for a transfer to the more convenient forum. If the law of forum 1 is more favorable to the plaintiff than the law of forum 2, then counsel might get the advantage of forum 1's law plus the advantage of forum 2's convenience, but only if the law of forum 1 follows the action to forum 2. The following chart shows how courts have responded, regarding the effect of transfer on the law applied to a diversity case, when confronted with precisely these tactics:

| Situation | Transfer? | By whom? | Law applied |
|---|---|---|---|
| 1) Forum 1 venue proper, but inconvenient. Personal jurisdiction satisfied | Yes—§ 1404 | Defendant, plaintiff, or court | Conflicts law of Forum 1 |
| 2) Forum 1 venue improper. Personal jurisdiction satisfied. | Yes—§ 1406 | Defendant, plaintiff, or court | Probably conflicts law of Forum 2 |
| 3) Forum 1 venue improper. No personal jurisdiction. | Yes—§ 1406 | Defendant, plaintiff, or court | Conflicts law of Forum 2 |
| 4) Forum 1 venue proper. No personal jurisdiction | Yes—§ 1404, § 1406, or gloss on both | Defendant, plaintiff, or court | Conflicts law of Forum 2 |

Note: For the third and fourth examples, the defendant must be served with process in forum 2. Also note that 28 U.S.C. § 1406 is primarily a *defense* tool, so that neither the court nor plaintiff is likely to invoke it, *if defendant does not* (plaintiff, after all, chose the forum, and defendant can waive both venue and personal jurisdiction objections). However, if defendant does object successfully to venue or personal jurisdiction *without* invoking 28 U.S.C. § 1406, i.e., through a 12(b) motion to dismiss, then plaintiff or the court conceivably could resort to § 1406 as authority to transfer, rather than dismiss, the action.

The Jurisdiction and Venue Clarification Act of 2011 includes significant changes to venue practice. First, the statute provides that 28 U.S.C. § 1391's venue rules do not displace any of the hundreds of specialized venue statutes that Congress has passed for special circumstances. Second, the statute repealed 28 U.S.C. § 1392, which previously limited certain actions regarding real property to the district in which the property was located. Third, the statute endorses a "unitary" approach to venue analysis in both diversity and federal question cases. See 28 U.S.C. § 1391(b)(3). The statute also permits the transfer of venue to any federal district court upon the consent of the parties. See 28 U.S.C. § 1404(a).

## 5. *Sua Sponte* Transfer

### *Republic of Bolivia v. Philip Morris Companies, Inc.*
39 F. Supp. 2d 1008 (S.D. Tex. 1999)

#### ORDER OF TRANSFER PURSUANT TO 28 U.S.C. § 1404(a)

KENT, District Judge.

Plaintiff, the Republic of Bolivia, brings this action to recover from numerous tobacco companies various health care costs it allegedly incurred in treating illnesses its residents suffered as a result of tobacco use. This action was originally filed in the District Court of Brazoria County, Texas, 239th Judicial District, and removed to this Court on February 19, 1999, by certain Defendants alleging jurisdiction under 28 U.S.C. § 1331 and 28 U.S.C. § 1332. For the following reasons, the Court exercises its authority and discretion pursuant to 28 U.S.C. § 1404(a) to *sua sponte* TRANSFER this case to the United States District Court for the District of Columbia.

This is one of at least six similar actions brought by foreign governments in various courts throughout the United States. The governments of Guatemala, Panama, Nicaragua, Thailand, Venezuela, and Bolivia have filed suit in the geographically diverse locales of Washington, D.C., Puerto Rico, Texas, Louisiana, and Florida, in both state and federal courts. Why none of these countries seems to have a court system their own governments have confidence in is a mystery to this Court. Moreover, given the tremendous number of United States jurisdictions encompassing fascinating and exotic places, the Court can hardly imagine why the Republic of Bolivia elected to file suit in the veritable hinterlands of Brazoria County, Texas. The Court seriously doubts whether Brazoria County has ever seen a live Bolivian . . . even on the Discovery Channel. Though only here by removal, this humble Court by the sea is certainly flattered by what must be the worldwide renown of rural Texas courts for dispensing justice with unparalleled fairness and alacrity, apparently in common discussion even on the mountain peaks of Bolivia! Still, the Court would be remiss in accepting an obligation for which it truly does not have the necessary resources. Only one judge presides in the Galveston Division—which currently has before it over seven hundred cases and annual civil filings exceeding such number—and that judge is presently burdened with a significant personal situation which diminishes its ability to always give the attention it would like to all of its daunting docket obligations, despite genuinely heroic efforts to do so. And, while Galveston is indeed an international seaport, the capacity of this Court to address the complex and sophisticated issues of international law and foreign relations presented by this case is dwarfed by that of its esteemed colleagues in the District of Columbia who deftly address such awesome tasks as a matter of course. Indeed, this Court, while doing its very best to address the more prosaic matters routinely before it, cannot think of a Bench better versed and more capable of handling precisely this type of case, which requires a high level of expertise in international matters. In fact, proceedings brought by the Republic of Guatemala are currently well underway in that Court in a related action, and there is a request now before the Judicial Panel on Multidistrict Litigation to transfer to the United States District Court for the District of Columbia all six tobacco actions brought by foreign governments, ostensibly for consolidated treatment. Such a Bench, well-populated with genuinely renowned intellects, can certainly better bear and share the burden of multidistrict litigation than this single judge division, where the judge moves his lips when he reads. . . .

Regardless of, and having nothing to do with, the outcome of Defendants' request for transfer and consolidation, it is the Court's opinion that the District of Columbia, located in this Nation's capital, is a much more logical venue for the parties and witnesses in this action because, among other things, Plaintiff has an embassy in Washington, D.C., and thus a physical presence and governmental representatives there, whereas there isn't even a Bolivian restaurant anywhere near here! Although the jurisdiction of this Court boasts no similar foreign offices, a somewhat dated globe is within its possession. While the Court does not therefrom profess to understand all of the political subtleties of the geographical transmogrifications ongoing in Eastern Europe, the Court is virtually certain that Bolivia is not within the four counties over which this Court presides, even though the words Bolivia and Brazoria are a lot alike and caused some real, initial confusion until the Court conferred with its law clerks. Thus, it is readily apparent, even from an outdated globe such as that possessed by this Court, that Bolivia, a hemisphere away, ain't in south-central Texas, and that, at the very least, the District of Columbia is a more appropriate venue (though Bolivia isn't located there either). Furthermore, as this Judicial District bears no significant relationship to any of the matters at issue, and the judge of this Court simply loves cigars, the Plaintiff can be expected to suffer neither harm nor prejudice by a transfer to Washington, D.C., a Bench better able to rise to the smoky challenges presented by this case, despite the alleged and historic presence there of countless "smoke-filled" rooms. Consequently, pursuant to 28 U.S.C. § 1404(a), for the convenience of parties and witnesses, and in the interest of justice, this case is hereby TRANSFERRED to the United States District Court for the District of Columbia.

*It is so ordered.*

## 6.  *Forum Non Conveniens*

When the forum chosen by the plaintiff is substantially inconvenient, and the correct forum is that of a different jurisdiction, the doctrine of *forum non conveniens* may require the court to dismiss the action. No transfer is possible, because the correct court is not within the same judicial system as the inconvenient court. Thus, if an action is filed in state court X, and if the substantially more convenient court is in state court Y, then the action must be dismissed by state X and refiled in state Y. Likewise, if the convenient court is in a foreign country, then the domestic state or federal court must dismiss the lawsuit, and it must be refiled in the foreign jurisdiction.

The following case deals with the doctrine of *forum non conveniens* and the factors that are relevant to the decision to dismiss an action on this basis.

### *Piper Aircraft Co. v. Reyno*
454 U.S. 235 (1981)

JUSTICE MARSHALL delivered the opinion of the Court.

These cases arise out of an air crash that took place in Scotland. Respondent, acting as representative of the estates of several Scottish citizens killed in the accident, brought wrongful death actions against petitioners in the United States District Court for the Middle District of Pennsylvania. Petitioners moved to dismiss on the ground of *forum non conveniens.* After noting that an alternative forum existed in Scotland, the District Court granted their motions. The United States Court of Appeals for the Third Circuit reversed. . . . [B]ecause we conclude that the District Court did not . . . abuse its discretion, we reverse.

# I

## A

In July 1976, a small commercial aircraft crashed in the Scottish highlands during the course of a charter flight from Blackpool to Perth. The pilot and five passengers were killed instantly. The decedents were all Scottish subjects and residents, as are their heirs and next of kin. There were no eyewitnesses to the accident. At the time of the crash the plane was subject to Scottish air traffic control.

The aircraft, a twin engine Piper Aztec, was manufactured in Pennsylvania by petitioner Piper Aircraft Company ("Piper"). The propellers were manufactured in Ohio by petitioner Hartzell Propeller, Inc. ("Hartzell"). At the time of the crash the aircraft was registered in Great Britain and was owned and maintained by Air Navigation and Trading Co., Ltd. ("Air Navigation"). It was operated by McDonald Aviation, Ltd. ("McDonald"), a Scottish air taxi service. Both Air Navigation and McDonald were organized in the United Kingdom. The wreckage of the plane is now in a hangar in Farnsborough, England.

The British Department of Trade investigated the accident several months after it occurred. A preliminary report found that the plane crashed after developing a spin, and suggested that mechanical failure in the plane or the propeller was responsible. At Hartzell's request, this report was reviewed by a three-member Review Board, which held a nine-day adversary hearing attended by all interested parties. The Review Board found no evidence of defective equipment and indicated that pilot error may have contributed to the accident. The pilot, who had obtained his commercial pilot's license only three months earlier, was flying over high ground at an altitude considerably lower than the minimum height required by his company's operations manual.

In July 1977, a California probate court appointed respondent Gaynell Reyno administratrix of the estates of the five passengers. Reyno is not related to and does not know any of the decedents or their survivors; she was a legal secretary to the attorney who filed this lawsuit. Several days after her appointment, Reyno commenced separate wrongful death actions against Piper and Hartzell in the Superior Court of California, claiming negligence and strict liability. Air Navigation, McDonald, and the estate of the pilot are not parties to this litigation. The survivors of the five passengers whose estates are represented by Reyno filed a separate action in the United Kingdom against Air Navigation, McDonald, and the pilot's estate.[2] Reyno candidly admits that the action against Piper and Hartzell was filed in the United States because its laws regarding liability, capacity to sue, and damages are more favorable to her position than are those of Scotland. Scottish law does not recognize strict liability in tort. Moreover, it permits wrongful death actions only when brought by a decedent's relatives. The relatives may sue only for "loss of support and society."

On petitioner's motion, the suit was removed to the United States District Court for the Central District of California. Piper then moved for transfer to the United States District Court for the Middle District of Pennsylvania, pursuant to 28 U.S.C. § 1404(a). . . . [T]he District Court . . . transferred the case to the Middle District of Pennsylvania. . . .

### B

In May 1978, after the suit had been transferred, both Hartzell and Piper moved to dismiss the action on the ground of *forum non conveniens.* The District Court granted these motions in October 1979. It relied on the balancing test set forth by this Court in Gulf Oil Corporation v. Gilbert, 330 U.S. 501 (1947), and its companion case, Koster v. Lumbermen's Mut. Cas. Co., 330 U.S. 518 (1947). In those decisions, the Court stated that a plaintiff's choice of forum should rarely be disturbed. However, when an alternative forum has jurisdiction to hear the case, and when trial in the chosen forum would "establish . . . oppressiveness and vexation to a defendant out of all proportion to plaintiff's convenience," or when the "chosen forum [is] inappropriate because of considerations affecting the court's own administrative and legal problems," the court may, in the exercise of its sound discretion, dismiss the case. To guide trial court discretion, the Court provided a list of "private interest factors" affecting the convenience of the litigants, and a list of "public interest factors" affecting the convenience of the forum.[6] . . .

In opposing the motions to dismiss, respondent contended that dismissal would be unfair because Scottish law was less favorable. The District Court

---

2. The pilot's estate has also filed suit in the United Kingdom against Air Navigation, McDonald, Piper, and Hartzell.

6. The factors pertaining to the private interests of the litigants included the "relative ease of access to sources of proof; availability of compulsory process for attendance of unwilling, and the cost of obtaining attendance of willing witnesses; possibility of view of premises, if view would be appropriate to the action; and all other practical problems that make trial of a case easy, expeditious and inexpensive." The public factors bearing on the question included the administrative difficulties flowing from court congestion; the "local interest in having localized controversies decided at home"; the interest in having the trial of a diversity case in a forum that is at home with the law that must govern the action; the avoidance of unnecessary problems in conflict of laws, or in the application of foreign law; and the unfairness of burdening citizens in an unrelated forum with jury duty.

explicitly rejected this claim. It reasoned that the possibility that dismissal might lead to an unfavorable change in the law did not deserve significant weight; any deficiency in the foreign law was a "matter to be dealt with in the foreign forum.". . .

## II

. . . The Court of Appeals erred in holding that plaintiffs may defeat a motion to dismiss on the ground of *forum non conveniens* merely by showing that the substantive law that would be applied in the alternative forum is less favorable to the plaintiffs than that of the present forum. The possibility of a change in substantive law should ordinarily not be given conclusive or even substantial weight in the *forum non conveniens* inquiry. . . .

The Court of Appeals' decision is inconsistent with this Court's earlier *forum non conveniens* decisions. . . . Those decisions have repeatedly emphasized the need to retain flexibility. In *Gilbert,* the Court refused to identify specific circumstances "which will justify or require either grant or denial of remedy." . . . Similarly, in *Koster,* the Court rejected the contention that where a trial would involve inquiry into the internal affairs of a foreign corporation, dismissal was always appropriate. "That is one, but only one, factor which may show convenience." . . . [I]n Williams v. Green Bay & Western R., 326 U.S. 549, 557 (1946), we stated that we would "not lay down a rigid rule to govern discretion," and that "each case turns on its facts." If central emphasis were placed on any one factor, the *forum non conveniens* doctrine would lose much of the very flexibility that makes it so valuable.

In fact, if conclusive or substantial weight were given to the possibility of a change in law, the *forum non conveniens* doctrine would become virtually useless. Jurisdiction and venue requirements are often easily satisfied. As a result, many plaintiffs are able to choose from among several forums. Ordinarily, these plaintiffs will select that forum whose choice of law rules are most advantageous. Thus, if the possibility of an unfavorable change in substantive law is given substantial weight in the *forum non conveniens* inquiry, dismissal would rarely be proper. . . .

The Court of Appeals' approach is not only inconsistent with the purpose of the *forum non conveniens* doctrine, but also poses substantial practical problems. If the possibility of a change in law were given substantial weight, deciding motions to dismiss on the ground of *forum non conveniens* would become quite difficult. Choice-of-law analysis would become extremely important, and the courts would frequently be required to interpret the law of foreign jurisdictions. First, the trial court would have to determine what law would apply if the case were tried in the chosen forum, and what law would apply if the case were tried in the alternative forum. It would then have to compare the rights, remedies, and procedures available under the law that would be applied in each forum. Dismissal would be appropriate only if the court concluded that the law applied by the alternative forum is as favorable to the plaintiff as that of the chosen forum. The doctrine of *forum non conveniens,* however, is designed in part to help courts avoid conducting complex exercises in comparative law. As we stated in *Gilbert,* the public interest factors point towards dismissal where the court would be required to "untangle problems in conflict of laws, and in law foreign to itself." 330 U.S., at 509.

Upholding the decision of the Court of Appeals would result in other practical problems. At least where the foreign plaintiff named an American manufacturer as defendant,[17] a court could not dismiss the case on grounds of *forum non conveniens* where dismissal might lead to an unfavorable change in law. The American courts, which are already extremely attractive to foreign plaintiffs,[18] would become even more attractive. The flow of litigation into the United States would increase and further congest already crowded courts.[19]

The Court of Appeals based its decision, at least in part, on an analogy between dismissals on grounds of *forum non conveniens* and transfers

---

17. In fact, the defendant might not even have to be American. A foreign plaintiff seeking damages for an accident that occurred abroad might be able to obtain service of process on a foreign defendant who does business in the United States. Under the Court of Appeals' holding, dismissal would be barred if the law in the alternative forum were less favorable to the plaintiff—even though none of the parties are American, and even though there is absolutely no nexus between the subject matter of the litigation and the United States.

18. First, all but 6 of the 50 American States—Delaware, Massachusetts, Michigan, North Carolina, Virginia, and Wyoming—offer strict liability. 1 CCH Prod. Liability Rep. § 4016. Rules roughly equivalent to American strict liability are effective in France, Belgium, and Luxembourg. West Germany and Japan have a strict liability statute for pharmaceuticals. However, strict liability remains primarily an American innovation. Second, the tort plaintiff may choose, at least potentially, from among 50 jurisdictions if he decides to file suit in the United States. Each of these jurisdictions applies its own set of malleable choice-of-law rules. Third, jury trials are almost always available in the United States, while they are never provided in civil law jurisdictions. G. Gloss, Comparative Law 12 (1979); J. Merryman, The Civil Law Tradition 121 (1969). Even in the United Kingdom, most civil actions are not tried before a jury. 1 G. Keeton, The United Kingdom: The Development of its Laws and Constitutions 309 (1955). Fourth, unlike most foreign jurisdictions, American courts allow contingent attorney's fees, and do not tax losing parties with their opponents' attorney's fees. R. Schlesinger, Comparative Law: Cases, Text, Materials 275-277 (3d ed. 1970); . . . Fifth, discovery is more extensive in American than in foreign courts. R. Schlesinger, supra, at 307, 310, and n.33.

19. In holding that the possibility of a change in law unfavorable to the plaintiff should not be given substantial weight, we also necessarily hold that the possibility of a change in law favorable to defendant should not be considered. Respondent suggests that Piper and Hartzell filed the motion to dismiss, not simply because trial in the United States would be inconvenient, but also because they believe the laws of Scotland are more favorable. She argues that this should be taken into account in the analysis of the private interests. We recognize, of course, that Piper and Hartzell may be engaged in reverse forum-shopping. However, this possibility ordinarily should not enter into a trial court's analysis of the private interests. If the defendant is able to overcome the presumption in favor of plaintiff by showing that trial in the chosen forum would be unnecessarily burdensome, dismissal is appropriate—regardless of the fact that defendant may also be motivated by a desire to obtain a more favorable forum. . . .

between federal courts pursuant to § 1404(a). In Van Dusen v. Barrack, 376 U.S. 612 (1964), this Court ruled that a § 1404(a) transfer should not result in a change in the applicable law. Relying on dictum in an earlier Third Circuit opinion interpreting *Van Dusen,* the court below stated that "this principle is no less applicable to a dismissal on *forum non conveniens* grounds." However, § 1404(a) transfers are different than dismissals on the ground of *forum non conveniens.*

Congress enacted § 1404(a) to permit change of venue between federal courts. Although the statute was drafted in accordance with the doctrine of *forum non conveniens,* . . . it was intended to be a revision rather than a codification of the common law. District courts were given more discretion to transfer under § 1404(a) than they had to dismiss on grounds of *forum non conveniens.*

The reasoning employed in Van Dusen v. Barrack is simply inapplicable to dismissals on grounds of *forum non conveniens.* That case did not discuss the common-law doctrine. Rather, it focused on "the construction and application" of § 1404(a). Emphasizing the remedial purpose of the statute, *Barrack* concluded that Congress could not have intended a transfer to be accompanied by a change in law. The statute was designed as a "federal housekeeping measure," allowing easy change of venue within a unified federal system. The Court feared that if a change in venue were accompanied by a change in law, forum-shopping parties would take unfair advantage of the relaxed standards for transfer. The rule was necessary to ensure the just and efficient operation of the statute.

We do not hold that the possibility of an unfavorable change in law should *never* be a relevant consideration in a *forum non conveniens* inquiry. Of course, if the remedy provided by the alternative forum is so clearly inadequate or unsatisfactory that it is no remedy at all, the unfavorable change in law may be given substantial weight; the district court may conclude that dismissal would not be in the interests of justice. In this case, however, the remedies that would be provided by the Scottish courts do not fall within this category. Although the relatives of the decedents may not be able to rely on a strict liability theory, and although their potential damage award may be smaller, there is no danger that they will be deprived of any remedy or treated unfairly.

## III

. . .

## B

The *forum non conveniens* determination is committed to the sound discretion of the trial court. It may be reversed only when there has been a clear abuse of discretion; where the court has considered all relevant public and private interest factors, and where its balancing of these factors is reasonable, its decision deserves substantial deference. . . .

In analyzing the private interest factors, the District Court stated that the connections with Scotland are "overwhelming." This characterization may be somewhat exaggerated. Particularly with respect to the question of relative ease of access to sources of proof, the private interests point in both directions. As respondent emphasizes, records concerning the design, manufacture, and testing of the propeller and plane are located in the United States. She would have greater access to sources of proof relevant to her strict liability and negligence theories if trial were held here.[25] However, the District Court did not act unreasonably in concluding that fewer evidentiary problems would be posed if the trial were held in Scotland. A large proportion of the relevant evidence is located in Great Britain.

The Court of Appeals found that the problems of proof could not be given any weight because Piper and Hartzell failed to describe with specificity the evidence they would not be able to obtain if trial were held in the United States. It suggested that defendants seeking *forum non conveniens* dismissal must submit affidavits identifying the witnesses they would call and the testimony these witnesses would provide if the trial were held in the alternative forum. Such detail is not necessary. Piper and Hartzell have moved for dismissal precisely because many crucial witnesses are located beyond the reach of compulsory process, and thus are difficult to identify or interview. Requiring extensive investigation would defeat the purpose of their motion. . . .

. . . As we stated in *Gilbert,* there is "a local interest in having localized controversies decided at home." [Gulf Oil Co. v. Gilbert, 330 U.S. 501, 509 (1947).] Respondent argues that American citizens have an interest in ensuring that American manufacturers are deterred from producing defective products, and that additional deterrence might be obtained if Piper and Hartzell were tried in the United States, where they could be sued on the basis of both negligence and strict liability. However, the incremental deterrence that would be gained if this trial were held in an American court is likely to be insignificant. The American interest in this accident is simply not sufficient to justify the enormous commitment of judicial time and resources that would inevitably be required if the case were to be tried here. . . .

[JUSTICE WHITE, concurring in part and dissenting in part, wrote a separate opinion. JUSTICE STEVENS, joined by JUSTICE BRENNAN, wrote in dissent.]

### Note: Placing Conditions on Dismissal

The defendants in *Piper* agreed that if the case were dismissed for *forum non conveniens* they would submit to the jurisdiction of the Scottish courts

---

25. In the future, where similar problems are presented, district courts might dismiss subject to the condition that defendant corporations agree to provide the records relevant to the plaintiff's claims.

and would waive any statute of limitations defense that might be available. Conditioning a *forum non conveniens* dismissal on steps to recompense in some measure the plaintiff's loss of her chosen forum is not unusual. The same judicial tactic for making the litigation more fair is used under § 1404.

The Supreme Court found in *Piper* that the defendants had described with sufficient detail the problems of proof that would confront them in Pennsylvania. In contrast, under § 1404 some courts have required detailed affidavits about the proof to be presented. See, e.g., Marbury-Patillo Constr. Co. v. Bayside Warehouse Co., 490 F.2d 155 (5th Cir. 1974). In McDonnell Douglas Corp. v. Polin, 429 F.2d 30 (3d Cir. 1970), the court ordered the trial judge, Judge Higginbotham, to limit discovery and rule on a transfer motion under § 1404 without further factual inquiry into the merits. This presented what the judge described as a difficult paradox:

> How can I ascertain whether the many purported "key" witnesses are really the *actual* "key" witnesses for the defense unless I accept either defendants' assertion that ninety "key" witnesses will be needed and called at trial . . . or plaintiff's assertion that the defendant has not sufficiently delineated the issues on which each witness will testify so as to enable me to ascertain whether or not any of the ninety witnesses is in reality a "key" witness[?] . . . Until there is some probe of the merits and of the defenses, how can I determine with reasonable precision whether merely hundreds or many thousands of documents will be required? How can I ascertain whether merely a few man hours or many thousands of man hours of testimony by key personnel would be required at trial?

Polin v. Conductron Corp., 340 F. Supp. 602, 607 (E.D. Pa. 1972). Cf. Sinochem Int'l Co. v. Malaysia Int'l Shipping Corp., 549 U.S. 422 (2007) (district court is not obliged to first establish its own jurisdiction before dismissing on grounds of *forum non conveniens*).

## Note: The Degree of Deference to Plaintiff's Choice

*Piper* correctly states the rule that "a plaintiff's choice of forum should rarely be disturbed." Should the degree of deference depend on whether there is evidence to suggest that plaintiff engaged in forum shopping? The Second Circuit has held that "circumstances may alter the degree of deference given the plaintiff's forum choice." Pollux Holding Ltd. v. The Chase Manhattan Bank, 329 F.3d 64, 71 (2d Cir. 2003). "Great deference" is accorded a plaintiff suing in her home forum "because it is presumed to be convenient." Id. However, less deference is accorded a foreign plaintiff suing in a United States forum because "it is more likely that forum-shopping for a higher damage award or for some other litigation advantage was the motivation for plaintiff's selection." Id. Do you agree?

In *Pollux*, Greek nationals used Liberian corporations as personal investment vehicles. When investments managed by Chase through its London office collapsed, plaintiffs filed suit in the Southern District of New York, defendant's home forum. The district court granted defendant's motion to dismiss on *forum non conveniens* grounds and the Second Circuit affirmed, reasoning that England provided an adequate alternate forum:

> Bearing in mind that litigants rarely are concerned with promoting their adversary's convenience at their own expense, a plaintiff's choice of the defendant's home forum over other fora where defendant is amenable to suit and to which the plaintiff and the circumstances or the case are much more closely connected suggests the possibility that plaintiff's choice was made for reasons of trial strategy.

*Pollux*, 329 F.3d at 71. See also Gross v. British Broad. Corp., 386 F.3d 224 (2d Cir. 2004) (discussing relevance of public and private interests as factors in *forum non conveniens* analysis); Carey v. Bayerische Hypo-Und Vereinsbank AG, 370 F.3d 234 (2d Cir. 2004) (observing that individual's choice of forum may receive more deference than choice of a large business because hardship on individual forced to litigate abroad is greater).

Are the concerns that animate hostility to domestic forum shopping applicable in the context of transnational litigation? See Pamela K. Bookman, The Unsung Virtues of Global Forum Shopping, 92 Notre Dame L. Rev. __ (forthcoming 2016). Should federal courts welcome or resist transnational litigation? On the one hand, these cases often present complex issues to already over-taxed federal courts, these cases do not necessarily fit the traditional expertise of federal judges, and there may be other more suitable fora for their adjudication. On the other hand, avoidance of transnational litigation is not without costs. See Pamela K. Bookman, Litigation Isolationism, 67 Stan. L. Rev. 1081 (2015).

### Note: Venue Transfers for Reasons Other Than Inconvenience

Goldlawr, Inc. v. Heiman, 369 U.S. 463 (1962), was an antitrust suit filed originally in the Eastern District of Pennsylvania. Several defendants moved to dismiss for improper venue and for lack of personal jurisdiction. The court, passing only on the venue contention, agreed that venue did not lie. But since the statute of limitations had run, the court did not dismiss the case, but instead transferred it to the Southern District of New York under 28 U.S.C. § 1406. The transferee court then dismissed because the Pennsylvania court had lacked personal jurisdiction.

The Supreme Court reversed, holding that the transfer enabled the plaintiff to cure defects in jurisdiction as well as venue. In dealing with the fact that one effect of transfers under § 1406 is to save claims from statutes of limitations and that it is arguably unfair to effect this saving by filing in a jurisdiction that has no power over the defendant, the Court wrote:

> The language of § 1406(a) is amply broad enough to authorize the transfer of cases, however wrong the plaintiff may have been in filing his case as to venue, whether the court in which it was filed had personal jurisdiction over

the defendants or not. This section is thus in accord with the general purpose which has prompted many of the procedural changes of the past few years—that of removing whatever obstacles may impede an expeditious and orderly adjudication of cases and controversies on their merits. When a lawsuit is filed, that filing shows a desire on the part of the plaintiff to begin his case and thereby toll whatever statute of limitations would otherwise apply. The filing itself shows the proper diligence on the part of the plaintiff which such statutes of limitations were intended to insure.

*Goldlawr*, 369 U.S. at 466-67. In dissent, Justices Harlan and Stewart wrote:

The notion that a District Court may deal with an in personam action in such a way as possibly to affect a defendant's substantive rights without first acquiring jurisdiction over him is not a familiar one in federal jurisprudence.

Id. at 467-68.

## Review Problem: Choosing Systems in a More Complex World

Return to our *Baites v. Froid* hypothetical in Chapter 1, section C(6), and recall the review problem based on it. Now test your skills by answering the following further questions.

A patient of a San Francisco–based psychiatrist injures his father, an Arizona resident, in Arizona. The father wishes to sue the California psychiatrist on the theory that she had a duty to warn the Arizonan of her patient's foreseeable violent acts toward his father. All therapy took place in California. The psychiatrist knew that her patient was going to visit his father in Arizona and increased his medication to ease the inevitable stress of family encounters.

1. Assuming that a federal court would have jurisdiction to hear the dispute, where within the federal system would venue be proper?
2. What law would govern Dr. Froid's liability—federal or state?
3. If the action is filed in federal court, what law will govern whether the plaintiff has the right to a trial by jury—federal or state? Statute of limitations? Burden of proof? Time within which defendant must answer the complaint?
4. Assuming that the action might be filed in either state or federal court, which one would you choose? Why?
5. If you chose to file the action in a state court in California, could Dr. Froid remove the action to federal court? Assume instead that you chose a state court in Arizona. Now can Dr. Froid remove the action to a federal court in Arizona?
6. If you file the action in a federal court in Arizona, could Dr. Froid move to transfer the action to a federal court in California? Would the court be inclined to grant the motion?

## B.   EXTENDING THE LAWSUIT: MORE ON JOINDER

### 1.   Joinder of Multiple Parties

In the next few pages, we will deal briefly with standing and capacity to sue, issues that assume greater significance as the lawsuit expands. This is not in any sense a full treatment of these complex topics, which are often a matter of substantive law. Rather, this will serve as background to our study of joinder of parties and the many rules that determine when others may, or must, be added to a lawsuit.

### Problem Case: A Woman Partner (Once Again)

Recall that Attorney Rosalind Shayes has sued her former partners in an action alleging sex discrimination under Title VII and (after timely amendment of the complaint) libel. The firm partners then counterclaimed for libel, alleging that Shayes had made fairly nasty comments about them that they claim are untrue and that caused damage to their professional reputations.

The counterclaim also alleges that Shayes's significant other, Graham Howard (who is also a prominent attorney), repeated Shayes's defamatory remarks to members of his firm. *Must* Howard be added as a party to the lawsuit? *Can* he be added, provided the partners seek some relief against him?

Assume further that the law firm has an insurance policy that arguably requires the insurance company to indemnify the partners for any recovery that Shayes wins against them. The insurance company, however, denies that the policy extends to the acts of discrimination alleged by Rosalind Shayes. May the partners join the insurance company in the lawsuit and litigate its potential liability on the policy?

Assume instead that Shayes questions several other women lawyers in the firm — past and present — and concludes that many of them also have been discriminated against in terms of promotion and pay. This prompts her to interview the female secretaries and legal assistants. She determines that many of them have been sexually harassed by male lawyers. Shayes now believes that the firm has a pattern or practice of discriminating against its women employees.

Can she expand her lawsuit into a class action suit against the firm, naming herself as the class representative for the 50 to 60 women she thinks were or are subject to unlawful discrimination? If not, could some of these women intervene in Shayes's lawsuit? Could they otherwise become involved in the litigation as parties?

Who can sue or be sued involves interesting questions about legal identity, responsibility, and injury. All litigation, of course, begins with a perceived injury. As modern society has become increasingly interdependent and interconnected, these perceived injuries often have a collective nature.

Mass production of goods, for instance, may lead to multiple victims. It also often means that a product is made by a chain of entities—the parts manufacturer, the assembly plant, the packager, the distributor, and the retailer—such that there are many possible defendants when a product is defective.

Determining the proper parties to a lawsuit is even more complex when the immediate entities involved in a dispute are not human beings. Assume, for example, that a client has been severely injured by a dish that melted in her hand. Who, exactly, made the product? Which party (or parties) at the manufacturer was responsible for any alleged defect? As you have seen, an incorrect decision about who to sue cannot always be fixed by amendment, especially after the statute of limitations has elapsed. Is a corporate parent responsible (and thus suable) for the negligence of a subsidiary? Should corporate officers and directors be named as defendants? Who is the proper defendant when the negligent party is "the state"? The state official who committed the negligence, the state itself, or both?

Likewise, determining whether a person or entity has capacity or standing to sue (or be sued) can become complicated. For example, if a public school teacher is negligent in supervising students on a field trip, should she be sued in her individual or official capacity? Does it matter to the outcome?

What about a party who wants to sue anonymously? Should this ever be permissible? What if it is a juvenile suing an adult for damages due to sexual abuse?

### a.   Real Party in Interest

To satisfy the requirement under Fed. R. Civ. P. 17(a) that "[a]n action must be prosecuted in the name of the real party in interest," the party must be one who, under the applicable substantive law, possesses the right sought to be enforced. See generally Jack H. Friedenthal, Mary Kay Kane, and Arthur R. Miller, Civil Procedure 327-37 (3d ed. 1999). Simply because one stands to gain from the litigation, however, does not necessarily mean that he is the real party in interest under the procedural code. Rather, "[t]he court first must ascertain the nature of the substantive right being asserted and then must determine whether the party asserting that right is recognized as the real party in interest under the forum's procedural code." Id. at 320. There is some debate about the need for the real party in interest rule, in that some observers argue that the rules of substantive liability alone should determine who is the real party in interest. In some jurisdictions, parallel real party in interest procedural rules have been abolished.

### b.   Capacity to Sue or Be Sued

A party must also have capacity to sue or be sued, which refers to an individual's ability to represent her interests in a lawsuit without the assistance of another. Fed. R. Civ. P. 17(b) provides that in federal court actions, capacity ". . . determined by the law of the individual's domicile." Where the party in question is a corporation, capacity "is determined . . . by the law under which [the corporation] was incorporated." See Friedenthal, Kane, and Miller, supra, at 332-34.

### c. Constitutional Limitations — Standing

In your constitutional law studies you will take up the issue of *standing*, which determines whether a party seeking to invoke federal court jurisdiction can satisfy the "case or controversy" requirement of Article III of the Constitution. Simply put, the party must demonstrate three things to have standing: 1) "injury in fact" — an invasion of a legally protected interest that is concrete, particularized, actual, and imminent, not conjectural or hypothetical; 2) a causal relationship between the injury and the challenged conduct, which means that the injury can fairly be traceable to the challenged action of the defendant and is not the result of the independent action of a third party not before the court; and 3) a likelihood that the injury will be redressed by a favorable decision, such that the prospect of relief is not too speculative. See Massachusetts v. Envtl. Prot. Agency, 549 U.S. 497 (2007); Lujan v. Defenders of Wildlife, 504 U.S. 555 (1992); Allen v. Wright, 468 U.S. 737 (1984); Valley Forge Christian Coll. v. Americans United for Separation of Church and State, Inc., 454 U.S. 464 (1982); Warth v. Seldin, 422 U.S. 490 (1975).

### d. Fictitious Names

Sometimes, a plaintiff may not know the names of the proper defendants, through no fault of his own. Some states allow the plaintiff to file an action against "John Doe" or "XYZ Corporation" defendants, in which he describes but does not name the parties. Once the plaintiff learns the names of the real defendants, he is allowed to amend the pleading. The principal benefit of such statutes is that the statute of limitations typically is deemed to be tolled by the filing of the original complaint, and the amendment relates back to this date.

### e. Anonymous Parties

On rare occasions the court may allow a plaintiff to proceed anonymously. These cases involve matters of special sensitivity, described by one court as "personal information of the utmost intimacy." See S. Methodist Univ. Assoc. of Women Law Students v. Wynne & Jaffe, 599 F.2d 707 (5th Cir. 1979). See also Doe v. Blue Cross & Blue Shield of R.I., 794 F. Supp. 72 (D.R.I. 1992) (approving transsexual's use of pseudonym in complaint against insurer). What policy reasons militate against allowing plaintiff anonymity? See generally Joan Steinman, Public Trial, Pseudonymous Parties: When Should Litigants Be Permitted to Keep Their Identities Confidential?, 37 Hastings L.J. 1 (1985).

## 2. The Rules of Party Joinder

### a. Permissive Joinder (Rule 20)

*Mosley v. General Motors Corp.*
497 F.2d 1330 (8th Cir. 1974)

Ross, Circuit Judge.

Nathaniel Mosley and nine other persons joined in bringing this action individually and as class representatives alleging that their rights guaranteed under 42 U.S.C. §§ 2000e et seq. and 42 U.S.C. § 1981 were denied by General Motors and Local 25, United Automobile, Aerospace and Agriculture Implement Workers of America (Union) by reason of their color and race. Each of the ten named plaintiffs had, prior to the filing of the complaint, filed a charge with the Equal Employment Opportunity Commission (EEOC) asserting the facts underlying these claims. Pursuant thereto, the EEOC made a reasonable cause finding that General Motors, Fisher Body Division and Chevrolet Division, and the Union had engaged in unlawful employment practices in violation of Title VII of the Civil Rights Act of 1964. Accordingly, the charging parties were notified by EEOC of their right to institute a civil action in the appropriate federal district court, pursuant to § 706(e) of Title VII, 42 U.S.C. § 2000e-5(e).

In each of the first eight counts of the twelve-count complaint, eight of the ten plaintiffs alleged that General Motors, Chevrolet Division, had engaged in unlawful employment practices by: "discriminating against Negroes as regards promotions, terms and conditions of employment"; "retaliating against Negro employees who protested actions made unlawful by Title VII of the Act and by discharging some because they protested said unlawful acts"; "failing to hire Negro employees as a class on the basis of race"; "failing to hire females as a class on the basis of sex"; "discharging Negro employees on the basis of race"; and "discriminating against Negroes and females in the granting of relief time." Each additionally charged that the defendant Union had engaged in unlawful employment practices "with respect to the granting of relief time to Negro and female employees" and "by failing to pursue 6a grievances." The remaining two plaintiffs made similar allegations against General Motors, Fisher Body Division. All of the individual plaintiffs requested injunctive relief, back pay, attorney's fees, and costs. Counts XI and XII of the complaint were class action counts against the two individual divisions of General Motors. They also sought declaratory and injunctive relief, back pay, attorney's fees and costs.

General Motors moved to strike portions of each count of the twelve-count complaint, to dismiss Counts XI and XII, to make portions of Counts I through XII more definite, to determine the propriety of Counts XI and XII as class actions, to limit the scope of the class purportedly represented, and to determine under which section of Rule 23 Counts XI and XII were maintainable as class actions. The district court ordered that "insofar as the first ten counts are concerned, those ten counts shall be severed into ten separate causes of action," and each plaintiff was directed to bring a separate action based upon his complaint, duly and separately filed. The court also ordered that the class action would not be dismissed, but rather would be left open "to each of the plaintiffs herein, individually or collectively . . . to allege a separate cause of action on behalf of any class of persons which such plaintiff or plaintiffs may separately or individually represent."

In reaching this conclusion on joinder, the district court followed the reasoning of Smith v. North American Rockwell Corp., 50 F.R.D. 515 (N.D. Okla. 1970), which, in a somewhat analogous situation, found there was no right to relief arising out of the same transaction, occurrence or series of transactions or occurrences, and that there was no question of law or fact common to all plaintiffs sufficient to sustain joinder under Federal Rule of Civil Procedure 20(a). Similarly, the district court here felt that the plaintiffs' joint actions against General Motors and the Union presented a variety of issues having little relationship to one another; that they had only one common problem, i.e., the defendant; and that as pleaded the joint actions were completely unmanageable. Upon entering the order, and upon application of the plaintiffs, the district court found that its decision involved a controlling question of law as to which there is a substantial ground for difference of opinion and that any of the parties might make application for appeal under 28 U.S.C. § 1292(b). We granted the application to permit this interlocutory appeal and for the following reasons we affirm in part and reverse in part.

Rule 20(a) of the Federal Rules of Civil Procedure provides:

> All persons may join in one action as plaintiffs if they assert any right to relief jointly, severally, or in the alternative in respect of or arising out of the same transaction, occurrence, or series of transactions or occurrences and if any questions of law or fact common to all these persons will arise in the action. . . .*

Additionally, Rule 20(b) and Rule 42(b) vest in the district court the discretion to order separate trials or make such other orders as will prevent delay or prejudice. In this manner, the scope of the civil action is made a matter for the discretion of the district court, and a determination on the question of joinder of parties will be reversed on appeal only upon a showing of abuse of that discretion. Chicago, R.I. & P.R.R. v. Williams, 245 F.2d 397, 404 (8th Cir.), *cert. denied,* 355 U.S. 855 (1957). To determine whether the district court's order was proper herein, we must look to the policy and law that have developed around the operation of Rule 20.

The purpose of the rule is to promote trial convenience and expedite the final determination of disputes, thereby preventing multiple lawsuits. 7 C. Wright, Federal Practice and Procedure § 1652 at 265 (1972). Single trials

---

* [The above quoted language from Rule 20(a) now appears as Rule 20(a)(1) following the restyling of the Civil Rules. — EDS.]

generally tend to lessen the delay, expense and inconvenience to all concerned. Reflecting this policy, the Supreme Court has said:

> Under the Rules, the impulse is toward entertaining the broadest possible scope of action consistent with fairness to the parties; joinder of claims, parties and remedies is strongly encouraged.

United Mine Workers of America v. Gibbs, 383 U.S. 715, 724 (1966).

Permissive joinder is not, however, applicable in all cases. The rule imposes two specific requisites to the joinder of parties: (1) a right to relief must be asserted by, or against, each plaintiff or defendant relating to or arising out of the same *transaction or occurrence, or series of transactions or occurrences;* and (2) some *question of law or fact common* to all the parties must arise in the action.

In ascertaining whether a particular factual situation constitutes a single transaction or occurrence for purposes of Rule 20, a case by case approach is generally pursued. 7 C. Wright, Federal Practice and Procedure § 1653 at 270 (1972). No hard and fast rules have been established under the rule. However, construction of the terms "transaction or occurrence" as used in the context of Rule 13(a) counterclaims offers some guide to the application of this test. For the purposes of the latter rule,

> "Transaction" is a word of flexible meaning. It may comprehend a series of many occurrences, depending not so much upon the immediateness of their connection as upon their logical relationship.

Moore v. New York Cotton Exchange, 270 U.S. 593, 610 (1926). Accordingly, all "logically related" events entitling a person to institute a legal action against another generally are regarded as comprising a transaction or occurrence. 7 C. Wright, Federal Practice and Procedure § 1653 at 270 (1972). The analogous interpretation of the terms as used in Rule 20 would permit all reasonably related claims for relief by or against different parties to be tried in a single proceeding. Absolute identity of all events is unnecessary.

This construction accords with the result reached in United States v. Mississippi, [380 U.S. 128 (1965)], a suit brought by the United States against the State of Mississippi, the election commissioners, and six voting registrars of the State, charging them with engaging in acts and practices hampering and destroying the right of black citizens of Mississippi to vote. The district court concluded that the complaint improperly attempted to hold the six country registrars jointly liable for what amounted to nothing more than individual torts committed by them separately against separate applicants. In reversing, the Supreme Court said:

> But the complaint charged that the registrars had acted and were continuing to act as part of a state-wide system designed to enforce the registration laws in a way that would inevitably deprive colored people of the right to vote solely because of their color. On such an allegation the joinder of all the

registrars as defendants in a single suit is authorized by Rule 20(a) of the Federal Rules of Civil Procedure. . . . These registrars were alleged to be carrying on activities which were part of a series of transactions or occurrences the validity of which depended to a large extent upon "questions[s] of law or fact common to all of them."

Id. at 142-143.

Here too, then, the plaintiffs have asserted a right to relief arising out of the same transactions or occurrences. Each of the ten plaintiffs alleged that he had been injured by the same general policy of discrimination on the part of General Motors and the Union. Since a "state-wide system designed to enforce the registration laws in a way that would inevitably deprive colored people of the right to vote" was determined to arise out of the same series of transactions or occurrences, we conclude that a company-wide policy purportedly designed to discriminate against blacks in employment similarly arises out of the same series of transactions or occurrences. Thus the plaintiffs meet the first requisite for joinder under Rule 20(a).

The second requisite necessary to sustain a permissive joinder under the rule is that a question of law or fact common to all the parties will arise in the action. The rule does not require that *all* questions of law and fact raised by the dispute be common. Yet, neither does it establish any qualitative or quantitative test of commonality. For this reason, cases construing the parallel requirement under Federal Rule of Civil Procedure 23(a) provide a helpful framework for construction of the commonality required by Rule 20. In general, those cases that have focused on Rule 23(a)(2) have given it a permissive application so that common questions have been found to exist in a wide range of contexts. 7 C. Wright, Federal Practice and Procedure § 1763 at 604 (1972). Specifically, with respect to employment discrimination cases under Title VII, courts have found that the discriminatory character of a defendant's conduct is basic to the class, and the fact that the individual class members may have suffered different effects from the alleged discrimination is immaterial for the purposes of the prerequisite. . . . In this vein, one court has said:

> [A]though the actual effects of a discriminatory policy may thus vary throughout the class, the existence of the discriminatory policy threatens the entire class. And whether the Damoclean threat of a racially discriminatory policy hangs over the racial class is a question of fact common to all the members of the class.

Hall v. Werthan Bag Corp., 251 F. Supp. 184, 186 (M.D. Tenn. 1966). . . .

The right to relief here depends on the ability to demonstrate that each of the plaintiffs was wronged by racially discriminatory policies on the part of the defendants General Motors and the Union. The discriminatory character of the defendants' conduct is thus basic to each plaintiff's recovery. The fact that each plaintiff may have suffered different effects from the alleged discrimination is immaterial for the purposes of determining the common question of law or fact. Thus, we conclude that the second requisite for joinder under Rule 20(a) is also met by the complaint.

For the reasons set forth above, we conclude that the district court abused its discretion in severing the joined actions. The difficulties in ultimately adjudicating damages to the various plaintiffs are not so overwhelming as to require such severance. If appropriate, separate trials may be granted as to any particular issue after the determination of common questions.

The judgment of the district court disallowing joinder of the plaintiff's individual actions is reversed and remanded with directions to permit the plaintiffs to proceed jointly. That portion of the district court's judgment that withholds determination of the propriety of the purported class until further discovery is affirmed. We consider the application of the appellants for attorney's fees on this appeal to be premature, and they will be denied without prejudice to their right to reassert that claim upon final disposition of the case.

## Note: Fraudulent Joinder

*Mosley* arose under federal law. Joinder can serve additional purposes in suits based on diversity of citizenship. Consider whether a plaintiff should be permitted to join in-state defendants to defeat a motion to remove a case from state to federal court where removal is predicated on diversity jurisdiction. Generally, in-state defendants can be joined (and the case will be remanded) as long as there is a reasonable possibility that state law will impose liability on the facts of the case. Absent such a showing, joinder is fraudulent and will not defeat removal to federal court. See Travis v. Irby, 326 F.3d 644, 647 (5th Cir. 2003); cf. Sweeney v. Sherwin Williams Co., 304 F. Supp. 2d 868 (S.D. Miss. 2004). See Note on Removal and Forum Shopping in section 3 of this chapter, supra.

## Note: Common Questions After Wal-Mart v. Dukes

*Mosley* reflects the traditional flexible approach toward assessing whether common questions of law and fact are present. The court draws on class action certification jurisprudence because Rule 23(a)(2) contains a parallel commonality requirement. The court emphasizes that different effects of discrimination do not make joinder improper as long as the cause of discrimination presents a common question. As we will see later in this chapter, the Supreme Court has recently imposed a stricter commonality requirement for certification of a class action. See Wal-Mart Stores, Inc. v. Dukes, infra, Section C.1. Whether and to what extent that case will affect joinder practice under Rule 20(a) remains to be seen. For evidence that lower courts remain committed to a flexible test of commonality in joinder, see Kassman v. KPMG LLP, 2013 WL 452913 (S.D.N.Y. Feb. 7, 2013). What differences between joinder and class litigation might support a more flexible test of commonality under Rule 20?

### b.    Compulsory Joinder (Rule 19)

*Temple v. Synthes Corp.*
498 U.S. 5 (1990)

Per Curiam.

Petitioner Temple, a Mississippi resident, underwent surgery in October 1986 in which a "plate and screw device" was implanted in his lower spine. The device was manufactured by respondent Synthes, Ltd. (U.S.A.) (Synthes), a Pennsylvania corporation. Dr. S. Henry LaRocca performed the surgery at St. Charles General Hospital in New Orleans, Louisiana. Following surgery, the device's screws broke off inside Temple's back.

Temple filed suit against Synthes in the United States District Court for the Eastern District of Louisiana. The suit, which rested on diversity jurisdiction, alleged defective design and manufacture of the device. At the same time, Temple filed a state administrative proceeding against Dr. LaRocca and the hospital for malpractice and negligence. At the conclusion of the administrative proceeding, Temple filed suit against the doctor and the hospital in Louisiana state court.

Synthes did not attempt to bring the doctor and the hospital into the federal action by means of a third-party complaint, as provided in Federal Rule of Civil Procedure 14(a). Instead, Synthes filed a motion to dismiss Temple's federal suit for failure to join necessary parties pursuant to Federal Rule of Civil Procedure 19. Following a hearing, the District Court ordered Temple to join the doctor and the hospital as defendants within 20 days or risk dismissal of the lawsuit. According to the court, the most significant reason for requiring joinder was the interest of judicial economy. The court relied on this Court's decision in Provident Tradesmen's Bank & Trust Co. v. Patterson, 390 U.S. 102 (1968), wherein we recognized that one focus of Rule 19 is "the interest of the courts and the public in complete, consistent, and efficient settlement of controversies." Id. at 111. When Temple failed to join the doctor and the hospital, the court dismissed the suit with prejudice.

Temple appealed, and the United States Court of Appeals for the Fifth Circuit affirmed. 898 F.2d 152 (1990). (judgt. order). The court deemed it "obviously prejudicial to the defendants to have the separate litigations being carried on," because Synthes' defense might be that the plate was not defective but that the doctor and the hospital were negligent, while the doctor and the hospital, on the other hand, might claim that they were not negligent but that the plate was defective. The Court of Appeals found that the claims overlapped and that the District Court therefore had not abused its discretion in ordering joinder under Rule 19. A petition for rehearing was denied.

In his petition for certiorari to this Court, Temple contends that it was error to label joint tortfeasors as indispensable parties under Rule 19(b) and to dismiss the lawsuit with prejudice for failure to join those parties. We agree. Synthes does not deny that it, the doctor, and the hospital are potential joint tortfeasors. It has long been the rule that it is not necessary for all joint tortfeasors to be named as defendants in a single lawsuit. See Lawlor v. National Screen Service Corp., 349 U.S. 322, 329-330 (1955); Bigelow v. Old Dominion Copper Mining & Smelting Co., 225 U.S. 111, 132 (1912). See also Nottingham v. General American Communications Corp., 811 F.2d 873, 880 (5th Cir.) (*per curiam*), *cert. denied*, 484 U.S. 854 (1987). Nothing in the 1966 revision of Rule 19 changed that principle. See *Provident Bank*, supra, at 116-117, n.12. The Advisory Committee Notes to Rule 19(a) explicitly state that "a tortfeasor with the usual 'joint-and-several' liability is merely a permissive party to an action against another with like liability." 28 U.S.C. App., p.595. There is nothing in Louisiana tort law to the contrary. See Mullin v. Skains, 252 La. 1009, 1014; La. Civ. Code Ann., Arts. 1794, 1795 (West 1987).

The opinion in *Provident Bank*, supra, does speak of the public interest in limiting multiple litigation, but that case is not controlling here. There, the estate of a tort victim brought a declaratory judgment action against an insurance company. We assumed that the policyholder was a person "who, under § (a), should be 'joined if feasible,'" 390 U.S. at 108, and went on to discuss the appropriate analysis under Rule 19(b), because the policyholder could not be joined without destroying diversity. Id. at 109-116. After examining the factors set forth in Rule 19(b), we determined that the action could proceed without the policyholder; he therefore was not an indispensable party whose absence required dismissal of the suit. Id. at 116, 119.

Here, no inquiry under Rule 19(b) is necessary, because the threshold requirements of Rule 19(a) have not been satisfied. As potential joint tortfeasors with Synthes, Dr. LaRocca and the hospital were merely permissive parties. The Court of Appeals erred by failing to hold that the District Court abused its discretion in ordering them joined as defendants and in dismissing the action when Temple failed to comply with the court's order. For these reasons, we grant the petition for certiorari, reverse the judgment of the Court of Appeals for the Fifth Circuit, and remand for further proceedings consistent with this opinion.

*It is so ordered.*

## Helzberg's Diamond Shops, Inc. v. Valley West Des Moines Shopping Center, Inc.
564 F.2d 816 (8th Cir. 1977)

ALSOP, DISTRICT JUDGE.

On February 3, 1975, Helzberg's Diamond Shops, Inc. (Helzberg), a Missouri corporation, and Valley West Des Moines Shopping Center, Inc. (Valley West), an Iowa corporation, executed a written Lease Agreement. The Lease Agreement granted Helzberg the right to operate a full line jewelry store at space 254 in the Valley West Mall in West Des Moines, Iowa. Section 6 of Article V of the Lease Agreement provides:

[Valley West] agrees it will not lease premises in the shopping center for use as a catalog jewelry store nor lease premises for more than two full line jewelry stores in the shopping center in addition to the leased premises. The clause shall not prohibit other stores such as department stores from selling jewelry from catalogs or in any way restrict the shopping center department stores.

Subsequently, Helzberg commenced operation of a full line jewelry store in the Valley West Mall.

Between February 3, 1975 and November 2, 1976, Valley West and two other corporations entered into leases for spaces in the Valley West Mall for use as full line jewelry stores. Pursuant to those leases the two corporations also initiated actual operation of full line jewelry stores.

On November 2, 1976, Valley West and Kirk's Incorporated, Jewelers, an Iowa corporation, doing business as Lord's Jewelers (Lord's), entered into a written Lease Agreement. The Lease Agreement granted Lord's the right to occupy space 261 in the Valley West Mall. Section 1 of Article V of the Lease Agreement provides that Lord's will use space 261

> only as a retail specialty jewelry store (and not as a catalogue or full line jewelry store) featuring watches, jewelry (and the repair of same) and incidental better gift items.

However, Lord's intended to open and operate what constituted a full line jewelry store at space 261.

. . . Valley West's motion to dismiss enters into and becomes a part of the District Court's order granting preliminary injunctive relief and because the granting of preliminary injunctive relief is itself appealable, we can and will review the order denying Valley West's motion to dismiss. See United States v. Fort Sill Apache Tribe, 507 F.2d 861 (Ct. Cl. 1974).

Rule 19, Fed. R. Civ. P. provides in pertinent part:

> (a) A person who is subject to service of process and whose joinder will not deprive the court of jurisdiction over the subject matter of the action shall be joined as a party in the action if (1) in his absence complete relief cannot be accorded among those already parties, or (2) he claims an interest relating to the subject of the action and is so situated that the disposition of the action in his absence may (i) as a practical matter impair or impede his ability to protect that interest or (ii) leave any of the persons already parties subject to a substantial risk of incurring double, multiple, or otherwise inconsistent obligations by reason of his claimed interest. . . .
>
> (b) If a person as described in subdivision (a)(1)-(2) hereof cannot be made a party, the court shall determine whether in equity and good conscience the action should proceed among the parties before it, or should be dismissed, the absent person being thus regarded as indispensable. The factors to be considered by the court include: first, to what extent a judgment rendered in the person's absence might be prejudicial to him or those already parties; second, the extent to which, by protective provisions in the judgment, by the shaping of relief, or other measures, the prejudice can be lessened or avoided; third, whether a judgment rendered in the person's absence will be adequate;

fourth, whether the plaintiff will have an adequate remedy if the action is dismissed for nonjoinder.*

Because Helzberg was seeking and the District Court ordered injunctive relief which may prevent Lord's from operating its jewelry store in the Valley West Mall in the manner in which Lord's originally intended, the District Court correctly concluded that Lord's was a party to be joined if feasible. *See* Rule 19(a)(2)(i).** Therefore, because Lord's was not and is not subject to personal jurisdiction in the Western District of Missouri, the District Court was required to determine whether or not Lord's should be regarded as indispensable. After considering the factors which Rule 19(b) mandates be considered, the District Court concluded that Lord's was not to be regarded as indispensable. We agree.

The determination of whether or not a person is an indispensable party is one which must be made on a case-by-case basis and is dependent upon the facts and circumstances of each case. Provident Tradesmen's Bank & Trust Co. v. Patterson, 390 U.S. 102 (1968); 7 C. Wright & A. Miller, Federal Practice & Procedure § 1607 (1972); 3A J. Moore, Federal Practice ¶ 19.07-2[0] (1976). An analysis of the facts and circumstances of the case before us leads us to conclude that Lord's was not an indispensable party and that, therefore, the District Court did not err in denying Valley West's motion to dismiss.

Rule 19(b) requires the court to look first to the extent to which a judgment rendered in Lord's absence might be prejudicial to Lord's or to Valley West. Valley West argues that the District Court's order granting preliminary injunctive relief does prejudice Lord's and may prejudice Valley West. We do not agree.

. . . Even if, as a result of the District Court's granting of the preliminary injunction, Valley West should attempt to terminate Lord's leasehold interest in space 261 in the Valley West Mall, Lord's will retain all of its rights under its Lease Agreement with Valley West. None of its rights or obligations will have been adjudicated as a result of the present proceedings, proceedings to which it is not a party. Therefore, we conclude that Lord's will not be prejudiced in a way contemplated by Rule 19(b) as a result of this action.

Likewise, we think that Lord's absence will not prejudice Valley West in a way contemplated by Rule 19(b). Valley West contends that it may be subjected to inconsistent obligations as a result of a determination in this action and a determination in another forum that Valley West should proceed in a fashion contrary to what has been ordered in these proceedings.

It is true that the obligations of Valley West to Helzberg, as determined in these proceedings, may be inconsistent with Valley West's obligations to Lord's. However, we are of the opinion that any inconsistency in those obligations will result from Valley West's voluntary execution of two Lease

---

* [Note that the restyled Federal Rules contain different section numbers and language for Rule 19.—Eds.]

** [This provision now appears as Rule 19(a)(1)(B)(i) in the restyled Federal Rules.—Eds.]

Agreements which impose inconsistent obligations rather than from Lord's absence from the present proceedings.

Helzberg seeks only to restrain Valley West's breach of the Lease Agreement to which Helzberg and Valley West were the sole parties. Certainly, all of the rights and obligations arising under a lease can be adjudicated where all of the parties to the lease are before the court. . . . Thus, in the context of these proceedings the District Court can determine all of the rights and obligations of both Helzberg and Valley West based upon the Lease Agreement between them, even though Lord's is not a party to the proceedings.

Valley West's contention that it may be subjected to inconsistent judgments if Lord's should choose to file suit elsewhere and be awarded judgment is speculative at best. In the first place, Lord's has not filed such a suit. Secondly, there is no showing that another court is likely to interpret the language of the two Lease Agreements differently from the way in which the District Court would. Therefore, we also conclude that Valley West will suffer no prejudice as a result of the District Court's proceeding in Lord's absence. Any prejudice which Valley West may suffer by way of inconsistent judgments would be the result of Valley West's execution of Lease Agreements which impose inconsistent obligations and not the result of the proceedings in the District Court.

Rule 19(b) also requires the court to consider ways in which prejudice to the absent party can be lessened or avoided. The District Court afforded Lord's an opportunity to intervene in order to protect any interest it might have in the outcome of this litigation. Lord's chose not to do so. In light of Lord's decision not to intervene we conclude that the District Court acted in such a way as to sufficiently protect Lord's interests. . . .

Similarly, we also conclude that the District Court's determinations that a judgment rendered in Lord's absence would be adequate and that there is no controlling significance to the fact that Helzberg would have an adequate remedy in the Iowa courts were not erroneous. It follows that the District Court's conclusion that in equity and good conscience the action should be allowed to proceed was a correct one.

In sum, it is generally recognized that a person does not become indispensable to an action to determine rights under a contract simply because that person's rights or obligations under an entirely separate contract will be affected by the result of the action. . . . This principle applies to an action against a lessor who has entered into other leases which also may be affected by the result in the action in which the other lessees are argued to be indispensable parties. . . . We conclude that the District Court properly denied the motion to dismiss for failure to join an indispensable party. . . .

*Affirmed.*

### Notes and Questions

1. *Joinder and Strategy.* Why did the plaintiff in *Temple* choose to sue the defendants separately? And why was plaintiff willing to take a dismissal

rather than comply with the court's demand, and then determined to press the point all the way to the Supreme Court?

2. *Compulsory Joinder and the Merits.* Isn't *Helzberg* a puzzling case? The court seems to discount the potential harm to Valley West should two lawsuits with inconsistent results occur. Has the court, in effect, peeked at the merits in deciding the joinder issue, such that it has prejudged Valley West's responsibility for the competing uses of space in the mall?

3. *Compulsory Joinder and Substantive Law.* Determinations about whether a party should be joined in a lawsuit are strongly influenced by substantive law that you may not yet have mastered. Consequently, the issue may have an especially abstract feel to it. But you do know something about tort law, joint and several liability, and contract law. What does this knowledge suggest about the result in *Temple*? In *Helzberg*? What about a class action suit brought by African-American firefighters who seek a determination that they were denied promotions on the basis of race? Are white firefighters who might be affected by any decree ordering promotion of the African-American firefighters necessary parties in the class action suit? See Martin v. Wilks, 490 U.S. 755 (1989), discussed later in this chapter.

4. *Compulsory Joinder and Complete Relief.* Can a plaintiff join a party under Rule 19 even if the relevant substantive law does not give the plaintiff a cause of action against that party? The Ninth Circuit, relying on International Bhd. of Teamsters v. United States, 431 U.S. 324 (1977), has said yes, where complete injunctive relief would otherwise be impossible. See EEOC v. Peabody Western Coal Co., 606 F.3d 1070, 1079 (9th Cir. 2010) (Rule 19 joinder of Navajo Nation appropriate where EEOC complaint for injunctive relief against mining company claims that maintaining a Navajo hiring preference at mines the company leases from the Navajo Nation discriminates against non-Navajo Native Americans; irrelevant that the EEOC cannot assert a cause of action against the Navajo Nation). But see Davenport v. Int'l Bhd. of Teamsters, AFL-CIO, 166 F.3d 356, 366 (D.C. Cir. 1999) (denying injunctive relief where flight attendant union members sued union for unfair representation and sought to join employer Northwest Airlines: "[W]hile Rule 19 provides for joinder of necessary parties, it does not create a cause of action against them. . . . It is not enough that plaintiffs 'need' an injunction against Northwest to obtain full relief. They must also have a right to such an injunction. . . ."), and Vieux Carre Prop. Owners, Residents & Assoc., Inc. v. Brown, 875 F.2d 453, 457 (5th Cir. 1989) (there must be a cause of action for or against party to be joined under Rule 19).

As *Temple* indicates, joint tortfeasors generally do not need to be joined under Rule 19(a)(1)(A) to ensure complete relief because complete relief can be had by the plaintiff against either defendant. But "there may be circumstances in which an alleged joint tortfeasor has particular interests that cannot be protected in a legal action unless it is joined under Rule 19(a)(1)(B)." Ward v. Apple Inc., 791 F.3d 1041, 1050-54 (9th Cir. 2015) (antitrust suit alleging conspiracy between Apple and AT&T; reversing district court's determination that AT&T was a required party; neither abstract risk of regulatory scrutiny, nor reputational harm, nor ambiguous evidence regarding

AT&T's contract rights of absent party constitute legally protected interests under Rule 19(a)(1)(B)).

### c.  Impleader (Rule 14)

*Toberman v. Copas*
800 F. Supp. 1239 (M.D. Pa. 1992)

RAMBO, CHIEF JUDGE.

Before the court is the motion of Third Party Defendants to dismiss, or in the alternative, for a more definite statement. The motion has been briefed and is ripe for disposition.

### Background

On May 6, 1992, Plaintiffs Jon and Carol Toberman filed a complaint against the captioned defendants. The complaint detailed counts of negligence and loss of consortium against each defendant, arising out of a motor vehicle accident which occurred on May 26, 1990 on the Pennsylvania Turnpike in Bedford County, Pennsylvania. Plaintiffs' complaint cited various injuries resulting from the accident, and provided some detail regarding the order of the events involved in the accident, the part played by each of the defendants, and specific conduct that was alleged to be negligent.

One of those defendants was Richard Menendez. On May 26, 1992, Menendez filed a Third Party Complaint against Timothy Swarthout and St. Johnsbury Trucking Company. It is this third party complaint that is the subject of the current motion.

### Discussion

The relevant portion of the Third Party complaint, for purposes of this motion, is paragraph four, which reads:

> If the Plaintiffs are entitled to recover for damages alleged and Defendant/ Third Party Plaintiff Menendez is held liable, which liability is expressly denied, then and in that event, and in the alternative, Defendant/Third Party Plaintiff Menendez believes and avers that all accidents, injuries, and/ or damages involved in this action were caused by and were the direct and proximate result of the negligence of the Third Party Defendants, Timothy Swarthout and St. Johnsbury Trucking Co., in this action, and that each of the Third Party Defendants in this action is solely liable to the Plaintiffs, or in the alternative, each Third Party Defendant is jointly and severally liable and Defendant/Third Party Plaintiff Menendez is entitled to contribution and/or indemnification from the Third Party Defendants.

Third party complaint at ¶ 4.

Third Party Defendants' motion to dismiss relies on Federal Rule of Civil Procedure 12(b)(1) and (b)(6). Specifically, Third Party Defendants argue that the third party complaint, as worded, does not fall within the court's ancillary jurisdiction and does not comport with the pleading require- ments of Federal Rule of Civil Procedure 8.

## I.  Is the Third Party Complaint a Proper Application of Rule 14?

Third Party Defendants argue that this court lacks jurisdiction over the third party claims that they are solely liable or jointly and severally liable to the Plaintiffs. After examining the issue, this court tends to agree, though not on exactly the same rationale presented by Third Party Defendants.

Third Party Defendants have been impleaded by defendant Menendez under Federal Rule of Civil Procedure 14. Rule 14 allows third-party com- plaints to be served by a defendant/third party plaintiff upon "a person not a party to the action who is or may be liable to the third-party plaintiff for all or part of the plaintiff's claim against the third-party plaintiff." Fed. R. Civ. P. 14(a).*

The underlying purpose of Rule 14 is to promote economy by avoiding the situation where a defendant has been adjudicated liable and then must bring a totally new action against a third party who may be liable to him for all or part of the original plaintiff's claim against him. Charles A. Wright, Arthur Miller & Mary Kane, 6 Federal Practice and Procedure ("Wright & Miller"), § 1441 at 289-90 (1990). True Rule 14 claims fall within "ancillary" or "supplemental" jurisdiction; the latter is a judicially developed concept under which a district court exercises jurisdiction over incidental matters raised by a case over which the court otherwise properly has jurisdiction. See id. § 1444 at 316. Rule 14 neither creates any legal causes of action, nor authorizes the use of impleader practice to violate the limits of federal juris- diction. Id. § 1442 at 293-94.

Rule 14 was amended in 1946, with the amended version becoming effec- tive in 1948; prior to that time, a defendant could also implead persons directly liable to the plaintiff. Id. § 1441 at 287-88. The 1948 amendment removed a serious jurisdictional issue that had arisen under Rule 14: if a defendant's impleader of a third party who was liable to the plaintiff under ancillary jurisdiction were allowed, this might sanction circumvention of federal jurisdictional requirements, like diversity of citizenship, by encour- aging collusion between the original plaintiff and the original defendant.[1]

---

* [This provision now appears in the restyled Federal Rules as Rule 14(a)(1). —Eds.]

1. Hence, before 1948, in cases like the captioned one, a defendant might have impleaded a third party who was allegedly directly liable to the plaintiff, but was not diverse in citi- zenship; the plaintiff could not have sued the third party in federal court, and to allow the third party's impleader would promote collusion to avoid the requirements of diversity jurisdiction.

Id. § 1444 at 320. The 1948 amendment was designed to totally eliminate the possibility of this occurring. Id. at 321.[2]

Courts have stringently followed the rule that a third party complaint may not set forth a claim of the third party defendant's liability to the plaintiff. It must set forth a claim of *secondary* liability such that, if the third party plaintiff is found liable, the third party defendant will be liable to him/her under a theory of indemnification, contribution, or some other theory of derivative liability recognized by the relevant substantive law. Jack Friedenthal, Mary Kane and Arthur Miller, Civil Procedure ("Friedenthal, Kane & Miller"), § 6.9 at 362. Any third party complaint which does not facially meet this test is not proper under Rule 14 and thus falls outside of this court's ancillary jurisdiction. A theory that another party is the correct defendant is not appropriate for a third party complaint.

> A defendant sued for negligence, for example, cannot implead a third party whose negligence was totally responsible for plaintiff's injury. When a third party's conduct furnishes a complete defense against the defendant's liability, the defendant may raise that conduct defensively in his answer but may not use it as a foundation for impleader.

Friedenthal, Kane & Miller, § 6.9 at 363.[3] See, e.g., Barab, 98 F.R.D. [455,] 456 [(E.D. Pa. 1983)] (even if third party defendant's contentions would constitute total defense, they were not proper basis to implead additional party under Rule 14); Donaldson v. United States Steel Corp., 53 F.R.D. 228, 230 (W.D. Pa. 1971) (proposed third party defendant's total responsibility for plaintiff's injuries was a defense, not grounds for third-party complaint).

In the captioned action, Third Party Defendants challenge the language in the third party complaint regarding their sole and direct liability to Plaintiffs. Given the foregoing discussion, this claim of sole and direct liability to Plaintiffs does not comprise a proper third party claim under Rule 14. Again, the third party complaint can only assert a theory of derivative liability to Third Party Plaintiff (recognized by Pennsylvania law) if he is found liable.

Third Party Defendants have raised no challenge to the remainder of the paragraph quoted above, regarding indemnity or contribution. However, there is no indication that the Third Party Plaintiff's theory of recovery is any different with regard to that remaining language. There is no allegation

---

2. See Fed. R. Civ. P. 14, Notes of Advisory Committee on Rules, 1946 Amendment.

3. The court would refer counsel to one particular text, Joseph W. Glannon's Civil Procedure, Examples & Explanations (Little, Brown, 1987). Glannon gives several instructive hypothetical examples regarding Rule 14, including one concerning "Dillinger," an apprehended robber, who sues "Officer Hayes" for assault in the process of arrest. "Officer Hayes" attempts to implead "Officer Kelly," claiming misidentification, that "Officer Kelly" was the actual arresting officer. However, he cannot do so. Either one officer or the other will be solely liable to the plaintiff; a defendant cannot use impleader merely to suggest new targets for the plaintiff. See Glannon at 150-51.

in the third party complaint that Third Party Defendants stand in a joint tortfeasor relationship to Third Party Plaintiff, or that there is any relationship of contribution or indemnity, which would trigger secondary liability under Pennsylvania law. The complaint merely says that Third Party Defendants are liable for indemnity or contribution to Third Party Plaintiff because they are wholly responsible for Plaintiff's injuries. As stated earlier, this is not an acceptable theory for third party liability under Rule 14.

Third Party Plaintiff will be given a chance to amend his third party complaint, if possible, to comport with the requirements of Rule 14. If he does not do so, the motion to dismiss will be granted. Of course, once an amended complaint is submitted, Third Party Defendants will be free to raise any appropriate challenges permitted by the Federal Rules. . . .

### *United States v. Joe Grasso & Son, Inc.*
380 F.2d 749 (5th Cir. 1967)

HUTCHESON, CIRCUIT JUDGE.

This is an interlocutory appeal growing out of a suit brought for the refund of federal employment taxes.

Joe Grasso & Son, Inc. owns seven shrimp boats used for commercial shrimp fishing in the Gulf of Mexico. Each of the boats is operated by a captain and usually two crewmen. The employment taxes were assessed against Grasso on the ground that it was the employer of these fishermen from the first quarter of 1959 through September 30, 1962. In its answer to Grasso's complaint for refund, the United States brought a third party complaint against the captains, alleging that if Grasso were able to put in issue facts proving that it was not the employer of the fishermen, then the same facts would demonstrate the liability of the captains for the taxes by showing an employer-employee relationship between the captains and the crewmen. The district court dismissed the third party complaint, made the appropriate certification for this appeal under 28 U.S.C. Sec. 1292(b), and placed the case on inactive status pending appeal. We affirm the order of the district court.

Whether the captains may be impleaded is controlled by the language of Fed. R. Civ. P. 14(a) which provides that a defendant may implead a person not a party to the action "who is or may be liable to him for all or part of the plaintiff's claim against him." Thus, in the instant case the government may implead the captains if it is found that the captains may be liable to the government for all or part of Grasso's claim against the government.

After carefully reviewing the nature and purpose of impleader under Rule 14, the district court concluded that it has been "strictly limited to situations where the very existence of potential liability in the third party defendant is dependent upon the outcome of the main claim." While the court agreed that both Grasso and the captains cannot be liable for the employment taxes, it rejected the government's contention that the captains' liability would automatically follow from proof of Grasso's nonliability since the court felt that a third finding is possible, i.e., that the crewmen are not employees of anyone. The court declared that the liability of the captains would not depend upon whether or not Grasso was an employer but only upon whether the government could establish facts bringing the captain-crew relationship within the applicable tax statutes. Of the view that the third party action therefore did not depend upon the outcome of the main claim, the court concluded that the complaint against the captains constituted a separate and independent claim. Accordingly, impleader was denied.

The main thrust of the government's attack is that the district court applied an unduly restrictive definition of the key word in Rule 14, *claim.* Arguing that *claim* refers to the "aggregate of operative facts which give rise to a right enforceable in the courts," the government insists that the operative facts constituting Grasso's claim will establish, if proved, that the captains are employers and self-employed persons who are liable to the government for all Grasso's claim, namely, the employment taxes due on the sums paid to the fishermen. For this to be so, it must be assumed that the crewmen are employed either by Grasso or by the captains.

We can agree with the general principle, as did the court below, that use of the word "claim" in Rule 14 avoids the narrow concepts of "cause of action" and employs instead the idea of the claim as a group of operative facts giving occasion for judicial action. See Dery v. Wyer, 265 F.2d 804, 807 (2d Cir. 1959). Cf. American Fid. & Cas. Co. v. Greyhound Corp., 232 F.2d 89, 92 (5th Cir. 1956). And it is true that when the defendant's right against the third party is merely an outgrowth of the same core of facts which determines the plaintiff's claim, impleader is properly used "to reduce litigation by having one lawsuit do the work of two." Falls Indus., Inc. v. Consolidated Chem. Indus., Inc., 258 F.2d 277, 283 (5th Cir. 1959). But we are also cognizant of the obverse rule, which the government seemingly ignores, that an entirely separate and independent claim cannot be maintained against a third party under Rule 14, even though it does arise out of the same general set of facts as the main claim. . . .

The question whether a defendant's demand presents an appropriate occasion for the use of impleader or else constitutes a separate claim has been resolved consistently by permitting impleader only in cases where the third party's liability was in some way derivative of the outcome of the main claim. In most such cases it has been held that for impleader to be available the third party defendant must be "liable *secondarily* to the original defendant in the event that the latter is held liable to the plaintiff" (emphasis added). Holtzoff, Entry of the Additional Parties in a Civil Action, 31 F.R.D. 101, 106 (1962). . . . Stating the same principle in different words, other authorities declare that the third party must necessarily be *liable over* to the defendant for all or part of the plaintiff's recovery, . . . or that the defendant must attempt to *pass on* to the third party all or part of the liability asserted against the defendant. . . . Whichever expression is preferred, it is clear that impleader under Rule 14 requires that the liability of the third party be dependent upon the outcome of the main claim.

Of course, the government does not contend that the case before us presents the usual situation where impleader is used, i.e., where the third party will be secondarily liable for the judgment against the original defendant. It tells us, however, that the liability of Grasso and the captains is so closely related that one of them will "in all likelihood" be liable for the employment taxes. The government is motivated to implead the captains by the fear that it will be whipsawed in separate trials in which both Grasso and the captains will escape liability by successfully arguing that the other is the employer.

We think that in order for the government to be able to implead the captains as third party defendants in this tax refund suit, it must appear that the liability of the two taxpayers is an either/or proposition as a result of the law or the facts. Such a requirement is consistent in principle with the rationale which underlies impleader as authorized by Rule 14. Although the government has been heard to contend that either Grasso or the captains must be found to be the employer of the crewmen, it has reluctantly conceded the distinct possibility that the crewmen are not employees of anyone but rather operate as independent contractors. Indeed, the government itself on a previous occasion has sought and obtained a finding that other shrimp fishermen were "independent businessmen engaged in business on their own account." Gulf Coast Shrimpers & Oysterman's Assn. v. United States, 236 F.2d 658, 662 n.7 (5th Cir. [1956]). And in Local 36, International Fishermen & Allied Workers of America v. United States, 177 F.2d 320 (9th Cir. 1949), it was found that the captains and the crewmen were joint venturers. Other decisions have found that the fishermen were not employees of the owners of the vessels but have not considered whether the crewmen were employees of the captains. See United States v. Crawford Packing Co., 330 F.2d 194 (5th Cir. 1964); Williams Packing & Nav. Co. v. Enochs, 176 F. Supp. 168 (S.D. Miss. 1959), *aff'd*, 291 F.2d 402 (5th Cir. 1961), *rev'd on jurisdictional grounds*, 370 U.S. (1962). Compare Cape Shore Fish Co., Inc. v. United States, 330 F.2d 961 (1964). These decisions illustrate that the determination of whether the crewmen are employees or not will turn on the facts of each case.

While we recognize that allowing impleader of the captains would expedite administratively the entire controversy, the government still has failed to show that the tax liability necessarily will fall upon either Grasso or the captains. The third party complaint against the captains is a separate claim for taxes, and as such must be denied. . . .

*The order of the district court is affirmed.*

### d.   Interpleader (Rule 22) and Statutory Interpleader: The Stakeholder's Remedy

Interpleader is a method of joining parties in cases where a stakeholder faces two potentially conflicting claims to the same stake. For example, an insurance company may recognize its obligation to pay insurance proceeds to "the wife of *A*" but may find that two women claim to be that person.

Interpleader allows the insurance company—the stakeholder—to interplead both putative spouses and thereby protect itself from conflicting claims to the same stake that might result if the women brought two separate actions.

Rule 22 (called Rule interpleader) is one means by which such interpleader can be effected. A far more useful device, however, is the Federal Interpleader Act, codified at 28 U.S.C. §§ 1335, 1397, and 2361. The latter (called statutory interpleader) is more useful than Rule interpleader because the Federal Interpleader Act permits minimal diversity (at least one claimant must be diverse from another claimant), requires only $500 in controversy, permits nationwide service of process, and has liberal venue requirements (venue is proper where one or more of the claimants reside). Likely the only context in which a stakeholder might use the Rule rather than statutory interpleader would be when all of the claimants are from the same state but are diverse from the stakeholder. In this case, statutory interpleader would be unavailable, as it requires diversity between at least two of the claimants.

Useful as the interpleader device may be, it is not an all-purpose "bill of peace," as the following case explains.

### *State Farm Fire & Casualty Co. v. Tashire*
386 U.S. 523 (1967)

JUSTICE FORTAS delivered the opinion of the Court.

Early one September morning in 1964, a Greyhound bus proceeding northward through Shasta Country, California, collided with a southbound pickup truck. Two of the passengers aboard the bus were killed. Thirty-three others were injured, as were the bus driver, the driver of the truck and its lone passenger. One of the dead and 10 of the injured passengers were Canadians; the rest of the individuals involved were citizens of five American States. The ensuing litigation led to the present case, which raises important questions concerning administration of the interpleader remedy in the federal courts.

The litigation began when four of the injured passengers filed suit in California state courts, seeking damages in excess of $1,000,000. Named as defendants were Greyhound Lines, Inc., a California corporation; Theron Nauta, the bus driver; Ellis Clark, who drove the truck; and Kenneth Glasgow, the passenger in the truck who was apparently its owner as well. Each of the individual defendants was a citizen and resident of Oregon. Before these cases could come to trial and before other suits were filed in California or elsewhere, petitioner State Farm Fire & Casualty Company, an Illinois corporation, brought this action in the nature of interpleader in the United States District Court for the District of Oregon.

In its complaint State Farm asserted that at the time of the Shasta County collision it had in force an insurance policy with respect to Ellis Clark, driver of the truck, providing for bodily injury liability up to $10,000 per person and $20,000 per occurrence and for legal representation of Clark in actions covered by the policy. It asserted that actions already filed in California and others which it anticipated would be filed far exceeded in aggregate damages sought, the amount of its maximum liability under the policy. Accordingly, it paid into court the sum of $20,000 and asked the court (1) to require all claimants to establish their claims against Clark and his insurer in this single proceeding and in no other, and (2) to discharge State Farm from all further obligations under its policy — including its duty to defend Clark in lawsuits arising from the accident. Alternatively, State Farm expressed its conviction that the policy issued to Clark excluded from coverage accidents resulting from his operation of a truck which belonged to another and was being used in the business of another. The complaint, therefore, requested that the court decree that the insurer owed no duty to Clark and was not liable on the policy, and it asked the court to refund the $20,000 deposit.

Joined as defendants were Clark, Glasgow, Nauta, Greyhound Lines, and each of the prospective claimants. Jurisdiction was predicated upon 28 U.S.C. § 1335, the federal interpleader statute and upon general diversity of citizenship, there being diversity between two or more of the claimants to the fund and between State Farm and all of the named defendants.

An order issued, requiring the defendants to show cause why they should not be restrained from filing or prosecuting "any proceeding in any state or United States Court affecting the property or obligation involved in this interpleader action, and specifically against the plaintiff and the defendant Ellis D. Clark." Personal service was effected on each of the American defendants, and registered mail was employed to reach the 11 Canadian claimants. Defendants Nauta, Greyhound, and several of the injured passengers responded, contending that the policy did cover this accident and advancing various arguments for the position that interpleader was either impermissible or inappropriate in the present circumstances. Greyhound, however, soon switched sides and moved that the court broaden any injunction to include Nauta and Greyhound among those who could not be sued except within the confines of the interpleader proceeding.

When a temporary injunction along the lines sought by State Farm was issued by the United States District Court for the District of Oregon, the present respondents moved to dismiss the action and, in the alternative, for a change of venue — to the Northern District of California, in which district the collision had occurred. After a hearing, the court declined to dissolve the temporary injunction, but continued the motion for a change of venue. The injunction was later broadened to include the protection sought by Greyhound, but modified to permit the filing — although not the prosecution — of suits. The injunction, therefore, provided that all suits against Clark, State Farm, Greyhound, and Nauta be prosecuted in the interpleader proceeding.

On interlocutory appeal, the Court of Appeals for the Ninth Circuit reversed. 363 F.2d 7. The court found it unnecessary to reach respondents' contentions relating to service of process and the scope of the injunction, for it concluded that interpleader was not available in the circumstances of this case. It held that in States like Oregon which do not permit "direct action" suits against insurance companies until judgments are obtained against the insured, the insurance companies may not invoke federal interpleader until the claims against the insured, the alleged tortfeasor, have been reduced to judgment. Until that is done, said the court, claimants with unliquidated tort claims are not "claimants" within the meaning of § 1335, nor are they "persons having claims against the plaintiff" within the meaning of Rule 22 of the Federal Rules of Civil Procedure.[3] Id., at 10. In accord with that view, it directed dissolution of the temporary injunction and dismissal of the action. Because the Court of Appeals' decision on this point conflicts with those of other federal courts, and concerns a matter of significance to the administration of federal interpleader, we granted certiorari. 385 U.S. 811 (1966). Although we reverse the decision of the Court of Appeals upon the jurisdictional question, we direct a substantial modification of the District Court's injunction for reasons which will appear. . . .

## I

. . .

## II

We do not agree with the Court of Appeals that, in the absence of a state law or contractual provision for "direct action" suits against the insurance company, the company must wait until persons asserting claims against its insured have reduced those claims to judgments before seeking to invoke the benefits of federal interpleader. That may have been a tenable position under the 1926 and 1936 interpleader statutes. These statutes did not carry forward the language in the 1917 Act authorizing interpleader where adverse claimants "may claim" benefits as well as where they "are claiming" them. In 1948, however, in the revision of the Judicial Code, the "may claim" language was restored. Until the decision below, every court confronted by the question has concluded that the 1948 revision removed whatever requirement there might previously have been that the insurance

---

3. We need not pass upon the Court of Appeals' conclusions with respect to the interpretation of interpleader under Rule 22, which provides that "(1) Persons having claims against the plaintiff may be joined as defendants and required to interplead when their claims are such that the plaintiff is or may be exposed to double or multiple liability. . . ." First, as we indicate today, this action was properly brought under § 1335. Second, State Farm did not purport to invoke Rule 22. Third, State Farm could not have invoked it in light of venue and service of process limitations. Whereas statutory interpleader may be brought in the district where any claimant resides (28 U.S.C. § 1397), Rule interpleader based upon diversity of citizenship may be brought only in the district where all plaintiffs or all defendants reside (28 U.S.C. § 1391(a)). And whereas statutory interpleader enables a plaintiff to employ nationwide service of process (28 U.S.C. § 2361), service of process under Rule 22 is confined to that provided in Rule 4. See generally 3 Moore, Federal Practice ¶ 22.04. . . .

company wait until at least two claimants reduced their claims to judgments. The commentators are in accord.

Considerations of judicial administration demonstrate the soundness of this view which, in any event, seems compelled by the language of the present statute, which is remedial and to be liberally construed. Were an insurance company required to await reduction of claims to judgment, the first claimant to obtain such a judgment or to negotiate a settlement might appropriate all or a disproportionate slice of the fund before his fellow claimants were able to establish their claims. The difficulties such a race to judgment pose for the insurer, and the unfairness which may result to some claimants, were among the principal evils the interpleader device was intended to remedy.

## III

The fact that State Farm had properly invoked the interpleader jurisdiction under § 1335 did not, however, entitle it to an order both enjoining prosecution of suits against it outside the confines of the interpleader proceeding and also extending such protection to its insured, the alleged tortfeasor. Still less was Greyhound Lines entitled to have that order expanded so as to protect itself and its driver, also alleged to be tortfeasors, from suits brought by its passengers in various state or federal courts. Here, the scope of the litigation, in terms of parties and claims, was vastly more extensive than the confines of the "fund," the deposited proceeds of the insurance policy. In these circumstances, the mere existence of such a fund cannot, by use of interpleader, be employed to accomplish purposes that exceed the needs of orderly contest with respect to the fund.

There are situations, of a type not present here, where the effect of interpleader is to confine the total litigation to a single forum and proceeding. One such case is where a stakeholder, faced with rival claims to the fund itself, acknowledges—or denies—his liability to one or the other of the claimants. In this situation, the fund itself is the target of the claimants. It marks the outer limits of the controversy. It is, therefore, reasonable and sensible that interpleader, in discharge of its office to protect the fund, should also protect the stakeholder from vexatious and multiple litigation. In this context, the suits sought to be enjoined are squarely within the language of 28 U.S.C. § 2361. . . .

But the present case is another matter. Here, an accident has happened. Thirty-five passengers or their representatives have claims which they wish to press against a variety of defendants: the bus company, its driver, the owner of the truck, and the truck driver. The circumstance that one of the prospective defendants happens to have an insurance policy is a fortuitous event which should not of itself shape the nature of the ensuing litigation. For example, a resident of California, injured in California aboard a bus owned by a California corporation should not be forced to sue that corporation anywhere but in California simply because another prospective defendant carried an insurance policy. And an insurance company whose maximum interest in the case cannot exceed $20,000 and who in fact asserts that it has no interest at all, should not be allowed to determine that dozens of tort plaintiffs must be compelled to press their claims—even those claims which are not against the insured and which in no event could be satisfied out of the meager insurance fund—in a single forum of the insurance company's choosing. There is nothing in the statutory scheme, and very little in the judicial and academic commentary upon that scheme, which requires that the tail be allowed to wag the dog in this fashion.

State Farm's interest in this case, which is the fulcrum of the interpleader procedure, is confined to its $20,000 fund. That interest receives full vindication when the court restrains claimants from seeking to enforce against the insurance company any judgment obtained against its insured, except in the interpleader proceeding itself. To the extent that the District Court sought to control claimants' lawsuits against the insured and other alleged tortfeasors, it exceeded the powers granted to it by the statutory scheme.

We recognize, of course, that our view of interpleader means that it cannot be used to solve all the vexing problems of multiparty litigation arising out of a mass tort. But interpleader was never intended to perform such a function, to be an all-purpose "bill of peace." Had it been so intended, careful provision would necessarily have been made to insure that a party with little or no interest in the outcome of a complex controversy should not strip truly interested parties of substantial rights—such as the right to choose the forum in which to establish their claims, subject to generally applicable rules of jurisdiction, venue, service of process, removal, and change of venue. None of the legislative and academic sponsors of a modern federal interpleader device viewed their accomplishment as a "bill of peace," capable of sweeping dozens of lawsuits out of the various state and federal courts in which they were brought and into a single interpleader proceeding. . . .

In light of the evidence that federal interpleader was not intended to serve the function of a "bill of peace" in the context of multiparty litigation arising out of a mass tort, of the anomalous power which such a construction of the statute would give the stakeholder, and of the thrust of the statute and the purpose it was intended to serve, we hold that the interpleader statute did not authorize the injunction entered in the present case. Upon remand, the injunction is to be modified consistently with this opinion.[18]

18. We find it unnecessary to pass upon respondents' contention, raised in the courts below but not passed upon by the Court of Appeals, that interpleader should have been dismissed on the ground that the 11 Canadian claimants are "indispensable parties" who have not been properly served. The argument is that 28 U.S.C. § 2361 provides the exclusive mode of effecting service of process in statutory interpleader, and that § 2361—which authorizes a district court to "issue its process for all claimants" but subsequently refers to service of "such process" by marshals "for the respective districts where the claimants reside or may be found"—does not permit service of process beyond the Nation's borders. Since our decision will require basic reconsideration of the litigation by the parties as well

**IV**

The judgment of the Court of Appeals is reversed, and the case is remanded to the United States District Court for proceedings consistent with this opinion.

*It is so ordered.*

JUSTICE DOUGLAS, dissenting in part.

. . . I feel that the use which we today allow to be made of the federal interpleader statute, 28 U.S.C. § 1335, is, with all deference, unwarranted. How these litigants are "claimants" to this fund in the statutory sense is indeed a mystery. . . .

This insurance company's policy provides that it will "pay on behalf of the insured all sums which the insured shall become legally obligated to pay." To date the insured has not become "legally obligated" to pay any sum to any litigant. Since nothing is owed under the policy, I fail to see how any litigant can be a "claimant" as against the insurance company. . . .

. . . Understandably, the insurance company wants the best of two worlds. It does not want an action against it until judgment against its insured. But, at the same time, it wants the benefits of an interpleader statute. Congress could of course confer such a benefit. But it is not for this Court to grant dispensations from the effects of the statutory scheme which Congress has erected. . . .

### Note: Transfer for Consolidation

Read 28 U.S.C. § 1407.

Passed in 1968, this legislation has resulted in thousands of cases being consolidated. Most typical are common disaster cases such as airplane crashes. In re Air Crash Disaster Near Dayton, Ohio, 310 F. Supp. 798 (J.P.M.L. 1970), is a good example. In that case, 13 actions had been filed in three federal district courts. The Judicial Panel on Multidistrict Litigation issued an order to show cause why the actions should not be transferred to a single district for coordinated and consolidated pretrial proceedings. Several plaintiffs and the Tann Corporation opposed transfer. Trans World Airlines and the United States supported it. As is typical in transfer disputes, the arguments made on the motion to transfer were highly practical.

---

as the lower courts, there appears neither need nor necessity to determine this question at this time. We intimate no view as to the exclusivity of § 2361, whether it authorizes service of process in foreign lands, whether in light of the limitations we have imposed on the interpleader court's injunctive powers the Canadian claimants are in fact "indispensable parties" to the interpleader proceeding itself, or whether they render themselves amenable to service of process under § 2361 when they come into an American jurisdiction to establish their rights with respect either to the alleged tortfeasors or to the insurance fund. . . .

The opponents of the motion argued that informal coordination of the pretrial proceedings was satisfactory, had already led to substantial discovery, and resulted in many settlements. In other words, they didn't need § 1407. Those supporting transfer countered that much discovery was still needed on the question of liability, and that it should be coordinated under the direction of one court.

In ordering a transfer, the Panel must make three findings: that there are one or more common questions of fact; that transfer will promote the just and efficient conduct of the individual suits; and that transfer will be for the convenience of the parties and witnesses. Usually, the transferee court is the one nearest the site of the disaster, or where the most cases are pending, or where there is a judge with unusual experience in mass litigation.

Although § 1407 speaks only to consolidation for pretrial purposes, a note writer in The Judicial Panel and the Conduct of Multidistrict Litigation, 87 Harv. L. Rev. 1001 (1974), found that "[i]n practice . . . the great majority of cases transferred by the Panel under § 1407 have been disposed of by transferee courts and not remanded to their original districts." Id. at 1001-02. This happens through the grant of partial or complete summary judgment as part of the pretrial proceedings, settlement, trial by agreement among the parties in the transferee forum, and the operation of collateral estoppel. The last of these has occurred most notably in multidistrict litigation in the patent field after Blonder-Tongue Laboratories, Inc. v. University Foundation, 402 U.S. 313 (1971). The Harvard note describes one such case:

> The history of the *Butterfield Patent* litigation, in which a patentee brought numerous infringement actions for relatively small amounts throughout the United States, illustrates both the strengths and weakness[es] of handling multidistrict patent litigation by a separate trial on validity followed by collateral estoppel. The Panel granted section 1407 transfer despite arguments by many of the 148 defendants that it would force on them a financial burden disproportionate to the small recoveries sought. [In re Butterfield Patent Infringement, 328 F. Supp. 513 (J.P.M.L. 1970).] Despite these fears about expense, the litigation was terminated in the amount of time about normal for one patent infringement case. Thirty-eight defendants agreed to a consolidated trial in the transferee court on the issue of validity. The court's finding of invalidity was then extended by collateral estoppel to 40 other defendants. However, before this scheme for the economical handling of the validity issue was worked out by the transferee court, 70 defendants had settled.

Note, supra, 87 Harv. L. Rev. at 1035-36.

See Note: The Aggregation Alternative in section 6 infra for more about the uses of § 1407.

For a mixed case involving 17 price-fixing suits filed around the country by more than 400 retail drug stores against drug manufacturers and wholesalers, see In re Brand-Name Prescription Drugs Antitrust Litigation, 264 F. Supp. 2d 1372 (M.D.L. Panel 2003) (the MDL panel upheld transferee court's decision to remand remaining individual suits after concluding common expert and fact discovery was complete and after granting summary judgment on the Sherman Act class action claims).

### e.   Intervention (Rule 24)

## *American Lung Ass'n v. Reilly*
962 F.2d 258 (2d Cir. 1992)

GEORGE C. PRATT, CIRCUIT JUDGE.

Sixty-seven electric utilities and three electric utility industry associations (collectively, "utilities") appeal from an order of the United States District Court for the Eastern District of New York, John R. Bartels, Judge, which denied their motion to intervene as of right as defendants in a citizen suit brought under the Clean Air Act, 42 U.S.C. §§ 7401 et seq., to compel the Environmental Protection Agency (EPA) to review and revise the national ambient air quality standards (NAAQSs) for ozone, 141 F.R.D. 19 (E.D.N.Y. 1992). We conclude that Judge Bartels acted within his discretion in denying the utilities' motion to intervene. We also determine that the district court had subject-matter jurisdiction of the action. Accordingly, we affirm.

### I

Under the Clean Air Act, EPA was required to make a final decision (either to revise the NAAQSs or retain the old ones) no later than December 31, 1990. Since EPA had not (and still has not) done so, plaintiffs filed this suit in the Eastern District of New York, alleging that it had breached its non-discretionary, statutory duty of reviewing (and if necessary revising), at five-year intervals, the NAAQSs for ozone, see 42 U.S.C. § 7409(d) (1977). Plaintiffs sought to compel EPA to perform its statutory duties. Specifically, the plaintiffs sought to compel EPA to (a) publish, within 180 days of the district court's order, either proposed revisions to the NAAQSs or a proposed decision formally declining to revise the NAAQSs, (b) provide the public with opportunity for notice and comment, and (c) promulgate final regulations thereafter.

The utilities moved to intervene as parties' defendant. Their proposed answer asserted two defenses: (1) that "[t]he complaint fails to state a claim against Defendants upon which relief can be granted," and (2) that the district court "lacks subject matter jurisdiction over the Plaintiff's complaint." Judge Bartels denied the motion to intervene, and the utilities filed a notice of appeal on February 27, 1992.

The next day, February 28, 1992, Judge Bartels signed a consent order and final judgment which, *inter alia*, ordered EPA, by August 1, 1992, to publish a proposed decision, made pursuant to notice and comment rulemaking procedures, to revise (or not) the existing NAAQSs for ozone. Judge Bartels also ordered EPA to allow a public comment period of at least 60 days, and then to publish a final decision by March 1, 1993.

## II

A denial of intervention as of right under Fed. R. Civ. P. 24(a)(2) is reviewed under an abuse of discretion standard, as only the district judge has the "feel of the case" necessary to "weigh the advantages to be derived from appellants' participation as intervenors." United States v. Hooker Chem. & Plastics Corp., 749 F.2d 968, 991 (2d Cir. 1984) (Friendly, J.). To merit consideration for intervention under rule 24(a)(2), a movant must (1) file a timely application, (2) claiming an interest relating to the property or transaction which is the subject of the action, (3) with the movant so situated that the disposition of the action may as a practical matter impair or impede the movant's ability to protect its interest, (4) unless the movant's interest is adequately represented by existing parties. . . .

Judge Bartels concluded that the motion was timely, but that the utilities fell short on the other three requirements of rule 24(a)(2). With respect to the second requirement, he saw the utilities' interest in the subject matter of the action as based on a "double contingency" of events: "first, the plaintiffs must prevail in this lawsuit and second, the defendants must then downwardly revise the NAAQS[s]." Thus, he concluded, the utilities' interests were too "remote from the subject matter of the proceeding" and too "contingent upon the occurrence of a series of events" (citing Washington Elec. [Coop., Inc. v. Mass. Mun. Wholesale Elec. Co.,] 922 F.2d [92,] 96 [2d Cir. 1990]). With respect to the third requirement, he concluded that since the utilities could participate in any NAAQS rulemaking ordered by the court, a judgment in favor of the plaintiffs could not as a practical matter impair the utilities' ability to challenge any defect of any subsequent rulemaking. As to the fourth requirement, Judge Bartels concluded that the utilities could not demonstrate an interest in the rulemaking schedule that would not be adequately represented by EPA.

On appeal the utilities claim primarily that their interest is not so much in the ultimate rule promulgated by the EPA, as Judge Bartels understood it to be, but in having an opportunity to help shape the schedule for this judicially-compelled rulemaking. The utilities argue that they might have insufficient time to prepare a response to any proposal or to submit comments during the judicially-established comment period. They further point out that absent intervention, they would have no standing to obtain an extension of the deadlines imposed by the district court. To this end, they inform us of numerous cases, mostly from district courts, that have allowed intervention in similar cases.

The utilities' arguments are inadequate to overcome the district court's discretionary denial of intervention. First, as the plaintiffs have correctly pointed out, the cases cited by the utilities that have allowed intervention are primarily cases involving the promulgation of rules for particular industries. In such cases, an industry applying for intervention would have a much less "remote" or "contingent" interest. See, e.g., ManaSota-88, Inc. v. Tidwell, 896 F.2d 1318, 1322 (11th Cir. 1990). Second, the utilities "have asked for little that is new or even particularly different" from the defenses asserted by EPA. Hooker Chem., 749 F.2d at 991. Third, even had EPA obeyed the schedule commanded by the statute, there would have been no guarantee that even the seven months prescribed by the district court's order would have been available for "meaningful and effective" comment. See 42 U.S.C. § 7409(d). Finally, the statute requires EPA to base its decisions on the latest scientific knowledge that bears upon a given NAAQS. 42 U.S.C. § 7409(b)(1). There is no reason to believe that EPA will shirk its statutory duty to solicit and consider such information, or that the utilities and their experts will not have adequate opportunity to present their views.

Judge Bartels acted within his discretion. "The circumstances that serve as a basis for decision [on motions to intervene] are so varied and random that the court would virtually need to create a new rule to describe each case." Gene R. Shreve, Questioning Intervention as of Right—Toward a New Methodology of Decisionmaking, 74 Nw. U. L. Rev. 894, 922-23 (1980) (footnotes omitted) (quoted in *Hooker Chem.*, 749 F.2d at 991 n.20). . . .

*The order of the district court is affirmed.*

## Notes and Questions

1. *Intervention and Subject Matter Jurisdiction.* As the Sixth Circuit has noted, "[i]ntervention cannot, as a general rule, create jurisdiction where none exists. Intervention 'presuppose[s] an action duly brought'; it cannot 'cure [the] vice in the original suit' and must 'abide the fate of that suit.' . . . In the absence of jurisdiction over the existing suit, a district court simply has no power to decide a motion to intervene; its only option is to dismiss." Vill. of Oakwood v. State Bank & Trust Co., 481 F.3d 364, 367 (6th Cir. 2007) (quoting United States ex rel. Tex. Portland Cement Co. v. McCord, 233 U.S. 157, 163-64 (1914)). In *Village of Oakwood*, depositors sued a bank in state court for improprieties while the bank was held in receivership by the Federal Deposit Insurance Corporation. The FDIC, which the complaint charged with breach of fiduciary duty but failed to name as a party, moved to intervene and then removed the case to federal court before the state court could resolve the motion to intervene. The depositors moved to remand for lack of diversity, but the trial court held onto the case by granting the FDIC's motion to intervene, reasoning that the case was now covered by the Financial Institutions Reform, Recovery, and Enforcement Act of 1989, 12 U.S.C. § 1819(b)(2), which "deems suits to which the FDIC is a party to arise under federal law." *Vill. of Oakwood*, 481 F.3d at 368.

The Sixth Circuit reversed. The court concluded that although there would be subject matter jurisdiction under § 1819(b)(2) and 28 U.S.C. § 1367(a) if the FDIC had substituted itself for the defendant bank under Rule 25(c), or even if the FDIC had been impleaded by the bank, intervention does not produce the same result because of the long-standing rule that "intervention cannot create jurisdiction where none existed." *Vill. of Oakwood*, 481 F.3 at 368-69. See also Allen v. FDIC, 710 F.3d 978 (9th Cir. 2013). But see Heaton v. Monogram Credit Card Bank, 297 F.3d 416, 426 (5th Cir. 2002) ("[T]he FDIC's attempt to intervene conferred on it sufficient 'party' status to bring this case within the federal court's jurisdiction under § 1819(b)(2)(A).").

2. *Making Decisions About Joinder.* Now that you have reviewed the basic party joinder rules in isolation, reconsider them as an array of devices available to the parties at the pleading stage. What factors, besides the technical aspects of the Rules themselves, are most likely to affect parties' decisions about joinder? A search for assets? Avoiding multiple liability? Convincing a jury to award a substantial verdict? Preventing same? Attracting media interest in the dispute?

If you believe, correctly, that all of these factors (and others not mentioned) may be relevant in at least some cases, then you can appreciate why the Rules are but a small part of the joinder story. Like many aspects of procedure, lawyers make joinder decisions based on a complex array of considerations that range from highly practical, concrete, and case-specific issues to very abstract, systemic issues of fundamental fairness and intelligent allocation of scarce public resources. Thus your ability to make competent joinder decisions will require practical experience, as well as the technical proficiency you can gain from this text.

3. *Restraints on Joinder.* It bears repeating (and we have repeated this) that the Federal Rules of Civil Procedure joinder rules are *not* the only constraints on party joinder in federal court. Subject matter jurisdiction, venue, and personal jurisdiction requirements must also be satisfied. For example, in an action based solely on diversity, a defendant can implead a party under Rule 14 only if the jurisdiction statutes—including the supplemental jurisdiction statute—permit it, and only if the court also has personal jurisdiction over the impleaded party. Likewise, the distinction between necessary and indispensable parties under Rule 19 cannot be made without knowing which persons can (or cannot) be made a party.

4. *Some Examples.* Test your comprehension of the joinder rules we have discussed thus far and federal subject matter jurisdiction requirements by asking whether each claim below could be heard in federal court. Analyze both the Federal Rules of Civil Procedure and subject matter jurisdiction aspects of each claim and—in general—the information you would need to determine each.

*Example 1*

P v. D

P claim (1)  +  P claim (2)  ⟶  D

Under what conditions may two or more claims of one plaintiff be asserted against one defendant? Consider both the joinder of claims requirements of the Fed. R. Civ. P. and subject matter jurisdiction requirements.

*Example 2*

P v. D

Under what conditions may the defendant assert one or more counter-claims against the plaintiff? Consider both the counterclaim and joinder of claims requirements of the Fed. R. Civ. P. and subject matter jurisdiction requirements.

*Example 3*

P v. D(1) and D(2)

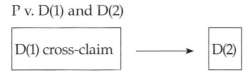

Under what conditions may one defendant assert one or more cross-claims against a codefendant? Consider both the cross-claim and joinder of claims requirements of the Fed. R. Civ. P. and subject matter jurisdiction requirements.

*Example 4*

P(1) v. D(1)
P(2) v. D(2)

Under what conditions may two plaintiffs join together in asserting claims against two defendants? Consider both the joinder of parties require-ments of the Fed. R. Civ. P. and subject matter jurisdiction requirements.

*Example 5*

P v. D

A (absentee)

a) Under what conditions may a nonparty A intervene in a suit? Consider both the intervention rules of the Fed. R. Civ. P. and subject matter jurisdic-tion requirements.

b) Under what conditions is joinder of nonparty A necessary before a lawsuit may proceed? Consider both the mandatory joinder requirements of the Fed. R. Civ. P. and subject matter jurisdiction requirements.

*Example 6*

P (stakeholder) v. D(1) (claimant 1)
and
D(2) (claimant 1)

Under what conditions may a stakeholder interplead claimants to a common fund or a "stake"? Consider both the statutory and Fed. R. Civ. P. interpleader requirements and subject matter jurisdiction requirements.

*Example 7*

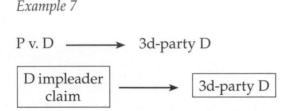

Under what conditions may a defendant implead a third-party defendant and assert one or more claims against the impleaded defendant? Consider the impleader and joinder of claims requirements of the Fed. R. Civ. P. and subject matter jurisdiction requirements.

5. *Who Are Persons "Affected"?* The joinder devices—especially mandatory joinder and intervention—force courts to consider the fundamental question of who is a person "affected" by the results of civil litigation, both directly and indirectly. In public law cases in particular, such as a school desegregation case, the court often must craft remedies that "involve the adjustment of many competing institutional and human interests, [such that] the decree in a public law case often looks like a discretionary regime addressing a problem governed by multiple and polycentric criteria." Melvin Aron Eisenberg, Participation, Responsiveness, and the Consultative Process: An Essay for Lon Fuller, 92 Harv. L. Rev. 410, 428 (1978). As such, the persons who may be "affected" by the litigation may include the whole community. What are the joinder implications of this feature of public law litigation? Does it point toward greater flexibility in adding parties or permitting absentees to intervene? See also Stephen C. Yeazell, Intervention and the Idea of Litigation: A Commentary on the Los Angeles School Case, 25 UCLA L. Rev. 244 (1977).

For example, must an intervenor have "standing" (that is, meet the applicable Article III requirements of concrete individualized injury), or may this be excused? Compare Ruiz v. Estelle, 161 F.3d 814 (5th Cir. 1998) (holding intervenors need not have Article III standing), with Mausolf v. Babbitt, 85 F.3d 1295, 1300 (8th Cir. 1996) (holding intervenors must have Article III standing). See also City of Chicago v. Fed. Emergency Mgmt. Agency,

660 F.3d 980, 984-85 (7th Cir. 2011) (gathering cases reflecting circuit split). The United States Supreme Court has reserved judgment on this point. See Diamond v. Charles, 476 U.S. 54, 68-69, n.21 (1986).

6. *Persons "Affected" and the "Limited Trough."* Persons who may be "affected" by litigation also include those who may be too late to recover assets from a corporation that is forced into bankruptcy by mass tort litigation. These "limited trough" cases present distributional justice issues that are particularly complex, as Thomas A. Smith explains in A Capital Markets Approach to Mass Tort Bankruptcy, 104 Yale L.J. 367 (1994).

The problem captured national attention when asbestos litigation in many forms and forums triggered a rush to the limited assets of the product manufacturers. Mass tort litigation in general raises the distributional justice issues most strikingly. Priorities of claims and the interests of future claimants are the most pressing of these.

Professor Smith proposes a novel capital markets approach to overcoming the distributional justice problems. Under his approach, the bankruptcy court would place the entire value of the defendant company in trust for the tort claimants, and the trust would use these assets to compensate present and future tort creditors under the following scheme: The trust would issue to the tort claimant a security that was designed to be traded on the capital market. The value of the security would be determined by the market, not the trust. Do you see any problems with this proposal? What are its strengths?

## C.   CLASS ACTIONS—AN INTRODUCTION (RULE 23)

### 1.   Introduction

In the last decades of the twentieth century, Rule 23 stirred more controversy, reaped larger financial rewards (often for lawyers), and pressed the federal justice system harder than any other rule in the history of procedural law. Whole legal practices and entire law school courses are devoted to this joinder device, which allows representatives to sue on behalf of large numbers of unnamed others, who will be bound by the judgment. Originally, Rule 23 reflected an ancient equitable practice for resolving multiple claims arising out of communal harms. Stephen C. Yeazell, in Group Litigation and Social Context: Toward a History of the Class Action, 77 Colum. L. Rev. 866 (1977), points out that the ancestor of the class action, the Bill of Peace, was an outgrowth of waning feudalism and typically involved a manor or parish in conflict with its lord or clergyman. Although villagers formed a cohesive "class," the status did not confer power or cement a group of strangers as it does in the modern class action. A few of the tenants or parishioners represented the group. The controversy to be settled was not a conflict over a sum of money that was owed according to settled substantive law. Rather, the parties came before the Chancellor to decide what had been the historical custom of the manor.

For instance, in Brown v. Vermuden, 22 Eng. Rep. 196 (1676), the parishioners of the village of Wem sued their vicar. The Chancellor was to determine whether the custom of the village required them to pay tithes on the coal they mined. Professor Yeazell describes the judgment in this case and others as follows:

> It is not difficult to understand why the chancellor in these cases did not award damages in the first instance. . . . [I]n these cases, he was engaged in a process that to a modern observer looks more like legislation than adjudication. A rule, generally applicable to a group of persons in particular social circumstances, was promulgated for the first time—a rule that, unlike a common law judgment, did not purport to result from simply applying a pre-existing legal standard to particular facts[.] The particularity of the custom, Chancery's power to alter in accordance with a vaguely defined standard of "reasonableness," and the chancellor's willingness to range far from the original issues posed by the parties in seeking a resolution of the dispute distinguished these cases from run-of-the-mill common law adjudication. Moreover, the decree governed future behavior of the parties, not merely in the sense that they could (as with any decided case) guide themselves by reference to its ratio decidendi, but because in its own terms it established the mode of their future conduct to one another; its command was explicit rather than implicit. . . .
>
> Understanding the relief sought and given in the early cases clarifies the apparent abandon with which courts bound absent group members. . . . Once one realizes that the relief sought was a declaration of custom, the problem seems far less urgent. Having one's day in court loses some of its significance if what the court does at the end of that day is simply to declare what shall be the law tomorrow, without retrospectively applying that law to a specific dispute.

Yeazell, supra, 77 Colum. L. Rev. at 890-91.

In a later article, From Group Litigation to Class Action, Part I: The Industrialization of Group Litigation, 27 UCLA L. Rev. 514 (1980), Professor Yeazell traced the mutations that occurred in group litigation as equity gradually bent the old feudal procedure to fit the litigation of industrial society. In place of the manorial or parochial community, there arose artificially created communities—the joint-stock companies and friendly societies (social organizations that served as primitive insurance companies). "Both were voluntary associations replacing an older, traditional, and smaller way of accomplishing the same thing—communal mutual assistance in the case of friendly societies and partnership in the case of joint-stock companies." Id. at 533. Since the beginning of the nineteenth century, "we have moved from a rural, customary, agricultural world to one that is urban, individualistic, entrepreneurial-capitalist. . . ." Id. at 521.

> No longer are the "multitude" who seek litigative recognition a social group. . . . The group is on its way to becoming a class—not a social organism but a number of individuals sharing some interest, here a straightforwardly

economic one. Moreover, the nature of the law applied to the dispute has changed, as has the remedy sought and administered. No longer do the plaintiffs seek a prospective declaration of reciprocal rights and duties that are to govern a continuing relation. Instead one sees the assimilation of group litigation to a more familiar legal model: acts in the past are measured against a previously existing legal standard and parties are amerced money damages for failure to comply. We are in a world recognizably "legal" and recognizably modern: group litigation has become one among many means of applying universally applicable rules of liability; it is no longer the peculiar procedure of a particularistic and moribund substantive law.

Id.

The Supreme Court sanctioned the class suit in America in Smith v. Swormstedt, 57 U.S. 288 (1853). That suit involved the Methodist church in schism over the issue of slavery. The ministers of the southern wing sued those of the northern wing to establish their right to share the proceeds of a pension fund provided by the church for "travelling and worn-out preachers." Although only nine individuals were joined as parties, the Court found that if the "persons brought on the record fairly represent[ed] the interest or right involved," the suit would be binding on the classes of 1,500 and 3,800 members. Id. at 302-03.

Following the merger of law and equity jurisdiction with the adoption of the Federal Rules in 1938, Rule 23 provided for three kinds of class actions: "true, spurious and hybrid," with the designation turning on whether absent parties were bound by the judgment. However, the Rule was little noted or used until 1966, when the present version was enacted in essentially the same form. In Class Action Dilemmas: Pursuing Public Goals for Private Gain (2000) (available at http://www.rand.org/pubs/monograph_reports/ MR969.html), Professor Deborah R. Hensler and her co-authors write about the impulses for changing Rule 23 in the 1960s. She quotes John Frank, an influential member of the Advisory Committee, as saying that "the race relations echo of that decade was always in the committee room." Id. at 12. This account of the modern class action finds its genesis in the need for more legal tools to fight discrimination, especially to make Brown v. Board of Education and the newly passed civil rights statutes practically effective. Others who were also at the inception deny the grand purposes and say the major impulses behind the changes were to simplify the Rule and make it generally more usable. Id. In either case, practice under the amended Rule has been a continuing source of controversy.

One of the classic arguments for Rule 23 is that it enables claims that would otherwise be too small for individuals to mount. Thus, class actions breathe life into rights that would otherwise go unvindicated. See Harry Kalven, Jr. & Maurice Rosenfield, The Contemporary Function of the Class Suit, 8 U. Chi. L. Rev. 684 (1941). Detractors point out that the device in effect may create rights and liabilities that would not otherwise exist — an argument you may recall Justice Ginsburg raised in her dissent in *Shady Grove*. Moreover, the same reasons that make it economically infeasible for the individuals to sue also make it impossible for them to monitor the litigation, supervise the attorney, and make decisions about whether to settle or continue—in short, to be a client. In the last section of our class action study, you will see how practice under Rule 23 arguably has created an alternative procedural universe where the focus of litigation is on the lawyer as entrepreneur. But we will start with the basics of the practice; instead of a problem case, we give you a district court judge walking through each step of the Rule as she decides whether to certify a class in a defective products case. As you read the case, consider what features, if any, are consistent with the historical features of group litigation.

## *In re Zurn Pex Plumbing Prod. Liab. Litig.*
267 F.R.D. 549 (D. Minn. 2010)

ANN D. MONTGOMERY, DISTRICT JUDGE.

### I.  Introduction

. . . Plaintiffs seek class certification of the following claims in the Second Amended Complaint . . . : violations of Minnesota consumer protection statutes (Counts I-IV), negligence (Count V), negligent failure-to-warn (Count VI), breach of implied warranty of merchantability (Count IX), and breach of express warranty (Count XII). For the reasons set forth below, Plaintiffs' Motion is granted in part and denied in part and Defendants' Motions to Exclude are denied.

### II.  Background

Defendant Zurn Pex, Inc. designs, manufactures, and sells plumbing products . . . .

Historically, potable water plumbing systems used copper pipes. In the 1990s, Zurn's predecessor, U.S. Brass Corporation, designed plumbing systems using polybutylene plastic. Complaint, ¶ 52. After a wave of litigation involving failed polybutylene plumbing systems, Zurn designed a cross-linked polyethylene plumbing system, commonly referred to as "pex," as an alternative to polybutylene systems and copper plumbing systems. Id. ¶¶ 57-59. The pex system purported to be easier to install, cheaper, and longer lasting than copper plumbing systems. Id. ¶ 62.

Zurn's pex plumbing system utilizes brass fittings and a crimp connection design. Id. ¶ 65. The brass fittings are secured by the use of a special tool to crimp copper rings around the outside of the pex tubing, creating a seal between the pex tubing and the brass fittings. Id. When the pex plumbing system is properly assembled, the crimp system design places stress on the brass fittings. Id. ¶ 66. Because the brass fittings used in Zurn's pex plumbing system were made from brass with a high zinc content, the fittings were claimed to be susceptible to premature failings due to phenomena such as dezincification and stress-corrosion cracking. Id. ¶¶ 68-69.

Plaintiffs are individuals who own a home with a Zurn pex plumbing system. Plaintiffs allege that defective fittings used in the pex system caused their plumbing systems to leak resulting in damage to their properties. Id. ¶ 27. Plaintiffs allege Zurn falsely represented the pex systems were of high quality, were reliable, and would last decades. Id. ¶¶ 30, 31, 79-90. Plaintiffs state that Zurn failed to adequately test the brass crimp fittings in their anticipated environments before marketing its product. Id. ¶¶ 75-78. Plaintiffs claim Zurn knew or should have known the brass crimp fittings were susceptible to premature failure from dezincification or stress corrosion and, therefore, knew or should have known these systems would fail. Id. ¶¶ 69-70. Plaintiffs assert pex systems are "doomed to leak within warranty" as they experience an unusually high failure rate. Pls'. Mem. in Supp. of Class Cert. at 12.

In July 2007, Denise and Terry Cox filed the first class action lawsuit in Minnesota state court for damages to their home from failed pex plumbing. Defendants removed the case to federal court. Beverly Barnes and Brian Johnston filed a similar lawsuit in the District of North Dakota. Several related lawsuits followed. On August 21, 2008, the Judicial Panel on Multi-District Litigation determined that the pex plumbing cases involved common questions of fact, and that centralization of the cases in Minnesota was appropriate. All Zurn Pex cases were transferred to the District of Minnesota for coordinated or consolidated pretrial proceedings and assigned to the undersigned United States District Judge. Plaintiffs now move the Court to certify this case as a class action.

## III.   Discussion

### A.   Motions to Exclude

Defendants move to exclude portions of the testimony of Plaintiffs' experts, Dr. Wallace Blischke and Dr. Roger Staehle under Federal Rule of Evidence 702 and Daubert v. Merrell Dow Pharmaceuticals, 509 U.S. 579 (1993). Rule 702, which governs the admissibility of expert testimony, provides:

> If scientific, technical, or other specialized knowledge will assist the trier of fact to understand the evidence or to determine a fact in issue, a witness qualified as an expert by knowledge, skill, experience, training, or education, may testify thereto in the form of an opinion or otherwise, if (1) the testimony is based upon sufficient facts or data, (2) the testimony is the product of reliable principles and methods, and (3) the witness has applied the principles and methods reliably to the facts of the case.

When evaluating the admissibility of expert testimony, a trial court serves as the "gatekeeper" to ensure the reliability and relevance of the expert testimony offered into evidence. Kumho Tire Co., Ltd. v. Carmichael, 526 U.S.

137 (1999). A court must exclude expert testimony if it is "so fundamentally unreliable that it can offer no assistance to the jury." Meterlogic, Inc. v. KLT, Inc., 368 F.3d 1017, 1019 (8th Cir. 2004). . . .

. . . The Eighth Circuit does not appear to expressly require district courts to engage in a full *Daubert* inquiry at the class certification stage. See Blades v. Monsanto, 400 F.3d 562, 565 (8th Cir. 2005) ("[W]e believe the district court's findings as to the experts' disputes were properly limited to whether, if [plaintiffs'] basic allegations were true, common evidence would suffice, given the factual setting of the case, to show class-wide injury."). Accordingly, the *Daubert* inquiry is tailored to the purpose for which the expert opinions are offered, e.g., Plaintiffs' claim that the action is capable of resolution on a class-wide basis and that the common defect in Zurn's brass fittings predominates over the class members' individual issues.

### 1.  Dr. Blischke

Defendants do not challenge Dr. Blischke's expert qualifications to analyze warranty claims data. Instead, Defendants argue that Dr. Blischke's calculation of the mean time to failure has no basis in fact and that, because he is not a metallurgist or chemist, Dr. Blischke's calculation should be disregarded.

Dr. Blischke, a statistician, performed an analysis of Zurn's warranty claims data and estimated that millions of Zurn's brass fittings will fail within the twenty-five year warranty period. He concluded that the fittings have a mean time to failure of 40 years, which means approximately half of the units will likely fail within 40 years and approximately half will fail after. . . .

. . . At his deposition, Dr. Blischke conceded that the usual statistical technique for obtaining the mean time to failure is to calculate it. . . . But, Dr. Blischke also testified that where, as here, the data is insufficient to calculate the value, estimating a value is a generally accepted methodology in the field. In addition, the 40 year estimate was based on a number of factors, including Zurn's own flow testing parameters, the testimony of other experts, and general information about the average lifetime of a plumbing system. . . . Dr. Blischke's analysis was circumscribed by the availability of warranty claims data. However, as merits discovery unfolds and more information becomes available, Dr. Blischke's 40 year estimate for the mean time to failure may or may not be admissible. . . . Based on the available information for class certification purposes, Dr. Blischke's expert opinion of a 40 year mean time to failure will not be stricken [now].

Turning to Defendants' argument that Dr. Blischke's opinion should be disregarded because he is not a metallurgist or chemist, and has little to no practical experience in plumbing products, Rule 702 establishes a background in one of the five areas of qualification—"knowledge, skill, experience, training, or education"—can be sufficient to qualify an expert. Dr. Blischke clearly possesses qualifications in some, if not all, of the five identified areas. "Gaps in an expert witness's qualifications or knowledge generally go to the weight of the witness's testimony, not its admissibility." Robinson v. GEICO Gen. Ins. Co., 447 F.3d 1096, 1100 (8th Cir. 2006). . . .

### 2.  Dr. Staehle

Defendants do not challenge Dr. Staehle's qualifications as an expert, but rather argue that he assumed an input factor in his testing that would result in stress corrosion cracking. Dr. Staehle conducted an initial round of testing known as bent beam testing, in which none of the crimped fittings cracked. He then conducted a second round of testing known as the U-bend test of brass specimens from Zurn's fittings. Defendants aver that the reliability of Dr. Staehle's U-bend testing was undermined by his use of an artificially-inflated level of strain. In particular, Defendants contest the correctness of Dr. Staehle's calculation of plastic strain. This is important, Defendants argue, because overstating the strain placed on the fittings due to the crimp yields test results that are unreliable. Accordingly, if the data used is incorrect, the determination regarding stress corrosion cracking necessarily will be flawed as well.

Defendants do not argue that U-bend testing is unreliable. Instead, Defendants argue that the specific number that Dr. Staehle used to estimate strain was wrong. Therefore, Defendants dispute the accuracy of Dr. Staehle's results, not the general scientific validity of his methods. The identification of inaccuracies in generally reliable scientific evidence is precisely the purpose of cross-examination. See generally *Daubert*, 509 U.S. at 596. The results of Dr. Staehle's U-bend testing lend support for Plaintiffs' claim that stress corrosion cracking is an inevitable result of Zurn's brass fittings. The Court has weighed and reviewed the expert opinions offered by both parties in determining whether class certification is warranted. At this stage of the proceedings, the Court declines to strike Dr. Staehle's testimony.

## B.  *Motion for Class Certification*

### 1.  Class Certification Standard

Plaintiffs seek certification of the following class:

> All persons and entities that own a structure located within the State of Minnesota that contains a Zurn Pex plumbing system with brass crimp fittings. The proposed class includes, without limitation, all such persons or entities who contacted Zurn or its representatives about their Zurn Pex plumbing system and were denied or partially denied warranty coverage for failure of the Zurn Pex plumbing system based on a claim that "corrosion" was not covered by the warranty or that other alleged warranty limitations applied. . . .

Rule 23 of the Federal Rules of Civil Procedure governs a district court's consideration of a motion for class certification. The class action serves to conserve the resources of the court and the parties by permitting an issue that may affect every class member to be litigated in an economical fashion. Gen. Tel. Co. of the Southwest v. Falcon, 457 U.S. 147, 155 (1982). The Plaintiff bears the burden of demonstrating that the requirements of Rule 23 are satisfied. Coleman v. Watt, 40 F.3d 255, 259 (8th Cir. 1994). Decisions on whether to certify a class action are entrusted to the discretion of the district court. See id. For class certification to be appropriate, a plaintiff must first establish the four prerequisites of Rule 23(a) of the Federal Rules of Civil Procedure. Class certification is proper when (1) the class is so numerous that joinder of all members is impracticable (numerosity); (2) there are questions of law or fact common to the class (commonality); (3) the claims or defenses of the representative party are typical of the class (typicality); and (4) the representative party will fairly and adequately protect the interests of the class (adequacy). Id. Upon satisfying the four requirements of Rule 23(a), a party seeking class certification must also demonstrate that the action falls within one of the three categories of Fed. R. Civ. P. 23(b). . . . Here, Plaintiffs seek certification pursuant to Rule 23(b)(3), which permits a class action to be maintained if two requirements are met: "Common questions of law or fact must 'predominate over any questions affecting only individual members'; and class resolution must be 'superior to other available methods for fairly and efficiently adjudicating the controversy.'" Amchem Prods., Inc. v. Windsor, 521 U.S. 591, 615 (1997) (quoting Fed.R.Civ.P. 23(b)).

When considering a motion for class certification, the court takes the substantive allegations in the plaintiff's complaint as true, as the issue is resolved, not by an investigation into the merits of the claim, but rather by consideration of the class certification criteria. . . . Nonetheless, a motion for class certification "generally involves considerations that are 'enmeshed in the factual and legal issues comprising the plaintiff's cause of action.'" Coopers & Lybrand v. Livesay, 437 U.S. 463, 469 (1978) (citation omitted). Only after a rigorous analysis of the proposed class and the requirements of Rule 23 may a court grant class certification. See Gen. Tel. Co. of the Southwest v. Falcon, 457 U.S. 147, 161 (1982).

### 2.  Scope of the Class

Before addressing the Rule 23(c) and Rule 23(b) requirements, there are two threshold issues. First, Defendants argue that the proposed class is overly broad because it includes persons who have not suffered or may never suffer any injury. Defendants urge that every class member must have suffered an actual injury to have a presently-existing, justiciable claim against them. Plaintiffs respond that it is not necessary for a person's home to have experienced water damage; the only prerequisite is that the class member own a home with a Zurn pex plumbing system. Because resolution of this dispute varies with respect to the type of claim, the scope of the class is addressed separately with respect to each claim.

Second, Zurn argues the class is unascertainable because it includes individuals who have a Zurn pex system but may not have used Zurn's brass crimp fittings to connect the piping. The Court agrees. However, this overbreadth in the proposed class definition is not fatal to certification. The Court has the authority to redefine a proposed class in such a way as to allow the class action to be maintained. Lamb v. Hamblin, 57 F.R.D. 58, 60-61 (D. Minn. 1972). Accordingly, the Court redefines the proposed class as follows:

> All persons and entities that own a structure located within the State of Minnesota that contains a Zurn Pex plumbing system with Zurn brass crimp fittings. The proposed class includes, without limitation, all such persons or entities who contacted Zurn or its representatives about their Zurn Pex plumbing system and were denied or partially denied warranty coverage for failure of the Zurn Pex plumbing system based on a claim that "corrosion" was not covered by the warranty or that other alleged warranty limitations applied.

### 3.   Rule 23(a) Factors

#### a.   *Numerosity*

The parties do not dispute that the class is so numerous that joinder of all members is impracticable. See Fed. R. Civ. P. 23(a)(1). The number of Zurn brass fittings that are known to have failed exceeds 800. Pls.' Memo. in Supp. of Class Cert. at 24. Plaintiffs project an early estimate of potential class members at 50,000. Id. Given the large number of purported class members, the Court finds joinder to be impracticable, fulfilling the numerosity requirement.

#### b.   *Commonality*

The second requirement is that there be "questions of law and fact common to the class." Fed. R. Civ. P. 23(a)(2). It is not necessary that all questions of law and fact are common to the class, rather the commonality requirement may be met where, for example, "the question of law linking the class members is substantially related to the resolution of the litigation even though the individuals are not identically situated." Paxton v. Union Nat'l Bank, 688 F.2d 552, 561 (8th Cir. 1982) (quotation omitted). In most cases, the commonality requirement is easily satisfied because it "requires only that the course of conduct giving rise to a cause of action affects all class members, and that at least one of the elements of that cause of action is shared by all class members." Egge v. Healthspan Servs. Co., 208 F.R.D. 265, 268 (D. Minn. 2002). . . .

The common legal questions are whether the Zurn pex plumbing system is defective, what Zurn knew about the allegedly defective brass fittings, and whether these facts give rise to claims for negligence, negligent failure to warn, breach of express warranty, and breach of implied warranty. These facts are constant among all class members. The proposed class definition unites plaintiffs with a common factual circumstance, namely, individuals who own property with an allegedly defective Zurn pex plumbing system. Accordingly, the putative class meets the commonality requirement. . . .

### c. *Typicality*

"[A] class representative must be part of the class and possess the same interest and suffer the same injury as the class members." *Gen. Tel. Co. of the Southwest*, 457 U.S. at 156 (citation omitted). "This requirement is generally considered to be satisfied if the claims or defenses of the representatives and the members of the class stem from a single event or are based on the same legal or remedial theory." *Paxton*, 688 F.2d at 561-62. The burden is "fairly easily met so long as other class members have claims similar to the named plaintiff." DeBoer v. Mellon Mortgage Co., 64 F.3d 1171, 1174 (8th Cir. 1995).

Like the proposed class members, the representative Plaintiffs in this action each own property that contains a Zurn pex plumbing system. The claims of the putative class arise from this common fact. Defendants argue that the named Plaintiffs' damages vary and determining damages will be very difficult, requiring consideration of the amount of damage to each Plaintiff and the appropriate reimbursement costs.

While the Court may have to make individualized determinations regarding damages, this alone does not preclude certification. *Midwestern Mach.*, 211 F.R.D. at 571 (D. Minn. 2001); In re Workers' Compensation, 130 F.R.D. 99, 110 (D. Minn. 1990). "Rule 23 explicitly envisions class actions with such individualized damage determinations." Gunnells v. Healthplan Servs., Inc., 348 F.3d 417, 428 (4th Cir. 2003). . . .

Defendants next argument is that the named representatives who allege injury do not, and cannot, represent the interests of proposed class members who have suffered no injury. Thus, Defendants' argument continues, their claims are not typical of the class and they will not adequately represent the class. However, as discussed in greater detail below, the interests of the named representatives are coextensive with that of the class with respect to the breach of warranty claim. The named representatives cannot represent the interests of the proposed class who have suffered no injury as to the negligence and negligent failure-to-warn claims.

### d. *Adequacy*

The focus of the adequacy requirement of Rule 23(a)(4) is whether: (1) the class representatives have common interests with the members of the class, and (2) whether the class representatives will vigorously prosecute the interest of the class through qualified counsel. *Paxton*, 688 F.2d at 562-63 (8th Cir. 1982). Defendants do not dispute that Plaintiffs' counsel are qualified, but argues that the named Plaintiffs are not adequate representatives. Defendants' argument on this issue restates the arguments asserted to oppose a finding of typicality. . . . In addition, there is no evidence that the named representatives would not vigorously litigate this claim on behalf of all class members.

### 4. Rule 23(b)(3) Factors

The final inquiry is whether class certification is appropriate under Rule 23(b)(3). In contrast to actions under Rules 23(b)(1) and (b)(2), Rule 23(b)(3) is designed for cases in which class action treatment is not clearly called for but "may nevertheless be convenient and desirable." *Amchem Prods.*, 521 U.S. at 615. . . .

#### a. Predominance

The question of predominance constitutes the core dispute between the parties. "The Rule 23(b)(3) predominance inquiry tests whether proposed classes are sufficiently cohesive to warrant adjudication by representation." *Amchem Prods.*, 521 U.S. at 623. In examining this requirement, the Court is to "conduct a limited preliminary inquiry, looking behind the pleadings . . . to determine whether, given the factual setting of the case, if the plaintiffs' general allegations are true, common evidence could suffice to make out a prima facie case for the class." Blades v. Monsanto Co., 400 F.3d 562, 566 (8th Cir. 2005) (internal citation omitted). "This necessarily requires an examination of the underlying elements necessary to establish liability for plaintiffs' claims," and the predominance standard is satisfied only if those elements "can be proven on a systematic, class-wide basis." Id. at 569 (citations omitted).

Defendants argue class certification is improper because individual issues abound. Specifically, Defendants contend that differences in water quality and installation techniques are necessarily individualized inquiries. With respect to water quality, Defendants state,

> [F]or each claim, the fact-finder must determine whether the failure was due to corrosive water conditions. That issue will vary from installation to installation. Was a homeowner advised by his well company to use orthophosphates for corrosion inhibitors, but failed to do it? Was a plumber oblivious to knowledge of other failures in the area? Did a plumber disregard specific recommendations not to use brass fittings in particular situations? Did a water softener manufacturer adequately warn of the effects of its product on corrosivity of water? Water quality is at the heart of this case, and the issues it raises cannot be litigated on a class-wide basis.

Defs'. Mot. in Opp. to Class Cert. at 40–41 (footnote omitted). With respect to installation, Defendants state:

> The potential for installation error presents another cause for failure and hence another individualized issue. Plumbers frequently fail to follow the manufacturer's installation instructions. When proper installation techniques are not followed, the failure of the PEX tube or fittings is not the responsibility of the tube and fitting manufacturer. The failure is directly related to the installation, and is the responsibility of the installation contractor.

Id. at 41.

In response, Plaintiffs argue that Defendants' attempt to defeat class certification by asserting predominance of individual water quality issues and installation practices fails because these issues are not factors in Plaintiffs' theory of the case. According to Plaintiffs, the brass crimp fittings used in the pex plumbing system suffer from an inherent design and manufacturing defect and are unsuitable as a plumbing product. Plaintiffs present evidence that because Defendants failed to adequately test the fittings, they are "substantially certain to fail within the 25 year express warranty provided by Zurn and/or the useful life of the fittings." 2d Am. Compl. ¶ 73.

### 1.  Consumer Protection Claims

In the briefing, Plaintiffs characterize their claims under Minnesota's Consumer Fraud, Unlawful Trade Practices, Deceptive Trade Practices, and False Advertising Acts as consumer protection claims, and Plaintiffs address predominance as it relates to those claims in one section. The Second Amended Complaint confirms that the claims are similar in that they sound in fraud and are based on alleged untrue statements of material fact, misrepresentations, material omissions, and other fraudulent and deceptive conduct.

Defendants argue that to prove their claims under Minnesota's consumer protection statutes, Plaintiffs must prove, among other elements, that they received the alleged misrepresentations and relied on them. . . . Defendants support their argument with the Eighth Circuit's conclusion in In re St. Jude Med., Inc., 522 F.3d 836 (8th Cir. 2008) ("*St. Jude II*"). In that case, the court cautioned that "[b]ecause proof often varies among individuals concerning what representations were received, and the degree to which individual persons relied on the representations, fraud cases often are unsuitable for class treatment." Id. at 838. The court in *St. Jude II* found the issues of receipt and reliance on alleged misrepresentations to be particularly problematic to class treatment of fraud-based claims under Minnesota's consumer protection laws. Id.

Plaintiffs counter that *St. Jude II* addressed only affirmative misrepresentations that were made and did not discuss material omissions. In this case, Plaintiffs' claims are based in part on alleged misrepresentations but also on Defendants' uniform failure to disclose to any and all members of the proposed class, facts which were material in the sense that no reasonable buyer would have purchased and installed Zurn's pex plumbing system had the omitted facts been disclosed. Therefore, although individual questions may exist regarding what representations each class member received and each member's reliance on those representations, there are no individual issues regarding the alleged omission of material information, which is an essential aspect of all Plaintiffs' claims.

. . . [However, in] Tuttle v. Lorillard Tobacco Co., the Eighth Circuit required that plaintiffs provide proof of reliance in omissions cases. 377 F.3d 917, 927 (8th Cir. 2004) ("Although Mrs. Tuttle need not present direct evidence of Tuttle's individual reliance, Mrs. Tuttle must establish some proof that the conduct of the smokeless tobacco manufacturers . . . in failing to warn caused consumers to continue using smokeless tobacco and to sustain physical injury in reliance on the defendants' conduct.").

. . . Since proof of reliance will likely vary among class members, and since *St. Jude II* confirms that Defendants are entitled to present individualized defenses to reliance, Plaintiffs have failed to show that the reliance component of their consumer protection claims can be proven by common evidence. Accordingly, class certification as to Plaintiffs' consumer protection claims is denied.

### 2. Warranty Claims

Plaintiffs allege that Defendants breached the implied warranty of merchantability and the express warranty. Plaintiffs assert that common issues of law and fact predominate on the warranty claims.

A claim for breach of warranty requires a plaintiff to show (1) the existence of a warranty, (2) breach of the warranty, and (3) a causal link between the breach and the alleged harm. Peterson v. Bendix Home Systems, 318 N.W.2d 50, 52-53 (Minn. 1982). To recover for breach of the implied warranty of merchantability, a plaintiff must demonstrate that a product is not suitable "for the ordinary purposes for which such goods are used." Minn. Stat. § 336.2-314(2)(c) . . . .

The warranty states in relevant part:

> Subject to the terms and conditions of this Limited Warranty, Zurn PEX Plumbing and Radiant Heating System warrants only to the owner of the real property when installed by licensed professional contractors or authorized distributors who purchase and properly install in a potable plumbing system and/or radiant heating system. . . .
>
> This warranty does not apply and you do not have a right of reimbursement if the failure or resulting damage is caused by . . . (V) exposure to harmful, unauthorized, or unanticipated chemicals or substances or corrosive water conditions; . . . (VIII) damage or wear from abnormal operating conditions, accident, abuse, misuse, or unauthorized alterations or repair. . . .

Because Zurn's warranty specifically excludes failures due to improper installation and corrosive water quality, individual questions of proximate cause may exist as to class members whose Zurn's brass crimp fittings have already failed and who have suffered resulting property damage.

However, . . . Plaintiffs contend that Zurn's "corrosive water conditions" exclusion is vague, unconscionable, and unenforceable. If Plaintiffs prevail on this threshold legal argument, individually litigating the issue of corrosive water for each class member will be unnecessary.

Second, the number of class members who have not yet suffered property damage, but rather seek replacement fittings, is far greater than those who have already suffered damage. As to these individuals, common questions predominate. As this Court recently explained: "for a breach of warranty claim, the breach occurs and thus the claim accrues when tender of delivery of a nonconforming good is made or, if the warranty explicitly extends to future performance, when discovery of the breach is or should have been made." McGregor v. Uponor, Inc., Civil No. 09-1136, 2010 WL 55985, *7 (D. Minn. Jan. 4, 2010). . . .

Individual issues of proximate cause may exist as to the much smaller number of Plaintiffs whose fittings have already leaked and, thus, seek damages to their property, not solely replacement of allegedly nonconforming goods. But again, if Plaintiffs can prove their theory of the case (that Zurn's brass fittings are inherently defective and will fail during its useful life), individual proximate cause determinations will not be relevant for the vast majority of class members who have not suffered property damage and seek only replacement of a nonconforming product. Plaintiffs intend to prove by expert testimony that Zurn's brass fittings are inherently defective and will fail during its useful life irrespective of water conditions or installation problems. Defendants intend to prove that the brass crimp fitting is not inherently defective and does not suffer from a manufacturing defect. Litigating this issue numerous times in different proceedings is neither practicable nor reasonable . . . .

. . . To the extent that different class members have warranties of different durations, a proposition disputed by Plaintiffs, the Court may create subclasses as necessary.

### a.   Scope of the Class

On the breach of warranty claim, Defendants' argument that the scope of the class is overly broad because it includes those who have not suffered any injury is unconvincing. As noted above, for a breach of warranty claim based on the delivery of a nonconforming product, Plaintiffs need only allege and prove that the brass fittings are defective and do not conform to the warranty. They are not required to allege and prove a manifestation of that defect. . . . Accordingly, the Court will certify the breach of express warranty and breach of implied warranty of merchantability class as follows:

> All persons and entities that own a structure located within the State of Minnesota that contains a Zurn Pex plumbing system with Zurn brass crimp fittings. The proposed class includes, without limitation, all such persons or entities who contacted Zurn or its representatives about their Zurn Pex plumbing system and were denied or partially denied warranty coverage for failure of the Zurn Pex plumbing system based on a claim that "corrosion" was not covered by the warranty or that other alleged warranty limitations applied.

### 3.   Negligence Claims

Negligent failure-to-warn claims are premised on a theory of negligence. Westerberg v. Sch. Dist. No. 792, 276 Minn. 1 (1967). In products liability cases, plaintiffs alleging negligent defective design must demonstrate the (1) product was in a defective condition unreasonably dangerous for its intended use, (2) the defect existed when the product left the manufacturer's control, and (3) the defect proximately caused the plaintiff's injuries. . . . In a products liability suit, to state a cause of action for failure to warn, the question of whether a duty to warn of a danger in a product exists is a matter of law. Germann v. F.L. Smithe Mach. Co., 395 N.W.2d 922, 924 (Minn. 1986). Whether a defendant has a duty to warn is dependent on the foreseeability of the injury. *Westerberg*, 148 N.W.2d at 317. . . .

Defendants renew their argument that proximate cause must be proven as to each class member and that individual issues regarding water quality and improper installation exist. . . . A fact question does exist as to whether the failures are due to a single cause or multiple causes. If Plaintiffs can prove that the crimp fittings suffer from a uniform, inherent design and manufacturing defect, and that the defect is the only cause of failure in the majority of the cases, then proximate cause will not involve predominately individual determinations, and resolution of that issue would be common [to] the class. For class certification purposes, the Court is convinced that Plaintiffs have adduced sufficient evidence to support their theory of the case.

Plaintiffs may or may not ultimately prove their negligence claims, but the facts they offer to prove their theory will be largely uniform for all class members. The central liability issues will pivot around what and when Zurn knew about the defects. The resolution of these common issues will resolve a significant portion of the case for all class members. The question of liability does not require the specific individually tailored examinations proposed by Zurn. That there may be some individualized issues does not outweigh the number, significance, and predominance of the common questions raised here. The Court finds that Plaintiffs have met the predominance requirement for their negligence claims.

### a.    Scope of the Class

. . . Defendants argue that the proposed class is overly broad because it includes persons who have not suffered or may never suffer any injury. . . .

. . . To state a negligence claim in Minnesota, Plaintiffs must allege a cognizable injury and a causal connection between that injury and Defendants' conduct. See Briehl v. Gen. Motors Corp., 172 F.3d 623, 627 (8th Cir. 1999) ("[L]iability does not exist in a vacuum; there must be a showing of some damage. . . . It is well established that purchasers of an allegedly defective product have no legally recognizable claim where the alleged defect has not manifested itself in the product they own."). The proposed class members own a Zurn pex plumbing system in which the alleged defect has not yet manifested and, thus, have not suffered an injury to support a legally cognizable negligence claim.

Plaintiffs argue that they "need only establish that future harm or injury to property is reasonably certain to occur." . . . Plaintiffs are correct that a person may recover damages for future harm, but in order to do so, the future harm must result from a present injury that indicates an increased risk of harm that is reasonably certain to occur in the future. See Dunshee

v. Douglas, 255 N.W.2d 42, 47 (Minn. 1977). Alone, however, "the threat of future harm, not yet realized, will not satisfy the damage requirement." Reliance Ins. Co. v. Arneson, 322 N.W.2d 604, 607 (Minn. 1982). Because some of the members of the proposed class have not suffered a present injury, the damages element of these Plaintiffs' negligence claims is not satisfied. Accordingly, the Court will certify the negligence class as follows:

> All persons and entities that own a structure located within the State of Minnesota that contains a Zurn Pex plumbing system with Zurn brass crimp fittings and who have suffered damage to their property caused by a failure in Zurn's brass crimp fittings. The proposed class includes, without limitation, all such persons or entities who contacted Zurn or its representatives about their Zurn Pex plumbing system and were denied or partially denied warranty coverage for failure of the Zurn Pex plumbing system based on a claim that "corrosion" was not covered by the warranty or that other alleged warranty limitations applied.

### b.   Superiority

Federal Rule of Civil Procedure 23(b)(3) also requires a court to find "that a class action is superior to other available methods for the fair and efficient adjudication of the controversy." Rule 23(b)(3) provides that the superiority analysis consider the following factors:

> (A) the interest of members of the class in individually controlling the prosecution or defense of separate actions;
> (B) the extent and nature of any litigation concerning the controversy already commenced by or against members of the class;
> (C) the desirability or undesirability of concentrating the litigation of the claims in the particular forum;
> (D) the difficulties likely to be encountered in the management of a class action.

With respect to the first factor, generally speaking, the members of the class do not appear interested in individually controlling separate actions. Plaintiffs assert that the size of each individual class member's loss is too small to warrant such individualized attention. In addition, Plaintiffs state that since any individual class member's recovery will be relatively modest, requiring each class member to bring an individual lawsuit against Zurn for damages is not economically feasible. As a result, Plaintiffs argue a class action is necessary so that class members can effectively redress their injuries.

Regarding the second factor, the extent of litigation concerning this controversy that has been commenced by or against members of this class is minimal. Only a small number of warranty claims have escalated into litigation, and those claims that are being litigated are brought by subrogated insurance companies rather than individual class members.

As to the third factor, concentrating this litigation will provide a remedy for those class members who might not otherwise seek a remedy due to the inherent difficulties associated with litigation. In addition, having one forum will avoid duplicative results and the potential for inconsistent judgments.

With respect to the fourth factor, the Court has found that common issues predominate over individualized questions, and therefore class-wide methods of proof are appropriate. At this point in the litigation, there is no reason to believe that Plaintiffs' proposed class action will be unmanageable.

## IV.   Conclusion

Based upon the foregoing, and all the files, records, and proceedings herein, it is hereby ordered that: [1. Defendants' Motions to Exclude Expert Testimony of Mr. Blischke and Mr. Staehle is Denied; and 2. Plaintiffs' motion for class certification is Granted in Part and Denied in Part.]

## Notes and Questions

1. *Complex Litigation.* At root, this is a fairly simple tort case. But once plaintiffs try to unite, aggregating their claims, procedural complexity emerges quickly. The court has to deal with expert evidence early on, instead of at the conclusion of discovery; the class definition varies, as does the court's certification analysis, for each cause of action; and the elements for certification under Rule 23(a) and Rule 23(b) seem to overlap and intersect (commonality is related to typicality, which is itself related to adequacy; predominance and superiority also relate to commonality in important ways). Moreover, the case is the product of an attempt to consolidate multiple suits using multi-district litigation coordination procedures; even after certification it may be necessary for the court to create further subclasses; and the entire certification decision seems heavily influenced by the judge's perception of the issue that will decide the merits (whether design defects, installation errors, poor water quality, or some combination of each of these factors cause or may cause the Zurn pex plumbing to fail).

You can anticipate, from the defendant's perspective, the enormous pressure to settle once a class is certified—at that point the possibility of paying damages for thousands or millions of claims at once looms over every subsequent stage in the litigation. And from the time and energy plaintiffs have spent on pre-certification discovery in *In re Zurn* (experts and expert reports do not come cheap), you can see the pressure to succeed in a motion for class certification. As Richard Marcus has put it, "[d]enial of class certification can be the 'death knell' of the case, and a grant supposedly can create such a death threat to the defendant that settlement is her only option." Richard Marcus, Reviving Judicial Gatekeeping of Aggregation: Scrutinizing the Merits, 79 Geo. Wash. L. Rev. 324, 325 (2011). The leverage a class action creates, and the cost of creating that leverage, are a large part of what makes class action litigation controversial.

2. *Consumer-Type Class Actions. In re Zurn* is not a paradigmatic example of a case where the potential gain is too small relative to the costs of litigation to make it worth filing an individual suit. Some kinds of plumbing repairs for residential and commercial real estate are expensive enough to attract attorneys working for contingency fees. The class probably contains a mix of plaintiffs whose claims would be sufficient to attract counsel for individual suits and others whose claims would not (perhaps especially those whose plumbing has not yet malfunctioned). Though admirers of the class action device think it is most suitable for aggregating small injuries that would otherwise go unremedied, there is not universal agreement even on this apparent purpose for Rule 23.

In a classic article, Professor Jonathan Landers attacked the use of class actions as a means of vindicating small claims:

> To consumerists, the consumer class action is an inviting procedural device to cope with frauds causing small damages to large groups. The slight loss to the individual, when aggregated in the coffers of the wrongdoers, results in gains which are both handsome and tempting. The alternatives to the class action—private suits or governmental actions—have been so often found wanting in controlling consumer frauds that not even the ardent critics of class actions seriously contend that they are truly effective. The consumer class action, when brought by those who have no other avenue of legal redress, provides restitution to the injured, and deterrence of the wrongdoer. Since both of these objectives are, at least partially, goals of the legal system itself, the class action device cannot be all bad.
>
> There is, however, another side of the coin. One can perceive the legal system as set up from a functional point of view to deter the bringing of small claims. Just as consumers have no effective redress within the legal system for small injuries in the absence of the class action device, business concerns are similarly afflicted. The business confronted with unpaid accounts or minor damage claims of a few dollars or even a few hundred dollars is no more able to sue than is the consumer. Many businesses regularly "write off" such small claims, and others turn such claims over to collection agencies which may retain 50 percent of an account in fees. Even those states which have small claims courts frequently prevent business use of the courts either by absolute prohibition, or by such methods as limiting the maximum number of suits which can be filed within a year. Hence, one might argue that in an increasingly complex, impersonal, and interdependent society, there will be an ever increasing number of small grievances and minor disputes, and that such matters are better handled by allowing the loss to lie where it falls than by trying to reallocate the loss though the legal system. In the case of widespread or recurrent situations, a combination of governmental action, criminal penalties, and remedial legislation could be employed.
>
> The consumer class action, as already noted, is seen as the savior for remedying instances of small injuries to large numbers of persons, and it has unquestionably been used in this role numerous times under Rule 23. It is not very clear, however, that the rule was ever intended to serve such a purpose. The Advisory Committee has stated that subsection 23(b)(3) "encompasses those cases in which a class action would achieve economies of time,

effort, and expense, and promote uniformity of decision as to persons similarly situated." Such a statement, standing alone, tends to suggest that the draftsmen conceived of the rule as an advanced joinder device to include in a single action all persons of a definable group in a situation where absent the class action at least a portion of the group both could and would sue as individuals. . . . Significantly, this literal reading of the Committee's class action comments would support the preclusion of class actions for large groups suing for small amounts. The dominant characteristic of such suits is that they do not involve combinations of persons who would sue anyway, but rather are actions on behalf of persons who, absent the class remedy, would not sue at all. In effect, then, the class action has not simply made an old remedy more efficient; in a realistic sense it has created a new remedy where none existed.

Jonathan M. Landers, Of Legalized Blackmail and Legalized Theft: Consumer Class Actions and the Substance-Procedure Dilemma, 47 S. Cal. L. Rev. 842, 845-847 (1974).

3. *Adequacy of Representation.* Perhaps the most crucial requirement under Rule 23 is that the class representative be "adequate." A class action permits a representative to litigate on behalf of people who are not parties in the usual sense anticipated by the adversary model. The rights of all class members who are properly represented nevertheless are resolved by the lawsuit, without their *own* day in court. Moreover, the rules do not allow represented parties to opt out of the class action in every instance. See Note 4 infra. Finally, the notice of the suit may not be actually received by all class members, to the extent that their whereabouts may be unknown or they may not receive or comprehend the notice given. Do you see the potential due process concerns? The authors of Note, Developments in the Law—Class Action, 89 Harv. L. Rev. 1318 (1976), argue that, by bringing the large number of interested parties in a controversy before the court all at once, there is the important substantive influence of forcing the court to see the situation in its entirety, rather than simply adjudicating between two of the many possible litigants. This aspect the authors call "the heuristic function" of class action. Is that benefit enough to outweigh the costs to individual rights of meaningful participation protected by the Due Process Clause?

Does a class action satisfy the individual's interest in autonomy and participation as fully as does a single-plaintiff or single-defendant lawsuit? Are deterrence, compensation, and distributional justice ends met adequately by the class action device? See Levell v. Monsanto Research Corp., 191 F.R.D. 543 (S.D. Ohio 2000) (rejecting proposed settlement agreement for favoring interests of current employees over past employees and retirees); Clement v. Am. Honda Fin. Corp., 176 F.R.D. 15 (D. Conn. 1997) (rejecting proposed settlement on ground that it shortchanged class members in favor of defendant car leasing company and the attorneys who negotiated the settlement); In re Telectronics Pacing Sys., Inc., 172 F.R.D. 271 (S.D. Ohio 1997) (re-certifying where class was divided into subclasses to take account of different applicable state laws).

For a discussion of the problem of intra-group political dissension and its implications for competing procedural and ethical models of class action representations, see William B. Rubenstein, Divided We Litigate: Addressing Disputes Among Group Members and Lawyers in Civil Rights Campaigns, 106 Yale L.J. 1623 (1997). Cf. Marcel Kahan & Linda Silberman, The Inadequate Search for "Adequacy" in Class Actions: A Critique of Epstein v. MCA, Inc., 73 N.Y.U. L. Rev. 765 (1998) (arguing that offering absent class members a broad right to collaterally attack the adequacy of representation is potentially wasteful and may invite forum shopping). See also Richard L. Marcus, Reexamining the Bendectin Litigation Story, 83 Iowa L. Rev. 231, 239 (1977) (reviewing Michael D. Green, Bendectin and Birth Defects: The Challenges of Mass Toxic Substances Litigation (1996), and noting that "critics of settlement classes can find considerable evidence for their fears in the Bendectin litigation story").

4. *Opting Out: Constitutionally Required?* Look carefully at Rule 23 to determine when a class member can "opt out" of a class action. How can this be squared with due process? Does it all depend on the adequacy of representation?

The issue continues to divide courts and commentators. In Ticor Title Ins. Co. v. Brown, 511 U.S. 117 (1994), the Court dismissed as "improvidently granted" a writ of certiorari granted to review a decision that due process bars giving preclusive effect to a judgment in a class action suit involving money damages against a plaintiff who had not been given an opportunity to opt out. The Court's refusal to hear the case leaves unresolved whether the non-opt-out provisions of Rules 23(b)(1) and 23(b)(2) are constitutional, though trial courts have discretion to require notice in these cases. See Rule 23(c)(2)(A). See also Steve Baughman, Note, Class Actions in the Asbestos Context: Balancing the Due Process Considerations Implicated by the Right to Opt Out, 70 Tex. L. Rev. 211 (1991). *In re Zurn* is a Rule 23(b)(3) suit as to which notice and the right to opt out are mandatory. See Rule 23(c)(2). Would you want to opt out if you were a class member in *In re Zurn*?

5. *Ascertainability.* Rule 23 sets out very specific requirements for certification. Although it is not written into the language of Rule 23, some courts have held that a 23(b)(3) class must be "ascertainable" at the moment of certification. This judicially created rule operates in concert with the requirement of Rule 23(c)(1)(B) that the definition of the class be sufficiently "clear" and "precise," and with the notice and opt out requirements of 23(b)(3) suits. Wachtel ex rel. Jesse v. Guardian Life Ins. Co. of Am., 453 F.3d 179, 187 (3d Cir. 2006). As the Third Circuit has put it, the "ascertainability" rule "requires something more than a class capable of clear definition by a court; it requires that the class's members be identifiable." Shelton v. Bledsoe, 775 F.3d 554, 560 (3d Cir. 2015) ("'If class members are impossible to identify without extensive and individualized fact-finding or 'mini-trials,' then a class action is inappropriate.'") (quoting Marcus v. BMW of N. Am., LLC, 687 F.3d 583, 593 (3d Cir. 2012)). But see Mullins v. Direct Digital, LLC, 795 F.3d 654, 658 (7th Cir. 2015) (rejecting heightened ascertainability

requirement in 23(b)(3) consumer class action on ground that it has "the effect of barring class actions where class treatment is often most needed: in cases involving relatively low-cost goods or services, where consumers are unlikely to have documentary proof of purchase").

The Supreme Court has not taken up the question explicitly. Moreover, the 1966 Advisory Committee Note to Rule 23 states that prototypical 23(b)(2) actions arise "in the civil rights field where a party is charged with discriminating unlawfully against a class, *usually one whose members are incapable of specific enumeration*" (emphasis added). Following this guidance, circuit courts have refused defendants' requests to assess 23(b)(2) actions for ascertainability. Most recently, the Third Circuit joined the First, Tenth, and Fifth Circuits in rejecting an ascertainability requirement for 23(b)(2) actions. See *Shelton*, 755 F.3d at 561-62 (citing and discussing cases from other circuits while analyzing a case challenging housing practices at a federal penitentiary that allegedly promoted inmate-on-inmate violence).

6. *Predominance of Class Questions and the Choice Between (b)(2) and (b)(3).* The requirement that common questions of law or fact should not merely exist, but predominate, has proved nettlesome in (b)(3) cases. It has been especially troublesome in cases that attempt to apply to large classes substantive law drafted with individual claims in mind. In particular, securities and antitrust class actions have absorbed much judicial energy as courts decide whether the elements of these causes of action can be applied to thousands of litigants in one suit without that suit splintering hopelessly into individual trials. Some courts have developed the bifurcated trial, in which elements of the action deemed sufficiently common are heard in one trial and other elements receive individual trial, e.g., Green v. Wolf, 406 F.2d 291, 301 (2d Cir. 1968), *cert. denied*, 395 U.S. 977 (1968). Other courts have simply dismissed the suit as unmanageable as a class action, e.g., Windham v. Am. Brands, Inc., 565 F.2d 59 (4th Cir. 1977). Still other courts have subtly modified the substantive law to accommodate mass claims, loosening or even omitting elements of the action that otherwise would have to be proven for each class member.

But as fact situations become more complex, it becomes impossible to prove the fact of injury for the whole class without separate trials. For instance, in Windham v. American Brands, Inc., 565 F.2d 59 (4th Cir. 1977), the plaintiff class alleged a price-fixing conspiracy in the sale of tobacco. The tobacco was classified into 161 grades, and price varied according to the grade and market at which the tobacco was sold. In order to prove the fact of injury, the plaintiffs would have had to show that the conspiracy affected the price of each grade and at each warehouse where class members bought tobacco. The plaintiffs urged the court to accept generalized proof of injury, but the court refused, finding the proposal an invitation to alter the substantive rights of the parties, in contravention of the command of the Rules Enabling Act. If the existence and extent of the injury could not be proven with any accuracy, the court would not award damages; the class certification was reversed. Accord Alabama v. Blue Bird Body Co., 573 F.2d 309 (5th Cir. 1978).

In contrast, other courts that are less concerned with precision have allowed injury to be inferred from the existence of a conspiracy and the purchase of the product in question. The Second Circuit in In re Master Key Antitrust Litigation, 70 F.R.D. 23, 26 n.3 (D. Conn. 1975), *appeal dismissed*, 528 F.2d 5 (2d Cir. 1975), stated: "If the plaintiffs introduce proof . . . that they bought master key systems and that the defendants engaged in a pervasive nationwide course of action that had the effect of stabilizing prices at supra-competitive levels, the jury may conclude that the defendants' conduct caused injury to each plaintiff." Other courts have gone even further to *presume* injury in such a situation, rather than merely allowing an inference of injury. E.g., In re Folding Carton Antitrust Litig., 75 F.R.D. 727, 734 (N.D. Ill. 1977). Thus, the burden of proof on one element of the claim has been shifted from plaintiff to defendant to accommodate the class action procedure.

Most recently, the Supreme Court has emphasized the importance of precision with respect to the "particular antitrust injury on which . . . liability . . . is premised." Comcast Corp. v. Behrend, 133 S. Ct. 1426, 1433 (2013) (rejecting regression model developed by plaintiffs' expert for measurement of damages across class; holding that individual issues predominate).

Predominance concerns arise in other contexts as well, perhaps none more controversial than class action suits alleging discrimination under Title VII. The costs of providing notice in Rule 23(b)(3) class actions, and the problem of proving that common questions of law or fact "predominate," create a strong incentive for discrimination plaintiffs to frame their suit under Rule 23(b)(1) or 23(b)(2) while still seeking to recover some form of monetary relief. Discrimination is precisely the sort of group-based conduct the Advisory Committee had in mind when it amended Rule 23(b)(2) in 1966. But plaintiffs often run into another "predominance" hurdle. What inference should be drawn from the fact that the Advisory Committee Notes say Rule 23(b)(2) is not intended to cover situations where the requested relief "relates exclusively or *predominantly* to money damages" (emphasis added)? For recent scholarship on these and other problems, see Richard A. Nagareda, Class Certification in the Age of Aggregate Proof, 84 N.Y.U. L. Rev. 97 (2009); Richard A. Nagareda, Embedded Aggregation in Civil Litigation, 95 Cornell L. Rev. 1105 (2010).

In the following case, the Supreme Court addressed both the commonality requirement and the limits on (b)(2) actions in a sex discrimination case.

## *Wal-Mart Stores, Inc. v. Dukes*
564 U.S. 338 (2011)

JUSTICE SCALIA delivered the opinion of the Court, in which THE CHIEF JUSTICE, JUSTICE KENNEDY, JUSTICE THOMAS, and JUSTICE ALITO joined, and, with respect to Parts I and III, in which JUSTICE GINSBURG, JUSTICE BREYER, JUSTICE SOTOMAYOR, and JUSTICE KAGAN joined.

We are presented with one of the most expansive class actions ever. The District Court and the Court of Appeals approved the certification of a class comprising about one and a half million plaintiffs, current and former female employees of petitioner Wal-Mart who allege that the discretion exercised by their local supervisors over pay and promotion matters violates Title VII by discriminating against women. In addition to injunctive and declaratory relief, the plaintiffs seek an award of backpay. We consider whether the certification of the plaintiff class was consistent with Federal Rules of Civil Procedure 23(a) and (b)(2).

## I

### A

Petitioner Wal-Mart is the Nation's largest private employer. It operates four types of retail stores throughout the country: Discount Stores, Supercenters, Neighborhood Markets, and Sam's Clubs. Those stores are divided into seven nationwide divisions, which in turn comprise 41 regions of 80 to 85 stores apiece. Each store has between 40 and 53 separate departments and 80 to 500 staff positions. In all, Wal-Mart operates approximately 3,400 stores and employs more than one million people.

Pay and promotion decisions at Wal-Mart are generally committed to local managers' broad discretion, which is exercised "in a largely subjective manner." 222 F.R.D. 137, 145 (N.D. Cal. 2004). Local store managers may increase the wages of hourly employees (within limits) with only limited corporate oversight. As for salaried employees, such as store managers and their deputies, higher corporate authorities have discretion to set their pay within pre-established ranges.

Promotions work in a similar fashion. Wal-Mart permits store managers to apply their own subjective criteria when selecting candidates as "support managers," which is the first step on the path to management. Admission to Wal-Mart's management training program, however, does require that a candidate meet certain objective criteria, including an above-average performance rating, at least one year's tenure in the applicant's current position, and a willingness to relocate. But except for those requirements, regional and district managers have discretion to use their own judgment when selecting candidates for management training. Promotion to higher office—*e.g.*, assistant manager, co-manager, or store manager—is similarly at the discretion of the employee's superiors after prescribed objective factors are satisfied.

### B

The named plaintiffs in this lawsuit, representing the 1.5 million members of the certified class, are three current or former Wal-Mart employees who allege that the company discriminated against them on the basis of their sex by denying them equal pay or promotions, in violation of Title VII of the Civil Rights Act of 1964, 42 U.S.C. § 2000e-1 *et seq.*

. . . [P]laintiffs, respondents here, do not allege that Wal-Mart has any express corporate policy against the advancement of women. Rather, they claim that their local managers' discretion over pay and promotions is exercised disproportionately in favor of men, leading to an unlawful disparate impact on female employees, see 42 U.S.C. § 2000e-2(k). And, respondents say, because Wal-Mart is aware of this effect, its refusal to cabin its managers' authority amounts to disparate treatment, see § 2000e-2(a). Their complaint seeks injunctive and declaratory relief, punitive damages, and backpay. It does not ask for compensatory damages.

Importantly for our purposes, respondents claim that the discrimination to which they have been subjected is common to *all* Wal-Mart's female employees. The basic theory of their case is that a strong and uniform "corporate culture" permits bias against women to infect, perhaps subconsciously, the discretionary decisionmaking of each one of Wal-Mart's thousands of managers—thereby making every woman at the company the victim of one common discriminatory practice. Respondents therefore wish to litigate the Title VII claims of all female employees at Wal-Mart's stores in a nationwide class action.

### C

. . . [R]espondents moved the District Court to certify a plaintiff class consisting of "'[a]ll women employed at any Wal-Mart domestic retail store at any time since December 26, 1998, who have been or may be subjected to Wal-Mart's challenged pay and management track promotions policies and practices.'" As evidence that there were indeed "questions of law or fact common to" all the women of Wal-Mart, as Rule 23(a)(2) requires, respondents relied chiefly on three forms of proof: statistical evidence about pay and promotion disparities between men and women at the company, anecdotal reports of discrimination from about 120 of Wal-Mart's female employees, and the testimony of a sociologist, Dr. William Bielby, who conducted a "social framework analysis" of Wal-Mart's "culture" and personnel practices, and concluded that the company was "vulnerable" to gender discrimination. 603 F.3d 571, 601 (9th Cir. 2010) (en banc).

Wal-Mart unsuccessfully moved to strike much of this evidence. It also offered its own countervailing statistical and other proof in an effort to defeat Rule 23(a)'s requirements of commonality, typicality, and adequate representation. Wal-Mart further contended that respondents' monetary claims for backpay could not be certified under Rule 23(b)(2), first because that Rule refers only to injunctive and declaratory relief, and second because the backpay claims could not be manageably tried as a class without depriving Wal-Mart of its right to present certain statutory defenses. With one limitation not relevant here, the District Court granted respondents' motion and certified their proposed class.

## D

A divided en banc Court of Appeals substantially affirmed the District Court's certification order. 603 F.3d 571. . . . With respect to the Rule 23(b)(2) question, the Ninth Circuit held that respondents' backpay claims could be certified as part of a (b)(2) class because they did not "predominat[e]" over the requests for declaratory and injunctive relief, meaning they were not "superior in strength, influence, or authority" to the nonmonetary claims. Id., at 616.

Finally, the Court of Appeals determined that the action could be manageably tried as a class action because the District Court could adopt the approach the Ninth Circuit approved in Hilao v. Estate of Marcos, 103 F.3d 767, 782-787 (1996). There compensatory damages for some 9,541 class members were calculated by selecting 137 claims at random, referring those claims to a special master for valuation, and then extrapolating the validity and value of the untested claims from the sample set. See 603 F.3d, at 625-26. The Court of Appeals "s[aw] no reason why a similar procedure to that used in *Hilao* could not be employed in this case." Id., at 627. It would allow Wal-Mart "to present individual defenses in the randomly selected 'sample cases,' thus revealing the approximate percentage of class members whose unequal pay or nonpromotion was due to something other than gender discrimination." Id., at n. 56.

We granted certiorari. . . .

## II

The class action is "an exception to the usual rule that litigation is conducted by and on behalf of the individual named parties only." Califano v. Yamasaki, 442 U.S. 682, 700-701 (1979). In order to justify a departure from that rule, "a class representative must be part of the class and 'possess the same interest and suffer the same injury' as the class members." East Tex. Motor Freight System, Inc. v. Rodriguez, 431 U.S. 395, 403 (1977). . . .

## A

The crux of this case is commonality—the rule requiring a plaintiff to show that "there are questions of law or fact common to the class." Rule 23(a)(2). That language is easy to misread, since "[a]ny competently crafted class complaint literally raises common 'questions.'" Nagareda, Class Certification in the Age of Aggregate Proof, 84 N.Y.U. L. Rev. 97, 131-32 (2009). For example: Do all of us plaintiffs indeed work for Wal-Mart? Do our managers have discretion over pay? Is that an unlawful employment practice? What remedies should we get? Reciting these questions is not sufficient to obtain class certification. Commonality requires the plaintiff to demonstrate that the class members "have suffered the same injury," [General Telephone Co. of Southwest v. Falcon, 457 U.S. 147, 157 (1982)]. This does not mean merely that they have all suffered a violation of the same provision of law. Title VII, for example, can be violated in many ways—by intentional discrimination, or by hiring and promotion criteria that result in disparate impact, and by the use of these practices on the part of many different superiors in a single company. Quite obviously, the mere claim by employees of the same company that they have suffered a Title VII injury, or even a disparate-impact Title VII injury, gives no cause to believe that all their claims can productively be litigated at once. Their claims must depend upon a common contention—for example, the assertion of discriminatory bias on the part of the same supervisor. That common contention, moreover, must be of such a nature that it is capable of classwide resolution—which means that determination of its truth or falsity will resolve an issue that is central to the validity of each one of the claims in one stroke. "What matters to class certification . . . is not the raising of common 'questions'—even in droves—but, rather the capacity of a classwide proceeding to generate common *answers* apt to drive the resolution of the litigation. Dissimilarities within the proposed class are what have the potential to impede the generation of common answers." Nagareda, supra, at 132.

Rule 23 does not set forth a mere pleading standard. A party seeking class certification must affirmatively demonstrate his compliance with the Rule—that is, he must be prepared to prove that there are *in fact* sufficiently numerous parties, common questions of law or fact, etc. We recognized in *Falcon* that "sometimes it may be necessary for the court to probe behind the pleadings before coming to rest on the certification question," 457 U.S., at 160, and that certification is proper only if "the trial court is satisfied, after a rigorous analysis, that the prerequisites of Rule 23(a) have been satisfied," id., at 161; see id., at 160 ("[A]ctual, not presumed, conformance with Rule 23(a) remains . . . indispensable"). Frequently that "rigorous analysis" will entail some overlap with the merits of the plaintiff's underlying claim. That cannot be helped. . . .

In this case, proof of commonality necessarily overlaps with respondents' merits contention that Wal-Mart engages in a *pattern or practice* of discrimination. That is so because, in resolving an individual's Title VII claim, the crux of the inquiry is "the reason for a particular employment decision," Cooper v. Federal Reserve Bank of Richmond, 467 U.S. 867, 876 (1984). Here respondents wish to sue about literally millions of employment decisions at once. Without some glue holding the alleged *reasons* for all those decisions together, it will be impossible to say that examination of all the class members' claims for relief will produce a common answer to the crucial question *why was I disfavored*.

## B

This Court's opinion in *Falcon* describes how the commonality issue must be approached. There an employee who claimed that he was deliberately denied a promotion on account of race obtained certification of a class comprising all employees wrongfully denied promotions and all applicants wrongfully denied jobs. 457 U.S., at 152. We rejected that composite class for lack of commonality and typicality, explaining:

> "Conceptually, there is a wide gap between (a) an individual's claim that he has been denied a promotion [or higher pay] on discriminatory grounds, and his otherwise unsupported allegation that the company has a policy of discrimination, and (b) the existence of a class of persons who have suffered the same injury as that individual, such that the individual's claim and the class claim will share common questions of law or fact and that the individual's claim will be typical of the class claims." Id., at 157-158.

*Falcon* suggested two ways in which that conceptual gap might be bridged. First, if the employer "used a biased testing procedure to evaluate both applicants for employment and incumbent employees, a class action on behalf of every applicant or employee who might have been prejudiced by the test clearly would satisfy the commonality and typicality requirements of Rule 23(a)." Id., at 159, n. 15. Second, "[s]ignificant proof that an employer operated under a general policy of discrimination conceivably could justify a class of both applicants and employees if the discrimination manifested itself in hiring and promotion practices in the same general fashion, such as through entirely subjective decisionmaking processes." Id. We think that statement precisely describes respondents' burden in this case. The first manner of bridging the gap obviously has no application here; Wal-Mart has no testing procedure or other companywide evaluation method that can be charged with bias. The whole point of permitting discretionary decisionmaking is to avoid evaluating employees under a common standard.

The second manner of bridging the gap requires "significant proof" that Wal-Mart "operated under a general policy of discrimination." That is entirely absent here. Wal-Mart's announced policy forbids sex discrimination,. . . and as the District Court recognized the company imposes penalties for denials of equal employment opportunity, 222 F.R.D., at 154. The only evidence of a "general policy of discrimination" respondents produced was the testimony of Dr. William Bielby, their sociological expert. Relying on "social framework" analysis, Bielby testified that Wal-Mart has a "strong corporate culture," that makes it "'vulnerable'" to "gender bias." Id., at 152. He could not, however, "determine with any specificity how regularly stereotypes play a meaningful role in employment decisions at Wal-Mart. At his deposition . . . Dr. Bielby conceded that he could not calculate whether 0.5 percent or 95 percent of the employment decisions at Wal-Mart might be determined by stereotyped thinking." 222 F.R.D. 189, 192 (N.D. Cal. 2004). The parties dispute whether Bielby's testimony even met the standards for the admission of expert testimony under Federal Rule of Evidence 702 and our *Daubert* case, see Daubert v. Merrell Dow Pharmaceuticals, Inc., 509 U.S. 579 (1993). The District Court concluded that *Daubert* did not apply to expert testimony at the certification stage of class-action proceedings. 222 F.R.D., at 191. We doubt that is so, but even if properly considered, Bielby's testimony does nothing to advance respondents' case. "[W]hether 0.5 percent or 95 percent of the employment decisions at Wal-Mart might be determined by stereotyped thinking" is the essential question on which respondents' theory of commonality depends. If Bielby admittedly has no answer to that question, we can safely disregard what he has to say. It is worlds away from "significant proof" that Wal-Mart "operated under a general policy of discrimination."

## C

The only corporate policy that the plaintiffs' evidence convincingly establishes is Wal-Mart's "policy" of *allowing discretion* by local supervisors over employment matters. On its face, of course, that is just the opposite of a uniform employment practice that would provide the commonality needed for a class action; it is a policy *against having* uniform employment practices. It is also a very common and presumptively reasonable way of doing business—one that we have said "should itself raise no inference of discriminatory conduct." Watson v. Fort Worth Bank & Trust, 487 U.S. 977, 990 (1988).

To be sure, we have recognized that, "in appropriate cases," giving discretion to lower-level supervisors can be the basis of Title VII liability under a disparate-impact theory—since "an employer's undisciplined system of subjective decisionmaking [can have] precisely the same effects as a system pervaded by impermissible intentional discrimination." Id., at 990-91. But the recognition that this type of Title VII claim "can" exist does not lead to the conclusion that every employee in a company using a system of discretion has such a claim in common. To the contrary, left to their own devices most managers in any corporation—and surely most managers in a corporation that forbids sex discrimination—would select sex-neutral, performance-based criteria for hiring and promotion that produce no actionable disparity at all. Others may choose to reward various attributes that produce disparate impact—such as scores on general aptitude tests or educational achievements, see Griggs v. Duke Power Co., 401 U.S. 424, 431-32 (1971). And still other managers may be guilty of intentional discrimination that produces a sex-based disparity. In such a company, demonstrating the invalidity of one manager's use of discretion will do nothing to demonstrate the invalidity of another's. A party seeking to certify a nationwide class will be unable to show that all the employees' Title VII claims will in fact depend on the answers to common questions.

Respondents have not identified a common mode of exercising discretion that pervades the entire company—aside from their reliance on Dr. Bielby's social frameworks analysis that we have rejected. In a company of Wal-Mart's size and geographical scope, it is quite unbelievable that all managers would exercise their discretion in a common way without some common direction. Respondents attempt to make that showing by means of statistical and anecdotal evidence, but their evidence falls well short.

The statistical evidence consists primarily of regression analyses performed by Dr. Richard Drogin, a statistician, and Dr. Marc Bendick, a labor economist. Drogin conducted his analysis region-by-region, comparing the number of women promoted into management positions with the percentage of women in the available pool of hourly workers. After considering regional and national data, Drogin concluded that "there are statistically significant disparities between men and women at Wal-Mart . . . [and] these disparities . . . can be explained only by gender discrimination." 603 F.3d, at 604 (internal quotation marks omitted). Bendick compared work-force data from Wal-Mart and competitive retailers and concluded that Wal-Mart "promotes a lower percentage of women than its competitors." Id.

Even if they are taken at face value, these studies are insufficient to establish that respondents' theory can be proved on a classwide basis. In *Falcon*, we held that one named plaintiff's experience of discrimination was insufficient to infer that "discriminatory treatment is typical of [the employer's employment] practices." 457 U.S., at 158. A similar failure of inference arises here. As Judge Ikuta observed in her dissent, "[i]nformation about disparities at the regional and national level does not establish the existence of disparities at individual stores, let alone raise the inference that a company-wide policy of discrimination is implemented by discretionary decisions at the store and district level." 603 F.3d, at 637. A regional pay disparity, for example, may be attributable to only a small set of Wal-Mart stores, and cannot by itself establish the uniform, store-by-store disparity upon which the plaintiffs' theory of commonality depends.

There is another, more fundamental, respect in which respondents' statistical proof fails. Even if it established (as it does not) a pay or promotion pattern that differs from the nationwide figures or the regional figures in *all* of Wal-Mart's 3,400 stores, that would still not demonstrate that commonality of issue exists. Some managers will claim that the availability of women, or qualified women, or interested women, in their stores' area does not mirror the national or regional statistics. And almost all of them will claim to have been applying some sex-neutral, performance-based criteria—whose nature and effects will differ from store to store. In the landmark case of ours which held that giving discretion to lower-level supervisors can be the basis of Title VII liability under a disparate-impact theory, the plurality opinion *conditioned* that holding on the corollary that merely proving that the discretionary system has produced a racial or sexual disparity *is not enough.* "[T]he plaintiff must begin by identifying the specific employment practice that is challenged." *Watson*, 487 U.S., at 994. . . . That is all the more necessary when a class of plaintiffs is sought to be certified. Other than the bare existence of delegated discretion, respondents have identified no "specific employment practice"—much less one that ties all their 1.5 million claims together. Merely showing that Wal-Mart's policy of discretion has produced an overall sex-based disparity does not suffice.

Respondents' anecdotal evidence suffers from the same defects, and in addition is too weak to raise any inference that all the individual, discretionary personnel decisions are discriminatory. In Teamsters v. United States, 431 U.S. 324 (1977), in addition to substantial statistical evidence of company-wide discrimination, the Government (as plaintiff) produced about 40 specific accounts of racial discrimination from particular individuals. See id., at 338. That number was significant because the company involved had only 6,472 employees, of whom 571 were minorities, id., at 337, and the class itself consisted of around 334 persons, United States v. T.I.M.E.-D.C., Inc., 517 F.2d 299, 308 (5th Cir. 1975), overruled on other grounds, *Teamsters*, supra. The 40 anecdotes thus represented roughly one account for every eight members of the class. Moreover, the Court of Appeals noted that the anecdotes came from individuals "spread throughout" the company who "for the most part" worked at the company's operational centers that employed the largest numbers of the class members. 517 F.2d, at 315, and n.30. Here, by contrast, respondents filed some 120 affidavits reporting experiences of discrimination—about 1 for every 12,500 class members—relating to only some 235 out of Wal-Mart's 3,400 stores. 603 F.3d, at 634 (Ikuta, J., dissenting). More than half of these reports are concentrated in only six States (Alabama, California, Florida, Missouri, Texas, and Wisconsin); half of all States have only one or two anecdotes; and 14 States have no anecdotes about Wal-Mart's operations at all. . . . Even if every single one of these accounts is true, that would not demonstrate that the entire company "operate[s] under a general policy of discrimination," *Falcon*, supra, at 159, n.15, which is what respondents must show to certify a companywide class. . . .

In sum, we agree with Chief Judge Kozinski that the members of the class: "held a multitude of different jobs, at different levels of Wal-Mart's hierarchy, for variable lengths of time, in 3,400 stores, sprinkled across 50 states, with a kaleidoscope of supervisors (male and female), subject to a variety of regional policies that all differed. . . . Some thrived while others did poorly. They have little in common but their sex and this lawsuit." 603 F.3d, at 652 (dissenting opinion).

## III

We also conclude that respondents' claims for backpay were improperly certified under Federal Rule of Civil Procedure 23(b)(2). Our opinion in Ticor Title Ins. Co. v. Brown, 511 U.S. 117, 121 (1994) (*per curiam*) expressed serious doubt about whether claims for monetary relief may be certified under that provision. We now hold that they may not, at least where (as here) the monetary relief is not incidental to the injunctive or declaratory relief.

## A

Rule 23(b)(2) allows class treatment when "the party opposing the class has acted or refused to act on grounds that apply generally to the class, so that final injunctive relief or corresponding declaratory relief is appropriate respecting the class as a whole." One possible reading of this provision is that it applies *only* to requests for such injunctive or declaratory relief and does not authorize the class certification of monetary claims at all. We need not reach that broader question in this case, because we think that, at a minimum, claims for *individualized* relief (like the backpay at issue here) do not satisfy the Rule. The key to the (b)(2) class is "the indivisible nature of the injunctive or declaratory remedy warranted—the notion that the conduct is such that it can be enjoined or declared unlawful only as to all of the class members or as to none of them." Nagareda, 84 N.Y.U. L. Rev., at 132. In other words, Rule 23(b)(2) applies only when a single injunction or declaratory judgment would provide relief to each member of the class. It does not authorize class certification when each individual class member would be entitled to a *different* injunction or declaratory judgment against the defendant. Similarly, it does not authorize class certification when each class member would be entitled to an individualized award of monetary damages.

That interpretation accords with the history of the Rule. Because Rule 23 "stems from equity practice" that predated its codification, Amchem Products, Inc. v. Windsor, 521 U.S. 591, 613 (1997), in determining its meaning we have previously looked to the historical models on which the Rule was based, Ortiz v. Fibreboard Corp., 527 U.S. 815, 841-45 (1999). As we observed in *Amchem,* "[c]ivil rights cases against parties charged with unlawful, class-based discrimination are prime examples" of what (b)(2) is meant to capture. 521 U.S., at 614. In particular, the Rule reflects a series of decisions involving challenges to racial segregation—conduct that was remedied by a single classwide order. In none of the cases cited by the Advisory Committee as examples of (b)(2)'s antecedents did the plaintiffs combine any claim for individualized relief with their classwide injunction. See Advisory Committee's Note, 39 F.R.D. 69, 102 (1966) (citing cases). . . .

Permitting the combination of individualized and classwide relief in a (b)(2) class is also inconsistent with the structure of Rule 23(b). Classes certified under (b)(1) and (b)(2) share the most traditional justifications for class treatment—that individual adjudications would be impossible or unworkable, as in a (b)(1) class, or that the relief sought must perforce affect the entire class at once, as in a (b)(2) class. For that reason these are also mandatory classes: The Rule provides no opportunity for (b)(1) or (b)(2) class members to opt out, and does not even oblige the District Court to afford them notice of the action. Rule 23(b)(3), by contrast, is an "adventuresome innovation" of the 1966 amendments, *Amchem,* 521 U.S., at 614, framed for situations "in which 'class-action treatment is not as clearly called for,'" id., at 615 (quoting Advisory Committee's Notes, 28 U.S.C. App., p. 697 (1994 ed.)). It allows class certification in a much wider set of circumstances but with greater procedural protections. . . .

Given that structure, we think it clear that individualized monetary claims belong in Rule 23(b)(3). . . .

## B

Against that conclusion, respondents argue that their claims for backpay were appropriately certified as part of a class under Rule 23(b)(2) because those claims do not "predominate" over their requests for injunctive and declaratory relief. They rely upon the Advisory Committee's statement that Rule 23(b)(2) "does not extend to cases in which the appropriate final relief relates *exclusively or predominantly* to money damages." 39 F.R.D., at 102 (emphasis added). The negative implication, they argue, is that it *does* extend to cases in which the appropriate final relief relates only partially and nonpredominantly to money damages. Of course it is the Rule itself, not the Advisory Committee's description of it, that governs. And a mere negative inference does not in our view suffice to establish a disposition that has no basis in the Rule's text, and that does obvious violence to the Rule's structural features. The mere "predominance" of a proper (b)(2) injunctive claim does nothing to justify elimination of Rule 23(b)(3)'s procedural protections: It neither establishes the superiority of *class* adjudication over *individual* adjudication nor cures the notice and opt-out problems. . . .

Respondents' predominance test, moreover, creates perverse incentives for class representatives to place at risk potentially valid claims for monetary relief. In this case, for example, the named plaintiffs declined to include employees' claims for compensatory damages in their complaint. That strategy of including only backpay claims made it more likely that monetary relief would not "predominate." But it also created the possibility (if the predominance test were correct) that individual class members' compensatory-damages claims would be *precluded* by litigation they had no power to hold themselves apart from. . . . That possibility underscores the need for plaintiffs with individual monetary claims to decide *for themselves* whether to tie their fates to the class representatives' or go it alone—a choice Rule 23(b)(2) does not ensure that they have.

The predominance test would also require the District Court to reevaluate the roster of class members continually. The Ninth Circuit recognized the necessity for this when it concluded that those plaintiffs no longer employed by Wal-Mart lack standing to seek injunctive or declaratory relief against its employment practices. The Court of Appeals' response to that difficulty, however, was not to eliminate *all* former employees from the certified class, but to eliminate only those who had left the company's employ by the date the complaint was filed. . . . As a consequence, . . . about half the members of the class approved by the Ninth Circuit have no claim for injunctive or declaratory relief at all. . . .

Finally, respondents argue that their backpay claims are appropriate for a (b)(2) class action because a backpay award is equitable in nature. The latter may be true, but it is irrelevant. The Rule does not speak of "equitable" remedies generally but of injunctions and declaratory judgments. As Title VII itself makes pellucidly clear, backpay is neither. See 42 U.S.C. §2000e-5(g)(2)(B)(i) and (ii) (distinguishing between declaratory and injunctive relief and the payment of "backpay," see § 2000e-5(g)(2)(A)).

## C

In *Allison v. Citgo Petroleum Corp.*, 151 F.3d 402, 415 (5th Cir. 1998), the Fifth Circuit held that a (b)(2) class would permit the certification of monetary relief that is "incidental to requested injunctive or declaratory relief," which it defined as "damages that flow directly from liability to the class *as a whole* on the claims forming the basis of the injunctive or declaratory relief." In that court's view, such "incidental damage should not require additional hearings to resolve the disparate merits of each individual's case; it should neither introduce new substantial legal or factual issues, nor entail complex individualized determinations." Id. We need not decide in this case whether there are any forms of "incidental" monetary relief that are consistent with the interpretation of Rule 23(b)(2) we have announced and that comply with the Due Process Clause. Respondents do not argue that they can satisfy this standard, and in any event they cannot.

Contrary to the Ninth Circuit's view, Wal-Mart is entitled to individualized determinations of each employee's eligibility for backpay. Title VII includes a detailed remedial scheme. . . .

We have established a procedure for trying pattern-or-practice cases that gives effect to these statutory requirements. . . .

The Court of Appeals believed that it was possible to replace such proceedings with Trial by Formula. A sample set of the class members would be selected, as to whom liability for sex discrimination and the backpay owing as a result would be determined in depositions supervised by a master. The percentage of claims determined to be valid would then be applied to the entire remaining class, and the number of (presumptively) valid claims thus derived would be multiplied by the average backpay award in the sample set to arrive at the entire class recovery—without further individualized proceedings. 603 F.3d, at 625-27. We disapprove that novel project. Because the Rules Enabling Act forbids interpreting Rule 23 to "abridge, enlarge or modify any substantive right," 28 U.S.C. § 2072(b); see *Ortiz*, 527 U.S., at 845, a class cannot be certified on the premise that Wal-Mart will not be entitled to litigate its statutory defenses to individual claims. And because the necessity of that litigation will prevent backpay from being "incidental" to the class-wide injunction, respondents' class could not be certified even assuming, *arguendo*, that "incidental" monetary relief can be awarded to a 23(b)(2) class.

The judgment of the Court of Appeals is *Reversed*.

JUSTICE GINSBURG, with whom JUSTICE BREYER, JUSTICE SOTOMAYOR, and JUSTICE KAGAN join, concurring in part, and dissenting in part.

The class in this case, I agree with the Court, should not have been certified under Federal Rule of Civil Procedure 23(b)(2). The plaintiffs, alleging discrimination in violation of Title VII, 42 U.S.C. § 2000e *et seq.*, seek monetary relief that is not merely incidental to any injunctive or declaratory relief that might be available. . . .

Whether the class the plaintiffs describe meets the specific requirements of Rule 23(b)(3) is not before the Court, and I would reserve that matter for consideration and decision on remand. The Court, however, disqualifies the class at the starting gate, holding that the plaintiffs cannot cross the "commonality" line set by Rule 23(a)(2). In so ruling, the Court imports into the Rule 23(a) determination concerns properly addressed in a Rule 23(b)(3) assessment.

I

A

Rule 23(a)(2) establishes a preliminary requirement for maintaining a class action: "[T]here are questions of law or fact common to the class." The Rule "does not require that all questions of law or fact raised in the litigation be common," 1 H. Newberg & A. Conte, Newberg on Class Actions § 3.10, pp. 3-48 to 3-49 (3d ed. 1992); indeed, "[e]ven a single question of law or fact common to the members of the class will satisfy the commonality requirement," Nagareda, The Preexistence Principle and the Structure of the Class Action, 103 Colum. L. Rev. 149, 176, n.110 (2003). See Advisory Committee's 1937 Notes on Fed. Rule Civ. Proc. 23, 28 U.S.C. App., p. 138 (citing with approval cases in which "there was only a question of law or fact common to" the class members).

A "question" is ordinarily understood to be "[a] subject or point open to controversy." American Heritage Dictionary 1483 (3d ed. 1992). See also Black's Law Dictionary 1366 (9th ed. 2009) (defining "question of fact" as "[a] disputed issue to be resolved . . . [at] trial" and "question of law" as "[a]n issue to be decided by the judge"). Thus, a "question" "common to the class" must be a dispute, either of fact or of law, the resolution of which will advance the determination of the class members' claims.

B

The District Court, recognizing that "one significant issue common to the class may be sufficient to warrant certification," 222 F.R.D. 137, 145 (N.D. Cal. 2004), found that the plaintiffs easily met that test. Absent an error of law or an abuse of discretion, an appellate tribunal has no warrant to upset the District Court's finding of commonality. See Califano v. Yamasaki, 442 U.S. 682, 703 (1979) ("[M]ost issues arising under Rule 23 . . . [are] committed in the first instance to the discretion of the district court."). . . .

Women fill 70 percent of the hourly jobs in the retailer's stores but make up only "33 percent of management employees." 222 F.R.D., at 146. "[T]he higher one looks in the organization the lower the percentage of women." Id., at 155. The plaintiffs' "largely uncontested descriptive statistics" also show that women working in the company's stores "are paid less than men in every region" and "that the salary gap widens over time even for men and women hired into the same jobs at the same time." Id. . . .

The District Court identified "systems for . . . promoting in-store employees" that were "sufficiently similar across regions and stores" to conclude that "the manner in which these systems affect the class raises issues that are common to all class members." 222 F.R.D., at 149. The selection of employees for promotion to in-store management "is fairly characterized as a 'tap on the shoulder' process," in which managers have discretion about whose shoulders to tap. Id., at 148. Vacancies are not regularly posted; from among those employees satisfying minimum qualifications, managers choose whom to promote on the basis of their own subjective impressions. Id.

Wal-Mart's compensation policies also operate uniformly across stores, the District Court found. The retailer leaves open a $2 band for every position's hourly pay rate. Wal-Mart provides no standards or criteria for setting wages within that band, and thus does nothing to counter unconscious bias on the part of supervisors. See id., at 146-47.

Wal-Mart's supervisors do not make their discretionary decisions in a vacuum. The District Court reviewed means Wal-Mart used to maintain a "carefully constructed . . . corporate culture," such as frequent meetings to reinforce the common way of thinking, regular transfers of managers between stores to ensure uniformity throughout the company, monitoring of stores "on a close and constant basis," and "Wal-Mart TV," "broadcas[t] . . . into all stores." Id., at 151-53.

The plaintiffs' evidence, including class members' tales of their own experiences, suggests that gender bias suffused Wal-Mart's company culture. Among illustrations, senior management often refer to female associates as "little Janie Qs." Plaintiffs' Motion for Class Certification in No. 3:01-cv-02252-CRB (N.D. Cal.), Doc. 99, p. 13. One manager told an employee that "[m]en are here to make a career and women aren't." 222 F.R.D., at 166. A committee of female Wal-Mart executives concluded that "[s]tereotypes limit the opportunities offered to women." Plaintiffs' Motion for Class Certification in No. 3:01-cv-02252–CRB (N.D. Cal.), Doc. 99, at 16.

Finally, the plaintiffs presented an expert's appraisal to show that the pay and promotions disparities at Wal-Mart "can be explained only by gender discrimination and not by . . . neutral variables." 222 F.R.D., at 155. Using regression analyses, their expert, Richard Drogin, controlled for factors including, *inter alia*, job performance, length of time with the company, and the store where an employee worked. Id., at 159.[5] The results, the District Court found, were sufficient to raise an "inference of discrimination." Id., at 155-60.

## C

The District Court's identification of a common question, whether Wal-Mart's pay and promotions policies gave rise to unlawful discrimination, was hardly infirm. The practice of delegating to supervisors large discretion to make personnel decisions, uncontrolled by formal standards, has long been known to have the potential to produce disparate effects. Managers,

---

5. The Court asserts that Drogin showed only average differences at the "regional and national level" between male and female employees. . . . In fact, his regression analyses showed there were disparities within stores. The majority's contention to the contrary reflects only an arcane disagreement about statistical method—which the District Court resolved in the plaintiffs' favor. 222 F.R.D. 137, 157 (N.D. Cal. 2004). Appellate review is no occasion to disturb a trial court's handling of factual disputes of this order.

like all humankind, may be prey to biases of which they are unaware.[6] The risk of discrimination is heightened when those managers are predominantly of one sex, and are steeped in a corporate culture that perpetuates gender stereotypes.

The plaintiffs' allegations resemble those in one of the prototypical cases in this area, Leisner v. New York Tel. Co., 358 F. Supp. 359, 364-65 (S.D.N.Y. 1973). In deciding on promotions, supervisors in that case were to start with objective measures; but ultimately, they were to "look at the individual as a total individual." Id., at 365. The final question they were to ask and answer: "Is this person going to be successful in our business?" Id. It is hardly surprising that for many managers, the ideal candidate was someone with characteristics similar to their own.

We have held that "discretionary employment practices" can give rise to Title VII claims, not only when such practices are motivated by discriminatory intent but also when they produce discriminatory results. See Watson v. Fort Worth Bank & Trust, 487 U.S. 977, 988, 991 (1988). . . . In *Watson*, as here, an employer had given its managers large authority over promotions. . . .

Aware of "the problem of subconscious stereotypes and prejudices," we held that the employer's "undisciplined system of subjective decisionmaking" was an "employment practic[e]" that "may be analyzed under the disparate impact approach." Id., at 990-91. . . .

The plaintiffs' allegations state claims of gender discrimination in the form of biased decisionmaking in both pay and promotions. The evidence reviewed by the District Court adequately demonstrated that resolving those claims would necessitate examination of particular policies and practices alleged to affect, adversely and globally, women employed at Wal-Mart's stores. Rule 23(a)(2), setting a necessary but not a sufficient criterion for class-action certification, demands nothing further.

## II

### A

. . . The Court blends Rule 23(a)(2)'s threshold criterion with the more demanding criteria of Rule 23(b)(3), and thereby elevates the (a)(2) inquiry so that it is no longer "easily satisfied," 5 J. Moore et al., Moore's Federal Practice § 23.23[2], p. 23-72 (3d ed. 2011). . . .

---

6. An example vividly illustrates how subjective decisionmaking can be vehicle for discrimination. Performing in symphony orchestras was long a male preserve. Goldin and Rouse, Orchestrating Impartiality: The Impact of "Blind" Auditions on Female Musicians, 90 Am. Econ. Rev. 715, 715-716 (2000). In the 1970's orchestras began hiring musicians through auditions open to all comers. Id., at 716. Reviewers were to judge applicants solely on their musical abilities, yet subconscious bias led some reviewers to disfavor women. Orchestras that permitted reviewers to see the applicants hired far fewer female musicians than orchestras that conducted blind auditions, in which candidates played behind opaque screens. Id., at 738.

The Court's emphasis on differences between class members mimics the Rule 23(b)(3) inquiry into whether common questions "predominate" over individual issues. And by asking whether the individual differences "impede" common adjudication, the Court duplicates 23(b)(3)'s question whether "a class action is superior" to other modes of adjudication. Indeed, Professor Nagareda, whose "dissimilarities" inquiry the Court endorses, developed his position in the context of Rule 23(b)(3). See 84 N.Y.U. L. Rev., at 131 (Rule 23(b)(3) requires "some decisive degree of similarity across the proposed class" because it "speaks of common 'questions' that 'predominate' over individual ones"). "The Rule 23(b)(3) predominance inquiry" is meant to "tes[t] whether proposed classes are sufficiently cohesive to warrant adjudication by representation." Amchem Products, Inc. v. Windsor, 521 U.S. 591, 623 (1997). If courts must conduct a "dissimilarities" analysis at the Rule 23(a)(2) stage, no mission remains for Rule 23(b)(3).

Because Rule 23(a) is also a prerequisite for Rule 23(b)(1) and Rule 23(b)(2) classes, the Court's "dissimilarities" position is far reaching. Individual differences should not bar a Rule 23(b)(1) or Rule 23(b)(2) class, so long as the Rule 23(a) threshold is met. For example, in Franks v. Bowman Transp. Co., 424 U.S. 747 (1976), a Rule 23(b)(2) class of African-American truckdrivers complained that the defendant had discriminatorily refused to hire black applicants. We recognized that the "qualification[s] and performance" of individual class members might vary. Id., at 772 (internal quotation marks omitted). "Generalizations concerning such individually applicable evidence," we cautioned, "cannot serve as a justification for the denial of [injunctive] relief to the entire class." Id.

### B

. . . Wal-Mart's delegation of discretion over pay and promotions is a policy uniform throughout all stores. The very nature of discretion is that people will exercise it in various ways. A system of delegated discretion, *Watson* held, is a practice actionable under Title VII when it produces discriminatory outcomes. 487 U.S., at 990-991; see supra, at 7-8. A finding that Wal-Mart's pay and promotions practices in fact violate the law would be the first step in the usual order of proof for plaintiffs seeking individual remedies for company-wide discrimination. Teamsters v. United States, 431 U.S. 324, 359 (1977); see Albemarle Paper Co. v. Moody, 422 U.S. 405, 415-423 (1975). That each individual employee's unique circumstances will ultimately determine whether she is entitled to backpay or damages, § 2000e-5(g)(2)(A) (barring backpay if a plaintiff "was refused . . . advancement . . . for any reason other than discrimination"), should not factor into the Rule 23(a)(2) determination.

The Court errs in importing a "dissimilarities" notion suited to Rule 23(b)(3) into the Rule 23(a) commonality inquiry. I therefore cannot join Part II of the Court's opinion.

## Notes and Questions

1. *Substance-Procedure Redux.* Justice Scalia and Justice Ginsburg obviously do not share the same theory of commonality. Is this a result of disagreement about Rule 23 or equally sharp differences of opinion about what constitutes unlawful sex discrimination? Revisit footnote 6 of Justice Ginsburg's opinion. Isn't commonality a lot easier to find if you accept that sex discrimination occurs with the kind of frightening efficiency revealed by that study? If you were counsel for plaintiffs in the case, what additional pre-certification discovery would you have conducted about Wal-Mart's culture and employment practices to establish a common question of law or fact?

Notice that both opinions, in their own ways, drift from asking whether there is a common *question* of law or fact into discussion of whether there is likely a common *answer*. Restricting the inquiry to whether there is a common question helps avoid speculating about the underlying merits, doesn't it? On increasing attention to the merits in class certification decisions, see Richard Marcus, Reviving Judicial Gatekeeping of Aggregation: Scrutinizing the Merits, 79 Geo. Wash. L. Rev. 324 (2011). On the overall effects of *Dukes* on class certification, see Elizabeth J. Cabraser, The Class Abides: Class Actions and the "Roberts Court," 48 Akron L. Rev. 757 (2015) (concluding that "the process of class certification has become more rigorous, more protracted, more expensive, and more uncertain," but that "the class action has survived and that its core functions, as well as its fundamental structure, are largely intact"); Michael Selmi & Sylvia Taskos, Employment Discrimination Class Actions After Wal-Mart v. Dukes, 48 Akron L. Rev. 803 (2015) (arguing that filings have decreased and that regional class actions have replaced nationwide suits).

2. Is the principal problem with certification the size of the class? Do you read the case as addressing distinctive concerns raised by class action suits in the context of discrimination? Some lower courts are applying the Court's new commonality jurisprudence and limitations on (b)(2) suits to much smaller class actions and to suits outside the context of discrimination. See, e.g., Manson v. GMAC Mortgage, LLC, 283 F.R.D. 20 (D. Mass. 2012). But see Wang v. Chinese Daily News, Inc., 737 F.3d 538 (9th Cir. 2013) (remanding for reconsideration of certification in light of *Dukes* but admonishing that "[*Dukes*] is factually distinguishable from our case. Most importantly, the class here is much smaller. It encompasses only about 200 employees, all of whom work or worked at the same . . . office. Plaintiffs' claims do not depend upon establishing commonalities among 1.5 million employees and millions of discretionary employment decisions."). In the context of discrimination claims, compare Scott v. Family Dollar Stores, Inc., 733 F.3d 105, 109 (4th Cir. 2013) (denying certification, pre-certification discovery, and amendment in light of *Dukes*), with Calibuso v. Bank of America Corp., 893 F. Supp 2d 374 (E.D.N.Y. 2012) (denying pre-certification motion to dismiss on ground that, notwithstanding *Dukes*, plaintiffs had alleged a "plausible" claim of commonality).

The Supreme Court also has rejected certification of an antitrust action in which plaintiffs relied on a regression model as evidence that damages could be measured by a common methodology across the class and that common questions of law or fact therefore predominated. Comcast Corp. v. Behrend, 133 S. Ct. 1426 (2013). Writing for a 5-4 majority, Justice Scalia again emphasized that the class action is "an exception to the usual rule" of individual litigation, that the certification analysis is supposed to be "rigorous," and that "[s]uch an analysis will frequently entail overlap with the merits of the plaintiff's underlying claim." 133 S. Ct. at 1432. Moreover, "Rule 23(b)(3)'s predominance criterion is even more demanding that Rule 23(a)." Id. Here, the plaintiffs' class action was improperly certified because the regression analysis failed to distinguish between legally viable and nonviable theories of antitrust market distortion in calculating the probable injury to consumer class members. The lower courts had not required that level of detail because they believed that doing so would involve impermissible consideration of the merits.

In light of the *Comcast* decision the Supreme Court has vacated and remanded circuit court decisions upholding certification of class actions and distinguishing *Dukes*. See, e.g., Ross v. RBS Citizens, N.A., 667 F.3d 900, 909 (7th Cir. 2012) ("Despite [Defendant's] best efforts to fit the present case into the *Dukes* mold, there are significant distinctions. Perhaps the most important distinction is the size of the class and the type of proof the *Dukes* plaintiffs were required to offer. . . . Here there are 1,129 Hourly class members and substantially fewer ABMs, all of whom are based only in Illinois. The plaintiffs' [wage law] claim requires no proof of discriminatory intent. . . . Although there might be slight variations in how [Defendant] enforced its overtime policy, both classes maintain a common claim that [Defendant] broadly enforced an unlawful policy denying employees earned-overtime compensation."), *vacated and remanded by* 133 S. Ct. 1722 (2013); Whirlpool Corp. v. Glazer, 678 F.3d 409 (6th Cir. 2012), *vacated and remanded by* 133 S. Ct. 1722 (2013). For another example of the constraining effect of the case, see Ochoa v. McDonalds Corp., 2016 WL 3648550 (N.D. Cal. July 7, 2016) (finding insufficient commonality in employee class action claim regarding certain workplace conditions).

More recently, the Court has distinguished *Dukes* in cases more modest in scale. See Tyson Foods, Inc. v. Bouaphakeo, 136 S. Ct. 1036, 1040 (2016) (upholding plaintiff employees' reliance on expert witness statistical estimation of average time employees spent donning and removing protective gear to demonstrate predominance; distinguishing *Dukes* because the Tyson Foods employees "worked in the same facility, did similar work, and were paid under the same policy"); see also Amgen Inc. v. Connecticut Ret. Plans & Trust Funds, 133 S. Ct. 1184 (2013) (Justice Ginsburg writing for a majority, taking a more generous approach to proving predominance).

Certification is obviously harder to secure in cases where the defendant has conferred discretion on relevant decision makers and where the evidence of discrimination is inferential. See Tabor v. Hilti, Inc., 703 F.3d 1206, 1229 (10th Cir. 2013) (class certification denied where plaintiffs "challenge a highly discretionary policy for granting promotions" and "the record suggests that Hilti failed to maintain the [promotion] system in any uniform manner"); Artis v. Yellen, No. 01-400 (EGS), 2014 WL 4801783, at *9-10 (D.D.C. 2014) (denying class certification to African American and Native American secretaries and clerical employees who alleged race discrimination under Title VII at the Federal Reserve; "the discrimination [plaintiffs] allege stems from an array of individualized decisions of low-level supervisors who operate with significant discretion to design subjective criteria for making personnel decisions. . . . Plaintiffs provide no evidence that could support an inference that the discretionary decisions they challenge are tied together by a common policy. . . . Nor do the plaintiffs supply evidence that supervisors exercise their discretion in a uniform manner. . . . 'Statistical disparities alone,' which might show that a particular group is underrepresented, 'generally are not proof that . . . the class as a whole . . . has been discriminated against'").

On the other hand, where both an illicit policy and causation can be established, courts are still granting certification. See Brown v. Nucor Corp, 785 F.3d 895 (4th Cir. 2015) (reversing denial of class certification where black employees alleged discriminatory job promotion practices and a racially hostile work environment; concluding that plaintiffs had satisfied the commonality requirement by providing: 1) statistics that indicate that promotions depended in part on whether an individual was black or white; 2) substantial anecdotal evidence suggesting discrimination in specific promotion decisions in multiple departments; and 3) significant evidence that promotion decisions were made in the context of a racially hostile work environment).

What about traditional Rule 23(b)(2) actions in which plaintiffs seek either no monetary relief or incidental equitable relief? Are these class actions less likely to be certified after Wal-Mart v. Dukes? In theory at least, Rule 23(a)(2) commonality should be easier to establish when the defendant's alleged wrongdoing is of a kind that makes the classic civil rights injunction appropriate. That is so because the defendant's conduct typically arises from an identifiable policy or practice affecting the class as a whole and because the remedy (typically a change in policy) redounds to the benefit of the entire class. See David Marcus, The Public Interest Class Action, 104 Geo. L.J. 777 (2016); Hernandez v. County of Monterey, 305 F.R.D. 132 (N.D. Cal. 2015) (unconstitutional prison conditions); Scott v. Clarke, 61 F. Supp. 3d 569 (W.D. Va. 2014) (Eighth Amendment deliberate indifference to medical needs of prisoners). For an example of a 23(b)(2) suit outside the civil right setting, see Sykes v. Mel S. Harris & Associates LLC, 780 F.3d 70 (2d Cir. 2015) (affirming certification of a class of debtors claiming a debt-buying company, law firm, and process server designed a fraudulent scheme to obtain debt judgments in civil court in violation of the FDCPA and RICO; noting that *Dukes* made clear that the certification of a class for injunctive relief is only appropriate where "'a single injunction . . . would provide relief to each member of the class'") (quoting Wal-Mart Stores, Inc. v. Dukes, 564 U.S., at 2557).

3. *Choice of Law and Class Actions After* Dukes. In a nationwide consumer class action, which state's substantive law should be applied? How can common questions of law or fact "predominate" if the injuries occurred in states with different consumer protection statutes? The Ninth Circuit confronted this question in Mazza v. American Honda Motor Co., 666 F.3d 581 (9th Cir. 2012), a nationwide consumer class action filed in California federal court against Honda for engaging in deceptive advertising of a $4,000 computerized "Collision Mitigation Braking System" sold as an option on Acura RLs. Plaintiffs alleged that in marketing the system Honda failed to warn consumers that the three-stem system (a collision warning light, preliminary braking with seat belt tightening, and increased braking) could all occur at once, could occur too late to avoid certain accidents, and could shut off in bad weather. California state law causes of action for deceptive advertising, unfair competition, and unjust enrichment were pled. The district court certified the class over Honda's objection that common issues did not predominate because California law conflicted with the laws of 43 other states in which class members were sold Acura RLs. On appeal, the Ninth Circuit reversed, finding that there were material differences between California consumer protection law and the laws of other relevant states with respect to scienter, reliance, and remedies. Id. at 590-91. "We conclude that these are not trivial or wholly immaterial differences. In cases where a defendant acted without scienter, a scienter requirement will spell the difference between the success and failure of a claim." Id. at 591.

A dissenting judge contended that the only "potentially material" conflict was between California and the pro-business statutes of six southern states. Id. at 597-98. She reasoned that while each state has an interest "in achieving the optimal balance between consumer protection and business friendliness," the conflict of laws question is "which state's interests would be more impaired if its policy were subordinated to the policy of the other state." Id. at 598. While the majority concluded that other states would be impaired in their ability to "foster commerce" if California consumer protection law applied and that California "has an attenuated interest in applying its law to nonresidents," the dissent argued that California actually has the greater interest in seeing its laws applied nationally in this case: "Honda is incorporated in California; the advertisements at issue emanated from the state [because Honda's PR firm is in California]. California has a compelling interest in regulating the conduct of corporations operating within the state and availing themselves of the state's privileges." Id.

We address the effect of nationwide and multistate class actions on personal jurisdiction and choice of forum later in this chapter, Phillips Petroleum Co. v. Shutts, 472 U.S. 797 (1985). For now, notice the parallels between the choice of law analysis here and what you learned about due process analysis for personal jurisdiction in Chapter 1. Federalism, fairness, and the degree of contact with a forum state all come into play. Notice too the sharp debate between the majority and the dissent about what makes a conflict "material" and how to assess the interest each state has in the application of its substantive law to conduct within its borders. The majority seems to assume that state-by-state class actions are the appropriate way to proceed. Even a class action restricted to California consumers may provide sufficient damages to give class action lawyers an incentive to bring suit and to deter Honda. Individual suits for $4,000 certainly would not. Do consumers in other states, where suit under their own state's consumer protection law would fail, have an interest in joining a nationwide class action under California's more consumer-friendly consumer protection laws? It would seem that their interest is linked to the fact that Honda and its PR firm are California companies. Framed this way, what is the federalism intrusion upon the interests of the states in which such consumers reside?

## Note: The Right to Jury Trial

Given the class action's roots in equity, one may assume that no jury trial right attaches when a case is filed as a class action. This, however, is not necessarily so.

In Ross v. Bernhard, 396 U.S. 531 (1970), the United States Supreme Court concluded that the right to trial by jury attaches to the issues in a class action—in *Ross* it was a shareholder's derivative suit—as to which the right to trial by jury would have attached if the parties had litigated the matter in individual actions, rather than through the collective action device of a class action. Thus a court must analyze the issues in a class action and determine whether they are "legal" or "equitable" in the manner described more fully in Chapter 5.

## Note: Tobacco-Related Class Actions and Their Progeny

Though consumer and employment discrimination class actions such as *In re Zurn* and *Dukes* have their detractors, the use of Rule 23 in mass tort cases is even more hotly debated. This is particularly true when the tort involves product liability rather than, for instance, some common disaster such as a plane crash. An early example was the Dalkon Shield litigation. Most of the several thousand cases against the defective birth control device were tort actions filed by women who used the device and suffered infertility or other injuries. In a bold and controversial move, a district court in California certified a nationwide class action in the Dalkon Shield mass tort cases, despite the protests of the defendants and many plaintiffs who preferred to litigate independently. The appellate court reversed the district court's certification. In re Northern District of California, Dalkon Shield IUD Products Liability Litigation, 693 F.2d 847 (9th Cir. 1982), *cert. denied*, A.H. Robins Co., Incorporated v. Abed, 459 U.S. 1171 (1983), *abrogation recognized by* Baxter Healthcare Corp. v. U.S. Dist. Court for Cent. Dist. of Cal., 121 F.3d 714 (9th Cir. 1997). Was this the sort of dispute Rule 23 was designed to cover? Isn't typicality a problem when the women each suffered distinctive injuries? Aren't mass torts presumptively inappropriate cases for class action treatment? How would you describe the competing interests at stake?

In addition to the Dalkon Shield cases, courts have been inundated with asbestos injury cases (more later on these), DES cases, Agent Orange cases, and—most prominently in the last two decades—cases filed against the tobacco industry. The tobacco industry cases have produced the most dramatic and far-reaching class actions to date. Of special concern to the industry was the chance of a nationwide or statewide class action suit succeeding. The first such case went to trial in July 1998. The class of plaintiffs included 100,000 to 200,000 people seeking $100 billion in compensatory and punitive damages. R.J. Reynolds Tobacco Co. v. Engle, 672 So. 2d 39 (Fla. Dist. Ct. App. 1996), *rev. denied*, 682 So. 2d 1100 (Fla. 1996) (approving certification of statewide class of tobacco smokers). But see Philip Morris, Inc. v. Angletti, 752 A.2d 200, 222 (Md. 2000) (reversing class certification and noting the nationwide trend of refusing to certify or uphold certification of class actions for mass tobacco litigation; finding that common issues did not predominate and that class litigation was not a superior method of adjudication).

A year before the *Engle* trial, defendant cigarette manufacturers reached a $300 million settlement with a nationwide class of nonsmoking flight attendants who claimed that their illnesses were the result of occupational exposure to secondhand smoke. Broin v. Philip Morris Cos., Fla. Cir. Ct. No. 91-49738CA(22), settlement agreement entered Oct. 10, 1997, and Ramos v. Philip Morris Cos., 743 So. 2d 24 (Fla. Dist. Ct. App. 1999). The agreement allowed attendants to bring individual actions for compensatory damages, with the defendant companies agreeing to assume the burden of proof on whether secondhand smoke was the cause of any number of medical conditions. The Florida Third District Court of Appeal upheld the settlement and described it as a "boon to the plaintiffs," Reuters, Tobacco Settlement Is Upheld in Florida, N.Y. Times, Mar. 25, 1999, at A20, but litigation involving the remedies in that settlement has continued well into the new century. See Broin v. Philip Morris Cos., 84 So. 3d 1107 (Fla. Dist. Ct. App. 2012), *quashed by* Young v. Achenbauch, 136 So. 3d 575 (Fla. 2014); Philip Morris, Inc. v. French, 897 So. 2d 480 (Fla. Dist. Ct. App. 2009) (jury award of $5.5 million reduced by judge on motion for remittitur to $500,000). These private suits prompted state attorneys general and the Department of Justice to sue the industry as well. See, e.g., United States v. Philip Morris USA, Inc., 566 F.3d 1095 (D.C. Cir. 2009).

## 2.   Appeal of Class Certification

### *Blair v. Equifax Check Services, Inc.*
181 F.3d 832 (7th Cir. 1999)

EASTERBROOK, Circuit Judge.

. . . Last year the Supreme Court promulgated Fed. R. Civ. P. 23(f), which reads: "A court of appeals may in its discretion permit an appeal from an order of a district court granting or denying class action certification under this rule if application is made to it within ten days after entry of the order. An appeal does not stay proceedings in the district court unless the district judge or the court of appeals so orders."

. . . [W]e have for consideration the first application filed in this circuit (and, so far as we can tell, the nation) under the new rule. A motions panel directed the parties to file briefs discussing the standard the court should employ to decide whether to accept appeals under this rule.

The Committee Note accompanying Rule 23(f) remarks: "The court of appeals is given unfettered discretion whether to permit the appeal, akin to the discretion exercised by the Supreme Court in acting on a petition for certiorari. . . . Permission to appeal may be granted or denied on the basis of any consideration that the court of appeals finds persuasive." . . . Although Rule 10 of the Supreme Court's Rules identifies some of the considerations that inform the grant of certiorari, they are "neither controlling nor fully measuring the Court's discretion." Likewise it would be a mistake for us to draw up a list that determines how the power under Rule 23(f) will be exercised. Neither a bright-line approach nor a catalog of factors would serve well—especially at the outset, when courts necessarily must experiment with the new class of appeals.

Instead of inventing standards, we keep in mind the reasons Rule 23(f) came into being. These are three. For some cases the denial of class status sounds the death knell of the litigation, because the representative plaintiff's claim is too small to justify the expense of litigation. Coopers & Lybrand v. Livesay, 437 U.S. 463 (1978), held that an order declining to certify a class is not appealable, even if that decision dooms the suit as a practical matter. Rule 23(f) gives appellate courts discretion to entertain appeals in "death knell" cases—though we must be wary lest the mind hear a bell that is not tolling. Many class suits are prosecuted by law firms with portfolios of litigation, and these attorneys act as champions for the class even if the representative plaintiff would find it uneconomical to carry on with the case. E.g., Rand v. Monsanto Co., 926 F.2d 596 (7th Cir. 1991). These law firms may carry on in the hope of prevailing for a single plaintiff and then winning class certification (and the reward of larger fees) on appeal, extending the victory to the whole class. A companion appeal, briefed in tandem with this one, presented just such a case. After class certification was denied, the plaintiff sought permission to appeal under Rule 23(f); although the remaining plaintiff has only a small stake, counsel pursued the case in the district court while we decided whether to entertain the appeal, and before the subject could be argued here the district judge granted summary judgment for the defendant. That plaintiff now has appealed on the merits and will seek to revive the class to boot. Many other cases proceed similarly; *Coopers & Lybrand* did not wipe out the small-stakes class action. But when denial of class status seems likely to be fatal, and when the plaintiff has a solid argument in opposition to the district court's decision, then a favorable exercise of appellate discretion is indicated.

Second, just as a denial of class status can doom the plaintiff, so a grant of class status can put considerable pressure on the defendant to settle, even when the plaintiff's probability of success on the merits is slight. Many corporate executives are unwilling to bet their company that they are in the right in big-stakes litigation, and a grant of class status can propel the stakes of a case into the stratosphere. In re Rhone-Poulenc Rorer, Inc., 51 F.3d 1293 (7th Cir. 1995), observes not only that class actions can have this effect on risk-averse corporate executives (and corporate counsel) but also that some plaintiffs or even some district judges may be tempted to use the class device to wring settlements from defendants whose legal positions are justified but unpopular. Empirical studies of securities class actions imply that this is common. Janet Cooper Alexander, Do the Merits Matter? A Study of Settlements in Securities Class Actions, 43 Stan. L. Rev. 497 (1991); Reinier Kraakman, Hyun Park and Steven Shavell, When Are Shareholder Suits in Shareholder Interests?, 82 Geo. L.J. 1733 (1994); Roberta Romano, The Shareholder Suit: Litigation Without Foundation?, 7 J.L. Econ. & Org. 55 (1991). Class certifications also have induced judges to remake some substantive doctrine in order to render the litigation manageable. See Hal S. Scott, The Impact of Class Actions on Rule 10b-5, 38 U. Chi. L. Rev. 337 (1971). This interaction of procedure with the merits justifies an earlier appellate look. By the end of the case it will be too late—if indeed the case has an ending that is subject to appellate review.

So, in a mirror image of the death-knell situation, when the stakes are large and the risk of a settlement or other disposition that does not reflect the merits of the claim is substantial, an appeal under Rule 23(f) is in order. Again the appellant must demonstrate that the district court's ruling on class certification is questionable—and must do this taking into account the discretion the district judge possesses in implementing Rule 23, and the correspondingly deferential standard of appellate review. However dramatic the effect of the grant or denial of class status in undercutting the plaintiff's claim or inducing the defendant to capitulate, if the ruling is impervious to revision there's no point to an interlocutory appeal.

Third, an appeal may facilitate the development of the law. Because a large proportion of class actions settles or is resolved in a way that overtakes procedural matters, some fundamental issues about class actions are poorly developed. Recent proposals to amend Rule 23 were designed in part to clear up some of these questions. Instead, the Advisory Committee and the Standing Committee elected to wait, anticipating that appeals under Rule 23(f) would resolve some questions and illuminate others. When an appellant can establish that such an issue is presented, Rule 23(f) permits the court of appeals to intervene. When the justification for interlocutory review is contributing to development of the law, it is less important to show that the district judge's decision is shaky. Law may develop through affirmances as well as through reversals. Some questions have not received appellate treatment because they are trivial; these are poor candidates for the use of Rule 23(f). But the more fundamental the question and the greater the likelihood that it will escape effective disposition at the end of the case, the more appropriate is an appeal under Rule 23(f). More than this it is impossible to say.

Judges have been stingy in accepting interlocutory appeals by certification under 28 U.S.C. § 1292(b), because that procedure interrupts the progress of a case and prolongs its disposition. That bogey is a principal reason why interlocutory appeals are so disfavored in the federal system. Disputes about class certification cannot be divorced from the merits—indeed, one of the fundamental unanswered questions is whether judges should be influenced by their tentative view of the merits when deciding whether to certify a class—and so this argument against interlocutory appeals carries some weight under Rule 23(f). But it has less weight than under § 1292(b), because Rule 23(f) is drafted to avoid delay. Filing a request for permission to appeal does not stop the litigation unless the district court or the court of appeals issues a stay—and a stay would depend on a demonstration that the probability of error in the class certification decision is high enough that the costs of pressing ahead in the district court exceed the costs of waiting. (This is the same kind of question that a court asks when deciding whether to issue a preliminary injunction or a stay of an administrative decision. See Illinois Bell Telephone Co. v. WorldCom Technologies, Inc., 157 F.3d 500 (7th Cir. 1998); American Hospital Supply Corp. v. Hospital Products Ltd., 780 F.2d 589, 593-594 (7th Cir. 1986).) We did not stay either of the two cases in which permission to appeal was sought; both continued in the district court and, as we related above, one already has been decided on the merits. Because stays will be infrequent, interlocutory appeals under Rule 23(f) should not unduly retard the pace of litigation.

So much for abstractions; what of this case? Equifax Check Services, which supplies a check-verification service to merchants, also attempts to collect fees imposed on dishonored checks. After we held that checks create "debts" within the meaning of the Fair Debt Collection Practices Act, 15 U.S.C. §§ 1692-1692o, see Bass v. Stolper, Koritzinsky, Brewster & Neider, S.C., 111 F.3d 1322 (7th Cir. 1997), many of Equifax's practices came under challenge. Until recently Equifax used a letter implying that it would refuse to verify checks written by anyone who had not paid all outstanding checks. Beverly Blair and Letressa Wilbon filed suits contending that this letter violated § 1692g of the Act because it did not adequately inform the recipients that they had 30 days within which to demand that Equifax obtain a verification of the debt from the merchant. Blair sought to represent a class of shoppers at Champs, and Wilbon a class of persons who had shopped at T.J. Maxx. The suits were consolidated and, after it became apparent that Equifax had sent the same letter to every person situated similarly to the plaintiffs, the district judge certified the case as a class action under Fed. R. Civ. P. 23(b)(3), defining the class as: "all Illinois residents (i) who were sent a demand letter by [Equifax] on or after a date one year prior to the filing of this action, (ii) in the form represented by Exhibit A . . . , (iii) in connection with an attempt to collect a check written to Champs or TJ Maxx for personal, family, or household purposes, where (iv) the letter was not returned by the Postal Service." 1999 U.S. Dist. LEXIS 2536, *21-22 (N.D. Ill. 1999). The court also certified a subclass of persons who received a particular follow-up letter less than 30 days after Equifax sent the first. Because plaintiffs sought only statutory penalties, the difficulties of proving individual loss did not block class treatment. Cf. Keele v. Wexler, 149 F.3d 589 (7th Cir. 1998). Equifax all but concedes that class certification was proper if the case is viewed in isolation, but it insists that what happened in another case requires a different outcome.

Several class actions against Equifax are pending in the Northern District of Illinois. On the same day Judge Plunkett certified the class in *Blair,* the plaintiffs in Crawford v. Equifax Check Services, Inc., No. 97 C 4240, which is pending before Magistrate Judge Schenkier, reached a settlement with Equifax. The class certified in *Crawford* is a superset of the class certified in *Blair,* and Equifax contends that as a result the terms of the *Crawford* settlement control here. A peculiar settlement it is. Equifax agreed to change the letters it sends in the future. Crawford personally receives $2,000. Members of the *Crawford* class get no relief for the letters sent to them, though Equifax agreed to donate $5,500 to Northwestern Law School's Legal Aid Clinic and (natch) [sic] the lawyers for the class receive fees for their work. According to the settlement, none of the class members will receive individual notice, and none will be offered the opportunity to opt out. The theory behind this is that the class was certified under Fed. R. Civ. P. 23(b)(2), even though it began as an action seeking damages. Finally, the settlement provides that all class members' claims for compensatory or statutory damages pass through the litigation unaffected and may be asserted elsewhere—but only in individual suits. The settlement forbids prosecution of any other case as a class action. It is this final feature of the *Crawford* settlement that Equifax contends should have led Judge Plunkett to decertify the *Blair-Wilbon* class. Maintaining *Blair* as a class action creates at least a possibility of inconsistent outcomes.

Judge Plunkett was not amused. He was piqued at Equifax's failure to ask the district court to consolidate *Crawford* with *Blair,* if indeed one comprises the other. He also concluded that the settlement in *Crawford* could not affect another pending suit. Because he deemed the *Crawford* settlement irrelevant, Judge Plunkett denied Equifax's motion for reconsideration of the class certification. This is the order Equifax wants to appeal under Rule 23(f). Before turning to that appeal, however, we need to describe additional proceedings before Magistrate Judge Schenkier.

Attorneys representing Blair and Wilbon were invited to a settlement conference in *Crawford* and there learned—for the first time, they say—that the *Crawford* class includes the *Blair* class. Counsel opposed the *Crawford* settlement as inadequate but did not persuade either Magistrate Judge Schenkier or Crawford's lawyers. Blair and Wilbon then sought to intervene in *Crawford* so that they would be able to appeal from final approval of the settlement, if their objections at the hearing under Rule 23(e) should be rejected. Magistrate Judge Schenkier denied the motion to intervene, concluding that counsel should have found out about the overlap and acted earlier. That decision is the subject of a separate appeal. . . .

. . . [T]he appeal is within our jurisdiction—if we choose to accept it.

We do accept it. This situation fits our third category of appropriate inter-locutory appeals. Equifax contends that it is entitled to be rid of multiple overlapping class actions. Questions concerning the relation among multiple suits may evade review at the end of the case, for by then the issue will be the relation among (potentially inconsistent) *judgments,* and not the management of pending litigation. That neither side can point to any precedent in support of its position implies that this is one of the issues that has evaded appellate resolution, and the issue is important enough to justify review now.

Because both sides favored us with their view of the merits of the appeal, as well as the question whether we should entertain it, we can bring matters to a swift conclusion. That the issue has evaded appellate resolution does not imply that it is difficult. Far from it. Judge Plunkett is plainly right—though not altogether for the reason he gave. We do not see any reason in principle why the disposition of the *Crawford* litigation cannot be conclusive on the plaintiffs in *Blair.* All members of the class certified in *Blair* also are members of the class certified in *Crawford;* a judgment binding on members of the *Crawford* class therefore will bind all members of the *Blair* class. See Tice v. American Airlines, Inc., 162 F.3d 966 (7th Cir. 1998). If the judgment binds them not to pursue class actions, then the class in *Blair* must be decertified. But it does not *yet* have this effect, and the district judge was not required to jump the gun just to avoid all possibility of inconsistent outcomes.

Parallel cases often seek the same relief. There's nothing peculiar about class actions. Sometimes the same plaintiff will file in two courts; sometimes different plaintiffs will seek equivalent relief in the same court. Our situation has a little of each, since Blair, Wilbon, and Crawford are not the same person, but they are in the same class. No mechanical rule governs the handling of overlapping cases. Judges sometimes stay proceedings in the more recently filed case to allow the first to proceed; sometimes a stay permits the more comprehensive of the actions to go forward. Cf. Colorado River Water Conservation District v. United States, 424 U.S. 800 (1976). But the judge hearing the second-filed case may conclude that it is a superior vehicle and may press forward. When the cases proceed in parallel, the first to reach judgment controls the other, through claim preclusion (res judicata). Davis v. Chicago, 53 F.3d 801 (7th Cir. 1995); Rogers v. Desiderio, 58 F.3d 299 (7th Cir. 1995). *Crawford* has yet to produce a final and binding decision, however, so Judge Plunkett was entitled to proceed with *Blair* in the interim.

On occasion it will be so clear that the first-filed suit is the superior vehicle that it would be an abuse of discretion for the court in the second-filed suit to press forward. This is not such a case, however. *Crawford* is far from decision on the merits; it has seen negotiation, not combat. It is not clear that *Crawford*'s settlement will beat *Blair* to finality even if *Blair* is fully litigated. As we have recounted, Blair and Wilbon have tried to intervene in *Crawford,* and they have appealed from the order denying that motion. We anticipate that they will appeal again from any order giving final approval to the *Crawford* settlement after the Rule 23(e) hearing. The latter appeal will of course be contingent on success in the intervention appeal, because only parties may appeal from an order settling a class action. See Felzen v. Andreas, 134 F.3d 873 (7th Cir. 1998), *affirmed by an equally divided Court under the name* California Public Employees' Retirement System v. Felzen, 525 U.S. 315 (1999). But if Blair and Wilbon persuade us that Magistrate Judge Schenkier erred in excluding them from *Crawford,* or if some other class member intervenes and appeals from approval of the settlement, then this court will have to address the propriety of that deposition.

Approval cannot be called a foregone conclusion. *Crawford* was settled for a pittance, plus attorneys' fees. Some cases settle for tiny sums because they have little chance of success; maybe *Crawford* is such a case. (We have resisted all temptation to peek at its merits.) But if the class in *Crawford* has such a weak position, why were the debtors' rights to compensatory and statutory damages preserved? If damages are at issue, how can Rule 23(b)(2) be used to avoid opt-outs and notice? If damages claims survive, what's wrong with pursuing them in a separate class action? We have never heard of a class action being settled on terms that amount to: "For $7,500 plus attorneys fees, the class is disestablished." When the individual claims are small, class actions are most useful. Perhaps Equifax found a plaintiff (or lawyer) willing to sell out the class—a possibility that we discussed most recently in Greisz v. Household Bank, 176 F.3d 1012 (7th Cir. 1999)—and then tried to use *Crawford* as a way to thwart parallel actions where the class had more vigorous champions. Then again, perhaps the deal in *Crawford* was the best the class could obtain. We do not prejudge that issue. Enough questions have been raised, however, to show that Judge Plunkett was entitled to keep the *Blair* class in place until final decision in *Crawford.*

When overlapping suits are filed in separate courts, stays (or, rarely, transfers) are the best means of coordination. But both *Crawford* and *Blair* were filed in the Northern District of Illinois. By far the best means of avoiding wasteful overlap when related suits are pending in the same court is to consolidate all before a single judge. Rules of the Northern District permit just such a process. At oral argument we asked the parties why this had not been done. Plaintiffs' counsel replied that until shortly before they attended the settlement conference in *Crawford* they believed that the classes did not overlap. Counsel say that they were shocked to learn that *Crawford* is much the larger case and that the *Blair* class is its subset. Lawyers representing Equifax say that *Blair*'s lawyers knew this all along or should have deduced it, and Magistrate Judge Schenkier agreed. We can't tell who is right, but surely Equifax knew from the get-go the relative sizes of, and relations among, the different class actions pending against it. Equifax could not plausibly explain at oral argument why *it* had not asked the district court to transfer all related actions to a single judge for decision. It is still not too late for the district court to accomplish this—although Magistrate Judge Schenkier will drop out of the picture if either case is transferred. Unanimous consent of the parties is required for a magistrate judge to enter final decision in a civil case, see 28 U.S.C. § 636(c), and it is obvious that Blair and Wilbon won't consent to that procedure. But both *Crawford* and

*Blair* easily could be handled by the same district judge—whether Judge Plunkett, to whom *Blair* is assigned, or Judge Andersen, to whom *Crawford* was initially assigned, does not matter for this purpose.

No matter what the district court does, we will do our own part to consolidate and expedite decision. *Crawford* is a related case for purposes of our Operating Procedure 6(b), so that any appeal in *Crawford,* and any further appeal in *Blair,* will come to this panel. For today, it is enough to hold that, until *Crawford* reaches final judgment, Judge Plunkett does not abuse his discretion by handling *Blair* as a class action.

*Affirmed.*

## Notes and Questions

1. *Appeals and Efficiency.* One of the reasons always given against allowing interlocutory appeals is the delay that ensues. Thus, though Rule 23(f) does not set any standards for when appeals should be taken, it does explicitly direct that the case should continue while the appeal is being decided, unless the trial or appellate court explicitly orders a stay. Isn't it likely, however, that trial judges will stay their orders pending appeal in most cases? Why spend time and effort on a case that may take an entirely different shape after the appeal is heard?

The court in *Blair* acted very expeditiously itself—hearing argument on the appeal in May and issuing a thoughtful and well-crafted opinion in June. The class certification occurred at the end of February. Another step promoting efficiency was the court's order that future appeals in these matters come back to the same panel (Judges Easterbrook, Posner, and Rovner). Briefing the certification issue on the merits at the same time appellate consideration was sought also promoted efficiency and is a practice that will probably be followed in most cases.

Yet for all its concern for expedition, the panel also held that the ten-day period for seeking an appeal specified in the rule could be extended by filing a motion to reconsider an adverse certification in the district court. Blair argued that an order denying reconsideration is not the kind of "order" to which Rule 23(f) refers; only the order granting or denying class action certification qualifies as a basis for appeal. But Judge Easterbrook held that the opportunity for the trial judge to correct her own errors would in the long run save time and effort. See Asher v. Baxter Int'l Inc., 505 F.3d 736 (7th Cir. 2007) (affirming and extending *Blair* to renewed motions for certification; concluding that the Rule 23(f) ten-day limit begins running after the first denial of certification, even if plaintiffs bring new motions for certification after changes in the lead plaintiff designation were made to satisfy concerns that drove the judge to deny the first certification).

Consider the approach of the Ninth Circuit to interlocutory review:

> Bearing in mind that many class certification decisions "present familiar and almost routine issues that are no more worthy of immediate appeal than

many other interlocutory rulings," Fed. R. Civ. P. 23(f), Advisory Committee Notes to 1998 Amendments, we adopt the following guidelines for consideration of Rule 23(f) petitions. Review of class certification decisions will be most appropriate when: (1) there is a death-knell situation for either the plaintiff or defendant that is independent of the merits of the underlying claims, coupled with a class certification decision by the district court that is questionable; (2) the certification decision presents an unsettled and fundamental issue of law relating to class actions, important both to the specific litigation and generally, that is likely to evade end-of-the-case review; or (3) the district court's class certification decision is manifestly erroneous.

Chamberlan v. Ford Motor Co., 402 F.3d 952, 959 (9th Cir. 2005) (holding that manifest error is sufficient, by itself, to warrant interlocutory review; observing that the three factors are "merely guidelines, not a rigid test"); id. at 960 (rejecting Ford's claim that this case falls within the "death knell" category because well over one hundred thousand class members were seeking an award of nearly $100 million; Ford failed to show that it lacks resources to defend or that defending "runs the risk of ruinous liability"). For discussion of other variations in the way circuits handle Rule 23(f) motions, see In re Lorazepam & Clorazepate Antitrust Litig., 289 F.3d 98 (D.C. Cir. 2002).

2. *Appeals and Reform.* The interlocutory type appeal under Rule 23(f) may result in a lot more appellate law on important class action issues. The fact that most class action cases settle (as do most cases in general) has meant that the definitive precedent has not developed at the same rate as the burgeoning use of the device. Because class actions can bind and affect so many people at once, the relatively stunted appellate case law in the area has, in the view of some, prevented needed improvement and reform in the administration of Rule 23. That is the import of *Blair*'s concern about issues that evade review as a main ingredient in allowing an appeal.

Coopers & Lybrand v. Livesay, discussed in *Blair*, held that a class certification order was not final, and also held that an appeal might be taken under 28 U.S.C. § 1292(b). 437 U.S. 463 (1978). That section requires that a "controlling question of law as to which there is a substantial ground for difference of opinion" be present and that an "immediate appeal from the order may materially advance the ultimate termination of the litigation." 28 U.S.C. § 1292(b). Are these reasons automatically sufficient under the new Rule 23(f)?

Another way in which appeals were gained before the passage of Rule 23(f) was through seeking an extraordinary writ of mandamus. In the Matter of Rhone-Poulenc Rorer Inc., 51 F.3d 1293 (7th Cir. 1995), was the best-known example of this tactic. Judge Posner decertified a class in that case, partly on the ground that there was an "undue and unnecessary risk of a monumental industry-busting error in entrusting the determination of potential multi-billion dollar liabilities to a single jury." Id. at 1304. Presumably, a case like *Rhone-Poulenc* would fit nicely into the requirements of Rule 23(f) for appeal.

3. *Appealing Certification of Defendant Classes.* Is the need for interlocutory appeal of certification orders any different for *defendant* classes? As the First Circuit observed in Tilley v. TJX Co., 345 F.3d 34, 37 (1st Cir. 2003), "[d]efendant classes are a relatively rare breed, and no court of appeals has had the opportunity to consider whether the same set of standards should apply to petitions for leave to appeal orders certifying (or refusing to certify) defendant classes." Noting the "special solicitude" owed to the "due process interests of absent members of defendant classes," the court accepted interlocutory appeal and reversed certification of a defendant class on the grounds that (1) Rule 23(b)(2) is an improper vehicle for defendant classes, and (2) the stare decisis effect of separate actions against individual defendants on subsequent cases would not "be dispositive of the interests of the other members" within the meaning of Rule 23(b)(1)(B). Id. at 37-41 (plaintiff named defendant class consisting of wholesaler and individual retailers who allegedly infringed her copyright in a wallpaper design).

## 3.   Who Is Bound?—Of Civil Rights and Class Actions

### Hansberry v. Lee
311 U.S. 32 (1940)

JUSTICE STONE delivered the opinion of the Court.

The question is whether the Supreme Court of Illinois, by its adjudication that petitioners in this case are bound by a judgment rendered in an earlier litigation to which they were not parties, has deprived them of the due process of law guaranteed by the Fourteenth Amendment.

Respondents brought this suit in the Circuit Court of Cook County, Illinois, to enjoin the breach by petitioners of an agreement restricting the use of land within a described area of the City of Chicago, which was alleged to have been entered into by some five hundred of the landowners. The agreement stipulated that for a specified period no part of the land should be "sold, leased to or permitted to be occupied by any person of the colored race," and provided that it should not be effective unless signed by the "owners of 95 per centum of the frontage" within the described area. The bill of complaint set up that the owners of 95 per cent of the frontage had signed; that respondents are owners of land within the restricted area who have either signed the agreement or acquired their land from others who did sign; and that petitioners Hansberry, who are Negroes, have, with the alleged aid of the other petitioners and with knowledge of the agreement, acquired and are occupying land in the restricted area formerly belonging to an owner who had signed the agreement.

To the defense that the agreement had never become effective because owners of 95 per cent of the frontage had not signed it, respondents pleaded that that issue was *res judicata* by the decree in an earlier suit. Burke v. Kleiman, 277 Ill. App. 519 [1934]. To this petitioners pleaded, by way of rejoinder, that they were not parties to that suit or bound by its decree, and that denial of their right to litigate, in the present suit, the issue of performance of the condition precedent to the validity of the agreement would be a denial of due process of law guaranteed by the Fourteenth Amendment. It does not appear, nor is it contended that any of petitioners is the successor in interest to or in privity with any of the parties in the earlier suit.

The circuit court, after a trial on the merits, found that owners of only about 54 per cent of the frontage had signed the agreement, and that the only support of the judgment in the *Burke* case was a false and fraudulent stipulation of the parties that owners of 95 per cent had signed. But it ruled that the issue of performance of the condition precedent to the validity of the agreement was *res judicata* as alleged and entered a decree for respondents. The Supreme Court of Illinois affirmed. 372 Ill. 369 [(1939)]. We granted certiorari to resolve the constitutional question. 309 U.S. 652 [(1940)].

The Supreme Court of Illinois, upon an examination of the record in Burke v. Kleiman, supra, found that that suit, in the Superior Court of Cook County, was brought by a landowner in the restricted area to enforce the agreement, which had been signed by her predecessor in title, on behalf of herself and other property owners in like situation, against four named individuals, who had acquired or asserted an interest in a plot of land formerly owned by another signer of the agreement; that, upon stipulation of the parties in that suit that the agreement had been signed by owners of 95 per cent of all the frontage, the court had adjudged that the agreement was in force, that it was a covenant running with the land and binding all the land within the described area in the hands of the parties to the agreement and those claiming under them, including defendants, and had entered its decree restraining the breach of the agreement by the defendants and those claiming under them, and that the appellate court had affirmed the decree. It found that the stipulation was untrue but held, contrary to the trial court, that it was not fraudulent or collusive. It also appears from the record in Burke v. Kleiman that the case was tried on an agreed statement of facts which raised only a single issue, whether by reason of changes in the restricted area, the agreement had ceased to be enforceable in equity.

From this the Supreme Court of Illinois concluded in the present case that Burke v. Kleiman was a "class" or "representative" suit and that in such a suit "where the remedy is pursued by a plaintiff who has the right to represent the class to which he belongs, other members of the class are bound by the results in the case unless it is reversed or set aside on direct proceedings"; . . . that petitioners in the present suit were members of the class represented by the plaintiffs in the earlier suit and consequently were bound by its decree, which had rendered the issue of performance of the condition precedent to the restrictive agreement *res judicata*, so far as petitioners are concerned. The court thought that the circumstance that the stipulation in the earlier suit that owners of 95 per cent of the footage had signed the agreement was contrary to the fact, as found in the present suit, did not militate against his conclusion, since the court in the earlier suit had jurisdiction to determine the fact as between the parties before it, and that its determination, because of the representative character of the suit, even though erroneous, was binding on petitioners until set aside by a direct attack on the first judgment.

State courts are free to attach such descriptive labels to litigations before them as they may choose and to attribute to them such consequences as they think appropriate under state constitutions and laws, subject only to the requirements of the Constitution of the United States. But when the judgment of a state court, ascribing to the judgment of another court the binding force and effect of *res judicata,* is challenged for want of due process it becomes the duty of this Court to examine the course of procedure in both litigations to ascertain whether the litigant whose rights have thus been adjudicated has been afforded such notice and opportunity to be heard as are requisite to the due process which the Constitution prescribes. . . .

It is a principle of general application in Anglo-American jurisprudence that one is not bound by a judgment *in personam* in a litigation in which he is not designated as a party or to which he has not been made a party by service of process. Pennoyer v. Neff, 95 U.S. 714 [(1877)]; 1 Freeman on Judgments (5th ed.), § 407. A judgment rendered in such circumstances is not entitled to the full faith and credit which the Constitution and statute of the United States, prescribe . . . and judicial action enforcing it against the person or property of the absent party is not that due process which the Fifth and Fourteenth Amendments require. . . .

To these general rules there is a recognized exception that, to an extent not precisely defined by judicial opinion, the judgment in a "class" or "representative" suit, to which some members of the class are parties, may bind members of the class or those represented who were not made parties to it. Smith v. Swormstedt, [57 U.S. 288 (1854)] . . . ; cf. Christopher v. Brusselback, 302 U.S. 500 [(1938)].

The class suit was an invention of equity to enable it to proceed to a decree in suits where the number of those interested in the subject of the litigation is so great that their joinder as parties in conformity to the usual rules of procedure is impracticable. . . .

It is evident that the considerations which may induce a court thus to proceed, despite a technical defect of parties, may differ from those which must be taken into account in determining whether the absent parties are bound by the decree or, if it is adjudged that they are, in ascertaining whether such an adjudication satisfies the requirements of due process and of full faith and credit. Nevertheless, there is scope within the framework of the Constitution for holding in appropriate cases that a judgment rendered in a class suit is *res judicata* as to members of the class who are not formal parties to the suit. Here, as elsewhere, the Fourteenth Amendment does not compel state courts or legislatures to adopt any particular rule for establishing the conclusiveness of judgments in class suits; . . . nor does it compel the adoption of the particular rules thought by this Court to be appropriate for the federal courts. With a proper regard for divergent local institutions and interests, . . . this Court is justified in saying that there has been a failure of due process only in those cases where it cannot be said that the procedure adopted, fairly insures the protection of the interests of absent parties who are to be bound by it.

It is familiar doctrine of the federal courts that members of a class not present as parties to the litigation may be bound by the judgment where they are in fact adequately represented by parties who are present, or where they actually participate in the conduct of the litigation in which members of the class are present as parties, . . . or where the interest of the members of the class, some of whom are present as parties, is joint, or where for any other reason the relationship between the parties present and those who are absent is such as legally to entitle the former to stand in judgment for the latter. Smith v. Swormstedt, supra; cf. Christopher v. Brusselback, supra, 503, 504 . . . and cases cited.

In all such cases, so far as it can be said that the members of the class who are present are, by generally recognized rules of law, entitled to stand in judgment for those who are not, we may assume for present purposes that such procedure affords a protection to the parties who are represented, though absent, which would satisfy the requirements of due process and full faith and credit. . . . Nor do we find it necessary for the decision of this case to say that, when the only circumstance defining the class is that the determination of the rights of its members turns upon a single issue of fact or law, a state could not constitutionally adopt a procedure whereby some of the members of the class could stand in judgment for all, provided that the procedures were so devised and applied as to insure that those present are of the same class as those absent and that the litigation is so conducted as to insure the full and fair consideration of the common issue. . . . We decide only that the procedure and the course of litigation sustained here by the plea of *res judicata* do not satisfy these requirements.

The restrictive agreement did not purport to create a joint obligation or liability. If valid and effective its promises were the several obligations of the signers and those claiming under them. The promises ran severally to every other signer. It is plain that in such circumstances all those alleged to be bound by the agreement would not constitute a single class in any litigation brought to enforce it. Those who sought to secure its benefits by enforcing it could not be said to be in the same class with or represent those whose interest was in resisting performance, for the agreement by its terms imposes obligations and confers rights on the owner of each plot of land who signs it. . . .

Because of the dual and potentially conflicting interests of those who are putative parties to the agreement in compelling or resisting its performance, it is impossible to say, solely because they are parties to it, that any two of them are of the same class. Nor without more, and with the due regard for the protection of the rights of absent parties which due process exacts, can some be permitted to stand in judgment for all.

It is one thing to say that some members of a class may represent other members in a litigation where the sole and common interest of the class in the litigation, is either to assert a common right or to challenge an asserted obligation. . . . It is quite another to hold that all those who are free alternatively either to assert rights or to challenge them are of a single class, so that any group, merely because it is of the class so constituted, may be deemed adequately to represent any others of the class in litigating their interests in either alternative. Such a selection of representatives for purposes of litigation, whose substantial interests are not necessarily or even probably the same as those whom they are deemed to represent, does not afford that protection to absent parties which due process requires. The doctrine of representation of absent parties in a class suit has not hitherto been thought to go so far. . . . Apart from the opportunities it would afford for the fraudulent and collusive sacrifice of the rights of absent parties, we think that the representation in this case no more satisfies the requirements of due process than a trial by a judicial officer who is in such situation that he may have an interest in the outcome of the litigation in conflict with that of the litigants. . . .

The plaintiffs in the *Burke* case sought to compel performance of the agreement in behalf of themselves and all others similarly situated. They did not designate the defendants in the suit as a class or seek any injunction or other relief against others than the named defendants, and the decree which was entered did not purport to bind others. In seeking to enforce the agreement the plaintiffs in that suit were not representing the petitioners here whose substantial interest is in resisting performance. The defendants in the first suit were not treated by the pleadings or decree as representing others or as foreclosing by their defense the rights of others; and, even though nominal defendants, it does not appear that their interest in defeating the contract outweighed their interest in establishing its validity. For a court in this situation to ascribe to either the plaintiffs or defendants the performance of such functions on behalf of petitioners here, is to attribute to them a power that it cannot be said that they had assumed to exercise, and a responsibility which, in view of their dual interests it does not appear that they could rightly discharge.

*Reversed.*

Justice McReynolds, Justice Roberts, and Justice Reed concur in the result.

### *Note:* Hansberry *and the Concept of Persons Whose Interests Are Affected by Litigation*

An important aspect of *Hansberry*, of course, is that the covenant in the case was a racially restrictive one. The family in the case was that of Lorraine Hansberry, who drew on the event in creating her well-known play *A Raisin in the Sun.* In her autobiography, *To Be Young, Gifted and Black* (1969), she described the psychic costs of the litigation to her father, the named plaintiff, and the whole family. More on the background of the case, especially on the prior litigation, Burke v. Kleiman, is explored in Allen R. Kamp, The History Behind *Hansberry v. Lee*, 20 U.C. Davis L. Rev. 481 (1987).

Eight years after *Hansberry*, the United States Supreme Court finally ruled that all racially restrictive covenants are unenforceable. Shelley v. Kraemer, 334 U.S. 1 (1948). It later ruled that all governmentally sanctioned racial discrimination violated the Constitution. But in 1940, the Court was writing in a period of transition from a society that tolerated race-conscious laws to one that deemed them presumptively intolerable and unlawful. *Hansberry* gave the Court in 1940 a means by which it could strike down the results of a racially restrictive covenant without confronting head-on the legal and social problem it later could not, or chose not, to avoid. Consider the following passage from Stephen C. Yeazell's influential work From Medieval Group Litigation to the Modern Class Action 231 (1987), in which he characterizes the impact of *Hansberry* on subsequent class action cases and the concept of "interest" within them:

> It may be that in situations of social flux the very concept of abstractly defined social interest dissolves, leaving only the individual as the definer of his good. It is less a question of whether or not the individual desires to assert his right, as the Court in *Hansberry* framed the question, than it is of figuring out the possible (and actual) combinations of economic and noneconomic, long-run and short-run interests. *Hansberry*'s power flows from the elevation to constitutional status of its struggle to define interests. It equates due process with representation of interest but then defines interest in terms of individually expressed desire to enforce rights. Commentators have been trying to read the entrails ever since.

To what extent do *Hansberry*, and class actions generally, compel courts to rethink the meaning of individual interests and to consider the social and systemic impact of what may at first blush appear to be a "private" dispute? Doesn't a neighborhood's decision to enforce a race-restrictive covenant have community-wide reverberations? What about an individual's or single corporation's decision to deposit toxic substances in a river or into the atmosphere?

### Note: Defendant Classes

Christopher v. Brusselback, 302 U.S. 500 (1938), held that a shareholder could not be subjected to personal liability by a judgment rendered against him in an action in which he was represented by a fellow shareholder but in which he was not personally joined as a party. Was that decision overruled by Hansberry v. Lee? It has been suggested that there is a difference between plaintiffs who may benefit from being represented in class actions and defendants who gain nothing from the representation. See, e.g., A. Peter Parsons & Kenneth W. Starr, Environmental Litigation and Defendant Class Actions: The Unrealized Viability of Rule 23, 4 Ecology L.Q. 881 (1975). The authors there suggest that the availability of the representative should be accepted as satisfying the requirements of due process, but only if the absent defendants are provided with notice and an opportunity to intervene.

### *Martin v. Wilks*
490 U.S. 755 (1989)

CHIEF JUSTICE REHNQUIST delivered the opinion of the Court.

A group of white firefighters sued the city of Birmingham, Alabama (City), and the Jefferson County Personnel Board (Board) alleging that they were being denied promotions in favor of less qualified black firefighters. They claimed that the City and the Board were making promotion decisions on the basis of race in reliance on certain consent decrees, and that these decisions constituted impermissible racial discrimination in violation of the Constitution and federal statutes. The District Court held that the white firefighters were precluded from challenging employment decisions taken pursuant to the decrees, even though these firefighters had not been parties to the proceedings in which the decrees were entered. We think this holding contravenes the general rule that a person cannot be deprived of his legal rights in a proceeding to which he is not a party.

The litigation in which the consent decrees were entered began in 1974, when the Ensley Branch of the National Association for the Advancement of Colored People and seven black individuals filed separate class-action complaints against the City and the Board. They alleged that both had engaged in racially discriminatory hiring and promotion practices in various public service jobs in violation of Title VII of the Civil Rights Act of 1964, 42 U.S.C. §§ 2000e *et seq.*, and other federal laws. After a bench trial on some issues, but before judgment, the parties entered into two consent decrees, one between the black individuals and the City and the other between them and the Board. These proposed decrees set forth an extensive remedial scheme, including long-term and interim annual goals for the hiring of blacks as firefighters. The decrees also provided for goals for promotion of blacks within the fire department.

The District Court entered an order provisionally approving the decrees and directing publication of notice of the upcoming fairness hearings. Notice of the hearings, with a reference to the general nature of the decrees, was published in two local newspapers. At that hearing, the Birmingham Firefighters Association (BFA) appeared and filed objections as *amicus curiae.* After the hearing, but before final approval of the decrees, the BFA and two of its members also moved to intervene on the ground that the decrees would adversely affect their rights. The District Court denied the motions as untimely and approved the decrees. United States v. Jefferson County, 28 FEP Cases 1834 (N.D. Ala. 1981). Seven white firefighters, all members of the BFA, then filed a complaint against the City and the Board seeking injunctive relief against enforcement of the decrees. The seven argued that the decrees would operate to illegally discriminate against them; the District Court denied relief.

Both the denial of intervention and the denial of injunctive relief were affirmed on appeal. United States v. Jefferson County, 720 F.2d 1511 (11th Cir. 1983). The District Court had not abused its discretion in refusing to let the BFA intervene, thought the Eleventh Circuit, in part because the fire-fighters could "institut[e] an independent Title VII suit, asserting specific violations of their rights." Id., at 1518. And, for the same reason, petition-ers had not adequately shown the potential for irreparable harm from the operation of the decrees necessary to obtain injunctive relief. Id., at 1520.

A new group of white firefighters, the *Wilks* respondents, then brought suit against the City and the Board in District Court. They too alleged that, because of their race, they were being denied promotions in favor of less qualified blacks in violation of federal law. The Board and the City admit-ted to making race-conscious employment decisions, but argued that the decisions were unassailable because they were made pursuant to the con-sent decrees. A group of black individuals, the *Martin* petitioners, were allowed to intervene in their individual capacities to defend the decrees.

The defendants moved to dismiss the reverse discrimination cases as impermissible collateral attacks on the consent decrees. The District Court denied the motions, ruling that the decrees would provide a defense to claims of discrimination for employment decisions "mandated" by the decrees, leaving the principal issue for trial whether the challenged promo-tions were indeed required by the decrees. After trial the District Court granted the motion to dismiss. The court concluded that "if in fact the City was required to [make promotions of blacks] by the consent decree, then they would not be guilty of [illegal] racial discrimination" and that the defendants had "establish[ed] that the promotions of the black individuals . . . were in fact required by the terms of the consent decree."

On appeal, the Eleventh Circuit reversed. It held that, "[b]ecause . . . [the *Wilks* respondents] were neither parties nor privies to the consent decrees, . . . their independent claims of unlawful discrimination are not precluded." In re Birmingham Reverse Discrimination Employment Litigation, 833 F.2d 1492, 1498 (1987). The court explicitly rejected the doctrine of "impermis-sible collateral attack" espoused by other Courts of Appeals to immunize parties to a consent decree from charges of discrimination by nonpar-ties for actions taken pursuant to the decree. Id. Although it recognized a "strong public policy in favor of voluntary affirmative action plans," the panel acknowledged that this interest "must yield to the policy against requiring third parties to submit to bargains in which their interests were either ignored or sacrificed." Id. The court remanded the case for trial of the discrimination claims, suggesting that the operative law for judging the consent decrees was that governing voluntary affirmative-action plans. Id., at 1497.

We granted certiorari, . . . and now affirm the Eleventh Circuit's judg-ment. All agree that "[i]t is a principle of general application in Anglo-American jurisprudence that one is not bound by a judgment *in personam* in a litigation in which he is not designated as a party or to which he has not been made a party by service of process." Hansberry v. Lee, 311 U.S. 32, 40

(1940). . . . This rule is part of our "deep-rooted historic tradition that everyone should have his own day in court." . . . A judgment or decree among parties to a lawsuit resolves issues as among them, but it does not conclude the rights of strangers to those proceedings.[2]

Petitioners argue that, because respondents failed to timely intervene in the initial proceedings, their current challenge to actions taken under the consent decree constitutes an impermissible "collateral attack." They argue that respondents were aware that the underlying suit might affect them, and if they chose to pass up an opportunity to intervene, they should not be permitted to later litigate the issues in a new action. The position has sufficient appeal to have commanded the approval of the great majority of the Federal Courts of Appeals, but we agree with the contrary view expressed by the Court of Appeals for the Eleventh Circuit in these cases.

We begin with the words of Justice Brandeis in Chase National Bank v. Norwalk, 291 U.S. 431[, 441] (1934):

> The law does not impose upon any person absolutely entitled to a hearing the burden of voluntary intervention in a suit to which he is a stranger. . . . Unless duly summoned to appear in a legal proceeding, a person not a privy may rest assured that a judgment recovered therein will not affect his legal rights.

While these words were written before the adoption of the Federal Rules of Civil Procedure, we think the Rules incorporate the same principle; a party seeking a judgment binding on another cannot obligate that person to intervene; he must be joined. See [Zenith Radio Corp. v.] Hazeltine, [395 U.S. 100,] 110 [1969] (judgment against Hazeltine vacated because it was not named as a party or served, even though as the parent corporation of one of the parties it clearly knew of the claim against it and had made a special appearance to contest jurisdiction). Against the background of permissive intervention set forth in *Chase National Bank,* the drafters cast Rule 24, governing intervention, in permissive terms. See Fed. Rule Civ. Proc. 24(a) (intervention as of right) ("Upon timely application anyone shall be permitted to intervene"); Fed. Rule Civ. Proc. 24(b) (permissive intervention) ("Upon timely application anyone may be permitted to intervene"). They

---

2. We have recognized an exception to the general rule when, in certain limited circumstances, a person, although not a party, has his interests adequately represented by someone with the same interests who is a party. See Hansberry v. Lee, 311 U.S. 32, 41-42 (1940) ("class" or "representative" suits); Fed. Rule Civ. Proc. 23 (same); Montana v. United States, 440 U.S. 147, 154-155 (1979) (control of litigation on behalf of one of the parties in the litigation). Additionally, where a special remedial scheme exists expressly foreclosing successive litigation by nonlitigants, as for example in bankruptcy or probate, legal proceedings may terminate preexisting rights if the scheme is otherwise consistent with due process. See NLRB v. Bildisco & Bildisco, 465 U.S. 513, 529-530, n.10 (1984) ("[P]roof of claim must be presented to the Bankruptcy Court . . . or be lost"); Tulsa Professional Collection Services, Inc. v. Pope, 485 U.S. 478 (1988) (nonclaim statute terminating unsubmitted claims against the estate). Neither of these exceptions, however, applies in these cases.

determined that the concern for finality and completeness of judgments would be "better [served] by mandatory joinder procedures." 18 Wright § 4452, p. 453. Accordingly, Rule 19(a) provides for mandatory joinder in circumstances where a judgment rendered in the absence of a person may "leave . . . persons already parties subject to a substantial risk of incurring . . . inconsistent obligations. . . ." Rule 19(b) sets forth the factors to be considered by a court in deciding whether to allow an action to proceed in the absence of an interested party.

Joinder as a party, rather than knowledge of a lawsuit and an opportunity to intervene, is the method by which potential parties are subjected to the jurisdiction of the court and bound by a judgment or decree.[6] The parties to a lawsuit presumably know better than anyone else the nature and scope of relief sought in the action, and at whose expense such relief might be granted. It makes sense, therefore, to place on them a burden of bringing in additional parties where such a step is indicated, rather than placing on potential additional parties a duty to intervene when they acquire knowledge of the lawsuit. The linchpin of the "impermissible collateral attack" doctrine — the attribution of preclusive effect to a failure to intervene — is therefore quite inconsistent with Rule 19 and Rule 24. . . .

Petitioners contend that a different result should be reached because the need to join affected parties will be burdensome and ultimately discouraging to civil rights litigation. Potential adverse claimants may be numerous and difficult to identify; if they are not joined, the possibility for inconsistent judgments exists. Judicial resources will be needlessly consumed in relitigation of the same question.

Even if we were wholly persuaded by these arguments as a matter of policy, acceptance of them would require a rewriting rather than an interpretation of the relevant Rules. But we are not persuaded that their acceptance would lead to a more satisfactory method of handling cases like these. It must be remembered that the alternatives are a duty to intervene based on knowledge, on the one hand, and some form of joinder, as the Rules presently provide, on the other. No one can seriously contend that an employer might successfully defend against a Title VII claim by one group of employees on the ground that its actions were required by an earlier decree entered in a suit brought against it by another, if the later group did not have adequate notice or knowledge of the earlier suit.

---

6. The dissent argues, on the one hand, that respondents have not been "bound" by the decree but, rather, that they are only suffering practical adverse effects from the consent decree. On the other hand, the dissent characterizes respondents' suit not as an assertion of their own independent rights, but as a collateral attack on the consent decrees which, it is said, can only proceed on very limited grounds. Respondents in their suit have alleged that they are being racially discriminated against by their employer in violation of Title VII: either the fact that the disputed employment decisions are being made pursuant to a consent decree is a defense to respondents' Title VII claims or it is not. If it is a defense to challenges to employment practices which would otherwise violate Title VII, it is very difficult to see why respondents are not being "bound" by the decree.

The difficulties petitioners foresee in identifying those who could be adversely affected by a decree granting broad remedial relief are undoubtedly present, but they arise from the nature of the relief sought and not because of any choice between mandatory intervention and joinder. Rule 19's provisions for joining interested parties are designed to accommodate the sort of complexities that may arise from a decree affecting numerous people in various ways. We doubt that a mandatory intervention rule would be any less awkward. . . .

Nor do we think that the system of joinder called for by the Rules is likely to produce more relitigation of issues than the converse rule. The breadth of a lawsuit and concomitant relief may be at least partially shaped in advance through Rule 19 to avoid needless clashes with future litigation. And even under a regime of mandatory intervention, parties who did not have adequate knowledge of the suit would relitigate issues. Additional questions about the adequacy and timeliness of knowledge would inevitably crop up. We think that the system of joinder presently contemplated by the Rules best serves the many interests involved in the run of litigated cases, including cases like the present ones.

Petitioners also urge that the congressional policy favoring voluntary settlement of employment discrimination claims, referred to in cases such as Carson v. American Brands, Inc., 450 U.S. 79 (1981), also supports the "impermissible collateral attack" doctrine. But once again it is essential to note just what is meant by "voluntary settlement." A voluntary settlement in the form of a consent decree between one group of employees and their employer cannot possibly "settle," voluntarily or otherwise, the conflicting claims of another group of employees who do not join in the agreement. This is true even if the second group of employees is a party to the litigation:

> [P]arties who choose to resolve litigation through settlement may not dispose of the claims of a third party . . . without that party's agreement. A court's approval of a consent decree between some of the parties therefore cannot dispose of the valid claims of nonconsenting intervenors.

Firefighters v. Cleveland, 478 U.S. 501, 529 (1986).

Insofar as the argument is bottomed on the idea that it may be easier to settle claims among a disparate group of affected persons if they are all before the court, joinder bids fair to accomplish that result as well as a regime of mandatory intervention.

For the foregoing reasons we affirm the decision of the Court of Appeals for the Eleventh Circuit. That court remanded the case for trial of the reverse discrimination claims. Birmingham Reverse Discrimination, 833 F.2d, at 1500-1502. Petitioners point to language in the District Court's findings of fact and conclusions of law which suggests that respondents will not prevail on the merits. We agree with the view of the Court of Appeals, however, that the proceedings in the District Court may have been affected by the mistaken view that respondents' claims on the merits were barred to the extent they were inconsistent with the consent decree.

*Affirmed.*

[The dissent of JUSTICE STEVENS, with whom JUSTICE BRENNAN, JUSTICE MARSHALL, and JUSTICE BLACKMUN join, is omitted.]

## Notes and Questions

1. *The Significance of Martin v. Wilks.* Shortly after the case was decided Congress enacted a statute designed to reverse the decision.

**Civil Rights Act of 1991**
Pub. L. No. 102. 166, § 402(a), 105 Stat. 1071, 1099,
reprinted at 42 U.S.C. § 2000e-2(n)(1) (Supp. V. 1993)

> § 108. [A]n employment practice that implements and is within the scope of a litigated or consent judgment or order that resolves a claim of employment discrimination under the Constitution or Federal civil rights laws may not be challenged . . . in a claim under the Constitution or federal civil rights laws:
>
> (i) by a person who, prior to the entry of the judgment or order . . . had—
>
> (1) actual notice of the proposed judgment or order sufficient to apprise such person that such judgment or order might adversely affect the interests and legal rights of such person and that an opportunity was available to present objections to such judgment or order by a future data certain; and
>
> (2) a reasonable opportunity to present objections to such judgment or order; or
>
> (ii) by a person whose interests were adequately represented by another person who had previously challenged the judgment or order on the same legal grounds and with a similar factual situation, unless there has been an intervening change in law or fact.

The statute does reverse *Wilks* on its facts, doesn't it? But what about a discrimination claim outside of the employment discrimination area? If, for instance, you were representing the plaintiffs in a claim charging housing discrimination, how would you proceed to frame your class action in light of *Wilks*? The effect of the case is to place the burden of joining all affected parties on the plaintiffs (and secondarily on the court). Think about using Rule 19 or 24, or about creating subclasses under Rule 23(c)(4). Think also about the management problems involved in having involuntary and opposing parties on the same side of the "versus."

2. *The Advantages of the Class Action.* Following are the first paragraphs of the introduction and the class action allegations in Rodriguez v. California Highway Patrol, 89 F. Supp. 2d 1131 (N.D. Cal. 2000). Employing what you know from *Wilks* and *Dukes*, do you think this is an appropriate kind of

case for class action treatment? What are the advantages of a class action in this situation?

1. This is a class action lawsuit seeking declaratory, injunctive, and monetary relief against the California Highway Patrol ("CHP") and the Bureau of Narcotics Enforcement ("BNE") for engaging in and condoning a continuing pattern and practice of race-based stops, detentions and searches of motorists of color traveling on the public streets and highways of the State of California. The specific abuses giving rise to this action occurred on or in the area of Highway 152 in California, including, but not limited to, the area where Highway 152 intersects with Interstate Highway 5.

2. Plaintiffs in this case, Curtis Rodriguez ("Rodriguez"), Jose Lopez ("Lopez"), MacArthur Washington ("Washington"), California Branches of the NAACP ("NAACP"), and California League of United Latin American Citizens ("LULAC"), represent a class of people of color who have been or will be subjected to the humiliation of being targeted, interrogated, detained and searched by defendants in the area of Highway 152 due to the defendants' policy and practice of what is commonly known as "racial profiling." The moment Mr. Rodriguez, Mr. Lopez and Mr. Washington were stopped by the defendants they became victims of what the United States Court of Appeals for the Ninth Circuit called "an all too familiar set of circumstances — an intrusive law enforcement stop and seizure of innocent persons on the basis of suspicions rooted principally in the race of 'the suspects.'" Washington v. Lambert, 98 F.3d 1181, 1182 (1996).

3. To any person of color, regardless of ethnic background, level of education, or economic station in life, the insidious problem of racial profiling by law enforcement officers is all too familiar. It is a continuing reminder that, despite popular notions of progress in race relations, racial discrimination remains a day-to-day reality in our society.

4. By the complaint in this case, plaintiffs seek judicial redress for violations of their civil rights due to racial profiling. But they also seek to confirm what everyone has a right to expect in the United States: that people of color may use the public streets and highways, just like anybody else, without having to suffer the indignities of racial discrimination at the hands of government officials.

5. Plaintiffs' claims are brought pursuant to the Fourth, Fifth and Fourteenth Amendments to the United States Constitution; Title VI of the Civil Rights Act of 1964 and its implementing regulations, 42 U.S.C. §§ 1982, 1983, 1985 and 1986; Article 1, Section 7(a) of the California Constitution; California Civil Code § 52.1; California Government Code § 11135. . . .

*Class Action Allegations*

64. For the purposes of all relief sought in this case, plaintiffs Rodriguez, Lopez and Washington bring this action pursuant to Federal Rule of Civil Procedure 23 on behalf of themselves and all other persons similarly situated. Each of these individual class representatives is a person of color who has been stopped, detained, interrogated and searched by CHP and/or BNE officers while travelling on or in the area of Highway 152. The class which plaintiffs seek to represent consists of all people of color who, since June 1998, have been or will be stopped, detained, interrogated and/or searched on Highway 152 or on any road or highway near 152 including, but not limited

to, Interstate Highway 5, by the CHP or the BNE. These class members are victims of the racially motivated and illegal pattern and practice of discrimination in the enforcement of traffic laws by the CHP and BNE.

65. The class of persons defined in paragraph 64 is so numerous that joinder of all members in one action is impracticable.

66. There are questions of law and fact common to all members of the class, because all class members have been, or will be, adversely affected by the challenged actions of the defendants. Common questions of fact and law include, but are not limited to: whether CHP and BNE officers target, stop, detain and/or search individual drivers in a racially discriminatory manner; and whether CHP and BNE officers are knowingly trained to employ methods that result in racial profiling and have an unjustified disparate impact on putative class members in violation of federal and state civil rights laws.

67. The claims of the representative plaintiffs are typical of the class as a whole who travel on or around Highway 152 and have been stopped, detained and/or searched by the defendants. The experiences of the plaintiffs at the hands of the defendants resulted from the defendants' policy and practice of discriminating on the basis of race and ethnicity, making their claims typical of those held by the class they seek to represent.

68. Plaintiffs can and will fairly and adequately protect the interests of the members of the class. Plaintiffs will be adequate representatives of the class in that all of the relevant questions of fact and law applicable to the class also apply to them.

69. Plaintiffs have retained counsel who are familiar with the applicable law and experienced in class action litigation, as well as litigation involving criminal law and civil rights. Counsel for plaintiffs have the resources necessary to pursue this litigation.

70. This action is properly maintained as a class action. The questions of law and fact common to the members of the class predominate over any questions affecting only individual members, and a class action is superior to other available methods for the fair and efficient adjudication of this controversy. Plaintiffs know of no difficulty to be encountered in the management of this action that would preclude its maintenance as a class action.

71. The prosecution of separate actions by individual class members would create a risk of inconsistent and varying adjudication concerning the subject of this action, and such adjudication could establish incompatible standards of conduct for defendants under the laws alleged herein.

## 4.   Notice and the Opportunity to Be Heard

### *Eisen v. Carlisle & Jacquelin*
417 U.S. 156 (1974)

JUSTICE POWELL delivered the opinion of the Court.

On May 2, 1966, petitioner filed a class action on behalf of himself and all other odd-lot[1] traders on the New York Stock Exchange (the Exchange).

---

1. Odd lots are shares traded in lots of fewer than a hundred. Shares traded in units of a hundred or multiples thereof are round-lots.

The complaint charged respondents with violations of the antitrust and securities laws and demanded damages for petitioner and his class. Eight years have elapsed, but there has been no trial on the merits of these claims. Both the parties and the courts are still wrestling with the complex questions surrounding petitioner's attempt to maintain his suit as a class action under Fed. Rule Civ. Proc. 23. We granted certiorari to resolve some of these difficulties. 414 U.S. 908 (1973).

## I

Petitioner brought this class action in the United States District Court for the Southern District of New York. Originally, he sued on behalf of all buyers and sellers of odd lots on the Exchange, but subsequently the class was limited to those who traded in odd lots during the period from May 1, 1962, through June 30, 1966. 52 F.R.D. 253, 261 (1971). Throughout this period odd-lot trading was not part of the Exchange's regular auction market but was handled exclusively by special odd-lot dealers, who bought and sold for their own accounts as principals. Respondent brokerage firms Carlisle & Jacquelin and DeCoppet & Doremus together handled 99% of the Exchange's odd-lot business. S.E.C., Report of Special Study of Securities Markets, H.R. Doc. No. 95, pt. 2¹, 88th Cong., 1st Sess., 172 (1963). They were compensated by the odd-lot differential, a surcharge imposed on the odd-lot investor in addition to the standard brokerage commission applicable to round-lot transactions. For the period in question the differential was 1/8 of a point (12 1/2¢) per share on stocks trading below $40 per share and 1/4 of a point (25¢) per share on stocks trading at or above $40 per share.

Petitioner charged that respondent brokerage firms had monopolized odd-lot trading and set the differential at an excessive level in violation of §§ 1 and 2 of the Sherman Act, 15 U.S.C. §§ 1 and 2, and he demanded treble damages for the amount of the overcharge. Petitioner also demanded unspecified money damages from the Exchange for its alleged failure to regulate the differential for the protection of investors in violation of §§ 6 and 19 of the Securities Exchange Act of 1934; 15 U.S.C. §§ 78f and 78s. Finally, he requested attorneys' fees and injunctive prohibition of future excessive charges.

A critical fact in this litigation is that petitioner's individual stake in the damages award he seeks is only $70. No competent attorney would undertake this complex antitrust action to recover so inconsequential an amount. Economic reality dictates that petitioner's suit proceed as a class action or not at all. Opposing counsel have therefore engaged in prolonged combat over the various requirements of Rule 23. The result has been an exceedingly complicated series of decisions by both the District Court and the Court of Appeals for the Second Circuit. To understand the labyrinthian history of this litigation, a preliminary overview of the decisions may prove useful.

In the beginning, the District Court determined that petitioner's suit was not maintainable as a class action. On appeal, the Court of Appeals issued two decisions known popularly as *Eisen I* and *Eisen II.* The first held that the District Court's decision was a final order and thus appealable. In the second the Court of Appeals intimated that petitioner's suit could satisfy the requirements of Rule 23, but it remanded the case to permit the District Court to consider the matter further. After conducting several evidentiary hearings on remand, the District Court decided that the suit could be maintained as a class action and entered orders intended to fulfill the notice requirements of Rule 23. Once again, the case was appealed. The Court of Appeals then issued its decision in *Eisen III* and ended the trilogy by denying class action status to petitioner's suit. . . .

Thus, after six and one-half years and three published decisions, the Court of Appeals endorsed the conclusion reached by the District Court in its original order in 1966—that petitioner's suit could not proceed as a class action. In its procedural history, at least, this litigation has lived up to Judge Lumbard's characterization of it as a "Frankenstein monster posing as a class action." *Eisen II,* 391 F.2d [555], 572 [(1968)].

## II

. . .

## III

Turning to the merits of the case, we find that the District Court's resolution of the notice problems was erroneous in two respects. First, it failed to comply with the notice requirements of Rule 23(c)(2), and second, it imposed part of the cost of notice on respondents.

## A

Rule 23(c)(2) provides that, in any class action maintained under subdivision (b)(3), each class member shall be advised that he has the right to exclude himself from the action on request or to enter an appearance through counsel, and further that the judgment, whether favorable or not, will bind all class members not requesting exclusion. To this end, the court is required to direct to class members "the best notice practicable under the circumstances, *including individual notice to all members who can be identified through reasonable effort.*" We think the import of this language is unmistakable. Individual notice must be sent to all class members whose names and addresses may be ascertained through reasonable effort.

The Advisory Committee's Note to Rule 23 reinforces this conclusion. See 28 U.S.C. App., p. 7765. The Advisory Committee described subdivision (c)(2) as "not merely discretionary" and added that the "mandatory notice pursuant to subdivision (c)(2) . . . is designed to fulfill requirements of due process to which the class action procedure is of course subject." Id., at 7768. The Committee explicated its incorporation of due process standards by citation to Mullane v. Central Hanover Bank & Trust Co., 339 U.S. 306 (1950), and like cases.

In *Mullane* the Court addressed the constitutional sufficiency of publication notice rather than mailed individual notice to known beneficiaries of a common trust fund as part of a judicial settlement of accounts. The Court observed that notice and an opportunity to be heard were fundamental requisites of the constitutional guarantee of procedural due process. It further stated that notice must be "reasonably calculated, under all the circumstances, to apprise interested parties of the pendency of action and afford them an opportunity to present their objections." Id., at 314. The Court continued:

> But when notice is a person's due, process which is a mere gesture is not due process. The means employed must be such as one desirous of actually informing the absentee might reasonably adopt to accomplish it. The reasonableness and hence the constitutional validity of any chosen method may be defended on the ground that it is in itself reasonably certain to inform those affected.

Id., at 315. The Court then held that publication notice could not satisfy due process where the names and addresses of the beneficiaries were known. In such cases, "the reasons disappear for resort to means less likely than the mails to apprise them of [an action's] pendency." Id. at 318.

In Schroeder v. City of New York, 371 U.S. 208 (1962), decided prior to the promulgation of amended Rule 23, the Court explained that *Mullane* required rejection of notice by publication where the name and address of the affected person were available. The Court stated that the "general rule" is that "notice by publication is not enough with respect to a person whose name and address are known or very easily ascertainable. . . ." Id. at 212-213. The Court also noted that notice by publication had long been recognized as a poor substitute for actual notice and that its justification was "'difficult at best.'" Id. at 213.

Viewed in this context, the express language and intent of Rule 23(c)(2) leave no doubt that individual notice must be provided to those class members who are identifiable through reasonable effort. In the present case, the names and addresses of 2,250,000 class members are easily ascertainable, and there is nothing to show that individual notice cannot be mailed to each. For these class members, individual notice is clearly the "best notice practicable" within the meaning of Rule 23(c)(2) and our prior decisions.

Petitioner contends, however, that we should dispense with the requirement of individual notice in this case, and he advances two reasons for our doing so. First, the prohibitively high cost of providing individual notice to 2,250,000 class members would end this suit as a class action and effectively frustrate petitioner's attempt to vindicate the policies underlying the antitrust and securities laws. Second, petitioner contends that individual notice is unnecessary in this case, because no prospective class member has a large enough stake in the matter to justify separate litigation of his individual claim. Hence, class members lack any incentive to opt out of the class action even if notified.

The short answer to these arguments is that individual notice to identifiable class members is not a discretionary consideration to be waived in a particular case. It is, rather, an unambiguous requirement of Rule 23. As the Advisory Committee's Note explained, the Rule was intended to insure that the judgment, whether favorable or not, would bind all class members who did not request exclusion from the suit. 28 U.S.C. App., pp. 7765, 7768. Accordingly, each class member who can be identified through reasonable effort must be notified that he may request exclusion from the action and thereby preserve his opportunity to press his claim separately or that he may remain in the class and perhaps participate in the management of the action. There is nothing in Rule 23 to suggest that the notice requirements can be tailored to fit the pocketbooks of particular plaintiffs.

Petitioner further contends that adequate representation, rather than notice, is the touchstone of due process in a class action and therefore satisfies Rule 23. We think this view has little to commend it. To begin with, Rule 23 speaks to notice as well as to adequacy of representation and requires that both be provided. Moreover, petitioner's argument proves too much, for it quickly leads to the conclusion that no notice at all, published or otherwise, would be required in the present case. This cannot be so, for quite apart from what due process may require, the command of Rule 23 is clearly to the contrary. We therefore conclude that Rule 23(c)(2) requires that individual notice be sent to all class members who can be identified with reasonable effort.

## B

We also agree with the Court of Appeals that petitioner must bear the cost of notice to the members of his class. The District Court reached the contrary conclusion and imposed 90% of the notice cost on respondents. This decision was predicated on the court's finding, made after a preliminary hearing on the merits of the case, that petitioner was "more than likely" to prevail on his claims. Apparently, that court interpreted Rule 23 to authorize such a hearing as part of the determination whether a suit may be maintained as a class action. We disagree.

We find nothing in either the language or history of Rule 23 that gives a court any authority to conduct a preliminary inquiry into the merits of a suit in order to determine whether it may be maintained as a class action. Indeed, such a procedure contravenes the Rule by allowing a representative plaintiff to secure the benefits of a class action without first satisfying the requirements for it. He is thereby allowed to obtain a determination on the merits of the claims advanced on behalf of the class without any assurance that a class action may be maintained. This procedure is directly contrary to the command of subdivision (c)(1) that the court determine whether a suit denominated a class action may be maintained as such "[a]s soon as practicable after the commencement of [the] action. . . ." In short, we agree with Judge Wisdom's conclusion in Miller v. Mackey International, 452 F.2d 424 (5th Cir. 1971), where the court rejected a preliminary inquiry into the merits of a proposed class action:

> In determining the propriety of a class action, the question is not whether the plaintiff or plaintiffs have stated a cause of action or will prevail on the merits, but rather whether the requirements of Rule 23 are met.

Id., at 427. Additionally, we might note that a preliminary determination of the merits may result in substantial prejudice to a defendant, since of necessity it is not accompanied by the traditional rules and procedures applicable to civil trials. The court's tentative findings, made in the absence of established safeguards, may color the subsequent proceedings and place an unfair burden on the defendant.

In the absence of any support under Rule 23, petitioner's effort to impose the cost of notice on respondents must fail. The usual rule is that a plaintiff must initially bear the cost of notice to the class. The exceptions cited by the District Court related to situations where a fiduciary duty preexisted between the plaintiff and defendant, as in a shareholder derivative suit. Where, as here, the relationship between the parties is truly adversary, the plaintiff must pay for the cost of notice as part of the ordinary burden of financing his own suit.

Petitioner has consistently maintained, however, that he will not bear the cost of notice under subdivision (c)(2) to members of the class as defined in his original complaint. See 479 F.2d at 1008; 52 F.R.D. at 269. We therefore remand the cause with instructions to dismiss the class action as so defined.

The judgment of the Court of Appeals is *vacated* and the cause *remanded.* . . .

JUSTICE DOUGLAS, with whom JUSTICE BRENNAN and JUSTICE MARSHALL concur, dissenting in part.

While I am in general agreement with the phases of this case touched on by the Court, I add a few words because its opinion does not fully explore the issues which will be dispositive of this case on remand to the District Court.

Federal Rule Civ. Proc. 23(c)(4) provides: "When appropriate (A) an action may be brought or maintained as a class action with respect to particular issues, or (B) a class may be divided into subclasses and each subclass treated as a class, and the provisions of this rule shall then be construed and applied accordingly."*

---

* [Rules 23(c)(4)(A) and 23(c)(4)(B) now appear as Rules (23)(c)(4) and 23(c)(5) in the restyled rules. — EDS.]

As Judge Oakes, speaking for himself and Judge Timbers, said below:

> The plaintiff class might, for example, be divided into much smaller sub-classes . . . of odd-lot buyers for particular periods, and one subclass treated as a test case, with the other subclasses held in abeyance. Individual notice at what would probably be a reasonable cost could then be given to all members of the particular small subclass who can be easily identified.

479 F.2d 1005, 1023 (dissenting from denial of rehearing en banc).

Or a subclass might include those on monthly investment plans, or payroll deduction plans run by brokerage houses.[1] The possibilities, though not infinite, are numerous.

The power to create a subclass is clear and unambiguous. Who should be included and how large it should be are questions that only the District Court should resolve. Notice to each member of the subclass would be essential under Rule 23(c)(2); and under Rule 23(c)(2)(A) any notified member may opt out. There would remain the question whether the subclass suit is manageable. But since the subclass could be chosen in light of the non-manageability of the size of the class whose claims are presently before us, there is no apparent difficulty in that sense. . . .

The class action is one of the few legal remedies the small claimant has against those who command the status quo. I would strengthen his hand with the view of creating a system of law that dispenses justice to the lowly as well as to those liberally endowed with power and wealth.

---

1. The parties and courts below concentrated on whether a class action could be sustained on behalf of all six million odd-lot investors, so that the record is limited in information bearing on what manageable subclasses could be created.

There is, nonetheless, indication that certain subclasses might be economically manageable. Counsel for respondent Carlisle & Jacquelin stated in oral argument before the Court of Appeals that 100,000 shareholders participate in his client's Monthly Investment Plan, and that Carlisle & Jacquelin corresponds with those investors. Merrill Lynch corresponds with 150,000 people participating in a pay-roll deduction investment plan. Whether Eisen or any other plaintiff who may come forward to intervene fits in such a subclass, we do not know. But if brokerage houses correspond regularly in the course of business with such odd-lot investors, the marginal cost of providing the individual notice required by Rule 23(c)(2) might be nothing more than printing and stuffing an additional sheet of paper in correspondence already being sent to the investor, or perhaps only programming a computer to type an additional paragraph at the bottom of monthly or quarterly statements regularly mailed by the brokers.

A subclass of those who had engaged in numerous transactions might also be defined, so that the recovery per class member might be large enough to justify the cost of notice and management of the action. A survey of only four of 14 wire firms revealed 2,000 customers with 10 or more transactions between 1962 and 1966. 52 F.R.D. 253, 259, 267, and n.10.

By defining more definite subclasses such as those discussed, moreover, the problems inherent in distributing an eventual judgment would be reduced. Class members would be more readily identifiable, with more readily accessible transaction records and individually provable damages.

## *Notes and Questions*

1. *The Centrality of Notice. Eisen* was the first big Supreme Court case after the revision of Rule 23 in 1966, and its weary path through the courts was not an inspiring example of the greater simplicity the new rule sought to promote. The case established the principle that new procedural tools must still adhere to due process fundamentals. A few years after *Eisen,* the court decided Oppenheimer Fund, Inc. v. Sanders, 437 U.S. 340 (1978), in which it held that the costs of providing notice to class members must be borne by the party seeking class treatment. Thus, if a plaintiff requests in discovery defendants' records in an effort to define and locate potential class members, the plaintiff may be required to bear the cost of producing such lists. Ordinarily, the party responding to a discovery request pays for the cost of responding; *Oppenheimer* suggests an exception to that general rule.

If, however, the plaintiff succeeds in the lawsuit, then the costs of notice can be deducted from the class recovery. Of course, when the notice costs are exceptionally high, this up-front expense can be an insurmountable obstacle for some litigants, despite the potential for reimbursement at litigation's close.

2. *Making Sense of Notice.* Professor Deborah Rhode cites the following responses to a notice advising potential class members of their right to opt out of a suit seeking damages from several drug companies. Do they suggest that notice may not be of much use in some situations?

> Dear Sir:
>
> I received your pamphlet on drugs, which I think will be of great value to me in the future.
>
> Due to circumstances beyond my control I will not be able to attend this class at the time prescribed on your letter due to the fact that my working hours are from 7:00 until 4:30.

> Dear Sir:
>
> Our son is in the Navy, stationed in the Caribbean some place. Please let us know exactly what kind of drugs he is accused of taking.
>
> From a mother who will help if properly informed.

> Dear Attorney General:
>
> . . . I received a card from you and I don't understand it, and my husband can't read his. Most of the time all I buy is olive oil for healing oil after praying over it, it is anointed with God's power and ain't nothing like dope.

Deborah L. Rhode, Class Conflicts in Class Actions, 34 Stan. L. Rev. 1183, 1235, 1235 n.212 (1983).

Consider also the following remarks by Professor Arthur R. Miller, the Reporter of the Judicial Conference's Advisory Committee on the Federal Civil Rules, in Problems of Giving Notice in Class Actions, 58 F.R.D. 313, 321-322 (1972), in connection with the intelligibility of notice:

> Obviously, the federal courts should not involve themselves in Madison Avenue activities. I am not advocating the use of gayly colored judicial mail

embossed: "Important! Open this envelope! You may be entitled to a cash reward!!" The courts cannot act as if they were hawking the *Reader's Digest.* Nevertheless, the notice-giving process under Rule 23 must be reasonably pragmatic. The sad truth is that notices issued by courts or attorneys typically are much too larded with legal jargon to be understood by the average citizen.

A good illustration of this also is offered by the tetracycline cases. The Attorney General of North Carolina sent notice of the action to citizens of his state who had paid income taxes during a particular period. The theory underlying this procedure was sound enough. Given the wide use of the medication it was important to send notice to a broadly based list of citizens. Some of the responses are worth reading because they are symptomatic of the difficulty with the wording of most notices and reflect the problem of communicating to lay people about legal matters.

Dear Mr. Clerk:

I have your notice that I owe you $300 for selling drugs. I have never sold any drugs, especially those you have listed; but I have sold a little whiskey once in a while.

Dear Sir:

I received this paper from you. I guess I really don't understand it, but if I have been given one of those drugs, nobody told me why. If it means what I think it does, I have not been with a man in nine years. . . .

Dear Mr. Attorney General:

I am sorry to say this, but you have the wrong John Doe, because in 1954, I wasn't but three years old and didn't even have a name. Mother named me when I got my driver's license. Up to then, they just called me Baby Doe.

3. *Sample Notice of Settlement in Securities Fraud Action.* Recall In re Time Warner, Inc. Sec. Litig., 9 F.3d 259 (2d Cir. 1993), which you encountered in connection with pleading specificity (Chapter 2, section B(1)(b) supra). Shortly after the major pleading issues were resolved, the parties settled. Below is a summary of the notice of that settlement. A longer, more detailed version was mailed to known interested parties. This shorter version was published in the newspaper.

UNITED STATES DISTRICT COURT
SOUTHERN DISTRICT OF NEW YORK

| IN RE TIME WARNER INC. ) | MASTER FILE NO. |
| SECURITIES LITIGATION ) | 91 CIV. 4081(MEL) |

*SUMMARY NOTICE OF PROPOSED SETTLEMENT
OF CLASS ACTION AND SETTLEMENT HEARING*

TO: ALL PERSONS WHO PURCHASED, OR OTHERWISE ACQUIRED FOR CONSIDERATION, COMMON STOCK (CUSIP NO. 887315109) OF TIME WARNER INC. ("TIME

WARNER") AT ANY TIME FROM APRIL 25, 1991 THROUGH
THE CLOSE OF TRADING ON JUNE 5, 1991 (THE "CLASS
PERIOD"), AND WHO SUFFERED A LOSS THEREBY,
EXCLUDING DEFENDANTS AND ANY MEMBERS OF THEIR
IMMEDIATE FAMILIES, ANY ENTITY IN WHICH THEY
HAVE A CONTROLLING INTEREST, AND THE LEGAL
REPRESENTATIVES, HEIRS, SUCCESSORS OR ASSIGNS OF
ANY SUCH EXCLUDED PERSON OR ENTITY (THE "CLASS").

YOU ARE HEREBY NOTIFIED, pursuant to Rule 23 of the Federal Rules of
Civil Procedure and an order of the United States District Court for the Southern
District of New York (the "Court") dated October 11, 1994, that a hearing will
be held on November 10, 1994 at 9:30 A.M., before the Court at the United States
Courthouse, Southern District of New York, 40 Centre Street, New York, New
York (the "Settlement Hearing"). The purpose of the Settlement Hearing is to
determine whether the proposed $5,500,000 settlement of the above-captioned
action against defendants should be approved by the Court as fair, reasonable
and adequate, whether the application for an award of attorneys' fees and reimbursement of costs and expenses should be approved, and whether the action
should be dismissed on the merits and with prejudice.

IF YOU PURCHASED SHARES OF COMMON STOCK OF TIME WARNER
(CUSIP NO. 887315109) DURING THE CLASS PERIOD YOUR RIGHTS
MAY BE AFFECTED BY THE ACTION AND YOU MAY BE ENTITLED
TO MONEY. If you purchased common stock during the Class Period and
have not yet received the "Notice of Pendency of Class Action and Proposed
Settlement And Settlement Hearing" (the "Settlement Notice") and accom-
panying "Proof of Claim," which describe the Settlement and your rights
and obligations thereunder in detail, you may obtain copies thereof by call-
ing (415) 461-0410 or by writing to Time Warner Securities Litigation, c/o
Gilardi & Co., P.O. Box 990, Corte Madera, CA 94976-0990. To participate
in the settlement, you must file a Proof of Claim no later than January 16,
1995. IF YOU DO NOT FILE A PROPER PROOF OF CLAIM FORM OR DO
NOT EXCLUDE YOURSELF FROM THE CLASS IN ACCORDANCE WITH
THE SETTLEMENT NOTICE'S INSTRUCTIONS, YOU WILL NOT SHARE
IN THE SETTLEMENT BUT YOU WILL BE BOUND BY THE FINAL
JUDGMENT OF THE COURT.

Bankers and/or brokers requesting materials should contact Time Warner
Securities Litigation, c/o Gilardi & Co., P.O. Box 990, Corte Madera, CA
94976-0990.

Bankers, brokers and/or other nominees will be entitled to reimbursement of the reasonable out-of-pocket expenses, service and research charges,
handling fees, postage and similar charges that they incur in connection
herewith.

PLEASE DO NOT CONTACT THE COURT OR THE CLERK'S OFFICE
FOR INFORMATION.

Dated: New York, New York        By Order of the United States
October 11, 1994                 District Court for the Southern District
                                 of New York

4. *Notice and Statutes of Limitation.* In a standard civil action, a plaintiff is barred from filing after the applicable statute of limitation has run. Statutes of limitation exist to protect defendants from stale claims, to prevent plaintiffs from sleeping on their rights, and to protect the integrity of the judicial process by ensuring that litigation occurs when memories are fresh and relevant evidence is more likely to be available. Normally, however, statutes of limitation are tolled while litigation is pending. How should statutes of limitation and tolling rules apply to class actions?

The Supreme Court has held that the filing of a class action automatically tolls the statute of limitations for putative class members, at least until class certification is denied. See Crown Cork & Seal Co. v. Parker, 462 U.S. 345 (1983); Am. Pipe & Constr. Co. v. Utah, 414 U.S. 538 (1974). A contrary rule, the Court observed in *Crown Cork & Seal*, would defeat the purposes of Rule 23—class members would have to file their own suits or intervene in the class suit to protect their rights, thereby inviting the very inefficiencies Rule 23 was designed to avoid. And as the Court emphasized in *American Pipe*, once a class action is filed, the defendants are on notice "not only of the substantive claims being brought against them, but also of the number and generic identities of the potential plaintiffs who may participate in the judgment." 414 U.S. at 554-55. Thus there is no harm to defendants in tolling the statute of limitations for class members.

The plaintiff in *Crown, Cork & Seal* was an African-American male fired by the defendant. He filed a charge of racial discrimination under Title VII with the EEOC which then issued him a "Notice of Right to Sue within 90 days." In the meantime, two other black employees filed a class action alleging discrimination under Title VII. Plaintiff, a putative member of the class suit, filed his individual claim nearly two years after the Notice of Right to Sue was issued, but within 90 days of the district court's decision denying class certification. The Supreme Court held that the 90-day statute of limitations was tolled while the unsuccessful class action was pending.

The courts of appeals have split, however, on whether tolling applies where class certification is denied in the first action and, rather than proceed individually, putative class members file a second class action suit. Can you see why it would be controversial to give plaintiffs the benefit of tolling to relitigate a denial of class certification? Justice Blackmun warned in *American Pipe* that the Court's decision to permit tolling in some circumstances "must not be regarded as encouragement to lawyers in a case of this kind to frame their pleadings as a class action, intentionally, to attract and save members of the purported class who have slept on their rights." 414 U.S. at 561 (Blackmun, J., concurring). The concern is that class members or their lawyers will "piggyback one class action onto another . . . and thereby engage in endless rounds of litigation" in an attempt to win certification. Griffin v. Singletary, 17 F.3d 356, 359 (11th Cir. 1994) (categorically disallowing tolling for successive class actions) (internal quotations omitted); cf. Yang v. Odom, 392 F.3d 97, 106 (3d Cir. 2004) ("While *Griffin*'s denial of tolling for all sequential class action plaintiffs has the virtue of clarity and ease of application, it is also characterized by a rigidity which we reject for at least three reasons.").

Are the grounds for the initial denial of class certification relevant to deciding whether tolling should apply? See Catholic Soc. Servs., Inc. v. I.N.S., 232 F.3d 1139 (9th Cir. 2000) (en banc). What if class certification is first denied on adequacy grounds because there is a problem with the class representative, but in the second suit the class members have cured the defect? See Yang v. Odom, 392 F.3d 97, 111 (3d Cir. 2004) (canvassing circuit split and holding that tolling is allowed).

What if class certification is first denied because of some deficiency in the class itself? See Basch v. Ground Round, Inc., 139 F.3d 6 (1st Cir. 1998) (no tolling for sequential class action where initial certification denied because the class members were not "similarly situated"); Korwek v. Hunt, 827 F.2d 874 (2d Cir. 1987) (no tolling where first class action failed because of manageability problems and intraclass conflicts); Salazar-Calderon v. Presidio Valley Farmers Ass'n, 765 F.2d 1334 (5th Cir. 1985) (tolling does not permit putative class members to file a subsequent class action where certification of first class denied because common questions did not predominate and class action was not a superior method for handling the controversy). If class members can take advantage of tolling to sue individually, why give them the option of filing another class action? Why allow two (or more) bites at the class certification apple?

## 5. Choice of Forum and Mode of Trial Issues: Personal Jurisdiction

### *Phillips Petroleum Co. v. Shutts*
472 U.S. 797 (1985)

JUSTICE REHNQUIST delivered the opinion of the Court.

Petitioner is a Delaware corporation which has its principal place of business in Oklahoma. During the 1970's it produced or purchased natural gas from leased land located in 11 different States, and sold most of the gas in interstate commerce. Respondents are some 28,000 of the royalty owners possessing rights to the leases from which petitioner produced the gas; they reside in all 50 States, the District of Columbia, and several foreign countries. Respondents brought a class action against petitioner in the Kansas state court, seeking to recover interest on royalty payments which had been delayed by petitioner. They recovered judgment in the trial court, and the Supreme Court of Kansas affirmed the judgment over petitioner's contentions that the Due Process Clause of the Fourteenth Amendment prevented Kansas from adjudicating the claims of all the respondents, and that the Due Process Clause and the Full Faith and Credit Clause of Article IV of the Constitution prohibited the application of Kansas law to all of the transactions between petitioner and respondents. 679 P.2d 1159 (1984). We granted certiorari to consider these claims. 469 U.S. 879 (1984). We reject petitioner's jurisdictional claim, but sustain its claim regarding the choice of law.

Because petitioner sold the gas to its customers in interstate commerce, it was required to secure approval for price increases from what was then the Federal Power Commission, and is now the Federal Energy Regulatory Commission. Under its regulations the Federal Power Commission permitted petitioner to propose and collect tentative higher gas prices, subject to final approval by the Commission. If the Commission eventually denied petitioner's proposed price increase or reduced the proposed increase, petitioner would have to refund to its customers the difference between the approved price and the higher price charged, plus interest at a rate set by statute. See 18 C.F.R. § 154.102 (1984).

Although petitioner received higher gas prices pending review by the Commission, petitioner suspended any increase in royalties paid to the royalty owners because the higher price could be subject to recoupment by petitioner's customers. Petitioner agreed to pay the higher royalty only if the royalty owners would provide petitioner with a bond or indemnity for the increase, plus interest, in case the price increase was not ultimately approved and a refund was due to the customers. Petitioner set the interest rate on the indemnity agreements at the same interest rate the Commission would have required petitioner to refund to its customers. A small percentage of the royalty owners provided this indemnity and received royalties immediately from the interim price increases; these royalty owners are unimportant to this case.

The remaining royalty owners received no royalty on the unapproved portion of the prices until the Federal Power Commission approval of those prices became final. Royalties on the unapproved portion of the gas price were suspended three times by petitioner, corresponding to its three proposed price increases in the mid-1970's. In three written opinions the Commission approved all of petitioner's tentative price increases, so petitioner paid to its royalty owners the suspended royalties of $3.7 million in 1976, $4.7 million in 1977, and $2.9 million in 1978. Petitioner paid no interest to the royalty owners although it had the use of the suspended royalty money for a number of years.

Respondents Irl Shutts, Robert Anderson, and Betty Anderson filed suit against petitioner in Kansas state court, seeking interest payments on their suspended royalties which petitioner had possessed pending the Commission's approval of the price increases. Shutts is a resident of Kansas, and the Andersons live in Oklahoma. Shutts and the Andersons own gas leases in Oklahoma and Texas. Over petitioner's objection the Kansas trial court granted respondents' motion to certify the suit as a class action under Kansas law. Kan. Stat. Ann. §§ 60-223 et seq. (1983). The class as certified was comprised of 33,000 royalty owners who had royalties suspended by petitioner. The average claim of each royalty owner for interest on the suspended royalties was $100.

After the class was certified respondents provided each class member with notice through first-class mail. The notice described the action and informed each class member that he could appear in person or by counsel; otherwise each member would be represented by Shutts and the Andersons, the named plaintiffs. The notices also stated that class members would be included in the class and bound by the judgment unless they "opted out" of the lawsuit by executing and returning a "request for exclusion" that was included with the notice. The final class as certified contained 28,100 members; 3,400 had "opted out" of the class by returning the request for exclusion, and notice could not be delivered to another 1,500 members, who were also excluded. Less than 1,000 of the class members resided in Kansas. Only a minuscule amount, approximately one quarter of one percent, of the gas leases involved in the lawsuit were on Kansas land.

After petitioner's mandamus petition to decertify the class was denied, Phillips Petroleum v. Duckworth, No. 82-54608 (Kan., June 28, 1982), *cert. denied,* 459 U.S. 1103 (1983), the case was tried to the court. The court found petitioner liable under Kansas law for interest on the suspended royalties to all class members. . . .

. . . The trial court did not determine whether any difference existed between the laws of Kansas and other States, or whether another State's laws should be applied to non-Kansas plaintiffs or to royalties from leases in States other than Kansas. 679 P.2d, at 1180.

Petitioner raised two principal claims in its appeal to the Supreme Court of Kansas. It first asserted that the Kansas trial court did not possess personal jurisdiction over absent plaintiff class members as required by International Shoe Co. v. Washington, 326 U.S. 310 (1945), and similar cases. Related to this first claim was petitioner's contention that the "opt-out" notice to absent class members, which forced them to return the request for exclusion in order to avoid the suit, was insufficient to bind class members who were not residents of Kansas or who did not possess "minimum contacts" with Kansas. Second, petitioner claimed that Kansas courts could not apply Kansas law to every claim in the dispute. The trial court should have looked to the laws of each State where the leases were located to determine, on the basis of conflict of laws principles, whether interest on the suspended royalties was recoverable, and at what rate.

The Supreme Court of Kansas held that the entire cause of action was maintainable under the Kansas class-action statute, and the court rejected both of petitioner's claims. 679 P.2d 1159 (1984). First, it held that the absent class members were plaintiffs, not defendants, and thus the traditional minimum contacts test of *International Shoe* did not apply. The court held that nonresident class-action plaintiffs were only entitled to adequate notice, an opportunity to be heard, an opportunity to opt out of the case, and adequate representation by the named plaintiffs. If these procedural due process minima were met, according to the court, Kansas could assert jurisdiction over the plaintiff class and bind each class member with a judgment on his claim. The court surveyed the course of the litigation and concluded that all of these minima had been met.

The court also rejected petitioner's contention that Kansas law could not be applied to plaintiffs and royalty arrangements having no connection with Kansas. The court stated that generally the law of the forum controlled all claims unless "compelling reasons" existed to apply a different law. The court found no compelling reasons, and noted that "[t]he plaintiff class members have indicated their desire to have this action determined under the laws of Kansas." 679 P.2d, at 1181. The court affirmed as a matter of Kansas equity law the award of interest on the suspended royalties, at the rates imposed by the trial court. . . .

## I

. . .

## II

Reduced to its essentials, petitioner's argument is that unless out-of-state plaintiffs affirmatively consent, the Kansas courts may not exert jurisdiction over their claims. Petitioner claims that failure to execute and return the "request for exclusion" provided with the class notice cannot constitute consent of the out-of-state plaintiffs; thus Kansas courts may exercise jurisdiction over these plaintiffs only if the plaintiffs possess the sufficient "minimum contacts" with Kansas as that term is used in cases involving personal jurisdiction over out-of-state defendants. E.g., International Shoe Co. v. Washington, 326 U.S. 310 (1945); Shaffer v. Heitner, 433 U.S. 186 (1977); World-Wide Volkswagen Corp. v. Woodson, 444 U.S. 286 (1980). Since Kansas had no prelitigation contact with many of the plaintiffs and leases involved, petitioner claims that Kansas has exceeded its jurisdictional reach and thereby violated the due process rights of the absent plaintiffs.

In *International Shoe* we were faced with an out-of-state corporation which sought to avoid the exercise of personal jurisdiction over it as a defendant by a Washington state court. We held that the extent of the dependant's due process protection would depend "upon the quality and nature of the activity in relation to the fair and orderly administration of the laws. . . ." 326 U.S., at 319. We noted that the Due Process Clause did not permit a State to make a binding judgment against a person with whom the State had no contacts, ties, or relations. Id. If the defendant possessed certain minimum contacts with the State, so that it was "reasonable and just, according to our traditional conception of fair play and substantial justice" for a State to exercise personal jurisdiction, the State could force the defendant to defend himself in the forum, upon pain of default, and could bind him to a judgment. Id., at 320.

The purpose of this test, of course, is to protect a defendant from the travail of defending in a distant forum, unless the defendant's contacts with the forum make it just to force him to defend there. As we explained in

*Woodson,* supra, the defendant's contacts should be such that "he should reasonably anticipate being haled" into the forum. 444 U.S., at 297. In Insurance Corp. of Ireland v. Compagnie des Bauxites de Guinee, 456 U.S. 694, 702-703, and n.10 (1982), we explained that the requirement that a court have personal jurisdiction comes from the Due Process Clause's protection of the defendant's personal liberty interest, and said that the requirement "represents a restriction on judicial power not as a matter of sovereignty, but as a matter of individual liberty." (Footnote omitted.)

Although the cases like *Shaffer* and *Woodson* which petitioner relies on for a minimum contacts requirement all dealt with out-of-state defendants or parties in the procedural posture of a defendant, cf. New York Life Ins. Co. v. Dunlevy, 241 U.S. 518 (1916); Estin v. Estin, 334 U.S. 541 (1948), petitioner claims that the same analysis must apply to absent class-action plaintiffs. In this regard petitioner correctly points out that a chose in action is a con-stitutionally recognized property interest possessed by each of the plain-tiffs. Mullane v. Central Hanover Bank & Trust Co., 339 U.S. 306 (1950). An adverse judgment by Kansas courts in this case may extinguish the chose in action forever through res judicata. Such an adverse judgment, petitioner claims, would be every bit as onerous to an absent plaintiff as an adverse judgment on the merits would be to a defendant. Thus, the same due process protections should apply to absent plaintiffs: Kansas should not be able to exert jurisdiction over the plaintiffs' claims unless the plain-tiffs have sufficient minimum contacts with Kansas.

We think petitioner's premise is in error. The burdens placed by a State upon an absent class-action plaintiff are not of the same order or magni-tude as those it places upon an absent defendant. An out-of-state defendant summoned by a plaintiff is faced with the full powers of the forum State to render judgment *against* it. The defendant must generally hire counsel and travel to the forum to defend itself from the plaintiff's claim, or suffer a default judgment. The defendant may be forced to participate in extended and often costly discovery, and will be forced to respond in damages or to comply with some other form of remedy imposed by the court should it lose the suit. The defendant may also face liability for court costs and attorney's fees. These burdens are substantial, and the minimum contacts require-ment of the Due Process Clause prevents the forum State from unfairly imposing them upon the defendant.

A class-action plaintiff, however, is in quite a different posture. The Court noted this difference in Hansberry v. Lee, 311 U.S. 32, 40-41 (1940), which explained that a "class" or "representative" suit was an exception to the rule that one could not be bound by judgment *in personam* unless one was made fully a party in the traditional sense. Id., citing Pennoyer v. Neff, 95 U.S. 714 (1878). As the Court pointed out in *Hansberry,* the class action was an invention of equity to enable it to proceed to a decree in suits where the number of those interested in the litigation was too great to permit join-der. The absent parties would be bound by the decree so long as the named parties adequately represented the absent class and the prosecution of the litigation was within the common interest. 311 U.S., at 41.

Modern plaintiff class actions follow the same goals, permitting litigation of a suit involving common questions when there are too many plaintiffs for proper joinder. Class actions also may permit the plaintiffs to pool claims which would be uneconomical to litigate individually. For example, this lawsuit involves claims averaging about $100 per plaintiff; most of the plaintiffs would have no realistic day in court if a class action were not available.

In sharp contrast to the predicament of a defendant haled into an out-of-state forum, the plaintiffs in this suit were not haled any-where to defend themselves upon pain of a default judgment. As commentators have noted, from the plaintiffs' point of view a class action resembles a "quasi-administrative proceeding, conducted by the judge." 3B J. Moore & J. Kennedy, Moore's Federal Practice ¶ 23.45 [4-5] (1984); [Benjamin] Kaplan, Continuing Work of the Civil Committee: 1966 Amendments to the Federal Rules of Civil Procedure (I), 81 Harv. L. Rev. 356, 398 (1967).

A plaintiff class in Kansas and numerous other jurisdictions cannot first be certified unless the judge, with the aid of the named plaintiffs and defendant, conducts an inquiry into the common nature of the named plaintiffs' and the absent plaintiffs' claims, the adequacy of representation, the jurisdiction possessed over the class, and any other matters that will bear upon proper representation of the absent plaintiffs' interest. See, e.g., Kan. Stat. Ann. § 60-223 (1983); Fed. Rule Civ. Proc. 23. Unlike a defendant in a civil suit, a class-action plaintiff is not required to fend for himself. See Kan. Stat. Ann. § 60-223(d) (1983). The court and named plaintiffs protect his interests. Indeed, the class-action defendant itself has a great interest in ensuring that the absent plaintiffs' claims are properly before the forum. In this case, for example, the defendant sought to avoid class certification by alleging that the absent plaintiffs would not be adequately represented and were not amenable to jurisdiction. . . .

The concern of the typical class-action rules for the absent plaintiffs is manifested in other ways. Most jurisdictions, including Kansas, require that a class action, once certified, may not be dismissed or compromised without the approval of the court. In many jurisdictions such as Kansas the court may amend the pleadings to ensure that all sections of the class are represented adequately. Kan. Stat. Ann. § 60-223(d) (1983); see also, e.g., Fed. Rule Civ. Proc. 23(d).

Besides this continuing solicitude for their rights, absent plaintiff class members are not subject to other burdens imposed upon defendants. They need not hire counsel or appear. They are almost never subject to counterclaims or cross-claims, or liability for fees or costs. Absent plaintiff class members are not subject to coercive or punitive remedies. Nor will an adverse judgment typically bind an absent plaintiff for any damages, although a valid adverse judgment may extinguish any of the plaintiff's claims which were litigated.

Unlike a defendant in a normal civil suit, an absent class-action plaintiff is not required to do anything. He may sit back and allow the litigation to run its course, content in knowing that there are safeguards provided for his protection. In most class actions an absent plaintiff is provided at least with an opportunity to "opt out" of the class, and if he takes advantage of that opportunity he is removed from the litigation entirely. This was true of the Kansas proceedings in this case. The Kansas procedure provided for the mailing of a notice to each class member by first-class mail. The notice, as we have previously indicated, described the action and informed the class member that he could appear in person or by counsel, in default of which he would be represented by the named plaintiffs and their attorneys. The notice further stated that class members would be included in the class and bound by the judgment unless they "opted out" by executing and returning a "request for exclusion" that was included in the notice.

Petitioner contends, however, that the "opt out" procedure provided by Kansas is not good enough, and that an "opt in" procedure is required to satisfy the Due Process Clause of the Fourteenth Amendment. Insofar as plaintiffs who have no minimum contacts with the forum State are concerned, an "opt in" provision would require that each class member affirmatively consent to his inclusion within the class.

Because States place fewer burdens upon absent class plaintiffs than they do upon absent defendants in nonclass suits, the Due Process Clause need not and does not afford the former as much protection from state-court jurisdiction as it does the latter. The Fourteenth Amendment does protect "persons," not "defendants," however, so absent plaintiffs as well as absent defendants are entitled to some protection from the jurisdiction of a forum State which seeks to adjudicate their claims. In this case we hold that a forum State may exercise jurisdiction over the claim of an absent class-action plaintiff, even though that plaintiff may not possess the minimum contacts with the forum which would support personal jurisdiction over a defendant. If the forum State wishes to bind an absent plaintiff concerning a claim for money damages or similar relief at law, it must provide minimal procedural due process protection. The plaintiff must receive notice plus an opportunity to be heard and participate in the litigation, whether in person or through counsel. The notice must be the best practicable, "reasonably calculated, under all the circumstances, to apprise interested parties of the pendency of the action and afford them an opportunity to present their objections." *Mullane,* 339 U.S. at 314-315; cf. Eisen v. Carlisle & Jacquelin, 417 U.S. 156, 174-175 (1974). The notice should describe the action and the plaintiffs' rights in it. Additionally, we hold that due process requires at a minimum that an absent plaintiff be provided with an opportunity to remove himself from the class by executing and returning an "opt out" or "request for exclusion" form to the court. Finally, the Due Process Clause of course requires that the named plaintiff at all times adequately represent the interests of the absent class members. *Hansberry,* 311 U.S. at 42-43, 45.

We reject petitioner's contention that the Due Process Clause of the Fourteenth Amendment requires that absent plaintiffs affirmatively "opt in" to the class, rather than be deemed members of the class if they do not "opt out." We think that such a contention is supported by little, if any precedent, and that it ignores the differences between class-action plaintiffs, on the one hand, and defendants in nonclass civil suits on the other. Any plaintiff may consent to jurisdiction. Keeton v. Hustler Magazine, Inc., 465 U.S. 770 (1984). The essential question, then, is how stringent the requirement for a showing of consent will be.

We think that the procedure followed by Kansas, where a fully descriptive notice is sent first-class mail to each class member, with an explanation of the right to "opt out," satisfies due process. Requiring a plaintiff to affirmatively request inclusion would probably impede the prosecution of those class actions involving an aggregation of small individual claims, where a large number of claims are required to make it economical to bring suit. See, e.g., *Eisen,* supra, at 161. The plaintiff's claim may be so small, or the plaintiff so unfamiliar with the law, that he would not file suit individually, nor would he affirmatively request inclusion in the class if such a request were required by the Constitution. If, on the other hand, the plaintiff's claim is sufficiently large or important that he wishes to litigate it on his own, he will likely have retained an attorney or have thought about filing suit, and should be fully capable of exercising his right to "opt out."

In this case over 3,400 members of the potential class did "opt out," which belies the contention that "opt out" procedures result in guaranteed jurisdiction by inertia. Another 1,500 were excluded because the notice and "opt out" form was undeliverable. We think that such results show that the "opt out" procedure provided by Kansas is by no means *pro forma,* and that the Constitution does not require more to protect what must be the somewhat rare species of class member who is unwilling to execute an "opt out" form, but whose claim is nonetheless so important that he cannot be presumed to consent to being a member of the class by his failure to do so. Petitioner's "opt in" requirement would require the invalidation of scores of state statutes and of the class-action provision of the Federal Rules of Civil Procedure, and for the reasons stated we do not think that the Constitution requires the State to sacrifice the obvious advantages in judicial efficiency resulting from the "opt out" approach for the protection of the *rara avis* portrayed by petitioner.

We therefore hold that the protection afforded the plaintiff class members by the Kansas statute satisfies the Due Process Clause. The interests of the absent plaintiffs are sufficiently protected by the forum State when those plaintiffs are provided with a request for exclusion that can be returned within a reasonable time to the court. See *Insurance Corp. of Ireland,* 456 U.S., at 702-703 and n.10. Both the Kansas trial court and the Supreme Court of Kansas held that the class received adequate representation, and no party disputes that conclusion here. We conclude that the Kansas court properly asserted personal jurisdiction over the absent plaintiffs and their claims against petitioner.

### Note: Venue in Class Actions

Should the venue requirement be fully satisfied if venue would be proper for an action against the class representative? For plaintiff classes, correct venue for the representative suffices for the absent parties, e.g., Research Corp. v. Pfister Assoc. Growers, 301 F. Supp. 497 (N.D. Ill. 1969).

For an isolated case holding that the defendant class judgment is not binding on members for whom the venue was improper, see Sperberg v. Firestone Tire & Rubber Co., 61 F.R.D. 70 (N.D. Ohio 1973).

### Note: Federal Jurisdiction in Class Actions

The United States Supreme Court held in Supreme Tribe of Ben-Hur v. Cauble, 255 U.S. 356 (1921), that only the citizenship of the named representatives of a class action suit based on diversity need be considered for jurisdictional purposes. Thus a class member whose citizenship was not diverse from all of the defendants nevertheless was bound by a prior decree, even though it would have destroyed diversity had he been a named class representative.

*Ben-Hur* may suggest that only the claims of the named representatives likewise should be considered in determining the amount-in-controversy requirement. Yet Snyder v. Harris, 394 U.S. 332 (1969), and Zahn v. International Paper Co., 414 U.S. 291 (1973), hold otherwise. The Court explained this result in *Zahn* as follows:

> None of the plaintiffs in Snyder v. Harris alleged a claim exceeding $10,000, but there is no doubt that the rationale of that case controls this one. As previously indicated, *Snyder* invoked the well-established rule that each of several plaintiffs asserting separate and distinct claims must satisfy the jurisdictional amount requirement if his claim was to survive a motion to dismiss: This rule plainly mandates not only that there may be no aggregation and that the entire case must be dismissed where none of the plaintiffs claims more than $10,000 but also requires that any plaintiff without the jurisdictional amount must be dismissed from the case, even though others allege jurisdictionally sufficient claims. . . .
>
> It also seems to us that the application of the jurisdictional amount requirement to class actions was so plainly etched in the federal courts prior to 1966 that had there been any thought of departing from these decisions and, in so doing, of calling into question the accepted approach to cases involving ordinary joinder of plaintiffs with separate and distinct claims, some express statement of that intention would surely have appeared, either in the amendments themselves or in the official commentaries. But we find not a trace to this effect. As the Court thought in Snyder v. Harris, the matter must rest there absent further congressional action.

414 U.S. at 300, 302. Justices Brennan, Marshall, and Douglas dissented, arguing that to assert ancillary jurisdiction over the claims that failed to satisfy the amount-in-controversy requirement would promote efficiency. In Justice Brennan's words,

> Class actions were born of necessity. The alternatives were joinder of the entire class, or redundant litigation of the common issues. The cost to the

litigants and the drain on the resources of the judiciary resulting from either alternative would have been intolerable. And this case presents precisely those difficulties: approximately 240 claimants are involved, and the issues will doubtless call for extensive use of expert testimony on difficult scientific issues.

It is, of course, true that an exercise of ancillary jurisdiction in such cases would result in some increase in the federal courts' workload, for unless the class action is permitted many of the claimants will be unable to obtain any federal determination of their rights. But that objection is applicable to every other exercise of ancillary jurisdiction. It should be sufficient answer that denial of ancillary jurisdiction will impose a much larger burden on the state and federal judiciary as a whole, and will substantially impair the ability of the prospective class members to assert their claims. . . .

Not only does the practical desirability of sustaining jurisdiction bring Rule 23(b)(3) class actions within the logic of our decisions, but the Court has long since recognized the fact, and has sustained ancillary jurisdiction over the nonappearing members in a class action who do not meet the requirements of [the] traditional rule of complete diversity laid down in Strawbridge v. Curtis, 3 Cranch 267 (1806). In Supreme Tribe of Ben-Hur v. Cauble, 255 U.S. 356 (1921), the Court not only held that only the original named plaintiffs and defendants had to satisfy the diversity requirements, but it also stated that intervention by nondiverse members of the class would not destroy the District Court's jurisdiction. Id., at 366. Particularly in view of the constitutional background on which the statutory diversity requirements are written, see Zahn v. International Paper Co., 469 F.2d 1033, 1038 ([2d Cir] 1972) (Timbers, J., dissenting), it is difficult to understand why the practical approach the Court took in *Supreme Tribe of Ben-Hur* must be abandoned where the purely statutory "matter in controversy" requirement is concerned.

Id. at 307-309 (Brennan, J., dissenting). Does the adoption of the supplemental jurisdiction statute (28 U.S.C. § 1367) alter this result? The Supreme Court has said "yes." See section A of this chapter, supra, for discussion of Exxon Mobil Corp. v. Allapattah Servs., Inc., 545 U.S. 546 (2005) (holding that § 1367 overrules *Zahn*; as long as the claims of one plaintiff satisfy the amount-in-controversy requirement, the court has supplemental jurisdiction over the claims of other class members).

Congress has also intervened, passing a major expansion of the original and removal jurisdiction of federal courts over "interstate" plaintiff class actions where the aggregate amount in controversy exceeds $5 million and the parties are minimally diverse. See The Class Action Fairness Act of 2005, Pub. L. No. 109-2; see especially 28 U.S.C. §§ 1332(d) and 1453. The Act's findings state that while class actions

are an important and valuable part of the legal system when they permit the fair and efficient resolution of legitimate claims of numerous parties . . . there have been abuses of the class action device that have . . . harmed class members with legitimate claims and defendants that have acted responsibly . . . [and] undermined public respect for our judicial system.

> Class members often receive little or no benefit from class actions, and are sometimes harmed, such as where (A) counsel are awarded large fees, while leaving class members with coupons or other awards of little or no value; (B) unjustified awards are made to certain plaintiffs at the expense of other class members; and (C) confusing notices are published that prevent class members from being able to fully understand and effectively exercise their rights. . . .
>
> Abuses in class actions undermine the national judicial system . . . and the concept of diversity jurisdiction as intended by the framers of the United States Constitution, in that State and local courts are (A) keeping cases of national importance out of Federal court; (B) sometimes acting in ways that demonstrate bias against out-of-State defendants; and (C) making judgments that impose their view of the law on other States and bind the rights of the residents of those States.

Pub. L. No. 109-2, § 2; 28 U.S.C. § 1711, Note. In addition to expanding federal court jurisdiction over class actions, the Act sets standards for "coupon settlements," see 28 U.S.C. §§ 1711-1712, requires evenhandedness in the distribution of awards, see 28 U.S.C. §§ 1713-1714, and mandates that defendants notify appropriate state and federal officials of proposed settlements. See 28 U.S.C. § 1715.

If state courts are in fact doing what Congress accuses them of doing in the third paragraph quoted above, expanding federal subject matter jurisdiction arguably is a legitimate response. But are federal courts in any better position to deal with the other alleged abuses?

## 6. Settlement

### *Amchem Products, Inc. v. Windsor*
521 U.S. 591 (1997)

JUSTICE GINSBURG delivered the opinion of the Court.

This case concerns the legitimacy under Rule 23 of the Federal Rules of Civil Procedure of a class action certification sought to achieve global settlement of current and future asbestos-related claims. The class proposed for certification potentially encompasses hundreds of thousands, perhaps millions, of individuals tied together by this commonality: each was, or some day may be, adversely affected by past exposure to asbestos products manufactured by one or more of 20 companies. Those companies, defendants in the lower courts, are petitioners here.

The United States District Court for the Eastern District of Pennsylvania certified the class for settlement only, finding that the proposed settlement was fair and that representation and notice had been adequate. That court enjoined class members from separately pursuing asbestos-related personal-injury suits in any court, federal or state, pending the issuance of a final order. The Court of Appeals for the Third Circuit vacated the District Court's orders, holding that the class certification failed to satisfy Rule 23's requirements in several critical respects. We affirm the Court of Appeals' judgment.

# I

## A

The settlement-class certification we confront evolved in response to an asbestos-litigation crisis. . . . A United States Judicial Conference Ad Hoc Committee on Asbestos Litigation, appointed by The Chief Justice in September 1990, described facets of the problem in a 1991 report:

> [This] is a tale of danger known in the 1930s, exposure inflicted upon millions of Americans in the 1940s and 1950s, injuries that began to take their toll in the 1960s, and a flood of lawsuits beginning in the 1970s. On the basis of past and current filing data, and because of a latency period that may last as long as 40 years for some asbestos-related diseases, a continuing stream of claims can be expected. The final toll of asbestos-related injuries is unknown. Predictions have been made of 200,000 asbestos disease deaths before the year 2000 and as many as 265,000 by the year 2015.
>
> The most objectionable aspects of asbestos litigation can be briefly summarized: dockets in both federal and state courts continue to grow; long delays are routine; trials are too long; the same issues are litigated over and over; transaction costs exceed the victims' recovery by nearly two to one; exhaustion of assets threatens and distorts the process; and future claimants may lose altogether. Report of The Judicial Conference Ad Hoc Committee on Asbestos Litigation 2-3 (Mar. 1991).

Real reform, the report concluded, required federal legislation creating a national asbestos dispute-resolution scheme. . . . To this date, no congressional response has emerged. . . .

. . . [T]he federal courts—lacking authority to replace state tort systems with a national toxic tort compensation regime—endeavored to work with the procedural tools available to improve management of federal asbestos litigation. . . . [T]he MDL [Multidistrict Litigation] Panel transferred all asbestos cases then filed, but not yet on trial in federal courts to a single district, the United States District Court for the Eastern District of Pennsylvania; pursuant to the transfer order, the collected cases were consolidated for pretrial proceedings before Judge Weiner. . . . The order aggregated pending cases only; no authority resides in the MDL Panel to license for consolidated proceedings claims not yet filed.

## B

After the consolidation, attorneys for plaintiffs and defendants formed separate steering committees and began settlement negotiations. . . . [S]ettlement negotiations included efforts to find a "means of resolving . . . future cases." . . .

Settlement talks thus concentrated on devising an administrative scheme for disposition of asbestos claims not yet in litigation. In these negotiations, counsel for masses of inventory plaintiffs endeavored to represent the interests of the anticipated future claimants, although those lawyers then had no attorney-client relationship with such claimants.

Once negotiations seemed likely to produce an agreement purporting to bind potential plaintiffs, CCR [the group defendants—a consortium of 20 former asbestos manufacturers] agreed to settle, through separate agreements, the claims of plaintiffs who had already filed asbestos-related lawsuits. . . .

### C

The class action thus instituted was not intended to be litigated. Rather, within the space of a single day, . . . the settling parties . . . presented to the District Court a complaint, an answer, a proposed settlement agreement, and a joint motion for conditional class certification.

The complaint identified nine lead plaintiffs, designating them and members of their families as representatives of a class comprising all persons who had not filed an asbestos-related lawsuit against a CCR defendant as of the date the class action commenced, but who (1) had been exposed—occupationally or through the occupational exposure of a spouse or household member—to asbestos or products containing asbestos attributable to a CCR defendant, or (2) whose spouse or family member had been so exposed. Untold numbers of individuals may fall within this description. All named plaintiffs alleged that they or a member of their family had been exposed to asbestos-containing products of CCR defendants. More than half of the named plaintiffs alleged that they or their family members had already suffered various physical injuries as a result of the exposure. The others alleged that they had not yet manifested any asbestos-related condition. The complaint delineated no subclasses; all named plaintiffs were designated as representatives of the class as a whole.

The complaint invoked the District Court's diversity jurisdiction and asserted various state-law claims for relief. . . .

A stipulation of settlement accompanied the pleadings; it proposed to settle, and to preclude nearly all class members from litigating against CCR companies, all claims not filed before January 15, 1993, involving compensation for present and future asbestos-related personal injury or death. . . . The stipulation describes four categories of compensable disease: mesothelioma; lung cancer; certain "other cancers" (colon-rectal, laryngeal, esophageal, and stomach cancer); and "non-malignant conditions" (asbestosis and bilateral pleural thickening). Persons with "exceptional" medical claims—claims that do not fall within the four described diagnostic categories—may in some instances qualify for compensation, but the settlement caps the number of "exceptional" claims CCR must cover. . . .

Class members are to receive no compensation for certain kinds of claims, even if otherwise applicable state law recognizes such claims.

Claims that garner no compensation under the settlement include claims by family members of asbestos-exposed individuals for loss of consortium, and claims by so-called "exposure-only" plaintiffs for increased risk of cancer, fear of future asbestos-related injury, and medical monitoring. "Pleural" claims, which might be asserted by persons with asbestos-related plaques on their lungs but no accompanying physical impairment, are also excluded. Although not entitled to present compensation, exposure-only claimants and pleural claimants may qualify for benefits when and if they develop a compensable disease and meet the relevant exposure and medical criteria. Defendants forgo defense to liability, including statute of limitations pleas.

Class members, in the main, are bound by the settlement in perpetuity, while CCR defendants may choose to withdraw from the settlement after ten years. A small number of class members—only a few per year—may reject the settlement and pursue their claims in court. Those permitted to exercise this option, however, may not assert any punitive damages claim or any claim for increased risk of cancer. Aspects of the administration of the settlement are to be monitored by the AFL-CIO and class counsel. Class counsel are to receive attorneys' fees in an amount to be approved by the District Court.

## D

. . . [A]s requested by the settling parties, the District Court conditionally certified, under Federal Rule of Civil Procedure 23(b)(3), an encompassing opt-out class. . . . In a separate order, Judge Weiner assigned to Judge Reed, also of the Eastern District of Pennsylvania, "the task of conducting fairness proceedings and of determining whether the proposed settlement is fair to the class." . . . Various class members raised objections to the settlement stipulation, and Judge Weiner granted the objectors full rights to participate in the subsequent proceedings. . . .

In preliminary rulings, Judge Reed held that the District Court had subject-matter jurisdiction, . . . and he approved the settling parties' elaborate plan for giving notice to the class. . . . The court-approved notice informed recipients that they could exclude themselves from the class, if they so chose, within a three-month opt-out period.

Objectors raised numerous challenges to the settlement. They urged that the settlement unfairly disadvantaged those without currently compensable conditions in that it failed to adjust for inflation or to account for changes, over time, in medical understanding. They maintained that compensation levels were intolerably low in comparison to awards available in tort litigation or payments received by the inventory plaintiffs. And they objected to the absence of any compensation for certain claims, for example, medical monitoring, compensable under the tort law of several States. Rejecting these and all other objections, Judge Reed concluded that the settlement terms were fair and had been negotiated without collusion. . . . He also found that adequate notice had been given to class members, . . . and that final class certification under Rule 23(b)(3) was appropriate. . . .

As to the specific prerequisites to certification, the District Court observed that the class satisfied Rule 23(a)(1)'s numerosity requirement, a matter no one debates. The Rule 23(a)(2) and (b)(3) requirements of commonality and preponderance were also satisfied, the District Court held. . . .

The District Court held next that the claims of the class representatives were "typical" of the class as a whole, a requirement of Rule 23(a)(3), and that, as Rule 23(b)(3) demands, the class settlement was "superior" to other methods of adjudication.

Strenuous objections had been asserted regarding the adequacy of representation, a Rule 23(a)(4) requirement. Objectors maintained that class counsel and class representatives had disqualifying conflicts of interests. In particular, objectors urged, claimants whose injuries had become manifest and claimants without manifest injuries should not have common counsel and should not be aggregated in a single class. Furthermore, objectors argued, lawyers representing inventory plaintiffs should not represent the newly-formed class.

Satisfied that class counsel had ably negotiated the settlement in the best interests of all concerned, and that the named parties served as adequate representatives, the District Court rejected these objections. . . . Subclasses were unnecessary, the District Court held, bearing in mind the added cost and confusion they would entail and the ability of class members to exclude themselves from the class during the three-month opt-out period. . . . Reasoning that the representative plaintiffs have a strong interest that recovery for *all* of the medical categories be maximized because they may have claims in *any*, or several categories, the District Court found "no antagonism of interest between class members with various medical conditions, or between persons with and without currently manifest asbestos impairment." . . . Declaring class certification appropriate and the settlement fair, the District Court preliminarily enjoined all class members from commencing any asbestos-related suit against the CCR defendants in any state or federal court. . . .

The objectors appealed. The United States Court of Appeals for the Third Circuit vacated the certification, holding that the requirements of Rule 23 had not been satisfied. . . .

### E

. . . While stating that the requirements of Rule 23(a) and (b)(3) must be met "without taking into account the settlement," . . . the Court of Appeals . . . closely considered the terms of the settlement as it examined aspects of the case under Rule 23 criteria. . . .

The Third Circuit, after intensive review, ultimately ordered decertification of the class and vacation of the District Court's anti-suit injunction. . . .

We granted certiorari, . . . and now affirm.

## II

Objectors . . . maintain that the settlement proceeding instituted by class counsel and CCR is not a justiciable case or controversy within the confines of Article III of the Federal Constitution. In the main, they say, the proceeding is a nonadversarial endeavor to impose on countless individuals without currently ripe claims an administrative compensation regime binding on those individuals if and when they manifest injuries. . . .

. . . We agree that "[t]he class certification issues are dispositive," . . . because their resolution here is logically antecedent to the existence of any Article III issues, it is appropriate to reach them first. . . . We therefore follow the path taken by the Court of Appeals, mindful that Rule 23's requirements must be interpreted in keeping with Article III constraints, and with the Rules Enabling Act, which instructs that rules of procedure "shall not abridge, enlarge or modify any substantive right," 28 U.S.C. § 2072(b). See also Fed. Rule Civ. Proc. 82 ("rules shall not be construed to extend . . . the [subject matter] jurisdiction of the United States district courts").

## III

. . . In addition to satisfying Rule 23(a)'s prerequisites, parties seeking class certification must show that the action is maintainable under Rule 23(b)(1), (2), or (3). . . .

In the 1966 class-action amendments, Rule 23(b)(3), the category at issue here was "the most adventuresome" innovation. See Kaplan, A Prefatory Note, 10 B.C. Indus. & Com. L. Rev. 497, 497 (1969) (hereinafter Kaplan, *Prefatory Note*). Rule 23(b)(3) added to the complex-litigation arsenal class actions for damages designed to secure judgments binding all class members save those who affirmatively elected to be excluded. . . .

Framed for situations in which "class-action treatment is not as clearly called for" as it is in Rule 23(b)(1) and (b)(2) situations, Rule 23(b)(3) permits certification where class suit "may nevertheless be convenient and desirable." Adv. Comm. Notes, 28 U.S.C.A. p. 697. To qualify for certification under Rule 23(b)(3), a class must meet two requirements beyond the Rule 23(a) prerequisites: Common questions must "predominate over any questions affecting only individual members"; and class resolution must be "superior to other available methods for the fair and efficient adjudication of the controversy." . . .

In the decades since the 1966 revision of Rule 23, class action practice has become ever more "adventuresome" as a means of coping with claims too numerous to secure their "just, speedy, and inexpensive determination" one by one. See Fed. Rule Civ. Proc. 1. The development reflects concerns about the efficient use of court resources and the conservation of funds to compensate claimants who do not line up early in a litigation queue. . . .

Among current applications of Rule 23(b)(3), the "settlement only" class has become a stock device. . . . Although all Federal Circuits recognize the utility of Rule 23(b)(3) settlement classes, courts have divided on the extent to which a proffered settlement affects court surveillance under Rule 23's certification criteria. . . .

A proposed amendment to Rule 23 would expressly authorize settlement class certification, in conjunction with a motion by the settling parties for Rule 23(b)(3) certification, "even though the requirements of subdivision (b)(3) might not be met for purposes of trial." Proposed Amendment to Fed. Rule Civ. Proc. 23(b), 117 S. Ct. No. 1 CXIX, CLIV to CLV (Aug. 1996) (Request for Comment). In response to the publication of this proposal, voluminous public comments—many of them opposed to, or skeptical of, the amendment—were received by the Judicial Conference Standing Committee on Rules of Practice and Procedure. . . . The Committee has not yet acted on the matter. We consider the certification at issue under the Rule as it is currently framed.

## IV

We granted review to decide the role settlement may play, under existing Rule 23, in determining the propriety of class certification. The Third Circuit's opinion stated that each of the requirements of Rule 23(a) and (b)(3) "must be satisfied without taking into account the settlement." . . . That statement, petitioners urge, is incorrect.

We agree with petitioners to this limited extent: Settlement is relevant to a class certification. The Third Circuit's opinion bears modification in that respect. But, as we earlier observed, the Court of Appeals in fact did not ignore the settlement; instead, that court homed in on settlement terms in explaining why it found the absentees' interests inadequately represented. . . . The Third Circuit's close inspection of the settlement in that regard was altogether proper.

Confronted with a request for settlement-only class certification, a district court need not inquire whether the case, if tried, would present intractable management problems, see Fed. Rule Civ. Proc. 23(b)(3)(D), for the proposal is that there be no trial. But other specifications of the rule—those designed to protect absentees by blocking unwarranted or overbroad class definitions—demand undiluted, even heightened, attention in the settlement context. Such attention is of vital importance, for a court asked to certify a settlement class will lack the opportunity, present when a case is litigated, to adjust the class, informed by the proceedings as they unfold. See Fed. Rule Civ. Proc. 23(c), (d).[16]

---

16. Portions of the opinion dissenting in part appear to assume that settlement counts only one way—in favor of certification. . . . To the extent that is the dissent's meaning, we disagree. Settlement, though a relevant factor, does not inevitably signal that class action certification should be granted more readily than it would be were the case to be litigated. For reasons the Third Circuit aired, . . . proposed settlement classes sometimes warrant more, not less caution on the question of certification.

And, of overriding importance, courts must be mindful that the rule as now composed sets the requirements they are bound to enforce. Federal Rules take effect after an extensive deliberative process involving many reviewers: a Rules Advisory Committee, public commenters, the Judicial Conference, this Court, the Congress. See 28 U.S.C. §§ 2073, 2074. The text of a rule thus proposed and reviewed limits judicial inventiveness. Courts are not free to amend a rule outside the process Congress ordered, a process properly tuned to the instruction that rules of procedure "shall not abridge . . . any substantive right." § 2072(b).

Rule 23(e), on settlement of class actions, reads in its entirety: "A class action shall not be dismissed or compromised without the approval of the court, and notice of the proposed dismissal or compromise shall be given to all members of the class in such manner as the court directs." This prescription was designed to function as an additional requirement, not a superseding direction, for the "class action" to which Rule 23(e) refers is one qualified for certification under Rule 23(a) and (b). . . .

The safeguards provided by the Rule 23(a) and (b) class-qualifying criteria, we emphasize, are not impractical impediments—checks shorn of utility—in the settlement class context. . . .

Federal courts, in any case, lack authority to substitute for Rule 23's certification criteria a standard never adopted—that if a settlement is "fair," then certification is proper. Applying to this case criteria the rulemakers set, we conclude that the Third Circuit's appraisal is essentially correct. Although that court should have acknowledged that settlement is a factor in the calculus, a remand is not warranted on that account. The Court of Appeals' opinion amply demonstrates why—with or without a settlement on the table—the sprawling class the District Court certified does not satisfy Rule 23's requirements.

### A

. . . The District Court concluded that predominance was satisfied based on two factors: class members' shared experience of asbestos exposure and their common "interest in receiving prompt and fair compensation for their claims, while minimizing the risks and transaction costs inherent in the asbestos litigation process as it occurs presently in the tort system." . . .

The predominance requirement stated in Rule 23(b)(3), we hold, is not met by the factors on which the District Court relied. The benefits asbestos-exposed persons might gain from the establishment of a grand-scale compensation scheme is a matter fit for legislative consideration, . . . but it is not pertinent to the predominance inquiry. That inquiry trains on the legal or factual questions that qualify each class member's case as a genuine controversy, questions that preexist any settlement. . . .

. . . Predominance is a test readily met in certain cases alleging consumer or securities fraud or violations of the antitrust laws. . . . Even mass tort cases arising from a common cause or disaster may, depending upon the circumstances, satisfy the predominance requirement. . . . The

Advisory Committee for the 1966 revision of Rule 23, it is true, noted that "mass accident" cases are likely to present "significant questions, not only of damages but of liability and defenses of liability, . . . affecting the individuals in different ways." . . . And the Committee advised that such cases are "ordinarily not appropriate" for class treatment. . . . But the text of the rule does not categorically exclude mass tort cases from class certification, and district courts, since the late 1970s, have been certifying such cases in increasing number. . . . The Committee's warning, however, continues to call for caution when individual stakes are high and disparities among class members great. . . . [T]he certification in this case . . . rests on a conception of Rule 23(b)(3)'s predominance requirement irreconcilable with the rule's design.

## B

Nor can the class approved by the District Court satisfy Rule 23(a)(4)'s requirement that the named parties "will fairly and adequately protect the interests of the class." The adequacy inquiry under Rule 23(a)(4) serves to uncover conflicts of interest between named parties and the class they seek to represent. . . .

As the Third Circuit pointed out, named parties with diverse medical conditions sought to act on behalf of a single giant class rather than on behalf of discrete subclasses. In significant respects, the interests of those within the single class are not aligned. Most saliently, for the currently injured, the critical goal is generous immediate payments. That goal tugs against the interest of exposure-only plaintiffs in ensuring an ample, inflation-protected fund for the future. . . .

The disparity between the currently injured and exposure-only categories of plaintiffs, and the diversity within each category are not made insignificant by the District Court's finding that petitioners' assets suffice to pay claims under the settlement. . . . Although this is not a "limited fund" case certified under Rule 23(b)(1)(B), the terms of the settlement reflect essential allocation decisions designed to confine compensation and to limit defendants' liability. For example, the settlement includes no adjustment for inflation; only a few claimants per year can opt out at the back end; and loss-of-consortium claims are extinguished with no compensation.

The settling parties, in sum, achieved a global compromise with no structural assurance of fair and adequate representation for the diverse groups and individuals affected. Although the named parties alleged a range of complaints, each served generally as representative for the whole, not for a separate constituency. . . .

## C

. . . Many persons in the exposure-only category, the Court of Appeals stressed, may not even know of their exposure, or realize the extent of the harm they may incur. Even if they fully appreciate the significance of class notice, those without current afflictions may not have the information or foresight needed to decide, intelligently, whether to stay in or opt out.

Family members of asbestos-exposed individuals may themselves fall prey to disease or may ultimately have ripe claims for loss of consortium. Yet large numbers of people in this category—future spouses and children of asbestos victims—could not be alerted to their class membership. And current spouses and children of the occupationally exposed may know nothing of that exposure.

Because we have concluded that the class in this case cannot satisfy the requirements of common issue predominance and adequacy of representation, we need not rule, definitively, on the notice given here. . . . [H]owever, we recognize the gravity of the question whether class action notice sufficient under the Constitution and Rule 23 could ever be given to legions so unselfconscious and amorphous.

## V

The argument is sensibly made that a nationwide administrative claims processing regime would provide the most secure, fair, and efficient means of compensating victims of asbestos exposure. Congress, however, has not adopted such a solution. And Rule 23, which must be interpreted with fidelity to the Rules Enabling Act and applied with the interests of absent class members in close view, cannot carry the large load CCR, class counsel, and the District Court heaped upon it. As this case exemplifies, the rulemakers' prescriptions for class actions may be endangered by "those who embrace [Rule 23] too enthusiastically just as [they are by] those who approach [the rule] with distaste." C. Wright, Law of Federal Courts 508 (5th ed. 1994). . . .

For the reasons stated, the judgment of the Court of Appeals for the Third Circuit is

*Affirmed.*

JUSTICE O'CONNOR took no part in the consideration or decision of this case.

JUSTICE BREYER, with whom JUSTICE STEVENS joins, concurring in part and dissenting in part.

Although I agree with the Court's basic holding that "settlement is relevant to a class certification," I find several problems in its approach that lead me to a different conclusion. First, I believe that the need for settlement in this mass tort case, with hundreds of thousands of lawsuits, is greater than the Court's opinion suggests. Second, I would give more weight than would the majority to settlement-related issues for purposes of determining whether common issues predominate. Third, I am uncertain about the Court's determination of adequacy of representation, and do not believe it appropriate for this Court to second-guess the District Court on the matter without first having the Court of Appeals consider it. Fourth, I am uncertain about the tenor of an opinion that seems to suggest the settlement is unfair. And fifth, in the absence of further review by the Court of Appeals, I cannot accept the majority's suggestions that "notice" is inadequate. . . .

## I

First, I believe the majority understates the importance of settlement in this case. Between 13 and 21 million workers have been exposed to asbestos in the workplace—over the past 40 or 50 years—but the most severe instances of such exposure probably occurred three or four decades ago. . . . This exposure has led to several hundred thousand lawsuits, about 15% of which involved claims for cancer and about 30% for asbestos. . . . . About half of the suits have involved claims for pleural thickening and plaques—the harmfulness of which is apparently controversial. . . . Some of those who suffer from the most serious injuries, however, have received little or no compensation. . . . These lawsuits have taken up more than 6% of all federal civil filings in one recent year, and are subject to a delay that is twice that of other civil suits. Judicial Conference Report 7, 10-11. . . .

. . . [T]he majority, in reviewing the District Court's determination that common "issues of fact and law predominate," says that the predominance "inquiry trains on the legal or factual questions that qualify each class member's case as a genuine controversy, questions that preexist any settlement." . . . If the majority means that these presettlement questions are what matters, then how does it reconcile its statement with its basic conclusion that "settlement is relevant" to class certification, or with the numerous lower court authority [sic] that says that settlement is not only relevant, but important? . . .

Nor do I understand how one could decide whether common questions "predominate" in the abstract—without looking at what is likely to be an issue in the proceedings that will ensue, namely, the settlement. . . . How can a court make a contextual judgment of the sort that Rule 23 requires without looking to what proceedings will follow? Such guideposts help it decide whether, in light of common concerns and differences, certification will achieve Rule 23's basic objective—"economies of time, effort, and expense." Advisory Committee's Notes on Fed. Rule Civ. Proc. 23(b)(3), 28 U.S.C.A., p. 697. . . .

The majority may mean that the District Court gave too much weight to the settlement. But I am not certain how it can reach that conclusion. It cannot rely upon the Court of Appeals, for that court gave no positive weight at all to the settlement. Nor can it say that the District Court relied solely on "a common interest in a fair compromise," for the District Court did not do so. Rather, it found the settlement relevant because it explained the importance of the class plaintiffs' common features and common interests. . . .

The settlement is relevant because it means that these common features and interests are likely to be important in the proceeding that would ensue—a proceeding that would focus primarily upon whether or not the proposed settlement fairly and properly satisfied the interests class members had in common. That is to say, the settlement underscored the importance of (a) the common fact of exposure, (b) the common interests in receiving *some* compensation for certain rather than running a strong risk of *no* compensation, and (c) the common interest in avoiding large legal fees, other transaction costs, and delays.

Of course, as the majority points out, there are also important differences among class members. Different plaintiffs were exposed to different products for different durations of time; each has a distinct medical history and a different history of smoking; and many cases arise under the laws of different States. The relevant question, however, is *how much* these differences matter in respect to the legal proceedings that lie ahead. Many, if not all, toxic tort class actions involve plaintiffs with such differences. And the differences in state law are of diminished importance in respect to a proposed settlement in which the defendants have waived all defenses and agreed to compensate all those who were injured. . . .

Third, the majority concludes that the "representative parties" will not "fairly and adequately protect the interests of the class." Rule 23(a)(4). . . .

I agree that there is a serious problem, but it is a problem that often exists in toxic tort cases. . . . And it is a problem that potentially exists whenever a single defendant injures several plaintiffs, for a settling plaintiff leaves fewer assets available for the others. With class actions, at least, plaintiffs have the consolation that a district court, thoroughly familiar with the facts, is charged with the responsibility of ensuring that the interests of no class members are sacrificed. . . .

Further, certain details of the settlement that are not discussed in the majority opinion suggest that the settlement may be of greater benefit to future plaintiffs than the majority suggests. . . .

I do not know whether or not the benefits are more or less valuable than an inflation adjustment. But I can certainly recognize an argument that they are. . . .

Fourth, I am more agnostic than is the majority about the basic fairness of the settlement. The District Court's conclusions rested upon complicated factual findings that are not easily cast aside. . . . I do not intend to pass judgment upon the settlement's fairness, but I do believe that these matters would have to be explored in far greater depth before I could reach a conclusion about fairness. And that task, as I have said, is one for the Court of Appeals.

Finally, I believe it is up to the District Court, rather than this Court, to review the legal sufficiency of notice to members of the class. . . .

## II

The issues in this case are complicated and difficult. The District Court might have been correct. Or not. Subclasses might be appropriate. Or not. I cannot tell. And I do not believe that this Court should be in the business of trying to make these fact-based determinations. That is a job suited to the district courts in the first instance, and the courts of appeal on review. But there is no reason in this case to believe that the Court of Appeals conducted its prior review with an understanding that the settlement could have constituted a reasonably strong factor in favor of class certification. For this reason, I would provide the courts below with an opportunity to analyze the factual questions involved in certification by vacating the judgment, and remanding the case for further proceedings.

## Notes and Questions

1. *Implications of* Amchem: *Ortiz v. Fibreboard Corp., 527 U.S. 815 (1999).* Post-*Amchem,* courts have shown far less appetite for settlement classes, and for broad-gauged mass tort class actions in general. See, e.g., Thomas v. Albright, 139 F.3d 227 (D.C. Cir. 1998) (ruling that *Amchem* did not invalidate an earlier holding that opt-outs are allowable, but concluding that the district court abused its discretion in allowing dissident class members to opt out in this Title VII race discrimination suit); Barnes v. American Tobacco Co., Inc., 984 F. Supp. 842 (E.D. Pa. 1997) (decertifying class); O'Connor v. Boeing North Am., Inc., 180 F.R.D. 359 (C.D. Cal. 1997) (denying class certification); Wilks v. Ford Motor Co., 174 F.R.D. 332 (D.N.J. 1997) (denying certification); Ford v. Murphy Oil USA, Inc., 703 So. 2d 542 (La. 1997) (decertifying an environmental toxic tort suit based on *Amchem*).

An important post-*Amchem* case suggests that the Court means business in demanding that settlement classes satisfy Rule 23 criteria. The background was the effort of a number of courts to find some path outside of Rule 23(b)(3) by which to establish a settlement class. In Flanagan v. Ahearn (In re Asbestos Litigation), 134 F.3d 668 (5th Cir. 1998), the Fifth Circuit held that a settlement class action was properly certified as a limited fund under 23(b)(1)(B), which does not require the "predominance" showing of 23(b)(3), and thus avoids some of the problems of *Amchem.* In Ortiz v. Fibreboard Corp., 527 U.S. 815 (1999), the Supreme Court reversed the Fifth Circuit's rationale and held that before a court can certify a mandatory settlement class on a limited fund rationale, it must assure the inadequacy of the fund to pay all claims. There was insufficient evidence in this case, the Court concluded, on which to base a finding that the fund was indeed inadequate.

Justice Souter, writing for the majority, laid out the history of class actions in general, and of the limited fund doctrine in particular. He concluded that "the limited fund cases . . . ensur[e] that the class as a whole [is] given the best deal; they [do] not give a defendant a better deal than seriatim litigation would have produced." 527 U.S. at 881. Rule 23(b)(1)(B) should be construed, according to the Court, in a way that "stay[s] close to the historical model." Id. at 817. The Court ultimately concluded that the applicability of Rule 23(b)(1)(B) to a fund and plan purporting to liquidate actual and potential tort claims was questionable in any case and improper in the case before it, where the fund was not shown to be limited "independently of the agreement of the parties to the action." Id. at 864. The Court thus intimated that bankruptcy may be a necessary precursor to invoking 23(b)(1)(B) on a limited fund rationale.

*Amchem*'s insistence on close adherence to Rule 23(a) and (b) criteria has not been interpreted to preclude the lower court practice of invoking 23(e)(5) as authority to allow dissident members to opt out of 23(b)(1) or (2) classes in "appropriate" cases, despite the absence of express opt-out authority under either section. See Thomas v. Albright, supra; see also Alex Raskolnikov, Note, Is There a Future for Future Claimants After Amchem Products, Inc. v. Windsor?, 107 Yale L.J. 2545 (1998) (arguing that a principal source of concern in *Amchem* was future claimants and that satisfaction of class action standards in mass tort cases thus will depend primarily on whether courts can devise a regime that would guarantee adequate protection for these claimants). See also Prof'l Firefighters Ass'n of Omaha, Local 385 v. Zalewski, 678 F.3d 640 (8th Cir. 2012) (distinguishing *Amchem* and *Ortiz* because relief sought was declaratory and injunctive, and because class members with potentially conflicting interests were twice given opportunity to opt out); id. at 647 ("We also do not believe . . . the stark conflicts of interest that the Supreme Court discerned in *Amchem* and *Ortiz* are present here. Though not entirely consistent, the interests of the active and retired city employees aligned in many significant ways, not the least of which was their driving interest to enjoin the city's enforcement" of an ordinance radically altering public employees' health care costs) (internal quotation marks and citations omitted).

The United States Supreme Court added another layer of protection against unfair class action settlements in Devlin v. Scardelletti, 536 U.S. 1 (2002). The Court held that non-named class members who object in a timely manner to approval of a settlement at a fairness hearing may bring an appeal without first intervening in the suit. The right to appeal in a class action is not restricted to named parties. The key is whether they are parties in the sense of being bound by the settlement, which non-named class members are.

For a recent class settlement centralizing hundreds of claims for economic loss and property damages arising from the Deepwater Horizon oil spill in the Gulf of Mexico, see In re Oil Spill by the Oil Rig Deepwater Horizon, 2012 WL 6652608 (E.D. La. Dec. 21, 2012) (certifying class for settlement purposes). See also Samuel Issacharoff and D. Theodore Rave, The BP Oil Spill Settlement and the Paradox of Public Litigation, 74 La. L. Rev. 397, 398-402 (2014) (comparing class action settlement with administrative process for settling claims arising from the Deepwater Horizon oil spill; "[i]n theory, the [administrative process] should have resolved the private claims against BP in a streamlined and efficient manner . . . allowing both claimants and BP to realize savings over traditional litigation. . . . [B]ut by all appearances, claimants will be receiving higher payments under the class settlement . . . and in some case much higher payments").

2. *Legislation and Rulemaking.* In *Ortiz*, Justice Souter said of the asbestos litigation that it "defies customary judicial administration and calls

for national legislation." 527 U.S. at 821. Though the Justice was probably thinking of legislation directed toward resolving such claims through an administrative process, as mentioned also by Justice Ginsburg, legislative exasperation was expended on the class action device itself. One bipartisan bill, for instance, the Class Action Fairness Act of 1999 (S. 353), would have altered class actions in several respects. (See also H.R. 1875.) For instance, notice of both the class action and of settlements was required to be given in easily understood terms. Settlement notices were to include the amount and source of attorneys' fees, among other information. The Act would also limit class action attorneys' fees to a reasonable percentage of actual damages paid to class members, the actual costs of complying with the terms of a settlement agreement, and any future financial benefits. In the alternative, the bill provided that, to the extent the law allows, fees would be based on a reasonable hourly rate.

Finally, it allowed removal from state court to federal court, either by a defendant, or an unnamed class member, and altered diversity of citizenship requirements to permit removal whenever the parties include citizens of different states. Cases would remain in state court, however, if the substantial majority of class and primary defendants were from the same state and that state's law would govern, or if the primary defendants were states and a federal court could not order the relief requested. See Stephen Labaton, Asbestos Cases in for Overhaul by Lawmakers, N.Y. Times, June 18, 1999, at A1.

Critics of the bill argued that it would unduly limit access to state court class actions and that there was inadequate evidence that state court class actions suffer from systematic problems that warrant the federalizing effect on class actions that would result from this last provision. Although the bill failed, possibly under the threat of a presidential veto, it was another indication of deep dissatisfaction with the efficacy of the class action device in mass tort situations.

*Amchem* came down just as the Advisory Committee was gearing up to add a new section to Rule 23, providing specifically for "settlement class actions." Specifically, the provision endorsed the much disputed practice of certifying a class under (b)(3) for settlement, even though it did not meet the requirements for trial. There were three main arguments against the new rule, which were basically the same as those made against the *Amchem* certification. First, the trial judge's discretion was unbounded as to when a settlement class was appropriate. Second, the legislation had potential constitutional flaws (violating due process, violating the case or controversy requirement for courts to act). There was also the argument, suggested in *Amchem*, too, that such a provision would encroach on the Rules Enabling Act by affecting substantive rights.

Needless to say, although *Amchem* did not hold settlement classes unconstitutional, it put a real crimp in an already-embattled rulemaking process. The new Rule 23(b)(4) was withdrawn. According to the Reporter of the Advisory Committee, Professor Edward Cooper, the committee thought that class action law would better develop through the ad hoc reforms enabled by the new provision, "allowing immediate appeals of certification rulings." 68 U.S.L.W. 2259, 2259-2260 (Nov. 9, 1999).

But the Advisory Committee did not leave the matters entirely to "ad hoc reforms" for long. In 2003, it returned to the general problem of managing class action settlements, promulgating new amendments to Rule 23 setting specific rules for court approval (including a requirement that the court provide a hearing on the settlement and specifically find it to be "fair, reasonable, and adequate"), notice to class members, and the right to object. See Rule 23(e).

The Advisory Committee also added two new subsections: Rule 23(g), which distinguishes scrutiny of the class representative (under Rule 23(a)(4)) from the process and standards for evaluation and appointment of class counsel, and Rule 23(h), which governs attorneys' fee awards. Significantly, Rule 23(g) requires that the court, not named plaintiffs, appoint counsel to represent the class in all federal class actions, and it lists factors that should bear on the court's decision, including the work the lawyer has done in identifying potential claims; the experience of the lawyer, particularly in handling class actions; and the resources the lawyer can commit to representing the class. Under Rule 23(h), any class member is entitled to object to a motion for an award of attorneys' fees.

As we discussed above in section A(d)(2), an even more comprehensive set of reforms was enacted by Congress in 2005. In specific settings, Congress has intervened to create alternatives to aggregate litigation of mass claims. The Deepwater Horizon case, discussed in Note 1, is one example. The administrative claims process established to pay $6.2 billion in compensation to over 220,000 claimants was structured according to the Oil Pollution Act of 1990, a statute passed after difficulties were encountered in administering compensation claims for victims of the 1989 Exxon-Valdez oil spill in Alaska. See Issacharoff and Rave, 74 La. L. Rev. at 399.

3. *Class Action Remainders.* In approving a class action settlement courts are often asked to review how the parties wish to handle money that goes unclaimed following distribution to class members who file claims as well as the disposition of money that, for one reason or another, cannot be distributed to individual class members. The latter circumstance is more common than you might think—quite often in consumer litigation the recovery of individual class members is so small that they do not take the time to file claims or it is too costly to distribute the funds. "There are several ways in which such funds can be distributed, including pro rata distribution to class members; reversion to the defendant; escheat to the government; or cy pres distribution." Kathryn Harrigan Christian et al., When The Cup Runneth Over: Cy Pres Distribution in Class Action Settlements, Bloomberg BNA, Mar. 11, 2013. None is ideal. Pro rata distribution can overcompensate known class members; reversion to the defendant can undermine the goal of full cost internalization for the harms caused; escheat to the state risks undercompensating victims and is unmoored from standard remedial objectives, unless the harm involved public costs and the state uses the money to address those costs; and cy pres—"a distribution for the indirect

prospective benefit of the class," id., such as a donation to a charity that serves a population or cause related to the injury the class members have suffered—has been criticized for providing windfall gains to non-class members.

Cy pres "originated as a rule of construction to save a testamentary charitable gift that would otherwise fail, allowing the next best use of the funds to satisfy the testator's intent as near as possible. The phrase 'cy pres' comes from the French Norman Expression 'cy pres comme possible,' meaning 'as near as possible.'" Id. As cy pres has become more common in class action settlements, criticism has also amplified. Chief Justice Roberts dissented from the denial of certiorari in a recent class settlement against Facebook for violating the privacy rights of consumers. He voiced concerns about the cy pres remedy in the case. See Marek v. Lane, 134 S. Ct. 8 (2013). Rather than compensate unnamed class members, two-thirds of the recovery was designated to the establishment of a "new charitable foundation that would help fund organizations dedicated to educating the public about online privacy." Id. at 9. An unnamed class member objected to the settlement on the ground that a senior Facebook officer would sit on the board of the new foundation, the board had "unfettered discretion" to determine fund recipients, and the foundation had no "proven track record" whatsoever. Id. The Chief Justice agreed that certiorari was improper in this case, but signaled interest in addressing

> more fundamental concerns surrounding the use of such remedies in class action litigation, including when if ever such relief should be considered; how to assess its fairness as a general matter; whether new entities may be established as part of such relief; if not, how existing entities should be selected; what the respective roles of the judge and parties are in shaping a cy pres remedy; how closely the goals of any organization must correspond to the interests of the class; and so on. This court has not previously addressed any of these issues. Cy pres remedies, however, are a growing feature of class action settlements. See Redish, Julian & Zyontz, Cy Pres Relief and the Pathologies of the Modern Class Action: A Normative and Empirical Analysis, 62 Fla. L. Rev. 617, 653-56 (2010). In a suitable case, this court may need to clarify the limits on the use of such remedies.

Id. See also Keepseagle v. Vilsack, 118 F. Supp. 3d 98 (D.D.C. 2015) (refusing to modify cy pres provision of civil rights settlement with Department of Agriculture for discrimination against Native American farmers after plaintiffs complained that more than half of the fund would be distributed in equal shares to charities).

4. *Lawyer's Ethics and Class Actions.* In *Amchem*, the Court did not examine the issues of the potential conflicts of interest between class counsel and the class itself, though these conflicts were of great concern in *Ortiz*. There Justice Souter warned that in drafting global settlement agreements especially, "Class counsel . . . had great incentive to reach any agreement . . . that they thought might survive a Rule 23(e) fairness hearing, rather than the best possible arrangement for the substantially unidentified global

settlement class." *Ortiz*, 527 U.S. at 818. Another ethical issue, one that often arises and is present but not mentioned in the Court's opinion in *Amchem*, is the possible collusion between the class counsel and the defendants, who (ironically, perhaps) sometimes turn out to desire class certification. Can you see why, especially if the settlement is "global" and binds future claimants as well as past ones? In *Amchem* in the lower court, the trial judge found specifically that neither of these potential ethical difficulties existed. Georgine v. Amchem Prods. Inc., 157 F.R.D. 246, 294-311 (E.D. Pa. 1994).

Professor Susan P. Koniak, who was an expert witness for the objectors, lays out the reasons she found such conflicts to exist. Without pulling punches, she charges that class counsel traded the interests of future claimants in order to obtain a better settlement for their "inventory clients" and higher fees for themselves. Feasting While the Widow Weeps: Georgine v. Amchem Products, Inc., 80 Com. L. Rev. 1045 (1995). See also Professor Carrie J. Menkel-Meadow, Ethics and the Settlement of Mass Torts: When the Rules Meet the Road, 80 Cornell L. Rev. 1159 (1995).

Most of the ethical dilemmas faced by class counsel arise because our professional norms and rules are based on a traditional bipolar lawsuit, where all lawyers know exactly whom they represent, and where the fee potential is related to the amount of work actually performed. Class actions in general, and especially settlement class actions, do not fit the traditional model at all. Perhaps most notably, and raising the greatest temptation, the class action lawyer is often less a representative of clients' interests than an entrepreneur, putting together a suit for himself.

Professor Judith Resnik describes the usual relationship of attorney and client as an unregulated, contractually bound unit. "Agent-principal relations are presumed sufficient [for regulation], in that the lawyer is imagined to be monitored by the client, and the charter for representation is assumed to be adequately controlled by the client." Money Matters: Judicial Market Interventions Creating Subsidies and Awarding Fees and Costs in Individual and Aggregate Litigation, 148 U. Pa. L. Rev. 2119, 2169 (2000). She argues that in *Amchem* and *Ortiz*, the Supreme Court refused to transpose this ethic into the mass tort context, and effectively calls for judicial intervention to make certain that not only individuals within the group litigation but also the group itself are fairly represented.

Also in the background of the class action lawyer's special ethical dilemmas is the fact that his interests and those of the clients may diverge very early in the case.

In particular, the lawyer may stand to profit from a large, early settlement in the dispute far more than the class members. The issue may be most visible in the arena of securities fraud litigation, where it has received extended treatment in the media, before Congress, and in academic journals. See, e.g., David Marcus, Some Realism About Mass Torts, 75 U. Chi. L. Rev. 1949 (2008); Jonathan R. Macey and Geoffrey P. Miller, The Plaintiffs' Attorney's Role in Class Action and Derivative Litigation: Economic Analysis and Recommendations for Reform, 58 U. Chi. L. Rev. 1 (1991); Janet Cooper Alexander, Do the Merits Matter? A Study of Settlements in Securities Class

Actions, 43 Stan. L. Rev. 497 (1991); Elliott J. Weiss and John S. Beckerman, Let the Money Do the Monitoring: How Institutional Investors Can Reduce Agency Costs in Securities Class Actions, 104 Yale L.J. 2053 (1995). See also Private Securities Litigation Reform Act of 1995, Pub. L. No. 104-67, § 102, 109 Stat. 737.

Consider the following materials addressing the ethical features of this problem, which appear in Deborah Rhode's Professional Responsibility: Ethics by the Pervasive Method 594-599 (1994):

> You work for Ford Motor Company's in-house general counsel. Assume that the following facts described in the American Lawyer are true. Would you recommend accepting the settlement? If the settlement is approved, what if any action would you recommend concerning Cohn's conduct?
>
> > Event 1: A lawyer [Cohn], using his partner's children as the aggrieved "shareholders," decides to bring a shareholders' derivative suit against a company, charging the chairman with stealing. The charges are so scandalous, and the company and its chairman so well known, that the suit makes big headlines.
> >
> > Event 2: After he files the suit he tells a reporter, as he waves various papers in the air, that he has "an open and shut" case on all the charges.
> >
> > Event 3: The suit has not been filed in the right jurisdiction. It is thrown out.
> >
> > Event 4: The lawyer vows to file the suit in the right jurisdiction.
> >
> > Event 5: Telling the other side that he plans to file again, and that this will mean a rehash of the charges in the press, the lawyer inquires if a "settlement" might be possible.
> >
> > Event 6: The company, which has denied all the charges but is beset by bad publicity on other fronts, including a criminal trial for allegedly having made dangerous products, gives the lawyer $100,000 in "legal fees" on the condition that he not bring the suit in the right jurisdiction.
> >
> > Event 7: The lawyer declares that "it now appears" that the company chairman was not guilty of any wrongdoing.
> >
> > The lawyer's supposed clients—the shareholders—get nothing. Nor do they give up anything: the shareholders can sue again on the same charges. It's just that the headline-making lawyer can't represent them. Contrary to what would be required in any other shareholders' suit, a judge does not have to approve this settlement. With the first suit thrown out and the second one only threatened, there is no suit pending and, therefore, no judge with jurisdiction.
> >
> > In short, the lawyer, having filed a claim in the wrong jurisdiction, having produced no proof, and having now admitted that the charges were unsupportable, gets $100,000 in return for dropping his client and not generating any more bad headlines.
> >
> > In many circles this would be called extortion. At Hughes Hubbard & Reed, it is called a "settlement." And Cohn's $100,000 is called "legal fees," although Hughes Hubbard lawyers say that his time and work were not documented in any way.
> >
> > How can it be a "settlement" if no suit was pending and if the shareholders can sue again on the same charges?

"Because we weren't buying off the lawsuit," says Hughes Hubbard senior partner Jerome Shapiro, who negotiated the deal with Cohn. "We were buying off Roy Cohn. It's Cohn we were interested in, and what he said he could do to us in the press if he started the suit again in Michigan [the correct jurisdiction]. Cohn has a special relationship with the press," Shapiro continues. "He can get a headline in The Wall Street Journal or The New York Times by picking up a phone. . . . These papers printed uncritical, big-headline accounts of Cohn's charges." . . .

"No, he doesn't deserve this as a fee, and it doesn't make me happy that he's received anything," Shapiro concludes. Then won't this just encourage him to go after other big-business targets? "Of course it will," Shapiro says, "but I represent the Ford Motor Company, not the next guy." . . .[20]

### Jonathan R. Macey and Geoffrey Miller, The Plaintiffs' Attorney's Role in Class Action and Derivative Litigation: Economic Analysis and Recommendations for Reform
58 U. Chi. L. Rev. 1, 22-26 (1991)

[C]onsider incentive effects in class and derivative litigation. The lack of monitoring [by nominal plaintiffs] . . . in these settings would not be especially problematic if the interests of plaintiffs' counsel were closely aligned with those of their clients. Unfortunately, there is a substantial deviation of interests between attorney and client. The nature of the conflict varies depending on the type of litigation involved and the procedure used in the jurisdiction for determining the attorney's fee. But at least under the existing regulatory system, the conflict remains significant in all cases.

In "common fund" cases, where the plaintiffs' attorney generates a fund for the benefit of the class, the majority of American courts award fees out of the fund based on the lodestar calculation. Under this approach, the hours reasonably expended by the lawyer are multiplied by the lawyer's reasonable hourly fee to calculate a lodestar. The lodestar is then adjusted by a multiplier to account for a variety of factors including [any unusual degree of skill, superior or inferior, and,] most significantly, the risk of the litigation. Attorneys in these cases thus have an incentive to run up excessive hours, delay the litigation unnecessarily, or even to exaggerate the number of hours expended in order to obtain a larger fee. Plaintiffs' attorneys may also wish to settle for a relatively low sum on the eve of trial, knowing that in so doing they obtain most of the benefits they can expect from the litigation while eliminating their downside risk. These abuses are checked, to a degree, by the required judicial scrutiny of fee awards and settlements in class and derivative litigation. Nevertheless, agency costs in cases where fees are calculated using the lodestar method are no doubt substantial.

---

20. Steven Brill, Roy Cohn Rides Again, Am. Law., Mar. 1980, at 5.

Further, plaintiffs' attorneys may sometimes substantially reduce their risk by reaching an understanding with defense counsel early on about the contours of the eventual settlement. Then they can expend a mutually acceptable number of additional hours on the case, charging them against the settlement fund under the lodestar calculation. The social disutility of this procedure is obvious; it represents an essentially meaningless exercise that ties up the resources of plaintiffs' counsel, defense counsel, and others such as witnesses who must submit to depositions that all parties understand will never be used in court. The principal losers are members of the plaintiff class who must pay over part of their recovery to counsel for work that serves no purpose other than to justify an enhanced attorney's fee.

The other method of calculating attorneys' fees in common fund cases, which has become more popular recently is the "percentage" method, in which fees are awarded based on some fixed percentage of the fund. There are obvious incentive problems with this arrangement as well. First, plaintiffs' attorneys will earn windfall profits, at the expense of the class members, in cases presenting large damages and low proof costs. . . .

The second incentive problem in percentage-of-the-recovery cases is settlement. Attorneys compensated on a percentage method have an incentive to settle early for an amount lower than what might be obtained by further efforts. The attorney who puts in relatively few hours to obtain an early settlement is likely to earn a much greater compensation per hour of effort than an attorney who expends greater efforts and litigates a case to the point where the plaintiffs' recovery is maximized. Again the plaintiff class loses.

Consider now common benefit . . . cases. Common benefit cases are typically shareholders' derivative suits in which the plaintiffs' attorney does not generate a fund, but rather causes the defendant to do something that confers a nonpecuniary benefit on the corporation. . . . In common benefit . . . cases the attorneys' fee comes from the defendant rather than from the class recovery. Unlike common fund cases, therefore, there is a counterparty in common benefit and fee-shifting cases with an incentive to bargain over the fee in order to keep it within reasonable limits.

This feature, however, does not effectively obviate the attorney-client conflict. Defendants in common benefit and fee-shifting cases typically wish to minimize the sum of three costs: the costs of the relief on the merits, the costs of their own attorney's fees, and the costs of the plaintiffs' attorney's fees. Defendants are typically indifferent about how the total cost of litigation is distributed among these elements. Plaintiffs' attorneys, on the other hand, have an interest in increasing their own fees, even at the expense of a reduction in the relief afforded to the putative client. Thus the conditions are present for a bargain under which the plaintiffs' attorneys agree to a lower overall settlement on the merits of the litigation in exchange for a higher fee.

A related problem occurs when the defendant offers a relatively generous settlement on the merits on condition that the plaintiffs' attorney agrees to waive any fee request (or to accept a low fee). This conflict has led some courts and commentators to call for a mandatory rule separating the fee negotiation from the settlement on the merits in fee-shifting cases. Whether such a rule could be effectively enforced is open to question, however. Moreover, separating the fee negotiation from the merits determination raises the possibility that plaintiffs' attorneys who believe that a favorable settlement will eventually be reached will string out litigation well past the point where settlement first becomes possible in order to justify a higher fee request. Splitting the fee and merits negotiations is no panacea for the agency problems in the common benefit and fee-shifting contexts.

### *Example: A Lawyer's Fairy Tale*

*A, B,* and *C* are three makers of widgets. Together, they have made and sold 100 million units a year for the last few decades.

Twelve years ago, the widget price went up from $1.00 to $1.20. There had been some rises in preceding years, and there have been some since, but this was the biggest single jump.

Two years ago, disgruntled former officers of *A* gave evidence that the 20¢ price increase was conspiratorial. This was hotly disputed. The Justice Department prosecuted and won. A fine in the amount of $50,000 was imposed on each of the companies.

Class Action I was brought on behalf of wholesalers against the three companies. The defendants conceded (as they could not dispute) that the government's judgment foreclosed litigation on the issue of liability. As to damages, however, they sought to prove that the price increase was largely, if perhaps not entirely, passed on to the retailers in higher wholesale prices. The jury found otherwise, ruling that the wholesalers had suffered a 20¢ loss on every widget for ten years. With the appropriate trebling, this resulted in a verdict of $600 million.

Class Action II was brought on behalf of retailers against the three companies. Again there was no issue as to liability. The plaintiffs offered substantially the same evidence on damages that the defendants had offered in Class Action I. This time the evidence was persuasive; the jury found that the retailers had, indeed, been caused to pay an extra 20¢ for each widget for ten years. The defendants' efforts to prove that the retailers had passed the price increase on to the consumers were unsuccessful. A second verdict and judgment in the amount of $600 million resulted.

Class Action III was brought on behalf of the consumers. Again there was no room for dispute as to liability; as to damages, the jury evaluated the conflicting testimony and concluded that consumers had, indeed, paid an extra 20¢ for each widget for ten years. Every consumer able to prove a purchase was held to be entitled to a 60¢ compensation.

Is there any question about the wisdom of this outcome? Is it required by the statute or by Rule 23? Is it unlikely that all three judgments can in fact be executed? If not, is there any priority among the payments from the assets of the three companies? If it were possible to satisfy all three judgments, is it not probable that the net worth of the lawyer representing the claimants would be greater than the net worth of the widget industry? Is this fairy tale a "miracle" of overstatement?

### Note: Rule 68, Class Actions, and Mootness

You have just read about the ethical dilemmas and temptations that plaintiff's-side lawyers face in the class action context. Defense lawyers are not without temptations in this setting. For decades one tactic used by defense lawyers prior to class certification was to make a Rule 68 offer to the named plaintiffs and then move to dismiss the case as moot on the ground that the named plaintiffs had no personal interest in the outcome of the litigation. Defense counsel employed this tactic even if the named plaintiffs refused the Rule 68 offer. See, e.g., Weiss v. Regal Collections, 385 F.3d 337, 345 (3d Cir. 2004) ("Allowing defendants to 'pick off' putative lead plaintiffs contravenes one of the primary purposes of class actions—the aggregation of numerous similar (especially small) claims in a single action. Moreover, a rule allowing plaintiffs to be 'picked off' at an early stage . . . may waste judicial resources by stimulating successive suits brought by others claiming aggrievement."). The Supreme Court has recently resolved a circuit split on the issue by holding that an unaccepted Rule 68 offer to named plaintiffs does not moot a class action case. Campbell-Ewald Co. v. Gomez, 136 S. Ct. 663 (2016) (consumer class action against advertiser for violations of the Telephone Consumer Protection Act by permitting third-party vendors to send unsolicited text messages to consumer's cellular phone; "an unaccepted settlement offer . . . does not moot a plaintiff's case. . . . We need not, and do not, now decide whether the result would be different if a defendant deposits the full amount of the plaintiff's individual claim in an account payable to the plaintiff, and the court then enters judgment for the plaintiff in that amount. That question is appropriately reserved for a case in which it is not hypothetical.").

What exactly is wrong with "picking off" named plaintiffs? After all, they are the class members most motivated to vindicate their rights and we know that many unnamed class members would not bother to sue. One concern is that an endless succession of suits will follow if Rule 68 offers to named plaintiffs can moot class relief, or that the "private attorney general" function of class actions will be undermined if defendants can avoid paying the full cost of their wrongdoing by buying off named plaintiffs. But if this is the driving concern, why should the named plaintiff have to decline the Rule 68 offer to prevent dismissal for mootness?

Is there anything ethically suspect about defeating an otherwise meritorious class action through a Rule 68 offer to the named plaintiff? Or is the real problem reconciling mootness doctrine with the complexities of interest representation—the fact that a named plaintiff sues not only to obtain individual relief but also to vindicate interests of the class?

## Note: Multidistrict Litigation—The Aggregation Alternative

Note that *Amchem* involved the transfer of cases from many forums to one court, effected under 28 U.S.C. § 1407. This aggregating of multiple claims has been used both as an alternative and accessory to class actions, and has aroused considerable commentary. As Andrew Brandt has observed, "Although the class-action structure seems increasingly untenable, the stresses on the system that create the need to aggregate have not disappeared. Given all this, it should also come as no surprise that multidistrict litigation, or 'MDL,' has stepped in to fill the void. . . . According to recent statistics . . . a third of all pending federal civil cases are part of an MDL, and over ninety percent of those cases are products-liability cases—exactly the sorts of cases that might have been nationwide class actions had choice-of-law issues not emerged as such a central obstacle." The Shortest Distance: Direct Filing and Choice of Law in Multidistrict Litigation, 88 Notre Dame L. Rev. 759, 761-762 (2012). See also Elizabeth Chamblee Burch, Judging Multidistrict Litigation, 90 N.Y.U. L. Rev. 71 (2015); Emery G. Lee III, Catherine R. Borden, Margaret S. Williams, and Kevin M. Scott, Multidistrict Centralization: An Empirical Examination, 12 J. of Empirical Legal Studies 211, 212 (2015) (finding that the probability of consolidation was 47 percent in 2013, compared with 38 percent in 1968; "the Panel is more likely to order centralization if the proceeding includes class allegations, and more likely to order centralization of proceedings raising air disaster, antitrust, intellectual property, products liability, and securities issues than proceedings raising other types of claims"); Andrew Brandt, The Multidistrict Litigation Act of 1968 (forthcoming 2015). For a discussion of the complexities in contemporary MDL litigation, see Eldon E. Fallon, Jeremey T. Grabill, and Robert Pitard Wynne, Bellwether Trials in Multidistrict Litigation, 82 Tulane L. Rev. 2323 (2008) (describing Vioxx litigation); Deborah R. Hensler, The Role of Multi-Districting in Mass Tort Litigation, 31 Seton Hall L. Rev. 883, 894 (2001).

After considering the policy issues, take any class action case or problem considered in this chapter and contemplate the possible application of § 1407. Imagine that several individual members of the classes have brought their own claims in different districts around the country. Perhaps some of these are class actions, and possibly multiple class actions with overlapping classes. Perhaps in some of these cases the plaintiffs are asserting multiple claims against the same defendants; in others, perhaps the defendants have asserted counterclaims.

It is possible in all of these situations that § 1407 might be applied. If none of the consolidated actions were previously class actions, the litigation would nevertheless begin to partake of some aspects of class litigation. There are, however, some important differences between multiple actions consolidated for pretrial under § 1407 and a class action proceeding under Fed. R. Civ. P. 23. The statute was enacted in 1968 for the purpose of enhancing efficiency in administration, inspired by an enormous saving achieved by voluntary consolidation of hundreds of duplicate antitrust suits in the electrical equipment industry.

In examining the text of the statute, consider the following questions:

1) Who decides whether an action should be transferred for consolidation?
2) Must the transfer be on motion of a party?
3) Can the panel select the transferee judge ad hominem?
4) Is there appellate review of panel decisions?
5) Does the transferee judge have authority under the statute to entertain a motion for summary judgment?
6) What are the choice of law advantages of MDL as compared to Rule 23?

On the MDL process, see Wahl v. Gen. Elec. Co., 786 F.3d 491 (6th Cir. 2015) (addressing determination of choice of law in MDL case transferred from MDL court back to plaintiff's home district); In re Volkswagen "Clean Diesel" Mktg., Sales Practices & Products Liab. Litig., 148 F. Supp. 3d 1367 (U.S. Jud. Pan. Mult. Lit. 2015) (consolidating actions in N.D. Cal. because one-fifth of all cases were filed in California, along with relevant documents and witnesses); Brandt, The Shortest Distance, 88 Notre Dame L. Rev. at 762.

One of the practices that grew up under § 1407 was for the transferee court, which had become familiar with the case through all the pretrial proceedings, to then assign the trial to itself under § 1404. But in Lexecon, Inc. v. Milberg, Weiss, Bershad, Hynes & Lerach, 523 U.S. 26 (1998), the United States Supreme Court unanimously disapproved the practice. According to the Court, the "plain meaning" of § 1407(a) requires that "[e]ach action so transferred shall be remanded by the [JPML] at or before the conclusion of such pretrial proceedings to the district [court] from which it was transferred unless it shall have been previously terminated." Id. at 35. In reversing the Ninth Circuit, the Court repudiated a practice followed by the appellate courts for over 30 years. Federal legislation subsequently was adopted that reinstates the practice of self-transfer and effectively undoes *Lexecon.* It also created a new 28 U.S.C. § 1369, which allows for original jurisdiction over single-event accidents in which there is minimal diversity between adverse parties, and at least 75 persons have died.

Another practice that has increased in recent years is for plaintiffs to file directly with the MDL court, rather than file in another preferred forum and be transferred to the MDL court. One effect of that practice, however, is to modify the choice of law portfolio of the MDL court, since by filing in the MDL court the plaintiff elects the choice of law rules of that forum. Can you see how this practice raises concerns similar to those at issue in *Amchem* and *Ortiz*? See also Thomas E. Willging and Emery G. Lee III, From Class Actions to Multidistrict Consolidations: Aggregate Mass-Tort Litigation After *Ortiz,* 58 U. Kan. L. Rev. 775, 801 (2010) ("[T]he MDL process has supplemented and perhaps displaced the class action device as a procedural mechanism for large settlements.").

The Supreme Court has not been as active in reviewing the function of MDL litigation as it has been in the class action context. One relatively minor exception is Gelboim v. Bank of Am. Corp., 135 S. Ct. 897 (2015). The case involves dozens of suits against banks alleged to have manipulated a benchmark interest rate that determines the interest rates for financial instruments around the world. The cases were consolidated for pretrial proceedings in the Southern District of New York. A class action under federal antitrust laws initially included in the MDL was dismissed with prejudice by the district court for failure to state a cognizable antitrust injury. The Second Circuit held that it had no jurisdiction under 28 U.S.C. § 1291 because the dismissal did not "'dispose of all claims in the consolidated action.'" Id. at 904. Over the banks' objection that consolidated cases must proceed as one unit for the duration of the consolidation unless the district court certifies appeal under Rule 54(b), the Supreme Court reversed. In a unanimous opinion, Justice Ginsburg reasoned that the district court's dismissal "had the hallmarks of a final decision. . . . As a result . . . petitioners are no longer participants in the consolidated proceedings. Nothing about the initial consolidation of their civil action with other cases in the [MDL] renders the dismissal of their complaint in any way tentative or incomplete. As is ordinarily the case, the § 1407 consolidation offered convenience for the parties and promoted efficient judicial administration, but did not meld the Gelboim-Zacher action and others in the MDL into a single unit." Id. at 905. In response to the banks' argument that weaker cases will therefore be appealable sooner, Justice Ginsburg noted that Rule 54(b) allows the district court to certify appeals to MDL plaintiffs who had antitrust claims dismissed but other claims that remained live. The decision may clear a path for more MDL appeals to reach the Supreme Court.

## 7.   Aggregation of Claims in Arbitration

### *AT&T Mobility v. Concepcion*
563 U.S. 333 (2011)

JUSTICE SCALIA delivered the opinion of the Court.

Section 2 of the Federal Arbitration Act (FAA) makes agreements to arbitrate "valid, irrevocable, and enforceable, save upon such grounds as exist at law or in equity for the revocation of any contract." 9 U.S.C. § 2. We consider whether the FAA prohibits States from conditioning the enforceability of certain arbitration agreements on the availability of classwide arbitration procedures.

I

In February 2002, Vincent and Liza Concepcion entered into an agreement for the sale and servicing of cellular telephones with AT&T Mobility

LCC (AT&T). The contract provided for arbitration of all disputes between the parties, but required that claims be brought in the parties' "individual capacity, and not as a plaintiff or class member in any purported class or representative proceeding."[2] The agreement authorized AT&T to make unilateral amendments, which it did to the arbitration provision on several occasions. . . .

The revised agreement provides that customers may initiate dispute proceedings by completing a one-page Notice of Dispute form available on AT&T's Web site. AT&T may then offer to settle the claim; if it does not, or if the dispute is not resolved within 30 days, the customer may invoke arbitration by filing a separate Demand for Arbitration, also available on AT&T's Web site. In the event the parties proceed to arbitration, the agreement specifies that AT&T must pay all costs for nonfrivolous claims; that arbitration must take place in the county in which the customer is billed; that, for claims of $10,000 or less, the customer may choose whether the arbitration proceeds in person, by telephone, or based only on submissions; that either party may bring a claim in small claims court in lieu of arbitration; and that the arbitrator may award any form of individual relief, including injunctions and presumably punitive damages. The agreement, moreover, denies AT&T any ability to seek reimbursement of its attorney's fees, and, in the event that a customer receives an arbitration award greater than AT&T's last written settlement offer, requires AT&T to pay a $7,500 minimum recovery and twice the amount of the claimant's attorney's fees.

The Concepcions purchased AT&T service, which was advertised as including the provision of free phones; they were not charged for the phones, but they were charged $30.22 in sales tax based on the phones' retail value. In March 2006, the Concepcions filed a complaint against AT&T in the United States District Court for the Southern District of California. The complaint was later consolidated with a putative class action alleging, among other things, that AT&T had engaged in false advertising and fraud by charging sales tax on phones it advertised as free.

In March 2008, AT&T moved to compel arbitration under the terms of its contract with the Concepcions. The Concepcions opposed the motion, contending that the arbitration agreement was unconscionable and unlawfully exculpatory under California law because it disallowed classwide procedures. The District Court denied AT&T's motion. It described AT&T's arbitration agreement favorably, noting, for example, that the informal dispute-resolution process was "quick, easy to use" and likely to "promp[t] full or . . . even excess payment to the customer *without* the need to arbitrate or litigate"; that the $7,500 premium functioned as "a substantial inducement for the consumer to pursue the claim in arbitration" if a dispute was not resolved informally; and that consumers who were members of a class

---

2. That provision further states that "the arbitrator may not consolidate more than one person's claims, and may not otherwise preside over any form of a representative or class proceeding."

would likely be worse off. Laster v. T-Mobile USA, Inc., 2008 WL 5216255, *11-*12 (S.D. Cal., Aug. 11, 2008). Nevertheless, relying on the California Supreme Court's decision in Discover Bank v. Superior Court, 113 P.3d 1100 (2005), the court found that the arbitration provision was unconscionable because AT&T had not shown that bilateral arbitration adequately substituted for the deterrent effects of class actions. . . .

The Ninth Circuit affirmed, also finding the provision unconscionable under California law as announced in *Discover Bank*. . . .

## II

The FAA was enacted in 1925 in response to widespread judicial hostility to arbitration agreements. See Hall Street Associates, L.L.C. v. Mattel, Inc., 552 U.S. 576, 581 (2008). Section 2, the "primary substantive provision of the Act," Moses H. Cone Memorial Hospital v. Mercury Constr. Corp., 460 U.S. 1, 24 (1983), provides, in relevant part, as follows:

> "A written provision in any maritime transaction or a contract evidencing a transaction involving commerce to settle by arbitration a controversy thereafter arising out of such contract or transaction . . . shall be valid, irrevocable, and enforceable, save upon such grounds as exist at law or in equity for the revocation of any contract." 9 U.S.C. § 2.

We have described this provision as reflecting both a "liberal federal policy favoring arbitration," *Moses H. Cone*, supra, at 24, and the "fundamental principle that arbitration is a matter of contract," Rent-A-Center, West, Inc. v. Jackson, 130 S. Ct. 2772, 2776 (2010). In line with these principles, courts must place arbitration agreements on an equal footing with other contracts, Buckeye Check Cashing, Inc. v. Cardegna, 546 U.S. 440, 443 (2006), and enforce them according to their terms, Volt Information Sciences, Inc. v. Board of Trustees of Leland Stanford Junior Univ. 489 U.S. 468, 478 (1989).

The final phrase of § 2, however, permits arbitration agreements to be declared unenforceable "upon such grounds as exist at law or in equity for the revocation of any contract." This saving clause permits agreements to arbitrate to be invalidated by "generally applicable contract defenses, such as fraud, duress, or unconscionability," but not by defenses that apply only to arbitration or that derive their meaning from the fact that an agreement to arbitrate is at issue. Doctor's Associates, Inc. v. Casarotto, 517 U.S. 681, 687 (1996). . . . The question in this case is whether § 2 preempts California's rule classifying most collective-arbitration waivers in consumer contracts as unconscionable. We refer to this rule as the *Discover Bank* rule.

Under California law, courts may refuse to enforce any contract found "to have been unconscionable at the time it was made," or may "limit the application of any unconscionable clause." Cal. Civ. Code Ann. § 1670.5(a) (West 1985). A finding of unconscionability requires "a 'procedural' and a 'substantive' element, the former focusing on 'oppression' or 'surprise' due to unequal bargaining power, the latter on 'overly harsh' or 'one-sided' results." Armendariz v. Foundation Health Pyschcare Servs., Inc., 6 P.3d 669, 690 (2000); accord, *Discover Bank,* 30 Cal. Rptr. 3d 76, 113 P.3d, at 1108.

In *Discover Bank,* the California Supreme Court applied this framework to class-action waivers in arbitration agreements and held as follows:

> "[W]hen the waiver is found in a consumer contract of adhesion in a set-
> ting in which disputes between the contracting parties predictably involve
> small amounts of damages, and when it is alleged that the party with the
> superior bargaining power has carried out a scheme to deliberately cheat
> large numbers of consumers out of individually small sums of money, then
> . . . the waiver becomes in practice the exemption of the party 'from respon-
> sibility for [its] own fraud, or willful injury to the person or property of
> another.' Under these circumstances, such waivers are unconscionable under
> California law and should not be enforced."

113 P.3d, at 1110 (quoting Cal. Civ. Code Ann. § 1668).

California courts have frequently applied this rule to find arbitration agreements unconscionable.

## III

### A

The Concepcions argue that the *Discover Bank* rule, given its origins in California's unconscionability doctrine and California's policy against exculpation, is a ground that "exist[s] at law or in equity for the revocation of any contract" under FAA § 2. . . .

When state law prohibits outright the arbitration of a particular type of claim, the analysis is straightforward: The conflicting rule is displaced by the FAA. Preston v. Ferrer, 552 U.S. 346, 353 (2008). But the inquiry becomes more complex when a doctrine normally thought to be generally applica-ble, such as duress or, as relevant here, unconscionability, is alleged to have been applied in a fashion that disfavors arbitration. In Perry v. Thomas, 482 U.S. 483 (1987), for example, we noted that the FAA's preemptive effect might extend even to grounds traditionally thought to exist "'at law or in equity for the revocation of any contract.'" Id., at 492, n. 9 (emphasis deleted). We said that a court may not "rely on the uniqueness of an agree-ment to arbitrate as a basis for a state-law holding that enforcement would be unconscionable, for this would enable the court to effect what . . . the state legislature cannot." Id.

An obvious illustration of this point would be a case finding unconscio-nable or unenforceable as against public policy consumer arbitration agree-ments that fail to provide for judicially monitored discovery. The rational-izations for such a holding are neither difficult to imagine nor different in kind from those articulated in *Discover Bank.* A court might reason that no consumer would knowingly waive his right to full discovery, as this would enable companies to hide their wrongdoing. Or the court might simply say that such agreements are exculpatory—restricting discovery would be of greater benefit to the company than the consumer, since the former is more likely to be sued than to sue. See *Discover Bank*, 113 P.3d, at 1109 (arguing that class waivers are similarly one-sided). And, the reasoning would continue, because such a rule applies the general principle of unconscionability or public-policy disapproval of exculpatory agreements, it is applicable to "any" contract and thus preserved by § 2 of the FAA. In practice, of course, the rule would have a disproportionate impact on arbitration agreements; but it would presumably apply to contracts purporting to restrict discovery in litigation as well.

Other examples are easy to imagine. The same argument might apply to a rule classifying as unconscionable arbitration agreements that fail to abide by the Federal Rules of Evidence, or that disallow an ultimate disposition by a jury (perhaps termed "a panel of twelve lay arbitrators" to help avoid preemption). Such examples are not fanciful, since the judicial hostility towards arbitration that prompted the FAA had manifested itself in "a great variety" of "devices and formulas" declaring arbitration against public policy. Robert Lawrence Co. v. Devonshire Fabrics, Inc., 271 F.2d 402, 406 (2d Cir. 1959). And although these statistics are not definitive, it is worth noting that California's courts have been more likely to hold contracts to arbitrate unconscionable than other contracts. Broome, An Unconscionable Applicable of the Unconscionability Doctrine: How the California Courts are Circumventing the Federal Arbitration Act, 3 Hastings Bus. L.J. 39, 54, 66 (2006); Randall, Judicial Attitudes Toward Arbitration and the Resurgence of Unconscionability, 52 Buffalo L. Rev. 185, 186-187 (2004).

The Concepcions suggest that all this is just a parade of horribles, and no genuine worry. "Rules aimed at destroying arbitration" or "demanding procedures incompatible with arbitration," they concede, "would be preempted by the FAA because they cannot sensibly be reconciled with Section 2." Brief for Respondents 32. . . .

We largely agree. . . . We differ with the Concepcions only in the application of this analysis to the matter before us. We do not agree that rules requiring judicially monitored discovery or adherence to the Federal Rules of Evidence are "a far cry from this case." The overarching purpose of the FAA, evident in the text of §§ 2, 3, and 4, is to ensure the enforcement of arbitration agreements according to their terms so as to facilitate streamlined proceedings. Requiring the availability of classwide arbitration interferes with fundamental attributes of arbitration and thus creates a scheme inconsistent with the FAA.

**B**

The "principal purpose" of the FAA is to "ensur[e] that private arbitration agreements are enforced according to their terms." *Volt*, 489 U.S., at 478. . . . This purpose is readily apparent from the FAA's text. Section 2 makes arbitration agreements "valid, irrevocable, and enforceable" as written (subject, of course, to the saving clause); § 3 requires courts to stay litigation of arbitral claims pending arbitration of those claims "in accordance with the terms of the agreement"; and § 4 requires courts to compel arbitration "in accordance with the terms of the agreement" upon the motion of either party to the agreement (assuming that the "making of the arbitration agreement or the failure . . . to perform the same" is not at issue). In light of these provisions, we have held that parties may agree to limit the issues subject to arbitration, Mitsubishi Motors Corp. v. Soler Chrysler-Plymouth, Inc., 473 U.S. 614, 628 (1985), to arbitrate according to specific rules, *Volt*, 489 U.S. at 479, and to limit with whom a party will arbitrate its disputes, *Stolt-Nielsen*, 130 S. Ct. at 1773.

The point of affording parties discretion in designing arbitration processes is to allow for efficient, streamlined procedures tailored to the type of dispute. It can be specified, for example, that the decisionmaker be a specialist in the relevant field, or that proceedings be kept confidential to protect trade secrets. And the informality of arbitral proceedings is itself desirable, reducing the cost and increasing the speed of dispute resolution. . . .

The dissent quotes Dean Witter Reynolds Inc. v. Byrd, 470 U.S. 213, 219 (1985), as "reject[ing] the suggestion that the overriding goal of the Arbitration Act was to promote the expeditious resolution of claims.'" Post, at 4. That is greatly misleading. After saying (accurately enough) that "the overriding goal of the Arbitration Act was [not] to promote the expeditious resolution of claims," but to "ensure judicial enforcement of privately made agreements to arbitrate," 470 U.S., at 219, *Dean Witter* went on to explain: "This is not to say that Congress was blind to the potential benefit of the legislation for expedited resolution of disputes. Far from it . . . ." Id., at 220. It then quotes a House Report saying that "the costliness and delays of litigation . . . can be largely eliminated by agreements for arbitration." Ibid. (quoting H.R. Rep. No. 96, 68th Cong., 1st Sess., 2 (1924)). The concluding paragraph of this part of its discussion begins as follows:

> We therefore are not persuaded by the argument that the conflict between two goals of the Arbitration Act—enforcement of private agreements and encouragement of efficient and speedy dispute resolution—must be resolved in favor of the latter in order to realize the intent of the drafters. 470 U.S., at 221.

In the present case, of course, those "two goals" do not conflict—and it is the dissent's view that would frustrate *both* of them.

. . . [I]n Preston v. Ferrer, holding preempted a state-law rule requiring exhaustion of administrative remedies before arbitration, we said: "A prime objective of an agreement to arbitrate is to achieve 'streamlined proceedings and expeditious results,'" which objective would be "frustrated" by requiring a dispute to be heard by an agency first. 552 U.S., at 357-358. That rule, we said, would "at the least, hinder speedy resolution of the controversy." Id., at 358.

California's *Discover Bank* rule similarly interferes with arbitration. Although the rule does not require classwide arbitration, it allows any party to a consumer contract to demand it *ex post*. The rule is limited to adhesion contracts . . . but the times in which consumer contracts were anything other than adhesive are long past . . . .[6] The rule also requires that damages be predictably small, and that the consumer allege a scheme to cheat consumers. . . . The former requirement, however, is toothless and malleable (the Ninth Circuit has held that damages of $4,000 are sufficiently small, see Oestreicher v. Alienware Corp., 322 Fed. Appx. 489, 492 (2009) (unpublished)), and the latter has no limiting effect, as all that is required is an allegation. Consumers remain free to bring and resolve their disputes on a bilateral basis under *Discover Bank*, and some may well do so; but there is little incentive for lawyers to arbitrate on behalf of individuals when they may do so for a class and reap far higher fees in the process. And faced with inevitable class arbitration, companies would have less incentive to continue resolving potentially duplicative claims on an individual basis.

Although we have had little occasion to examine classwide arbitration, our decision in *Stolt-Nielsen* is instructive. In that case we held that an arbitration panel exceeded its power under § 10(a)(4) of the FAA by imposing class procedures based on policy judgments rather than the arbitration agreement itself or some background principle of contract law that would affect its interpretation. 130 S. Ct. at 1773-76. We then held that the agreement at issue, which was silent on the question of class procedures, could not be interpreted to allow them because the "changes brought about by the shift from bilateral arbitration to class-action arbitration" are "fundamental." Id., at 1776. This is obvious as a structural matter: Classwide arbitration includes absent parties, necessitating additional and different procedures and involving higher stakes. Confidentiality becomes more difficult. And while it is theoretically possible to select an arbitrator with some expertise relevant to the class-certification question, arbitrators are not generally knowledgeable in the often-dominant procedural aspects of certification, such as the protection of absent parties. The conclusion follows that class arbitration, to the extent it is manufactured by *Discover Bank* rather than consensual, is inconsistent with the FAA.

First, the switch from bilateral to class arbitration sacrifices the principal advantage of arbitration—its informality—and makes the process slower, more costly, and more likely to generate procedural morass than final judgment. "In bilateral arbitration, parties forgo the procedural rigor and appellate review of the courts in order to realize the benefits of private dispute resolution: lower costs, greater efficiency and speed, and the ability to choose expert adjudicators to resolve specialized disputes." 130 S. Ct. at 1775. But before an arbitrator may decide the merits of a claim in

---

6. Of course States remain free to take steps addressing the concerns that attend contracts of adhesion—for example, requiring class-action-waiver provisions in adhesive arbitration agreements to be highlighted. Such steps cannot, however, conflict with the FAA or frustrate its purpose to ensure that private arbitration agreements are enforced according to their terms.

classwide procedures, he must first decide, for example, whether the class itself may be certified, whether the named parties are sufficiently representative and typical, and how discovery for the class should be conducted. A cursory comparison of bilateral and class arbitration illustrates the difference. According to the American Arbitration Association (AAA), the average consumer arbitration between January and August 2007 resulted in a disposition on the merits in six months, four months if the arbitration was conducted by documents only. AAA, Analysis of the AAA's Consumer Arbitration Caseload, online at http://www.adr.org/si.asp?id=5027 (all Internet materials as visited Apr. 25, 2011, and available in Clerk of Court's case file). As of September 2009, the AAA had opened 283 class arbitrations. Of those, 121 remained active, and 162 had been settled, withdrawn, or dismissed. Not a single one, however, had resulted in a final award on the merits. Brief for AAA as Amicus Curiae in *Stolt-Nielsen*, O.T. 2009, No. 08-1198, pp. 22-24. For those cases that were no longer active, the median time from filing to settlement, withdrawal, or dismissal—not judgment on the merits—was 583 days, and the mean was 630 days. Id., at 24.

Second, class arbitration *requires* procedural formality. The AAA's rules governing class arbitrations mimic the Federal Rules of Civil Procedure for class litigation. . . . And while parties can alter those procedures by contract, an alternative is not obvious. If procedures are too informal, absent class members would not be bound by the arbitration. For a class-action money judgment to bind absentees in litigation, class representatives must at all times adequately represent absent class members, and absent members must be afforded notice, an opportunity to be heard, and a right to opt out of the class. Phillips Petroleum Co. v. Shutts, 472 U.S. 797, 811-12 (1985). At least this amount of process would presumably be required for absent parties to be bound by the results of arbitration.

We find it unlikely that in passing the FAA Congress meant to leave the disposition of these procedural requirements to an arbitrator. Indeed, class arbitration was not even envisioned by Congress when it passed the FAA in 1925; as the California Supreme Court admitted in *Discover Bank*, class arbitration is a "relatively recent development." 113 P.3d, at 1110. And it is at the very least odd to think that an arbitrator would be entrusted with ensuring that third parties' due process rights are satisfied.

Third, class arbitration greatly increases risks to defendants. Informal procedures do of course have a cost: The absence of multilayered review makes it more likely that errors will go uncorrected. Defendants are willing to accept the costs of these errors in arbitration, since their impact is limited to the size of individual disputes, and presumably outweighed by savings from avoiding the courts. But when damages allegedly owed to tens of thousands of potential claimants are aggregated and decided at once, the risk of an error will often become unacceptable. Faced with even a small chance of a devastating loss, defendants will be pressured into settling questionable claims. Other courts have noted the risk of "in terrorem" settlements that class actions entail, see, e.g., Kohen v. Pacific Inv. Management Co. LLC, 571 F.3d 672, 677-78 (7th Cir. 2009), and class arbitration would be no different.

Arbitration is poorly suited to the higher stakes of class litigation. In litigation, a defendant may appeal a certification decision on an interlocutory basis and, if unsuccessful, may appeal from a final judgment as well. Questions of law are reviewed *de novo* and questions of fact for clear error. In contrast, 9 U.S.C. § 10 allows a court to vacate an arbitral award *only* where the award "was procured by corruption, fraud, or undue means"; "there was evident partiality or corruption in the arbitrators"; "the arbitrators were guilty of misconduct in refusing to postpone the hearing . . . or in refusing to hear evidence pertinent and material to the controversy[,] or of any other misbehavior by which the rights of any party have been prejudiced"; or if the "arbitrators exceeded their powers, or so imperfectly executed them that a mutual, final, and definite award . . . was not made." The AAA rules do authorize judicial review of certification decisions, but this review is unlikely to have much effect given these limitations; review under § 10 focuses on misconduct rather than mistake. And parties may not contractually expand the grounds or nature of judicial review. *Hall Street Assocs.*, 552 U.S., at 578. We find it hard to believe that defendants would bet the company with no effective means of review, and even harder to believe that Congress would have intended to allow state courts to force such a decision.[8]

The Concepcions contend that because parties may and sometimes do agree to aggregation, class procedures are not necessarily incompatible with arbitration. But the same could be said about procedures that the Concepcions admit States may not superimpose on arbitration: Parties could agree to arbitrate pursuant to the Federal Rules of Civil Procedure, or pursuant to a discovery process rivaling that in litigation. Arbitration is a matter of contract, and the FAA requires courts to honor parties' expectations. *Rent-A-Center*, 130 S. Ct. 2772, 2774. But what the parties in the aforementioned examples would have agreed to is not arbitration as envisioned by the FAA, lacks its benefits, and therefore may not be required by state law.

The dissent claims that class proceedings are necessary to prosecute small-dollar claims that might otherwise slip through the legal system. But States cannot require a procedure that is inconsistent with the FAA, even if it is desirable for unrelated reasons. Moreover, the claim here was most unlikely to go unresolved. As noted earlier, the arbitration agreement provides that AT&T will pay claimants a minimum of $7,500 and twice their

---

8. The dissent cites three large arbitration awards (none of which stems from classwide arbitration) as evidence that parties are willing to submit large claims before an arbitrator. Those examples might be in point if it could be established that the size of the arbitral dispute was predictable when the arbitration agreement was entered. Otherwise, all the cases prove is that arbitrators can give huge awards—which we have never doubted. The point is that in class-action arbitration huge awards (with limited judicial review) will be entirely predictable, thus rendering arbitration unattractive. It is not reasonably deniable that requiring consumer disputes to be arbitrated on a classwide basis will have a substantial deterrent effect on incentives to arbitrate. . . .

attorney's fees if they obtain an arbitration award greater than AT&T's last settlement offer. The District Court found this scheme sufficient to provide incentive for the individual prosecution of meritorious claims that are not immediately settled, and the Ninth Circuit admitted that aggrieved customers who filed claims would be "essentially guarantee[d]" to be made whole, 584 F.3d, at 856, n. 9. Indeed, the District Court concluded that the Concepcions were *better off* under their arbitration agreement with AT&T than they would have been as participants in a class action, which "could take months, if not years, and which may merely yield an opportunity to submit a claim for recovery of a small percentage of a few dollars." *Laster,* 2008 WL 5216255, at *12.

* * *

Because it "stands as an obstacle to the accomplishment and execution of the full purposes and objectives of Congress," Hines v. Davidowitz, 312 U.S. 52, 67 (1941), California's *Discover Bank* rule is preempted by the FAA. The judgment of the Ninth Circuit is reversed, and the case is remanded for further proceedings consistent with this opinion.

*It is so ordered.*

JUSTICE THOMAS, concurring.

. . . If § 2 means anything, it is that courts cannot refuse to enforce arbitration agreements because of a state public policy against arbitration, even if the policy nominally applies to "any contract." There must be some additional limit on the contract defenses permitted by § 2. . . .

I write separately to explain how I would find that limit in the FAA's text. . . .

Reading §§ 2 and 4 harmoniously, the "grounds . . . for the revocation" preserved in § 2 would mean grounds related to the making of the agreement. This would require enforcement of an agreement to arbitrate unless a party successfully asserts a defense concerning the formation of the agreement to arbitrate, such as fraud, duress, or mutual mistake. . . . Contract defenses unrelated to the making of the agreement—such as public policy—could not be the basis for declining to enforce an arbitration clause.

## II

. . . [T]he *Discover Bank* rule does not concern the making of the arbitration agreement. Exculpatory contracts are a paradigmatic example of contracts that will not be enforced because of public policy. 15 G. Giesel, Corbin on Contracts §§ 85.1, 85.17, 85.18 (rev. ed. 2003). Indeed, the [California] court explained that it would not enforce the agreements because they are "'against the policy of the law.'" *Discover Bank,* 113 P.3d, at 1108 (quoting Cal. Civ. Code Ann. § 1668). . . . Refusal to enforce a contract for public-policy reasons does not concern whether the contract was properly made.

Accordingly, the *Discover Bank* rule is not a "groun[d] . . . for the revocation of any contract" as I would read § 2 of the FAA in light of § 4. . . .

JUSTICE BREYER, with whom JUSTICE GINSBURG, JUSTICE SOTOMAYOR, and JUSTICE KAGAN join, dissenting.

. . . California law sets forth certain circumstances in which "class action waivers" in *any* contract are unenforceable. In my view, this rule of state law is consistent with the federal Act's language and primary objective. It does not "stan[d] as an obstacle" to the Act's "accomplishment and execution." Hines v. Davidowitz, 312 U.S. 52, 67 (1941). And the Court is wrong to hold that the federal Act pre-empts the rule of state law.

## I

. . . The *Discover Bank* rule does not create a "blanket policy in California against class action waivers in the consumer context." Provencher v. Dell, Inc., 409 F. Supp. 2d 1196, 1201 (C.D. Cal. 2006). Instead, it represents the "application of a more general [unconscionability] principle." Gentry v. Superior Ct., 165 P.3d 556, 564 (2007). Courts applying California law have enforced class-action waivers where they satisfy general unconscionability standards. . . . And even when they fail, the parties remain free to devise other dispute mechanisms, including informal mechanisms, that, in context, will not prove unconscionable. . . .

## II

### A

The *Discover Bank* rule is consistent with the federal Act's language. It "applies equally to class action litigation waivers in contracts without arbitration agreements as it does to class arbitration waivers in contracts with such agreements." 113 P.3d, at 1112. Linguistically speaking, it falls directly within the scope of the Act's exception permitting courts to refuse to enforce arbitration agreements on grounds that exist "for the revocation of *any* contract." 9 U.S.C. § 2 (emphasis added). The majority agrees.

### B

The *Discover Bank* rule is also consistent with the basic "purpose behind" the Act. Dean Witter Reynolds Inc. v. Byrd, 470 U.S. 213, 219 (1985). We have described that purpose as one of "ensur[ing] judicial enforcement" of arbitration agreements. Ibid. . . .

Congress was fully aware that arbitration could provide procedural and cost advantages. The House Report emphasized the "appropriate[ness]" of making arbitration agreements enforceable "at this time when there is so much agitation against the costliness and delays of litigation." Id., at 2. And this Court has acknowledged that parties may enter into arbitration agreements in order to expedite the resolution of disputes. See Preston v. Ferrer, 552 U.S. 346, 357 (2008) (discussing "prime objective of an agreement to arbitrate"). . . .

But we have also cautioned against thinking that Congress' primary objective was to guarantee these particular procedural advantages. Rather, that primary objective was to secure the "enforcement" of agreements to arbitrate. *Dean Witter*, 470 U.S., at 221. See also id., at 219 (we "reject the suggestion that the overriding goal of the Arbitration Act was to promote the expeditious resolution of claims"); id., at 219, 217-218 ("[T]he intent of Congress" requires us to apply the terms of the Act without regard to whether the result would be "possibly inefficient"); cf. id., at 220 (acknowledging that "expedited resolution of disputes" might lead parties to prefer arbitration). The relevant Senate Report points to the Act's basic purpose when it says that "[t]he purpose of the [Act] *is clearly set forth in section 2,*" S. Rep. No. 536, at 2 (emphasis added) . . . .

Thus, insofar as we seek to implement Congress' intent, we should think more than twice before invalidating a state law that does just what § 2 requires, namely, puts agreements to arbitrate and agreements to litigate "upon the same footing."

## III

The majority's contrary view (that *Discover Bank* stands as an "obstacle" to the accomplishment of the federal law's objective) rests primarily upon its claims that the *Discover Bank* rule increases the complexity of arbitration procedures, thereby discouraging parties from entering into arbitration agreements, and to that extent discriminating in practice against arbitration. These claims are not well founded.

For one thing, a state rule of law that would sometimes set aside as unconscionable a contract term that forbids class arbitration is not (as the majority claims) like a rule that would require "ultimate disposition by a jury" or "judicially monitored discovery" or use of "the Federal Rules of Evidence." Ante. Unlike the majority's examples, class arbitration is consistent with the use of arbitration. It is a form of arbitration that is well known in California and followed elsewhere. See, e.g., Keating v. Superior Ct., 167 Cal. Rptr. 481, 492 (1980) (officially depublished); American Arbitration Association (AAA), Supplementary Rules for Class Arbitrations (2003); JAMS, The Resolution Experts, Class Action Procedures (2009). . . . Indeed, the AAA has told us that it has found class arbitration to be "a fair, balanced, and efficient means of resolving class disputes." Brief for AAA as Amicus Curiae in Stolt-Nielsen S.A. v. AnimalFeeds Int'l Corp., O.T. 2009, No. 08-1198, p. 25. And unlike the majority's examples, the *Discover Bank* rule imposes equivalent limitations on litigation; hence it cannot fairly be characterized as a targeted attack on arbitration.

Where does the majority get its contrary idea—that individual, rather than class, arbitration is a "fundamental attribut[e]" of arbitration? The majority does not explain. And it is unlikely to be able to trace its present view to the history of the arbitration statute itself.

When Congress enacted the Act, arbitration procedures had not yet been fully developed. Insofar as Congress considered detailed forms of arbitration at all, it may well have thought that arbitration would be used primarily where merchants sought to resolve disputes of fact, not law, under the customs of their industries, where the parties possessed roughly equivalent bargaining power. See *Mitsubishi Motors*, supra, at 646 (Stevens, J., dissenting); Joint Hearings on S. 1005 and H.R. 646 before the Subcommittees of the Committees on the Judiciary, 68th Cong., 1st Sess., 15 (1924); Hearing on S. 4213 and S. 4214 before a Subcommittee of the Senate Committee on the Judiciary, 67th Cong., 4th Sess., 9-10 (1923); Dept. of Commerce, Secretary Hoover Favors Arbitration—Press Release (Dec. 28, 1925), Herbert Hoover Papers—Articles, Addresses, and Public Statements File—No. 536, p. 2 (Herbert Hoover Presidential Library); Cohen & Dayton, The New Federal Arbitration Law, 12 Va. L. Rev. 265, 281 (1926); AAA, Year Book on Commercial Arbitration in the United States (1927). This last mentioned feature of the history—roughly equivalent bargaining power—suggests, if anything, that California's statute is consistent with, and indeed may help to further, the objectives that Congress had in mind.

Regardless, if neither the history nor present practice suggests that class arbitration is fundamentally incompatible with arbitration itself, then on what basis can the majority hold California's law pre-empted?

For another thing, the majority's argument that the *Discover Bank* rule will discourage arbitration rests critically upon the wrong comparison. The majority compares the complexity of class arbitration with that of bilateral arbitration. And it finds the former more complex. But, if incentives are at issue, the *relevant* comparison is not "arbitration with arbitration" but a comparison between class arbitration and judicial class actions. After all, in respect to the relevant set of contracts, the *Discover Bank* rule similarly and equally sets aside clauses that forbid class procedures—whether arbitration procedures or ordinary judicial procedures are at issue.

Why would a typical defendant (say, a business) prefer a judicial class action to class arbitration? AAA statistics "suggest that class arbitration proceedings take more time than the average commercial arbitration, but may take *less time* than the average class action in court." AAA *Amicus* Brief 24 (emphasis added). Data from California courts confirm that class arbitrations can take considerably less time than in-court proceedings in which class certification is sought. . . . And a single class proceeding is surely more efficient than thousands of separate proceedings for identical claims. Thus, if speedy resolution of disputes were all that mattered, then the *Discover Bank* rule would reinforce, not obstruct, that objective of the Act.

The majority's related claim that the *Discover Bank* rule will discourage the use of arbitration because "[a]rbitration is poorly suited to . . . higher stakes" lacks empirical support. Ante. Indeed, the majority provides no convincing reason to believe that parties are unwilling to submit high-stake disputes to arbitration. And there are numerous counterexamples. Loftus, Rivals Resolve Dispute Over Drug, Wall Street Journal, Apr. 16, 2011, p. B2 (discussing $500 million settlement in dispute submitted to arbitration); Ziobro, Kraft Seeks Arbitration In Fight With Starbucks Over Distribution, Wall Street Journal, Nov. 30, 2010, p. B10 (describing initiation of an arbitration in which the payout "could be higher" than $1.5 billion); Markoff, Software Arbitration Ruling Gives I.B.M. $833 Million From Fujitsu, N.Y. Times, Nov. 30, 1988, p. A1 (describing both companies as "pleased with the ruling" resolving a licensing dispute).

Further, even though contract defenses, e.g., duress and unconscionability, slow down the dispute resolution process, federal arbitration law normally leaves such matters to the States. Rent-A-Center, West, Inc. v. Jackson, 130 S. Ct. 2772, 2775 (2010) (arbitration agreements "may be invalidated by 'generally applicable contract defenses'"). . . . A provision in a contract of adhesion (for example, requiring a consumer to decide very quickly whether to pursue a claim) might increase the speed and efficiency of arbitrating a dispute, but the State can forbid it. See, e.g., Hayes v. Oakridge Home, 908 N.E.2d 408, 412 (Ohio 2009) ("Unconscionability is a ground for revocation of an arbitration agreement"); In re Poly-America, L.P., 262 S.W.3d 337, 348 (Tex. 2008) ("Unconscionable contracts, however—whether relating to arbitration or not—are unenforceable under Texas law"). The *Discover Bank* rule amounts to a variation on this theme. California is free to define unconscionability as it sees fit, and its common law is of no federal concern so long as the State does not adopt a special rule that disfavors arbitration . . . .

[T]he majority highlights the disadvantages of class arbitrations, as it sees them. See ante (referring to the "greatly increase[d] risks to defendants"; the "chance of a devastating loss" pressuring defendants "into settling questionable claims"). But class proceedings have countervailing advantages. In general agreements that forbid the consolidation of claims can lead small-dollar claimants to abandon their claims rather than to litigate. I suspect that it is true even here, for as the Court of Appeals recognized, AT&T can avoid the $7,500 payout (the payout that supposedly makes the Concepcions' arbitration worthwhile) simply by paying the claim's face value, such that "the maximum gain to a customer for the hassle of arbitrating a $30.22 dispute is still just $30.22." Laster v. AT&T Mobility LLC, 584 F.3d 849, 855, 856 (9th Cir. 2009).

What rational lawyer would have signed on to represent the Concepcions in litigation for the possibility of fees stemming from a $30.22 claim? See, e.g., Carnegie v. Household Int'l, Inc., 376 F.3d 656, 661 (7th Cir. 2004) ("The *realistic* alternative to a class action is not 17 million individual suits, but zero individual suits, as only a lunatic or a fanatic sues for $30"). In California's perfectly rational view, nonclass arbitration over such sums will also sometimes have the effect of depriving claimants of their claims (say, for example, where claiming the $30.22 were to involve filling out many forms that require technical legal knowledge or waiting at great length while a call is placed on hold). *Discover Bank* sets forth circumstances in which the California courts believe that the terms of consumer contracts can be manipulated to insulate an agreement's author from liability for its own frauds by "deliberately cheat[ing] large numbers of consumers out of individually small sums of money." 113 P.3d, at 1110. Why is this kind of decision—weighing the pros and cons of all class proceedings alike—not California's to make?

Finally, the majority can find no meaningful support for its views in this Court's precedent. The federal Act has been in force for nearly a century. We have decided dozens of cases about its requirements. We have reached results that authorize complex arbitration procedures. E.g., *Mitsubishi Motors*, 473 U.S., at 629 (antitrust claims arising in international transaction are arbitrable). We have upheld nondiscriminatory state laws that slow down arbitration proceedings. E.g., *Volt Information Sciences*, 489 U.S., at 477-79 (California law staying arbitration proceedings until completion of related litigation is not pre-empted). But we have not, to my knowledge, applied the Act to strike down a state statute that treats arbitrations on par with judicial and administrative proceedings. Cf. *Preston*, 552 U.S., at 355-56 (Act pre-empts state law that vests primary jurisdiction in state administrative board).

At the same time, we have repeatedly referred to the Act's basic objective as assuring that courts treat arbitration agreements "like all other contracts." Buckeye Check Cashing, Inc. v. Cardegna, 546 U.S. 440, 447 (2006). . . . And we have recognized that "[t]o immunize an arbitration agreement from judicial challenge" on grounds applicable to all other contracts "would be to elevate it over other forms of contract." Prima Paint Corp. v. Flood & Conklin Mfg. Co., 388 U.S. 395, 404, n. 12 (1967); see also Marchant v. Mead-Morrison Mfg. Co., 169 N.E. 386, 391 (N.Y. 1929) (Cardozo, C.J.) ("Courts are not at liberty to shirk the process of [contractual] construction under the empire of a belief that arbitration is beneficent any more than they may shirk it if their belief happens to be the contrary"). . . .

These cases do not concern the merits and demerits of class actions; they concern equal treatment of arbitration contracts and other contracts. Since it is the latter question that is at issue here, I am not surprised that the majority can find no meaningful precedent supporting its decision.

# IV

By using the words "save upon such grounds as exist at law or in equity for the revocation of any contract," Congress retained for the States an important role incident to agreements to arbitrate. 9 U.S.C. § 2. Through those words Congress reiterated a basic federal idea that has long informed the nature of this Nation's laws. . . . [F]ederalism is as much a question of deeds as words. It often takes the form of a concrete decision by this Court that respects the legitimacy of a State's action in an individual case. Here, recognition of that federalist ideal, embodied in specific language in this particular statute, should lead us to uphold California's law, not to strike it down. . . .

With respect, I dissent.

## Notes and Questions

1. Are class action waivers in arbitration agreements now bulletproof? In a divided decision, again authored by Justice Scalia, the Court reaffirmed its commitment to strict enforcement of a clause barring arbitration of claims "on a class action basis." American Express Co. v. Italian Colors Restaurant, 133 S. Ct. 2304 (2013) (rejecting plaintiffs' argument that "requiring them to litigate their claims individually . . . would contravene the policies of the antitrust laws" and "prevent the 'effective vindication' of a federal statutory right" by removing any economic incentive to sue). The Court again emphasized that class arbitration would undermine the goal of expeditious resolution of claims in arbitration. In 2016 the Court reaffirmed *Concepcion*.

2. In a recent article, Thomas J. Stipanowich argues that *Concepcion* and other recent arbitration decisions by the Supreme Court "express[] a national policy that vastly expands the power of companies to impose and control arbitration procedures while tying the hands of state legislatures and courts." The Third Arbitration Trilogy: *Stolt-Nielsen, Rent-A-Center, Concepcion* and the Future of American Arbitration, 22 Am. Rev. of Int'l Arb. 323, 324 (2011). The California courts, for their part, have not behaved as though their hands are tied—at least with respect to the use of unconscionability doctrine to review individual arbitration agreements. See generally Salvatore U. Bonaccorso, State Court Resistance to Federal Arbitration Law, 67 Stan. L. Rev. 1145 (2015); cf. Vargas v. Sai Monrovia B., 356 P.3d 778 (Cal. 2015); Brown v. S.C. (Morgan Tire & Auto), 331 P.3d 1274 (Cal. 2014).

Federal district courts in California are divided about whether to follow this approach. Compare Mohamed v. Uber Technologies, Inc., No. C-14-5200 EMC, 109 F. Supp. 3d 1185 (N.D. Cal. 2015) (striking down mandatory arbitration clause in employment contract between Uber and its drivers; holding that, despite *Concepcion*, the FAA did not preempt California's Private Attorneys General Act and that the arbitration provision found in Uber's employment contracts was "permeated with unconscionability"), appeal filed, No. 15-16250 (9th Cir. June 23, 2015), with Ortiz v. Hobby Lobby, 52 F. Supp. 3d 1070 (E.D. Cal 2014) (refusing to allow an individual claim under PAGA).

The Supreme Court has not given the California courts free rein. In 2016 it again overruled the California courts' attempt to protect the right to aggregate adjudication. DɪʀᴇᴄTV, Inc. v. Imburgia, 136 S. Ct. 463 (2016). Amy Imburgia filed a class action in California state court against DirecTV, claiming that the company charged early termination fees on its consumer contracts without justification. In the wake of the Supreme Court's decision in *Concepcion*, DirecTV moved to compel arbitration. The trial court denied the motion and the California Court of Appeals affirmed, on the ground that the arbitration clause provided that if class arbitration was not permitted under state law, the arbitration clause was void. The arbitration clause states:

> "Special Rules . . . Section 9: Neither you nor we shall be entitled to join or consolidate claims in arbitration by or against other individuals or entities, or arbitrate any claim as a representative member of a class or in a private attorney general capacity. Accordingly, you and we agree that the JAMS Class Action Procedures do not apply to our arbitration. *If, however, the law of your state would find this agreement to dispense with class arbitration procedures unenforceable, then this entire Section 9 is unenforceable.*
>
> Section 10: 'Applicable Law': The interpretation and enforcement of this Agreement shall be governed by the rules and regulations of the Federal Communications Commission, other applicable federal laws, and the laws of the state and local area where Service is provided to you. This Agreement is subject to modification if required by such laws. Notwithstanding the foregoing, Section 9 shall be governed by the Federal Arbitration Act."

Reviewing this language, the state appellate court concluded that Section 9's reference to "the law of your state" is an explicit exception to the agreement's general adoption of the FAA in Section 10 and denied DirecTV's motion to compel individual arbitration. The United States Supreme Court reversed, finding that the California courts had not given due weight to the federal policy favoring arbitration.

3. Consider the majority opinions in *Dukes* and *Concepcion* as expressing a specific idea of what the modern class action is. How does that idea differ from or draw upon ideas expressed in earlier cases such as *Hansberry, Eisen,* and *Wilks*? Does it square with your reading of Rule 23? With the views expressed by the Advisory Committee in its notes to the 1966 amendments that gave us modern class action procedure?

# 7   Repose: Ending Disputes

In this chapter we address direct and collateral post-trial avenues by which a party may seek to overturn a judgment or to give it preclusive effect in another, collateral lawsuit, and the procedural rules and decisional law that apply to these strategies. Before turning to the technical aspects of these maneuvers, however, consider the policy reasons why even an incorrect judgment nevertheless might be hard to overturn. The most obvious one is that disputes should end, and that even an incorrect outcome has in its favor that it concludes the dispute. Just as obvious, however, is that incorrect judgments are a strain on a judicial process that prides itself on arriving at just—which must mean reasonably accurate—outcomes. Yet, given the impressive array of procedural devices already available to litigants to question outcomes—such as the motions for judgment as a matter of law and for a new trial, and especially the opportunity to appeal—are any *other* means of challenging or avoiding these judgments necessary?

We first take up the subject of direct attacks on judgments. Read Fed. R. Civ. P. 60, which lists conditions under which a party may attack a judgment rendered by a federal judge. Then consider the following cases that construe the Rule and its limits.

## A.   DIRECT ATTACKS ON JUDGMENTS

### Problem Case: A Time to Reconsider

For some years, the school board encouraged teachers and others employed at Senior High School to attend home football and basketball games, to sit in assigned areas among the students, and thus to assist in crowd control. Free tickets and free refreshments were provided, and those who regularly attended were warmly praised by school administrators for their loyalty and professionalism.

As counsel for 15 teachers led by Aldrich, Olvida filed an action in the county court against the school district, alleging that the plaintiffs were coerced to attend games and thus performed overtime work without overtime pay, in violation of the Federal Fair Labor Standards Act. The plaintiffs sought double damages, as provided by § 16(b) of the Act, and also an injunction against further violations of federal law by the school board.

The school board, through its counsel, Elder, answered and denied that any of the plaintiffs had been coerced.

At pretrial, the county judge questioned whether he had the power to issue an injunction against a local school board to enforce a federal law in a suit brought by a private plaintiff. Responding to this concern, Olvida contended that the applicability of this federal law to local school districts was controlled by Maryland v. Wirtz, 392 U.S. 183 (1968), and that injunctions to enforce the Act are authorized by § 17 of the Act. Elder contested neither of these statements.

At trial, the plaintiffs each testified to some form of coercion brought to bear upon them to assure their attendance at games. The defense witnesses denied each of the coercive acts .

The county judge found that there was at least implicit coercion, entitling the plaintiffs to double damages and an injunction. The school board did not appeal, and satisfied the money judgments.

Two years later, Elder retired. In reviewing the files, his successor, Newman, encountered the case. Newman is aware that Maryland v. Wirtz was overruled in National League of Cities v. Usery, 426 U.S. 833 (1976), which held that the Fair Labor Standards Act cannot constitutionally be applied to local governments. He is also aware that the Act authorizes injunctive relief only in suits brought by the Department of Labor, e.g., Roberg v. Henry Phipps Estate, 156 F.2d 958 (2d Cir. 1946). And Newman is now informed by Bailey, one of the claimants in the action, that Bailey is prepared to recant his testimony, which was given only on the assurance of Aldrich that all of the plaintiffs would give similar false testimony. Bailey has, indeed, refunded to the school district the money received in satisfaction of the judgment, and has voluntarily paid interest on that amount.

What action should Newman recommend on behalf of the school board?

## 1.   Judgments of Courts Lacking Jurisdiction

### *Durfee v. Duke*
375 U.S. 106 (1963)

JUSTICE STEWART delivered the opinion of the Court.

The United States Constitution requires that "Full Faith and Credit shall be given in each State to the . . . judicial Proceedings of every other State." The case before us presents questions arising under this constitutional provision and under the federal statute enacted to implement it.[2]

---

2. "The Acts of the legislature of any State, Territory or Possession of the United States, or copies thereof, shall be authenticated by affixing the seal of such State, Territory or Possession thereto.

The records and judicial proceedings of any court of any such State, Territory or Possession, or copies thereof, shall be proved or admitted in other courts within the United States and its Territories and Possessions by the attestation of the clerk and

In 1956 the petitioners brought an action against the respondent in a Nebraska court to quiet title to certain bottom land situated on the Missouri River. The main channel of that river forms the boundary between the States of Nebraska and Missouri. The Nebraska court had jurisdiction over the subject matter of the controversy only if the land in question was in Nebraska. Whether the land was Nebraska land depended entirely upon a factual question—whether a shift in the river's course had been caused by avulsion or accretion. The respondent appeared in the Nebraska court and through counsel fully litigated the issues, explicitly contesting the court's jurisdiction over the subject matter of the controversy. After a hearing the court found the issues in favor of the petitioners and ordered that title to the land be quieted in them. The respondent appealed, and the Supreme Court of Nebraska affirmed the judgment after a trial de novo on the record made in the lower court. The State Supreme Court specifically found that the rule of avulsion was applicable, that the land in question was in Nebraska, that the Nebraska courts therefore had jurisdiction of the subject matter of the litigation, and that title to the land was in the petitioners. Durfee v. Keiffer, 95 N.W.2d 618 [(Neb. 1959)]. The respondent did not petition this Court for a writ of certiorari to review that judgment.

Two months later the respondent filed a suit against the petitioners in a Missouri court to quiet title to the same land. Her complaint alleged that the land was in Missouri. The suit was removed to a Federal District Court by reason of diversity of citizenship. The District Court after hearing evidence expressed the view that the land was in Missouri, but held that all the issues had been adjudicated and determined in the Nebraska litigation, and that the judgment of the Nebraska Supreme Court was res judicata and "is now binding upon this court." The Court of Appeals reversed. . . . 308 F.2d 209. We granted certiorari. . . . 371 U.S. 946. For the reasons that follow, we reverse. . . .

It is not questioned that the Nebraska courts would give full res judicata effect to the Nebraska judgment quieting title in the petitioners. It is the respondent's position, however, that whatever effect the Nebraska courts might give to the Nebraska judgment, the federal court in Missouri was free independently to determine whether the Nebraska court in fact had

---

seal of the court annexed, if a seal exists, together with a certificate of a judge of the court that the said attestation is in proper form.

Such Acts, records and judicial proceedings or copies thereof, so authenticated, shall have the same full faith and credit in every court within the United States and its Territories and Possessions as they have by law or usage in the courts of such State, Territory or Possession from which they are taken." Act of June 25, 1948, c. 646, 62 Stat. 947, 28 U.S.C. § 1738.

The progenitor of the present statute was enacted by the First Congress in 1790. 1 Stat. 122. "The Act extended the rule of the Constitution to all courts, federal as well as state. Mills v. Duryee, [11 U.S.] 7 Cr. 481, 485 [(1813)]." Davis v. Davis, 305 U.S. 32, 40 [(1938)].

jurisdiction over the subject matter, i.e., whether the land in question was actually in Nebraska.

In support of this position the respondent relies upon the many decisions of this Court which have held that a judgment of a court in one State is conclusive upon the merits in a court in another State only if the court in the first State had power to pass on the merits — had jurisdiction, that is, to render the judgment. As Mr. Justice Bradley stated the doctrine in the leading case of Thompson v. Whitman, [85 U.S.] 18 Wall. 457 [(1873)],

> we think it clear that the jurisdiction of the court by which a judgment is rendered in any State may be questioned in a collateral proceeding in another State, notwithstanding the provision of the fourth article of the Constitution and the law of 1790, and notwithstanding the averments contained in the record of the judgment itself. [18 Wall. at 469.]

The principle has been restated and applied in a variety of contexts.

However, while it is established that a court in one State, when asked to give effect to the judgment of a court in another State, may constitutionally inquire into the foreign court's jurisdiction to render that judgment, the modern decisions of this Court have carefully delineated the permissible scope of such an inquiry. From these decisions there emerges the general rule that a judgment is entitled to full faith and credit — even as to questions of jurisdiction — when the second court's inquiry discloses that those questions have been fully and fairly litigated and finally decided in the court which rendered the original judgment.

With respect to questions of jurisdiction over the person,[8] this principle was unambiguously established in Baldwin v. Iowa State Traveling Men's Assn., 283 U.S. 522 [(1931)]. There it was held that a federal court in Iowa must give binding effect to the judgment of a federal court in Missouri despite the claim that the original court did not have jurisdiction over the defendant's person, once it was shown to the court in Iowa that the question had been fully litigated in the Missouri forum. "Public policy," said the Court,

> dictates that there be an end of litigation; that those who have contested an issue shall be bound by the result of the contest, and that matters once tried shall be considered forever settled as between the parties. We see no reason why this doctrine should not apply in every case where one voluntarily appears, presents his case and is fully heard, and why he should not, in the absence of fraud, be thereafter concluded by the judgment of the tribunal to which he has submitted his cause. [283 U.S. at 525-526.]

---

8. It is not disputed in the present case that the Nebraska courts had jurisdiction over the respondent's person. She entered a general appearance in the trial court, and initiated the appeal to the Nebraska Supreme Court.

Following the *Baldwin* case, this Court soon made clear in a series of decisions that the general rule is no different when the claim is made that the original forum did not have jurisdiction over the subject matter. Davis v. Davis, 305 U.S. 32 [(1938)]; Stoll v. Gottlieb, 305 U.S. 165 [(1938)]; Treinies v. Sunshine Mining Co., 308 U.S. 66 [(1939)]; Sherrer v. Sherrer, 334 U.S. 343 [(1948)]. In each of these cases the claim was made that a court, when asked to enforce the judgment of another forum, was free to retry the question of that forum's jurisdiction over the subject matter. In each case this Court held that since the question of subject-matter jurisdiction had been fully litigated in the original forum, the issue could not be retried in a subsequent action between the parties. . . .

The reasons for such a rule are apparent. In the words of the Court's opinion in Stoll v. Gottlieb, supra,

> We see no reason why a court, in the absence of an allegation of fraud in obtaining the judgment, should examine again the question whether the court making the earlier determination on an actual contest over jurisdiction between the parties, did have jurisdiction of the subject matter of the litigation. . . . Courts to determine the rights of parties are an integral part of our system of government. It is just as important that there should be a place to end as that there should be a place to begin litigation. After a party has his day in court, with opportunity to present his evidence and his view of the law, a collateral attack upon the decision as to jurisdiction there rendered merely retries the issue previously determined. There is no reason to expect that the second decision will be more satisfactory than the first. [305 U.S. at 172.]

It is argued that an exception to this rule of jurisdictional finality should be made with respect to cases involving real property because of this Court's emphatic expressions of the doctrine that courts of one State are completely without jurisdiction directly to affect title to land in other States. This argument is wide of the mark. Courts of one State are equally without jurisdiction to dissolve the marriages of those domiciled in other States. But the location of land, like the domicile of a party to a divorce action, is a matter "to be resolved by judicial determination." Sherrer v. Sherrer, 334 U.S. at 349. The question remains whether, once the matter has been fully litigated and judicially determined, it can be retried in another State in litigation between the same parties. Upon the reason and authority of the cases we have discussed, it is clear that the answer must be in the negative.

It is to be emphasized that all that was ultimately determined in the Nebraska litigation was title to the land in question as between the parties to the litigation there. Nothing there decided, and nothing that could be decided in litigation between the same parties or their privies in Missouri, could bind either Missouri or Nebraska with respect to any controversy they might have, now or in the future, as to the location of the boundary between them, or as to their respective sovereignty over the land in question. Fowler v. Lindsey, 3 Dall. 411 [(1799)]; New York v. Connecticut, 4 Dall. 1 [(1799)]; Land v. Dollar, 330 U.S. 731, 736-737 [(1947)]. Either State may at any time protect its interest by initiating independent judicial proceedings here. Cf. Missouri v. Nebraska, 196 U.S. 23 [(1904)].

For the reasons stated, we hold in this case that the federal court in Missouri had the power and, upon proper averments, the duty to inquire into the jurisdiction of the Nebraska courts to render the decree quieting title to the land in the petitioners. We further hold that when that inquiry disclosed, as it did, that the jurisdictional issues had been fully and fairly litigated by the parties and finally determined in the Nebraska courts, the federal court in Missouri was correct in ruling that further inquiry was precluded. Accordingly the judgment of the Court of Appeals is *reversed*, and that of the District Court is *affirmed*.

*It is so ordered.*

### Note: Failure to Challenge Jurisdiction in the First Litigation

What if facts necessary to a court's subject matter jurisdiction were not challenged in the first proceeding? Should a party be allowed to question those facts, and thereby the validity of the judgment, in a subsequent case? In Sherrer v. Sherrer, 334 U.S. 343, 351-352 (1948), the Supreme Court held:

> [T]he requirements of full faith and credit bar a defendant from collaterally attacking a divorce decree on jurisdictional grounds in the courts of a sister State where there has been participation by the defendant in the divorce proceedings, where the defendant has been accorded full opportunity to contest the jurisdictional issues, and where the decree is not susceptible to such collateral attack in the courts of the State which rendered the decree. . . . If respondent failed to take advantage of the opportunities afforded him, the responsibility is his own.

The Court stressed the interests of finality:

> It is just as important that there should be a place to end as that there should be a place to begin litigation. After a party has his day in court, with opportunity to present his evidence and his view of the law, a collateral attack upon the decision as to jurisdiction there rendered merely retries the issue previously determined. There is no reason to expect that the second decision will be more satisfactory than the first.

Id. at 350.

What if jurisdiction was not adjudicated in the first proceeding, or a party to be bound by a judgment was not involved in the first proceeding? See Tennessee ex rel. Sizemore v. Surety Bank, 200 F.3d 373, 380-381 (5th Cir. 2000) (distinguishing *Sherrer* and *Durfee*; "The constitutional command of full faith and credit does not compel Texas courts to defer to a Tennessee court's exercise of jurisdiction where the issue was neither fully and fairly litigated nor involved the same parties as the Texas litigation.").

## 2.   Judgments Obtained by Fraud or Mistake

### *Kupferman v. Consolidated Research & Mfg. Co.*
459 F.2d 1072 (2d Cir. 1972)

[Kupferman was the receiver of an insolvent underwriter, Vickers, Christy & Co. Among the assets of Vickers, Christy were 12,500 shares of stock in Consolidated acquired pursuant to a 1960 underwriting agreement. By 1962, these shares were diminished in value. Kupferman brought this action against Consolidated, alleging that it had violated the underwriting agreement by its inadequate compliance with SEC filing requirements. Ross, Kupferman's attorney, had in his possession a copy of a release executed in 1961 by Vickers, Christy that purported to absolve Consolidated for any breach of the underwriting agreement. Purcell, the lawyer for Consolidated, did not discover the release, although he had a copy of a letter of February 3, 1961, referring to it. The release was not pleaded as a defense. The trial resulted in a judgment for the plaintiff receiver in 1962.

When the judgment against Consolidated proved unenforceable because of the absence of corporate assets, Kupferman brought an action in state court against its monied directors, asserting that their mismanagement of Consolidated gave rise to the loss resulting in the adverse judgment. In this litigation, Jacobsen, one of the defendant directors, discovered the release in 1971, and thereupon filed a motion in the court that had rendered the 1962 judgment, seeking a vacation of that judgment. — EDS.]

FRIENDLY, CHIEF JUDGE. . . .

Fed. R. Civ. P. 60(b) authorizes a court on motion to "relieve a party or his legal representative from a final judgment" for "(1) mistake, inadvertence, surprise, or excusable neglect" or "(3) fraud (whether heretofore denominated intrinsic or extrinsic), misrepresentation, or other misconduct of an adverse party." However, motions seeking relief under these broad provisions may not be made "more than one year after judgment was entered." Any rights of appellant to have the 1962 judgment vacated must therefore stem from the saving clause in Rule 60(b): "This rule does not limit the power of a court to entertain an independent action to relieve a party from a judgment . . . or to set aside a judgment for fraud upon the court."*

Since appellant has not initiated an independent action for fraud *inter partes*, he can prevail only upon a showing that Ross practiced "fraud upon the court" by not disclosing the release.

The meaning of the quoted phrase has not been much elucidated by decisions. Obviously it cannot be read to embrace any conduct of an adverse party of which the court disapproves; to do so would render meaningless the one-year limitation on motions under Fed. R. Civ. P. 60(b)(3). See

---

* [See Rule 60(d) in the restyled rules. — EDS.]

7 Moore, *Federal Practice* 60.33 at 511 (1971 ed.). Professor Moore submits that the concept should "embrace only that species of fraud which does or attempts to, defile the court itself, or is a fraud perpetrated by officers of the court so that the judicial machinery cannot perform in the usual manner its impartial task of adjudging cases that are presented for adjudication." Id. at 515. . . . We accepted that formulation in Martina Theatre Corp. v. Schine Chain Theatres, Inc., 278 F.2d 798, 801 (2d Cir. 1960). Professor Moore explains Hazel-Atlas Glass Co. v. Hartford-Empire Co., 322 U.S. 238 (1944), setting aside a judgment on motion because of conduct which, shocking as it was, was a shade less flagrant than that held insufficient to sustain a plenary action in United States v. Throckmorton, 98 U.S. 61 (1878), largely on the basis, claimed by appellant to be presented here, that an attorney was implicated in perpetrating the fraud. While an attorney

> should represent his client with singular loyalty that loyalty obviously does not demand that he act dishonestly or fraudulently; on the contrary his loyalty to the court, as an officer thereof, demands integrity and honest dealing with the court. And when he departs from that standard in the conduct of a case he perpetrates a fraud upon the court. [7 Moore, supra, at 513.]

If there were no facts other than those stated up to this point, it would be hard to resist the conclusion that the case came within the boundaries of the concept of fraud upon the court which this court recognized in *Martina Theatre,* supra, 278 F.2d at 801, strict as these are. Contrary to views intimated by the district court, Purcell's negligent failure to discover the release would not of itself operate against such a conclusion if Ross had instituted, or allowed a judgment to be recovered in, an action to which he knew there was a complete defense. Hazel-Atlas Glass Co. v. Hartford-Empire Co., supra, 322 U.S. at 246. However, the full story has not yet been told; when it has been, Ross' conduct appears in a different light. . . . In his affidavit opposing the instant motion he averred that, pursuant to court order, he had been examining Vickers under oath from time to time in an endeavor to obtain evidence that would assist the receiver in carrying out his duties.

On May 10, 1962, Ross interrogated Vickers about the release. Vickers answered that the release, prepared by Friedman & Friedman, had been signed at the closing in Consolidated's office in Connecticut; that its purpose was simply to show "that Vickers, Christy & Co., Inc., had actually received the 12,500 shares"; and that Mr. Friedman "had given that as the reason for asking him to sign it." While it is hard to square this explanation with the [general language] of the release, particularly when that is read in light of the letter of February 3, Ross was not aware of the latter, and Vickers' construction gained credence from Consolidated's failure promptly to reject his demands. . . . Ross cannot therefore be criticized for *continuing* to prosecute the litigation after learning of the release; he could have expected that his adversary would also be armed with such knowledge and that the court would have to determine whether the release meant what it said or only what Vickers alleged he had been told.

The crucial question thus becomes whether it was fraud upon the court for Ross to fail to disclose the release when, as the trial came to an end, Purcell had said nothing about it. . . .

If this had been a criminal case, such nondisclosure by a prosecutor of a piece of evidence that might have been so material to the defense would almost certainly have afforded ground for collateral attack. See United States v. Keogh, 391 F.2d 138, 147-48 (2d Cir. 1968). But it was not. Neither was this a case where Ross and his client stood in a fiduciary relation to Consolidated or were under any order to produce all relevant documents. Cf. Alleghany Corp. v. Kirby, 333 F.2d 327, 341-43 (2d Cir. 1964) (dissenting opinion), aff'd by an equally divided court, 340 F.2d 311 (2d Cir. 1965). . . . Although Judge Frank said in Phelan v. Middle States Oil Corp., 154 F.2d 978, 991-92 (2d Cir. 1946), that a receiver "is a trustee with the highest kind of fiduciary obligations," the next sentence of the opinion makes clear that these obligations are those that run "to all persons interested in the receivership estate," and the many illustrations given relate to failure to discharge such duties, the issue there before the court, not to proceedings against adversaries. The duty of a receiver's attorney, when seeking to recover monies for the estate, like that of all other attorneys, is the high one of "integrity and honest dealing with the court," 7 Moore, supra, at 513, not something vaguely higher.

Whether Ross' failure to apprise the court of the release before the trial ended was such a breach of that duty as to constitute a fraud upon the court is not altogether easy to decide. Doubtless the highest standards of professional conduct would have suggested that he should have sought counsel from the judge . . . concerning where his duty lay. However, it is all too easy to fall into the error of condemning conduct with the aid afforded by the bright glare of hindsight—specifically our knowledge of Purcell's ignorance of the release and of the contents of the February letter. Ross had to make his decision without benefit of such knowledge. He could hardly have supposed that so experienced a lawyer as Purcell would have failed to contact the attorneys who had represented Consolidated when the sale of the 12,500 shares was consummated and obtain the papers Ross had secured for the asking. He could have thought not unreasonably, particularly in light of Friedman's letter of August 8, that such inquiry had been made but had resulted in Friedman's confirming the construction of the release to which Vickers had testified, and that therefore Purcell had made a tactical decision to defend on another ground.

Broad statements that a trial is a search for the truth must be read in the context that, under our legal system, the method for reaching this goal is a properly conducted adversary proceeding. The vague requirement of "candor and fairness" in the Canons of Professional Ethics in force in 1962 could hardly be read as requiring Ross to make certain that his opponent was fully aware of every possible defense that could be advanced. The present Code of Professional Responsibility does not advance matters greatly when it tells us that a lawyer shall not "conceal or knowingly fail to disclose that which he is required by law to reveal," D.R. [Disciplinary Rule] 7-102(A)(3) (1970). So far as we can see, Ross made no misrepresentations: it would be going too far to characterize as "fraud upon the court" his failure to disclose an instrument which he could have supposed reasonably—although, as it now appears, erroneously—to have been known to his adversary. . . .

The order denying the motion to vacate the judgment is *affirmed.*

## Note: *Rozier v. Ford Motor Co., 573 F.2d 1332 (5th Cir. 1978)*

Return to Chapter 3 and review *Rozier* now with the Rule 60(b)(3) aspect of the case in mind. The appellate court in *Rozier* held that the trial court had abused its discretion in denying plaintiff's 60(b)(3) motion, and that a new trial was necessary. Was this a sound result? See also Summers v. Howard Univ., 374 F.3d 1188 (D.C. Cir. 2004) (attempting to conceal filing of related action qualifies as misconduct but does not warrant setting aside consent decree); Cummings v. General Motors Corp., 365 F.3d 944 (10th Cir. 2004) (failure to produce videos not misconduct when not specifically requested; distinguishing *Rozier*), *abrogated on other grounds by* Unitherm Food Sys., Inc. v. Swift-Eckrich, Inc., 546 U.S. 394 (2006).

## Note: Extrinsic Fraud

In Dowdy v. Hawfield, 189 F.2d 637 (D.C. Cir. 1951), it was held that an independent action requires proof of "extrinsic fraud." An early description of the term appears in United States v. Throckmorton, 98 U.S. 61, 65-66 (1878):

> Where the unsuccessful party has been prevented from exhibiting fully his case by fraud or deception practiced on him by his opponent, as by keeping him away from court, a false promise or compromise; or where the defendant never had knowledge of the suit, being kept in ignorance by the acts of the plaintiff or where an attorney fraudulently or without authority assumes to represent a party or connives at his defeat; or where the attorney regularly employed corruptly sells out his client's interest to the other side—these and similar cases which show that there never has been a real contest in the trial or hearing of the case, are reasons for which a new suit may be sustained to set aside and annul the former judgment or decree, and open the case for a new and fair hearing.

The distinction was repudiated in Publicker v. Shallcross, 106 F.2d 949 (3d Cir. 1939). But it was applied in Salvation Army v. Morris, 421 F.2d 805, 808 (10th Cir. 1970). Note that it is explicitly inapplicable to motions under Rule 60(b)(3); see Tate v. Equity Brokerage Corp., 506 A.2d 201, 201 (D.C. 1986). One reason for doubt about the value of the distinction is the curious results it may produce. New York Life Ins. Co. v. Nashville Trust Co., 292 S.W.2d 749 (Tenn. 1956), is a case in which the insurer recovers the proceeds of a life insurance policy when the insured reappears. The fraud was extrinsic because the "widow" was also deceived by the disappearance. The implication is that she would have been able to keep the money if she had proved her own complicity, because the fraud would then be intrinsic.

Despite these sorts of unwelcome consequences, many states still observe the elusive distinction between extrinsic and intrinsic fraud, and deem only extrinsic fraud to be a valid basis for overturning a judgment.

## 3.   Judgments Contrary to Law

*Pierce v. Cook & Co.*
518 F.2d 720 (10th Cir. 1975)

BREITENSTEIN, Circuit Judge.

Plaintiffs-appellants have moved for relief under Rule 60(b), Fed. R. Civ. P., from a judgment of this court. The problem is that the same vehicular accident has produced divergent results in federal and state courts. We grant the motion and remand the case to the district court with directions.

Edwards, the owner and driver of a tractor-trailer combination, was hauling wheat for defendant-appellee Cook. On January 11, 1968, Edwards' rig collided on an Oklahoma highway with a car driven by Ted Pierce. Pierce was killed and passengers in his car were injured. Claudiatte Pierce brought suit in an Oklahoma state court for herself as surviving widow of Ted and for their minor daughter Letitia. Similar state suits were brought against Cook by Stephen Ellenwood and Mike Davis, passengers in the Pierce car.

On the motion of defendant Cook each case was removed to federal court on diversity grounds. The *Mike Davis* case was dismissed by the federal court on the motion of the plaintiff. It was later refiled in state court by coguardians of Mike, a minor. The guardianship maneuver apparently destroyed diversity and prevented removal.

The federal district court granted defendant Cook summary judgment on the ground that under the Oklahoma decision in Marion Machine, Foundry & Supply Co. v. Duncan, 101 P.2d 813 [(1940)], the shipper, Cook, was not liable for the torts of the independent contractor, Edwards.

Claudiatte Pierce and Ellenwood appealed. They conceded the effect of the *Marion Machine* decision and argued that, because of the Motor Carrier Act, 49 U.S.C. §§ 301 et seq., federal common law controlled. We held that the Motor Carrier Act did not indicate a congressional intent to supersede state tort law with respect to liability of a shipper, and concluded that Oklahoma law controlled. Pierce v. Cook & Co., 10th Cir., 437 F.2d 1119 [(1970)].

In the *Mike Davis* case the Oklahoma state court gave summary judgment for Cook on the basis of the *Marion Machine* decision. The case then went to the Oklahoma Supreme Court which specifically overruled *Marion Machine* and said, Hudgens v. Cook Industries, Inc., 521 P.2d 813, 816 [(1974)]:

> Where there is foreseeable risk of harm to others unless precautions are taken, it is the duty of one who is regularly engaged in a commercial enterprise which involves selection of motor carriers as an integral part of the business, to exercise reasonable care to select a competent carrier. Failure

to exercise such care may create liability on the part of the employer for the negligence of the carrier.

The court remanded the case for jury trial. The case was then settled favorably to the plaintiff.

The Tenth Circuit decision became final in January, 1971. The Oklahoma Supreme Court decision became final in May, 1974. In November, 1974, Claudiatte Pierce and Ellenwood filed the pending Rule 60(b) motion for relief from judgment.

The first question is the propriety of consideration of the motion by the court of appeals. Movants seek relief as a matter of law from a judgment of this court. This is not a case like Wilkin v. Sunbeam Corporation, 10th Cir., 405 F.2d 165 [(1968)], where a motion was filed in the court of appeals for leave to file in the district court a Rule 60(b) motion on the grounds of newly discovered evidence and fraud. Saying that the district court was in a better position to decide the issues presented, we held that the motion was unnecessary. The procedural problems involved have been the subject of much discussion. . . . Because our judgment is final and mandate issued, the trial court could well believe that it is without power to determine a legal question contrary to the decision of the court of appeals. Accordingly, we shall consider the motion.

Rule 60(b) provides that a court may grant relief from a judgment on five stated grounds and then says: "(6) any other reason justifying relief from the operation of the judgment." The one-year limitation provided in the rule does not apply to (6).

An adjudication must at some time become final. We recognized this principle in the *Collins* litigation. There, the plaintiffs attacked the constitutionality of a Kansas statute and lost. Collins v. City of Wichita, Kansas, 10th Cir., 225 F.2d 132 [(1955)]. A year later in an unrelated case the Supreme Court held the Kansas statute unconstitutional. Plaintiffs then sought Rule 60(b)(6) relief which we denied, Collins v. City of Wichita, Kansas, 10th Cir., 254 F.2d 837, 839 [(1958)], saying (1) "in extraordinary situations, relief from final judgments may be had under Rule 60(b)(6), when such action is appropriate to accomplish justice," and (2) "[a] change in the law or in the judicial view of an established rule of law is not such an extraordinary circumstance which justifies such relief." *Collins* differs from the instant case in that there the decisional change came in an unrelated case. Here it came in a case arising out of the same accident as that in which the plaintiffs now before us were injured. The question is whether we have here an extraordinary situation justifying Rule 60(b)(6) relief.

Our attention is called to no case considering the situation before us. Plaintiffs were forced into federal court by Cook's removal of their state court actions on diversity grounds. They lost because state law controls and the *Marion Machine* decision defeated their claims as a matter of law. Another party, exercising a stratagem not shown to be available to these plaintiffs, obtained the reversal of the *Marion Machine* decision and a settlement thereafter.

Research has disclosed only one case considering divergent results from a common vehicular accident and it afforded relief to the previously unsuccessful party. Gondeck v. Pan American World Airways, Inc., 382 U.S. 25 [(1965)], was concerned with a claim for death benefits under the Longshoremen's and Harbor Workers' Compensation Act. Two men were killed in the same accident. An award made by the Department of Labor to the survivors of one of the men was set aside in the United States District Court for the Southern District of Florida. The Fifth Circuit affirmed. United States v. Pan American World Airways, Incorporated, 5th Cir., 299 F.2d 74 [(1962)]. The Supreme Court denied certiorari, 370 U.S. 918, and on October 8, 1962, denied rehearing, 371 U.S. 856.

The survivors of a second man killed in the same accident litigated in the Eastern District of Virginia and lost but the Fourth Circuit reversed and upheld the right to recover. Pan American World Airways, Incorporated v. O'Hearne, 4th Cir., 335 F.2d 70 [(1964)].

The survivors of the first then went back to the Supreme Court in 1965 with a petition for rehearing. The Supreme Court granted the rehearing, granted certiorari, and reversed the Fifth Circuit court of appeals. In so doing, it said, 382 U.S. 25, 27, . . . "since, of those eligible for compensation from the accident, this petitioner stands alone in not receiving it, 'the interests of justice would make unfair the strict application of our rules.'"

The reasons for relief in the instant case are more compelling than those in *Gondeck*. There two federal courts differed as to the construction and application of a federal statute. We are concerned with an action in which federal jurisdiction depends on diversity. In diversity jurisdiction cases the results in federal court should be substantially the same as those in state court litigation arising out of the same transaction or occurrence. Erie Railroad Co. v. Tompkins, 304 U.S. 64, 74-75 [(1938)]; Guaranty Trust Co. v. York, 327 U.S. 99, 109 [(1945)]; Hanna v. Plumer, 380 U.S. 460, 468 [(1965)]; and Merchants Transfer & Warehouse Co. v. Ragan, 10th Cir., 170 F.2d 987, 991 [(1948)], *aff'd*, 337 U.S. 530 [(1949)]. Here they were not.

The unusual combination of events which have occurred make the situation extraordinary. The federal courts in which plaintiffs were forced to litigate have given them substantially different treatment than that received in state court by another injured in the same accident. The outcome determination principle mandated by Erie v. Tompkins has been violated.

Relief under Rule 60(b)(6) "is appropriate to accomplish justice" in an extraordinary situation. *Collins*, 254 F.2d 837, 839. Accordingly, our judgment heretofore entered in this case is vacated and the case is remanded. We do not set aside the judgment of the trial court. If plaintiffs file a Rule 60(b)(6) motion for relief from the trial court's judgment, that court shall consider the motion, and any response thereto, in the light of the *Hudgens* opinion, and of this opinion and shall make such determination as it deems proper.

*Motion granted and case remanded with directions.*

BARRETT, CIRCUIT JUDGE (concurring in the result).

I concur in the result reached by the majority. Notwithstanding my strong disinclination to disturb a final judgment, I conclude that under the circumstances of this case that such is necessary in order to effect fundamental justice, thus justifying application of Rule 60(b)(6), Fed. R. Civ. P. on behalf of plaintiffs-appellants (hereinafter referred to as Pierce-Ellenwood). . . .

In my view, Rule 60(b)(6) should always be applied in order to relieve a party who did not invoke the jurisdiction of the federal court in a diversity suit from a judgment adverse to that which would otherwise have been favorable in the state court forums. One who invokes the jurisdiction of the federal court when the diversity requirements are present should pay the consequences of that election. A change in state law should not be cause for relief to one who has voluntarily selected that forum. Such a litigant is not entitled to the proverbial "two bites at the apple." Furthermore, such application should do much to promote and strengthen proper Federal-State court relations.

LEWIS, CHIEF JUDGE, with whom SETH, CIRCUIT JUDGE, joins, dissenting.

I am completely uncertain as to what impact the ruling of the majority has, or is intended to have, on established procedural and substantive law or in the administration of justice generally. The opinion would appear to recognize that relief under Rule 60(b) is directed to the sound discretion of the trial court (except in this case) and remands the case to the trial court for consideration under Rule 60(b)(6) but in accord with the views expressed in the opinion. There is, of course, no existent motion under Rule 60(b)(6), or any motion under Rule 60(b)(6), or any motion at all, before the trial court but the majority suggests to plaintiffs that one be filed. This unusual judicial direction is surprising especially since the case was presented to this court in reliance upon Rule 60(b)(5) and counsel for plaintiffs expressly disavowed reliance on Rule 60(b)(6) during oral argument. The impact, if any, of Rule 60(b)(6) was neither argued nor briefed for this court and the authorities cited in the majority opinion appear in the case for the first time. . . .

The factual background of this case is based on a common disaster and, although the majority opinion does not specifically so state, I assume that the majority ruling is intended to be limited by this "extraordinary circumstance." But the driving force of the ruling, the desire to obtain consistent results in state and federal cases involving state law, to me, seems equally applicable to identical accidents and even to such instances as this court considered in Collins v. City of Wichita, 254 F.2d 837 [(10th Cir. 1958)].

Perhaps such a breakthrough would be desirable; perhaps not, for consistency, even in criminal cases, is not an invariable exaction of the law. United States v. Cudd, 10th Cir., 499 F.2d 1239, 1242 [(1974)]. In any event, I do not agree that the court has properly exercised its appellate function in this case and accordingly I dissent and join with Judge Seth in his expressed views. . . .

In Ackerman v. United States, 340 U.S. 193 (1950), the petitioner's citizenship had been revoked in a case joined with that of his brother-in-law, Keilbar. Keilbar appealed, but Ackerman did not, on the advice of an officer of the Immigration and Naturalization Service and because his attorney told him that he would have to sell his house to pay the cost of an appeal. When Keilbar's case was reversed, Ackerman sought relief under 60(b)(6) and was denied. The Supreme Court wrote:

> Petitioner made a considered choice not to appeal. . . . His choice was a risk, but calculated and deliberate and such as follows a free choice. Petitioner cannot be relieved of such a choice because hindsight seems to indicate to him that his decision not to appeal was probably wrong. . . . There must be an end to litigation someday, and free, calculated, deliberate choices are not to be relieved from.

Id. at 198.

## Notes and Questions

1. *Finality and "the Law."* The federal courts have been reluctant to find changes in law to be a reason to set aside a judgment as void. As the First Circuit explained in Lubben v. Selective Service System Local Bd. No. 27, 453 F.2d 645, 649 (1st Cir. 1972), "[a] void judgment is one which, from its inception, was a complete nullity and without legal effect. In the interest of finality, the concept of void judgments is narrowly construed. . . . Only in the rare instance of a clear usurpation of power will a judgment be rendered void." Cf. Ungar v. Palestinian Liberation Organization, 599 F.3d 79, 84 (1st Cir. 2010) (holding that "extraordinary circumstances" may warrant vacating a default judgment against a "willfully defaulting party"); United States v. Roberson, 752 F.3d 517, 524 (1st Cir. 2014) (declining to follow *Lubben* on other grounds).

Nevertheless, the presumption in favor of finality can be overcome by a subsequent change in the law when especially compelling public policy reasons so dictate. See, e.g., Moch v. East Baton Rouge Parish School Bd., 548 F.2d 594, 598 (5th Cir. 1977) (holding that a judgment could be set aside where it had the effect of allowing to continue "ad infinitum a constitutionally infirm [school] system outlawed everywhere else"); but see Celestine v. Petroleos de Venezuela, 108 Fed. App'x 180, 184 (5th Cir. 2004) (change in decisional law is not an extraordinary circumstance in itself; distinguishing *Pierce* on ground that the divergent judgments did not arise out of the same transaction); Blue Diamond Coal Co. v. Trustees of UMWA Combined Ben. Fund, 249 F.3d 519, 525-526 (6th Cir. 2001) (distinguishing *Pierce* as involving "transactions with a much tighter nexus of common activity, common rights, and common liability"); Norgaard v. DePuy Orthopaedics, Inc., 121 F.3d 1074, 1078 (7th Cir. 1997) ("If Congress cannot tell a federal court to reopen a judgment in order to give the losing side the benefit of a change of law, neither may a state. Legitimate interests in finality also counsel against revision. Thus it can be no surprise that other circuits have not followed *Pierce*.").

Notably, the United States Supreme Court took the 60(b) route to revising Aguilar v. Felton, 473 U.S. 402 (1985), in Agostini v. Felton, 521 U.S. 203 (1997). In *Aguilar,* New York City taxpayers complained of a program that sent public school teachers to various schools to provide remedial education for disadvantaged children. Since some of the qualifying disadvantaged children attended parochial schools, this meant that city funds were paying for classes in parochial schools, a practice that the Supreme Court held entangled church and state. On remand, the district court issued a permanent injunction preventing the city from sending public school teachers to teach remedial classes in parochial schools. Twelve years later, the Court in *Agostini* held that *Aguilar* was inconsistent with subsequent Supreme Court Establishment Clause decisions and that petitioners thus were entitled to 60(b)(5) relief from the prospective injunction issued earlier by the district court judge in *Aguilar.* Although the majority expressly rejected the dissent's argument that its approach could inspire a flurry of 60(b)(5) motions arguing that the applicable law has changed, *Agostini* does seem to invite such a response. As the dissent emphasizes, the factual conditions of *Aguilar* had not changed, and *Aguilar* itself had not been formally overruled when the district court acted.

Implicated by these results is an interesting and quite basic question about what the law is, or should be. At a superficial level, law is simply whatever rules are in force at the time of a decision. To disrupt a result simply because that law later changes in no way undermines the correctness of the result, provided it was consistent with the law of its time. By permitting such results to be disrupted — even if rarely — aren't courts suggesting that "law" is sometimes found outside the controlling cases and statutes, such that this superficial definition of law is misleading?

2. *Default Judgments.* One important caveat to the general principle that Rule 60(b) motions tend not to succeed is that the motion applies to default judgments as well as to judgments after appearance by a defendant. As you might imagine, motions to set aside a default judgment are far more likely to prevail than ones filed after a trial. Indeed, the motion's likely success may be a reason not to take a default judgment, lest the judgment simply be set aside later, and the expenses of this process be added to other expenses of pursuing the case.

3. *Appeal Versus Rule 60(b).* The courts' interpretation of Rule 60(b) must be evaluated in light of the alternatives available to a litigant who is unhappy with a judgment. The most important of these, of course, is the right to appeal. As the courts have repeatedly observed, "Rule 60(b) was not intended to provide relief for error on the part of the court or to afford a substitute for appeal." Title v. United States, 263 F.2d 28, 31 (9th Cir.), *cert. denied,* 359 U.S. 989 (1959).

4. *Independent Actions.* Note that Rule 60 also anticipates the possibility of an independent action to challenge a judgment. When might such an action be filed? Isn't allowing such challenges a waste of judicial resources that runs counter to the efficiency concerns that tend to govern rulings on Rule 60(b) motions?

Another question raised by Rule 60 challenges is whether this independent action requires an independent source of jurisdiction. The United States Supreme Court held in United States v. Beggerly, 524 U.S. 38 (1998), that an independent action to set aside a judgment under 60(b) does not require this independent jurisdiction. *Beggerly* also discussed the history of the Rule preserving such independent actions and stressed their rarity:

> [A]n independent action should be available only to prevent a grave miscarriage of justice. In this case, it should be obvious that respondents' allegations do not nearly approach this demanding standard. Respondents allege only that the United States failed to "thoroughly search its records and make full disclosure to the Court" regarding the Boudreau grant. Whether such a claim might succeed under Rule 60(b)(3), we need not now decide; it surely would work no "grave miscarriage of justice," and perhaps no miscarriage of justice at all, to allow the judgment to stand.

Id. at 47.

An example of the rare case justifying an independent action is Marshall v. Holmes, 141 U.S. 589 (1891), in which the underlying judgment was based on forged evidence.

## B.   COLLATERAL EFFECTS OF JUDGMENTS—CLAIM AND ISSUE PRECLUSION

Res judicata (or "thing(s) decided") is the doctrine determining when and how a judgment in one action will be dispositive in a second, later action. Essentially, it is a doctrine of repose, reflecting the belief that part of due process is closure—that is, that a litigation system should be able to bring a matter to an end.

Because of the increased burden on courts and litigants, and the increased chance for varying results, our system has always resisted relitigation of claims. The legal vessels for this resistance are the ancient, much respected, though little loved, doctrines of res judicata and collateral estoppel. In modern parlance, "res judicata" means claim preclusion and "collateral estoppel" means issue preclusion.

The trend in the federal cases and in general is to impose strict requirements on litigants that force them to raise as many issues and facts as they can in the first litigation forum. In fact, courts seem to be moving toward a rule that would require a plaintiff not only to raise as many transactionally related claims as she can in the first forum, but also to choose the forum that allows her to raise the greatest number of claims—lest she be deemed to have waived those claims that cannot be heard in her chosen forum.

In the following sections, we explore claim and issue preclusion and the growing significance of both doctrines. Before turning to these materials, however, you should distinguish the preclusion doctrines from stare decisis, double jeopardy, and the law of the case. Professors Friedenthal, Kane, and Miller explain the distinctions as follows:

> Stare decisis describes the effect of previous judicial decisions on present litigation. Stare decisis principles, also referred to as the doctrine of precedent, dictate that like cases should be decided alike by courts in a single jurisdiction. To adhere to precedent is a fundamental doctrine of Anglo-American law. Like former adjudication, stare decisis has the task of ensuring stability and consistency in judicial decisions, allowing people to plan their conduct. The law must appear to be rationally consistent if it is to be accepted as an impersonal arbiter of disputes. . . .
>
> Res judicata effect is given to any valid judgment, civil or criminal, that is final and on the merits. Double jeopardy depends on the concept of "jeopardy," which is unique to criminal cases. Jeopardy attaches to a criminal proceeding when the accused is in imminent danger of conviction. Once this has occurred, double jeopardy forbids the prosecution from renewing the same charges in a second proceeding no matter how the case was dealt with in the original court. Ordinarily, jeopardy is deemed to have attached when the jury is sworn, or a witness examined. Because res judicata and double jeopardy rely on different standards, one can imagine criminal cases in which one doctrine would apply but not the other. For example, if a criminal prosecution is dismissed before a jury is empaneled on a finding that the relevant statute of limitations has expired, the defendant has not yet been placed in jeopardy. Nevertheless, he might avoid later prosecution for the same offense by invoking res judicata.
>
> The last doctrine to be distinguished from former adjudication is "law of the case." Law of the case refers to the principle that issues once decided in a case that recur in later stages of the same case are not to be redetermined. Thus, just as notions of collateral estoppel prevent the relitigation of the same issues in successive suits, this doctrine limits relitigation in successive stages of a single suit. For example, law of the case will apply when an issue in the case is decided by the trial court and appealed. If the appellate court reverses and rules on the law to be applied and how it affects certain issues of the case, those findings will be binding on the trial court when the action is remanded for a new trial. In practice, the doctrine is not enforced with the rigor that attends the rules of res judicata and collateral estoppel. As noted by the Supreme Court, it "merely expresses the practice of courts generally to refuse to reopen what has been decided, not a limit on their power." [Messinger v. Anderson, 225 U.S. 436, 444 (1912).]

Jack Friedenthal, Mary Kay Kane, and Arthur R. Miller, Civil Procedure 629-631 (3d ed. 1993).

## Note: *Planned Parenthood v. Casey*

The United States Supreme Court relied heavily on stare decisis in reaching its controversial decision not to overrule Roe v. Wade, 410 U.S. 113 (1973).

Consider the following excerpts of Planned Parenthood v. Casey, 505 U.S. 833, 854-855 (1992), in which the Court expands on the force and limits of precedent:

> The obligation to follow precedent begins with necessity, and a contrary necessity marks its outer limit. With Cardozo, we recognize that no judicial system could do society's work if it eyed each issue afresh in every case that raised it. See B. Cardozo, The Nature of the Judicial Process 149 (1921). Indeed, the very concept of the rule of law underlying our own Constitution requires such continuity over time that a respect for precedent is, by definition, indispensable. See Powell, Stare Decisis and Judicial Restraint, 1991 Journal of Supreme Court History 13, 16. At the other extreme, a different necessity would make itself felt if a prior judicial ruling should come to be seen so clearly as error that its enforcement was for that very reason doomed.
>
> Even when the decision to overrule a prior case is not, as in the rare, latter instance, virtually foreordained, it is common wisdom that the rule of stare decisis is not an "inexorable command," and certainly it is not such in every constitutional case, see Burnet v. Coronado Oil & Gas Co., 285 U.S. 393, 405-411 (1932) (Brandeis, J., dissenting). . . . Rather, when this court reexamines a prior holding, its judgment is customarily informed by a series of prudential and pragmatic considerations designed to test the consistency of overruling a prior decision with the ideal of the rule of law, and to gauge the respective costs of reaffirming and overruling a prior case. Thus, for example, we may ask whether the rule has proved to be intolerable simply in defying practical workability, Swift & Co. v. Wickham, 382 U.S. 111, 116 (1965); whether the rule is subject to a kind of reliance that would lend a special hardship to the consequences of overruling and add inequity to the cost of repudiation, e.g., United States v. Title Ins. & Trust Co., 265 U.S. 472, 486 (1924); whether related principles of law have so far developed as to have left the old rule no more than a remnant of abandoned doctrine, see Patterson v. McLean Credit Union, 491 U.S. 164, 173-174 (1989); or whether facts have so changed, or come to be seen so differently, as to have robbed the old rule of significant application or justification, e.g., Burnet, supra, 285 U.S. at 412 (Brandeis, J., dissenting).

Applying these factors, the Court concluded that the central holding of *Roe*—that viability of the fetus marks the earliest point at which the State's interest in fetal life is sufficient to justify a legislative ban on nontherapeutic abortions—was still valid and should be given stare decisis effect. The Court further justified its conclusion by underlining the importance of preserving the Court's authority. To overrule precedent on such a divisive issue, it argued, might create the appearance of a Court that acts not for legally principled reasons, but in response to political pressure. When the arguments for the debatable precedent on a hotly contested issue are at least as strong as those against it, the Court should not risk its authority by overruling precedent. Rather, "the justification claimed must be beyond dispute. The Court must take care to speak and act in ways that allow people to accept its decisions on the terms the Court claims for them, as grounded truly in principle, not as compromises with social and political pressures having, as such, no bearing on the principled choices that the Court is obliged to make." Id. at 865-866.

## 1.  Claim Preclusion

### a.  In General

"Claim preclusion" means that a party may not relitigate all or part of a previously litigated claim. It prevents plaintiffs from splitting a cause of action into two separate claims, in effect precluding them from raising in a second action not only what they *actually* raised in the first, but *issues they could have raised* as well.

There are policy exceptions to what can operate as a harsh rule, but courts are becoming less and less forgiving as they feel the pressure for efficiency. As we shall see in Federated Department Stores v. Moitie, infra, the Court even has refused to excuse the only plaintiff in a multiparty case who failed to appeal a judgment against them all. Moitie simply wanted to join in the retrial that his coplaintiffs had won, but the Court invoked res judicata to bar him from further action.

The terms "merger" and "bar" have been much fussed over by courts and commentators. Simply put: If plaintiff wins in the first suit, claim preclusion acts as a merger, such that all causes are merged in the judgment and cannot be split. If plaintiff loses in the first suit, then the judgment acts as a bar to bringing a second action on the same claim.

An example of "merger" is the following verbatim account of a case from King's Bench in 1697, Fetter v. Beale, 91 Eng. Rep. 1122, a res judicata classic:

> Plaintiff had brought an action for battery against defendant and recovered. *Subsequently* "part of his skull by reason of the said battery came out of his head," and plaintiff brought another action. Plaintiff's counsel argued that "this action differed from the nature of the former . . . because the recovery in the former action was only for the bruise and battery, but here there is a mayhem by the loss of the skull."
>
>  [T]he jury in the former action considered the nature of the wound, and gave damages for all the damages that it had done to the plaintiff; and therefore a recovery in the said action is good here. And *it is the plaintiff's fault, for if he had not been so hasty, he might have been satisfied for this loss of the skull also.* Judgment for the defendant. . . .

In general, then, a plaintiff cannot sue again on the same matter, alleging a new theory, new type of relief, or extension of damages. In Fetter v. Beale, the plaintiff sought an extension of the damages.

## b.   Conditions of Claim Preclusion

The conditions of claim preclusion are sometimes summarized as follows:

1. Valid final judgment in forum 1:
   - Notice
   - Subject matter jurisdiction
   - Personal jurisdiction
2. Same parties
3. Same claim

As a matter of due process, a person cannot be bound by a judgment unless made a party thereto (or represented, as in a class action). See, e.g., South Central Bell Telephone Co. v. Alabama, 526 U.S. 160 (1999), in which the Court held that where a prior case involving different plaintiffs and tax years was not a class action and had entailed no privity or special relationship between the plaintiffs in the prior case and the one at hand, no claim or issue preclusion from the first case could bar the second action, as the plaintiffs in the second action were "strangers" to the earlier suit. A corollary is that a judgment has preclusive effect only for the parties to the judgment. The major exception to this rule occurs when a person is a successor in interest to a party in a previous lawsuit, for example, when he inherits the land from a party. He then may be bound by any previous judgment that touched on the land.

Much trickier is the requirement that for res judicata to apply, the *same claim* must be involved. Many jurisdictions, though not all, define a claim from the standpoint of transactional relatedness.

As modern procedural rules have become more flexible in defining the outer contours of a "claim" and in allowing a joinder of claims and parties, there has been a corresponding expansion of the preclusive effects of a judgment. When you add to this joinder flexibility the expanded federal subject matter jurisdiction (through supplemental jurisdiction), you find a much broader definition of what "claim" is precluded.

Gone are the days when, in Yogi Berra's immortal words, "It ain't over 'til it's over." It may be over a lot sooner than that.

## Problem Case: A Woman Partner (Yet Again)

Return now to the problem case from Chapter 2, Shayes v. McKenzie, Brachman, et al. In summary, Rosalind Shayes sued her former law partners in federal court for sex discrimination. In the course of discovery, she learns that defendants are writing vicious things about her. She moves to amend her complaint to add a claim for libel.

a) Would the court allow her to amend the complaint? This would be influenced partly by its assessment of the res judicata effect of failure to raise the claim in this case. This in turn depends on how closely it is related to the sex discrimination claim in the original complaint. If it is found to be very closely related, then if this sex discrimination claim goes to judgment first, Shayes will be barred by res judicata from suing for libel.

b) Does the possible res judicata effect of the amendment mean that the trial judge *must* grant the motion to add the libel claim? Practically speaking, this factor is a strong motivator for the judge unless he thought that Shayes had deliberately sat on the claim until late in the proceedings for some strategic reason, such as delay or limiting discovery time for the defendants.

c) Assume that McKenzie argued against the libel amendment on the ground that it would delay the proceedings and the court refused to allow the libel claim. Shayes then filed a libel suit in state court. The federal case went to trial and Shayes lost and the defendants move to dismiss the state case on grounds of res judicata. (Note that they would argue that she was barred from the claim.)

In ruling on the motion, the state court would probably apply its own preclusion law, though this approach is questionable. Can you see why a judgment's reach should be governed by the law of the rendering forum? For a cogent discussion of claim and issue preclusion effects of a judgment on subsequent judicial proceedings in another jurisdiction, see Howard M. Erichson, Interjurisdictional Preclusion, 96 Mich. L. Rev. 945 (1998), concluding, based on a study of several hundred cases, that state courts typically, but improperly, apply their own preclusion law.

Whatever law it applied, however, the state court would be making some of the same determinations that the federal court considered in ruling on the motion to amend. How closely related is it to the original sex discrimination claim? Under one view the libel claim is transactionally related because it arose out of the partnership dissolution. But a state court might find that Shayes was nevertheless not barred because here the defendants specifically denied the relationship of the claims in opposing the motion to amend, and because that motion was argued without any discussion or warning of a possible res judicata effect. As with everything that is judge-made and controlled, there is a great expanse for the play of discretion. And more and more, appellate courts are deferring to the discretion of trial judges on these matters.

## *McConnell v. Travelers Indemnity Co.*
346 F.2d 219 (5th Cir. 1965)

WISDOM, CIRCUIT JUDGE.

This hard case involving, for the plaintiff, disastrous effects from splitting his cause of action, is an invitation to make bad law. We decline the invitation.

Mr. and Mrs. Archie McConnell, Louisiana residents, were both injured in an automobile accident. Under Louisiana community property law, the wife's claim for personal injuries is her separate property; the husband's claim for personal injuries belongs to the community. Claims for medical expenses for either spouse also belong to the community. LSA-Civil Code, Article 2334 and 2402. As head and master of the community, only the husband may sue on claims belonging to the community. LSA-Code of Civil Procedure, Article 686. . . .

In August 1960 Mrs. McConnell brought suit against the Travelers Indemnity Company and Employers Casualty Company in the 24th Judicial District Court for the Parish of Jefferson, State of Louisiana, to recover damages of $8500 for personal injuries.[2] Her husband joined in the suit seeking recovery of $362.50 he had paid for medical expenses for treatment of Mrs. McConnell's injuries. A week later, Mr. McConnell filed the present suit in the district court to recover $85,000 for his personal injuries and $352.75 for his medical expenses. The state court suit was submitted in May 1963. In June 1963 the defendants filed a motion in the district court for a summary judgment of dismissal based upon the contention that the plaintiff had split his cause of action by filing suit in the state court for medical expenses; that under Article 425 of the LSA-Code of Civil Procedure the plaintiff is precluded from splitting a cause of action. While this motion was under submission, the plaintiff moved in the state court to dismiss his suit "with prejudice." That court therefore dismissed his claim for $362.50, with prejudice and at his cost. The district court then denied the motion for summary judgment in the instant case. The defendants then filed in the district court a renewed motion for summary judgment, contending that the plaintiff could have pursued his claim for personal injuries only by amending his petition in the state court; but that since that court had dismissed the action with prejudice, the dismissal was a final judgment of his entire claim, and was res judicata as to his action in the United States district court. The trial judge granted the motion and dismissed the complaint.

"Under Louisiana law, the splitting of tort claims is forbidden and the effect of such a split is to waive the right to recover the excess." Comment, 30 Tul. L. Rev. 462, 469 (1956). . . .

[Art. 425 provides:]

> An obligee cannot divide an obligation due him for the purpose of bringing separate actions on different portions thereof. If he brings an action to enforce only a portion of the obligation, and does not amend his pleading to demand the enforcement of the full obligation, he shall lose his right to enforce the remaining portion. . . .

Although there is no Louisiana case dealing specifically with the type of action-splitting this case presents, there is little doubt that a Louisiana court would hold that Mr. McConnell did indeed split his action. Louisiana courts hold that a plaintiff cannot split his claims for personal injuries and

---

2. The suits were brought under the Louisiana Direct Action Statute, LSA-R.S. 22:655.

property damage arising from the same accident. Fortenberry v. Clay, 68 So. 2d 133 [(La. Ct. App. 1953)]; Thompson v. Kivett & Reel, Inc., 25 So. 2d 124 [(La. Ct. App. 1946)]. In addition, in wrongful death cases courts forbid the survivor to split his damages and the decedent's damages. . . .

We are aware that the result we reach produces an anomaly. The husband and wife may split their tort claims, but the husband's lawsuit must include any claim for the wife's medical expenses. In effect, therefore, the parties may twice litigate the issue of the wife's injuries. On the other hand, the plaintiff's theory of the case would also produce an anomaly. The purpose of the tort claims is compensation. Under Louisiana law the community of acquets [i.e., property that has been acquired by purchase, gift, or otherwise rather than by succession] and gains suffers the injury. The plaintiff's theory would divide community damages among several potential lawsuits. It is the Louisiana community property system that causes the anomaly, not the rules of res judicata. This Court must apply the Louisiana law as the Court finds it.

The judgment is *affirmed.*


### Consumers Union of United States v. Consumer Product Safety Commission
590 F.2d 1209 (D.C. Cir. 1978)

Spottswood W. Robinson, III, Circuit Judge.

At the core of this litigation is appellants' challenge under the Freedom of Information Act (FOIA) to the Consumer Product Safety Commission's failure to disclose data concerning accidents attributable to the operation of television sets. When their cause was first before us, we reversed the District Court's ruling that no case or controversy was presented. That determination had been premised on the Commission's acknowledged willingness to release the data save for a ban imposed thereon by a preliminary injunction awarded television manufacturers by the District Court for the District of Delaware in a reverse-FOIA suit involving the same information. We held that the Delaware action, to which appellants were not parties, was no obstacle to their effort in the District Court here. We reasoned that a preliminary injunction is designed merely to preserve the status quo ante pending final decision, and "is not an adjudication of rights in any proper sense of the term. . . ." [Consumers Union v. Consumer Prod. Safety Comm'n, 561 F.2d 349, 356 (D.C. Cir. 1977).] Because the Delaware court had entered an order "closing out" the case before any final stage had been reached, we concluded that the Delaware proceeding was not "an insuperable barrier to the suit at bar." [Id.] . . .

Our prior opinions spurred the manufacturers to renew vigorously their pursuit of a judgment on the merits in Delaware, and appellants made no effort to have the District Court here enjoin them from that course. And the Commission, at long last, moved in the Delaware court for a change of venue to the District of Columbia, but added no alternative motion to join the FOIA requesters in the Delaware case—in which, we are now told, their rights have been fully and finally adjudicated. The Delaware court denied transfer primarily on the ground that, though the Commission faced the possibility of inconsistent outcomes on the merits, "[t]he time for the Commission to have moved for a transfer of these cases was in the early stages of this litigation in 1975 before all the effort and work had been expended here." [GTE Sylvania, Inc. v. Consumer Prod. Safety Comm'n, 438 F. Supp. 208, 212 (D. Del. 1977).]

While a petition to the Supreme Court for a writ of certiorari in this case was pending, the Delaware court issued a permanent injunction. The Supreme Court subsequently granted certiorari and remanded the case to us "for further consideration in light of the permanent injunction." [GTE Sylvania, Inc. v. Consumers Union, 434 U.S. 1030 (1978).] Thus we are now brought face-to-face with the issue we had earlier reserved: Does a judgment in favor of information-suppliers in a reverse-FOIA suit bar requesters not parties thereto from litigating their contention that the Freedom of Information Act mandates disclosure? The answer, we think, becomes clear once one investigates the interrelationship of the Act and reverse-FOIA suits in light of traditional principles governing preclusion of subsequent litigation.

Before the Freedom of Information Act was adopted, official dissemination of information was frequently marked by caprice, and suits to obtain information or to forestall its release met with "far from uniform" judicial treatment. [I.K. Davis, Administrative Law Treatise § 3.13, at 227 (1958).] The Act was intended to rationalize agency disclosure policies by providing a mechanism for balancing the public's "right to know" against the agency's interest in preserving confidentiality. If a court finds that the Act applies to material for which a request has been properly made, that is the end of the matter; the material *must* be disclosed, for the Act effectuates a congressional judgment that in those circumstances no public or private interest in secrecy outweighs the benefits attending public access. Moreover, in determining whether the Act is operative, the legislative command that disclosure be the rule and exemptions be narrowly construed must be sedulously observed. But Congress in the same breath specified classes of information to which the Act—and its policy of openness—"do[] not apply." [5 U.S.C. § 552(b) (1976).] When a court finds that requested material falls into one of these categories, and resultantly that its divulgence is not compelled by the Act, the propriety of voluntary disclosure by the agency must hinge on reconciliation with such other law as is pertinent—whether statute, regulation, the administrative "common law" or general principles of equity.

Some of these residual legal rules may endow private parties with legally cognizable interests in the confidentiality of exempted information; others may bestow on some a greater entitlement to information than the Act itself gives the general public. Since the agency's purposes will only coincidentally correspond with those of nongovernmental parties, it would be folly to entrust these often-critical private interests to unreviewable bureaucratic discretion. This court has accordingly held that when an agency asserts its intention to comply with a demand for information, parties who would be aggrieved by compliance may sue for a declaration whether that release would be lawful. But such litigants must first pass through the needle's eye of the Freedom of Information Act, for if the Act calls for disclosure they have, of course, no right whatsoever to confidentiality. Only if the Act does not govern need the court examine other sources of law—which may prohibit dissemination, give the agency judicially reviewable or unreviewable discretion to release or retain, or even mandate disclosure, depending on the circumstances. . . .

Federal courts in different jurisdictions may sometimes reach conflicting conclusions on the duties of an administrative agency, but normally without placing it in an impossible dilemma or bringing on a direct clash of judicial power. A serious conundrum, however, arises when, as here, the subject matter is information and the dispute is over whether it should be disclosed to the public. Once released pursuant to judicial decree, the data cannot be bottled up within the court's geographical area; with modern communications, information made public at any one point may soon be available throughout the country, often within moments. By the same token, when a court orders an agency to retain information, its edict is absolutely useless unless it stops agency action everywhere. Consequently, the first court to decide—in either a FOIA or a reverse-FOIA suit—will have pronounced a judgment that might reach across the Nation, or, on the other hand, might not have any practical effect even in its own jurisdictional domain.

That is exactly the situation here. The Delaware proceeding began, and the Commission was temporarily enjoined, before the appellant-requesters filed their own action in the District of Columbia seeking disclosure. By the time appellants sued, the District Court here knew that should the litigation before it continue, a decision contrary to that of the Delaware court might be reached, and that the Commission could not possibly comply with each of the conflicting orders.

Thus focused, the issue is the proper response of the court chronologically second. We earlier rejected one solution—dismissal for absence of a case or controversy—and we adhere to that position for the reasons then stated. That still leaves other alternatives—dismissal on a theory of stare decisis, collateral estoppel or comity, or continuation of the suit in some manner. For more than ample reason, we have chosen the latter course.

## A.  Stare Decisis

We surely do not gainsay that "the doctrine of stare decisis is still a powerful force in our jurisprudence." [United States v. Maine, 420 U.S. 515, 527 (1975).] So, a court resolving a FOIA claim may choose to defer to a previous judicial decision that the Act does or does not apply to particular documents, whether the prior action sought disclosure or restraint. It has not, however, been our experience that federal judges are either careless or timorous. The notion that any would defer on stare decisis grounds to a decision by a co-ordinate court with which he disagreed is unworthy of comment.

## B. Collateral Estoppel

Furthermore, the doctrine of collateral estoppel, which does bind parties to a previous suit to such determinations of material issues as are encompassed in the judgment, only rarely precludes nonparties from litigating the same issues afresh. If the FOIA applicant has neither been a party nor otherwise represented in a prior successful reverse-FOIA suit, he will not be blocked from taking his controversy to the courts.

The only parties here who were litigants in Delaware are the Consumer Product Safety Commission and the manufacturers who sought to prevent disclosure of materials that the Commission was prepared to turn over to appellants. An agency's interests in FOIA suits of either stripe diverge markedly from private interests, and raise serious doubt whether the agency could ever be deemed to represent members of the public. Indeed, congressional appreciation of that divergence underlies the Act. The institutional predilections that distinguish the agency's position from the citizens argue against permitting the Commission to do via litigation what it may not do by agreement—to bar applicants from information to which the Act mandates access. Far less do they justify departure from the rule, articulated in the milieu of antitrust enforcement, that "just as the Government is not bound by . . . litigation to which it is a stranger, so private parties, similarly situated, are not bound by government litigation." [Sam Fox Publ'g Co. v. United States, 366 U.S. 683, 690 (1961).]

Nor can the agency's role in reverse-FOIA litigation be likened to that of the named representative of a class in a defendant class action, and thus raise the spectre that a judgment against the agency would extend to bind all putative members of the hypothetical class it supposedly represents. At the outset, the clash of purposes would render the bureaucracy suspect as a representative of any class composed of FOIA requesters. Even passing that, when—as in the present circumstances—no class has been convened, no preclusive effect can possibly follow, and the public's right to know remains secure.

## C. Comity

That brings us lastly to comity, here reflected in the principle that "[o]rdinarily, the court first acquiring jurisdiction of a controversy should be allowed to proceed with it without interference from other courts under suits subsequently instituted." [Carbide & Carbon Chem. Corp. v. United States Indus. Chem. Co., 140 F.2d 47, 49 (4th Cir. 1944).] . . . Created to assure judicial efficiency and to reflect abiding respect for other courts, the doctrine surely does not contemplate that fundamental rights of citizens will be adjudicated in forums from which they are absent. . . .

The decisions invoking the principle involve circumstances in which the plaintiff in the later federal suit was a party to the earlier action involving the same issues and subject matter. When everyone with an interest could have had his claim resolved in one court, it would be senseless to allow some of the parties to initiate concurrent litigation over the same dispute. But that is not this case. Some—at least appellants—with a stake in the controversy were not before the Delaware court, and accordingly the principle of comity is inapplicable. Even if comity might be thought at all relevant, it would not outweigh the nonparties' right, guaranteed by the Act and the Constitution, to have their claims adjudicated.

The sum of the foregoing is that none of the familiar anti-relitigation doctrines operates to deprive nonparty requesters of their right to sue for enforcement of the Freedom of Information Act; rather, they remain unaffected by prior litigation solely between the submitters and the involved agency. One obvious consequence is that federal agencies that are prey to reverse-FOIA suits may by that token find themselves subject to the possibility of inconsistent judgments. Threats of that nature are not unprecedented, however, and there are procedural devices aplenty designed to avoid the hazard of conflicting obligations. Resort to them in the present context, moreover, would have brought about representation of all interests before the court that first addressed the merits, and thereby would have eliminated the problem completely.

Another consequence is that reverse-FOIA plaintiffs may find that, to prevent judgments in their favor from becoming nugatory, they must join in their lawsuits anyone whose request for information quickened the submitter's controversy with the agency—or perhaps even, by way of a defendant class action, all those who likely may subsequently make such requests. That, too, can only be salutary, for it will assure that the public's interest will be represented by at least one of its own. It will also relieve courts of the temptation—to which we earlier succumbed—to undertake a critique of the agency's litigative strategy.

The manufacturer-plaintiffs could have named appellant-requesters as defendants in the Delaware lawsuit, or they could have maintained it as a defendant class action against the Commission and all possible requesters. They did not. The Commission, with some creativity, could have filed an interpleader counterclaim and joined the requesters on the theory that otherwise the Commission might be exposed to multiple accountability and that, in a dispute over disclosure, information is an indivisible res over which the parties contest. It did not. At the very least, the Commission could have urged that the requesters were parties whose joinder was required under Civil Rule 19. But no consideration was given to the mandates of that rule, though, as we now elucidate, its applicability could hardly have been questioned.

If, as the manufacturers and the Commission assert, the Delaware reverse-FOIA suit so affected appellants' interest in disclosure of the information sought that they are now barred from litigating it in the District

Court here, the Delaware action certainly could have been said, in the words of Rule 19, "as a practical matter [to] impede [their] ability to protect that interest or . . . [to] leave [the agency] subject to a substantial risk of incurring double, multiple, or otherwise inconsistent obligations by reason of [appellants'] claimed interest." [Fed. R. Civ. P. 19(a).] Indeed, the concept of joinder was created to resolve the problem of conflicting exercise of equity jurisdiction. . . . In our view, those factors, had anyone in the Delaware action paused to look at them, surely demanded dismissal of the manufacturers' Delaware suit, or at least an injunction shaped to impact to the smallest possible extent upon the absent requesters' interest.

Joinder of the requesters would have been the better course, for it would have avoided the duplicative litigation in which we now are unfortunately entangled, but it was not the only solution. A well-crafted judgment in Delaware could have steered clear of any embarrassment to appellants' claim. Indeed, the inherent tension between reverse-FOIA and FOIA suits could often be mitigated by a rule that, unless the party resisting disclosure joins in his reverse-FOIA suit those seeking release, any injunction therein must be drafted to halt only voluntary disclosure by the agency, and to leave unaffected the requesters' right to seek a subsequent judicial determination that the Act mandates disclosure.

Appellant requesters were not made parties to the Delaware action, and the effect of that omission on this litigation is, to us, indisputable. A judgment cannot bind those who were not before the court either in person or through some sort of representative. . . . This basic tenet of due process can hardly be circumvented through the ritualistic invocation of "comity." The manufacturers have no valid objection to relitigation of disclosure of this information "for clearly the plaintiff [in the earlier suit], who himself chose both the forum and the parties defendant, will not be heard to complain about the sufficiency of the relief obtain[ed] against them." [Provident Tradesmens Bank & Trust Co. v. Patterson, 390 U.S. 102, 111 (1968).] Nor can the Commission legitimately bemoan the threat of inconsistent obligations since it never attempted to foreclose that possibility by seeking the joinder of appellants in Delaware.

The only factor even remotely capable of preventing appellants from prosecuting their FOIA suit toward a result contrary to the broad Delaware reverse-FOIA injunction is their failure to intervene in the proceeding there. We believe, however, that appellants, and perhaps information-requesters generally, should not suffer from bypasses of this sort. To decide otherwise would force them to accept the choice of a forum possibly sympathetic to the submitter and surely inconvenient or impossible for the requester. Congress specified the sites proper for judicial consideration of FOIA claims; to allow submitters to force FOIA litigation to occur in other arenas would free the tail to wag the dog.

This, in our opinion, is the type of "undue hardship" expressly discountenanced by the Advisory Committee when it discussed amended Rule 19 in 1966. The rule puts the burden on existing parties and the court to bring in those whose presence is necessary or desirable, and to work out a fair solution when joinder is jurisdictionally impossible. A generally applicable theory of waiver by one who declines to voluntarily step into the proceeding would abrogate the rule and its purpose completely. It is the party's—not the nonparty's—responsibility to make certain that the court has before it all those needed to enable it to serve the ends of justice. And if the essential nonparty cannot, for reasons of personal jurisdiction, be joined in the suit, then the litigation must proceed elsewhere, if at all.

This case, therefore, must finally continue toward a decision on the merits in the District Court for the District of Columbia. Its first task is to analyze closely the Delaware court's reasoning, for it may turn out that the court here will agree with the Delaware court. Should, however, the court decide that the failure to release the information was indeed improper, it will have to ascertain the relief appropriate in the circumstances. Since the manufacturers are party-defendants, it might consider enjoining them from enforcing their Delaware judgment against the Commission. In short, our decision is a narrow one—that this litigation is not prohibited by the earlier action—and we have not attempted to decide whether or not actual disclosure should be the final result.

*Remanded.*

### Note: *GTE Sylvania, Inc. v. Consumers Union*

Notwithstanding the D.C. Circuit's assurance that its decision was both "narrow" and "indisputable," the Supreme Court reversed. GTE Sylvania, Inc. v. Consumers Union, 445 U.S. 375 (1979). Without any discussion of necessary parties, mandatory intervention, or due process, the Court held that disclosure could not be ordered under the FOIA:

> The issue squarely presented is whether the Court of Appeals erred in holding that the requesters may obtain the accident reports under the Freedom of Information Act when the agency with possession of the documents has been enjoined from disclosing them by a Federal District Court. The terms of the Act and its legislative history demonstrate that the court below was in error.
>
> The Freedom of Information Act gives federal district courts the jurisdiction "to enjoin the agency from withholding agency records and to order the production of any agency records improperly withheld." 5 U.S.C. § 552(a)(4)(B). This section requires a showing of three components: the agency must have (1) improperly (2) withheld (3) agency records. Kissinger v. Reporters Committee for Freedom of the Press, [445 U.S. 136, 150 (1980)]. In this case the sole question is whether the first requirement, that the information has been "improperly" withheld, has been satisfied. . . .
>
> The CPSC has not released the documents sought here solely because of the orders issued by the Federal District Court in Delaware. At all times since the filing of the complaint in the instant action the agency has been subject to a temporary restraining order or a preliminary or permanent injunction barring disclosure. . . .

To construe the lawful obedience of an injunction issued by a federal district court with jurisdiction to enter such a decree as "improperly" withholding documents under the Freedom of Information Act would do violence to the common understanding of the term "improperly" and would extend the Act well beyond the intent of Congress.

We conclude that the CPSC has not "improperly" withheld the accident reports from the requesters under the Freedom of Information Act.

Id. at 384, 386-387. What happened? Who should have done what to whom to prevent it from happening? Why didn't they?

## Federated Department Stores v. Moitie
452 U.S. 394 (1981)

JUSTICE REHNQUIST delivered the opinion of the Court.

The only question presented in this case is whether the Court of Appeals for the Ninth Circuit validly created an exception to the doctrine of res judicata. The court held that res judicata does not bar relitigation of an unappealed adverse judgment where, as here, other plaintiffs in similar actions against common defendants successfully appealed the judgments against them. We disagree with the view taken by the Court of Appeals for the Ninth Circuit and reverse. . . .

In 1976 the United States brought an antitrust action against petitioners, owners of various department stores, alleging that they had violated § 1 of the Sherman Act, 15 U.S.C. § 1, by agreeing to fix the retail price of women's clothing sold in Northern California. Seven parallel civil actions were subsequently filed by private plaintiffs seeking treble damages on behalf of proposed classes of retail purchasers, including that of respondent Moitie in state court (*Moitie I*) and respondent Brown (*Brown I*) in the United States District Court for the Northern District of California. Each of these complaints tracked almost verbatim the allegations of the Government's complaint, though the *Moitie I* complaint referred solely to state law. All of the actions originally filed in the District Court were assigned to a single federal judge, and the *Moitie I* case was removed there on the basis of diversity of citizenship and federal question jurisdiction. The District Court dismissed all of the actions "in their entirety" on the grounds that plaintiffs had not alleged an "injury" to their "business or property" within the meaning of § 4 of the Clayton Act, 15 U.S.C. § 15. Weinberg v. Federated Department Stores, 426 F. Supp. 880 (N.D. Cal. 1977).

Plaintiffs in five of the suits appealed that judgment to the Court of Appeals for the Ninth Circuit. The single counsel representing Moitie and Brown, however, chose not to appeal and instead refiled the two actions in state court, *Moitie II* and *Brown II*. Although the complaints purported to raise only state-law claims, they made allegations similar to those made in the prior complaints, including that of the Government. Petitioners removed these new actions to the District Court for the Northern District of California and moved to have them dismissed on the ground of res judicata. In a decision rendered July 8, 1977, the District Court first denied respondents' motion to remand. It held that the complaints, though artfully couched in terms of state law, were "in many respects identical" with the prior complaints, and were thus properly removed to federal court because they raised "essentially federal law" claims. The court then concluded that because *Moitie II* and *Brown II* involved the "same parties, the same alleged offenses, and the same time periods" as *Moitie I* and *Brown I,* the doctrine of res judicata required that they be dismissed this time. Moitie and Brown appealed.

Pending that appeal, this Court on June 11, 1979, decided Reiter v. Sonotone Corp., 442 U.S. 330, . . . holding that retail purchasers can suffer an "injury" to their "business or property" as those terms are used in § 4 of the Clayton Act. On June 25, 1979, the Court of Appeals for the Ninth Circuit reversed and remanded the five cases which had been decided with *Moitie I* and *Brown I,* the cases that had been appealed, for further proceedings in light of *Reiter.*

When *Moitie II* and *Brown II* finally came before the Court of Appeals for the Ninth Circuit, the court reversed the decision of the District Court dismissing the cases. 611 F.2d 1267.[2] Though the court recognized that a "strict application of the doctrine of res judicata would preclude our review of the instant decision," id. at 1269, it refused to apply the doctrine to the facts of this case. It observed that the other five litigants in *Weinberg* cases had successfully appealed the decision against them. It then asserted that "non-appealing parties may benefit from a reversal when their position is closely interwoven with that of appealing parties," and concluded that "because the instant dismissal rested on a case that has been effectively overruled," the doctrine of res judicata must give way to "public policy" and "simple justice." Id. at 1269-1270. We granted certiorari . . . to consider the validity of the Court of Appeals' novel exception to the doctrine of res judicata. . . .

. . . As this Court explained in Baltimore Steamship Co. v. Phillips, 274 U.S. 316, 325 (1927), an "erroneous conclusion" reached by the court in the first suit does not deprive the defendants in the second action

---

2. The Court of Appeals also affirmed the District Court's conclusion that *Brown II* was properly removed to federal court, reasoning that the claims presented were "federal in nature." We agree that at least some of the claims had a sufficient federal character to support removal. As one treatise puts it, courts "will not permit plaintiff to use artful pleading to close off defendant's right to a federal forum . . . [and] occasionally the removal court will seek to determine whether the real nature of the claim is federal, regardless of plaintiff's characterization." 14 C. Wright, A. Miller, & E. Cooper, Federal Practice and Procedure § 3722, pp. 564-66 (1976) (citing cases) (footnote omitted). The District Court applied that settled principle to the facts of this case. After "an extensive review and analysis of the origins and substance of" the two Brown complaints, it found, and the Court of Appeals expressly agreed, that respondents had attempted to avoid removal jurisdiction by "artful[ly]" casting their "essentially federal law claims" as state-law claims. We will not question here that factual finding.

of their right to rely upon the plea of *res judicata*. . . . A judgment merely voidable because based upon an erroneous view of the law is not open to collateral attack, but can be corrected only by a direct review and not by bringing another action upon the same cause [of action].

We have observed that "[t]he indulgence of a contrary view would result in creating elements of uncertainty and confusion and in undermining the conclusive character of judgments, consequences which it was the very purpose of the doctrine of res judicata to avert." Reed v. Allen, 286 U.S. 191, 201 (1932). . . . [T]his Court recognizes no general equitable doctrine, such as that suggested by the Court of Appeals, which countenances an exception to the finality of a party's failure to appeal merely because his rights are "closely interwoven" with those of another party. . . . Respondents here seek to be the windfall beneficiaries of an appellate reversal procured by other independent parties, who have no interest in respondents' case. . . . Moreover . . . it is apparent that respondents here made a calculated choice to forego their appeals. . . .

The Court of Appeals also rested its opinion in part on what it viewed as "simple justice." But we do not see the grave injustice which would be done by the application of accepted principles of res judicata. "Simple justice" is achieved when a complex body of law developed over a period of years is evenhandedly applied. The doctrine of res judicata serves vital public interests beyond any individual judge's ad hoc determination of the equities in a particular case. There is simply "no principle of law or equity which sanctions the rejection by a federal court of the salutary principle of *res judicata*." Heiser v. Woodruff, 327 U.S. 726, 733 (1946). The Court of Appeals' reliance on "public policy" is similarly misplaced. This Court has long recognized that "[p]ublic policy dictates that there be an end of litigation; that those who have contested an issue shall be bound by the result of the contest, and that matters once tried shall be considered forever settled as between the parties." Baldwin v. [Iowa] Traveling Men's Association, 283 U.S. 522, 525 (1931). We have stressed that "the doctrine of *res judicata* is not a mere matter of practice or procedure inherited from a more technical time than ours. It is a rule of fundamental and substantial justice, 'of public policy and of private peace,' which should be cordially regarded and enforced by the courts. . . ." Hart Steel Co. v. Railroad Supply Co., 244 U.S. 294, 299 (1917). The language used by this Court half a century ago is even more compelling in view of today's crowded dockets:

> "The predicament in which respondent finds himself is of his own making. . . . [W]e cannot be expected, for his sole relief, to upset the general and well-established doctrine of res judicata, conceived in the light of the maxim that the interest of the state requires that there be an end to litigation—a maxim which comports with common sense as well as public policy. And the mischief which would follow the establishment of precedent for so disregarding the salutary doctrine against prolonging strife would be greater than the benefit which would result from relieving some case of individual hardship." Reed v. Allen, 286 U.S. at 198-199.

Respondents . . . argue that "the District Court's dismissal on grounds of res judicata should be reversed, and the District Court directed to grant respondents' motion to remand to the California State Court." In their view, *Brown I* cannot be considered res judicata as to their *state* law claims, since *Brown I* raised only federal law claims and *Brown II* raised additional state law claims not decided in *Brown I*, such as unfair competition, fraud and restitution.

It is unnecessary for this Court to reach that issue. It is enough for our decision here that *Brown I* is res judicata as to respondents' federal law claims. Accordingly, the judgment of the Court of Appeals is reversed, and the cause remanded for proceedings consistent with this opinion.

*It is so ordered.*

JUSTICE BLACKMUN, with whom JUSTICE MARSHALL joins, concurring in the judgment. . . .

I would flatly hold that *Brown I* is res judicata as to respondents' state law claims. Like the District Court, the Court of Appeals found that those state law claims were simply disguised federal claims; since respondents have not cross-petitioned from that judgment, their argument that this case should be remanded to state court should be itself barred by res judicata. More important, even if the state and federal claims are distinct, respondents' failure to allege the state claims in *Brown I* manifestly bars their allegation in *Brown II*. The dismissal of *Brown I* is res judicata not only as to all claims respondents actually raised, but also as to all claims that could have been raised. See Commissioner v. Sunnen, 333 U.S. 591, 597 (1948). . . . Since there is no reason to believe that it was clear at the outset of this litigation that the District Court would have declined to exercise pendent jurisdiction over state claims, respondents were obligated to plead those claims if they wished to preserve them. . . . Because they did not do so, I would hold the claims barred.

JUSTICE BRENNAN, dissenting. . . .

Respondent Floyd R. Brown filed this class action lawsuit (*Brown II*) against petitioners in California state court. The complaint stated four state law causes of action: (1) fraud and deceit, (2) unfair business practices, (3) civil conspiracy, and (4) restitution. . . . *All four* of the causes of action rested wholly on California statutory or common law; *none* rested in any fashion on federal law. . . . Removability depends solely upon the nature of the plaintiff's complaint: an action may be removed to federal court only if a "right or immunity created by the Constitution or laws of the United States [constitutes] an element, and an essential one, of the plaintiff's cause of action." Gully v. First National Bank in Meridian, 299 U.S. 109, 112 (1936). . . .

An important corollary is that "the party who brings a suit is master to decide what laws he will rely upon and therefore does determine whether he will bring a 'suit arising under' the . . . law[s] of the United States" by the allegations in his complaint. The Fair v. Kohler Die & Specialty Co., 228

U.S. 22, 25 (1913). . . . Where the plaintiff's claim might be brought under either federal or state law, the plaintiff is normally free to ignore the federal question and rest his claim solely on the state ground. If he does so, the defendant has no general right of removal. La Chemise Lacoste v. Alligator Co., 506 F.2d 339, 346 (3d Cir. 1974) (other citations omitted).

This corollary is well grounded in principles of federalism. So long as States retain authority to legislate in subject areas in which Congress has legislated without preempting the field, and so long as state courts remain the preferred forum for interpretation and enforcement of state law, plaintiff must be permitted to proceed in state court under state law. It would do violence to state autonomy were defendants able to remove state claims to federal court merely because the plaintiff *could have* asserted a federal claim based on the same set of facts underlying his state claim. . . .

The Court relies on what it calls a "factual finding" by the District Court, with which the Court of Appeals agreed, that "respondents had attempted to avoid removal jurisdiction by 'artfully' casting their 'essentially federal law claims' as state-law claims." . . . But this amounts to no more than a pejorative characterization of respondents' decision to proceed under state, rather than federal, law. "Artful" or not, respondents' complaints were not based on any claim of a federal right or immunity, and were not, therefore, removable. . . .

Even assuming that this Court and the lower federal courts have jurisdiction to decide this case, however, I dissent from the Court's disposition of the res judicata issue. . . .

Like Justice Blackmun, I would hold that the dismissal of *Brown I* is res judicata not only as to every matter that was actually litigated, but also as to every ground or theory of recovery that might also have been presented. . . .

I therefore respectfully dissent. . . .

### Note: Pleading and Preclusion

Post-*Moitie*, courts and commentators had struggled over the meaning of footnote 2, in which the Court discussed "artful pleading" used by plaintiffs to close off defendant's right to a federal forum. One influential observer concluded that the Court in *Moitie* had "departed from the traditional scope of the artful-pleading doctrine." Arthur R. Miller, Artful Pleading: A Doctrine in Search of a Definition, 76 Tex. L. Rev. 1781, 1802 (1998). In Rivet v. Regions Bank, 522 U.S. 470, 478 (1998), however, a unanimous Supreme Court stated that "*Moitie* did not create a preclusion exception to the rule, fundamental under currently governing legislation, that a defendant cannot remove on the basis of a federal defense. In sum, claim preclusion by reason of a prior federal judgment is a defensive plea that provides no basis for removal under § 1441(b). Such a defense is properly made in the state proceedings, and the state courts' disposition of it is subject to this Court's ultimate review."

## Note: Are Defects in Subject Matter Jurisdiction
## *Ever Res Judicata?*

Recall that subject matter jurisdiction defects can be raised at any time, as we saw in *Belleville Catering.* See Chapter 2. How should an appellate court treat lack of diversity when a case settles, the settlement agreement is incorporated into the trial court's judgment disposing of the case, and one side then raises a defect in subject matter jurisdiction for the first time as part of an appeal of the trial court's enforcement of terms of the settlement? Normally, a settlement is just a private contract and enforcing it requires an entirely new lawsuit for breach of contract. However, when the court that entertained the original suit incorporates the agreement into its judgment, the agreement becomes enforceable by that court. Rather than file a new action, parties can just go back to the original court with proof of breach and request a remedy.

In Baella-Silva v. Hulsey, 454 F.3d 5 (1st Cir. 2006), an attorney sued his co-counsel when co-counsel refused to pay his fees under a fee-sharing agreement. The parties settled and the district court agreed to incorporate the agreement into its judgment. No objection was raised to the agreement and no appeal was taken from the judgment.

When the attorney later breached the terms of the settlement, defendants moved the district court to award the liquidated damages provided for in the contract. The court imposed the sanctions and the attorney appealed. In the First Circuit, for the first time, the attorney argued that there was incomplete diversity in the original action for attorneys' fees. The First Circuit rejected the argument. To be sure, the court conceded, "a lack of complete diversity between the parties deprives the federal courts of jurisdiction over the lawsuit," id. at 9 (quoting Casas Office Machs., Inc. v. Mita Copystar Am., Inc., 42 F.3d 668, 673 (1st Cir. 1994)) (internal quotation marks omitted), but "[w]eighing against this seemingly 'inflexible' jurisdictional requirement . . . is a strong interest in the finality of judgments," id. (quoting Fafel v. DiPaola, 399 F.3d 403, 410 (1st Cir. 2005)) (internal quotation marks omitted). "A district court's express or implicit determination that it has jurisdiction is open to direct review, but it is res judicata when collaterally attacked." Id. at 9. Thus as long as "the record supports an 'arguable basis' for concluding that subject-matter jurisdiction existed, a final judgment cannot be collaterally attacked." Id. at 9-10.

Here, the court concluded, there was evidence that the nondiverse parties may have been fraudulently joined. Id. at 10. The court viewed Baella-Silva's attempt to raise the subject matter jurisdiction issue for the first time on appeal of the enforcement of the settlement agreement as "collateral" because neither he nor defendants "[brought] a direct appeal challenging the district court's jurisdiction or any other aspect of the settlement judgment within the time period provided for appeal." Id. at 9. Thus Baella-Silva's collateral attack on the trial court's jurisdiction was analogous to "an appeal from the denial of a motion for relief from a void judgment pursuant to Federal Rule of Civil Procedure 60(b)(4)." Id. at 10.

Isn't a settlement agreement over which the trial court retains enforcement jurisdiction quite different from a final judgment as to which no appeal is taken? Surely the interest in finality is not identical in the two cases. The First Circuit noted the traditional doctrine that "[a] court without subject-matter jurisdiction may not acquire it by consent of the parties," id. at 9 (quoting Fafel v. DiPaola, 399 F.3d at 410) (internal quotation marks omitted), but isn't that precisely the result the court sanctions in this case?

## Note: Subject Matter Jurisdiction and Remedies

What happens if a plaintiff fails to request an available remedy in her first suit, say, damages for emotional distress, and wants to file a new suit to recover these damages? The answer is the same as it would be if the plaintiff omitted an available cause of action arising from the same transaction or occurrence—res judicata bars relitigation.

Matters are different, however, if the subject matter jurisdiction of the court in which the plaintiff first sued is limited in such a way that damages for emotional distress are not available.

Gale Nestor worked as a machinist for Pratt & Whitney for 20 years until she was fired in 1992 following an altercation with a male employee. She filed a complaint with the Connecticut Commission on Human Rights and Opportunities alleging that she had been terminated because of sex discrimination in violation of Title VII and parallel state law. Nestor v. Pratt & Whitney, 466 F.3d 65 (2d Cir. 2006). The Commission informed Nestor that it could not award compensatory damages, just back pay, and that proceedings before the Commission include representation by staff counsel at a reduced fee, "flexible evidentiary rules . . . and speedy proceedings." Id. at 68. The proceedings were not, in fact, speedy; they took six years. But the Commission eventually returned a finding for Nestor and awarded her back pay. Pratt appealed to the Connecticut courts, the state courts upheld the award, and Pratt eventually paid the judgment with interest.

In 2003, the federal Equal Employment Opportunity Commission issued Nestor a right-to-sue letter, and she promptly filed suit against Pratt seeking remedies available under Title VII, including compensatory damages, punitive damages, attorneys' fees, and prejudgment interest. Pratt moved for summary judgment on the theory that res judicata barred Nestor's federal suit. Recognizing a division of authority in the circuit courts, compare Jones v. Am. State Bank, 857 F.2d 494 (8th Cir. 1988) (state administrative litigation does not preclude Title VII suit for attorneys' fees); Patzer v. Bd. of Regents of Univ. of Wis. Sys., 763 F.2d 851 (7th Cir. 1985) (state administrative litigation upheld by state courts does not bar Title VII action for additional relief), with Chris v. Tenet, 221 F.3d 648 (4th Cir. 2000) (federal court cannot entertain Title VII action to recover attorneys' fees incurred in prior state administrative proceeding), the Second Circuit held that a plaintiff who prevails in state administrative proceedings can "subsequently file suit in federal court seeking relief that was *unavailable* in the state proceedings."

*Nestor,* 466 F.3d at 69 (emphasis added). The Ninth Circuit has since adopted the position taken by the Eighth Circuit in *Jones.* See Porter v. Winter, 603 F.3d 1113 (9th Cir. 2010) (federal courts have jurisdiction to hear claims brought solely to recover attorneys' fees incurred in Title VII administrative proceedings).

Reasoning that the result would be the same under either federal or Connecticut preclusion law, the court rejected Pratt's argument that it was "unfair to allow plaintiff to (in effect) re-litigate damages while binding the defendant to liability findings, particularly when (as here) liability was decided in an administrative forum that did not afford such basic procedures as discovery." *Nestor,* 466 F.3d at 73. According to New York Gaslight Club, Inc. v. Carey, 447 U.S. 54 (1980), a prevailing plaintiff in state administrative proceedings is entitled to pursue supplemental relief afforded by Title VII—the federal statute operates as "a 'supplement' to state remedies 'when the State does not provide prompt or complete relief.'" Id. at 71. And Connecticut preclusion doctrine, the court explained, follows the Restatement (Second) of Judgments § 26(1)(c), see infra, page 1219, in recognizing an exception to res judicata "for later actions that assert claims or seek relief that could not have been pressed or recovered in the prior proceeding." Id. at 74.

### c. Counterclaims and Cross-Claims

Remember that res judicata (claim preclusion) applies not only to issues that were raised but also to issues that could or should have been raised in the prior lawsuit. Thus we bring in the compulsory counterclaim rules—Fed. R. Civ. P. 13(a) and many similar state provisions.

If a counterclaim was compulsory, then by definition it could and should have been raised in the first suit and is precluded. In fact, courts may even bar a party from later raising a transactionally related counterclaim when the defendant defaulted on the claim. See Todd David Peterson, The Misguided Law of Compulsory Counterclaims in Default Cases, 50 Ariz. L. Rev. 1107 (2008). But what if a jurisdiction does *not* have a compulsory counterclaim rule, or if an action is dismissed before the counterclaim rule kicks in? The answer is that the action may still be barred based on an unasserted counterclaim if it would completely contradict the result in the first action. This is sometimes called the "logical inconsistency" exception.

Here is an example of how this works.

*A* sues *B* in state court for damages resulting from an automobile accident. The jury returns a verdict for *B*. *B* then sues *A* in federal court (diversity) for damages *B* incurred in the same accident. What result:

a) if state court has a procedural rule identical to Rule 13(a)? (precluded)
b) if state has no compulsory counterclaim rule? (This depends on whether it fits the logical inconsistency exception. For example, might this happen if the result for *B* occurred in the first action because *A* and *B* were equally negligent?)

## Problem Case: A Woman Partner (One More Time)

Return again to Shayes v. McKenzie, Brachman. Assume that Shayes brings a civil rights suit in federal court and amends her complaint to include a claim of libel. If McKenzie, Brachman wants to assert a libel claim — that she said equally horrible things about the firm — *must it do so in the original suit?* In other words, is McKenzie, Brachman's libel action a compulsory counterclaim?

It is a compulsory counterclaim under Rule 13(a) if it arose out of the same transaction or occurrence. "Compulsory" means that if McKenzie does not raise libel as a counterclaim, it will be precluded from bringing a separate libel suit later; that is, a final judgment in Shayes v. McKenzie, Brachman will preclude the libel claim, *even if it was never asserted.* Rule 13(a) refers, by definition, to claims that *should have been asserted.*

The interests of efficiency are likely to override those that deal with McKenzie's right to choose his own forum for his claims. If his libel claim sheds any light on the plaintiff's sex discrimination claim (for example, "This is not sex discrimination — I disliked her because of the outrageous things she said about the firm"), a court ruling on whether he must assert it now would be strongly inclined to say it grows out of the same transaction or occurrence. Once more: If it is a compulsory counterclaim, McKenzie will be barred from bringing any later state claim regardless of the outcome in federal court.

Could McKenzie choose to bring a separate libel claim in state court while the Shayes case is pending in federal courts? Technically yes, since only valid final judgments have res judicata effect. Thus even if the counterclaim is "compulsory," there is nothing to prevent McKenzie from entering this inefficient and potentially nasty situation. The solution is for either court to "stay" or "abate" its proceedings pending resolution of the other suit. Most likely the court in the later-filed action will do so, which means that when two feuding parties have competing claims against one another, either of which might be a compulsory counterclaim to the other, there may be an unseemly race to the courthouse to attain choice of forum.

## *Martino v. McDonald's System, Inc.*
598 F.2d 1079 (7th Cir. 1979)

PELL, CIRCUIT JUDGE.

The plaintiffs, Louis J. Martino and McDonald's Drive-In of Ottumwa, Iowa, Inc. (McDonald's Ottumwa), appeal from the district court's entry of summary judgment against them on one count of their two count antitrust complaint against the defendants, McDonald's System, Inc. (McDonald's System) and Franchise Realty Interstate Corporation (FRIC). The only issue before this court is whether a 1973 consent judgment against Martino precludes the cause of action set forth in Count I of the present complaint. The district court held that both res judicata and the compulsory counterclaim rule of Fed. R. Civ. P. 13(a) barred the plaintiffs from suing on their first cause of action. Martino v. McDonald's System, Inc., 432 F. Supp. 499 (N.D. Ill. 1977).

In 1962 the plaintiff Louis Martino and three brothers not involved in this action entered into a franchise and lease agreement with the defendants. Martino and his brothers then organized McDonald's Ottumwa, the corporate plaintiff here, to operate the business. The contract to which Martino and the defendants were parties provided that neither Martino nor a member of his immediate family would acquire a financial interest in a competing self-service food business without the written consent of McDonald's System and FRIC. In 1968 Martino's son purchased a Burger Chef franchise in Pittsburg, Kansas. Martino financed this transaction.

On the basis of this transaction FRIC and McDonald's System brought a federal diversity action in Iowa against Martino and his three brothers, charging that Martino had violated the contract provision restricting acquisitions described above. This lawsuit, commenced in 1972, ended in 1973 with a consent judgment to which the district court appended findings of fact and conclusions of law. The court order also provided that the parties had entered an agreement for the sale of McDonald's Ottumwa franchise to FRIC for $140,000. The sale was completed according to the terms of the agreement. Martino's brothers later cancelled their stock in McDonald's Ottumwa, leaving Martino as the sole shareholder.

Martino and McDonald's Ottumwa brought this action in 1975. Count I of their complaint alleges that the enforcement of the restriction on acquisition in the franchise and lease agreements violated Section 1 of the Sherman Act, 15 U.S.C. § 1. As a basis for damages, Martino claims profits he would have earned as owner of the McDonald's franchise. Both plaintiffs claim damages for having had to sell the franchise, allegedly below its market value.

The defendants have presented two theories for barring Count I of the plaintiffs' antitrust complaint. The first theory is based on the preclusive effect of Fed. R. Civ. P. 13(a), applying to compulsory counterclaims. The second theory is based on the principle of res judicata. We shall now consider the merits of each theory.

The defendants argue that the district court correctly held that Count I is precluded by Fed. R. Civ. P. 13(a). Claims coming within the definition of "compulsory counterclaim" are lost if not raised at the proper time. Baker v. Gold Seal Liquors, Inc., 417 U.S. 467, 469 n.1 (1974); Fagnan v. Great Central Insurance Co., 577 F.2d 418 (7th Cir.), *cert. denied,* 439 U.S. 1004 (1978). According to the defendants, Rule 13(a) required Martino to raise this antitrust challenge to the contract provision in the earlier suit based on the same provision. If Rule 13(a) were applicable to these facts, the defendants' argument might have merit. Rule 13(a), however, by its own terms does not apply unless there has been some form of pleading.

The rule expressly says that "a *pleading* shall state as a counterclaim any claim which at the time of serving the *pleading* the *pleader* has against any opposing party. . . ." (Emphasis added.) In the prior Iowa action at issue here, Martino filed no pleading as the word is defined in Fed. R. Civ. P. 7(a). For this reason, Martino argues that we must not apply Rule 13(a) to the claim stated in Count I of his complaint. We agree.

Rule 13(a) is in some ways a harsh rule. It forces parties to raise certain claims at the time and place chosen by their opponents, or to lose them. The rule, however, is the result of a balancing between competing interests. The convenience of the party with a compulsory counterclaim is sacrificed in the interest of judicial economy. See Southern Construction Co. v. Pickard, 371 U.S. 57 (1962); Dindo v. Whitney, 451 F.2d 1, 3 (1st Cir. 1971). We do not believe that the drafters of Rule 13 chose the term "pleading" unadvisedly. It no doubt marks, although somewhat arbitrarily, a point at which the judicial burden of the earlier lawsuit outweighs the opposing party's interest in bringing an action when and where it is most convenient. The earlier action between these parties was terminated by a consent judgment before the answer was filed. We see little sense in applying the broad bar established in Rule 13(a) to an action that ended with virtually no burden on the judicial calendar.

McDonald's System and FRIC emphasize, however, that the deadline for filing the answer in the earlier action had passed[5] and that Rule 13(a) should therefore apply regardless of the absence of a responsive pleading. Citing as support several cases construing rules similar to Rule 13(a), . . . McDonald's System and FRIC argue that to hold otherwise is to reward noncompliance with the Federal Rules. We believe that this argument exaggerates the effect of not applying Rule 13(a). The Rules themselves provide for default judgments against a party for failure to plead, Fed. R. Civ. P. 55, and the effect of such a judgment as res judicata . . . prevents the nonpleading party from profiting as the result of his noncompliance. . . .

Although Rule 13(a) does not dispose of Martino's antitrust claim, longstanding principles of res judicata establish a narrowly defined class of "common law compulsory counterclaims." . . . We hold that the antitrust claim set forth in Count I of Martino's complaint falls within this narrow class of claims and that the res judicata effect of the earlier consent judgment is a bar to raising it now.

The principle of res judicata at issue here treats a judgment on the merits as an absolute bar to relitigation between the parties and those in privity with them of every matter offered and received to sustain or defeat the claim or demand and to every matter which might have been received for that purpose. Commissioner v. Sunnen, 333 U.S. 591, 597 (1948); Chicot County Drainage District v. Baxter State Bank, 308 U.S. 371, 375 (1940); Cromwell v. County of Sac, 94 U.S. 351, 352 (1876).

The conclusion of the earlier contract lawsuit with a consent judgment does not prevent the earlier judgment from having a res judicata effect. . . . The plaintiffs argue that the former judgment has no res judicata effect

---

5. Almost immediately after the complaint was filed, the parties entered into settlement negotiations. The resulting consent judgment was entered before Martino filed an answer.

because the parties did not sign mutual releases. We recognize that if a consent decree is expressly entered without prejudice or reserving rights the decree will not have a preclusive effect. . . . The mere absence of releases, however, is insufficient to indicate the unambiguous intent of the parties to counteract what would otherwise be the preclusive effect of the judgment. Although the earlier judgment at issue here was entered pursuant to the agreement of the parties, it was accompanied by judicial findings of fact and conclusions of law that go to the merits of the controversy. The court described Martino's actions as "a material breach of the agreements sufficient to justify termination."[8] The trial "court is not properly a recorder of contracts, but is an organ of government constituted to make judicial decisions and when it has rendered a consent judgment it has made an adjudication." 1B Moore's Federal Practice ¶ 0.409[5] at 1030 (2d ed. 1974).

Having determined that the prior consent judgment is an adjudication on the merits, we conclude that this judgment precludes Count I of this antitrust action. As a predicate for our discussion of the res judicata effect of the prior judgment we turn to the basis of Martino's present antitrust claim.

The gravamen of Count I of Martino's antitrust complaint is the 1973 lawsuit. In paragraph 12 of Count I, the complaint describes the 1973 lawsuit seeking termination of the franchise. Paragraph 13 continues, describing the personal pressures on Martino to settle the suit.[9] Paragraph 15 alleges that

> By enforcing the provisions of the franchise agreement and the sublease that prohibited the acquisition of any financial interest in a non-McDonald's self-service food and beverage establishment against plaintiffs, defendants discouraged competition and unreasonably restrained trade and commerce in violation of Section 1 of the Sherman Act (15 U.S.C. § 1).

Paragraph 16 concludes Count I, alleging that Martino lost profits he would have earned as owner of the McDonald's franchise and that Martino was forced to sell the franchise at below its market value.

It is impossible to interpret this count as anything but a direct challenge to the outcome of the 1973 lawsuit. The 1973 lawsuit concluded that termination was justified. The plaintiff now contends that termination was not justified, because the federal antitrust laws forbade it. If Martino's antitrust

---

8. The court held that "the defendant, Louis J. Martino, or a member of his immediate family, has violated the terms of the sublease and the franchise agreement by engaging in a business in which food and beverages are dispensed other than [at] the location covered by the agreements without the prior consent of Franchise Realty or McDonald's System, and that such action constitutes a material breach of agreement sufficient to justify termination."

9. The personal pressures were not attributable to the defendants but were in part from his brothers who owned other McDonald's franchises which they feared might be jeopardized by fighting the lawsuit and in part from the recent death of his wife.

theory had merit, it would have been a defense in 1973, changing the outcome of the litigation. Milsen Company v. Southland Corporation, 454 F.2d 363 (7th Cir. 1971).

The well-settled rule for the purpose of determining the res judicata effect of a judgment is that a "cause of action" comprises defenses, such as the alleged antitrust violation here, that were or might have been raised. As the Supreme Court said long ago:

> [A judgment on the merits] is a finality as to the claim or demand in controversy, concluding parties, and those in privity with them, not only as to every matter which was offered and received to sustain or defeat the claim or demand, but as to any other admissible matter which might have been offered for that purpose. Thus, for example, a judgment rendered on a promissory note is conclusive as to the validity of the instrument and the amount due upon it, although it be subsequently alleged that perfect defenses actually existed, of which no proof was offered, such as forgery, want of consideration, or payment. If such defenses were not presented in the action, and established by competent evidence, *the subsequent allegation of their existence is of no consequence.* [Cromwell v. County of Sac, 94 U.S. 351, 352 (1876) (emphasis added). See Chicot County Drainage District v. Baxter State Bank, 308 U.S. 371, 375 (1940); Lambert v. Conrad, 536 F.2d 1183, 1185 (7th Cir. 1976).]

Because the alleged antitrust violation constitutes a separate ground for recovery as well as a defense to the suit to terminate the franchise, however, Martino argues that Count I of this action constitutes a different "cause of action" for the purpose of res judicata and that the prior judgment does not preclude relitigation of the defendants' termination rights under the antitrust laws. For cases like this one, to which Rule 13(a) is inapplicable, Martino's argument correctly states the general rule. When facts form the basis of both a defense and a counterclaim, the defendant's failure to allege these facts as a defense or a counterclaim "does not preclude him from relying on those facts in an action subsequently brought by him against the plaintiff." . . . Virginia-Carolina Chemical Co. v. Kirven, 215 U.S. 252 (1909); [Austin Wakeman] Scott, Collateral Estoppel by Judgment, 56 Harv. L. Rev. 1, 27 (1942). The logic of this rule in circumstances not subject to Rule 13(a) is manifest. Should the earlier litigation end in its very first stage, no great burden on the courts results from permitting a counterclaim to be raised at a more convenient time and place. Notions of judicial economy give way to fairness. The defendant in the earlier action has his day in court when and where he sees fit.

The rule is not absolute, however. Both precedent and policy require that res judicata bar a counterclaim when its prosecution would nullify rights established by the prior action. Judicial economy is not the only basis for the doctrine of res judicata. Res judicata also preserves the integrity of judgments and protects those who rely on them. McDonald's System and FRIC have terminated and repurchased Martino's franchise in reliance on the trial court's 1973 judgment telling them they were justified in doing so. Now Martino seeks to impose significant financial liability on the defendants for these actions. We cannot hold that the counterclaim exception to the res judicata rule, based merely on notions of convenience, permits the plaintiff here to wage this direct attack on the rights established by the prior judgment.

A comparison between two Supreme Court decisions illustrates the rule and the exception to the rule we have discussed. In Chicot County Drainage District v. Baxter State Bank, 308 U.S. 371 (1940), a case similar in relevant respects to the one before us, the Supreme Court applied res judicata to preclude a claim. In *Chicot County* the Court held that a judgment effecting a plan of readjustment of indebtedness, resulting in a cancellation of certain bonds, precluded a subsequent suit on the same bonds. The subsequent suit on the bonds alleged the unconstitutionality of the 1934 Readjustment Act which was the basis of the prior action. Although the question of constitutionality in *Chicot County,* like the antitrust issue here, was not actually litigated in the earlier action, and although the suit to recover on the bonds, like the antitrust claim here, was a different cause of action, the Supreme Court applied the principle of res judicata to bar the second action. . . .

. . . In contrast, in Virginia-Carolina Chemical Co. v. Kirven, 215 U.S. 252 (1909), a purchaser sued for damages to his crops caused by the defendant's fertilizer. The defendant chemical company argued that its earlier successful suit against the purchaser for the price was a bar to the present suit. The Supreme Court held that the purchaser was entitled to bring the action for damages, drawing a distinction between claims which is crucial to the result in this case. A claim for crop damage in the earlier action for the purchase price would merely have effected a set-off to the Chemical Company's recovery of the purchase price. The claim for crop damage "[did not] go to the validity of the [Chemical Company's] demand [for the price] in its inception . . . such as . . . forgery, want of consideration, or payment." 215 U.S. at 257. Concluding that Martino's claim set forth in Count I of his complaint is a direct attack on the termination rights established in the earlier judgment, we hold that Martino is barred from raising that claim. . . .

Accordingly, the judgment of the district court is *affirmed.* . . .

### d. Sources of Preclusion Law

Claim and issue preclusion law is judge-made. Rules and cases vary from jurisdiction to jurisdiction. Since it is considered substantive on the whole, rather than procedural, federal courts follow state law on this matter in diversity actions.

But procedural rules about whether claims are compulsory or not may enter the picture, and federal courts follow their own rules about what is a compulsory counterclaim while taking into account the possible claim-preclusive effects of their decisions on joinder.

Though there are many cases on both issue and claim preclusion, and both doctrines arise often in practice, the major source of the law is the Restatement of Judgments, major excerpts of which appear below. Produced by the American Law Institute, a group of distinguished lawyers and judges, the Restatement is an influential document often followed by both courts and legislators.

## Restatement (Second) of Judgments
§§ 17-29, 86-87

### § 17. Effects of Former Adjudication—General Rules

A valid and final personal judgment is conclusive between the parties, except on appeal or other direct review, to the following extent:

(1) If the judgment is in favor of the plaintiff, the claim is extinguished and merged in the judgment and a new claim may arise on the judgment (see § 18);

(2) If the judgment is in favor of the defendant, the claim is extinguished and the judgment bars a subsequent action on that claim (see § 19);

(3) A judgment in favor of either the plaintiff or the defendant is conclusive, in a subsequent action between them on the same or a different claim, with respect to any issue actually litigated and determined if its determination was essential to that judgment (see § 27).

### § 18. Judgment for Plaintiff—The General Rule of Merger

When a valid and final personal judgment is rendered in favor of the plaintiff:

(1) The plaintiff cannot thereafter maintain an action on the original claim or any part thereof, although he may be able to maintain an action upon the judgment; and

(2) In an action upon the judgment, the defendant cannot avail himself of defenses he might have interposed, or did interpose, in the first action.

### § 19. Judgment for Defendant—The General Rule of Bar

A valid and final personal judgment rendered in favor of the defendant bars another action by the plaintiff on the same claim.

### § 20. Judgment for Defendant—Exceptions to the General Rule of Bar

(1) A personal judgment for the defendant, although valid and final, does not bar another action by the plaintiff on the same claim:

(a) When the judgment is one of dismissal for lack of jurisdiction, for improper venue, or for nonjoinder or misjoinder of parties; or

(b) When the plaintiff agrees to or elects a nonsuit (or voluntary dismissal) without prejudice or the court directs that the plaintiff be nonsuited (or that the action be otherwise dismissed) without prejudice; or

(c) When by statute or rule of court the judgment does not operate as a bar to another action on the same claim, or does not so operate unless the court specifies, and no such specification is made.

(2) A valid and final personal judgment for the defendant, which rests on the prematurity of the action or on the plaintiff's failure to satisfy a precondition to suit, does not bar another action by the plaintiff instituted after the claim has matured, or the precondition has been satisfied, unless a second action is precluded by operation of the substantive law.

## § 21. Judgment for Defendant on His Counterclaim

(1) Where the defendant interposes a counterclaim on which judgment is rendered in his favor, the rules of merger are applicable to the claim stated in the counterclaim, except as stated in Subsection (2).

(2) Where judgment on a counterclaim is rendered in favor of the defendant, but he is unable to obtain full recovery in the action because of the inability of the court to render such a judgment and the unavailability of such devices as removal to another court or consolidation with another action in the same court, the defendant is not precluded from subsequently maintaining an action for the balance due on the claim stated in the counterclaim.

## § 22. Effect of Failure to Interpose Counterclaim

(1) Where the defendant may interpose a claim as a counterclaim but he fails to do so, he is not thereby precluded from subsequently maintaining an action on that claim, except as stated in Subsection (2).

(2) A defendant who may interpose a claim as a counterclaim in an action but fails to do so is precluded, after the rendition of judgment in that action, from maintaining an action on the claim if:

(a) The counterclaim is required to be interposed by a compulsory counterclaim statute or rule of court, or

(b) The relationship between the counterclaim and the plaintiff's claim is such that successful prosecution of the second action would nullify the initial judgment or would impair rights established in the initial action.

## § 23. Judgment for Plaintiff on Defendant's Counterclaim

Where the defendant interposes a claim as a counterclaim and a valid and final judgment is rendered against him on the counterclaim, the rules of bar are applicable to the judgment.

## § 24. Dimensions of "Claim" for Purposes of Merger or Bar—General Rule Concerning "Splitting"

(1) When a valid and final judgment rendered in an action extinguishes the plaintiff's claim pursuant to the rules of merger or bar (see §§ 18, 19), the claim extinguished includes all rights of the plaintiff to remedies against the defendant with respect to all or any part of the transaction, or series of connected transactions, out of which the action arose.

(2) What factual grouping constitutes a "transaction," and what groupings constitute a "series," are to be determined pragmatically, giving weight to such considerations as whether the facts are related in time, space, origin, or motivation, whether they form a convenient trial unit, and whether their treatment as a unit conforms to the parties' expectations or business understanding or usage.

## § 25. Exemplifications of General Rule Concerning Splitting

The rule of § 24 applies to extinguish a claim by the plaintiff against the defendant even though the plaintiff is prepared in the second action

(1) To present evidence or grounds or theories of the case not presented in the first action, or

(2) To seek remedies or forms of relief not demanded in the first action.

## § 26. Exceptions to the General Rule Concerning Splitting

(1) When any of the following circumstances exists, the general rule of § 24 does not apply to extinguish the claim, and part or all of the claim subsists as a possible basis for a second action by the plaintiff against the defendant:

(a) The parties have agreed in terms or in effect that the plaintiff may split his claim, or the defendant has acquiesced therein; or

(b) The court in the first action has expressly reserved the plaintiff's right to maintain the second action; or

(c) The plaintiff was unable to rely on a certain theory of the case or to seek a certain remedy or form of relief in the first action because of the limitations on the subject matter jurisdiction of the courts or restrictions on their authority to entertain multiple theories or demands for multiple remedies or forms of relief in a single action, and the plaintiff desires in the second action to rely on that theory or to seek that remedy or form of relief; or

(d) The judgment in the first action was plainly inconsistent with the fair and equitable implementation of a statutory or constitutional scheme, or it is the sense of the scheme that the plaintiff should be permitted to split his claim; or

(e) For reasons of substantive policy in a case involving a continuing or recurrent wrong, the plaintiff is given an option to sue once for the total harm, both past and prospective, or to sue from time to time for the damages incurred to the date of suit, and chooses the latter course; or

(f) It is clearly and convincingly shown that the policies favoring preclusion of a second action are overcome for an extraordinary reason, such as the apparent invalidity of a continuing restraint or condition having a vital relation to personal liberty or the failure of the prior litigation to yield a coherent disposition of the controversy.

## § 27. Issue Preclusion — General Rule

When an issue of fact or law is actually litigated and determined by a valid and final judgment, and the determination is essential to the judgment, the determination is conclusive in a subsequent action between the parties, whether on the same or a different claim.

## § 28. Exceptions to the General Rule of Issue Preclusion

Although an issue is actually litigated and determined by a valid and final judgment, and the determination is essential to the judgment, relitigation of the issue in a subsequent action between the parties is not precluded in the following circumstances:

(1) The party against whom preclusion is sought could not, as a matter of law, have obtained review of the judgment in the initial action; or

(2) The issue is one of law and (a) the two actions involve claims that are substantially unrelated, or (b) a new determination is warranted in order to take account of an intervening change in the applicable legal context or otherwise to avoid inequitable administration of the laws; or

(3) A new determination of the issue is warranted by differences in the quality or extensiveness of the procedures followed in the two courts or by factors relating to the allocation of jurisdiction between them; or

(4) The party against whom preclusion is sought had a significantly heavier burden of persuasion with respect to the issue in the initial action than in the subsequent action; the burden has shifted to his adversary; or the adversary has a significantly heavier burden than he had in the first action; or

(5) There is a clear and convincing need for a new determination of the issue (a) because of the potential adverse impact of the determination on the public interest or the interests of persons not themselves parties in the initial action, (b) because it was not sufficiently foreseeable at the time of the initial action that the issue would arise in the context of a subsequent action, or (c) because the party sought to be precluded, as a result of the conduct of his adversary or other special circumstances, did not have an adequate opportunity or incentive to obtain a full and fair adjudication in the initial action.

## § 29. Issue Preclusion in Subsequent Litigation with Others

A party precluded from relitigating an issue with an opposing party, in accordance with §§ 27 and 28, is also precluded from doing so with another person unless the fact that he lacked full and fair opportunity to litigate the issue in the first action or other circumstances justify [sic] affording him an opportunity to relitigate the issue. The circumstances to which considerations should be given include those enumerated in § 28 and also whether:

(1) Treating the issue as conclusively determined would be incompatible with an applicable scheme of administering the remedies in the actions involved;

(2) The forum in the second action affords the party against whom preclusion is asserted procedural opportunities in the presentation and determination of the issue that were not available in the first action and could likely result in the issue being differently determined;

(3) The person seeking to invoke favorable preclusion, or to avoid unfavorable preclusion, could have effected joinder in the first action between himself and his present adversary;

(4) The determination relied on as preclusive was itself inconsistent with another determination of the same issue;

(5) The prior determination may have been affected by relationships among the parties to the first action that are not present in the subsequent action, or apparently was based on a compromise verdict or finding;

(6) Treating the issue as conclusively determined may complicate determination of issues in the subsequent action or prejudice the interests of another party thereto;

(7) The issue is one of law and treating it as conclusively determined would inappropriately foreclose opportunity for obtaining reconsideration of the legal rule upon which it was based;

(8) Other compelling circumstances make it appropriate that the party be permitted to relitigate the issue.


## § 86. Effect of State Court Judgment in a Subsequent Action in Federal Court

A valid and final judgment of a state court has the same effects under the rules of res judicata in a subsequent action in a federal court that the judgment has by the law of the state in which the judgment was rendered, except that:

(1) An adjudication of a claim in a state court does not preclude litigation in a federal court of a related federal claim based on the same transaction if the federal claim arises under a scheme of federal remedies which contemplates that the federal claim may be asserted notwithstanding the adjudication in state court; and

(2) A determination of an issue by a state court does not preclude relitigation of that issue in federal court if according preclusive effect

to the determination would be incompatible with a scheme of federal remedies which contemplates that the federal court may make an independent determination of the issue in question.

### § 87. Effect of Federal Court Judgment in a Subsequent Action

Federal law determines the effects under the rules of res judicata of a judgment of a federal court.

---

## *Notes and Questions*

1. *Raise It or Waive It.* Given the principles of claim preclusion, the merger of law and equity, the expansion of federal courts' supplemental jurisdiction, and the liberal joinder of parties and claims now permitted by the Federal Rules of Civil Procedure and most states' rules of procedure, the most prudent step for trial lawyers is to raise anything in the first litigation that arguably may be deemed res judicata in a second litigation, or risk being precluded from asserting the matter. As was true with counterclaims that are arguably compulsory, the safest course is to raise it, lest you waive it. The trial judge then may exercise discretion to sever some matters and try them separately, if warranted. See Fed. R. Civ. P. 42(b).

2. *Mechanics of Preclusion.* By what procedural move does a party raise the issues of claim or issue preclusion? See Rule 8(c). Can it be waived? If it can, how does the doctrine promote judicial efficiency, versus the parties' interest in repose?

3. *Defining "Same Claim."* Determining what constitutes one "claim" for purposes of claim preclusion can be quite difficult. Different tests have been proposed—such as the same cause of action test, the same evidence test, and the same transaction or occurrence test—yet none is entirely satisfactory or workable in all cases. As was true with joinder and subject matter jurisdiction, the key seems to be transactional relatedness such that matters that logically belong together should be tried together. The test inevitably must consider context, and thus cannot avoid the fuzziness and flexibility that seem to undermine the parties' interest in predictability. As the Ninth Circuit has described its approach:

> We have long recognized the flexibility inherent in the res judicata determination with respect to identity of claims. See Costantini v. Trans World Airlines, 681 F.2d 1199, 1202 n.7 (9th Cir. 1982) ("[I]dentity of causes of action cannot be determined precisely by mechanistic application of a simple test"). To decide identity of claims, we have applied four criteria: "(1) whether rights or interests established in the prior judgment would be destroyed or impaired by prosecution of the second action; (2) whether

substantially the same evidence is presented in the two actions; (3) whether the two suits involve infringement of the same right; and (4) whether the two suits arise out of the same transactional nucleus of facts." Id. at 1201-1202. The fourth criterion—the same transactional nucleus of facts—is the most important.

United States v. Liquidators of European Federal Credit Bank, 630 F.3d 1139, 1150-1151 (9th Cir. 2011) (citations omitted) (internal quotation marks omitted). See also Whole Woman's Health v. Hellerstedt, 136 S. Ct. 2292, 2305 (2016) (litigation of as-applied challenge to Texas restrictions on admitting privileges at abortion clinics is not barred where several plaintiffs had previously brought facial challenge prior to the enforcement of the restrictions; "where 'important human values—such as the lawfulness of continuing personal disability or restraint—are at stake, even a slight change of circumstances may afford a sufficient basis for concluding that a second action may be brought.'") (quoting Restatement (Second) of Judgments § 24 cmt. f).

4. *Defining "On the Merits."* Reread Restatement (Second) of Judgments § 20. This section summarizes courts' general approach to determinations of whether a prior judgment was "on the merits" or addressed only a threshold issue that should not bar relitigation. Reconsider the various procedural objections that a defendant can assert under Rule 12 in a pre-answer motion to dismiss. Which of these would bar a plaintiff from relitigating the same claim in a different forum? Which would not? What about a default judgment? Voluntary dismissal after an out of court settlement? A consent judgment? See Jack H. Friedenthal, Mary Kay Kane, and Arthur R. Miller, Civil Procedure 667-673 (4th ed. 2005). See also Semtek Int'l Inc. v. Lockheed Martin Corp., 531 U.S. 497 (2001) (adjudication "on the merits" in Rule 41(b) does not necessarily mean that the judgment has claim-preclusive effect; dismissal "with prejudice" on statute of limitations grounds bars refiling in federal court, but it may or may not preclude relitigation in another forum); Legnani v. Alitalia Linee Aeree Italiane S.p.A., 400 F.3d 139 (2d Cir. 2005) (res judicata does not bar a second action concerning a transaction that occurred after the commencement of the first litigation; failed attempt to add the claim to the first action is without consequence); Styskal v. Weld Cty. Bd. of Cty. Comm'rs, 365 F.3d 855, 859 (10th Cir. 2004) (dismissal with prejudice for want of supplemental jurisdiction over state law claims under 28 U.S.C. § 1367 bars refiling in federal court: "The state court's decision regarding whether claim preclusion prevents a state lawsuit will depend upon the basis of the federal court's dismissal, not the nomenclature employed by the federal court to describe the dismissal."), distinguished in Brereton v. Bountiful City Corp., 434 F.3d 1213, 1218 (10th Cir. 2006) ("*Styskal* . . . could not have and did not purport to overrule our prior, long-standing line of cases requiring that a dismissal for lack of jurisdiction be without prejudice. We read *Styskal* only to say that where a federal court erroneously dismisses 'with prejudice' a claim over which it lacks jurisdiction, a state court need not be blinded by this nomenclature into barring a subsequent action on the same claim that is properly brought within its jurisdiction.").

5. *Contract Issues and Claim Preclusion.* Claim preclusion in contract matters operates under the general principle that one contract will support only one cause of action. See, e.g., Pakas v. Hollingshead, 77 N.E. 40 (N.Y. 1906). When the contract is an installment contract, however, then the contract is considered severally, such that breach of one installment does not necessarily breach the whole contract. See Uniform Commercial Code § 2-612(3). Courts nevertheless have developed the rule that a party who sues for breach of an installment contract must raise (or waive) all claims that arose before the time that the suit is brought. Thus, if a party to an installment contract brings suit after unsatisfactory performance of the first installment, she is still free to sue for any subsequent installments that are unsatisfactory. But if she sues on the fifth installment but fails to raise any complaints about the first four installments, she waives these claims.

## 2.  Issue Preclusion

### Problem Case: Using a Friendly Decision

Bob Hesse recently was fired from his management job at ABC Photos, Inc., a corporation that provides driver's license image machines to state agencies. The reason for his termination was that Hesse, along with other corporate officials, was responsible for alleged questionable financial dealings by the corporation.

Hesse filed an arbitration proceeding against the company, claiming that his termination violated the employment agreement with ABC. ABC filed a complaint in the state district court to stay the arbitration proceedings on the ground that there was no employment agreement. In response to the state court action, Hesse filed a motion for partial summary judgment, alleging that ABC was estopped from relitigating the existence of an employment agreement, given a recent decision against ABC in the federal district court. The federal court action was filed by a fellow management employee, Adrian Spears. In that suit, one of the issues litigated was the existence of an employment agreement that entitled Spears to executive retirement plan benefits, unreimbursed expenses, and stock funds. The federal court concluded there was such an agreement. Hesse testified in the action, but was not a party in it. The federal case is now on appeal.

Can Hesse invoke this prior federal court judgment against ABC to bar relitigation of the employment agreement issue in the state court action? Should the federal court judgment have any stare decisis effect in the state court action? For a case based on similar facts, see Tofany v. NBS Imaging Systems, Inc., 616 N.E.2d 1034 (Ind. 1993).

### a.  In General

Issue preclusion, also called "collateral estoppel," prevents a party who has had a full and fair opportunity to litigate a question from relitigating the same matter. This branch of preclusion law applies *only* to issues that were actually litigated and determined in the first lawsuit, *not* matters that could have been raised but were not.

Thus, if a defendant chooses to assert a cross-claim against a codefendant (which she is not required to do under any pleading or procedural rules), then the defendant is bound by the outcome on the issue and cannot raise it in a subsequent suit.

Unlike claim preclusion, issue preclusion does not require that the claim in the first suit be the same as that asserted in the second suit.

Rather, the conditions of issue preclusion, generally stated, are as follows: 1) An issue of fact that 2) was actually litigated, and that was afforded 3) a full and fair opportunity to be litigated, received 4) a final and valid judgment, and 5) the issue to be precluded was essential to that judgment.

Issue preclusion can be asserted defensively or offensively. Defensive collateral estoppel occurs when a defendant asserts estoppel to prevent a plaintiff from relitigating issues. Offensive collateral estoppel occurs when a plaintiff uses it against a defendant to prevent relitigation of issues.

## Examples

a) Assume that *P* sues *D* claiming that *D*'s product infringes her patent. The court decides that *P*'s patent is invalid. If *P* later sues *D*(2) claiming that *D*(2)'s product infringes the same patent, then *D*(2) would invoke *defensive collateral estoppel (issue preclusion)*.

b) Assume that *P* sues *D*, claiming *D*'s mass-produced product is defective and that *D* knew of the defect. *P* wins. If *P*(2) now sues *D*, making the same claims and invoking the prior determination of the issue of knowledge against *D*, *this is offensive collateral estoppel (issue preclusion)*.

### Commissioner of Internal Revenue v. Sunnen
333 U.S. 591 (1948)

[Respondent taxpayer made gifts to his wife of various patent license contracts during the years 1937-1941. The Tax Court held that, with one exception, all the royalties paid to the wife during those years were part of the taxpayer's taxable income. The one exception involved royalties paid in 1937 under a 1928 contract. In an earlier proceeding, the Board of Tax Appeals had concluded Sunnen could not be taxed on the royalties he had received during the years 1929-1931 on the 1928 contract. This determination led the Tax Court to apply res judicata to bar a different result for the royalties received in 1937 on the same contract.—EDS.]

Opinion of the Court by JUSTICE MURPHY. . . .

Relying upon its own prior decision in Estate of Dodson v. Commissioner, 1 T.C. 416 [(1943)], the Tax Court held that, with one exception, all the royalties paid to the wife from 1937 to 1941 were part of the taxable income of the taxpayer. 6 T.C. 431. The one exception concerned the royalties of $4,881.35 paid in 1937 under the 1928 agreement. In an earlier proceeding in 1935, the Board of Tax Appeals dealt with the taxpayer's income tax liability for the years 1929-1931; it concluded that he was not taxable on the royalties paid to his wife during those years under the 1928 license agreement. This prior determination by the Board caused the Tax Court to apply the principle of res judicata to bar a different result as to the royalties paid pursuant to the same agreement during 1937.

The Tax Court's decision was affirmed in part and reversed in part by the Eighth Circuit Court of Appeals, 161 F.2d 171 [(8th Cir. 1947)]. . . .

We then brought the case here on certiorari. . . .

If the doctrine of res judicata is properly applicable so that all the royalty payments made during 1937-1941 are governed by the prior decision of the Board of Tax Appeals, the case may be disposed of without reaching the merits of the controversy. We accordingly cast our attention initially on that possibility, one that has been explored by the Tax Court and that has been fully argued by the parties before us.

It is first necessary to understand something of the recognized meaning and scope of res judicata, a doctrine judicial in origin. The general rule of res judicata applies to repetitious suits involving the same cause of action. It rests upon considerations of economy of judicial time and public policy favoring the establishment of certainty in legal relations. The rule provides that when a court of competent jurisdiction has entered a final judgment on the merits of a cause of action, the parties to the suit and their privies are thereafter bound "not only as to every matter which was offered and received to sustain or defeat the claim or demand, but as to any other admissible matter which might have been offered for that purpose." Cromwell v. County of Sac, 94 U.S. 351, 352 [(1876)]. The judgment puts an end to the cause of action, which cannot again be brought into litigation between the parties upon any ground whatever, absent fraud or some other factor invalidating the judgment. . . .

But where the second action between the same parties is upon a different cause or demand, the principle of res judicata is applied much more narrowly. In this situation, the judgment in the prior action operates as an estoppel, not as to matters which might have been litigated and determined, but "only as to those matters in issue or points controverted, upon the determination of which the finding or verdict was rendered." Cromwell v. County of Sac, supra, [94 U.S. at] 353. . . . Since the cause of action involved in the second proceeding is not swallowed by the judgment in the prior suit, the parties are free to litigate points which were not at issue in the first proceeding, even though such points might have been tendered and decided at that time. But matters which were actually litigated and determined in the first proceeding cannot later be relitigated. Once a party has fought out a matter in litigation with the other party, he cannot later renew that duel. In this sense, res judicata is usually and more accurately referred to as estoppel by judgment, or collateral estoppel. . . .

These same concepts are applicable in the federal income tax field. Income taxes are levied on an annual basis. Each year is the origin of a new liability and of a separate cause of action. Thus if a claim of liability or nonliability relating to a particular tax year is litigated, a judgment on the merits is res judicata as to any subsequent proceeding involving the same claim and the same tax year. But if the later proceeding is concerned with a similar or unlike claim relating to a different tax year, the prior judgment acts as a collateral estoppel only as to those matters in the second proceeding which were actually presented and determined in the first suit. Collateral estoppel operates, in other words, to relieve the government and the taxpayer of "redundant litigation of the identical question of the statute's application of the taxpayer's status." Tait v. Western Md. R. Co., 289 U.S. 620, 624 [(1933)]. . . .

It is readily apparent in this case that the royalty payments growing out of the license contracts which were not involved in the earlier action before the Board of Tax Appeals and which concerned different tax years are free from the effects of the collateral estoppel doctrine. That is true even though those contracts are identical in all important respects with the 1928 contract, the only one that was before the Board, and even though the issue as to those contracts is the same as that raised by the 1928 contract. For income tax purposes, what is decided as to one contract is not conclusive as to any other contract which is not then in issue, however similar or identical it may be. In this respect, the instant case thus differs vitally from Tait v. Western Md. R. Co., supra, where the two proceedings involved the same instruments and the same surroundings facts.

A more difficult problem is posed as to the $4,881.35 in royalties paid to the taxpayer's wife in 1937 under the 1928 contract. Here there is complete identity of facts, issues and parties as between the earlier Board proceeding and the instant one. The Commissioner claims, however, that legal principles developed in various intervening decisions of this Court have made plain the error of the Board's conclusion in the earlier proceeding, thus creating a situation like that involved in Blair v. Commissioner, [300 U.S. 5 (1937)]. This change in the legal picture is said to have been brought about by such cases as Helvering v. Clifford, 309 U.S. 331 [(1940)]; Helvering v. Horst, 311 U.S. 112 [(1940)]; Helvering v. Eubank, 311 U.S. 122 [(1940)]; Harrison v. Schaffner, 312 U.S. 579 [(1941)]; Commissioner v. Tower, 327 U.S. 280 [(1946)]; and Lusthaus v. Commissioner, 327 U.S. 293 [(1946)]. These cases all imposed income tax liability on transferors who had assigned or transferred various forms of income to others within their family groups, although none specifically related to the assignment of patent license contracts between members of the same family. It must therefore be determined whether this *Clifford-Horst* line of cases represents an intervening legal development which is pertinent to the problem raised by the assignment of the 1928 agreement and which makes manifest the error of the result reached in 1935 by the Board. If that is the situation, the doctrine of collateral estoppel becomes inapplicable. A different result is then permissible as to the royalties paid in 1937 under the agreement in question. . . .

. . . True, [the *Clifford-Horst*] cases did not originate the concept that an assignor is taxable if he retains control over the assigned property or power to defeat the receipt of income by the assignee. But they gave much added emphasis and substance to that concept, making it more suited to meet the "attenuated subtleties" created by taxpayers. So substantial was the amplification of this concept as to justify a reconsideration of earlier Tax Court decisions reached without the benefit of the expanded notions, decisions which are now sought to be perpetuated regardless of their present correctness. Thus in the earlier litigation in 1935, the Board of Tax Appeals was unable to bring to bear on the assignment of the 1928 contract the full breadth of the ideas enunciated in the *Clifford-Horst* series of cases. And . . . a proper application of the principles as there developed might well have produced a different result, such as was reached by the Tax Court in this case in regard to the assignments of the other contracts. Under those circumstances collateral estoppel should not have been used by the Tax Court in the instant proceeding to perpetuate the 1935 viewpoint of the assignment. . . .

. . . The transactions were simply a reallocation of income within the family group, a reallocation which did not shift the incidence of income tax liability.

The judgment below must therefore be reversed and the case remanded for such further proceedings as may be necessary in light of this opinion.

*Reversed.*

JUSTICE FRANKFURTER and JUSTICE JACKSON believe the judgment of the Tax Court is based on substantial evidence and is consistent with the law, and would affirm that judgment. . . .

## Allen v. McCurry
449 U.S. 90 (1980)

JUSTICE STEWART delivered the opinion of the Court. . . .

In April 1977, several undercover police officers, following an informant's tip that McCurry was dealing in heroin, went to his house in St. Louis, Mo., to attempt a purchase. Two officers, petitioners Allen and Jacobsmeyer, knocked on the front door, while the other officers hid nearby. When McCurry opened the door, the two officers asked to buy some heroin "caps." McCurry went back into the house and returned soon thereafter, firing a pistol at and seriously wounding Allen and Jacobsmeyer. After a gun battle with the other officers and their reinforcements, McCurry retreated into the house; he emerged again when the police demanded that he surrender. Several officers then entered the house without a warrant, purportedly to search for other persons inside. One of the officers seized drugs and other contraband that lay in plain view, as well as additional contraband he found in dresser drawers and in auto tires on the porch.

McCurry was charged with possession of heroin and assault with intent to kill. At the pretrial suppression hearing, the trial judge excluded the evidence seized from the dresser drawers and tires, but denied suppression of the evidence found in plain view. McCurry was convicted of both the heroin and assault offenses.

McCurry subsequently filed the present § 1983 action for $1 million in damages against petitioners Allen and Jacobsmeyer, other unnamed individual police officers, and the city of St. Louis and its police department. The complaint alleged a conspiracy to violate McCurry's Fourth Amendment rights, an unconstitutional search and seizure of his house, and an assault on him by unknown police officers after he had been arrested and handcuffed. The petitioners moved for summary judgment. The District Court apparently understood the gist of the complaint to be the allegedly unconstitutional search and seizure and granted summary judgment, holding that collateral estoppel prevented McCurry from relitigating the search and seizure question already decided against him in the state courts. [McCurry v. Allen,] 466 F. Supp. 514 (E.D. Mo. 1978).

The Court of Appeals reversed the judgment and remanded the case for trial. McCurry v. Allen, 606 F.2d 795 (8th Cir. 1979). . . .

This Court has never directly decided whether the rules of res judicata and collateral estoppel are generally applicable to § 1983 actions. But in Preiser v. Rodriguez, 411 U.S. 475, 497 [(1973)], the Court noted with implicit approval the view of other federal courts that res judicata principles fully apply to civil rights suits brought under that statute. . . . And the virtually unanimous view of the Court of Appeals since *Preiser* has been that § 1983 presents no categorical bar to the application of res judicata and collateral estoppel concepts. These federal appellate court decisions have spoken with little explanation or citation in assuming the compatibility of § 1983 and rules of preclusion, but the statute and its legislative history clearly support the courts' decisions.

Because the requirement of mutuality of estoppel was still alive in the federal courts until well into this century, see Blonder-Tongue Laboratories, Inc. v. University of Illinois Foundation, [402 U.S. 313] at 322-23 [(1971)],* the drafters of the 1871 Civil Rights Act, of which § 1983 is a part, may have had less reason to concern themselves with rules of preclusion than a modern Congress would. Nevertheless, in 1871 res judicata and collateral estoppel could certainly have applied in federal suits following state-court litigation between the same parties or their privies, and nothing in the language of § 1983 remotely expresses any congressional intent to contravene the common law rules of preclusion or to repeal the express statutory requirements

---

* [Mutuality of estoppel required that for a prior judgment to be determinative of an issue in current litigation, both parties must have been involved in the earlier suit. *Blonder-Tongue* severely undercut the doctrine of mutuality by holding that a defendant could raise collateral estoppel to a charge of patent infringement that was based on an earlier determination that the patent was invalid in a suit to which he was not a party. For a further discussion of the doctrine of mutuality, see Parklane Hosiery Co. v. Shore, 429 U.S. 322 (1979), infra.—Eds.]

of the predecessor of 28 U.S.C. § 1738. . . . Section 1983 creates a new federal cause of action. It says nothing about the preclusive effect of state-court judgments.

Moreover, the legislative history of § 1983 does not in any clear way suggest that Congress intended to repeal or restrict the traditional doctrines of preclusion. . . .

To the extent that it did intend to change the balance of power over federal questions between the state and federal courts, the 42d Congress was acting in a way thoroughly consistent with the doctrines of preclusion. . . .

The . . . basis of the Court of Appeals' holding appears to be a generally framed principle that every person asserting a federal right is entitled to one unencumbered opportunity to litigate that right in a federal district court, regardless of the legal posture in which the federal claim arises. But the authority for this principle is difficult to discern. It cannot lie in the Constitution, which makes no such guarantee, but leaves the scope of the jurisdiction of the federal district courts to the wisdom of Congress. And no such authority is to be found in § 1983 itself. For reasons already discussed at length, nothing in the language or legislative history of § 1983 proves any congressional intent to deny binding effect to a state court judgment or decision when the state court, acting within its proper jurisdiction, has given the parties a full and fair opportunity to litigate federal claims, and thereby has shown itself willing and able to protect federal rights. And nothing in the legislative history of § 1983 reveals any purpose to afford less deference to judgments in state criminal proceedings than to those in state civil proceedings. There is, in short, no reason to believe that Congress intended to provide a person claiming a federal right an unrestricted opportunity to relitigate an issue already decided in state court simply because the issue arose in a state proceeding in which he would rather not have been engaged at all.

Through § 1983, the 42d Congress intended to afford an opportunity for legal and equitable relief in a federal court for certain types of injuries. It is difficult to believe that the drafters of that Act considered it a substitute for a federal writ of habeas corpus, the purpose of which is not to redress civil injury, but to release the applicant from unlawful physical confinement. . . .

The only other conceivable basis for finding a universal right to litigate a federal claim in a federal district court is hardly a legal basis at all, but rather a general distrust of the capacity of the state courts to render correct decisions on constitutional issues. . . .

. . . Accordingly, the judgment is reversed, and the case is remanded to the Court of Appeals for proceedings consistent with this opinion.

*It is so ordered.*

JUSTICE BLACKMUN, with whom JUSTICE BRENNAN and JUSTICE MARSHALL join, dissenting. . . .

. . . The Court repeatedly has recognized that § 1983 embodies a strong congressional policy in favor of federal courts' acting as the primary and final arbiters of constitutional rights. In Monroe v. Pape, 365 U.S. 167 (1961), the Court held that Congress passed the legislation in order to substitute a federal forum for the ineffective, although plainly available, state remedies:

> It is abundantly clear that one reason the legislation was passed was to afford a federal right in federal courts because, by reason of prejudice, passion, neglect, intolerance or otherwise, state laws might not be enforced and the claims of citizens to the enjoyment of rights, privileges, and immunities guaranteed by the Fourteenth Amendment might be denied by the state agencies. [Id. at 180.]

. . . The Court's conclusion was that this remedy was to be available no matter what the circumstances of state law:

> It is no answer that the State has a law which if enforced would give relief. The federal remedy is supplementary to the state remedy, and the latter need not be first sought and refused before the federal one is invoked. Hence the fact that Illinois by its constitution and laws outlaws unreasonable searches and seizures is no barrier to the present suit in the federal court. [Id. at 183.] . . .

One should note also that in England v. Medical Examiners, 375 U.S. 411 (1964), the Court had affirmed the federal courts' special role in protecting constitutional rights under § 1983. In that case it held that a plaintiff required by the abstention doctrine to submit his constitutional claim first to a state court could not be precluded entirely from having the federal court, in which he initially had sought relief, pass on his constitutional claim. The Court relied on "the unqualified terms in which Congress, pursuant to constitutional authorization, has conferred specific categories of jurisdiction upon the federal courts," and on its "fundamental objections to any conclusion that a litigant who has properly invoked the jurisdiction of a federal district court to consider federal constitutional claims can be compelled, without his consent and through no fault of his own, to accept instead a state court's determination of those claims." Id. at 415. The Court set out its understanding as to when a litigant in a § 1983 case might be precluded by prior litigation, holding that

> if a party freely and without reservation submits his federal claims for decision by the state courts, litigates them there, and has them decided there, then — whether or not he seeks direct review of the state decision in this Court — he has elected to forgo his right to return to the District Court. [Id. at 419.]

I do not understand why the Court today should abandon this approach. . . .

In this case, the police officers seek to prevent a criminal defendant from relitigating the constitutionality of their conduct in searching his house, after the state trial court had found that conduct in part violative of the defendant's Fourth Amendment rights and in part justified by the circumstances. I doubt that the police officers, now defendants in the § 1983 action, can be considered to have been in privity with the State in its role as prosecutor. Therefore, only "issue preclusion" is at stake.

The following factors persuade me to conclude that this respondent should not be precluded from asserting his claim in federal court. First, at the time § 1983 was passed, a nonparty's ability, as a practical matter, to invoke collateral estoppel was nonexistent. One could not preclude an opponent from relitigating an issue in a new cause of action, though that issue had been determined conclusively in a prior proceeding, unless there was "mutuality." Additionally, the definitions of "cause of action" and "issue" were narrow. As a result, and obviously, no preclusive effect could arise out of a criminal proceeding that would affect subsequent *civil* litigation. Thus, the 42d Congress could not have anticipated or approved that a criminal defendant, tried and convicted in state court, would be precluded from raising against police officers a constitutional claim arising out of his arrest.

Also, the process of deciding in a state criminal trial whether to exclude or admit evidence is not at all the equivalent of a § 1983 proceeding. The remedy sought in the latter is utterly different. In bringing the civil suit the criminal defendant does not seek to challenge his conviction collaterally. At most, he wins damages. In contrast, the exclusion of evidence may prevent a criminal conviction. A trial court, faced with the decision whether to exclude relevant evidence, confronts institutional pressures that may cause it to give a different shape to the Fourth Amendment right from what would result in civil litigation of a damages claim. Also, the issue whether to exclude evidence is subsidiary to the purpose of a criminal trial, which is to determine the guilt or innocence of the defendant, and a trial court, at least subconsciously, must weigh the potential damage to the truth-seeking process caused by excluding relevant evidence. See Stone v. Powell, 428 U.S. 465, 489-495 (1976). . . .

A state criminal defendant cannot be held to have chosen "voluntarily" to litigate his Fourth Amendment claim in the state court. The risk of conviction puts pressure upon him to raise all possible defenses. He also faces uncertainty about the wisdom of forgoing litigation on *any* issue, for there is the possibility that he will be held to have waived his right to appeal on that issue. The "deliberate bypass" of state procedures, which the imposition of collateral estoppel under these circumstances encourages, surely is not a preferred goal. To hold that a criminal defendant who raises a Fourth Amendment claim at his criminal trial "freely and without reservation submits his federal claims for decision by the state courts," see England v. Medical Examiners, 375 U.S. at 419, is to deny reality. The criminal defendant is an involuntary litigant in the state tribunal, and against him all the forces of the State are arrayed. To force him to a choice between forgoing either a potential defense or a federal forum for hearing his constitutional civil claim is fundamentally unfair.

I would affirm the judgment of the Court of Appeals.

### b.   Mutuality of Estoppel

Mutuality is an old rule on its way out, though a few jurisdictions still follow it. Essentially, it says that no party can benefit from a judgment in which she was not also at risk. If she stood to lose nothing, she should likewise be unable to gain. Thus where *P*(2) sues a defendant who previously was found in a different lawsuit to have been liable, she would be invoking nonmutual offensive collateral estoppel. She was not a party to the original lawsuit, so could not be hurt by it. Likewise, a second defendant on the patent would be invoking nonmutual defensive estoppel.

Most courts would allow issue preclusion in both of these nonmutual examples. Mutuality requirements have been much relaxed over the years, especially in defensive estoppel cases.

Parklane Hosiery Co. v. Shore, 439 U.S. 322 (1979), is the leading federal case on offensive collateral estoppel. In brief, it holds that courts should weigh numerous factors in deciding whether issue preclusion is fair, and should not simply apply the old doctrines of mutuality.

## *Parklane Hosiery Co. v. Shore*
439 U.S. 322 (1979)

JUSTICE STEWART delivered the opinion of the Court.

This case presents the question whether a party who has had issues of fact adjudicated adversely to it in an equitable action may be collaterally estopped from relitigating the same issues before a jury in a subsequent legal action brought against it by a new party.

The respondent brought this stockholder's class action against the petitioners in a Federal District Court. The complaint alleged that the petitioners, Parklane Hosiery Co., Inc. (Parklane), and 13 of its officers, directors, and stockholders, had issued a materially false and misleading proxy statement in connection with a merger. The proxy statement, according to the complaint, had violated §§ 14(a), 10(b), and 20(a) of the Securities Exchange Act of 1934, 48 Stat. 895, 891, 899, as amended, 15 U.S.C. §§ 78n(a), 78j(b), and 78t(a), as well as various rules and regulations promulgated by the Securities and Exchange Commission (SEC). The complaint sought damages, rescission of the merger, and recovery of costs.

Before this action came to trial, the SEC filed suit against the same defendants in the Federal District Court, alleging that the proxy statement that had been issued by Parklane was materially false and misleading in essentially the same respects as those that had been alleged in the respondent's complaint. Injunctive relief was requested. After a four-day trial, the District Court found that the proxy statement was materially false and misleading in the respects alleged, and entered a declaratory judgment to that effect. SEC v. Parklane Hosiery Co., 422 F. Supp. 477 [(1976)]. The Court of Appeals for the Second Circuit affirmed this judgment. 558 F.2d 1083 [(1977)].

The respondent in the present case then moved for partial summary judgment against the petitioners, asserting that the petitioners were collaterally estopped from relitigating the issues that had been resolved against them in the action brought by the SEC. The District Court denied the motion on the ground that such an application of collateral estoppel would deny the petitioners their Seventh Amendment right to a jury trial. The Court of Appeals for the Second Circuit reversed. . . . [W]e granted certiorari, 435 U.S. 1006 [(1978)].

The threshold question to be considered is whether, quite apart from the right to a jury trial under the Seventh Amendment, the petitioners can be precluded from relitigating facts resolved adversely to them in a prior equitable proceeding with another party under the general law of collateral estoppel. Specifically, we must determine whether a litigant who was not a party to a prior judgment may nevertheless use that judgment "offensively" to prevent a defendant from relitigating issues resolved in the earlier proceeding.

Collateral estoppel, like the related doctrine of res judicata, has the dual purpose of protecting litigants from the burden of relitigating an identical issue with the same party or his privy and of promoting judicial economy by preventing needless litigation. Blonder-Tongue Laboratories, Inc. v. University of Illinois Foundation, 402 U.S. 313, 328-329 [(1971)]. Until relatively recently, however, the scope of collateral estoppel was limited by the doctrine of mutuality of parties. Under this mutuality doctrine, neither party could use a prior judgment as an estoppel against the other unless both parties were bound by the judgment. Based on the premise that it is somehow unfair to allow a party to use a prior judgment when he himself would not be so bound, the mutuality requirement provided a party who had litigated and lost in a previous action an opportunity to relitigate identical issues with new parties.

By failing to recognize the obvious difference in position between a party who has never litigated an issue and one who has fully litigated and lost, the mutuality requirement was criticized almost from its inception. Recognizing the validity of this criticism, the Court in Blonder-Tongue Laboratories, Inc. v. University of Illinois Foundation, supra, abandoned the mutuality requirement, at least in cases where a patentee seeks to relitigate the validity of a patent after a federal court in a previous lawsuit has already declared it invalid. The "broader question" before the Court, however, was "whether it is any longer tenable to afford a litigant more than one full and fair opportunity for judicial resolution of the same issue." 402 U.S. at 328. The Court strongly suggested a negative answer to that question:

> In any lawsuit where a defendant, because of the mutuality principle, is forced to present a complete defense on the merits to a claim which the plaintiff has fully litigated and lost in a prior action, there is an arguable misallocation of resources. To the extent the defendant in the second suit may not win by asserting, without contradiction, that the plaintiff had fully and fairly, but unsuccessfully, litigated the same claim in the prior suit, the

defendant's time and money are diverted from alternative uses—productive or otherwise—to relitigation of a decided issue. And, still assuming that the issue was resolved correctly in the first suit, there is reason to be concerned about the plaintiff's allocation of resources. Permitting repeated litigation of the same issue as long as the supply of unrelated defendants holds out reflects either the aura of the gaming table or "a lack of discipline and of disinterestedness on the part of the lower courts, hardly a worthy or wise basis for fashioning rules of procedure." Kerotest Mfg. Co. v. C-O-Two Co., 342 U.S. 180, 185 (1952). Although neither judges, the parties, nor the adversary system performs perfectly in all cases, the requirement of determining whether the party against whom an estoppel is asserted had a full and fair opportunity to litigate is a most significant safeguard. [Id. at 329.]

The *Blonder-Tongue* case involved defensive use of collateral estoppel—a plaintiff was estopped from asserting a claim that the plaintiff had previously litigated and lost against another defendant. The present case, by contrast, involves offensive use of collateral estoppel—a plaintiff is seeking to estop a defendant from relitigating the issues which the defendant previously litigated and lost against another plaintiff. In both the offensive and defensive use situations, the party against whom estoppel is asserted has litigated and lost in an earlier action. Nevertheless, several reasons have been advanced why the two situations should be treated differently.

First, offensive use of collateral estoppel does not promote judicial economy in the same manner as defensive use does. Defensive use of collateral estoppel precludes a plaintiff from relitigating identical issues by merely "switching adversaries." Bernhard v. Bank of America Nat. Trust & Savings Assn., 122 P.2d at 895 [(1942)]. Thus defensive collateral estoppel gives a plaintiff a strong incentive to join all potential defendants in the first action if possible. Offensive use of collateral estoppel, on the other hand, creates precisely the opposite incentive. Since a plaintiff will be able to rely on a previous judgment against a defendant but will not be bound by that judgment if the defendant wins, the plaintiff has every incentive to adopt a "wait and see" attitude, in the hope that the first action by another plaintiff will result in a favorable judgment. . . . Thus offensive use of collateral estoppel will likely increase rather than decrease the total amount of litigation, since potential plaintiffs will have everything to gain and nothing to lose by not intervening in the first action.

A second argument against offensive use of collateral estoppel is that it may be unfair to a defendant. If a defendant in the first action is sued for small or nominal damages, he may have little incentive to defend vigorously, particularly if future suits are not foreseeable. The Evergreens v. Nunan, 141 F.2d 927, 929 (2d Cir. [(1944)]); cf. Berner v. British Commonwealth Pac. Airlines, 346 F.2d 532 (2d Cir. [(1965)]) (application of offensive collateral estoppel denied where defendant did not appeal an adverse judgment awarding damages of $35,000 and defendant was later sued for over $7 million). Allowing offensive collateral estoppel may also be unfair to a defendant if the judgment relied upon as a basis for the estoppel is itself inconsistent with one or more previous judgments in favor of the defendant. Still another situation where it might be unfair to apply offensive estoppel is where the second action affords the defendant procedural opportunities unavailable in the first action that could readily cause a different result.

We have concluded that the preferable approach for dealing with these problems in the federal courts is not to preclude the use of offensive collateral estoppel, but to grant trial courts broad discretion to determine when it should be applied. The general rule should be that in cases where a plaintiff could easily have joined in the earlier action or where, either for the reasons discussed above or for other reasons, the application of offensive estoppel would be unfair to a defendant, a trial judge should not allow the use of offensive collateral estoppel.

In the present case, however, none of the circumstances that might justify reluctance to allow the offensive use of collateral estoppel is present. The application of offensive collateral estoppel will not here reward a private plaintiff who could have joined in the previous action, since the respondent probably could not have joined in the injunctive action brought by the SEC even had he so desired. Similarly, there is no unfairness to the petitioners in applying offensive collateral estoppel in this case. First, in light of the serious allegations made in the SEC's complaint against the petitioners, as well as the foreseeability of subsequent private suits that typically follow a successful Government judgment, the petitioners had every incentive to litigate the SEC lawsuit fully and vigorously. Second, the judgment in the SEC action was not inconsistent with any previous decision. Finally, there will in the respondent's action be no procedural opportunities available to the petitioners that were unavailable in the first action of a kind that might be likely to cause a different result.[19]

We conclude, therefore, that none of the considerations that would justify a refusal to allow the use of offensive collateral estoppel is present in this case. Since the petitioners received a "full and fair" opportunity to litigate their claims in the SEC action, the contemporary law of collateral estoppel leads inescapably to the conclusion that the petitioners are collaterally estopped from relitigating the question of whether the proxy statement was materially false and misleading.

The question that remains is whether, notwithstanding the law of collateral estoppel, the use of offensive collateral estoppel in this case would violate the petitioners' Seventh Amendment right to a jury trial. . . .

Recognition that an equitable determination could have collateral-estoppel effect in a subsequent legal action was the major premise of this Court's decision in Beacon Theatres, Inc. v. Westover, 359 U.S. 500 [(1959)].

In that case the plaintiff sought a declaratory judgment that certain arrangements between it and the defendant were not in violation of the

---

19. It is true, of course, that the petitioners in the present action would be entitled to a jury trial. . . . But the presence or absence of a jury as fact finder is basically neutral, quite unlike, for example, the necessity of defending the first lawsuit in an inconvenient forum.

antitrust laws, and asked for an injunction to prevent the defendant from instituting an antitrust action to challenge the arrangements. The defendant denied the allegations and counterclaimed for treble damages under the antitrust laws, requesting a trial by jury of the issues common to both the legal and equitable claims. The Court of Appeals upheld denial of the request, but this Court reversed, stating:

> [T]he effect of the action of the District Court could be, as the Court of Appeals believed, "to limit the petitioner's opportunity fully to try to a jury every issue which has a bearing upon its treble damage suit," for determination of the issue of clearances by the judge might "operate either by way of res judicata or collateral estoppel so as to conclude both parties with respect thereto at the subsequent trial of the treble damage claim." [Id. at 504.]

It is thus clear that the Court in the *Beacon Theatres* case thought that if an issue common to both legal and equitable claims was first determined by a judge, relitigation of the issue before a jury might be foreclosed by res judicata or collateral estoppel. To avoid this result, the Court held that when legal and equitable claims are joined in the same action, the trial judge has only limited discretion in determining the sequence of trial and "that discretion . . . must, wherever possible, be exercised to preserve jury trial." Id. at 510.

Both the premise of *Beacon Theatres,* and the fact that it enunciated no more than a general prudential rule were confirmed by this Court's decision in Katchen v. Landy, 382 U.S. 323 [(1966)]. In that case the Court held that a bankruptcy court, sitting as a statutory court of equity, is empowered to adjudicate equitable claims prior to legal claims, even though the factual issues decided in the equity action would have been triable by a jury under the Seventh Amendment if the legal claims had been adjudicated first. The Court stated: "Both *Beacon Theatres* and *Dairy Queen* recognize that there might be situations in which the Court could proceed to resolve the equitable claim first even though the results might be dispositive of the issues involved in the legal claim." Id. at 339. Thus the Court in Katchen v. Landy recognized that an equitable determination can have collateral-estoppel effect in a subsequent legal action and that this estoppel does not violate the Seventh Amendment. . . .

The petitioners have advanced no persuasive reason . . . why the meaning of the Seventh Amendment should depend on whether or not mutuality of parties is present. A litigant who has lost because of adverse factual findings in an equity action is equally deprived of a jury trial whether he is estopped from relitigating the factual issues against the same party or a new party. In either case, the party against whom estoppel is asserted has litigated questions of fact, and has had the facts determined against him in an earlier proceeding. In either case there is no further factfinding function for the jury to perform, since the common factual issues have been resolved in the previous action. . . .

The Seventh Amendment has never been interpreted in the rigid manner advocated by the petitioners. On the contrary, many procedural devices developed since 1791 that have diminished the civil jury's historic domain have been found not to be inconsistent with the Seventh Amendment. See Galloway v. United States, 319 U.S. 372, 388-393 [(1943)]. . . .

The *Galloway* case is particularly instructive. There the party against whom a directed verdict had been entered argued that the procedure was unconstitutional under the Seventh Amendment. In rejecting this claim, the Court said:

> The Amendment did not bind the federal courts to the exact procedural incidents or details of jury trial according to the common law in 1791, any more than it tied them to the common-law system of pleading or the specific rules of evidence then prevailing. Nor were "the rules of the common law" then prevalent, including those relating to the procedure by which the judge regulated the jury's role on questions of fact, crystallized in a fixed and immutable system. . . .
>
> The more logical conclusion, we think, and the one which both history and the previous decisions here support, is that the Amendment was designed to preserve the basic institution of jury trial in only its most fundamental elements, not the great mass of procedural forms and details, varying even then so widely among common-law jurisdictions. [319 U.S. at 390, 392 (footnote omitted).]

The law of collateral estoppel, like the law in other procedural areas defining the scope of the jury's function, has evolved since 1791. Under the rationale of the *Galloway* case, these developments are not repugnant to the Seventh Amendment simply for the reason that they did not exist in 1791. Thus if, as we have held, the law of collateral estoppel forecloses the petitioners from relitigating the factual issues determined against them in the SEC action, nothing in the Seventh Amendment dictates a different result, even though because of lack of mutuality there would have been no collateral estoppel in 1791.

The judgment of the Court of Appeals is *affirmed*.

JUSTICE REHNQUIST, dissenting. . . .

. . . Neither respondent nor the Court doubts that at common law as it existed in 1791, petitioners would have been entitled in the private action to have a jury determine whether the proxy statement was false and misleading in the respects alleged. The reason is that at common law in 1791, collateral estoppel was permitted only where the parties in the first action were identical to, or in privity with, the parties to the subsequent action. It was not until 1971 that the doctrine of mutuality was abrogated by this Court in certain limited circumstances. Blonder-Tongue Laboratories, Inc. v. University of Illinois Foundation, 402 U.S. 313 [(1971)]. But developments in the judge-made doctrine of collateral estoppel, however salutary, cannot, consistent with the Seventh Amendment, contract in any material fashion the right to a jury trial that a defendant would have enjoyed in 1791. In the instant case, resort to the doctrine of collateral estoppel does more than merely contract the right to a jury trial: It eliminates the right entirely and therefore contravenes the Seventh Amendment.

The Court responds, however, that at common law "a litigant was not entitled to have a jury [in a subsequent action at law between the same parties] determine issues that had been previously adjudicated by a chancellor in equity," and that "petitioners have advanced no persuasive reason . . . why the meaning of the Seventh Amendment should depend on whether or not mutuality of parties is present." . . . But that is tantamount to saying that since a party would not be entitled to a jury trial if he brought an equitable action, there is no persuasive reason why he should receive a jury trial on virtually the same issues if instead he chooses to bring his lawsuit in the nature of a legal action. The persuasive reason is that the Seventh Amendment requires that a party's right to jury trial which existed at common law be "preserved" from incursions by the government or the judiciary. Whether this Court believes that use of a jury trial in a particular instance is necessary, or fair or repetitive is simply irrelevant. If that view is "rigid," it is the Constitution which commands that rigidity. To hold otherwise is to rewrite the Seventh Amendment so that a party is guaranteed a jury trial in civil cases unless this Court thinks that a jury trial would be inappropriate. . . .

Even accepting, arguendo, the majority's position that there is no violation of the Seventh Amendment here, I nonetheless would not sanction the use of collateral estoppel in this case. The Court today holds:

> The general rule should be that in cases where a plaintiff could easily have joined in the earlier action or where, either for the reasons discussed above or for other reasons, the application of offensive estoppel would be unfair to a defendant, a trial judge should not allow the use of offensive collateral estoppel.

In my view, it is "unfair" to apply offensive collateral estoppel where the party who is sought to be estopped has not had an opportunity to have the facts of his case determined by a jury. Since in this case petitioners were not entitled to a jury trial in the Securities and Exchange Commission (SEC) lawsuit[,] I would not estop them from relitigating the issues determined in the SEC suit before a jury in the private action. I believe that several factors militate in favor of this result.

First, the use of offensive collateral estoppel in this case runs counter to the strong federal policy favoring jury trials, even if it does not, as the majority holds; violate the Seventh Amendment. The Court's decision in Beacon Theatres, Inc. v. Westover, 359 U.S. 500 (1959), exemplifies that policy. . . . Today's decision will mean that in a large number of private cases defendants will no longer enjoy the right to jury trial. Neither the Court nor respondent has adverted or cited to any unmanageable problems that have resulted from according defendants jury trials in such cases. I simply see no "imperative circumstances" requiring this wholesale abrogation of jury trials.

Second, I believe that the opportunity for a jury trial in the second action could easily lead to a different result from that obtained in the first action before the Court and therefore that it is unfair to estop petitioners from relitigating the issues before a jury. This is the position adopted in the Restatement (Second) of Judgments, which disapproves of the application of offensive collateral estoppel where the defendant has an opportunity for a jury trial in the second lawsuit that was not available in the first action. The Court accepts the proposition that it is unfair to apply offensive collateral estoppel "where the second action affords the defendant procedural opportunities unavailable in the first action that could readily cause a different result." . . . Differences in discovery opportunities between the two actions are cited as examples of situations where it would be unfair to permit offensive collateral estoppel. . . . But in the Court's view, the fact that petitioners would have been entitled to a jury trial in the present action is not such a "procedural opportunit[y]" because "the presence or absence of a jury as factfinder is basically *neutral,* quite unlike, for example, the necessity of defending the first lawsuit in an inconvenient forum." . . . (emphasis added).

As is evident from the prior brief discussion of the development of the civil jury trial guarantee in this country, those who drafted the Declaration of Independence and debated so passionately the proposed Constitution during the ratification period, would indeed be astounded to learn that the presence or absence of a jury is merely "neutral," whereas the availability of discovery, a device unmentioned in the Constitution, may be controlling. It is precisely because the Framers believed that they might receive a different result at the hands of a jury of their peers than at the mercy of the sovereign's judges, that the Seventh Amendment was adopted. And I suspect that anyone who litigates cases before juries in the 1970's would be equally amazed to hear of the supposed lack of distinction between trial by court and trial by jury. The Court can cite no authority in support of this curious proposition. The merits of civil juries have been long debated, but I suspect that juries have never been accused of being merely "neutral" factors. . . .

The ultimate irony of today's decision is that its potential for significantly conserving the resources of either the litigants or the judiciary is doubtful at best. That being the case, I see absolutely no reason to frustrate so cavalierly the important federal policy favoring jury decisions of disputed fact questions. The instant case is an apt example of the minimal savings that will be accomplished by the Court's decision. As the Court admits, even if petitioners are collaterally estopped from relitigating whether the proxy was materially false and misleading, they are still entitled to have a jury determine whether respondent was injured by the alleged misstatements and the amount of damages, if any, sustained by respondent. . . . Thus, a jury must be impaneled in this case in any event. The time saved by not trying the issue of whether the proxy was materially false and misleading before the jury is likely to be insubstantial. It is just as probable that today's decision will have the result of coercing defendants to agree to consent orders or settlements in agency enforcement action in order to preserve their right to jury trial in the private actions. In that event, the Court, for no compelling reason, will have simply added a powerful club to the administrative agencies' arsenals that even Congress was unwilling to provide them.

## Notes and Questions

1. *Implications of* Parklane. The factors to consider in whether there was a full and fair opportunity for litigation in the first suit and whether the claim may be asserted in the second suit now are:

a) Size of claim. If the first lawsuit was for $1,000 and the second for $100,000, there may be a real difference in how the parties litigate. In *Parklane*, the parties knew the importance of the SEC suit, so they litigated the suit flat out.
b) Forum of first suit. Is there any indication that the first forum had odd procedures, discovery, or other limitations that make preclusion unfair? In *Parklane*, the first forum was the federal court.
c) Extent of litigation. Was the matter given full adversarial attention?
d) Competence and experience of counsel in first action.
e) New evidence or changed circumstances that have developed since the first trial.
f) Differences in applicable law.
g) Foreseeability of future litigation.
h) Whether the party who now seeks to use the previously adjudicated case is a "wait and see" plaintiff. Could she have joined the first case? In *Parklane*, definitely not.
i) Public interest. Is there a public interest in allowing relitigation of the claims?

2. *Prediction and Issue Preclusion.* After you review the list of factors in Note 1 supra, the following question should seem inevitable: How workable is a doctrine of repose that depends on such a flexible, multifactored test for determining when an issue can be relitigated? Indeed, both claim and issue preclusion are highly context-dependent. Does the uncertainty that goes with such fact-bound inquiries cut against the policy interest that underlies a doctrine of repose? See In re Microsoft Corp. Antitrust Litigation, 355 F.3d 322 (4th Cir. 2004) (limiting nonmutual offensive collateral estoppel to previously litigated facts that are "critical and necessary" to, not just "supportive" of, the result).

3. *Policy Factors Revisited.* What is wrong with being a "wait and see" plaintiff anyway? Isn't this prudent behavior that promotes judicial economy? Are the policy factors invoked by the Court as reasons not to permit nonmutual estoppel persuasive?

4. *Inscrutable Verdicts and Issue Preclusion.* Another way in which jury trials play into the application of collateral estoppel is that the verdicts of juries are often "inscrutable." A general verdict may mean many things, none of them clearly. Consider the following examples:

a) *P* sues *D* for negligence. Jury enters a general verdict for *D*. What issue-preclusive effect does this judgment have if *P* then wants to sue *D*(2) for negligence in the same accident? None, because the general verdict could mean that 1) the jury found *P* contributorily negligent, 2) *P* has assumed the risk, or 3) *P* suffered no damages, and thus the verdict is inscrutable.

(b) *P*, the owner of a building, sues *D*, a gas utility, and *D*(2), a contractor doing repair work on the building, contending that through the negligence of both, a gas line in the building was ruptured, resulting in an explosion that demolished the building. *D* and *D*(2) each contend that he was not negligent and that the other was. If they have a full and fair opportunity to litigate these contentions, a judgment in favor of *P* against *D*(2) but in favor of *D* is preclusive of the issue that *D* was not negligent in a subsequent action between *D*(2) and *D*.

5. *Preclusion in Alternative Dispute Resolution.* As arbitration and other forms of alternative dispute resolution grow increasingly common, courts have extended the doctrine of collateral estoppel to these new contexts, holding that where the prerequisites for collateral estoppel are satisfied, arbitrators must give preclusive effect to prior federal judgments. See, e.g., Collins v. D.R. Horton, Inc., 505 F.3d 874, 882 (9th Cir. 2007); Aircraft Braking Sys. Corp. v. Local 856, 97 F.3d 155, 159 (6th Cir. 1996); Miller v. Runyon, 77 F.3d 189, 193 (7th Cir. 1996); see also Miller Brewing Co. v. Fort Worth Distrib. Co., 781 F.2d 494, 499 (5th Cir. 1986) ("Since an arbitration award involves the entry of judgment by a court, parties should be barred from seeking relief from arbitration panels when, under the doctrine of res judicata, they would be barred from seeking relief in the courts."); cf. Hancock Fabrics, Inc. v. Rowdec, LLC, 126 F. Supp. 3d 784, 791 (N.D. Miss. 2015).

Should arbitrators have the same broad discretion as district courts in determining when to apply offensive nonmutual collateral estoppel? Will they have the same expertise as trial judges in making such determinations? See *Collins*, 505 F.3d at 882 (holding that arbitrators should have the same discretion possessed by district courts in applying the *Parklane* factors to determine whether offensive nonmutual collateral estoppel is appropriate). In *Collins*, the Ninth Circuit affirmed the arbitrators' refusal to give collateral estoppel effect to a district court decision that was pending on appeal. Unlike an Article III court's judgment, the arbitrators reasoned, an arbitration award cannot normally be corrected on appeal if the decision to which it gives collateral estoppel effect is later reversed. Interestingly, this suggests that collateral estoppel will be less binding before arbitrators, at least in part because their own awards are so binding. Finality cuts both ways.

6. *Preclusion Resulting from Administrative Adjudication.* The New Deal greatly expanded adjudication before administrative agencies. A common question is whether agency decisions should have preclusive effect in any parallel or subsequent federal court litigation. In B&B Hardware, Inc. v. Hargis Indus., Inc., 135 S. Ct. 1293 (2015), the Supreme Court held that trademark registration proceedings before the Trademark Trial and

Appeal Board may have preclusive effect in federal court litigation for trademark infringement. Generally a trademark cannot be registered if it "so resembles" another mark as to "cause confusion." Parties who oppose registration of a mark may initiate opposition proceedings before the Board. The Board follows the Federal Rules of Civil Procedure, but there is no live testimony or jury trial. All proceedings before the Board are in writing. After a Board decision, a party can seek review in the Federal Circuit or file a new action in which the record will be reviewed de novo in district court.

In *B&B Hardware*, the manufacturer of a "Sealtight" screw used in aerospace engineering challenged Hargis Industries' registration of a "Sealtite" screw used in building construction. B&B Hardware, the maker of the aerospace screw, already had a trademark registration for its Sealtight mark. The Board concluded that Hargis could not register its mark because of the risk of confusion. In a parallel trademark infringement suit between the parties, B&B then sought to preclude Hargis from relitigating the likelihood of confusion. The district court denied collateral estoppel on the ground that the Board's decisions are not entitled to preclusive effect because it is not an Article III court. The Eighth Circuit affirmed on the separate ground that the Board uses different factors than it does for analyzing the likelihood of confusion.

The Supreme Court reversed, emphasizing that courts should presume preclusion rules apply unless the relevant statute indicates otherwise:

> [B]ecause the principle of issue preclusion was so "well established" at common law, in those situations in which Congress has authorized agencies to resolve disputes, "courts may take it as given that Congress has legislated with the expectation that the principle [of issue preclusion] will apply except when a statutory purpose to the contrary is evident." [Astoria Fed. Sav. & Loan Ass'n v. Solimino, 501 U.S. 104, 108 (1991)]. This reflects the Court's longstanding view that "'[w]hen an administrative agency is acting in a judicial capacity and resolves disputed issues of fact properly before it which the parties have had an adequate opportunity to litigate, the courts have not hesitated to apply res judicata to enforce repose.'" University of Tenn. v. Elliott, 478 U.S. 788, 797-98 (1986) (quoting United States v. Utah Constr. & Mining Co., 384 U.S. 394, 422 (1966)).

Id. at 1303. The Court brushed aside concerns that the Board considers only whether the marks resemble each other, whereas infringement litigation considers resemblance and "use" of the marks in commerce not encompassed by the registration materials. If this difference is relevant in an individual case, the Court noted, collateral estoppel would not be warranted because the issues are not identical. The Court also dismissed the Eighth Circuit's concern about different factors applied by the Board, stressing that the underlying statutory standard is the same, and "if federal law provides a single standard, parties cannot escape preclusion simply by litigating anew in tribunals that apply that one standard differently.

A contrary rule would encourage the very evils that issue preclusion helps to prevent." Id. at 1307. Finally, the Court held that procedural differences between an agency adjudication and adjudication in an Article III court are only relevant if the "procedures used in the first proceeding [are] fundamentally poor, cursory, or unfair." Id. at 1309. The Court remanded to the Eighth Circuit to reconsider the case in light of ordinary preclusion rules.

Justice Ginsburg concurred, emphasizing that differences between a mark's registration and its actual commercial use will often make issue preclusion inappropriate. Justice Thomas, joined by Justice Scalia, dissented on the ground that giving preclusive effect to agency decisions raises serious constitutional concerns. First, Justice Thomas argued that at common law, doctrines of repose applied only to decisions of a "'court of competent jurisdiction'"—meaning, "courts of law, courts of equity, admiralty courts, and foreign courts." Id. at 1312. The distinction between these true courts and agencies, he continued, "stems from the Constitution itself, which vests the 'judicial Power' not in administrative agencies, but in federal courts, whose independence is safeguarded by certain constitutional requirements." Id. at 1313. In light of that history, Justice Thomas found no grounds for a presumption in favor of giving agency decisions preclusive effect. Second, Justice Thomas argued that the private property rights at issue in trademark disputes are the kind of rights traditionally decided by full Article III courts. Displacing Article III adjudication by giving preclusive effect to Board decisions "raises serious questions" regarding separation of powers. Id. at 1318.

Finally, Justice Thomas attached greater significance than did the majority to the fact that the Lanham Act provides de novo review of Board decisions in federal district courts. Congress thus refused to give any deference to Board decisions subject to direct federal judicial review. Justice Thomas concluded that it would be odd, given this lack of deference, to interpret the statute as supporting collateral estoppel—itself a kind of deference to a prior adjudicator. All the more so given that Congress passed the Lanham Act the same year it passed the Administrative Procedure Act, "following a lengthy period of disagreement in the courts about what deference administrative findings of fact were entitled to receive on direct review." Id. at 1315. Congress clearly understood how to provide for finality of agency decisions when it wanted to. It seems to have done just the opposite in the Lanham Act.

7. *Preclusion in Litigation with Nonparties.* Can a person or entity who was *not* a party (or represented as in a class action) in an earlier action ever be precluded from relitigating matters there decided? Due process would seem to require that a nonparty should be allowed to relitigate the issue, because the nonparty had no opportunity to be heard in the first place. But see Robert G. Bone, Rethinking the "Day in Court" Ideal and Nonparty Preclusion, 67 N.Y.U. L. Rev. 193 (1992) (arguing against the general rule that a nonparty may relitigate a matter). Review this question after you have read Montana v. United States.

## *Montana v. United States*
440 U.S. 147 (1979)

JUSTICE MARSHALL delivered the opinion of the Court.

The State of Montana imposes a one percent gross receipts tax upon contractors of public, but not private, construction projects. Montana Rev. Codes Ann. § 84-3505 (Supp. 1977). A public contractor may credit against the gross receipts tax its payments of personal property, corporate income, and individual income taxes. Any remaining gross receipts liability is customarily passed on in the form of increased construction costs to the governmental unit financing the project. At issue in this appeal is whether a prior judgment by the Montana Supreme Court upholding the tax precludes the United States from contesting its constitutionality and if not, whether the tax discriminates against the Federal Government in violation of the Supremacy Clause.

In 1971, Peter Kiewit Sons' Co., the contractor on a federal dam project in Montana, brought suit in state court contending that the Montana gross receipts tax unconstitutionally discriminated against the United States and the companies with which it dealt. The litigation was directed and financed by the United States. Less than a month after the state suit was filed, the Government initiated this challenge to the constitutionality of the tax in the United States District Court for the District of Montana. On stipulation by the parties, the instant case was continued pending resolution of the state-court litigation.

That litigation concluded in a unanimous decision by the Montana Supreme Court sustaining the tax. Peter Kiewit Sons' Co. v. State Board of Equalization, 505 P.2d 102 (1973) (*Kiewit I*). The court found the distinction between public and private contractors consistent with the mandates of the Supremacy and Equal Protection Clauses. Id. at 108-10. The contractor subsequently filed a Notice of Appeal to this Court, but abandoned its request for review at the direction of the Solicitor General. . . . It then instituted a second action in state court seeking a refund for certain tax payments different from those involved in *Kiewit I*. On determining that the contractor's second legal claim was, in all material respects, identical to its first, the Montana Supreme Court invoked the doctrines of collateral estoppel and res judicata to affirm the dismissal of the complaint. Peter Kiewit Sons' Co. v. Department of Revenue, 531 P.2d 1327 (1975) (*Kiewit II*).

After the decision in *Kiewit II*, a three-judge District Court heard the instant case on the merits. In a divided opinion, the court concluded that the United States was not bound by the *Kiewit I* decision, and struck down the tax as violative of the Supremacy Clause. 437 F. Supp. 354 ([D. Mont.] 1977). . . .

We noted probable jurisdiction. 436 U.S. 916 (1978). Because we find that the constitutional question presented by this appeal was determined adversely to the United States in a prior state proceeding, we reverse on grounds of collateral estoppel without reaching the merits.

A fundamental precept of common-law adjudication, embodied in the related doctrines of collateral estoppel and res judicata, is that a "right, question or fact distinctly put in issue and directly determined by a court of competent jurisdiction . . . cannot be disputed in a subsequent suit between the same parties or their privies. . . ." Southern Pacific R. Co. v. United States, 168 U.S. 1, 48-49 (1897). . . .

. . . To preclude parties from contesting matters that they have had a full and fair opportunity to litigate protects their adversaries from the expense and vexation attending multiple lawsuits, conserves judicial resources, and fosters reliance on judicial action by minimizing the possibility of inconsistent decisions.

These interests are similarly implicated when nonparties assume control over litigation in which they have a direct financial or proprietary interest and then seek to redetermine issues previously resolved. As this Court observed in Souffront v. Compagnie des Sucreries, 217 U.S. 475, 486-87 (1910), the persons for whose benefit and at whose direction a cause of action is litigated cannot be said to be

> strangers to the cause. . . . [O]ne who prosecutes or defends a suit in the name of another to establish and protect his own right, or who assists in the prosecution or defense of an action in aid of some interest of his own . . . is as much bound . . . as he would be if he had been a party to the record.

See Schnell v. Peter Eckrich & Sons, Inc., 365 U.S. 260, 262 n.4 (1961); cf. Zenith Radio Corp. v. Hazeltine Research, Inc., 395 U.S. 100, 111 (1969). Preclusion of such nonparties falls under the rubric of collateral estoppel rather than res judicata because the latter doctrine presupposes identity between causes of action. And the cause of action which a nonparty has vicariously asserted differs by definition from that which he subsequently seeks to litigate in his own right. . . .

That the United States exercised control over the *Kiewit I* litigation is not in dispute. The Government has stipulated that it:

(1) required the *Kiewit I* lawsuit to be filed;
(2) reviewed and approved the complaint;
(3) paid the attorneys' fees and costs;
(4) directed the appeal from state district court to the Montana Supreme Court;
(5) appeared and submitted a brief as *amicus* in the Montana Supreme Court;
(6) directed the filing of a Notice of Appeal to this Court; and
(7) effectuated Kiewit's abandonment of that appeal on advice of the Solicitor General . . .

Thus, although not a party, the United States plainly had a sufficient "laboring oar" in the conduct of the state-court litigation to actuate principles of estoppel. . . .

To determine the appropriate application of collateral estoppel in the instant case necessitates three further inquiries: first, whether the issues presented by this litigation are in substance the same as those resolved against the United States in *Kiewit I;* second, whether controlling facts or legal principles have changed significantly since the state-court judgment; and finally, whether other special circumstances warrant an exception to the normal rules of preclusion.

A review of the record in *Kiewit I* dispels any doubt that the plaintiff there raised and the Montana Supreme Court there decided the precise constitutional claim that the United States advances here. . . .

Relying on Commissioner v. Sunnen, 333 U.S. 591 (1948), the United States argues that collateral estoppel extends only to contexts in which "the controlling facts and applicable legal rules remain unchanged." Id. at 600. In the Government's view, factual stasis is missing here because the contract at issue in *Kiewet I* contained a critical provision which the contracts involved in the instant litigation do not.

Under its contract with the Army Corps of Engineers, Kiewit was unable to take advantage of the credit provisions of the gross receipts tax. In 1971, however, the United States altered its policy and has since required Montana contractors to seek all available refunds and credits. . . . But we do not construe the opinion in *Kiewit I* as predicated on the factual assumption that the gross receipts tax would cancel out if public contractors took all available refunds and credits. . . .

Thus, unless there have been major changes in the law governing intergovernmental tax immunity since *Kiewit I,* the Government's reliance on Commissioner v. Sunnen, 333 U.S. 591 (1948), is misplaced. . . . No such considerations obtain here. The Government does not contend and the District Court did not find that a change in controlling legal principles had occurred between *Kiewit I* and the instant suit. That the Government's amended complaint in this action replicates in substance the legal argument advanced by the contractor's complaint in *Kiewit I* further suggests the absence of any major doctrinal shifts since the Montana Supreme Court's decision.

Because the factual and legal context in which the issues of this case arise has not materially altered since *Kiewit I,* normal rules of preclusion should operate to relieve the parties of "redundant litigation [over] the identical question of the statute's application to the taxpayer's status." Tait v. Western Maryland R. Co., 289 U.S. 620, 624 (1933). . . .

The sole remaining question is whether the particular circumstances of this case justify an exception to general principles of estoppel. Of possible relevance is the exception which obtains for "unmixed questions of law" in successive actions involving substantially unrelated claims. United States v. Moser, 266 U.S. 236, 242 (1924). As we recognized in *Moser*:

> Where, for example, a court in deciding a case has enunciated a rule of law, the parties in a subsequent action *upon a different demand* are not estopped from insisting that the law is otherwise, merely because the parties are the same in both cases. But a *fact, question* or *right* distinctly adjudged in the original action cannot be disputed in a subsequent action, even though the determination was reached upon an erroneous view or by an erroneous application of the law. [Id. (emphasis added.)]

Thus, when issues of law arise in successive actions involving unrelated subject matter, preclusion may be inappropriate. . . . This exception is of particular importance in constitutional adjudication. Unreflective invocation of collateral estoppel against parties with an ongoing interest in constitutional issues could freeze doctrine in areas of the law where responsiveness to changing patterns of conduct or social mores is critical. To be sure, the scope of the *Moser* exception may be difficult to delineate, particularly where there is partial congruence in the subject matter of successive disputes. But the instant case poses no such conceptual difficulties. Rather, as the preceding discussion indicates, the legal "demands" of this litigation are closely aligned in time and subject matter to those in *Kiewit I.*

Nor does this case implicate the right of a litigant who has "properly invoked the jurisdiction of a Federal District Court to consider federal constitutional claims," and who is then "compelled, without his consent . . . , to accept a state court's determination of those claims." England v. Medical Examiners, 375 U.S. 411, 415 (1964) (footnote omitted). As we held in *England,* abstention doctrine may not serve as a vehicle for depriving individuals of an otherwise cognizable right to have federal courts make factual determinations essential to the resolution of federal questions. Id. at 417. See NAACP v. Button, 371 U.S. 415, 427 (1963). However, here, as in *England,* a party has "freely and without reservation submitt[ed] his federal claims for decision by the state courts . . . and ha[d] them decided there. . . ." England v. Medical Examiners, supra, 375 U.S. at 419. Considerations of comity as well as repose militate against redeterminations of issues in a federal forum at the behest of a plaintiff who has chosen to litigate them in state court.

Finally, the Government has not alleged unfairness or inadequacy in the state procedures to which it voluntarily submitted. We must conclude therefore that it had a full and fair opportunity to press its constitutional challenges in *Kiewit I.* Accordingly, the Government is estopped from seeking a contrary resolution of those issues here.

The judgment of the District Court is *reversed.*

## Notes and Questions

1. *Revisiting* Sunnen. The Court in *Montana* carefully distinguishes *Sunnen.* Is *Sunnen* still good law? Consider the analysis of the D.C. Circuit in a case involving a challenge by hospitals against the Secretary of Health, Education and Welfare regarding eligibility for Medicare reimbursement for specific reporting periods. The hospitals argued that the Secretary was collaterally estopped from withholding reimbursements for certain costs that had been deemed reimbursable in earlier litigation in the Court of Claims:

> The Secretary insists that an estoppel is foreclosed by the Supreme Court's decision in Commissioner v. Sunnen three decades ago. That argument, at

first glance, seems persuasive. So long as the facts in two cases are formally "separable," the *Sunnen* Court declared, it is inappropriate to use a judgment in the first to estop a party on a legal point in the second . . . .

This prong of *Sunnen* has never been popular with commentators—who maintain that formal separability of facts, without some difference pertinent to the first decision, does not justify denial of preclusive effect to the initial adjudication—and has also been less scrupulously applied by the courts. If valid, however, *Sunnen*'s separable-facts doctrine would, as the Secretary suggests, appear to control here, for the Court of Claims' litigation involved different years—and hence a different, though for all relevant purposes an identical, bundle of facts—from those in the case at bar.

There is, however, no need to wrestle with the intricacies of this problem, for the controversial aspect of *Sunnen* is no longer good law. In one of its most recent analyses of collateral estoppel, the Supreme Court allowed a judgment predicated upon one set of contracts to estop litigation of legal issues in another case dealing with a similar, though unrelated, set of contracts, because there had been no "changes in facts essential to [the] judgment." [Montana v. United States, 440 U.S. 147, 159 (1979).] The first ruling had not been "predicated" on facts peculiar to the contracts there in issue, so that differences in the documents were not of "controlling significance." [*Montana*, 440 U.S. at 159-160.] While the Court did not expressly overrule the separable-facts doctrine, it characterized *Sunnen* as holding simply "that modifications in 'controlling legal principles' . . . could render a previous determination inconsistent with prevailing doctrine"; "unless there have been major changes in the law," the Court said, *Sunnen* is inapplicable. [Id. at 161.] Since this cannot be squared with *Sunnen*'s declaration that "the legal matter raised in the second proceeding must involve the same set of events or documents" as that involved in the first, [Comm'r v. Sunnen, 333 U.S. 591, 601-602 (1948),] it seems clear that "*Sunnen* was limited by the Court . . . to cases in which there had been a significant 'change in the legal climate. . . .'" [Starker v. United States, 602 F.3d 1341, 1347 (9th Cir. 1979)]. Plainly that is not the case here.

Am. Med. Int'l, Inc. v. Sec'y of Health, Educ. & Welfare, 677 F.2d 118, 119-121 (D.C. Cir. 1981). See also Vetrano v. Comm'r of Internal Revenue, 116 T.C. 272, 280 (2001) (discussing abrogation of *Sunnen* by statute).

2. *Stare Decisis Versus Collateral Estoppel.* Even a judgment that does not qualify for issue-preclusive effect may nevertheless be pesky for a party seeking to avoid its adverse consequences. After all, if the issue is very similar, and a prior court ruled against another litigant on very similar facts, then stare decisis may make it difficult to avoid a similar fate in the subsequent action. For a case that addresses the differences between issue preclusion and stare decisis, see Meredith v. Beech Aircraft Corp., 18 F.3d 890 (10th Cir. 1994).

3. *Preclusion and Criminal Actions.* Should issues resolved against a party in a civil action be used against her in a criminal action? How about the reverse scenario? The standard of proof differences obviously play a role here, such that—stated generally—the answer to the first question is "no," whereas the answer to the second is "yes." Similarly, acquittal in a criminal trial will not insulate the defendant from a civil suit based on the same facts. Do you see why? See Restatement (Second) of Judgments § 28(4), supra.

4. *Alternative Grounds and Preclusion.* If a judge provides alternative grounds for a holding in an action, should both receive preclusive effect? Neither? The Restatement (Second) of Judgments § 27 holds that alternative grounds should not be given preclusive effect unless an appeal is taken and the appellate court affirms the judgment on both grounds. The rationale is that neither alternative ground can be said to be "essential to the judgment." Moreover, a party may lack an incentive to appeal when she disagrees with only one of the alternative grounds, and there is also the risk that each ground was not weighed as carefully in conjunction with the other as it might have been in isolation. For a contrary view, see Winters v. Lavine, 574 F.2d 46 (2d Cir. 1978), in which the court concluded that it should be presumed that the judge considered fully all issues raised by the parties, and that the parties would have appealed if they disagreed with the holding.

5. *Identity and Privity: Limits on Binding Strangers to the Cause.* The Court in *Montana* thought the government had "a sufficient 'laboring oar' . . . to actuate principles of estoppel." What facts other than having a controlling hand might establish "privity"? What if the nonparty's interests align with those of a party to the original suit such that one could say its interests were effectively represented in the original suit? Would that suffice? What if a "horse-switching" attorney refiles the same legal claims against the same defendant on behalf of a different plaintiff?

*Martino* and the dissenters in *Allen* and *Parklane* all mention the privity rule. In the following case, the Supreme Court addressed its outer boundaries.


*Taylor v. Sturgell*
553 U.S. 880 (2008)


JUSTICE GINSBURG delivered the opinion of the Court.

"It is a principle of general application in Anglo-American jurisprudence that one is not bound by a judgment *in personam* in a litigation in which he is not designated as a party or to which he has not been made a party by service of process." Hansberry v. Lee, 311 U.S. 32, 40 (1940). Several exceptions, recognized in this Court's decisions, temper this basic rule. In a class action, for example, a person not named as a party may be bound by a judgment on the merits of the action, if she was adequately represented by a party who actively participated in the litigation. See id., at 41. In this case, we consider for the first time whether there is a "virtual representation" exception to the general rule against precluding nonparties. Adopted by a number of courts, including the courts below in the case now before us, the exception so styled is broader than any we have so far approved.

The virtual representation question we examine in this opinion arises in the following context. Petitioner Brent Taylor filed a lawsuit under the Freedom of Information Act seeking certain documents from the Federal Aviation Administration. Greg Herrick, Taylor's friend, had previously brought an unsuccessful suit seeking the same records. The two men have no legal relationship, and there is no evidence that Taylor controlled, financed, participated in, or even had notice of Herrick's earlier suit. Nevertheless, the D.C. Circuit held Taylor's suit precluded by the judgment against Herrick because, in that court's assessment, Herrick qualified as Taylor's "virtual representative."

We disapprove the doctrine of preclusion by "virtual representation," and hold, based on the record as it now stands, that the judgment against Herrick does not bar Taylor from maintaining this suit.

# I

The Freedom of Information Act (FOIA or Act) accords "any person" a right to request any records held by a federal agency. 5 U.S.C. § 552(a)(3)(A) (2006 ed.). No reason need be given for a FOIA request, and unless the requested materials fall within one of the Act's enumerated exemptions, see § 552(a)(3)(E), (b), the agency must "make the records promptly available" to the requester, § 552(a)(3)(A). If an agency refuses to furnish the requested records, the requester may file suit in federal court and obtain an injunction "order[ing] the production of any agency records improperly withheld." § 552(a)(4)(B).

The courts below held the instant FOIA suit barred by the judgment in earlier litigation seeking the same records. Because the lower courts' decisions turned on the connection between the two lawsuits, we begin with a full account of each action.

# A

The first suit was filed by Greg Herrick, an antique aircraft enthusiast and the owner of an F-45 airplane, a vintage model manufactured by the Fairchild Engine and Airplane Corporation (FEAC) in the 1930's. In 1997, seeking information that would help him restore his plane to its original condition, Herrick filed a FOIA request asking the Federal Aviation Administration (FAA) for copies of any technical documents about the F-45 contained in the agency's records.

To gain a certificate authorizing the manufacture and sale of the F-45, FEAC had submitted to the FAA's predecessor, the Civil Aeronautics Authority, detailed specifications and other technical data about the plane. Hundreds of pages of documents produced by FEAC in the certification process remain in the FAA's records. The FAA denied Herrick's request, however, upon finding that the documents he sought are subject to FOIA's exemption for "trade secrets and commercial or financial information obtained from a person and privileged or confidential," § 552(b)(4). In an administrative appeal, Herrick urged that FEAC and its successors had waived any trade-secret protection. The FAA thereupon contacted FEAC's corporate successor, respondent Fairchild Corporation (Fairchild). Because

Fairchild objected to release of the documents, the agency adhered to its original decision.

Herrick then filed suit in the U.S. District Court for the District of Wyoming. Challenging the FAA's invocation of the trade-secret exemption, Herrick placed heavy weight on a 1955 letter from FEAC to the Civil Aeronautics Authority. The letter authorized the agency to lend any documents in its files to the public "for use in making repairs or replacement parts for aircraft produced by Fairchild." Herrick v. Garvey, 298 F.3d 1184, 1193 (C.A.10 2002). This broad authorization, Herrick maintained, showed that the F-45 certification records held by the FAA could not be regarded as "secre[t]" or "confidential" within the meaning of § 552(b)(4).

Rejecting Herrick's argument, the District Court granted summary judgment to the FAA. Herrick v. Garvey, 200 F. Supp. 2d 1321, 1328-1329 (D. Wyo. 2000). The 1955 letter, the court reasoned, did not deprive the F-45 certification documents of trade-secret status, for those documents were never in fact released pursuant to the letter's blanket authorization. See id., at 1329. The court also stated that even if the 1955 letter had waived trade-secret protection, Fairchild had successfully "reversed" the waiver by objecting to the FAA's release of the records to Herrick. Ibid.

On appeal, the Tenth Circuit agreed with Herrick that the 1955 letter had stripped the requested documents of trade-secret protection. See *Herrick*, 298 F.3d, at 1194. But the Court of Appeals upheld the District Court's alternative determination—i.e., that Fairchild had restored trade-secret status by objecting to Herrick's FOIA request. Id., at 1195. On that ground, the appeals court affirmed the entry of summary judgment for the FAA.

In so ruling, the Tenth Circuit noted that Herrick had failed to challenge two suppositions underlying the District Court's decision. First, the District Court assumed trade-secret status could be "restored" to documents that had lost protection. Id., at 1194, n.10. Second, the District Court also assumed that Fairchild had regained trade-secret status for the documents even though the company claimed that status only "after Herrick had initiated his request" for the F-45 records. Ibid. The Court of Appeals expressed no opinion on the validity of these suppositions. See id., at 1194-1195, n. 10.

### B

The Tenth Circuit's decision issued on July 24, 2002. Less than a month later, on August 22, petitioner Brent Taylor—a friend of Herrick's and an antique aircraft enthusiast in his own right—submitted a FOIA request seeking the same documents Herrick had unsuccessfully sued to obtain. When the FAA failed to respond, Taylor filed a complaint in the U.S. District Court for the District of Columbia. Like Herrick, Taylor argued that FEAC's 1955 letter had stripped the records of their trade-secret status. But Taylor also sought to litigate the two issues concerning recapture of protected status that Herrick had failed to raise in his appeal to the Tenth Circuit.

After Fairchild intervened as a defendant,[1] the District Court in D.C. concluded that Taylor's suit was barred by claim preclusion; accordingly, it granted summary judgment to Fairchild and the FAA. The court acknowledged that Taylor was not a party to Herrick's suit. Relying on the Eighth Circuit's decision in Tyus v. Schoemehl, 93 F.3d 449 (1996), however, it held that a nonparty may be bound by a judgment if she was "virtually represented" by a party. . . .

The record before the District Court in Taylor's suit revealed the following facts about the relationship between Taylor and Herrick: Taylor is the president of the Antique Aircraft Association, an organization to which Herrick belongs; the two men are "close associate[s]"; Herrick asked Taylor to help restore Herrick's F-45, though they had no contract or agreement for Taylor's participation in the restoration; Taylor was represented by the lawyer who represented Herrick in the earlier litigation; and Herrick apparently gave Taylor documents that Herrick had obtained from the FAA during discovery in his suit.

Fairchild and the FAA conceded that Taylor had not participated in Herrick's suit. The D.C. District Court determined, however, that Herrick ranked as Taylor's virtual representative because the facts fit each of the other six indicators on the Eighth Circuit's list. Accordingly, the District Court held Taylor's suit, seeking the same documents Herrick had requested, barred by the judgment against Herrick.

The D.C. Circuit affirmed. It observed, first, that other Circuits "vary widely" in their approaches to virtual representation. Taylor v. Blakey, 490 F.3d 965, 971 (2007). In this regard, the D.C. Circuit contrasted the multifactor balancing test applied by the Eighth Circuit and the D.C. District Court with the Fourth Circuit's narrower approach, which "treats a party as a virtual representative only if the party is 'accountable to the nonparties who file a subsequent suit' and has 'the tacit approval of the court' to act on the nonpart[ies'] behalf." Ibid. (quoting Klugh v. United States, 818 F.2d 294, 300 (C.A.4 1987)).

Rejecting both of these approaches, the D.C. Circuit announced its own five-factor test. The first two factors—"identity of interests" and "adequate representation"—are necessary but not sufficient for virtual representation. . . .

Applying this test to the record in Taylor's case, the D.C. Circuit found both of the necessary conditions for virtual representation well met. As to identity of interests, the court emphasized that Taylor and Herrick sought the same result—release of the F-45 documents. Moreover, the D.C. Circuit observed, Herrick owned an F-45 airplane, and therefore had "if anything, a stronger incentive to litigate" than Taylor, who had only a "general

---

1. Although Fairchild provided documents to the Wyoming District Court and filed an amicus brief in the Tenth Circuit, it was not a party to Herrick's suit.

interest in public disclosure and the preservation of antique aircraft heritage." Id., at 973.

Turning to adequacy of representation, the D.C. Circuit acknowledged that some other Circuits regard notice of a prior suit as essential to a determination that a nonparty was adequately represented in that suit. See id., at 973-974 (citing Perez v. Volvo Car Corp., 247 F.3d 303, 312 (C.A.1 2001), and Tice v. American Airlines, Inc., 162 F.3d 966, 973 (C.A.7 1998)). Disagreeing with these courts, the D.C. Circuit deemed notice an "important" but not an indispensable element in the adequacy inquiry. The court then concluded that Herrick had adequately represented Taylor even though Taylor had received no notice of Herrick's suit. For this conclusion, the appeals court relied on Herrick's "strong incentive to litigate" and Taylor's later engagement of the same attorney, which indicated to the court Taylor's satisfaction with that attorney's performance in Herrick's case. See 490 F.3d, at 974-975.

The D.C. Circuit also found its "close relationship" criterion met, for Herrick had "asked Taylor to assist him in restoring his F-45" and "provided information to Taylor that Herrick had obtained through discovery"; furthermore, Taylor "did not oppose Fairchild's characterization of Herrick as his 'close associate.'" Id., at 975. . . .

We granted certiorari, 552 U.S. 1136 (2008), to resolve the disagreement among the Circuits over the permissibility and scope of preclusion based on "virtual representation."

## II

The preclusive effect of a federal-court judgment is determined by federal common law. See Semtek Int'l Inc. v. Lockheed Martin Corp., 531 U.S. 497, 507-08 (2001). For judgments in federal-question cases—for example, Herrick's FOIA suit—federal courts participate in developing "uniform federal rule[s]" of res judicata, which this Court has ultimate authority to determine and declare. Id., at 508. The federal common law of preclusion is, of course, subject to due process limitations. See Richards v. Jefferson County, 517 U.S. 793, 797 (1996). . . .

### A

. . . A person who was not a party to a suit generally has not had a "full and fair opportunity to litigate" the claims and issues settled in that suit. The application of claim and issue preclusion to nonparties thus runs up against the "deep-rooted historic tradition that everyone should have his own day in court." *Richards*, 517 U.S., at 798. Indicating the strength of that tradition, we have often repeated the general rule that "one is not bound by a judgment *in personam* in a litigation in which he is not designated as a party or to which he has not been made a party by service of process." *Hansberry*, 311 U.S., at 40.

## B

Though hardly in doubt, the rule against nonparty preclusion is subject to exceptions. For present purposes, the recognized exceptions can be grouped into six categories.[6]

First, "[a] person who agrees to be bound by the determination of issues in an action between others is bound in accordance with the terms of his agreement." 1 Restatement (Second) of Judgments § 40, p. 390 (1980). For example, "if separate actions involving the same transaction are brought by different plaintiffs against the same defendant, all the parties to all the actions may agree that the question of the defendant's liability will be definitely determined, one way or the other, in a 'test case.'" D. Shapiro, Civil Procedure: Preclusion in Civil Actions 77-78 (2001). See also California v. Texas, 459 U.S. 1096, 1097 (1983) (dismissing certain defendants from a suit based on a stipulation "that each of said defendants . . . will be bound by a final judgment of this Court" on a specified issue).

Second, nonparty preclusion may be justified based on a variety of pre-existing "substantive legal relationship[s]" between the person to be bound and a party to the judgment. Shapiro 78. See also *Richards*, 517 U.S., at 798. Qualifying relationships include, but are not limited to, preceding and succeeding owners of property, bailee and bailor, and assignee and assignor. See 2 Restatement §§ 43-44, 52, 55. These exceptions originated "as much from the needs of property law as from the values of preclusion by judgment." 18A C. Wright, A. Miller, & E. Cooper, Federal Practice and Procedure § 4448, p. 329 (2d ed. 2002).[8]

Third, we have confirmed that, "in certain limited circumstances," a nonparty may be bound by a judgment because she was "adequately represented by someone with the same interests who [wa]s a party" to the suit. *Richards*, 517 U.S., at 798. Representative suits with preclusive effect on nonparties include properly conducted class actions, see [Martin v. Wilks, 490 U.S. 755, 762, n.2 (1989)], and suits brought by trustees, guardians, and other fiduciaries, see Sea-Land Services, Inc. v. Gaudet, 414 U.S. 573, 593 (1974). See also 1 Restatement § 41.

Fourth, a nonparty is bound by a judgment if she "assume[d] control" over the litigation in which that judgment was rendered. [Montana v. United States, 440 U.S. 147, 154 (1979)]. See also 1 Restatement § 39. Because such a person has had "the opportunity to present proofs and argument,"

---

6. The established grounds for nonparty preclusion could be organized differently. . . . The list that follows is meant only to provide a framework for our consideration of virtual representation, not to establish a definitive taxonomy.

8. The substantive legal relationships justifying preclusion are sometimes collectively referred to as "privity." See, e.g., Richards v. Jefferson County, 517 U.S. 793, 798; 2 Restatement § 62, Comment a. The term "privity," however, has also come to be used more broadly, as a way to express the conclusion that nonparty preclusion is appropriate on any ground. See 18A Wright & Miller § 4449, pp. 351-53, and n.33 (collecting cases). To ward off confusion, we avoid using the term "privity" in this opinion.

he has already "had his day in court" even though he was not a formal party to the litigation. Id., Comment a, p. 382.

Fifth, a party bound by a judgment may not avoid its preclusive force by relitigating through a proxy. Preclusion is thus in order when a person who did not participate in a litigation later brings suit as the designated representative of a person who was a party to the prior adjudication. See Chicago, R.I. & P.R. Co. v. Schendel, 270 U.S. 611, 620, 623 (1926). And although our decisions have not addressed the issue directly, it also seems clear that preclusion is appropriate when a nonparty later brings suit as an agent for a party who is bound by a judgment.

Sixth, in certain circumstances a special statutory scheme may "expressly foreclos[e] successive litigation by nonlitigants . . . if the scheme is otherwise consistent with due process." *Martin*, 490 U.S., at 762, n.2. Examples of such schemes include bankruptcy and probate proceedings, see ibid., and quo warranto actions or other suits that, "under [the governing] law, [may] be brought only on behalf of the public at large," *Richards*, 517 U.S., at 804.

## III

Reaching beyond these six established categories, some lower courts have recognized a "virtual representation" exception to the rule against nonparty preclusion. Decisions of these courts, however, have been far from consistent. See 18A Wright & Miller § 4457, p. 513 (virtual representation lacks a "clear or coherent theory"; decisions applying it have "an episodic quality"). Some Circuits use the label, but define "virtual representation" so that it is no broader than the recognized exception for adequate representation. See, e.g., Becherer v. Merrill Lynch, Pierce, Fenner & Smith, Inc., 193 F.3d 415, 423, 427 (C.A.6 1999) (en banc). But other courts, including the Eighth, Ninth, and D.C. Circuits, apply multifactor tests for virtual representation that permit nonparty preclusion in cases that do not fit within any of the established exceptions.

The D.C. Circuit, the FAA, and Fairchild have presented three arguments in support of an expansive doctrine of virtual representation. We find none of them persuasive.

## A

The D.C. Circuit purported to ground its virtual representation doctrine in this Court's decisions stating that, in some circumstances, a person may be bound by a judgment if she was adequately represented by a party to the proceeding yielding that judgment. See 490 F.3d, at 970-71. But the D.C. Circuit's definition of "adequate representation" strayed from the meaning our decisions have attributed to that term.

In *Richards*, we reviewed a decision by the Alabama Supreme Court holding that a challenge to a tax was barred by a judgment upholding the same tax in a suit filed by different taxpayers. 517 U.S., at 795-97. The plaintiffs in the first suit "did not sue on behalf of a class," their complaint "did not purport to assert any claim against or on behalf of any nonparties," and the judgment "did not purport to bind" nonparties. Id., at 801. There was no indication, we emphasized, that the court in the first suit "took care to protect the interests" of absent parties, or that the parties to that litigation "understood their suit to be on behalf of absent [parties]." Id., at 802. In these circumstances, we held, the application of claim preclusion was inconsistent with "the due process of law guaranteed by the Fourteenth Amendment." Id., at 797.

The D.C. Circuit stated, without elaboration, that it did not "read *Richards* to hold a nonparty . . . adequately represented only if special procedures were followed [to protect the nonparty] or the party to the prior suit understood it was representing the nonparty." 490 F.3d, at 971. As the D.C. Circuit saw this case, Herrick adequately represented Taylor for two principal reasons: Herrick had a strong incentive to litigate; and Taylor later hired Herrick's lawyer, suggesting Taylor's "satisfaction with the attorney's performance in the prior case." Id., at 975.

The D.C. Circuit misapprehended *Richards*. As just recounted, our holding that the Alabama Supreme Court's application of res judicata to nonparties violated due process turned on the lack of either special procedures to protect the nonparties' interests or an understanding by the concerned parties that the first suit was brought in a representative capacity. See *Richards*, 517 U.S., at 801-02. *Richards* thus established that representation is "adequate" for purposes of nonparty preclusion only if (at a minimum) one of these two circumstances is present.

We restated *Richards'* core holding in South Central Bell Telephone Co. v. Alabama, 526 U.S. 160 (1999). In that case, as in *Richards*, the Alabama courts had held that a judgment rejecting a challenge to a tax by one group of taxpayers barred a subsequent suit by a different taxpayer. See 526 U.S., at 164-65. In *South Central Bell*, however, the nonparty had notice of the original suit and engaged one of the lawyers earlier employed by the original plaintiffs. See id., at 167-68. Under the D.C. Circuit's decision in Taylor's case, these factors apparently would have sufficed to establish adequate representation. See 490 F.3d, at 973-75. Yet *South Central Bell* held that the application of res judicata in that case violated due process. Our inquiry came to an end when we determined that the original plaintiffs had not understood themselves to be acting in a representative capacity and that there had been no special procedures to safeguard the interests of absentees. See 526 U.S., at 168.

Our decisions recognizing that a nonparty may be bound by a judgment if she was adequately represented by a party to the earlier suit thus provide no support for the D.C. Circuit's broad theory of virtual representation.

## B

Fairchild and the FAA do not argue that the D.C. Circuit's virtual representation doctrine fits within any of the recognized grounds for nonparty preclusion. Rather, they ask us to abandon the attempt to delineate discrete grounds and clear rules altogether. Preclusion is in order, they contend, whenever "the relationship between a party and a non-party is 'close enough' to bring the second litigant within the judgment." Courts should make the "close enough" determination, they urge, through a "heavily fact-driven" and "equitable" inquiry. Only this sort of diffuse balancing, Fairchild and the FAA argue, can account for all of the situations in which nonparty preclusion is appropriate.

We reject this argument for three reasons. First, our decisions emphasize the fundamental nature of the general rule that a litigant is not bound by a judgment to which she was not a party. See, e.g., *Richards*, 517 U.S., at 798-99; *Martin*, 490 U.S., at 761-62. Accordingly, we have endeavored to delineate discrete exceptions that apply in "limited circumstances." Id., at 762, n.2. Respondents' amorphous balancing test is at odds with the constrained approach to nonparty preclusion our decisions advance.

Resisting this reading of our precedents, respondents call up three decisions they view as supportive of the approach they espouse. Fairchild quotes our statement in Coryell v. Phipps, 317 U.S. 406, 411 (1943), that privity "turns on the facts of particular cases." That observation, however, scarcely implies that privity is governed by a diffuse balancing test. Fairchild also cites Blonder-Tongue Laboratories, Inc. v. University of Ill. Foundation, 402 U.S. 313, 334 (1971), which stated that estoppel questions turn on "the trial courts' sense of justice and equity." This passing statement, however, was not made with nonparty preclusion in mind; it appeared in a discussion recognizing district courts' discretion to limit the use of issue preclusion against persons who *were* parties to a judgment. See *Blonder-Tongue*, 402 U.S., at 334.

The FAA relies on United States v. Des Moines Valley R. Co., 84 F. 40 (C.A.8 1897). . . . *Des Moines Valley* was a quiet title action in which the named plaintiff was the United States. The Government, however, had "no interest in the land" and had "simply permitted [the landowner] to use its name as the nominal plaintiff." 84 F., at 42. The suit was therefore barred, the appeals court held, by an earlier judgment against the landowner. As the court explained: "[W]here the government lends its name as a plaintiff . . . to enable one private person to maintain a suit against another," the government is "subject to the same defenses which exist . . . against the real party in interest." Id., at 43. *Des Moines Valley*, the FAA contended at oral argument, demonstrates that it is sometimes appropriate to bind a nonparty in circumstances that do not fit within any of the established grounds for nonparty preclusion. Properly understood, however, *Des Moines Valley* is simply an application of the fifth basis for nonparty preclusion described above: A party may not use a representative or agent to relitigate an adverse judgment. We thus find no support in our precedents for the lax approach to nonparty preclusion advocated by respondents.

Our second reason for rejecting a broad doctrine of virtual representation rests on the limitations attending nonparty preclusion based on adequate representation. A party's representation of a nonparty is "adequate" for preclusion purposes only if, at a minimum: (1) the interests of the non-party and her representative are aligned, see *Hansberry*, 311 U.S., at 43; and (2) either the party understood herself to be acting in a representative capacity or the original court took care to protect the interests of the nonparty, see *Richards*, 517 U.S., at 801-02. In addition, adequate representation sometimes requires (3) notice of the original suit to the persons alleged to have been represented, see *Richards*, 517 U.S., at 801. In the class-action context, these limitations are implemented by the procedural safeguards contained in Federal Rule of Civil Procedure 23.

An expansive doctrine of virtual representation, however, would "recogniz[e], in effect, a common-law kind of class action." *Tice*, 162 F.3d, at 972. That is, virtual representation would authorize preclusion based on identity of interests and some kind of relationship between parties and nonparties, shorn of the procedural protections prescribed in *Hansberry*, *Richards*, and Rule 23. These protections, grounded in due process, could be circumvented were we to approve a virtual representation doctrine that allowed courts to "create de facto class actions at will." *Tice*, 162 F.3d, at 973.

Third, a diffuse balancing approach to nonparty preclusion would likely create more headaches than it relieves. Most obviously, it could significantly complicate the task of district courts faced in the first instance with preclusion questions. An all-things-considered balancing approach might spark wide-ranging, time-consuming, and expensive discovery tracking factors potentially relevant under seven- or five-prong tests. And after the relevant facts are established, district judges would be called upon to evaluate them under a standard that provides no firm guidance. See *Tyus*, 93 F.3d, at 455 (conceding that "there is no clear test for determining the applicability of" the virtual representation doctrine announced in that case). Preclusion doctrine, it should be recalled, is intended to reduce the burden of litigation on courts and parties. Cf. *Montana*, 440 U.S., at 153-54. "In this area of the law," we agree, "'crisp rules with sharp corners' are preferable to a round-about doctrine of opaque standards." Bittinger v. Tecumseh Products Co., 123 F.3d 877, 881 (C.A.6 1997).

## C

Finally, relying on the Eighth Circuit's decision in *Tyus*, 93 F.3d, at 456, the FAA maintains that nonparty preclusion should apply more broadly in "public law" litigation than in "private law" controversies. To support this position, the FAA offers two arguments. First, the FAA urges, our decision in *Richards* acknowledges that, in certain cases, the plaintiff has a reduced interest in controlling the litigation "because of the public nature of the right at issue." When a taxpayer challenges "an alleged misuse of public funds" or "other public action," we observed in *Richards*, the suit "has only an indirect impact on [the plaintiff's] interests." 517 U.S., at 803. In actions of this character, the Court said, "we may assume that the States have wide latitude to establish procedures . . . to limit the number of judicial proceedings that may be entertained." Ibid.

Taylor's FOIA action falls within the category described in *Richards*, the FAA contends, because "the duty to disclose under FOIA is owed to the public generally." The opening sentence of FOIA, it is true, states that agencies "shall make [information] available to the public." 5 U.S.C. § 552(a) (2006 ed.). Equally true, we have several times said that FOIA vindicates a "public" interest. E.g., National Archives and Records Admin. v. Favish, 541 U.S. 157, 172 (2004). The Act, however, instructs agencies receiving FOIA requests to make the information available not to the public at large, but rather to the "person" making the request. § 552(a)(3)(A). Thus, in contrast to the public-law litigation contemplated in *Richards*, a successful FOIA action results in a grant of relief to the individual plaintiff, not a decree benefiting the public at large.

Furthermore, we said in *Richards* only that, for the type of public-law claims there envisioned, States are free to adopt procedures limiting repetitive litigation. See 517 U.S., at 803. In this regard, we referred to instances in which the first judgment foreclosed successive litigation by other plaintiffs because, "under state law, [the suit] could be brought only on behalf of the public at large." Id., at 804.[12] *Richards* spoke of state legislation, but it appears equally evident that *Congress*, in providing for actions vindicating a public interest, may "limit the number of judicial proceedings that may be entertained." Id., at 803. It hardly follows, however, that *this Court* should proscribe or confine successive FOIA suits by different requesters. Indeed, Congress' provision for FOIA suits with no statutory constraint on successive actions counsels against judicial imposition of constraints through extraordinary application of the common law of preclusion.

The FAA next argues that "the threat of vexatious litigation is heightened" in public-law cases because "the number of plaintiffs with standing is potentially limitless." FOIA does allow "any person" whose request is denied to resort to federal court for review of the agency's determination. 5 U.S.C. § 552(a)(3)(A), (4)(B) (2006 ed.). Thus it is theoretically possible that several persons could coordinate to mount a series of repetitive lawsuits.

But we are not convinced that this risk justifies departure from the usual rules governing nonparty preclusion. First, *stare decisis* will allow courts swiftly to dispose of repetitive suits brought in the same circuit. Second, even when *stare decisis* is not dispositive, "the human tendency not to waste money will deter the bringing of suits based on claims or issues that have already been adversely determined against others." Shapiro 97. This intuition seems to be borne out by experience: The FAA has not called our attention to any instances of abusive FOIA suits in the Circuits that reject the virtual representation theory respondents advocate here.

12. Nonparty preclusion in such cases ranks under the sixth exception described above: special statutory schemes that expressly limit subsequent suits.

## IV

For the foregoing reasons, we disapprove the theory of virtual representation on which the decision below rested. The preclusive effects of a judgment in a federal-question case decided by a federal court should instead be determined according to the established grounds for nonparty preclusion described in this opinion.

Although references to "virtual representation" have proliferated in the lower courts, our decision is unlikely to occasion any great shift in actual practice. Many opinions use the term "virtual representation" in reaching results at least arguably defensible on established grounds. See 18A Wright & Miller § 4457, pp. 535-539, and n.38 (collecting cases). In these cases, dropping the "virtual representation" label would lead to clearer analysis with little, if any, change in outcomes. See *Tice*, 162 F.3d, at 971 ("[T]he term 'virtual representation' has cast more shadows than light on the problem [of nonparty preclusion].").

In some cases, however, lower courts have relied on virtual representation to extend nonparty preclusion beyond the latter doctrine's proper bounds. We now turn back to Taylor's action to determine whether his suit is such a case, or whether the result reached by the courts below can be justified on one of the recognized grounds for nonparty preclusion.

## A

It is uncontested that four of the six grounds for nonparty preclusion have no application here: There is no indication that Taylor agreed to be bound by Herrick's litigation, that Taylor and Herrick have any legal relationship, that Taylor exercised any control over Herrick's suit, or that this suit implicates any special statutory scheme limiting relitigation. Neither the FAA nor Fairchild contends otherwise.

It is equally clear that preclusion cannot be justified on the theory that Taylor was adequately represented in Herrick's suit. Nothing in the record indicates that Herrick understood himself to be suing on Taylor's behalf, that Taylor even knew of Herrick's suit, or that the Wyoming District Court took special care to protect Taylor's interests. Under our path-marking precedent, therefore, Herrick's representation was not "adequate." See *Richards*, 517 U.S., at 801-02.

That leaves only the fifth category: preclusion because a nonparty to an earlier litigation has brought suit as a representative or agent of a party who is bound by the prior adjudication. Taylor is not Herrick's legal representative and he has not purported to sue in a representative capacity. He concedes, however, that preclusion would be appropriate if respondents could demonstrate that he is acting as Herrick's "undisclosed agen[t]."

Respondents argue here, as they did below, that Taylor's suit is a collusive attempt to relitigate Herrick's action. The D.C. Circuit considered a similar question in addressing the "tactical maneuvering" prong of its virtual representation test. See 490 F.3d, at 976. The Court of Appeals did not, however, treat the issue as one of agency, and it expressly declined to reach any definitive conclusions due to "the ambiguity of the facts." Ibid. We therefore remand to give the courts below an opportunity to determine whether Taylor, in pursuing the instant FOIA suit, is acting as Herrick's agent. Taylor concedes that such a remand is appropriate.

We have never defined the showing required to establish that a nonparty to a prior adjudication has become a litigating agent for a party to the earlier case. Because the issue has not been briefed in any detail, we do not discuss the matter elaboratively here. We note, however, that courts should be cautious about finding preclusion on this basis. A mere whiff of "tactical maneuvering" will not suffice; instead, principles of agency law are suggestive. They indicate that preclusion is appropriate only if the putative agent's conduct of the suit is subject to the control of the party who is bound by the prior adjudication. See 1 Restatement (Second) of Agency § 14, p. 60 (1957) ("A principal has the right to control the conduct of the agent with respect to matters entrusted to him.").[13]

## B

On remand, Fairchild suggests, Taylor should bear the burden of proving he is not acting as Herrick's agent. When a defendant points to evidence establishing a close relationship between successive litigants, Fairchild maintains, "the burden [should] shif[t] to the second litigant to submit evidence refuting the charge" of agency. Fairchild justifies this proposed burden-shift on the ground that "it is unlikely an opposing party will have access to direct evidence of collusion."

We reject Fairchild's suggestion. Claim preclusion, like issue preclusion, is an affirmative defense. See Fed. Rule Civ. Proc. 8(c); *Blonder-Tongue*, 402 U.S., at 350. Ordinarily, it is incumbent on the defendant to plead and prove such a defense, and we have never recognized claim preclusion as an exception to that general rule, see 18 Wright & Miller § 4405, p. 83 ("[A] party asserting preclusion must carry the burden of establishing all necessary elements."). We acknowledge that direct evidence justifying nonparty preclusion is often in the hands of plaintiffs rather than defendants. See, e.g., *Montana*, 440 U.S., at 155 (listing evidence of control over a prior suit). But "[v]ery often one must plead and prove matters as to which his

---

13. Our decision in Montana v. United States, 440 U.S. 147 (1979), also suggests a "control" test for agency. In that case, we held that the United States was barred from bringing a suit because it had controlled a prior unsuccessful action filed by a federal contractor. See id., at 155. We see no reason why preclusion based on a lesser showing would have been appropriate if the order of the two actions had been switched—that is, if the United States had brought the first suit itself, and then sought to relitigate the same claim through the contractor. See *Schendel*, 270 U.S., at 618 ("[I]f, in legal contemplation, there is identity of parties" when two suits are brought in one order, "there must be like identity" when the order is reversed.).

adversary has superior access to the proof." 2 K. Broun, McCormick on Evidence § 337, p. 475 (6th ed. 2006). In these situations, targeted interrogatories or deposition questions can reduce the information disparity. We see no greater cause here than in other matters of affirmative defense to disturb the traditional allocation of the proof burden.

\* \* \*

. . . [T]he judgment of the District of Columbia Circuit Court is vacated, and the case is remanded for further proceedings consistent with this opinion.

*It is so ordered.*

## Notes and Questions

1. As you can see from *Taylor*, there is a danger of endless litigation if privity is too narrowly defined. On the other hand, if privity is too broadly defined—if future litigants stand in privity with prior litigants whose purely legal interests align—a great deal of public law litigation would be precluded. Indeed, as the Court warns, privity would function as a kind of common law class action rule, binding strangers to the litigation who were "virtually" represented in only the most trivial sense. And yet the Court appears to endorse a broader approach in public interest cases. What is the justification for this? For analysis of the case, see Martin H. Redish & William J. Katt, Taylor v. Sturgell, Procedural Due Process, and the Day-in-Court Ideal: Resolving the Virtual Representation Dilemma, 84 Notre Dame L. Rev. 1877 (2009).

2. Even before *Taylor*, courts were reluctant to find privity on the basis that the same attorney represented parties with similar claims in different cases. See Headwaters Inc. v. U.S. Forest Service, 399 F.3d 1047, 1053-54 (9th Cir. 2005) (reversing district court's application of privity doctrine to two environmental organizations who had not before litigated the validity of certain timber sales where counsel for the organizations, a year earlier, signed a dismissal with prejudice of a similar suit); see id. at 1050, 1054-1056 (privity doctrine only applies if "the present plaintiffs were adequately represented in the prior suit" but "parallel legal interests alone, identical or otherwise, are not sufficient to establish privity, or to bind a plaintiff to a decision reached in another case involving another plaintiff"; remanding for reconsideration and a fact hearing on the ties between plaintiffs in the two suits and whether the first suit was "structured so as to protect 'strangers' to that case").

3. What about the preclusive effect of an injunction upon dissolution of the organization bound? Can members who form related new organizations be bound? See Nat'l Spiritual Assembly of Baha'is of U.S. Under Hereditary Guardianship, Inc. v. Nat'l Spiritual Assembly of Baha'is of U.S., Inc., 628 F.3d 837 (7th Cir. 2010) (following *Taylor* and upholding denial of contempt motion brought against new religious corporation formed after

dissolution of an earlier one; "To find privity based on 'adequate representation' here would treat every suit by an organization as having res judicata and contempt implications for the organization's members *individually.*").

4. Recall the note after Martin v. Wilks in Chapter 6 describing the intervention of Congress in 1991 to insulate a "judgment or order that resolves a claim of employment discrimination" from collateral attack by a person who had "actual notice" of the proposed judgment and an "opportunity . . . to present objections," where that person's interests were "adequately represented by another." After white firefighters outperformed minority candidates on promotion exams in 2003, the city of New Haven decided not to certify the results because it feared that doing so would be a basis for *disparate impact* liability under Title VII. Eighteen firefighters (all but one of them white) then sued the city's civil service board on the ground that refusing to certify the results was illegal *intentional* discrimination under Title VII. The Supreme Court agreed in Ricci v. DeStefano, 557 U.S. 557 (2009). Anticipating that minority firefighters might bring disparate impact suits against the city after the test results were certified, the Supreme Court emphasized:

> If, after it certifies the test results, the City faces a disparate-impact suit, then in light of our holding today it should be clear that the City would avoid disparate-impact liability based on the strong basis in evidence that, had it not certified the results, it would have been subject to disparate-treatment liability.

Id. at 593. In a subsequent disparate impact suit by an African-American firefighter not a party to *Ricci*, the district court dismissed the case on the ground that *Ricci* had preclusive effect and that if the plaintiff wanted to protect his rights he should have intervened in *Ricci*. The Second Circuit reversed, relying on *Taylor* and the 1991 Civil Rights Act to support its conclusion that the plaintiff's disparate impact claims were not precluded. Briscoe v. City of New Haven, 654 F.3d 200 (2d Cir. 2011), *cert. denied*, 132 S. Ct. 2741 (2012). The court treated the above quoted phrase from *Ricci* as mere dicta.

The core of the *Ricci* case was about whether the city could take the possibility of disparate impact liability into account in making a decision to use or reject its test scores. The *Ricci* test requires a high degree of confidence that disparate impact liability will in fact follow. The *Ricci* Court's anticipation of "reverse-*Ricci*" scenarios quoted above flips that test around, suggesting that the city could defend against disparate impact liability in the future by showing that it would have been liable for intentional discrimination if it failed to use the test scores. That inquiry is clearly outside the facts of *Ricci* and properly treated as dicta. Can you see other reasons to distinguish *Ricci* from *Briscoe*? It matters, doesn't it, that evidence of intentional discrimination is generally much less objective than evidence supporting a claim of disparate impact?

5. State courts have not uniformly followed the narrow approach to virtual representation taken by the Supreme Court in *Taylor*. See City of Chicago v. St. John's United Church of Christ, 935 N.E.2d 1158, 1168 (Ill. App. 2010) ("A nonparty may be bound pursuant to privity if his interests are so closely aligned to those of a party that the party is the 'virtual representative' of the nonparty. . . . *Taylor* in no way addressed, let alone overruled, this state's common law regarding privity."); Exec. Risk Indem., Inc. v. Jones, 89 Cal. Rptr. 3d 747, 760 n.12 (App. 2009).

## 3. Preclusion in a Federal System

Among the most complicated issues within the complex field of claim and issue preclusion are the effects of judgments by state courts in federal court and vice versa. Below we introduce these problems of inter-sovereign relations, though an appreciation of their fuller dimension will come through your future work in courses on constitutional law, federal courts, conflicts, and complex litigation. The decisions demonstrate how powerful, conflicting ideals for full hearings and forum choice on the one hand, and for efficiency and repose on the other, can make for hard cases. This is an area of the law to which you will often return.

### a. State Court Judgments in Federal Courts

*Kremer v. Chemical Corp.*
456 U.S. 461 (1982)

JUSTICE WHITE delivered the opinion of the Court.

As one of its first acts, Congress directed that all United States courts afford the same full-faith-and-credit to state court judgments that would apply in the state's own courts. Act of May 26, 1790, ch. 11, 1 Stat. 122, 28 U.S.C. § 1738 [(1976)]. More recently, Congress implemented the national policy against employment discrimination by creating an array of substantive protections and remedies which generally allows federal courts to determine the merits of a discrimination claim. Title VII of the Civil Rights Act of 1964, 78 Stat. 253, as amended, 42 U.S.C. §§ 2000e et seq. (1976). The principal question presented by this case is whether Congress intended Title VII to supersede the principles of comity and repose embodied in § 1738. Specifically, we decide whether a federal court in a Title VII case should give preclusive effect to a decision of a state court upholding a state administrative agency's rejection of an employment discrimination claim as meritless when the state court's decision would be res judicata in the state's own courts. . . .

Petitioner Rubin Kremer emigrated from Poland in 1970 and was hired in 1973 by respondent Chemical Corporation ("Chemico") as an engineer. Two years later he was laid off, along with a number of other employees. Some of these employees were later rehired, but Kremer was not although he made several applications. In May 1976, Kremer filed a discrimination charge with the Equal Employment Opportunity Commission (EEOC), asserting that his discharge and failure to be rehired was due to his national origin and Jewish faith. Because the EEOC may not consider a claim until a state agency having jurisdiction over employment discrimination complaints has had at least 60 days to resolve the matter, § 706(c), 42 U.S.C. § 2000e-5(c), the Commission referred Kremer's charge to the New York State Division of Human Rights ("NYHRD"), the agency charged with enforcing the New York law prohibiting employment discrimination. N.Y. Exec. Law §§ 295(6), 296(1)(a) (McKinney 1972 and Supp. 1981-1982).

After investigating Kremer's complaint, the NYHRD concluded that there was no probable cause to believe that Chemico had engaged in the discriminatory practices complained of. The NYHRD explicitly based its determination on the finding that Kremer was not rehired because one employee who was rehired had greater seniority, that another employee who was rehired filled a lesser position than that previously held by Kremer, and that neither Kremer's creed nor age was a factor considered in Chemico's failure to rehire him. The NYHRD's determination was upheld by its Appeal Board as "not arbitrary, capricious, or an abuse of discretion." Kremer again brought his complaint to the attention of the EEOC and also filed, on December 6, 1977, a petition with the Appellate Division of the New York Supreme Court to set aside the adverse administrative determination. On February 21, 1978, five justices of the Appellate Division unanimously affirmed the Appeal Board's order. Kremer could have, but did not seek review by the New York Court of Appeals.

Subsequently, a District Director of the EEOC ruled that there was no reasonable cause to believe that the charge of discrimination was true and issued a right-to-sue notice. The District Director refused a request for reconsideration, noting that he had reviewed the case files and considered the EEOC's disposition as "appropriate and correct in all respects."

Kremer then brought this Title VII action in District Court, claiming discrimination on the basis of national origin and religion. . . .

. . . The District Court . . . dismissed the complaint on grounds of res judicata. 477 F. Supp. 587 (S.D.N.Y. 1979). The Court of Appeals [affirmed]. 623 F.2d 786 ([2d Cir.] 1980).

. . . [P]etitioner filed for a writ of certiorari. We issued the writ . . . to resolve [an] important issue of federal employment discrimination law over which the Courts of Appeals are divided. We now *affirm.* . . .

Section 1738 requires federal courts to give the same preclusive effect to state court judgments that those judgments would be given in the courts of the state from which the judgments emerged. Here the Appellate Division of the New York Supreme Court has issued a judgment affirming the decision of the NYHRD Appeals Board that the discharge and failure to rehire Kremer were not the product of the discrimination that he had alleged. There is no question that this judicial determination precludes Kremer from bringing "any other action, civil or criminal, based upon the same grievance" in the New York courts. N.Y. Exec. Law § 300 (McKinney 1972).

By its terms, therefore, § 1738 would appear to preclude Kremer from reliti-gating the same question in federal court.

Kremer offers two principal reasons why § 1738 does not bar this action. First, he suggests that in Title VII cases Congress intended that federal courts be relieved of their usual obligation to grant finality to state court decisions. . . .

Allen v. McCurry, 449 U.S. 90, 99 (1980), made clear that an exception to § 1738 will not be recognized unless a later statute contains an express or implied partial repeal. There is no claim here that Title VII expressly repealed § 1738; if there has been a partial repeal, it must be implied. "It is, of course, a cardinal principle of statutory construction that repeals by implication are not favored." Radzanower v. Touche Ross & Co., 426 U.S. 148, 154 (1976); United States v. United Continental Tuna Corp., 425 U.S. 164, 168 (1976), and whenever possible, statutes should be read consistently.

. . . Congress enacted Title VII to assure equality of employment opportu-nities without distinction with respect to race, color, religion, sex, or national origin. Alexander v. Gardner-Denver Co., 415 U.S. 36, 44 (1974); McDonnell Douglas Corp. v. Green, 411 U.S. 792, 800 (1973). To this end the EEOC was created and the federal courts were entrusted with ultimate enforcement responsibility. State anti-discrimination laws, however, play an integral role in the Congressional scheme. Whenever an incident of alleged employment discrimination occurs in a state or locality which by law prohibits such discrimination and which has established an "authority to grant or seek relief from such [discrimination] or to institute criminal proceedings with respect thereto," no charge of discrimination may be actively processed by the EEOC until the state remedy has been invoked and at least 60 days have passed, or the state proceedings have terminated. § 706(c), 42 U.S.C. § 2000e-5(c). Only after providing the appropriate state agency an opportunity to resolve the complaint may an aggrieved individual press his complaint before the EEOC. In its investigation to determine whether there is reason-able cause to believe that the charge of employment discrimination is true, the Commission is required to "accord substantial weight to final findings and orders made by State and local authorities in proceedings commenced under State or local law" pursuant to the limited deferral provisions of § 706, but is not bound by such findings. Alexander v. Gardner-Denver Co., [415 U.S.] at 48, n.8. If the EEOC finds reasonable cause to believe that dis-crimination has occurred, it undertakes conciliation efforts to eliminate the unlawful practice; if these efforts fail, the Commission may elect to bring a civil action to enforce the Act. If the Commission declines to do so, or if the Commission finds no reasonable cause to believe that a violation has occurred, "a civil action" may be brought by an aggrieved individual. § 706(f)(1); 42 U.S.C. § 2000e-5(f)(1).

No provision of Title VII requires claimants to pursue in state court an unfavorable state administrative action, nor does the Act specify the weight a federal court should afford a final judgment by a state court if such a remedy is sought. While we have interpreted the "civil action" authorized to follow consideration by federal and state administrative *agencies* to be a "trial de novo," Chandler v. Roudebush, 425 U.S. 840, 844-845 (1976); Alexander v. Gardner-Denver Co., [415 U.S.] at 38; McDonnell Douglas Corp. v. Green, [411 U.S.] at 798-799, neither the statute nor our decisions indicate that the final judgment of a state *court* is subject to redetermination at such a trial. Similarly, the Congressional directive that the EEOC should give "substantial weight" to findings made in state proceedings, § 706(b), 42 U.S.C. § 2000e-5(b), indicates only the minimum level of deference the EEOC must afford all state determinations; it does not bar affording the greater preclusive effect which may be required by § 1738 if judicial action is involved. To suggest otherwise, to say that either the opportunity to bring a "civil action" or the "substantial weight" requirement implicitly repeals § 1738, is to prove far too much. For if that is so, even a full trial on the merits in state court would not bar a trial *de novo* in federal court and would not be entitled to more than "substantial weight," before the EEOC. The state courts would be placed on a one-way street; the finality of their decisions would depend on which side prevailed in a given case. . . .

At the time Title VII was written, over half of the states had enacted some form of equal employment legislation. . . . Senator Humphrey, an advocate of strong enforcement, emphasized the state role under the legislation:

> We recognized that many States already have functioning antidiscrimination programs to insure equal access to places of public accommodation and equal employment opportunity. We sought merely to guarantee that these States — and other States which may establish such programs — will be given every opportunity to employ their expertise and experience without premature interference by the Federal Government. [110 Cong. Rec. 12725 (1964).]

Indeed, New York's fair employment laws were referred to in the Congressional debates by proponents of the legislation as an example of existing state legislation effectively combatting employment discrimination. . . .

Because Congress must "clearly manifest" its intent to depart from § 1738, our prior decisions construing Title VII in situations where § 1738 is inapplicable are not dispositive. They establish only that *initial resort* to state administrative remedies does not deprive an individual of a right to a federal trial *de novo* on a Title VII claim. In McDonnell Douglas Corp. v. Green, 411 U.S. 792 (1973) and Chandler v. Roudebush, 415 U.S. 820 (1976), we held that the "civil action" in federal court following an EEOC decision was intended to be a trial de novo. This holding, clearly supported by the legislative history, is not a holding that a prior state court judgment can be disregarded.

The petitioners and the Courts of Appeals which have denied res judicata effect to such judgments rely heavily on our statement in Alexander v. Gardner-Denver, that "final responsibility for enforcement of Title VII is vested with federal courts." 415 U.S. at 44. We did not say, and our language should not be read to imply, that by vesting "final responsibility" in one forum, Congress intended to deny finality to decisions in another. The context of the statement makes this clear. In describing the operation of Title

VII, we noted that the EEOC cannot adjudicate claims or impose sanctions; that responsibility, the "final responsibility of enforcement," must rest in federal court.

The holding in *Gardner-Denver* was that a private arbitration decision concerning an employment discrimination claim did not bind the federal courts. Arbitration decisions, of course, are not subject to the mandate of § 1738. Furthermore, unlike arbitration hearings under collective bargaining agreements, state fair employment practice laws are explicitly made part of the Title VII enforcement scheme. Our decision in *Gardner-Denver* explicitly recognized the "distinctly separate nature of these contractual and statutory rights." Id. at 50. Here we are dealing with a state statutory right, subject to state enforcement in a manner expressly provided for by the federal Act. . . .

Finally, the comity and federalism interests embodied in § 1738 are not compromised by the application of res judicata and collateral estoppel in Title VII cases. Petitioner maintains that the decision of the Court of Appeals will deter claimants from seeking state court review of their claims ultimately leading to a deterioration in the quality of the state administrative process. On the contrary, stripping state court judgments of finality would be far more destructive to the quality of adjudication by lessening the incentive for full participation by the parties and for searching review by state officials. Depriving state judgments of finality not only would violate basic tenets of comity and federalism, Board of Regents v. Tomanio, 446 U.S. 478, 488, 491-492 (1980), but also would reduce the incentive for states to work towards effective and meaningful anti-discrimination systems. . . .

The petitioner nevertheless contends that the judgment should not bar his Title VII action because the New York courts did not resolve the issue that the District Court must hear under Title VII—whether Kremer had suffered discriminatory treatment—and because the procedures provided were inadequate. Neither contention is persuasive. Although the claims presented to the NYHRD and subsequently reviewed by the Appellate Division were necessarily based on New York law, the alleged discriminatory acts are prohibited by both federal and state laws. The elements of a successful employment discrimination claim are virtually identical; petitioner could not succeed on a Title VII claim consistently with the judgment of the NYHRD that there is no reason to believe he was terminated or not rehired because of national origin or religion. The Appellate Division's affirmance of the NYHRD's dismissal necessarily decided that petitioner's claim under New York law was meritless, and thus it also decided that a Title VII claim arising from the same events would be equally meritless.

The more serious contention is that even though administrative proceedings and judicial review are legally sufficient to be given preclusive effect in New York, they should be deemed so fundamentally flawed as to be denied recognition under § 1738. We have previously recognized that the judicially created doctrine of collateral estoppel does not apply when the party against whom the earlier decision is asserted did not have a "full and fair opportunity" to litigate the claim or issue, Allen v. McCurry, 449

U.S. at 95; Montana v. United States, 440 U.S. 147, 153 (1979); Blonder-Tongue Laboratories, Inc. v. University of Illinois Foundation, 402 U.S. 313, 328-329 (1971). "Redetermination of issues is warranted if there is reason to doubt the quality, extensiveness, or fairness of the procedures followed in the prior litigation." Montana v. United States, [440 U.S.] at 164 n.11. Cf. Gibson v. Berryhill, 411 U.S. 564 (1973). . . .

We have little doubt that Kremer received all the process that was constitutionally required in rejecting his claim that he had been discriminatorily discharged contrary to the statute. We must bear in mind that no single model of procedural fairness, let alone a particular form of procedure, is dictated by the Due Process Clause. Mitchell v. W. T. Grant Co., 416 U.S. 600, 610 (1974); Inland Empire Council v. Millis, 325 U.S. 697, 710 (1945). "'The very nature of due process negates any concept of inflexible procedures universally applicable to every imaginable situation.'" Mitchell v. W.T. Grant Co., [416 U.S.] at 610 (quoting Cafeteria Workers v. McElroy, 367 U.S. 886, 895 (1961)). Under New York law, a claim of employment discrimination requires the NYHRD to investigate whether there is "probable cause" to believe that the complaint is true. Before this determination of probable cause is made, the claimant is entitled to a "full opportunity to present on the record, though informally, his charges against his employer or other respondent, including the right to submit all exhibits which he wishes to present and testimony of witnesses in addition to his own testimony." State Div. of Human Rights v. New York State Drug Abuse Commn., 59 A.D.2d 332, 336 (1977). The complainant also is entitled to an opportunity "to rebut evidence submitted by or obtained from the respondent." 9 N.Y.C.R.R. § 465.6 (1977). He may have an attorney assist him and may ask the division to issue subpoenas. 9 N.Y.C.R.R. § 465.12(c) (1977).

If the investigation disclosed probable cause and efforts at conciliation fail, the NYHRD must conduct a public hearing to determine the merits of the complaint. N.Y. Exec. Law § 297(4)(a) (McKinney Supp. 1981-1982). A public hearing must also be held if the Human Rights Appeal Board finds "there has not been a full investigation and opportunity for the complainant to present his contentions and evidence, with a full record." State Div. of Human Rights v. New York State Drug Abuse Commn., [59 A.D.2d] at 337. Finally, judicial review in the Appellate Division is available to assure that a claimant is not denied any of the procedural rights to which he was entitled and that the NYHRD's determination was not arbitrary and capricious. N.Y. Civ. Prac. Law § 7803 (McKinney 1981). . . .

We have no hesitation in concluding that this panoply of procedures, complemented by administrative as well as judicial review, is sufficient under the Due Process Clause. Only where the evidence submitted by the claimant fails, as a matter of law, to reveal any merit to the complaint may the NYHRD make a determination of no probable cause without holding a hearing. Flah's, Inc. v. Schneider, 71 A.D.2d 993 (1979). . . . And before that determination may be reached, New York requires the NYHRD to make a full investigation, wherein the complainant has full opportunity to present his evidence, under oath if he so requests. State Div. of Human Rights v.

New York State Drug Abuse Control Commission, [59 A.D.2d] at 336. The fact that Mr. Kremer failed to avail himself of the full procedures provided by state law does not constitute a sign of their inadequacy. Cf. Judice v. Vail, 430 U.S. 327, 337 (1977). . . .

In our system of jurisprudence the usual rule is that merits of a legal claim once decided in a court of competent jurisdiction are not subject to redetermination in another forum. Such a fundamental departure from traditional rules of preclusion, enacted into federal law, can be justified only if plainly stated by Congress. Because there is no "affirmative showing" of a "clear and manifest" legislative purpose in Title VII to deny res judicata or collateral estoppel effect to a state court judgment affirming that a claim of employment discrimination is unproved, and because the procedures provided in New York for the determination of such claims offer a full and fair opportunity to litigate the merits, the judgment of the Court of Appeals is

*Affirmed.*

JUSTICE BLACKMUN, with whom JUSTICE BRENNAN and JUSTICE MARSHALL join, dissenting. . . .

Title VII provides that no charge may be filed until 60 days "after proceedings have been commenced under the State or local law, unless such proceedings have been earlier terminated." § 706(c), 42 U.S.C. § 2000e-5(c). After a charge is filed, the Equal Employment Opportunity Commission (EEOC) may take action and, eventually, the complainant may file suit, §§ 706(b) and (f)(1). By permitting a charge to be filed after termination of state proceedings, the statute expressly contemplates that a plaintiff may bring suit despite a state finding of no discrimination.

This fact is also made clear by § 706(b). In 1972, by Pub. L. 92-261, § 4, 86 Stat. 104, Congress amended that section by directing that the EEOC "accord substantial weight to final findings and orders made by State or local authorities in proceedings commenced under State or local law." If the original version of Title VII had given the outcomes of state "proceedings" preclusive effect, Congress would not have found it necessary to amend the statute in 1972 to direct that they be given "substantial weight." And if in 1972 Congress had intended final decisions in state "proceedings" to have preclusive effect, it certainly would not have instructed that they be given "substantial weight."

Thus, Congress expressly recognized in both § 706(b) and § 706(c) that a complainant could bring a Title VII suit in federal court despite the conclusion of state "proceedings." . . .

Yet the Court nevertheless finds that petitioner's Title VII suit is precluded by the termination of state "proceedings." In this case, the New York State Division of Human Rights (NYHRD) found no probable cause to believe that petitioner had been a victim of discrimination. Under the Court's own rule, that determination in itself does not bar petitioner from filing a Title VII suit in federal district court. According to the Court, however, petitioner lost his opportunity to bring a federal suit when he unsuccessfully sought review of the state agency's decision in the New York courts. As the

Court applies preclusion principles to Title VII, the state court affirmance of the state agency decision—*not* the state agency decision itself—blocks any subsequent Title VII suit. . . .

State court review is merely the last step in the administrative process, the final means of review of the state *agency's* decision. For instance, in New York, the NYHRD "is primarily responsible for administering the law and to that end has been granted broad powers to eliminate discriminatory practices." Imperial Diner, Inc. v. State Human Rights Appeal Bd., 52 N.Y.2d 72, 77 (1980). When, as in this case, the NYHRD finds no probable cause, a reviewing court must affirm the division's decision unless it is "arbitrary, capricious or characterized by abuse of discretion or clearly unwarranted exercise of discretion," see N.Y. Exec. Law § 297-a(7)(e) (McKinney 1972), that is, unless the decision is "devoid of a rational basis." State Office of Drug Abuse Servs. v. State Human Rights Appeal Bd., 48 N.Y.2d 276, 284 (1979). If the agency decides to hold a hearing, its decision must be affirmed if it is "supported by substantial evidence on the whole record." N.Y. Exec. Law § 297-a(7)(d) (McKinney Supp. 1981). . . .

This review therefore, is not de novo in the state courts. When it affirms the agency's decision, the reviewing court does not determine that the division was correct. In fact, the court may not "substitute its judgment for that of the [NYHRD]," State Division of Human Rights v. Mecca Kendall Corp., 53 App. Div. 2d 201, 203-204 (1976); the court is "not empowered to find new facts or take a different view of the weight of the evidence if the [NYHRD's] determination is supported by substantial evidence," State Division of Human Rights v. Columbia University, 39 N.Y.2d 612, 616 (1976). . . . In affirming, the reviewing court finds only that the agency's conclusion "was a reasonable one and thus may not be set aside by the courts although a contrary decision may 'have been reasonable and also sustainable.'" Imperial Diner, Inc. v. State Human Rights Appeal Bd., 52 N.Y.2d at 79 (quoting Mize v. State Division of Human Rights, 33 N.Y.2d 53, 56 (1973)).

The Court purports to give preclusive effect to the New York court's decision. But the Appellate Division made no finding one way or the other concerning the *merits* of petitioner's discrimination claim. The NYHRD, not the New York court, dismissed petitioner's complaint for lack of probable cause. In affirming, the court merely found that the *agency's* decision was not arbitrary or capricious. Thus, although it claims to grant a state *court* decision preclusive effect, in fact the Court bars petitioner's suit based on the state *agency's* decision of no probable cause. The Court thereby disregards the express provisions of Title VII, for, as the Court acknowledges, Congress has decided that an adverse state agency decision will not prevent a complainant's subsequent Title VII suit.

Finally, if the Court is in fact giving preclusive effect only to the state *court* decision, the Court misapplies 28 U.S.C. § 1738 by barring petitioner's suit. The state reviewing court never considered the merits of petitioner's discrimination claim, the subject matter of a Title VII suit in federal court. It is a basic principle of preclusion doctrine . . . that a decision in one judicial proceeding cannot bar a subsequent suit raising issues that were not relevant to the first decision. . . . Here, the state court decided only whether the state agency decision was arbitrary or capricious. Since the discrimination claim, not the validity of the state agency's decision, is the issue before the federal court, under § 1738 the state court's decision by itself cannot preclude a federal Title VII suit.

Thus, the Court is doing one of two things: either it is granting preclusive effect to the state agency's decision, a course that it concedes would violate Title VII, or it is misapplying § 1738 by giving preclusive effect to a state court decision that did not address the issue before the federal court. . . .

The Court's decision is directly contrary to . . . congressional intent. The lesson of the Court's ruling is: *An unsuccessful state discrimination complainant should not seek state judicial review.* If a discrimination complainant pursues state judicial review and loses—a likely result given the deferential standard of review in state court—he forfeits his right to seek redress in a federal court. If, however, he simply bypasses the state courts, he can proceed to the EEOC and ultimately to federal court. Instead of a deferential review of an agency record, he will receive in federal court a de novo hearing accompanied by procedural aids such as broad discovery rules and the ability to subpoena witnesses. Thus, paradoxically, the Court effectively has eliminated state reviewing courts from the fight against discrimination in an entire class of cases. Consequently, the state courts will not have a chance to correct state agency errors when the agencies rule against discrimination victims, and the quality of state agency decisionmaking can only deteriorate. It is a perverse sort of comity that eliminates the reviewing function of state courts in the name of giving their decision due respect.

. . . Invariably, there will be some complainants who will not be aware of today's decision. The Court has thus constructed a rule that will serve as a trap for the unwary pro se or poorly represented complainant. For these complainants, their sole remedy lies in the state administrative processes. Yet, inevitably those agencies do not give all discrimination complaints careful attention. Often hampered by "inadequate procedures" or "an inadequate budget," see 110 Cong. Rec. 7205 (1964), the state antidiscrimination agency may give a discrimination charge less than the close examination it would receive in federal court. When, as in this case, the state agency dismisses for lack of probable cause, the discrimination complainant is particularly at risk, because inadequate staffing of state agencies can lead to "a tendency to dismiss too many complaints for alleged lack of probable cause." Though state courts may be diligent in reviewing agency dismissals for no probable cause, the nature of the agency's deliberations combined with deferential judicial review can lead only to discrimination charges receiving less careful consideration than Congress intended when it passed Title VII. The Court's decision thus cannot be squared with the congressional intent that the fight against discrimination be a policy "of the highest priority." Newman v. Piggie Park Enterprises, 390 U.S. 400, 402 (1968). . . .

I dissent.

### Note: *England v. Louisiana State Board of Medical Examiners,*
### 375 U.S. 411 (1964)

Chiropractors brought an action challenging the Louisiana Medical Practice Act as applied to them by the Louisiana State Board of Medical Examiners, who had decided that the practice of chiropractic is the practice of medicine and requires full compliance with the educational requirements of the Act. The plaintiffs sought an injunction, claiming that the interpretation violated the Fourteenth Amendment. The district court abstained from deciding the federal constitutional issue, pending state court review of the board's action to determine its legality under the Act and the Louisiana Constitution.

Plaintiffs proceeded then to present their challenge in state court, arguing that the board's action was a violation of the Act, the Louisiana Constitution, and the Fourteenth Amendment. The Louisiana courts upheld the board. Plaintiffs then returned to the district court and sought federal court consideration of the federal constitutional challenge. The district court held that the Louisiana state court judgment was a bar to further litigation inasmuch as the plaintiffs had submitted the federal challenge to the state court. The proper remedy, if any, for possible error by the Louisiana courts should be sought in the Supreme Court of the United States.

Plaintiffs then appealed to the Supreme Court from this federal judgment. The Court indicated that the district court was correct in the view that an unreserved submission of the federal constitutional challenge to the state court should serve as a bar to further litigation. But, the Court cautioned, it was also correct that the Louisiana court was entitled to hear argument on the federal constitutional issue as a means of interpreting the state law, which it would, of course, normally prefer to interpret in a way that would avoid serious constitutional challenge. Inasmuch as these chiropractors may have been confused by Supreme Court cases making this distinction, and may have unreservedly submitted the issue to state court in the mistaken belief that this was required, they should be given another chance to present their federal constitutional argument. But now that the Supreme Court has clarified the law in this regard, other litigants will not be permitted to avail themselves of two opportunities to make unreserved presentations of constitutional arguments to both state and federal courts.

For discussion and application of *England*, see DLX Inc. v. Kentucky, 381 F.3d 511 (6th Cir. 2004).

### Note: *Matsushita Electrical Indus. Co. v. Epstein,*
### 516 U.S. 367 (1996)

The Court held that where a claim would have been barred by Delaware law, the statutory version of the Full Faith and Credit Clause (28 U.S.C. § 1738) required federal courts to give the same preclusive effect to the claims as Delaware law would give it. The case involved a shareholders' derivative suit filed in Delaware state court based on state law, and a class action suit filed in federal court based on federal law, over which federal courts had exclusive jurisdiction. The parties in the Delaware suit reached a global settlement, which stated that the parties gave up all state and federal claims. The court approved and entered judgment on the settlement. The defendant in the federal action then invoked the settlement as preclusive of the then-pending federal claims. Even though these federal claims could *not* have been filed in Delaware court, the Supreme Court held that they were barred in federal court, because under Delaware law the unasserted claims would have been barred.

On remand from the Supreme Court, the Ninth Circuit held that "the Delaware judgment was not constitutionally infirm and must be accorded full faith and credit" notwithstanding the claim that representation was inadequate in the state proceeding. Epstein v. MCA, Inc., 179 F.3d 641, 650 (9th Cir. 1999). A dissenting judge insisted that there were "significant structural conflicts" in the class, and "[b]ecause these conflicts were unresolved, the class representation was constitutionally infirm and cannot bind absent class members." Id. at 653. "Thus, the Epstein plaintiffs are entitled as a matter of federal law to assert their claims in this action." Id. at 654. Cf. Gooch v. Life Inv'rs Ins. Co., 672 F.3d 402 (6th Cir. 2012) (state court class action settlement entitled to preclusive effect); see also Stephenson v. Dow Chem. Co., 273 F.3d 249, 261 (2d Cir. 2001), *aff'd in part, vacated in part*, 539 U.S. 111 (2003) (concluding that applying res judicata to bar plaintiffs' claims would violate their due process rights because plaintiffs were inadequately represented).

### Note: Effect of Res Judicata on Amount in Controversy

Generally, "waivable affirmative defenses" may not be used "to whittle down the amount in controversy." Scherer v. Equitable Life Assurance Soc'y of U.S., 347 F.3d 394, 397 (2d Cir. 2003). This means that the res judicata effect of a prior state court judgment against a plaintiff cannot be used in a subsequent federal suit to establish that the amount in controversy is below the jurisdictional limit. Id. at 399 (reversing 12(b)(1) dismissal of federal suit for insurance benefits covering the period after plaintiff's earlier suit for benefits in state court).

### Brown v. Felsen
442 U.S. 127 (1979)

JUSTICE BLACKMUN delivered the opinion of the Court. . . .

Petitioner G. Garvin Brown III was a guarantor for respondent Mark Paul Felsen and Felsen's car dealership, Le Mans Motors, Inc. Petitioner's guaranty secured a bank loan that financed the dealership's trading in

Lotus, Ferrari, and Lamborghini automobiles. In 1975, the lender brought a collection suit against petitioner, respondent, and Le Mans in Colorado state court. Petitioner filed an answer to the bank's complaint, and a cross-claim against respondent and Le Mans. The answer and the cross-claim, by incorporating the answer, alleged that respondent and Le Mans induced petitioner to sign the guaranty "by misrepresentations and nondisclosures of material facts." . . . The suit was settled by a stipulation. It provided that the bank should recover jointly and severally against all three defendants, and that petitioner should have judgment against respondent and Le Mans. Neither the stipulation nor the resulting judgment indicated the cause of action on which respondent's liability to petitioner was based. Because the case was settled, respondent's sworn deposition was never made part of the court record.

A short time later, respondent filed a petition for voluntary bankruptcy and sought to have his debt to petitioner discharged. Through discharge the Bankruptcy Act provides "a new opportunity in life and a clear field for future effort, unhampered by the pressure and discouragement of pre-existing debt," Local Loan Co. v. Hunt, 292 U.S. 234, 244 (1934). By seeking discharge, however, respondent placed the rectitude of his prior dealings squarely in issue, for, as the Court has noted, the Act limits that opportunity to the "honest but unfortunate debtor." Ibid. Section 14 of the Act, 11 U.S.C. § 32, specifies that a *debtor* may not obtain a discharge if he has committed certain crimes or offenses. Section 17a, the focus of this case, provides that certain *types* of debts are not affected by a discharge. These include, under § 17a(2), "liabilities for obtaining money or property by false pretenses or false representations . . . or for willful and malicious conversion of the property of another" and, under § 17a(4), debts that "were created by his fraud, embezzlement, misappropriation, or defalcation while acting as an officer or in any fiduciary capacity."

In the bankruptcy court petitioner sought to establish that respondent's debt to petitioner was not dischargeable. Petitioner alleged that the guaranty debt was the product of respondent's fraud, deceit, and malicious conversion and so came within §§ 17a(2) and 17a(4). Petitioner contended that respondent had prepared false title certificates, sold automobiles out of trust, and applied the proceeds to private purposes. Respondent answered and moved for summary judgment. Respondent said that the prior state-court proceeding did not result in a finding of fraud, and contended that res judicata barred relitigation of the nature of respondent's debt to petitioner, even though the application of § 17 had not been in issue in the prior proceeding.

Before 1970, such res judicata claims were seldom heard in federal court. Traditionally, the bankruptcy court determined whether the debtor merited a discharge under § 14, but left the dischargeability under § 17 of a particular debt to the court in which the creditor sued, after bankruptcy, to enforce his prior judgment. Typically, that court was a state court. In 1970, however, Congress altered § 17 to require creditors to apply to the bankruptcy court for adjudication of certain dischargeability questions, including those arising under §§ 17a(2) and 17a(4). . . .

The bankruptcy court here . . . confined its consideration to the judgment, pleadings, exhibits, and stipulation which were in the state-court record. It declined to hear other evidence, and it refused to consider respondent's deposition that had never been made part of that record. The court concluded that, because neither the judgment nor the record showed that petitioner's allegation of misrepresentation was the basis for the judgment on the cross-claim against respondent, the liability had not been shown to be within §§ 17a(2) and 17a(4). The court granted summary judgment for respondent and held that the debt was dischargeable.

Both the United States District Court for the District of Colorado and the United States Court of Appeals for the Tenth Circuit affirmed. . . . We granted certiorari. . . .

Bankruptcy often breeds litigation, and respondent contends that the policy of repose which underlies res judicata has particular force here. Respondent argues that petitioner chose not to press the question of fraud in the state-court proceeding even though an adjudication of fraud would have entitled petitioner to extraordinary remedies such as exemplary damages and body execution.[5] Respondent says that because petitioner did not obtain a stipulation concerning fraud in the prior state-court proceeding, he is now barred from litigating matters that could have been concluded in the consent judgment. See United States v. Armour & Co., 402 U.S. 673, 681-82 (1971). Applying res judicata in bankruptcy court, it is argued, prevents a creditor from raising as an afterthought claims so insubstantial that they had previously been overlooked. In respondent's view, res judicata stops harassment and promotes the orderly processes of justice by encouraging the consolidation of the entire dispute between debtor and creditor into one prior proceeding.

Because res judicata may govern grounds and defenses not previously litigated, however, it blockades unexplored paths that may lead to truth. For the sake of repose, res judicata shields the fraud and the cheat as well as the honest person. It therefore is to be invoked only after careful inquiry. Petitioner contends, and we agree, that here careful inquiry reveals that neither the interests served by res judicata, the process of orderly adjudication in state courts, nor the policies of the Bankruptcy Act would be well served by foreclosing petitioner from submitting additional evidence to prove his case.

. . . [P]etitioner readily concedes the prior decree is binding. That is the cornerstone of his claim. He does not assert a new ground for recovery, nor does he attack the validity of the prior judgment. Rather, what he is attempting to meet here is the new defense of bankruptcy which respondent has interposed between petitioner and the sum determined to be due him. A substantial minority of state-court decisions, particularly those following

---

5. In Colorado, body execution is a statutory remedy which, under certain circumstances, permits a creditor to have a tortious judgment debtor imprisoned at the creditor's expense. See Hershey v. People, 12 P.2d 345 ([Colo.] 1932); Colo. Rev. Stat. § 13-59-103 (1973).

Fidelity & Casualty Co. v. Golombosky, 50 A.2d 817, 819-20 ([Conn.] 1946) (Maltbie, C.J.), have recognized this distinction and have refused to apply res judicata in determining the dischargeability of debts previously reduced to judgment. Respondent has upset the repose that would justify treating the prior state-court proceeding as final, and it would hardly promote confidence in judgments to prevent petitioner from meeting respondent's new initiative. . . .

Respondent contends that the § 17 questions raised here, or similar issues of state law, could have been considered in the prior state-court proceeding and therefore are not "new." Respondent argues that the state-court collection suit is the appropriate forum for resolving all debtor-creditor disputes, including those concerning dischargeability. While in some circumstances the consolidation of proceedings may be desirable, here consolidation would undercut a statutory policy in favor of resolving § 17 questions in bankruptcy court, and would force state courts to decide these questions at a stage when they are not directly in issue and neither party has a full incentive to litigate them. See In re Pigge, 539 F.2d 369, 371-72 (4th Cir. 1976).

. . . Considerations material to discharge are irrelevant to the ordinary collection proceeding. The creditor sues on the instrument which created the debt. Even if an issue similar to those created by § 17 should arise, the state-law concept is likely to differ from that adopted in the federal statute. . . . For example, in Davis v. Aetna Acceptance Co., 293 U.S. 328 (1934), the Court held that a mere technical conversion by a bankrupt dealer in automobiles was not "willful and malicious" within the meaning of § 17 by virtue of being actionable under state law, nor was a misappropriation of funds, held pursuant to a "trust receipt," a breach of an express trust sufficient to constitute an act done "as an officer or in any fiduciary capacity."

When § 17 issues are not identical to those arising under state law, the parties have little incentive to litigate them. In the collection suit, the debtor's bankruptcy is still hypothetical. The rule proposed by respondent would force an otherwise unwilling party to try § 17 questions to the hilt in order to protect himself against the mere possibility that a debtor might take bankruptcy in the future. In many cases such litigation would prove, in the end, to have been entirely unnecessary, and it is not surprising that at least one state court has expressly refused to embroil itself in an advisory adjudication of this kind. See Pioneer Finance & Thrift Co. v. Powell, 443 P.2d 389 ([Utah] 1968). And absent trial on the merits, there is no particular reason to favor extraneous facts thrown into a record for § 17 purposes over facts adduced before the bankruptcy court.

. . . If a state court should expressly rule on § 17 questions, then giving finality to those rulings would undercut Congress' intention to commit § 17 issues to the jurisdiction of the bankruptcy court. The 1970 amendments eliminated postbankruptcy state-court collection suits as a means of resolving certain § 17 dischargeability questions. In those suits, creditors had taken advantage of debtors who were unable to retain counsel because bankruptcy had stripped them of their assets. Congress' primary purpose was to stop that abuse. A secondary purpose, however, was to take these § 17 claims away from state courts that seldom dealt with the federal bankruptcy laws and to give those claims to the bankruptcy court so that it could develop expertise in handling them. By the express terms of the Constitution, bankruptcy law is federal law, U.S. Const., Art. I, § 8, cl. 4, and the Senate Report accompanying the amendment described the bankruptcy court's jurisdiction over these § 17 claims as "exclusive," S. Rep. No. 91-1173, p. 2 (1970). While Congress did not expressly confront the problem created by prebankruptcy state-court adjudications, it would be inconsistent with the philosophy of the 1970 amendments to adopt a policy of res judicata which takes these § 17 questions away from bankruptcy courts and forces them back into state courts. . . .

. . . Respondent . . . contends that petitioner had an adequate incentive to prove state-law fraud, which might have entailed proof identical to that required by § 17. Petitioner, however, rejected whatever lure exemplary damages and body execution may have provided. That rejection does not conclusively show that petitioner thought respondent was innocent of fraud. Petitioner may have thought those remedies would not be advantageous to him.[8] While respondent is certainly entitled to claim that res judicata would bar further pursuit of those extraordinary remedies in state court, their hypothetical desirability provides no basis for preventing petitioner from recovering on the debt, the remedy he elected from the beginning. . . .

Refusing to apply res judicata here would permit the bankruptcy court to make an accurate determination whether respondent in fact committed the deceit, fraud, and malicious conversion which petitioner alleges. These questions are now, for the first time, squarely in issue. They are the type of question Congress intended that the bankruptcy court would resolve. That court can weigh all the evidence, and it can also take into account whether or not petitioner's failure to press these allegations at an earlier time betrays a weakness in his case on the merits. . . .

The judgment of the Court of Appeals is *reversed*.

---

8. So long as a debtor is solvent, the debtor and creditor alike may prefer a simple contract suit to complex tort litigation. Default and consent judgment are common in collection proceedings. For the creditor, the prospect of increased attorneys' fees and the likelihood of driving the debtor into bankruptcy may offset the advantages of exemplary damages or other extraordinary remedies. Bankruptcy deprives the debtor of his creditworthiness and so impairs his ability to repay. In the words of a Shakespearean creditor, fearing the worst: "When every feather sticks in his own wing, Lord Timon will be left a naked Gull, Which flashes now a Phoenix." Timon of Athens, Act 2, Scene 1, in VII The Works of Shakespeare 294 (Henley ed. 1903). Nor does body execution aid in the collection of a debt if the creditor needs to be out of jail in order to earn the money to repay the debt.

## *Baker v. General Motors Corporation*
522 U.S. 222 (1998)

Justice Ginsburg delivered the opinion of the Court.

This case concerns the authority of one State's court to order that a witness' testimony shall not be heard in any court of the United States. In settlement of claims and counterclaims precipitated by the discharge of Ronald Elwell, a former General Motors Corporation (GM) engineering analyst, GM paid Elwell an undisclosed sum of money, and the parties agreed to a permanent injunction. As stipulated by GM and Elwell and entered by a Michigan County Court, the injunction prohibited Elwell from "testifying, without the prior written consent of [GM], . . . as . . . a witness of any kind . . . in any litigation already filed, or to be filed in the future, involving [GM] as an owner, seller, manufacturer and/or designer. . . ." GM separately agreed, however, that if Elwell were ordered to testify by a court or other tribunal, such testimony would not be actionable as a violation of the Michigan court's injunction or the GM-Elwell agreement.

After entry of the stipulated injunction in Michigan, Elwell was subpoenaed to testify in a product liability action commenced in Missouri by plaintiffs who were not involved in the Michigan case. The question presented is whether the national full faith and credit command bars Elwell's testimony in the Missouri case. We hold that Elwell may testify in the Missouri action without offense to the full faith and credit requirement.

## I

Two lawsuits, initiated by different parties in different states, gave rise to the full faith and credit issue before us. One suit involved a severed employment relationship, the other, a wrongful-death complaint. We describe each controversy in turn.

## A

### *The Suit Between Elwell and General Motors*

Ronald Elwell was a GM employee from 1959 until 1989. For fifteen of those years, beginning in 1971, Elwell was assigned to the Engineering Analysis Group, which studied the performance of GM vehicles, most particularly vehicles involved in product liability litigation. Elwell's studies and research concentrated on vehicular fires. He assisted in improving the performance of GM products by suggesting changes in fuel line designs. During the course of his employment, Elwell frequently aided GM lawyers engaged in defending GM against product liability actions. Beginning in 1987, the Elwell-GM employment relationship soured. GM and Elwell first negotiated an agreement under which Elwell would retire after serving as a GM consultant for two years. When the time came for Elwell to retire, however, disagreement again surfaced and continued into 1991.

In May 1991, plaintiffs in a product liability action pending in Georgia deposed Elwell. The Georgia case involved a GM pickup truck fuel tank that burst into flames just after a collision. During the deposition, and over the objection of counsel for GM, Elwell gave testimony that differed markedly from testimony he had given when serving as an in-house expert witness for GM. Specifically, Elwell had several times defended the safety and crashworthiness of the pickup's fuel system. On deposition in the Georgia action, however, Elwell testified that the GM pickup truck fuel system was inferior in comparison to competing products.

A month later, Elwell sued GM in a Michigan County Court, alleging wrongful discharge and other tort and contract claims. GM counterclaimed, contending that Elwell had breached his fiduciary duty to GM by disclosing privileged and confidential information and misappropriating documents. In response to GM's motion for a preliminary injunction, and after a hearing, the Michigan trial court, on November 22, 1991, enjoined Elwell from

> consulting or discussing with or disclosing to any person any of General Motors Corporation's trade secrets[,] confidential information or matters of attorney-client work product relating in any manner to the subject matter of any products liability litigation whether already filed or [to be] filed in the future which Ronald Elwell received, had knowledge of, or was entrusted with during his employment with General Motors Corporation. Elwell v. General Motors Corp., No. 91-115946NZ (Wayne Cty.) (Order Granting in Part, Denying in Part Injunctive Relief, pp. 1-2), App. 9-10.

In August 1992, GM and Elwell entered into a settlement under which Elwell received an undisclosed sum of money. The parties also stipulated to the entry of a permanent injunction and jointly filed with the Michigan court both the stipulation and the agreed-upon injunction. . . .

. . . Elwell and GM included in their separate settlement agreement a more general limitation. If a court or other tribunal ordered Elwell to testify, his testimony would "in no way" support a GM action for violation of the injunction or the settlement agreement:

> It is agreed that [Elwell's] appearance and testimony, if any, at hearings on Motions to quash subpoena or at deposition or trial or other official proceeding, if the Court or other tribunal so orders, will in no way form a basis for an action in violation of the Permanent Injunction or this Agreement. [Settlement Agreement, at 10, as quoted in 86 F.3d 811, 820, n.11 (8th Cir. 1996).]

In the six years since the Elwell-GM settlement, Elwell has testified against GM both in Georgia (pursuant to [an agreed-upon] exception contained in the injunction) and in several other jurisdictions in which Elwell has been subpoenaed to testify.

*B*

*The Suit Between the Bakers and General Motors*

Having described the Elwell-GM employment termination litigation, we next summarize the wrongful-death complaint underlying this case. The decedent, Beverly Garner, was a front-seat passenger in a 1985 Chevrolet S-10 Blazer involved in a February 1990 Missouri highway accident. The Blazer's engine caught fire, and both driver and passenger died. In September 1991, Garner's sons, Kenneth and Steven Baker, commenced a wrongful death product liability action against GM in a Missouri state court. The Bakers alleged that a faulty fuel pump in the 1985 Blazer caused the engine fire that killed their mother. GM removed the case to federal court on the basis of the parties' diverse citizenship. On the merits, GM asserted that the fuel pump was neither faulty nor the cause of the fire, and that collision impact injuries alone caused Garner's death.

The Bakers sought both to depose Elwell and to call him as a witness at trial. GM objected to Elwell's appearance as a deponent or trial witness on the ground that the Michigan injunction barred his testimony. In response, the Bakers urged that the Michigan injunction did not override a Missouri subpoena for Elwell's testimony. The Bakers further noted that, under the Elwell-GM settlement agreement, Elwell could testify if a court so ordered, and such testimony would not be actionable as a violation of the Michigan injunction.

After *in camera* review of the Michigan injunction and the settlement agreement, the Federal District Court in Missouri allowed the Bakers to depose Elwell and to call him as a witness at trial. Responding to GM's objection, the District Court stated alternative grounds for its ruling: (1) Michigan's injunction need not be enforced because blocking Elwell's testimony would violate Missouri's "public policy," which shielded from disclosure only privileged or otherwise confidential information; (2) just as the injunction could be modified in Michigan, so a court elsewhere could modify the decree.

At trial, Elwell testified in support of the Bakers' claim that the alleged defect in the fuel pump system contributed to the post-collision fire. In addition, he identified and described a 1973 internal GM memorandum bearing on the risk of fuel-fed engine fires. Following trial, the jury awarded the Bakers $11.3 million in damages, and the District Court entered judgment on the jury's verdict.

The United States Court of Appeals for the Eighth Circuit reversed the District Court's judgment, ruling, *inter alia,* that Elwell's testimony should not have been admitted. 86 F.3d 811 (8th Cir. 1996). Assuming, *arguendo,* the existence of a public policy exception to the full faith and credit command, the Court of Appeals concluded that the District Court erroneously relied on Missouri's policy favoring disclosure of relevant, nonprivileged information, see id. at 818-819, for Missouri has an "equally strong public policy in favor of full faith and credit," id. at 819.

The Eighth Circuit also determined that the evidence was insufficient to show that the Michigan court would modify the injunction barring Elwell's testimony. See id. at 819-820. The Court of Appeals observed that the Michigan court "has been asked on several occasions to modify the injunction, [but] has yet to do so," and noted that, if the Michigan court did not intend to block Elwell's testimony in cases like the Bakers', "the injunction would . . . have been unnecessary." Id. at 820.

We granted certiorari to decide whether the full faith and credit requirement stops the Bakers, who were not parties to the Michigan proceeding, from obtaining Elwell's testimony in their Missouri wrongful death action. 520 U.S. 1142 (1997).

## II

### A

The Constitution's Full Faith and Credit Clause provides:

Full Faith and Credit shall be given in each State to the public Acts, Records, and judicial Proceedings of every other State. And the Congress may by general Laws prescribe the Manner in which such Acts, Records and Proceedings shall be proved, and the Effect thereof. [U.S. Const., Art. IV, § 1.]

Pursuant to that Clause, Congress has prescribed:

Such Acts, records and judicial proceedings or copies thereof, so authenticated, shall have the same full faith and credit in every court within the United States and its Territories and Possessions as they have by law or usage in the courts of such State, Territory or Possession from which they are taken. [28 U.S.C. § 1738.]

The animating purpose of the full faith and credit command, as this Court explained in Milwaukee County v. M.E. White Co., 296 U.S. 268 (1935),

was to alter the status of the several states as independent foreign sovereignties, each free to ignore obligations created under the laws or by the judicial proceedings of the others, and to make them integral parts of a single nation throughout which a remedy upon a just obligation might be demanded as of right, irrespective of the state of its origin. [Id. at 277.]

Our precedent differentiates the credit owed to laws (legislative measures and common law) and to judgments. "In numerous cases this Court has held that credit must be given to the judgment of another state although the forum would not be required to entertain the suit on which the judgment was founded." *Milwaukee County,* 296 U.S. at 277. The Full Faith and Credit Clause does not compel "a state to substitute the statutes of other states for its own statutes dealing with a subject matter concerning which it is competent to legislate." Pacific Employers Ins. Co. v. Industrial Accident Comm'n, 306 U.S. 493, 501 (1939); see Phillips Petroleum Co. v. Shutts, 472 U.S. 797, 818-819 (1985). Regarding judgments, however, the full faith and credit obligation is exacting. A final judgment in one State, if rendered by a court with adjudicatory authority over the subject matter and persons governed by the judgment, qualifies for recognition throughout the land. For claim and issue preclusion (res judicata) purposes, in other words, the judgment of the rendering State gains nationwide force.

A court may be guided by the forum State's "public policy" in determining the law applicable to a controversy. See Nevada v. Hall, 440 U.S. 410, 421-424 (1979). But our decisions support no roving "public policy exception" to the full faith and credit due *judgments.* See [Estin v. Estin, 334 U.S. 541, 546 (1948)] (Full Faith and Credit Clause "ordered submission . . . even to hostile policies reflected in the judgment of another State, because the practical operation of the federal system, which the Constitution designed, demanded it."); Fauntleroy v. Lum, 210 U.S. 230, 237 (1908) (judgment of Missouri court entitled to full faith and credit in Mississippi even if Missouri judgment rested on a misapprehension of Mississippi law). In assuming the existence of a ubiquitous "public policy exception" permitting one State to resist recognition of another State's judgment, the District Court in the Bakers' wrongful-death action, see supra, at 662, misread our precedent. "The full faith and credit clause is one of the provisions incorporated into the Constitution by its framers for the purpose of transforming an aggregation of independent, sovereign States into a nation." Sherrer v. Sherrer, 334 U.S. 343, 355 (1948). We are "aware of [no] considerations of local policy or law which could rightly be deemed to impair the force and effect which the full faith and credit clause and the Act of Congress require to be given to [a money] judgment outside the state of its rendition." Magnolia Petroleum Co. v. Hunt, 320 U.S. 430, 438 (1943).

The Court has never placed equity decrees outside the full faith and credit domain. Equity decrees for the payment of money have long been considered equivalent to judgments at law entitled to nationwide recognition. We see no reason why the preclusive effects of an adjudication on parties and those "in privity" with them, *i.e.,* claim preclusion and issue preclusion (res judicata and collateral estoppel), should differ depending solely upon the type of relief sought in a civil action. . . .

Full faith and credit, however, does not mean that States must adopt the practices of other States regarding the time, manner, and mechanisms for enforcing judgments. Enforcement measures do not travel with the sister State judgment as preclusive effects do; such measures remain subject to the even-handed control of forum law. . . .

Orders commanding action or inaction have been denied enforcement in a sister State when they purported to accomplish an official act within the exclusive province of that other State or interfered with litigation over which the ordering State had no authority. Thus, a sister State's decree concerning land ownership in another State has been held ineffective *to transfer title,* see Fall v. Eastin, 215 U.S. 1 (1909), although such a decree may indeed preclusively adjudicate the rights and obligations running between the *parties* to the foreign litigation, see e.g., Robertson v. Howard, 229 U.S. 254, 261 (1913) ("[I]t may not be doubted that a court of equity in one State in a proper case could compel a defendant before it to convey property situated in another State."). And antisuit injunctions regarding litigation elsewhere, even if compatible with due process as a direction constraining parties to the decree, . . . in fact have not controlled the second court's actions regarding litigation in that court. . . . Sanctions for violations of an injunction, in any event, are generally administered by the court that issued the injunction. . . .

### B

. . . What matters did the Michigan injunction legitimately conclude? As earlier recounted, . . . the parties before the Michigan County Court, Elwell and GM, submitted an agreed-upon injunction, which the presiding judge signed. While no issue was joined, expressly litigated, and determined in the Michigan proceeding, that order is *claim* preclusive between Elwell and GM. Elwell's claim for wrongful discharge and his related contract and tort claims have "merged in the judgment," and he cannot sue again to recover more. See Parklane Hosiery Co. v. Shore, 439 U.S. 322, 326, n.5 (1979) ("Under the doctrine of res judicata, a judgment on the merits in a prior suit bars a second suit involving the same parties or their privies based on the same cause of action."); see also Restatement (Second) of Judgments § 17 (1980). Similarly, GM cannot sue Elwell elsewhere on the counterclaim GM asserted in Michigan. See id., § 23, Comment *a*, p. 194 ("A defendant who interposes a counterclaim is, in substance, a plaintiff, as far as the counterclaim is concerned, and the plaintiff is, in substance, a defendant.").

Michigan's judgment, however, cannot reach beyond the Elwell-GM controversy to control proceedings against GM brought in other States, by other parties, asserting claims the merits of which Michigan has not considered. Michigan has no power over those parties, and no basis for commanding them to become intervenors in the Elwell-GM dispute. See Martin v. Wilks, 490 U.S. 755, 761-63 (1989). Most essentially, Michigan lacks authority to control courts elsewhere by precluding them, in actions brought by strangers to the Michigan litigation, from determining for themselves what witnesses are competent to testify and what evidence is relevant and admissible in their search for the truth. . . .

As the District Court recognized, Michigan's decree could operate against Elwell to preclude him from *volunteering* his testimony. But a Michigan court cannot, by entering the injunction to which Elwell and GM stipulated, dictate to a court in another jurisdiction that evidence relevant in the Bakers' case — a controversy to which Michigan is foreign — shall be inadmissible. This conclusion creates no general exception to the full faith and credit command, and surely does not permit a State to refuse to honor a sister state judgment based on the forum's choice of law or policy preferences. Rather, we simply recognize that, just as the mechanisms for enforcing a judgment do not travel with the judgment itself for purposes of Full Faith and Credit, . . . and just as one State's judgment cannot automatically transfer title to land in another State, . . . similarly the Michigan decree cannot determine evidentiary issues in a lawsuit brought by parties who were not subject to the jurisdiction of the Michigan court. . . .

In sum, Michigan has no authority to shield a witness from another jurisdiction's subpoena power in a case involving persons and causes outside Michigan's governance. Recognition, under full faith and credit, is owed to dispositions Michigan has authority to order. But a Michigan decree cannot command obedience elsewhere on a matter the Michigan court lacks authority to resolve.

For the reasons stated, the judgment of the Court of Appeals for the Eighth Circuit is reversed, and the case is remanded for further proceedings consistent with this opinion.

*It is so ordered.*

JUSTICE KENNEDY, with whom JUSTICES O'CONNOR and THOMAS join, concurring in the judgment.

. . . In my view the case is controlled by well-settled full faith and credit principles which render the majority's extended analysis unnecessary and, with all due respect, problematic in some degree. This separate opinion explains my approach.

## I

The majority, of course, is correct to hold that when a judgment is presented to the courts of a second State it may not be denied enforcement based upon some disagreement with the laws of the State of rendition. Full faith and credit forbids the second State from questioning a judgment on these grounds. . . . We have often recognized the second State's obligation to give effect to another State's judgments even when the law underlying those judgments contravenes the public policy of the second State. . . .

My concern is that the majority, having stated the principle, proceeds to disregard it by announcing two broad exceptions. First, the majority would allow courts outside the issuing State to decline to enforce those judgments "purport[ing] to accomplish an official act within the exclusive province of [a sister] State." . . . Second, the basic rule of full faith and credit is said not to cover injunctions "interfer[ing] with litigation over which the ordering State had no authority." . . . The exceptions the majority recognizes are neither consistent with its rejection of a public policy exception to full faith and credit nor in accord with established rules implementing the Full Faith and Credit Clause. As employed to resolve this case, furthermore, the exceptions to full faith and credit have a potential for disrupting judgments, and this ought to give us considerable pause.

Our decisions have been careful not to foreclose all effect for the types of injunctions the majority would place outside the ambit of full faith and credit. These authorities seem to be disregarded by today's holding. For example, the majority chooses to discuss the extent to which courts may compel the conveyance of property in other jurisdictions. That subject has proven to be quite difficult. Some of our cases uphold actions by state courts affecting land outside their territorial reach. . . . Nor have we undertaken before today to announce an exception which denies full faith and credit based on the principle that the prior judgment interferes with litigation pending in another jurisdiction. . . . As a general matter, there is disagreement among the state courts as to their duty to recognize decrees enjoining proceedings in other courts.

Subjects which are at once so fundamental and so delicate as these ought to be addressed only in a case necessarily requiring their discussion, and even then with caution lest we announce rules which will not be sound in later application. . . . We might be required to hold, if some future case raises the issue, that an otherwise valid judgment cannot intrude upon essential processes of courts outside the issuing State in certain narrow circumstances, but we need not announce or define that principle here. Even if some qualification of full faith and credit were required where the judicial processes of a second State are sought to be controlled in their procedural and institutional aspects, the Court's discussion does not provide sufficient guidance on how this exception should be construed in light of our precedents. . . . The Court's reliance upon unidentified principles to justify omitting certain types of injunctions from the doctrine's application leaves its decision in uneasy tension with its own rejection of a broad public policy exception to full faith and credit. . . .

In any event, the rule would be an exception. Full faith and credit requires courts to do more than provide for direct enforcement of the judgments issued by other States. It also "requires federal courts to give the same preclusive effect to state court judgments that those judgments would be given in the courts of the State from which the judgments emerged." Kremer v. Chemical Constr. Corp., 456 U.S. 461, 466 (1982). Through full faith and credit, "the local doctrines of res judicata, speaking generally, become a part of national jurisprudence. . . ." Riley v. New York Trust Co., 315 U.S. 343, 349 (1942). And whether or not an injunction is enforceable in another State on its own terms, the courts of a second State are required to honor its issue preclusive effects.

## II

[T]he Bakers were neither parties to the earlier litigation nor subject to the jurisdiction of the Michigan courts. The majority pays scant attention to this circumstance, which becomes critical. . . . In our most recent full faith and credit cases, we have said that determining the force and effect of a judgment should be the first step in our analysis. . . . A conclusion that the issuing State would not give the prior judgment preclusive effect ends the inquiry, making it unnecessary to determine the existence of any exceptions to full faith and credit. We cannot decline to inquire into these state-law questions when the inquiry will obviate new extensions or exceptions to full faith and credit.

If we honor the undoubted principle that courts need give a prior judgment no more force or effect than the issuing State gives it, the case before us is resolved. Here the Court of Appeals and both parties in their arguments before our Court seemed to embrace the assumption that Michigan would apply the full force of its judgment to the Bakers. Michigan law does not appear to support the assumption.

The simple fact is that the Bakers were not parties to the Michigan proceedings, and nothing indicates Michigan would make the novel assertion that its earlier injunction binds the Bakers or any other party not then before it or subject to its jurisdiction. For collateral estoppel to apply under Michigan law, "the same parties must have had a full opportunity to litigate the issue, and there must be mutuality of estoppel." Nummer v. Treasury Dept., 533 N.W.2d 250, 253 [Mich.] [internal quotations omitted], *cert. denied,* 516 U.S. 964 (1995). Since the Bakers were not parties to the Michigan proceedings and had no opportunity to litigate any of the issues presented, it appears that Michigan law would not treat them as bound by the judgment. . . .

It makes no difference that the judgment in question is an injunction. The Michigan Supreme Court has twice rejected arguments that injunctions have preclusive effect in later litigation, relying in no small part on the fact that the persons against whom preclusion is asserted were not parties to the earlier litigation. Bacon v. Walden, 152 N.W. 1061, 1063 (1915) ("Defendant was not a party to [the prior injunctive] suit and was not as a matter of law affected or bound by the decree rendered in it."); Detroit v. Detroit Ry., 95 N.W. 992, 993 (1903) ("[T]he fact that defendant was in no way a party to the record is sufficient answer to the contention that the holding of the circuit judge in that [prior injunctive] case is a controlling determination of the present."). . . .

Although inconsistent on this point, GM disavows its desire to issue preclude the Bakers. . . . This is difficult to accept because in assessing the preclusive reach of a judgment we look to its practical effect. Despite its disclaimer, GM seeks to alter the course of the suit between it and the Bakers by preventing the Bakers from litigating the admissibility of Elwell's testimony. Furthermore, even were we to accept GM's argument that the Bakers are essentially irrelevant to this dispute, GM's argument is flawed on its own terms. Elwell, in the present litigation, does not seek to relitigate anything; he is a witness, not a party.

In all events, determining as a threshold matter the extent to which Michigan law gives preclusive effect to the injunction eliminates the need to decide whether full faith and credit applies to equitable decrees as a general matter or the extent to which the general rules of full faith and credit are subject to exceptions. Michigan law would not seek to bind the Bakers to the injunction and that suffices to resolve the case.

What about parties who lose in state court but believe the state court's decision violates federal constitutional law? Do the federal district courts have authority to entertain such claims or is an appeal to the United States Supreme Court the only option? Take a look at 28 U.S.C. § 1257. It provides a clear answer, doesn't it?

But what if the state court decision is quasi-legislative? And what is the effect of a state judgment on a related and still pending federal case? These issues converged in the following case interpreting the so-called *Rooker-Feldman* doctrine.

### *ExxonMobil Corp. v. Saudi Basic Indus. Corp.*
544 U.S. 280 (2005)

JUSTICE GINSBURG delivered the opinion of the Court.

This case concerns what has come to be known as the *Rooker-Feldman* doctrine, applied by this Court only twice, first in Rooker v. Fidelity Trust Co., 263 U.S. 413 (1923), then, 60 years later, in District of Columbia Court of Appeals v. Feldman, 460 U.S. 462 (1983). Variously interpreted in the lower courts, the doctrine has sometimes been construed to extend far beyond the contours of the *Rooker* and *Feldman* cases, overriding Congress' conferral of federal-court jurisdiction concurrent with jurisdiction exercised by state courts, and superseding the ordinary application of preclusion law pursuant to 28 U.S.C. § 1738. See, e.g., Moccio v. New York State Office of Court Admin., 95 F.3d 195, 199-200 (2d Cir. 1996).

*Rooker* was a suit commenced in Federal District Court to have a judgment of a state court, adverse to the federal court plaintiffs, "declared null and void." 263 U.S. at 414. In *Feldman*, parties unsuccessful in the District of Columbia Court of Appeals (the District's highest court) commenced a federal-court action against the very court that had rejected their applications. Holding the federal suits impermissible, we emphasized that appellate jurisdiction to reverse or modify a state-court judgment is lodged, initially by § 25 of the Judiciary Act of 1789, 1 Stat. 85, and now by 28 U.S.C. § 1257, exclusively in this Court. Federal district courts, we noted, are empowered to exercise original, not appellate, jurisdiction. Plaintiffs in *Rooker* and *Feldman* had litigated and lost in state court. Their federal complaints, we observed, essentially invited federal courts of first instance to review and reverse unfavorable state-court judgments. We declared such suits out of bounds, i.e., properly dismissed for want of subject-matter jurisdiction.

The *Rooker-Feldman* doctrine, we hold today, is confined to cases of the kind from which the doctrine acquired its name: cases brought by state-court losers complaining of injuries caused by state-court judgments rendered before the district court proceedings commenced and inviting district court review and rejection of those judgments. *Rooker-Feldman* does not otherwise override or supplant preclusion doctrine or augment the circumscribed doctrines that allow federal courts to stay or dismiss proceedings in deference to state-court actions.

In the case before us, the Court of Appeals for the Third Circuit misperceived the narrow ground occupied by *Rooker-Feldman*, and consequently erred in ordering the federal action dismissed for lack of subject-matter jurisdiction. We therefore reverse the Third Circuit's judgment.

## I

In Rooker v. Fidelity Trust Co., 263 U.S. 413, the parties defeated in state court turned to a Federal District Court for relief. Alleging that the adverse state-court judgment was rendered in contravention of the Constitution, they asked the federal court to declare it "null and void." Id. at 414-415. This Court noted preliminarily that the state court had acted within its jurisdiction. Id. at 415. If the state-court decision was wrong, the Court explained, "that did not make the judgment void, but merely left it open to reversal or modification in an appropriate and timely appellate proceeding." Id. Federal district courts, the *Rooker* Court recognized, lacked the requisite appellate authority, for their jurisdiction was "strictly original." Id. at 416. Among federal courts, the *Rooker* Court clarified, Congress had empowered only this Court to exercise appellate authority "to reverse or modify" a state-court judgment. Id. Accordingly, the Court affirmed a decree dismissing the suit for lack of jurisdiction. Id. at 415, 417.

Sixty years later, the Court decided District of Columbia Court of Appeals v. Feldman, 460 U.S. 462. The two plaintiffs in that case, Hickey and Feldman, neither of whom had graduated from an accredited law school, petitioned the District of Columbia Court of Appeals to waive a court Rule that required D.C. bar applicants to have graduated from a law school approved by the American Bar Association. After the D.C. court denied their waiver requests, Hickey and Feldman filed suits in the United States District Court for the District of Columbia. Id. at 465-473. The District Court and the Court of Appeals for the District of Columbia Circuit disagreed on the question whether the federal suit could be maintained, and we granted certiorari. Id. at 474-475.

Recalling *Rooker*, this Court's opinion in *Feldman* observed first that the District Court lacked authority to review a final judicial determination of the D.C. high court. "Review of such determinations," the *Feldman* opinion reiterated, "can be obtained only in this Court." 460 U.S. at 476. The "crucial question," the Court next stated, was whether the proceedings in the D.C. court were "judicial in nature." Id. Addressing that question, the Court concluded that the D.C. court had acted both judicially and legislatively.

In applying the accreditation Rule to the Hickey and Feldman waiver petitions, this Court determined, the D.C. court had acted judicially. Id. at 479-482. As to that adjudication, *Feldman* held, this Court alone among federal courts had review authority. Hence, "to the extent that Hickey and Feldman sought review in the District Court of the District of Columbia Court of Appeals' denial of their petitions for waiver, the District Court lacked subject-matter jurisdiction over their complaints." Id. at 482. But that determination did not dispose of the entire case, for in promulgating the bar admission rule, this Court said, the D.C. court had acted legislatively, not judicially. Id. at 485-486. "Challenges to the constitutionality of state bar rules," the Court elaborated, "do not necessarily require a United States district court to review a final state-court judgment in a judicial proceeding." Id. at 486. Thus, the Court reasoned, 28 U.S.C. § 1257 did not bar District Court proceedings addressed to the validity of the accreditation Rule itself. *Feldman,* 460 U.S. at 486. The Rule could be contested in federal court, this Court held, so long as plaintiffs did not seek review of the Rule's application in a particular case. Id.

The Court endeavored to separate elements of the Hickey and Feldman complaints that failed the jurisdictional threshold from those that survived jurisdictional inspection. Plaintiffs had urged that the District of Columbia Court of Appeals acted arbitrarily in denying the waiver petitions of Hickey and Feldman, given that court's "former policy of granting waivers to graduates of unaccredited law schools." Id. That charge, the Court held, could not be pursued, for it was "inextricably intertwined with the District of Columbia Court of Appeals' decisions, in judicial proceedings, to deny [plaintiffs'] petitions." Id. at 486-487.

On the other hand, the Court said, plaintiffs could maintain "claims that the [bar admission] rule is unconstitutional because it creates an irrebuttable presumption that only graduates of accredited law schools are fit to practice law, discriminates against those who have obtained equivalent legal training by other means, and impermissibly delegates the District of Columbia Court of Appeals' power to regulate the bar to the American Bar Association," for those claims "do not require review of a judicial decision in a particular case." Id. at 487. The Court left open the question whether the doctrine of res judicata foreclosed litigation of the elements of the complaints spared from dismissal for want of subject-matter jurisdiction. Id. at 487-488.

Since *Feldman,* this Court has never applied *Rooker-Feldman* to dismiss an action for want of jurisdiction. The few decisions that have mentioned *Rooker* and *Feldman* have done so only in passing or to explain why those cases did not dictate dismissal. See Verizon Md. Inc. v. Public Serv. Comm'n of Md., 535 U.S. 635, 644, n.3 (2002) (*Rooker-Feldman* does not apply to a suit seeking review of state agency action); Johnson v. De Grandy, 512 U.S. 997, 1005-1006 (1994) (*Rooker-Feldman* bars a losing party in state court "from seeking what in substance would be appellate review of the state judgment in a United States district court, based on the losing party's claim that the state judgment itself violates the loser's federal rights," but the doctrine has no application to a federal suit brought by a nonparty to the state suit.); Howlett v. Rose, 496 U.S. 356, 369-370, n.16 (1990) (internal citations omitted); ASARCO Inc. v. Kadish, 490 U.S. 605, 622-623 (1989) (If, instead of seeking review of an adverse state supreme court decision in the Supreme Court, petitioners sued in federal district court, the federal action would be an attempt to obtain direct review of the state supreme court decision and would "represent a partial inroad on *Rooker-Feldman*'s construction of 28 U.S.C. § 1257.");

Pennzoil Co. v. Texaco Inc., 481 U.S. 1, 6-10 (1987) (abstaining under *Younger v. Harris,* 401 U.S. 37 (1971), rather than dismissing under *Rooker-Feldman,* in a suit that challenged Texas procedures for enforcing judgments); 481 U.S. at 18 (Scalia, J., concurring) (The "so-called *Rooker-Feldman* doctrine" does not deprive the Court of jurisdiction to decide Texaco's challenge to the Texas procedures.); id. at 21 (Brennan, J., concurring in judgment) (*Rooker* and *Feldman* do not apply; Texaco filed its federal action to protect its "right to a meaningful opportunity for appellate review, not to challenge the merits of the Texas suit."). But cf. 481 U.S. at 25-26 (Marshall, J., concurring in judgment) (*Rooker-Feldman* would apply because Texaco's claims necessarily called for review of the merits of its state appeal). See also Martin v. Wilks, 490 U.S. 755, 783-784, n.21 (1989) (Stevens, J., dissenting) (it would be anomalous to allow courts to sit in review of judgments entered by courts of equal, or greater, authority [internal citations omitted]).

## II

In 1980, two subsidiaries of petitioner ExxonMobil Corporation (then the separate companies Exxon Corp. and Mobil Corp.) formed joint ventures with respondent Saudi Basic Industries Corp. (SABIC) to produce polyethylene in Saudi Arabia. 194 F. Supp. 2d 378, 384 (D.N.J. 2002). Two decades later, the parties began to dispute royalties that SABIC had charged the joint ventures for sublicenses to a polyethylene manufacturing method. 364 F.3d 102, 103 (3d Cir. 2004).

SABIC preemptively sued the two ExxonMobil subsidiaries in Delaware Superior Court in July 2000 seeking a declaratory judgment that the royalty charges were proper under the joint venture agreements. 194 F. Supp. 2d at 385-386. About two weeks later, ExxonMobil and its subsidiaries countersued SABIC in the United States District Court for the District of New Jersey, alleging that SABIC overcharged the joint ventures for the sublicenses. Id. at 385; App. 3. ExxonMobil invoked subject-matter jurisdiction in the New Jersey action under 28 U.S.C. § 1330 which authorizes district courts to adjudicate actions against foreign states. 194 F. Supp. 2d at 401.

In January 2002, the ExxonMobil subsidiaries answered SABIC's state-court complaint, asserting as counterclaims the same claims ExxonMobil had made in the federal suit in New Jersey. 364 F.3d, at 103. The state suit went to trial in March 2003, and the jury returned a verdict of over $400 million in favor of the ExxonMobil subsidiaries. Id.; Saudi Basic Industries Corp. v. Mobil Yanbu Petrochemical Co., 866 A.2d 1, 11 (Del. 2005). SABIC appealed the judgment entered on the verdict to the Delaware Supreme Court.

Before the state-court trial, SABIC moved to dismiss the federal suit, alleging, *inter alia,* immunity under the Foreign Sovereign Immunities Act of 1976, 28 U.S.C. §§ 1602 *et seq.* (2000 ed. and Supp. II). The Federal District Court denied SABIC's motion to dismiss. 194 F. Supp. 2d, at 401-407, 416-417. SABIC took an interlocutory appeal, and the Court of Appeals heard argument in December 2003, over eight months after the state-court jury verdict. 364 F.3d at 103-104.

The Court of Appeals, on its own motion, raised the question whether "subject matter jurisdiction over this case fails under the *Rooker-Feldman* doctrine because ExxonMobil's claims have already been litigated in state court." Id. at 104. The court did not question the District Court's possession of subject-matter jurisdiction at the outset of the suit, but held that federal jurisdiction terminated when the Delaware Superior Court entered judgment on the jury verdict. Id. at 104-105. The court rejected Exxon-Mobil's argument that *Rooker-Feldman* could not apply because ExxonMobil filed its federal complaint well before the state-court judgment. The only relevant consideration, the court stated, "is whether the state judgment precedes a federal judgment on the same claims." 364 F.3d at 105. If *Rooker-Feldman* did not apply to federal actions filed prior to a state-court judgment, the Court of Appeals worried, "we would be encouraging parties to maintain federal actions as 'insurance policies' while their state court claims were pending." 364 F.3d at 105. Once ExxonMobil's claims had been litigated to a judgment in state court, the Court of Appeals held, *Rooker-Feldman* "preclude[d] [the] federal district court from proceeding." 364 F.3d at 104 (internal quotation marks omitted).

ExxonMobil, at that point prevailing in Delaware, was not seeking to overturn the state-court judgment. Nevertheless, the Court of Appeals hypothesized that, if SABIC won on appeal in Delaware, ExxonMobil would be endeavoring in the federal action to "invalidate" the state-court judgment, "the very situation," the court concluded, "contemplated by *Rooker-Feldman*'s 'inextricably intertwined' bar." Id. at 106.

We granted certiorari, 543 U.S. 924 (2004), to resolve conflict among the Courts of Appeals over the scope of the *Rooker-Feldman* doctrine. We now reverse the judgment of the Court of Appeals for the Third Circuit.

## III

*Rooker* and *Feldman* exhibit the limited circumstances in which this Court's appellate jurisdiction over state-court judgments, 28 U.S.C. § 1257, precludes a United States district court from exercising subject-matter jurisdiction in an action it would otherwise be empowered to adjudicate under a congressional grant of authority, e.g., § 1330 (suits against foreign states), § 1331 (federal question), and § 1332 (diversity). In both cases, the losing party in state court filed suit in federal court after the state proceedings ended, complaining of an injury caused by the state-court judgment and seeking review and rejection of that judgment. Plaintiffs in both cases, alleging federal-question jurisdiction, called upon the District Court to overturn an injurious state-court judgment. Because § 1257, as long interpreted, vests authority to review a state court's judgment solely in this Court, e.g., *Feldman*, 460 U.S. at 476; Atlantic Coast Line R. Co. v. Locomotive Engineers, 398 U.S. 281, 286 (1970); *Rooker*, 263 U.S. at 416, the District Courts in *Rooker* and *Feldman* lacked subject-matter jurisdiction. See *Verizon Md. Inc.*, 535 U.S. at 644, n.3 ("The *Rooker-Feldman* doctrine merely recognizes that 28 U.S.C. § 1331 is a grant of original jurisdiction, and does not authorize district courts to exercise appellate jurisdiction over state-court judgments, which Congress has reserved to this Court, see § 1257(a).").[8]

When there is parallel state and federal litigation, *Rooker-Feldman* is not triggered simply by the entry of judgment in state court. This Court has repeatedly held that "the pendency of an action in the state court is no bar to proceedings concerning the same matter in the Federal court having jurisdiction." McClellan v. Carland, 217 U.S. 268, 282 (1910); accord Doran v. Salem Inn, Inc., 422 U.S. 922, 928 (1975); *Atlantic Coast Line R. Co.*, 398 U.S. at 295. Comity or abstention doctrines may, in various circumstances, permit or require the federal court to stay or dismiss the federal action in favor of the state-court litigation. See, e.g., Colorado River Water Conservation Dist. v. United States, 424 U.S. 800 (1976); Younger v. Harris, 401 U.S. 37 (1971); Burford v. Sun Oil Co., 319 U.S. 315 (1943); Railroad Comm'n of Tex. v. Pullman Co., 312 U.S. 496 (1941). But neither *Rooker* nor *Feldman* supports the notion that properly invoked concurrent jurisdiction vanishes if a state court reaches judgment on the same or related question while the case remains *sub judice* in a federal court.

Disposition of the federal action, once the state-court adjudication is complete, would be governed by preclusion law. The Full Faith and Credit Act, 28 U.S.C. § 1738 originally enacted in 1790, ch. 11, 1 Stat. 122, requires the federal court to "give the same preclusive effect to a state-court judgment as another court of that State would give." Parsons Steel, Inc. v. First Alabama Bank, 474 U.S. 518, 523 (1986). Preclusion, of course, is not a jurisdictional matter. See Fed. Rule Civ. Proc. 8(c) (listing res judicata as an affirmative defense). In parallel litigation, a federal court may be bound to recognize the claim- and issue-preclusive effects of a state-court judgment, but federal jurisdiction over an action does not terminate automatically on the entry of judgment in the state court.

Nor does § 1257 stop a district court from exercising subject-matter jurisdiction simply because a party attempts to litigate in federal court a matter previously litigated in state court. If a federal plaintiff "present[s] some independent claim, albeit one that denies a legal conclusion that a state court has reached in a case to which he was a party . . . , then there is jurisdiction and state law determines whether the defendant prevails under principles of preclusion." GASH Assocs. v. Village of Rosemont, 995 F.2d 726, 728 (7th Cir. 1993).

This case surely is not the "paradigm situation in which *Rooker-Feldman* precludes a federal district court from proceeding." 364 F.3d at 104. ExxonMobil plainly has not repaired to federal court to undo the Delaware

---

8. Congress, if so minded, may explicitly empower district courts to oversee certain state-court judgments and has done so, most notably, in authorizing federal habeas review of state prisoners' petitions. 28 U.S.C. § 2254(a).

judgment in its favor. Rather, it appears ExxonMobil filed suit in Federal District Court (only two weeks after SABIC filed in Delaware and well before any judgment in state court) to protect itself in the event it lost in state court on grounds (such as the state statute of limitations) that might not preclude relief in the federal venue. Tr. of Oral Arg. 46; App. 35-36.[9] *Rooker-Feldman* did not prevent the District Court from exercising jurisdiction when ExxonMobil filed the federal action, and it did not emerge to vanquish jurisdiction after ExxonMobil prevailed in the Delaware courts.

For the reasons stated, the judgment of the Court of Appeals for the Third Circuit is reversed, and the case is remanded for further proceedings consistent with this opinion.

*It is so ordered.*

## b. Federal Court Judgments in State Courts

The following case involves the reverse scenario from that of Kremer v. Chemical Corp. Here the court is a state court, and it must determine the preclusive effects of a prior federal court judgment. But the case also raises several procedure issues from earlier chapters: adequacy of service of process, the scope of Article III, the contours of a claim, and the reach of federal subject matter jurisdiction under the supplemental jurisdiction statute. The decision therefore offers an excellent opportunity to review these concepts and to admire your progress. Many once-familiar and elusive aspects of procedure are now well within your grasp. These pieces now should fit together in a sturdy procedure framework that you will spend a career filling in, remodeling, and critiquing.

### *Watkins v. Resorts International Hotel and Casino, Inc.*
591 A.2d 592 (N.J. 1991)

POLLOCK, J.

This appeal concerns the preclusive effect of a federal judgment in a state court. Specifically, it requires us to decide whether state law claims

---

9. The Court of Appeals criticized ExxonMobil for pursuing its federal suit as an "insurance policy" against an adverse result in state court. 364 F.3d 102, 105-106 (3d Cir. 2004). There is nothing necessarily inappropriate, however, about filing a protective action. See, e.g., Rhines v. Weber, 544 U.S. 269 (2005) (permitting a federal district court to stay a federal habeas action and hold the petition in abeyance while a petitioner exhausts claims in state court); Union Pacific R. Co. v. Dept. of Revenue of Ore., 920 F.2d 581, 584, and n.9 (9th Cir. 1990) (noting that the railroad company had filed protective actions in state court to prevent expiration of the state statute of limitations); Government of Virgin Islands v. Neadle, 861 F. Supp. 1054, 1055 (M.D. Fla. 1994) (staying an action brought by plaintiffs "to protect themselves" in the event that personal jurisdiction over the defendants failed in the United States District Court for the Virgin Islands); see also England v. Louisiana Bd. of Medical Examiners, 375 U.S. 411, 421 (1964) (permitting a party to reserve litigation of federal constitutional claims for federal court while a state court resolves questions of state law).

brought in a state court are precluded by a prior federal court judgment dismissing federal law claims based on the same facts, if the federal claims were dismissed for insufficient service of process and for lack of standing.

Plaintiffs, Murrell Watkins and Abraham McDaniel and their wholly-owned company, sued Resorts International (Resorts), Bally's Park Place Casino (Bally's), and other defendants in federal district court, claiming that as minority bus-line owners they had been the targets of discriminatory practices. The claims, which sought relief pursuant to 42 U.S.C. sections 1981, 1983, 1985(3), and 1988, were dismissed on motion for various reasons, including insufficient service of process and lack of standing.

Relying on state law, Watkins and McDaniel then filed this action in the Superior Court based on the same allegations of discrimination that underlay their federal claims. The Law Division granted defendants' motion to dismiss, on the ground that plaintiffs were barred by the entire controversy doctrine from relitigating the same cause of action that had already been decided in federal court. In an unreported decision, the Appellate Division affirmed on grounds of res judicata, collateral estoppel, and the entire controversy doctrine. We granted certification, 584 A.2d 253 (1990), and now reverse the judgment of the Appellate Division and remand the matter to the Law Division. Although state courts must honor judgments of federal courts, dismissals for insufficient service of process or lack of standing do not preclude relitigation. Consequently, the federal judgments against Watkins and McDaniel do not bar their state claims.

## I

For purposes of this appeal, we accept the facts as alleged in the complaint. . . . Plaintiff Watkins and his wife were the sole shareholders in Ocean Breeze Transit Company (Ocean Breeze), a bus company that operated service to Atlantic City casinos. Plaintiff McDaniel owned Cobra Coach Lines, Inc. (Cobra), which also operated bus service to Atlantic City. Plaintiffs, who are black, allege that Resorts and Bally's discriminated against them by interfering with their efforts to operate bus lines to the casinos. . . .

On August 27, 1984, Watkins, McDaniel, Ocean Breeze, and Cobra filed suit in the United States District Court for the District of New Jersey, claiming civil rights violations under 42 U.S.C. sections 1981, 1983, 1985(3), and 1988. The complaint named the same defendants as in the instant matter: Resorts, Bally's, McClain, McDermott, the DOT, and Fitzsimmons. Plaintiffs did not assert any pendent state claims. Eventually, the federal court dismissed all of the claims. First, on June 12, 1985, the court dismissed plaintiffs' section 1983 claim. Plaintiffs stipulated to a dismissal with prejudice of their section 1983 claim, leaving only the section 1985 claim and the derivative section 1981 claim for attorneys' fees. Then, on November

27, 1985, the court dismissed the complaint against Bally's for insufficient service of process under Federal Rule of Civil Procedure 4(j).* Specifically, the court dismissed the complaint without prejudice because plaintiffs had failed to serve the summons and complaint on Bally's within 120 days of filing the complaint, contrary to Federal Rule of Civil Procedure 4(j). Plaintiffs voluntarily dismissed their complaint against DOT. . . .

Shortly thereafter, Watkins and McDaniel brought suit in the Law Division. As in the federal action, they claimed that as minority bus-line owners they were the targets of discrimination by the two casinos, their employees, and DOT. Plaintiffs alleged the same facts as those in their federal complaint. Instead of alleging violations of federal anti-discrimination laws, however, plaintiffs founded their claims entirely on state law. . . .

Resorts moved to dismiss the complaint, arguing that the entire controversy doctrine, res judicata, or collateral estoppel precluded plaintiffs' action. It argued that no private cause of action existed under the Casino Control Act. The court agreed that the state cause of action was essentially the same as the federal action, and that the entire controversy doctrine barred plaintiffs from relitigating the matter. The trial court therefore granted the motion to dismiss. As to DOT, the court dismissed plaintiffs' complaint for failure to state a claim.

Before the Appellate Division, plaintiffs argued that the federal court had not determined the matter on its merits and that therefore neither res judicata, collateral estoppel, nor the entire controversy doctrine should bar the state court action. The Appellate Division disagreed, and affirmed the dismissal. As to Resorts, the court viewed the dismissal for lack of standing as a resolution on the merits, stating that the district court's "holding was that the claims which the individual plaintiffs were asserting belonged solely to their corporations and, therefore, the individuals were not entitled to redress." The court held that plaintiffs' claims against Resorts were barred by res judicata or collateral estoppel. As to Bally's, the court affirmed the dismissal on the ground of the entire controversy doctrine. The court determined that although the federal dismissal for insufficient service of process was not on the merits and therefore did not itself preclude the state suit, Bally's was a necessary party and the dismissal of the federal suit against Resorts barred a later action against Bally's.

## II

A fundamental feature of the relationship between state and federal courts is that the courts of each system must respect the judgments of courts of the other system. That respect is essential to the fair and efficient functioning of our federalist system of justice. The rule that state courts must

---

* [The provision of Rule 4 to which the court refers now appears as 4(m), not 4(j). — Eds.]

accord preclusive effect to prior federal court judgments is . . . settled. . . . This case requires that we search for the reasons beneath the rule.

Our inquiry begins with the full faith and credit clause of the United States Constitution, which provides that "[f]ull Faith and Credit shall be given in each State to the public Acts, Records, and judicial Proceedings of every other State." U.S. Const. art. IV, § 1. That clause directs the courts of each state to give preclusive effect to the judgments of a sister state. The clause, however, does not expressly require state courts to accept the judgments of a federal court.

Nor does the federal full faith and credit statute, 28 U.S.C.A. § 1738, impose that requirement. The statute provides that

> judicial proceedings [of any State, Territory or Possession of the United States] . . . shall have the same full faith and credit in every court within the United States and its Territories and Possessions as they have by law or usage in the courts of such State, Territory or Possession from which they are taken.

Because they are included in "every court within the United States," federal courts are required to give full faith and credit to the judgments defined in the statute. The judgments so defined, however, are those "of any State, Territory, or Possession of the United States," not those of the federal courts. Thus, the statute does not compel state courts to give preclusive effect to judgments of the federal courts. In sum, neither the constitutional full faith and credit clause nor the corresponding federal statute solves the problem.

Some older cases purported to find the answer in the full faith and credit clause of the federal constitution. See Bigelow v. Old Dominion Copper Mining & Smelting Co., 225 U.S. 111, 129 (1912) (addressing federal-state preclusion issue as one governed by the full faith and credit clause and its implementing statute, and holding that a federal court judgment "is entitled to the same sanction which would attach to a like judgment of a court of the state"); National Foundry & Pipe Works v. Oconto City Water Supply Co., 183 U.S. 216, 233 (1902) (holding that state court's failure to give due effect to federal court decree raises federal question [internal citations omitted]). Courts also looked to the federal full faith and credit statute or its predecessor. . . . As previously noted, however, neither the full faith and credit clause of the Constitution nor the corresponding federal statute applies. In brief, positive law does not expressly mandate that state courts give preclusive effect to the judgments of federal courts.

Generally without analysis, state courts have accepted federal court judgments as binding. [Ronan E.] Degnan, [Federalized Res Judicata,] 85 Yale L.J. [741,] 744 n.17 [(1976)]. In the absence of any such analysis, respected scholars have theorized about the basis for the preclusive effect in state courts of federal court judgments. For example, Professor Charles Alan Wright, drawing on an explanation of Professor Ronan Degnan, states

> Article III limits the federal judicial power to cases and controversies. To decide a case or controversy implies some binding effect. Proceedings that

do not have at least the potential effect of precluding later relitigation of the same claims and issues would constitute something other than the exercise of the judicial power. Once it is accepted that Article III and its implementing legislation have created courts with the power to issue judgments that will have preclusive effects in other litigation, the Supremacy Clause of Article VI mandates that those preclusive effects are binding on state courts. [C. Wright, The Law of Federal Courts 694-695 (4th ed. 1983) (internal citations omitted).]

See also Degnan, supra, 85 Yale L.J. at 772-73 (federal-state preclusion "will have to be placed forthrightly on the ground that the integrity of the federal judicial power is at stake"); cf. Burbank, Interjurisdictional Preclusion, Full Faith and Credit and Federal Common Law: A General Approach, 71 Cornell L. Rev. 733, 753-55 & n.92 (1986) (questioning how far Professor Degnan's article III analysis can go, but acknowledging article III's significance in imposing basic obligation to respect federal judgments). Professor Wright's analysis echoes the earlier analysis in Dupasseur v. Rochereau, 88 U.S. (21 Wall.) 130 (1875), in which the United States Supreme Court held that a state court's failure to honor a federal court judgment constituted a federal question triggering the jurisdiction of the Supreme Court.

By insulating courts from the relitigation of claims, res judicata prevents the judicial inefficiency inherent in multiplicitous litigation. At some point litigation over a particular controversy should end. By preventing harassment of parties, preclusion serves the interest of fairness. Preclusion further protects the integrity of the judgments of state and federal courts. The strength of a judgment derives from the expectation that it will be binding. Essential to the proper functioning of state and federal courts is the principle that a disappointed litigant may not circumvent a judgment entered in one system by relitigating the claim or the decided issues in the other system. Generally speaking, whether started in state or federal courts, the determination of a case in one system should conclude the matter.

Beyond the general policy favoring finality, interjurisdictional preclusion serves the vital function of unifying the nation. The United States Supreme Court, this Court, and scholars have recognized that the full faith and credit clause, by obliging each state to enforce the judgments of another state, fulfills this function. As the United States Supreme Court has written,

[t]he full faith and credit clause like the commerce clause thus became a nationally unifying force. It altered the status of the several states as independent foreign sovereignties, each free to ignore rights and obligations created under the laws or established by the judicial proceedings of the others, by making each an integral part of a single nation, in which rights judicially established in any part are given nation-wide application. [Magnolia Petroleum Co. v. Hunt, 320 U.S. 430, 439 (1943).]

Just as cohesion between state courts is necessary for national unity, cohesion between state and federal courts is necessary for the continuing vitality of the federalist system. Maintaining a cohesive federal system requires not only that federal courts honor state court judgments, as mandated by 28 U.S.C. § 1738, but also that state courts honor federal court judgments. . . .

Plaintiffs ordinarily have one chance to prove their case. Overlapping jurisdiction frequently gives plaintiffs the option of suing in either the state or the federal system. The availability of alternative forums should not give plaintiffs the additional luxury of suing first in one system and then in the other.

When a state court considers the binding effect of a federal court judgment, nothing less is at stake than the integrity of federal judicial power and the coherence of the federalist judicial system. See Degnan, supra, 85 Yale L.J. at 773. So viewed, state courts are bound by federal court judgments, just as they are bound by the judgments of sister states. Consequently, a cause of action finally determined on the merits by a competent federal court cannot be relitigated by the same parties or their privies in a state court.

We now consider the question of what law governs the preclusive effect of a federal judgment in state court. In general, the binding effect of a judgment is determined by the law of the jurisdiction that rendered it. Restatement (Second) of Conflict of Laws § 95 comment e (1971). This rule applies not only when considering the preclusive effect of a judgment of one state court on the courts of another state, but also when determining the preclusive effect in a state court of a federal court judgment. The Restatement (Second) of Judgments . . . § 87, states the rule plainly: "Federal law determines the effects under the rules of res judicata of a judgment of a federal court."

In principle, the preclusive effect of a judgment is the logical consequence of the procedures of the issuing court. See id. Introduction at 6-13. "Within the constitutional limits, the contours of res judicata are determined by the particulars of the opportunity to litigate afforded by the system of procedure in question." Id. at 7. The underlying consideration is whether the contending party in the second forum was accorded a "full and fair" opportunity to litigate in the first forum. Id. at 9.

It follows that ordinarily a federal court judgment would be neither more nor less binding in the courts of this State than it would be in the federal courts. The reason is that the preclusive effect of the judgment is a function of the procedures of the federal court that rendered it. Id. at 5. These considerations affect the applicability of the entire controversy doctrine, on which the Appellate Division relied. That doctrine, like res judicata, advances the goals of fairness, efficiency, and finality. In limited circumstances, the entire controversy doctrine may preclude an action that is not otherwise precluded by the federal law of res judicata. We note in this context the decision of the Appellate Division in Blazer Corp. v. New Jersey Sports & Exposition Authority, 488 A.2d 1025 (1985). There, the court relied on the entire controversy doctrine to bar a Superior Court action that "formed the foundation," id. at 1025, of a previously dismissed federal action. Our reading of that opinion leads us to conclude that the Appellate Division may not have sufficiently considered the federal law of claim preclusion in resorting to the entire controversy doctrine.

We turn therefore to the federal law of claim preclusion. Federal law requires the same three basic elements as New Jersey law: (1) the judgment in the prior action must be valid, final, and on the merits; (2) the parties in the later action must be identical to or in privity with those in the prior action; and (3) the claim in the later action must grow out of the same transaction or occurrence as the claim in the earlier one. Federated Dept. Stores v. Moitie, 452 U.S. 394, 398 (1981).

Claim preclusion applies not only to matters actually determined in an earlier action, but to all relevant matters that could have been so determined. For the purposes of res judicata, causes of action are deemed part of a single "claim" if they arise out of the same transaction or occurrence. Restatement (Second) of Judgments, supra, § 24. If, under various theories, a litigant seeks to remedy a single wrong, then that litigant should present all theories in the first action. Otherwise, theories not raised will be precluded in a later action. Thus, if a federal court in a prior action would have exercised pendent jurisdiction over related state claims that were not asserted, a final judgment on the merits by the federal court precludes raising those claims in a subsequent action in state court. Federated Dept. Stores, supra, 452 U.S. at 404 (Blackmun, J., concurring).

If, on the other hand, a claim could not have been presented in the first action, then it will not be precluded in a later action. The Restatement (Second) of Judgments explains:

> When the plaintiff brings an action on the claim in a court, either state or federal, in which there is no jurisdictional obstacle to his advancing both theories or grounds, but he presents only one of them, and judgment is entered with respect to it, he may not maintain a second action in which he tenders the other theory or ground. If, however, the court in the first action would clearly not have had jurisdiction to entertain the omitted theory or ground (or, having jurisdiction, would clearly have declined to exercise it as a matter of discretion), then a second action in a competent court presenting the omitted theory or ground should be held not precluded. [§ 25 comment e.]

See also id. § 26(1)(c) (subject matter jurisdiction exception to rule against claim splitting). If the plaintiffs could not have asserted both state and federal claims in a single forum, it would be unfair to force them to sacrifice the claims that could not be so asserted in order to bring a single action in one forum.

In the present case, therefore, we must determine whether the federal district court had jurisdiction to entertain plaintiffs' omitted state law claims. A federal court can hear pendent state claims when the state and federal claims "derive from a common nucleus of operative fact." United Mine Workers of Am. v. Gibbs, 383 U.S. 715, 725 (1966). In cases asserting violations of civil rights, federal courts routinely exercise pendent jurisdiction over state claims. E.g., Hayden v. Chrysler Corp., 486 F. Supp. 557, 558

(E.D. Mich. 1980). Some scholars believed that the Supreme Court's decision in Finley v. United States, 490 U.S. 545 (1989), spelled the demise of pendent and ancillary jurisdiction. See [Thomas M.] Mengler, The Demise of Pendent and Ancillary Jurisdiction, 1990 BYU L. Rev. 247; [Wendy Collins] Perdue, Finley v. United States: Unstringing Pendent Jurisdiction, 76 Va. L. Rev. 539 (1990). Congress, however, rescued the doctrines by passing the Judicial Improvements Act of 1990. None of this affects our resolution of the present case, however, because the federal action at issue here occurred before *Finley* and the Act.

Here, defendants argue that because plaintiffs could have appended their state claims to the federal action, the federal dismissal precludes presentation of those claims. In reply, plaintiffs argue that the federal court dismissal of their federal claims does not preclude the present action because the federal court would have declined to exercise pendent jurisdiction over their state claims. A federal court may choose not to exercise jurisdiction over pendent state claims when the federal claims have been dismissed before trial. *Gibbs,* supra, 383 U.S. at 726. In such a case, perhaps plaintiffs should not be precluded from later asserting their state claims in a state court. Restatement (Second) of Judgments, supra, § 25 comment e, illustration 10 (state action barred "unless it is clear that the federal court would have declined as a matter of discretion to exercise that jurisdiction (for example, because the federal claim, though substantial, was dismissed in advance of trial)"); Note, The Res Judicata Implications of Pendent Jurisdiction, 66 Cornell L. Rev. 608, 621-24 (1981) (generally, if federal claims dismissed before trial, then later court should presume federal court would not have invoked pendent jurisdiction despite common nucleus of operative fact, and therefore should hold omitted state claims not precluded). We need not decide that issue, however, because we conclude that even if plaintiffs could have asserted all their claims in federal court, the federal court's determination of the federal claims was not of such a nature as to preclude plaintiffs' subsequent assertion of their state claims in the state courts.

Only a judgment "on the merits" will preclude a later action on the same claim. Respected authorities reject the phrase "on the merits" as "question-begging," C. Wright, supra, at 679 [internal quotations omitted], and "possibly misleading," Restatement (Second) of Judgments, supra, § 19 comment a. Because "on the merits" may connote too limited a view of judgments that are entitled to preclusive effect, the Restatement (Second) of Judgments avoids the phrase. Compare Restatement (First) of Judgments § 48 (1942) ("Where a valid and final personal judgment is rendered on the merits in favor of the defendant, the plaintiff cannot thereafter maintain an action on the original cause of action.") with Restatement (Second) of Judgments, supra, § 19 ("A valid and final personal judgment rendered in favor of the defendant bars another action by the plaintiff on the same claim."). Semantics aside, the rule remains that a dismissal based on a court's procedural inability to consider a case will not preclude a subsequent action on the same claim, Restatement (Second) of Judgments, supra, § 19 comment a,

§ 20, but a judgment can be preclusive even if it does not result from a plenary hearing on the substantive claims. For example, in Velasquez [v. Franz,] 589 A.2d [143,] 151-52 [(1991)], we recently recognized the preclusive effect of a federal court dismissal based on a dissolved corporation's lack of capacity to be sued, although the federal court did not reach the facts underlying plaintiff's tort claim. In the present case, the issue is whether federal court dismissals for insufficient service of process and lack of standing preclude subsequent actions.

Concerning the dismissal for insufficient service of process, Federal Rule of Civil Procedure 4(j) provides that if service is not made on a defendant within 120 days after the filing of the complaint, and no good reason is given for the delay, "the action shall be dismissed as to that defendant without prejudice." Cf. Degnan, supra, 85 Yale L.J. at 763 ("To the extent, then, that the Federal Rules of Civil Procedure do speak about the preclusive effect of federal adjudications, they speak authoritatively, and determinations based upon them are entitled to res judicata effect or full faith and credit. They have been given that effect by state and federal courts alike." (footnote omitted)). Consequently, the November 27, 1985, federal court order dismissing Watkins' and McDaniel's individual claims against Bally's was necessarily "without prejudice." . . .

## III

Plaintiff's state court and federal court actions arose from the same factual occurrences. Hence, they constitute the same claim for res judicata purposes. Although the corporations, which were plaintiffs in the federal action, do not join as plaintiffs in the state action, the individual plaintiffs and all defendants are identical. Thus, two of the requirements for claim preclusion, identity of parties and of claim, are satisfied.

In the federal courts, however, the complaint against Bally's was dismissed for insufficient service of process under Federal Rule of Civil Procedure 4(j). A dismissal on that ground is not a judgment on the merits for res judicata purposes. Rule 4(j) specifically provides for dismissal "without prejudice." Moreover, the opinion on which the order is based states that "plaintiffs will not be barred from refiling the action," and that the claim against Bally's "shall be dismissed, without prejudice, in accord with Fed. R. Civ. P. 4(j)." Consequently, we conclude that the federal dismissal of the complaint against Bally's is not entitled to claim preclusive effect. . . .

Initially, the federal courts dismissed the claims of the individual plaintiffs against Bally's and Resorts for improper service and lack of standing. The subsequent dismissal "with prejudice" on May 27, 1987, applied only to those claims remaining at that time, the claims of the corporate plaintiffs. Thus, the provision in the May 27, 1987, order that the dismissal is "with prejudice" could not affect the previously dismissed claims of the individual plaintiffs.

To conclude, the only issue precluded by the federal court judgment is the standing of the individual plaintiffs to maintain an action under federal law. The federal courts did not resolve the question whether Watkins and McDaniel have standing under the New Jersey Constitution, the Casino Control Act, and the Law Against Discrimination. Plaintiffs deserve the opportunity to be heard on that issue. We state no view concerning plaintiffs' standing or concerning the merits of their claims. Our opinion goes no further than holding that because the federal court judgment was not on the merits, it does not preclude plaintiffs from raising their state claims in state court.

The judgment of the Appellate Division is *reversed*, and the matter is remanded to the Law Division.

## Notes and Questions

1. *Federal Judgments in State Court.* The foregoing cases construe Article IV, § 1 of the United States Constitution and § 1738 of the United States Code. Review both provisions carefully. Notice that neither provides any obligation for state courts to respect federal judgments. Nevertheless, as *Watkins* demonstrates, the obligation is well recognized. What arguments support this practice? What exceptions might there be to this general obligation to respect the judgments of another sovereign?

2. *Policy Bars to Respect for the Judgments of Other States.* Should marriage be considered a judicial act subject to the Full Faith and Credit Clause of the federal constitution? In Baehr v. Lewin, 852 P.2d 44 (Haw. 1993), *aff'd sub nom.* Baehr v. Miike, 910 P.2d 112 (Haw. 1996), the Hawaii Supreme Court held that the Hawaii constitution required that the state justify its proscription of same-sex marriage with compelling reasons, a difficult standard to meet. In another landmark decision, the Massachusetts Supreme Judicial Court held that the state "failed to identify any constitutionally adequate reason for denying civil marriage to same-sex couples." Goodridge v. Dep't of Pub. Health, 798 N.E.2d 941, 948 (Mass. 2003).

The California Supreme Court followed suit several years later, holding that "the state interest in limiting the designation of marriage exclusively to opposite-sex couples . . . cannot properly be considered a compelling state interest for equal protection purposes." In re Marriage Cases, 183 P.3d 384, 451 (Cal. 2008). In the November 2008 election, however, California voters responded by adopting a ballot measure altering the state constitution to provide that "[o]nly marriage between a man and a woman is valid or recognized in California." Cal. Const. art. I, § 7.5. Gay and lesbian couples promptly filed a federal lawsuit asserting that the state constitutional amendment violates the federal constitutional guarantee of equal protection of the laws. The district court entered judgment for plaintiffs after a lengthy trial and the Ninth Circuit affirmed. Perry v. Brown, 671 F.3d 1052 (9th Cir. 2012). Defendants appealed to the United States Supreme Court.

The Supreme Court declined to reach the merits, holding that once "the District Court issued its order, respondents no longer had any injury to redress, and the state officials chose not to appeal. The only individuals who sought to appeal [interveners who proposed Proposition 8 as a ballot initiative] . . . had not been ordered to do or refrain from doing anything. Their only interest was to vindicate the constitutional validity of a generally applicable California law. As this Court has repeatedly held, such a 'generalized grievance'—no matter how sincere—is insufficient to confer standing." Hollingsworth v. Perry, 133 S. Ct. 2652, 2656 (2013).

In 2015, the Court finally addressed the merits of the claim that bans on same-sex marriage violate the Fourteenth Amendment, holding that the right to marry is a fundamental liberty interest of every person and that the Due Process and Equal Protection Clauses protect the right of couples of the same sex to marry. Obergefell v. Hodges, 135 S. Ct. 2584, 2604 (2015). The Court further held that states must recognize same-sex marriages that were validly performed in other states. Id. at 2607-2608. The Court's second holding did not explicitly rely on the Full Faith and Credit Clause. Instead, the majority simply noted that given that states must issue same-sex marriages "on the same terms as accorded to couples of the opposite sex[,] . . . the Court also must hold . . . that there is no lawful basis for a State to refuse to recognize a lawful same-sex marriage performed in another State on the ground of its same-sex character." Id. at 2607-2608. The decision thus appears to foreclose a state from arguing that it may refuse to recognize a same-sex marriage license issued by another state because of a "legitimate public policy" under Nevada v. Hall, 440 U.S. 410 (1979). As the Court put it, "if States are required by the Constitution to issue marriage licenses to same-sex couples, the justifications for refusing to recognize those marriages performed elsewhere are undermined." Obergefell, 135 S. Ct. at 2607.

After the ruling, government officials in Alabama, Texas, Arkansas, and Kentucky resisted issuing same-sex marriage certificates, either by specifically denying marriage certificates to same-sex couples or by halting the issuance of marriage certificates altogether. At least two counties in Kentucky were not issuing marriage licenses to same-sex couples as of July 17, 2015, excluding counties that were not issuing licenses because of paperwork or technical delays. In Alabama, 12 of 53 counties were not issuing any marriage licenses, and in both Texas and Arkansas, one county was not issuing licenses to same-sex couples. Moreover, the Texas state Attorney General issued an advisory opinion suggesting that county clerks may have a religious right to refuse to issue same-sex marriage licenses. These counties will likely face additional litigation. In Kentucky, the ACLU has already brought a Fourteenth Amendment claim against a county clerk who refused to issue marriage licenses. For detailed statistics on state responses to Obergefell, see http://ballotpedia.org/Local_government_responses_to_Obergefell_v._Hodges#tab=Alabama (includes a state-by-state breakdown).

What does Baker v. General Motors Corp. suggest about the obligation of sister courts to respect other states' decisions to recognize same-sex marriage? What, if anything, does the federal Defense of Marriage Act (DOMA), 1 U.S.C. § 7 (1997), 28 U.S.C. § 738C, which specifically provides that no state "shall be required to give effect to any public act, record, or judicial proceeding between persons of the same sex that is treated as a marriage under the laws of such other State," add to this full faith and credit analysis? Is a marriage a judicial act within the meaning of the Full Faith and Credit Clause?

What weight should the courts give to congressional input in deciding whether a judicial act should receive full faith and credit? Recall that in the text immediately following the Full Faith and Credit Clause, U.S. Const. art. IV, § 1 gives Congress the power to "prescribe the manner in which such Acts, Records and Proceedings shall be proved, and the Effect thereof." DOMA did not invalidate same-sex marriages in states that permit them, but it did exclude such marriages from recognition under more than a thousand federal statutes and programs that are administered on the basis of marital status, including veterans benefits, immigration petitions involving spouses, tax breaks, educational loan programs, federal employee benefits, etc. In 2013, the Supreme Court held that DOMA was unconstitutional under the Due Process Clause of the Fifth Amendment as applied to lawful same-sex marriages recognized by the states. United States v. Windsor, 133 S. Ct. 2675, 2696 (2013) ("[N]o legitimate purpose overcomes the purpose and effect to disparage and to injure those whom the State, by its marriage laws, sought to protect in personhood and dignity.").

More recently, the Court has held that a final judgment of the Georgia courts, making a same-sex partner a legal parent of children that she and the biological mother raised together since birth, may be enforced in an Alabama court. V.L. v. E.L., 136 S. Ct. 1017, 1020 (2016). The Alabama courts had refused to grant the adoptive parent custody or visitation rights to which she was entitled on the theory that the Georgia court lacked subject matter jurisdiction over the adoption. The Supreme Court reversed, reasoning that under the Full Faith and Credit Clause and its precedents, "[w]here a judgment indicates on its face that it was rendered by a court of competent jurisdiction, such jurisdiction 'is to be presumed unless disproved.' There is nothing here to rebut that presumption." Id. at 1021 (citation omitted).

3. *The "One Bite" Test in a Federal System.* If a party files an action in state court when she could have filed in federal court, should she subsequently be precluded from litigating a claim related to the original action that is within the exclusive jurisdiction of the federal courts? She clearly could not have raised that issue in state court; should she nevertheless be precluded from litigating it later on the theory that she chose the forum with narrower jurisdiction and should get only one bite at the apple? The United States Supreme Court confronted the issue in Marrese v. American Academy of Orthopaedic Surgeons, 470 U.S. 373 (1985), and concluded that the answer

depends on the state's law of preclusion. If it precludes subsequent litigation of issues that the party could not have raised in an earlier suit for jurisdictional reasons, then the federal claim is precluded. What arguments might support preclusion in such a case? What reasons can you offer in support of no preclusion? Cf. Czarniecki v. City of Chicago, 633 F.3d 545, 548-549 n.3 (7th Cir. 2011) ("[W]hen the issue is whether an earlier *federal* judgment has preclusive effect on a subsequent federal claim, we apply federal res judicata principles.") (emphasis in the original).

# Table of Cases

*Principal cases are indicated by italics.*

# Table of Federal Rules of Civil Procedure

# Table of Judicial Code Citations — U.S. Code

# Index